T0180284

Lecture Notes in Computer Science   10058

Commenced Publication in 1973
Founding and Former Series Editors:
Gerhard Goos, Juris Hartmanis, and Jan van Leeuwen

More information about this series at http://www.springer.com/series/7409

Marinos Ioannides · Eleanor Fink
Antonia Moropoulou · Monika Hagedorn-Saupe
Antonella Fresa · Gunnar Liestøl
Vlatka Rajcic · Pierre Grussenmeyer (Eds.)

Digital Heritage

Progress in Cultural Heritage: Documentation, Preservation, and Protection

6th International Conference, EuroMed 2016
Nicosia, Cyprus, October 31 – November 5, 2016
Proceedings, Part I

 Springer

Editors

Marinos Ioannides
Cyprus University of Technology
Limassol
Cyprus

Eleanor Fink
Arlington, VI
USA

Antonia Moropoulou
National Technical University of Athens
Athens
Greece

Monika Hagedorn-Saupe
Institut für Museumsforschung
Berlin
Germany

Antonella Fresa
Promoter s.r.l.
Peccioli
Italy

Gunnar Liestøl
University of Oslo
Oslo
Norway

Vlatka Rajcic
University of Zagreb
Zagreb
Croatia

Pierre Grussenmeyer
INSA
Strasbourg
France

ISSN 0302-9743   ISSN 1611-3349 (electronic)
Lecture Notes in Computer Science
ISBN 978-3-319-48495-2   ISBN 978-3-319-48496-9 (eBook)
DOI 10.1007/978-3-319-48496-9

Library of Congress Control Number: 2016956494

LNCS Sublibrary: SL3 – Information Systems and Applications, incl. Internet/Web, and HCI

This Springer imprint is published by Springer Nature
The registered company is Springer International Publishing AG
The registered company address is: Gewerbestrasse 11, 6330 Cham, Switzerland

Preface

Welcome to the proceedings of EuromedMed 2016, the biennial scientific event which this year was held in the capital city of Cyprus, the island that has always been a bridge to three continents in the world going back to the origins of civilization. It is a place where the fingerprints of several ancient cultures and civilizations on earth can be found, with a wealth of historical sites recognized and protected by UNESCO.

Several organizations and current EU projects (such as the Marie Sklodowska-Curie Fellowship project on Digital Heritage Marie Sklodowska-Curie FP7-PEOPLE ITN-DCH, the Marie Sklodowska-Curie FP7-IAPP 4D-CH-WORLD, the FP7-CIP ICT-PSP EuropeanaSpace, the H2020 Reflective 7 - INCEPTION, the H2020 CSA Virtual Museums ViMM, the Research Infrastructure DARIAH-EU ERIC and DARIAH-CY) as well as the Innovation in Intelligent Management of Heritage Buildings (i2MHB) decided to join EuroMed2016 and continue cooperating together in order to create an optimal environment for the discussion and explanation of new technologies, the exchange of modern innovative ideas, and in general to allow the transfer of knowledge between a large number of professionals and academics during one common event.

The main goal of the event is to illustrate the programs underway, whether organized by public bodies (e.g., UNESCO, European Union, National States, etc.) or by private foundations (e.g., Getty Foundation, World Heritage Foundation, etc.) in order to promote a common approach to the tasks of recording, documenting, protecting, and managing world cultural heritage. The 6th European-Mediterranean Conference (EuroMed 2016) was definitely a forum for sharing views and experiences, discussing proposals for the optimum approach as well as the best practice and the ideal technical tools to preserve, document, manage, present/visualize and disseminate the rich and diverse cultural heritage of mankind.

This conference was held during the mid-term of the new Framework Programme, Horizon 2020, which is the largest in the world in terms of financial support on research, innovation, technological development, and demonstration activities. The awareness of the value and importance of heritage assets has been reflected in the financing of projects since the first Framework Programme for Research & Technological Development (FP1, 1984–87) and continues into current HORIZON 2020 that follows FP7 (2007–13). In the past 30 years, a large community of researchers, experts, and specialists have had the chance to learn and develop the transferable knowledge and skills needed to inform stakeholders, scholars, and students. Europe has become a leader in heritage documentation, preservation, and protection science, with COST Actions adding value to projects financed within the FP and EUREKA programme and transferring knowledge to practice and supporting the development of SMEs.

The EuroMed 2016 agenda focused on enhancing and strengthening of international and regional cooperation and promoting awareness and tools for future innovative research, development, and applications to protect, preserve, and document the

European and world cultural heritage. Our ambition was to host an exceptional conference by mobilizing also policy makers from different EU countries, institutions (European Commission, European Parliament, Council of Europe, UNESCO, International Committee for Monuments and Sites ICOMOS, the International Committee for Documentation of Cultural Heritage CIPA, the International Society for Photogrammetry and Remote Sensing ISPRS, the International Centre for the study of the Preservation and Restoration of Cultural Property ICCROM, and the International Committee for Museums ICOM), professionals, as well as participants from all over the world and from different scientific areas of cultural heritage.

Protecting, preserving, and presenting our cultural heritage are actions that are frequently interpreted as change management and/or changing the behavior of society. Joint European and international research produce the scientific background and support for such a change. We are living in a period characterized by rapid and remarkable changes in the environment, in society, and in technology. Natural changes, war conflicts, and man-made changes, including climate, as well as technological and societal changes, form an ever-moving and colorful stage and a challenge for our society. Close cooperation between professionals, policy makers, and authorities internationally is necessary for research, development, and technologica advancements in the field of cultural heritage.

Scientific projects in the area of cultural heritage have received national, European Union, or UNESCO funding for more than 30 years. Through financial support and cooperation, major results have been achieved and published in peer-reviewed journals and conference proceedings with the support of professionals from many countries. The European Conferences on Cultural Heritage research and development and in particular the biennial EuroMed conference have become regular milestones on the never-ending journey in the search for new knowledge of our common history and its protection and preservation for the generations to come. EuroMed also provides a unique opportunity to present and review results as well as to draw new inspiration.

To reach this ambitious goal, the topics covered include experiences in the use of innovative technologies and methods and how to take best advantage to integrate the results obtained to build up new tools and/or experiences as well as to improve methodologies for documenting, managing, preserving, and communicating cultural heritage.

In these proceedings we present 105 papers, selected from 504 submissions, which focus on interdisciplinary and multidisciplinary research concerning cutting-edge cultural heritage informatics, physics, chemistry, and engineering and the use of technology for the representation, documentation, archiving, protection, preservation, and communication of cultural heritage knowledge.

Our Keynote speakers, Prof. Dr. Antonia Moropoulou (NTUA and Technical Chamber of Greece), Prof. Dr. Dieter Fellner (Director of FhD/IGD and TU Darmstadt, Germany), Prof. Dr. Wolfgang Kippes (University for Applied Arts Vienna and Donau University Krems, Austria), Prof. Dr. Sarah Whatley (Director of Centre for Dance Research, UK), Prof. Dr. Mustafa Erdik (Bogazici University of Instabul, Turkey), Mr. Jean-Pierre Massué (Senate Member of the European Academy of Sciences and Arts/COPRNM, France), Mr. Axel Ermert (Institute for Museum Research SMB/PK of Berlin, Germany), Mrs. Rosella Caffo (Director of the Central Institute for the Union

Catalogue of the Italian Libraries (ICCU), Italy), Mr. Vasco Fassina (President of the European Standardization Commission CEN/TC 346: Conservation of Cultural Heritage, Italy), Mrs. Maria P. Kouroupas (Director Cultural Heritage Center, US Department of State), Mrs. France Desmarais (ICOM), Dr. Thomas R. Klein (Counsel, Andrews Kurth LLP), Françoise Bortolotti (Criminal Intelligence Officer, Works of Art Unit, Interpol) and Prof. Dr. Markus Hilgert (Director, Vorderasiatisches Museum im Pergamonmuseum Staatliche Museen zu Berlin - Preußischer Kulturbesitz and Project Leader, ILLICID) are not only experts in their fields, but also visionaries for the future of cultural heritage protection and preservation. They promote the e-documentation and protection of the past in such a way for its preservation for the generations to come.

We extend our thanks to all authors, speakers, and those persons whose labor, financial support, and encouragement made the EuroMed 2016 event possible. The International Program Committee—whose members represent a cross-section of archaeology, physics, chemistry, civil engineering, computer science, graphics and design, library, archive and information science, architecture, surveying, history and museology—worked tenaciously and finished their work on time. The staff of the IT department at the Cyprus University of Technology helped with their local ICT and audio visual support, especially Mr. Filippos Filippou, Mr. Costas Christodoulou, and Mr. Stephanos Mallouris. We would also like to express our gratitude to all the organizations supporting this event and our co-organizers, the European Commission scientific and policy officers of the H2020 Marie Skłodowska-Curie Programme, the director general of Europeana, Mrs. Jill Cousins, the Getty Conservation Institute and World Monuments Fund, the Cyprus University of Technology, the Ministry of Energy, Commerce, Industry, and Tourism. Especially the permanent secretary and Digital Champion Dr. Stelios Himonas and Mr. Nikos Argyris, the Ministry of Education and Culture and particularly Minister Dr. Costas Kadis, the director of Cultural Services Mr. Pavlos Paraskevas, the Department of Antiquities in Cyprus, all the members of the Cypriot National Committee for E-Documentation and E-Preservation in Cultural Heritage, and finally our corporate sponsors, CableNet Ltd., the Cyprus Tourism Organization, the Cyprus Postal Services, the Cyprus Handicraft Center, and Dr. Kyriacos Themistocleous from the Cyprus Remote Sensing Society, who provided services and gifts in kind that made the conference possible.

We express our thanks and appreciation to Dr. Nikos Grammalides from CERTH in Greece and Dr. Sander Münster, the Dresden University of Technology, Germany, as well as the board of the ICOMOS Cyprus Section for their enthusiasm, commitment, and support for the success of this event. Most of all we would like to thank the organizations UNESCO, European Commission, CIPA, ISPRS, and ICOMOS Europa Nostra that entrusted us with the task of organizing and undertaking this unique event.

September 2016

Marinos Ioannides
Eleanor Fink
Antonia Moropoulou
Monika Hagedorn-Saupe
Antonella Fresa
Gunnar Liestøl
Vlatka Rajcic
Pierre Grussenmeyer

Acknowledgments and Disclaimer

The EuroMed 2016 conference was partly supported by the Republic of Cyprus, the Cyprus University of Technology, the Cyprus Tourism Organization, the CableNet Ltd., by CIPA (http://cipa.icomos.org/), ISPRS, ICOMOS, Europa Nostra the EU projects FP7 PEOPLE ITN2013 ITN-DCH and IAPP2012 4D-CH-WORLD, the DARIAH-EU ERIC and DARIAH-CY, the FP7-ICT-2011 i-Treasures, the CIP ICT-PSP EuropeanaSpace and H2020 INCEPTION and H2020-ViMM projects.

However, the content of this publication reflects only the authors' views; the European Commission, the Republic of Cyprus, CIPA, ISPRS, ICOMOS, Europa Nostra, Cyprus University of Technology and the EU projects FP7 PEOPLE ITN2013 ITN-DCH and IAPP2012 4D-CH-WORLD, the DARIAH-EU ERIC and DARIAH-CY, the FP7-ICT-2011 i-Treasures, the CIP ICT-PSP EuropeanaSpace and H2020-INCEPTION and H2020-ViMM are not liable for any use that may be made of the information contained herein.

Organization

Conference Chairs

Marinos Ioannides
Eleanor Fink
Antonia Moropoulou
Monika Hagedorn-Saupe
Antonella Fresa
Gunnar Liestøl
Vlatka Rajcic
Pierre Grussenmeyer

Paper Review Chair

Pavlos Chatzigrigoriou

Local Organizing Committee

Agapiou, Athos
Chatzigrigoriou, Pavlos
Eliades, Ioannis
Gkanetsos, Theodoros
Leventis, Georgios
Marina, Christodoulou
Nikolakopoulou, Vasiliki

Nobilakis, Elias
Papageorgiou, Eirini
Skriapas, Konstantinos
Yianni, Stephanie
Stylianou, Georgios
Themistocleous, Kyriacos
Athanasiou, Vasilios

International Scientific Committee

Agapiou, Athos	Cyprus	Caliandro, Rocco	Italy
Albertson, Lynda	Italy	Callet, Patrick	Italy
Angeletaki, Alexandra	Norway	Chatzigrigoriou, Pavlos	Greece
Balet, Olivier	France	Colla, Camilla	Italy
Barcelo, Juan	Spain	Corsi, Cristina	Italy
Bebis, George	USA	Cuca, Branca	Serbia
Belgiorno, Maria-Rosaria	Italy	Dallas, Costis	Canada
Bellini, Francesco	Italy	De Jong, Annemieke	Netherlands
Berni, Marco	Italy	De Kramer, Marleen	Austria
Bockholt, Ulrich	Germany	De Leeuw, Sonja	Netherlands
Bryan, Paul	UK	De Masi, Alessandro	Italy

De Niet, Marco	Netherlands	Liestøl, Gunnar	Norway
De Polo Saibanti, Andrea	Italy	Lobovikov Katz, Anna	Israel
Degraeve, Ann	Belgium	Lonnqvist, Minna	Lichtenstein
Dobreva, Milena	Malta	Lopez-Menchero Bendicho,	Italy
Domajnko, Matevz	Slovenia	Victor	
Doneus, Michael	Austria	Madija, Lidija	Serbia
Doulamis, Anastasios	Greece	Maietti, Federica	Italy
Doulamis, Nikolaos	Greece	Makantasis, Konstantinos	Greece
Drap, Pierre	France	Marcella, Stefano	Italy
Eppich, Rand	USA	Martins, Joao	Portugal
Farrag, Maged	Egypt	Masini, Nicola	Italy
Filin, Sagi	Israel	Mate, Toth	Hungary
Fouseki, Kalliopi	UK	Michail, Harris	Cyprus
Fresa, Antonella	Italy	Moropoulou, Antonia	Greece
Frick, Jürgen	Germany	Munster, Sander	Germany
Gebhardt, Andreas	Germany	Nanetti, Andrea	Singapore
Giannoulopoulos,	Spain	Nikolakopoulou, Vasiliki	Greece
Giannoulis Georgios		Nurminen, Antti	Finland
Giuliano, Angele	Italy	Nys, Karin	Belgium
Graf, Holger	Germany	Ouimet, Christian	Canada
Grammalidis, Nikos	Greece	Papageorgiou, Dimitris	Greece
Grosset, Marie	France	Papageorgiou, Eirini	Greece
Grussenmeyer, Pierre	France	Papagiannakis, George	Greece
Gutierrez, Mariano Flores	Spain	Petrelli, Daniela	UK
Gutiérrez Meana, Javier	Spain	Pietro, Liuzzo	Germany
Hagedorn-Saupe, Monika	Germany	Potsiou, Chryssy	Greece
Hanke, Klaus	Austria	Protopapadakis, Eftychios	Greece
Ibáñez, Francisco	Spain	Radoslav, Pavlov	Bulgary
Ioannidis, Charalambos	Greece	Rajcic, Vlatka	Hungary
Jabi, Wassim	UK	Rodriguez-Echavarria,	UK
Kersten, Thomas	Germany	Karina	
Klein, Michael	Austria	Roko, Zarnic	Slovenia
Klein, Reinhard	Germany	Ronchi, Alfredo	Italy
Kolias, Stefanos	Greece	Saleh, Fathi	Egypt
Koukios, Emmanuel	Greece	Sánchez Andreu, Joan	Spain
Koutsabasis, Panayiotis	Greece	Santana, Mario	Canada
Kuroczyński, Piotr	Germany	Santos, Pedro	Germany
Kyriakaki, Georgia	Greece	Schindler, Mathias	Germany
Landes, Tania	France	Sempere, Isabel Martínez	Spain
Lange, Guus	Belgium	Shang, Jin	China
Laquidara, Giuseppe	Italy	Snyders, Marius	Netherlands
Leissner, Johanna	Germany	Stork, Andre	Germany
León, Alfredo Grande	Spain	Tapinaki, Sevasti	Greece
Lerma, José Luis	Spain	Themistocleous, Kyriacos	Cyprus
Leventis, Georgios	Greece	Thwaites, Harold	MY
Liarokapis, Fotis	Greece	Tsai, Fuan	Taiwan

Tsapatsoulis, Nicolas	Cyprus	Vermeulen, Frank	Belgium
Tsiafaki, Despoina	Greece	Vosinakis, Spyros	Greece
Tsoupikova, Daria	USA	Walczak, Krzysztof	Poland
Uueni, Andres	Estonia	Wallace, Manolis	Greece
Vander Vorst, Daniel	Spain	Wehr, Aloysius	Germany
Vassilara, Archontoula	Greece	Wilk, Christian	Germany
Vavalis, Manolis	Greece	Yen, Alex	Taiwan

The Icons of the Chapel of Saint Jacob

The icon shown on the cover of LNCS 10058 (Part I) depicts the scene of the Enthroned Virgin Mary with Child together with Saint John the Evangelist, while the icon shown on the cover of LNCS 10059 (Part II) illustrates Jesus Christ on a throne together with Saint John the Baptist. The icons are dated back to 1620 A.D. and were painted by the artist Meletios from Crete. These icons were stolen from the iconostasis of the chapel of Saint Jacob in Trikomo (Famagusta district) after the Turkish invasion of 1974. Saint Jacob's chapel had no frescoes but it was decorated with colorful plates of traditional folk art.

The icon illustrating Jesus Christ and Saint John the Baptist is 110 × 128 cm in size and close to the feet of the latter there is the inscription "XEIP MEΛETIOϒ TOϒ ΚΡΙΤΟΣ AXK(= 1620) X(ριστο) ϒ. M(ηνος) αυγούστου)," which includes the name of the artist as well as the date. The icon of Mary, Mother of Jesus, together with Saint John the Evangelist is 114 × 134 cm in size. Both of them were in the possession of the Russian–Jewish art dealer Alexander Kocinski, until their confiscation by the Swiss Police in Zurich in 2007. The only documentation available to recover these stolen icons from abroad was a paper published in the *Proceedings of the International Cretan Conference* in 1976 by the former director of the Department of Antiquities of Cyprus, Mr. Athanasios Papageorgiou.

The icons were tracked down in 2007 in Christie's Auction House in London, from where they were withdrawn after actions by Kykkos Monastery. Following information by the bishop of Kykkos Monastery, representatives of the monastery traveled to Zurich to meet the owner of the icons; however, it was not possible to persuade him to return the icons to the lawful owners and therefore the authorities of Cyprus were informed. A written complaint by the Byzantinologist of Kykkos Monastery, Dr. C. Chotzakoglou, to the Cypriot Police and to Interpol in Cyprus initiated the repatriation procedure of the icons, eventually leading to their confiscation by the Swiss Interpol.

By means of a new testimony from Dr. C. Chotzakoglou, in addition to a full documentation of the Cypriot origin of the icons and their looting after the Turkish invasion in northern Cyprus, the Supreme Court of Famagusta, based in Larnaca, took legal measures against the owner of the icons, who was convicted. The verdict of the Cypriot Supreme Court was subsequently used in the Swiss Court, leading to the signing of a compromise settlement between the Church of Cyprus and Kocinski for the return of the icons to Cyprus.

Dr. Ioannis A. Eliades,
Director,
Byzantine Museum and Art Galleries,
Archbishop Makarios III Foundation,
Arch. Kyprianos sqr., P.O. Box 21269,
CY-1505 Nicosia, CYPRUS

Contents – Part I

**Full Paper: Innovative Methods on Risk Assesment, Monitoring
and Protection of Cultural Heritage**

Full Paper: Intangible Cultural Heritage Documentation

**Full Paper: Digital Applications for Materials' Preservation
and Conservation in Cultural Heritage**

Full Paper: Non-destructive Techniques in Cultural Heritage Conservation

Full Paper: Visualisation, VR and AR Methods and Applications

Full Paper: The New Era of Museums and Exhibitions: Digital Engagement and Dissemination

Full Paper: Digital Cultural Heritage in Education, Learning and Training

Project Paper: Data Acquisition, Process and Management in Cultural Heritage

Project Paper: Data, Metadata, Semantics and Ontologies in Cultural Heritage

Project Paper: 3D Reconstruction and 3D Modelling

Project Paper: Heritage Building Information Models (HBIM)

Project Paper: Novel Approaches to Landscapes in Cultural Heritage

**Project Paper: Innovative Methods on Risk Assessment, Monitoring
and Protection of Cultural Heritage**

**Project Paper: Digital Applications for Materials' Preservation
and Conservation in Cultural Heritage**

Project Paper: Serious Games for Cultural Heritage

Project Paper: Digital Cultural Heritage in Education, Learning and Training

Contents – Part II

**Innovative Methods on Risk Assessment, Monitoring and Protection
of Cultural Heritage**

Intangible Cultural Heritage Documentation

**Digital Applications for Materials' Preservation and Conservation
in Cultural Heritage**

Visualisation, VR and AR Methods and Applications

The New Era of Museums and Exhibitions: Digital Engagement and Dissemination

Digital Cultural Heritage in Education, Learning and Training

Full Paper: 3D Reconstruction and 3D Modelling

Implementation and Usage Scenarios of a Participatory Platform for Cultural Environments

Zois Koukopoulos and Dimitrios Koukopoulos[✉]

Department of Cultural Heritage Management and New Technologies,
University of Patras, Agrinio, Greece
(zkoukopu,dkoukopoulos)@upatras.gr

Abstract. Raising audience awareness over the creation and evolution of a cultural participatory digital platform is a critical point for its acceptance. The proposed platform adopts user involvement in the content collection level through the implementation of a mobile application easily downloadable to the user's smartphone and the use of a web portal application. Complementary web portal permits the management of the collected content in a trustworthy manner adopting an extended role-based access control model for authorization purposes. Users can formulate private groups to contribute and share content. Platform guarantees the soundness of contributed content through an auditing procedure requested by the contributors and conducted by experts selected randomly. In order to stress the applicability of our platform to various cultural environments, we present a number of usage scenarios targeting various stakeholders from specialists and museum curators to students, teachers and simple enthusiasts aiming in the development of coherent narrations.

Keywords: Participatory platform · Cultural content · Web portal · Mobile application

1 Introduction

Cultural heritage is useful as a means to highlight common origins and achievements among nations around the world. Cultural heritage management tries to reveal and present our common origins and cultural achievements, more than any other way [16]. Through cultural heritage management, international structures like the European Union try to reach the target of Europeanization, the inculcation of the European Idea among the nations of Europe [6]. The explosion of Internet use around the world provides the essential background to amateurs and enthusiasts of culture to search for cultural content or collect and publish their own content [1–3]. This trend poses a series of questions regarding the quality and the usefulness of such content, in the case it is contributed by non-experts. Is the contributed content sound or can it be beneficial to specific communities? Answering these questions is not a simple task. As the volume of digital cultural content rises and the technological resources are evolving in terms of efficiency and availability, the need for cultural data management becomes a priority. New mechanisms and systems need to be proposed and implemented to manage the produced, vast

M. Ioannides et al. (Eds.): EuroMed 2016, Part I, LNCS 10058, pp. 3–14, 2016.
DOI: 10.1007/978-3-319-48496-9_1

amounts of cultural data. Participatory platforms are such systems where data are being contributed by users in smaller or larger amounts, collected, organized and presented to the public. Users can range from established scholars and university professors, to simple enthusiasts of cultural heritage or professionals in the cultural market.

In recent years, several participatory systems are trying to open new ways in cultural heritage digital management [1–3]. Also there are others that exploit the notion of open participation, complementary [6]. The first experience from those systems indicates that not only a participatory system needs to be interactive, dynamic and easy to use, but also to constantly urge users in involving more and more with the platform and integrate new services based on participant feedback. Here we propose a participatory system design oriented to user needs, experts or not, concerning content contribution and authoring. We involve modern mobile devices in the digitization and content collection procedures, along with content visualization functionalities through cultural maps. Our main goal is two-fold: the provision of a learning tool for culture, and a dissemination tool for expert and public communities to communicate cultural content they create or collect in a trustworthy manner.

The proposed system design guided the implementation of Culture Gate, a participatory platform that aspires to become a fundamental digital platform that will receive cultural heritage content from different sources (scientists, artists, the public etc.), preserve and digitize it, organize it in widely accepted ways and present it to the online users in a friendly, modern and innovating manner. By making scientific information public, we allow users to correct, update or enrich cultural content leading in more qualitative data. Our implementation is oriented to satisfy typical usage scenarios concerning cultural content searching, viewing, uploading and authoring, that may be applicable to various groups of users like experts, artists, educators, tour operators, public authorities or simple enthusiasts. Culture Gate takes special care to protect sensitive data (like user credentials and contributed material) through a suitable authorization mechanism based on the extension of role-based access control model (RBAC model [17]).

The platform offers a dedicated smartphone application which the users can use to collect cultural content and store it to the system. This capability offers users the opportunity to capture tangible or intangible cultural content in real-time and share their findings with the community in an open or private manner. Field scientists are extremely benefited by such a service since they could digitize their findings, immediately and store them in a secure environment for further management.

2 Related Work

Participatory digital platforms implement the participatory action research theory in the digital domain [8]. Oomen and Aroyo in [18] propose specific classifications of cultural heritage crowdsourcing platforms: correction and transcription platforms and projects [7], contextualization [9], complementing collections [10], classification [11] and co-curation [12]. There are platforms that support content contribution as a key functionality [1–3], while others support only complementary and occasionally the creation of crowdsourcing exhibitions where any user can be a contributor [6]. Moreover, some platforms host information about tangible cultural content [1, 3] while others deal with intangible content [2] or both [6] and platforms that support mobile applications to view and search content [3, 6], like Muse [3] which hosts native iPad apps for digital libraries with cultural heritage content. Current trends in cultural heritage management platforms dictate the integration of mobile services within participatory platforms [1, 3, 9]. MQUADRO offers a dedicated tablet application [1], Muse hosts native iPad apps for digital libraries with cultural heritage content [3], while an application for android and iPhone is being used in a portal dedicated to storytelling in Denmark [9].

Security is a critical point concerning the public acceptance of a cultural heritage management and dissemination system [4]. An important aspect of security in cultural heritage platforms is the limitation of the user access to sensitive content. An RBAC based authorization mechanism for secure mobile services used in archaeological excavations is presented in [19], while an authorization model for musical heritage archives is described in [20]. A guiding services platform presented in [21] supports trustworthy content dissemination through an extended RBAC model.

Participatory platforms are gaining ground to market sectors like tourism or social sectors like education and sociology. TripAdvisor [13] is a successful participatory platform where users contribute content about sites, locations or businesses that interest tourists and visitors of a place. The amount of information contributed by users is so vast and rich that no dedicated project team would ever accomplish the task of collecting these data. Second Life [14] is a participatory platform that simulates an alternative 3D world where everyone you see is a real person and all content is produced by users. Users interact with each other, solve problems and build a collaborative environment, of mutual learning, achieving the creation a functional society, without supervision of certified professors or teachers [15].

3 System Architecture and Implementation Technologies

Culture Gate is a general purpose platform that implements various services in order to support multiple objectives. Platform design addresses several quality issues like scalability, security, concurrency, integration of third party software, low resource cost and adaptability to several computational systems (mobile devices or traditional computers), in a participatory environment.

- Participation: The design should support multiple user roles with different permission levels that implement a wide range of activities, like content contribution or system monitoring.
- Scalability: The system needs to be able to support new functionalities and procedures in order to offer new services or enrich the existing ones, periodically. A static system is threatened to become out of date very quickly.
- Security: The users that contribute content must be sure that their intellectual property is protected and editable only by themselves. Also the system must protect the daily use, from malicious attacks (bots or hackers).
- Concurrency: As a participatory platform, the design should support multiple users simultaneously.

- Third Party Software Integration: Since the platform wishes to host artwork from artists or experts, the design must be able to support efficiently various software implementations with different technologies.
- Low Cost: The design must use limited resources in equipment, software and human dynamic to become viable and extend its lifecycle.
- Adaptability: The platform should be accessible both from traditional computational systems (desktops, laptop) and mobile devices (smartphones, tablets).

In order to support all the above design goals, the platform uses a modular architecture consisting of several modules (Fig. 1):

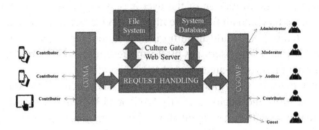

Fig. 1. Culture Gate system architecture

Culture Gate Mobile Application (CGMA). Smartphone application that collects cultural content from indoor or outdoor locations, in real-time and stores it in platform database and file system. CGMA feeds the system with cultural data.

Culture Gate Online Web Portal (CGOWP). Web interface where users can submit content or search and view cultural information. CGOWP presents the cultural content to the broad public.

Web Server. Supports the necessary tools for multiple operations like request handling from CGMA and CGOWP, hosting and managing system database and file system.

Request Handler. Implements scripts that get data from CGMA and CGOWP content contributors perform insert/update/search/delete operations to system database, create responses to send encoded data to CGMA users and displays user requested content.

File System. All files are stored in the platform file system. The files vary from php, html, xml scripts and apache files to directories with audiovisual material from users' contributions (CGMA and CGOWP). This system is isolated from all the other modules, except the handler, which is the only module that has permission to interact with the file system, for security reasons.

System Database. Stores all information concerning application data (including user credentials) and cultural data, contributed by the users.

The system follows RBAC model in order to classify users to several roles/groups (administrator, moderator, auditor, contributor, guest). Each user can have more than one role. Furthermore, platform users can be registered users (moderator, auditor, contributor), simple users (guest) or members of the project team (administrator, moderator). In Table 1, we present user roles, types and their permitted operations.

Table 1. User groups/roles.

Role	Type	Operations
Administrator	Project team	Supervises every technical procedure, checks system integrity, assigns moderator roles to users, administers system database and file system, views all content (published and unpublished), deletes users
Moderator	Project team – registered user	Assigns user roles, creates user private groups, views all content, checks for offensive content and warns or bans users for this purpose
Auditor	Registered user	Views private content after assignment, informs contributors for the required content modifications
Contributor	Registered user	Views public content and private content of his group, uploads content. A contributor can modify only the content he contributes
Guest	Unregistered user	A nomadic user who views and searches public content

Platform supports different types of content (text, audio, images, video and multimedia). Text content can be content description, notes, event announcements, historical background information, theatrical plays and scripts, literary works or reviews and references. Images can be site and artifact pictures or depictions (like drawings, pictures, notes, sketch). Video can be animation or live activities like excavation or a folk dance. Audio content can be narrations, storytelling, interviews and vocal guides. Multimedia files can be a full demo package with all kinds of data types.

The basic entity of contributed content is the cultural item which is characterized by three categories of attributes: content-based, context-based and model-based attributes. Content-based attributes include thematic ones like title and description, and disciplines where the contribution belongs to. Context-based attributes include featured image (contribution's most representative image), files (multimedia files corresponding to the contribution), location (region's geographical coordinates where the contribution was uploaded), digitization equipment (equipment used to collect the data) and date (date and time of the contribution). Model-based attributes include the permitted operations on the specific item by specific user roles (like authoring or content visibility).

Culture Gate platform uses several technologies to implement all its modules: Apache Web Server, PHP scripts, MySQL database, Google Maps API and Android operating system (JAVA, JSON, XML). For the implementation of CGOWP we used a Windows 10, intel core i7-2600, 8 GB RAM at 1866 MHz system. For CGMA implementation we used Android Studio as the IDE, target SDK version 23 and minimum SDK version 8 and Samsung Galaxy Grand Neo to test the resulted application (Fig. 2).

Fig. 2. Cultural listings table schema (MySQL workbench)

4 Platform Services

Platform services are classified in three categories according to the sub-system they refer to: core, mobile and web portal services.

Core Services. *Security:* We propose an extended RBAC model (implemented by Request Handler) for authorization purposes. Platform supports five user roles with different authorization privileges to platform's content (administrator, moderator, auditor, contributor and guest). User passwords are encrypted (PKI) and disclosed only to the user. Several programming techniques are applied to encounter security breaches. Coding techniques used for security reasons are: input validation, compiler warnings heeding, simple security design, default denying, sanitizing data sent to other systems and effective assurance techniques. *Registration:* Creation of a new user account. Users complete fields like username, email, password and discipline. *Moderation:* The platform allows registered users with elevated permissions to monitor the daily procedures and keep the platform live (like monitoring disciplines, CGMA monitoring, cultural information uploading and management). *Authoring:* Guarantees that platform content is sound and up-to-date. After assignment to a specific contribution by the moderator, the auditor checks the validity of the contributed content and informs the contributor for the needed changes. *Group formation:* When a registered user wants to formulate a private group to share content, in a protected manner, with other users, he communicates with a moderator. This user must provide a clear group description (like a class of students that implements an educational virtual tour to a museum) and a list of platform users who will serve as group members. This user will be the group leader and will be responsible for the content each member of the group uploads. This content will be private and restricted only to the group members for viewing. A group member that uploads private content must declare that this content is only available for the group members. A group of colleagues could create a private user group to share real-time content with each other. *Personalization:* The platform displays to a user, information according to his interests. User chooses fields of interest during registration procedure.

Mobile Services. CGMA's main task is to collect and upload digitized cultural content. CGMA offers three different services that can be used by several user groups to store real-time data. *Field service:* Capturing audiovisual content from an outdoor uncharted location (like an excavation point) and sending it with its coordinates and notes to the web server. Users complete fields like: Title, Description, Discipline, Audio/Video/Image Files. CGMA sends geographical data automatically during the uploading procedure. *Street service:* Capturing audiovisual content from an outdoor charted location (like a city street) and sending it with its coordinates and notes to the web server. *Indoor service:* Sending text content related to a tangible cultural item (like an artifact in a museum), along with notes or audiovisual files to the web server.

Web Portal Services. CGOWP supports management, presentation and dissemination services. *Content organization:* When a user uploads content from data submission screens, he makes a series of choices that give semantics to each new record (like discipline). User has the ability to view related content to a specific point in cultural map. *Content viewing:* A user has two choices in order to view content: geographical map or list. *Content searching:* A user has several choices in order to search content: keywords, disciplines and geo-location data or their combinations. Dissemination and User attraction: calendar of events, news, serious games implementation, 3D representations, smartphone applications and time-lapse videos.

5 Usage Scenarios

Culture Gate is a collector, organizer and presenter of cultural heritage content. In order to highlight the platform capabilities, we present specific scenarios based on the used service carrier: web portal or mobile device.

Web Portal Based Scenarios

Guest Searching and Viewing. User accesses a cultural map where he views all content as pins on a geographical map and lists of cultural information, organized per discipline. The map displays every public listing, contributed by registered users, as a pin. Pins are grouped by discipline and can be filtered by keywords or disciplines (one or more). Every discipline has a different color and icon for its pin. Figure 3 displays the cultural map with all information and Fig. 4 shows a filtered version of the map with the keyword "Acropolis" and the discipline "Museology". When the user clicks on a pin, an information box is displayed with some information. If the user clicks on the information he will be transferred to listing's dedicated webpage where he can find all the needed information (Fig. 5).

Fig. 3. Unfiltered view of cultural map

Fig. 4. Filtered view of map with keyword "Acropolis" and discipline "Museology"   **Fig. 5.** "Acropolis Museum" listing page

Registration. Every user can register to Culture Gate by accessing the "User Registration" screen. The user submits credentials (username, password) and information about the discipline he serves mandatory. Optionally, user declares specialty and fields of interest. This procedure is vital for system, to personalize the presented content according to user interests and draw information to formulate the auditor pool.

Authoring. When a registered user makes a content contribution and marks it as "Needs Authoring" then the system initializes the authoring procedure, which is a comprehensive way to check the soundness of platform's content. After contributor request, the content moderator chooses one of the auditors with related specialty randomly to audit the content. If the auditor accepts the invitation, he proceeds to the submitted content checking. Afterwards, the auditor sends the content back to the contributor with the proposed modifications. When the contributor makes the appropriate modifications, the auditor gives his approval for the content to be published as audited. If an auditor rejects invitation, another auditor is chosen.

Moderation. Culture Gate uses a decentralized model to administer platform content and everyday use. Administrator chooses the users that will become moderators from a pool of registered users that have shown interest for this role. According to the assigned duties (like monitoring disciplines or contributed content), the administrator gives the corresponding elevated permissions. For example, if a user is chosen to become a content moderator, the administrator will allow him to moderate contributions, create private user groups or ban users, but he will not be able to moderate content assigned to another moderator.

Registered User Public Content Uploading and Managing. A registered user is permitted to upload cultural content through the "Add Listing" screen. Users contribute content filling out fields like title, description, discipline, featured image, multimedia files, location, date or keywords. Users can click the "Review your Listing" button and see the way the content will be displayed. If the content is compliant to platform's terms and conditions, the information is being published. When the uploading procedure terminates, the content becomes available to the public (Fig. 3).

Registered User Private Content Uploading and Viewing. A registered user that uploads content has full ownership over the content. The user can declare his content public (for everyone to see) or private (can be seen by him or a certain user group). When a registered user wants to formulate a private group to share content, in a protected manner, with other users, he informs a moderator. The user must provide a clear group description (like a class of students that implements an educational virtual tour to a museum) and a list of users who will serve as group members. The first user will be the group leader and will be responsible for the content each member of the group uploads. This content will be private and restricted only to the group members for viewing. A group member that uploads private content must declare that this content is only available for the group members.

Mobile Based Scenarios. CGMA offers an extremely useful functionality to scientists of cultural heritage, especially those working in the field. These experts can capture tangible and intangible cultural content and store it immediately and easily to a web server. This procedure gives them the opportunity to secure their findings, digitize content and preserve it, share their content with colleagues in real-time and exchange information with them. Every new finding, is enriched with several other information, automatically, like the coordinates of the location that the discovery have been made and annotations about the finding that enrich the content of the discovery.

Field Use - Archaeological Excavation Site. A team of archaeologists works on an uncharted area. At least one member of the team has an android smartphone with CGMA installed in it. This smartphone must have an internet connection when CGMA is being used. The user clicks and opens the application. If he has already used the application or has an account, he can sign in immediately. Otherwise he must register using the "Sign Up" screen (Fig. 6) submitting username, password, email and discipline. After signing in the system, the user navigates to "Field Functionality" screen (Fig. 7) and submits contribution title, description and the concerning discipline (in this case "Archaeology"). User can take a photo, record video or audio. When the user clicks the "Send Cultural Data" button, the system sends the collected data along with the excavation point's geographical coordinates to the web server.

Fig. 6. CGMA "Sign Up" screen   **Fig. 7.** CGMA "Field Functionality" screen

Indoor Use - Museum School Visit. A class teacher decides to visit the city museum with his students and communicates with a moderator in order to create a private user group for the class, with him as a group leader. Moreover, he asks from every student to install CGMA to their smartphones and create accounts. The teacher informs the moderator about the user accounts to be added to the user group. When the class visits the museum, the teacher informs the students to sign in Culture Gate and navigate to "Indoor Functionality" screen and start using CGMA's indoor service. He consults them to capture artifacts, make notes stating their point of view and send them to Culture Gate. The teacher can use CGMA to record an audio file with museum's conducted guide. When the visit is over, the teacher accesses the content contributed by students and reviews it. Then, he publishes the content with visibility only to group members. In the next lesson, he will be able to discuss this museum visit with the students and publish the corresponding virtual tour to the public.

Street Use - Cultural Event. A user is watching a religious ceremony in a city street. The user signs in the system and navigates to the "Street Functionality" screen. In order to capture a video he must submit title, description, discipline and click the corresponding button to capture a video. After the video is recorded and stored to the smartphone, it is ready to be transferred along with geographical coordinates to Culture Gate web server by clicking the "Send Cultural Data" button (Fig. 8).

Fig. 8. Religious ceremony in Arta, Greece – video capture

6   Discussion and Future Work

In this work we address the problem of provisioning digital tools that support public participation in evolving cultural projects. Digital tools are implemented through a participatory platform where users collect and disseminate cultural information. Since May 2016 the platform is accessible for the broad public [5]. Web portal services (content organization, viewing, searching, dissemination and user attraction) have been well - received by the rapidly growing Culture Gate Community. Most of platform's core services (access control, registration, moderation, authoring, group formation, personalization) have been successfully implemented and tested, except issues related to intellectual property, which are in design phase. Concerning CGMA, we distributed the application to a group of application developers to express their opinion about several technical issues like network connectivity or big data uploading. Simultaneously, CGMA was distributed to cultural experts to notify us about the application's usability and user friendliness. We plan specific activities for elementary and secondary education to test the acceptance of the proposed platform as an education tool. In this direction we have already come in contact with school teachers. Those activities will give us feedback for the improvement of our system.

Alongside with the platform development strategy, we follow an operational strategy with the formulation of project teams, which consist primarily of interested cultural heritage academic students, which undertake daily tasks and help in maintaining the platform. Culture Gate could be commercially exploited in many ways as it can have a significant social impact in sectors like tourism or cultural heritage market. Museum curators can promote museum collections by uploading information about them to the platform. Tour operators or Public authorities could use Culture Gate to highlight certain cultural heritage spots and attract new clients and tourists, thus helping local and national markets. Organizers of cultural events have the opportunity to advertise their events to an immense and targeted public. Moreover, CGMA could contribute revenue in two different ways: the free version could host advertisements while a premium version with additional features could become available for downloading for a small price. In order to handle intellectual property rights we will enhance our platform with watermarking services for image, audio and video that will be available with a small fee to any contributor upon the uploading of his contribution. For images, we plan to offer a service based on a watermarking scheme that guarantees efficient and fast embedding and detection of watermarks [22]. For MP3 audio files, we will provide a service based on an algorithm that supports watermarks with semantic meaning and it is fast and reliable for online use [23]. For video files, the selection of an efficient scheme will be a goal for future work.

References

1. Lacedelli, S.Z., Pompanin, G.: MQUADRO: a platform model for cultural heritage. In: 104th Annual Conference of the College Art Association, Washington (2016)
2. The Prow. http://www.theprow.org.nz/
3. Muse Platform. http://muse-opensource.org/

4. Arnold, D.: Pasteur's quadrant: cultural heritage as inspiration for basic research. ACM J. Comput. Cult. Heritage **1**(1), 1–10 (2008)
5. Culture Gate Web Portal. http://www.culture-gate.com
6. EUROPEANA. http://strategy2020.europeana.eu/
7. Transcribe Bentham Project. http://blogs.ucl.ac.uk/transcribe-bentham/
8. Rahman, M.A.: People's Self-development: Perspectives on Participatory Action Research: A Journey Through Experience. Zed Books, London (1993)
9. Stories of Denmark. http://www.kulturarv.dk/1001fortaellinger/en_GB
10. UK_Soundmap Project. http://sounds.bl.uk/sound-maps/uk-soundmap
11. Flickr: The Commons. https://www.flickr.com/commons
12. Click! A Crowd-Curated Exhibition. https://www.brooklynmuseum.org/exhibitions/click/
13. TripAdvisor. http://www.tripadvisor.com
14. Second Life. http://secondlife.com/
15. Ondrejka, C.: Education unleashed: participatory culture, education, and innovation in second life. In: Salen, K. (ed.) The Ecology of Games: Connecting Youth, Games, and Learning, pp. 229–252. MIT Press, Cambridge (2008)
16. Michigan State University: Department of Anthropology Cultural Heritage Informatics Initiative (2010). http://chi.anthropology.msu.edu/program/
17. Ferraiolo, D., Kuhn, R.: Role-based access controls. In: 15th NIST-NCNC National Computer Security Conference, Baltimore, pp. 554–563 (1992)
18. Oomen, J., Aroyo, L.: Crowdsourcing in the cultural heritage domain: opportunities and challenges. In: 5th International Conference on Communities and Technologies, pp. 138–149. ACM Press, Brisbane (2011)
19. Koukopoulos, D., Tsolis, D., Gazis, M., Skoulikari, A.I.: Secure mobile services for on-going archaeological excavations management and dissemination. In: 6th International Conference of Information, Intelligence, Systems and Applications, pp. 1–6. IEEE Press, Kerkyra (2015)
20. Koukopoulos, D., Tsolis, D., Heliades, G.: Ionian music archive: application of digitization, management and dissemination technologies for musical cultural heritage. In: 5th International Conference of Information, Intelligence, Systems and Applications, pp. 239–244. IEEE Press, Chania (2014)
21. Koukopoulos, D., Styliaras, G.: Design of trustworthy smartphone-based multimedia services in cultural environments. Electron. Commer. Res. **13**(2), 129–150 (2013)
22. Tsolis, D., Sioutas, S., Papatheodorou, T.: A multimedia application for watermarking digital images based on a content based image retrieval technique. Multimedia Tools Appl. **47**(3), 581–597 (2010)
23. Koukopoulos, D., Stamatiou, Y.: An efficient watermarking method for MP3 audio files. In: International Enformatika Conference, pp. 154–159. Enformatika, Prague (2005)

Benchmarking Close-range Structure from Motion 3D Reconstruction Software Under Varying Capturing Conditions

Ivan Nikolov[(✉)] and Claus Madsen

Architecture, Design and Media Technology, Aalborg University,
Rendsburggade 14, 9000 Aalborg, Denmark
{iani,cbm}@create.aau.dk
http://www.aau.dk/

Abstract. Structure from Motion 3D reconstruction has become widely used in recent years in a number of fields such as industrial surface inspection, archeology, cultural heritage preservation and geomapping. A number of software solutions have been released using variations of this technique. In this paper we analyse the state of the art of these software applications, by comparing the resultant 3D meshes qualitatively and quantitatively. We propose a number of testing scenarios using different lighting conditions, camera positions and image acquisition methods for the best in-depth analysis and discuss the results, the overall performance and the problems present in each software. We employ distance and roughness metrics for evaluating the final reconstruction results.

Keywords: Multi-view 3D reconstruction · Structure from Motion (SfM) · Photogrammetry · Software comparison · Benchmark

1 Introduction

Structure from Motion (SfM) for 3D reconstruction has come a long way in recent years. The technology is at a point where a multitude of commercial and free packages exist, enabling non-experts to quickly and easily capture high quality models from uncalibrated images. An example is given in Fig. 1.

Most of these packages are used for landscape reconstruction, creation of orthomosaics and large scale reconstructions. They can be also used for close-range reconstructions. This makes them perfect for use in cultural heritage preservation, artifact digitalization, virtual museums and others. However, many of these solutions come with high initial and upkeep monetary costs. This makes choosing the one most suitable for a specific task an important first step for each project relying on 3D reconstruction - both in result accuracy, resource requirements and performance across varying conditions. Such an endeavour can require a large investment of time. This is why in our paper we provide an in-depth overview of the newest and most widely used commercial software

© Springer International Publishing AG 2016
M. Ioannides et al. (Eds.): EuroMed 2016, Part I, LNCS 10058, pp. 15–26, 2016.
DOI: 10.1007/978-3-319-48496-9_2

Fig. 1. Example of 4 out of N input images, taken from different view points and the resulting camera position triangulation and dense point cloud creation. The view is from Agisoft PhotoScan.

solution tested across various conditions. We concentrate on close-range SfM, as opposed to aerial or long-range.

Six commercial 3D reconstruction software solutions are chosen for testing in the paper. Each of the solutions takes an unordered list of images as input, extracts features and creates a sparse point cloud, triangulating the camera positions. A dense point cloud and a mesh are created by interpolating the sparse point cloud. Texture of the reconstructed object is also created.

Six different objects are used for the reconstructions, depicted in Fig. 2. They are selected according to their varying reconstruction difficulty and different problems that they present like textureless surfaces, repeatable patterns, symmetrical objects, glossiness, etc. Objects are scanned with a white light scanner for evaluating the meshes produced by the SfM packages.

Six different scenarios are tested. These scenarios cover different lighting, positioning and shooting setups. These experiments show that the environmental conditions have a noticeable impact on the final reconstruction and affect some software solutions more than others.

For verifying the accuracy of the output meshes from the different programs, two qualitative methods are chosen: (1) calculating the signed distance between ground truth objects and the reconstructions; (2) comparing the local roughness profiles between the ground truth objects and the reconstructions. The results show that some of the tested packages have more problems reconstructing glossy, symmetrical and textureless surfaces, than others, resulting in complete failures. Some programs sacrifice details for a less noisy final mesh, while others capture more detail, but are very sensitive to noise. A moving camera setup with uniform lighting also gives higher reconstruction accuracy than a turntable setup.

2   Related Work

SfM is just one of many techniques for 3D reconstruction of objects and artifacts. Other techniques are beyond the scope of the paper, but for a quick overview the work in stereo-vision reconstruction [13], structured light [8] or laser scanning [14] is available for reference.

For SfM reconstruction most resources for benchmarks and comparisons are either from archaeological context [15] or from geomapping context [16]. These give valuable information, but are mostly focused on one type of surfaces and

Table 1. Tested software solutions with some of their most important characteristics. In the output column the shortened names denote: dense point cloud (DPC), sparse point cloud (SPC). The price is given for both standard and pro versions. Bolded font denotes the one used for testing.

Program	Outputs	Online/Offline	OS	Scripting	Price (USD)
ContextCapture	Mesh/Texture/DPC	Offline	Win	Yes	N/A
Memento	Mesh/Texture	Online/Offline	Win/Mac	No	**Free**/190 annual
PhotoScan	Mesh/Texture/SPC/DPC	Offline	Win/Mac/Linux	Yes	**179**/3499
Reality Capture	Mesh/Texture/SPC/DPC	Offline	Win	Yes	**110**/8351 annual
3DF Zephyr	Mesh/Texture/SPC/DPC	Offline	Win	No	**199**/3200
Pix4D	Mesh/Texture/DPC	Offline	Win/Mac	No	**3222** annual

objects to reconstruct under a more limited set of environment conditions. Other resources [9,17] give more in-depth comparison using both their own datasets and freely available ones, but lack the comparison for a larger number of software solutions.

3   Tested Software

We have chosen six of the state of the art software packages for 3D reconstruction. These products are *Agisoft PhotoScan Pro* [3], *Bentley ContextCapture* [1], *Autodesk Memento (ReMake)* [2], *Pix4D* [5], *3Dflow 3DF Zephyr Pro* [6] and *Reality Capture* [4]. For more information on some of the important features each of the selected software solutions has, please refer to Table 1. The prices are subject to change and are given as they are in the time of writing this paper and converted to dollars. In the output column four of the most widely used ones for close-range photogrammetry are given to preserve space - 3D mesh, texture, sparse point cloud, dense point cloud. Additional outputs like orthophotos, orthomosaic, fly-through videos, depth and normal maps, etc. are supported by many of the programs, but are out of the scope of this paper.

4   Datasets

The six chosen objects are shown in Fig. 2. These objects are selected based on a number of criteria concerning the properties of the materials that they are made of. These criteria are used to judge the capability of each software to handle different difficult cases, which are considered weak points for SfM. The criteria are as follows - *glossy/smooth surfaces, monochrome colors, very dark/black color, repeating patterns, partial occlusions, symmetrical surfaces*. They may result in failures in reconstruction, decreased overall accuracy, cause holes and noise in the resultant point clouds and mesh [20,21].

As an initial observation the objects are divided into two groups depending on their perceived reconstruction difficulty. The easy to reconstruct objects - angel statue, sea vase and bird bath and the hard to reconstruct objects - black vase, plastic vase and owl statue. The angel statue and sea vase are perceived as easy because they have a lot of surface detail and features, both global and local, which should make them easy to reconstruct by all the programs. They also have some partial self occlusion, which will be tested. The bird bath is also feature rich and has both very smooth and glossy surface parts, as well as rough ones. The black and plastic vases are perceived as hard, because of their color, glossiness and repeated patterns. The owl statue is chosen as an intermediate object, which has a lot of glossiness and feature poor parts, as well as non-glossy more feature-rich ones.

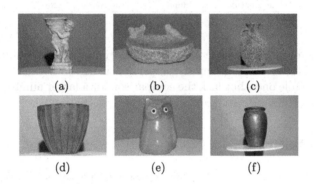

Fig. 2. Testing objects: (a) angel statue, (b) bird bath, (c) sea vase, (d) plastic vase, (e) owl statue, (f) black vase. Typical size of the objects is between 25 and 60 cm

The input images are taken using a *Canon 6D* camera at maximum resolution of *5472 × 3648*. A zoom lens with focal length of 70–300 mm is used to accommodate the different zoom levels needed for the different objects. The reconstructions are carried out on a stand alone laptop equipped with *Intel Core i7 - 4710HQ at 2.50 GHz, 16 Gb of RAM and a GeForce GTX 970M*. The operating system is Windows 8.1. Each of the six objects has been scanned with a high resolution, high accuracy white light scanner from *Aicon*. These scans are considered detailed enough to be used as a benchmark for the performance. To demonstrate the accuracy and detail of the scans, a cube with known dimensions is also scanned and the measurement of the 3D model's sides are compared to the real world ones. The two differ by an average of 1.03 mm/1.12 mm/0.93 mm in width/height/depth. Henceforth these scans will be referred to as ground truth objects, while the outputs from each of the tested programs will be referred to as reconstructed objects.

5   Testing Scenarios and Results

5.1   Main Test Scenario

All six objects are used in the initial test scenario, together with all the tested programs. The distance between the reconstructed and ground truth objects is calculated, together with the local roughness. The scenario aims to determine how are the selected programs fairing when tested with both easy and hard to reconstruct objects, as well as noting their speed, accuracy and robustness against noise. The test also aims to determine the object factors which make reconstruction hardest for each of the programs.

The test scenario uses photos captured in an indoor controlled environment. The image capturing algorithm is as follows - the captured object is positioned on a turntable; the camera on a tripod is facing the object and is lower than it for capturing the first set of images at lower angle; one light is positioned on a stand above the camera so it shines directly at object; a photo is taken and the turntable is turned 20°; this is done 18 times, so the object is captured from all sides; the camera on the tripod is then repositioned higher two times, each time 18 more photos are taken; a total of 54 photos of the three different height sets. The $CanonD6$ camera is used for taking photos as it gives high detail photos, without straining the hardware of the testing machine.

The total processing time of creating the 3D model is noted for each program. For the online version of Memento, the processing time does not give a proper estimate of the working time. It is given just for a more full presentation of the data. This data is given in Table 2. A course visual inspection is done on the created model, focusing on severe problems with the objects.

Table 2. Processing time in seconds for each of the six objects by the tested software solutions. Models which contain problems like missing sides, broken parts, floating noise, etc. are marked with red. Models which could not be reconstructed are given an N/A notation.

Program	Angel	Bird bath	Owl	Sea vase	Plastic vase	Black vase
ContextCapture	2820 s	3600 s	N/A	3780 s	3060 s	N/A
Memento Online	4860 s	4920 s	5160 s	4440 s	4260 s	5340 s
PhotoScan	4020 s	4500 s	3780 s	4560 s	4740 s	3480 s
RealityCapture	5220 s	6480 s	N/A	6720 s	2820 s	N/A
3DF Zephyr	3720 s	4440 s	4140 s	4860 s	3060 s	4680 s
Pix4D	4140 s	3240 s	N/A	4860 s	3960 s	3720 s
Memento Offline	11520 s	9360 s	7140 s	10320 s	7980 s	N/A

All packages, except Memento offline have comparable processing times, which depend on the complexity of the reconstructed object. Memento online, PhotoScan and 3DF Zephyr could reconstruct all objects, while ContextCapture, Reality Capture and Pix4D experienced the most problems. The coarse visual inspection is followed by a more qualitative inspection, using the ground truth scanner data for comparison. The idea suggested by Schning and Heidemann [17] is used for this part of the test scenario. In their paper they conclude that each tested program produces 3D models and point clouds of different density, which also may contain parts of the background or noise particles. Therefore, it is better to use the reconstructed models as reference and compare the ground truth data to each, noting the difference. In addition their idea of using the meshes for comparison is used, as opposed to using the point cloud. This gives the possibility to test signed distances using the model's pre-calculated normals.

The comparison between the reconstruction and the scanned data is done using the free open source software *CloudCompare* [7]. The reconstructed models are scaled to the absolute scale of the ground truth and registered to it using an iterative closest point algorithm (ICP) by Besl and McKay [18]. Once the models are registered the distances between the triangles of the reconstructions and the ground truth is calculated. Using the normals of the meshes the distance is calculated as signed. These distances are visualized as pseudo color heat map. The pseudo color maps for the angel statue can be seen in Fig. 3. The maps are filtered removing distances outside the interval of $[-0.3\,\text{mm}; 0.3\,\text{mm}]$, for easier visualization. From the distances, the mean and standard deviation of the distance distribution for the whole object are calculated. A Gaussian normal distribution is assumed for the modelling of the distance distribution between the ground truth and the reconstruction. The mean and standard deviation are given in Table 3 for the easy to reconstruct objects - angel statue, bird bath and sea vase, together with the Gaussian distributions for them in Fig. 4. For the hard to reconstruct objects - the plastic vase, owl and black vase the data is given in Table 4 and Fig. 5, respectively.

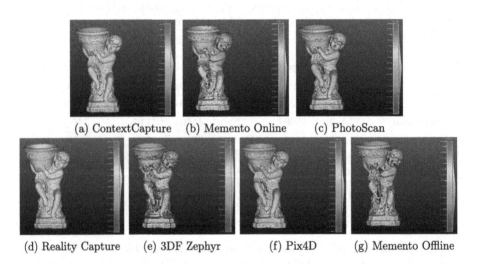

(a) ContextCapture   (b) Memento Online   (c) PhotoScan

(d) Reality Capture   (e) 3DF Zephyr   (f) Pix4D   (g) Memento Offline

Fig. 3. Pseudo color distance maps between the ground truth and the reconstructed objects. Red colors indicate distances above the ground truth, blue colors indicate distances below the ground truth and green colors indicate where the surfaces coincide. (Color figure online)

Table 3. Mean value (μ) in mm and standard deviation (σ) in mm^2 of the distance metric for each software solution for the three objects selected as easy to reconstruct

	Angel	Bird bath	Sea vase
	Mean/Variance	Mean/Variance	Mean/Variance
ContextCapture	−0.024/0.703	−0.030/0.588	−0.245/2.016
Memento Online	−0.089/0.438	−0.039/0.382	−0.408/2.277
PhotoScan	−0.109/0.805	0.034/0.175	−0.463/2.321
Reality Capture	−0.038/0.486	−0.006/0.143	−0.481/2.421
3DF Zephyr	−0.040/1.020	−0.045/1.537	−0.911/3.514
Pix4D	−0.194/1.124	−0.060/0.668	−0.425/2.419
Memento Offline	−0.080/0.569	−0.046/0.40	−0.255/2.983

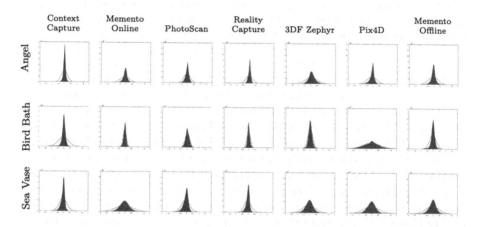

Fig. 4. Histograms of the Gaussian distribution characterizing the distances between the ground truths and the three easy objects. All the histograms are scaled the same.

Table 4. Mean value (μ) in mm and standard deviation (σ) in mm^2 of the distance metric for each software solution for the three objects selected as hard to reconstruct

	Plastic vase	Owl	Black vase
	Mean/Variance	Mean/Variance	Mean/Variance
ContextCapture	−2.512/10.601	N/A	N/A
Memento Online	−3.450/6.697	−0.937/3.318	−4.549/5.886
PhotoScan	−3.791/7.027	0.371/6.806	−4.331/5.758
Reality Capture	−4.395/7.222	N/A	N/A
3DF Zephyr	−4.814/7.471	0.169/3.191	−4.035/5.933
Pix4D	−3.782/7.187	N/A	−4.794/6.027
Memento Offline	−5.074/7.429	−0.929/0.977	N/A

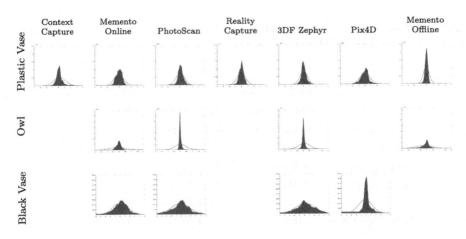

Fig. 5. Histograms of the Gaussian distribution characterizing the distances between the ground truths and the three hard objects. The missing histograms are programs which failed to reconstruct the object. All the histograms are scaled the same.

The initial speculation dividing the objects into easy and hard ones is proven by the amount of reconstruction failures. Both the black vase and the owl statue, experience much higher number of failures, compared to the other objects. The plastic vase fairs better, but because of its symmetrical featureless and dark surface, the reconstruction suffers from improperly placed geometry. This can also be seen from the Gaussian histogram distributions in Fig. 5, where the distributions for both the black vase and the plastic vase are much wider, showing larger divination distances from the ground truth. The owl statue has less noisy histogram, but it suffers from holes in the reconstruction. ContextCapture and Reality Capture demonstrate the overall smallest mean and variance deviations from the ground truth for the easy objects, but both programs completely or partially fail when the surfaces are not optimal. 3DF Zephyr, Memento Online and PhotoScan on the other hand are much more consistent and have a more graceful degradation of performance, but tend to miss smaller details and have an overall high variance in the distance distribution. From here another observation can be made - the programs can be roughly divided into ones that capture a lot of small detail at the price of noise and easier failures - Context Capture, Reality Capture, Memento Offline and the ones that are more consistent and robust, but fail to capture details - Memento Online, 3DF Zephyr, PhotoScan. Pix4D is mainly aimed at aerial photos and this clearly shows, as the program is much noisier in all instances.

To determine the amount of noise and over-smoothing of features in the reconstructions compared to the ground truth, a second metric is introduced. The local roughness of both the reconstructions and the ground truth is calculated using the Gaussian curvature of the models, which is normalized to give proper weights to rough patches and smooth patches near edges. The method is introduced by Wang et al. [19] for assessment of mesh visual quality.

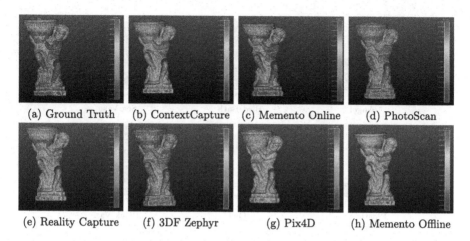

(a) Ground Truth   (b) ContextCapture   (c) Memento Online   (d) PhotoScan

(e) Reality Capture   (f) 3DF Zephyr   (g) Pix4D   (h) Memento Offline

Fig. 6. Pseudo color roughness maps of the ground truth and reconstructed meshes. The colors go from red to blue through green, depending on how rough the surface is. (Color figure online)

The method is useful in the case of our paper as it generates an accurate roughness map, which can give both visual and more quantitative information for the success of the reconstruction. The roughness map is also visualized as a pseudo color map, which is given in Fig. 6.

From the local roughness map, the histograms of both the ground truth and the reconstructions is calculated. Using these histograms the Kullback-Leibler distances [22] between the ground truth and reconstructions are calculated. This gives a measurement of the similarity between the two, which penalizes deviations from the roughness of the ground truth both caused by introduction of noise in the reconstructed mesh and in over-smoothing details in it. Figure 7 has the results from the roughness histogram distances, where smaller values give more faithful reconstructions, roughness-wise.

The results from the roughness metric support the division of the programs. Pix4D introduces a lot of noise and smooths details. This can be seen in both Figs. 6 and 7, where it has clear disadvantage in many of the cases. Figure 6 also shows that Pix4D, Memento Offline and Reality Capture have introduced a lot of noise on the smoother parts of the angel, compared to the ground truth, like the stomach and legs, while Memento Online, 3DF Zephyr and PhotoScan have smoothed out small features in the face and hair of the angel. Memento Offline, Reality Capture and PhotoScan manage to capture most of the detail on the easier to reconstruct objects like the angel and the bird bath, without introducing too much noise as evidenced by the smaller histogram distances. However they fail on the smoother objects like the plastic vase and the owl, where they introduce uncertainty noise. Memento Online and 3DF Zephyr tend to over-smooth the surfaces as evidenced by the bar chart of the sea vase.

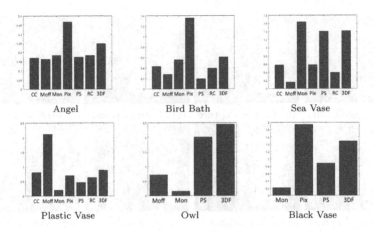

Angel   Bird Bath   Sea Vase

Plastic Vase   Owl   Black Vase

Fig. 7. Bar chart visualizing the calculated Kullback-Leibler distances between the roughness histogram of the ground truth and the reconstructed objects. The tested software is denoted with short names - *Context Capture (CC)*, *Memento Online (Mon)*, *PhotoScan(PS)*, *Reality Capture (RC)*, *3DF Zephyr (3df)*, *Pix4d (Pix)* and *Memento Offline (Moff)*.

5.2 Follow Up Test Scenarios

One of the best performing objects - the bird bath is tested in a number of follow up scenarios under different capturing conditions. This is done to determine the effect of capturing conditions on the reconstruction results. Five follow up experiments are carried out focusing on different combinations of conditions. First tested condition is the effect of rotating the camera to capture images from different views, as opposed to using a turntable to rotate the object and keep the camera stationary. This test aims to assess if a moving background and completely static lighting will help with reconstruction process, as opposed to the lighting which "moved" with the object in the case of using a turntable. The second tested condition is using multiple light sources for a more even lighting, as opposed to one directional light. The third condition is using different number of photo positions, combined into bands of photos, with varying height. Five and three bands of photos are created. The first two contain 18 photos each taken in 20° intervals, the next two contain 9 photos in 40° and the final one contain 4 images. The setup also aims to test if introducing information from more angles can help the feature point matching algorithm of the tested software solutions. The same analysis pipeline is used as with the main experiment, using the ground truth scans to compare with. The results from the different combination of conditions are given in Table 5.

The tests show that using static lighting and moving background without a turntable yields a higher accuracy, with lower mean and standard deviation values, compared to the turntable results. There is also a difference between using multiple light sources and just one directional one, with the latter introducing more noise, which can be seen by the higher standard deviation in the table

Table 5. Mean value (μ) in mm and standard deviation (σ) in mm^2 of the distance metric for the bird bath object for each of the tested software solution from the five tested shooting scenarios.

	No turntable		Turntable		
	Multiple lights		One light	Multiple lights	
	Five bands	Three bands	Five bands	Five bands	Three bands
	$(\mu)/(\sigma)$	$(\mu)/(\sigma)$	$(\mu)/(\sigma)$	$(\mu)/(\sigma)$	$(\mu)/(\sigma)$
ContextCapture	$-7.167/13.289$	$-4.147/8.052$	N/A	N/A	N/A
Memento	$-0.209/2.028$	$-0.094/1.306$	$-0.366/2.148$	$-0.947/3.826$	$-0.309/2.305$
PhotoScan	$-0.283/2.312$	$-0.240/2.685$	$0.206/1.982$	$-0.212/2.410$	$-0.167/1.159$
Reality Capture	$-0.031/0.284$	$-0.014/0.689$	N/A	$0.108/1.710$	N/A
3DF Zephyr	$-0.039/0.584$	$0.011/0.411$	$-0.308/2.035$	$-0.372/2.712$	$-0.165/0.922$
Pix4D	$-0.169/0.407$	$-0.166/1.911$	$-5.023/12.401$	$-0.204/1.520$	$0.061/1.674$
Memento Offline	$-0.105/1.355$	$-0.071/1.118$	$-1.135/4.253$	$-0.389/2.262$	$-0.114/1.552$

above. This shows that if higher accuracy is necessary, a capturing process without a turntable and with uniform lighting and more diverce camera positions need to be used, even if this will cost more time and resources.

6   Conclusion and Future Work

Our paper presents a head to head comparison of the state of the art SfM 3D reconstruction software solutions. As part of the research we tested six programs - ContextCapture, PhotoScan, Memento, Reality Capture, Pix4D and 3DF Zephyr. We tests the programs on both a variety of challenging objects and on images taken from different capturing conditions. Reconstruction results were evaluated against ground truth objects on the basis of distance measurement and roughness comparison.

We demonstrated that programs can be roughly divided in two groups - ones that are more robust to sub-optimal objects and capturing conditions, but do not manage to capture smaller details and ones that can capture high amount of details, but degrade in performance and introduce a lot of noise, once the optimal conditions are not met. Additionally we show that using a turntable can have a negative effect on the accuracy of the reconstructed objects, as well as using a single light source. For optimal capture conditions a moving camera, multiple lights and images taken from multiple locations and angles are recommended.

As an extension to this paper we propose introducing prior information to the programs like - camera positions, feature points, markers, etc., as well as combining multiple software solutions in a pipeline for achieving better results and helping failed reconstruction attempts on hard to reconstruct objects.

References

1. Bentley: ContextCapture, May 2016. https://www.bentley.com/en/products/brands/contextcapture
2. Autodesk: ReMake, May 2016. https://remake.autodesk.com/about

3. Agisoft: PhotoScan, May 2016. http://www.agisoft.com/
4. CapturingReality: Reality Capture, May 2016. https://www.capturingreality.com/
5. Pix4D, May 2016. https://pix4d.com/
6. 3DFlow: 3DF Zephyr, May 2016. http://www.3dflow.net/
7. CloudCompare, May 2016. http://www.cloudcompare.org/
8. Izadi, S., Kim, D., Hilliges, O., Molyneaux, D., Newcombe, R., Kohli, P., Fitzgibbon, A.: KinectFusion: real-time 3D reconstruction and interaction using a moving depth camera. In: Proceedings of the 24th Annual ACM Symposium on User Interface Software and Technology, pp. 559–568. ACM (2011)
9. Singh, S.P., Jain, K., Mandla, V.R.: 3D scene reconstruction from video camera for virtual 3D city modeling. Am. J. Eng. Res. 3(1), 140–148 (2014)
10. Smith, M.W., Carrivick, J.L., Quincey, D.J.: Structure from motion photogrammetry in physical geography. In: Progress in Physical Geography (2015)
11. Yilmaz, O., Karakus, F. Stereo and Kinect fusion for continuous 3D reconstruction and visual odometry. In: 2013 International Conference on Electronics, Computer and Computation (ICECCO), pp. 115–118. IEEE (2013)
12. Schning, J., Heidemann, G.: Taxonomy of 3D sensors. Argos 3, P100 (2016). VISIApp
13. Ahmadabadian, A.H., Robson, S., Boehm, J., Shortis, M., Wenzel, K., Fritsch, D.: A comparison of dense matching algorithms for scaled surface reconstruction using stereo camera rigs. ISPRS J. Photogram. Remote Sens. 78, 157–167 (2013)
14. Kaartinen, H., Hyypp, J., Kukko, A., Jaakkola, A., Hyypp, H.: Benchmarking the performance of mobile laser scanning systems using a permanent test field. Sensors 12(9), 12814–12835 (2012)
15. Nex, F., Gerke, M., Remondino, F., Przybilla, H.J., Bumker, M., Zurhorst, A.: ISPRS benchmark for multi-platform photogrammetry. ISPRS Ann. Photogram. Remote Sens. Spat. Inf. Sci. 2(3), 135 (2015)
16. Koutsoudis, A., Vidmar, B., Ioannakis, G., Arnaoutoglou, F., Pavlidis, G., Chamzas, C.: Multi-image 3D reconstruction data evaluation. J. Cult. Heritage 15(1), 73–79 (2014)
17. Schning, J., Heidemann, G.: Evaluation of multi-view 3D reconstruction software. In: Azzopardi, G., Petkov, N. (eds.) CAIP 2015. LNCS, vol. 9257, pp. 450–461. Springer, Switzerland (2015). doi:10.1007/978-3-319-23117-4_39
18. Besl, P.J., McKay, N.D.: Method for registration of 3-D shapes. In: Robotics-DL tentative, International Society for Optics and Photonics, pp. 586–606 (1992)
19. Wang, K., Torkhani, F., Montanvert, A.: A fast roughness-based approach to the assessment of 3D mesh visual quality. Comput. Graph. 36(7), 808–818 (2012)
20. Guidi, G., Gonizzi, S., Micoli, L.L.: Image pre-processing for optimizing automated photogrammetry performances. ISPRS Ann. Photogram. Remote Sens. Spat. Inf. Sci. 2(5), 145 (2014)
21. Nicolae, C., Nocerino, E., Menna, F., Remondino, F.: Photogrammetry applied to problematic artefacts. Int. Arch. Photogram. Remote Sens. Spat. Inf. Sci. 40(5), 451 (2014)
22. Kullback, S., Leibler, R.A.: On information and sufficiency. Ann. Math. Stat. 22(1), 79–86 (1951)

Proportional Systems in the Design of the Cathedral of St. George of the Greeks, Cyprus

Douglas Cawthorne[✉] and Romylos Irodotou

The Digital Building Heritage Group, De Montfort University, The Gateway,
Leicester, LE1 9BH, UK
DCawthorne@dmu.ac.uk, romilosh@msn.com

Abstract. The cathedral of St. George of the Greeks was built in the 14th–15th c. in Famagusta, Cyprus to accommodate the religious needs of the Greek orthodox community living under a Frankish aristocracy. Its design is a hybrid of western European and Greek orthodox architectural traditions which reflect the political and social circumstances of its creation. This paper examines the degree to which the underlying design methods employed can be extrapolated from the physical remains of the building, the historical sources bearing upon its interpretation and comparisons with related structures. Results are presented of a recent (2016) photogrammetric survey of the building and a new digital reconstruction of the church derived from it. These are used to quantify, assess and illustrate a three dimensional armature of regulatory proportions which it is proposed for reasons of ecclesiastical philosophy and practical execution, were employed to shape the building's physical form.

Keywords: Proportions · Medieval · Architecture · Photogrammetry · Geometry · Masons · Pell Numbers · Root two · Armature

1 Introduction

The Cathedral of St. George of the Greeks is the largest Orthodox Church from the Lusignan period (circa 1191–1489) in Cyprus and is of an architectural style that might best be described as Franco-Byzantine. Now ruinous it was begun probably in the mid to late fourteenth century as an addition to the much older and smaller Hagios Epiphanios which adjoins it on the south side. St George's can be viewed as an orthodox alternative and some might say a competitor to the Latin cathedral of St. Nicholas, which is situated a mere 150 m away. St George's combination of a Latin basilica and sculptural detailing with Byzantine centralized planning and byzantine religious art raises a number of questions about its provenance and the motivations and preoccupations of its architects. In this regard the circumstances of its invention are germane. Until the Crusades in the twelfth century AD medieval Cyprus was culturally and religiously Byzantine albeit with a substantial Arab influence. This changed in the 1190's when the English King Richard I gave the island as a fiefdom to Guy de Lusignan a long time vassal who had been ousted from his position as king of Jerusalem after the death of his wife Sybilla [1]. Although described by his peers as "simple and unsophisticated" ("simplex et minus

© Springer International Publishing AG 2016
M. Ioannides et al. (Eds.): EuroMed 2016, Part I, LNCS 10058, pp. 27–38, 2016.
DOI: 10.1007/978-3-319-48496-9_3

astutus") [2] Guy de Lusignan succeeded in holding Cyprus by means of a series of military and political stratagems (Fig. 1).

Fig. 1. Left - the West end of the Cathedral of St George of the Greeks showing the rose window/ oculus. Right - the East end of the Cathedral showing the three apses, lancet windows and flying buttresses supporting the clerestory.

In doing so he founded a dynasty of Frankish rulers and fundamentally recast Cypriot society in a European feudal mold. Guy de Lusignan died in 1194 and was succeeded by his brother Amaury who obtained a crown from the Holy Roman Emperor, Henry VI becoming in 1197 the first Lusignan king of Cyprus. Of importance here is that Amaury took steps to displace the Orthodox Church by introducing the Roman communion, a process that was continued by his successors with papal assistance. Cyprus became the center of European trade with Africa and Asia after the fall of Acre in 1291 and this brought the kings of Cyprus into conflict with Italian merchants who dominated trade in the eastern Mediterranean. This led to a Genoese occupation of Famagusta in 1372. The kingdom was then made a tributary to the Mameluke state in 1426 and the succeeding monarchs gradually lost almost all independence until the last Queen, Catherine Cornaro, was forced to sell the island to Venice in 1472. The Genoese occupation of Famagusta from 1372 and later the Venetian Republic from 1472 allowed the Orthodox Church to regain a position it did not have during the feudal kingdom of the Lusignans, thus despite the absence of evidence regarding its foundation and commissioning, it has generally been assumed that the building of St George of the Greeks was started during or shortly after this recrudescence of Eastern Orthodoxy in the mid-fourteenth century under the influence of the Genoese [3]. However, as Jeffery noted of this period in Famagusta's history in 1918 *"not a single monument of importance can be identified with any certainty as belonging to the period of the Genoese Occupation of the city"* [4, p. 103]. It is within this prolonged condition of uncertainty that we approached research into the intentions of the architects of the cathedral of St George of the Greeks.

2   The Surviving Fabric of St George of the Greeks

The Cathedral of St George of the Greeks is in a ruinous, roofless condition and lies in the south eastern quarter of the old walled city of Famagusta, close to the Latin Cathedral of St. Nicholas. Unlike St. Nicholas's which is still in use, now as a mosque, St George's retains some of its original internal wall decoration and is largely unmodified, since it was severely damaged by an earthquake in 1735 and has been a recorded as ruin for at least the past one hundred and fifty years. Over this period it has received intermittent academic attention. It was noted by the Marquis de Vogüé and Baron Emmanuel Guillaume Rey in 1860, and was visited by the British architects Edward I' Anson and Sydney Vacher in 1882–1883 though it was drawings of the West and South elevations of the Cathedral of St Nicholas in Famagusta that Vacher exhibited at the Royal Academy in 1882. It was not until 1900 that the physical remains of the Cathedral of St George of the Greeks was first reported to scholarly audiences by the French architectural historian Camille Enlart who visited Cyprus in 1896 under the auspices of the Ministère de l'Instruction Publique et des Beaux-Arts. He drew several medieval structures dating from the period of the Crusades (including St George of the Greeks) from which were produced engravings which were published in his *L'art gothique et la renaissance en Chypre* [5]. In 1919 George Everett Jeffery published an account of the building noting that both St Nicholas and St George were *"were undoubtedly erected between the years 1373 and 1571"* [4] therefore between the start of the Genoese occupation and the end of Venetian rule, a view which still persists in many quarters. It should be noted that both Enlart and Jeffery were not able to record the cathedral's lower details fully, as it was still covered with debris from the collapsed vaults [6, p. 169]. The basic plan layout of St. George comprises a nave divided from two side aisles of equal length by two rows of four columns unequally spaced such that a square is defined by four columns at the midpoint of the nave. At the eastern end of the nave and each aisle there is a semicircular apse covered by semi domes that formed the raised sanctuary or bema. Flying buttresses supported the upper clerestory walls of the main aisle and it is believed a hemispherical dome on a short cylindrical tower existed above the central crossing, which was observed and drawn by Cornelis De Bruyn in 1683 [7, pp. 185–186, Fig. 25]. The austere, unarticulated external wall surfaces at the east end are pierced only by two-centered arch windows. The western end of the church, with the three doorways still retains a rose window above the central one. The building is made entirely from high quality ashlar limestone masonry. Stylistically it has been argued that St George's presents closer parallels with churches in the Crusader mainland states than with Frankish or German counterparts in mainland Europe, which if true may reflect the origins of the citizens its served [8, pp. 309–310].

3 The Photogrammetric Survey

Several methods exist for the accurate capture of the 3D form of buildings [9]. Unlike laser scanning which was considered as an alternative means of data capture for this project [10, pp. 1–25] stereo photogrammetry requires little specialist equipment and so does not require special customs security clearance or transportation and tends to take less time. It does require careful planning and execution on the ground but for the purposes of this study its advantages of simplicity were overriding factors in its selection as the preferred technique. Stereo photogrammetry uses a series of photographs of the building taken from different angles and positions that are then processed through specialized software to produce a detailed 3D surface model and photographic textures overlaid upon it. It is not the purpose of the discussion here to rehearse photogrammetric methodology, this can be found well described comprehensively elsewhere [11–13]. However the capture of textures in particular for this project is of some consequence. One of the major advantages of stereo photogrammetry over laser scanning is the ability to generate photorealistic continuous colour textures precisely mapped onto the 3D point-cloud geometric data (Fig. 2).

Fig. 2. Left – the 3D digital model of the Cathedral as it exists from the North West showing the photo-textures overlaid upon the surface of the geometric model. Right – the 3D digital model without photo-textures, viewed from the south east.

This means that images of internal surface decoration like wall paintings are pre-mapped to their respective points and are as complete as the original photographs. This potentially allows the religious frescoes and other iconography and their state of preservation to be considered simultaneously along with the 3D form of the building, thus providing a contextually more complete, richer and more integrated data set for examination. It also gives the data set a potential use beyond this study firstly for preservation and conservation of the building and secondly for developing more effective heritage interpretation material. St. George's interior surfaces would originally have been substantially covered with frescoes of ecclesiastical scenes, only some of which still survive in a faded and damaged state in some of the tombs' arches and between the registers of the three apses with pointed semi-domes in the eastern end. Discussion of the narrative arc of the interior decorative schema is beyond the scope of this study but photogrammetric recording of its current state carried out for this study may assist in doing so in the future. For this study the photogrammetric and texture data has been used to generate orthographic 2D scale drawings of the building which have been the principal vehicle for examining the dimensional and proportional relationships of the design (Fig. 3.).

As noted above previous plans of the building were known to have significant inconsistencies so the 3D point cloud model was horizontally sectioned at 1 m above nave floor level to give an accurate floor plan that conformed exactly to the elevations and sections. From these a reconstruction was developed based on the photogrammetric survey, careful on-site measurement and recording of molding profiles and previous

Fig. 3. A longitudinal section of the existing remains of the interior wall of the south aisle with a reconstruction based on proportional analysis of the arcuation of the nave, clerestory and cupola superimposed upon it.

interpretation. In this regard we looked to Theophilus A.H. Mogabgab's extensive study and restorations of the historic buildings in Famagusta between 1937 and 1939 [14]. He photographically recorded much of the fabric of St George of the Greeks at this time but he also made a reconstruction of the windows which we have used here in reconstructing the elevations. It is notable that the remains of a surviving clerestory window on the south nave wall, instead of being smaller as one might expect, in fact has exactly the same height as those on the side aisles' walls. In addition, both groups have the same distance between their sills and the decorative string-course separating the registers. All have hood moldings which in wetter climates serve to direct rainwater away from the window opening, but in Cyprus are functionally anachronistic.

4   Dimensions, Geometry and Proportions

The practical or operative craft of masonry has always relied upon geometry for its effective execution. It was inevitable that this became imbued with meanings and symbolism, particularly in temples and churches and so by implication the importance of an internally coherent geometrical schema for religious buildings was often an essential part of their perceived spiritual efficacy as well as an aesthetic goal of elegance, repose and unity in design. The most ancient, and in the fifteenth and sixteen centuries most revered western authority on architectural design was the first century BC Roman author Vitruvius who states: *"The architect's greatest care must be that his buildings should have their design determined by the proportions of a fixed unit. When therefore account has been taken of the symmetries of the design and the dimensions have been worked out by calculation, it is then the business of his skill ... to produce a proper balance by adjustment, adding or subtracting from the symmetry of the design ..."* [15, p. III. 1. 1.16]. Here symmetry is used not in the modern axial sense but instead to mean a balance of proportion by use of geometry. Metaphysically this preoccupation with proportional design became attached to the Christian doctrine of the affinity of souls. This was a philosophical concept that led firstly to the idea that an inborn sense makes us aware of harmony, in other words that the perception of harmony through the senses is possible by virtue of the affinity of our souls. Secondly as articulated by Leon Battista Alberti (1404–1472) it led to the idea that that a harmonic balance of proportions through geometry in a building would more effectively convey the communion of ones soul through prayer to heaven and allow the soul to partake of the vital force which lay behind all matter and which bound the universe together [16]. This was an old and much venerated Aristotelian idea and Fra Luca Bartolomeo de Pacioli (c. 1447–1517) in the second half of the Quattrocento went so far as to say in his book De Divina Proportione (On the Divine Proportion) published in Venice in 1509 but written between 1496–1498 that divine functions are of little value if the church (temple) has not been built 'with correct proportions' ('con debita proportione'). He goes on to say that perfect proportions must be applied to churches, whether or not the exact relationships are manifest to the 'outward' eye [17]. Beyond this the fabric of the well-proportioned late medieval/early modern church was not only seen as an amplifier of ones prayers it was also a palimpsest of metaphor and symbolism which was open to those who understood through spiritual and moral guidance how to interpret and learn from it. For instance at an elementary level the geometry of the circle representing heaven and the square representing earth and the geometric union of these two figures in their correct relative vertical positions in the central crossing and dome of the church was a symbol of heavenly perfection on earth. From this background the starting point for proportional analysis of this, or indeed any late medieval or early modern ecclesiastical building is normally detection of the module, the fundamental unit (mentioned by Vitruvius) used to regulate the dimensions of the building. Usually this is a divisor of the wall thickness of the nave which itself is often a multiple of the local unit of measure. At St George of the Greeks the wall thickness ranges between 1375 mm and 1400 mm. A Lombardic/Venetian foot = 347.73 mm, therefore four Lombardic/Venetian feet = 1390.92 mm, which is within a 1.1 % error of the lower range of 1375 mm and 0.5 % of the upper range of 1400 for the main east-west wall of the nave. The byzantine foot was 312.3 mm (but could be between 308 mm and 320 mm) which does not give a good multiple fit to the known wall thickness. We have no data on a Genoese foot but the Genoese palmo = 248 mm again does not yield plausible whole multiples to fit the wall dimension. However the French ell [aune] (1372 mm) lies dimensionally very close to the lower limit of the wall thickness. The French ell was mainly used as a cloth measure and it would be unusual to find it deliberately applied within an architectural context and so for the purposes of this study we discount it. The columns of the nave originally had the same thickness as the walls (1400 mm) but were later reinforced with an additional shell of masonry in 1491 after an earthquake [6, p. 190]. This increased the diameter to ~2300 mm. The triplet colonettes on the nave wall oppose each column are 680–690 mm (~2 Venetian feet). Given the above it is recognized here that the closeness of fit of the wall and column dimensions to Lombardic/Venetian feet may not necessarily indicate a post 1372 date (i.e. after the Genoese occupation of Famagusta) but could do and could also indicate a design created by a northern Italian master mason some time before this. In an attempt to reconcile or "harmonise" the available historical evidence for the building of the new Cathedral of St George of the Greeks Kaffenberger places its erection between 1350 and 1374 and states that it was "probably begun in around the 1360 s at the very latest" [6, p. 179] and suggests citizens' piety following a plague of 1349 as a possible motivating factor in the Cathedral's inception. He also notes both that there were substantial dona-tions towards the building of the Orthodox cathedral documented in the year 1363 [6, p. 180] and that, "…in the 1360s, the city was already suffering from a commercial decline, which would have slowly decreased the availability of financial resources necessary to start large scale building projects" [6, p. 181]. He also notes that if the cathedral were finished before the Genoese takeover of Famagusta in 1374 this would mean a construction duration of 25 years, 10 of which in the (1360's) may have been in a period of economic hardship, but during which donations were received. Twenty five years is a short period of time to complete a building of this size and Kaffenberger suggests between 50–100 years as realistic for the Latin cathedrals of Famagusta and Nicosia [18]. One might therefore reasonably assume a similar construction period for St George of the Greeks, in which case a completion date somewhere in the 1390's or 1400's at the earliest might be realistic. This would place its completion squarely within the Genoese occupation of Famagusta which began in 1372. Paschali gives a date range of between the late 1360's and ca. 1400 for the completion of the late Byzantine wall paintings which covered the two lowest registers of the central apse and the three lowest registers of the south apse [19, p. 282] (Fig. 4).

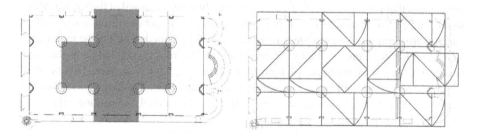

Fig. 4. Plans of St George of the Greeks: Left - showing the symmetrical central crossing. Right – the proportional arrangement of root two ($\sqrt{2}$) rectangles in process of quadrature which define the plan and the intercolumniation of the church.

Irrespective of the provenance of the unit of measure the plan conforms to medieval architectural practice insofar as it appears to be extrapolated from the wall width. The width across the cathedral between inner wall surfaces is 21.0 m or 15 × the wall module. The interior length of the nave from the west door to the iconostasis is 22 modules, the bema has a length of 5 modules from west to east, (excluding the apses). The square at the central crossing is 7 modules on each side from the column centers, and 6 modules wide from the inner faces of the original columns (before they were thickened). The bays in the nave are 5 modules long (west to east) by 7 modules wide between column centers and those in the aisles are 5 modules long by 4 modules wide from the column center to the internal surface of the wall (Fig. 5).

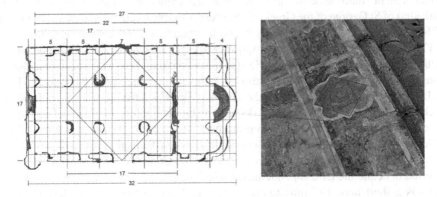

Fig. 5. Left - plan of the Cathedral derived from the photogrammetry survey overlaid with the module grid and Pell Numbers. Right - the quadrature motif, one of a number of representations of this very specific geometric figure which appear on the internal walls of the church (authors' emphasis in red lines). (Color figure online)

The use of whole number units in the plan is philosophically attractive in an Aristotelian sense, and would have had a number of practical advantages for the builders during the cathedral's construction. However the choice of numbers of units is not arbitrary because they have been selected to give close approximations to the irrational dimensions that naturally arise from the use of root two, the diagonal of the square. Many are in fact Pell Numbers which asymptotically approximate root two ratios as their values tend towards infinity. An example here is the body of the cathedral before the iconostasis an area which is 15 units wide by 22 units long. A true root two rectangle of the same width of 15 units would have a length of 21.21 units… 3.7 % shorter. This is small enough to be undetectable to the human eye but not an insignificant deviation from the geometric ideal. On the one hand the approximation of irrational dimensions with whole number ratios in this way has a long history in architectural theory and historical practice and their use at St George of the Greeks may have been a purely practical one in a perfectly normal inherited technical tradition which accepted this degree of approximation. On the other hand it is clear from the extant fabric that the geometric ideal was well understood. The plan form has at its heart the square as the generative geometric figure but the arms of the cross-in-square plan it produces are clearly not squares but are root two ($\sqrt{2}$) rectangles, whose long sides are equal to the diagonal of the central square. This ancient form of geometric rather than arithmetic extrapolation from one figure to another has a number of well-known properties of self-similarity (it is the basis of the widely used A paper size system), and traditionally is produced using compass and squares in a method known as quadrature, involving the rotation of a square about its center. Intriguingly in the south apse of the sanctuary of St George's there exist some of the better-preserved frescoes in the first and second register representing the Deposition and Entombment on the left side of the window and the Anastasis and Holy Women at the Empty Tomb on the right. A close inspection of the geometric motif that runs around the window and at the edges shows a repeating image of the quadrature or rotating squares. The use of a motif (in this case the quadrature) as a semiotic clue to the underlying geometry of the design of the fabric of the building as whole is a common architectural trope intended to assist a viewer who had been suitably instructed to better appreciate or "read" the building as a message of overall coherence, integration and unity of design intended by the church architects as a reflection of divine creation. Symbols and signs were central to Christian thought and so a late medieval Christian would be alert to their presence and receptive to the messages like this one that they were intended to convey. But of principal interest here is the coherent way in which a bilaterally symmetrical Orthodox centralized plan form has been extended through the consistent use of repeating root two geometry to create a three aisled (one nave and two aisles) Franco-Byzantine basilica plan form. We suggest here that it indicates that the intention to unify these two traditions of Christian architectural design was not an afterthought or whim but was encoded from the outset in the "genes" of the design when the architect first started drawing its basic plan form. The mechanics of the process of extending that initial centralized square to create the basilica plan and maintain the high degree of proportional unity and coherence in it is only possible because of the unique properties of self-similarity of the root two rectangle, properties with which medieval master masons and later architects were entirely familiar both in the Christian west and the Orthodox east. It is suggested here that it is the use of *ad quadratum* root two proportional geometry, which was common to both traditions, that is the real unifying factor in this building's design (Fig. 6).

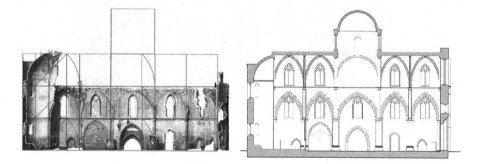

Fig. 6. Left – the internal south wall of the nave taken at the mid line longitudinal section of the church showing the root ($\sqrt{2}$) rectangles extrapolated upwards to form a three dimensional armature. Right – the same section reconstructed based on the root two proportions on the left.

This coherence also extend upwards in the third dimension to the elevational and sectional arrangement of the design through a relatively straightforward repetition of identical root two rectangles. The degree of fit between photogrammetry data and armature is very good, the height of the registers defined by the decorative string course that separates the wall into three vertical registers or stories very closely align with multiples of a five module square giving a good alignment with the top to the springing of the vaulting. Each of the bays of the vault are of course one × five module squares wide. The height of the side aisle fits exactly within two × five module squares and the middle bay within three × $\sqrt{2}$ rectangular modules. The total height of the nave fits within three 5 × 5 module squares which is equal to the total interior width of the church which is three by five module squares wide. In order to clarify the overall composition of these proportional arrangements we recreated them as a three dimensional armature to overlay upon the 3D data from the photogrammetry as an aid in the digital reconstruction of the cathedral. It is highly probable that the architects responsible for the design of St George of Greeks conceived their initial ideas for the building in this way too, as an armature, a simplified mental model if you like, aided in memory by remembering a few of the whole number dimensions (lengths, breadth heights and so on) of the armature. From these key dimensions and the visual picture of their relationships between one another the architect could extrapolate detail as required, though the property of self similarly of the root two geometry and the *ad quadratum* method (Fig. 7).

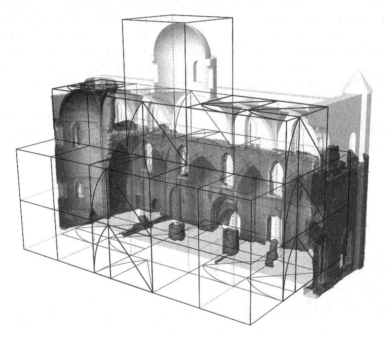

Fig. 7. The 3D armature of root two ($\sqrt{2}$) proportions superimposed upon the photogrammetry data and the reconstruction of the cathedral.

5   Conclusions

The use of root two ($\sqrt{2}$) geometry and its arithmetical approximation in church architecture is by no means unique to St George of the Greeks in Famagusta. Derived from antecedents in Roman building practice these properties may be found both in western European church architecture and in churches in the Byzantine world. It was a method of design shared by medieval and early modern master masons and architects of both the Orthodox and Latin architectural traditions. It is suggested here that the use of *ad quadratum* (the utilization of root two geometry for developing internally coherent architectural designs) was the key underlying unifying factor in the design of the Cathedral of St George of the Greeks and that it was recognized as such by the architects. It shaped the overall form and provided a unifying framework of proportionally related regulatory lines of control to allow firstly a mathematically and architecturally meaningful union of orthodox cross-in-square plan with a Latin basilica plan and secondly an armature on which to place the architectural elements. The method of *ad quadratum* was philosophically attractive because through the concept of idealized architectural proportions it supported the Platonic concept of the affinity of souls and therefore the efficacy of prayer. There is evidence that a modular system of measurement was used and that this was applied as arithmetic whole number multiples (Pell Numbers) of the module to approximate the irrational numbers that naturally arise from the use of root two geometry. This may have been practically useful during construction but would also have been philosophically attractive in terms of the Christian interpretation of Aristotelian atomism and the indivisibility of the fundamental unit. There is also evidence from the surviving wall paintings that this program of design was meant to be understood by audiences other than the architects, in this case the clerics who served in the sanctuary beyond the iconostasis. There remains much to discover in the Franco-Byzantine churches of the Eastern Mediterranean surrounding the role of proportional systems in religious belief. We would suggest that the approach described briefly here can be usefully and more fully extended to other buildings of this type to do so.

Acknowledgements. The authors wish to acknowledge the technical and equipment support of De Montfort University in undertaking this research.

References

1. Flori, J.: Richard the Lionheart: King and Knight. Edinburgh University Press, Edinburgh (2006). 464 pages
2. Hill, G.F.S.: A History of Cyprus. Cambridge University Press, Cambridge (1972). 554 pages
3. Luttrell, A.: The Latin church in Cyprus, 1195–1312. J. Ecclesiastical Hist. **50** (1999). Routledge. 380 pages
4. Jeffery, G.E.: A Description of the Historic Monuments of Cyprus. Studies in the Archæology and Architecture of the Island with Illustrations and Plans, etc., 1918. W. J. Archer, Nicosia (1919)
5. Enlart, C.: L'art gothique et la renaissance en Chypre: illustré de 34 planches et de 421 figures. E. Leroux, Paris (1899)
6. Walsh, M.J.K., Kiss, T. Coureas, N. (eds.): The Harbour of all this Sea and Realm: Cusader to Venetian Famagusta, pp. 171–191. Department of Medieval Studies, Central European University Press, Budapest, New York (2014)
7. Kaffenberger, T.A., Walsh, M.J.K., Norris, S.J.: Visualising Famagusta: The Virtual Archaeology of the Orthodox Cathedral of St George of the Greeks, Cyprus (2012)

8. Pringle, D.: Gothic architecture in the Holy Land and Cyprus: from Acre to Famagusta. Levant **47**(3), 293–315 (2015)

9. Andrews, D.D., et al.: Measured and Drawn: Techniques and Practice for the Metric Survey of Historic Buildings, 2nd edn. English Heritage, Swindon (2009). xii, 70 ill. (chiefly col.); 28 cm pages

10. Remondino, F.: Heritage recording and 3D modeling with photogrammetry and 3D scanning. Remote Sens. **3**(6), 1104 (2011)

11. Baltsavias, M., et al. (eds.): Recording, Modeling and Visualization of Cultural Heritage. Taylor & Francis, London (2006). Edited by E.P. Baltsavias. 528 pages

12. Sapirstein, P.: Accurate measurement with photogrammetry at large sites. J. Archaeol. Sci. **66**, 137–145 (2016)

13. Balletti, C., et al.: 3D integrated methodologies for the documentation and the virtual reconstruction of an archaeological site. In: The International Archives of the Photogrammetry, Remote Sensing and Spatial Information Sciences, vol. XL-5/W4, pp. 215–222 (2015)

14. Mogabgab, T.A.H., Excavations and improvements in Famagusta. Report of the Department of Antiquities Cyprus (RDAC), Department of Antiquities Cyprus, pp. 181–90 (1951)

15. Henderson, J., Goold, G.P.: Vitruvius, Vitruvius on Architecture Books I-V. The Loeb Classical Library, vol. 1. Harvard University Press, London (2002). 322 pages

16. Alberti, L.B., et al.: On the Art of Building in Ten Books, 1st edn. MIT Press, Cambridge (1988). xxiii, 442 ill.; 27 cm pages

17. Pacioli, L., Da Vinci, L.: De Divina Proportione (On the Divine Proportion): Facsimile (in Black and White) of the Original Version of 1509. CreateSpace Independent Publishing Platform (2009). 322 pages

18. Walsh, M.J.K., Edbury, P.W., Coureas, N. (eds.): Medieval and Renaissance Famagusta: Studies in Architecture. Art and History. Ashgate, Farnham (2012)

19. Paschali, M.: Negotiating identities in fourteenth-century Famagusta: Saint George of the Greeks, the Liturgy and the Latins, in identity/identities in late medieval Cyprus. Papers given at the ICS Byzantine Colloquium, pp. 281–301. Centre for Hellenic Studies/Cyprus Research Centre, King's College London, Nicosia, London (2014)

The Reconstruction – Argumentation Method

Proposal for a Minimum Standard of Documentation in the Context of Virtual Reconstructions

Mieke Pfarr-Harfst[(⊠)] and Marc Grellert

Digital Design Unit, Technische Universität Darmstadt,
El-Lissitzky-Str. 1, 64287, Darmstadt, Germany
{pfarr, grellert}@dg.tu-darmstadt.de

Abstract. Virtual reconstructions exist for around 25 years. A documentation of the process of reconstructions was rarely made – a deficit from a scientific standpoint. One reason was that this was a relatively new discipline and there was a lack of agreement as to standards and methods. Another was that in many cases the client did not provide separate funds for a documentation and also did not require or request them.

In the meantime, many involved parties have become aware of the problem of the lack of documentation and standards. Besides good scientific practice, also the guarantee to have access to knowledge embedded in reconstructions should be realized. However, up to now the proposals orientate themselves rather on extensive maximal solutions, often coupled with complex data bank applications, possibly also with annotations to 3D models, which in reality in most projects would present big challenges as far as usability and available resources are concerned.

Thus it seemed more constructive to develop a minimal standard, which in practice would be manageable. The goal of the proposal presented is to compare images of the reconstruction with the sources and to link them to a written text (argumentation), which explains upon what basis, including sources, analogies etc. the reconstruction was made. The core is therefore the triad – "Reconstruction – Argumentation – Source". In addition there exists the possibility to also depict variants for the different areas of a reconstructed building.

The advantage of such a documentation method is that it would be theoretically useable for every kind of architectural reconstruction and thus also for haptic models, reconstruction drawings or actually built structures. The technical goal is a web-linked database that can serve as a platform for work, publication and discussion. The method can also be implemented as a simple text document with a series of images.

Keywords: Virtual reconstruction · Documentation · Standards · Knowledge · Digital cultural heritage · Cultural heritage · Visualisation · Digital 3D reconstruction

© Springer International Publishing AG 2016
M. Ioannides et al. (Eds.): EuroMed 2016, Part I, LNCS 10058, pp. 39–49, 2016.
DOI: 10.1007/978-3-319-48496-9_4

1   Introduction and Statement of the Problem

At the intersection of architecture, archaeology and architectural history, reconstructions are a recognised method of visualising and communicating knowledge and the latest state of research. Classic forms of visualisations include drawings and sketches as well as haptic models. These have been revolutionised by the rise and steady advance of the new information and communication technologies. For the last twenty-five years and more, digital 3D computer model, generally referred to as virtual reconstructions, have dramatically changed the way reconstructions are done in the cultural heritage sector. Virtual reconstructions can be seen as direct successors to the traditional methods of reconstruction, using the new digital media and tools. In the cultural heritage sector of the humanities, digital processes and applications have become standard. But virtual reconstructions as a method of visualisation have not only gained widespread acceptance in the realm of education and knowledge transfer, they have also become an increasingly widely used research tool in their own right.

The pervasive ubiquity of these digital applications brings with it a new and unprecedented challenge, namely the long-term storage and protection of this growing body of digitally stored knowledge and information. The UNESCO [1] spells out the task in its "Charter on the Preservation of Digital Heritage" [1], warning "that this digital heritage is at risk of being lost and that its preservation for the benefit of present and future generations is an urgent issue of worldwide concern" [1].

Similarly, in its "Memorandum zur Langzeitverfügbarkeit digitaler Informationen in Deutschland" ('Memorandum on the long-term availability of digital information Germany'), the Federal Ministry of Education and Research (BMBF) [2] describes the "preservation of digital objects" as an "undertaking of national significance within the international context". It demands that "digital long-term archiving [should encompass] the entire spectrum of digital objects" and that "transparency of information in the shape of knowledge mapping should be promoted" [2].

Virtual reconstructions can be seen as both repositories of knowledge and knowledge models, because they bring together knowledge from heterogeneous sources and data. The translation of information into 3D calls for a continual concretisation in the interpretation of the underlying facts and assumptions. This interdisciplinary process generates new knowledge by means of virtual reconstructions; the models become carriers and repositories of knowledge. What's more, they represent the fusion of different kinds of knowledge that can be described as primary and secondary sources. Primary sources are findings from excavations; secondary sources comprise excerpts from literature, topographical surveys, plans, sketches, comparable structures and, above all, the knowledge accrued by individuals. More often than not, it is this individual knowledge that is indispensable for the creation of virtual reconstructions.

Based on Mahr [3] it is possible to distinguish three types of knowledge that grow out of the reconstruction process:

Knowledge inherent in the model: stored knowledge from different sources translated and transferred into 3D.

Knowledge around the model: knowledge that comprises the context of the model, important background information about the project, project partners, technical systems, intention and goals – all of which are factors that have an indirect influence on the model and the final result.

Knowledge arising from the model: new knowledge that was generated by the translation into 3D and the bringing together of the different sources [4].

Like all digital data, virtual reconstructions and the multifaceted knowledge they contain can easily be lost without strategies for their preservation and storage. Even if the 3D data of the physical model survive, it is safe to assume that the knowledge basis on which the model had been constructed can no longer be accessed, and that earlier findings are no longer transparent or comprehensible. To safeguard the sustainability of the model, it is vital to preserve the technical accessibility of the underlying datasets as well as the wealth of knowledge on which they were based.

Safeguarding the accessibility of the datasets is a question of sustained backup strategies and hardware. Moreover, the accessibility and legibility of datasets is predicated on their unbroken migration from one generation of hard- and software to the next. This first area of sustainability is not central to this paper, as it is an area that has to be tackled by computer scientists working closely with the users and creators of 3D models.

This paper, by contrast, addresses the challenges presented by the second area, namely the preservation of the knowledge that underlies the digital dataset and that primarily underpins its geometry and texture. The focus here is on the preservation of the underpinnings in the shape of the heterogeneous sources and on the visualisation of the process and the decisions that informed it. Drawing on the demands of the London [5] and Seville Charters [6], appropriate documentation methods and strategies have to be developed for virtual reconstructions to safeguard the underlying knowledge as well as the sustainability and verifiability of the models.

More often than not, however, these efforts are jeopardised by insufficient funding and personnel shortages, which constitute a key reason for the looming loss of knowledge. Another threat is posed by the lack of uniform documentation systems and methods. It is here that action is needed. We need to develop everyday methods that can easily be integrated into the work process, methods that lend themselves to the annotation of the reconstructed architecture with "footnotes".

Usability, the simple and effective integration of the method into everyone's everyday practice and research, is of paramount importance and has to be integral to the strategy or system. At the same time, the general accessibility of the documentation and of the tools developed should be safeguarded, for example through an open access scheme.

It should be emphasised that the development of documentation standards is indispensable in two areas of virtual reconstructions: in keeping the knowledge up to date with the latest findings and in upholding academic standards of best practice.

Virtual reconstructions allow for easy updating whenever new data becomes available, but updating requires the earlier reconstruction process to be traceable and comprehensible.

If we conceive of virtual reconstructions as a tool of the humanities, the demand for comprehensive documentation is simply integral to academic standards of best practice. As in every academic and scientific discipline, good practice requires findings to be documented to make them comprehensible and available to succeeding generations as the basis of further research.

2 Status Quo

The exhortation to document the knowledge contained in virtual reconstructions is not new. The subject has preoccupied the humanities for several years. In light of the current situation, we can assume that the knowledge that underpins most virtual reconstructions is not transparent and cannot be accessed or traced. Publications that document the path of investigation, the findings, the methodology and the sources – i.e. publications that bear comparison with the documentation of findings in the natural sciences – are few and far between [7].

In the current research landscape, virtual reconstructions fall within the purview of the digital humanities, a relatively new area of interdisciplinary enquiry at the intersection of computing and the humanities that draws on the steady rise of new information and communication technologies in the humanities and the neighbouring disciplines. Whereas the digital humanities are already well-established in the UK and the USA, the field is still relatively new in the German academic landscape. The current state of research can therefore be described as heterogeneous [8].

While the virtual reconstructions as typologies form a subcategory in the field of the digital humanities, the question of documentation systems or standards is to be understood as a subtopic of virtual reconstructions.

As early as 2003, the UNESCO Charter on the Preservation of Digital Heritage [1] called on the research community to develop strategies and solutions to prevent the loss of knowledge. In the current research landscape, two types of approaches to this problem can be distinguished. On the one hand, approaches that deal with the problem on an epistemological level and on the other hand, those that annotate the 3D model itself with the relevant information and references.

The London [5] and Seville Charters [6] can be read as following the epistemological approach and classified as theoretical position papers, neither of which presents concrete solutions. Moreover, because of their limited relevancy to practice thus far neither charter has taken root and become fully established. Nevertheless, both charters played an important role in highlighting the problems surrounding virtual reconstructions and the concomitant lack of rigorous documentation strategies.

There are very few publications that address the subject on an epistemological basis. A few conference papers touch on it, foregrounding aspects such as hypothesis and findings and the evidence that underpins them through universally accepted modelling and notation [9]. What all of these theoretical discussion papers have in common is that they call for minimum standards of transparency in the documentation of the processes and sources that underpin virtual reconstructions and for the direct link of that information with the reconstruction [9, 10].

The doctoral thesis "Dokumentationssystem für Digitale Rekonstruktionen am Beispiel der Grabanlage Zhaoling" ('Documentation system for virtual reconstructions using the example of the Zhaoling burial site', 2010, Technical University, Darmstadt, Department of Information and Communication Technology in Architecture) [11] also belongs to the epistemological line of studies. Starting with the principles of academic documentation and the special requirements of virtual reconstructions, the author developed a best practice strategy. The documentation system, which can also be described as four-level system, covers all important levels for a valid, transparent and editable documentation. It records not only the context and background of the project, but also the underlying sources and the reconstruction process. On the evidence level, the sources are linked to the relevant digital model; the method catalogue presents the process as an input-output principle. Thus the different states of the model and the relevant decisions and reasoning that underpins them are made transparent. This theoretical system was then tested on a concrete example, giving rise to one of the first comprehensively documented virtual reconstructions [11, 12].

The research project "Digitales Forum Romanum ('Digital Forum Romanum')" of the Winckelmann-Institut of the Humboldt-Universität of Berlin is an example for making a virtual reconstruction understandable". Here the virtual reconstruction of different time periods of Forum Romanum are linked with a WIKI, in which the basis of the reconstructions is publicly accessible [13].

Alongside the epistemological approach, the current research landscape also features projects that investigate the potential of annotating the 3D model with the relevant information. The spectrum of objectives and themes is wide, but all are driven by the ambition to find a paradigmatic solution.

The project "Virtual reconstructions in transnational research environments – the web portal Palaces and Parks in former East Prussia" [14] funded by the Leibnitz Association uses the 3D model as an interface for navigation, linking it to an underlying database by means of semantic annotation and the integration of a wide range of meta and paradata. This database stores all of the sources and contributors and every step of the process. Information is entered via complex input masks that draw on an ontology developed especially for this project [14, 15].

Another, recently completed project in this context is the "DokuVis" [16] documentation system of the Dresden Technical University. Based on CIDOC CRM [17], a dedicated cultural heritage ontology, it too is concerned with the annotation of 3D models with information about sources and the reconstruction process [16].

In this context, we should also mention the "Oplontis project" at King's College in London [18], which is based on the same principles, and the reconstruction of the cloister of Saint-Guilhem-le-Désert [19]. The latter offers an interesting way of documenting individual architectural elements, their historical context and their position in a 3D model. For example, it is annotated with information on the current whereabouts of original architectural fragments of the monastery. A system of colour coding links the fragment with the museum in which it is now preserved.

It must be noted that most publications tend to treat the subject of documentation in the context of the project they deal with. They are less concerned with trying to formulate a proposal for standards of documentation that would serve as a basis for discussion.

Numerous projects, which aim for the comprehensive annotation of the 3D model, are based on highly complex systems, e.g. annotated systems [20, 21] or principles of BIM [22] and ontologies. Although these processes run in the background, the necessary datasets for information about sources, process protocols etc. have to be entered into the system during the reconstruction process by members of the project team. Complex input masks with specialised terms and concepts often stand in the way of quick and efficient data entering and require additional funding and staff. This form of documentation is only viable in well-funded research projects.

Whether the approach of comprehensive, global standardisation can be shown to work with ontologies – for example in the context of the Semantic Web – remains, we believe, debatable. Even advocates of this approach such as Doerr and Iorizzo [23] stress that 'solutions' have to be 'scalable'. 'A global model must be relevant, small and manageable' [23]. It goes without saying that it is sensible to make the documentation of the reconstruction process in addition to the reconstruction results and, possibly, the model itself available to national or European platforms, for example Europeana, as the EU stipulates [24]. But for the documentation to make sense, it must be based on a process of consultation. It is only through broad acceptance and practicable approaches that documentation can be established at all and that, in a second step, the digital cultural heritage contained in the documentation can be preserved and made accessible in the long term.

3   New Approach Towards a Minimum Standard of Documentation - The 'Reconstruction - Argumentation Method'

Based on the analysis of the status quo, it appears sensible to develop a minimum standard that is achievable in everyday practice. The approach presented here aims to link screenshots or renderings of the virtual reconstruction with the relevant underlying source information and to tie them together with an explanatory text (argumentation). The text provides explanations about the bases, sources and analogies used in the reconstruction. At the heart of this approach is the triad of 'Reconstruction - Argumentation - Source' (Figs. 2 and 3). Each area of the reconstructed building is linked with such a triad. Each of the different areas is tagged and positioned on an overview images. In addition, there is the option of visualising variants for any number of the areas. Each 'Reconstruction - Argumentation - Source' triad is assigned a value on an evaluation scale ranging from 'substantiated' to 'probable', 'possible' and 'hypothetical'. The following diagram illustrates the structure of the documentation method:

Project

- Area 1
    Variant 1 Reconstruction - Argumentation - Source
- Area 2
    Variant 1 Reconstruction - Argumentation - Source
    Variant 2 Reconstruction - Argumentation - Source
    Variant …
- Area 3
    Variant 1 Reconstruction - Argumentation - Source
- Area …

This type of documentation method has the advantage of being applicable to any kind of architectural reconstruction, be that a haptic model, a reconstruction drawing or an actual built structure. It would place the discourse about the scholarly documentation of reconstruction projects on a broader, more generally accessible foundation. A documentation method such as this – applicable to all kinds of architectural reconstructions, image-centred and comparatively undemanding in terms of information technology – may also help to dispel reservations against virtual reconstructions as opposed to traditional reconstructions.

The scope of the documentation – in the sense of the number of areas covered – can be individually defined and adapted to the available resources in terms of time, funding and personnel.

The technical goal is a web-linked database that can serve as a platform for work, publication and discussion. In addition to the database application, the method can also be implemented as a simple text document with a series of images.

Decisions as to which pieces of information should serve as the minimum basis are facilitated by a combination of data fields and free text input. The latter provides the opportunity to add any amount of further information. The focus is on textual information. The following schematic provides an overview of the information the documentation should supply.

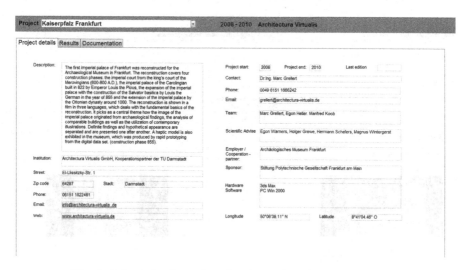

Fig. 1. Information for each project (example Kaiserpfalz Frankfurt)

Project (Fig. 1):

- Project name
- Runtime of the project
- Institution, under whose umbrella the reconstruction was undertaken
- Person/persons responsible
- Scientific advice
- Contracting body/co-operation partner(s)
- Sponsor

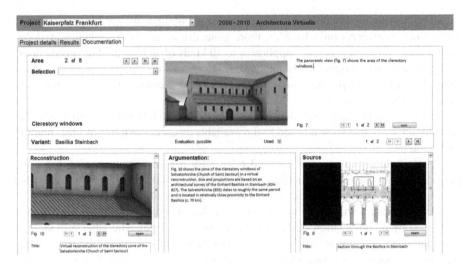

Fig. 2. 'Reconstruction - Argumentation - Source' triad for the area 'Clerestory windows' (Kaiserpfalz Frankfurt, Church of Saint Saviour)

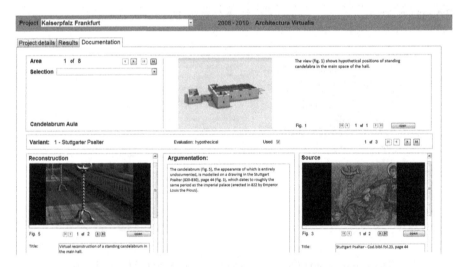

Fig. 3. 'Reconstruction - Argumentation - Source' triad for the area 'Candelabrum Aula' (Kaiserpfalz Frankfurt, imperial hall)

- Hardware and software used
- Geographic coordinates of the reconstructed building or urban environment
- Project website
- Name(s) of the contact(s) with email address and phone number
- Further information about the institution: email address, phone number, website, address and acronym of the institution
- Renderings of the completed project (Fig. 4)

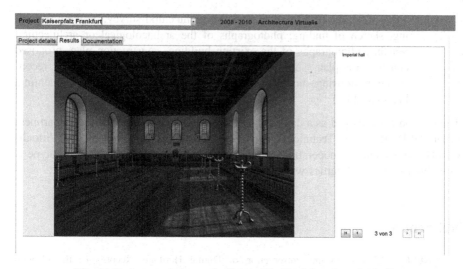

Fig. 4. Project result (example Kaiserpfalz Frankfurt, imperial hall)

Areas

- Number of areas (1: n)
- Name of the area
- Overview image in which the area is mapped, caption
- Number of variants of an individual area (1: n)

Variants

- Name of the variant (standard name '1')
- Assessment of the variants as 'substantiated', 'probable', 'possible' or 'hypothetical'
- Indication whether or not the variant is part of the final presentation of the project
- Reconstruction – Argumentation – Source
    Reconstruction
    – Screenshot/rendering (1: n)
    – Caption
    Argumentation
    – Free text input
    Source
    – Illustration (1: n)
    – Caption
    – Author
    – Date of origin
    – Archive
    – Signature
    – Copyright
    – Direct URL if available
    – Personal comment for further information

- Type of source (3D Laser scan, SFM architectural survey, drawing of finding, sketch of finding, photographs of the archaeological or architectural remains, photographs of the existing building, construction plan, proposed construction plan, survey drawings, haptic reconstruction model, reconstruction drawing, textual source, historical drawing, historical painting, historical film)

The method is developed as a database prototype and will be tested at the Department of Digital Design at the Technical University Darmstadt and by Architectura Virtualis GmbH, a university's cooperation partner, in the summer of 2016. The prototype is available to interested parties who wish to trial it.

References

1. UNESCO: Charter on the Preservation of Digital Heritage, Records of the General Conference, Paris, 29 September–17 October 2003
2. BMBF und Nestor (eds.): Memorandum zur Langzeitverfügbarkeit digitaler Informationen in Deutschland (2003). http://www.zlb.de/aktivitaeten/bd_neu/heftinhalte2006/DigitaleBib010506.pdf
3. Mahr, B.: Das Wissen im Modell. http://www.tu-berlin.de/fileadmin/fg53/KIT-Reports/r150.pdf
4. Pfarr-Harfst, M.: Typical workflows, documentation approaches and principles of 3D digital reconstruction of cultural heritage. In: Münster, S., Pfarr-Harfst, M., Kuroczynski, P., Ioannides, M. (eds.) 3D Research Challenges in Cultural Heritage. How to Manage Data and Knowledge Related to Interpretative Digital 3D Reconstructions of Cultural Heritage, vol. 2, Heidelberg (forthcoming)
5. Denard, H.: The London Charter for the computer-based Visualisation of cultural heritage. Draft 2.1, 7 February 2009. http://www.londoncharter.org/fileadmin/templates/main/docs/london_charter_2_1_en.pdf
6. International Forum of Virtual Archaeology (eds.): Principles of Seville. International Principles of Virtual Archaeology, Sevilla (2014). http://www.arqueologiavirtual.com/carta/?page_id=437
7. Münster, S.: Entstehungs- und Verwendungskontexte von 3D-CAD-Modellen in den Geschichtswissenschaften. In: Meissner, K., Engelien, M. (eds.) Virtual Enterprises, Communities and Social Networks, pp. 99–108. TUDpress, Dresden (2011)
8. Sander, M. (eds.): Aktuelle Herausforderungen im Kontext digitaler Rekonstruktion. Beitrag der Arbeitsgruppe Digitale Rekonstruktion des Digital Humanities im deutschsprachigen Raum e.V. zum Agendaprozess, "Zukunft sichern und gestalten" des BMBF. Dresden (2014). http://digitale-rekonstruktion.info/wp-content/uploads/2015/01/140831_Herausforderungen_Digitaler_Rekonstruktion.pdf
9. Grellert, M., Haas, F.: Sharpness versus uncertainty in 'complete models'. Virtual reconstructions of the Dresden castle in 1678. In: Hoppe, S., Breitling, S. (eds.) Virtual Palaces, Part II Lost Palaces and their Afterlife, Virtual Reconstruction between Science and Media, Munich, pp. 119–148 (2016). http://www.courtresidences.eu/index.php/publications/e-Publications/#Volume%203
10. Bentkowska-Kafel, A., Denard, H., Baker, D. (eds.): Paradata and Transparency in Virtual Heritage. Ashgate, Farnham (2012)

11. Pfarr, M.: Dokumentationssystem für digitale Rekonstruktionen am Beispiel der Grabanlage Zhaoling, Provinz Shaanxi, China. TUprints, Darmstadt (2010). http://tuprints.ulb.tu-darmstadt.de/2302/

12. Pfarr-Harfst, M.: A new documentation system in the context of cultural heritage. In: Verhagen, P.U.A. (eds.) Across Space and Time. Proceedings of the 41th International Conference on Computer Applications and Quantitative Methods in Archaeology (CAA), Perth, Australia

13. Digitales Forum Romanum. http://www.digitales-forum-romanum.de/

14. Virtual reconstructions in transnational research environments - The portal: palaces and parks in the former East Prussia. http://www.herder-institut.de/index.php?id=585

15. Kuroczyński, P., Hauck; O., Dworak, D.: Digital reconstruction of cultural heritage – questions of documentation and visualisation standards for 3D content. In: 5th International Euro-Mediterranean International Conference on Cultural Heritage (EuroMed 2014), Cyprus, Heidelberg (2014). http://www.academia.edu/9189049/

16. Bruschke, J., Wacker, M.: Neuartige Werkzeuge für die Entwicklung und Dokumentation digitaler Rekonstruktionen. In: TU Dresden Forschungsförderung und Transfer, TechnologieZentrumDresden GmbH, Industrie- und Handelskammer Dresden, GWT-TUD GmbH (eds.) Dresdner Transferbrief, p. 9. TUDpress, Dresden (2015)

17. The CIDOC Conceptual Reference Model. http://www.cidoc-crm.org/

18. The Oplontis Visualization Project. http://www.oplontisproject.org/index.php/people/the-oplontis-visualization-project/

19. De Luca, L.: A complete methodology for the virtual assembling of dismounted historic buildings. Int. J. Interact. Des. Manuf. (IJIDeM) (2014). Heidelberg

20. MayaArch3D. http://www.mayaarch3d.org/language/en/sample-page/

21. VSim. https://idre.ucla.edu/research/active-research/vsim

22. Fai, S., Graham, K., Duckworth, T., Wood, N., Attar, R.: Building Information Modelling and heritage Documentation (2011). https://pdfs.semanticscholar.org/b76a/6be1ab4c5c14 8757eac8c73dc7a5c2995999.pdf

23. Doerr, M., Iorizzo, D.: The dream of a global knowledge network - a new approach. Comput. Cult. Heritage **1**(1), 1–23 (2008)

24. European Commission (eds.): European Commission's Report on Digitisation, Online Accessibility and Digital Preservation of Cultural Material (2014). https://ec.europa.eu/digital-single-market/en/news/european-commissions-report-digitisation-online-accessibility-and-digital-preservation-cultural

Multi-scale 3D Modelling of Damaged Cultural Sites: Use Cases and Image-Based Workflows

Styliani Verykokou[✉], Anastasios Doulamis, George Athanasiou,
Charalabos Ioannidis, and Angelos Amditis

Institute of Communication and Computer Systems, Athens, Greece
st.verykokou@gmail.com, doulamisanastasios@gmail.com,
ioannidis.charalabos@gmail.com,
{george.athanasiou,a.amditis}@iccs.gr

Abstract. The creation of 3D models of Cultural Heritage (CH) sites that have undergone a severe disaster due to a catastrophic incident (e.g., earthquake, explosion, terrorist attack) is of great importance for several use cases. Different actors, like Urban Search and Rescue crews, structural, civil and surveying engineers, people in charge of restoration plans, archaeologists, architects, reporters, television presenters and computer engineers, may exploit the 3D information in a different way. Hence, each of them needs models of different scales/levels of detail and under different time constraints. In this paper the need for multi-scale 3D models of severely damaged or collapsed CH sites is addressed and various use cases are discussed. Also, image-based workflows are established for creating multi-scale 3D products via UAV images of a damaged church due to an earthquake. The models of different scales require very different amounts of time for their generation and may be used for search and rescue, damage assessment, geometric documentation, planning of repair works and simple visualization.

Keywords: 3D model · Multi-scale model · Image-based modelling · Cultural heritage · Disaster · Search and rescue · Photogrammetry

1   Introduction

Up to now, considerable research has been conducted on 3D modelling of Cultural Heritage (CH) sites using various methods. Terrestrial laser scanning in combination with photogrammetric and surveying techniques have been extensively used for the creation of detailed 3D models of historic monuments, heritage works of art and cultural sites [1–10], for their geometric recording and documentation. Also, thanks to recent developments in photogrammetry and computer vision, which permit the automated processing of image datasets, several papers have dealt with image-based 3D modelling of CH sites without the use of laser scanning technologies, via terrestrial images and/or imagery from Unmanned Aerial Vehicles (UAVs) [11–13], as well as using large web-based collections of images [14, 15]. Moreover, some research has been conducted towards the detection and evaluation of structural damages and surface weathering damages in CH sites via 3D modelling [16–20]. However, state-of-the-art automated

© Springer International Publishing AG 2016
M. Ioannides et al. (Eds.): EuroMed 2016, Part I, LNCS 10058, pp. 50–62, 2016.
DOI: 10.1007/978-3-319-48496-9_5

techniques have not been applied for 3D modelling of severely damaged or collapsed CH sites due to a natural or man-made disaster (e.g., earthquake, explosion, terrorist attack); such incidents may cause large-scale damages in CH sites and their 3D recording is of great importance for several applications.

The most important use case of 3D models of CH sites that have undergone a destructive incident is the assistance of the work of first responders and Urban Search and Rescue (USaR) crews in an emergency scenario, in order to detect and locate possible entrapped victims. It is true that CH sites are highly visited places that attract a great number of tourists; thus, the availability of a rescue plan in case of an emergency is particularly important for such sites. The 3D model of a disaster scene may aid the localization of trapped humans, according to the operations framework proposed by the EU FP7 project INACHUS [21]. Except for USaR support, the 3D models of damaged CH sites may be used for damage assessment, geometric documentation, planning of the restoration processes and simple visualization. In this paper the need for 3D models of severely damaged CH sites is highlighted and various use cases are discussed.

Furthermore, different actors, like USaR crews, engineers and archaeologists, who exploit the 3D information of disaster CH scenes in a different way, need 3D models of different scales/levels of detail, under different time constraints. Image-based modelling workflows are established for the creation of products at various scales, adapted to the needs of different professionals. Whereas 3D models can be created using other techniques as well, like surveying methods and laser scanning technologies, in combination with image-based processes, emphasis is given on the proper parameterization of the image-based workflow that leads to the generation of multi-scale 3D models.

2   Use Cases of 3D Models of Damaged Cultural Sites

In this section, the use cases of 3D models of CH sites affected by a disaster are presented, giving emphasis on the most important one, which lies in the field of USaR.

2.1   Urban Search and Rescue

The most important and immediate need for 3D modelling of CH sites affected by natural hazards (e.g., a severe earthquake) or man-made disasters with lots of damages and injured people lies in the fields of disaster response and USaR. CH places (e.g., old churches, ancient odeons, archaeological sites, historical buildings) are centers of attraction for tourists, usually being visited by a great number of people every day. Thus, in case of a catastrophic incident, there is a high possibility of trapped people. In such an emergency situation, USaR crews have to make quick decisions under stress to determine the location of any trapped alive humans, with the intent of saving lives. The fast creation of the 3D model of a damaged CH site would significantly assist the work of USaR teams, increasing their effectiveness in locating people under rubble piles.

This innovative idea is the basic concept of the EU FP7 project INACHUS, which aims at achieving significant time reduction in the USaR phase by establishing a system that provides wide-area situation awareness solutions for improved detection and localization of trapped victims, assisted by simulation tools for predicting structural failures and a holistic decision support mechanism incorporating operational procedures and resources of relevant actors. A fundamental part of the INACHUS framework is the 3D modelling of partially or fully collapsed buildings and, generally, disaster scenes, using UAV images in combination with terrestrial and airborne laser scanning techniques. Whereas a live video from a UAV camera could also aid the work of USaR crews, the 3D models generated in near real-time additionally enable comparison of the actual disaster scene with simulation results (i.e., a library of collapsed building models) in order to find possible survival spaces and rescue paths, thereby facilitating the prioritization and planning of USaR activities. These outputs may be used by human operators for visual inspection in order to identify main disaster areas and make critical decisions with the aim of rapidly locating and saving trapped victims. In parallel with this macroscopic surveillance of the crisis area via simulation tools, imaging techniques and photogrammetric workflows, a further decrease in the overall rescue time of USaR operations in a microscopic/per-building level can be achieved by using sensors that are able to penetrate deeper into the rubble cavities, like autonomous snake robots with thermal cameras that provide preliminary indication of presence of trapped victims. Other methods for prioritization of search areas by means of triangulating the location of radiation originating from personal handsets (mobile phones) buried under rubble can also be implemented. Hence, the smart combination of 3D modelling pipelines, building damage simulations, sophisticated data fusion techniques and intelligent inference methods may help to quickly gain an overview of the actual damage and identify possible survival spaces. Also, in combination with complementary technologies, USaR forces can make well-educated decisions and efficiently perform their tasks. More information on the INACHUS approach can be found in [22].

This idea may be of great significance in CH sites which attract many people and may collapse partially or fully due to a devastating incident. In such a situation, the near real-time 3D modelling of a destroyed heritage site may enhance the operational effectiveness of all those involved in the complex USaR and first response activities, in combination with other techniques, as part of the INACHUS operations framework.

2.2   Post-disaster Damage Assessment

Another use case of 3D models of damaged CH sites is structural damage assessment, which is always a priority after the detection and rescue of any trapped victims, especially in CH sites of high significance. It has been shown that geometric parameters derived from 3D point clouds of damaged structures can reveal damage indicators that are difficult to be detected via the original images, assisting the identification of severely damaged or completely destroyed buildings [23]. The identification of damage in buildings based on gaps in point clouds has also been addressed for damage assessment [24]. This research is conducted as part of the EU FP7 project RECONASS [25], aiming at the assessment of the structural condition of facilities after a disaster. The structural seismic damage assessment is conducted via multi-perspective oblique airborne images [26]; such kind of images is preferred in comparison with vertical ones for damage assessment, as they provide visual information for both horizontal and vertical structures

[27]; thus, current research focuses on their metric exploitation, both in terms of exterior orientation estimation [28] and Dense Image Matching [29]. In this context, 3D modelling via UAV oblique images, could also be applied for structural damage analysis of damaged CH sites, following various types of catastrophic events.

2.3   Geometric Documentation

The detailed 3D geometric documentation of damaged CH sites may be used as a background by engineers and other scientists in order to find the reasons to what caused the destruction of structures and draw general conclusions. The 3D geometric documentation is indispensable for the full registration of the structure deformations [30] and has to be conducted after the crucial near real-time support of rescue forces and the subsequent damage assessment, also aiding the planning of restoration works (Sect. 2.4).

2.4   Planning of the Restoration Process

The precise 3D modelling of damaged CH sites is essential for planning repair works and may assist the decision making process concerning the restoration actions to be undertaken. The availability of a 3D model of a CH site depicting its actual situation after a severe disaster would assist architects and engineers in charge of restoration and rehabilitation works. The planning of the restoration process aided by the 3D modelling products is a significant task for the preservation of the built CH, preventing its loss.

2.5   Photorealistic Visualization

The textured 3D mesh model of a damaged CH site may be used for photorealistic visualization by newscasts and information programs in television. The fast access of the viewers to such a model could inform them in a realistic manner about the magnitude and the extent of the disaster. A photorealistic 3D model of a damaged CH site may also be used in an augmented reality application [31] for the interactive visualization of different states of the site throughout the years, e.g., before the disaster, just after the disaster and the present situation, which ideally corresponds to the reconstructed site. Similarly, such a model may be used in a virtual reality application or for simple visualization. These applications are of less importance compared to USaR assistance, damage assessment, geometric documentation and planning of reconstruction works; however, they cannot be ignored in today's multimedia and visualization era.

3   Multi-scale 3D Modelling

Taking into account the different use cases of 3D models of damaged CH sites, it is evident that several actors of various specialties require such products, including first responders in an emergency scenario, USaR teams, structural, civil and surveying engineers, archaeologists, architects, reporters, television presenters, computer engineers, graphic designers, etc. Each one has diverse requirements and information needs concerning the resolution and the accuracy of the 3D model as well as the timescale. Thus, the scale dimension needs to be handled as well in the modelling of damaged CH sites. The concept of multi-dimensional modelling has already been introduced in literature, mainly concerning Land Information Systems [32, 33]; also, its use has been proposed for large-scale CH resources [34]. In this paper, the scale dimension is proposed to be integrated in the modelling of damaged CH sites. Models of different scales correspond to different accuracy, point cloud density and number of triangles or polygons and may have been produced via different methodologies; e.g., combination of surveying, laser scanning and photogrammetric techniques for the derivation of a high accuracy 3D model for geometric documentation or image-based techniques for the creation of a non-georeferenced 3D model of arbitrary scale, for visualization purposes.

3.1 Different Levels of Detail

Whereas the establishment of a categorization of levels of details (LoDs) for CH sites requires the cooperation of scientists of various specialties, being out of the scope of this paper, an indicative differentiation of LoDs for CH sites of the same type as the case study (i.e., churches, historical buildings, etc.) is proposed, using five LoDs. LoD0 is proposed to represent the volume of the CH building or its rubble if it has collapsed, without texture or differentiated surfaces (e.g., openings, columns). LoD1 may represent a rough 3D textured model, encompassing roof structures, openings and the basic shape of the rubble. LoD2 may correspond to a low-scale textured 3D model representing the walls, columns, spaces and other basic structures of the monument. LoD3 is proposed to represent a medium-scale textured model comprising 3D information about component elements of columns, doors, floor, roof and other architectural elements, also allowing more precise identification of the rubble and damaged items. Finally, LoD4 may represent a large-scale textured 3D model of a CH site with all the architectural details, depicting even the smallest cracks and damages caused by a catastrophic incident. The models of different LoDs may be organized in a database, possibly in a multi-level pyramid framework, each one corresponding to a different user's category.

   LoD0 models of damaged CH sites are not useful for the aforementioned applications, as they can only serve for a very rough estimation of the volume and location of the rubble. LoD1 and LoD2 models may be useful for a refined estimation of the volume and position of the rubble as well as for USaR tasks, because of the short time required for their generation. LoD2 and LoD3 models may be used for visualization purposes, as they have a relatively small size. LoD4 models are needed for geometric documentation, damage assessment and planning of repair works.

3.2 Image-Based Modelling Workflow

Multi-scale models may be produced via different parameterization of the automated image-based 3D modelling workflow. Its first step is the Structure from Motion (SfM) method, which refers to the process of simultaneously recovering the camera poses and 3D structure from a 2D image sequence. Feature extraction and matching algorithms are applied, usually combined with a sequential algorithm for metric reconstruction, in case of known interior orientation, or projective reconstruction, in case of uncalibrated cameras; in the latter case, an auto-calibration process is applied. The final step of the SfM process is usually a bundle adjustment. The georeferencing of the SfM sparse point cloud and the camera projection centers is generally performed by estimating the 3D similarity transformation between the arbitrary SfM coordinate system and the world reference system via control points and/or GPS measurements. The generation of a dense point cloud using the SfM results is accomplished through Dense Image Matching (DIM), via a stereo or a multi-view approach. Finally, the dense point cloud may be converted into a 3D mesh model, which can be textured via the oriented images.

4   Case Study: The Church of Saint Paul in Mirabello

In this section, an example of 3D modelling at various scales via photogrammetric techniques is presented. The case study is the Church of Saint Paul in Mirabello, Italy, built in 1795–1804, demolished in 1929, reconstructed in 1943 and partially collapsed due to the earthquake of May 20, 2012 that hit the Emilia-Romagna region of Italy. Emphasis is given on the image-based automated 3D modelling workflow and the parameterization that leads to the creation of models of various LoDs. Surveying methods, possibly laser scanning techniques and a thorough editing of the resulting point cloud and mesh are also required for creating accurate models of non-arbitrary scale, combined with photogrammetric methods. However, such techniques are out of the scope of this paper, which examines the possibility of automatic image-based creation of 3D models at various LoDs via different parameters, using the same dataset. The modelling pipeline using UAV images of the Church and the parameters used for the creation of models of different resolutions are established using one of the most commonly used software.

4.1   Data Capturing and Processing

Dataset Description. A dataset of images (Fig. 1) depicting the Church of Saint Paul in Mirabello, acquired using a VTOL (vertical take-off and landing) UAV after the earthquake of 2012 in Northern Italy, was used. The dataset consists of 131 low-height images from several perspectives (subset 1) and 79 mainly vertical aerial images (subset 2), captured by an Olympus E-P2 digital camera featuring a 12.3-megapixel sensor (4032 × 3024 pixels), corresponding to a focal length of 17 mm. The fact that the flight planning and the planning of image capturing are performed quickly and under stress in such situations may result in incomplete datasets. The specific dataset lacks of completeness, as it does not include any oblique images to provide a connection between the low-height (almost horizontal) and vertical images. Also, the images do not have GPS/INS information; hence, the generated models are not georeferenced. However, the availability of such datasets up to now is quite rare and the specific one provides a representative instance of multi-scale image-based 3D modelling of disaster CH sites.

Used Software and Computer Equipment. The Agisoft PhotoScan software [35] (professional edition, version 1.2.3) was used for the 3D modelling of the damaged

Fig. 1. Images from subsets 1 (top) and 2 (bottom)

Church of Saint Paul; it is a stand-alone commercial software that generates 3D models from images. Recent research that focused on the evaluation of commercial and open-source software for 3D modelling of disaster scenes [36] has shown that PhotoScan leads to satisfactory results in a small time period. It relies on SfM and DIM techniques to generate a dense point cloud of the scene and applies meshing and texture mapping algorithms for the creation of complete photorealistic 3D surface models. In addition, it includes limited point cloud and mesh editing capabilities. The tests were performed on a 64-bit Intel Core i7-4700MQ 2.40 GHz laptop computer with 24 GB of RAM.

4.2 Image-Based 3D Modelling at Different Scales

In this section, the workflow and the parameterization applied for image-based modelling at various scales via the PhotoScan software are presented and the corresponding use cases, depending on the resolution of the 3D model, are outlined.

Workflow and Parameter Tuning. 3D point clouds of the two image subsets are generated independently from each other, because not enough tie points are detected between them, making it impossible to create a 3D model of the whole Church in one go. This problem could be solved if oblique imagery were also captured. The dense clouds are aligned and merged for the generation of a complete model of the Church.

Alignment of Images. The first step is the alignment of images; it is a SfM process that generates a sparse point cloud of the scene and computes the camera interior and exterior orientation of every image. A modification of the SIFT algorithm [37] is used for the extraction of interest points. The alignment of the images of both subsets is performed using the lowest (ALL), low (AL) and medium (AM) accuracy options available in PhotoScan for the generation of LoD1, LoD2 and LoD3 3D models respectively, as well as the high (AH) and highest (AHH) settings for the creation of LoD4 models. ALL causes image downscaling by a factor of 64 (8 times by each side); at AL the images are downscaled by a factor of 16; at AM they are downscaled by a factor of 4; at AH the images of original dimensions are used; at AHH the images are upscaled by a factor of 4. The latter setting is used for more accurate localization of tie points. Higher accuracy settings are used for more accurate orientation estimation, whereas lower accuracy options are used to obtain rough camera parameters in a shorter period of time. In order to speed up the alignment process, the "generic" pair preselection mode is chosen, according to which the overlapping image pairs are selected via an initial matching process with a lower accuracy setting. The maximum number of feature points and tie points on every image is set to 40000 and 1000 respectively.

Dense Point Cloud Generation. The generation of a dense point cloud using the estimated camera poses is the second step. PhotoScan calculates depth information for each camera and combines it into a single dense cloud. The dense point cloud creation using both subsets of images is performed via the lowest (DLL) quality setting for the generation of LoD1 and LoD2 3D models, the low (DL) quality setting for the generation of a LoD3 model as well as the medium (DM) and high (DH) options for creating LoD4 models. DLL implies image size downscaling by a factor of 256 (16 times by each side); DL downscales images by a factor of 64; at DM images are downscaled by a factor of 16; DH downscales images by a factor of 4.

Merging of "Chunks". Six common points are manually measured in five images of each subset for the alignment (A) of the "chunks" of images and the dense point clouds via the estimation of the 3D similarity transformation between them. Some wrong and noisy cloud points are manually deleted, to obtain a cleaner mesh in the subsequent stage of meshing. The aligned "chunks" are merged, resulting into 210 oriented images in a common coordinate system; according to this process (M), the point clouds are combined into a single dense cloud.

Meshing. The multi-scale dense point clouds are transformed into meshes. The "arbitrary" surface type is chosen for all models and the maximum number of polygons is set to 1/5 of the number of dense cloud points, using the "high" setting (MH). The interpolation mode is enabled to automatically fill some holes in areas without points.

Texture Mapping. Texture mapping is the final step. The "generic" mapping mode, which does not make any assumptions on the scene type, and the "mosaic" mode, which performs blending of the low frequency component for overlapping images and uses the high frequency component from one image, are applied. Color correction is disabled. The texture size is set to 5000×5000 pixels for the LoD1, LoD2 and LoD3 models (T5) and 15000×15000 for the LoD4 models (T15). According to the aforementioned steps, the multi-scale model of the damaged Church is created. Specifically, five 3D models of different scale that correspond to LoD1 – LoD4 are generated using the same dataset; the parameterization used is summarized in Table 1.

Table 1. Parameterization used for the generation of 3D models at different LoDs

LoD	Parameterization
LoD1	ALL + DLL + A + M + MH + T5
LoD2	AL + DLL + A + M + MH + T5
LoD3	AM + DL + A + M + MH + T5
LoD4	AH + DM + A + M + MH + T15 / AHH + DH + A + M + MH + T15

Results and Discussion. The computational time of the first two steps (i.e., alignment of images and DIM), which are the most time consuming ones, and the number of dense cloud points for each subset of images are presented in the form of clustered bar charts in logarithmic scale in Fig. 2 (top). Figure 2 (bottom) indicates the total computational time of 3D modelling for the combined image subsets (entire dataset) in logarithmic scale. Both the computational time of SfM and DIM as well as the total 3D modelling time and the number of generated points increase approximately exponentially in each higher parameterization setting. The effectiveness in terms of time is very crucial for emergency situations, like the one addressed by the INACHUS project. In such situations, a coarse model of the scene has to be created in a very short time period in order to be used by USaR teams to locate survivors, in combination with other techniques. Thus, the 3D model generated via the ALL + DLL + A + M + MH + T5 settings in near real-time can be used as a first rough LoD1 model; subsequently, the AL + DLL + A + M + MH + T5 parameters may be used for the creation of a low-scale LoD2 model in a short time period. The creation of a LoD3 model for such situations is advised if a powerful computer is used, only after the faster generation of a LoD2 model. LoD2 and LoD3 models may also be used for visualization purposes, e.g., for newscasts and augmented reality applications; especially, the latter types of applications need models of small size, i.e., low resolution, because of their requirement for real-time rendering. LoD4 models (e.g., via the AH + DM + A + M + MH + T15 settings) may be used for damage assessment and LoD4 models of the highest possible resolution (e.g., via the AHH + DH + A + M + MH + T15 settings) may be used for geometric documentation of damaged CH sites and planning of restoration works. In any case, much attention has to be paid in the image acquisition process, which has to be held by a professional, so that complete datasets are obtained, avoiding data redundancy; the latter is very crucial for near real-time applications (e.g., USaR). Figure 3 shows details of the dense point

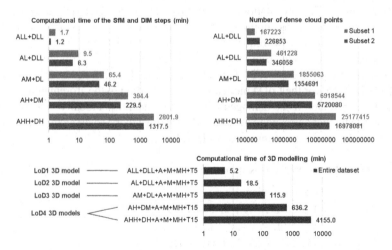

Fig. 2. Bar charts indicating the computational time of the SfM and DIM steps for each subset of images (top, left), the number of generated cloud points for each subset (top, right) and the computational time required for the generation of a textured 3D model (bottom) via different settings

clouds used for the creation of the multi-scale model of the Church of Saint Paul. Figure 4 illustrates views of the non-textured and textured meshes of the Church at different LoDs.

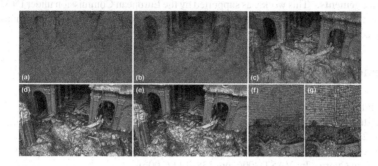

Fig. 3. (a)–(e): Views of the 3D dense point clouds of increasing scale (ALL + DLL, AL + DLL, AM + DL, AH + DM, AHH + DH) used for the creation of the multi-scale 3D model of the damaged Church of Saint Paul; (f)–(g): details of the AH + DM (f) and AHH + DH (g) dense point clouds

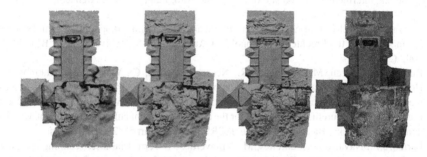

Fig. 4. 3D models of the damaged Church of Saint Paul at different scales; from left to right: LoD2 model (AL + DLL + A + M + MH), LoD3 model (AM + DL + A + M + MH), LoD4 model (AH + DM + A + M + MH), LoD4 textured model (AH + DM + A + M + MH + T15)

5   Conclusions

In this paper the generation of multi-scale 3D models of CH sites seriously damaged due to a catastrophic incident has been addressed. The most important use case of such models lies in the field of search and rescue during an emergency scenario. CH sites are highly visited by many people, so the detection of possible victims has to be held using a well-defined plan; the 3D model of the disaster scene may contribute significantly to the localization of entrapped humans. Other use cases lie in the fields of damage assessment, geometric documentation, planning of repair operations and photorealistic visualization. Image-based 3D modelling workflows have been established for the aforementioned use cases, resulting in models of different scales, which require very different amounts of computational time for their generation. All the 3D models of different scales of the same CH site form a multi-scale model of the site, which encompasses various levels of detail, each one corresponding to a different application.

Acknowledgements. This work was supported by the European Commission under INACHUS, a collaborative project, part of the FP7 for research, technological development and demonstration (grant agreement no. 607522).

References

1. Ioannidis, C., Tsakiri, M.: Laser scanning and photogrammetry for the documentation of a large statue - experiences in the combined use. In: CIPA XIX International Symposium, pp. 517–523 (2003)
2. Sofocleous, E., Ioannides, M., Ioannidis, C.: The geometric documentation of the Asinou Church in Cyprus. In: VAST 2006, pp. 138–144 (2006)
3. Guarnieri, A., Remondino, F., Vettore, A.: Digital photogrammetry and TLS data fusion applied to cultural heritage 3D modeling. ISPRS Arch. **36**(Part 5) (2006). 6 pages
4. Lambers, K., Eisenbeiss, H., Sauerbier, M., Kupferschmidt, D., Gaisecker, T., Sotoodeh, S., Hanusch, T.: Combining photogrammetry and laser scanning for the recording and modelling of the late intermediate period site of Pinchango Alto, Palpa. Peru. J. Archaeol. Sci. **34**(10), 1702–1712 (2007)
5. Remondino, F., El-Hakim, S., Baltsavias, E., Picard, M., Grammatikopoulos, L.: Image-based 3D modeling of the Erechteion, Acropolis of Athens. ISPRS Archives **37**(Part B5), 1083–1092 (2008)
6. Rüther, H., Chazan, M., Schroeder, R., Neeser, R., Held, C., Walker, S.J., Matmon, A., Horwitz, L.K.: Laser scanning for conservation and research of African cultural heritage sites: the case study of Wonderwerk Cave. South Africa. J. Archaeol. Sci. **36**(9), 1847–1856 (2009)
7. Fregonese, L., Taffurelli, L.: 3D model for the documentation of cultural heritage: the wooden domes of St. Mark's Basilica in Venice. ISPRS Arch. **38**(Part 5) (2009). 6 pages
8. Lerma, J.L., Navarro, S., Cabrelles, M., Villaverde, V.: Terrestrial laser scanning and close range photogrammetry for 3D archaeological documentation: the upper Palaeolithic Cave of Parpalló as a case study. J. Archaeol. Sci. **37**(3), 499–507 (2010)
9. Ioannidis, C., Valanis, A., Tapinaki, S., Georgopoulos, A.: Archaeological documentation and restoration using contemporary methods. In: CAA2010, pp. 1–4 (2010)
10. Lerma, J. L., Seguí, A. E., Cabrelles, M., Haddad, N., Navarro, S., Akasheh, T.: Integration of laser scanning and imagery for photorealistic 3D architectural documentation. In: Wang, C.C. (ed.) Laser Scanning, Theory and Applications, pp. 414–430. InTech (2011)
11. Alsadik, B., Gerke, M., Vosselman, G., Daham, A., Jasim, L.: Minimal camera networks for 3D image based modeling of cultural heritage objects. Sensors **14**(4), 5785–5804 (2014)
12. Themistocleous, K., Ioannides, M., Agapiou, A., Hadjimitsis, D.G.: The methodology of documenting cultural heritage sites using photogrammetry, UAV, and 3D printing techniques: the case study of Asinou Church in Cyprus. In: RSCy2015, pp. 953510-1–953510-7 International Society for Optics and Photonics (2015)
13. Alsadik, B., Gerke, M., Vosselman, G.: Efficient use of video for 3D modelling of cultural heritage objects. ISPRS Ann. **2**(3/W4), 1–8 (2015)
14. Kyriakaki, G., Doulamis, A., Doulamis, N., Ioannides, M., Makantasis, K., Protopapadakis, E., Hadjiprocopis, A., Wenzel, K., Fritsch, D., Klein, M., Weinlinger, G.: 4D reconstruction of tangible cultural heritage objects from web-retrieved images. Int. J. Herit. Digit. Era **3**(2), 431–451 (2014)

15. Makantasis, K., Doulamis, A., Doulamis, N., Ioannides, M.: In the wild image retrieval and clustering for 3D cultural heritage landmarks reconstruction. Multimed. Tools Appl. **75**(7), 3593–3629 (2014)
16. Arias, P., Herraez, J., Lorenzo, H., Ordonez, C.: Control of structural problems in cultural heritage monuments using close-range photogrammetry and computer methods. Comput. Struct. **83**(21), 1754–1766 (2007)
17. San José, J.I., Fernández Martín, J.J., Pérez Moneo, J.D., Finat, J., Martínez Rubio, J.: Evaluation of structural damages from 3D laser scans. In: XXI CIPA International Symposium (2007)
18. Alshawabkeh, Y., Bal'awi, F., Haala, N.: 3D digital documentation, assessment, and damage quantification of the Al-Deir monument in the ancient city of Petra, Jordan. Conserv. Manage. Archaeol. Sites **12**(2), 124–145 (2010)
19. Crespo, C., Armesto, J., González-Aguilera, D., Arias, P.: Damage detection on historical buildings using unsupervised classification techniques. ISPRS Arch. **38**(Part 5) (2010)
20. Bhadrakom, B., Chaiyasarn, K.: As-built 3D modeling based on structure from motion for deformation assessment of historical buildings. Int. J. GEOMATE **11**(24), 2378–2384 (2016)
21. INACHUS, http://www.inachus.eu
22. Athanasiou, G., Amditis, A., Riviere, N., Makri, E., Bartzas, A., Anyfantis, A., Werner, R., Axelsson, D., di Girolamo, E., Balet, O., Schaap, M., Kerle, N., Bozabalian, N., Marafioti, G., Berzosa, J., Gustafsson, A.: INACHUS: Integrated wide area situation awareness and survivor localisation in search and rescue operations. In: GiT4NDM (2015)
23. Kerle, N., Fernandez Galarreta, J., Gerke, M.: Urban structural damage assessment with oblique UAV imagery, object-based image analysis and semantic reasoning. In: 35th Asian conference on remote sensing (2014)
24. Vetrivel, A., Gerke, M., Kerle, N., Vosselman, G.: Identification of damage in buildings based on gaps in 3D point clouds from very high resolution oblique airborne images. ISPRS J. Photogramm. Remote Sens. **105**, 61–78 (2015)
25. RECONASS, http://www.reconass.eu
26. Gerke, M., Kerle, N.: Automatic structural seismic damage assessment with airborne oblique Pictometry imagery. Photogramm. Eng. Remote Sens. **77**(9), 885–898 (2011)
27. Verykokou, S., Ioannidis, C.: Metric exploitation of a single low oblique aerial image. In: FIG Working Week (2015)
28. Verykokou, S., Ioannidis, C.: Exterior orientation estimation of oblique aerial imagery using vanishing points. ISPRS Arch. **41**(B3), 123–130 (2016)
29. Gerke, M.: Dense matching in high resolution oblique airborne images. ISPRS Arch. **38**(Part 3/W4), 77–82 (2009)
30. Lambrou, E., Pantazis, G.: Geometric documentation of structures after an earthquake. In: FIG Working Week (2004)
31. Verykokou, S., Ioannidis, C., Kontogianni, G.: 3D visualization via augmented reality: the case of the Middle Stoa in the Ancient Agora of Athens. In: Ioannides, M., Magnenat-Thalmann, N., Fink, E., Žarnić, R., Yen, A.-Y., Quak, E. (eds.) EuroMed 2014. LNCS, vol. 8740, pp. 279–289. Springer, Heidelberg (2014). doi:10.1007/978-3-319-13695-0_27
32. Ioannidis, C., Verykokou, S., Soile, S., Potsiou, C.: 5D multi-purpose land information system. In: Biljecki, G., Tourre, V. (eds.) Eurographics Workshop on Urban Data Modelling and Visualisation, pp. 19–24. The Eurographics Association (2015)
33. Ioannidis, C., Potsiou, C., Soile, S., Verykokou, S., Mourafetis, G., Doulamis, N.: Technical aspects for the creation of a multi-dimensional land information system. ISPRS Arch. **41**(B2), 115–122 (2016)

34. Doulamis, A., Doulamis, N., Ioannidis, C., Chrysouli, C., Grammalidis, N., Dimitropoulos, K., Potsiou, C., Ioannides, M.: 5D modelling: an efficient approach for creating spatiotemporal predictive 3D maps of large-scale cultural resources. ISPRS Ann. **2**(5/W3), 61–68 (2015)
35. Agisoft, http://www.agisoft.com
36. Verykokou, S., Doulamis, A., Athanasiou, G., Ioannidis, C., Amditis, A.: UAV-based 3D modelling of disaster scenes for urban search and rescue. In: IEEE IST (2016)
37. Lowe, D.G.: Distinctive image features from scale-invariant keypoints. Int. J. Comput. Vision **60**(2), 91–110 (2004)

Low Cost Technique for Accurate Geometric Documentation of Complex Monuments by Non-experts

Charalabos Ioannidis$^{(\boxtimes)}$, Sofia Soile, and Styliani Verykokou

School of Rural and Surveying Engineering,
National Technical University of Athens, Athens, Greece
{cioannid,ssoile}@survey.ntua.gr, st.verykokou@gmail.com

Abstract. This paper proposes the technique of stereo-orthoimage for reliable and accurate identification and digitization of complex features of cultural heritage (CH) monuments (e.g., edges, outlines, damages, holes, cracks) in the context of large-scale geometric and damage documentation. It is a low cost technique, which can be implemented by non-experts (architects, archaeologists, etc.). A developed plugin, named OrthoSteroMate (OSM), for the open-source GIS system QGIS that implements the stereo-orthoimage technique is presented. It introduces stereo-orthoimages in GIS environments, as complements to conventional orthoimages, allowing better interpretation of the details of built CH and enabling more accurate digitization, taking advantage of stereoscopic observation when no special equipment or photogrammetric knowledge are needed. The application of the plugin along with QGIS tools for the restitution of two CH monuments were made, yielding satisfying results and proving the applicability of the proposed low-cost method for complex CH documentation.

Keywords: Anaglyph image · Artificial x-parallax · Geometric documentation · Orthoimage · Stereo-mate · Stereo-orthoimage

1 Introduction

The geometric documentation of monuments requires the acquisition, processing, presentation and recording of the necessary data for the determination of their position and their form, shape and size in the 3D space at a particular moment in time [1]. It forms the necessary background not only for the studies of their past, but also for their preservation and protection as well as the studies of their future. The usual products for the geometric documentation of monuments consist of orthoimages, 2D vector drawings and 3D models having metric properties [2]. Orthoimages, generally created by photogrammetrists, are extensively used as a background by professionals of various specialties, like architects and archaeologists, for the digitization of damages of monuments, broken edges and cracks in addition to the typical digitization of monuments for the production of 2D vector drawings. Cultural damage digitization is a prerequisite for the detection of deformations and cracks [3] and vector drawings indicating damages may be used as inputs in a monument damage information system [4] as well as in GIS systems, supporting strategic planning of possible conservation interventions for the

© Springer International Publishing AG 2016
M. Ioannides et al. (Eds.): EuroMed 2016, Part I, LNCS 10058, pp. 63–75, 2016.
DOI: 10.1007/978-3-319-48496-9_6

protection, management and sustainable development of built cultural heritage (CH) [5]. However, the fact that the surfaces of monuments are usually complex, with intense anaglyph, makes the 2D digitization process via orthoimagery a rather difficult task, which may end up in mistakes. Thus, for complex monuments with irregular edges and damages, the possibility for 3D stereoscopic observation would significantly facilitate the digitization process and contribute to more accurate products.

This paper proposes the technique of stereo-orthoimage for use in the digitization process of monuments with complex features and damages, as it combines the advantages of both the orthoimage and 3D observation, enabling accurate identification of complex features. In cases of monuments with intense anaglyph and various damages, the stereoscopic observation could allow efficient monitoring of the digitized edges and detection of the digitization errors, which can be easily corrected through stereoscopic measurements. The stereo-orthoimage based digitization does not require specific photogrammetric knowledge and specialized equipment, thus being a low-cost technique that can be adopted even by non-experts.

The concept of stereo-orthoimage was introduced at the end of the 1960s [6] with applications in the areas of Cadastre and medium scale mapping. The theory of stereo-orthoimages and their applications, concerning the updating of maps and cadastral diagrams, are presented in [7]. The Ortho Stereo Mate (OSM) technique, that is, the artificial creation of a "partner" (mate) orthoimage in order to enable stereoscopic observation, was proposed in 1976 [8, 9] for use in developing countries, for easy mapping and accurate photo interpretation of large areas, achieving a significant improvement in the quality of the final products. However, the limitations of this technique, that is, the fact that is uses a derivative product of original images (i.e., orthoimages) and its lack of adaptation in the instruments and techniques of the analog and analytical photogrammetry, led to the reduction of its use during the 1980s and 1990s.

During the last 20 years, the interest towards the stereo-orthoimage technique was revitalized using digital methods [10–12] in combination with GIS systems [13–16], as the latter ones have a large number of users of various scientific fields and disciplines, for whom the orthoimages are products with high metric and photointerpretation value. However, current research is more focused in airborne applications and the potential of stereo-orthoimages in close-range applications with architectural or archaeological interest has not been fully exploited yet. In this context, the purpose of this paper is the introduction of stereo-orthoimages in GIS environments as complements to conventional orthoimages to allow better interpretation of the details of complex and damaged CH monuments even by non-experts. Thus, a free plugin for an open-source GIS, QGIS, was developed; it implements the stereo-orthoimage technique enabling stereoscopic observation with the use of color-coded anaglyph glasses.

2 Geometric Documentation of Monuments Using 2D and 3D Techniques and Products

The geometric documentation of CH monuments may be performed via simple topometric methods, if the complexity of the monument allows it, or, usually, via the combination of surveying and photogrammetric methods. The latter ones rely on direct measurements, both in the field and using images, for the creation of 2D products, like orthoimages and vector drawings (e.g., horizontal sections, cross-sections), and 3D outputs, like point clouds and textured meshes. The photogrammetric methods for geometric documentation of monuments may be categorized into monoscopic (e.g., orthoimage, projective rectification for flat surfaces), stereoscopic (e.g., stereo-restitution) and multi-image (e.g., image-based 3D modelling) [2]. The use of terrestrial laser scanners (TLS), in most cases in combination with photogrammetric and surveying techniques, may yield impressive results on 3D documentation of complex monuments [17]. However, laser scanning is a rather costly solution that may be replaced by image-based 3D point cloud generation via dense image matching techniques [18].

The introduction of contemporary techniques and tools (TLS, computer vision algorithms, multi-view systems, etc.) in CH documentation, allows the collection of large volumes of 3D data (images and point clouds) and the creation of 3D models of monuments using automated procedures. On the other hand, architects and other CH professionals continue to use mainly 2D vector drawings on their studies, as the 3D viewers do not have yet the flexibility or the tools needed for these studies, and the 3D (image) processing software is expensive and complex in use. So, the orthoimages which can be produced easily from the 3D models, are the best background for the 2D digitization of monuments by professionals without particular photogrammetric knowledge. However, as they do not allow stereoscopic observation, the resulting vector drawings may contain digitization errors and inaccuracies, especially in cases of complex monuments with damages and intense relief, where the identification of edges is a challenging task, mainly for non-experts. In such cases, stereo-orthoimages would be low-cost photogrammetric products that do not require specialized equipment and permit accurate documentation thanks to stereoscopic observation.

3   The Proposed Method

The proposed method for the geometric documentation of complex and damaged monuments requires the performance of three fundamental steps: (a) Digital Surface Model (DSM) creation, (b) orthoimage or orthomosaic creation and (c) stereo-orthoimage generation. The input data consist of multiple overlapping terrestrial and UAV imagery and ground control points (GCPs) acquired via topographic methods.

3.1   DSM and Orthoimage or Orthomosaic Generation

The DSM of a monument is used both for the orthoimage or orthomosaic creation and the generation of the stereo-orthoimage. The image-based creation of a DSM requires the implementation of two fundamental techniques, that is, Structure from Motion (SfM) and Dense Image Matching (DIM). SfM is a low-cost technique that refers to the process of recovering the 3D structure and the camera poses (i.e., the camera exterior orientation) from a 2D image sequence [19]. The extraction of feature points in each image, followed by the matching of the descriptors of the feature points, using the criterion of a minimum distance measure and techniques for outlier removal, are the first steps of the SfM process. In the case of non-calibrated cameras, a projective reconstruction is applied and is transformed into a metric one via auto-calibration. In the case of calibrated cameras, a metric reconstruction is directly obtained. The final step of the SfM process is usually a bundle adjustment. The georeferencing of the SfM point cloud and the camera projection centers is generally performed via the computation of the 3D similarity transformation between the arbitrary SfM coordinate system and the world reference system via GCPs. DIM using the camera external parameters estimated by SfM is applied for the creation of the DSM of the monument of interest. Several DIM algorithms may be implemented using either a stereo or a multi-view approach, according to which, the DSM may be generated at a resolution which corresponds to the ground sampling distance of the original images [20]. A review and analysis of DIM algorithms can be found in [21].

Finally, the creation of an orthoimage or othomosaic of a monument or part of a monument (e.g., front or top view) is accomplished through differential rectification. It requires the knowledge of the camera interior orientation, the exterior orientation of the image or images used for the generation of the orthoimage or mosaic respectively and the DSM of the region depicted in the image(s). A commercial (e.g., Agisoft PhotoScan, Pix4Dmapper, iWitness, ContextCapture, SURE) or open-source (e.g., MicMac, VSfM) software package may be used for the creation of a DSM and orthoimage or orthomosaic of CH monuments for being used in the proposed stereo-orthoimage technique via the developed QGIS plugin.

3.2   The Stereo-Orthoimage Technique

The basic concept of the stereo-orthoimage technique is the creation of a stereo-pair consisting of orthoimages, which enables stereoscopic observation. The ortho stereo-pair consists of an orthoimage, which may have been produced from the left or the right image of the pair of original images, and the Ortho Stereo Mate (OSM), that is, the "partner" (mate) orthoimage, which has been artificially created in order to allow stereoscopic observation. The generation of the OSM is achieved by introducing artificial x-parallax in each pixel of the orthoimage. The stereo-orthoimage technique is illustrated in Fig. 1.

Artificial Parallax Calculation. The artificial x-parallaxes include information about the third dimension and their introduction to the orthoimage creates a new image; the latter along with the orthoimage constitute the ortho stereo pair. The artificial x-parallax for every pixel is calculated as a function of its third dimension, derived from the DSM of the monument, which has also been used for the orthoimage production. Several methods for calculating the artificial x-parallax have been proposed (e.g., the parallel projection method, the logarithmic method, the non-parallel projection method) [16]. The non-parallel projection method is proposed in this paper, because the calculated artificial x-parallax is, by definition, of the same size as the "original" one. According to this method, the x-parallax is calculated by Eq. (1):

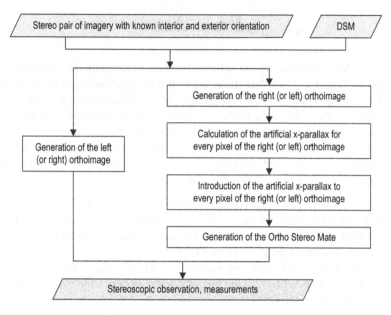

Fig. 1. The stereo-orthoimage technique

$$P = \frac{B \cdot Z}{H} \tag{1}$$

where B is the base of the stereo pair of orthoimages, Z is the third dimension of the point, the x-parallax (P) of which is calculated, and H is the "flying" height, that is, the distance between the camera and the reference level of the monument.

Ortho Stereo Mate Generation. The initial data required for the creation of the OSM include an orthoimage, its corresponding DSM, the base of the generated stereo pair of imagery and the "flying" height. The horizontal ground coordinates of every pixel of the orthoimage are calculated using the georeferencing information stored in the world file of the orthoimage. The elevation of every pixel is calculated through the bilinear interpolation in the DSM. The artificial x-parallax for every pixel is computed according to Eq. (1). The abscissas of the OSM are computed via the calculation of the new positions where the geodetic X coordinates of the orthoimage have to be moved, because of the introduction of the artificial x-parallax, according to Eq. (2):

$$X_{OSM} = X_{ortho} - P. \tag{2}$$

The X coordinates of the OSM along with the ordinates of the orthoimage and their corresponding Z values form a 3D point cloud. The OSM has the same pixel size as the orthoimage, in order to allow stereoscopic observation. The number of rows (height) of this image is the same as the number of rows of the orthoimage. However, the number of columns (width) of these images, differs, because of the introduction of the artificial x-parallax. The number of columns of the OSM is given by Eq. (3):

$$\text{cols}_{\text{OSM}} = \frac{X_{\text{OSM,max}} - X_{\text{OSM,min}}}{\text{cell}_{\text{ortho}}}. \tag{3}$$

Only the blue and green channel of the orthoimage are used for the OSM generation. Points having bigger Z value than the Z value of their neighboring ones are displayed to the left of their neighbors with lower elevation and smaller abscissa. Thus, the geodetic X coordinates of the cells of the OSM are stored in ascending order in every row and their initial position in the row (i.e., the number of their initial column) is also stored. The cells with smaller initial column number than the one after the ordering are deleted and black cells cover the OSM in these areas. The color value of each cell of the OSM is determined according to the following assumptions [16]:

- if the pixel of the OSM fully coincides with a "shifted" cell of the orthoimage or partially coincides with a "shifted" cell of the orthoimage and the rest of it lies in an area without cells (color values), the color value of the corresponding pixel of the orthoimage is given to the pixel of the OSM;
- if the pixel of the OSM covers two or more "shifted" cells of the orthoimage, the color value of the pixel having the bigger Z value between the two nearest ones is given to the pixel of the OSM;
- if the pixel of the OSM lies in a region that is not covered by any "shifted" cell of the orthoimage, the black color (zero tone) is given to it.

The stereo-orthoimage, that is, the anaglyph image, is generated via the composition of the red channel of the orthoimage and the blue and green channel of the OSM; it enables stereo observation, provided that the operator is equipped with special color-coded anaglyph glasses, which are usually red and cyan.

3.3   Digitization of Complex Monuments

OSM Plugin for QGIS. QGIS, developed by the Open Source Geospatial Foundation (OSGeo), is a free and open source GIS used by scientists of various disciplines. A QGIS plugin, named OrthoStereoMate (OSM), was developed, implementing the stereo-orthoimage technique (Fig. 2); it expands the functions of QGIS and covers the constraints of current software solutions regarding stereoscopic observation and digitization. For instance, ArcScene enables stereoscopic observation and digitization via the creation of an anaglyph image; however, some tests conducted revealed a practical weakness for points with high relief, as the allowable range of motion to eliminate the x-parallax is not sufficient. Also, although stereoscopic observation is possible through ERDAS Imagine, via the creation of a color anaglyph simulation of the terrain in three dimensions, the digitization process is not feasible.

The OSM plugin was developed in the Python programming language and its graphical user interface (GUI) was developed via the Qt cross-platform application framework, through Python bindings for Qt (PyQt) using the integrated development environment Qt Creator. The fact that the whole QGIS code depends on Qt libraries allows the seamless integration of PyQGIS (Python bindings for QGIS) with PyQt. The necessary files of the Python plugin were created according to the directory structure defined

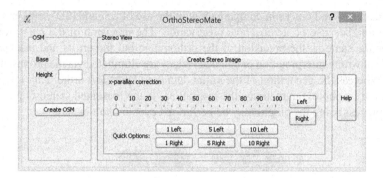

Fig. 2. OrthoSteroMate plugin GUI

by the QGIS Project. The OSM plugin requires the addition of two raster layers in QGIS environment: the orthoimage and the DSM. The base between the orthoimage and the OSM image, and the distance between the camera and the reference level of the monument have to be specified in the corresponding input widgets of the plugin. Then, the OSM can be created, via the corresponding button, and is automatically added as a raster layer in QGIS. The next step is the creation of the anaglyph image (stereo-orthoimage) via the corresponding button; this image enables 3D observation, with the use of anaglyph glasses. Similarly, the anaglyph image is added as a raster layer. The x-parallax correction in the anaglyph image may be accomplished via the appropriate buttons, which move the right orthoimage 1, 5 or 10 pixels to the left or right, and recreate the anaglyph image. Alternatively, if the predefined number of pixels (1, 5 and 10) does not meet the requirements of the application, the x-parallax correction is accomplished by moving the horizontal slider to the target number of pixels by which the right orthoimage has to be moved and recreating the anaglyph image via the appropriate button. Finally, the user may create or load vector layers in QGIS and start digitizing using the available QGIS tools. At any time, the x-parallax can be corrected locally in the relief image, via the OSM plugin.

Digitization of Complex Monuments Using the OSM Plugin and QGIS Tools. The stereo-orthoimage generated via the OSM plugin may be used:

- For stereoscopic observation and checking of the digitization errors arisen due to 2D recording of edges, outlines, damages, cracks, holes, cavities, etc. using conventional orthoimages and stereoscopic re-digitization in areas with errors;
- For stereoscopic digitization of features non-easily identifiable in 2D orthoimages;
- For complete stereoscopic digitization of complex and damaged monuments without the use of 2D orthoimagery.

Figure 3 illustrates the proposed stereoscopic digitization procedure using QGIS and the OSM plugin. Stereo orthoimages generated via the plugin may be used for the creation of detailed 2D vector drawings of damaged monuments, which consist of irregular or unclear edges that cannot be easily identified using conventional orthoimages. The proposed procedure results into better, more reliable and accurate recording of outlines, edges, damages and cracks in comparison with the use of a single (2D) orthoimage for digitization, because of stereoscopic observation. The precision of the measurements remains the same as the precision of the orthoimage but the errors and inaccuracies because of wrong interpretation of damaged edges are eliminated via the proposed technique. Whereas the generation of the initial data (i.e., DSM and orthoimage) has to be carried out by photogrammetrists, the restitution via the presented stereoscopic digitization process using the plugin may be performed even by non-experts.

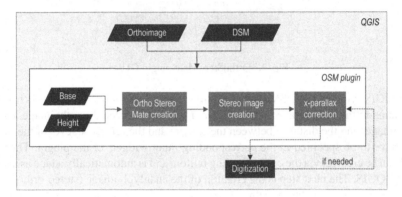

Fig. 3. Damage digitization using the OSM plugin and QGIS tools

4   Applications

The OSM plugin was used along with QGIS tools for the geometric documentation of a variety of CH monuments with different size, construction era, style, from all over Greece; the common characteristic of all these monuments was the significant damage of their materials. In the following, two of the monuments are described as case studies.

4.1   Data Description and Processing

The first case study concerns the ruins of a stone ancient tower, which was a part of an ancient wall in Attica, Greece. The remaining part of the tower has an intense relief of 2.5 m, with stones which have irregular edges and suffer from corrosion and material damages. This monument is located in the internal area of a contemporary building, structural elements of which (such as walls and columns) are in contact with the stones of the ancient wall. Terrestrial images were acquired by a Canon EOS 5 Mark II camera with a 21.1-megapixel sensor and a prime lens of 24 mm. They were captured from distances ranging from 3 to 6 m from several perspectives, with large overlap between them. GCPs were also measured. The DSM and the orthoimage of the top view of the tower corresponding to an area of 70 m^2 were created through Agisoft PhotoScan, corresponding to a pixel size of 7.5 mm and a cell size of 3 mm respectively (Fig. 4 left).

The second application concerns the restitution of the crepidoma (a platform constructed of three steps on which the superstructure of the building is erected) of an

Fig. 4. Orthoimages of the top view of the ancient tower (left) and the facade of the crepidoma of the temple (right)

ancient temple in Athens, Greece, made of marble, having an anaglyph variation of 80 cm. Several damages, corrosion and irregular edges are present in this part of the monument. Terrestrial images were acquired by a Canon EOS 5 Mark II camera with a lens of 24 mm. The images were captured from distances ranging from 5 to 7 m from several perspectives and correspond to 80 % overlap. GCPs were also measured in the field. The DSM and the orthoimage of the front view of the crepidoma were created via Agisoft PhotoScan, corresponding to a pixel size of 3 mm and a cell size of 3 mm respectively (Fig. 4 right).

4.2 Digitization Processes

For each case study, the orthoimage and the DSM were inserted into QGIS. The distance (H) between the camera and the reference level of the monument, and the base (B) of the stereo-pair of orthoimages were specified using the OSM plugin. Ratios B/H ranging from 0.15 to 0.2 were used. Figure 5 top shows a view of the 3D model of the tower and the stereo-anaglyph developed via the OSM plugin; the extensive damages of the stones, especially in the front façade, that make the digitization via a 2D orthoimage difficult, are shown here. Figure 5 bottom shows the produced stereo-anaglyph of part of the crepidoma, which illustrates the intense anaglyph, the cracks and the missing material that creates rough and uneven edges, which cannot be identified correctly or at all through mono-image digitization.

For comparison reasons, for each case study two independent detailed digitizations were performed; the first one was carried out in AutoCAD environment using the 2D conventional orthoimages and the second one was performed through 3D observation and digitization of stereo-orthoimages using the QGIS tools and the OSM plugin for x-parallax correction. Figure 6 shows the environment where the digitization process has been performed using the stereo-orthoimages of the ancient tower.

The digitization results derived from both techniques (using orthoimages and stereo-orthoimages) were superimposed on one another and comparative studies were performed. Most differences were observed in areas with strong elevation variations and particularly in damaged and irregular edges. The restitution results derived from stereo-digitization in QGIS – OSM environment are more reliable than the products generated through mono-digitization of orthoimages and include more details.

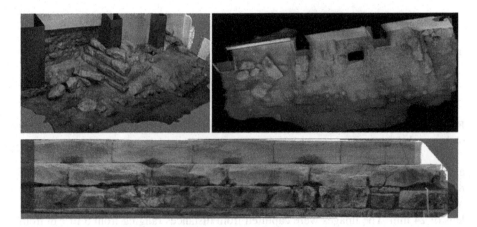

Fig. 5. 3D model and stereo anaglyph of the ancient tower (top); stereo-anaglyph of the crepidoma of the temple (bottom)

The products of the mono-digitization process include outliers, which are due to the difficulty of edge recognition; thus, either edges are omitted (successive stones are not distinguished from each other or the edges that are created due to a broken stone or missing material are not digitized) or non-existent false edges are added (e.g., there is a sense that an edge is there due to lighting difference). Figure 7 illustrates the digitization outputs of both techniques superimposed on one another; at the tower less edges than the existing number have been digitized using the mono-digitization process, because the stones suffer from extended corrosion (Fig. 7 top), while at the crepidoma many details of the stones have not been digitized (Fig. 7 bottom).

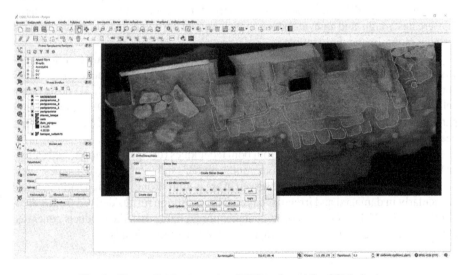

Fig. 6. Stereo-digitization using QGIS tools and the OSM plugin

Fig. 7. 2D digitization (blue color) and stereo-digitization (magenta color) outputs superimposed on one another (Color figure online)

One weakness of the stereo-digitization process is the fact that additional time is needed for the correction of the x-parallax. What is more, the restitution through mono-digitization is easier to be performed by non-experts. However, the option to combine the two technical methods for digitization in QGIS environment leads to a minimization of such weaknesses. Thus, in areas where the edges are unclear, 2D digitization may be applied via the user-friendly tools of QGIS and the OSM plugin may be used at the remaining areas or just for checking the correctness of digitization.

5   Conclusions

This paper proposes the technique of stereo-orthoimage for use in the digitization of complex monuments with damages and irregular edges. This low-cost technique enables accurate identification of complex features and eliminates digitization errors and inaccuracies arising from 2D observation of conventional orthoimages, which are the most common product of geometric documentation used as a background by architects and archaeologists. A plugin for the QGIS (an open source software) was developed and used along with QGIS tools for stereo-restitution purposes; there is no need for any expensive hardware or software component. A comparative study on two CH monuments was performed, proving that the proposed technique improves the reliability, accuracy and completeness of the digitization products in comparison with the use of simple 2D orthoimages, in areas with intense relief, cracks, holes and damaged edges.

References

1. United Nations Educational, Scientific and Cultural Organization: Photogrammetry applied to the survey of Historic Monuments, of Sites and to Archaeology. UNESCO Editions (1972)
2. Georgopoulos, A., Ioannidis, C.: Photogrammetric and surveying methods for the geometric recording of archaeological monuments. In: FIG Working Week (2004)
3. Cheng, H.M.: The workflows of 3D digitizing heritage monuments. In: Munoz, J.A. (ed.) Laser Scanner Technology. InTech Open Access Publisher (2012)
4. Cacciotti, R., Valach, J., Kuneš, P., Cernanský, M., Blaško, M., Kremen, P.: Monument damage information system (MONDIS): an ontological approach to cultural heritage documentation. ISPRS Ann. Photogramm. Remote Sens. Spat. Inf. Sci. 2(5), 55–60 (2013)
5. Moropoulou, A., Labropoulos, K.C., Delegou, E.T., Karoglou, M., Bakolas, A.: Non-destructive techniques as a tool for the protection of built cultural heritage. Constr. Build. Mater. 48, 1222–1239 (2013)
6. Collins, S.: The stereorthophoto pair. Photogramm. Eng. 38(12), 1195–1202 (1972)
7. Blachut, T.J.: Mapping and photointerpretation system based on stereo-orthophotos. Doctoral dissertation, Institute of Geodesy and Photogrammetry, ETH Zürich (1971)
8. Blachut, T.J.: Results of the International orthophoto experiment 1972-1976. Photogramm. Eng. Rem. Sens. 42(12), 1483–1498 (1976)
9. Kraus, K., Otepka, G., Lottsc, J., Haitzmann, H.: Digitally controlled production of orthophotos and stereo-orthophotos. Photogramm. Eng. Rem. Sens. 45(10), 1353–1362 (1979)
10. Damen, M.C.J., Smit, G.S., Verstappen, H.T.: Remote sensing for resources development and environmental management. In: 7th International Symposium on Remote Sensing for Resources Development and Environmental Management (1986)
11. Domik, G., Leberl, F., Cimino, J.: Multiple incidence angle SIR-B experiment over Argentina: generation of secondary image products. IEEE Trans. Geosci. Remote Sens. 24(4), 492–497 (1986)
12. Chang, H., Yu, K., Joo, H., Kim, Y., Kim, H., Choi, J., Han, D.Y., Eo, Y.D.: Stereo-mate generation of high resolution satellite imagery using a parallel projection model. Can. J. Remote Sens. 34(2), 57–67 (2008)
13. Baltsavias, E.P.: Integration of ortho-images in GIS. In: Optical Engineering and Photonics in Aerospace Sensing, pp. 314–324. SPIE (1993)
14. Baltsavias, E.P.: Digital ortho-images – a powerful tool for the extraction of spatial-and geo-information. ISPRS J. Photogramm. Remote Sens. 51, 63–67 (1996)
15. Pyka, K., Slota, M., Twardowsk, I.M.: Usage of stereo orthoimage in GIS: old concept, modern solution. In: The International Archives of the Photogrammetry, Remote Sensing and Spatial Information Sciences, vol. XXXIX-B4, pp. 379–383 (2012)
16. Soile, S., Verykokou, S., Ioannidis, C.: Stereo-orthoimage as a GIS tool for reliable restitution of Cultural Monuments. Int. J. Heritage Digit. Era 4(3–4), 275–294 (2015)
17. Remondino, F.: Heritage recording and 3D modeling with photogrammetry and 3D scanning. Remote Sens. 3(6), 1104–1138 (2011)
18. Kersten, Thomas, P., Lindstaedt, M.: Image-based low-cost systems for automatic 3D recording and modelling of archaeological finds and objects. In: Ioannides, M., Fritsch, D., Leissner, J., Davies, R., Remondino, F., Caffo, R. (eds.) EuroMed 2012. LNCS, vol. 7616, pp. 1–10. Springer, Heidelberg (2012). doi:10.1007/978-3-642-34234-9_1

19. Remondino, F., Pizzo, S., Kersten, T.P., Troisi, S.: Low-cost and open-source solutions for automated image orientation – a critical overview. In: Ioannides, M., Fritsch, D., Leissner, J., Davies, R., Remondino, F., Caffo, R. (eds.) EuroMed 2012. LNCS, vol. 7616, pp. 40–54. Springer, Heidelberg (2012). doi:10.1007/978-3-642-34234-9_5

20. Haala, N: The landscape of dense image matching algorithms. In: Fritsch, D. (ed.) Photogrammetric Week 2013, pp. 271–284. Wichmann/VDE Verlag, Belin & Offenbach (2013)

21. Remondino, F., Spera, M.G., Nocerino, E., Menna, F., Nex, F., Gonizzi-Barsanti, S: Dense image matching: comparisons and analyses. In: Digital Heritage International Congress, vol. 1, pp. 47–54 (2013)

Full Paper: Heritage Building Information Models (HBIM)

Implementation of Scan-to-BIM and FEM for the Documentation and Analysis of Heritage Timber Roof Structures

Maarten Bassier[1]([✉]), George Hadjidemetriou[1], Maarten Vergauwen[1],
Nathalie Van Roy[2], and Els Verstrynge[2]

[1] Department of Civil Engineering, TC Construction – Geomatics, KU Leuven,
Leuven, Belgium
{maarten.bassier,maarten.vergauwen}@kuleuven.be,
georgios.hadjidemetriou@student.kuleuven.be
[2] Building Materials and Building Technology Division, Department of Civil
Engineering, KU Leuven, Leuven, Belgium
{nathalie.vanroy,els.verstrynge}@kuleuven.be
http://www.kuleuven.be

Abstract. Current heritage analysis applications and documentation techniques for timber roof structures rely on manual measurements to provide the spatial data. Major simplifications are made to document these structures efficiently. However, these simplified geometric models provide less reliable results. Therefore, the need exists for more realistic models. Additionally, the exchangeability of information between varying parties is paramount. Hence, the construction elements should be defined in a Building Information Model (BIM). This allows users to reuse the model, allowing the distribution of information throughout the project. The goal of our research is to create a realistic BIM model of a complex heritage roof structure employing dense point clouds. The comparison of our complex geometric model to a traditional wire-frame model proves that our approach provides more reliable results in terms of geometry and structural behaviour. Our work covers the acquisition, the modelling and the structural analysis of timber roof structures.

Keywords: Cultural heritage · BIM · Structural analysis · Modelling · Timber roof structures

1 Introduction

Built heritage is an integral part of our history and its conservation is important. To preserve these assets, qualitative as well as quantitative information about the structure is needed throughout the conservation process. The acquired data is used for the documentation, analysis and exchange of the cultural heritage. Current heritage projects are struggling with such data management. For instance, the spatial measurements of heritage monuments prove problematic due to the complexity of these structures. This is particularly true for timber roof structures. Subsequently, the metric data is used to

© Springer International Publishing AG 2016
M. Ioannides et al. (Eds.): EuroMed 2016, Part I, LNCS 10058, pp. 79–90, 2016.
DOI: 10.1007/978-3-319-48496-9_7

create geometric models. The quality of these models have a major impact on the structural analysis of the structure. Less realistic geometry provide less accurate results.

Another major factor in the data management process is data homogeneity. The information at consecutive stages of the process should be accessible by the varying stakeholders. However, due to software incompatibility, the data exchange between parties is flawed or non-existent. As a result, specialists have to revisit the site and reacquire the scene over and over again.

The goal of our research is to provide the heritage industry with a workflow that will allow for more comprehensive documentation, the creation of more realistic geometric models and the improvement of interoperability between parties. This paper is organised as follows. Subsections 1.1, 1.2 and 1.3 give detailed information about the state of the art of heritage documentation, analysis and data exchange. Section 2 elaborates on the methodology. Sections 3 and 4 respectively discuss the test design and results. In Sect. 5, the conclusions are presented.

1.1 Data Acquisition

Traditionally, hand measurements and visual inspections are employed to document cultural heritage. Such measurements, for instance, serve as a basis to create geometric models used in structural analysis. However, the sparsity and inaccuracy of hand measurements only allow for the creation of simplistic models. Denser and more accurate data is required to create more realistic geometric models.

An increasingly popular data acquisition tool is Terrestrial Laser Scanning (TLS). The static scanning instrument is capable of capturing accurate 3D point measurements of an entire scene in a matter of minutes. The result is a geometric point cloud containing tens of millions of points with high accuracy. An example of a scanned roof structure is shown in Fig. 1.

Terrestrial Laser Scanning and point cloud data have been used in several heritage projects [1]. In addition to TLS data, photogrammetric point clouds are also used [2]. In our research, we prefer to use TLS data over photogrammetric point clouds because of

Fig. 1. Overview heritage roof structure: image (left), point cloud (right).

the size of the heritage site. Research indicates that Terrestrial Laser Scanning, while being more expensive, scales better with the size of the project in terms of accuracy and density [3].

1.2 Geometric Models for Structural Analysis

The analysis of the structural behaviour is crucial to the assessment and preservation of built heritage [4]. The aim of this analysis is appropriate damage therapy and strengthening measures. Currently, basic wire-frame models based on hand measurements are employed for the geometric representation. These simplistic models are error prone and provide only a rough approximation of the real conditions. Therefore, the analysis is less reliable.

Several researchers have proposed more complex geometric models. A promising approach is the use of solid models [5]. Castellazzi presented such models based on voxel elements [6]. Their semi-automated procedure has shown promising results compared to traditional CAD-based models. Also constructive solid geometry (CSG) has been considered [7]. They state that solid approaches are to be preferred over wire-frame models for mass calculations and structural behaviour. In our research, we also employ a volume based representation of the geometry. This allows for a more realistic representation of the structural elements.

1.3 Data Exchange

Data heterogeneity is a major obstacle in the heritage industry. During a project, data is stored in different software specific formats conform varying data models. The data is not interoperable with other applications. To facilitate the data transfer throughout the conservation process, the need exist for a uniform data model and an exchangeable format. An innovative technology is Building Information Models (BIM). These models constitute a digital representation of a structure with all its metric, non-metric and semantic data. The data is stored in a format called Industry Foundation Classes (IFC), an open standard for the exchange of BIM information between different software. In our research, we employ IFC to store the geometry of structural elements.

Research has been performed on the integration of BIM in the cultural heritage industry [8–10]. In addition, heritage BIM library projects such as HBIM provide a set of reusable heritage objects [11–13]. BIM has also been used as a basis for the structural analysis of heritage buildings [14]. This field is still ongoing research.

2 Methodology

In this paper we propose an approach to create realistic BIM objects of structural elements based on point cloud data and apply these BIM objects as a base for structural analysis. More specifically, we create a model for the evaluation of a heritage timber roof structure. Our approach consists of two phases. The Scan to BIM phase covers the data acquisition, modelling of the elements and their representation in a BIM

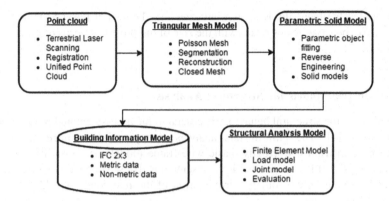

Fig. 2. Workflow for Scan-to-BIM and structural analysis.

environment. The structural analysis phase covers the exchange of the model to a Structural Analysis software and the evaluation of the model's behaviour. An overview of the intermediate stages is depicted in Fig. 2. Our model is compared to a traditional geometric wire-frame model, which functions as a benchmark.

2.1 Scan to BIM

For the data acquisition, we employ a static terrestrial laser scanner to acquire a dense 3D point cloud of the structure. Leica Cyclone is utilized to process the data. First, cloud-to-cloud constraints are defined for the coarse alignment of each scan. Subsequently, an Iterative Closest Point (ICP) Algorithm computes a fine alignment between the data sets.

After the registration, the unified point cloud is exported to 3D Reshaper for further modelling (Fig. 3a). In this software, watertight meshes are computed for each element based on the point cloud. The software employs a coarse to fine meshing approach. The coarse meshing computes a rough shape representation to acquire the initial shape. The fine meshing refines the initial geometry to better approximate the point cloud. Both stages are an implementation of a Poisson meshing algorithm [15] (Fig. 3b). Second, the mesh is interpolated to create a watertight mesh (Fig. 3c). Third, the mesh is segmented per element and closed (Fig. 3d). For structural analysis, it is imperative that the connections between elements are consistent so they are able to transfer forces correctly. At this stage, the data is defined by a non-parametric representation. While this representation is adequate for simple evaluations, applications that interact with the geometry prefer parametric data representations.

The closed meshes serve as a basis for the parametric reconstruction of the beams. The objects are imported in the SolidWorks software (Fig. 4a). The built-in *ScanTo3D* function allows for the semi-automated reverse engineering of closed meshes. This function operates as follows. First, the mesh is represented by a set of surface patches to approximate the exact geometry (Fig. 4b). The user can influence the settings of the reconstruction algorithm to alter the level of detail. This has a direct impact on the

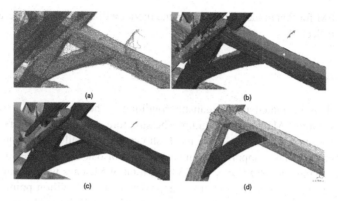

Fig. 3. Overview stages of the modelling process in 3D Reshaper: point cloud (a), Poisson mesh (b), watertight mesh (c), segmented mesh (d).

number of generated patches. Next, the user is able to adjust topological errors present in the patch representation (Fig. 4c). Finally, the software calculates the parametric volumetric representation of the given patches (Fig. 4d). After the modelling, the objects are exported to the IFC 2 × 3 format, which is exchangeable with BIM software such as Revit.

2.2   Structural Analysis

A Finite Element Model (FEM) is defined for the structural analysis. In addition to the geometry, this model encompasses loads, material properties and joint definitions. These parameters are derived from varying standards [16–20]. The Finite Element Analysis (FEA) is performed in the ANSYS software. Quadratic triangular volume elements are used to represent the geometry [21]. A 3D solid analysis method is chosen to perform the evaluation. For comparison purposes, a wire-frame model of the roof structure is created from manual measurements. The same method is employed to

Fig. 4. Overview stages of the modelling process in SolidWorks: triangulated mesh (a), surface patches on normal LOD (b), surface patches on high LOD (c), solid parametric model (d).

define the FEM for this model. The wire-frame model will function as a reference in the evaluation in Sect. 4.

3   Test Design

Our approach is evaluated using realistic conditions. The test site is a small castle located in the city of Mechelen, Belgium. The structure is nearly 400 years old and is heavily deteriorated [22]. The roof itself shows major deflections and damaged structural members. The supporting elements consist of oak beams. The structure was scanned employing a FARO Focus 3D X330. A total of 54 scans were acquired to map the building, resulting in a point cloud of approximately 540 million points. The roof itself was acquired with 16 scans. A scanning resolution of 12.5 mm/10 m was used to ensure a high density point cloud of the beam elements [23].

3.1   Building Information Model

One section of the roof was modelled and 11 beams were isolated represented by 40 million points. The total beam length is approximately 26 m. After filtering stray points, the point cloud of the section was unified with an average spacing of 3 mm, resulting in 6 million points or 230 thousand points per meter. The Poisson meshing in 3D Reshaper was performed using the two step meshing algorithm explained in Sect. 2. A sampling size of 5 mm was applied for the meshing. A total of 1.2 million triangular surfaces were constructed, approximately 40 thousand triangles per meter. The meshes were manually segmented. For computational efficiency, the mesh complexity was reduced. A maximal deviation of 1 mm was allowed on the decimation, resulting in 50 thousand triangles. An average deviation of 0.35 mm was computed for the entire data set.

The meshes were reverse engineered to solid models employing the *ScanTo3D* function in SolidWorks. On average, the elements were created with a 0.02 mm deviation from the mesh model. The parametric objects were exported to IFC 2 × 3 without any loss of data. Within this model, additional non-metric properties can be defined by the user.

For the wire-frame model, hand measurements were acquired at the best suited location for the accessible elements. For the inaccessible elements, total station measurements were used. Rectangular beams were employed to best approximate the structural elements. Also, the elements are linear and are located in the same plane.

3.2   Structural FEM-Based Model

A structural analysis model is defined for the evaluation. The varying parameters such as material properties will be determined based on the European Standards. Both geometric models will be evaluated with the same parameters.

Material. Code-based values are assumed as a first approximation since a detailed assessment of the timber's strength properties, e.g. by means of non-destructive techniques (NDT) and minor-destructive testing (MDT), is not the focus of this paper. Therefore, rheological phenomena in timber are currently not taken into account. The material properties are derived from the EN 338 standard for the strength categorisation of structural timber [16]. The roof elements are macroscopically identified as hardwood oak with an assumed strength class of *D*30 and an orthotropic behaviour (Table 1).

Table 1. D30 properties from EN 338 [16]

General	Strength properties [N/mm^2]						Stiffness properties [kN/mm^2]				Density [kg/m^3]	
Material	Class	$f_{m,k}$	$f_{t,0,k}$	$f_{t,90,k}$	$f_{c,0,k}$	$f_{c,90,k}$	$f_{v,k}$	$E_{m,0,mean}$	$E_{m,0,k}$	$E_{m,90,mean}$	G_{mean}	ρ_k	ρ_{mean}
Hardwood oak	D30	30	18	0.6	24	5.3	3.9	11	9.2	0.73	0.69	530	640

The material properties are affected by the duration of the load and the moisture content. Factor *kmod* is introduced to deal with these effects. In our test design, the roof structure is assumed to be service class 2, which corresponds to an average working temperature of 20° and a relative humidity more than 85 % for only a few weeks per year [18]. The matching k_{mod} is 0.6 and 0.9 for the permanent and short-term load durations respectively. The reduced characteristic strength value X_d is calculated using Eq. (1). γ_M is the partial factor for the material property which is 1.3 for solid timber.

$$X_d = k_{mod} \frac{X_k}{\gamma_M} \tag{1}$$

Joints. Varying types of connections are present in the roof structure: mortise and tenon joints, and dovetail half lapped joints. Both are constructed with wooden dowels. While these connections can resist normal forces, they have limited rotational stiffness. Therefore, the connections are designed as perfect hinges. The joints that connect the roof to the building are modelled as fixed joints. This decision is supported by field observations. Also, the use of perfect hinges simplifies the calculations and overestimates the bending moment and deflections, resulting in a conservative analysis [24].

Loads. The different loads imposed on the roof structure are the self-weight, the imposed loads, the wind loads and the snow loads. The self-weight is considered the dead load of the structure. The permanent load consists of the roof frame (rafters and battens) and the tiles. The imposed load is neglected because of the inaccessibility of the roof.

For the snow and wind loads, the angle of the roof is required. From the laser scan data is derived that the roof has an angle of 58°. The Eurocode EN 1991-1-3 [19] specifies that snow loads on such steep roofs can be neglected. For the wind load, only the forces in the plane with the considered roof truss are considered. The wind pressure is obtained using Eq. (2) [20]. q_p is the peak velocity pressure, z_e is the reference height for the external pressure and C_{pe} is the coefficient for the external pressure. Category III best fits the terrain category of the test site. The wind pressure on the strong side of the section mounts up to 0.41 kN/m². On the weak side a suction force of −0.51 kN/m² is calculated.

$$W_e = q_p(z_e) * C_{pe} \qquad (2)$$

The roof is connected to the structural elements by purlins. Therefore, the varying loads are represented by concentrated forces located perpendicular to the purlins at their respective connections. Figure 5 shows the roofs connections in detail as well as the location of the varying loads split into the vertical and horizontal components.

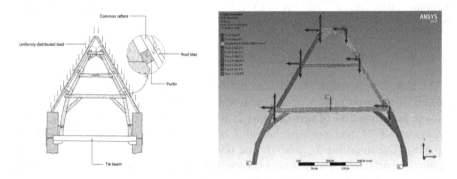

Fig. 5. Load model: the forces are transmitted from the rafters to the beams trough the purlins (left). The wind load and the permanent load of the roof are depicted in red. The self weight of the structural elements is shown in yellow (right). (Color figure online)

Structural Analysis. Both structural models are tested in the Serviceability Limit State (SLS), which calculates the overall deformations of the structure [18]. It applies to structures, components and connections with the assumption of a linear relationship between the subjected actions and the corresponding deformations. The total deformation is calculated for the worst combination of the loads.

4 Experimental Results

The comparison between the two models is performed in two stages. First a metric comparison is made. Second, a structural analysis comparison is made.

Geometry. To compare both geometric models, a million sample points are generated on the surface of the models. The shortest euclidean distance between the two geometries is calculated in the CloudCompare software. The results are shown in Fig. 6. A mean distance of 20 mm with a standard deviation of 40 mm is calculated between both data sets. This results in a mean difference in profile area of 15 % and in volume of 12.5 %. These numbers indicate a major discrepancy between both data sets. The complex model has more weight because the modelling in the wire-frame model is based on the smallest section. The mass discrepancy both affects the load from self weight and the structural behaviour of the beams. Figure 6 shows that the largest deviations are located in the more complex areas. These differences are the result of the abstractions made by hand measurements. Moreover, the wire-frame model does not encompass geometries such as complex connections, non-rectangular and varying sections, non-linear beams and out of the plane elements. The difference in geometry is expected to have a major impact on the structural analysis.

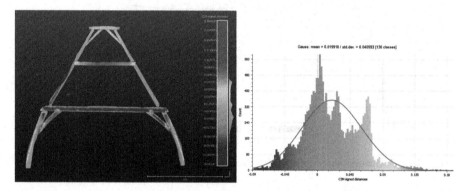

Fig. 6. Overview metric comparison: the smallest euclidean distance between both data sets at each location (left), and the histogram of the errors (right).

Structural Analysis. Both models are tested with the same material parameters and external loads specified in Sect. 3. Figures 7 and 8 depict the results from the SLS analysis. They show the deformations of the elements for the varying loads on the structure. The discrepancy in deformation between the models is very noticeable. The complex model shows deformations up to three times larger than the maximum deformation in the wire-frame model. This is partially caused by a difference in weight and section profiles, as well as the difference in modelling between the two structural models. As stated in the geometry comparison, the complex model consists of non-rectangular beams that connect to the joints in varying angels at different locations. This causes forces to be transferred sub-optimal. Also, the location of the loads has a major impact. In the complex model, the loads are placed more accurately, causing a difference in stress concentration.

In addition to an increased stress in the beams, both models behave differently. For instance, the main deformation is located elsewhere in both models. In the wire-frame model it is located on in the left upper beam, while in the complex model it is located in the right upper beam. This is caused by the behaviour of the central horizontal beam. From Fig. 7 is derived that in the wire-frame model, the horizontal beam in the middle of the structure is a crucial component to transfer forces from the right to the upper left side of the structure. In the complex model, this is not the case. If the deformations are

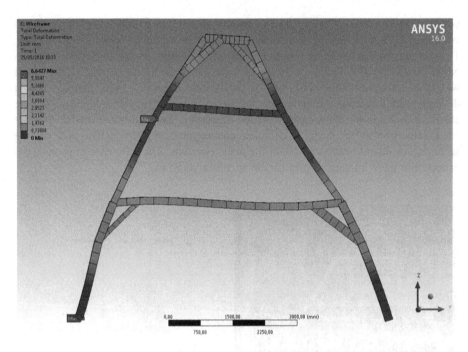

Fig. 7. Deformation wire-frame model. Largest deformation located in upper left beam.

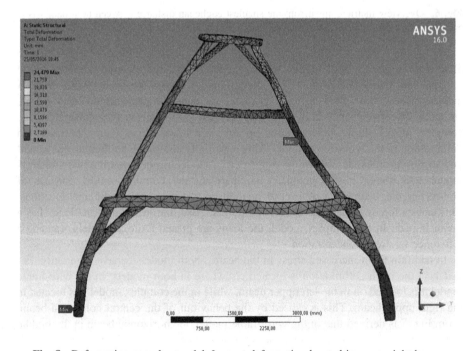

Fig. 8. Deformation complex model. Largest deformation located in upper right beam.

compared to the deviations in the modelling (Fig. 6), it is revealed that this beam shows the largest discrepancies. This is caused by a difference in modelling. In the wire-frame model, this beam was modelled straight and fitted between the vertical beams. In the complex model, this beam is out of the section plane in accordance with the real conditions. Hence, the beam cannot transfer forces as efficiently in the complex model. As a result, the peak deformation is located elsewhere in both models (Fig. 8).

5   Conclusion

In this paper we presented a method to create realistic BIM objects of heritage roof elements and subsequently apply the geometric model as input for structural modelling. Instead of utilising traditional wire-frame models, we used more complex solid models. By employing accurate dense point clouds, we were able to construct as-built models of the structural elements of a building. The test results proved that with our approach, volumes are estimated 12.5 % more accurately and profile areas 15 % more accurately. Furthermore, the complex solid model was able to encompass complex geometries such as complex connections, non-rectangular and varying sections, non-linear beams and out of the plane elements. The simulation results from the structural analysis showed that these differences in geometry have a significant impact on the structural behaviour of the timber roof truss. Deformations up to three times larger than the value of the maximum deformation in the wire-frame model were measured in the complex models. These observations are crucial in the preservation process. Additionally, our method provides a solution to deal with data heterogeneity. By creating BIM objects, we allow the exchange of data between different software and stakeholders in the heritage process.

Acknowledgement. The research group Geomatics of the Department of Civil Engineering, TC Construction and the support of the Raymond Lemaire International Center for Conservation, KU Leuven are gratefully acknowledged.

References

1. Castagnetti, C., Bertacchini, E., Capra, A., Dubbini, M.: Terrestrial Laser Scanning for Preserving Cultural Heritage: Analysis of Geometric Anomalies for Ancient Structures, TS08C-Laser Scanners II, 6031 (2012)
2. Arias, P., Armesto, J., Lorenzo, H., et al.: Digital photogrammetry, GPR and finite elements in heritage documentation: geometry and structural damages. In: ISPRS Commission V Symposium 'Image Engineering and Vision Metrology' DIGITAL (2012)
3. Bassier, M., Yousefzadeh, M., Van Genechten, B.: Evaluation of data acquisition techniques and workflows for scan to BIM. In: Proceedings of Geobussiness (2015)
4. Van Roy, N., Verstrynge, E., Brosens, K., Van Balen, K.: Quality management of structural repair of traditional timber roof structures. In: Structural Analysis of Historical Constructions, Anamnesis, Diagnosis, Therapy, Controls (2016)

5. Mngumi, E.A., Ruther, H.: Solid modeling for heritage documentation. In: Workshop – Archaeological Surveys, WSA2 Modelling and Visualization (2004)
6. Castellazzi, G., Altri, A.M.D., Bitelli, G., Selvaggi, I., Lambertini, A.: From laser scanning to finite element analysis of complex buildings by using a semi-automatic procedure. Sensors 15, 18360–18380 (2015)
7. Son, H., Hwang, N., Kim, C., Kim, C.: Rapid and automated determination of rusted surface areas of a steel bridge for robotic maintenance systems. Autom. Constr. 42, 13–24 (2014)
8. Saygi, G., Agugiaro, G., Hamamcolu-Turan, M., Remondino, F.: Evaluation of GIS and BIM roles for the information management of historical buildings. ISPRS Ann. Photogramm. Remote Sens. Spat. Inf. Sci. 2, 283–288 (2013)
9. Garagnani, S., Manferdini, M.: Parametric accuracy: building information modelingprocess applied to the cultural heritage preservation. In: International Archives of the Photogrammetry, Remote Sensing and Spatial Information Sciences, vol. XL-5/W1 (2013)
10. Logothetis, S., Delinasiou, A., Stylianidis, E.: Building information modelling for cultural heritage: a review. ISPRS Ann. Photogramm. Remote Sens. Spat. Inf. Sci. II-5/W3, 177 (2015)
11. Murphy, M., McGovern, E., Pavia, S.: Historic building information modelling-adding intelligence to laser and image based surveys of European classical architecture. ISPRS J. Photogramm. Remote Sens. 76, 89–102 (2013)
12. Dore, C., Murphy, M., McCarthy, S., Brechin, F., Casidy, C., Dirix, E.: Structural simulations and conservation analysis-historic building information model (HBIM). ISPRS Int. Arch. Photogramm. Remote Sens. Spat. Inf. Sci. XL-5/W4, 351–357 (2015)
13. Oreni, D., Brumana, R., Della Torre, S., Banfi, F., Previtali, M.: Survey turned into HBIM: the restoration and the work involved concerning the Basilica di Collemaggio after the earthquake (L'Aquila). ISPRS Ann. Photogramm. Remote Sens. Spat. Inf. Sci. 5, 267–273 (2014)
14. Barazzetti, L., Banfi, F., Brumana, R., Gusmeroli, G., Previtali, M., Schiantarelli, G.: Cloud-to-BIM-to-FEM: structural simulation with accurate historic BIM from laser scans. Simul. Model. Pract. Theor. 57, 71–87 (2015)
15. Kazhdan, M., Bolitho, M., Hoppe, H.: Poisson surface reconstruction. ACM Trans. Graph. 32(3), 1–13 (2013)
16. European Committee for Standardisation, EN 338: Structural timber-Strength classes (2016)
17. European Committee for Standardisation, EN 1991-1-1: Eurocode 1: Actions on structures - Part 1-1: General actions - Densities, self-weight, imposed loads for buildings (2002)
18. European Committee for Standardisation, EN 1995-1-1: Eurocode 5: Design of timber structures - Part 1-1: General - Common rules and rules for buildings (2014)
19. European Committee for Standardisation, EN 1991-1-3: Eurocode 1: Actions on structures - Part 1-3: General actions - Snow loads (2015)
20. European Committee for Standardisation, EN 1991-1-4: Eurocode 1: Actions on structures - Part 1-4: General actions - Wind actions (2005)
21. ANSYS, Inc.: ANSYS Modeling and Meshing Guide (2005)
22. Verstrynge, E., Kips, G.: Exploitation of 3D laser scanning data to generate FEM structural models of historical timber roof structures (2016)
23. Bassier, M., Vergauwen, M., Van Genechten, B.: Standalone terrestrial laser scanning for Effciently capturing AEC buildings for as-built BIM. ISPRS Ann. Photogramm. Remote Sens. Spatial. Inf. Sci. III-6, 49–55 (2016). doi:10.5194/isprs-annals-III-6-49-2016
24. Branco, J., Varum, H.: Behaviour of Traditional Portuguese Timber Roof Structures (2006)

Implementation Analysis and Design for Energy Efficient Intervention on Heritage Buildings

Elena Gigliarelli[✉], Filippo Calcerano, and Luciano Cessari

National Research Council CNR, Institute for Technologies Applied to Cultural Heritage ITABC,
Via Salaria km. 29.300, 00016 Monterotondo, Italy
{elena.gigliarelli,filippo.calcerano,
luciano.cessari}@itabc.cnr.it

Abstract. The study focuses on a multi-scale and multi-disciplinary approach, for energy efficient intervention on the historic centre and buildings of a town in southern Italy. The methodology involves the use of numerical simulations and building information modeling for the management optimisation of the analysis and design phases. The energy analyses are carried out with experimental measurements and numerical simulations and are integrated with traditional historical, typological and architectural analyses. The study confirms the optimal behaviour of historic settlement principle against new urbanisation and proposes a series of specific solutions to be implemented on the buildings based on improving energy efficiency and sustainability of interventions, compatibility with the restoration charts and with the historical and microclimate context of reference. The study highlighted a number of limitations still present in the interoperability between software that future research developments will have to overcome in order to improve the practical applicability of the approach.

Keywords: Cultural heritage · Building performance simulation · Numerical simulation · BIM · Diagnostic · Urban historic fabric · Energy analysis

1 Introduction

1.1 Cultural Heritage and Sustainable Development

The energy consumption of buildings in Europe is about 40 % [1] of total energy demand and about 36 % of total CO2 emissions [2] and a large part of this consumption (over 80 %) is due to the buildings during their life cycle and do not depends on their construction [3]. In Europe more than 40 % of the building stock was built before 1960, in the absence of laws on energy efficiency [2], and the average amount of investment in new construction accounts for about 1 % of total investments in the construction sector [4]. There is therefore a need to act according to the principles of sustainability and energy efficiency even on existing buildings [5] to make the historic fabric of European cities less energy-intensive and more resilient to climate change [6, 7].

© Springer International Publishing AG 2016
M. Ioannides et al. (Eds.): EuroMed 2016, Part I, LNCS 10058, pp. 91–103, 2016.
DOI: 10.1007/978-3-319-48496-9_8

1.2   Conservation and Energy Revitalization Trend of Historic Architecture

Cultural heritage preservation and energy savings are two important issues for Europe but at the moment there isn't a strong coordinated action on the matter [8]. Energy building retrofit is the application of the best set of technologies to achieve the greatest reduction in energy consumption while maintaining satisfactory internal comfort conditions under certain operating constraints [5]. For proper energy efficient and sustainable design of the built heritage conservation, in the decision making are added the issues of the compatibility of the interventions and materials with the restoration charts and regulations in force and the evaluation of the intervention in its whole life cycle along with its the socio-economic and environmental impacts [9]. The European Commission has taken several actions to reduce energy consumption in buildings, through two directives on the energy performance [1, 10], but the difficulties in finding energy efficiency measures that do not compromise the architectural, historical and cultural values of the built heritage has led lawmakers to exclude it from the laws on energy efficiency [11]. Nevertheless minor and moderate interventions on historic buildings are growing and are characterized by a significant potential for the reduction of energy consumption as demonstrated in the European project SECHURBA [12]. The energy efficiency of the cultural heritage is finally starting to get out of a "regulatory" dimension in contrast with the professional practice and is becoming a strategy to protect the built heritage that in any case is subordinated to its preservation [13, 14].

Generally the approach is characterized by two different scales: at the urban scale are performed expeditious analyses on the fabric, while at the building scale are performed detailed surveys and analyses and more accurate and targeted interventions though they are often decontextualised from the microclimate reference condition [15]. For a proper energy efficient and sustainable design, the approach should instead be simultaneous. The relationship between buildings and climatic and microclimatic context is undeniable in historical architecture, both in construction materials and methods and in the morphology of settlement and building typologies which are determined by biophysical and bioclimatic conditions. Investigating and designing these historical fabrics also from a bioclimatic point of view means not only to improve them from an energy standpoint, but also to rebuild the natural functioning processes of historical and architectural structures enhancing at the same time their distinctive characteristics and identities linked to the conditions of the local microclimate [16]. Moreover, if the approach is also used for newly urban portions it allows for a better harmonization with the historical part.

1.3   Change to the Methods and Tools for Numerical Simulation and Assessment

An integrated and holistic multi-scalar approach requires new methodologies and management tools. The research is then oriented towards the use of numerical simulation (NS), and the integration of the various disciplinary contributions into a single IT platform.

The urban morphology has a substantial effect on the microclimate. Within the Urban Canopy Layer (UCL) there is an interrelation between indoor and outdoor thermo-hygrometric condition which reflects on the building energy balance and consumption [17]. A quantitative study identifies energy savings achievable in buildings by optimizing the external microclimate between 20 and 30 % of the total [18]. Microclimate numerical simulations allow to investigate the ante-operam conditions and to evaluate and compare the performances of different design alternatives. It is still difficult to directly transfer these results to specific Building Performance Simulation (BPS) that are the creation of a "behavioural model" of a building, reduced to a certain level of abstraction of the physical real world entities and connected phenomena [19], and this issue is currently the subject of innovative research insights [20].

For the integrated management of traditional and simulative analyses, some research experiences has started to use Building Information Modeling, that is an additional instrument for the design, representation, production and management of the built environment [21], declined in the field of cultural heritage (HBIM).

The interpretation of HBIM proposed in this study points to an integration in the BIM environment of the geometric complexity of a building or historic fabric (only partly achievable with parametric object libraries derived from manuals and historical data), along with all the multidisciplinary data resulting from the aforementioned design approach of sustainable and energy efficient conservation interventions, which includes the experimental data and energy modeling, configuring then a Historic Energy BIM (HEBIM).

2 Methodology

2.1 The Advantages and Limits of Numerical Simulations and Historic BIM in the Regeneration Process

Numerical simulations are now recognized as a key tool for the energy retrofit of the building stock and the consequent reduction of greenhouse gas emissions because they treat the buildings as a system of interrelated elements that can be optimized and not as the sum of a number of separately designed and optimized sub-systems or components [22]. The purpose of the simulations is to pursue the understanding of passive and active behaviour of the buildings in its microclimatic context [23], thus accelerating the analysis and increasing the efficiency of the design process, and enabling at the analytical stage the understanding of a greater range of design variables, in the design phase the quantitative verification of the effectiveness of the design alternatives through retroactive feedback [19]. The application of numerical simulations in historical contexts triggers a tremendous increase in complexity and at present, few studies focus on the numerical simulation of historic buildings and their calibration [24]. The difficulties mainly depend on the constructive and geometric specificity stratified over the years and on the need to apply dynamic simulations, both for the study of the inertial behaviour that usually historic buildings have, and for the study in the summer season where the simplifications of the steady or quasi-steady-state currently used in energy efficiency regulations are likely to produce misleading results.

The integration between numerical simulations and BIM, due to a lack of standardization of the modeling process of numerical simulation [25] and interoperability limits of current BIM platforms [26], it is still a complex process, that is not automated and heavily dependent on manual steps [27, 28]. Despite the views of the scientific community about the possible future integration of numerical simulation and BIM are still discordant [26, 29], especially on the timing within which this integration will be sufficiently automated, it is now clear that the research should produce the greatest efforts in the direction of this integration [23]. Pursuing this scope applying NS and BIM in historical contexts allows to test the limits and potential of current approaches, offering the possibility of promoting their evolution towards a more effective practical application.

2.2   NS and HBIM Integration Workflow (HEBIM)

From the analysis of the most recent applications of BIM to the cultural heritage, with a majority of case studies in Italy [30, 31], emerges a common approach based on data collection (generally through 3D laser scanner survey), then processed for the acquisition into the BIM environment, to which then follows each time the creation of a custom "mini-library" of parametric "historic objects" which are then related to the virtual geometric model [32]. Then to the objects are added properties concerning the data relating to historical, structural [33] or energy analysis [34], even if the energy analysis is generally performed with simplified software integrated in the same BIM tool. For an optimised Historic Energy BIM (HEBIM) workflow it is instead necessary to integrate the best simulation software (typically external to the BIM tools), taking care not to increase the parallel geometric modeling, caused by low interoperability of software, while increasing at the same time the degree of model flexibility and feedback between NS and BIM.

3   Application

3.1   Selection of a Sustainable Heritage Case. The Town of Frigento

This integrated approach made up of urban regeneration and energy and sustainable redevelopment strategies and methodologies has been applied in the development of the Project METRICS "Methodologies and Technologies for the Management and Requalification of Historic Centres and Buildings". METRICS is an industrial research project funded by the PON Research and Competitiveness 2007-2013, which aims to develop methodologies and innovative and sustainable technologies in historic city centres, for energy and environmental requalification of historic buildings and to study the resilience of urban systems. The research was carried out by a team of scientific institutions and companies led from the Campanian high technology research centre for sustainable construction STRESS.

Frigento, a historic town in the province of Avellino characterized by a strong seismic activity was chosen as a case study and a demonstrator project. In 1980 the earthquake that swept across the territory of Irpinia caused massive damage to Frigento, still noticeable through numerous voids inside the urban fabric. To repair the damage, several actions were planned and implemented concerning demolition works, structural rein-forcement and even numerous reconstructions that have led to a transformation of some parts of the urban fabric.

The old town is now depopulated and features a mix of original and reconstructed buildings that mimic the historical forms with new materials and technologies. Some of these works along with a new expansion have extended the urban fabric along the main roads, according to settlement principles different than the traditional ones.

As a research guideline on the historic fabric, it was decided to operate both at the urban scale, focusing the analysis on a homogeneous and most populated construction sector, and at building scale by working on two of the most representative monumental buildings of Frigento and two smaller buildings with less historic and architectural value.

Testa-Cipriano palace, an elegant building with courtyard currently inhabited by the owners, and De Leo palace that today houses the archaeological museum, the municipal library, a conference room and a multifunctional area, were chosen as examples of the monumental buildings of Frigento.

As regards the buildings characterized by minor historic architectural value, a four-block area in the heart of the town has been identified after several inspections and following careful analysis of maps and documentation, supported by meetings with local experts and technical staff of the municipality. Within the area the investigation was deepened on two terraced residential buildings. The first building has withstood the earthquake and has undergone seismic upgrading works, the other the second was the subject of heavy reconstruction by replacement of the original structure which was in masonry with a new reinforced concrete (Fig. 1).

Fig. 1. Frigento, vico San Giovanni, volumetric assumption previous the earthquake of 1980 on the left and current situation on the right

3.2 From the Survey to the Models: Data Integration of Energy and Restoration Documentation

For the project, a multi-scale approach was adopted to integrate all the collected infor-mation in a series of federated models in HEBIM environment.

On the urban scale, historical, architectural, typological and microclimate studies have been carried out with a first simulation run concerning the sunshine and microclimate conditions (using computing fluid dynamic simulations for analysing the microclimate) (Figs. 2 and 3).

Fig. 2. Solar radiation winter season

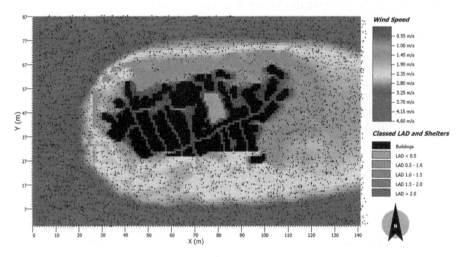

Fig. 3. Winter average wind speed simulation, typical design day: 2017.02.07, h: 14:00

On the identified area further investigations have been developed. As shown in the diagram below, from a 3D laser scanner survey (Figs. 4 and 5), geometric modeling has been developed for BIM (Fig. 6). Inside the BIM an optimized database (Fig. 7) containing historical and urban planning information has been linked to the geometry

(Fig. 6). The geometry was then adapted (simplified) to the level of detail required by energy simulation, eliminating elements of excessive detail arising from the point cloud of the laser scanner survey, or elements of the BIM environment too burdensome for the simulation (such as the trees of BIM libraries, replaced with simplified forms). The geometry was then sent to the simulative analysis of the external microclimate, from which came back the graphical output to be displayed in the BIM model (Fig. 8).

Fig. 4. Workflow scheme (geometric flows highlighted in green, data flows in orange), 3D laser scanning of the area (STRESS) (Color figure online)

Fig. 5. Stages of exploratory and diagnostic investigations: 3D laser scanning survey (STRESS); heat flow analysis (STRESSS – TRE); environmental monitoring (STRESS, ITABC and IRISS CNR, ETT, TRE, TME)

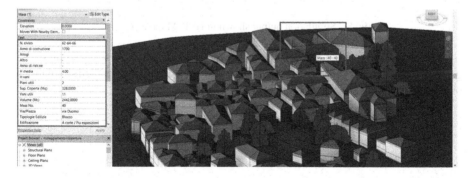

Fig. 6. HBIM modeling with integration of the urban plan in force

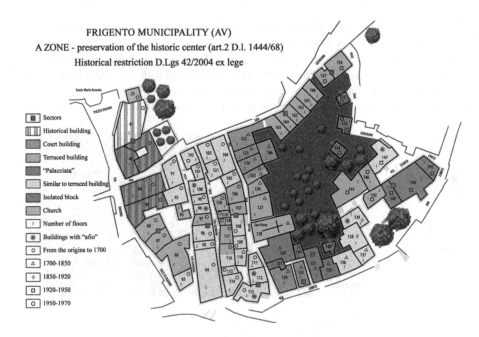

Fig. 7. Urban plans and typological and historical analysis of the reference area

Fig. 8. Simulation output shown in HEBIM environment

The modeling was then deepened over the selected buildings by associating to the geometry functional layers, heat flow and thermographic survey and detailed simulations of solar radiation on the surfaces (Figs. 9 and 10).

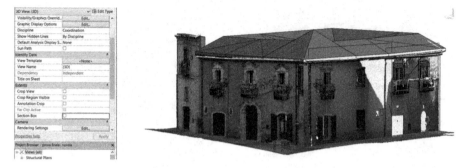

Fig. 9. HBIM model of one of the selected historic buildings

Fig. 10. Thermographic survey and sunshine radiation simulation shown in HEBIM

At the same time a research for energy efficient and sustainable materials and technologies was carried out. The individual elements of the database have been assigned scores by a team of experts according to their potential for improving energy performance of the building, resource consumption, affordability and compatibility with the restoration charts. The survey was then used as a decision support for selecting the retrofit solutions for the selected buildings in order to achieve and surpass the Italian regulatory standards aiming at an environmental sustainability of the intervention including life-cycle cost analysis and social and environmental impacts.

4   Findings and Discussion

4.1   Energy Performance at Historic Urban Level

The results of the microclimate simulations confirm that the old urban fabric is organised for an optimized seasonal behaviour, sheltering the prevailing winds and improving solar exposure in the winter season. On the contrary, the areas of new construction are exposed to the prevailing winds and with poor sun exposure in the cold season (Fig. 11).

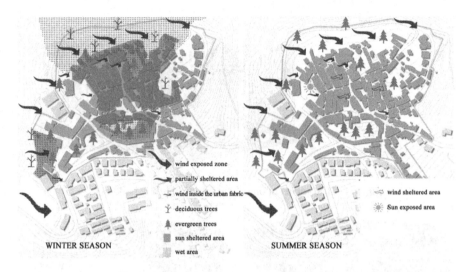

Fig. 11. Summary of environmental performance of the municipality of Frigento in the winter and summer seasons.

4.2 Energy Performance of Heritage Buildings

In all investigated buildings, the analyses have shown poor energy performance due to poor insulation of the envelopes and ground floors of the buildings, poor moisture management and inefficient systems. The envelopes of the historic buildings are slightly less isolated but can count on a better thermal mass that provides better performances in summer season.

For one of the investigated case studies, a retrofit intervention has been proposed with the following design solution:

- the improvement of the envelope and roof insulation through natural sustainable materials that do not hinder the normal transpiration of the building;
- the realisation of a photovoltaic field on the roof made of local innovative photovoltaic and photocatalytic tiles produced with sustainable production processes;
- the substitution of the existing boiler with high efficiency condensing boiler and the realisation of an insulated radiant floor system for the ground floor.

5 Conclusion

5.1 Evaluation

The study, with a multi-scale and multi-disciplinary approach, focused on the application of new tools both for investigation and assessment of the conservation design management in a town in southern Italy. The urban and building scales have been integrated in a progressive deepening of the investigation always able to maintain a strong link between the different levels of the research.

The energy analyses have been carried out both with experimental measurements and with numerical simulations and have been integrated with the traditional historical-typological and architectural analysis.

The data produced were then integrated into a HEBIM platform to facilitate and optimize their management and consulting. The study made it possible to test an innovative workflow showing the potential of a simultaneous analysis and design methodology and highlighting a number of pending limits concerning interoperability between software.

5.2 Future Research

Future research developments will concern the use of dynamic building performance simulations on case studies in order to test and increase interoperability among numerical simulations and BIM both in terms of geometry modeling and in terms of data visualisation of the simulation output inside the BIM environment.

Acknowledgments. This research is funded by the PON Campania Research and Competitiveness 2007–2013. We also thank our colleagues from the research team led from the Campanian high technology research centre for sustainable construction STRESS.

References

1. European Parliament: Directive 2010/31/EU of the European Parliament and of the Council of 19 May 2010 on the Energy Performance of Buildings (2010)
2. Economidou, M., Atanasiu, B., Despret, C., Maio, J., Nolte, I., Rapf, O.: Europe's buildings under the microscope. A country-by-country review of the energy performance of buildings. Buildings Performance Institute Europe, BPIE (2011)
3. Menassa, C.C.: Evaluating sustainable retrofits in existing buildings under uncertainty. Energy Build. **43**, 3576–3583 (2011)
4. Baek, C.-H., Park, S.-H.: Changes in renovation policies in the era of sustainability. Energy Build. **47**, 485–496 (2012)
5. Ma, Z., Cooper, P., Daly, D., Ledo, L.: Existing building retrofits: methodology and state-of-the-art. Energy Build. **55**, 889–902 (2012)
6. IPCC: 2014: Summary for policymakers. In: Field, C.B., Barros, V.R., Dokken, D.J., Mach, K.J., Mastrandrea, M.D., Bilir, T.E., Chatterjee, M., Ebi, K.L., Estrada, Y.O., Genova, R.C., Girma, B., Kissel, E.S., Levy, A.N., MacCracken, S., Mastrandrea, P.R., White, L.L. (eds.) Climate Change 2014: Impacts, Adaptation, and Vulnerability. Part A: Global and Sectoral Aspects. Contribution of Working Group II to the Fifth Assessment Report of the Intergovernmental Panel on Climate Change (2014). http://www.ipcc.ch/pdf/assessment-report/ar5/wg2/ar5_wgII_spm_en.pdf
7. Leissner, J., Kilian, R., Kotova, L., Jacob, D., Mikolajewicz, U., Broström, T., Ashley-Smith, J., Schellen, H.L., Martens, M., van Schijndel, J., Antretter, F., Winkler, M., Bertolin, C., Camuffo, D., Simeunovic, G., Vyhlídal, T.: Climate for culture: assessing the impact of climate change on the future indoor climate in historic buildings using simulations. Herit. Sci. **3**, 38 (2015)

8. Mazzarella, L.: Energy retrofit of historic and existing buildings. The legislative and regulatory point of view. Energy Build. **95**, 23–31 (2015)
9. Moropoulou, A., Labropoulos, K.C., Delegou, E.T., Karoglou, M., Bakolas, A.: Non-destructive techniques as a tool for the protection of built cultural heritage. Constr. Build. Mater. **48**, 1222–1239 (2013)
10. European Commission: Directive 2002/91/EC of the European Parliament and of the Council of 16 December 2002 on the Energy Performance of Buildings (2003)
11. Martínez-Molina, A., Tort-Ausina, I., Cho, S., Vivancos, J.-L.: Energy efficiency and thermal comfort in historic buildings: a review. Renew. Sustain. Energy Rev. **61**, 70–85 (2016)
12. Cessari, L., Gigliarelli, E.: Heritage-led eco-regeneration: the case of Zhejiang water towns protection, restoration and preservation. In: Ioannides, M., Fritsch, D., Leissner, J., Davies, R., Remondino, F., Caffo, R. (eds.) Progress in Cultural Heritage Preservation, pp. 369–377. Springer, Heidelberg (2012)
13. Carbonara, G.: Energy efficiency as a protection tool. Energy Build. **95**, 9–12 (2015)
14. De Santoli, L.: Reprint of "guidelines on energy efficiency of cultural heritage". Energy Build. **95**, 2–8 (2015)
15. Davoli, P., Belpoliti, V., Boarin, P., Calzolari, M.: Innovative methods for a sustainable retrofit of the existing building stock a cross-path from social housing to the listed heritage. In: TECHNE 08 (2014)
16. Baiani, S.: I criteri per il progetto, Cultural Technology. E Progetto Sostenibile Idee E Propos, Ecocompatibili (2010)
17. Bouyer, J., Inard, C., Musy, M.: Microclimatic coupling as a solution to improve building energy simulation in an urban context. Energy Build. **43**, 1549–1559 (2011)
18. de la Flor, F.S., Domínguez, S.A.: Modelling microclimate in urban environments and assessing its influence on the performance of surrounding buildings. Energy Build. **36**, 403–413 (2004)
19. Augenbroe, G.: Trends in building simulation. Build. Environ. **37**, 891–902 (2002)
20. Calcerano, F., Martinelli, L.: Numerical optimisation through dynamic simulation of the position of trees around a stand-alone building to reduce cooling energy consumption. Energy Build. **112**, 234–243 (2016)
21. Murphy, M., McGovern, E., Pavia, S.: Historic building information modelling – adding intelligence to laser and image based surveys of European classical architecture. ISPRS J. Photogramm. Remote Sens. **76**, 89–102 (2013)
22. Hensen, J.L.M.: Towards more effective use of building performance simulation in design. In: Leeuwen, J.P., Van Timmermans, H.J.P. (eds.) Proceeding of 7th International Conference Design and Decision Support Systems in Architecture and Urban Planning, 2–5 July 2004. Eindhoven University of Technology, Eindhoven (2004)
23. Clarke, J.A., Hensen, J.L.M.: Integrated building performance simulation: progress, prospects and requirements. Build. Environ. **91**, 294–306 (2015)
24. Roberti, F., Oberegger, U.F., Gasparella, A.: Calibrating historic building energy models to hourly indoor air and surface temperatures: methodology and case study. Energy Build. **108**, 236–243 (2015)
25. Hitchcock, R.J., Wong, J.: Transforming IFC architectural view BIMs for energy simulation. In: Proceedings of Building Simulation 2011: 12th Conference of International Building Performance Simulation Association, 14–16 November 2011
26. Ivanova, I., Kiesel, K., Mahdavi, A.: BIM-generated data models for EnergyPlus: a comparison of gbXML and IFC Formats. In: Proceedings of Building Simulation Applications, BSA 2015 - 2nd IBPSA-Italy Conference, Bozen-Bolzano, 4th – 6th February 2015 (2015)

27. Maile, T., O'Donnell, J., Bazjanac, V., Rose, C.: BIM-Geometry modelling guidelines for building energy performance simulation. In: Proceedings of BS2013: 13th Conference of International Building Performance Simulation Association, Chambéry, France, 26–28 August 2013
28. O'Donnell, J., Maile, T., Rose, C., Marazovic, N., Morrissey, E., Regnier, C., Parrish, K., Bazjanac, V.: Transforming BIM to BEM: generation of building geometry for the NASA Ames sustainability base BIM (2013)
29. Bazjanac, V.: IFC BIM-based methodology for semi-automated building energy performance simulation. In: 25th International Conference on Information Technology in Construction (2011)
30. Logothetis, S., Delinasiou, A., Stylianidis, E.: Building Information modelling for cultural herigate: a review. In: 25th International CIPA Symposium 2015, ISPRS Annals of the Photogrammetry, Remote Sensing and Spatial Information Sciences, vol. II-5W3, Taipei, Taiwan, 31 August – 04 September 2015 (2015)
31. Garagnani, S., Manferdini, A.M.: Parametric accuracy: building information modeling process applied to the cultural heritage preservation. ISPRS Int. Arch. Photogramm. Remote Sens. Spat. Inf. Sci. 5, 87–92 (2013)
32. Dore, C., Murphy, M., McCarthy, S., Brechin, F., Casidy, C., Dirix, E.: Structural simulations and conservation analysis -historic building information model (HBIM). In: International Archives of the Photogrammetry, Remote Sensing and Spatial Information Sciences, vol. XL-5W4 2015, 3D Virtual Reconstruction and Visualization of Complex Architectures, Avila Spain, 25–27 February 2015 (2015)
33. Oreni, D., Brumana, R., Della Torre, S., Banfi, F., Barazzetti, L., Previtali, M.: Survey turned into HBIM: the restoration and the work involved concerning the Basilica di Collemaggio after the earthquake (L'Aquila). In: ISPRS Annals of the Photogrammetry, Remote Sensing and Spatial Information Sciences, vol. II-5, 2014, ISPRS Technical Commission V Symposium, 23 – 25 June 2014, Riva del Garda, Italy (2014)
34. Brumana, R., Oreni, D., Raimondi, A., Georgopoulos, A., Bregianni, A.: From survey to HBIM for documentation, dissemination and management of built heritage: the case study of St. Maria in Scaria d'Intelvi. In: Digital Heritage International Congress (Digital Heritage), pp. 497–504 (2013)

Historic BIM in the Cloud

Luigi Barazzetti$^{(\boxtimes)}$, Fabrizio Banfi, and Raffaella Brumana

Department of Architecture, Built Environment and Construction
Engineering (ABC), Politecnico di Milano, Via Ponzio 31, 20133 Milan, Italy
{luigi.barazzetti,fabrizio.banfi,
raffaella.brumana}@polimi.it

Abstract. In this paper, we present a procedure which makes available an accurate historic BIM (HBIM) in the cloud. Data processing is carried out with a NURBS-based strategy to reduce the size of the final HBIM derived from images and laser scans, providing an accurate and reliable 3D model with limited memory occupation. This guarantees a remote access with PCs and mobile devices connected through a cloud service.

Keywords: Accuracy · AEC industry · BIM · Cloud · Interoperability · NURBS

1 Introduction

Building Information Modeling (BIM) is becoming more and more important in the Architecture, Engineering and Construction industry [1, 2, 7]. CAD-based drawings (such as plans, sections, elevations generated by architects, engineers, designers, ...) are replaced by a three dimensional model of the building, from which standard 2D project boards are automatically extracted. On the other hand, BIM is much more than a 3D model. BIM requires parametric models where objects have relationships to other objects (e.g. a door fits into a wall) and attributes (e.g. thermal properties, materials, etc.) [9, 13].

Historic Building Information Modeling (HBIM) is a novel approach for documentation, conservation and assessment of historic buildings. It refers to the use of BIM technology for modeling historic structures surveyed with laser scans and photogrammetric methods [10, 14]. The aim of this work is to illustrate a procedure for HBIM generation and the following use with a cloud service (Fig. 1).

The complexity of historic structures makes (parametric) modeling very difficult for the lack of algorithms and procedures able to accurately reconstruct 3D shapes. Generating and managing an accurate HBIM can become a challenge when complex elements cannot be simplified with basic geometric shapes [3]. In fact, most 3D reconstruction approaches tend to generate meshes from point clouds to create a 3D model from photogrammetric and laser scanning data. On the other hand, 3D reconstructions based only on meshes are not optimal for BIM because of problems with mesh parametrization [6, 8, 11, 12, 15, 18, 20, 21] and memory occupation.

A mesh is mainly defined as a set of connected 3D points. It is a static concept that does not satisfy all the requirements of BIM projects. In addition, huge point clouds can be needed in large construction projects, from which huge meshes can be generated.

© Springer International Publishing AG 2016
M. Ioannides et al. (Eds.): EuroMed 2016, Part I, LNCS 10058, pp. 104–115, 2016.
DOI: 10.1007/978-3-319-48496-9_9

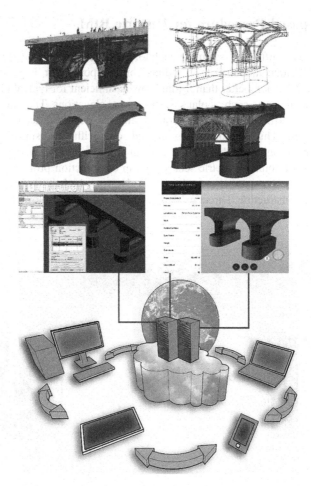

Fig. 1. HBIM generated from point clouds is managed by project teams with centralized access to the project data in the cloud.

The proposed approach focuses on NURBS rather than meshes. NURBS are mathematical functions defined in parametric form and can be interactively manipulated to reconstruct complex shapes. The goal of this work is the use of models based on NURBS curves and surfaces for HBIM to provide an efficient solution that takes into consideration the basic requirements of the surveying project (metric scale, accuracy, level of detail, etc.). At the same time, it provides an efficient solution for the use of the model in interactive 3D modeling environments.

Finally, the proposed approach allows one to exploit cloud computing solutions. The reduced size of the model based on a NURBS objects allows a fluid visualization when users interact with the model, so that architects, engineers, conservators, archeologist, etc., can collaborate in a single, central workspace.

2   The Proposed Procedure for Historic BIM

The use of phase-shift laser scanning technology for digital surveying allows the acquisition of a huge amount of 3D points (billion points for large and complex projects) with a precision better than 5 mm. This is sufficient for typical project boards used in the AEC industry, such as plans, sections, and elevations. The translation of the point cloud into a BIM is carried out considering the expected accuracy at a given metric scale (m). This evaluation is carried out with the simple relationship $E = 0.2m$ (from cartography) that results in 1 cm at the scale 1:50, and 2 cm at 1:100. These are the most common metric scales used in construction projects.

Figure 2 shows the span of a mediaeval bridge, in which it is clear the irregular geometry of the construction. Direct modeling from point clouds allows one to generate

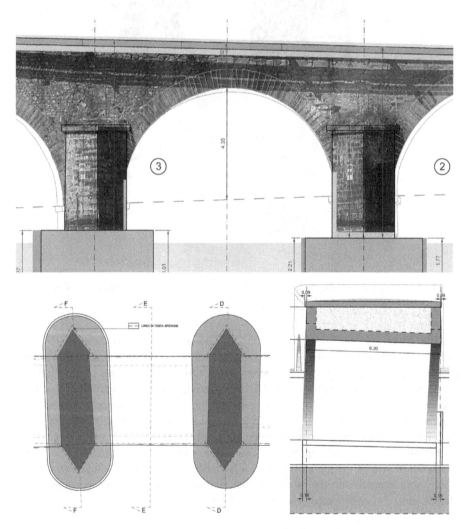

Fig. 2. The case study used in this paper is a span of a medieval bridge. The figure shows an orthophoto of the front (top), a plan (bottom-left) and a section (bottom-right).

a reconstruction based on curves that follows laser scanning data, but BIM software have not libraries able to provide accurate reconstruction of the unique geometry of the bridge.

For this reason, the procedure presented by [5], that exploit NURBS curves and surfaces [16], is used to create 3D parametric objects of the different structural elements of the bridge. Figure 3 shows the NURBS-based modeling results for the intrados of the vault compared to the laser scanning point cloud. The overall discrepancy in terms of RMS is about 5 mm, that is more than sufficient for the metric scale 1:50. In this case, the vault cannot be approximated with simple elements available in BIM packages (e.g. arches) because of the operational requirements of the project.

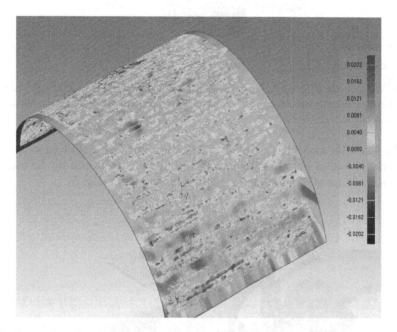

Fig. 3. Comparison between the point cloud and the NURBS surface generated with the proposed procedure. The overall discrepancy is 5 mm in terms of RMS.

The NURBS surface was then parametrized by means of an offset [17] of the intrados, so that the original NURBS surface is preserved and a dynamic object-based representation of the complete object (including semantics and attributes) is achieved (Fig. 4). This last step, i.e. the creation of the final BIM objects, is carried out by exploiting both geometrical and functional requirements, in which the geometrical problem is solved through a multilayer structure with multiple offsets of the intrados.

The reconstruction of the whole span was carried out with the proposed NURBS based procedure with the identification of the different constructive elements. This is a fundamental step for the creation of accurate object-based reconstructions that will be used by different specialists.

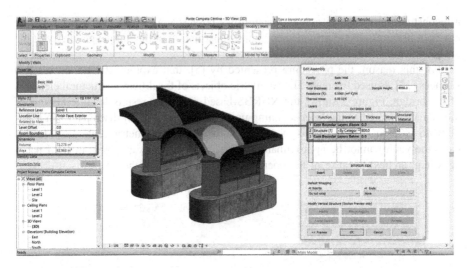

Fig. 4. The dynamic BIM representation of the vault. The intrados surveyed through laser scans has a new parametric representation in which the thinness is interactively modified in the software database.

The final BIM model has a size of 17 MB when imported and saved in Autodesk Revit. The choice of Autodesk Revit as final software is motivated by the need of a single platform for all the specialists involved in the project (Fig. 5).

Fig. 5. The final HBIM of the span is made up of several BIM objects for the different constructive elements.

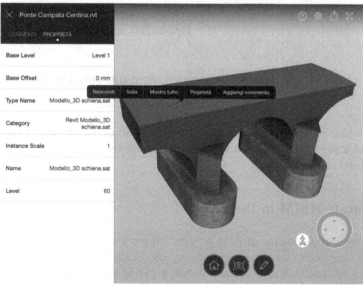

Fig. 6. HBIM simultaneously available in multiple devices thanks to A360 cloud technology (top). Object properties are still available so that the database is (partially) preserved.

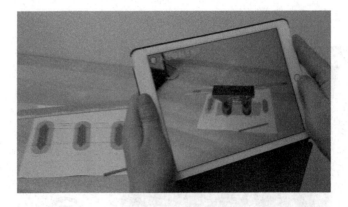

Fig. 7. Technical drawings available for the users involved in the project become the marker for triggering AR apps.

The reader is referred to [19] for more details about the presented case study. Additional images illustrating the work carried out for the whole bridge are shown in Fig. 9, at the end of the paper.

3 Accurate HBIM in the Cloud

Because basic requirements of BIM projects require a collaborative environment for architects, engineers, customers, producers, etc., cloud-BIM is a very promising technology to simultaneously connect people avoiding the release of multiple project versions with possible inconsistencies. A centralized version of the model can be remotely accessed by multiple operators who can view, inspect, and edit project files without expensive hardware and software. Real-time communication can be carried out between multiple specialists through chat and email notifications. Such solution is

Fig. 8. AR allows one to see hidden elements, such as foundations, riverbed, and a digital reconstruction of the possible wooden structure used to build the vault.

already available in some cloud-based platforms, allowing multiple specialists to work inside a highly collaborative environment.

On the other hand, cloud-BIM is still a relatively new technology with a limited use in practical applications. The first scientific papers on cloud-BIM were published in 2011. The number of available systems has rapidly increased, leading to the actual avaibility of several platforms such as Autodesk 360, BIM9, BIMServer, BIMx, etc. As things stand at the present, cloud-BIM is mainly used for the design and construction phase of the building, with limited application to maintenance, building lifecycle, facility management and demolition.

In this work Autodesk® 360 (A360) was used to use the bridge project in the cloud. Only a span of the bridge was considered and future work will focus on the whole model. Autodesk 360 is defined as "a cloud-based platform that gives you access to storage, a collaboration workspace, and cloud services to help you dramatically improve the way you design, visualize, simulate, and share your work with others anytime, anywhere". The system provides 3 GB of free storage space, whereas a monthly, quarterly or annual subscription includes 25 GB and the access to cloud computing services for rendering, optimization, energy analysis and structural analysis. The file size limit is 2 GB per file.

The supported web browsers are Google Chrome, Mozilla Firefox, Microsoft Internet Explorer for 2D visualization (plans, sections, elevations, …), whereas 3D

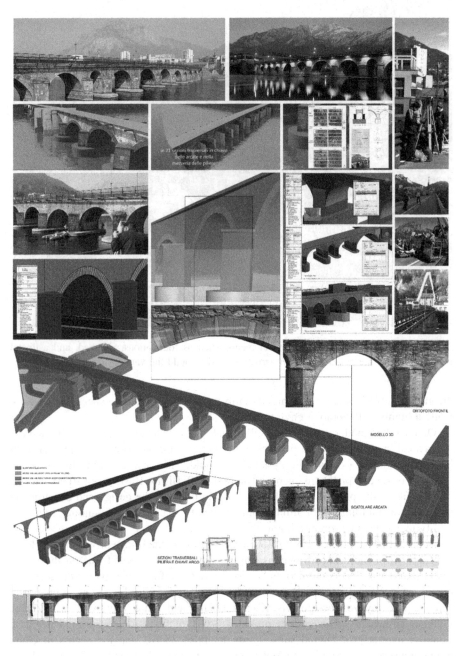

Fig. 9. The BIM project of the whole bridge, more details about the reconstruction process are illustrated in [19]. The work presented in this paper was carried out with a single span.

viewing is only supported by Google Chrome and Mozilla Firefox (Fig. 6 – top). A mobile application was also developed to bridge the gap between the office and field. The mobile app supports more than 100 file formats used in the AEC industry including 2D and 3D (e.g. dwg, dwf, ipt, iam, idw, rvt, sldprt, sldasm, asm, nwd, nwc, catpart, catproduct, f3d, etc.). It can access email attachments and files from Dropbox, Box, Google Drive, OneDrive, iCloud, Buzzsaw, etc. Basic functions are available for reviewing and navigating models through intuitive touch-based navigation (zoom, pan, rotate) as well as tools for annotation, markup, and comment. It should be mentioned that operations are not carried out by simply visualizing the geometry of a 3D model. Objects properties (level, type, category, ...) are provided by selecting the different objects, so that the project database remains available.

4   Conclusions and Outlooks

HBIM in the cloud is probably one of the future developments of BIM technology. The avaibility of the model in mobile devices, as well as functions and tools for navigating and editing, is potentially able to bridge the gap between office and construction site. As things stand at the present, only PCs with reasonable screen size can be used for effective work in which the model and its database are handled. On the other hand, mobile applications can have a primary role for in-situ productive work, where digital documentation is today substituted by printed project boards. The development of cloud-based solutions and the use of tablets will integrate (not substitute) the traditional use of paper. Cloud technology requires also a particular attention on security issues. The presented A360 application is provided through a protected infrastructure for cloud computing, in which both individuals and companies can securely access data stored or data in transit.

As data are immediately available in 3D, cloud BIM opens new opportunities also for augmented and virtual reality (AR and VR). IN particular, AR allows a direct connection of projects boards with the 3D model available in mobile devices. Figure 7 shows the plan of the span with the 3D model, both inspected inside the office.

Marker-less AR represents a real challenge with formidable expected results during on-site exploitation. Parts that are not visible (foundations and river bed, i.e. covered by water), as well as elements that are no longer available (the wooden structure used during the construction of the vault), can be reviewed (Fig. 8). The potential for generic construction sites relies on the visualization of hidden elements (e.g. MEP) or the progressive construction stages of the construction, among the others.

A significant difference between the BIM available in the cloud and that used in the AR examples is relating to information loss. The model for AR is no longer a BIM. It is turned into a static model without attributes, i.e. it requires a preliminary conversion in common formats for direct 3D modeling. The avaibility of a complete BIM also in AR apps is a possible future innovation to make BIM technology directly available.

References

1. Arayici, Y.: Towards building information modelling for existing structures. Struct. Surv. **26**, 210–222 (2008)
2. Azhar, S., Khalfan, M.: MAQSOOD: building information modeling (BIM): now and beyond. Australas. J. Constr. Econ. Build. **12**(4), 15–28 (2012)
3. Baik, A., Alitany, A., Boehm, J., Robson, S.: Jeddah historical building information modelling "JHBIM" – object library. ISPRS Ann. Photogramm. Remote Sens. Spat. Inf. Sci. **2**(5), 41–47 (2014)
4. Barazzetti, L.: Parametric as-built model generation of complex shapes from point clouds. Adv. Eng. Inform. **30**, 298–311 (2016)
5. Barazzetti, L., Banfi, F., Brumana, R., Previtali, M.: Creation of parametric BIM objects from point clouds using NURBS. Photogramm. Rec. **30**(152), 339–362 (2015)
6. Barazzetti, L., Banfi, F., Brumana, R., Gusmeroli, G., Oreni, D., Previtali, M., Roncoroni, F., Schiantarelli G.: BIM from laser clouds and finite element analysis: combining structural analysis and geometric complexity. In: International Archives of Photogrammetry, Remote Sensing and Spatial Information Sciences, vol. 40(5/W4), pp. 345–350 (2015)
7. Bryde, D., Broquetas, M., Volm, J.M.: The project benefits of building information modelling (BIM). Int. J. Project Manage. **31**(7), 971–980 (2013)
8. Brumana, R., Oreni, D., Raimondi, A., Georgopoulos, A., Breggiani, A.: From survey to HBIM for documentation, dissemination and management of built heritage: the case study of St. Maria in Scaria d'Intelvi. In: Digital Heritage International Congress, Marseille, France, pp. 497–504 (2013)
9. Eastman, C., Teicholz, P., Sacks, R., Liston, K.: BIM Handbook: A Guide to Building Information Modeling for Owners, Managers, Designers, Engineers and Contractors, 2nd edn. Wiley, Hoboken (2011). 626 pages
10. Fai, S., Graham, K., Duckworth, T., Wood, N., Attar, R.: Building information modeling and heritage documentation. In: 23rd International CIPA Symposium (2011). 8 pages
11. Fai, S., Filippi, M., Paliaga, S.: Parametric modelling (BIM) for the documentation of vernacular construction methods: a BIM model for the Commissariat Building, Ottawa, Canada. In: ISPRS Annals of Photogrammetry, Remote Sensing and Spatial Information Sciences, vol. 2(5/W1), pp. 115–120 (2013)
12. Fai, S., Rafeiro, J.: Establishing an appropriate level of detail (LoD) for a building information model (BIM) – West Block, Parliament Hill, Ottawa, Canada. ISPRS Ann. Photogramm. Remote Sens. Spat. Inf. Sci. **2**(5), 123–130 (2014)
13. Kensek, K., Noble, D.: Building Information Modeling: BIM in Current and Future Practice. Wiley, Hoboken (2014). 432 pages
14. Murphy, M., Mccgovern, E., Pavia, S.: Historic building information modelling (HBIM). Struct. Surv. **27**(4), 311–327 (2009)
15. Oreni, D., Brumana, R., Cuca, B.: Towards a methodology for 3D content models. the reconstruction of ancient vaults for maintenance and structural behaviour in the logic of BIM management. In: 18th International Conference on Virtual Systems and Multimedia - Virtual Systems in the Information Society, Milan, Italy, pp. 475–482 (2012)
16. Piegl, L., Tiller, W.: The NURBS Book. Monographs in Visual Communication. Springer, Heidelberg (2012). 646 pages. ISBN 978-3-642-97385-7
17. Piegl, L., Tiller, W.: Computing offsets of NURBS curves and surfaces. Comput. Aided Des. **31**, 147–156 (1999)
18. Thomson, C., Boehm, J.: Automatic geometry generation from point clouds for BIM. Remote Sens. **7**(9), 11753–11775 (2015)

19. Barazzetti, L., Banfi, F., Brumana, R., Previtali, M., Roncoroni, F.: BIM from laser scans… not just for buildings: NURBS-based parametric modeling of a medieval bridge. ISPRS Ann. Photogramm. Remote Sens. Spat. Inf. Sci. **III-5**, 51–56 (2016). doi:10.5194/isprs-annals-III-5-51-2016

20. Georgopoulos, A., Oreni, D., Brumana, R., Cuca, B.: HBIM for conservation and management of built heritage: towards a library of vaults and wooden beam floors. In: Proceeding of XXIV International CIPA Symposium (2013)

21. Oreni, D.: From 3D content models to HBIM for conservation and management of built heritage. In: Murgante, B., Misra, S., Carlini, M., Torre, C.M., Nguyen, H.-Q., Taniar, D., Apduhan, B.O., Gervasi, O. (eds.) ICCSA 2013. LNCS, vol. 7974, pp. 344–357. Springer, Heidelberg (2013). doi:10.1007/978-3-642-39649-6_25

Building Information Modelling – A Novel Parametric Modeling Approach Based on 3D Surveys of Historic Architecture

Fabrizio Banfi[✉]

Department of Architecture, Built Environment and Construction Engineering (ABC),
Politecnico di Milano, Via Ponzio 31, 20133 Milan, Italy
fabrizio.banfi@polimi.it

Abstract. Building Information Modelling (BIM) appears to be the best answer to simplify the traditional process of design, construction, management and maintenance. On the other hand, the intricate reality of the built heritage and the growing need to represent the actual geometry using 3D models collide with the new paradigms of complexity and accuracy, opening a novel operative perspective for restoration and conservation. The management of complexity through BIM requires a new management approach focused on the development of improve the environmental impact cost, reduction and increase in productivity and efficiency the Architecture, Engineering and Construction (AEC) Industry. This structure is quantifiable in morphological and typical terms by establishing levels of development and detail (LoDs) and changes of direction (ReversLoDs) to support the different stages of life cycle (LCM). Starting from different experiences in the field of HBIM, this research work proposes a dynamic parametric modeling approach that involves the use of laser scanning, photogrammetric data and advanced modelling for HBIM.

Keywords: BIM · Complexity · LoD · NURBS · Point clouds

1 Introduction

The innovation and development of Information Communication Technology (ICT) in support of the Architecture, Engineering industry, Construction and Operations (AECO) is characterized by the growing use of BIM [9, 12].

The digitized management of historic buildings, infrastructure and complex systems bases its foundation on theoretical and operational processes in continuous development. In this process, the level of transmissibility of knowledge is fragmented and not fully assimilated by the professionals involved. Their software and support tools are not able to accommodate the correct level of complexity causing the generation of simplified 3D models (not corresponding to the as-built) or complex BIM for a subsequent management.

Research and introduction of new paradigms as complexity for the built heritage is a basic need to develop operative aspects to support identification, assimilation and

© Springer International Publishing AG 2016
M. Ioannides et al. (Eds.): EuroMed 2016, Part I, LNCS 10058, pp. 116–127, 2016.
DOI: 10.1007/978-3-319-48496-9_10

transmission of useful and valuable information for the preservation of cultural heritage [2, 7]. Each application requires geometric and technical characteristics defined by advanced modeling procedures that could lead to data loss if not property tuned. Nowadays, modeling requires long generative practices and specific computer skills that correctly interpret the complexity of the buildings, and then transmit them within an operating process that consists of different interdisciplinary teams [3, 5].

The complexity is a fundamental prerogative for high transmissibility of the information [10]. It results essential to enhance the vast number of technical analyses for all types of buildings [1, 14]. It can become a definable standard parameter addressed to European and global directives for the next years in favor of BIM integration in design and construction processes.

The objectives of this research are:

- Integrate 3D survey techniques and advanced parametric modelling, providing a real starting point for the creation of as-built BIMs with different LoDs.
- Argue the usefulness of a methodological advanced modelling approach that automates the generative process of HBIM favouring the control, management and transmissibility of the information collected during the building's life cycle.
- Show how BIM can support the process of designing, building, restructuring, maintenance and analyses, through three case studies aimed at different ReversLoDs approach for historic buildings.
- To discuss, analyse, identify gaps in the work carried out, and propose possible future research lines.

The process is based on research work carried out in recent years in the field of HBIMs of great historical value buildings in the Italian territory. It was supported by public institutions, multinational companies and research groups that have made possible a sensitive scientific growth in the protection of architectural heritage. The Italian case studies which will be described are the Basilica of Collemaggio in L'Aquila, Castel Masegra in Sondrio and finally the Azzone Visconti Bridge in Lecco. The chronologic order imposed in this paper follows the creation of models, from oldest to most current BIM, in order to highlight the improvement of the interchangeability with different LoDs obtained from 2013 to 2016.

2   A Novel Parametric Modeling Approach

This research proposes a dynamic methodological approach based on the management of complex 3D shapes managed and manipulated with a new initial LoDs obtained from the 3D survey and with bidirectional levels of complexity (ReversLods) which provides the integration of NURBS modeling and parametric applications to support life cycle management (LCM). HBIM increased the level of knowledge of the building through the integrated use of various applications, which can be mainly divided into two macro families: pure modeling software like MC Neel® Rhinoceros, and Autodesk® Autocad 3DS MAX, which are able to fully investigate the morphological appearance of the building, and BIM Platforms such as Autodesk® Revit and ArchiCAD Graphisoft®, where the typological differentiation and the ability to associate additional information is the basic logic. The first family is characterized by a free modeling approach that generates 3D elements and surfaces able to reproduce complex forms. The user can create surfaces and solids starting from the basic generative elements like lines, NURBS (Non Uniform Basis Splines) [11], and mesh [16]. The disadvantage is the absence of tools that allow the parameterization of the elements. The second family is characterized instead by an internal structure made up of a database with families of objects. These objects represent the architectural elements that form a building. Each element is adjustable in its sub components, the parameterization of the dimensional components can be adjusted and the type of each element can be edited through the use of settable parameters (before and after) [6]. The main disadvantage that impedes the use of BIM for historic buildings is the modeling of complex shapes: only through hard, long and complex modeling practices it is possible to reach a sufficient level of detail. In historic buildings morphological and typological aspects are not aligned. This is a fundamental problem for the creation of HBIMs derived from 3D surveying techniques. The interoperability of modeling software is a crucial aspect in order to optimize the peculiarities of the two modeling families.

The transition from pure modeling software like Rhinoceros, AutoCAD to Revit depended on the determination of the complexity and the level of accuracy of BIM. Modeling must adapted to the information collected during the survey, allowing the association of data to 3D parametric objects [4]. The advantage of combining these two macro families with a survey based laser scanner (*integration*) could develop new methodological approaches to investigate the accuracy of existing assets and the overall control over the entire design process as well as construction, maintenance of building (Fig. 1).

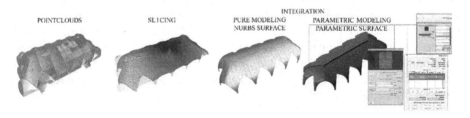

Fig. 1. Generation process characterized by the integration of pure modeling (NURBS) with the parametric modeling in BIM application.

For this reason, the 3D model must guarantee in terms of morphological features and reality and then know how to steer a specific LoD [8]. The peculiarities of an existing building, complex shapes of architectural and structural elements can be properly interpreted, generated and represented by generative advanced modeling tools based on NURBS technology.

The technological advancement requires continuous adaptation of the various standards. In recent years, new parameters have been defined to assess the level of the 3D model in geometrical terms and its associated information.

The management of CAD formats presupposes a development of interoperability techniques to convey the totality of information available. This integration requires an orientation of the models based on different LoDs of BIM, guaranteeing the new hierarchy of the model. This means that the use of the information associated with the parametric model determines level of transmissibility of information of the building. Consequently, transmission of knowledge is determined by the modeling of each element and by the level of complexity transmitted during the process. Figure 2 shows the integration process used to generate HBIM.

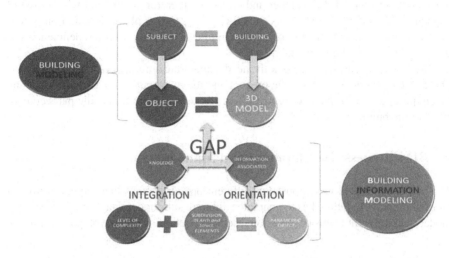

Fig. 2. The proposed parametric modeling approach – integration of pure and parametric modeling in order to improve the transmission of complexity, information and knowledge of the building

3   LoD Level of Development and Detail

LoDs allow us to measure the reliability and security of information associated to the BIM during the building process: starting from planning and construction to maintenance [8]. From an operational point of view, the advantages in the built environment can be substantial especially in terms of time in the implementation phase of the 3D model. LoDs are divided into a first 'not modeled' Conceptual representation (100), a second level with the general requirements and the main quantities (200), a third level to support the detailed design, a fourth level 'manufacture/install' in support of construction planning (400), and a fifth and final level 'as-built' in support of a Asset management (500).

In most cases, a 300-definition level can be a good initial compromise to manage a new building. It is possible to pass to the next levels following the requirements of the design and the following integration in the building process. It is sometimes impossible to define a correct LoD for existing and historic buildings. For example: the use of a laser scanner does not allow the automatic recognition of materials and elements.

On the other hand, the protection and conservation of the built heritage requires, (during the survey) to use non-invasive methodologies. The use of destructive techniques, such as core drilling, is not permitted in order to protect the building. Therefore, the materials used and the construction techniques are unknown in the early stages of laser scanner survey. The survey of the building can reveal morphological and typological aspects even after years. However it is sometimes necessary to decrease the level of definition of the model obtained, reversing the accuracy of the model to support the design process. Consequently, it is not possible to define a clear LoD during the initial agreement between BIM developer and customer; therefore the model will consist of elements with different LoDs. This should require a further phase of definition of not-modeled objects. The transmission clearly implies a duty to report the deficiencies of the model in terms of quality and quantity.

The following case studies show the need to integrate different LoD in the generation phase of the models to support the process and the importance of advanced modeling that requires to invert the level of modelling (ReverseLoDs) for specific parts/components of the building.

4   BIM Process: Development and Management

The proposed method is composed at different operative steps that required different types of model. Modelling has to guarantee different sub-models starting from the same model with different levels of precision, accuracy, definition and development (Fig. 3).

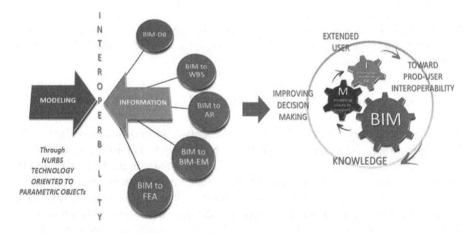

Fig. 3. Orientation model based on the integration of advanced modeling to improve the transferability of knowledge in BIM

The generation of complex elements such as vaults, arches, domes and walls damaged capable of represent the laser data requires complex modeling practices.

Figure 4 describes the process in its analytic and operative phases. It shows the required model and the ReverseLoDs approach:

Fig. 4. BIM Implementation: different type of model in life cycle

The key idea is based on both interoperability and integrated use of development levels, as well as definition (for each building) should be targeted of specific analyses. The analysis software must be viewed from the point of view of an advanced modelling practice, that is a constraint in which the first modeling step must be oriented to the correct reading of the BIM. It must to update and change throughout the process and this requires an improvement of knowledge of the modeling techniques. This requires a model that must allow an increase or decrease (ReverseLoD) in the level of complexity. The new paradigm of Orientation of model/modelling is crucial to achieve such particular type of analyses [15].

5 Case Study 1: Bidirectional Generative Process to Support the Restoration Project of Basilica of Collemaggio in L'Aquila

In 2009 the Aquila's earthquake severely damaged the apse of the basilica, leading to the collapse of the roof. The pillar of the transept completely collapsed. Their supported the weight of the vault and the covering system. Naves have suffered subsidence in the north wall (out of plumb of about 40 cm) and in the pillars. This case study shows that the levels used in the model are different because they had to support different phases of the restoration project. Specifically, the generative phase resulted in an HBIM and its use in the restoration project, with a special attention to procedures used to preserve the complexity of photogrammetry and laser scanning data and not always suit the design phase. The 3D survey of the basilica required integration of detection techniques (Fig. 5) that could restore the morphological complexity of the construction.

Fig. 5. 3D survey campaign with UAV, total station and laser scanner 3D

The geodetic network was measured with a Leica® TS30 total station, with a level of precision on the measurement of 0.6 mm and 0.15 mgon on measures of azimuth and zenith angles. The number of scans was 182 collected, with a resolution of 44 million points. The UAV survey with Astec Falcon 8 equipped with RGB camera Sony NEX - 5N photogrammetrically calibrated performed have allowed us to use a powerful tool to inspect the condition of the roof in 2013, providing useful data for the generation of as-built model of the basilica.

The morphological complexity of the Basilica was the key to refine modelling techniques oriented to the generation of a BIM that represent the actual reality of the building adapted to project requirements. The main objective was to define a high level of detail of the constructive elements of the basilica and achieve an accuracy of modeling with parametric surfaces and objects with a LoD 500. The architectural elements generated from point clouds were characterized obtaining semi-automatic generative profiles through the integrated use of software McNeel® Rhinoceros and plug-in Pointools. This is a support for managing and editing the clouds to proceed to the realization of 2D drawings (plans, elevations and sections) and then the model. Figure 6 shows the generation process: the slice extraction procedure from point clouds led automatic generation of NURBS surfaces and solids. They were obtained by a preliminary morphological quantification corresponding to a LoD 300.

Fig. 6. Generative process. From pointclouds to 3D model the pillars defined by each single stone. The HBIM reaches LoD 500

The flexibility of the method, has allowed transferring each element generated with the pure modeling at a LoD 400, except the excavations, cellars and external parts still characterized by a LoD 200 for a lack of data on the environments, resulting in a lack of thickness of the walls and only a 3D generation of intrados surfaces. Starting from the use of Autodesk® Revit, the HBIM of the Basilica was able to associate useful information to the next steps. Direct survey was essential to determine each sub stone form. Each pillar is composed of a certain number of courses; each course is composed of a variable number of stone blocks (Fig. 6). The definition of the laser scanner survey did not allow detecting the joints of connections of the various segments because of the safety straps covering each pillar, so the direct survey allowed migrating the main geometric information of the blocks in the HBIM with LoD 500.

Subsequently, the level of definition achieved exceeded the real needs for the Construction Site (4D) of this phase [13]. The simplification required a LoD 200/300/400.

Finally, the flexibility of the 3D model allowed the updating of the project requests in the preliminary and final phase thanks to 3D rendering and digital video simulations generated with the application Abvent® Artlantis. As shown in Fig. 7,

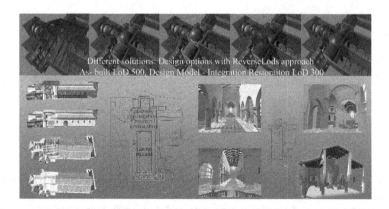

Fig. 7. Comparing as/built and project. Through different LoDs it was possible to integrate BIM (LoD 500) with 3D design integration of the Basilica with a LoD 300.

through ReverseLods it was possible to integrate design assumptions (LoD 300) to LoD 500 (as-built) of the basilica, supporting the design choices during life cycle of project restoration.

6   Case Study 2: Modelling, NURBS-Mesh Technology, LoDs and HBIM of Masegra Castel in Sondrio

This case study involved the construction of a HBIM of Castel Masegra in Sondrio by laser scanner and photogrammetric data. The objective of this project is to preserve the architectural and landscape heritage of Valtellina and Valposchiavo, sharing activities, knowledge and methodologies using the most advanced techniques for diagnostics, restoration, maintenance and management of cultural heritage, which were developed by interpreting the preservation as a long-term process. The 3D survey has produced 176 scans for a total of 7.5 Billion of points with a resolution greater than 3 mm by using a Faro® Laser Scanner Focus 3D and Leica® TS30 total station. Each scan was composed of 44 million points. A robust geodetic network controlled the large amount of data collected with laser scanner.

The modeling phase is based on a generative approach of the various elements surveyed with the laser scanner. The integrated use of Autodesk® AutoCAD and McNeel® Rhinoceros allowed us to generate 3D profiles for the generation of NURBS surfaces able to follow the clouds of points with an average deviation of around 2, 3 mm. Specific tools for point cloud management were recently included in AutoCAD2015. The integrated use of the Pointools plugin in McNeel® Rhinoceros and Autodesk® ReCap have greatly shortened the generative process of the model. Cloud management was carried out through the new .rcp format, which can index and group all the scans. New cleaning tools of point clouds have determined the area of interest directly in AutoCAD, without using other plugins. The case study of the umbrella vault at the second floor exploited the entire method applied to the Basilica of Collemaggio (Fig. 8).

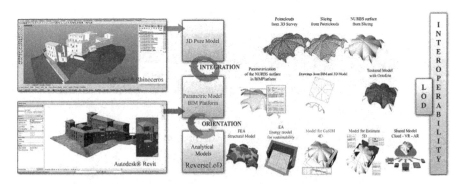

Fig. 8. Modeling process – integration, orientation, LoD and interoperability of 3D model

The combined use of laser scanning data and Agisoft® PhotoScan gave an orthophoto that highlights the morphological complexity of the vault. It was generated by the alignment of 34 photos and a total of 95110 points. The use of a total station allowed to define 9 control points and correctly georeferenced the photogrammetric model with the laser point clouds. The integration of these two techniques allowed us to reprocess data collected directly in Rhinoceros and model the data by importing the mesh generated in Agisoft® PhotoScan through the obj file format. Through this format all the information can be listed for the definition of lines, polygons and curves and complex surfaces. 3D mesh generation led to determine a number of profiles and control sections of the complex geometry of the vault in McNeel® Rhinoceros. To avoid possible geometrical deviations, each profile was used with the ReverseLoDs approach, for the next portion of the vaults.

Thanks to the dynamic offset, it was possible to automatically parameterize surfaces with a LoD 400. Figure 9 describes the modelling process used: the transformation of wall surfaces allowed the integration of physical information, for materials with LoD 500 and the orientation the model for different analyses.

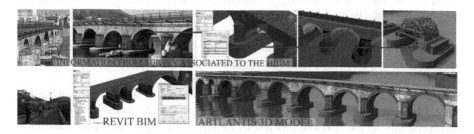

Fig. 9.   From 3D survey to BIM LoD 500 and an example of historical rib

7   Case Study 3: LoD 500 for Defining the HBIM of a Mediaeval Infrastructure - Visconti Bridge in Lecco, Italy

The third case study is the HBIM of the medieval bridge Azzone Visconti in Lecco. This is still under investigation by the public administration of the town of Lecco. The main objective of the research was to create a model that can accommodate the maximum amount of information collected by other research groups (geologists, structural engineers, historians etc.) to monitor and preserve the bridge.

The survey campaign involved the generation of a geodetic network of 77 scans obtained with a Faro Focus 3D. The total number of laser scanning points was more than 2.5 billions, with an average precision of ±3 mm achieved by using chessboard targets detected with the total station and additional scan-to-scan correspondence (spherical targets). Photogrammetry has allowed the realization of number orthophotos of the 11 arches of the bridge and its fronts.

The purpose of modeling was to achieve a LoD 500 and implement the method of the two cases previous studies. The scans of the bridge have been transferred directly into the Mc Neel® Rhinoceros. The NURBS technology (due to its ability to interpolate points) allowed us, to generate surfaces that follow the data laser without geometric deviations. The creation of the wall partitions in Autodesk® Revit carried out through the automatic parameterization of the NURBS surfaces using the tools Wall By Face and Edit Profile. Thanks to the resolution of the point clouds has been possible to get an example of historical rib with LoD500. The putlog hole have determined the thickness of the various wooden elements of the rib. With the 3D Augmented app you can directly simulate the insertion of the rib on the river bridge.

A comprehensive database (LoD 500) for objects and share information for portable devices was created with Autodesk® A360. Finally, Abvent® Artlantis and iVisit 3D allowed us to created a virtual simulation of the medieval system of construction. The transmission of information to structural engineers, geologists and supervisors can take place by importing the whole model in a cloud service with the automatic ReverseLoDs approach at the level 500.

8   Results and Discussion

The HBIM the Basilica of Collemaggio can directly demonstrate the general complexity of geometric model through different LoDs, which avoids simplified representations that do not match the actual complexity of the building. In the Concept and Design phase the model can receive changes in certain areas of the building to support different design solutions. The inversion of LoDs of these areas can be useful for modelling practices in terms of time and design simulations at lower or higher levels.

The modellative practices of Castel Masegra have been optimized trying to reduce processing time, costs related to the generation of the model and increase its level of interoperability for the next maturity level. Starting on the experience of the Basilica of Collemaggio, it was useful to set a proper general LoDs. The large size of an HBIM required ReverseLoDs practices to guide the extrados and intrados surfaces of the vaults.

The HBIM model of Visconti Bridge showed the morphological features of a medieval infrastructure bypassing the generative phase of 2D drawings, thanks to a LoD 500 supporting the entire decision-making process, facilitated the sharing of information in different interdisciplinary groups for the protection and preservation of a historical bridge. Shared knowledge phase provides a process of simplification of the model for mobile devices and clouds in the web. The reversal definition 'ReverseLoDs' may provide a selection of the information shared to improve the size of the model, the navigation and its simulation.

9   Conclusion

Thanks to laser scanning technology for a modeler is easier to reconstruct the complexity of the building. Simplifications of the model based on personal interpretive logic is still mandatory of complex projects. This paper presents an advanced modeling technique for historic buildings, which integrate the pure modelling and NURBS technology with additional parametrization to orientate the models to the correct level of complexity. The levels of development for the HBIM must ensure a bidirectionality in favor of updates of the constructive elements of the building realized in digital environment for different types of analyses. The ReverseLoDs approach for historic buildings can support the process of designing, building, restructuring, maintenance and analyses.

Finally, these techniques highlight the need to introduce a hierarchy of new levels of accuracy of HBIM models giving a certified quality value of the generated model.

References

1. Azhar, S., Brown, J., Farooqui, R.: BIM-based sustainability analysis: an evaluation of building performance analysis software. In: Proceedings of the 45th ASC Annual Conference, Gainesville, Florida (2009)
2. Barazzetti, L.: Parametric as-built model generation of complex shapes from point clouds. Adv. Eng. Inform. **30**, 298–311 (2016)
3. Barazzetti, L., Banfi, F., Brumana, R., Gusmeroli, G., Oreni, D., Previtali, M., Roncoroni, F., Schiantarelli, G.: BIM from laser clouds and finite element analysis: combining structural analysis and geometric complexity. In: International Archives of Photogrammetry, Remote Sensing and Spatial Information Sciences, vol. 40(5/W4), pp. 345–350 (2015)
4. Barazzetti, L., Banfi, F., Brumana, R., Previtali, M.: Creation of parametric BIM objects from point clouds using nurbs. Photogramm. Rec. **30**(152), 339–362 (2015)
5. Brumana, R., Oreni, D., Cuca, B., Binda, L., Condoleo, P., Triggiani, M.: Strategy for integrated surveying techniques finalized to interpretive models in a byzantine church, Mesopotam, Albania. Int. J. Archit. Heritage **8**, 886–924 (2014)
6. Eastman, C., Teicholz, P., Sacks, R., Liston, K.: BIM Handbook: A Guide to Building Information Modeling for Owners, Managers, Designers, Engineers and Contractors, 2nd edn. Wiley, Hoboken (2011). 626 pages
7. Fai, S., Graham, K., Duckworth, T., Wood, A.: Building information modelling and heritage documentation. In: XXIII CIPA International Symposium, Prague, Czech Republic (2011)
8. Fai, S., Rafeiro, J.: Establishing an appropriate level of detail (LoD) for a building information model (BIM) – West Block, Parliament Hill, Ottawa, Canada. ISPRS Ann. Photogramm. Remote Sens. Spat. Inf. Sci. **2**(5), 123–130 (2014)
9. Johnson, R.E., Clayton, M.J.: The impact of information technology in design and construction: the owner's perspective. Autom. Constr. **8**(1), 3–14 (1998)
10. Oreni, D., Brumana, R., Banfi, F., Bertola, L., Barazzetti, L., Cuca, B., Previtali, M., Roncoroni, F.: Beyond crude 3D models: from point clouds to historical building information modeling via NURBS. In: Ioannides, M., Magnenat-Thalmann, N., Fink, E., Žarnić, R., Yen, A.-Y., Quak, E. (eds.) EuroMed 2014. LNCS, vol. 8740, pp. 166–175. Springer, Heidelberg (2014). doi:10.1007/978-3-319-13695-0_16
11. Piegl, L.A., Tiller, W.: The NURBS Book. Monographs in Visual Communication. Springer, Heidelberg (1997). 646 pages
12. Succar, B.: Building information modelling framework: a research and delivery foundation for industry stakeholders. Autom. Costr. **3**, 357–375 (2009)
13. Trani, M., Cassano, M., Todaro, B., Bossi, B.: BIM level of detail for construction site design. In: 4th Creative Construction Conference, Krakow, Poland (2015)
14. Aravici, Y.: Towards building information modelling for existing structures. Struct. Surv. **26**, 210–222 (2008)
15. Zhanga, J.P., Hub, Z.Z.: BIM- and 4D-based integrated solution of analysis and management for conflicts and structural safety problems during construction: 1. Principles and methodologies. Autom. Constr. **20**(2), 155–166 (2011)
16. Zvietcovich, F., Castañeda, B., Perucchio, R.S., Morales, R., Uceda, S.: A methodology for updating 3D solid models of complex monumental structures based on local point-based meshes. In: 1st International Congress on Digital Heritage, DigitalHeritage, Marseille, France (2013)

Full Paper: Innovative Methods on Risk Assesment, Monitoring and Protection of Cultural Heritage

Applicability of 3DVE Indicator for Cultural Heritage Landscape Management

Jaeyong Lee[✉] and Youngmo Kim

Department of Heritage Conservation and Restoration,
Graduate School of Convergence Cultural Heritage,
Korea National University of Cultural Heritage,
Buyeo-gun, Chungcheongnam-do, Korea
{headoz,ymkim1683}@nuch.ac.kr

Abstract. Uniformly control of the height of buildings owned by individuals to protect cultural heritage landscape causes social conflicts. Thus, it is necessary to introduce an indicator that can simultaneously evaluate the criteria for control of the height of buildings (CCBH) for urban development and cultural heritage landscape management. We developed 3D Visual Exposure (3DVE) as a useful indicator to review the validity of the CCBH around cultural heritage. By using the 3DVE, it was possible to calculate visibility and we succeeded in mapping the opportunity of view on 3D geospatial information and evaluating landscape variation with statistics through changing building heights around cultural heritage. We predict that the 3DVE presented in this study will have high utilization as an indicator for the cultural heritage landscape management.

Keywords: Visible intensity evaluation · Historic landscape conservation · Building height control · Digital terrain model

1 Introduction

1.1 Background and Aims of the Study

Urban development and expansion form a contrasting relation against the protection of cultural heritage. An urban management plan is established, using data on population, atmosphere, transportation and facilities. Quantitative data are analyzed, and criteria are prepared to control urban development capacities such as land use, building coverage rate, building height, floor area ratio and green area ratio. In the meantime, a landscape management plan for cultural heritage, too, begins with preparing criteria for control of the height and usage of the surrounding buildings. In a city of which a cultural heritage is its landmark, like St. Paul's Cathedral, London, the CCBH are set up through view corridor [4]. Most cities use a method of maintaining the line of sight to the cultural heritage from a main view point.

On the other hand, in a radical or randomly developed city where cultural heritage is not the landmark anymore, it is not easy to set up the CCBH for the cultural heritage landscape management. Since 2007, in order to protect cultural heritage and harmonize with the landscape of neighboring areas, the CCBH has been established by Cultural

© Springer International Publishing AG 2016
M. Ioannides et al. (Eds.): EuroMed 2016, Part I, LNCS 10058, pp. 131–143, 2016.
DOI: 10.1007/978-3-319-48496-9_11

Properties Protection Law in South Korea. The goals of the building height control are to prevent cultural heritage from diminution, preserve skyline and background land-scape and secure view (Fig. 1). However, no reasonable methods for the setting of the CCBH have not been prepared, which may cause the excessive infringement of private ownership of property.

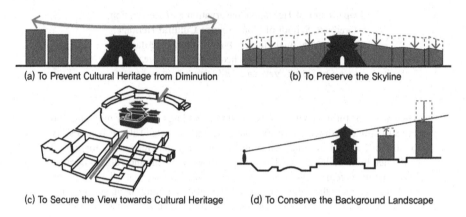

(a) To Prevent Cultural Heritage from Diminution   (b) To Preserve the Skyline

(c) To Secure the View towards Cultural Heritage   (d) To Conserve the Background Landscape

Fig. 1. Purposes of the CCBH by cultural properties protection law in South Korea

In urban areas, social conflicts are caused by the overlapping regulations on building height according to Urban Planning Law as well as Cultural Properties Pro-tection Law. In order to solve this problem, it is necessary to measure changes in landscape and prepare assessment methods. Especially, a quantitative landscape indi-cator has high potential to be used as an important factor of urban planning along with various development factors of the urban environment.

We attempted to develop a useful indicator in setting up the CCBH for urban planning and cultural heritage landscape protection. For this purpose, we used the 3DVE to calculate visibility frequency quantitatively. We also evaluated changes in the opportunity of view with the Pungnam Gate (Cultural Heritage) and its surrounding areas in Jeonju, where the CCBH is applied redundantly. In addition, by mapping the 3DVE results of view point and cultural heritage including its surrounding buildings on 3D geospatial information, this study expressed changes in landscape and sought to estimate statistics for comparison.

1.2   Related Works

From the urban planner's point of view, the visibility issues become significant in establishing policy [2, 3, 15, 19]. Many researchers have developed visual indicators which human visual senses were taken into account focusing on city developments and planning [16]. The process of the visibility analysis enables planners to identify potential landscape character and its changes [12, 14]. Still, attempt to quantify the amount of vision in architecture or urban space is actively in progress (Table 1).

Schroder et al. (2006) estimated the visible area two-dimensionally through an analysis of the line of sight of the corners of the building. However, 3D topography has not been considered. Yang et al. (2007) estimated viewed surface from a view point by using buildings modeled with digital vector data. By measuring the visibility of the building, the CCBH was proposed. Through simplified modeling of the building, alternatives for control of building height were compared. However, like Schroder et al., the topography of the actual study site was not reflected.

Bartie et al. (2010) analyzed the visibility of a wide range of areas by using data surveyed with LiDAR. It was time-saving for a rough analysis of the visibility of a wide range of areas. However, since the precision of the building data obtained from a satellite was low, it did not materialize the shape of the building in detail, and there was a limitation that alternatives according to changes in building height could not be compared. It is noted that raster dataset based Visual Exposure is not suitable for urban areas where built up structures are dominant [10–12].

Kim et al. (2015) developed a nurbs data-driven 3D visual analysis method and proposed a method of overcoming the limitation of the visibility analysis by ArcView. An et al. (2015) showed the usability of 3DVE indicator in quantifying the reduction of the view chance in neighboring houses according to the construction of apartment houses using Rhino 5.0 and Grasshopper.

Therefore, it is important to develop a vector data driven 3D visibility analysis program in order to increase accuracy of the analysis [10, 11, 13] and it is need to consider the possibility of the vector data based visibility analysis [5, 6].

Table 1. Comparison of related works

Previous studies	Terrain (elevation) modelling	Detailed building modelling	Building facade visibility evaluation	Controlling landscape variation	Processing speed	Work efficiency	Cost
Schroder et al. (2006)	X	X	X	O	Slow	Low	Low
Yang et al. (2007)	X	O	O	O	Fast	Low	High
Bartie et al. (2010)	O	X	X	X	Normal	High	High
Kim et al. (2015)	O	O	X	O	Fast	Low	Low
An et al. (2015)	O	O	O	O	Fast	Low	Low

1.3 Fundamentals of 3DVE

Visual Access and Exposure (VAE) model is a method of measuring the amount of vision, developed by Archea (1984) for the first time [1]. The VAE model is an indicator that divides a space into the grid, adds up the frequency seen in the horizontal vision from the level of human eyes or estimates the visibility from a certain view point.

We brought about this analysis and measurement method to a 3D urban space. The 3DVE is adding up the amounts of view point (road, square and park, etc.) from which cultural heritage is visible within a certain range (Fig. 2(a)). Of course, a place with high 3DVE can be one easily seen from the vicinities. By applying this estimation method, we can find out the main parts of cultural heritage which can be seen best from multi-view points (Fig. 2(a)) and the view point where cultural heritage can be seen most (Fig. 2(b)). If you use this, you can find out the view point with excellent view of the object.

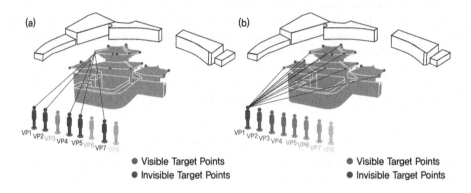

Fig. 2. Calculation of 3DVE cultural heritage (a) and 3DVE view point (b)

Therefore, it is possible to review whether the view towards cultural heritage is secured or not according to the changes of view point and visible areas of cultural heritage. In addition, we can check skyline infringement and relative diminution of cultural heritage against its surrounding buildings through a comparison of the visibility intensity between cultural heritage and buildings in its background.

2 Methodology and Study Site

2.1 Process

The research was conducted in 4 steps.

In Step 1, the 3DVE analysis program was produced. It was developed with Visual C++ so that it could operate in MS Windows. On the 3DVE, functions such as data input, screen operation, analysis execution, analysis result checking and statistical data storage were loaded.

In Step 2, a 3D DTM and building models were drawn up, using the data such as topography, the height and the shape of buildings and cultural heritage in the study site. For the drawing, a digital terrain map with the scale of 1/1,000 was used. As the cultural heritage for which the visibility would be reviewed, the Pungnam Gate was modeled. The Pungnam Gate (W45 × D32 × H16 m) was drawn up with mesh on AutoCAD 2016. The maximum range to which the CCBH is applied by the Cultural Properties Protection Law is within 500 m radius from the cultural heritage. Thus, the area and buildings within 500 m radius from the Pungnam Gate were modeled. The area is 1.4 km^2, which includes a river and mountain. 4,479 buildings were modeled in the form of a simple cube, ignoring the shape of the roof.

In Step 3, the CCBH were collected, which were applied to the study site according to the Urban Planning Law and the Cultural Properties Protection Law. Referring to the collected data, a present condition and two development scenarios (A and B) to compare the landscape were prepared. Present Condition reproduces the current building height and form (Fig. 3(a)). Scenario A is the landscape assuming the maximum development according to CCBH in the Urban Planning Law (Fig. 3(b)) while Scenario B is the landscape assuming the maximum development according to CCBH in the Cultural Properties Protection Law (Fig. 3(c)). At this time, the floor area of the building was fixed, and the building height only was changed to adjust the development capacity.

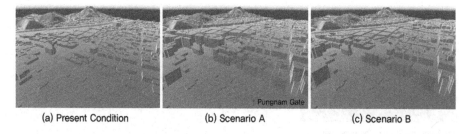

(a) Present Condition   (b) Scenario A   (c) Scenario B

Fig. 3. Landscape modeling of present condition and two development scenarios

In Step 4, to use in a 3D analysis, a total of 1,769 target points[1] were extracted from the primary outline of the Pungnam Gate (Fig. 4(a)). 26,517 view points were selected from road, square and park within 500 m radius from the cultural heritage (Fig. 4(b)). From the surrounding buildings of the Pungnam Gate, 30,458, 89,538 and 61,520 target points were extracted from Present Condition, Scenarios A and B, respectively.

---

[1] In order to calculate the visibility quickly, multiple 'points' should be selected from the important parts of the object (We call this 'target point'). Since no more than two sides of a building are seen simultaneously, target points were calculated with 884, ½ of the 1,769 target points extracted.

(a) Target Points Selected from the Pungnam Gate   (b) View Points Selected from Road, Suqare, etc.

Fig. 4. Examples of selected target points and view points

2.2   Value of Study Site and Landscape Control

The target of the research was the Pungnam Gate (Treasure No. 308) in Jeonju has a relatively high importance among the cultural heritages designated by the state (Fig. 5 (a), (b)). The Pungnam Gate is the landmark of the city because it is a point-shaped cultural heritage in which visibility as a target should be secured and also it takes advantage of analyzing the view and its surrounding areas (Fig. 5(c)).

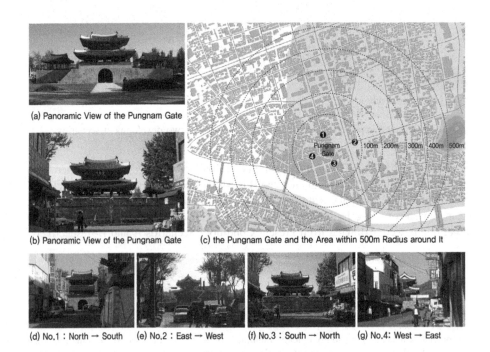

(a) Panoramic View of the Pungnam Gate

(b) Panoramic View of the Pungnam Gate   (c) the Pungnam Gate and the Area within 500m Radius around It

(d) No.1 : North → South   (e) No.2 : East → West   (f) No.3 : South → North   (g) No.4: West → East

Fig. 5. Study site

The Pungnam Gate and its surrounding area have been controlled by the Urban Planning Law. The area within 30 m radius around the Pungnam Gate was designated as the Historic Cultural Aesthetic District, which is regulated at the maximum building height less than 6 m. The main road in the east of the Pungnam Gate is the Center Aesthetic District, which is regulated at the minimum building height of 9 m (3-story); the 1st Class Residential District, at the building height of 15 m; and the 2nd Class Residential District in the south, at the building height of 21 m. In addition, the other areas are Commercial Districts, for which the building height is regulated to less than 21 m (Fig. 6(a)).

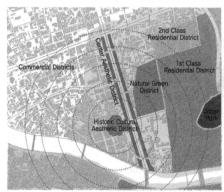 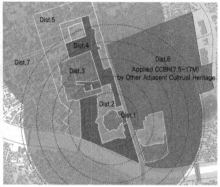

(a) CCBH by Urban Planning Law   (b) CCBH by Cultural Properties Proctection Law

Fig. 6. Two CCBHs of the study site

On the other hand, the height of buildings in the area within 500 m radius around the Pungnam Gate differ according to seven districts by the Cultural Properties Protection Law: District 1 is the whole area to the east within 30 m radius around the Pungnam Gate, which is, in principle, for the preservation of the original topography, and all actions of construction are subject to be reviewed by the Cultural Heritage Committee. District 2 is the area within 50 m radius around the Pungnam Gate, in which the maximum building height is regulated to less than 12 m (2-story) for the buildings with pitched roof.

District 3 is the area within 200 m radius around the Pungnam Gate, in which the maximum building height is regulated to less than 15 m (3-story). The regulations on District 4 are the same as those on District 3. District 5 is the area extended to the north more than 500 m radius around the Pungnam Gate, in which the maximum building height is regulated to less than 18 m (4-story). District 6 is the area to the east with 300 to 500 m radius around the Pungnam Gate, to which the CCBH according to the nearby cultural heritage is applied. District 7 is an area extended to the north-west south towards more than 500 m radius around the Pungnam Gate, to which the level of control of buildings is applied according to the Urban Planning Law (Fig. 6(b)).

3 3DVE Analysis Results

3.1 Changes of View Points

The 3DVE analysis result for view points is high around the square where the Pungnam Gate is located and the whole area of the road traversing from east to west in three landscape modellings. It is noted that the view opportunity of the Pungnam Gate is high only on the axis of the road from east to west and from the square while there are almost no points on the adjacent main roads from which it is seen (Fig. 7). As for the 3DVE of the road in Present Condition, 53.9 points (6.1 %) on average and up to 668 points (75.6 %) could be seen out of 884 target points of the Pungnam Gate (Table 2).

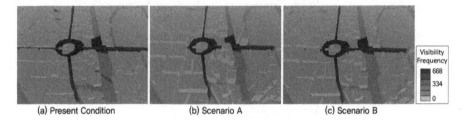

(a) Present Condition   (b) Scenario A   (c) Scenario B

Fig. 7. 3DVE analysis results for view points

Table 2. Statistics of View Point 3DVE (left) and Result of Paired T-Test (right)

	Present	Scenario A	Scenario B	Assuming Equal Variances	Scenario A	Scenario B
std	141.7	139.7	140.0	Mean	46.865	47.064
avg	53.9(6.1%)	46.9(5.3%)	47.1(5.3%)	Variance	19509.737	19595.583
max	668(75.6%)	668	668	Observations	26516	26516
				Hypothesized Mean Diff.	19552.660	
				df	53030	
				t Stat	-0.164	
				tCritcal two-tail	1.960	
				Significant	0.05	

In the meantime, in the two scenarios, the 3DVE slightly decreases as compared to Present Condition (Fig. 7(b), (c)). It is expected that similar landscape will be formed in the two scenarios (As a result of a paired t-test, it was not possible to say that the two were different at the level of significance of 95 %). It decreases by 46.9 and 47.1, respectively, but there is no change in the maximum value. The 3DVE decreased slightly, which means that the view from the road was not affected by the increase of building height. In addition, the maximum value is maintained the same since there is no change in the view from the vicinity of the square (Table 2).

Also, that there is no difference in the 3DVE in two scenarios means that the CCBH, which was set up by the Cultural Properties Protection Law to protect cultural heritage landscape, does not have an influence. In other words, even if the CCBH set up by the Cultural Properties Protection Law are excluded and development by urban planning is made, there is no impact on the view.

3.2   Visibility Intensity of Cultural Heritage (The Pungnam Gate)

As a result of the 3DVE analysis, in Present Condition, the Pungnam Gate was seen from 341.6 view points on average (Table 3). The point best seen was seen from 2,749 view points. In the result of 3DVE mapping, the part best seen is the top of the roof to the east of the Pungnam Gate (Left upper part in the Fig. 8).

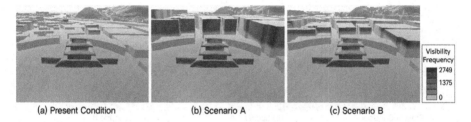

(a) Present Condition   (b) Scenario A   (c) Scenario B

Fig. 8. 3DVE analysis results for the north side of the Pungnam gate

Table 3. Statistics of the Pungnam Gate 3DVE (left) and Result of Paired T-Test (right)

	Present	Scenario A	Scenario B	Assuming Equal Variances	Scenario A	Scenario B
std	502.6	456.7	457.0	Mean	292.698	293.8105
avg	341.6	292.5	293.6	Variance	208629.2	208917
max	2749	2276	2276	Observations	1768	1768
				Hypothesized Mean Diff.	208773.1	
				df	3534	
				t Stat	-0.0724	
				tCritcal two-tail	1.960 635	
				Significant	0.05	

There is no meaningful difference in the 3DVE of the Pungnam Gate between the two development scenarios (Fig. 8(b), (c)). The average decreases to 292.5 and 293.6, respectively, and the maximum value decreases to 2,276, which is the same. There are no differences in standard deviation (456.7 and 457) and mean (292.5 and 293.6) in two scenarios. As a result of a paired t-test of the distribution value of the two scenarios, the similarity was very high (Table 3). This means that, even if the CCBH is different, there is the same effect on preserving the view of the Pungnam Gate. In other words, even if the heights of the surrounding buildings increase, the CCBH by the Cultural Properties Protection Law does not affect practically. In addition, this suggests that, even if the heights of buildings around the Pungnam Gate increase by the Urban Planning Law, a situation which interfering the view of the cultural heritage does not occur.

3.3   Visibility Intensity of Buildings Near Cultural Heritage

There was a tendency in the 3DVE of the buildings near the Pungnam Gate, very different from that of cultural heritage or view points (Fig. 9). The 3DVE average of the buildings around the Pungnam Gate was similar in Present Condition (7.6) and Scenario B (8.4). The maximum value, too, shows similarity at 1,284 and 1,350, respectively (Table 4).

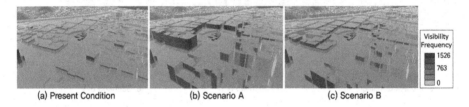

(a) Present Condition   (b) Scenario A   (c) Scenario B

Fig. 9. 3DVE analysis results for building in the area within 100 m radius around the Pungnam gate

Table 4. Statistics of Buildings 3DVE (left) and Result of Paired T-Test (right)

	Present	Scenario A	Scenario B	Assuming Equal Variances	Scenario A	Scenario B
std	53.3	80.1	61.6	Mean	7.54247	8.3555
avg	7.6	13.2	8.4	Variance	2792.715	3763.316
max	1284	1526	1350	Observations	30457	61519
				df	69364	
				t Stat	-2.079	
				tCritcal two-tail	1.960	
				Significant	0.05	

As a result of a paired t-test assuming heterogeneous dispersion since the target points differ as the building heights are different, it turned out that the 3DVE was not the same in Present Condition and Scenario B at a significant of 95 %. In other words, this means that, in spite of similarity, the two landscapes may have different views.

In the meantime, in Scenario A with large development capacity (Fig. 9(b)), the 3DVE of the surrounding buildings increases almost more than two times on average from Present Condition (Table 4). The 3DVE result of the buildings near a cultural heritage is high and this means that they may be seen better than the cultural heritage. In other words, the possibility of weakening the identification of a cultural heritage can be measured when the buildings form a landscape with it.

3.4   Skyline Changes of Cultural Heritage

The 3DVE result of Scenario B shows a noticeably lower distribution than that of Scenario A and at the same time the distribution similar to the Present Condition, which means that the CCBH by the Cultural Properties Protection Law is powerful. The control of the surrounding building height affects the protection of the skyline with a cultural heritage as background.

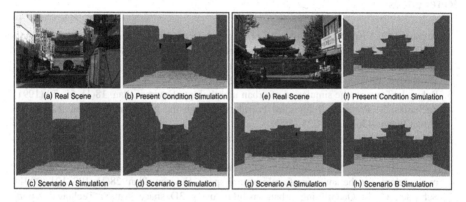

Fig. 10. Comparison of landscape simulations ((a)–(d): no. 1 north to south, (e)–(h): no. 2 south to north)

In order to review the effect, landscape simulations were produced for comparison. In the Fig. 10, buildings located at the back of the Pungnam Gate in Scenario A ((c) and (g)) intrude the skyline while buildings located at the back of the Pungnam Gate in Scenario B ((d) and (h)) does not intrude the skyline. Therefore, it is expected that the 3DVE will be able to evaluate the effect on the protection of the background and skyline of cultural heritage.

4   Conclusions and Outlook

Controlling the capacity of urban planning properly is the main interest of urban planning. In this situation, the landscape recognized as an important factor of the city has not been treated carefully in the process of establishing a plan due to the difficulty of measurement. With reaching the maximum capacity of urban planning, utilizing simulation data that maintain the 3DVE to an appropriate level can contribute to drawing effective measures for control of building height near cultural heritage.

Especially, cities holding cultural heritages have perceived the importance of the landscape and set up a system to protect them; however, since no proper indicator for measuring the landscape has been prepared, there was limitation in testing the reliability and validity of their effects. The 3DVE proposed in this study showed a possibility as an indicator that could assess the protection and infringement of the view of cultural heritage and the intrusion of the skyline by the surrounding buildings.

A merit of the 3DVE is that it can intuitively judge the elements affecting landscape by mapping the estimated results on the building elevation and the position of the view point. In addition, it is expected that it would contribute to drawing the optimum plan, comparing alternatives of the various CCBH by providing statistical analysis data.

References

1. Archea, J.C.: Visual access and exposure: an architectural basis for interpersonal behavior. Ph.D. thesis, The Pennsylvania State University, Pennsylvania (1984)
2. Quintrand, P., Zoller, J., de Fillppo, R., Faure, S.: A model for the representation of urban knowledge. Environ. Plan. **18**(1), 71–83 (1991)
3. Rabie, J.: Towards the simulation of urban morphology. Environ. Plan. **18**(1), 57–70 (1991)
4. Zacharias, J.: Preferences for view corridors through the urban environment. Landscape Urban Plann. **43**(4), 217–225 (1999)
5. O'Sulivan, D., Turner, A.: Visibility graphs and landscape visibility analysis. Int. J. Geogr. Inf. Sci. **15**(3), 221–237 (2001)
6. Turner, A., Doxa, M., O'Sullivan, D., Penn, A.: From isovists to visibility graphs: a methodology for the analysis of architectural space. Environ. Plan. **28**(1), 103–121 (2001)
7. Schroder, C. J.: Quantifying urban visibility using 3D space syntax: Technical report, Unpublished MSc thesis, University of Edinburgh, Edinburgh (2006)
8. Yang, P.P., Putra, S.Y., Li, W.: Viewsphere-a GIS-based 3D visibility analysis for urban design evaluation. Environ. Plan. B Plan. Des. **34**(6), 971–992 (2007)
9. Bartie, P., Reitsma, F., Kingham, S., Mills, S.: Advancing visibility modelling algorithms for urban environments. Environ. Urban Syst. **34**(6), 518–531 (2010)
10. Domon, G.: Landscape as resource: consequences, challenges and opportunities for rural development. Landscape Urban Plann. **100**(1), 338–340 (2011)
11. Jorgensen, A.: Beyond the view: future directions in landscape aesthetics research. Landscape Urban Plann. **100**(1), 353–355 (2011)
12. Domingo-Santos, J., Villarán, R.F., Rapp-Arrarás, Í., Provens, E.C.: The visual exposure in forest and rural landscapes: an algorithm and a GIS tool. Landscape Urban Plann. **101**(1), 52–58 (2011)
13. Kirkpatrick, J.B., Daniels, G.D., Davison, A.: Temporal and spatial variation in garden and street trees in six eastern australian cities. Landscape Urban Plann. **101**(3), 244–252 (2011)
14. Park, B., Furuya, K., Kasetani, T., Takayama, N., Kagawa, T., Miyazaki, Y.: Relationship between psychological responses and physical environments in forest settings. Landscape Urban Plann. **102**(1), 24–32 (2011)
15. Anastasopoulos, P., Islam, M., Perperidou, D., Karlaftis, M.: Hazard-based analysis of travel distance in urban environments: longitudinal data approach. J. Urban Plann. Dev. **138**(1), 53–61 (2012)
16. Zheng, Z., Bohong, Z.: Study on spatial structure of Yangtze river delta urban agglomeration and its effects on urban and rural regions. J. Urban Plann. Dev. **138**(1), 78–89 (2012)

17. An, K., Ko, H., Kim, C.: Development and implementation of visual exposure indicator for residential development. Int. J. Smart Home **9**(2), 1–10 (2015)
18. Kim, C., Ko, H., An, K.: Development and 3D visibility analysis models using NURBS in a residential development. Int. J. Smart Home **9**(1), 151–160 (2015)
19. Jie, H., Tsou, J.: GIS-based visual perception analysis of urban natural landscape for urban planning supporting: a case study of Jinzishan Hill region. In: 19th eCAADe Conference Proceedings, pp. 505–510. eCAADe Press, Helsinki (2001)
20. Schroder, C., Mackaness, W., Reitsma, F.: Quantifying urban visibility using 3D space syntax. In: Geographical Information Science Research UK Conference, pp. 359–366. GISRUK Press, Kildare (2007)

Taking the Next Step in Digital Documentation of Historic Cities

How HERMeS Evolved in an Open Data Digital Library of Historic Buildings

Pavlos Chatzigrigoriou[✉]

Cyprus University of Technology, CY 3036 Limassol, Cyprus
p.chatzigrigoriou@cut.ac.cy

Abstract. When a long-term research finishes, there is always a question about implementation and further development. In the case of HER.M.e.S, the Digital Heritage Management System of the Historic City of Hermoupolis, in a Greek Aegean Island, Syros, it was also a question about raising awareness. The research proved that 2.4 historic buildings collapse every year, as a result of abandonment. This phenomenon was intensified by the severe economic crisis in Greece. The research proposed an optimal conservation plan for the city, after carefully evaluating variables through a multi-criteria model using GIS and an innovating point system. But in order to apply this plan, we need to be able to update the data, as buildings are constantly changing through time. Updating a database with more than 1000 historic buildings, with no funds, is a huge challenge. Soon, we decided that the only way to go is to use a crowdsourcing method. Developing a digital heritage collection portal, using free open source software and serving crucial data for every building, was the answer to our problem. We asked citizens to check the data base, report mistakes, updates, stories, photographs and use the portal to learn about their city. This effort led us to a big digitization project, with up to 1290 historic buildings, 14.400 geo-tagged photos and more than 15.000 fields of information. The project HERMeS, as a conservation plan and a heritage digitization project won the 2015 European Union Europa Nostra Award in Category Research & Digitalisation.

Keywords: Conservation · Digital documentation · GIS · Heritage · Buildings pathology · Historic city · Open data

1 Introduction

Because of the severe economic crisis, Greek historic heritage is at risk. However, historic cities like Hermoupolis, were dealing with this threat years before the crisis. The current situation needs drastic action, with innovative low cost ideas. The main objective of this research is to evaluate the vulnerability of historic buildings and to propose a decision-making model that ranks the need of intervention in a historic building stock. In order to achieve this, it is essential to design a digital database system that enables the recording and indexing of the historic buildings pathology profile.

© Springer International Publishing AG 2016
M. Ioannides et al. (Eds.): EuroMed 2016, Part I, LNCS 10058, pp. 144–156, 2016.
DOI: 10.1007/978-3-319-48496-9_12

Apart from pathology data, historic buildings are classified in terms of architecture style and type, historic importance and spatial data (position in the city). Digital monitoring building's pathology profile has many positive impacts, such as knowing the building's conservation status, the need for intervention, and the risk of collapsing. In a historic building stock, the safety assessment of buildings is a major research goal. It needs a rational and quantitative evaluation, which usually involves six steps: information acquisition, data processing, numerical modeling, evaluation of potential scenarios, risk analysis, decision-making [1].

The city of Hermoupolis was chosen because of its uniqueness that can be traced on its intact conservation almost as a hole until today. In Greece, there are only a few cities that have managed to remain unharmed and even less are those that have endured the unbearable pressures of "land granting". In addition, the global interest for this city by dozens of travellers for over 200 years, has maintained its physiognomy alive through a number of literature works and manuscripts, which served as a protective shield for its uniqueness. This protection endures until today in the consciousness of the inhabitants as well as the visitors of Hermoupolis, and has produced many supporters of its physiognomy ready to take action in case of its endangerment. Therefore, it should come as no surprise that Hermoupolis presents a uniform image that cannot be found anywhere else in Greece [2].

2 Theoretical Approach

Buildings express the society and people that constructed them. They are testimonies of the cultural and social changes; the way and the time that buildings were designed, constructed, used, abandoned and ultimately destroyed indicate the prime and decline of a society. In that sense, the conservation of buildings as part of the cultural inheritance of a place is of crucial importance because it helps us arrive to many conclusions about the development of our civilization. All cities may be characterized as large scale "works of art". However, this kind of art has a temporary nature, it cannot be controlled and does not progress in the rhythm that other form of arts can, such as music for example. In the course of time, various people may experience a city in totally different ways [3]. Ingold, professor of Anthropology in the University of Aberdeen, mentions in his book "The Perception of the Environment: Essays in livelihood, dwelling and skill" that *"building is a constantly continuing process, for as long as people inhabit a certain space. It doesn't have a clear starting point based on a design that we have previously fashioned and it doesn't conclude in a ready object. The "final form" is only momentary...."* [4]. Since human beings reside in a city only for a really brief period of time compared to the lifespan of the city itself, they should not impose predetermined schemes on it and its environment, rather, they should integrate to the city, develop it according to the environment's demands and inherit it to succeeding inhabitants.

Every facet of human activity has its Monuments charging them with important historical memories. Therefore, Monuments may appear as formations in time (buildings, cities, natural elements, or even music works), as points of reference (e.g. March 25th, 1821), or even as prescribed behaviors (e.g. the New Year's Gala in Vienna). However, when it comes to structured environments, a monument has an even more essential role, which is to stimulate people's memory and to function as a connecting link between the past and the future. Indeed, this role is dual, since the monument provides answers to problems of the present, while retaining the memories of the past. When the monument is placed in an urban area, it charges memories, excites imagination, and creates a certain mindset to human beings [5, 6]. The monument as a work of art is perceptible only in a specific cultural milieu, not everywhere, not always, and certainly not by everybody. Heidegger uses the word "Bewahrung", which means "conservation", but shares the same root with the word "Warheit", which means "truth", denoting in the term conservation the conservation of the "truth" of the monument [7].

Buildings have their own circle of life; they get older, have their own pathology, are restored (sometimes poorly), abandoned and ultimately-at the end of their life-they collapse [8]. Buildings have three different ages: The age based on the date they were built, the age based on their materials condition and the age based on economic and service factors [9]. The aging/deterioration

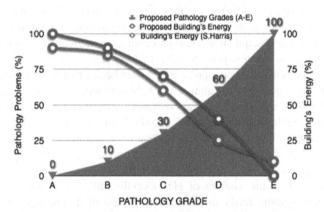

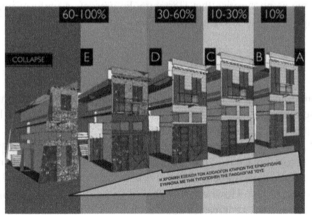

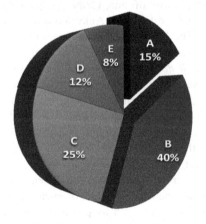

Fig. 1. Pathology grades and building's energy

process of buildings is a complicated procedure where a lot of research is taking place. Samuel Harris in his book "Buildings Pathology" (pages 16–23) in order to describe the deterioration mechanism, is viewing the building as an energy model and the he uses the Second Law of Thermodynamics: Energy flows from higher (ordered) state to a lower (random) state, increasing its "entropy". Keeping in mind the First Law of Thermodynamics (the building is a "closed" energy system), Harris is proposing that the deterioration mechanism is inherently an exothermic process and the deterioration is entropic (Fig. 1) [10].

To predict the life span of a building, one should be able to identify with certainty all the variables involved in the deterioration model. Considering that it is simple to identify the properties of a single material, one realizes the complexity of the issue when it comes to buildings, where hundreds of different materials are involved. It is also very likely in the same building to evolve two and more deterioration mechanisms simultaneously, which further complicates the prediction process. Therefore, identification of materials, their properties and damage-suffered buildings from the environment is the first step to approach a complex interdisciplinary problem as that of determining the mechanism of deterioration and collapse of buildings. This matter concerns the engineers of all disciplines.

With regard to the issue of rescuing interventions, building pathology as well as the monitoring of building pathology, are of major importance. It's a fact that when a building is abandoned it runs into trouble. The first signs of humidity activate dozens of wearing/erosion mechanisms on the building materials. Shortly after, they all start to rot and collapse, one after the other. As soon as a building is categorized as "dangerous" in the consciousness of the neighborhood tenants, it becomes a target for demolishment [8]. This practice has been confirmed on many different occasions also in the present study. Therefore, the objective is to monitor the pathology of buildings – monuments, and to primarily help the ones that are in the process of being stigmatized as dangerous.

The use of the Information and Communication Technologies can be decisive towards that direction. On a scientific level of the protection of architectural inheritance, the contribution of information science was and continues to be of outmost importance. It provides us with answers and solutions for the difficulties and problems that arise during the evaluation process of the subordinate state of buildings, as well as their monitoring and managing. From the relevant theoretical overview, it is concluded that Planning Support Systems infiltrate remarkably slow mainly due to their limited dissemination, their weakness in the choice of appropriate tools, their incomplete -for their ability- update and the non-projection of good practices. This is a phenomenon that can be traced in general in the distribution of new technologies [11, 12].

3 Methodology

First, a field research was conducted by a team of trained inspectors (civil engineers and architects). Specifically, nine hundred and twenty-four (924) buildings were recorded, creating inventories with one hundred and ninety-two (192) fields for each of the examined building. The author trained the inspectors. The author answered any questions or problems and the same guidelines were given to all inspectors, in order to increase the credibility of the collected data. The field research took place in years 2004 and 2005. For this research, "recording" of a historic building is a holistic process in order for the building to join the system HERMeS in a reliable and functional way. This recording process was designed in a structured and simplified manner so as to minimize the factors that may affect the reliability of the survey.

Before starting the recording process, the tool that was used for the required purpose, has the form of a questionnaire. The design of the questionnaire is a very important part of the development process of database systems HERMeS. This is because the items included in the questionnaire are in fact the database fields and from processing them one gets the research findings. Considering the above, a lot of thought was spent for each section of the questionnaire in order to integrate important data for the building, but with no unnecessary fields that could increase the recording time and the size of the database. Special attention was given to pathology data recording, as this is the primer research purpose. Every historic building was divided in sub-structural units, considering what Greek and international bibliography propose [13–18]. In this research a historic building is divided in ten (10) sub structural units (Fig. 2). Recording pathology problems in a historic building is complicated, because it is difficult to measure those problems. In order to simplify the process, a five (5) grade scale was used in every pathology problem (Fig. 1): from grade "A" (it means that there is no pathology problem) to grade "E" (crucial pathology problem). Pathology data reliability is extremely important for developing a reliable conservation plan. This is why there is a pathology profile picture for every single building (Fig. 2) and HERMeS uses an algorithm to mass check all 924 buildings, for common errors during pathology recording (Fig. 3). Regarding earthquake damages, the conservation state documentation recorded all pathology data of the buildings, including -plausible-earthquake cracks. Since HERMeS is applied in the same historic city, earthquake risk is the same for all buildings. The variable of this risk is covered by the total pathology grade of the building. Having said that, one can try multiple scenarios using only the pathology grade of bearing walls, since they play a crucial role for complete failure (collapse) of buildings during earthquakes.

The Database of HERMeS is originally designed according to user requirements and needs of the present research. The main objective is to record all the pathology data of "historic building", architectural and historical data and any other information that helps to protect the building in long-term. The data fed to HERMeS are spatial, which vary both in space and time. Specifically, it is predicted in advance that the data collected from evaluations of engineers in the field, will be associated with the Geographic Information System (GIS) HERMeS, and thus the database developed in to a Geographic Database [19]. The spatial dimension serves many variables, especially when assessing the risk of a building (e.g. location of the building in the city and distance from a school).

The objective of the conservation of the physiognomy of Hermoupolis by protecting important building's shells will not be achieved without ensuring mechanisms slowing deterioration of buildings and making the necessary interventions to prevent their collapse. In this respect, a key role has the GIS of HERMeS in combination with the information provided by the database.

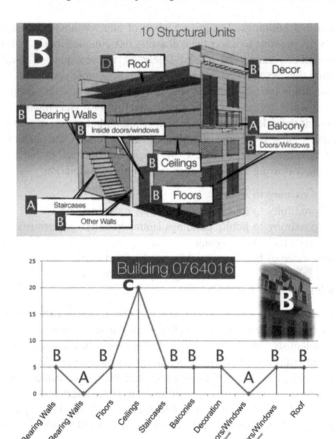

Fig. 2. Analyzing pathology profile in buildings, in order to increase the reliability of the data.

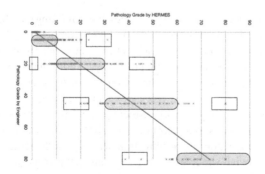

Fig. 3. An Algorithm checked all 924 buildings, for recording pathology errors.

By recording the pathology, HERMeS identifies the buildings at danger via an appropriate algorithm. In the first application of the system those buildings were 160 from a total of 924 buildings. The prioritization of interventions in these buildings is critical, as it is not possible to lower the collapsing risk simultaneously in 160 buildings and the interventions cannot be judged solely by the reactions of local residents. Bearing in mind the fact that one, given the current economic conditions, has to make best use of the funds for this purpose, it is proved that the relevant decision requires multi-criteria analysis method of prioritizing interventions. Specifically, the analysis takes into account the risk of collapse for each building, but in connection with a series of other variables, such as the role of building in Hermoupolis, the position in the city, the influence in other areas of interest, the social impact etc. In the case study of Hermoupolis the following variables were taken into consideration:

- Buildings' proximity to schools
- Buildings' proximity to touristic sites (harbor, museums, etc.)
- Buildings' proximity to public buildings (municipalities, government offices etc.)
- Buildings' proximity to city center
- The historic value of buildings (architectural importance)
- The lack of interest to restore buildings (by the owners)
- The pathology state of buildings

A team of experts was chosen to evaluate and classify the six (6) variables starting with the most important variable and ending with the less important. The team consisted of 30 scientists, architects and civil engineers, having a minimum of ten (10) years of experience in the field of buildings' conservation. Five (5) of the team members were academics. The evaluation of the variables was conducted on-line via an Internet survey process. The results were adjusted to percentages and then weighted on a scale of 1 to 1000. The seventh variable (severity of building's pathology) was weighted equally with the average of the other six factors (143/1000) in order to avoid chances of overruling.

4 Results

The multi-criteria model presented here is flexible. Buildings pathology grades are changing constantly due to interventions and deterioration mechanisms. Schools, touristic sites and other criteria are also subject to change. HERMeS is able to process the updated data, in a fast and user-friendly way. Additionally, a tool in GIS was developed to apply the multi-criteria model on the historic city building stock and export an updated version of ranked risk assessment buildings.

Building's pathology is a quality assessment factor, but it is not sufficient enough to evaluate and rate building's risk hazard. The above-proposed multi-criteria model based on pathology indicators in combination with the architectural quality ones, as well as with other social variables such as the area, the density, the usage of near buildings, the tourist attraction, etc. can produce a hierarchy list of risk assessment (Fig. 4). The point system leads to a Conservation Plan for the city of Hermoupolis, giving the hierarchy of interventions that must be done in order to save the maximum architecture heritage with the minimum funds, postponing the risk of collapsing. With

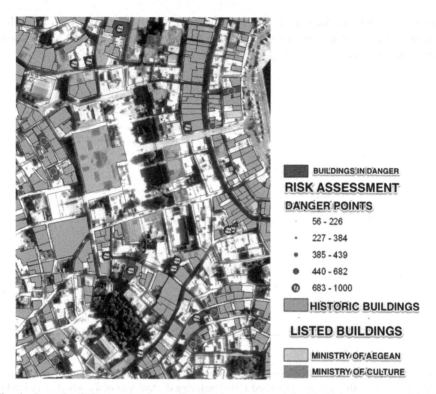

BUILDINGS IN DANGER

RISK ASSESSMENT
DANGER POINTS

- 56 - 226
- 227 - 384
- 385 - 439
- 440 - 682
- 683 - 1000

HISTORIC BUILDINGS

LISTED BUILDINGS

MINISTRY OF AEGEAN
MINISTRY OF CULTURE

Fig. 4. Part of a GIS map; the threat of collapsing is measured with "risk assessment points".

this in mind, the Municipality of Hermoupolis started applying this strategy as a Conservation Plan.

The final resulted historic buildings' ranking catalogue was proposed to the municipality of Hermoupolis as the optimal strategy for protecting the physiognomy of the city, with low cost and gentle maintenance techniques to be applied on the historic buildings. It is noteworthy to indicate that the municipality has already adopted this strategy and implemented on six (6) buildings. So far, the results have been encouraging since the deterioration process has been delayed and the risk hazard has been reduced. These results validate the model developed in the present study.

Finally, the achievement of the documentation and management of important building stock in Hermoupolis as implemented in this research, enrich the design of the proposal for the inclusion of Hermoupolis in the list of monuments and sites of World Heritage by UNESCO.

The research model has a huge social impact. For the first time in the history of Hermoupolis, people are not afraid of their buildings. They know that there is a monitoring system; they see that there is a conservation plan aiming to support specific historic buildings. They also started to accept the historic value of buildings at risk, giving information to the municipality in order to index them in HERMeS model. The implementation of the research has an environmental value. Rescuing the Historic

Buildings at risk, we are reusing space and the city is not expanding. With HERMeS model, we can evaluate the amount of space that is lost because of the lack of conservation and reuse of space (Fig. 5).

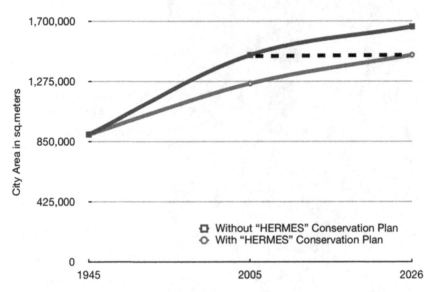

Fig. 5. The impact of research's conservation plan on City expansion (environmental value). The city in sixty (60) years, has expanded 110 % reducing the free area of the island. An island is a "closed system", surrounded by the sea. The free space is important as an environmental value. Applying the Proposed Conservation Plan, we could reduce the need for expansion, because we are saving historic building and we reuse the space. As shown at the graph, if the conservation plan was used from 1945, Hermoupolis would be at today's size, in 2026.

5   The Evolution

When this research ended, the author started thinking of how we will use all these digital data in the future. It was a problem known in literature as "big data", a term used for collection of data sets so large and complex that is becomes difficult to process using traditional data processing applications. The challenges include analysis, capture, cu-ration, search, sharing, storage, transfer, visualization, and privacy violations. We divided our data in smaller sets and we estimated what kind of information we can release, who is going to benefit and what we expect from the data sharing. Then, we researched the software more suitable for our project; a free, flexible and open source web-publishing platform. We used OMEKA (www.omeka.org), an open-source software platform developed by the Center for History and New Media at George Mason University (Fig. 6). As a "web-based publishing platform for scholars, librarians, archivists, museum professionals, educators, and cultural enthusiasts" (Omeka About Page, 2009), Omeka resembles WordPress, with its plugins and themes, but is a very different platform.

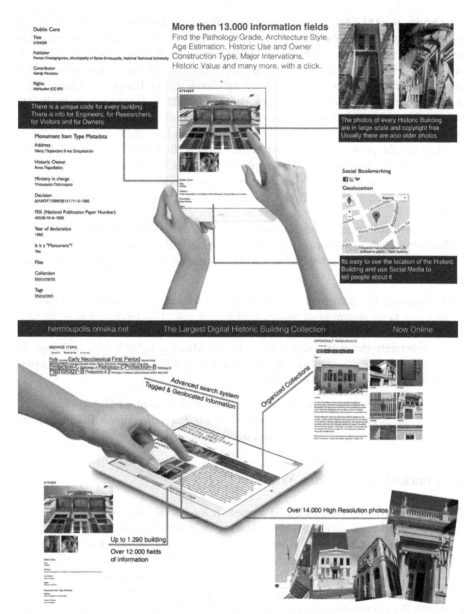

Fig. 6. Omeka is a free open source software for digital collections. Thinking "out of the box", we verged HERMeS not as a Conservation Plan any more, but as a big data digital collection. It was the only way to ensure awareness, updating and enrichment for our Database. The Omeka free software provides also the option of "Omeka.net" a low budget hosting. We choose this plan in order to minimize the demands for support and web hosting. HERMeS is currently the biggest online historic buildings digital collection. It has 5.550 unique visitors and 5–20 visits per day. Architects, engineers, citizens of Hermoupolis, tourist offices and tourists use it every day for information. The contributions are low, but after the Europa Nostra Award we predict a deeper evolvement of local habitants.

Omeka is OAI-PMH compliant, and is based on Dublin Core. It can ingest metadata in both CSV format and in XML. Point it at open access repository and it can import collections whose XML is exposed for harvesting. The author developed a web site hermoupolis.omeka.net using omeka and omeka.net hosting. More than 14.000 High Definition geotagged photos were uploaded, 1.290 Historic Buildings (and adding more), more than 20 core data fields per building, summing up to 36.000 information objects. The buildings were tagged with info such as pathology grades, architecture style, usage, size, historic value, protection laws etc.

Adding old photos (digitized) of these Historic Buildings was crucial for the Historic Value of this project. We used photos from 1995, 2005 and 2014 (and adding more). Researchers, Architects and Students can search, discover and learn about Neoclassicism, an important Architectural Period in Europe, from this Digitization Project.

The metadata are following International Standards and most of the information is in English, in order to accommodate foreign users and Europeans.

Now, HERMeS is a complicated scientific system with two unique and prototype pillars:

- It measures the pathology and estimates social factors in order to provide an innovate point system to all historic buildings at risk. This point system is the base of the conservation plan
- It deliberately shares the most important fields (data) of 1.290 historic buildings, in a free open source web platform, providing useful information and asking peoples feedback, in order to update its data.

Because of the above approach to the complicated problem of Historic City Conservation, in 2015 HERMeS is honored with the European Union Europa Nostra Award, in the category of "research and digitization".

6 Conclusions – Future Work

This Digitization Project is based on a research for a solid conservation plan for the Historic City of Hermoupolis. Serving historic "Big Data" online makes this project special. It adds to the Historic Value of Europe, because it presents live (online) and organized an important part of European History; the Neoclassicism, as a movement with all its aspects, in one city. The goal of this digital preservation is the accurate rendering of authenticated content over time. At the same time, we still update our HERMeS data, preventing the ageing of the Historic Buildings, following our bigger Conservation Plan.

People are using HERMeS for different purposes:

(1) Scholars, use HERMeS to learn, for an essay or for a dissertation, to share collections and collaborate with others in the creation of a project for scholarships.
(2) Educators use HERMeS to build inquiry-based tasks for students, create lesson plans or build learning modules with their team.

(3) Architects use HERMeS to study Neoclassicism, to understand the different styles, to find out the history of specific buildings and discover old photos.

(4) Engineers use HERMeS to understand Pathology, to find out the Pathology Grade of their project and to learn about the past of Historic Buildings.

(5) Citizens use HERMeS to find out useful information about their buildings, to learn about the pathology grades and of course to contribute stories for Historic Buildings.

At the end, HERMeS is a Digitization Project of Cultural Heritage with a double conservation aim: (i) Digital Preservation of the History (tangible and intangible) and (ii) Conservation of Historic Buildings. This double aiming (a "Lighter" Portal and a "Heavy" Scientific System) makes this project unique and challenging.

In the future HERMeS can adopt the know-how from 4D-CH world project and develop more in the "timeline" of historic buildings [20, 21]. Using technology for creating 3D reconstructed models and applying the digital data in an engaging way is one of the goals. Another goal is to connect tangible and intangible heritage [22], a challenge that HERMeS is already answering through a postdoc research.

Acknowledgments. **4DCH** (http://www.4d-ch-world.eu/) project has received funding from the European Union's Seventh Framework program for research, technological development and demonstration under GA no 324523.

EU Prize for Cultural Heritage/Europa Nostra Awards (http://www.europanostra.org) was launched in 2002 by the European Commission and has been organised by Europa Nostra since then. The Prize celebrates and promotes best practices related to heritage conservation, management, research, education and communication. In this way, it contributes to a stronger public recognition of cultural heritage as a strategic resource for Europe's society and economy.

References

1. Zonta, D., Pozzi, M., Zannon, P.: Managing the historical heritage using distributed technologies. Int. J. Archit. Heritage **3**, 200–225 (2008)
2. Travlos, I., Kokkou, A.: Hermoupolis. Commercial Bank of Greece, Athens (1980)
3. Lynch, K.: The Image of the City. MIT Press, Cambridge (1960)
4. Ingold, T.: The perception of the environment: essays in livelihood, dwelling and skill. Routledge, London and New York (2000)
5. Stefanou, J.: The concept of the monument and the ideology of protection, Athens. University publishing, N.T.U.A. (2004)
6. Papalexopoulos, D., Kalafati, E., Papadopoulos, S.: Building memory. In: Proceedings of the 2001 Conference on Virtual Reality, Archaeology, and Cultural Heritage, VAST 2001, pp. 27–32. ACM, New York (2001)
7. Lefas, P.: Architecture and Inhabitation: From Heidegger to Koolhaas. Plethron, Athens (2008)
8. Brand, S.: How Buildings Learn: What Happens After They Are Built. Penguin Books, USA (1995)
9. Levy, M., Salvadori, M.: Why Buildings Fall Down. WW Norton & Company, New York (2002)

10. Harris, S.: Building Pathology, Detioration, Diagnostics and Intervantion. Wiley, New York (2001)
11. Darzentas, D., Darzenta, J., Spyroy, T.: Choosing appropriate tools by means of intelligent decision support. In: JDS, pp. 1–17 (1997)
12. Vonk, G., Geertman, S., Schot, P.: Usage of planning support systems. In: Leeuwen, J.P.V., Timmermans, H.J.P. (eds.) Design & Decision Support Systmes in Architecture and Urban Planning. Springer, The Netherlands (2006)
13. Antonakakis, D., Tsiomis, I.: Conservation study for restoration of the historic center of Hermoupolis, Athens (1996)
14. Stefanou, J.: The Urban Planning of Hermoupolis: A Pilot Urban Study of a Historic City. National Technical University, Athens (2003)
15. Organization for Anti Seismic Planning and Protection. Checking Structural Venerability, Ministry of Environment. http://www.oasp.gr/node/76
16. Spanos, Ch., Spithakis, M., Trezos, K.: Methods for On-Site Valuation of Material's Characteristics. TEE, Athens (2006)
17. Watt, D.: Building Pathology. Blackwell, Oxford (2007)
18. Thornes, R., Bold, J.: Documenting the Cultural Heritage. Getty Information Institute, Los Angeles (1998). European Foundation for Heritage Skills
19. Koutsopoulos, K.: Geographic Information Systems. Papasotiriou Press, Athens (2005)
20. Kyriakaki, G., Doulamis, A., Doulamis, N., Ioannides, M., Makantasis, K., Protopapadakis, E., Hadjiprocopis, A., Wenzel, K., Fritsch, D., Klein, M., Weinlinger, G.: 4D reconstruction of tangible cultural heritage objects from web-retrieved images. Int. J. Herit. Digit. Era. **3**, 431–451 (2014)
21. Ioannides, M., Hadjiprocopi, A., Doulamis, N., Doulamis, A., Protopapadakis, E., Makantasis, K., Santos, P., Fellner, D., Stork, A., Balet, O., Julien, M., Weinlinger, G., Johnson, P. S., Klein, M., Fritsch, D.: Online 4D reconstruction using multi-images available under open access. ISPRS Ann. Photogramm. Remote Sens. Spatial Inf. Sci. **II-5/W1**, 169–174 (2013). doi:10.5194/isprsannals-II-5-W1-169-2013
22. Cacciotti, R., Valach, J., Kuneš, P., Čerňanský, M., Blaško, M., Křemen, P.: Monument damage information system (Mondis): an ontological approach to cultural heritage documentation. In: ISPRS Annals of the Photogrammetry, Remote Sensing and Spatial Information Sciences, vol. II-5/W1, 2013 XXIV International CIPA Symposium, 2–6 September 2013, Strasbourg, France

Risk Analysis and Vulnerability Assessment of Archeological Areas for the Preventive Conservation

Giuliana Quattrone[✉]

National Council of Research CNR, Institute of Atmospheric Pollution Research,
UNICAL-Polifunzionale, 87036 Rende, Italy
g.quattrone@iia.cnr.it

Abstract. The territorial structure of archaeological sites is often compromised by a variety of factors which, over time, can contribute to aggravate the deteriorating conditions of the archaeological areas. Natural disasters, often, have caused irreversible damage (crashes, loss of finds, etc.) at the archeological sites. The paper shows the results of research aimed at developing an innovative risk assessment model, oriented to sustainability criteria, that can provide help in making decisions process about the protection, conservation and valorisation of archaeological areas. The proposed work presents a logical and operative model suitable to estimate the actual risk condition for archeological sites developed by integrating the information concerning vulnerability of archeological areas and the danger condition of the sites upon which they are located. The determination of the risk, derived from the evaluation of potential co-presence of independent sources of danger within a given geographical area, has been modeled by a type of approach multi hazard.

The methodology is applied at the case study of archaeological area of Sybari in Calabria Region, in south of Italy, where tried to develop an integrated and coordinated cognitive methodology - evaluation within an overall information system for assessing the vulnerability of archaeological heritage and environmental dangerousness in order to identify the level of risk which is under the archaeological area in relation to the territory of reference.

The results obtained allow to relate the risk with the risk factors, the detection of damage on archaeological heritage in question, determine the tolerance threshold within which it is possible the preservation of goods and to propose a synthesis strategy between environmental protection and sustainable exploitation.

Keywords: Archaeological areas · Risk management · Vulnerability · Territorial planning · Resilience · Environmental sustainability

1 Introduction

The paper describe the results of the research aimed to establish the level of risk of an archaeological resource in a particular area (geo-referenced), applying a comparative evaluation based on the characteristics of the goods valued in relation to the reference

© Springer International Publishing AG 2016
M. Ioannides et al. (Eds.): EuroMed 2016, Part I, LNCS 10058, pp. 157–168, 2016.
DOI: 10.1007/978-3-319-48496-9_13

context, compared with the degree of dangerousness of the territory, on the basis of a shared taxonomy territorial and a preventive spatial assessment designed to measure the definition of the threshold of tolerance within which it is possible the recovery and preservation of goods and cultural areas also with respect to their environmental sustainability.

The analysis of the degree of conservation/degradation of the natural heritage and environmental components, is conducted considering interactions respect to a qualitative measurement scale and depending on some variables: the probability, the duration, the frequency and the reversibility of impacts.

The research work is based on methodological approaches that seek to develop innovative methods of analysis and risk assessment to improve the effectiveness of mitigation actions and management in the territory and to improve vulnerability assessment and risk level to which the cultural heritage is subjected in relation to the territorial context y of reference. In this context, the archaeological heritage of the area of Sybaris, in the first instance, was known and subsequently assessed, using several criteria to recognize the cultural value and to assess the risk in an ordinal and comparative ranking (rank order). This rank was achieved through multi-dimensional evaluations [8].

The demonstration of the level of risk is related to the phases of the "life cycle" of the urban area and the territory in general, and also is related to the type and quality of settlement of historic centers, as well as the recognition of the specific categories of obsolescence that determine the asset depreciation (the loss of intrinsic economic value and value in use). The risk is analyzed according to three profiles: the probability that a risk event to occur; the consequences if the risk event occurs; the necessary measures to prevent or minimize the expected consequences [8].

The research work was carried out within the SI.MO.NA Project, "Systems and technologies for the Monitoring of cultural areas in the marine and terrestrial environment" with financial supporter of the Operational Regional Project of Calabria Region, FERS 2007/2013 and with technical supporter of Institute of Atmospheric Pollution Research and Culture and innovation consortium of Calabria Region.

2   Vulnerability and Danger in the Archaeological Areas

The local risk is measured using a model that takes into account the local variation range of dangerousness present in a given territory and the state of conservation of the properties examined. The overall risk derives from valuation of the potential co-presence, within a given geographical area, of independent sources of dangerousness. In order to identify which parts of the territory to secure for to protect the integrity of the existing cultural heritage it is necessary to determine the local risk associated with each asset and also the global risk [4].

The preventive estimate of the risk, the prevention of damage and conse-lowing reduction of possible degradation factors on capital, are based on a knowledge of the environmental and territorial phenomena and assets to be protected.

As an alternative to the restoration which occurs at the expense occurred, this address proposes to develop, through the intervention of conservation and maintenance of the goods, a strategy based on prevention of the damage from the prevention of the degradation process through the environmental control and land control [5].

The model developed in the research and presented in this paper is a logical model which takes account the local variation of the dangers present in a given territory and the state of conservation of the properties examined. Appropriately crossing the hazard data with vulnerability data of cultural heritage, it is possible to calculate, for each asset located in a specific area of the territory, the value of the Global Risk associated with the good as a whole. This risk dependes from the assessment of the potential co-presence, within a given geographical area, of independent sources of danger.

The determination of the model has been shaped by a multi hazard approach or "cross-cutting risks". the risk is the product of two terms: hazard and vulnerability

$$R = V \times P \qquad (1)$$

The vulnerability (V) of the cultural property, is a function that indicates the level of exposure of a given good to aggression of territorial environmental factors, the territorial hazard (P), is a function that indicates the level of potential pressure characteristic of a given territorial area, regardless of the presence or not of the goods [4].

Two other variables are also considered:

"Resilience", defined as the ability, refers to any body, individual or organization, to cope and to recover from the effect of perturbing action produced by a negative event, which depends on the capacity of adaptation and intrinsic regeneration to the system;

The "Resistance", is the attitude of imperturbability of system [7].

Vulnerability and resilience depend on the interaction of socio-economic elements and fragility and ecosystem elements and on political and institutional determinants of land (aspects not yet systematically covered in the construction of synthetic indexes). Dimensioning the model, territorial unit corresponds to the wide area conterminous to the archaeological area, or a good part of the municipal area.

Through an Overlay Mapping method, the model seeks to relate the hazards factors existing on the territory and the conditions of the archaeological area vulnerability, trying to arrive at a definition and quantification of the objective factors of hazardous agents on individual assets. Obviously assuming the municipal area as the territorial reference unit will have an effect of generalization of the "dangerousness values" modeled due to the fact of heterogeneity of sources and to the different factors hazard detection systems [12]. The risk is determined by this model using a multi hazard approach (or "cross-cutting risks" or "interdisciplinary risks") taking into account a large number of variables and interaction of potentials independent events. In this sense, the developed model allows to account of how effectively the different localized contexts affect the actual state of risk to which an asset is subjected, from its current state of conservation.

The risk is considered to be a function of two different sizes, the danger that is the presence or likelihood of damaging events, and the vulnerability, that is the attitude of the asset to be damaged [1].

The vulnerability of an asset is concretely manifested in his state of conservation: it is therefore a measurable dimension through the various aspects of degradation. More a good is wasted, more it is vulnerable to the aggression of the environment [7].

3   The Study Area

The archaeological site of Sybaris is located on the Ionian coast of Calabria, at a short distance from the mouth of the Crati river. This part of the Calabrian territory, topographically known as Sybaritid, saw the birth, expansion an decline of the great poleis of Sybaris. After the destruction of the Greek town, the Hellenist centre of Thurii first and then the Roman town called Copia were built on its ruins. Such exceptional stratification made Sybaris one of the widest and most important Archaic and Classical Age archaeological sites of the Mediterranean [6].

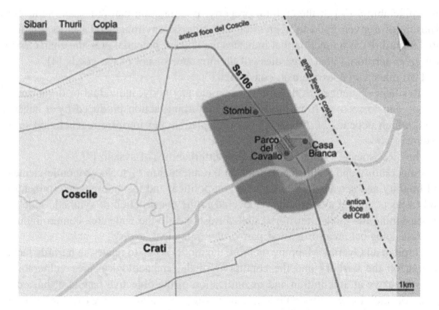

Fig. 1. Locational scheme of archeological area of Sibari

The history of the site starts in 720 B.C. with the foundation of the Achaean colony of Sybaris. In 510 B.C. the town was destroyed by Croton but was rebuilt in 444–443 B.C. as the Panhellenic city of Thurii. In 193 B.C. the Roman colony of Copia was founded on that same site; it was turned into a Roman "municipium" in 84 B.C.

During the Imperial age, from the 1st to the 3rd century A.D., the town knew a period of prosperity, but the marshy nature of the land led to a slow decay and gradual abandon in the 5th and 6th century A.D. The site was abandoned definitively in the 7th century [6].

For the taxonomy of resources were used the data of filing of the assets of the Archaeological Superintendence of Calabria and the results of excavation carried out by the Italian Archaeological School of Athens in 2013.

Starting from the 19th century, the growing interest for the still unknown and mysterious history of Sybaris allowed to locate the site of the ancient settlement and finally start the excavations in the '30s, after several decades of investigations based solely on the topographical directions provided by historical sources. The great archaeological campaigns of the '60s and those of the following decades, however, only allowed to explore a small part of the large area of Sybaris, mostly unearthing ruins connected to Copia and the Roman Age [6].

The area of the archaeological park covers 168 hectares and is divided into sectors, each of which is identified with the name of the excavations: "Parco del Cavallo", "Prolungamento strada", "Casabianca" and "Stombi".

With specific reference to the Archaeological Park area, research has highlighted a subsidence phenomenon evidenced by the presence of three overlaid cities: Sybaris (720–510 BC), Thurii (444–285 BC) and Copiae (193 BC). The rate of subsidence has gone reducing, but in recent decades the rate of subsidence has also become important for anthropogenic causes, due to the archaeological excavations and the deeper aquifer withdrawals, particularly in the levels high permeability below. The several problems concerning the excavations in the area the alluvial layers covering the ruins, the overlapping foundations of the three towns, the water table hindering the archaeological operations required an accurate planning of the archaeological interventions.

4 Problems Related to the Degradation and Management of the Archaeological Areas

The flooding of the Crati, due to the breaking of the banks, a few years ago, did arrive in the archaeological area about 200 thousand cubic meters of water and debris that have flooded completely five hectares provoking several damage. For the mud we have

Fig. 2. Plan of the archeological excavations

had to clean up the street and, above all, to clean and restore the area of the theater, of the Thermae and the Roman houses.

The structures of the various areas of Sybaris Archaeological Park, are located at a lower level to the level of the aquifer water and therefore it is need a pump system that provides the lowering of the aquifer water under the floor of the structures [10]. The well-points system, active 24/24 h and whose management is contracted out to external companies, is subject to occasional malfunctions, influenced by weather conditions, which cause periodic rises of the water level inside the archeological area.

Fig. 3. The archeological area of Sibary after the flooding of the Crati river

The structures are therefore subjected to a stress due to the presence of water. Two are the most immediate consequences caused by humidity the growth of vegetation which with its own root system damages the structures; the erosion of incoherent soil, on which rest the old structures [9].

Some interventions, completed in 2012, have made a significant contribution to minimize humidity damage:

– Were made same metal fences containing soil subject to erosion underliving to the mausoleums of the Roman period, fate, in fact, on top of a layer of soil accumulated over the Hellenistic structures;
– Are punctual works were started filling in depressed areas without archaeological structures, reducing the areas where water stagnates so as to inhibit the growth of wetland vegetation.

The amount of filling and leveling works with soil are not yet concluded and it is necessary to provide for additional works of fill with soil to eliminate the remaining areas subject to the waterlogging.

A separate problem concerns the degradation of limestone blocks of Hellenistic structures, mainly due to phenomena of degradation of the stone disintegration, accentuated by repeated cycles of wet and dry, which inevitably affects the structures. In addition, the pre-Hellenistic walls feel considerable damage due to the disintegration caused by the action of atmospheric agents; the eastern sector of the area, is often occupied by water due to the inability of the current system to ensure a continuous and effective drainage [11].

Many of the ancient walls, finally, require integrations and completions, with adequate restorations, to facilitate the readability of the architectural complex.

5   The Risks Identification

The risk factors considered in the model are several and cover the aspects more specifically related to environmental risk, the aspects related to the structural risk, those related to the risk due to the use, the aspects related to the risk due to malicious acts, or, more generally, to anthropic risk or economic risk.

The assessment was developed through the following phases:

- Analysis: Identification of important periods from an archaeological and historical point of view, regarding the geographical area considered.
- Sensitivity: Definition qualitative/quantitative sensitivity of the historic period.
- Risk Assessment: definition qualitative/quantitative of the risk level.

This is a type of probabilistic and presumptive evaluation having to define ex ante the territorial mutations, over time.

From a theoretical and methodological point of view, the "value", which can be identified by term "sensitivity" (S), of a component, is the result of the product of the fragility (f) inherent in the component, and its vulnerability (v).

$$S = f.v \tag{2}$$

Where the fragility is the characteristic of a component and the vulnerability is the probability that this component can be "assalted" by an external pressure source [1].

The indicators used to define the archaeological sensitivity are: Uniqueness, Rarity, Antiquity, Conservation Status, Artistic Merit.

The characteristics of each indicator were represented through four hierarchical levels of quality, which is assigned a numeric value from 1 to 4, except for the Uniqueness indicator, which may be present or absent.

The vulnerability to the archaeological areas is represented by a global index expressed by a growing number from 0 to 10, where increasing of the index corresponds the higher vulnerability. The vulnerability was calculated, statistically, on a significant number of variables that precisely describe the state of preservation of the archaeological area.

The acquisition of information about the vulnerability of archaeological heritage took place through a phase of cataloging that has provided a metric assessment of individual elements that can be each real estate (foundations, high, slab structures,

Constructive and decorative elements	Uniqueness,		Antiquity	Rarity	Conservation Status						Artistic Merit
	Original Element	No Original Element	Historical period	Level	Structural damage	Disintegration	Humidity	Biological attacks	Alteration surface layers	Accretions remakes	Level
Foundations	4		4	3	3	3	3	2	2	3	0
Struttures in elevation	4		4	3	4	3	3	2	1	3	0
Horizontal Struttures o	0	0	0	0	0	0	0	0	0	0	0
Covers	0	0	0	0	0	0	0	0	0	0	0
Vertical connections	0	0	0	0	0	0	0	0	0	0	0
floors	4		3	2	0	3	1	1	2	0	3
Coatings and decorations	4		2	2	0	3	2	2	2	0	3
Use	3										
Maintenance and protection systems	3				3	1	1	1	1	0	3
Security systems	1										
Sistema deflusso acque	2				1	2	2	2	1	0	2
Scooping water disposal systems	2				1	2	2	2	1	0	2
Protective covers	0	0	0	0	0	0	0	0	0	0	0

Fig. 4. Sensitivity matrix

stairs and vertical connections, covers, floors, walls) present in the archaeological area, the forms of alteration observed, and an estimated of the extension and severity of the degradation [3].

In the study of Sybaris area we tried to analyze every constructive and decorative element, of the area of domus, of the are of excavation of the Cavallo Park by relating the damage found to the techniques and materials that constitute them. A same form of alteration, in fact, can take a meaning and a different valence depending on the material used and the manner in which this is put in place in the structures. The mechanical characteristics, the shape, the size and the material constitute further elements of assessment in the analysis of archaeological vulnerability.

For to calculate the vulnerability also we have tried to collect the information on other specific aspects. In many cases, the possibility of conservation of the ruins is not only a function of the conditions of the physical characteristics of the materials, but is also determined by a number of factors, extrinsic to its physicality, but who have a direct feedback on its possible decline. In other words the judgment on the status of an archaeological monument conservation, not only based on the semiotics of traditional damage, must also occur to verify:

- the presence, the effectiveness, the adequacy and the maintenance of the architectural protection artifacts;
- the existence and the effectiveness of out flow systems and drainage of rain waters devices;
- the presence, the effectiveness and the adequacy of the partial or seasonal protection measures (e.g. the waterproofing of walls filled or the floor covers during the fall and winter);
- the existence of a routine maintenance program and weeding;
- the presence and the efficiency of security and surveillance devices (such as the guard, the fences, etc.),
- the compatibility of the possible uses of the ancient structures.

To calculate the vulnerability indicator, a statistical - descriptive approach was used, in which each considered information is fed back to a limited number of sortable categories according to a scale of increasing value. The model for the calculation has been set considering each archaeological resource analyzed as a statistical unit "complete" regardless of the number and the type of the elements that constitute it.

Information processed are those arising from the analysis of the seven constitutive and decorative elements, implemented, taking as additional parameters, the following categories:

- Use,
- maintenance,
- security systems,
- Installations water drainage system
- Disposal system water/water-scooping,
- Protective covers

The set of the parameters described contributes to the calculation of the vulnerability index and hazard, but each information intervenes in different measure, on the basis of an appropriate "weights" system. The state of conservation of the building blocks is given more weight than the other considered variables (use, maintenance, protection systems, installations). But even among these there are differences that have led to a hierarchy of weights. The roof structures are analyzed, also the architectural structure in the individual components of the artifact are analized by evaluating for each the adequacy and efficiency in relation also to the type of the various structural parts and materials used.

The information so collected are properly reprocessed and evaluated according to specific qualitative relations with the aid of statistical methods.

The sensitivity level for the archaeological site of Sybaris is placed in a medium-high range.

From the reading of the environmental analysis we can draw the hazard matrix. With the level of risk means the likelihood that the risks could interfere, generating a negative impact on the presence of objects and artifacts airborn present in the archaeological area. It can define the level of risk within a range from 0 to 3, or:

- Risk Null (numeric value 0).
- Risk Low (numerical value 1).

Presence of the risk	High	Medium	Low	Null
Hydrogeological Risk	X			
Erosion Risk	X			
Pollution Risk				X
Earthquake Risk		X		
Desertification Risk	X			
Fire Risk			X	
Subsidence Risk	X			
Sinkholes Risk		X		
Environmental Risk	X			
Human Pressure Risk		X		
Total Risk	15	6	1	0

Fig. 5. Hazard matrix

- Medium Risk (numerical value 2).
- High Risk (numeric value 3).

The level of risk to the archaeological site of Sybaris is 22 that is placed in the high range.

At this point, pondering of the archaeological component, performed through the definition of the environmental sensitivity, on the basis of the discoveries and information in the literature, assessing the value of different historical periods, in comparative way, and risk identification, such as probabilistic factor, capable of generating a negative impact on the presence of objects and artefacts of archaeological interest allow us to proceed to the final evaluation.

Assessment is carried out through the use of a matrix that calculate the total cumulative risk that you might have on the archaeological site and define preventive actions to be activated in the archaeological field.

6 Conclusions

The inferential evaluation systems for multi-dimensional estimation (Inferrential Evaluation Engine) of cultural heritage (archaeological areas) are, in many respects, very important for the current and future compatible use of cultural heritage, especially if managed with geographic software inferential, as well as methods of support to the decisions, because they allow to switch from a simultaneous vision to a synthetic vision [2].

However the intervention and enhancement choices they must carried out starting from the type of quantitative/qualitative considerations mainly related to the level of deterioration of the asset beyond the reference context. The demonstration of the level of risk is related to the phases of the "life cycle" of the urban area and the territory in general, to the type and quality of settlement of historic centers, and to the recognition of the specific categories of obsolescence that determine the asset depreciation. Starting from the case study of the archeological area of Sibari has been developed an innovative risk assessment model, by a type of approach multi hazard, oriented to sustainability criteria, that can provide help in making decisions process about the protection, conservation and valorisation of archaeological areas. The model allows to estimate the actual risk condition for archeological sites through integrating informations concerning vulnerability of archeological areas and the danger condition of the sites upon which they are located. The determination of the risk, derived from the evaluation of potential co-presence of independent sources of danger within a given geographical area within an overall information system for assessing the vulnerability of archaeological heritage and environmental dangerousness in order to identify the level of risk which is under the archaeological area in relation to the territory of reference. The results obtained allow to relate the risk with the risk factors, the detection of damage on archaeological heritage in question, determine the tolerance threshold within which it is possible the preservation of goods and to propose a synthesis strategy between environmental protection and sustainable exploitation.

References

1. Abhas, K.J.: Cultural heritage conservation. In: World Bank, Safer Homes, Stronger Communities: A Handbook for Reconstructing after Natural Disasters, Washington, pp. 173–79 (2010)
2. Canuti, P., Margottini, C., Fanti, R., Bromhead, E.N.: Cultural heritage and landslides: research for risk prevention and conservation. In: Sassa, K., Canuti, P. (eds.) Landslides-Disaster Risk Reduction. Springer, Berlin (2009)
3. Campeol, G., Pizzinato, C.: Metodologia per la valutazione dell'impatto archeologico. Archeologia e Calcolatori **18**, 273–292 (2007)
4. Corcelli, A., Ioannilli, M., Cacace, C.: Progettazione e sperimentazione di un modello di analisi Multi–hazard per la valutazione del rischio locale dei beni culturali. In: Atti della 12° Conferenza Nazionale ASITA, pp. 839–846 (2008)
5. Ferroni, A., Cacace, C.: Carta del rischio: la vulnerabilità archeologica. http://www.icr. beniculturali.it/documenti/allegati/Vulnerabilità_archeologica

6. Ministero dei beni e attività culturali - Sopraintendenza Archeologica della Calabria. http://www.archeocalabria.beniculturali.it/archeovirtualtour/calabriaweb/sitoparco.htm

7. Graziano, P.: Rischio, vulnerabilità e resilienza territoriale. In: Quaderni del Dipartimento di scienze economiche e sociali, dell'Università Cattolica del Sacro Cuore di Piacenza, serie rossa economia, quaderno, no. 87, pp. 1–32 (2012)

8. Quattrone, G.: Protocollo definizione e mitigazione dei livelli di rischio dei beni, report della ricerca CNR-IIA (WP7) per il progetto SIMONA SIstemi e tecnologie per il MONitoraggio di Aree culturali in ambiente subacqueo e terrestre, POR Calabria FESR 2007/2013 (2015)

9. Quattrone, G.: Planning religious tourist routes for the development of Calabria territory. In: Trono, A. (ed.) Sustainable Religious Tourism. Esperidi Ed. Lecce (2012)

10. Taboroff, J.: Cultural heritage and natural disasters: incentives for risk management and mitigation. In: Kreimer, A., Arnold, M. (eds.) Managing Disaster Risk in Emerging Economies, the World Bank, Washington, pp. 233–240 (2000)

11. Teti, M.A.: La pianificazione delle aree archeologiche. Carta dei vincoli archeologici della Calabria (1912–1992). Gangemi editore, Roma (1993)

12. Will, T., Meier, H.R.: Cultural Heritage and Natural Disasters: Risk Preparedness and the Limits of Prevention ICOMOS. Heritage At Risk, Dresden (2007). Special Edition

Full Paper: Intangible Cultural Heritage Documentation

Parameterizing the Geometry and Visualizing the Lighting Method of Byzantine Church Domes

Wassim Jabi[1(✉)] and Iakovos Potamianos[2]

[1] Welsh School of Architecture, Cardiff University, Cardiff, UK
jabiw@cardiff.ac.uk
[2] Faculty of Fine Arts, School of Drama,
Aristotle University of Thessaloniki, Thessaloniki, Greece
ipota@thea.auth.gr

Abstract. This paper introduces a computer-based tool for the analysis of the geometry and the daylighting of Byzantine church domes to facilitate experimentation with a number of cases before any fieldwork is undertaken. Starting with a geometric derivation of the relationship between dome parameters, the digital tool builds an interactive three-dimensional model of a Byzantine church dome. The model allows the user to input the properties of the dome, the drum, any windows, and the slope of their sills. The model allows the user to define the dome using three different curvatures since such a case was identified in a Mistras church. A custom ray-tracing algorithm visualizes the path of light rays falling on the windowsills and their reflections within the dome. It was found that several parameters are interrelated and that an optimal set of proportions must be established to achieve the expected behavior of light within the dome.

Keywords: Byzantine domes · Lighting simulation · Parametric models · Natural daylighting

1 Introduction

In many Byzantine churches the dome appears to be uniformly illuminated even though logically it could not be since the windows are located at the lower part of the dome and the sunrays always point downwards (Fig. 1). According to our studies this phenomenon was first posed and solved as a problem of solid geometry by Anthemius of Tralles presumably to achieve the unique lighting of the Hagia Sophia dome, his life masterpiece. Anthemius was an important geometer who was well versed in "catoptrics", a science, which captured the interest of mathematicians since classical antiquity. While the problem was clearly posed by Anthemius, there is no record that the combination of forms he invented was known or followed in subsequent churches. However, although later churches adopted a quite different geometry, the phenomenon of a highly lit dome persisted. In order to understand the manner in which a byzantine dome was lit, we have attempted several studies and simulations [1–5], of which the one appearing in this paper constitutes a new development.

© Springer International Publishing AG 2016
M. Ioannides et al. (Eds.): EuroMed 2016, Part I, LNCS 10058, pp. 171–183, 2016.
DOI: 10.1007/978-3-319-48496-9_14

Fig. 1. Dome of the Iveron monastery church, Mount Athos, 11th c.

The dome of Hagia Sophia of Istanbul, as has been established in our previous studies, had been designed as a combination of two curved mirrors (Fig. 2) of different curvature [1, 2]. These mirror designs were found in the architect's own extant writings [6]. The manner in which these two mirrors were combined has been shown in previous studies (Fig. 3), and the impression generated has been described by Procopius, the historian eye-witness of the effect. This hypothesis can be considered largely proven in terms of geometric, topographic and textual evidence [1].

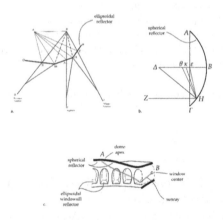

Fig. 2. a. Anthemius's ellipsoidal reflector, b. Anthemius's spherical reflector (i.e. the shallow dome itself), c. Sketch showing the location of the reflectors.

The most persistent questions posed, whenever these findings had been presented in academic fora, were the following: "Hagia Sophia is a unique case. How would domes of lesser church examples achieve a similar visual effect? Since their form is quite different than Hagia Sophia's and thereby could not have employed the same method of illumination, how did they achieve the constantly and uniformly luminous effect which is common among them?"

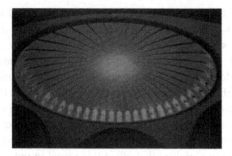

Fig. 3. Computer model of the original dome of Hagia Sophia with the two mirrors in place (from an earlier simulation).

2   The Case of Other Byzantine Churches

Any attempt to answer the above questions tends to become particularly complex. The reason is that one is not dealing with a single building, which may be studied exhaustively from a number of different aspects. Instead, one has to investigate many different buildings of various eras. Therefore, the enormity of the problem requires a carefully planned strategy.

A highly and quite uniformly lit dome in lesser Byzantine church examples is a persistent phenomenon. This is not something expected or occurring in all domed churches. If there had been no lighting planning, a different portion of the dome would be lit depending on the position of the sun in the sky (Fig. 4) while the rest of the dome would remain darker. Instead, a Byzantine dome is uniformly lit and the brightest spot is usually found at the apex (Fig. 1). Therefore, it may be assumed that there must be a certain lighting system at work in the domes of lesser Byzantine churches as well. This system is what we set out to discover and to this purpose we thought that we could take advantage of the method of parametric modeling before we move into actual field work.

Fig. 4. Drawing of the original Hagia Sophia dome by E. Antoniades, showing a bright spot in the dome, located off center [8]. This image would be created if the lighting had not been carefully planned.

Following the construction of the parametric model one could then resort to surveys of existing domes. In typical surveys of Byzantine churches, published in various specialized articles, books, and dissertations, some basic, easily measurable variables are already available. Thus, one would have a significant amount of elementary measurements, (i.e. dome height, drum height, number and dimensions of dome windows) to begin with, before travelling to the monument site. One would then have to observe whether the dome of the monument is luminous, using existing photographs, and would manipulate the subtler variables of the parametric model in order to achieve the effect. Once the luminous effect had been achieved in the model one would already have a fair estimate of the variables that affect this visual impression. As a result, only those variables of the actual form would have to be measured that made sense in terms of the model. Strategically, this would be the most effective procedure.

3   Geometric Principles of the Parametric Model

The Byzantine church domes vary considerably. They are made up of various parts. Often, there is an upright standing tube-like part, which may be cylindrical or polygonal, called the "drum". On top of it a roughly semispherical dome is placed. On the drum several openings are pierced which differ in number from six to eight to twelve to forty. However, the closer one looks at that geometry the more variations one discovers to this basic scheme.

Below, certain general observations and principles are outlined which lie behind the construction of the model. First, the drum is not always of the same height and its proportions are related to the scale of the dome ensemble (i.e., the diameter of the dome in plan) as well as to the total height. A general proportioning rule is that a greater dome radius corresponds to a lower drum height. This rule has not yet been established as a strict mathematical proportional relationship.

In some cases, the drum disappears completely. This is the case, for instance, of the original dome of Hagia Sophia in Istanbul (Fig. 3), while in the church of Saints Sergius & Bacchus – which served as a model for the design of the former - the drum is quite low. In the church of Hagia Eirini, of the same city, while a substantial drum is visible from the outside, in the interior the smooth curvature of the dome blends in with the drum and makes the drum invisible as if it were part of the dome. This difference is visible in most churches of later periods as well. While the drum is clearly articulated as a form from the exterior, it loses all articulation and blends in with the curvature of the dome as it is seen from the inside. Architecturally, the exterior and the interior seem as belonging to two different aesthetic approaches. This phenomenon requires a special investigation, which, however, is not the focus of this paper. What we might retain from this observation for now is that for some reason this sense of transition from one geometric form to another, so that the composite form appears unified, as seen from the inside, constituted an essential goal.

Second, the size of the windows piercing the drum depend on the drum's height. The taller the drum the greater the height of the windows and the slenderer their proportions become. This proportional relationship appears to be consistent. However, as we have already mentioned, the drum in some cases may not exist at all. In these cases, the window height acquires a proportional relationship to the sum of the circular segments length. Therefore, the possibility of inserting windows on the dome curvature should be incorporated in the model. The window height does have an effect on the manner in which light is reflected towards the dome. In a taller drum the rays seem to be able to be reflected more vertically while in a shorter drum the window header limits the reflected rays to more oblique angles.

Third, it has been noticed that the dome may not be necessarily semispherical. What has been observed in Hagia Sophia is that a very shallow curvature was employed. Such shallow curvatures have been observed in various other churches as well. Similar shallow curvatures were not limited to the dome but were employed also in vertical wall surfaces such as the one above the main gate of the church of Hagia Sophia, which seems to be responsible for the concentration of light so that the image of Christ, located on that surface, becomes suddenly lit at a certain distance [7]. Shallow curvatures, in general, seem to be connected to the impression of a uniformly lit dome. A shallow curvature has the ability to trap light and distribute it uniformly onto its surface, as long as light enters the curvature obliquely. This particular characteristic would render the shallow curvature invaluable to a dome designer. Therefore, our parametric model has the capability of incorporating a shallow dome curvature.

Fourth, a sunray passing through a dome window must somehow be reflected in order to reach the interior of the dome. The windowsill may provide such a surface. Anthemius especially designed such a surface for this location [1, 4]. However, this design, placed on the dome windowsill was conceived as a concave surface, which sloped inward. For the case of Hagia Sophia, of which the original dome had no drum, this windowsill design and slope was reasonable. For a dome with a drum, however, the same principle would tend to produce an outward sloping windowsill. We have found evidence of such treatment on the dome windowsills of the Monastery of Iveron church, which has a particularly bright and uniformly lit dome (Fig. 1). Based on these observations, the model has the capability of manipulating the windowsills by changing their slope and curvature.

Fifth, if not planned carefully, the reflected ray, once it reached the dome, would most probably hit it once and then be reflected downward to the floor. The point on which it hit would vary depending on the position of the sun in the sky. This means that a luminous point in the dome would appear at different positions while the rest of the dome would remain dim (Fig. 4). It appears that the only way to create a uniformly and constantly luminous dome would be to trap the light in it. This can happen if two conditions are met. First, if a shallow reflective surface for the interior of the dome itself is employed. Second, if a windowsill with a slope is employed so as to send the rays into the dome in such a way that further reflections continue to remain entrapped within the dome. Then, we could expect that most ordinary churches may incorporate not one but two or even three curvatures within the dome. The upper curvature of the dome may have to be deeper when a drum exists and be proportional to its height. The idea of a tri-partite dome was conceived based on the observation of an existing dome, of the Metropolis church of Mistras (Fig. 5).

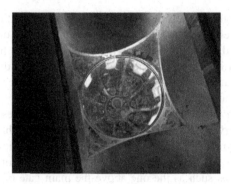

Fig. 5. Dome of Metropolis church, Mistras, 13th c.

3.1   Derivation of the Geometric Relationships

The purpose of this section is to provide a geometric proof of the derivation of the two other radii (called middle dome radius and upper dome radius) given the first radius of the lower/main dome and a set of input parameters. This derivation forms the basis of the algorithms and the parametric calculations based on user input in the interactive graphical interface. Please refer to the diagram below for reference to the named vertices (Fig. 6).

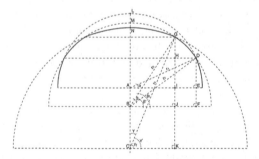

Fig. 6. Drawing showing the section of the dome which is composite of three circular curvatures. This drawing shows the fundamental variables of the dome introduced into the model.

Before we start the derivation, it is important to note that the naming of the domes (lower, middle, and upper), refers to the end result after its construction. These domes are shown in dashed lines in the figure above. The actual domes need to be vertically stacked in the opposite direction to achieve that end result (shown in a solid line). The lower dome arc has the smallest radius (*r1*) and the highest vertical position for its center (*A*), followed by the middle dome with a larger radius (*r2*) and a lower vertical position of its center (*B*), and ending with the upper dome with the largest radius (*r3*) and the lowest vertical position of its center (*C*).

We will mainly use Pythagoras's theorem which defines the relation in Euclidean geometry among the three sides of a right triangle. It states that the square of the hypotenuse (the side opposite the right angle) is equal to the sum of the squares of the other two sides. In addition, we will use trigonometric functions to derive the angles subtended by the arcs we are calculating. The calculated lengths and angles will allow us to geometrically create the necessary arcs of any desired dimension while maintaining consistent parametric relationships in the overall geometry.

Given parameters

The derivation assumes a set of given parameters:

1. r_1 is the radius of the lower dome. This is the main interior radius of the dome as perceived from the bottom at the "springing" point of the dome.
2. AB is the vertical distance from the centre of the lower dome to the centre of the middle dome
3. BC is the vertical distance from the centre of the middle dome to the centre of the upper dome.
4. ED is the vertical height of the lower dome portion. Above that height, the dome arcs according to the middle dome radius (r_2).
5. HG is the vertical height of the middle dome portion. Above that height, the dome arcs according to the upper dome radius (r_3).

Derivation of the radius of the middle dome (r2)

$$r_1^2 = AE^2 + ED^2 \tag{1}$$

Since ED and $r1$ are given, we can derive AE.

$$AE = \sqrt{(r_1^2 - ED^2)} \tag{2}$$

$$BF = AE \tag{3}$$

AE is calculated in (2)

$$FD = FE + ED \tag{4}$$

Both FE (AB) and ED are given, so we can calculate FD.

$$r_2^2 = BF^2 + FD^2 \tag{5}$$

Since BF and FD have been calculated above in (3) and (4), we can derive r_2.

$$r_2 = \sqrt{(BF^2 - FD^2)} \tag{6}$$

Derivation of the radius of the upper dome (r3)

$$JG = JI + IH + HG \tag{7}$$

$$JI = AB, IH = ED \therefore JG = AB + ED + HG \tag{8}$$

AB, ED, and HG are given therefore we can derive JG.

$$r2^2 = JG^2 + BJ^2 \therefore BJ = \sqrt{(r_2^2 - JG^2)} \tag{9}$$

Since r2 and JG have been calculated above, we can derive BJ.

$$CK = BJ \tag{10}$$

BJ is calculated in (9).

$$KG = KJ + JI + IH + HG \tag{11}$$

$$KJ = BC, JI = AB, IH = ED \therefore KG = BC + AB + ED + HG \tag{12}$$

BC, AB, ED, and HG are given, therefore we can derive KG.

$$r3^2 = CK^2 + KG^2 \therefore r3 = \sqrt{(CK^2 + KG^2)} \tag{13}$$

CK and KG have been calculated in (10) and (11) respectively, therefore we can derive r3.

Thus, given the radius of the lower dome, the vertical position of the centres of the three domes and the vertical height of the lower and the middle dome portions, we can derive the radii of the lower and higher domes and construct a complex dome curvature made out of three arcs that can have a significantly lower apex (N) compared to that of a single-radius dome (L), or a double-radius dome (M).

Derivation of the angles
The construction of the curves of the parametric dome also depend on discovering the subtended angles for the lower, middle, and upper dome. In the figure above, these angles are <EAD (α), <DBG (β), and <GCN (γ) respectively. Using trigonometry, we can find these angles. Specifically, we can use the definition of the *sin* of an angle as the division of the opposite side divided by the hypotenuse in a right-angled triangle. Space limitations prevent us from including the full derivation in this paper.

4   Computer Implementation

In order to investigate these hypotheses, we created a computer script within Autodesk 3 ds Max 3D that generates a three-dimensional solid model of a dome (Fig. 7).

The parametric model presented here has been constructed with the capability of representing a dome created with three different arcs above the drum. The dome can

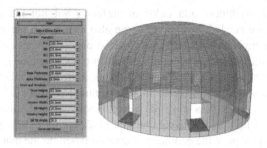

Fig. 7. Parametric dome model and associated input parameters.

acquire any radius and wall thickness. The lower and upper curvatures of the dome can vary in terms of their vertical height; thus creating different composite curvatures while maintaining a consistent geometric relationship between them. Any number of windows, of any width and height, can be incorporated into the drum or into the lower curvature of the dome. The windowsill can be made to slope inward or outward.

Once the dome has been created, we created a custom ray-tracing algorithm to simulate the behavior of light and reflection to visualize a representation of the sunrays as they hit the windowsill and reflect multiple times inside the dome (Fig. 8). This methodology is similar to the ones used for acoustic analysis [9]. The accuracy of the computer modelling has previously been verified [10]. In the image below, two sub-cases are presented simultaneously, one with a semispherical upper dome and another with a shallower upper dome in order to compare the manner in which light is reflected in each. The light is reflected in such a way that it washes the entire dome surface. This light behavior guarantees the uniform illumination of the entire dome.

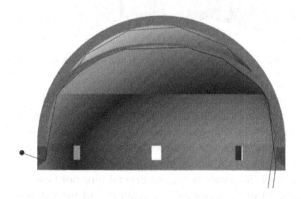

Fig. 8. Computer model comparing a semispherical and a tri-spherical dome

We decided that the most effective method to study the behavior of the multiple reflections within the dome was to calculate and visualize the line vectors that represent the direction of a sunray. It is important to note here that the built-in ray-tracing capabilities of the software environment were of no use to us at this stage as they only represent the final brightness and color of surfaces, but not the light ray vectors themselves which we needed. Furthermore, we also abandoned the use of the built-in physics simulation engine as reported in a previous paper. The reason for developing a ray-tracing algorithm rather than rely on the built-in physics engine is to eliminate data noise present in the physics simulation that takes into consideration the friction of surfaces, bounciness and other forces. In light-simulation, these forces do not exist. Thus, the enhanced script uses pure 3D vector geometry and rules of reflection to calculate the path of light as it reflects multiple times within the dome. While outside the scope of this paper, once the geometry is derived based on the mathematics of light, additional visual studies of texture and spatial perceptions can be undertaken following the examples in the project "Virtual Hagia Sophia" at MIRALab [11]. Similarly, high-dynamic-range (HDR) imaging can be used as a good method to present a similar range of luminance to that experienced through the human eye and has been used to better visualize light beams in existing buildings [12].

By varying the input parameters and re-running the ray-tracing algorithm, we were able to simulate multiple incidence angles and derive the appropriate parameters that can achieve the desired light path and therefore luminous effect through the entrapment of light within the dome (Fig. 9).

Fig. 9. Computer model of a dome with drum and a convex parabolic windowsill.

In addition to the parametric script that creates the main geometry of the dome, we enhanced our work with an additional script that allows us to generate and test the effect of parabolic surfaces. The script accurately creates a parabolic surface based on the location of a "focus" point and a "directrix" line. This three-dimensional parabolic surface can then be placed on top of the sill window and incorporated in the dome geometry. The axis of the parabola (i.e. its general direction) can be oriented in any angle. The orientation of the main axis of symmetry of the parabola determines the direction of reflections for any ray that falls on the exterior surface of the parabola and passes through its focus if extended to the other side of the parabola. However, parallel rays that hit the surface in other areas will reflect in different and non-parallel directions because they do not pass through the focus if extended. Using these scripts, we were able to simulate and visualize the behavior of several parallel light rays coming in at a steep angle as can be seen in (Fig. 9). The two rays in the above figure, the first exiting downwards on the right side (indicated in red) and the second exiting the window on the right side (indicated in blue), are close to each other and thus behave in a similar fashion. These two rays enter the dome space at a steeply vertical angle which causes them to reflect along the surface of the dome in a tangential matter. Other parallel rays that do not pass through the focus of the parabola are reflected in other directions — mainly back to the exterior of the dome. With the introduction of these additional scripts and the refined ray-tracing algorithm, we now have more accurate tools to further study different reflecting geometries and propose possible methods used to light the apex of the dome.

5 Summary of Findings

So far we have established the following:

1. In order to generate a light wash of the dome surface the rays must enter the concave surface as laterally to the dome curvature as possible. In a dome with a drum, this lateral introduction of the reflected ray corresponds to the vertical direction.
2. The taller the drum the more possible it is for the reflected ray to enter the dome at a more vertical angle.
3. The variable that is most important for the upward lateral direction of the reflected sunray is the slope of the windowsill of the dome windows. In a dome with a drum the windowsill must slope outwards while in the absence of a drum it must slope inwards.
4. In order for the reflected sunrays to acquire the same upward direction regardless of the position of the sun in the sky, the windowsill must be curved and most probably convex, acquiring the form of a parabola.
5. Both a semispherical dome as well as a tri-spherical one will generate consecutive reflections within it, given the appropriate windowsill shape.
6. In a tri-spherical dome the transition from one curvature to the next must be as gradual as possible in order for the reflections to follow the dome curvature closely.
7. The difference in a tri-spherical dome appears to be that more reflections are concentrated toward the upper parts of the dome.
8. Various parameters are interrelated. The height of the drum to the number and radius of the curvatures of the dome as well as to the rotation of the central axis of the convex parabolic windowsill.
9. Every sunray that falls in the direction of the focus of the parabola is reflected upwards within the dome and begins travelling along its curvature.
10. The closer the first reflection is to the vertical the greater the entrapment of the reflections within the dome.
11. Most of the sunrays that do not align with the parabola focus are reflected back out. Therefore, this type of curvature creates a highly selective and exclusive windowsill.

6   Conclusions and Future Work

Byzantine church domes are paradoxically brighter than all surrounding surfaces. This phenomenon has been investigated in previous work for the case of the dome of Hagia Sophia of Istanbul. The lighting of this dome had been resolved by the combination of two reflectors designed by Anthemius. In order to understand the dome design methods employed in lesser church examples, where a luminous dome effect is achieved, a parametric model was constructed which gave us the opportunity to experiment with a number of parameters influencing the behavior of light within the dome before we test any particular church case. It has been found that several of the parameters are inter-related, as for instance, the height of the drum, the slope of the windowsill and the height of the three curvatures of the dome. Depending on the various forms constituting the dome an optimal set of proportions must be established for the behavior of light within the dome. It is probable that there is a precise mathematical relationship governing these factors. This is an area to be investigated in future work. Such an investigation is valuable along with archaeological evidence to the restoration of domes of Byzantine churches of various periods. Contingent on the availability of funding, we plan to use advanced laser scanning and photogrammetry techniques on site to document the geometry of selected domes and their windowsills to verify our parametric model findings. Given the height of windowsills, we anticipate the need for aerial-based photogrammetry (e.g. using quadcopter drones equipped with cameras and 3D laser scanning equipment). Ultimately, we would like to study the experiential qualities achieved through the manipulation of light and its interaction with the architecture.

References

1. Potamianos, I.: Light into architecture: the evocative use of natural light as related to liturgy in Byzantine Churches. Ph.D. dissertation, Doctoral Program in Architecture, University of Michigan, Ann Arbor (1996)
2. Jabi, W., Potamianos, I.: A parametric exploration of the lighting method of the Hagia Sophia Dome. In: Proceedings of 2006 7th International Conference on Virtual Reality, Archaeology and Intelligent Cultural Heritage, pp. 257–265 (2006)
3. Jabi, W., Potamianos, I.: Geometry, light, and cosmology in the church of Hagia Sophia. Int. J. Architectural Comput. 5(2), 303–319 (2007)
4. Potamianos, I., Jabi, W.: A parametric model of Byzantine church domes. In: Proceedings of the 6th Balkan Light Conference, pp. 13–17 (2015)
5. Jabi, W., Potamianos, I.: Interactive parametric design and the role of light in Byzantine Churches. In: Proceedings of 24th eCAADe Conference, pp. 798–803 (2006)
6. Huxley, G.L.: Anthemius of Tralles: A Study of Later Greek Geometry. Eaton Press, Cambridge (1959)
7. Mathew, G.: Byzantine Aesthetics. Viking Press, New York (1964)
8. Antoniades, E.: Ekphrasis tes Hagias Sophias (1905)

9. Turner, J., Hall, T.W.: An application of geometric modeling and ray tracing to the visual and acoustical analysis of a municipal open-air auditorium. In: Proceedings of ACADIA 1990, pp. 173–185 (1990)
10. Taengchum, T., Chirarattananon, S.: Ray tracing method of light through rectangular light pipe with bends. Energy Procedia **79**(2), 791–798 (2015)
11. Foni, A., Papagiannakis, G., Cadi-Yazli, N., Magnenat Thalmann, N.: Time-dependant illumination and animation of virtual Hagia-Sophia. Int. J. Architectural Comput. (IJAC) (IF: 1.144) **5**(2), 284–301 (2007). Multi-Science Publishing
12. Happa, J., Artusi, A., Czanner, S., Chalmers, A.: High dynamic range video for cultural heritage documentation and experimental Archaeology. In: Proceedings of 2010 VAST 2010 the 11th International Symposium on Virtual Reality, Archaeology and Cultural Heritage (2010)

Digital and Handcrafting Processes Applied to Sound-Studies of Archaeological Bone Flutes

Etienne Safa[1], Jean-Baptiste Barreau[2,3], Ronan Gaugne[4],
Wandrille Duchemin[6], Jean-Daniel Talma[7], Bruno Arnaldi[3],
Georges Dumont[5], and Valérie Gouranton[3(✉)]

[1] Université de Bourgogne/ArTeHiS UMR 6298, Dijon, France
[2] CNRS/CReAAH UMR 6566, Rennes, France
[3] INSA de Rennes/IRISA UMR 6074/Inria-Rennes, Rennes, France
`Valerie.Gouranton@irisa.fr`
[4] Université de Rennes 1/IRISA UMR 6074/Inria-Rennes, Rennes, France
[5] ENS de Rennes/IRISA UMR 6074/Inria-Rennes, Rennes, France
[6] LBBE UMR CNRS 5558, University of Lyon 1, Lyon, France
[7] Atelier El Bock, Chatel-Montagne, France

Abstract. Bone flutes make use of a naturally hollow raw-material. As nature does not produce duplicates, each bone has its own inner cavity, and thus its own sound-potential. This morphological variation implies acoustical specificities, thus making it impossible to handcraft a true and exact sound-replica in another bone. This phenomenon has been observed in a handcrafting context and has led us to conduct two series of experiments (the first-one using handcrafting process, the second-one using 3D process) in order to investigate its exact influence on acoustics as well as on sound-interpretation based on replicas. The comparison of the results has shed light upon epistemological and methodological issues that have yet to be fully understood.

This work contributes to assessing the application of digitization, 3D printing and handcrafting to flute-like sound instruments studied in the field of archaeomusicology.

Keywords: Acoustics · Statistics · Handcrafting · Raw-materials · Digitization · 3D printing · Music archaeology

1 Introduction

Elaborating a research project in close collaboration with a craftsman and a research team dedicated to digitization of cultural heritage was the trigger point to different kinds of experiments meant to investigate the morphological variability of bones and its influence on the emitted sounds when carved as flutes. Dealing with this "Sound-morphology" is the main part of a craftsman's work, which is why it was decided to run the project of an apprenticeship that would last for one year [18]. During this time, particular attention was paid to the creation and use of prototypes, i.e. a bone flute manufactured in order to try

© Springer International Publishing AG 2016
M. Ioannides et al. (Eds.): EuroMed 2016, Part I, LNCS 10058, pp. 184–195, 2016.
DOI: 10.1007/978-3-319-48496-9_15

and understand the sound specificities of a particular bone, and then used as a guide in order to ease the adaptation process. Indeed, each bone has its own morphology and needs to be considered as an individual. The flute-maker proceeds then with a precise observation of each individual and takes every morphological specificity into consideration in order to craft series of bone flutes with similar sounds and identical tuning, even if this has to result in objects that do not look the same. Otherwise, he would risk to create an inefficient object, or a completely different flute.

These observations have raised specific issues regarding the use of bone flute's replicas for tone scales interpretations in archaeological surveys, as their manufacture never seems to take into consideration the bone's morphology as part of its acoustical specificities [6, 8, 16]. They have also led us to conduct "twin experiments" in the hope of reaching consistent results that would spare no methodological tracks (past, actual and yet-to-come sound-reconstruction methods) in order to explore their limitations as well as their potential. This way, we hope to contribute to better the epistemological landscape of archaeological flute's research.

The work presented in this paper focuses on the comparison of the sound results given by both series of experiments.

2   Context of the Work

2.1   Approach

Flutes are not all the same. They are grouped into several kinds which are distinguished by the way the air stream is directed toward the edge. Each kind has its own sound aesthetics, but gives also more or less freedom to the flute-player in choosing the pitch and the sound's characteristics, thanks to the blowing angle variability (Fig. 1). Oblique-, pan-, vessel- and transverse-flutes are amongst the most malleable kinds of flutes. We chose duct-flutes as they are the opposite.

In term of organology, these objects can be mentioned as 421.221.12 in the S/H classification system (Sachs/Hornbostel), which means: Internal duct-flute (straight and single) with finger holes and an open end.

Fig. 1. Blowing angle variations regarding two different organological kinds of flutes: (a) oblique flute, (b) duct-flute

2.2 Partnership

This "two-front approach" demands to assemble a consistent amount of knowledge, which can only be achieved through partnership.

- **Handcrafting process:** the work gathered a traditional flute-maker and a statistician in computational biology.
- **3D process:** the work was based on an existing collaboration between archaeologists and computer scientists on advanced imaging for archaeology, the CNPAO [2]

2.3 Terminology

This paper will use the following terminology according to the acoustical specificities of bone flutes:

- **Morphology:** refers to the natural inner and outer shapes of the bone.
- **Geometry:** refers to the handcrafted inner and outer shapes carved deliberately or not onto the bone's surface.
- **Sound-morphology:** refers to the acoustical sections of the morphology, which define the sound potential of the bone (i.e. the inner cavity). By definition, each bone has a different sound-morphology.
- **Sound-geometry:** refers to the acoustical sections of the geometry, which are involved in the definition of the instrument's final sound, whether they were meant (deliberately carved) or not (unintentional and/or unconscious geometry). As an example: the shapes of the internal duct, of the edge, of the finger holes, etc. By definition, the sound-geometry rules out the outer shaping as long as it does not change the finger holes depth.
- **T0, T1, T2, etc.:** refers to the finger holes' combination. T0 means all holes closed. T1 means that the lower finger hole (the first one) is open. T2 means that the two lower finger holes (the first and the second one) are open, etc.
- **F0, F1, F2, etc.:** systematic identification numbers of the experimental flutes. F0 refers to the control flute, whereas F1, F2, F3, etc. refers to each replica copying the control flute.

2.4 Related Works

Nowadays, 3D technologies allow outer and inner contact-free investigation on complex geometries [15]. As such they contribute to answer both preservation and sound studies issues and are more and more used in the actual archaeomusicological research. If their consequences on our interpretations are still to be defined, they allow different kind of approaches and studies that aim to get a better understanding of ancient sounds. They can be applied to any organological material [10], such as string instruments [4,13,20,21] but also aerophones [3,8, 9,11], among which archaeological "flutes", and objects presumed to be flutes, figure [1,14,22,23].

Eventually, the music-archaeology research may even explore new possibilities in sound reconstruction studies, as its data can be applied to sound simulators and sound-scape reconstructions [7,12,24].

3   The Sound-Morphology Principle

Naturally hollow rawmaterials, such as bones, hornes, shells or reeds, present a morphological variability between one individual and another. Those variations can be observed both regarding their shapes, their scale and their volumetric and spatial configuration (Fig. 2). Some of them are involved in the sound-morphology. For example, a larger bone will produce a lower pitch for the same length. Likewise, an important and sudden increase or decrease of the bone's conicity tends to distort the efficiency of a close-range finger-hole.

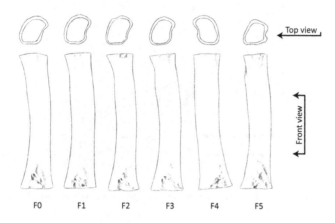

Fig. 2. Morphological variations between bones used for crafting F0 to F5 in the Hand-crafting process experiments explained below. Deer femurs show several constants, such as a bulge characterizing the distal part of the epiphysis, a triangular and irregular depression characterizing its proximal part, and a slimming zone in the concave area of the bone's bean-like cross-section. Despite those constants, there never are two identical bones.

In order to illustrate this phenomenon, we chose to handcraft a unique replica of a bone flute in another similar bone (Fig. 3).

The control flute was made in a goat's tibia. It was made very simply, using only steel knife and file, evoking archaeological flutes found in northern Europe for medieval period [5]. The handmade replica was made very carefully, using several measurement tools (caliper, compass, etc.). Also, as the depth of the block changes the pitch, we chose depth 0 (Fig. 4). This calibration is easier to reproduce. We also tried our best to give both blocks a similar soil angle. As a result, the two flutes gave different sounds, with a deviation going from half a tone to more than one tone, increasing as we open the finger holes (Figs. 9 and 10).

This replication test shows how much the sound of a bone flute replica may be deviant from the sound of the control flute it's related to. This phenomenon illustrates the notion of "sound-morphology" as it reveals that every bone has a sound-potential of its own.

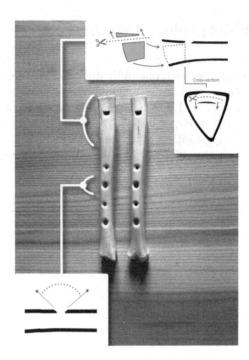

Fig. 3. The control flute (left) and its replica (right) both made out of goat's tibias.

4   Handcrafting Experiments

4.1   Handcrafting Replication Process and Technical Specifications

- **Objectives:** those experiments aim to define the extent of the limitation caused by sound-morphology, as well as to explore the acoustical specificities of this phenomenon. The approach is then different from what we can see in experimental archaeology, as we need here a well-known, functional and replicable bone flute in order to compare its actual sounds with our interpretations.
- **Control and sample:** we chose 6 similar deer femurs with morphological variations. 5 replicas is the minimum sample required for statistical analysis.
- **Chosen sound-geometry:** inner duct-flute with rectangular opening and straight edge (Fig. 5). Combined with a straight geometry, this configuration creates powerful blowing constraints and is easier to reproduce.
- **Manufacture:** handcrafted in January 2016.
- **Sound capture and analysis:** because of lack of means, we had to use a common recording device (smartphone) and a free software (audacity). Having no mechanical blower nor anechoic chamber available at the time, we had to record the sound using natural blowing (as homogeneous as possible) and the same context (a chosen room). Thankfully, the studied phenomenons are contrasting enough to be well illustrated even with a lack of technical means.

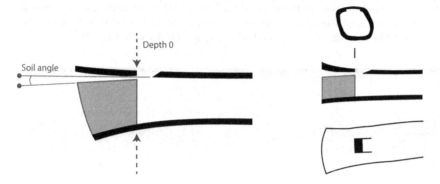

Fig. 4. Illustration of Depth 0 and soil angle

Fig. 5. Depiction of the sound-geometry used for the handcrafting experiments

4.2 Sound Results

The diagrams in Fig. 8 represent the results of basic acoustical analysis of the control flute and its 5 replicas. They obviously show that each individual is different from the control flute.

4.3 Statistics and Discussion

The table (Table 1) represents statistical analysis made on the recorded frequencies. In order to compare them properly, we had to translate them from Hertz to logarithmic scale (base 2 logarithm).

This table shows heterogeneous frequencies and intervals deviations comparing the sample to the control flute, as well as between each individual from the sample itself. Even if the frequency deviations are mostly non-significant regarding statistics (T0 is the only one being significant), the sound estimation they produce is not satisfying for the ear (about one quarter-tone). However, intervals deviations are really small in comparison (about $1/20^{th}$ of a tone), which is extremely accurate.

The following facts should also be considered regarding those results:

1. The lower end of the flute was one of the most variable areas and it was then difficult to reproduce an exact geometry in a changing trabecular bone. This could explain T0 deviation.
2. The small sample size is probably involved in those statistical results: a larger sample (20 to 30 replicas) should help us to get better results and thus assess if whether or not this incredibly accurate estimation of intervals is exact. It should also explain the difference between a satisfying intervals reproduction and an unsatisfying frequencies reproduction.
3. The human blow should be ruled out and replaced by a mechanical blower in order to ensure the accuracy of the sound-capture.

Table 1. Statistical analysis of frequencies emitted by F0 to F5 while playing successively T0, T1 and T2. Differences are expressed in semi-tones ("−1" equals "1 semi-tone lower"). The right columns show intervals deviations (T0–T1 and T1–T2).

	Hz T0	log T0	Diff 1/2 ton	Hz T1	log T1	Diff 1/2 ton	Hz T2	log T2	Diff 1/2 ton			Diff 1/2			Diff 1/2
Flute 0	1051	10.03745		1176	10.19967		1372	10.38651			-0.162125	-1.845905		-0.168834	-2.026009
Flute 1	1004	9.971544	-0.792041	1133	10.14593	-0.644882	1269	10.30948	-0.708361		-0.174389	-2.092663		-0.163544	-1.96253
Flute 2	1048	10.03342	-0.049487	1194	10.22159	0.262977	1350	10.39874	0.362847		-0.188164	-2.257969		-0.177157	-2.125879
Flute 3	1011	9.981567	-0.671756	1132	10.14466	-0.660169	1269	10.30948	-0.708361		-0.163091	-1.957092		-0.164818	-1.977817
Flute 4	995	9.958553	-0.947931	1115	10.12283	-0.922132	1247	10.28425	-1.011129		-0.164275	-1.971303		-0.161418	-1.937013
Flute 5	1027	10.00422	-0.399918	1145	10.16113	-0.462486	1290	10.33316	-0.424213		-0.156911	-1.882937		-0.172023	-2.064282
Average		9.989961			10.15923			10.32702			-0.169086	-2.032193		-0.167792	-2.013504
Standard deviation		0.029531			0.037438			0.043667			0.012237	0.146847		0.006579	0.078945
table student n=6 & alpha=0.95		2.571			2.571			2.571			2.571	2.571		2.571	2.571
Confidence interval 96 %		0.031951			0.043045			0.050202			0.01919	0.168843		0.007563	0.090773
minimum confidence interval		9.955907			10.11618			10.27681			-0.183436	-2.201236		-0.175356	-2.104274
maximum confidence interval		10.02262			10.20227			10.37728			-0.155299	-1.86355		-0.160228	-1.92273
Flute 0 in the confidence interval range ?		NO			YES			YES						YES		YES
deviation comparing to Flute 0 (Log2)		-0.047686			-0.040445			-0.041487							
deviation comparing to Flute 0 (semi-tone)		-0.572227			-0.485338			-0.497844				0.069888			-0.012505

5   3D Experiments

5.1   CT-scanning

There exist several possibilities in matter of 3D image acquisition, but CT-scanning was the only viable option because of the very nature of flutes: inner shapes are drastically important and their acoustical properties are extremely sensitive. We needed then a technology that would be able to capture high resolution images both inside and outside of the objects. μ-tomography, also known as μCT, was then the perfect tool. This technology uses X-rays in order to recreate high resolution 3D internal views of an object by compiling the acquired images and is mainly used in medical imaging and industries.

5.2   3D Replication Process and Technical Specifications

- **Objectives:** those experiments aim to question the sound-replication capability of 3D technologies in order to define whether or not they may allow us to pass beyond the sound-morphology limitation endured by handcrafting process. They also aim to assess their own limitations and potential as a sound-reconstruction method.
- **Technologies used:**
    1. **μCT-scanning:** the machine is an X-ray microfocus CT system General Electric (formerly Phoenix) v—tome—x 240D from CRT Morlaix, a resources center dedicated to metrology (http://www.crt-morlaix.com/). In the set-up, the sample is placed on a rotating table, and the X-ray source and detector are stationary.
    2. **3D wire and resin printing:** the machines are a MakerBotReplicator2 from IUT Le Creusot, and a Stratasys Mojo from ENS Rennes. The resin model was printed on a 3D Objet by a contractor.
- **Scanned object:** we chose to scan the control flute used in the sound-morphology principle (the one made from a goat's tibia) in order to compare the 3D results to the handmade replica. The flute was scanned in three parts in order to get a precision of less than 50μ. The reassembly was processed

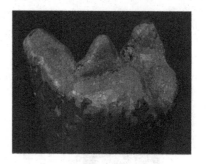

Fig. 6. Disconnected objects (yellow) in the area of the trabecular bone. (Color figure online)

Fig. 7. 3D sculpted patch (transparent gray) on Blender (based on the geometry of the cloud).

with the software Autodesk Meshmixer. Also, as the trabecular bone renders through μ-CT scanning as a cloud of 600+ tiny objects, it cannot be directly printed (Fig. 6). We chose to explore two possibilities: simply removing the objects in one case, and integrating them as a 3D sculpted "patch" in the other (Fig. 7). We used Meshlab and Blender in order to get ready-to-print 3D models.

- **Replicas:** F1 refers to the handmade replica. F2 refers to the 3D orange wire replica (with 3D sculpted "patch", no post-printing treatments). F3 refers to the 3D white wire replica (without the trabecular bone, acetone bath and ultrasounds post-printing treatment). F4 refers to the 3D white resin replica (better printing resolution, with 3D sculpted "patch", no post-printing treatments).
- **Printings:** printed between January and May 2016.
- **Sound capture and analysis:** same context than for the handcrafting process.

5.3 Sound Results

The diagrams in Fig. 9 represent the results of basic acoustical analysis of the control flute and its four replicas.

5.4 Analysis and Discussion

The following tables represent sound-comparisons between the control flute and its replicas using the recorded frequencies translated from Hertz to base 2 logarithm (Table 2).

As we expected, this table shows that 3D printed replicas are globally closest to the original than the handmade one. This is due to the absence of the bone's morphological variability that would occur from using several bones. However, they are not identical between each other (Fig. 10).

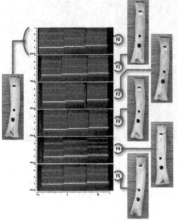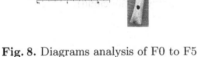

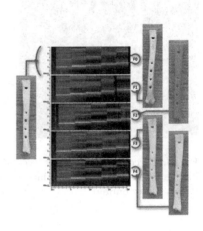

Fig. 8. Diagrams analysis of F0 to F5

Fig. 9. Diagrams analysis of F0 to F4

Table 2. Comparison between frequencies (top)/intervals (bottom) emitted by F0 to F4 while playing successively T0, T1, T2, T3 and T4. Green cells indicate a sound-reproduction precision of $1/20^{th}$ of a tone or less.

objet	hz T0	log2 T0	Diff 1/2	hz T1	log2 T1	Diff 1/2	hz T2	log2 T2	Diff 1/2	hz T3	log2 T3	Diff 1/2	hz T4	log2 T4	Diff 1/2
Flute 0	1088	10,087		1208	10,238		1300	10,344		1489	10,54		1649	10,687	
Flute 1 (hand-made)	1124	10,134	0,56	1277	10,319	0,96	1401	10,452	1,30	1659	10,696	1,87	1854	10,856	2,03
Flute 2 (orange wire)	1055	10,043	-0,53	1176	10,2	-0,46	1287	10,33	-0,17	1497	10,548	0,09	1658	10,695	0,09
Flute 3 (white wire)	1083	10,081	-0,08	1187	10,213	-0,30	1271	10,312	-0,39	1455	10,507	-0,40	1624	10,665	-0,26
Flute 4 (white resin)	1084	10,082	-0,06	1203	10,232	-0,07	1296	10,34	-0,05	1491	10,542	0,02	1656	10,693	0,07

objet	T0-T1	1/2 ton	Diff 1/2	T1-T2	1/2 ton	Diff 1/2	T2-T3	1/2 ton	Diff 1/2	T3-T4	1/2 ton	Diff 1/2
Flute 0	0,15	1,81		0,11	1,27		0,20	2,35		0,15	1,77	
Flute 1 (hand-made)	0,18	2,21	0,40	0,13	1,60	0,33	0,24	2,93	0,58	0,16	1,92	0,16
Flute 2 (orange wire)	0,16	1,88	0,07	0,13	1,56	0,29	0,22	2,62	0,27	0,15	1,77	0,00
Flute 3 (white wire)	0,13	1,59	-0,22	0,10	1,18	-0,09	0,20	2,34	-0,01	0,16	1,90	0,14
Flute 4 (white resin)	0,15	1,80	-0,01	0,11	1,29	0,02	0,20	2,43	0,08	0,15	1,82	0,05

In Fig. 10, both orange and white wire flutes present a significant but different deviation regarding their emitted frequencies, whereas the resin flute is the most accurate of them all. Indeed, it reaches the sounds of the original with a precision of less than $1/20^{th}$ of a tone.

As it appears, acoustical phenomenons related to 3D printed replicas seem to be quite intricate. The following facts should thus be considered regarding those results:

1. 3D wire-printing is processed by fusing a plastic filament which is then deposited by layers, and finally cools down and solidifies. The cooling process comes with a shrinking phenomenon which extent depends on the wire itself as well as on the cooling context (hygrometry and temperature) [17]. Furthermore, these deformations may occur in an irregular way. In other words, 3D wire-printing has a morphological variability of its own.

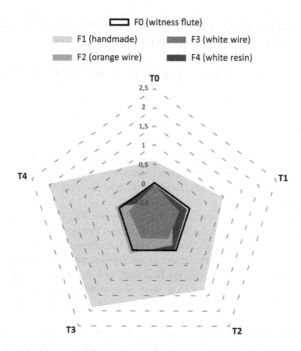

Fig. 10. Diagram representing the sound proximity of each replica comparing to the control flute, for each finger hole (numeric scale in semi-tones). The 0 line represents the control flute. The colored areas represent the replicas' sounds. The more the colored area fills the 0 line, the closest the replica is to the control flute.

2. 3D resin-printing on the other hand does not work the same and thus does not have the same sources of error [19]: it uses a laser impact which solidifies a gelatinous resin. This technology is more accurate than 3D wire-printing and gives different physical results (smoother state of surface, solid 3D printings). That explains why this replica is much more accurate than the other ones.
3. Once again, human blow should be replaced by a mechanical blower.

6   Conclusion

Handcrafting and 3D replication processes illustrate the acoustical complexity of bone flutes, as well as they raise most important epistemological and methodological issues. Succinctly, these results advise of the dangers of sound-interpretations regarding ancient flutes when dealing with replicas. They demonstrate the complexity of the acoustical phenomenons related to naturally hollow raw-materials. They also demonstrate that 3D imagery is not as precise and trustworthy as we would think it would be. However, the use of statistics and of high-precision 3D printers seems to offer a promising track to continue this research. Although there is still much work to do in order to reach a better understanding of this situation, at least we now know that archaeological bone flutes sounds should always be interpreted with caution. In any case, this research will try and go deeper in the epistemological and methodological issues.

Acknowledgments. This project was partially funded by the french CNRS ImagIn IRMA project.

References

1. Avanzini, F., Canazza, S., De Poli, G., Fantozzi, C., Pretto, N., Roda, A., Menegazzi, A.: Archaeology and virtual acoustics - a pan flute from ancient Egypt. In: Proceedings of the 12th International Conference on Sound and Music Computing, pp. 31–36 (2015)
2. Barreau, J.B., Gaugne, R., Bernard, Y., Le Cloirec, G., Gouranton, V.: The West Digital Conservatory of Archaelogical Heritage Project, DH, Marseille, France. Digital Heritage International Congress, pp. 1–8, November 2013
3. Bellia, A.: The virtual reconstruction of an ancient musical instrument: the aulos of selinus. In: Proceedings of Digital Heritage, vol. 1, pp. 55–58 (2015)
4. Borman, T., Stoel, B.: Review of the uses of computed tomography for analyzing instruments of the violin family with a focus on the future. J. Violin Soc. Am. VSA Papers **22**(1), 1–12 (2009)
5. Brade, C.: Die mittelalterlichen Kernspaltflöten Mittel-und Nordeuropas, Ein Beitrage zur Überlieferung prähistorischer und zur Typologie mittelalterlicher Kernspaltflöten, Band. 14, Neumünster, Wachholtz (1975)
6. Clodor-Tissot, T.: Fiche témoins sonores du Néolithique et des Âges des métaux, Industrie de l'os préhistorique. Instruments sonores du Néolithique à l'aube de l'Antiquité, XII (2009)
7. Causs, R., Mille, B., Piechaud, R.: Restitution sonore numérique des cornua de Pompei, Sound Making: Handcraft of Musical Instruments in Antiquity, video recordings of the third IFAO conference, IRCAM (2016). http://medias.ircam.fr/x27292e
8. Garca, B.C., Alcolea, M., Mazo, C.: Experimental study of the aerophone of Isturitz: Manufacture, use-wear analysis and acoustic tests. Quaternary International (2015). doi:10.1016/j.quaint.2015.11.033
9. Garca, B.C.: Methodology for the reconstruction of prehistoric aerophones made of hard animal material, Actas das IV Jornadas de Jovens em Investigação Arqueológica, pp. 411–416 (2011)
10. Gattoni, F., Melgara, C., Sicola, C., Uslenghi, C.M.: Unusual application of computerized tomography: the study of musical instruments. Radiol. Med. **97**(3), 170–173 (1999)
11. Hagel, S.: The meroë pipes: a musical jigsaw puzzle, sound making: handcraft of musical instruments in antiquity, video recordings of the third IFAO conference, IRCAM (2016). http://medias.ircam.fr/x9e8e19
12. Hawkins, J., Jacobson, J., Franklin, J.: Greco-Roman Music in Context; Bringing Sound and Music to Virtual Pompeii, World Conference on E-Learning in Corporate, Government, Health Care, and Higher Education (2011)
13. Koumartzis, N., Tzetzis, D., Kyratsis, P., Kotsakis, R.G.: A new music instrument from ancient times: modern reconstruction of the greek lyre of hermes using 3D laser scanning, advanced computer aided design and audio analysis. J. New Music Res. **44**(4), 324–346 (2015)

14. Kunej, D., Turk, I.: New perspectives on the beginnings of music: archaeological and musicological analysis of a middle Paleolithic bone "flute". In: The Origins of Music, pp. 235–268 (2000)

15. Laycock, S., Bell, G., Mortimore, D., Greco, M., Corps, N., Finkle, I.: Combining x-ray Micro-CT technology and 3D printing for the digital preservation and study of a 19th century cantonese chess piece with intricate internal structure. ACM J. Comput. Cultl. Heritage 5(4), 1–7 (2012)

16. Münzel, S.C., Seeberger, F., Hein, W.: The Geissenklösterle flute: discovery, experiments, reconstruction, Studien zur Musikarchäologie. Archäologie früher Klangerzeugung und Tonordnung, Rahden, Verlag M. Leidorf, pp. 107–118 (2002)

17. Pierce, L.B.: Hacking the Digital Print: Alternative image capture and printmaking processes with a special section on 3D printing, New Riders, Voices That Matter, p. 262 (2015)

18. Safa, E.: Handcrafting in archaeomusicological research: record of a one-year apprenticeship alongside a traditional-flute-maker and its application to sound archaeology, Sound Making: Handcraft of Musical Instruments in Antiquity, video recordings of the third IFAO conference, IRCAM (2016). http://medias.ircam.fr/xcf6cf9

19. Sculpteo: 3D Printing Material: PolyJet Resin, Sculpteos website (2016). https://www.sculpteo.com/en/materials/polyjet-resin-material/

20. Sirr, S.A., Waddle, J.R.: CT analysis of bowed stringed instruments. Radiology 203(3), 801–805 (1997)

21. Sodini, N., Dreossi, D., Chen, R., Fioravanti, M., Giordano, A., Herrestal, P., Zanini, F.: Non-invasive microstructural analysis of bowed stringed instruments with synchrotron radiation X-ray microtomography. J. Cultl. Heritage 13(3), S44–S49 (2012)

22. Tuniz, C., Bernardini, F., Turk, I., Dimkaroski, L., Mancini, L., Dreossi, D.: Did Neanderthals play music? X-ray computed micro-tomography of the Divje Dabe 'flute'. Archaeometry 54(3), 581–590 (2012)

23. Turk, I., Blackwell, B.A., Turk, J., Pflaum, M.: Results of computer tomography of the oldest suspected flute from Divje bab I (Slovenia) and its chronological position within global palaeoclimatic and palaeoenvironmental change during last glacial. Anthropologie 110(3), 293–317 (2006)

24. Tzevelekos, P., Georgaki, A., Kouroupetroglou, G.: HERON: a zournas digital virtual musical instrument. In: Proceedings of the 3rd International Conference on Digital Interactive Media in Entertainment and Arts, pp. 352–359, September 2015

Full Paper: Digital Applications for Materials' Preservation and Conservation in Cultural Heritage

Evolution of Building Materials and Philosophy in Construction: A Process of Digitalization and Visualization of the Accumulated Knowledge

Ioanna Papayianni and Vasiliki Pachta[✉]

Laboratory of Building Materials,
Department of Civil Engineering, Aristotle University Thessaloniki,
Thessaloniki, Greece
{papayian, vpachta}@civil.auth.gr

Abstract. The long-term research on the constructional materials and techniques of monuments and historic buildings, allowed the accumulation of significant knowledge which could be further disseminated. The masons of antiquity followed principles in designing and building, established by their intuition and experience. The selection of raw materials, the way they upgraded them in constructing foundations, walls, domes, is still remarkable. In the paper, a process of using digital technology tools for making knowledge acquisition attractive is presented. By developing a specific platform, all relevant scientific knowledge can be sorted, while with a series of digital applications, the diachronic principles of construction, the ancient technology and the achievements of the past can be exploited in a friendly and interactive environment. By this way it is expected that the values of building philosophy in the context of safety, sustainability and economy will be forwarded to new generations.

Keywords: Monumental heritage · Building materials · Constructions · Evolution · Mortars

1 Introduction

It has been well established by the history of humanity that civilization proceeds in parallel to building materials' innovations. From the very first time man built a shelter for protection, he realized that he could improve his life. He slowly, by practical experience, acquired the necessary knowledge and elementary principles of building. He used locally available materials (stone, clay) from nearby deposits and tried to treat or mix them with straw and sand to make them more resistant to natural environment. For centuries, masons invested in details and created some of the master pieces of architecture and engineering, such as Pantheon and Hagia Sophia, still alive.

The selection of the topography of the place and the geometry of the buildings' ground plan were carefully made, so as the structure to cooperate with natural environment by arranging the openings for ventilation and lightening.

M. Ioannides et al. (Eds.): EuroMed 2016, Part I, LNCS 10058, pp. 199–208, 2016.
DOI: 10.1007/978-3-319-48496-9_16

These are some of the principles followed in the past constructions. Studying the materials of monuments, a treasure of knowledge and masons' dexterities is revealed. For example, in ancient Olynthos (4th century BC) they used mud mortar for the construction of stone walls, but they plastered the walls for functioning in moisture with thick lime-pozzolan mortar plasters (Fig. 1) [1].

Fig. 1. Macroscopic and microscopic figure of plaster from the archaeological site of Olynthos

Some writers of antiquity like Vitruvius and Plenius [2] have included in their treatises precious practical instructions on preparing building materials and using them, but after Roman period the knowledge transfer was limited [3].

During the recent past, for the needs of restoration, the ancient materials were studied and analyzed systematically and many philosophical principals on which building was based were recognized [4–6]. At the same time, huge data bases have been developed at Research Centers containing real treasures of knowledge concerning building materials, without any beneficial for the society exploitation [6–8].

Nowadays, the advances in building materials (high performance and strength concrete) lead to the construction of skyscrapers, expressing the spirit of modern society. However, under the prism of sustainability (saving energy, reducing environmental footprint, recycling), building materials and technology are reconsidered. The science of building materials provides the knowledge at all levels of controlling and increasing the potential of them and allows understanding how materials work in the structure.

While architecture in construction has drawn the interest of society, building materials and technological evolution have not appeared in museum exhibitions at European level and all concepts and philosophy of building have not been highlighted to gain educational value, to offer multi-level and multidisciplinary readings and inspire new generations for a better future in building.

On the other hand, there is an increase of research interest on the application of Information and Communications Technology (ICT) tools in Cultural Heritage, such as Historic Building Information Modelling (HBIM), development of virtual museums and exhibitions, visualization of objects and artifacts, development of 3D environments and experiences [9–11].

Under these aspects, the paper focuses on an attempt to gather, evaluate and finally visualize scientific results on the building materials and techniques used in constructions during the last four millenniums, starting from prehistory until nowadays. The study aims at covering a significant gap of knowledge, regarding the technological evolution of structures and developing a dynamic platform by processing, disseminating and promoting knowledge regarding:

- The significant role of building materials in the development of the architecture and civilization of an area
- The evolution of the building materials technology from the past (2nd millennium BC) until nowadays (advances of concrete)
- The diachronically valid principles of sustainability, durability and economy in construction
- The proper materials and techniques for the restoration of monuments and historic buildings.

2 Principles and Objectives

ICT (information and communications technology) is an umbrella term including many applications and during the last decade is interrelated with multiple research sectors in order to promote and disseminate scientific knowledge [12–14].

The use of ICT tools in understanding and promoting specific aspects of Cultural Heritage has been studied by many researchers [15–17] and applied by various Organizations, museums and galleries. On the other hand, the need of digitalizing and visualizing archives and collections is increased.

The idea of developing of a dynamic platform on building materials and techniques from the past up to nowadays emerged from the weakness of relevant museums of Architecture or monuments' exhibition to cover material's aspects, the inadequacy of education on these topics, as well on the lack of finding concentrated scientific knowledge on the evolution of constructional technology.

The invention of cement and the continuous evolution of concrete technology of nowadays, demonstrate the close relation of modern society with building materials and technology and lead to the adoption of the basic environmental issues (i.e. saving energy, reducing environmental footprint, recycling in construction).

Furthermore, it is of great importance to make people think and be conscious about building, since construction is the sector that mostly influences the economy of natural sources and environment, in other words the future of humanity. If people choose for building their houses local materials of high ecological profile, the CO_2 footprint of human activities could be reduced.

The proposed platform aims at managing, exploiting and disseminating a large volume of scientific knowledge regarding the evolution, characteristics and effectiveness of different building materials and technologies. Earth, stone, bricks, limes, pozzolans, cements, mortars and concretes that have dominated in housing for four millenniums are addressed, showing the entity of building the space with materials taken from the Earth.

The innovation of the platform is that such a museum dedicated to the common European building materials and technology, does not exist either in virtual or in conventional form. In relevant contemporary museums and exhibitions of architecture, there are very limited references to the building materials and technology of specific historic periods and regions. Therefore, a holistic approach on the evolution of building materials and technology is not provided to visitors. Philosophical aspects (such as functionality, sustainability) and their diachronicity in construction are also not revealed to visitors.

3 Process Followed

The proposed dynamic platform will provide the opportunity for visitors to acquire, extend or deepen their knowledge on building materials and techniques, through story-telling authoring tools and digital creations such as virtual reality and 3D experiences.

Different aspects on the technology of building materials, such as structural types, selection of raw materials, manufacture and application of materials, properties and characteristics, damages and repair of structures, will be presented under the prism of sustainability and economy in construction, covering a historical period of more than 4 millenniums.

Scientific knowledge on building materials will be combined with ICT technology, in order to facilitate the access of all levels of users. Best practices will be presented, highlighting that the science of building materials provides the knowledge of controlling and increasing their potential, as well as understanding how materials work in each structure.

It is expected that a consciousness about cost-effective and "green" building will be developed in the users of the coming generations.

The Process followed could be distinguished in specific tasks, including:

- Management of a large volume of scientific knowledge, regarding research analysis results of building materials (mortars, stones, bricks, concrete technology) and critical review of relevant literature concerning the types and characteristics of building materials used in constructions for millenniums.
- Development of a flexible and easily comprehensive platform for the management and dissemination of all information that could be moderated according to future needs. The platform will have a dual performance, referring to the input of all data and the narrative and virtual representation of the information to users, according to their needs.
- Visualization of all data through the development of architectural designs, structural representations, 3D animations and videos. Story-telling digital tools will be used for the dissemination of knowledge. For example, interactive maps will indicate structures of specific type (i.e. adobe masonry) with emerging information on historic, architectural and morphological issues (Fig. 3). Narrative three dimensional environments with specialized information (in different forms, such as diagrams, tables, photos) regarding the characteristics and properties of specific building materials and structural systems will be developed.

The schematic diagram of the process is depicted in Fig. 2.

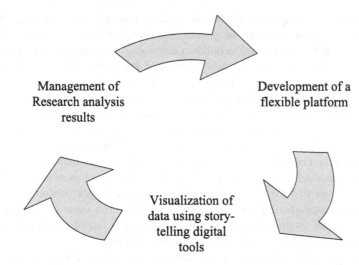

Management of
Research analysis
results

Development of a
flexible platform

Visualization of
data using story-
telling digital
tools

Fig. 2. Schematic diagram of the process followed

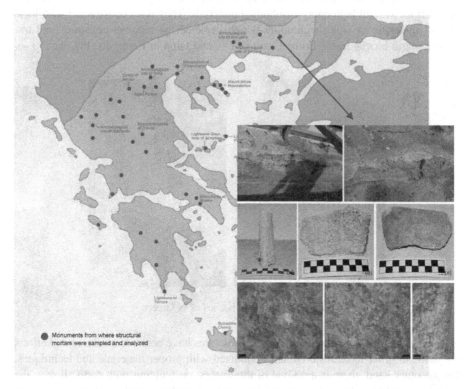

Fig. 3. Interactive map with indicative structural types. Sanctuary of Dionysus, archaeological site of Maronia (4th cent. BC)

4   Data Input

As it has been described, the evolution of building materials and techniques has not been adequately interrelated with the growth of civilizations and architecture, although all innovations and achievements in building technology have been implemented with materials. Therefore, there is a significant lack of knowledge regarding the role of structural materials in developing European society and economy.

Moreover, the strong influence of built environment to the nature has not been sufficiently understood by society. The comprehension of the philosophy of building in the past highlights the principles of building, such as how the local environment was taken into account, as well as the economy in using natural resources.

Under the prism of sustainability, building materials and technology are nowadays reconsidered, since it has been well proved by the experience of great catastrophes due to climatic change that the sector of constructions is the major consumer of natural resources and sustainable building is one way road to limit these phenomena. As a result, the research on upgrading local building materials is cutting edge technology and billions of euros are annually invested to that direction.

For example, earth structures which concern the primer constructional system found, have been continuously used in construction from prehistory until nowadays (33 % of worldwide houses are still built with earth), due to their low cost and easy production, without high energy embodied materials. They were constructed with local clayish materials by using techniques which depicted the regional constructional traditions (earth-blocks in SE Europe, cob in UK and taipa in Portugal) (Fig. 4).

Fig. 4. Earth-block houses of N Greece

Under the light of sustainability, these structures have been reconsidered and efforts are made in order to be restored and revitalized with proper materials and techniques. On the other hand, there is a revival of the interest on building with earth all over the world (i.e. France, Germany), due to the constructional, economic and environmental benefits [20].

Fig. 5. Various structural systems used in constructions

Through the platform these aspects will be highlighted in order to offer multidisciplinary readings and inspire users for a better future in building. Apart from increasing the dissemination potential of knowledge about the evolution of building materials, the scientific experience and knowledge will be presented under the concepts of effectiveness, economy, sustainability and environmental protection.

Well documented knowledge has been accumulated by the Laboratory of Building Materials of the Aristotle University of Thessaloniki during the last 25 years of continuous work with Ephorates of Antiquities in studying the building materials of historic structures [4, 6, 18, 19].

According to a systematic evaluation of the analysis results, many conclusions can be asserted regarding multiple aspects, such as the type of building materials used diachronically, the constructional types encountered, as well as their correlation to the specific characteristics of each era and region (socio-economic, cultural and environmental aspects).

In the proposed platform, the research results will be presented under specific axes, regarding:

- the main structural types found diachronically in constructions (rubble masonry, ashlar masonry, adobe, brick masonry, contemporary concrete structures) (Fig. 5)
- the characteristics and technological evolution of building materials and techniques (Fig. 6)
- the wider historic, cultural, environmental and socio-economic aspects of each region and era
- the background and educational level of the user (general public, students, professionals, scientists, stake holders).

Historic period	Monument/ Date	Monument	Macroscopic figure	Microscopic figure
Prehistoric	Toumpa, Thessaloniki / 1200BC			
Helenistic	Ancient theatre of Argos / 3rd cent. BC			
Roman	Galerius Palace / 3rd cent. AD			
Byzantine	Early Cristian Basilica C', Filippoi / 6th cent. AD			
Ottoman	Pazar Hamam, Thessaloniki 1500			
19th–20th century	Koligospita Zografou / 1845			
	Administrati n building o Allatini / 1879			

Fig. 6. Macroscopic and microscopic figures of mortars from various monuments of Greece

5 Conclusions

As it is formerly stated, the technological evolution of building materials has not been yet adequately acknowledged and interrelated with the development of civilizations and advances in construction. Therefore, there is a gap of knowledge related to the significant role of building materials and philosophy of construction in creating the built environment in Europe.

On the other hand, under the prism of sustainability, the comprehension of the diachronic principles of constructions could contribute to maximizing the effectiveness of the contemporary building materials and minimizing their cost and environmental footprint.

To this direction, the development of a flexible platform providing input to many digital applications concerning building materials and constructional techniques would contribute to forward the messages to the next generations:

- the significant role of building materials in the development of the architecture and civilization of a region,
- the evolution of the building materials technology from the past (2nd millennium BC) until nowadays (advances of concrete),
- the diachronically valid principles of sustainability, durability and economy in construction,
- the proper materials and techniques for the restoration of monuments and historic buildings.

References

1. Papayianni, I., Stefanidou, M.: Durability aspects of Ancient Mortars of the archeological site of Olynthos. J. Cult. Heritage **8**, 193–196 (2007)
2. Morgan, M.H.: Vitruvius: The Ten Books of Architecture. Dover Publications Inc., New York (1960)
3. Palladio, A.: The Four Books of Architecture. Dover Publications Inc., New York (1965). Unabridged republication of the work first published by Ware I in 1938
4. Papayianni, I.: The longevity of old mortars. Appl. Phys. A Mater. Sci. Process. **83**, 685–688 (2006)
5. Middendorf, B., Hughes, J.J., Callebaut, K., Baronio, G., Papayianni, I.: Investigative methods for the characterisation of historic mortars-Part 1: mineralogical characterization. Mater. Struct. **38**, 761–769 (2005). RILEM TC 167-COM: 'Characterisation of Old Mortars with Respect to their Repair'
6. Pachta, V.: Study of the Technological Evolution of Mortars, Dissertation. Aristotle University of Thessaloniki, Thessaloniki (2011)
7. Papayianni, I., Pachta, V., Iliadou, K.: A data base system for managing information concerning historical mortars. In: Ioannides, M., Addison, A., Georgopoulos, A., Kalisperis L. (eds.) VSMM 2008, pp. 271–277 (2008)

8. Moropoulou, A., Polikreti, K., Bakolas, A., Michailidis, P.: Correlation of physicochemical and mechanical properties of historical mortars and classification by multivariate statistics. Cem. Concr. Res. **33**, 891–898 (2003)
9. Athanasiou, G.S., Michail, H.E., Gregoriades, A., Ioannides, M.: Evolution of the e-Museum concept through exploitation of cryptographic algorithms. In: Ioannides, M., Fritsch, D., Leissner, J., Davies, R., Remondino, F., Caffo, R. (eds.) EuroMed 2012. LNCS, vol. 7616, pp. 291–300. Springer, Heidelberg (2012). doi:10.1007/978-3-642-34234-9_29
10. Kiourt, C., Koutsoudis, A., Pavlidis, G.: DynaMus: a fully dynamic 3D virtual Museum framework. J. Cult. Heritage. http://dx.doi.org/10.1016/j.culher.2016.06.007
11. Robles-Ortega, M.D., Feito, F.R., Jiménez, J.J., Segura, R.J.: Web technologies applied to virtual heritage: an example of an Iberian Art Museum. J. Cult. Heritage **13**, 326–331 (2012)
12. Ashlock, D.: Evolutionary Computation for Modelling and Optimization. Springer, New York (2006)
13. Comby-Peyrot, I., Bernard, F., Bouchard, P.O., Bay, F., Garcia-Diaz, E.: Development and validation of a 3D computational tool to describe concrete behaviour at mesoscale. application to the alkali-silica reaction. Comput. Mater. Sci. **46**, 1163–1177 (2009)
14. Donga, S., Wang, X., Xu, S., Wu, G., Yin, H.: The development and evaluation of Chinese digital science and technology Museum. J. Cult. Heritage **12**, 111–115 (2011)
15. Donga, S., Xu, S., Wu, G.: Earth Science Digital Museum (ESDM): toward a new paradigm for Museums. Comput. Geosci. **32**, 793–802 (2006)
16. Pavlidis, G., Koutsoudis, A., Arnaoutoglou, F., Tsioukas, V., Chamzas, C.: Methods for 3D digitization of cultural heritage. J. Cult. Heritage **8**, 93–98 (2007)
17. Sylaiou, S., Liarokapis, F., Kotsakis, K., Patias, P.: Virtual Museums, a survey and some issues for consideration. J. Cult. Heritage **10**, 520–528 (2009)
18. Pachta, V., Stefanidou, M., Konopissi, S., Papayianni, I.: Technological evolution of historic structural mortars. J. Civ. Eng. Architect. **8**(7), 846–854 (2014)
19. Stefanidou, M., Papayianni, I., Pachta, V.: Evaluation of inclusions in mortars of different historic periods from Greek monuments. Archaeometry **54**, 737–751 (2012)
20. Papayianni, I., Pachta, V.: Earth block houses of historic centers. a sustainable upgrading with compatible repair materials. Procedia Environ. Sci. (in press)

A Study of 3D Digital Simulation Analysis of Fire Charring Degree of Wood Construction of Chinese Traditional Architecture

Tsung Chiang Wu[(⊠)]

Department of Civil Engineering and Engineering Management,
National Quemoy University, 89250 Kinmen, Taiwan
tsung_chiang@nqu.edu.tw

Abstract. For the Chinese traditional architecture which uses wood construction in large quantities, the fire often causes irreversible disasters, and the cultural heritage may be lost in a flash. According to Taiwan Cultural Assets Preservation Act, the historic monuments restoration must uphold the spirit of "Restoring the Old as the Old", so the structural safety assessment is a necessary program for what can be restored after disaster. Traditionally, the char depth data of the wood construction after fires are obtained by pore-drilling measurement. Therefore, the detection positions and quantity are determined according to the post-disaster condition. The weak structure often fails to be measured, so that the evaluation result is likely to be distorted. This study uses dynamic fire simulation theory, and takes a Chinese traditional architecture, Potzu Pei-tian Temple in Chiayi, Taiwan as an example for experiment, trying to build a digital char depth virtual detection model. The research findings show that this conception can build a virtual detection mode, which may provide more comprehensive char depth information than traditional method, assisting the safety assessment operation of post-disaster restored structures effectively.

Keywords: Digital simulation · Charring degree · Dynamic fire simulation theory · Virtual detection mode

1 Introduction

The "fires" will cause irrecoverable results of cultural heritage preservation and inheritance, the intelligence and sequence of thought transferred by ancient people for hundreds of years may be destroyed and eliminated in a short period of time. However, if a fire happens unfortunately, for the restorable case, the situation shall be assessed efficiently and accurately before related restoration plans are made, so as to avoid further losses. Before dawn on March 26, 2013, the 330 years old historic monument, Potzu Pei-tian Temple of Chiayi, Taiwan fired, the wood construction-based main hall was burnt down, including numerous historic relics, the loss was heavy. It is so regrettable that on November 15, 2012, a grand ceremony for the completion of Pei-tian Temple which cost 4 years and NT$120 million was held. The fire burnt down the four years' efforts, and caused irrecoverable losses of Taiwan's cultural heritage. In order to push the subsequent maintenance work, the post-disaster on-scene safety

© Springer International Publishing AG 2016
M. Ioannides et al. (Eds.): EuroMed 2016, Part I, LNCS 10058, pp. 209–216, 2016.
DOI: 10.1007/978-3-319-48496-9_17

assessment is the first work. Therefore, the structural safety of the burnt heavy timber construction and the charring degree of beam columns must be further detected. The old charring degree detection methods used tube sample boring for actual measurement, related samples were insufficient, or the positions were inappropriate, the evaluation result was likely to be distorted. If there are too many holes drilled, there is a high risk of secondary damage to the post-disaster remnant. Therefore, how to take sufficient samples and reduce the risk of secondary damage shall be thought over and studied.

This study tries to integrate digital building and digital fire simulation techniques for virtual simulation of the process of fire. The wood construction is taken as an example, referring to the experience in the study of charring rate estimation model [1] and the study of wood characteristics [2], the temperature change withstood by the wood construction in the fire simulation results is analyzed. Afterwards, the charring degree in relative position of wood construction is estimated according to the "relationship between temperature and charring degree" established in laboratory [3]. In this conception, the spatial pattern of the distressed architectural space is built by 3D digital modeling, and the fire is simulated by FDS (Fire Dynamics Simulator) software. The 3D realistic fire simulation technique will be used to preliminarily detect and estimate the wood construction char depth of the distressed building, and the quantity of drill samples may be reduced, so as to analyze the wood construction char depth rapidly.

2 Method

Potzu Pei-tian Temple, Chiayi, Taiwan is taken as an example for virtual simulation and detection of the char depth of the wood construction of the burnt main hall space. The research process and the outcomes are detailed below:

2.1 Collect and Integrate the Data of Study Case

This study case is Potzu Pei-tian Temple, Chiayi, Taiwan (Fig. 1 left). The temple is registered as a county historic monument of Taiwan, it has very high historic significance and cultural value. Pei-tian Temple was founded in the 26th year of Kangxi of the Qing Dynasty (1687). It was built for the fourth time during the Japanese occupation in 1915, under the charge of Ying-bin Chen, a famous master from Zhangzhou, China. The "opposite construction" was adopted, and it was the first temple in Taiwan subsidized by Japanese authority [4]. The latest construction was completed in 2012, but the main hall was burnt down in 2013 (Fig. 1 right). In order to probe into the historical evolution and building maintenance history of the study case, the historical documents, investigation reports, planning and design, rehab works reports, architectural drawings and records of interview with the parties concerned about the temple are collected.

Fig. 1. Potzu Pei-tian Temple, Chiayi, Taiwan (left), main hall burnt (right)

2.2 Build Spatial 3D Digital Model of the Burnt Main Hall

As the scene of the burnt main hall was messy, there was no spatial information obtained from the scene. Therefore, the 3D digital model of the burnt main hall was built (Fig. 2 right) by using SketchUp according to the collected architectural drawing (Fig. 2 left) and related image data as the FDS software.

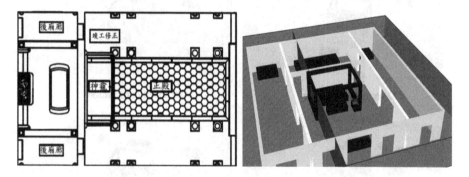

Fig. 2. Architectural drawing (left), 3D digital model of main hall (right)

2.3 Construction of Attribute Data of Burnt Main Hall

The materials and size of the space must be given for FDS. Therefore, the material and size of the main hall wood construction are given referring to related architectural drawing, investigation and research reports and restoration design planning data. The wood construction material of this study case is fir.

2.4 FDS Test

For accurate FDS, the input conditions must match current condition as possible, and the simulation environment shall be tested by appropriate 3D simulation grid and the digital thermometer shall be selected and mounted [5] before FDS test. The settings of environmental parameters must match the research purpose. As the FDS space in this study is an indoor confined space, when the FDS is used for calculation, relevant parameters must be set. This step analyzes the effect of the precision of spatial layout and size of fire scene on the fire simulation result, so the spacing between digital space nodes is set as 25 cm in x, y and z directions. According to the equation $Q = \alpha t^2$ of "t-squared fires" [6], where Q is the heat release rate, α is the fire burning rate, the growth time t is defined as the time for active combustion to grow to $1,055\,kw$ $(1,000\,Btu/s)$. The heat release rate of the fire source at initial stage of fire is set according to t^2 swift growth, the burning rate α is $0.01689\,kw/s^2$, the peak of fire heat release rate is $10,000\,kw$ [7, 8]. After the aforesaid data are imported and the environmental parameters are set, the FDS is implemented. The total time of the simulated burning process is accelerated, the simulation is finished in 10 min. The simulated burning process is shown in Fig. 3 including 420 s, 480 s, 540 s and 600 s of combustion.

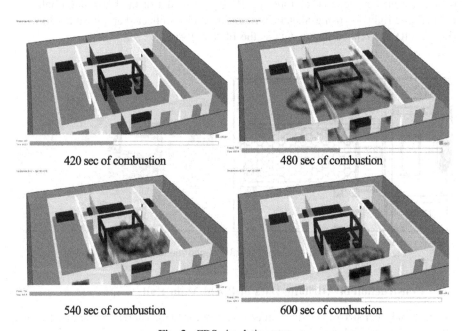

420 sec of combustion   480 sec of combustion

540 sec of combustion   600 sec of combustion

Fig. 3. FDS simulating process

2.5   Analysis of Wood Construction Component Temperature Change

FDS provides the function of digital thermometer, which can be mounted on the 3D digital model surface. There are 14 digital thermometers located on the main hall structure components, coded A1, A2, A3, B1, B2, B3, C1, C2, C3, D1, D2, D3, E1 and G1. The locations are shown in Fig. 4. The temperature-time change values of digital thermometers on the wood construction are obtained after FDS. The temperature

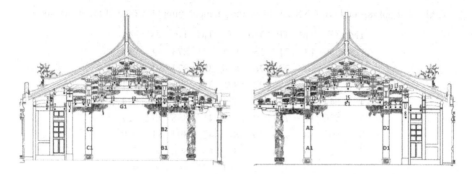

Fig. 4. 14 digital thermometers located on main hall components

changes of wood construction, such as beams and columns of main hall, in the fire simulation process are analyzed. The maximum combustion temperatures in the positions detected by the 14 digital thermometers are listed in Table 1.

Table 1. Maximum temperatures recorded by 14 digital thermometers

Position code	Detected maximum temperature (°C)	Position code	Detected maximum temperature (°C)
A1	460	C1	1110
A2	460	C2	1120
A3	460	C3	465
B1	1180	D1	465
B2	1225	D2	470
B3	460	D3	470
E1	470	G1	1240

2.6   Comparative Analysis of Charring Data

Referring to the look-up table of CNS 12514 heating temperature and time (Table 2), the regression curve of heating temperature and time is calculated (Fig. 5), the temperature and time are calculated, the burning duration in 14 positions is obtained. The regression equation is calculated according to the look-up table of CNS 12514 heating char depth and charring rate of fir material in Table 3 (Fig. 6), the burning duration, char depth and charring rate are compared, so as to analyze the values of char depth and charring rate.

Table 2. Look-up table of CNS 12514 heating temperature(TP, °C) and time(TM, sec.)

TM	TP	TM	TP	TM	TP	TM	TP	TM	TP
1	349	13	717	25	815	37	873	49	915
2	445	14	728	26	820	38	877	50	918
3	502	15	739	27	826	39	881	51	921
4	544	16	748	28	832	40	885	52	924
5	576	17	757	29	837	41	888	53	927
6	603	18	766	30	842	42	892	54	930
7	626	19	774	31	847	43	896	55	932
8	645	20	781	32	851	44	899	56	935
9	663	21	789	33	856	45	902	57	938
10	678	22	796	34	860	46	906	58	940
11	693	23	802	35	865	47	909	59	943
12	705	24	809	36	869	48	912	60	945

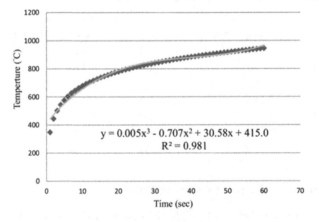

$$y = 0.005x^3 - 0.707x^2 + 30.58x + 415.0$$
$$R^2 = 0.981$$

Fig. 5. CNS 12514 standard heating temperature and time regression curve and equation

Table 3. Look-up table of fir heating time and char depth of CNS 12514 [9]

Tree species	Heating time (sec.)	Char depth (mm)
Fir	1800	21.3(2.6)
	2700	26.8(3.6)
	3600	43.4(5.7)

Brackets(): standard deviation

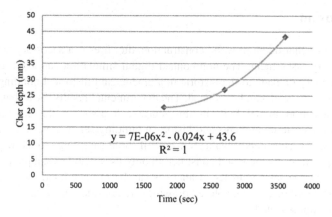

Fig. 6. Regression curve and equation of fir heating time and char depth

3   Discussion

The outcomes obtained by the wood construction char depth simulation detection model built in this study are shown in Table 4. The detection positions B1, B2 and G1 are nearby the fire source, receiving higher temperature, so the char depths are greater than 41.55 mm; the char depths in the other positions are 10.00 mm $\sim$ 11.00 mm.

Table 4. Detection results of wood construction char depth simulation detection model

Detection position	Simulated combustion temperature (°C)	Corresponding burning duration (sec)	Corresponding char depth (mm)
A1	460	135.6	10.57
A2	460	135.6	10.57
A3	460	135.6	10.57
B1	1180	>3600.00	>41.55
B2	1225	>3600.00	>41.55
B3	460	135.6	10.57
C1	1110	>3600.00	>41.55
C2	1120	>3600.00	>41.55
C3	465	143.4	10.61
D1	465	143.4	10.61
D2	470	151.2	10.61
D3	470	151.2	10.61
E1	470	151.2	10.61
G1	1240	>3600.00	>41.55

4   Conclusion

The detection of char depth of wood construction after fires is a necessary procedure of structural safety assessment. The non-contact digital simulation can avoid the drilling causing secondary damage to the historic monuments and historical buildings, and the risk of assessors in work can be reduced. The experimental results show that the digital simulation detection model built in this study can assist in the structural safety assessment of historic monuments and historical buildings after fires, and can make up the deficiencies in char depth evaluation by drill hole sampling, so as to perfect the evaluation operation. As the wood construction only uses wood as sample parameter, if the actual wood species parameter of analysis can be provided and the water content and surface material (e.g. paint, colored drawing) are considered, the model built in this study will be sophisticated.

Acknowledgments. This research was supported by the Taiwan Ministry of Science and Technology "A study of analyzing carbonized degree of historical sites' timbers using 3D realistic simulation of fire scene" (Project No. 103-2410-H-507-006-).

References

1. White, R.H., Dietenberger, M.A.: Wood handbook-wood as an engineering material, Chap. 17. In: Fire Safety. Forest Products Laboratory (1999)
2. Njankouo, J.M., Dotreppe, J.-C., Franssen, J.-M.: Experiment study of the charring rate of tropical hardwoods. Fire Mater. **28**(1), 15–24 (2004)
3. Schaffer, E.: State of structural timber fire endurance. Wood Fiber Sci. **19**(2), 145–170 (1977)
4. Bureau of Cultural Heritage, MOC, Taiwan website. http://www.boch.gov.tw/
5. McGrattan, K., Klein, B., Hostikka, S., Floyd, J.: Fire: dynamics simulator (Version 5) user's guid. NIST Spec. Publ. 1019–5 (2007)
6. Milke, J.A.: Smoke management for covered malls and atria. Fire Technol. **26**(3), 223–243 (1990)
7. Spearpoint, M.J.: Predicting the ignition and burning rate of wood in the Cone Calorimeter using an integral model. NIST GCR, 99–775 (1999)
8. Spearpoint, M.J., Quintiere, J.G.: 2001, Predicting the ignition of wood in the Cone Calorimeter - effect of species, grain orientation and heat flux. Fire Saf. J. **36**(4), 391–415 (2001)
9. Wang, S.-Y.: Fire behavior and fire protection procedures for wooden historical buildings. J. Cult. Property Conserv. **1**(1), 18–26 (2007). (in Chinese)

Full Paper: Non-destructive Techniques in Cultural Heritage Conservation

Recovering Historical Film Footage by Processing Microtomographic Images

Chang Liu[1,2], Paul L. Rosin[2(✉)], Yu-Kun Lai[2], Graham R. Davis[3], David Mills[3], and Charles Norton[4]

[1] School of Astronautics, Beihang University, Beijing, China
[2] School of Computer Science & Informatics, Cardiff University, Cardiff, UK
paul.rosin@cs.cf.ac.uk
[3] Institute of Dentistry, Queen Mary University of London, London, UK
[4] BBC Archive Development, London, UK

Abstract. 1960s film was typically printed on tri-acetate film base. If not preserved properly, such material breaks down at a chemical level, which is a non-stoppable process that permanently fuses the film so that it essentially becomes a lump of solid plastic. Recently, some precious films, such as the only known copy of the earliest surviving episode of 'The Morecambe and Wise Show' have been discovered, but they are in poor condition. They will eventually turn into a pool of sticky liquid and be gone forever. In this paper, as proof of concept, we use X-ray microtomography to provide 3D imaging of a test film of similar vintage, and propose an automatic method to extract footage from it.

Keywords: Tri-acetate film · X-ray microtomography · 3D imaging

1   Introduction

In 1968, Eric Morecambe and Ernie Wise came to London to make a new light entertainment series for BBC 2, which would come to dominate the UK light entertainment landscape for the next 15 years. Sadly, the BBC never formally archived that very first season of 'The Morecambe and Wise Show'. Before the advent of commercial video exploitation (DVDs, iplayer etc.), bodies like the BBC saw little purpose in maintaining a large and expensive collection of programming. 'The Morecambe and Wise Show' (like almost all UK comedy broadcasts of the time) was recorded to and transmitted from videotape. After being broadcasted, the master-tape would be stored for a limited period of time for potential re-use and eventually cleared for wiping.

A programme *might* still survive, but only if it was deemed likely to be popular overseas. Around the time of broadcast, many BBC programmes would also be copied to 16 mm black and white film via a process called telerecording. A master-tape would be played on a special flat cathode ray tube screen. A 16 mm film camera was pointed at this screen and filmed the programme. These film recordings were made for international syndication, and, since most countries

© Springer International Publishing AG 2016
M. Ioannides et al. (Eds.): EuroMed 2016, Part I, LNCS 10058, pp. 219–231, 2016.
DOI: 10.1007/978-3-319-48496-9_18

were able to play 16 mm film, this became the standard format for the marketing of BBC programmes overseas.

All of the episodes of that first season of 'The Morecambe and Wise Show' were telerecorded to black and white film. Rather than having multiple film prints created for each episode, it was routine for prints to be shared. When the episodes had been screened by everyone who wanted them, the last network in the chain would be asked to send the film back to BBC Enterprises in London or for the films to be destroyed (to stop them being screened without permission). By the late 1970s, series one of 'The Morecambe and Wise Show' had reached Nigeria, in the film stores of a broadcaster called RKTV.

At some point prior to 1978 BBC Enterprises decided that there was no need to retain their black and white negatives of 'The Morecambe and Wise Show' since colour television had become established across the world. They destroyed the films, and along with the destruction of their master-tapes some years before, this now meant that the BBC no longer held any recordings of the first series of 'The Morecambe and Wise Show'.

Then in 2012, a freelance film researcher called Philip Morris gained rare access to the RKTV vault, which consisted of a hot, poorly ventilated outbuilding in a small settlement called Jos in the heart of Nigeria. The area suffers from high-humidity in the rainy season and a desert of drought at all other times. The often poor state of the films in the archive reflects these harsh conditions. Philip Morris' trip to the RKTV vault was worthwhile, as it turned out RKTV held unique film recordings of various BBC programmes that were not known to exist elsewhere in the world, including episodes of both 'Doctor Who', 'The Sky at Night' and finally also 'The Morecambe and Wise Show'. RKTV now retained only one episode of 'The Morecambe and Wise Show', but it was still an important find. On a single 16 mm film spool, RKTV had the earliest surviving episode of 'The Morecambe and Wise Show' and the earliest surviving footage of the double act working for the BBC.

However, there was a problem: the Nigerian Morecambe and Wise film was in an advanced state of decay. The episode was on a form of film stock (i.e. the flexible ribbon of transparent plastic backing onto which the image is printed) not used nowadays called cellulose acetate, and was suffering from 'tri-acetate film base degradation' – a film 'disease' that can cause film to rot away to nothing. If kept in humid conditions for any prolonged period of time, the tri-acetate can begin to break down at a chemical level, leading to a runaway reaction. At a molecular level, as the plastic increases in temperature, the acetate breaks down releasing a vapour of acetic acid, which further breaks down the plastic by eating away at the film, through general acidic corrosion. The process only stops when there is no more acetate left to be converted [4].

The RKTV Morecambe and Wise film had been stored in exactly the wrong sort of conditions for an acetate roll: a humid atmosphere with poor ventilation and a cracked film can that did not shield the film from sunlight. As the acid has eaten away at the surface of the film, the roll has become sticky, thinner and lacking in overall structural integrity. Every layer of film on the Morecambe and Wise roll has now permanently fused itself with every adjacent layer of film, so that all of the pictures are now sealed inside a solid lump of plastic. Since the film is sitting in a self-sustaining vapour of corrosive acid, eventually this priceless roll will turn into soup. There is nothing we can do to stop that rot.

The BFI film archives recommended its destruction since the sheer quantity of acid vapour being produced by the film made it a hazard to other rolls in the BFI's collection. The risk of 'infection' is always high with this kind of stock.

There is a long history of film restoration [1], and many techniques have been developed [6,7]. Much of that work involves applying image processing techniques to enhance existing footage, whereas for the Morecambe and Wise film that footage needs to be first recovered from the acetate roll. In this paper we describe a radically different approach to dealing with the film, inspired by work in other areas of culture heritage.

In 2012, archaeologists embarked on a project to examine the Antikythera mechanism – a Greek navigational calculator constructed around the end of the second century BC. High-resolution X-ray tomography enabled them to analyse the inner workings of the device, without breaking the item apart [5]. Recently, several of the authors of the current paper have worked on the task of reading historical scrolled parchment documents which have been damaged due to fire or water. Such damage makes the document fragile, and often impossible to open without causing considerable further damage. It was demonstrated that using high-resolution X-ray tomography it was possible to virtually unroll a parchment from the X-ray volume, and recover its written contents [9].

Any roll of film is essentially just a strip of plastic with a picture printed onto one side of it, which for a monochrome image is always applied in the same basic way. The image layer is called the emulsion layer and the key component of black and white emulsion is silver oxide. The metal content in silver oxide emulsion is very high. This suggested that it should be possible to apply X-ray microtomography to obtain images from a roll of black and white film.

As a study of feasibility, in this paper we use the film of 'Snow White and the Seven Dwarfs', a black and white film on tri-acetate stock of roughly the same vintage as 'Morecambe and Wise'. It was an 8 mm silent black and white digest print from the 1970s containing the 1965 American dubbed version of the 1955 German film 'Schneewittchen'. We first introduce how the film was scanned and some early effort to construct the footage, which involved user interaction. We then introduce a novel *automatic* algorithm to reconstruct the footage. This is followed by experimental results and discussions.

2   Film Scanning and Early Effort of Reconstruction

Prior to tomographic scanning, a single thickness of 8 mm silent black and white film (extracted from Snow White) was X-rayed at 40 kV and 405 μA, using a 0.5 mm Al filter. Although this X-ray energy was far too high for optimal contrast, it was necessary in order to penetrate even a small roll of film. The MuCAT 2 X-ray microtomography scanner at Queen Mary University of London [2] was used, which employs time delay integration to obtain very high contrast images. But even with an equivalent exposure time of 40 s, little image contrast could be seen. Given the poor image contrast, a long exposure time was set for the tomographic scan. This was also performed at 40 kV and 405 μA. A length of the film was rolled and inserted into a 27 mm internal diameter plastic container. 2115 projections were recorded with an equivalent exposure time of 20 seconds per projection to ensure a high SNR. The voxel size was 20 μm.

The reconstructed film scan showed good signal to noise ratio. Streak artefacts were present, due to tangential X-ray paths passing through relatively long lengths of silver. For future scans, these can be reduced in severity by increasing the number of projections (the exposure time can be reduced to keep the same total acquisition time).

The recent work in [3] demonstrated the possibility of recovering footage from XMT scanned data. The method however requires manual interaction and assumes uniform structure of the film. Moreover, it would be difficult to generalise such methods to a highly damaged dataset.

3   Method for Image Recovery from Film

In this work, we will describe an *automatic* approach to footage recovery. We first introduce the method to recover the image printed on the film and in the next section, the method to create the video footage from such images.

3.1   Preprocessing and Initialisation

An example slice of the Snow White film is shown in Fig. 1. It looks similar to parchments which our previous research has developed several effective methods to deal with [8–10]. However, the methods for parchment unrolling fail on this data because they assume that the parchment layers are mostly separated by at least a small gap, whereas the film is more tightly rolled. On the other hand, film is more uniform than parchment. Thus, in this work we focus on modelling the appearance of the film, for which we use image intensity ridges [11], while making no assumptions about any background gaps. Ideally, the ridges should form a continuous spiral curve, but they are often incomplete. There also exist artifacts, false positive responses which should be discarded. Based on the fact that adjacent slices have similar images and hence similar ridge locations, we semi-automatically correct the first slice, and automatically propagate the ridges across slices, using the previous slice to constrain the linking of the next slice.

3.2   Propagation

Because of the large similarity between two adjacent images, if the ridge sections in the previous image have been correctly linked, so that there exists an entire ridge in the previous image, we can use the previous ridge image as a reference to connect the ridge sections in the current image. In Fig. 2(a), the blue spiral

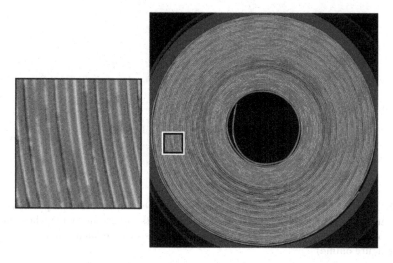

Fig. 1. An X-ray image of Snow White film. A section is shown zoomed in.

represents the previous ridge, i.e. the reference ridge; the red curves are some ridge fragments in the current image. Generally, if a fragment is a section of the film ridge rather than an artifact, it should be very close to the reference ridge. By means of this condition, we check whether a fragment is a ridge part or not in the following way. Let points v_1 and v_2 be the two endpoints of a fragment and their nearest points on the reference ridge be points p_1 and p_2 respectively. l_1 is the length of the path p between p_1 and p_2 on the reference ridge, l_2 is the length of the fragment, and d_i is the distance between v_i and p_i, $i = 1, 2$, and t_1 and t_2 are thresholds. We will consider this fragment as an artifact instead of a ridge section, thus deleting this fragment if one of the following conditions is true: $\max\left(\frac{l_1}{l_2}, \frac{l_2}{l_1}\right) > t_1$, or $d_1 + d_2 > t_2$. The former states that the lengths l_1 and l_2 differ too much and the latter states that the endpoints of the fragment are too far away from the closest ridge. Otherwise, we will keep the fragment, and delete the pixels between p_1 and p_2 along p. After dealing with all the fragments in the current image, the reference ridge becomes the form shown in Fig. 2(b). It can be readily found from Fig. 2(b) that the original entire reference ridge has been broken into several segments, and it is noteworthy that the two endpoints of two different fragments in the current image should be linked only if their nearest points on the reference ridge are the endpoints of the same segment. Therefore we can merge the ridge parts in the current image together using this criterion.

3.3   Linking Method

Based on the aforementioned criterion, we can easily select the two endpoints which should be linked and then connect them by a curve parallel to their adjacent ridge. First of all, we find the closest ridge for each endpoint. As illustrated

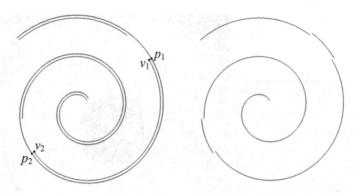

Fig. 2. Determining which two endpoints should be linked. (a) The previous ridge image and the current ridge image. (b) The endpoints in current image whose nearest points on the reference ridge are the two endpoints of a segment should be linked. (Color figure online)

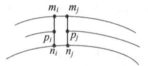

Fig. 3. Linking the two endpoints which should be linked.

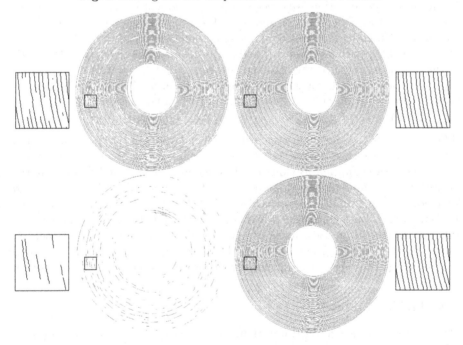

Fig. 4. Getting the entire ridge. (a) The current ridge image. (b) The previous ridge image. (c) An intermediate result. (d) The final result

in Fig. 3, given an endpoint p_i, a line which passes through p_i and is perpendicular to the orientation at p_i meets the upper closest ridge at m_i, and the lower closest ridge at n_i. The ridge where m_i or n_i lies are the closest ridge of p_i. Providing that there exist two endpoints p_i and p_j which ought to be linked, they can be linked on condition that they have at least one same closest ridge. As depicted in Fig. 3, p_i and p_j have two same closest ridges. We first generate a curve Q_1 which is as parallel to curve $m_i m_j$ as possible to connect p_i and p_j, and then check if this curve intersects the existing ridges at any places other than p_i and p_j. If not, Q_1 can be used to link p_i and p_j together, so if p_i and p_j only have one same closest ridge, we will connect p_i and p_j by Q_1 and then begin to check other endpoint pairs. If p_i and p_j have another same closest ridge, as shown in Fig. 3, we will use $n_i n_j$ to generate another as-parallel-as-possible curve Q_2 in the same way, and evaluate Q_1 and Q_2 by the following equation:

$$H_1 = 1 - \frac{\min(m_i p_i, m_j p_j)}{\max(m_i p_i, m_j p_j)}, \quad H_2 = 1 - \frac{\min(n_i p_i, n_j p_j)}{\max(n_i p_i, n_j p_j)}. \tag{1}$$

Equation 1 reflects the similarity of the distances from p_i and p_j to their closest ridge. The smaller H_1 (respectively H_2) means p_i and p_j are at a more similar distance to $m_i m_j$ (respectively $n_i n_j$) than to $n_i n_j$ (respectively $m_i m_j$), so it is more suitable to use the curve generated from $m_i m_j$ (respectively $n_i n_j$) to link p_i and p_j. Eventually the curve which has smaller H-value will be chosen to connect p_i and p_j together. We repeatedly use this algorithm to process all pairs of endpoints which should be linked until no pair of endpoints should be linked in the current image.

3.4   Ridge Propagation Result

We show a result of ridge propagation. We set $t_1 = 4$ and $t_2 = 10$ in our experiments. The current ridge image (Fig. 4(a)) consists of many fragments. The reference ridge image, i.e. the previous ridge image, is shown in Fig. 4(b). These are used by the propagation method in Sect. 3.2 to produce the result in Fig. 4(c). The endpoint pairs in Fig. 4(a) corresponding to the two endpoints of a segment in Fig. 4(c) are connected by the method in Sect. 3.3. The final result is displayed in Fig. 4(d), in which all the fragments in Fig. 4(a) have been correctly merged together, producing an entire film ridge in the current image.

Once the ridges are recovered, we use the ink projection method in [8, 10] to obtain a flattened image, which contains all the frames of the footage (see Fig. 5(top)). Since the ridges contain the footage frames, when performing projection only a thin layer close to the ridges need to be considered (the maximum displacement in either direction is set to 2 pixels).

4   Extracting Frames

Once the reconstructed image containing the film strip has been obtained, the final task is to extract the individual frames so that they can be reassembled as a

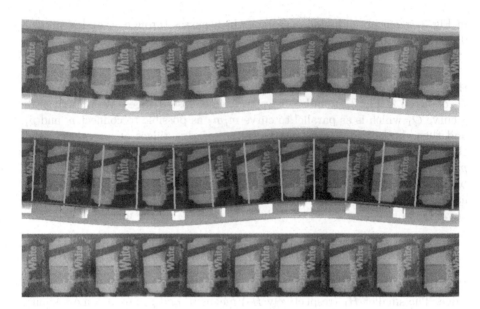

Fig. 5. Straightening a section of reconstructed film strip. (a) initial reconstructed film strip showing sinusoidal deformation, (b) sinusoid fitted to the boundary curves (shown in green) and sampled normals (shown in red), (c) film strip after warping and cropping. (Color figure online)

video. As can be seen in Fig. 5a there is an approximately sinusoidal oscillation, the period of which increases by a factor of about 2.7 from the beginning to the end of the reconstructed film strip. This oscillation is due to the film not being aligned perfectly vertically when placed in the X-ray scanner, while the increasing period is a consequence of the spiral roll of the film. To simplify subsequent processing, the film strip is straightened to correct for the oscillation.

First, the boundaries of the central part of the film strip that contains the images is extracted. Since the area of the image outside this area is relatively bright a simple approach is sufficient. The height H of a single frame[1] is manually determined, and then for each column in the image the range $[i_c, i_c + H]$ that minimises the summed intensities $i_c = argmin_r \sum_{r=i}^{i+H} I[r][c]$ is considered as the frame. The set of frame boundaries $i_c; c = 1 \ldots n$ provides the upper boundary for the film strip. Since each point along the boundary is estimated independently, they can be noisy, so robust smoothing is applied to the boundary which down-weights the effect of outliers.

The boundary is modelled as piecewise sinusoidal (with a fixed frequency per section). Since a sinusoidal function is non-linear, fitting to data tends to be unreliable unless a good initialisation is provided. The amplitude is already known from the height H of a single frame, and the mean height of the bound-

---

[1] Height H refers to the height of the frame which is in the film strip, and is therefore rotated $90°$ to the normal viewing position.

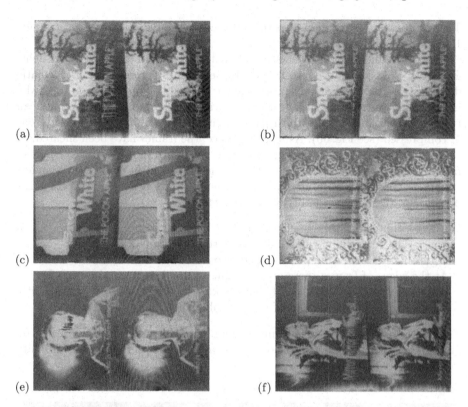

Fig. 6. Examples of problems for segmentation of film strip into frames. (a) nonlinear stretching of frame, (b) nonlinear compression of frame, (c) first frame smaller than second frame, (d) two frames with weak frame boundary, (e) first frame contains reconstruction artifact, (f) bright patches.

ary curve provides the offset. The frequency is determined by computing the autocorrelation of the sampled boundary function, and finding the lag that produces the first peak in the autocorrelation function. Finally, the first peak in the boundary function is detected, providing the phase.

This procedure is applied to small sections (5000 pixels long) of the film strip to estimate the upper boundary curve. The lower boundary is taken as the same curve vertically shifted by H. Figure 5b shows the fitted curves for a part of a section. A sparse set of corresponding points are found in the upper and lower curves by computing the normals from the sinusoidal function, and projecting them from the upper curves towards the lower curves. A thin plate spline warp is applied to the image using the endpoints of the normals in the source image which are mapped to a set of vertically aligned normals, separated by the arc-length along the sinusoid, in the target image. Figure 5c shows the warped image (after cropping) which has effectively straightened that section of the film strip.

The results for the individual sections are concatenated back to form a single 150336×281 pixel image.

Once the film strip has been straightened and cropped it should be straightforward to split the image into frames. However, in practice this is problematic due to several factors. First the process of recovering the film strip from the XMT image volume introduces nonlinear deformations in the geometry. Examples can be seen clearly in Fig. 6, in which parts of the image are stretched (see Fig. 6a) or compressed (see Fig. 6b). As a consequence, the frames have been sheared, so that the vertical frame border has become diagonal. Figure 6c shows a pair of frames in which there has been a 10 % change in width. In addition, the image quality is poor. Not only are the images noisy and low resolution (213×281 pixels), but there are several types of artifacts:

– Due to the partial volume effect banding is visible in many of the frames in Fig. 6. The curved film surface results in the curvature of the bands.
– Figure 6e shows an example of image reconstruction errors (in the face).
– At the edges of frames there are sometimes some bright patches, e.g. Fig. 6a and f. The film tends to be a little wrinkled at the edges, and consequently these are also manifestations of the partial volume effect.

Finally, the boundary between frames is often not evident. For instance in Fig. 6d and e most of the boundary does not contain any significant vertical discontinuity in intensity or texture.

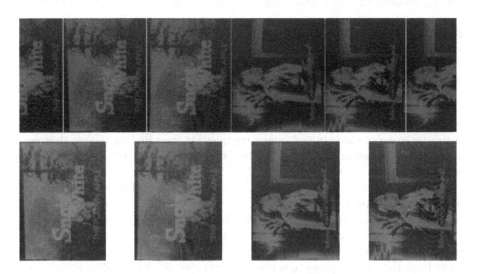

Fig. 7. Extracting frames. The green lines indicate estimated regular frame boundaries, while the red lines show the keyframes that were determined to start a new shot. The extracted frames are shown below after resizing to a common width (Color figure online)

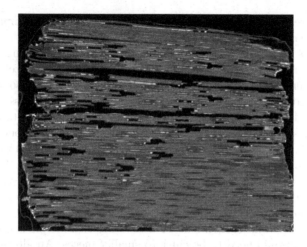

Fig. 8. An X-ray image of a section of 'The Morecambe and Wise Show'.

To split the film we provide the width W of the first frame F_1 in the film strip. All other frames will be resized to this width. The next frame F_2 is assumed to follow, but may have width $W \pm w$. The set of possible frames F_2 are compared against F_1 and the one maximising a normalised cross-correlation score is selected. Once frame F_i is found it is used to estimate the width of the next frame F_{i+1}. In addition, a threshold on the normalised cross-correlation score is used to check that the match is sufficiently good. Otherwise there may be substantial distortion between frames F_i and F_{i+1}. Alternatively, there could be substantial change in appearance between the frames, either from a fast moving object, sudden changes in lighting, or a cut between scenes. This would make the estimation of the width of F_{i+1} unreliable, and so it is re-estimated by comparing it against the currently undetermined F_{i+2}. Both the widths of F_{i+1} and F_{i+2} are optimised using normalised cross-correlation. This process is demonstrated in Fig. 7. Note the width of the second frame of the woman shot has been correctly estimated although it is more than 10 % narrower than the keyframe.

5   Conclusions and Future Work

In this paper we have shown the feasibility of a primarily automatic method for recovering the contents of lost films from source acetate rolls by performing a virtual unrolling of a 3D tomographic scan of the film. Our approach involved first generating the film reel by extracting lines (intensity ridges) along the film layers, connecting disconnected lines, aligning the lines from across the X-ray scans, and finally projecting densities along normals to the lines to measure the response of the silver content in the film. Finally, frames were extracted from the film reel, and reassembled into a video. Difficulties were encountered in the final stage due to stretching artifacts in the alignment stage of the virtual unrolling.

Nevertheless, reasonable results were obtained, which could be improved in the future by better flattening methods.

The success of recovering this short section of film from a tomographic scan gives hope for recovery of large, damaged film reels. Unfortunately, the X-ray dose requirement increases dramatically with increasing size, so upscaling is problematic and even impossible to the degree that would be necessary for recovery of a 30 cm diameter film reel. Not only would it be necessary to increase the detector array size to around 20,000 pixels across, but the number of recorded photons per pixel would also have to increase by thousands. This would require an, as yet unconceived, detector with a massive dynamic range. Furthermore, acquiring such a photon count in a reasonable amount of time would require such an intense X-ray beam that heating would be a problem, bearing in mind that any dimensional change should be much less than 1 in 20,000. Conceivably, the smallest 8 mm reels might be able to be scanned in one go, whereas larger film reels would need to be cut into smaller pieces. An alternative might be tomosynthesis, which would avoid the necessity of an X-ray path that passes diametrically through the film; however it is unlikely that this could produce a reconstructed image of sufficient quality.

Returning to the rediscovered episode of 'The Morecambe and Wise Show', its rapid degradation, along with the above limitations, meant that the only feasible solution was to cut the film into smaller sections which could then be scanned using the MuCAT 2 X-ray microtomography scanner at QMUL. Figure 8 shows a single image from one such section. The quality is significantly poorer than the Snow White scan, as it contains many holes and also some local deformations. We are just starting to work on this more challenging data, and we believe that our processing pipeline can cope since it was adapted from the pipeline developed for damaged historical scrolled parchments [8,10], and that these documents also contained many artifacts such as holes, delaminations, geometric distortions, etc.

Acknowledgments. We thank Paul Vanezis (BBC) and Ulrich Reudel (BFI).

References

1. Binder, M.: A Light Affliction: A History of Film Preservation and Restoration (2015). Lulu.com
2. Davis, G.R., Evershed, A.N.Z., Mills, D.: Quantitative high contrast X-ray microtomography for dental research. J. Dent. **41**(5), 475–482 (2013)
3. Davis, G.R., Mills, D.: Brute force absorption contrast microtomography. In: Proceedings of SPIE: Developments in X-Ray Tomography IX, vol. 9212 (2014)
4. Macchia, A., et al.: Characterization and weathering of motion-picture films with support of cellulose nitrate, cellulose acetate and polyester. Procedia Chem. **8**, 175–184 (2013)
5. Freeth, T., et al.: Decoding the ancient Greek astronomical calculator known as the Antikythera Mechanism. Nature **444**, 587–591 (2006)
6. Enticknap, L., Restoration, F.: The Culture and Science of Audiovisual Heritage. Palgrave Macmillan, New York (2013)

7. Kokaram, A.C.: Motion Picture Restoration: Digital Algorithms for Artefact Suppression in Degraded Motion Picture Film and Video. Springer, London (2013)
8. Liu, C., Rosin, P.L., Lai, Y.-K., Hu, W.: Robust segmentation of historical parchment XMT images for virtual unrolling. In: Digital Heritage, pp. 11–18 (2015)
9. Mills, D., Curtis, A., Davis, G., Rosin, P.L., Lai, Y.-K.: Apocalypto: revealing the Bressingham roll. J. Pap. Conserv. 15(3), 14–19 (2014)
10. Samko, O., Lai, Y.-K., Marshall, D., Rosin, P.L.: Virtual unrolling and information recovery from scanned scrolled historical documents. Pattern Recogn. 47(1), 248–259 (2014)
11. Steger, C.: An unbiased detector of curvilinear structures. IEEE Trans. Pattern Anal. Mach. Intell. 20(2), 113–125 (1998)

Multi-spectral Imaging System (IWN) for the Digitization and Investigation of Cultural Heritage

Ibrahim El-Rifai[1(✉)], Hend Mahgoub[2], and Ari Ide-Ektessabi[1]

[1] Advanced Imaging Technology Lab, Graduate School of Engineering,
Kyoto University, Kyoto, Japan
ibrahimeg@yahoo.com, ide.ari.4n@kyoto-u.ac.jp
[2] Institute for Sustainable Heritage, University College London, London, UK
hend.mahgoub.13@ucl.ac.uk

Abstract. This research focuses on the digitization and investigation of cultural heritage liaised with the practical requirements of conservators and museum curators. Different types of information are extracted about the physical characteristics of the artifacts, pigments preliminary identification and pigments distribution in addition to the colorimetric information. In this regard, a multi-spectral digitization system – named as "iwn" was developed to collect the required information from the cultural heritage objects. The system is portable, customizable, easy to use, in-situ, non-invasive and relatively not expensive. This paper will describe the specifications of the system showing its functions and capabilities through few case studies.

Keywords: Digitization · Multi-spectral imaging · Pigment identification and distribution · Spectral reflectance reconstruction

1 Introduction

The digital era introduced several e-preservation and investigation systems for heritage objects, such systems have been developed with variety of setups and features, ranged from large systems [1–4] to portable and small ones [5–9]. The cost of such systems varies significantly according to the functions and requirements.

This research aims to introduce a multi-spectral imaging system which is portable, in-situ, non-invasive, relatively not expensive. It is designed to extract sufficient information from the surface and also from other layers of artworks through imaging in the visible, very near infrared (IR) and near ultraviolet (UV) regions to enrich its documentation and conservation plans.

The system also is using a method for spectral reflectance reconstruction named as Adaptive pseudo inverse (API) [10, 11] to improve the accuracy of the colorimetric measurements.

© Springer International Publishing AG 2016
M. Ioannides et al. (Eds.): EuroMed 2016, Part I, LNCS 10058, pp. 232–240, 2016.
DOI: 10.1007/978-3-319-48496-9_19

2 Experimental MSI System (IWN)

The multispectral imaging (MSI) system will be referred to as "iwn" throughout the following text which is an ancient Egyptian term for color 𓈖𓏤 ⁓ 𓏏𓏛 [12, 13].

IWN (Fig. 1) consists of two motorized stages for the X and Y directions, two filter wheels facing each other, and various light sources with an ability to use different imaging sensors. Ball screw motion is being used for the X and Y movement controlled by stepper motors that gives movement of 5 mm translation for a full revolution about 25 μ per a single step with an option to go down to 1.5 μ movement in the micro-stepping mode.

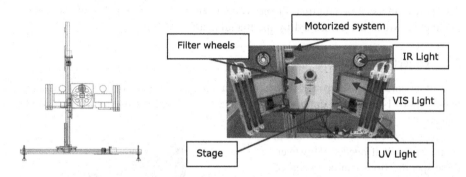

Fig. 1. IWN System CAD drawing (Left) and its components (Right). (Color figure online)

2.1 System Specifications

2.1.1 Lights

Different light sources are used to cover the required regions; six Ultraviolet (UV) lamps (Mini Blacklight - 6 W UV-A), two infrared (IR) Led light (850 nm) sources and two Visible (VIS) led Light (5000k) sources.

2.1.2 Filter Wheels

Two filters wheels are used to host different combinations of filters. The first wheel is designed to host 7 filters (Fujifilm BandPass) covering the visible spectrum in; 420, 450, 500, 530, 550, 600 and 640 nm which can be replaced with other filters as required. The second wheel hosts 3 filters; IR reflected filter (B + W 093), UV reflected filter (B + W 403) and IR/UV block filter - hot mirror (B + W 486). The wheel is used to pass either infrared or ultraviolet only or block both to pass only the visible radiation. The second wheel can be replaced by another filter wheel that can host either another 7 filters in the visible range to achieve 14 different filters combinations or a range of IR filters from 700–960 nm as needed.

2.1.3   Imaging Sensors

IWN can be used with either a monochromatic or DSLR cameras. The monochromatic sensor is an area camera Artray ArtCam-150PIII with c-mount to f-mount adapter to allow the use of Nikon 35 mm f/2D lens.

Many modified DSLR cameras can be installed with the system which are sensitive to the UVA and NIR radiation. A modified Fuji FinePix S5 camera with a sensitivity range from 380–1000 nm was used in some cases.

2.1.4   Software

A software was developed to control IWN system in two modes; full control mode or DSLR mode. The full control mode controls the whole system (X and Y motion, filter wheels and the different types of lights) in addition to the monochromatic camera. The DSLR mode also controls all the system parameters except the DSLR camera parameters which are controlled by the manufacturer software.

2.2   Object Specifications

The monochromatic setup of IWN allows capturing an object of 2 × 1.5 cm and a maximum of 14.5 × 10.5 cm in size on a distance of 12–80 cm from the object. Wider objects can be captured using the motorized system that moves 60 cm in the X and Y if needed. However, these specifications can be increased with the use of DSLR camera or the use of different lenses.

The system can be installed in different ways to allow for horizontal or vertical imaging. It also can be attached to linear guide rails to give the ability of capturing longer objects like papyrus and manuscripts (Fig. 2).

Fig. 2. IWN on linear guide rails for investigation of long objects (Color figure online)

2.3   System Calibration

Different calibration targets (i.e. Labsphere white reference and X-Rite color checker passport) are used to improve the accuracy and reproducibility of the system. In addition to the collection of dark, bias frames and flat field frames. An image reduction process also is used to remove the noise from the electronics or from the system optics. The removal of the dust from the CCD and the calculations of system gain and signal to noise ratio are performed regularly to insure the stability of the system.

3   Case Studies

3.1   Spectral Reflectance Reconstruction

A test painting was captured using IWN to reconstruct the spectral reflectance of the different colors from the multi-spectral data. An area (12 × 10 cm) was selected (Fig. 3) for the experiment.

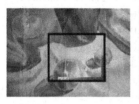 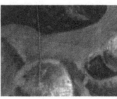 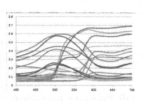

Fig. 3. Oil Painting (test painting). Black square represents the selected area for investigation (Left), Monochromatic image of the selected area showing the 21 selected positions of the training set (Middle) and the colorimetric measurements of these positions. (Color figure online)

In this experiment, 7 filters were used in the range of 420–700 nm (Fujifilm BPB42, BPB45, BPB50, BPB55, BPB60, SC64, SC70) accompanied by UV/IR block filter. The acquisition was conducted in a dark room. 21 positions (Fig. 3) were selected for the training dataset. The reflectance of these positions was measured by X-Rite eXact colorimeter and re-sampled in the range of 400–700 nm with 10 nm interval. Spectral data from the positions were collected in two modes; one pixel and region of interest (ROI) with an average area of 4 mm similar to the size of the colorimeter scan area.

All the measurements were used to reconstruct spectral reflectance using two estimation methods for comparison; the pseudo inverse (PI) [14] and the adaptive pseudo inverse method (API) [10]. The results of the comparison (Table 1) were assessed by the mean squared error equation for spectral error between the actual and the estimated spectral reflectance and the equation of $\Delta E2000$ obtained from the formula of CIEDE2000 [15, 16] under the CIE D65 as a standard illuminant for colorimetric error.

The proposed method API is showing noticeable improvement over the PI method in both modes (one pixel and ROI).

It should be considered that the data was not acquired from a standard color chart with a homogeneous color patches so it is expected to find a mixture of pigments or at least average of different intensity levels of the same pigment, which is reflected in the values of the standard deviation in spectral and colorimetric errors. The new method is showing a potential to be used to improve the accuracy of color reconstruction but further work is needed which is the focus of our further research.

Table 1. Spectral and colormetric errors for the 21 positions of two spectral reflectance construction methods in two modes; one pixel and region of interest (4 mm) – ROI. The table is showing the spectral RMS and colorimetric errors including the mean, standard deviation and maximum error of the tested methods for the 21 positions dataset.

21 positions		One pixel			ROI		
		API	PI	Diff.	API	PI	Diff.
RMSE	Mean	0.0026	0.0043	−0.0017	0.0019	0.0039	−0.0019
	STD	0.0032	0.0027	0.0005	0.0037	0.0041	−0.0004
	Max	0.0114	0.0104	0.0011	0.0157	0.0184	−0.0027
ΔE_{00} under D65	Mean	0.0844	0.1455	−0.0611	0.0507	0.1250	−0.07438
	STD	0.0909	0.0988	−0.0079	0.0864	0.1431	−0.0567
	Max	0.2537	0.3905	−0.1368	0.3446	0.6370	−0.2924

3.2 Oil Painting Investigation

Multispectral imaging has been used intensively in the investigation of paintings [17–22] due to its effectiveness and valuable results. In this section a painting from the storage of the Egyptian geographic society will be presented as a case study for investigating paintings using IWN (Fig. 4). The painting is suffering from many deterioration aspects and was found without frame or information about the portrayed figure. Comparing the painting with other portraits in the geographic society, it was suggested that this frameless portrait belongs to one of the famous figures of the geographic society with no more information.

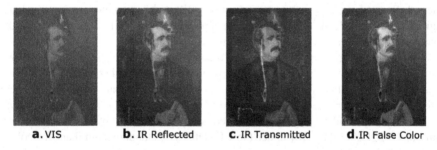

a. VIS   **b.** IR Reflected   **c.** IR Transmitted   **d.** IR False Color

Fig. 4. Unknown oil painting from the Egyptian geographic society (Color figure online)

The painting (verso and recto) was digitized in the visible, near IR and UV ranges followed by various post-processes to explore any features or hidden remarks that could lead to know the depicted person in addition to the documentation of the painting condition.

The initial inspection of the images revealed a change in the composition in the left arm of the man, which was assumed positioned behind his back. Through multispectral imaging, it is now clear that the artist painted the left arm in the original composition (Fig. 5), then removed it intentionally. This worked as a guide to search for a pioneer who had a problem with his left arm which did not take too long to be revealed "Dr. Livingstone".

David Livingstone (19 Mar. 1813–1 May 1873) is a famous European explorer who was seriously wounded and had a disability of his arm after being attacked by a lion in one of his expeditions [23].

It is believed that the portrait was painted from an engraving made by D. J. Pound on 1857 from a photograph by J.J. Edwin Mayall [24].

A previous conservation also is observed around the head (Fig. 4.d)

Fig. 5. Details of the painting (Visible and IR images of the left arm) (Color figure online)

which shows the different degradation rate of pigments between the original and the retouched.

Unfortunately, there is no signature or date for this painting but it is estimated to be painted at the end of the 19th century.

3.3   Pigments Preliminary Identification and Distribution

MSI proved to be useful for pigments preliminary identification [25–31]. 9 pigments were selected to test the ability of IWN to identify and differentiate between the different pigments; Lapis Lazuli, Ultramarine, Egyptian Blue, Azurite, Smalt, Malachite, Verdigris, Viridian, Cadmium Red and Cadmium Yellow (L. Cornelissen & son [32]).

Pigments reaction were investigated under several multi-spectral imaging modes of acquisition such as: Visible, Visible induced IR (VIL / IRF), UV reflected, UV fluorescence, and IR reflected in addition to producing UV and IR false color images.

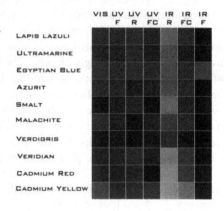

Fig. 6. Pigments reaction under multispectral acquisition. (Color figure online)

Observations:

Blue Pigments

Egyptian blue has a unique infrared luminescence property when excited with the visible light and captured using infrared filter. Thus, it is easily identified among other pigments [29, 30]. Azurite also reacted similarly to Egyptian blue under the different modes except for the infrared luminescence mode.

Smalt and Azurite can be differentiated by observing the IR false color image as smalt appears red while Azurite is purple.

Ultramarine and Lapis Lazuli have similar responses under MSI technique which is expected as both are chemically similar [33]. Both can be differentiated to Azurite by IR false color image.

Green pigments

Green pigments gave different responses as seen in Fig. 6. Malachite turns yellow in the UV false color and blue in the IR false color. On the other hand, Viridian turns yellowish in the UV false color while Verdigris gives greenish color. Also, Viridian can be identified by the pink or reddish color in the IR false color while Verdigris turns dark.

Cadmium pigments: (Red and Yellow)

Cadmium pigments can be identified by the faint glow or fluorescence in the VIL mode, Moreover, cadmium yellow gives red color in the UV false color while cadmium red becomes dark. Cadmium red also gives orange-yellowish color in the IR false color.

4   Conclusions

This research presented a multispectral imaging system (IWN) which is portable, customizable, in-situ, non-invasive and relatively not expensive. The system is working in the range of 380–1000 nm. It is developed with the practical requirements of museum curators and conservators in mind which they need a fast tool to digitize and investigate cultural heritage objects. The system has the ability to acquire color information with the potential to improve the accuracy of the reconstruction of colors through the use of modified spectral reflectance reconstruction method (Adaptive Pseudo-inverse - API). The system is also capable of the digitization and investigation in the visible, near infrared and near ultraviolet regions which are imaging techniques proved its usefulness/utility in the investigation of different artifacts such as oil paintings in addition to the potential of preliminary identification of early pigments.

Acknowledgement. This research is partially funded and supported by Prof. Ide-Ektessabi Laboratory, Advanced Imaging Technology, Graduate School of Engineering, Kyoto University as part of a PhD research.

References

1. Martinez, K., Cupitt, J., Saunders, D., Pillay, R.: Ten years of art imaging research. Proc. IEEE **90**, 28–41 (2002)
2. Ribés, A., Schmitt, F., Pillay, R., Lahanier, C.: Calibration and spectral reconstruction for cristatel: an art painting multispectral acquisition system. J. Imaging Sci. Technol. **49**, 563–573 (2005)

3. Christens-Barry, W.A., Boydston, K., France, F.G., Knox, K.T., Easton Jr., R.L., Toth, M. B.: Camera system for multispectral imaging of documents. In: Proceedings of SPIE 7249, Sensors, Cameras, and Systems for Industrial/Scientific Applications X, 724908, 27 January 2009. doi:10.1117/12.815374

4. Easton Jr., R.L., Knox, K.T., Christens-Barry, W.A.: Multispectral imaging of the Archimedes palimpsest. In: Applied Imagery Pattern Recognition Workshop Proceedings, pp. 15–17 (2003)

5. Costas, B., et al.: A novel hyper-spectral imaging apparatus for the non-destructive analysis of objects of artistic and historic value. J. Cult. Heritage **4**, 330s–337s (2003)

6. Novati, G., Pellegri, P., Schettini, R.: An affordable multispectral imaging system for the digital museum. Int. J. Digit. Libr. **5**, 167–178 (2005)

7. Pelagotti, A., Del Mastio, A., De Rosa, A., Piva, A.: Multispectral imaging of paintings. IEEE Sign. Process. Mag. **25**, 27–36 (2008)

8. Berns, R.S., Taplin, L.A., Urban, P., Zhao, Y.: Spectral color reproduction of paintings. In: Proceedings of the Fourth European Conference on Color in Graphics, Imaging and Vision, Barcelona, Spain, pp. 484–488 (2013)

9. Bearman, G.H., Spiro, S.I.: Archaeological applications of advanced imaging techniques. Biblical Archaeologist **59**(1), 56–66 (1996)

10. El-Rifai, I., Mahgoub, H., Magdy, M., Toque, J.A., Ide-Ektessabi, A.: Enhanced spectral reflectance reconstruction using pseudo-inverse estimation method. Int. J. Image Process. (IJIP) **7**(3), 278–285 (2013)

11. Ohno, Y.: CIE fundamentals for color measurements. In: International Conference on Digital Printing Technology, NIP 2016, Vancouver, Canada, pp. 540–545 (2016)

12. Faulkner, R.O.: A Concise Dictionary of Middle Egyptian Oxford, p. 13. Oxford University Press, London (1991)

13. Gardiner, A.: Egyptian Grammar: Being an Introduction to the Study of Hieroglyphs, 3rd edn, p. 552. Oxford University Press, London (1966)

14. Barata, J., Hussein, M.: The moore-penrose pseudoinverse: a tutorial review of the theory. Braz. J. Phys. **42**(1–2), 146–165 (2012)

15. ASTM International: Standard Practice for Computing the Colors of Objects by Using the CIE System, ASTM Standard E308-08, West Conshohocken, United States (2008). www.astm.org

16. Luo, M.R., Cui, G., Rigg, B.: The development of the CIE 2000 colour-difference formula: CIEDE2000. Color Res. Appl. **26**(5), 340–350 (2001). (Special Issue on Color Difference)

17. El-Rifai, I., Ezzat, H., Mahgoub, H., Bebars, Y., Ide-Ektessabi, A.: Artwork digitization and investigation a case study of the loom weaver, oil painting by Hosni El-Bannani. Int. Sci. J. Mediterr. Archaeol. Archaeometry **13**(2), 21–29 (2013). Greece

18. René de la Rie, E.: Fluorescence of paint and varnish layers (part I). Stud. Conserv. **27**(1), 1–7 (1982). doi:10.2307/1505977

19. René de la Rie, E.: Fluorescence of paint and varnish layers (part III). Stud. Conserv. **27**(3), 102–108 (1982)

20. Walmsley, E., Metzger, C., Delaney, J.K., Fletcher, C.: Improved visualization of under drawings with solid-state detectors operating in the infrared. Stud. Conserv. **39**, 217–231 (1994)

21. Aldrovandi, A., Buzzegoli, E., Keller, A., Kunzelman, D.: Investigation of painted surfaces with a reflected UV false color technique. In: 8th International Conference on Non Destructive Investigations and Micronalysis for the Diagnostics and Conservation of the Cultural and Environmental Heritage, Lecce, art 2005, Italy (2005)

22. Pelagotti, A., Del Mastio, A., De Rosa, A., Piva, A.: Multispectral imaging of paintings. IEEE Sign. Process. Mag. **25**, 27–36 (2008)

23. Livingstone, D.: Encyclopaedia Britannica Online (2016). www.britannica.com/biography/David-Livingstone. Accessed June 2016
24. Pound, D.J.: The Drawing-Room of Eminent Personages, vol. 2. Mayall, London (1857). John Jabez Edwin Paisley. npg.org.uk/collections/search/portrait/mw40836/David-Livingstone?
25. Toque, J.A., Sakatoku, Y., Ide-Ektessabi, A.: Pigment identification by analytical imaging using multispectral images. In: 2009 16th IEEE International Conference on Image Processing (ICIP), Cairo, pp. 2861–2864 (2009)
26. Delaney, J.K., Walmsley, E., Berrie, B.H., Fletcher, C.F.: Multispectral Imaging of Paintings in the Infrared to Detect and Map Blue Pigments. National Academy of Sciences. (Sackler NAS Colloquium) Scientific Examination of Art: Modern Techniques in Conservation and Analysis. The National Academies Press, Washington, DC (2005). doi:10.17226/11413
27. Delaney, J.K., Walmsey, E., Berrie, B.H., Fletcher, C.F.: Multispectral imaging of paintings in the infared to detect and map blue pigments. In: Proceedings of the National Academy of Sciences, pp. 120–136 (2003)
28. Smith, G.D., et al.: Inexpensive, near-infrared imaging of artwork using a night-vision webcam for chemistry-of-art courses. J. Chem. Educ. **86**(12), December 2009. Verri, "The spatially resolved characterization of Egyptian blue."
29. Verri, G.: The spatially resolved characterization of Egyptian blue, Han blue and Han purple by photo-induced luminescence digital imaging. Anal. Bioanal. Chem. **394**(4), 1011–1021 (2009). doi:10.1007/s00216-009-2693-0
30. Accorsi, G., Verri, G., Bolognesi, M., Armaroli, N., Clementi, C., Miliani, C., Romani, A.: The exceptional near-infrared luminescence properties of cuprorivaite (Egyptian blue). Chem. Commun. **23**, 3392–3394 (2009). doi:10.1039/B902563D
31. Cosentino, A.: Identification of pigments by multispectral imaging a flowchart method. Heritage Sci. **2**(8) (2014). doi:10.1186/2050-7445-2-8
32. L. Cornelissen & Son, London: www.cornelissen.com
33. Sackler Colloquia: Scientific Examination of Art: Modern Techniques in Conservation and Analysis, Arthur M. Sackler Colloquia of the National Academy of Sciences, National Academies Press, Washington, D.C. (2003)

Diagnostic Activities for the Planned and Preventive Conservation of Mosaic Pavements: The Case Study of the Triclinium of the Villa Romana del Casale (Sicily)

Antonella Versaci[1], Alessio Cardaci[2(✉)], and Luca R. Fauzia[1]

[1] Faculty of Engineering and Architecture, University of Enna KORE, Enna, Italy
{antonella.versaci,luca.fauzia}@unikore.it
[2] School of Engineering, University of Bergamo, Bergamo, Italy
alessio.cardaci@unibg.it

Abstract. The *Villa Romana del Casale* at Piazza Armerina, Sicily is known for the richness of the mosaic pavements that decorate almost every room. They are the finest mosaics from the Roman world and, even because of their exceptional extent, the Villa was declared a UNESCO World Heritage site in 1997. Their *in situ* conservation advocated by Cesare Brandi in the late 1950s, an exception to the typical treatment of excavated mosaics of the time, requires a regular monitoring of the physical condition and the establishment of mitigation strategies, however, difficult to implement especially for economic and technical reasons. In this sense, this paper intends to propose an innovative and user-friendly procedure based on laser scanning and thermo-hygrometric investigations able to assess the *tessellatum* status through time and to evaluate the maintenance work's efficiency, which could be included in a long-term and sustainable approach to preserving our ancient mosaic heritage.

Keywords: Mosaics · Preventive conservation · Diagnostics · Piazza Armerina

1 Introduction

The mosaics, one of the main wealth of the Mediterranean area, represent a treasure of extreme delicacy, often endangered by both the neglect and the deficiency of economic resources, if not subverted by other ever-increasing man-made disasters such as wars and terrorist attacks. The *in situ* conservation of mosaic decorations is at present a largely privileged cultural choice, which, in concert with the site's documentation and valorisation, requires, since the time of excavation, to study and implement a series of coordinated and systematic acts to counter the decline of their physical and chemical state, as well as the growing of instability phenomena. Too often, however, the carelessness of preliminary investigations, the absence of timely and appropriate conservation/maintenance measures, the inadequacy of the protection systems from the major climatic factors, the indiscriminate influx of tourists and even the consequences of intrusions, theft and vandalism, often favoured by the failure of tools and security/surveillance activities, cause irreversible damages. In order to oppose the destruction of this precious

© Springer International Publishing AG 2016
M. Ioannides et al. (Eds.): EuroMed 2016, Part I, LNCS 10058, pp. 241–253, 2016.
DOI: 10.1007/978-3-319-48496-9_20

heritage, it appears necessary to develop a culture of planning and protection, which could finally supplant that of emergency and improvisation; i.e. to establish principles able to improve an idea of well-structured preservation. Nevertheless, for this to happen, despite the progress made by the matter for the past sixty years, it is still essential to operate "a profound change in mentality" [1], from how to why heritage should be preserved [2], both in the operators and administrations.

Today, conservation techniques seem having definitively abandoned the practice of mosaics detachment long-followed and motivated by a desire to safeguard only their image, paying little attention to their material consistency and heedless of their three-dimensional values [3, 4]. Nonetheless, the maintaining in the original location first demands a great ethical consciousness, as well as specific operational and management capacities. In most cases nowadays, the mosaic is restored *in situ*, without altering the final appearance of the surfaces, respecting the traces of the past and the historical/artistic values of the good and its archaeological field. Conservation practice does not in fact solely apply to mosaic but goes further to the analysis of its context, the building that it covers and to which is intimately linked, the landscape and highly considers the significance of the work itself. Major new activities are then entrusted to the restorer, now necessarily part of a multidisciplinary team composed of engineers, chemists, physicists, biologists, mineralogists, etc. Starting from a deep knowledge of the mosaic, its functionality, techniques of execution, original materials and those used in previous restorations and from the documentation of its state of preservation, he plans the intervention to be executed [5]. He also studies the measures to be taken for the future protection of the property: indirect interventions on the environment [6], monitoring and prevention seen as "a mode that maximizes the permanence of authenticity (material, of course) of architectural object" [7]. These devices, critical to secure a future to works that are an expression of art, technology and building expertise and a privileged source of knowledge related to ancient civilizations, still seem hard to implement, mainly due to both the lack of adequate resources and technological skills. They demand a full awareness of the numerous meanings embodied in cultural heritage even in users and authorities that should be understood as owners/managers of the properties, fully involved in their conservation through on-going maintenance programs.

In this framework, the control activities on the mosaics of the Roman Villa in Piazza Armerina, which this work illustrates, have been planned and implemented. The monument includes "the largest and comprehensive set of mosaics ever discovered in a single monument, and mosaics in a state of preservation, if not perfect, some very considerable" [8]. It is known for the complexity of figurative themes, which are very important for the historical and aesthetical values and a cultural testimony of late imperial Rome in the heart of the Mediterranean (Fig. 1).

Characterized by a nearly 4,000 m^2 extension, the site must deal with the complex issues of iconography's conservation, public enjoyment and appreciation that inevitably play an essential role in all management decisions [9]. The case study, therefore, aims to contribute to the preservation of a priceless heritage, through the design and execution of simple, low-cost monitoring actions, to ensure early detection of possible anomalies and related causes, as well as of the onset of degradation phenomena and damages.

Fig. 1. Plan of the Villa Romana del Casale (left) and its famous mosaic known as "The Bikini Girls", early 4th century A.D. (right)

2   The Villa Romana del Casale and Its Mosaics

The *Villa Romana del Casale* is part of a wider geographical and cultural area, in which the historical factors that have produced countless goods spread throughout the territory are intimately connected to the magnificent characteristics of landscape, shaping today's morphology. Little or poorly studied by the admirers of classical antiquity and the ancient surveyors, it is only in the second half of 18th century that, with the start of *Grand Tours*, descriptions of the city and its monuments appeared. The first complete portrait of Piazza Armerina dates back to 1761 by Arcangelo Leanti that puts the old town in a countryside named 'the Casale', close to the ruins of what will prove to be an imposing Roman villa. He depicts the surrounding lands as pleasant and delightful as later will appear in one of the illustrations of the *Voyage pittoresque* by Jean Claude Richard de Saint-Non. This image of a cosy and lush place, well away from the collective belief of a barren and desolate inland Sicily, becomes recurring in the reports of following travellers such as the Dutch classicist Jacques-Philippe D'Orville (1727), the great geologist Déodat de Dolomieu (1781), the German poet Augusto Von Platen (1835). They returned a vision of the place of exceptional interest, so to affirm that this spatial feature has favoured in the 4th century AD the construction of the *Villa del Casale*, not far from the *Itinerarium Antonini*, which linked Catania to Agrigento [10].

The imposing late-antique building, a "unicum in the monumental and figurative heritage of the past" [11], was built on pre-existing structures, probably a *villa rustica*. It belonged to a member of the Roman senatorial aristocracy, maybe a governor; or, according to some scholars, it was commissioned and improved by a personality of imperial rank, perhaps Maxentius [12]. Traces of it were found from the late 18th century when clandestine excavations had already drawn fully from the precious heritage of archaeological finds hidden underground. At the beginning of the 19th century, confused and hasty researches were initiated by careless diggers or antique dealers, who caused serious harm to mosaic floors. Sabatino Del Muto, on behalf of Roberto Fagan, British Consul-General in Sicily, performed the first authorised excavations. However, illicit activities continued in the following years in the absence of an effective protection system, often only delegated to the good will of some wardens.

It was after the unification of Italy that more systematic explorations started. In 1881, excavations were indeed conducted, under the ministerial aegis, by the engineer Luigi Pappalardo, the inspector of monuments and excavations of antiquities of Caltanissetta district [13]. Pappalardo will raise the issue of mosaics' protection since the discovery of the first fragments of 'the twelve labours of Hercules', which took place following the opening of the first trench in the central part of the *triclinium*. It soon became clear, in fact, the danger to which the *tesserae* will encounter after the removal of the thick layer of soil that had protected them all along the centuries, both because of the weather and the action of treasure hunters. The preservation of the mosaic will be assigned to a shelter designed by the famous architect-restorer Piero Gazzola with "the task of transferring a precious fragment from the past (a three-apsed hall with rich mosaic floors) to the present times" [14]. The enormous roofing made by "wooden trusses, with terracotta tiles, supported by massive brick pillars [...] that adulterated so the appearance of the ruin, to make it similar to a barn instead of a sumptuous room as it should be" [8], built in the years 1941–42, was not however able to protect the mosaics by wind and heavy weather. The fact that visitors could walk on them had caused the lifting of large parts and the detachment of numerous *tesserae*. Moreover, erroneous cleanings made by hydrochloric acid treatments had resulted in a deterioration of cohesion mortars.

New interventions were executed between 1942 and 1949 for the restoration of the mosaic carpet. Nevertheless, it was only after the excavations carried out by Gino Vinicio Gentili in 1950 that the architect Franco Minissi will be charged with the design of a new protective shelter. A roof that, giving to Cesare Brandi, at that time director of the *Istituto Centrale del Restauro*, should have been characterised by a non-monumental proposal, leaving the ruins clearly visible. The design of Minissi, implemented in a first phase in the years 1957–1960, to which followed new shelters for the basilica (1977), the 'corridor of the big hunt' and the *triclinium* (1978), consisted of a lightweight steel skeleton sheathed with translucent panels of plastic material (a slightly clouded Perspex laminate, 3.2 mm thick). His aims were to protect the mosaics while retaining the maximum light, to permit visitors to see the interior of the villa from above, without walking upon the mosaic floors and to create new volumes suggesting the missing ones with a modern material, while safeguarding the integrity of the ancient. The intent was "to reform not rebuild" and to reintegrate the architectural image of the villa without "imitating the original" [8]. For this reason was approved by Cesare Brandi who considered it the 3D translation of that technique of *tratteggio* he was advocating for the integration of losses in paintings and polychrome sculptures [17].

This solution guaranteed the maintenance of the mosaics *in situ* and their fruition by millions of visitors, representing a milestone in the history of restoration and museum display in the archaeological field because of the sensitivity and the ability to dialogue with the landscape. However, the rapid deterioration of the materials did not respond the expectations of the same designer, showing major limitations in the conservation of the decorations. Compromised by serious degradation problems in the 1970s, perhaps also due to an unexceptional realization, it was subjected to subsequent adjustment and protection interventions in the years 1985–88, planned by Minissi. He replaced the original Perspex 'blinds' for perimeter shielding of pavilions with Visarm glass sheets 12 mm thick and the original Perspex ceilings and roofs with other similar laminates in acrylic material, as well as the opening of Vasistas windows.

In the 1990s, however, the entire mosaic decorations was in a state of extreme disrepair. The deterioration of roofing and metal supports, the lack of constant maintenance, along with a variety of events (vandalism, percolation and stagnant waters rain, moisture in the walls and floors, thermal imbalance and humidity inside the rooms, the biodeteriogens organisms attack, etc.) asked for targeted interventions in the site. They then became mandatory by the heavy rains of October 1991 that flooded the Villa extensively. Therefore, the *Regional Center for Planning and Restoration* undertook new studies. It was suggested implementing a number of measures primarily aimed at first regiment the waters for the purpose of a hygrometer soil stabilization of the villa's premises because the changed moisture conditions could lead to further and more serious deformations of the mosaic floors. In particular, it was denounced the use of cement and iron bands both for the reconstruction and consolidation of vertical structures and the restoration of the mosaics that had already caused efflorescence on the plaster and masonry, as well as internal tensions with consequent fractures, lifting and material explosions. It was then required the almost surgical removal of such elements, replacing them with mortars, kicks and stones having historical and material legitimacy [16, 17].

In the 1998–2002 years, new scientific surveys were accomplished by ENEA and the Central Institute of Restoration, highlighted several problems related to environmental comfort, attributable to incorrect maintenance solutions. The research conclusions pointed out that in the absence of opaque closures, including the use of new-generation transparent commercially available materials, microclimatic parameters could not be effectively controlled [18]. It then made its way the idea of a divestiture of Minissi's shelters, which will become effective with the guidelines for the design, which Vittorio Sgarbi, High Commissioner for the Villa of Piazza Armerina, will in 2005 (Fig. 2).

Fig. 2. The *triclinium*'s shelters: Piero Gazzola's project (left), Franco Minissi's project (center) and the new project by Guido Meli (left).

Despite numerous appeals by the international scientific world, the "rusty scrap metal" will be removed [19]. In order to improve living conditions and thus promote the conservation of the decorations, a new project designed by architect Guido Meli will be realized in 2012. It will give up the transparency of the materials as considered unreliable for the proper maintenance and inadequate for the use [17] and will provide for important recovery activities of the mosaics. The new roofing system will be made by a steel frame and laminated wood, with cladding made of panels in polystyrene layers, stucco and aluminium plastered outside and ventilated copper roofs. It will concern the entire monumental site except, even if foreseen by the program, the *frigidarium* and the *triclinium*; a structure, this latter, which lies today almost abandoned.

3   The Triclinium: Reasons for a Case Study

Minissi's shelters that still remains on the *Triclinium*, causes considerable problems that are accelerating degradation processes already in place. While waiting for the construction of the new structure, this large three-apsed hall has been forbidden to visitors, both due to the precarious condition of the path along the wall tops and the fragile state of conservation of mosaics. The room consists of a square central atrium of about 12 m per side, with an inlet at west punctuated by two columns, which leads to the ovoid peristyle. On the other three sides are three semi-circular apses with a radius of almost 4 m, each one preceded by a threshold were the traces of two pillars are still visible.

This environment, together with the adjacent peristyle (*xystus*), was erected in a later stage than the rest of the villa, maybe in Theodosian era [20]. This is evidenced by stylistic and iconological assessments of mosaics and by some findings of recent excavations, as well as by the presence of thicker walls (perhaps made in this way to deal with the structural problems that in the basilica and other settings imposed the subsequent construction of buttresses). This part of the Villa was supposed to host banquets offered by the owner to his guests, who were welcomed in a gorgeous environment suited to the fun and carefree, with mosaics that often refer to the cult of Dionysus. The mosaic of the large central atrium represents 'the twelve labours of Hercules' and develops along five bands parallel to the entrance. In the scene, unfortunately, today very deficient in the west part, the ninth labour - the Girdle of Hippolyte - is missing [10]. In the mosaic bands used as thresholds to the three *exedrae*, the art historian Salvatore Settis recognized a thread around the theme of metamorphosis that makes immortal: Daphne and Cyparissus on the south side, Andromeda and Endymion on the east side, perhaps Ampelos and Kissos on the north side [11]. The mosaic on the left of the *exedra* is the apotheosis of Hercules; the central apse, the only one where there are no gaps and which can still be appreciated in its entirety, shows anguiped giants pierced by the arrows of Hercules. Finally, the right *exedra* displays the Ambrosia nymph rescued by Dionysus from the assault of King Lycurgus.

The metal and glass structure, which now covers this environment, makes the reading of the mosaics extremely difficult, because of the shadows cast on all surfaces. It also causes the greenhouse effect that exposes the mosaic pavements to both high summer heat and low winter temperatures.

The lack of adequate air conditioning system does not, therefore, protect the mosaics from both the risks of a high thermal stress and the consequences of the condensation that arises on the surfaces in conditions, alas, frequently, in the cold months. The shelter also presents several shortcomings, opening access routes to the birds 'living' undisturbed this environment, tainting of guano the mosaics and significantly contributing to their biodeterioration. In addition, the roofing structure and the runway are highly oxidized and the rainwater disposal plant is ineffective because one of the drainpipes is broken and another has been removed.

This precarious situation that has continued for several years, now strongly contrasts with the overall state of conservation of the site. Although lacking in a maintenance program which still needs to be approved due to inexplicable bureaucratic reasons (it has to be remembered that the site is in the UNESCO World Heritage List since 1997 and subjected to a strict management plan), the Villa seems having largely benefited from the new roofing systems. Despite the still ongoing controversy on the overall concept of the architectural project, it has allowed, to date, a better preservation of the mosaic decorations and a more user-friendly fruition.

Conversely, in the triclinium, although restored in 2007 there has been a clear deterioration of the mosaics, which has sought the opening of new investigations (Fig. 3). These have been studied in accordance with a clear desire for simplification of the monitoring activities aimed at prevention of decay's phenomena, also sustainable from the economic point of view.

Fig. 3. Major vulnerabilities on the *triclinium*.

The goal of the experiment is not to confirm the ineffectiveness of a shelter, already clearly compromised by tampering made during the years and by the total absence of maintenance. It rather aims at contributing to the formulation of simple procedures for early detection of degradation that could become part of specific protocols for preventive and planned conservation of the whole complex.

4   Mosaics Monitoring Activities Through 3D Survey and Thermoygrometric Analysis

The conservation of a delicate heritage as floor mosaics are, especially when preserved on site, requires regular maintenance to reduce the impact of destructive environmental forces. Maintenance consists of a series of operations that includes a preliminary study, pre-consolidation work, and periodic inspections followed, if needed, by planned interventions to protect and stabilize it. Control activities cannot be occasional and episodic but must be done in a methodical and structured manner. They begin with collecting data about the mosaic, its condition, and previous interventions.

The metric survey and diagnostic analysis, if regularly taken, are powerful tools for checking goods state. The survey on the spatial surface of *tessellatum*, in order to identify the changes in the geometry (new depressions, punctual elevations or areas where the tiles rotate moving away), offers insight into the variation that has suffered over the centuries compared to a presumed initial arrangement. It also can help in attesting the existence of any ongoing action, responsible for alignment's changes.

However, the diagnostic analysis is able to return an overall picture of the geophysical situation of substratum (presence and level of groundwater, soil's imbibition, etc.) and the microclimate just above the decorated squares (temperature, relative and absolute humidity) that can help in understanding the causes of degenerative phenomena in place. Actually, the *tesserae* can break away because of the mechanical actions generated by the movement of the mantle or even for physical and chemical reasons (the presence of water and/or high-temperature excursions) which attack the mortar binders.

The Metric Survey and Diagnostic Tests (Microclimate and IR Analysis). The analytical investigations carried out through metric, material, and colorimetric observation, are able to provide clear guidance on both structural instabilities underway and the progression/regression of degradation phenomena over time. The close range acquisitions - terrestrial 3D laser scanning and photogrammetric 3D image-based reconstruction - allow accurate and not expensive measurements, both in terms of cost and time. The two technologies are suitable for iterative activities, thanks to their flexibility, speed, and automation. The 3D laser scanning, in particular, is able to return in an expeditious manner and in the form of a point clouds a very accurate three-dimensional model. On the other hand, the photogrammetry allows creating a more simplified digital artefact but with a very high colour rendering. The two techniques, if integrated, can deliver a result characterised by the metric precision granted by the optically active sensors and the high detail of the colour information instead possible with passive optical sensors. In addition, compared to other traditional systems for precise monitoring, they are non-contact measurement instruments that do not require targets anchored with adhesives and/or silicone materials, whose application and removal could damage mosaics. The surveys planning, in fact, founded on dense acquisitions at close range from the pavement, allows an appropriate resolution, which can ensure the virtual reconstruction of the individual tiles [9, 21]. The use of a normal equipment typically allows obtaining a polygon model with a distance between each vertex of 4–5 mm to which is projected a texture with an interval between two sequential pixels of less than 1–2 mm.

With this in mind, the *triclinium* was the subject of a number of survey campaigns that have been programmed, initially, on an annual basis: the first was undertaken in July 2015, the second in June 2016. The acquisitions were executed from 15 stations (the same for each survey campaign, 3 stations on the *lacunae* and 12 along the perimeter of the walkway). They allowed obtaining, in addition to the plans at various altitudes and sections/elevations, the mapping of geometric discontinuities of the surface and height variations, with respect to a horizontal plane taken as the reference. The final model has been produced thanks to the overrun, on the geometry acquired with 3D laser scanning, of a single high-resolution photomapping, the result of digital photogrammetry activities. In both tests, shots were performed in the early morning, in diffuse light conditions (to avoid the projection of the metal roof's shadows on the mosaic surfaces).

The processing phase has enabled the creation of models with common checkpoints, orthographic projections, sections and mapping of the anomalies with the indication of levels and the tracking of the contour lines. An open and flexible planning marked these activities, as considered essential to compare data acquired at different times, and frame them into a single global coordinate system, independent from the tools and the methods adopted. Different formats, in fact, must be able to be 'read' by various operating systems and software as well as to allow a suitable data compression to reduce storage space and to be consulted/managed online also by remote devices.

The comparison between the two models, geo-referenced into a single global system based on 4 marked summits on the walls (which supposedly will remain unvaried over the years) has permitted to ascertain the differences between relative movements of the mosaic in the time elapsed between the two experiences. The anomalies have been represented by the map of the relative deviations, considering only major differences of ± 0.5 mm, as related to an effective geometric alteration and not the 'disorders' due to the digital noise. The diagrams highlighted some punctual areas, with maximum values of ± 4–5 cm, showing a detachment of the *tesserae* and the consequent creation of new gaps. Given the existence of a relatively rapid progression of the lifting phenomena, as agreed with Villa's management authorities, the operations will be repeated every four months in the future. Following the replacement of the current shelter with the new one, it would be also possible to check the eventual improvement of the mosaic conditions that now requires preservation actions that cannot be anymore delayed. The analyses of the geometry and of the discontinuities have allowed obtaining the framework of decay actions in place but nothing says about the causes. It is an analysis on the surface depicting the status of the mosaics but which provides no information on possible reasons. The metric survey was then integrated with a microclimate monitoring and the study of the physical and mechanical characteristics of the soil conducted by thermographic surveys. The implemented diagnostic activities took into due consideration previous analyses, which have allowed knowing the maximum environmental excursions, both daily and seasonally, while omitting an important factor: the ground temperature [17, 22, 23].

The current shelter of the *triclinium*, in fact, does not prevent the mosaics are directly affected by sunlight and this determines high temperatures on the surface, as revealed by these tests, of about 15°–20 °C higher than that of air. Measurements were performed by placing the sensor - the first time at sunrise and again in the mid-afternoon - in

12 points at about 30–50 cm above the floor. Data were then processed by a gridding and contouring software (for thermal maps and humidity distribution production) and then superimposed to the orthographic projection. The comparison between ground temperature values and the analysis of geometric deformations allowed verifying that the most damage corresponds to thermal singularities. In detail, the campaign conducted in the early hours of the morning showed that colder areas - due to increased walls imbibition - are placed near the corners between the central and the two lateral apses. Actually, on the left, masonry borders with a damp embankment (as evidenced by the spontaneous and lush flora that covers it), while on the right side, there is a rain gutter and a manhole, alas, both badly damaged. The distribution maps of the temperatures measured at the hottest times, however, have led to the conclusion that because of the absence of shielding in the entrance, the solar radiation, especially in the area close to the peristyle, causes a strong surface's heating, which extends along the longitudinal axis until the central apse. This is, in fact, the most damaged portion of mosaic, even because of the smaller resistance and elasticity of the mortar due to strong environmental changes. The passive thermography confirmed the assumptions of the microclimate monitoring and completed surveys in areas at risk. They have given clear indications about the *tesserae* detachments, gaps and/or the presence of underground water [9]. Cold areas in the zones where the geometric analysis had highlighted swellings, in fact, show the presence of air between the backing and the *tesserae*'s layer. A dangerous situation that, if not quickly and properly addressed, will accelerate the mosaics detachment (Figs. 4 and 5).

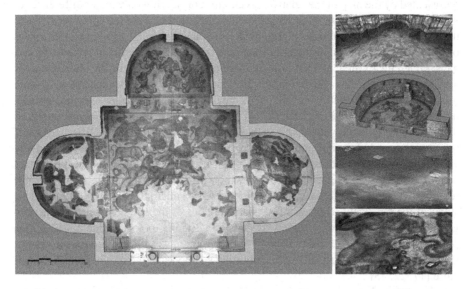

Fig. 4. Metric survey: 3D rendering model and orthographic projection (survey 2015).

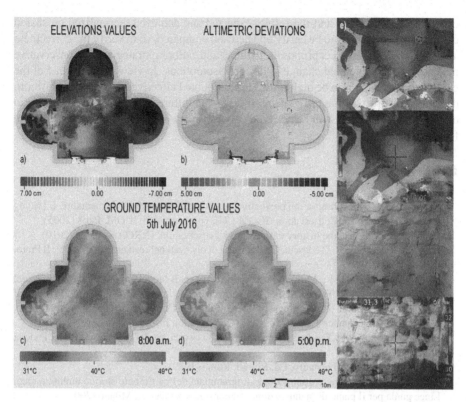

Fig. 5. Comparison between (a) elevations values and (b) altimetric deviations resulted from the surveys of 2015 and 2016; (c) and (d) mapping of the ground temperature and (e) IR analysis.

5   Conclusions

The activities carried out on the *triclinium* of the Villa del Casale in Piazza Armerina intend to provide a quick and low-cost methodology for the planned and preventive checking of the mosaics preserved *in situ*. Certainly, only monitoring does not guarantee the goods maintenance but can facilitate conservation status diagnosis thanks to the structured recording of the knowledge acquired over time. It is the first step in a preparatory process towards prevention practices to implement before reaching a limit situation. Diagnostic analyses conducted with light and relatively not too much expensive instruments are suitable to be repeated at regular intervals, providing an updated overview of the health status of the mosaics, useful to promptly direct any further investigations and therefore to make the right intervention. This will avoid incurring in superficial and hasty assessments and then in designing wrong solutions.

This procedure integrates the first critical analysis on the mosaics in its environment with surveying - used in an innovative way - and diagnostics technologies. It develops a codified path having specific timelines related to the intensities and dynamics of examined objects and factors at play. The acquired data will then converge in a database of the methods adopted and the results expected and achieved, normalized on shared computerized language, to be easily updated and compared, so to verify the correctness and effectiveness of project proposals, to direct and calibrate strategies and conservative methods and any eventual change in design assumptions. In view of the spread of the experimental data, it is to be highlighted the undoubted effectiveness of a web platform, developed by diversifying the contents access from different users. The open-access to diagnostic data acquired will be reserved only for specialists, so becoming a useful tool for the site management[1].

References

1. De Guichen, G.: La conservation préventive: un changement profond de mentalité. In: Study series. Committee for Conservation (ICOM-CC), vol. 1, pp. 4–5. ICOM, Paris (2005)
2. Lambert, S.: Italy and the history of preventive conservation. CeROAr **6**, 1–15 (2010)
3. Fiori, C., Riccobene, R., Tedeschi, C.: Tecniche di distacco nel restauro dei mosaici. Il Prato, Padova (2008)
4. De Guichen, G., Nardi, R.: Mosaic conservation: fifty years of modern practice. In: Ben Abed, A., Demas, M., Roby, T. (eds.) Lessons Learned: Reflecting on the Theory and Practice of Mosaic Conservation, Proceedings of the 9th ICCM Conference, Hammamet, Tunisia, November 29–December 3, pp. 9–14. Getty Conservation Institute, Los Angeles (2008)
5. Fiori, C., Vandini, M.: Teoria e tecniche per la conservazione del mosaico. Il Prato, Padova (2002)
6. Basile, G.: Che cos'è il restauro, Ed. Riuniti, Roma (1989)
7. Della Torre, S. (ed.): La conservazione programmata del patrimonio storico architettonico. Linee guida per il piano di manutenzione e il consuntivo. Guerini, Milano (2003)
8. Brandi, C.: Archeologia Siciliana. Bollettino dell'ICR 27–28, 93–100 (1956)
9. Michaelides D. (ed.): La conservazione. Uno strumento di conoscenza. In: 10a Conferenza del comitato Internazionale per la Conservazione dei Mosaici (ICCM), Palermo, 20–26 October 2008. Regione Siciliana, Palermo (2014)
10. Gentili, G.V.: La villa romana di Piazza Armerina. Palazzo Erculio, Osimo (1999)
11. Settis, S.: Per l'interpretazione di Piazza Armerina. In: Mélanges de l'Ecole française de Rome, Antiquité, vol. 87, no. 2, pp. 873–994 (1975)
12. Kähler, H.: Die Villa des Maxentius bei Piazza Armerina (Monumenta Artis Romanae xii). G. Mann Verlag, Berlin (1973)
13. Vitale, M.R.: Un progetto "stratificato". Pensieri e azioni per la tutela, il restauro e la protezione della Villa romana del Casale di Piazza Armerina. In: Nigrelli, F.C., Vitale, M.R. (eds.) Piazza Armerina. Dalla villa al parco. Studi e ricerche sulla villa romana del casale e sul fiume Gela. Biblioteca del Cenide, Villa S. Giovanni, pp. 97–161 (2010)
14. Stanley-Price, N.: The Roman Villa at Piazza Armerina. In: de la Torre, M. (ed.) The Conservation of Archaeological Sites in the Mediterranean Region, Los Angeles, pp. 65–84 (1997)

---

[1] A. Versaci and A. Cardaci who shared methodological principles and finalities coordinated this research. In detail, paragraphs 1 and 2 were developed by A. Versaci, 3 by L.R. Fauzia, 4 and 5 by A. Cardaci. Authors are very grateful to arch. Rosa Oliva, former director of the Villa Romana del Casale Regional Museum for her trust in them and for her kind and precious cooperation.

15. Oteri, M.A.: «a copertura l'azzurra volta del cielo». Il progetto di Piero Gazzola per la conservazione a rudere della chiesa di S. Maria degli Alemanni a Messina (1940–41). Quaderni del dipartimento patrimonio architettonico e urbanistico, 37–40, 223–230 (2010)

16. Scognamiglio, M.: Emergency intervention on flooded mosaic at Piazza Armerina. Newslett. Int. Committee Conserv. Mosaics **9**, 17–18 (1992)

17. Meli, G. (ed.): Progetto di recupero e conservazione della Villa Romana del Casale di Piazza Armerina. I Quaderni di Palazzo Montalbo, vol. 12. Regione Siciliana, Palermo (2007)

18. Vivio, B.A.: Franco Minissi. Musei e restauri. La trasparenza come valore. Gangemi, Roma (1991)

19. Ranellucci, S.: Conservazione e musealizzazione nei siti archeologici. Gangemi, Roma (2012)

20. Pensabene, P.: I mosaici della villa romana del Casale: distribuzione, programmi iconografici, maestranze. In: Lentini, M.C. (ed.) Mosaici Mediterranei, pp. 87–116. Paruzzo, Caltanissetta (2009)

21. Inglese, C.: Il rilievo integrato dei mosaici pavimentali nelle ville romane di Terme Vigliatore e di piazza della Vittoria a Siracusa. Disegnare idee immagini **44**, 80–91 (2012)

22. Bernardi, A.: Microclimate inside cultural heritage buildings. Il prato, Padova (2008)

23. Lucchi, E., Pracchi, V. (eds.): Efficienza energetica e patrimonio costruito. La sfida del miglioramento delle prestazioni nell'edilizia storica. Maggioli Editore, Milano (2013)

Full Paper: Visualisation, VR and AR Methods and Applications

A Mobile, AR Inside-Out Positional Tracking Algorithm, (MARIOPOT), Suitable for Modern, Affordable Cardboard-Style VR HMDs

Paul Zikas[1,2(✉)], Vasileios Bachlitzanakis[1,2], Margarita Papaefthymiou[1,2], and George Papagiannakis[1,2]

[1] Foundation for Research and Technology Hellas, Heraklion, Greece
{mpapae02,papagian}@ics.forth.gr
[2] University of Crete, Heraklion, Greece
{zikas,csd3058}@csd.uoc.gr

Abstract. Smartphone devices constitute a low-cost, mainstream and easy to use h/w for VR rendering and main component for modern, mobile VR Head-Mounted-Displays (HMDs). They support rotational tracking from on board sensors to manage orientation changes, via their Inertial Measurement Units (IMUs), but they lack positional tracking to reflect head translational movements, a key feature that modern, desktop VR HMDs nowadays provide out-of-the-box. Taking advantage of the RGB camera sensor that each modern mobile device is equipped, we describe a novel combination of inside-out AR tracking algorithms based on both marker and markerless tracking systems to provide the missing positional tracking for mobile HMDs. We employed this system as an affordable, low-cost VR visualization h/w and s/w method, for heritage professionals to employ it for VR archeological sites and Cultural Heritage related monuments interactive walk-throughs. We also compared our results with a recent holographic AR headset (Meta AR-glasses) that supports gesture recognition and interaction with the virtual objects via its RGB-D camera sensor and integrated IMU.

Keywords: Mixed reality · Positional tracking · Monument visualization · Mobile VR · Marker and markerless tracking

1 Introduction

Most of Head Mount Displays (HMDs) support the basic three Degrees Of Freedom (DOF) that includes roll, pitch and yaw. The calculation of those can be achieved by onboard Inertial Measurement Unit (IMU) sensors which determine the orientation of the camera in space. However, in order to track positional movements, we need an additional external point of reference. This is usually implemented only in desktop VR HMDs, with the use of a camera placed in the external environment (outside–in tracking) or on-top or inside the HMD (inside-out tracking).

Positional tracking is the ability to determine the absolute position of the user's HMD within a three-dimensional space. By incorporating this feature into a VR headset we

© Springer International Publishing AG 2016
M. Ioannides et al. (Eds.): EuroMed 2016, Part I, LNCS 10058, pp. 257–268, 2016.
DOI: 10.1007/978-3-319-48496-9_21

can represent these missing three more DOF in a total of 6. Originally Most HMDs could track only head rotation, providing 3 DOF (e.g. Oculus DK1). The updated Oculus Rift DK2 and current CV1 has an outside-in system for positional tracking with an external camera placed on top of the monitor to track the position of the headset. Other commercial HMDs follow similar tracking approaches. Studies showed [14] that positional tracking reduces the motion sickness these HMDs suffer as the orientation of the virtual world is very similar to the real one. However, all current desktop-VR HMDs need to be connected by cable to a computer. In contrast, smartphones provide a mainstream and easy to use mobile VR platform but they lack positional tracking. Visual Markers seems ideal for such low cost, mobile systems [16] that need a distinct visual sing to determine a static position from camera. By placing a marker in front of our desk we are simply define a static point in the real world in order to collect information about the relative position of the marker and our camera. Although markers are easy to use it is not very convenient to attach a marker everywhere we need positional tracking features. To overcome this limitation, we can use a markerless, SLAM-based AR tracking system. The main principles remain the same as we have to scan the environment to track visual features and extract a 3D map of the surroundings. Later we will use this mapping as a 3D marker to calculate the position of the camera like before.

For the above reasons we introduce two different ways of positional tracking with both marker and markerless implementations. For the needs of this project we developed a virtual reality navigation in the Palace of Knossos. User can navigate his way through the archeological site by rotating his head and leaning back and forwards or left and right as positional tracking is supported. To the best of our knowledge this is the first time in bibliography that AR inside-out positional tracking enhance conventional IMU sensor tracking in mobile VR.

In the following sections we present MARIOPOT for both marker and markerless implementations. In more detail, in Sect. 2 we describe the previous work in the area indicating AR and VR applications which appeared useful. Afterwards (Sect. 3) we fully describe MARIOPOT for both approaches (marker and markerless) by presenting the methodology, the needed calculations and the used matrixes. The next two paragraphs describe both the marker and markerless implementation of our application by pointing out the differences in each approach. In Sect. 6 we compare our results with Meta AR-glasses using marker based positional tracking with and gesture based interaction to handle and examine the archeological site of Knossos. Finally, we present the conclusions of our work and the future work-research that can be done.

2   Previous Work

When reconstructing a digital model of an archeological site it needs to be as accurate as possible [1] to improve the user experience (UX). For this reason, the model of Knossos we used is a realistic representation of the Palace as it stands today [11]. In recent years VR approaches for educational purposes have introduced a didactic potential in the area of cultural heritage. As [3] states, there are various VR systems available for cultural heritage purposes to enhance the interest of the general public. The benefit of an immersive and interactive simulation imparts knowledge and further motivation for great interest and research in the area of cultural heritage.

Both marker and markerless tracking intensify the basic features of augmented reality applications. [2] presents an AR application with markerless tracking about a quiz based on a museum visit. Another notable approach was done in [10] where a markerless system with automatically recover from features loss, runs an AR application for the maintenance of a car's engine. A robust authoring of life-sized AR characters for mobile devices was presented in [12], where a fast pipeline based on Metaio was used to populate AR scenes. The work featured an easy to use method for rendering AR characters with a novel pipeline in under one-minute process. The tracking of the area was done beforehand with Metaio to export a 3D mapping of the scene that will be later used for the character's authoring. The augmented characters were able to perform various animations, gestures and speech with the use of SmartBody library. This SLAM tracking method allows the augmentation of any indoors or outdoors scene capable of generate a decent number of features that will export the 3D map.

The importance of an easy to use AR mobile tracking system is emphasized in [7]. Daniel Wagner et al. present an accurate 6DOF pose tracking system that tracks conventional markers to render augmented content. Since most mobile devices have a build in camera they provide a complete tracking platform able to manage marker based tracking with the least effort. There is also an interesting apposition of the performance each mobile device had after a series of tests, providing a more technical view of the research. Moreover, [13] proposed a robust tracking system to determine the position of a mobile device in space using the build-in GPS sensor. A careful study on the energy consumption of different GPS based techniques is presented in parallel with their accuracy and efficiency. Mobile devices have limited power supplies requiring such systems to tackle this issue and manage the energy consumption to the point they reduce their impact on it.

In this work we have used the open source OpenGL Geometric Application (glGA) framework [8] implemented for IOS mobile devices. More specifically, glGA framework is a shader based computer graphics framework supported by desktops and mobile devices. The architectural structure of glGA provides the basic functionalities of OpenGL applications like loading and rendering both static and rigged 3D meshes, compiling and loading shaders, load textures and play animations.

3   Our Mobile, AR Inside-Out Positional Tracking (MARIOPOT) Algorithm

For the complete 6 DOF movement we need two main components: (1) The rotation of our device to determine the orientation of HMD in space and (2) its position to compute the translation in the digital scene. In our application we integrate the basic functionalities of cardboard SDK to get the rotation values as reflected from the orientation sensors. These values appear as a 3×3 matrix that from which we constructed the final view matrix of our application. Except from the rotations we also need the camera's translation. This is the reason we used a marker to provide the translation values. The position of the camera is a vector with three elements that defines the translation of the camera in all three axes.

From the extraction of these two components we have to construct the view matrix of the application. To make the transformations work properly we should not apply the matrix directly to our object as this will cause malfunctions in the visualization process, especially when the marker is no longer in sight. We have to construct a custom LookAt matrix from the extracted values as we need to rotate the world from the point of camera and not from the position of Knossos. By doing this we eliminate an issue that positional tracking brings about when the camera is changing position. We have to take in consideration the position of the camera in every frame as we always want to rotate the scene according to this specific point.

Below there is a brief explanation of the needed calculations to export the final view matrix.

Camera's Position. The position of the mobile device we are using can be represented as a three-dimensional vector. In both cases (marker and markerless) we extract the positional vector from the computed model matrices OpenCV and Metaio provide, saving only the last column of the matrix which holds the camera's position.

For the Marker implementation we used the detection mechanism [6] proposed to get the transformation values. After we calculate the marker's position we use the positional values to generate the application's Model Matrix as seen below.

```
m_transformations = markDetect->getTransformations();
//getTransformation() implemented in [6]

for (size_t i=0; i<m_transformations.size(); i++){
  const Transformation& t = m_transformations[i];
  Matrix44 glMatrix = transformation.getMat44();
  glm::mat4 initial = glm::make_mat4(glMatrix.data);
  MarkerMatrix[3][1]=initial[3][0]/initial[3][2];
  MarkerMatrix[3][0]=initial[3][1]/initial[3][2];
  MarkerMatrix[3][2]=initial[3][2];
  //For scaling we divide by the z transformation

}
```

The Markerless approach differentiate on the calculation of positional values made by Metaio. The code below shows the construction of the transformation matrix in each frame.

```
void MainSystem::update() {
    metaioSDK->requestCameraImage();
    metaioSDK->render();
    TrackingValues tr = metaioSDK->getTrackingValues(1);
    //If tracking quality is sufficient
    if (metaioSDKReady && (tr.quality > 0)){
        float modelMatrix2[16];
        metaioSDK->getTrackingValues(1, m2, false, true);
        float metaioMat[16];
        metaioSDK->getProjectionMatrix(metaioMat, true);
        mat4 projectionMatrix = make_mat4(metaioMat);
        modelMatrix = make_mat4(m2);
        //modelMatrix contains the transformations needed
    }

}
```

Camera's Rotation. The next step is to calculate the orientation of our mobile device. For both implementations we used CardboardSDK to extract the desired rotational values. The SDK provides build-in functions to get the head matrix of cardboard that represents the orientation of our device.

```
const GLKMatrix4 head_from_start_matrix = [headTransform
headPoseInStartSpace];
```

From the rotational matrix we have to compute three vectors that will constitute the orientation of our camera in all three axes. In order to create a functional camera matrix, we also need to determine the eye position which describes the position of our camera in virtual space. The eye position is defined from the rotational values and the position of our camera as follows.

$$eye_x = -dot(xaxis, position)$$
$$eye_y = -dot(yaxis, position)$$
$$eye_z = -dot(zaxis, position)$$

Final Matrix. The final LookAt matrix is computed by combining the above vectors of rotational and positional values. Our custom LookAt matrix will be used to compute the final view matrix of our application. It is important to notice that we have to take care of the matrix order while working with matrices from different systems or SDKs as the default order for OpenGL is column-major whereas Cardboard represents matrices in row-major order (Fig. 1).

However, there is a major issue with inside-out tracking when combining rotational tracking from cardboard and positional tracking using marker of markerless implementation. When we rotate the camera of our device we have two data inputs: (1) Cardboard SDK calculates the change of mobile's orientation. (2) From the point of marker it seems the model has changed position. This not accurate as we have a conflict between these

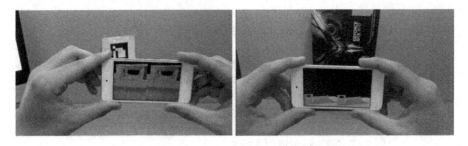

Fig. 1. Positional tracking in both marker and markerless implementation.

two data streams. Only if we use the marker for both rotational and positional tracking the visualization seems correct. To make things more clear, if we keep our device static and rotate it to the left while keeping contact with the marker, our virtual world will simultaneously rotate to the right (from Cardboard) and translate to the right (from marker) as from the camera's feedback the marker seems to move also to right. This is incorrect as we want our world to remain static but the camera will catch the marker moving to right and change the position of our virtual camera too. To reduce this effect we have to separate the two movements (rotation and translation) for both marker and markerless implementation. We provide a demonstration of this implementation in the next section (Fig. 2).

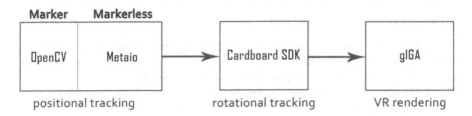

Fig. 2. The architectural diagram of our application

4   AR Positional Tracking with Markers

In order to determine the position of the camera we need to define a reference point in space. Marker based tracking is an efficient, low cost and easy to use method to achieve this result. To detect possible markers, we need to enable the camera of our mobile device and collect the data from live image streaming. Since every mobile device has an onboard camera there is no need for an additional sensor or active tracker to determine the position of the device. We used OpenCV image recognition patterns [6] to compute the position of our maker [9]. The detection of markers requires a pipeline of image processing that begins with the definition of existing candidates and finishes with the determination of the actual markers. The vector extracted from this method containing the positions in three-dimensional space will set the camera's translation in our virtual scene (Fig. 3).

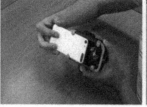

Fig. 3. Setting the marker and our HMD for marker based positional tracking

Marker based tracking has the limitation of a reference point that always need to be in camera's sight. If the marker is no longer in contact with camera the mobile device will stop calculating its position in the virtual scene as there will be no point of reference in the real world. The small field of view most mobile phones have will cause even more marker losses after an amount of rotation or translation. In our case, when the marker is out of reach of camera, the rotational tracking is applied to the last known position of the mobile device. This is achieved by saving the position we lost track with the marker and continue calculate the orientation values from the cardboard SDK. This implementation provides a smooth rotation even if the marker is not in sight and in the situation of the marker loss, the application continues to be functional with rotational tracking. When the camera tracks again the marker, we start computing again the transformation values and the positional tracking is enabled from the new position.

As mentioned before, we have to separate the positional and the rotational tracking to perform rotations without unwanted positional changes by the moving marker. To manage this issue we had to deactivate the marker when our mobile device overcomes a fixed angular threshold. By doing this the virtual scene will stop moving in a static rotation indicated incorrectly from the marker as the marker will no longer affect the position of the camera. We will activate the marker again when the mobile device reaches again lower angles and the computation of positional tracking will start again.

5   Markerless Positional Tracking

Unlike conventional tracking with markers, markerless tracking is definitely more flexible and reliable. To implement markerless AR camera tracking we employed Metaio SDK and the Toolbox. Both applications make markerless tracking an easy task by simplifying the process of capturing features and generating the final view matrix of the visualization. The procedure of markerless tracking is more complicated than placing a marker in front of your desk but it can track large areas (e.g. small rooms) providing user with more space to move around. With the markerless approach we have the opportunity to leave our desk to walk freely in a room and still receiving positional feedback from the 3D mapping we tracked (Fig. 4).

Fig. 4. The process from capturing features with Toolbox to markerless positional tracking.

To implement markerless tracking we need a 3D map of the area we are about to run the application. A 3D map is actually a file that contains the positions of district features in the environment and works the same way as a typical marker. We create this file by using Toolbox application. To make the file we run the application and scan the environment to capture visual features, the more features the better. After saving the 3D map we have to transfer it to the same folder our VR applications runs in order to detect the physical environment as a 3D marker.

Markerless implementation for positional tracking has the same methodology as marker based ones. We have to calculate again the rotational matrix form cardboard SDK and the translation matrix from Metaio SDK. The positional vector extracted from Metaio it is still a three-dimensional vector but the origin of tracking in 3D space is represented by a 3D marker (e.g. a box on top of our desk) and not by a 2D sign as marker based approach does. However, with markerless tracking we have a greater area of possible movements thus we have to scale the translation matrix accordingly to maintain the proportions of real and the virtual world translations. When the camera loses visibility of the features we maintain the last known position of the mobile phone and from there user can perform head rotations without having the ability to move to another position. After features become visible again user can start again moving around the virtual scene.

6   Comparison with Meta AR Glasses

Since we had our first results from the positional tracking we implemented this method with a different HMD that utilizes an RGB-D camera sensor. The main motivation behind this comparison is due to the fact that many forthcoming smartphones will feature such an RGB-D camera as part of their standard configuration h/w and we wanted to be the first to study their use and draw a comparison.

We reproduced our methodology in Meta AR-glasses, a holographic, see-through headset with gesture recognition. Wearing Meta AR-glasses gives user the ability to interact with holographic objects by using basic gestures [5]. Holographic headsets constitute an ideal HMD to experiment with novel AR applications [4]. Meta AR-glasses support rotational tracking from onboard sensors but they lack of positional tracking due to the absence of an external camera. However, we can utilize the embedded marker recognition mechanism to introduce positional tracking functionality (Fig. 5).

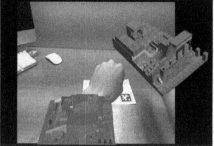

Fig. 5. Interaction using markers and hand gestures.

Meta use markers to attach holograms onto them but we used them in a different way. As mentioned earlier, we need to have a point of reference in the real world to manage the translations in the virtual one. To implement this idea we have to attach our virtual scene to the marker. By doing this we will enable positional tracking for Meta glasses. We need to compare applications with similar content to have more accurate results so for the Meta application we used again the model of Knossos. As indicated in [15] the two technologies have some basic differences in immersion, interaction and in the scale of the digital environment but the tracking mechanism remains the same. The positional tracking was of the same quality as it was implemented with the same principles. In general, by introducing positional tracking is Meta AR-glasses we were able to zoom in and out the palace of Knossos and see the model in more detail than previously when the only way to handle the model was with hand gestures.

While mobile VR applications have the advantage of generating an immersive experience, Meta headset with gesture recognition enhances the interaction between user and the hologram he sees. Interaction in game based applications has great importance as user is no longer an observer, he is able to handle holographic objects with native hand movements. In cultural heritage we can use this feature of Meta AR-glasses to handle and examine known monuments or important buildings from a different perspective.

In order to compare the user experience of Meta glasses and our mobile tracking system, we conducted an experiment to evaluate the use of both technologies. The participants were 7 in total (6 male, 1 female). For the mobile orientation demo participants had to navigate through the palace of Knossos by making head movements. In this way we were able to test if the navigation system was simple and easy to use. Most of the participants performed well as they managed to find their way in the ruins within less than a minute. After a while they were more confident and start to explore the archeological site in detail by zooming at point of great interest (e.g. the Prince with the lilies fresco). However, half of the participants complained about dizziness which was something expected as it takes time to get used to virtual reality. Another think that needs to be mentioned is that most of the participants had problems with the interruption of positional tracking caused by the loss of visual contact with the marker. As was shown by the process this was the most common issue we faced at the experiment.

For Meta AR glasses the participants had to handle a building of the archeological site with the marker provided. In addition to the previous experiment we enhanced the user experience with gesture based interaction to find out if there will be any significant change to the final remarks. We asked the participants to zoom in specific points of the building as well to rotate, translate and scale it with their hands. Most of the participants had a serious problem with gesture handling as they couldn't manage to grab the building correctly. Besides this, the marker based handling of the building was a task that completed successfully from all the participants. About this, there were few complains referring to the limited field of view Meta AR glasses provide as the building was cropped from being too close to the headset leading to the failure of the immersion. As a final remark, the participants were satisfied from the HMD's orientation capabilities that were enhanced with the use of positional marker based tracking.

To conclude, both HMDs perform well in the positional tracking and orientation in general. Our mobile implementation had better results considering the immersion of the archeological site as the participants were in a fully virtual environment unlike Meta glasses. Since we used conventional markers in both methods to provide positional tracking they had very similar results in accuracy and performance. An extra feature we used with Meta headset was the gesture handling they support but we faced poor results as it was difficult for most of our participants to successfully perform the correct gestures for the device to recognize (Fig. 6).

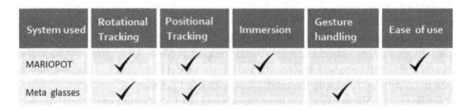

Fig. 6. Comparison table of MARIOPOT and Meta AR glasses.

7   Conclusions and Future Work

In this work we presented a low cost and easy to use implementation of positional tracking for mobile device-based, cardboard-style VR HMDs that are ideal to be used as affordable visualization for cultural heritage professionals and sites. It is the first time in bibliography that such a hybrid orientation system is presented, combining sensor and camera tracking. With the contribution of positional on-top of rotational tracking in mobile VR, we were able to zoom in and out not only to change our orientation but also our translational position in a virtual world and thus appreciate the presented 3D monuments in better detail, with less motion sickness effects. The presented algorithm can improve the visualization of digitized archeological finds (e.g. pottery, frescos, and coins) instead of using conventional software methods. Since the digitization process in Cultural Heritage is used frequently, we have to develop the appropriate tools to make better use of those findings. A VR demonstration of monuments and historical buildings is without a doubt the best way of visualization as the immersion generated from this technology can really make the difference. Mobile AR, inside-out Positional tracking can extend the basic limits of VR and especially when implemented with markerless tracking in room sized areas as user will not only be an observer of the monument but he will actually walk and explore the site on his own. Such technology can be used in museum galleries and expeditions to attract the interest of general public and to inform users about the importance and the benefits of digital preservation.

In the future we aim to replace the Metaio SLAM-based markerless tracking with OpenCV. We are also planning to enhance the visualization of Knossos with gamification elements to constitute a fully interactive experience of the archeological site. Serious game industry expands rapidly over the last years introducing new ways of learning through gaming. Cultural heritage applications can definitely benefit from a more interactive environment that will augment their efficiency.

Acknowledgements. The research leading to these results has received partial funding from the European Union People Programme (FP7- PEOPLE- 2013-ITN) under grant agreement No. 608013 and from the European Union Horizon2020 Programme (H2020-SC6-CULT-COOP-9 – CSA) under grant agreement No. 727107. Special thanks also to ARdictive (www.ardictive.com) and its CEO & founder Nils Huebner for the MetaAR glasses.

References

1. Foni, A., Papagiannakis, G., Magnenat-Thalmann, N.: A taxonomy of visualization strategies for cultural heritage applications. ACM J. Comput. Cult. Heritage **3**(1), 1–21 (2010)
2. Yudiantika, A.R., Sulistyo, S., Hantono, B.S.: The development of mobile augmented reality quiz visualization methods based on markerless tracking for museum learning application. Disampaikan pada seminar "The International Forum on Strategic Technology (IFOST)", June 2015
3. Gaitatzes, A., Christopoulos, D., Roussou, M.: Reviving the past: cultural heritage meets virtual reality. In: Proceedings of the 2001 Conference on Virtual Reality, Archeology, and Cultural Heritage (VAST 2001), pp. 103–110. ACM, New York (2001)
4. Billinghurst, M., Clark, A., Lee, G.: A survey of augmented reality. Found. Trends Hum. Comput. Interact. **8**(1), 1–202 (2015)
5. Billinghurst, M.: Gesture based AR interaction research at the HIT Lab NZ. Presentation (2015)
6. Baggio, D.L., Emami, S., Escrivá, D.M., Ievgen, K., Mahmood, N., Saragih, J., Shilkrot, R.: Mastering OpenCV with Practical Computer Vision Projects
7. Wagner, D., Schmalstieg, D.: ARToolKitPlus for pose tracking on mobile devices. In: Grabner, M., Grabner, H. (eds.) Computer Vision Winter Workshop 2007, St. Lambrecht, Austria, 6–8 February 2007. Graz Technical University (2007)
8. Papagiannakis, G., Papanikolaou, P., Greasidou, E., Trahanias, P.: glGA: an OpenGL geometric application framework for a modern, shader-based computer graphics curriculum. In: Eurographics 2014, pp. 1–8 (2014)
9. Kato, H., Billinghurst, M.: Marker tracking and HMD calibration for a video-based augmented reality conferencing system. In: Proceedings of the IEEE International Workshop on Augmented Reality, pp. 125–133 (1999)

10. Platonov, J., Heibel, H., Meier, P., Grollmann, B.: A mobile markerless AR system for maintenance and repair. In: Proceedings of the 5th IEEE and ACM International Symposium on Mixed and Augmented Reality (ISMAR 2006), pp. 105–108. IEEE Computer Society, Washington, DC (2006)

11. Kateros, S., Georgiou, S., Papaefthymiou, M., Papagiannakis, G., Tsioumas, M.: A comparison of gamified, immersive VR curation methods for enhanced presence and human-computer interaction in digital humanities. Int. J. Heritage Digit. Era 4(2), 221–233 (2015)

12. Papaefthymiou, M., Feng, A., Shapiro, A., Papagiannakis, G.: A fast and robust pipeline for populating mobile AR scenes with gamified virtual characters. In: SIGGRAPH Asia 2015 Mobile Graphics and Interactive Applications (SA 2015). ACM, New York (2015). Article 22, 8 pages

13. Kjærgaard, M.B., Langdal, J., Godsk, T., Toftkjær, T.: EnTracked: energy-efficient robust position tracking for mobile devices. In: Proceedings of the 7th International Conference on Mobile Systems, Applications, and Services (MobiSys 2009), pp. 221–234. ACM, New York (2009)

14. Desai, P. R., Desai, P. N., Ajmera, K. D., Mehta, K.: Int. J. Eng. Trends Technol. (IJETT) 13(4) (2014)

15. Zikas, P., Bachlitzanakis, V., Papaefthymiou, M., Kateros, S., Georgiou, S., Lydatakis, N., Papagiannakis, G.: Mixed reality serious games and gamification for smart education. In: 10th European Conference on Games Based Learning (ECGBL), October 2016

16. Zhang, X., Fronz, S., Navab, N.: Visual marker detection and decoding in AR systems: a comparative study. In: Proceedings of the 1st International Symposium on Mixed and Augmented Reality (ISMAR 2002), p. 97. IEEE Computer Society, Washington, DC (2002)

Virtual and Augmented Reality Tools to Improve the Exploitation of Underwater Archaeological Sites by Diver and Non-diver Tourists

Fabio Bruno[1(✉)], Antonio Lagudi[1], Loris Barbieri[1], Maurizio Muzzupappa[1], Gerardo Ritacco[1], Alessandro Cozza[2], Marco Cozza[2], Raffaele Peluso[2], Marco Lupia[3], and Gianni Cario[3]

[1] Department of Mechanical, Energy and Management Engineering (DIMEG), University of Calabria, Rende, CS, Italy
{f.bruno,antonio.lagudi,loris.barbieri,
muzzupappa,gerardo.ritacco}@unical.it
[2] 3D Research S.r.l., Rende, CS, Italy
{a.cozza,m.cozza,r.peluso}@3dresearch.it
[3] Applicon S.r.l., Rende, CS, Italy
{m.lupia,g.cario}@applicon.it

Abstract. The underwater cultural heritage is an immeasurable archaeological and historical resource with huge, but yet largely unexploited, potentials for the maritime and coastal tourism.

In this regard, in the last years, national and international government authorities are supporting and strengthening research activities and development strategies, plans and policies to realize a more sustainable, responsible and accessible exploitation of the underwater cultural heritage.

To this end, the paper presents the architecture of a new system that, taking advantage of the modern virtual and augmented reality technologies, allows diver and non-diver tourists to make a more engaging and educational experience of the underwater archaeological sites.

This system has been developed and tested in the VISAS project (www.visas-project.eu) that aims to the enhancement of the cultural and tourist offer related to the underwater archaeology through innovation of modes of experience, both on site and remote, of the underwater environments of archaeological interest.

Keywords: Underwater cultural heritage · VR systems · AR systems · Underwater 3D reconstruction

1 Introduction

The underwater cultural heritage (UCH) is an extensive and varied asset with wide potentials for the development, but in return it needs protection, care and investment. These potentials could be exploited in a fruitful and efficient way especially in the tourism sector, which enables high profit margins for an unlimited range of time. But most importantly, in addition to the economic return, the exploitation of the UCH

M. Ioannides et al. (Eds.): EuroMed 2016, Part I, LNCS 10058, pp. 269–280, 2016.
DOI: 10.1007/978-3-319-48496-9_22

provides also an immediate value creation in terms of entertainment and learning experience, for the cultural enrichment of the individual, and of reputation and notoriety of a location, for the local identity that makes a place unique and can direct tourism streams.

The tourism is clearly an important economic activity, especially in many maritime and coastal regions. In fact, every EUR invested in heritage increases economic activity around it by up to 12, on the contrary, heritage destruction decrease the value of its location [1].

Considerable improvements are going on in the UCH field especially thanks to an articulated implementation of the Unesco conventions 1970 (prevention of illicit traffic), 1972 (World Cultural and National Heritage), and 2001 (Underwater Cultural Heritage). In particular, the 2001 Unesco Convention on the Protection of the Underwater Cultural Heritage [2] has represented important achievements in the field of submerged archaeological site safeguarding that have led to the rise of a plethora of innovative methods and tools that cover a wide range of applications [3–8] for this burgeoning sector.

In addition to the work carried out by National Commissions for Unesco other national and international organizations and government bodies are already moving in the same direction to make the underwater archaeological sites' exploitation more sustainable and accessible to large-scale tourism. It is worth to mention the European Commission that has set-up the EU's Blue Growth strategy [9] for the cooperation among research institutes, museums, tourism companies and other stakeholders in order to develop innovative and sustainable solutions and products, with a maximum use of information technology, to boost the tourism in coastal destinations.

In accordance to these recommendations, the paper presents a new system that, taking advantage of the modern virtual and augmented reality technologies, allows diver and non-diver tourists to make a more engaging and educational experience of the underwater archaeological sites. In fact, this system, on the one hand, promotes the diving tourism by improving the divers' experience in the underwater site, and, on the other hand, promotes the induced tourist activity through the development of an innovative virtual tour of the site.

In particular, a virtual reality (VR) tool allows non-diver tourists to live a virtual experience inside the reconstructed 3D model of the underwater archaeological site. The VR tool provides also an interactive navigation within the virtual environment to plan the guided dives. Instead, an augmented reality (AR) tool is intended for diver tourists that visit the underwater site, allowing them to have a virtual guide that provides specific information about the artifacts and the area they are visiting. The AR tool is based on a tablet properly equipped with a waterproof case and an integrated system for acoustic localization and inertial navigation.

This system has been developed and tested in the VISAS project (Virtual and augmented exploitation of Submerged Archaeological Sites - http://www.visas-project.eu) that is a collaborative research project funded by MIUR (Italian Ministry of Education, University and Research); it has started on 1st April 2014 and will end on 30th September 2016.

The VISAS project aims to the development of tools for improving the visitor's experience of underwater archaeological sites by making it more interesting, charming, and effective [10]. The VISAS project architecture is depicted in Fig. 1. The process starts with the acquisition of optical and acoustic data. The first can be carried out by scuba divers or by Remotely Operated underwater Vehicles (ROVs), the second by multibeam sonar system mounted on the bottom of a survey vessel. Downstream of the process, there is the opto-acoustic 3D reconstruction from which the multi-resolution textured 3D models of underwater archaeological sites are generated. These models are stored into a database and made available to the diver and non-diver tourists by means of the VR and AR diving tools.

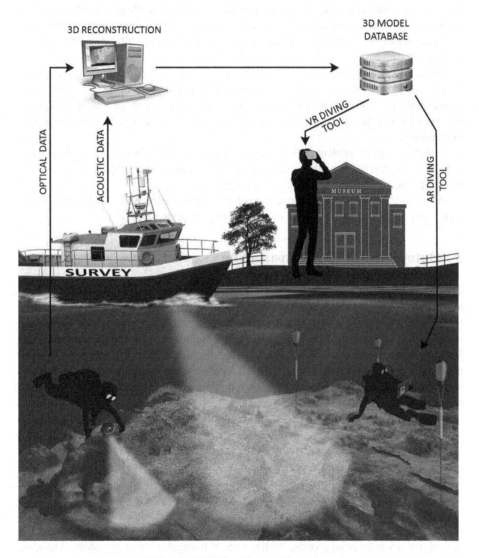

Fig. 1. VISAS project architecture

2   UCH Exploitation by Means of VR and AR Technologies

The virtual reality and augmented reality technologies have demonstrated to ensure a good effectiveness in increasing the value of cultural heritage [11–15], but the possible applications for underwater archaeology have not been sufficiently investigated. The potentialities of these 3D graphics techniques in the cultural heritage exploitation are related to the possibility to de-materialize the heritage itself, so that it can be enjoyed without any constraint given by distance or time, giving also the possibility to live an impressive learning experience with a high emotional impact. These potentialities may be also more important for the exploitation of the underwater cultural and naturalistic heritage, because its accessibility is limited to diver tourists.

For a few years now, various researches are investigating and proposing different frameworks for the reconstruction, collection and visualization of the UCH but these results limit the exploitation to the single underwater archaeological remain [16] or are more oriented to the digitization for scientific purposes [17–21] instead for the tourist exploitation.

This lack is more evident in the case of AR technology, in fact, at the moment there is only a research that proposes the adoption of an underwater tablet but its usage is limited to the geolocation and diver monitoring [22].

As a result, the VR and AR applications for the exploitation of the UCH are still few, with many shortcomings and huge development potentials.

3   Opto-acoustic 3D Reconstruction

The 3D reconstruction of the underwater archaeological site is worth a particular attention because of the long and articulated process. In fact, the creation of a multi-resolution textured 3D model of the underwater archaeological site requires various steps with an integrated adoption of both optical and acoustic techniques [23–26]. In particular, the VISAS project proposes a method to merge the high resolution data acquired through photogrammetric techniques with acoustic microbathymetric maps to obtain a complete representation of the underwater scene and to geo-localize the optical 3D model using the acoustic bathymetric map as a reference.

After a first inspection of the site and a calibration of the optical and acoustic equipment, the photogrammetric acquisition process is performed according to standard aerial photography layouts that consist of overlapping straight lines and also cross lines with oblique poses to minimize the occluded areas.

The acoustic acquisition process is performed thanks to a high frequency multibeam equipment that allows to obtain an acoustic bathymetry of the seabed.

Custom opto-acoustic markers, placed on the seabed and whose number depends by the extension of the site, are used to accurately compute the registration between the optical and acoustic point clouds. While, a set of triangular target are adopted to scale the optical 3D model.

The last steps of the process consist of meshing and texturing the opto-acoustic point cloud of the underwater archaeological site. The meshing step is carried out using a dedicated software, which has the ability to create a mesh by using an efficient multi-resolution algorithm and to perform further refinements of the model by using the point cloud as reference, so that the model reconstruction is performed in a coarse-to-fine fashion.

A technique based on the projection and blending of 2D images on the 3D surface has been adopted in order to place textures on the 3D model. In particular, since the camera poses are known downstream of the optical 3D reconstruction process, the high resolution images are mapped on the portion of the 3D surface of the model representing the archaeo-logical remains. The low-resolution polygonal mesh of the seabed is in turn obtained from the acoustic bathymetry and textured with a tile-based texture mapping approach that just requires to set some sample images of texture tiles instead of a large texture.

4   VR Diving Tool

The VR tool is a virtual diving exhibit that allows non-diver tourists to live a virtual experience and learn both general information and historical-cultural contents related to the specific archaeological site. In particular, thanks to the VR tool, tourists are able to explore the 3D reconstruction of the underwater site and to receive historical and archaeological information about the submerged exhibits and structures of the site, but flora and fauna are also described, with a particular attention on their interaction with the submerged artifacts.

The VR tool can be also used by diver tourists because of its capability to make a detailed planning of the operations and of the itinerary to carry out in the underwater archaeological site. The tool indeed represents a reliable instrument to plan and simulate the tourist itinerary that is performed at a later time in the real submerged environment.

The VR diving tool has been implemented by means of the cross-platform game engine Unity in order to take full advantage of its capability to program software that can be used and communicate on the web. In fact, a web service software represents the key element of the software architecture because it provides the linking between the database and a scene development environment. The development environment is composed of two modules, i.e., an editor and an interaction module. The scene editor module allows to compose the virtual scene by integrating 3D objects and multimedia information stored in the database. The main elements of a virtual scene are: the 3D texturized model of the underwater archaeological site; 3D models of the flora and fauna; the Points of Interest (POI) that contain educational textual, visual and audio information related to a specific underwater area or a specific kind of archaeological artifact. Further-more, depending on the type of the element, other metadata are integrated into the scene, such as the color and luminosity for the lights. Once the scene is created the interaction module is adopted to implement the logics of the virtual scenario defining the physics of the elements that belongs to the scene. Furthermore, it loads from the database the graphical assets of the submerged, terrestrial and aerial environments, such as, refrac-tions, fog, caustics of the particulate, etc.

The interaction module is used also to perform the exploration within the virtual scenario according to the user input get by means of the controller.

From the user's point of view, the VR diving tool presents two different possible embodiments each one characterized by the type of devices, the provided levels of immersion, interaction and presence.

4.1 Semi-immersive VR Environment

The VR tool can involve tourists in a semi-immersive visualization by means of a full HD monitor based on passive 3D technology (Fig. 2). The passive technology has been preferred to the active one because active 3D glasses are expensive and need batteries to work. Furthermore, passive 3D glasses are inexpensive, lighter and more comfortable.

Fig. 2. Tourist engaging with the VR tool in the semi-immersive environment (a). POI's information provided by the VR diving tool (b)

Tourists interact with the system by means of a multi-touch tablet featuring a user interface (UI) that provides all the input functionalities needed to explore the 3D environment and get access to the multimedia data. In particular, as shown in Fig. 2a, the UI provides to the tourist two large command buttons, respectively, to go back and forth and to rotate the camera's point of view. While, on the top left side of the UI, a slider controls the depth of the camera view from the water surface. A set of option buttons, placed in the center of the UI, are dedicated to the dive planning. In particular, the tourist can load or close a path and play, pause, or resume an automatic flight of the planned dive session which is later performed in the real underwater archaeological site. On the top part of the UI a detail disclosure button opens a modal view, depicted in Fig. 2b, containing additional textual, graphical and audio information related to a specific POI.

4.2 Immersive VR Environment

The immersive diving environment is provided by the VR tool to the tourists by means of HMD (head mounted display) technology. The HMD isolates the user from the distractions of the actual physical environment and encompasses the entire field of view, including the peripheral space. The navigation in the virtual environment is performed by the tourist by moving his/her head and interacting with a single wireless handheld controller (Fig. 3). In particular, a HTC Vive [27] has been used to implement the immersive environment.

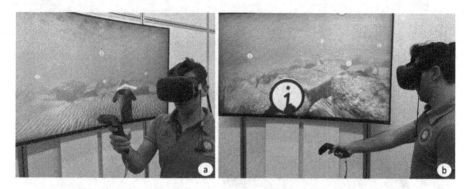

Fig. 3. Tourist engaging with the VR tool in the immersive environment

When the tourist wears the HMD he/she experiences the immersive virtual environment from the scuba diving viewpoint simulating a real diving session. Then the scenario that appears to the tourist, at the beginning of the virtual experience, is above the water surface in the point of immersion. Once he/she dives in the submerged virtual environment, he/she is guided by a directional 3D arrow (Fig. 3a) to the archaeological underwater site. When the tourist arrives to the site the 3D arrow disappears and lets him/her free to interact with the 3D POIs to discover historical and archaeological information (Fig. 3b).

Compared to the semi-immersive environment, which relies on monitors for the visualization, in the immersive environment tourists receive audio contents instead of visual information when interacting with 3D objects and POIs.

5   AR Diving Tool

The AR tool consists in an underwater tablet equipped with an underwater positioning and orientation system that guides the diver tourists during the diving session while providing information about the archaeological artifacts spotted during the visit.

The underwater positioning and orientation system is performed by means of an acoustic modem, integrated to the underwater tablet, which estimate the position of the receiver by computing the distance from at least three fixed transmitters (beacons) placed on the seabed (LBL - Long BaseLine technique) (Fig. 4). In order to improve the accuracy and increase the robustness in case of loss of signal from one or more beacons, the tablet is also equipped with an inertial platform and a depth sensor. The data coming from the various sensors are processed through data fusion and error estimation algorithms.

The tracking system on the tablet sends a query to the beacons and computes the distance from each of them. These data are used by the data fusion algorithm to correct the estimate on the position obtained through the inertial system and the pressure sensor.

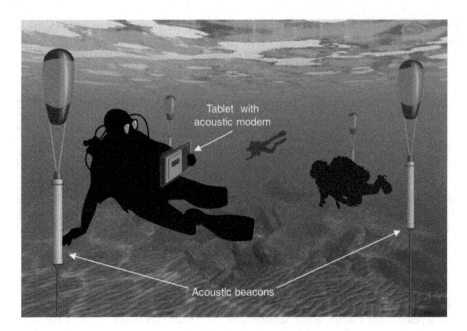

Fig. 4. Augmented diving system architecture

The navigation software receives this information and shows the location of the tablet on a 3D map of the underwater archaeological site.

Each beacon contains an electronic board to drive the piezoelectric transducer. It operates at 25–30 kHz frequency band. The beacon is equipped with a battery pack, which enables up to five hours of use, and with anchor rings used to fix it on the buoy cable. The beacons are positioned in known geographical points using a mooring post and a surface buoy that facilitates their recovery.

The tablet is composed of two major parts: a fully functional underwater touchscreen housing and a waterproof case for the electronics of the tracking system. The two devices are connected using a Bluetooth Low Energy (BLE) interface.

The tablet updates the diver's position on the 3D map at a frequency of 50 Hz. The current position is estimated through an Extended Kalman Filter that uses the distances from each beacon, the depth provided by a pressure sensor, the accelerations along the three axes (x, y, z), and the orientations provided by an inertial platform.

In order to compute the distance between the tablet and a beacon, the simplest way is to compute the time-of-fly of the acoustic wave. To this end, the acoustic modem on the tablet sends a two-way range (TWR) command to the remote beacon and starts an internal timer. When the tablet receives the response message sent by the beacon, the timer is stopped. The position system sends cyclically a TWR to all beacons. The tablet position is calculated within the Kalman filter using a trilateration algorithm.

The user interface (Fig. 5) of the augmented navigation system guides the diver along the selected track inside the archeological site. It has been implemented by means of the cross-platform game engine Unity. Using the tablet position and orientation, the AR tool shows a 3D map representing the environment around the diver, adding useful

Fig. 5. UI of the AR diving tool

information about underwater artifacts and structures. Moreover, some additional data are displayed: system status, battery charge, water temperature, and depth. The diver can also change the view mode or open the camera device to shoot photos that are automatically geo-referenced.

6   Results

The paper has presented an innovative system that fits the Unesco's recommendations for a respectful exploitation of the underwater cultural heritage and represents a concrete and efficient response to the challenge proposed by the European Parliament for a smart, sustainable and inclusive growth of the maritime and coastal tourism.

In particular, this system, developed in the VISAS project, integrates virtual and augmented reality technologies to make more engaging, attractive and educative the exploitation, both inside and outside, of the underwater archaeological sites. In fact, if on one side the AR tool improves the diver tourists' experience in the submerged archaeological site, on the other the VR tool provides to non-diver tourists a 3D virtual tour of the underwater cultural heritage.

The VISAS project will end in September 2016 and the remaining activities are focusing on the experimentation and user studies of the developed tools. The VR diving tool has been showcased at BPER Optimist European Championship 2016, which has been held in Crotone, Italy, on July 16–22, 2016 (Fig. 6a). After exposure to the system, users completed standardized satisfaction questionnaires that confirmed the positive benefits and added value that VR technologies can bring in the exploitation of underwater archaeology sites. About the AR diving tool experimentation activities have been carried out in the underwater archaeological site of Punta Scifo, located in the East coast

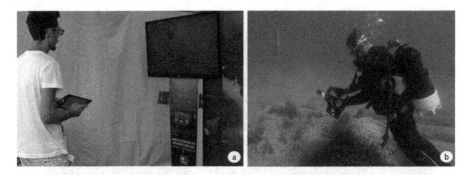

Fig. 6. User interacting with the virtual diving tool (a) and testing the augmented diving tool in the underwater site of Punta Scifo (b)

of Calabria at 10 km far from Crotone, where raw and semi-finished marble products, transported by Roman cargo ships, lay on the seabed at a depth of 7 m (Fig. 6b).

Acknowledgements. The VISAS Project (Ref. Start-Up PAC02L2-00040), has been financed by the MIUR under the PAC Programme. The authors would like to thank the Marine Protected Area of Capo Rizzuto, the Soprintendenza per i Beni culturali e ambientali del Mare della Sicilia for the permission to conduct the experimentation in the sites of Cala Minnola and the Soprintendenza per i Beni Archeologici della Calabria for the site of Punta Scifo.

References

1. Guérin, U.: Underwater cultural heritage and its potentials for sustainable maritime and coastal tourism. UNESCO Convention on the Protection of the Underwater Cultural Heritage (2001)
2. Unesco 2001: Convention on the protection of the underwater cultural heritage, 2 November 2001. http://www.unesco.org
3. Bruno, F., Gallo, A., Barbieri, L., Muzzupappa, M., Ritacco, G., Lagudi, A., La Russa, M.F., Ruffolo, S.A., Crisci, G.M., Ricca, M., Comite, V., Davidde, B., Di Stefano, G., Guida, R.: The CoMAS project: new materials and tools for improving the in-situ documentation, restoration and conservation of underwater archaeological remains. Mar. Technol. Soc. J. **50**(4), 108–118 (2016)
4. Bruno, F., Muzzupappa, M., Gallo, A., Barbieri, L., Spadafora, F., Galati, D., Petriaggi, B.D., Petriaggi, R.: Electromechanical devices for supporting the restoration of underwater archaeological artefacts. In: Proceedings of IEEE/MTS OCEANS 2015 Conference, Genova (Italy), 18–21 May 2015
5. Bruno, F., Muzzupappa, M., Lagudi, A., Gallo, A., Spadafora, F., Ritacco, G., Angilica, A., Barbieri, L., Di Stefano, G., Guida, R., Di Lecce, N., Saviozzi, G., Laschi, C.: A ROV for supporting the planned maintenance in underwater archaeological sites. In: Proceedings of IEEE/MTS OCEANS 2015 Conference, Genova (Italy), 18–21 May 2015
6. Skarlatos, D., Demestiha, S., Kiparissi, S.: An 'open' method for 3D modelling and mapping in underwater archaeological sites. Int. J. Heritage Digit. Era **1**(1), 1–24 (2012)
7. Pearson, C.: Conservation of Marine Archaeological Objects. Elsevier, Burlington (2014)
8. Davidde, B.: Underwater archaeological parks: a new perspective and a challenge for conservation—the Italian panorama. Int. J. Nautical Archaeol. **31**(1), 83–88 (2002)

9. European Commission Directorate General for Maritime Affairs and Fisheries: A European Strategy for more Growth and Jobs in Coastal and Maritime Tourism. Communication from the commission to the European Parliament, the council, the European and economic and social committee and the committee of the regions, 20 February 2014

10. Bruno, F., Lagudi, A., Muzzupappa, M., Lupia, M., Cario, G., Barbieri, L., Passaro, S., Saggiomo, R.: Project VISAS – virtual and augmented exploitation of Submerged Archaeological Sites: overview and first results. Mar. Technol. Soc. (MTS) J. **50**(4), 119–129 (2016)

11. Barceló, J.A, Forte, M., Sanders D.H.: Virtual Reality in Archaeology. BAR International Series, vol. 843. Archeopress, Oxford (2000). Edited by Sanders, D.H., Forte, M.

12. Pavlidis, G., Koutsoudis, A., Arnaoutoglou, F., Tsioukas, V., Chamzas, C.: Methods for 3D digitization of cultural heritage. J. Cult. Heritage **8**(1), 93–98 (2007)

13. Bruno, F., Bruno, S., De Sensi, G., Luchi, M.L., Mancuso, S., Muzzupappa, M.: From 3D reconstruction to virtual reality: a complete methodology for digital archaeological exhibition. J. Cult. Heritage **11**(1), 42–49 (2010)

14. Barbieri, L., Bruno, F., Mollo, F., Muzzupappa, M.: User-centered design of a Virtual Museum system: a case study. In: Eynard, B., Nigrelli, V., Oliveri, S,M., Peris-Fajarnes. G., Rizzuti, S. (eds.) Advances on Mechanics, Design Engineering and Manufacturing. LNME, pp. 155–165. Springer, Heidelberg (2017). doi:10.1007/978-3-319-45781-9_17

15. Almeida, L.: Archeoguide: an augmented reality guide for archaeological sites. IEEE Comput. Graph. Appl. (2002)

16. Varinlioğlu, G.: Data collection for a virtual museum on the underwater survey at Kaş, Turkey. Int. J. Nautical Archaeol. **40**(1), 182–188 (2011)

17. Chapman, P., Conte, G., Drap, P., Gambogi, P., Gauch, F., Hanke, K., Richards, J.: Venus, virtual exploration of underwater sites. In: Proceeding of Joint Event CIPA/VAST/EG/Euro-Med (2006)

18. Haydar, M., Roussel, D., Maïdi, M., Otmane, S., Mallem, M.: Virtual and augmented reality for cultural computing and heritage: a case study of virtual exploration of underwater archaeological site. Virtual Reality **15**(4), 311–327 (2011)

19. Chapman, P., Roussel, D., Drap, P., Haydar, M.: Virtual exploration of underwater archaeological sites: visualization and interaction in mixed reality environments, pp. 141–148 (2008)

20. Gallo, A., Angilica, A., Bianco, G., De Filippo, F., Muzzupappa, M., Davidde, B., Bruno, F.: 3D reconstruction and virtual exploration of submerged structures: a case study in the underwater archaeological site of Baia (Italy). In: The 13th International Symposium on Virtual Reality, Archaeology and Cultural Heritage VAST (2012)

21. Katsouri, I., Tzanavari, A., Herakleous, K., Poullis, C.: Visualizing and assessing hypotheses for marine archaeology in a VR CAVE environment. J. Comput. Cult. Heritage (JOCCH) **8**(2), 10 (2015)

22. Leinikki, J., Kanerva, J., Panu Oulasvirta, P., Syvärant, J.: Personal underwater tablets bring new possibilities to data collection, communication, geolocation and diver monitoring. In: Lang, M.A., Sayer, M.D.J. (eds.) Proceedings of the 2013 AAUS/ESDP Curaçao Joint International Scientific Diving Symposium, Curaçao, 24–27 October 2013, pp. 163–166. American Academy of Underwater Sciences, Dauphin Island (2013)

23. Lagudi, A., Bianco, G., Muzzupappa, M., Bruno, F.: An alignment method for the integration of underwater 3D data captured by a stereovision system and an acoustic camera. Sensors **16**(4), 536 (2016)

24. Bruno, F., Lagudi, A., Passaro, S., Saggoimo, R.: Opto-acoustic 3D reconstruction of the "Punta Scifo D" shipwreck. In: 1st IMEKO TC4 International Workshop on Metrology for Geotechnics, MetroGeotechnics 2016, pp. 327–333 (2016)
25. Bruno, F., Lagudi, A., Gallo, A., Muzzupappa, M., Petriaggi Davidde, B., Passaro, S.: 3D documentation of archeological remains in the underwater park of Baiae. Int. Arch. Photogrammetry Remote Sens. Spat. Inf. Sci. **40**(5), 41 (2015)
26. Rende, S.F., Irving, A.D., Bacci, T., Parlagreco, L., Bruno, F., De Filippo, F., Montefalcone, M., Penna, M., Trabucco, B., Di Mento, R., Cicero, A.M.: Advances in micro-cartography: a two-dimensional photo mosaicing technique for seagrass monitoring. Estuar. Coast. Shelf Sci. **167**, 475–486 (2015)
27. HTC Vive. https://www.htcvive.com

Interacting with Simulated Archaeological Assets

Arian Goren[1]($\boxtimes$), Kay Kohlmeyer[1], Thomas Bremer[2], Susanne Brandhorst[2],
Arie Kai-Browne[1], Felix Balda[2], David Strippgen[3], and Sebastian Plesch[3]

[1] Landscape Archaeology,
University of Applied Sciences Berlin, Berlin, Germany
`ariangoren@gmail.com`, {`Kay.Kohlmeyer,`
`Arie.Kai-Browne`}`@HTW-Berlin.de`
[2] Game Design, University of Applied Sciences Berlin, Berlin, Germany
{`Thomas.Bremer,Susanne.Brandhorst,Felix.Balda`}`@HTW-Berlin.de`
[3] Computer and Media Sciences, University of Applied Sciences Berlin, Berlin, Germany
{`David.Strippgen,Sebastian.Plesch`}`@HTW-Berlin.de`

Abstract. Digital and 3D data are common components in current archaeological work, and expectations regarding their utilization in contextualizing archaeological knowledge are steadily on the rise. The rapid progress in real-time rendering software and more accessible computational power enables integrated data-sets to (re)gain relevance in the process of interpreting archaeological contexts. Retaining high level of details and correct geometric relations of a complex scene while reconciling inherent variations in the scale, format, and resolution of input data (including 2D legacy data and 3D field recordings) has been already successfully achieved in the simulation of the Temple of the Storm God of Aleppo, realized by an interdisciplinary working group in the HTW Berlin. The current paper addresses the modification of virtual and immersive environments within the field of cultural heritage, and evaluating their potential as tools in interpretative archaeological processes. Based on widely available game technology, two applications are presented, supporting real-time interaction and collaborative work within a single modeled space.

1 Introduction

Incorporating 3D data capturing tools has become a common practice in archaeological work worldwide, making archaeological data more available for post-processing and presentation, but also much more voluminous than ever before. Also the array of data formats, the variety of processing tools, and the range of devices enabling presentation of digital and digitized data is much wider. The challenge, therefore, modern archaeologists face is setting proper standards regarding data-sets manipulation, sophisticated visualizations, and flexible data application. To meet the rise in expectations, co-operating with other researchers or specialists in interdisciplinary frameworks gathers momentum. This underlines a need to articulate the imperatives for engaging in an archaeological research, and carefully employ techniques which are relevant to chosen archaeological analysis and work methodologies. Increased incorporation of advanced computer and game technologies does not only expand an archaeologist's toolkit, but also encourages re-thinking work procedures and work assumptions. In particular,

© Springer International Publishing AG 2016
M. Ioannides et al. (Eds.): EuroMed 2016, Part I, LNCS 10058, pp. 281–291, 2016.
DOI: 10.1007/978-3-319-48496-9_23

virtual environments (VE) and virtual reality (VR) can be utilized to experiment with new approaches to interpret archaeological assets and provide new means, for both the public as well as scholars, to re-engage with cultural heritage knowledge. Contrary to the more common hyper-realistic nature of 3D simulations associated with popular culture, when purposed for scientific use it is essential to maintain the correct relations between different data-sets and varying resolutions involved in assembling archaeological information systems.

A recently developed application evaluates the potential of VR platforms and immersive devices as ground-braking tools in interpretative archaeological research. The application allows for real-time interaction with a modeled space and its assets, and supports remote collaborative work within a single simulated space. Demonstrated on the game engine generated 3D simulation of the Temple of the Storm God in Aleppo, purposing immersive devices to the field of cultural heritage is explored.

2   Implementing and Manipulating Integrated Data in Virtual Environments

A viable 3D simulation of the Temple of the Storm God and its assets, which correctly visualize the various temple components, was constructed through workflows compiled by members of a dedicated interdisciplinary working group [1]. These workflows describe the steps taken to properly convert the various inputs comprising the virtual scene. The datasets used to compile the virtual scene include data captured originally in 3D in the temple compound itself in 2010, available satellite imagery, and 2D legacy data. Prior to compiling the virtual scene, processing these varied inputs for further manipulation followed specific pipelines in order to meet the project objectives and while taking methodological concerns into account [1]. The resulting product is a detailed and multi-scalar simulation of the temple compound with its architectural elements and finely carved inscriptions. The geometrical relations of the objects were accurately maintained despite rigorous file size reduction, achieved by implementing decimation algorithms [1–4]. Using capabilities offered by media design and game technology, a 3D simulation of the temple was embedded in a VE, facilitated with interactive functionality and displayable on both desktop as well as immersive devices, such as head mounted displays (HMD).

Several aspects need to be considered when implementing 3D scientific data in VR platforms. Technical issues might be the most obvious ones. From our experience with several game engines, achieving high representational fidelity is much more a matter of the engine's architecture and the quality and Level of Details (LoD) it supports rather than the quality and accuracy of the fed data. As programming a costume game engine is not part of the project goals, and in order to keep costs low, a strategic decision was taken to generate the simulation on available gaming platforms (several cost-free platforms available for non-commercial use were tested. In this paper the Unreal Engine 4 is referred to). Formerly, relying on cost-free development kits restricted the range of available game engines to those offering only limited access to code-editing and asset manipulation. This approach substantially constrains the ability to simulate complex scenes comprising multiple assets with a wide range of LoDs. Fortunately, game technology is a rapidly developing industry. Newer versions of game engines are regularly released to the market, implementing better rendering algorithms, deeper development kits, and higher representational fidelity. Once the groundwork is set and the required 3D data is processed, converting the simulated scene to another game engine or a newer version is relatively simple, without apparent loss of details or data quality. Nonetheless, this step should be supported with hardware components which correspond to the system's requirements.

Technical issues are only the backstage to other fundamental concerns regarding content and functionality. The potential affordances of a certain VE are prompted through several factors, determine the user's experience and perception of the environment. Such factors can be, for example, the scene's design, smoothness of display, choice of interface, or type and range of user allocated actions [5, 6]. In the developed applications presented here, navigational tools were implemented, meant to enhance an exploratory affordance and help the user to develop a better sense of presence and spatial acquaintance with the modeled environment. It is important to note the difference between a sense of presence, or embodiment - the reaction a user might develop while experiencing a VE - and the notion of spatial immersion, which can be described as the constellation of components and characteristics comprising a certain VE [6]. While the latter depends on system architecture and hardware configuration, the former has to do with the content and actions embedded in the VE. Whether an immersive system will encourage a user to develop a sense of presence depends on the system's configuration and the representational fidelity of the environment. However, whether a user will be motivated to engage with the VE and the assets in it has much to do with the affordances offered by the VE. An effective immersive system should convince us, that is our perception, in the real-life properties of the virtual simulation we are experiencing.

The challenges in reconciling between the different methodologies of game technology and archaeology are made more clear when trying to adjust game engines to produce complex multi-scalar and visually versatile virtual simulations. By their nature, game engines are constructed to deliver first-person experience and are optimal for presenting vivid representations of a (virtual) world from a subjective point of view. Hence, some game engines offer better rendering when the simulated scenes are spatially limited. Although it is usually possible to depict endless simulated plains, distant objects will be often simplified as a "backdrop" to the main scene.

3   Virtually Re-contextualizing the Temple of the Storm God

The created VE depicts a 3D simulation of the Temple of the Storm God in Aleppo, a compound measuring 42×42 m with an interior cella of approximately 27×17 m, dated to the 1st half of the 2nd millennium BCE [7]. The modeling of the temple was created with common 3D processing software [1], rendered in the Unreal Engine. The resulting simulation retains the temple's floor plan in several scales while maintaining accurate geometric relations of the architectural elements (Fig. 1). A key aspect in modeling the temple is the ability to distinguish various spatial levels, such as very fine chisel marks and hieroglyphic inscriptions from remote mountain ranges.

Fig. 1. The virtual simulation of the Temple of the Storm God compound rendered in the Unreal Engine 4.

Two types of applications were tested in the virtual simulation, both well established in the world of game technology and immersive environments. One of the applications uses an HMD. By nature, such devices are designed to generate a highly immersive environment, which can induce users to very vivid reactions and a strong sense of presence, mimicking an illusory sense of body ownership [8–10 and references therein].

The other application refers to Multiplayer Computer (Online) Games (MCG/MOG), among the most widely distributed types of popular entertainment. Research on online game addiction [11, 12] indicates the profound immersive quality MOGs can have, even though - contrary to games played using immersive devices such as HMDs - for the most part they are played in front of a computer screen. Research on the educational and sociological aspects of computer and online games [13–15] reveals that such games provide users valuable opportunities to engage in social interactions. MCGs and MOGs are powerful platforms, motivating participants to fulfill effective learning tasks and encouraging them to explore, communicate, and collaborate.

4 Interactively Exploring the Temple of the Storm God

Having user experience in mind, this application implements an Oculus Rift DK2 HMD device to the virtual simulation of the temple compound (Fig. 2), with free movement in the modeled space, and direct access to interaction being emphasized. Enabling these actions aims to facilitate spatial affordances - high degree of acquaintance with the temple compound and its layout, and consistent assessment of scales and measures from different locations within the compound. However, a learning affordance was also assessed through enabling the interaction with archaeological content, in this case the temple's decorated reliefs.

Fig. 2. The hardware setup used in the HMD application implemented in the virtual environment of the temple. The user wears an Oculus Rift DK2 HMD device. Movement in the virtual environment is controlled through a hand held XBox 360 controller. The user's movements are captured through an external Oculus positional tracking camera positioned in front of the user.

Nonetheless, several limitations and challenges are inevitable when using immersive devices such as HMDs, relating to representation of the virtual avatar and to navigation in the VE. Motion sickness (or simulator sickness) is the most prominent challenge to be addressed in this context. A variety of factors could trigger this phenomenon. Some refer to the construction of the system, such as frame rate, navigation speed, or display characteristics. Other factors are rather subjective and depend on individual circumstances, such as age, previous experience with VE systems, or medical condition [16–18]. The most common occurrence of motion sickness are instances of spatial disorientation or general discomfort, triggered by the effects that an immersive experience has on the proprioceptive system. Movement is one of the most obvious examples of motion sickness: while the physical body of a user is stationary in the real world (s)he experiences its virtual representation, or virtual avatar, as moving or flying without any corresponding vestibular or kinesthetic cues.

A possible way to reduce some of these disorienting effects is to bridge the gap between the physical gestures of a user and those of the virtual counterpart. A solution implemented in the tested HMD application was to allow the user to control navigation in the modeled space with a hand held controller (here an XBox 360 joystick). However, in order to do so, first the movements of the user need to be captured and mapped on to the gestures of the avatar in the VE. A basic HMD configuration positions only a single tracking device. The tracking camera provided with the Oculus Rift device, which was used as a default for the temple's virtual scene (Fig. 2), tracks only the position of the HMD and not that of the full body. However, movement mapping does not need to be perfect, suffice it when gestures of movement or directions are generally simulated in order for a user to develop a sense of presence and experience embodiment [6].

Stepping out of the range of the tracking device pauses the motion tracking and the display fades to black. This pre-defined characteristic could also induce motion sickness. But more importantly, this action deeply effects the user's movement, in the physical world as well as in the virtual space. Extending the tracking volume (of both the user and the avatar) can be rather easily achieved with additional devices/detectors, or by switching to technologies using motion capture systems or magnetic based tracking (trading-off a light-weight single laptop and HMD with a much less portable system). However, even if systems are switched or tracking devices are added, the user will still be literally confined to staying on ground level. Performing a flight, for example in order to observe objects from above, will still, in most likelihood, induce motion sickness, since it can be simulated virtually but not tracked physically.

Reconciling between system mobility and limited tracking volume was settled in the developed application through implementing a virtual dynamic platform, on which the avatar is placed. In fact, this solution improves user experience in a twofold way. On the one hand, the tracking volume is substantially extended. The user is granted with an almost unlimited range of movement in the simulated temple, and so the risk of stepping out of the scene is reduced. In addition, also motion sickness is reduced by overcoming the discrepancy between the physical movement and its simulation in the temple.

Fig. 3. A virtual movable dynamic platform and visualization of tracking volume boundaries. (a) The user's representation in the VE (as an avatar) is visualized on the dynamic platform, while the user's body (here slightly crouching) is approximated from the position of the HMD respective the tracking device. (b) Schematic depiction of the tracking volume covered by the tracking device positioned in front of the user. (c) The walls of the confining box blend in front of the user/the avatar when approaching the limits of the tracking volume, signaling the need to re-position.

The virtual platform, designed to resemble a "flying carpet" (Fig. 3a), is visible to the user and semi-transparent to not distract the view. The platform's position in the VE is manipulated by the user through a hand held controller, allowing to actively explore the entire modeled temple and approach objects from multiple angles.

The platform is structured as a confining box with dynamically changing walls. In a static position, only a subset of the platform is visible at the feet of the user (as seen in Fig. 3a). When the limits of the tracking volume are approached (Fig. 3b), a colored wall appears in front of the user, signaling a need to reposition (Fig. 3c). Moving the dynamic platform results in the re-positioning of the tracking volume within the virtual space, and does not require to re-position the avatar (essentially negating the need to physically move in the real world). The confining box becomes visible also when the platform is shifted in the virtual space. The user thus can have a better spatial reference and can apprehend that the platform (or avatar) is what being moved rather than its own physical body.

5   Remote Collaboration in a Shared Virtual Space

Another tested application builds on the concept of multi-user systems, or multiplayer gaming platforms. Whether played online or implemented in VEs, multi-user systems demonstrate powerful immersive characteristics. Such systems can support basic features, such as location, orientation, agency, and communication [9, 19]. These features are capable of inducing a strong sense of embodiment and participation, albeit the fundamental difference in their configuration compared to other immersive VEs, such as HMDs or DIVE/CAVE systems [13, 20].

Running on the same virtual simulation of the temple, the system is configured to support a first-person point of view and the scene is displayed on a screen. Similar to the HMD application, the temple compound can be actively explored and the different assets can be approached from up close. Also the avatar movements and parts of the virtual body representation are visible to the user, encouraging a sense of orientation and direction in the VE. The main difference compared to the user-oriented HMD application, is the design of this tested multi-user system, which aims to enhance producer expertise. In order to reach that goal an innovative approach was taken, maximizing real-time interaction and knowledge sharing between peers using common interfaces, such as desktop PC.

The concept of the application's design follows two key objectives: real-time communication and interactive cooperation, both are essential properties in conducting meaningful collaborations in VEs [19, 20]. The platform offers participants to carry out remote work sessions, thus supporting knowledge transfer between professionals and decision makers. Using the application, multiple users can conduct remote work sessions in a faster and more efficient way while sitting in front of their personal computer screens.

During a work session, participants can operate two main types of user-asset interaction. They can open information pop-ups (Fig. 4), containing information regarding the characteristics of a certain object. Additionally, assets in the virtual scene can be edited and manipulated on-the-fly (Fig. 5a), while these and other actions are evaluated in real time through verbal communication.

Fig. 4. Informational pop-ups regarding the properties of specific objects can be activated by the user when approaching an object.

Fig. 5. The virtual simulation of the Temple of the Storm God as seen from the point of view of a single participant in the multi-user application. (a) A modeled wall added to the virtual scene as part of testing a suggested reconstruction of the pedestal wall in the Temple's compound. (b) The avatar of another participant is seen while inspecting the cult images of the Storm God and King Taita of Philistin to his right.

The temple compound can be navigated and explored simultaneously by multiple participants (Fig. 5b). The properties of existing objects (for example its spatial position or physical measures) can be edited, and new objects can be added to the scene, however only one object can be manipulated by a single user at a time. While an editing action takes place, the object is highlighted so other peer(s) can be aware of changes made to the scene. Object manipulation in the application is based on an underlying database, containing the model and its assets. Establishing a direct link to the underlying database allows to access assets in real-time without the need to recompile the entire application after each editing task.

Enabling an advanced asset-interaction is particularly important in order to organize and carry out tasks successfully in a shared virtual space. The developed user-asset interactions specifically aim to open up new approaches to re-contextualize cultural heritage knowledge, for example when testing assumptions regarding architectural reconstructions of both diachronic and synchronic implications. However, much as in real-life, peer communication and collaboration are essential to support a sense of co-presence in VE, and can be decisive factors in carrying out joint tasks successfully [19, 20]. Hence, both written and verbal communication options are offered in the application, as embedded text messaging or via VoIP technology offered by third-party services.

Different from the HMD application, some prerequisites need to be met in order to operate the multi-user system. Participating in a session requires internet accessibility in order to connect to the server hosting the VE and the temple's simulation. Hardware configuration (in particular graphic card performance) as well as system and network stability (which are dependent on the available client/server infrastructure) might also present limiting factors to carrying out a successful collaborative session. At the moment, the design of the application requires all participants to load the same model version on their respective PC in order to share the same simulated space. Designing a peer-to-peer (P2P) configuration and connecting to a shared asset database can improve some of these issues and provide better application flexibility and increased stability. Further aspects that can be improved in future versions of the application relate to physical properties and sense of embodiment in the VE. These, however, are more so dependent on the state of game technology available in the market. Developments in the field are anticipated in the coming future with the introduction of advanced tactile user-interfaces and newer versions of end-user immersive devices.

6   Closing Remarks

Taking advantage of capabilities offered by media design and game technology, dedicated applications were implemented on a 3D simulation of the Temple of the Storm God in Aleppo. The 3D model of the temple compound and its assets are generated in a game engine, and based on data integrated from diverse sources with varying scales. The purpose of the presented applications is to allow real-time interaction with the virtual temple space and its assets. While an HMD application emphasizes user experience, a multi-user system addresses scientist and professionals in the fields of archaeology and cultural heritage. In particular, the multi-user system enables conducting a remote collaborative work within a single shared space. Both applications facilitate interactive functionalities and are displayable on PC desktop as well as immersive devices. In general, virtual environments can be very effective tools in inducing a strong sense of presence and embodiment, and motivate engagement with individual as well as joint tasks. Both applications implement further advanced functions which allow to directly manipulate and edit assets in real-time. The work of an interdisciplinary group of archaeologists, media designers, and computer scientists presented in the paper lays ground for meaningful remote collaborative work, where peers can act and communicate in the same virtual space. Such capabilities are particular interest also for professionals seeking to engage in re-thinking work procedures as well as re-contextualizing cultural heritage knowledge. With future developments in game technology and newer versions of immersive devices released to the market, soft-spots such as motion sickness and tactile feedback are expected to be improved.

Acknowledgements. Former sponsors of the project and related fieldwork are: the IFAF Institute Berlin, the World Monuments Fund, the German Research Foundation, the Gerda Henkel Foundation, TOPOI Cluster of Excellence at the Free University of Berlin.

References

1. Goren, A., Kohlmeyer, K., Bremer, T., Kai-Browne, A., Bebermeier, W., Öztürk, D., Öztürk, S., Müller, T.: The virtual archaeology project – towards an interactive multi-scalar 3D visualisation in computer game engines. In: Traviglia, A. (ed.) Across Space and Time, Selected Papers from the 41st Computer Applications and Quantitative Methods in Archaeology Conference, Perth, WA, 25–28 March 2013, pp. 386–400. Amsterdam University Press (2015)
2. Alliez, P., Ucelli, G., Gotsman, C., Attene, M.: Recent advances in remeshing surfaces. In: De Floriani, L., Spangnulo, M. (eds.) Shape Analysis and Structuring, pp. 53–82. Springer, Heidelberg (2008)
3. Merlo, A., Dalcò, L., Fantini, F. Game engine for cultural heritage: new opportunities in the relation between simplified models and database. In: Guidi, G., Addison, A.C. (eds.) 18th International Conference on Virtual Systems and Multimedia (VSMM), Proceedings of the VSMM 2012 Virtual Systems in the Information Society, Milan, Italy, 2–5 September 2012, pp. 623–628. Institute of Electrical and Electronics Engineers (IEEE), Piscataway (2012)
4. Merlo, A., Sánchez Belenguer, C., Vendrell Vidal, E., Fantini, F, Alipetra, A.: 3D model visualization enhancements in real-time game engines. In: Bohem, J., Remondion, F., Kersten, T., Fuse, T., Gonzalez-Aguilera, D. (eds.) 5th International Workshop 3D-Arch 2013: Virtual Reconstruction and Visuzlization of Complex Architectures, Trento, Italy, 25–26 February 2013, vol. XL-5/W1, pp. 181–188. International Archives of the Photogrammetry, Remote Sensing and Spatial Information Sciences (ISPRS) (2013)
5. Dalgarno, B., Lee, M.J.: What are the learning affordances of 3-D virtual environments? Br. J. Educ. Technol. **41**(1), 10–32 (2010)
6. Slater, M.: A note on presence terminology. Presence Connect **3**(3), 1–5 (2003)
7. Kohlmeyer, K.: Der Tempel des Wettergottes von Aleppo. Baugeschichte und Bautyp, räumliche Bezüge, Inventar und bildliche Ausstattung. In: Kamlah, J. (ed.) Temple Building and Temple Cult, pp. 55–78. Harrassowitz Verlag, Wiesbaden (2012)
8. Ehrsson, H.H.: The experimental induction of out-of-body experiences. Science **317**(5841), 1048 (2007)

9. Kilteni, K., Groten, R., Slater, M.: The sense of embodiment in virtual reality. Presence Teleop. Virtual Environ. **21**(4), 373–387 (2012)
10. Slater, M., Perez-Marcos, D., Ehrsson, H.H., Sanchez-Vives, M.V.: Inducing illusory ownership of a virtual body. Front. Neurosci. **3**(2), 214–220 (2009)
11. Kuss, D.J., Griffiths, M.D.: Internet gaming addiction: a systematic review of empirical research. Int. J. Mental Health Addict. **10**(2), 278–296 (2012)
12. Lee, Z.W.Y., Cheung, C.M.K., Chan, T.K.H.: Massively multiplayer online game addiction: instrument development and validation. Inf. Manag. **52**(4), 413–430 (2015)
13. De Freitas, S.: Learning in Immersive Worlds. Joint Information Systems Committee, London (2006)
14. Steinkuehler, C.A.: Massively multiplayer online games. Paper Presented at the Proceedings of the 6th International Conference on Learning Sciences: ICLS 2004: Embracing Diversity in The Learning Sciences, University of California, Los Angeles, Santa Monica, CA, 22–26 June 2004 (2004)
15. Steinkuehler, C.A., Williams, D.: Where everybody knows your (screen) name: online games as "Third Places". J. Comput. Mediated Commun. **11**(4), 885–909 (2006)
16. Kolasinski, E.M.: Simulator Sickmess in Virtual Environments. DTIC, U.S. Army Research Unit (1995)
17. Moss, J.D., Muth, E.R.: Characteristics of head-mounted displays and their effects on simulator sickness. Hum. Fact. J. Hum. Facto. Ergon. Soc. **53**(3), 308–319 (2011)
18. So, R.H.Y., Lo, W.T., Ho, A.T.K.: Effects of navigation speed on motion sickness caused by an immersive virtual environment. Hum. Fact. J. Hum. Facto. Ergon. Soc. **43**(3), 452–461 (2001)
19. Mortensen, J., Vinayagamoorthy, V., Slater, M., Steed, A., Lok, B., Whitton, M.: Collaboration in tele-immersive environments. In: Stürzlinger, W., Müller, S. (eds.) Proceedings of the Eighth Eurographics Workshop on Virtual Environments 2002. Eurographics Association, Aire-la-Ville (2002)
20. Benford, S., Bowers, J., Fahlen, L.E., Greenhalgh, C., Snowdon, D.: User embodiment in collaborative virtual environments. In: Proceedings of the SIGCHI Conference on Human Factors in Computing Systems, pp. 242–249. Addison-Wesley Publishing Co. (1995)

Virtual Reconstruction 3.0: New Approach of Web-based Visualisation and Documentation of Lost Cultural Heritage

Daniel Dworak[1,2]($\boxtimes$) and Piotr Kuroczyński[3]

[1] Institute of Information Technology, Lodz University of Technology, Łódź, Poland
daniel.dworak@dokt.p.lodz.pl
[2] Center for Media and Interactivity, Justus Liebig University Giessen,
Giessen, Germany
[3] Herder Institute for Historical Research on East Central Europe,
Marburg, Germany
piotr.kuroczynski@herder-institut.de

Abstract. The paper presents the project entitled "Virtual Reconstructions in Transnational Research Environments the Portal: 'Palaces and Parks in former East Prussia'" in the light of the Semantic Web and Open Source technologies. The researches are focused on certification, classification, annotation, storage and visualisation of 3D data sets, proposing methodology of the computer-based 3D computer reconstruction of Cultural Heritage, which are still lacking. The multinational and interdisciplinary project with interactive 3D models being part of a semantic data model, is concerned with designing a Virtual Research Environment. Our approach affects the entire process of digital 3D reconstruction with the development of an XML schema called Cultural Heritage Markup Language as a groundwork for an application ontology.

The results bring new insights into areas such as effective data acquisition, documentation, semantic 3D modelling and visualisation and data management. They may be useful for the creation of Virtual Environments and other forms of Cultural Heritage's interactive presentation that employ open source visualisations standards (e.g. WebGL technology). An aspect that needs to be improved concerns coding and uploading large 3D data sets using alternative formats, with an emphasis on art and architectural models. We have developed a technique for coding, long-term storing and decoding 3D geometrical data in 2D PNG files, which are characterised by small size and lossless compression.

1 Introduction

The art and architectural representation, as well as the research in the field of art history, are traditionally based on iconographic sources and 3D models. The development of the Computer Aided Design software accompanied by the potential growth of the counting performance of the computers led to increased

© Springer International Publishing AG 2016
M. Ioannides et al. (Eds.): EuroMed 2016, Part I, LNCS 10058, pp. 292–306, 2016.
DOI: 10.1007/978-3-319-48496-9_24

application of so called Virtual Reconstruction in research projects and for dissemination purposes in the Cultural Heritage sector, in particular museums exhibitions.

Since 1990s we have observed an increased application of Virtual Reconstruction based on the enthusiasm for innovative visualisation possibilities and (hyper)realistic representations (renderings) of destroyed or never realised art an architecture. One of the early academic centres for the Virtual Reconstruction since the beginning of 1990s was established by Prof. Manfred Koob (2011) at the Darmstadt University of Technology (Faculty of Architecture). The projects reflect the development and application of the digital 3D reconstruction throughout two decades [13]. Since then all the involved researchers on the one hand have recognized the potentials of the new "holistic approach" in the data processing, on the other hand they have pointed out the drawbacks of (hyper)realistic visualisation and the lack of documentations standards [4]. The treachery of images highlights the gap between the image, language and the meaning.

In general, the result of a Virtual Reconstruction is an animation (renderings) the recipients are confronted with. The images suggest an imaginary picture of lasting effect in the sense of "A picture says more than 1000 words!". The unsolved questions how to record the interpretative creation process of the model and preserve a scholarly approved information lead to a critical attitude towards digital 3D models. Beside internationally-recognised principles for the use of computer-based visualisation by researchers, educators and cultural heritage organisations, like London Charter, there is no documentation, visualisation and preservation standard for digital 3D models in the above-mentioned scientific context [3].

Besides, the museums are currently confronted with the challenges of the mass digitisation of the 3D artefacts (collections), the scientific approach and digital preservation. There are several documentation standards for digital 3D models resulting in data models. The XML metadata schemas, like CARARE 2.0, captures the machine-driven process of 3D scanning and the context of the artefact, and enable rudimentary publishing to digital libraries, e.g. Europeana [1]. The digital 3D reconstruction (Virtual Reconstruction) differs from the 3D digitisation, because normally there are no remains that could be scanned. The digital 3D reconstruction refers to heterogenous sources and is highly interpretative (human-driven). The London Charter introduces the "paradata" (data about the creative processes of human interpretation and 3D modelling) to capture the essential process of the digital 3D reconstruction.

To ensure the academic acceptance of digital 3D reconstruction as scholarly productions, contributing "comprehensive historical digital 3D models", a customised data model is of outstanding importance. Collecting, transforming and managing the data as central part of the digital 3D reconstruction force us to consider the formal structure of the data. Otherwise we risk to lose the data that leads to the final result the digital 3D representation of the research issue. In a row leaving the 3D visualisation (renderings) stand alone without context and without scientifically required "digital footnotes." Additionally, the long-term storage of the information and a scholarly approved visualisation of the 3D models plays a significant role for the acceptance.

2   Designing a Virtual Research Environment for Digital 3D Reconstructions

The ongoing project "Virtual reconstructions in transnational research environments the web portal 'Palaces and Parks in former East Prussia'" [9] focuses on the challenges concerned with the data processing, documentation and visualisation. The core aim of the project is the design of a data model in reference to existing documentation standards and the development of a Virtual Research Environment (VRE) for spatial research projects [7]. As the groundwork serves the "Cultural Heritage Markup Language" (CHML), a data model in XML-format specified for the needs of a digital 3D reconstruction [6]. The implementation and further development of the data model in E-CRM/OWL DL results in an application ontology, compliant with the ISO 21127:2006 (CIDOC CRM) [5]. The current state of the CHML application ontology.

The collaborative VRE is set up upon the "Scientific Communication Infrastructure" (WissKI) [10]. The innovative approach of WissKI is the marriage between the open-source Content Management System (Drupal) and the graph database with a triple-store based on E-CRM/OWL DL. The system enables the usage of easy to handle field-based entries and free-text annotations. All entries create RDF-triples following the Semantic Web requirements. The free-text annotation allows the semantic keywording. The project processed data is Linked Data.

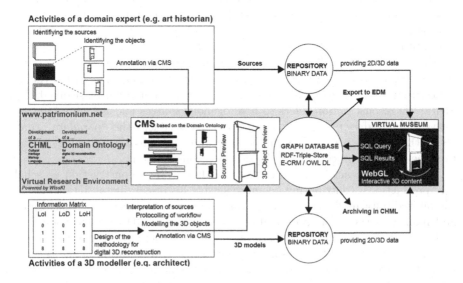

Fig. 1. Graphical abstract of the project (Color figure online)

The VRE enables the involved, multidisciplinary research team to acquire data sets and to semantically enrich the records, 3D models included. While recording and editing the data, the system semi-automatically expands the graph database, interlinking the data with internal records of the database and with external Linked Data addressed by the SPARQL Endpoint. The graphical abstract reveals the centralised backbone of the project, represented by the red background (Fig. 1).

The activities of the domain expert (e.g. art historian) evaluate the sources and identify the objects for further 3D reconstruction. Activities, sources and objects are embedded and annotated within the VRE. The 3D modeller (e.g. architect) interprets the registered information and creates the digital 3D reconstruction. Ideally, in result, every identified object includes an interpretative (hypothetical) 3D representation. The creative provenance of the digital 3D model (paradata) is annotated by the architect during the modelling process. All field-based entries and the semantically enriched free-text annotations within the VRE results in a graph data. The integration of 3D scenes by queries take place in the prototype of the "Virtual Museum" (VM), an immersive and interactive web-based 3D environment (WebGL). The VM combines the semantic data model with the 3D visualisation providing transparency and validity of information.

In the following the project-based approach for the web-based 3D visualisation as well the customised integration of semantically enriched and scholarly approved 3D models will be explained from the technological point of view.

3   Challenges for 3D Visualisation

The beginnings of 3D graphics on the Internet dates back to the mid-90s when it began to exploit the potential of graphics accelerators, also in Web browsers. In 2005, there has also been developed Adobe Papervision3D, which revolutionized the real-time 3D graphics on the Internet. Further technological development occured with the publication of the latest implementation of the HTML5 standard. It introduced the possibility to draw graphics using scripts (mostly using Javascipt) on the $< canvas >$ element simply called canvas. Consortium Khronos Group (including Intel, NVIDIA, Google, Sony, Apple, Samsung, IBM) proposed a completely innovative project, developing the extension of JavaScript that have an access to the 3D API called WebGL [14] with usage of Web browser.

WebGL uses the OpenGL ES 2.0 instructions and allows to view three-dimensional elements using the element canvas. In order to ensure smooth animation, WebGL provides hardware supported rendering using graphics card (GPU), and in the case of hardware incompatibility - rendering on a CPU. Currently, WebGL is supported by all the latest desktop browsers, even mobile ones. There are many libraries using the capabilities of WebGL (GLGE, C3DL, Copperlicht, SpiderGL, SceneJS or Three.js), without installing additional software or plugins - it is only needed to install a supported browser.

3.1   Storing 3D Geometry

There are formats that are optimized and supposed to be more efficient in Web appliance (Table 1). Many Internet technologies support COLLADA (DAE) [2] format because of variety of information that can be stored in one file. This XML-based format is also supported by various software like the Maya, the 3ds Max, the SketchUP or the Blender 3D. This format can be sufficient for the models with small number of vertices, but according to our test model, .DAE was the biggest one with 480 MB file's size. The JSON format (JavaScript Object Notation) is an open standard format with user-friendly notation (e.g. readable text) and is used to transmit data from server to client easily. It allows to store huge data sets like vertices, normals, texture coordinates, faces and textures' names. Although the Web technologies decode JSON files faster than OBJ, due to specific way of storing geometry with the similar size as OBJ format.

Table 1. Size comparison for different file formats - 1.5 M and 76,625 vertices geometry.

Vertices	DAE	FBX	WRL	OBJ	JSON
1.5 M	480 MB	41.3 MB	176 MB	267 MB	230 MB
76,625	19.80 MB	3.10 MB	8.28 MB	6.95 MB	6.55 MB

There are also challenges with users hardware, platforms, browsers and computing power. The main problem for 3D graphics in the Web are huge 3D data sets, which contain 3D models, in particular art and architectural models, terrain and vegetation models. Transmission of such data via network requires wideband Internet connection and transmission formats. There are standarized transmission formats for Audio (MP3), Video (H.264), and images (JPEG, PNG) but no transmission format exists for 3D computer graphics yet [12]. Popular 3D data formats like FBX, OBJ, WRL, COLLADA (DAE), DWG are too heavy to send them via Internet in real time. An aspect that needs to be improved concerns coding and uploading large 3D data sets using alternative formats, with an emphasis on art and architectural models. First steps were aimed to the way of saving and storing 3D models data. This problem is being tried to be solved by Khronos Organization [12] using content pipeline: Collada − > glTF − > Open GL, OpenGL ES, or WebGL. A glTF asset is represented by JSON file (for node hierarchy, materials, and cameras), binary files (geometry and animations), JPEG and PNG image files (textures), and GLSL text file (shaders). Another idea, that seemed to be worth considering is coding 3D data sets to 2D binary PNG files. We have developed a technique for storing 3D geometrical data in 2D PNG files, which are characterised by small sizes and lossless compression (Fig. 2). Additionally, the PNG compression can be used for long-term preservation purposes, due to its portable and standardised form. Our research has shown that the 3D data encoding in PNG file reduces its size and time needed to transfer them via Internet.

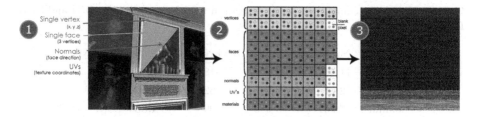

Fig. 2. (1) Prototype of the Virtual Museum: elements of geometry - vertices, faces, normal and UV's, (2) structure of PNG file with geometry (vertices, faces, normals, UV's and materials) and (3) PNG output file with geometry for testing model of fireplace.

Basically, there are five types of data to define 3D model: vertices (space coordinates x, y and z), faces (set of vertices' indices which creates single polygon), normals (vectors of surface's orientation for lighting calculations), texture's coordinates (called UV's), material properties (like color coefficients and images for texture). It have been decided to use JSON (JavaScript Object Notation) format for storing 3D data. This format is an open standard with user-friendly notation (e.g. readable text) and is used to transmit data from server to client easily. The conception of conversion JSON to PNG files is based on saving any 3D data to RGB channels of 2D image (Fig. 2). Then, every value (vertex, normal, UV's) is splitted into integer and fractional parts and stored in R, G, B channels. The Alpha channel (A) identifies kind of data: vertex ($A = 128$), faces ($A = 100$), normal ($A = 50$), texture coordinate ($A = 25$), material ($A = 255$). At the end of PNG file, information about materials are saved. There has been proposed JSON based sequence of properties like: materials' name, colors, textures' names or transparency. A textual information (for example the name of a texture map) is stored in ASCII code - one character in single pixel's channel but material's colors - as RGB pixels.

We have decided to use PNG file, because it supports lossless data compression and was designed for transferring it over the Internet. The compression algorithm implemented for PNG file is called DEFLATE and it builds a data dictionary of information occurring in an original stream. This method eliminates redundant data, because, when any part of data occurs once, it may be used many times. This is an important point in our research, because many art and architectural models are symmetrical and tend to have a lot of common vertices, faces and other characteristics. This approach is likely to help to decrease the size of files (Table 2). For example, in case of raw 3D data with 550,000 vertices stored in OBJ we have 79 MB file. After saving it as PNG we only have approximately 11.5 MB. There is also an improvement for small objects (35,000 vertices) OBJ file was about 3.5 MB, and a PNG file was only 0.76 MB (780 KB). Moreover, modern web technologies are optimised for streaming pictures and movies. This reduces the uploading time of a PNG file, compared to OBJ file.

Table 2. Files' size comparison for architectural models, according to OBJ and PNG format.

Model	No. vertices	OBJ [KB]	PNG [KB]	Ratio OBJ:PNG
Portrait	11 439	2 124	518	**4,1**
Chairs	12 618	2 098	462	**4,54**
Column	17 901	3 083	709	**4,35**
Sala001	24 958	3 727	807	**4,62**
Sala002	28 480	12 971	2 334	**5,56**
Sala112	39 202	6 882	1 370	**5,02**
Stairways	44 525	9 246	1 372	**6,74**

It has been proposed to use a GPU rendering pipeline, supported by WebGL technology, to decode large two-dimensional data sets to tridimensional geometry. Our researches revealed that a model with 77,407 vertices saved in OBJ file (13 MB) downloads about 25 s, while model encoded by authors' algorithm in PNG (2.25 MB) only 4.5 s. For the same PNG file, a period of time that is needed to decode a data set is also short (less than 1 s), but GPU decoding is nine times faster than CPU due to calculation's parallelism.

4   Integration of 3D Content Within WebGL and WissKI

At the beginning of the project, there has been proposed ways of storing, placing and giving names for 3D models. The whole scene is splitted into smaller parts, familiar to the hierarchical structure of the spatial artefacts and architectural ensembles and objects. It means the "Manor House" hasPart "Facades", "Roof", "Storages", etc. The storage (e.g.: 1. floor) hasPart "room no. 1" hasPart "Wall" hasPart "Fireplace" hasPart "Portrait A. And the other way around: the "Fireplace" is a part of the "Wall". It makes it possible to store, annotate and retrieve information about every model apart. What is more, there is also an opportunity to receive data about "Fireplace" while asking only about "Wall" as it is a part of it. The challenge occurs in the final scene's creation while having many separate 3D models. The origin point $(0, 0, 0)$ is set to the entrance of the Palace. Then, each 3D model is put in the right place, according to the basic model of facade, which makes it fast and simple to build the scene (with every model).

Every 3D model is stored in triplestore database as the result of *Activity* event and the "3D reconstruction" process, for example modelling one. It means that every object has its own and unique URI with accesible website. It provides the way of describing every needed aspect, like topic, title set (in different languages), timespan, actor, sources used, additional events (creation, modification or destruction), rich text annotations and much more (Fig. 3). The file with geometry is attached by modeller and placed in *Geometry* field.

The customized WissKI system also provides a way of storing, describing and displaying data saved in a variety of modern formats. They are accesible

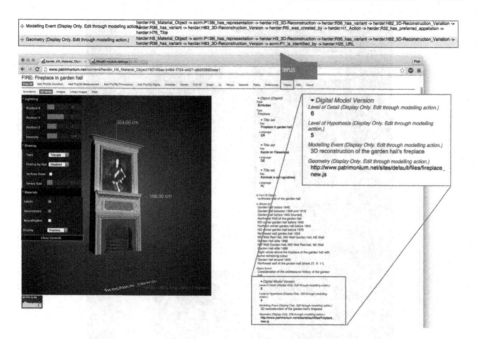

Fig. 3. The element *"ModellingEvent"* within the object view and the RDF-triples of *"Modelling Event"*

via WebGL based canvas: for 2D files (JPEG, TIFF, PNG) and 3D (OBJ, DAE, JSON, 3dPNG) as well. While creating the 3D scene, the algorithm filters the extensions of formats and decides what kind of data should be prepared. For example, it creates two-dimensional camera and different tools for pictures and for triangulated geometry. Furthermore, it supports point clouds formats saved in PLY and XYZ formats, with complete color information. Attaching six JPEG files with proper names (directions like _bottom, _right etc.) results in creation of cubic view with panoramic view, based on those files.

Window with 2D & 3D data consists of GUI controller and main view with the loaded source. When having more than one geometry object in the same Activity (at different level of detail), it loads the newest one, but it is possible to change displayed model from drop-down menu. Additionally, the user can control the settings of lightning, show geometry faces and vertices or change material's properties in real time.

Moreover, we designed a technique of describing those 3D objects and 2D sources in WebGL canvas in three-dimensional space. It is possible to create (a triangle, quad or any shape) or choose (from existing faces) an area that should be featured. It is helpful for modellers or historians to highlight any interesting part of the model. Then, they can annotate it because of possible doubts, questions or additional data to be modelled, which can be connected with events in database.

Fig. 4. Activity event during fireplace's annotation.

5 Guidelines for 3D Modelling and Texturing

There are many different software products for 3D modelling, what causes a lot of problems to be solved. First of all, there are many ways of calculating and saving geometry's properties like normals or faces. What is more, during exporting/importing, the pivots of the scene are positioned differently due to changed Y and Z axes. Some of the 3D software are allowed to store negative texture's coordinates, what is not appropriate for Web technologies.

We prepared the requirements for 3D modelling with an emphasis on Internet applications.

– Due to backward hardware compatibility (16-bit vertex buffer), it is recommended to not exceed the number of 65,536 vertices per model's segment. Splitting large models (e.g. >2 M vertices) into few smaller segments (eg. file that contains of palace's faade and roof could be splitted into north & south parts of faade and roof separately) is worth considering. It makes much faster and more convenient to store every object separately, because of describing and displaying in real time.
– It is needed to export object with normals and texture coordinates. Modeller should render an item to check if normals and textures are prepared well.

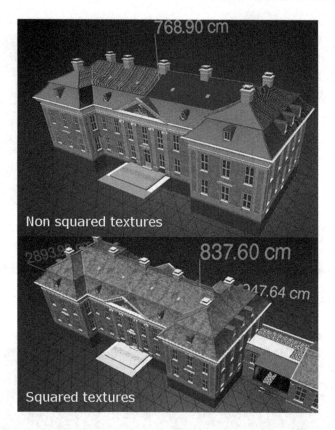

Fig. 5. The influence of texture's dimensions on textured object.

- Triangulated mesh or polygons are necessary to display an object properly. Interchargable formats (as OBJ) are not allowed to use quads or parametric meshes.
- WebGL supports squared textures with dimensions of power of 2 ($n \times n$, where n^2), see: Fig. 5.
- There is also prepared nomenclature for unique objects's names. It stores the data about main topic and what the part it is (e.g. Friedrichstein_Manor-House_Roof − > F_MANH_ROOF). The directory and texture's names are also given: NameOfModel_Date_Version_Textures/NameOfModel_Date_Version_TypeOfMaterial   e.g.:   F_MANH_ROOF_16-04-04_Ver2_Textures/F_MANH_ROOF _16-04-04_Ver2_Tiles.jpg
- While using SketchUP, it usually gives improper results after exporting to OBJ file. We found out that COLLADA is more accurate for SketchUP based geometry, neverless it is much more complex to display and retrieve such geometry.

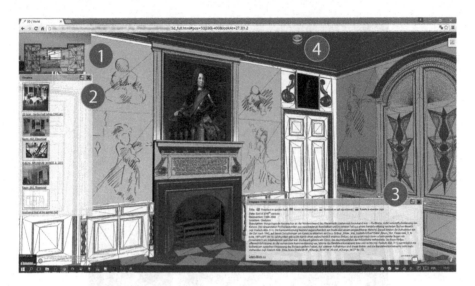

Fig. 6. Prototype of the Virtual Museum: integration of interactive semantic 3D objects in WebGL.

Fig. 7. Prototype of the Virtual Museum. Foreground: interactive, procedural real time generated trees; background: billboarding trees.

6   Virtual Museum

The Virtual Museum (VM) connects many techniques and standards that are commonly used in virtual reconstructions. There are existing and ready-made solutions like X3D, which allow to create a virtual world. Regardless, the possibilities of such one are not enough for our researches and limited by external

Fig. 8. Rendered realistic scene with 3D models of Schlodien Palace (LumenRT).

libraries. However, there are no attempts to create a container for 3D geometry that would compress needed files, reduce the time of decoding such data or complexity of existing models. In fact, our solution also uses a lot of authors' ideas that were prepared for "virtual reconstructions" and solve the problems mentioned before. This approach exemplifies the adoption of new web standards and gaming technologies, such as WebGL or Stage 3D, that extend the possibilities of visualisation of 3D data, among others.

VM's interactive form allows to visit non-existing places like Garden Room in the destroyed manor house Schlodien (Fig. 6). The real-time displayed map (1) with surroundings, supports the navigation and orientation on the user side. The whole scene is composed of actual 3D geometry (saved in PNG file by author's algorithm) with textures. After picking some interesting (for user) element, e.g. Fireplace, the semantically enriched content is loaded from the graph database. As Fig. 6 point (2) shows there is a visual information (images, movies used for the 3D reconstruction by the modeller) connected with this specific element. Moreover, there is a paradata (the data describing the intellectual process during the interpretation and computer-based reconstruction), medadata and textual content (3) with complex data about historical background, names in different languages and a link that directs to database's page of this model within the VRE www.patrimonium.net. Some of the places are associated with a panoramic view (4) of existing state what makes it possible to compare past and digital 3D representation with present outlook. There is also a list of initially prepared "Point of Interest" which can be changed/generated by the user (add or remove) for future use. In fact, if the user wants to share some view with others or come back to the same place with same view, the website link contains a position and look at vector, which is called Deep Linking.

The technique of splitting models with a huge number of vertices is frequently used to reduce the file size; then a portalling method [8] can be applied. There is also a LoD method [11], which requires few representations of the same object with different number of vertices. If the user is far away from the model, algorithm loads the object with the smallest number of vertices. When this distance is decreasing, a model with more vertices should be loaded.

We have tested the LoD method in combination with a matrix of Level of Information (in reference to the detail of sources) and Level of Hypothesis. However a promising implementation still needs to be improved [7].

Prepared models for real-time calculated scenes can be also used for high resolution rendered images and movies (Fig. 8). For this purpose we use LumenRT software, which allows to create more realistic environment with authentic objects that has been measured and examined by art historians, architects and 3D modellers. There has been used more advanced light and shadow effects, more complex vegetation and living animals. It is not possible to reach such results in real-time with modern Web technologies on an ordinary computer. Previously prepared and rendered images or movies can be easily used during exploring WebGL environment, which appears to be a golden mean between quality and efficiency.

7   3D Modelling of the Park and the Landscape

According to well known WebGL restrictions and hardware compatibility, we also decided to generate trees in real time. It has been decided to use Open Source library called proctree.js which generates complicated trees using GLGE - library for direct access to OpenGL. Every tree's type is described by 25 parameters (including height, size of leaves, root, drop amount, twig scale, textures etc.) and its position. An average number of vertices per one object is about 4 000, depending on it's parameters.

The whole prototype of Schlodien VM consists of about 350 trees what leads to great number of vertices in this case. It is not possible to display that complicated geometry in real time, so we used conjunction of two well known techniques: billboarding (two crossed textures) and LoD (Level of Detail). Basic version of LoD technique needs to load whole geometry at the beginning and hide or display necessary ones at demand. It also caused displaying problems on average laptop and stopped working while displaying about 60 trees. This lead to introduce modified LoD technique that we called Progressive LoD (PLoD) which bases on billboardings that are swapped by more complicated, real time generated objects while going closer to them (Fig. 7). It appeared to be very efficient method, allowing great interactive and seems to be golden meaning between performance and appearance.

The terrain placed in Schlodien VM is based on actual cartographic map, prepared by specialists. We have prepared high poly representation of the map with usage of height map technique. It built high resolution model with real dimensions and curvature of space according to map's colors. Then, there has been created few geometries at different levels of detail. It has been decided to use the terrain model at low level of complexity due to restrictions of Web technologies.

8   Conclusions for Combined Schema and Prospects on Common Application Ontology

The increased digitisation efforts within the CH sector (e.g. in museums, archives, libraries, research institutions, etc.) request strategies for extended documentation standards serving the transparency (validity), interoperability, long-term access and preservation of the information, in particular of the 3D data sets.

Beside domain-driven documentation standards in museums, archives and libraries, applied documentation standards for "digital 3D preservation", specialised to capture and express a broad range of requirements for 3D digitisation, already exists. At present we recognise the lack of documentation standards for "digital 3D reconstruction", based on a different procedure in data acquisition and data processing, and leading to various 3D visualisation application.

The interactive visualisation of integrated 3D point clouds and hand-modelled 3D data sets accompanied by the "semantic 3D annotations" tool (under development) will have a significant impact on immediate research on 3D data sets, the documentation and dissemination of our common "Digital Heritage" as the representation of the CH in the broader means. The mid-term challenge is to improve the documentation of the provenace and paradata, recently expressed in the WissKI "field-based entry" and the "free text input".

Our proposed solutions for the interactive integration of semantic 3D objects are under development, but reached results promise to solve current problems with transferring 3D data sets in real time. There are many reasons to continue researches in this way, but Internet technologies (like WebGL) are demanding, needing many techniques of optimization to reach the main aim.

Acknowledgments. We would like to thank our project partners, in particular Oliver Hauck, Martin Scholz and Mark Fichtner for the cooperation in the design of the data model and the VRE.

The international, collaborative research project and the resulting Virtual Research Environments (patrimonium.net) under discussion, as well as the findings concerned with the prototype of the Virtual Museum, are funded by the German Leibniz Association from 2013 to 2016.

References

1. 3D-Icons: 3D-icons   guidelines   (2015).   http://3dicons-project.eu/eng/Guidelines-Case-Studies/Guidelines2
2. COLLADA: Documentation (2016). http://www.khronos.org/collada

3. Denard, H.: A new introduction to the London Charter. In: Bentkowska-Kafel, A., Baker, D., Denard, H. (eds.) Paradata and Transparency in Virtual Heritage, Ashgate, pp. 57–71 (2012)

4. Favro, D.: Se non vero, ben trovato (If not true, it is well conceived): digital immersive reconstructions of historical environments. J. Soc. Arch. Hist. 1, 273–277. University of California Press 71.3 (2012). Special Issue on Architectural Representations

5. Görz, G., Schiemann, B., Oischinger, M.: An implementation of the CIDOC conceptual reference model (4.2.4) in OWL-DL (2015). http://erlangen-crm.org/docs/crm_owl_cidoc2008.pdf

6. Hauck, O., Kuroczyński, P.: Cultural heritage markup language - designing a domain ontology for digital reconstructions. In: Proceedings of the 2nd International Conference on Virtual Archaeology, Hermitage Museum, St. Petersburg/Russia, pp. 250–255 (2015). http://www.virtualarchaeology.ru/pdf/281_va_book2015.pdf

7. Kuroczyński, P.: Virtual museum of destroyed cultural heritage 3D documentation, reconstruction, visualization in the semantic web. In: Proceedings of the 2nd International Conference on Virtual Archeology, The State Hermitage, St. Petersburg/Russia, pp. 54–61 (2015). http://www.virtualarchaeology.ru/pdf/281_va_book2015.pdf

8. Lowe, N., Datta, A.: A technique for rendering complex portals. IEEE Trans. Vis. Comput. Graph. 11(2005), 81–90 (2005)

9. Patrimonium: Virtual reconstructions (2015). http://www.herder-institut.de/go/dp-962a8d

10. Scholz, M., Goerz, G.: WissKI: a virtual research environment for cultural heritage. In: De Raedt, L., et al. (eds.) 20th European Conference on Artificial Intelligence, ECAI 2012, Proceedings. IOS Press, Amsterdam (2012). http://wisski.eu/, http://www.dh.cs.fau.de/IMMD8/staff/Goerz/ecai2012.pdf

11. Tan, K., Daut, D.: A review on level of detail. In: Computer Graphics, Imaging and Visualization, pp. 70–75 (2004)

12. Trevett, N.: 3D transmission format. In: NVIDIA (2013)

13. TUD: Technical University of Darmstadt, Digitale Rekonstruktionen (2016). http://www.dg.architektur.tu-darmstadt.de/dg/forschung_dg/digitale_rekonstruktionen/projekte.de.jsp

14. WebGL: Documentation (2016). http://www.chromeexperiments.com/webgl

Full Paper: The New Era of Museums and Exhibitions: Digital Engagement and Dissemination

CultureCam: An Interactive Search Tool for Small Image Galleries

Sergiu Gordea[1]([✉]), Michela Vignoli[1], and Sanna Marttila[2]

[1] AIT Austrian Institute of Technology, 1220 Vienna, Austria
{sergiu.gordea,michela.vignoli}@ait.ac.at
[2] Aalto University, Helsinki, Finland
sanna.marttila@aalto.fi

Abstract. As a result of digitization initiatives in recent years, most galleries hold digital copies of their masterpieces. In order to attract more visitors, public galleries are interested in advertising their content on websites and tourist-centric applications deployed in public spaces. The online version of CultureCam has the goal of stimulating the reuse of cultural heritage content by creative designers. In this paper, we present the Interactive Installation version of CultureCam tool, which has the goal of attracting the interest of public users when exploring public galleries. It concentrates on enhancing the user experience, by offering access to the images in an immersive environment, using an intuitive, easy-to-use tool that supports touch free interaction with the gallery content. A novel image similarity search algorithm was developed in order to adapt to user expectations when searching in small image datasets. The user feedback collected from exhibitions in different European cities indicates a very high acceptance of the CultureCam tool by the public. The intuitive and seamless interaction with the tool, as well as the automation and enhancement of the search algorithm are the main improvements over the previous version of CultureCam.

Keywords: CultureCam · Interactive exploration · User experience · Similarity search · Cultural heritage

1 Introduction

CultureCam is an image similarity search tool, developed within the context of the Europeana Creative project[1]. The prototype has been designed to support creative designers, and to increase the re-use of visual content that has a great potential to inspire creation of new artifacts. The online version of the Culture-Cam tool[2] makes Europeana public domain image content easily accessible for the open craft and media designer communities. By employing a search using query by example approach we aim to overcome the limitations of free text search

---

[1] http://pro.europeana.eu/web/europeana-creative.
[2] http://culturecam.eu.

© Springer International Publishing AG 2016
M. Ioannides et al. (Eds.): EuroMed 2016, Part I, LNCS 10058, pp. 309–321, 2016.
DOI: 10.1007/978-3-319-48496-9_25

(e.g. lack of descriptive metadata, semantic miss-match, complex search queries) and offer an effective solution for visual content retrieval.

The visual artworks, which compose the dataset and are made accessible online through image search, were manually curated by professional designers according to their quality and reusability criteria. The relatively small dataset used within the tool includes 3500+ artifacts selected from bio-diversity collections, illustrations from old books, portrait and landscape paintings, as well as various design and poster artifacts. The user evaluation presented in [vignoli2015] indicates that the tool was found to be quite useful and appreciated by the professional designers for exploring reusable and inspiring image content. However, in order to improve the effectiveness of the proposed approach for a larger public, the search scenario needs to be adapted to the requirements and expectations of regular users [gordea2014]. Additionally, the input used by the search algorithm needs to be acquired in a more controlled environment, in order to reduce the negative influence of background colors and the variation of light exposure on the search precision.

The Interactive Installation version of the CultureCam tool presented in this paper aims at enhancing the user experience in a scenario that concentrates on interactive exploration of image content available in small visual art galleries. In comparison to the online version of the tool, the new prototype introduces important enhancements by providing:

- An intuitive and engaging interaction using a Kinect device. The users are invited to explore the gallery through a seamless search and to play with the content using a touch free user-system interaction;
- An immersive user experience using high quality projections on large surfaces in a dark room;
- An efficient color based search algorithm using HSV image Histograms.

The concrete solutions proposed for addressing these challenges are described in the main part of the paper, which is organized as follows: Sect. 2 presents the related work, describing concepts and artifacts that are reused in CultureCam. The detailed description of the proposed approach, the CultureCam prototype and the concrete solutions contributed by this paper are presented Sect. 3. The image search algorithm specially designed to comply with the requirements of the Interactive Installation version of CultureCam is presented in Sect. 4, while preliminary user feedback on the tool is discussed in Sect. 5.2. The conclusions of this paper and the future work are summarized in Sect. 6.

2   Related Work

Given the contributions of the current paper, the related work is structured in three categories, presenting similar approaches employed for: user experience improvement, advanced image visualization techniques, and similar image retrieval algorithms.

User experience. Van der Sluis, van den Broek and van Dijk state that an Information Retrieval system should be human-centered, as it solves the information need of its user, with its user [sluis2010]. They suggest a Human-Centered Model of Information Retrieval eXperience (IRX), which incorporates different features into a coherent relevance model. They approach IR from a User eXperience framework (UX) perspective with a special focus on the emotional factors. UX is a fuzzy concept and is often defined as *technology use beyond its instrumental value* [sluis2010]. Hassenzahl and Tractinsky divide UX in three factors: Aesthetic and hedonic factors, emotional factors, and experiential factors [hassenzahl2015]. All these factors should be taken into consideration when designing an IR system. Van der Sluis, van den Broek and van Dijk stress that users develop negative emotions if they experience difficulties with the search task. Thus IR systems should be user-friendly and meet their expectations in order to be successful. To meet this requirement, CultureCam was build after organizing a so-called co-creation workshop in which the requirements and needs of professional designers were collected. Furthermore the selection of the image dataset was guided by the professional designers.

Visualization. Many visualization approaches create static compositions of various images. For instance, Manovich analyzed and visualized over 50.000 Instagram photographs shared in Tokyo over a few consecutive days [manovich2014]. The progression of activities by the people during the day is reflected by varying colours and brightness of the images. The visualization creates an "aggregated documentary" constructed from thousands of activities documented on Instagram.

Other projects like RockViz offer a more interactive content visualization. The project combined data of about 1994 significant Rock albums from Rovi and visual analysis data from the gathered album covers. The images were organised in various experimental web-based image plots. The user can filter the images by group, title, or year, and click on the images for a larger view and details [garcia2014].

In collaboration with Gravity Lab, the Software Studies Initiative developed an interactive media visualization software running on the visual super computer HIPerSpace [yamaoka2011]. The software can load up to 10.000 images and interactively create a variety of media visualizations in real time. The images can be analyzed and displayed in (multiple) image plots or scatterplots. This technology allows analysis of single or multiple datasets and has been successfully applied to large collections with hundreds of data sets, e.g. a collection of 883 manga titles with more than 1 million images [yamaoka2011].

Image retrieval. The diversity and heterogeneity of the Europeana collections as well as poor textual descriptions of individual collections make a targeted text-based search challenging. In terms of image items the content and particularities of the represented objects are poorly described, which limits the possible text-based search output considerably [gordea2014].

Content-based retrieval services such as the CultureCam provide complementary solutions to overcome the limits of text-based search. The tool follows a search by example approach and includes a *tactile* centric interface for interactively browsing a curated dataset with pre-selected images from the Europeana image collection. The dataset is composed of items available in higher resolution and without copyright restrictions, as this would otherwise prevent their re-use. Also, the images contain rare patterns as well as beautiful shapes and colours. With the online version of CultureCam the user can take a picture of an object with the computer's or a mobile device's webcam, whereupon the application searches the index for images with similar colours, shapes and patterns [vignoli2015].

In the tool, a nearest neighborhood algorithm is used to reduce the search space and improve the execution performance at runtime. This is achieved by selecting a pivot set and computing the distances between each indexed image and the pivots. At runtime, the search results are ordered by their similarity relative to the pivot set. A detailed description of the feature extraction and indexing process is available in [amato2011]. The new search algorithm introduced in Sect. 4 follows the same indexing approach, but it uses a clustering approach based on the centroids of non-uniform color beans in HSV space. 54 Color clusters and 4 grayscale clusters were empirically defined basing on the visual representation of the 6 main color sections of HSV space.

3   Interactive Installation Approach

As explained above, CultureCam offers a more straightforward and intuitive way of exploring image content than the more traditional text based search on the Europeana portal. It stimulates and offers new possibilities for creative re-use of Europeana content, and facilitates the creation of new content visualizations with shapes and patterns, which have only a small probability of arising in other frameworks [dorin2009]. The followup Interactive Installation version of Culture-Cam brings the content closer to public user and public spaces and extends the image content exploration to a physical, touch free, and immersive user experience.

The objectives of the prototype were to create an experience-based (i.e. through stimulation of emotions like fun, fascination, intrigue) version of CultureCam tool tailored for public or private exhibition spaces. It is designed as a stand-alone system, which can be easily adapted to specific collections and venues. The prototype presented here uses the same image dataset as the online version. However, the tool was designed to easily change the image content and create exhibitions of existing digital collections of galleries or museums.

3.1   An Immersive User Experience

The overview of the physical system is presented in Fig. 1. A high definition projector is used to present the image content on large surfaces in order to place the user in an immersive environment. When projecting on a surface like large walls in public institutions, the projector is typically placed behind the user at a height that eliminates the obstruction of the projection by the human body. The exploration of the image content is triggered by the automatic capture of pictures with the camera of the Kinect device[3]. The movement sensors are used to detect when the user enters a square which is marked on the floor as being the focus position of the camera. The image search service and the interactive image rendering application, run on a commodity computer that is connected with the projector and the Kinect device.

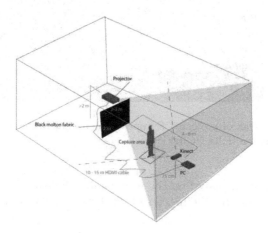

Fig. 1. Culture Cam: physical system

In order to reduce the influence of background colors, a black molton fabric is placed behind the user, and the black color is weighted to narrow scores by the image search algorithm. As seen in the sketch, the Kinect device is in front of the user, at a distance that takes pictures of the upper part of the user's body. Consequently the captured images will represent the pullovers and shirts worn by the human user. However, different artifacts like scarfs or images printed on paper can be used by users to explore different subsets of the image collections. The most impressive user experience is obtained in dark rooms, simulating the cinema environment (see Fig. 2). In this case a source of directed light needs to be placed near the Kinect to ensure the required light exposure for capturing decent quality pictures.

The Kinect device is not only used for capturing images of one person at a time. The Interactive Installation also features gesture-based interaction for other visitors who want to interact with the image search results displayed on the wall. Specifically movements of the hands and feet are captured by the Kinect device. By pointing to a certain area of the wall, the images in that area are enlarged and animated in a three-dimensional fashion giving the user the feeling of touching or getting closer to the images. As a further visual effect all the

---

[3] http://www.xbox.com/en-US/xbox-one/accessories/kinect-for-xbox-one.

Fig. 2. Gallery wall of projected Europeana images in National Gallery of Denmark. Photo by Christina Holm CC BY-SA 4.0

images currently displayed on the wall rotate when the Kinect captures a new image, which indicates the process of similarity search for a new set of images.

3.2 Touch-Free and Engaging Interaction

As explained above, the user can interact with the CultureCam via a Kinect sensor covered by a black box, which scans/photographs the visitor. Once the motion sensor of the Kinect has detected a person standing on the marked "scanning spot", a picture is taken and analyzed in order to retrieve Europeana images matching the colors and patterns in the photo. In a larger area around the "scanning spot" up to six people can interact with the projected images by making movements to enlarge and animate the images. All in all the installation gives the users a highly dynamic and spatial experience (see Fig. 3).

For the exhibition at the National Gallery of Denmark 3,231 public domain and CC0 licensed images from the Europeana collection were used. Due to the large size of the wall, the relatively small data set, and the impact of the similarity functionality the images were repeated to fill out the projection area on the wall as well as to provide the audience with a clear and immediate visual understanding of the colour similarity concept of CultureCam. The interface of the installation resembles the online version of CultureCam: the captured photo of the person is displayed in a circular shape area in the center of the screen.

A more comprehensive report on the CultureCam product prototypes and their evaluation can be found in the Europeana Creative deliverable *D4.6 Delivery of the Design Pilot* [marttila2015].

Fig. 3. Museum visitors interacting with the CultureCam installation using props

4 Efficient Search Algorithm Using HSV Color Histograms

The novel search algorithm designed to serve the Interactive Installation is based on HSV Color Histogram. The HSV representation of the color space is more intuitive and easier to be sampled in color bins that have a clear functional meaning for human user. However, as with most color representation models, HSV is not a uniform color space[4]. For computation of the color histogram the color space was divided in 54 color bins and 4 grayscale bins.

4.1 Image Descriptor

The grayscale bins contains all colors with the saturation (S) and/or value (V) smaller that 32, with the meaning of grouping values close to *white, black, light gray* and *dark gray* colors. The color bins are built using the 6 base colors of the HSV space: *red, yellow, green, cyan, blue, magenta*. Given that the lower values for H and V are distributed over the grayscale bins, the rest of the values are grouped in 3 bins for each. Consequently, the resulting bins include 54 sets of colors (i.e. 6H * 3S * 3V).

The HSV Color Histogram of an image is computed by counting the number of pixels that belong to each color bin. Given that the input images and the bin are not of equal size, the image descriptor used for indexing and search purposes is using the normalized HSV histogram ($NH(i)$), see Eq. 1. The normalization of the histogram values ($normScore(b_i)$) is computed by multiplying the ratio of pixels from each bin (i.e. computed as percentage) in the picture with the entropy of each bin. The bin entropy is the inverse ratio between the size of individual bins to the average bin size, see Eq. 2.

---

[4] https://en.wikipedia.org/wiki/HSL_and_HSV#HSV.

$$NH(i) = \{normScore(b_i))|b_i \in B, I\} \tag{1}$$

$$normScore(b_i) = \frac{count(p_i \in b_i) * avgSize(b) * 100}{size(b_i) * size(i)}, \tag{2}$$

Where b_i represents a color bin of image I, with regard to the bin definitions B. $normScore(b_i)$ represents the normalized score for bin b_i to which the pixels p_i are assigned. $avgSize(b)$ is the average size of all b bin definitions computed as number or pixels, $size(b_i)$ counts the number of pixels p_i associated to bin b_i, and $size(i)$ represents the size of the image i computed in pixels.

4.2 Indexing and Search Algorithm

For building the image search index, we adopt a similar approach as Amato et al. [amato2011]. We aim at taking the benefits of the advanced technologies developed for supporting high-performance and scalable search services for text documents, for which Lucene library is the most frequently used implementation.

The normalized color histogram descriptor is represented as a map, in which the hexa representations of the color bin centroids are used as keys and the normalized scores represent the values. This is an equivalent representation to the bag of words used for text indexing, where the integer value of the normalized score serves as term frequency. Consequently, the descriptors or all images in the dataset are used to build the image index. In the same way, the descriptors or query images are converted to text search queries, in which the normalized scores are used for boosting terms in the search queries. At runtime the similarities between the query image and the dataset items is computed using the cosine similarity as shown in Eq. 3.

$$similarity(q, x) = \sum_{c \in hist(q)} (tf(c \in hist(x)) * boost(c \in hist(q)) * idf(c)^2), \tag{3}$$

Here the $similarity(q, x)$ represents the similarity between the query image q and the indexed image x. c represents the identifiers of color bin centroids in the normalized color histogram of query image q (i.e. $hist(q)$). The $tf(c \in hist(x))$ represents the term frequency of color bin centroid c in the color histogram of image x, and it is computed using the normalized score of the color bin (i.e. see Eq. 2). Also the boost of the centroid c in the color histogram of the query image q is computed using the normalized score for the given bin. While $idf(c)$ represents the inverse (document) frequency of centroid c and it is an index constant. This constant has a marginal influence on the ranking of the search results, therefore, implementations may set this to 1, which is equivalent to a uniform distribution of centroids over the indexed documents.

5 User Experience Evaluation

5.1 User Experience for Online Version

The user experience testing for the online version of CultureCam was carried out in a controlled environment using professionals from the creative design domain.

browser **camera** clear easy expect **icon** laptop middle **mobile** navigate **picture** result **screen** **search** sharing site tablet **text** url **zoom**

Fig. 4. TagCloud: Criticism

bigger **button** camera **clicking** culture **desktop** display **images** inspiration **mobile** original **pinterest** possible **results search** share tool **version** visual work

Fig. 5. TagCloud: Enhancement suggestions

The goal was to verify to which extent the tool satisfies the expectations and needs of users and what kind of new functionality the users would recommend for subsequent versions. The user feedback was collected in a two step process including:

- An online survey collecting structured information regarding the usability and efficiency of the tool
- User interviews collecting explicit feedback regarding the user experience and ideas for further improvements

There were 10 users who took part in the evaluation, 4 of them in Barcelona/Spain and 6 in Helsinki/Finland. They were active professionals having the following roles in their daily work: graphic designer, illustrator, visual artist, art director, editorial designer, architect. The users were provided with objects regularly used by designers and they were also encouraged to use their own artifacts for evaluating the value of CultureCam with regard to their daily work. The results of the online survey show that the great majority of the users had a positive user experience. The negative feedback was related to the navigation and the limited interaction with the image content (for more details on the evaluation see evaluation report [senabre2015]).

The narrative feedback collected was divided in tree categories, positive feedback, criticism and enhancement suggestions. The TagCloud representation including the top 20 words for the criticisms and enhancement suggestions are visually presented in Figs. 4 and 5 respectively. This type of feedback was particularly important for development of the follow-up version of the tool, which is the Interactive Installation. The criticism of the interaction with the tool was mainly related to the handling of the camera, the low resolution of the thumbnails and the lengthy way of accessing higher quality images. There were also criticisms regarding the layout, the tooltip texts and the navigation icons. Suggestions for further enhancement of the Culture cam tool were collected and they include requests for functionality like:

- Storing navigation history and enhancing the sharing functionality (e.g. adding possibility to share with pinterest, sharing images, more share buttons)
- Requirements for improving the relevance of search results
- Support for more interaction with search results, like and grouping images in mood boards

The testers gave clear affirmative answers to the questions related to the product's new way of approaching and re-using digital heritage. In particular, the testers confirmed that the platform makes re-usable high quality content for designers available and accessible, and that the product compiles already existing content in a uniquely and easily navigable platform, encouraging creative re-use. Two users compared it to Shazam[5], a music exploration tool, but for images. One user indicated that CultureCam offers many opportunities for museums, and another user liked the idea behind the tool, but he was puzzled that the results shown by the tool when capturing images of the same scene (with the same or with different devices) are not always the same ones.

5.2   User Experience Observations for Interactive Installation Version

The Interactive Installation version of the CultureCam was implemented to address the weaknesses of the online version, to enhance the user experience, and to bring it closer to public users. This version was not evaluated in a controlled environment, however it was presented at various events. In May 2015 the interactive CultureCam was installed at the National Gallery of Denmark at the *Set art free!* Open Culture event. The visitors of the exhibition could interact with the tool by standing in front of a black box covering a Kinect motion sensor, which scans/photographs the visitor. The installation projected CultureCam's search results based on the interacting person's clothes on a large wall in the gallery. Because of the enormous projection, which filled the whole wall, the individual experience of the visitors triggering the search turned into a shared experience by the audience [marttila2015].

The CultureCam installation was well attended during the *Set art free!* event. People of all ages were attracted due to the high degree of playfulness of the installation. Two large posters introducing the CultureCam prototype as well as the Europeana Creative project in Danish and English were displayed. The interaction and subsequent response to human movements on the wall were intuitively understood by the audience. Some assistance was requested to understand exactly why and when certain positions/movements trigger specific reactions by the tool. In particular questions related to the exact positions in regards of the Kinect to get the best capture result were posed by the visitors.

The installation stimulated visitors' emotional responses and added a unique aesthetic value to exhibition space and experience. The visitors seemed amazed about and overwhelmed by the transformation of the gigantic wall of e.g. entirely

---

[5] http://www.shazam.com.

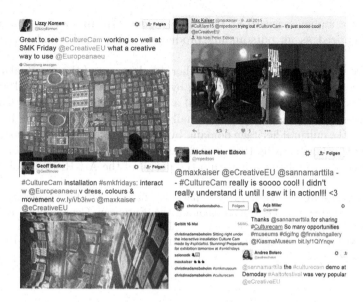

Fig. 6. Selected online user feedback

blue images to entirely red ones. For this event the a new search algorithm was developed which use only color descriptors, as the shape similarities are not well enough described by global image descriptors. This improved the intuitiveness of the installation dramatically leading to the result mentioned above. Another factor was the influence on the projections by the decreasing natural light in the room, which led to an aesthetical transition of the installation during the evening. The aesthetic impact played a significant role in the total user experience. The CultureCam installation generated very positive user feedback in social media, in which the users characterized the installation as cool, stunning, and popular (see Fig. 6).

6 Conclusions and Future Work

This paper presents the CultureCam tool that makes visual navigation through selected image content in Europeana as simple and intuitive as possible. The current version of CultureCam uses a collection of 3700 items that were curated to be freely reusable and inspiring for creative designers, as well as to stimulate the interest of public users of digital cultural heritage content. Within this paper we focus on the user experience improvements, which were implemented in the Interactive Installation version of the tool. Following the user feedback collected on the previous version of the tool, different techniques were integrated to enhance user experience, including: presentation of cultural heritage content in an immersive environment, touch free interaction, and a specialized image search algorithm. The tool was exhibited at a couple of events in different European cities, where the new version of the tool was very appreciated. Besides

winning the audience award at the *Culture Jam* 2015 in Vienna, CultureCam
was categorized as an outstanding product in social media and various blog
posts[6]).

Future work will concentrate of further development of the search algorithms
to enhance the precisions of the search, by integrating the usage of MPEG local
descriptors (i.e. ISO/IEC CD 15938-13) and deep learning models for classification, clustering and indexing. Additionally, we aim at enhancing the impact of
the tool in the cultural heritage domain, by deploying the Interactive Installation
in different Galleries, using their own datasets. For the online version of the tool
the ambition is to integrate it within the portal of the Art-History Collection.

Acknowledgments. This work was partially funded by the EuropeanaCreative
project, co-funded by the Commission of the European Communities under the
ICT Policy Support Programme (ICT PSP). This publication reflects only the
author's/authors' views and the European Union is not liable for any use that might
be made of information contained therein.

References

[gordea2014] Gordea, S.: An image similarity search for the European digital
library and beyond. In: TPDL 2013 Selected Workshops, Communications in Computer and Information Science, vol. 416, pp. 190–196
(2014)

[amato2011] Amato, G., Bolettieri, P., Falchi, F., Gennaro, C., Rabitti, F.: Combining local and global visual feature similarity using a text search
engine. In: Content-Based Multimedia Indexing (CBMI), pp. 49–54
(2011)

[dorin2009] Dorin, A., Korb, K.: Improbable creativity. In: Dagstuhl Seminar
Proceedings of Computational Creativity: An Interdisciplinary Approach, nr. 09291 (2009)

[vignoli2015] Gordea, S., Vignoli, M.: Culturecam: visual exploration of cultural
heritage content by professional designers. In: Multimedia Expo
Workshops (ICMEW), pp. 1–6 (2015)

[hassenzahl2015] Hassenzahl, M., Tractinsky, N.: User experience-a research agenda.
Behav. Inf. Technol. **25**(2), 91–97 (2015)

[manovich2014] Manovich, L.: Watching the world. In: Aperture, nr. 214 (2014)

[marttila2015] Marttila, S., Holm, C., Hyypp, K., Gordea, S., Laakso, N., Stokes, L.,
Senabre-Hidalgo, E.: Delivery of the design pilot. Technical report
(2015).   http://pro.europeana.eu/files/Europeana_Professional/
Projects/Project_list/Europeana_Creative/Deliverables/eCreative_
D4.6_NISV_v1.0.pdf

[garcia2014] Reyes-Garcia, E.: Explorations in media visualization. In: Extended
Proceedings of the 25th ACM Conference on Hypertext and Hypermedia Hypertext. ACM Press, New York (2014)

---

[6] https://twitter.com/hashtag/culturecam.

[senabre2015] Senabre, E., Utratel, A.: Pilot and infrastructure evaluation report. Technical report (2015). http://pro.europeana.eu/files/ Europeana_Professional/Projects/Project_list/Europeana_Creative/ Deliverables/eCreative_D6.3_platoniq_v1.0.pdf

[sluis2010] van der Sluis, F., van den Broek, E., van Dijk, B.: Information retrieval eXperience (IRX): towards a human-centered personalized model of relevance. In: Web Intelligence and Intelligent Agent Technology (WI-IAT), vol. 3, pp. 322–325 (2010)

[yamaoka2011] Yamaoka, S., Manovich, L., Douglass, J., Kuester, F.: Cultural analytics in large-scale visualization environments. Computer **44**(12), 39–48 (2011)

Learning Algorithms for Digital Reconstruction of Van Gogh's Drawings

Yuan Zeng[(✉)], Jiexiong Tang, Jan C.A. van der Lubbe, and Marco Loog

Delft University of Technology, 2628 CD Delft, The Netherlands
{Y.Zeng,J.Tang-5,J.C.A.vanderLubbe,M.Loog}@tudelft.nl

Abstract. Many works of Van Gogh's oeuvre, such as letters, drawings and paintings, have been severely degraded due to light exposure. Digital reconstruction of faded color can help to envisage how the artist's work may have looked at the time of creation. In this paper, we study the reconstruction of Vincent van Gogh's drawings by means of learning schemes and on the basis of the available reproductions of these drawings. In particular, we investigate the use of three machine learning algorithms, k-nearest neighbor (kNN) estimation, linear regression (LR), and convolutional neural networks (CNN), for learning the reconstruction of these faded drawings. Experimental results show that the reconstruction performance of the kNN method is slightly better than those of the CNN. The reconstruction performance of the LR is much worse than those of the kNN and the CNN.

Keywords: Van Gogh's drawing · Drawing reconstruction · Reproduction · Machine learning

1 Introduction

Van Gogh is famous for his canvas paintings, but the largest part of his oeuvre consists of works of art on paper [1]. For this he used different instruments and materials: pencil, crayon, ink, watercolor and oil paint, often in combination. However, many drawings of Van Gogh have dramatically deteriorated over the last century. This especially holds for the ink drawings, where degradation is caused by ink fading due to light exposure among others. An dramatic example can be found in Fig. 1, where the entire original drawing has been faded. In addition to ink fading there are also other types of color changes. Many drawings, which now have a brown color, were originally black, blue, or purple. In Fig. 1(b) the original purple color is visible in the margin, since it was occluded by a frame and therefore largely protected from the influence of light.

One of the goals of the interdisciplinary REVIGO-project (REassessing VIncent van GOgh, funded by the Netherlands Organization for Scientific Research NWO) is to predict the original and future appearances of art works by means of advanced digital methods that integrate the results of both in-depth studies of the colors used and their discoloration over time. This will help to envisage how

© Springer International Publishing AG 2016
M. Ioannides et al. (Eds.): EuroMed 2016, Part I, LNCS 10058, pp. 322–333, 2016.
DOI: 10.1007/978-3-319-48496-9_26

the artist's works of art may have looked at the time of creation. Furthermore, it will help for the identification of appropriate conservation and restoration treatment strategies as well as of implications for future preservation and display. Although in this paper the focus is on Van Gogh, the problem of fading and discoloration holds for most works of art on paper and manuscripts from the 19th century.

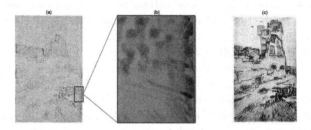

Fig. 1. (a) Reproduction of the present state of "*Montmajour*", made by Van Gogh in 1888; (b) The original aniline ink color in the margin of the present "*Montmajour*"; (c) Reproduction of "*Montmajour*" which was made in 1928. (Color figure online)

This paper can be considered as an initial study of the possibility of digital reconstruction based on reproductions of the original drawings in combination with state-of-the-art supervised learning techniques.

In the course of the 20th century, many reproductions were made of Van Gogh's drawings, i.e., photographs, facsimiles, stencils, and so on. In some cases, e.g., for the fountain (1889) and La Crau (1888), there are at least 10 to 20 high quality reproductions dating from 1910 to 1928. Especially the early reproductions are important because they show the unfaded drawing. Most reproductions, however, are black and white. Only from a limited selection of drawings and watercolors colored facsimiles exist. Nevertheless, these reproductions contain a large amount of information that could be exploited in reconstructing the original works based on their present degraded appearance. The idea is that based on various examples of degraded appearances and their corresponding original (or at least less degraded) appearances, it may very well be possible to learn the inverse process, at least partly. If so, also for unseen works, for which no reproductions are known, reconstructions of their past appearance may be possible. In this paper, a first step is made to exploit the information content of reproductions for the digital reconstruction of drawings.

Three machine learning algorithms are considered. As a simple baseline, linear regression (LR) [2] is considered. The more powerful, nonlinear methods considered are k-nearest neighbor regression (kNN) [3,4] and convolutional neural networks (CNN) [5–7]. In this paper, next to the question to what extent reconstruction might be possible at all, we are also interested in the performance of a CNN in comparison with more traditional methods like LR and kNN.

2   Data

For this initial study, a single faded present-day Van Gogh drawing together with one reproduction has been chosen. The latter is a reproduction from the 20th century for which the content and color are faded less and which is closer to the original drawing. The drawing and the reproduction are obtained from the Van Gogh Museum collection. In general, one drawing may have several reproductions, and those reproductions can be categorized based on two aspects: degradation level and reproduction method. Reproductions made with the same method but different degradation level can show the degradation process over time. However, reproductions with different methods can severely affect the reconstruction process, and thus affect estimation performance of the learning algorithms, since color or even content of reproductions made with different methods can be differ from each other. In this work we want to find out what is at all possible in a simple prediction setting and therefore we study a basic setting with one input (faded original) and one output (close to non-degraded original) image. Later this work can be extended to one drawing and multiple reproductions.

For the data, we consider two images of the same drawing, where one is the present faded version and the other is the reproduction. $\mathbf{x}$ and $\mathbf{x}'$ are parts of the faded image and the reproduction, respectively, which are used as training images. $\mathbf{y}$ and $\mathbf{y}'$ are corresponding parts in the faded image and the reproduction, respectively, which are used as test images. Then, given a test image $\mathbf{y}$, the object of learning algorithms is to learn the degradation process of $\mathbf{x}'$ and $\mathbf{x}$, and thus predict $\mathbf{y}'$, where the degradation between $\mathbf{y}'$ and $\mathbf{y}$ is the same as the degradation between $\mathbf{x}'$ and $\mathbf{x}$.

3   Methods

In this section, we introduce framework for learning the degradation process between $\mathbf{x}'$ and $\mathbf{x}$, and predicting target image $\mathbf{y}'$ by using three different machine learning algorithms, which are the linear regression (LR), the k-nearest neighbor estimation (kNN) and the convolutional neural networks (CNN).

3.1   Linear Regression

Let us consider $I \times J$ dimensional training images $\mathbf{x}$ and $\mathbf{x}'$. Then, the learning process of simple linear regression is given by

$$x'_{ij} = a_0 + a_1 x_{ij} + \epsilon_{ij}, \tag{1}$$

where $i = \{1, \cdots, I\}$ is the row index, $j = \{1, \cdots, J\}$ is the column index, x_{ij} is the RGB value of the ith row and jth column pixel in $\mathbf{x}$ and ϵ_{ij} is the estimation error. Then parameters a_0 and a_1 can be estimated by minimizing the square value of estimation error, that is

$$\min_{a_0, a_1} \sum_{i=1}^{I} \sum_{j=1}^{J} \epsilon_{ij}^2. \tag{2}$$

Later, given a test image $\mathbf{y}$, a target image $\mathbf{y}'$ can be estimated as $\hat{\mathbf{y}}' = a_0 + a_1 \mathbf{y}$.

3.2 k-nearest Neighbor Estimation

The basic idea of the method in this subsection for estimating the target image $\mathbf{y}'$ is per-pixel k-nearest neighbor estimation. Assuming that a test image $\mathbf{y}$ consists of $R \times C$ pixels. Then, for each pixel $\hat{y}'_{rc}$ with row index $r = \{1, \cdots, R\}$ and column index $c = \{1, \cdots, C\}$, we first search the k nearest pixels in $\mathbf{x}'$ and then predict the pixel $\hat{y}'_{rc}$ via simply averaging the k nearest pixels, i.e.,

$$\hat{y}'_{rc} = \frac{1}{k} \sum_{i=1}^{k} x'_{p_i}, \tag{3}$$

where $\mathbf{p} = [p_1, \cdots, p_k]$ is the index of the k closest pixels. The method for searching the k nearest pixels in $\mathbf{x}'$ for each pixel $\hat{y}'_{rc}$ is based on measuring the closeness between feature vector of the corresponding pixel y_{rc} and feature vectors of all pixels in $\mathbf{x}$. The searching method can be described as follows:

1. For each pixel x_{ij}, based on s neighboring pixels of the pixel x_{ij}, we construct a feature vector $F_{x_{ij}} = [x_{i-s,j-s}, \cdots, x_{i,j}, \cdots, x_{i+s,j+s}]$. In this case, we can construct a $s^2 \times (I \times J)$ dimensional feature matrix $\mathbf{F_x}$ of the training image $\mathbf{x}$.
2. For the test pixel y_{rc}, similar as the step 1), we construct a $s^2 \times 1$ dimensional feature vector $F_{y_{rc}}$ based on the s neighboring pixels of y_{rc}.
3. Measure the closeness between the feature vector $F_{y_{rc}}$ and the feature matrix $\mathbf{F_x}$ via the standard Euclidean distance as

$$\mathbf{D} = \|F_{y_{rc}} \mathbf{I} - \mathbf{F_x}\|^2, \tag{4}$$

where $\mathbf{I}$ is a $1 \times (I \times J)$ dimensional vector with all ones, and $\mathbf{D}$ is a $(I \times J) \times 1$ dimensional vector.
4. Based on the index $\mathbf{p} = [p_1, \cdots, p_k]$ of the k smallest values in $\mathbf{D}$, select the k pixels $[x'_{p_1}, \cdots, x'_{p_k}]$ in the training image $\mathbf{x}'$ as the k nearest pixels of the estimated pixel $\hat{y}'_{rc}$.

Here we mainly present the framework of the kNN for color reconstruction, while the detailed theoretical basis and convergence properties of the kNN regression is given in [3].

3.3 Convolutional Neural Networks

A typical single layer CNN consists of three basic parts: convolution, non-linear mapping and pooling. It can be denoted as

$$a_{ij}^l = \text{Pool}\left(\text{ReLU}\left((\mathbf{W}^l * a_{ij}^{l-1}) + b^l\right)\right), \tag{5}$$

where a_{ij}^l is the activation from lth feature maps with row and column indexes (i, j). And if this is the input layer, the a_{ij}^{l-1} are the pixels of input images $\mathbf{x}$. And if it is output layer, a_{ij}^{l-1} are pixels of the predicted images $\mathbf{x}'$. $\mathbf{W}^l$ and b^l are learned weights and bias of convolution filters, respectively. $*$ is the convolution operation. ReLU $(\mathbf{x}) = \max(0, \mathbf{x})$ refers to the non-linear transform of a rectified linear unit (ReLU). Pool $(\cdot)$ is the pooling operator for down-sampling the image with certain strategy, e.g., Max Pooling and Average Pooling, which uses the max or average value to replace the pixels of the same local region.

Based on the basic structure introduced above, in this paper, the specification of the CNN layers for reconstruction of the drawings could be seen in Fig. 2. Please note that, every convolution layer before pooling and the fully connected layers are with ReLU layers on top, they are not explicitly shown here. Firstly, the typical structure is stacked three times to detect different details from multiple views. Specifically, the convolution is implemented twice before pooling. Then, the fully connected layers are followed to further encode the high level features. Since the convolution combined with pooling will gradually down-sample the input, three deconvolution layers are build on top the fully connected layer, they will reconstruct the image with its original resolution. The deconvolution is the inverse transform of convolution, it inserts pixels with learned weight and bias based on the value in each location. Finally, the square loss is used to measure the distance between prediction from current drawing and its reproduction.

In general, the CNN treats the reconstruction as a pixel-level regression which is performed by using three procedures: convolution, encoding and deconvolution. Proposed structure uses the current drawing images as input and directly output the prediction. The function of overall degradation is expected to be learned during the optimization rather than be formulated explicitly.

4   Experiments

In this section, we illustrate the estimation performance of the three machine learning algorithms, which are the LR, the kNN and the CNN. First, we analyze the trade-off between the estimation performance of the kNN method and the three parameters (i.e., the amount of training data $|\mathbf{x}|$, the amount of neighboring pixels for constructing feature vector s and the number of nearest pixels k). After that, the estimation performance comparison between the LR, the kNN and the CNN is given.

To use the reproduction in Fig. 3(b) for reconstruction of the present state drawing in Fig. 3(a), we first use control point registration method to align the present drawing and its reproduction. This indicates that the registration performance depends on the amount of and the accuracy of selected control points, where more accurate control points leads to better registration performance. Although the registration accuracy can be improved via selecting hundreds or even thousands control points with enough accuracy, it is very difficult to obtain perfect alignment of the drawing and its reproduction, since digital information of the drawing and digital information of its reproduction are collected by

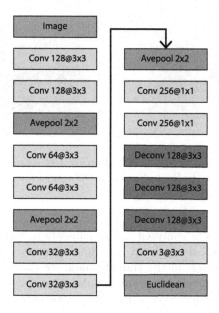

Fig. 2. Layer specification

using different devices. In this work, we focus on the study of reconstruction of drawings via different machine learning algorithms, we thus simply register the drawing in Fig. 3(a) and its reproduction in Fig. 3(b) with 30 manually selected control points and use the as such aligned images for our study. In addition, the dimension of the drawing in Fig. 3(a) and its reproduction in Fig. 3(b) is 6132 × 8176. To remove blank margin, we use effectively 5000 × 6500 pixels of both the drawing and its reproduction in our experiments. The mean square-error (MSE) is used as a measure to assess the estimation performance of the learning algorithms. The MSE between the estimated image $\hat{\mathbf{y}}'$ and the target image $\mathbf{y}'$ is given by

$$\text{MSE} = \frac{1}{RC} \sum_{r=1}^{R} \sum_{c=1}^{C} |\hat{y}'_{rc} - y'_{rc}|^2. \tag{6}$$

In the following experiments, the 5000 × 6500 dimensional drawing and its reproduction are divided into 50 × 50 sub-images, respectively. Three-quarters of the 2500 sub-images are randomly selected as training images (in total 1875) and the remaining sub-images are divided into validation set (70 sub-images) and test set (555 sub-images).

4.1 Parameter Estimation

Since the estimation performance of the kNN method depends on the three parameters: $|\mathbf{x}|$, s and k, the trade-off between the estimation performance and

Fig. 3. (a) Present version of Van Gogh's drawing *Old vineyard with peasant woman* with size 44.3 cm × 54 cm; (b) Reproduction of *Old vineyard with peasant woman* which made in 1928 with size 41.9 cm × 51 cm.

those three parameters is analyzed in this subsection. Since the computational complexity of the kNN depends on the dimensionality of feature vectors and thus the amount of pixels in the training data, we construct training data by randomly selecting n pixels per training sub-image ($|\mathbf{x}| = n \times 1875$), and the test data in this experiment is constructed by randomly selecting 1×10^4 pixels from the validation set.

Firstly, we evaluate the MSE as a function of the n and the s with fixed $k = 12$. Figure 4(a) shows the simulation results in terms of MSE between the estimated image $\hat{\mathbf{y}}'$ and the target image $\mathbf{y}'$, where the MSE is decreased with increasing n from 1 to 150, and the MSE is decreased with increasing the s from 1 to 9, but it is increased with s larger than 9. This indicates that the optimal setup of the s is 9. Next, to evaluate the MSE as a function of the n and the k, we set $s = 9$. The experimental results in Fig. 4(b) show that the MSE is decreased with increasing k from 1 to 15, and it is decreased slowly when k is larger than 10.

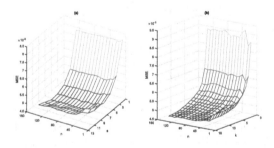

Fig. 4. (a) MSE versus the n and the s; (b) MSE versus the n and the k.

To further show how the three parameters affect the estimation performance of the kNN, we randomly select one sub-image from the validation set as test image $\mathbf{y}$ and its corresponding image from the reproduction as target image $\mathbf{y}'$. We then evaluate the estimation performance of the kNN with eight different

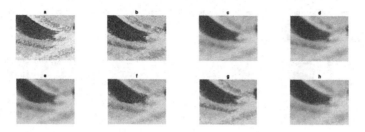

Fig. 5. (a) Test image $\mathbf{y}$; (b) target image $\mathbf{y}'$; (c) $\hat{\mathbf{y}}'$ with $n = 5$, $s = 9$ and $k = 10$, and the MSE = 0.0061; (d) $\hat{\mathbf{y}}'$ with $n = 45$, $s = 9$ and $k = 10$, and the MSE = 0.0060; (e) $\hat{\mathbf{y}}'$ with $n = 145$, $s = 9$ and $k = 10$, and the MSE = 0.0058; (f) $\hat{\mathbf{y}}'$ with $n = 145$, $s = 9$ and $k = 3$, and the MSE = 0.0084; (g) $\hat{\mathbf{y}}'$ with $n = 145$, $s = 3$ and $k = 10$, and the MSE = 0.0125; (h) $\hat{\mathbf{y}}'$ with $n = 45$, $s = 13$ and $k = 10$, and the MSE = 0.0073.

setups of the n, the s and the k. The simulation results in Fig. 5 are consistent with the analysis in Fig. 4, where MSE is decreased with increasing either the n from 5 to 145, the s from 3 to 9 or the k from 3 to 10. In the following experiments, we use $n = 150$, $s = 9$ and $k = 10$ for the kNN estimation.

4.2 Comparison Experiments

Here, we compare reconstruction process of the LR, the kNN and the CNN in terms of MSE. In order to show visible estimation results, we first carefully select 8 representative sub-images (e.g., images with different patterns, color and texture) from the test set.

Figure 6 shows the comparison between the LR, the kNN and the CNN outputs of the 8 sub-images. Visually, we observe that in general the estimation outputs of both the CNN and the kNN are much better than the LR method. This is reasonable since the LR method uses a simple linear function to model the relation between the outputs and the inputs, whereas the relation between the drawing and its reproduction is not linear, see Fig. 7. Furthermore, the estimation results for the sub-images (1), (2), (3) and (6) show that the CNN can learn textural information and provide better visual outputs, while the kNN method smoothly predicts output by averaging k nearest neighbors and thus loses textural details. The CNN also works much better than the kNN for estimating the sub-image (8). This is because the kNN is based on local pixel-level optimization, and thus the estimation performance of the kNN can be worse if pixels with close RGB values in training data $\mathbf{x}$ relates to pixels with two or several different RGB values in $\mathbf{x}'$. However, the estimation results of the CNN for the sub-image (3), (4), (5) are worse than the kNN method. This can partly explained by the fact that the contour of the local blobs in those sub-images could barely be seen due to degradation, the CNN seems fail to detect the specific structure and shape, i.e., the faded yellow half circles. From the perspective of the MSE in Table 1, it is observed that both the kNN and the CNN predict better than the LR, and the kNN performs better than the CNN for the sub-image (2), (3), (4), (5) and (6).

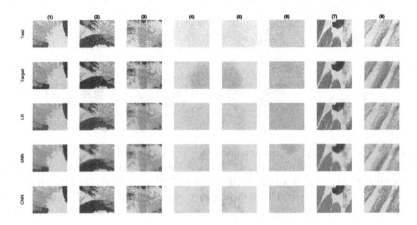

Fig. 6. Estimation performance comparison between the LR, the kNN and the CNN.

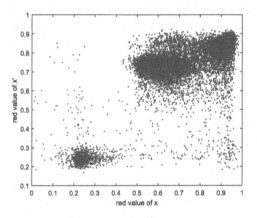

Fig. 7. Red value of a sub-image in the drawing and its corresponding sub-image in the reproduction.

Next, to compare general performance between the three learning algorithms, we test all sub-images in test set and assess the estimation performance of the three learning algorithms by averaging MSE (AMSE) of the $M = 555$ estimations, that is

$$\text{AMSE} = \frac{1}{M} \sum_{m=1}^{M} \text{MSE}_m, \tag{7}$$

where MSE_m is the mean square-error between the mth estimated sub-image and the mth target sub-image and can be computed via Eq. (6). To assess the estimation performance for each color channel, we denote AMSE_R, AMSE_G and AMSE_B as the AMSE of red, green and blue channel, respectively. The simulation results are given in Table 2, where the estimation performance of the kNN

Table 1. Estimation performance comparison between the LR, the kNN and the CNN in terms of MSE.

	(1)	(2)	(3)	(4)	(5)	(6)	(7)	(8)
MSE_{LR}	0.0039	0.0068	0.0105	0.0008	0.0011	0.0023	0.0377	0.0033
MSE_{kNN}	0.0047	0.0042	0.0078	0.0004	0.0005	0.0036	0.0015	0.0024
MSE_{CNN}	0.0034	0.0065	0.0099	0.0005	0.0020	0.0044	0.0015	0.0018

Table 2. The AMSE of the LR, the kNN and the CNN.

	LR	kNN	CNN
AMSE_R	0.0113	0.0067	0.0093
AMSE_G	0.0113	0.0068	0.0094
AMSE_B	0.0112	0.0068	0.0092

and the CNN is much better than the LR, and the kNN performs better than the CNN.

5   Discussion and Conclusions

In this paper, we introduced three classic machine learning algorithms for reconstructing faded color of Van Gogh's drawings: the linear regression (LR), the k-nearest neighbor estimation (kNN) and the convolutional neural networks (CNN). We first analyzed the trade-off between the estimation performance of the kNN as function of the three parameters (e.g., the amount of training data, the dimensions of feature vector and the k). The experiments have shown that better reconstruction performance is obtained by using the estimated optimal parameters for the kNN. Furthermore, we compared the reconstruction performance between the three learning algorithms. The experimental results have shown that the reconstruction performance of the LR method is worse than the kNN and the CNN, and that the kNN and the CNN have comparable capability for learning the degradation process of the drawings. In addition, the kNN method generally performs better than the CNN for color reconstruction, while the CNN performs better than the kNN for estimating textural information.

This work presented here is based on the assumption that the degradation between test images and target images is in the same way as in the training images. However, in practice, different drawings and their reproductions were made in different reproduction methods and with different degradation level. Thus, in this work we illustrate the use of learning algorithms to learn degradation process between sub-images of a drawing and its reproduction, and later test the estimation performance via different sub-images of the drawing and its reproduction. Although the current research work in this paper considers only one drawing and one of its reproductions, it can also be explored to estimate the original drawing by using multiple reproductions and when more research results about the instruments of drawings from other side, such as chemical, are available. On the basis of the composition of purple inks in some of Van Goghs drawing [8], it is possible to reproduce representative purple inks according to contemporary 19th century recipes. In an experimental context Van Gogh like drawings with this new ink can be made and with them the effect of exposure to light up to 60 museum years can be simulated [9,10]. This approach can lead to a set of reference images: original and several discolored ones (i.e. before and after aging). This reference set can be used for the generation of a mathematical model for fading and color changes. The inverse model can then be applied to the discolored drawing.

The comparison experiments in this paper have shown that the estimation performance of the simple linear regression method is very limited, since the degradation process is not linear. Comparable estimation results were obtained by using the kNN and the CNN. The estimation in the CNN is based on both local and global information of the drawing, while the kNN is based on comparing the distance between pixel-level features and predicts the target image pixel by pixel. Furthermore, to obtain sufficient estimation accuracy, the kNN method should use all pixels in training images, which will lead to extremity high computational complexity. Thus, due to limited computational time, we use approximately one tenth training data in the kNN method in this work. As a matter of fact the estimation performance of kNN can be improved by using more training data. Another possible approach to improve the estimation performance of kNN and reduce its computational complexity is to use well constructed features, such as scale-space features [11], instead of raw pixels value. Moreover, since the CNN is good at using local and global information for estimation, while the advantage of the kNN is using detail information of local pixels, for future research work it will be interesting to investigate how to combine the CNN with the kNN to further improve color reconstruction performance.

Acknowledgments. This research is a part of the REVIGO project, supported by the Netherlands Organisation for scientific research (NWO; grant 323.54.004) in the context of the Science4Arts research program.

References

1. Vellekoop, M., Jansen, L., Geldof, M., Hendriks, E., de Tagle, A.: Van Goghs Studio Practice. Van Gogh Museum, Brussels (2013)
2. Edwards, A.L.: Multiple Regression and the Analysis of Variance and Covariance. W.H. Freeman, San Francisco (1979)
3. Devroye, L., Gyrfi, L., Lugosi, G.: A Probabilistic Theory of Pattern Recognition. Springer, New York (1996)
4. Loog, M., van Ginneken, B., Schilham, A.M.R.: Filter learning: application to suppression of bony structures from chest radiographs. Med. Image Anal. **10**(6), 826–840 (2006)
5. Simonyan, K., Zisserman, A.: Very deep convolutional networks for large-scale image recognition. In: Proceedings of ICLR 2015 (2015)

6. Zhou, B., Lapedriza, A., Xiao, A., Torralba, J., Oliva, A.: Learning deep features for scene recognition using places database. In: Proceedings of NIPS 2014 (2014)
7. Ren, S., He, K., Girshick, R., Sun, J.: Faster R-CNN: towards real-time object detection with region proposal networks. In: Proceedings of NIPS 2015 (2015)
8. Neevel, H., van Bommel, M., Vellekoop, M., Lingbeek, N.: From purple to brown analysis of Van Goghs drawing inks; non-invasive identification of inks on Van Goghs drawings and letters. In: Proceedings of the 15th Triennial Conference, vol. 15, pp. 278–284 (2008)
9. Geerts, J.: Light damage on paper objects with coloured media; towards a differential sensitivity classification, MA thesis (2010)
10. Reissland, B., Geerts, J., Confortin, D., Neevel, J.G., van Velzen, B., Ligterink, F.: Deep purple? Visualizing the alarming low lightfastness of crystal violet inks. In: XIIth Congress of the International Association of Book and Paper Conservators, p. 37, August 2011
11. Van Vliet, L.J., Young, I.T., Verbeek, P.W.: Recursive Gaussian derivative filters. In: Proceedings of ICPR 1998 (1998)

Full Paper: Digital Cultural Heritage in Education, Learning and Training

"Human" Technology in the Digital Era: Freehand Images and Analysis of Cultural Heritage – The Know-How and Its Applications

Anna Lobovikov-Katz[✉]

Faculty of Architecture and Town Planning, Technion - Israel Institute of Technology,
Technion City, 32000 Haifa, Israel
anna@technion.ac.il

Abstract. Rapidly developing advanced methods and techniques often displace the traditional ones. But might such "traditional" perception of the "old" as hopelessly outdated cause us to overlook its intrinsic qualities? Could a relevance for actual disadvantages be suggested, could a traditionally time-consuming technology be transformed into an effective one, with its original values preserved? This paper reconsiders the role of *freehand sketching* in modern conservation of cultural heritage by shifting the main focus from the **result** to the **process**. It presents a method, combined with the rapid learning methodology for achieving this traditional artistic ability, and examines its focused application to the visual analysis of cultural heritage by non-artist users. This paper demonstrates its wide accessibility to the general public and conservation experts, and examines its uses in modern multi-and interdisciplinary conservation of built heritage through recent results of the application of the method in national and international projects.

Keywords: Freehand sketching · Visual analysis · Conservation of cultural heritage (CCH) · Learning methodology · Documentation · Cultural heritage (CH)

1 Introduction: Structure of the Problem

Freehand images are traditionally associated with arts and art-related areas. Sometimes, historic images are used as an auxiliary source of information about historic monuments. However, active use of conservation-focused modern freehand image is not part of the methods presently applied to the contemporary conservation of cultural heritage. Exclusion of freehand images from this field might be understandable, due to several common assumptions:

(A) The use of freehand methods cannot produce precise and detailed results, compared to images produced by the use of high-technology techniques;
(B) Producing a freehand image is traditionally thought to be time consuming;
(C) Acquiring an acceptable skill in freehand sketching requires much time, effort and aptitude, which reduces its application to a very limited number of experts.

© Springer International Publishing AG 2016
M. Ioannides et al. (Eds.): EuroMed 2016, Part I, LNCS 10058, pp. 337–349, 2016.
DOI: 10.1007/978-3-319-48496-9_27

Are these A-B-C assumptions real? Can a proper solution be found to overcome the difficulties? Let us cast a fresh analyzing glance at the role of freehand sketching in the modern conservation of cultural heritage (CCH), and focus on the following questions which this paper addresses:

- *What* uses of freehand sketching and freehand images are relevant in the contemporary highly-technological field of conservation of CH;
- *How* can they be applied;
- *Who* can benefit from CCH sketches and sketching?

Actually, the above A-B-C assumptions focus on the outcome qualities, while they miss its *purposes*. In this paper, the sketch (image) is approached as part of the sketching process.

The paper presents the method of "Focusing the Eye" (FtE) on conservation-related data of each specific CH object. Combined with "Rapid Learning Methodology in Freehand Sketching" (RaLeMeFS), it can serve as a powerful tool for the analysis of CH objects for conservation purposes. The approach is based on methods initially developed, applied and introduced by the author in 2002, 2003, 2009 [1–3].

[FtE] + [RaLeMeFS] = [Visual Analysis Tool for CCH through Sketching]

The paper presents the results of recent development and application of the above methods in national and international projects. It demonstrates the easy applicability of the method, and exemplifies the results of its application by diverse types of users who had little or no experience in arts before the application period.

2   WHAT: Freehand Image as an Engine of Conservation Analysis

In the past, freehand sketching and drawing were an integral part of architectural education, and they were traditionally applied in conservation of built heritage [4, 5]. Architectural curricula produced the main heritage conservation expert force—conservation/ restoration architects, and included a significant number of courses in drawing, painting and sculpture, with many sources available [6–8]. Since the closing decades of the 20th century, the important development of advanced methods and techniques for collection, processing and production of visual and multi-dimensional data has led to a wide replacement of freehand techniques in both architectural and engineering education, and in the field of recording and survey of historic buildings. At the same time, the understanding of specific and unique values of freehand applications for architects, engineers and scientists is gaining more attention, and sometimes originates from the ICT community [9]. The role and uses of sketching as an instrument for creative synthesis in various areas of design have been profoundly studied over the decades [10–13]. Moreover, recent developments in sketch-based modeling are opening new opportunities of integration of freehand sketches as free input in computer-aided design [14–16]. However, the majority of architects and engineers seem to no longer possess the freehand drawing ability. Some developments, aimed at providing a short path to successful drawing, are mostly addressed to general public [17], or non-conservation architects [18], but they don't have heritage conservation in mind.

In the context of CH conservation, the production and application of freehand images are commonly seen as fossils, with unchangeable properties. However, if we approach them as flexible and goal-adjustable, the spectrum of their uses may be extended significantly. This also allows reconsidering the A-B-C Assumptions.

With regards to *Assumption B: producing a freehand image is time consuming*; - indeed, it takes far more time to produce a free hand image than e.g. to take a photograph. But what are the aims of each action? Freehand drawing and precise imaging, produced with the aid of advanced technologies, differ by their driving forces. While advanced technologies provide a wide range of methods and equipment for data collection and multi-layer analysis, usually by means of pre-developed processes, a freehand image has a first-hand connection with the brain of its human producer. A freehand image is flexible and is produced through the immediate contact, reflection and reaction to the experience, perception, knowledge and understanding of its maker in real time (Fig. 1).

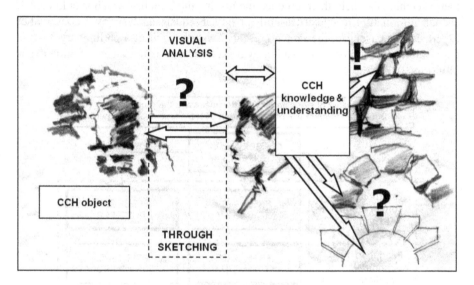

Fig. 1. CCH - targeted sketching process visual analysis © A. Lobovikov-Katz

In conservation of CH, a freehand image is more useful for analysis and decision making than for the accumulation of precise data. In many cases it is simply unnecessary to produce a detailed image which can be obtained by the use of advanced technologies. A sketch serves as a self-focusing instrument for its producer. Such a sketch should not be significantly time-consuming. In this context, the terms "image" and "produce" lose their original role, because the main focus here is shifted *from the result to the process of understanding and analyzing.* This is the major contribution of freehand sketching to CCH.

With regard to *Assumption A: the use of freehand methods cannot produce accurate and detailed results*, - accuracy can be achieved when a sufficient level of proficiency in sketching is achieved through the learning process [19]. Now, let us focus on *Assumption C* which claims that acquiring an acceptable skill in freehand sketching requires much time, effort and aptitude, which reduces its application to a very limited number of experts. The major aim of "Rapid Learning Methodology in Freehand Sketching" is precisely to do this - to shorten the duration of the learning period needed to attain a sufficient level in freehand sketching. In this way, it allows practically everybody to quickly acquire a sketching ability, and open up sketch-powered visual analysis to wide range of users within and beyond the heritage conservation community.

Different types of conservation-focused sketchers might use freehand sketches in different ways. Conservation experts are capable of immediately understanding the conservation implications of their discoveries made through sketching, and the major outcome might be operational conclusions, rather than the sketch itself. However, sketchers who are not trained in conservation, but who produce a sketch with a specific focus on its contribution to CCH, cannot achieve full-scale conclusions resulting from their sketching process. In this case, the process of understanding which occurs during their sketching can help them produce the result - the sketch, - which should contain enough information to make it useful for its subsequent analysis by a conservation expert. In this case also, the sketch presents a visual result of a preliminary analysis purposefully focused on conservation by a sketcher who is not a conservation expert [20] (Fig. 2).

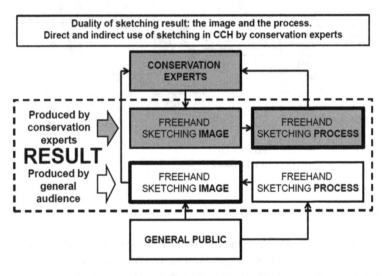

Fig. 2. Duality of sketching result: the image and the process. Direct and indirect use of sketching in CCH by conservation experts © A. Lobovikov-Katz

As demonstrated in the course of different educational heritage studying frameworks, sketching can be used to a varying extent and purpose at different levels of CH expertise, but they have a common basis - visual analysis, powered by the sketching process, activating deeper levels of understanding than by merely looking at a monument.

3   HOW: Focusing the Eye - CCH-Focused Visual Analysis in Sketching

Two skills are required from a sketcher for a successful representation for CCH:

- to perform an educated visual analysis of CCH objects:
- to produce an image of a CCH object.

This section focuses on the first skill as part of the sketching process - the ability to understand the visual data of a heritage object perceived by the sketcher. As shown in the European project ELAICH (Educational Linkage Approach In Cultural Heritage) that was carried out in the framework of the Euromed Heritage Programme 4 (2009–2012) - ELAICH ENPI-2008/150-583, it is possible to educate in a relatively short time an audience, non-trained in CCH, - to achieve a good level of understanding of CCH basic problems, by the use of "ELAICH Methodology" [21]. However, to enable a sketcher to produce a sketch of conservational analytical value, it is necessary to train his eye and mind to capture the multilayered data on site. To become effective for actual sketching, CCH focus should be formulated as simply as possible. At the same time, focus definition should not overlook the essence of CCH. This includes the efforts to understand and preserve a unique complex of values of each heritage object; the efforts on its recovering (to possible limits) from deterioration and preventing further decay, through respect to authenticity, taking into consideration methodologies, principles and the development of criteria. In this context, CCH is formulated as *reaching a balance between the values (positive) and the deterioration (negative) of CH objects* (Fig. 3). This simplified formula is the basis for focusing the Eye (FtE) of non-trained sketchers and it can be of use to both CCH experts and the general public in the real time of in-situ sketching.

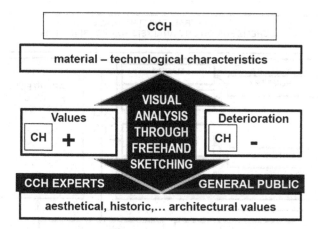

Fig. 3. Focusing the eye: capturing the characteristics of both the values and the deterioration of CH © A. Lobovikov-Katz

While conservation experts are highly knowledgeable in their CCH area, they still need to sharpen their skills in the unfamiliar area of CCH sketching. It is not easy for an untrained-in-the-art sketcher to capture and transmit to/by sketch many of the visual characteristics of a sketched object. This might be caused not merely by the complexity of the sketching process, but also in the difficulty to combine analytical thinking with creative processes. Furthermore, experts from many areas of science and technology are involved in the contemporary conservation of cultural heritage, and some of them do not deal with the analysis of historic buildings or sites on a daily basis, e.g. experts in analytical chemistry need to develop different skills for sketching than those required in their laboratory.

For the general public, who are not conservation experts, such guidance is indispensable. For them, it is necessary to go further, and get more into details, such as learning to perceive an entire edifice as an entity combined of its integral parts: geometry (shape, space) and materials [22]. Both geometry and materials play an active role in solving contradictions frequently encountered on historic monuments, such as between the urge to preserve an architectural value of a building or a detail, versus its poor physical state. The difficulty of conservation decisions and interventions may be rooted in the fine geometry of an authentic detail and the inability to preserve it due to lost geometry of its present state, while geometry is lost through the loss of material, and possibly - the loss of structural stability. Developing awareness and understanding of such problems sharpens and educates the visual focus of general public sketchers. Their efforts in actual sketching are based on this solid intellectual basis - not just looking at a building but to know where to look and what to look for.

In Fig. 4, macro geometry relates to a large-scale built heritage object, - the entire architectural ensemble, structure, building or its large parts. Micro geometry relates to elementary single units, e.g. a single stone, column capital, etc., with attention to both

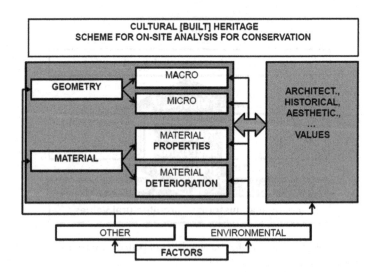

Fig. 4. Focusing the eye: capturing the characteristics of both the values and the deterioration of CH - between geometry, material and environment © A. Lobovikov-Katz

material properties and material deterioration. This simple scheme demonstrates the interconnection between environment, geometry and material, with regard to both the values and the deterioration, e.g. the original architectural choice of building material depends on its availability, and at the same time its original material properties predetermine its durability under specific environmental conditions.

"Focusing the eyes" of CCH sketchers should be undertaken before the start of their actual on-site sketching of historic buildings. This should be combined with introducing the actual methodology for freehand sketching based on the author's Rapid Learning Methodology in Freehand Sketching.

4 WHO: Accessibility of the Method, Its Uses and Application Examples

In order to sketch, a basic proficiency in freehand sketching is needed. The method is accessible to practically everybody, through the Rapid Learning Methodology in Freehand Sketching. This section of the paper presents several examples of its application combined with FtE - "focusing the eye" on CCH. Different types of participants, from high school students to conservation experts took part in the sessions given by author, in the framework of several projects. The majority of all participants had no experience in freehand sketching before the sessions. Duration of learning-sketching sessions was different for each group, as was the relative duration of introducing the sketching methodology (RaLeMeFS) and the "focusing the eye" on CCH.

4.1 Case Study 1: The Use of CCH Freehand Sketching by CCH Experts

This example demonstrates the use of CCH freehand sketching in the course of a pilot learning experience undertaken in sessions on "Understanding cultural heritage through sketching – rapid learning methodology" as part of the Training School, organized by COST i2MHB and the Fundación Santa María la Real del Patrimonio Histórico on its premises in Aguilar de Campoo in Spain, January 27–29, 2016.

As part of the Training School, sketching sessions (2 h lecture and demonstration; home work; 2.5 h practical application on a historic site; 1 h conclusion and analysis of results) were given by the author to a group of experts, MSc and PhD students from the following areas of CH conservation: history, archaeology, architecture, art history, sociology, cultural heritage, conservation of cultural heritage, civil eng., building pathology, chemistry, electrical eng., economics, management. Some participants came from a combined educational background in several areas, i.e. BSc., MSc., and PhD in different fields. Only a small number of participants were architects.

At the conclusion of the sessions, participants filled in questionnaires. Of 22 participants, 8 had no experience in freehand drawing, sketching or painting before the sessions, 2 had "almost none" or "very little" experience (45 % altogether), while 12 participants had experience in this area.

There was very little difference between the two types of participants with regard to the main difficulties during the sessions. As reported by the participants, many difficulties were related to capturing "perspective" and "proportions". 50 % of the participants with no or very little experience in sketching wrote that "everybody can learn to draw", as an answer to their summing up of the session.

72 % of all participants answered that sketching is useful for every expert in this field. Majority of participants were interested in further learning of sketching. 86 % of all participants were planning to use sketching in their main field of work. According to participants' answers, a wide range of possible general uses of sketching in conservation of cultural heritage could be possible. The participants provided interesting and often unusual answers. One answer expresses the essence and relevance of sketching for understanding and preserving of cultural heritage. This was provided as an answer to the question: Q: "What can be the use of sketching in conservation of cultural heritage in general (if any?)". A: "To sketch what you do not see". This quotation puts in a nutshell the great value of sketching as a tool for deepening the understanding and discovering the data which is often "invisible" to a non-sketching observer.

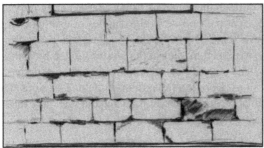 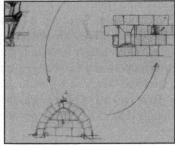

Fig. 5. Sketches, produced by two conservation experts - participants of practical session on "Understanding cultural heritage through sketching", as part of the COST i2MHB Training School, Fundación Santa María la Real del Patrimonio Histórico, Spain, 2016: FtE and RaLeMeFS were applied. Both participants (D.Sc., construction economist (left) and MSc, building engineer; restorer (right)) had no previous experience in sketching, painting or freehand drawing before the session. Nevertheless, the sketches demonstrate accurate graphic analysis of geometry and material, including visible diverse degrees of deterioration.

After the lecture and demonstration, during the practical part of the session at the historic site, the participants were asked to pick a detail or a small portion of a wall or structure on which to focus their sketching. In spite of the short duration of the practical session, some participants without previous experience in sketching showed very good results. Some sketches of "newcomers to the art" demonstrated attentive visual analysis of conservation problems of a historic monument. At first, many participants experienced difficulty with proportions and perspective. However, many quickly grasped the rules and discarded their mistakes already by the end of the 2-hour sketching session. At the same time, they apparently enjoyed "understanding heritage through sketching", which possibly helped them to persist until completing their task in the severe winter cold of Northern Spain. To conclude this specific experience, the main value of CCH sketching by conservation experts is "fueling" the process of their analytical understanding rather than the production of a detailed sketch. At the same time, FtE-aided sketcher-sketch analytical dialogue should be based on an acceptable level of sketching which can be achieved by RaLeMeFS (Fig. 5).

4.2 Case Study 2: The Use of CCH Freehand Sketching by General Public - The Case of High School Students

This example presents a very short session given by author to a group of some 25 students of the Ben Zvi high school at Kiriat Ono, with the support of and at the premises of the Society for Preservation of Israel Heritage Sites (SPIHS) at the Mikveh Israel School Visitor Centre in Tel Aviv, Israel, in May 2016.

The students had several introductory meetings to the conservation of cultural heritage provided by the SPIHS experts before this session. They had no previous experience in sketching. The session duration was about 1.5 h. It included the "Focusing the Eye" part and a short review of different types or projections; a very brief explanation and demonstration on sketching methodology (RaLeMeFS); and about 20 min of practical sketching of historic buildings or their elements. Introduction to and practicing RaLeMeFS were too short (about 40 min altogether) to prevent mistakes in proportions and perspective, which affected negatively the reliability of many sketches.

However, students' choice of their sketching subjects demonstrated their ease and success with using FtE. Right from the start of the practical part of the session, as they stepped from the classroom into the historic compound, they "focused their eyes" on conservation problems and values, e.g.: artistic values and material deterioration of specific architectural elements, material deterioration problems of plaster; cracks in buildings and supporting walls; etc (Fig. 6).

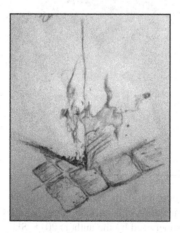

Fig. 6. Fast on-site sketch by a high-school student at a practical part of a lesson on understanding historic sites through sketching: material deterioration of a ground storey corner of a historic building, and pavement.

4.3   Case Study 3: The Use of CCH Freehand Sketching by Non-conservation Architecture Students

These architecture students had no previous course in conservation. Some of them took a course in architectural drawing assisted by RaLeMeFS. Freehand sketch demonstrated here was produced in the framework of the course in documentation and survey of historic buildings and sites. The course was given by the author at the Faculty of Architecture and Town Planning, Technion – Israel Institute of Technology in Haifa. It consisted of lessons in a university classroom, exercise in Haifa, and three to four days of precise measurements on a World Heritage site in Acre (Akko) with the help of simple equipment supplied by the Transportation and Geo-Information Engineering section of the Faculty of Civil Engineering. This course had a strictly precise orientation. At the end of the course, students had to produce several layers of mapping according to guidelines. Freehand sketching was not required. Furthermore, CAD disciplines dominate the faculty curriculum, with a very limited number of freehand-related, not obligatory courses. Nevertheless, the few participants who succeeded to acquire basic sketching skills before this course used sketching to the benefit of their documentation teams. Furthermore, the sketch of a heavily deteriorated column capital, presented here, helped

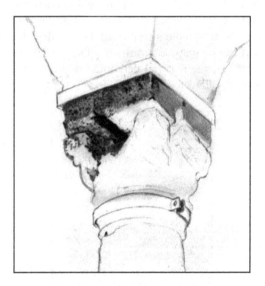

Fig. 7. Sketch from a field book, part of the teamwork in students' documentation and mapping project, in the course "Documentation of historic building and sites" Faculty of Architecture and Town Planning, Technion, (supervised by the author) 2011. Sketch by Ori Roll. This freehand sketch focuses on severe deterioration of the column's capital. It also points out the initial visible stage of detachment of a stabilizing metal brace beneath it; and hints at material deterioration of an arch above the capital, on the left. Basing his opinion on this sketch, a conservation expert might recommend urgent engineering investigation of such details of the courtyard in order to examine their material deterioration and structural stability altogether. In the specific context of this students' project, the sketch helped them to discover and analyze the main natural deterioration cause on this part of the monument.

them to formulate the right questions and reach correct conclusions about the main deterioration causes, their geometrical distribution on the monument, and relative dating of the capitals of the courtyard (Fig. 7).

As demonstrated by these examples, on-site sketching brings the sketching person to deeper levels of understanding than by merely looking at the monument. This is true for both high school students and conservation experts, though their use of sketching differs.

5   Conclusions

Human visual system is able to process complex data, including information on both geometry and materials of complex objects. Combining this natural ability with a focus on conservation data and problems of an observed cultural heritage object with the help of FtE (Focusing the Eye), and at the same time activating the process of visual analysis through sketching, can be an invaluable aid to the conservation of cultural heritage. FtE, supported by RaLeMeFS, allows for the inclusion of traditional freehand sketching into modern interdisciplinary and multidisciplinary conservation research and practice. Due to its simplicity, the method can be used by the general public and therefore enable large numbers of historic monuments to be studied and monitored regularly on a basic level. The results of such wide active visual observation can be used by conservation experts. Furthermore, conservation experts can use this method directly, to effectively enhance their process of visual analysis of historic buildings and sites under study or conservation. This method can be also applied by other heritage-related communities, who have become more involved in conservation in recent decades, e.g. archaeologists.

Activating visual analysis by FtE and RaLeMeSF, successful results of involving e-learning in the education of the general public for CCH [23–25], and the rise of interest and achievements of the digital community in the development of sketch-based modeling in the recent decade [26] add new dimensions to an old traditional, two-dimensional technique of freehand sketching.

Acknowledgements. The author would like to express her appreciation to all organizers and participants of training and learning activities, for their support and enthusiasm, especially COST TD1406 (I2MHB) - Innovation in the intelligent management of heritage buildings; Fundación Santa María la Real del Patrimonio Histórico, Aguilar de Campoo, Spain; Society for Preservation of Israel Heritage Sites (SPIHS); Technion-Israel Institute of Technology.

References

1. Lobovikov-Katz, A.: A new teaching methodology in freehand drawing and painting and its application to the field of conservation of monuments. In: Galan, E.M., Zezza, F. (eds.) Protection and Conservation of the Cultural Heritage of the Mediterranean Cities, Proceedings of the 5th International Symposium on the Conservation of Monuments in the Mediterranean Basin, Sevilla, Spain, 5–8 April 2000, pp. 593–597. Swets & Zeitlinger, Lisse (2002)
2. Lobovikov-Katz, A.: Heritage education for heritage conservation (contribution of educational codes to study of deterioration of natural building stone in historic monuments). Strain Int. J. Exp. Mech. **45**(5), 480–484 (2009)

3. Lobovikov-Katz, A.: Renovation approach to the role and methodology of teaching graphic disciplines as an integral part of education of architects for conservation (comprehensive teaching program approach). In: Proceedings of the Scientific Congress: 7th International Symposium of the Organization of World Heritage Cities, (Keeping Heritage Alive – Education and Training for the Preservation of Cultural Heritage), Rhodes, 23–26 September 2003 (2003)

4. Feilden, B.M.: Conservation of Historic Buildings. Butterworth Scientific, London (1982)

5. Burns, J.A.: Recording Historic Structures: Historic American Buildings Survey, Historic American Engineering Record. American Institute of Architects Press, Washington, D.C. (1989)

6. Alberti, L.B.: Ten books on architecture. The Academy of Architecture of the USSR, Moscow MCMXXXV (Леон Баттиста Альберти: Десять Книг о Зодчестве, Издательство Всесоюзной Академии Архитектуры, Москва) (1935)

7. Vasari, G.: Vasari On Technique: Being the Introduction to the Three Arts of Design, Architecture, Sculpture and Painting, Prefixed to the Lives of the Most Excellent Painters, Sculptors and Architects. Dover, New York (1960)

8. Tichonov, S., Demijanov, V., Podrezkov, V.: Drawing. Moscow, Stroiizdat (Тихонов, С.В., Демьянов, В.Г., Подрезков, В.Б.: Рисунок, Москва Стройиздат) (1983)

9. Duhovnik, J., Demsar, I., Drešar, P.: Technical freehand sketching, Chap. 2: In: Duhovnik, J., Demsar, I., Drešar, P. (eds.) Space Modeling with SolidWorks and NX, vol. XIV. Springer, Cham (2015)

10. Goldschmidt, G.: The dialectics of sketching. Creativity Res. J. **4**, 123–143 (1991)

11. Lane, D., Seery, N., Gordon, S.: A paradigm for promoting visual synthesis through freehand sketching. Des. Technol. Educ. **15**(3), 2010 (2010)

12. Verstijnen, I.M., van Leeuwen, C., Goldschmidt, G., Hamel, R., Hennessey, J.M.: Sketching and creative discovery. Des. Stud. **19**(4), 519–546 (1998)

13. Goldschmidt, G.: On visual design thinking: the vis kids of architecture. Des. Stud. **15**(2), 158–174 (1994)

14. Olsen, L., Samavati, F., Sousa, M.C., Jorge, J.: A taxonomy of modeling techniques using sketch-based interfaces. Eurograph. State Art Rep. **1**(1–4), 1 (2008)

15. Kondo, K.: Interactive geometric modeling using freehand sketches. J. Geom. Graph. **13**(2), 195–207 (2009)

16. Olsen, L., Samavati, F., Sousa, M.C., Jorge, J.: Sketch-based modeling: a survey. Comput. Graph. **33**, 85–103 (2009)

17. Edwards, B.: The New Drawing on the Right Side of The Brain. Tarcher/Putnam, New York (1999)

18. Yee, R.: Architectural Drawing: A Visual Compendium of Types and Methods. Wiley, New York (1997)

19. Lobovikov-Katz, A.: Freehand sketching in the contemporary conservation of monuments, water and cultural heritage. In: Zezza, F., Perthuisot, V., Plancon, A. (eds.) Proceedings of the 7th International Symposium on the Conservation of Monuments in the Mediterranean Basin, Orleans, France, June 2007 (2008)

20. Lobovikov-Katz, A., Moropoulou, A., Konstanti, A., Calderón, P.O., Grieken, R., Worth, S., Cassar, J., Angelis, R., Biscontin, G., Izzo, F.C.: Tangible versus intangible in e-Learning on cultural heritage: from online learning to on-site study of historic sites. In: Ioannides, M., Magnenat-Thalmann, N., Fink, E., Žarnić, R., Yen, A.-Y., Quak, E. (eds.) EuroMed 2014. LNCS, vol. 8740, pp. 819–828. Springer, Heidelberg (2014). doi:10.1007/978-3-319-13695-0_84

21. Lobovikov-Katz, A., Konstanti, A., Labropoulos, K., Moropoulou, A., Cassar, J., Angelis, R.: The EUROMED 4 project "ELAICH": e-Tools for a teaching environment on eu mediterranean cultural heritage. In: Ioannides, M., Fritsch, D., Leissner, J., Davies, R., Remondino, F., Caffo, R. (eds.) EuroMed 2012. LNCS, vol. 7616, pp. 710–719. Springer, Heidelberg (2012). doi:10.1007/978-3-642-34234-9_75

22. Lobovikov-Katz, A.: The correlation between the technological and conservation aspects and those of urban appearance in a stone-built environment: an evaluation approach, Chap. 4.2. In: Kourkoulis, S. (ed.) Fracture and Failure of Natural Building Stones – Applications in the Restoration of the Ancient Monuments, pp. 201–215. Springer, Dordrecht (2006)

23. Lobovikov-Katz, A.: The virtual and the real: e-learning in interdisciplinary education – the case of cultural heritage. In: The 13th Annual MEITAL National Conference "New Technologies and Their Evaluation in Online Teaching and Learning", Technion - Israel Institute of Technology, Haifa, June 2015. http://meital.iucc.ac.il/conf2015/papers15/A3_3.pdf

24. Lobovikov-Katz, A., et al. (eds.): ELAICH (Educational Linkage Approach in Cultural Heritage) Manual. Technion (2012). http://www.elaich.technion.ac.il/e-learning

25. ELAICH e-learning platform. http://www.elaich.technion.ac.il/e-learning

26. Kazmi, IK., You, L., Zhang, J.J.: A survey of sketch based modeling systems. In: 11th International Conference on Computer Graphics, Imaging and Visualization (CGIV) (2014)

Adult and Children User Experience with Leap Motion in Digital Heritage: The Cycladic Sculpture Application

Panayiotis Koutsabasis[(⊠)] and Spyros Vosinakis

Interactive Systems Design Lab, Department of Product and Systems Design Engineering,
University of the Aegean, Syros, Greece
{kgp,spyrosv}@aegean.gr

Abstract. Recent advances in low-cost sensor technologies, such as Microsoft Kinect and Leap Motion allow kinaesthetic interactions with interactive 3D applications. Museums and heritage institutions can significantly benefit from kinaesthetic applications that provide a more experiential approach for learning about cultural heritage; however detailed evaluations of the user experience are still scarce. This paper presents the development and user-centred evaluation of a cultural heritage application about sculpturing Cycladic figurines, which places users in the role of an ancient craftsman or sculptor who progressively creates a statue by selecting and applying the appropriate tools with bare-hand interactions tracked by the Leap Motion sensor. The evaluation of the user experience of ten adults and ten children in two subsequent studies reveals that users find the experience very positive and engaging but usability and tracking issues remain. We identify these issues and propose design guidelines to address them.

Keywords: Cultural heritage · Kinaesthetic interaction · User experience · Adults · Children · Concurrent think-aloud · Usability testing · Leap Motion

1 Introduction

The dissemination of cultural heritage has gained significant benefits from digital technology. Various digital applications related to both tangible and intangible cultural heritage have been made available to the public, which rest on various established trends in entertainment software [1], such as Virtual Worlds [16], Serious Games, Interactive Storytelling, Location-based Games, Augmented Reality, etc.

Recent advances in sensor technology have led to novel low-cost devices that can track human body motion which allow the user to make use of their body movements and gestures to interact with digital content. Notable examples are the Microsoft Kinect, which can track the position and movement of the whole body and recognize user gestures and the Leap Motion which tracks the placement and motion of the hands only.

The possibility of kinaesthetic interactions may expand the potential of digital heritage applications into new paradigms. The kinaesthetic approach is considered an important pedagogy for museum education [5], especially for highlighting intangible aspects of cultural heritage, e.g. habits, rituals, everyday activities of the past, etc. Additionally, gesture-based interactions are generally more suitable input methods for 3D

© Springer International Publishing AG 2016
M. Ioannides et al. (Eds.): EuroMed 2016, Part I, LNCS 10058, pp. 350–361, 2016.
DOI: 10.1007/978-3-319-48496-9_28

digital heritage environments because they involve natural motion in three dimensions. Last but not least natural and intuitive interactions may make the user experience more fun and, as such, retain user interest and engagement for a longer period of time [6].

Up to now, there are limited digital heritage kinaesthetic applications, but there seems to be a growing interest in this direction of research and development. In addition, the impact of kinaesthetic heritage applications on the visitor user experience is largely unknown. There are too few reasonably detailed studies of their usability and impact on the user experience, which poses the question of whether kinaesthetic digital heritage applications provide valuable and usable experiences to users.

In this paper we present the design, development and user-centred evaluation of a kinaesthetic digital heritage application that provides users with simplified virtual sculpting of Cycladic figurines which is exercised by applying respective gestures with their bare hands. We also present the results of a detailed evaluation of the user experience with the participation of ten adults and ten children in two subsequent studies that included both formative and summative assessments based on the concurrent think-aloud protocol, performance measurements and a short questionnaire. The evaluation results indicate that users gain an engaging and educational user experience through kinaesthetic interactions, however various usability and tracking issues remain.

2   Background and Related Work

Kinaesthetic or embodied interaction [2] is about exploiting any type of user movements to interact with a computer, a distant display, projected content or a technologically enhanced room or environment. This is a distinguishable style of natural human-computer interaction which has materialized in further areas including: whole-body interaction [3], which refers to the use of body movements and postures; mid-air inter-action [7], which refers to the use of (whole) hand gestures in the mid-air in order to interact with distant displays; and bare-hands interaction [14], which refers to the use of the hand palms and fingers mainly for desktop or kiosk-oriented interactions.

Kinaesthetic interaction has not yet substantially developed into a considerable corpus of applications in cultural heritage. In [11], a number of large-scale virtual reality installations of whole-body interactions with projected 3D content in museums are presented, supported by the Kinect sensor. A user can made simple moves into the physical space to control her avatar inside an Etruscan grave. A user could also apply mid-air gestures to interact with digital objects, but would need to learn a gesture vocabulary.

The installation of [4] comprises of a Kinect-based installation with which a user may navigate in restored sites of ancient Rome, and a kiosk-based application in which another user may inspect digital artefacts with bare-hand interactions supported by the Leap Motion. The evaluation results are encouraging, but it is reported that users required to guess for the appropriate manipulations regarding the kiosk-based application.

In the Leap Motion app store [8], the applications related to cultural heritage are underdeveloped. From the total of 230 apps, 99 are free of charge and only one is about cultural heritage, 'TomBraining, the Gallery', which offers a virtual tour to a collection of 250 paintings. Users use the Leap motion controller to travel in the virtual world using respective gestures.

3   The Cycladic Sculpture Application

3.1   Main Sources of Information

The process of Cycladic figurine creation has been documented on an illustrative book regarding the Cycladic sculpture process officially distributed by the museum of Cycladic art [10]. We have made interviews with the author who is the curator of the respective exhibition at the museum of Cycladic art as well as field visits in the museum. Respective information is also provided in the museum's Web site [9].

3.2   User Tasks and Challenges

The Cycladic sculpting application places the user in the role of the ancient craftsman or sculptor. When the program starts, the user finds himself immersed in the sculptor's workspace and can see his 'virtual hands' i.e. the 3D representation of their hands in the scene. Then, the user has to go through three main stages of constructing the figurine, by selecting the appropriate tool and imitating the task of using it (Fig. 1). Throughout the process the user sees the sculpture in a 3D form starting from a piece of marble and slowly taking the form of the figurine.

(a)   (b)   (c)

Fig. 1. Screenshots of Cycladic sculpture application. A girl user performs (a) carving, (b) smoothing, (c) engraving.

Each of the identified stages has two phases: the selection of the tool and its application with corresponding gestures. In the selection phase, the user has to identify the correct tool that matches the requested task. By lowering his hand, the camera is rotated down, and he can see the three tools arranged in front of the statue (Fig. 1a). When he brings the hand above a tool, it is being highlighted, and its name is displayed. To select a tool, the user has to perform a grasping gesture with his hand. If a grasping gesture is detected and the user's virtual hand collides with the tool, the tool is appropriately attached to his hand, as if he is actually holding it. If the user selects a wrong tool, the application provides feedback explaining why the tool is not appropriate for this task. In that case the tool automatically leaves his hand and returns to its starting position.

In the task phase, the user has to use the tool appropriately on the statue mimicking sculpting movements with his hand in order to complete the stage. Initially, the application presents a message and an animated clip to explain how the user should perform the task in that stage. Then, the user is applying the tool on the sculpture and sees the impact of his actions on the form of the model. While performing, the user receives feedback about his progress through a progress bar and about his errors through warning messages and designated sounds. Finally, when the task is completed, the user is notified with a message and a music clip that the stage is over, and the application progresses to the next one.

The main stages of interaction are carving, smoothing and engraving.

During carving, the user has to remove the exterior pieces of marble using the emery tool (Fig. 1a). The outline of the target shape is visualized so that the user knows which are the correct places to hit. Using the information provided from leap motion sensor, the system attempts to detect fast hand motion towards the statue. If the edge of the tool collides with the marble with a relatively fast speed, the marble shows a crack, a sound of carving stone is played and a particle system generates the effect of small pieces of marble falling on the ground. Then, a second hit on the same piece results in the piece detaching from the statue and falling down. If the user hits three times inside the target shape, it is marked as an error and appropriate feedback is produced.

During smoothing, the user has to rub the exterior part of the statue with the pumice stone, in order to transform the crude edges into more detailed surfaces (Fig. 1b). The outline of the target shape is visualized, so the user has to rub all the pieces outside this. To detect the rubbing process, the system checks whether the tool collides with the exterior parts, and, if so, it has to detect quite fast hand motion. A respective sound is played, and a particle system visually indicates the process. When a piece of marble is being rubbed, it initially becomes semi-transparent, so that the user is informed that he is making progress, and then it fully disappears. An error is marked if rubbing motion is detected in parts of the statue that must not be removed for one second.

During engraving, the user has to engrave the marked areas of the statue using the pointy obsidian tool to add finer detail in the nose, the hands and feet (Fig. 1c). The process of engraving requires slower and more focused hand movements. Therefore, the user perspective changes, and the program zooms in the statue, so that the hand motions can be mapped to smaller movements. The process is split in three parts: the face, the body and the legs. When the user completes a part, the game progresses to the next one, and the camera zooms to the respective area of the statue. Each part that needs to be engraved is a thick line segment, in some cases slightly curved. The user has to bring the pointy edge of the obsidian tool on the segment and move the tool slowly and repeatedly across it in order to be engraved. The segments to be engraved are designated with blue colour to be easily recognized on the statue. Technically, each segment that has to be removed is split into multiple (usually two or three) objects. When each of these objects detects engraving motion, it is removed, and the engraved part of the statue is revealed. When the engraving task is detected, a respective sound and particle system is being visualized to give feedback that the tool is actually touching the statue. If an engraving process outside the designated segments is detected continuously for more than one second, the system considers it an error.

After all three stages are completed, the statue is replaced by a detailed 3D model of an actual figurine with a similar shape and size, which makes the user understand how the final statue would look like. The user can freely rotate the statue using hand gestures in order to be able to carefully observe it from various angles.

3.3   3D Modelling

The application development involved a series of 3D modelling stages starting from the final statue and resulting to the unprocessed piece of marble. Initially, the detailed 3D model of the figurine was created by 3D scanning a replica of a known Cycladic figurine. Then, following the generic shape features of the figurine, a second, abstract version of the model was created by flattening the surfaces in the z-dimension (depth) and simplifying the geometry. The latter would be the final model after the three stages had been completed. Then, we added extra geometry to re-generate its form prior to the execution of each of the three stages. First we filled the engraved parts with pieces of marble to generate the form of the statue before engraving. Then, we added extra pieces of marble to the exterior surface of the statue (only in the XY-plane) to generate the rough shape of the statue before smoothing. And finally we added a number of larger pieces of marble to generate the original piece that surrounds the statue. All these additions have been unified under a single transformation tree.

This 3D model serves a basis to produce the response of the marble to user actions in each of the three stages. In each stage there are a number of objects that need to be removed by applying each technique. Collision detection tests combined with the identification of the tool movement allows the system to determine if the technique is correctly applied. If successfully applied, respective feedback is triggered, and the object is removed. The number of remaining objects divided by their total number results to the completion rate of that stage, which is visualized in the progress bar.

The Cycladic sculpture application has been implemented in Unity Game engine using Leap Motion Orion SDK. In its current version it supports only interactions with the right hand and has been tested in a desktop setup. The prototype implementation is part of a larger project intended to be installed as a public installation for children and adults in exhibition halls related to Cycladic art.

4   Evaluation Method

4.1   Procedure

We followed a mixed evaluation approach, in two subsequent studies with adults and children, that enabled us to identify UX issues as well as to measure user performance. We asked users to: (a) think-aloud during familiarizing with the use of the app, (b) perform the tasks without being interrupted, and (c) provide final remarks and fill-in a short questionnaire. The results of the first study concerned adult users and were documented in detail in [15]. In this paper we present the results of the second study with children and we provide a comparative account.

4.2 Participants and Apparatus

The first study involved ten (10) users (nine men, one woman, av. age: 27); all right-handed; seven were students of design engineering and three were faculty. Seven participants had limited prior experience with the Leap Motion. The second study involved ten (10) children (seven girls, three boys, av. age: 10.4) all right handed. All were of the fourth grade of elementary school and they were acquainted with Cycladic figurines from their history class. One had limited previous experience with the Leap Motion.

The application was installed on a computer with i7 2.50 GHz CPU, 16 GB RAM and nVidia GTX 850 M graphics card. The Leap motion controller was positioned in front of the user at the centre of the desk, at a distance of approximately 10 cm from the screen and another 10 cm from the edge of the desk. Users were seated during the test.

4.3 Measures

The measures collected in these studies were:

- UX issues: they were mainly identified during the think-aloud session, but also during play (from observation) and from post-test remarks (self-reported). After the end of all tests, UX issues were processed and coded: this included rewriting (so that a single statement resulted to the same issue), identifying common issues among users and matching issues into wider UX and usability principles.
- Spontaneous verbal comments; they were recorded during the think-aloud phase.
- Performance metrics: task time and errors, measured by the application during the play phase. Errors were of the following types: to select the wrong tool, to apply the tool on an incorrect area, to perform an inappropriate gesture repeatedly.
- Questionnaire responses. Both adults and children filled in the fun toolkit [12], which is a simple and validated instrument to assess the user experience in child-computer interaction. An additional question was added that asked users to match tools (emery, pumice rock, obsidian rock) for operations.

5 Results

5.1 Overall Impressions

To obtain a "bird's eye view" of the overall impression of participants for the Cycladic sculpture app, we asked them what they thought about this application (Table 1). All participants provided positive responses with children being more satisfied than adults. In particular six children found the app 'brilliant' and the rest of them found it 'really good', while there was one adult who found it 'brilliant', six of them found it 'really good' and three 'good'. There were no negative responses.

Table 1. Participant responses about their overall impression of the application.

What do you think about this app?	Adults	Children
Brilliant	1	6
Really good	6	4
Good	3	0
Not very good	0	0
Awful	0	0

Furthermore, after the test there was unanimous remembrance of all ancient tools operations. Although this may be considered simple to learn and remember, an interesting question (that can be investigated in future work) would be if they would have recalled these after a traditional visit to the museum and without the use of the app.

5.2 User Performance

The average time to task (Fig. 2, left) was faster for adults for carving (adults: 48.8 s, children: 65.2 s) and significantly faster for engraving (adults: 193.9 s, children: 284 s). However, children were faster on smoothening (children: 67.1 s, adults: 77.4 s), which is very interesting since that most adults had some prior experience with the Leap Motion device, while for all but one children this was a totally new experience. This can be attributed to some extent to that adult users had some occlusion issues during smoothening caused by their hand size and placement (see later on Sect. 5.3) that children did not face since that their hands are smaller.

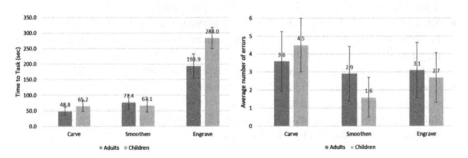

Fig. 2. Left: Average time to task. Right: Average errors per task.

Another measure of performance is average number of errors (Fig. 2, right). Adults performed with fewer errors in carving (adults: 3.6 errors; children 4.5), while children performed with fewer errors in both smoothening (adults: 2.9, children 1.6) and engraving (adults 3.1, children 2.7). This is also an interesting result: children may perform with fewer errors with this technology even when they do not have prior experience! This result may seem inconsistent provided that children performed considerably slowly in engraving, but it is not so: we observed that children were highly focused during engraving which eventually resulted in fewer errors.

5.3 Particular User Experience Issues

A detailed view on particular UX issues was obtained during the think-aloud session and the post-test interview. A total of 197 verbal comments were obtained (104 from adults and 93 from children). The analysis of the verbal comments was made as follows:

- Firstly, the verbal comments were categorized into UX issues (75 for adults, 77 for children) and other comments (29 for adults, 16 for children).
- Then, we examined each UX issue to identify uniqueness (Table 2). Some issues were re-written to be better reflected. A total of 36 unique UX issues were identified (26 were unique for adults and another 26 issues were unique for children).
- Finally, we mapped UX issues into design and usability principles for 3D interactions (Fig. 3). We identified eight (8) principles in which the identified issues fall into: Look & Feel, Feedback, Tracking, Gesturing, User Positioning, Gamification, Control/Reach and Visibility. These are 'working' categorizations to enable sense-making, based on our experience as UX designers and researchers and not any kind of a formal classification.

Physical setup issues severely affected the UX of the app. These include tracking (14.7 % for adults; 20.3 % for children) and user positioning (13.3 % for adults, 6.3 % for children). More specifically, these refer to the quality of hand tracking by the Leap in relation to the user positioning, the placement of the controller and the screen. Most users experienced some kind of a tracking issue, which was either that the Leap lost hand tracking (6/10 adults; 2/10 children), or that the hand colouring changed unexpectedly (3/10 adults; 5/10 children), or that the tracked virtual hand moved or took stances different from user moves (2/10 adults; 4/10 children). All these effects occurred for a few seconds but interrupted the user flow resulting to an unpleasant UX.

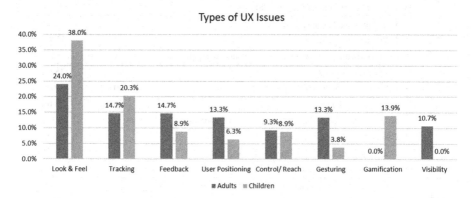

Fig. 3. Types of UX issues identified from think-aloud.

Furthermore, most users – especially adults - felt uneasy with the positioning of their body or hands during interaction. This happened often when they needed to perform operations at the limits of the tracking area (which generally corresponded to the edges of the scene). Some users felt they wanted to stand up (3/10 adults, 3/10 children) in

Table 2. User experience issues identified by participants (adults and children) with occurrences and frequency, classified into more general issues.

	#	UX Issue	A	C	Freq.
Look & Feel	1	Not good perception of depth	4	9	65.0%
	2	Fatigue during engraving	5	7	60.0%
	3	Engraving takes too long	3	6	45.0%
	4	Hand passes through the statue	2	5	35.0%
	5	Not sure what the problem is (during unsuccessful operations)	2	1	15.0%
	6	User requests to add music (overall)	1	2	15.0%
	7	Vertical engraving seems to work better	1	0	5.0%
Tracking	8	Lost hand tracking (hand disappears from scene for a while)	6	2	40.0%
	9	Leap switches between right/left hand unexpectedly	3	5	40.0%
	10	The virtual hand does not follow my own moves	2	4	30.0%
	11	Tool drops from hand	0	3	15.0%
	12	Rotating hand does not show well	0	2	10.0%
Feedback	13	Audio feedback does not differentiate	5	4	45.0%
	14	Feedback required on gesture rhythm or velocity	4	0	20.0%
	15	Low visibility of progress during engraving	2	1	15.0%
User Positioning	16	User stands up (to better position the hand)	3	3	30.0%
	17	User places hand at an unusual orientation for better view	2	2	20.0%
	18	User keeps both hands in scene to avoid possible tracking loss	2	0	10.0%
	19	User places elbow on table to apply gestures	2	0	10.0%
	20	The Leap is better positioned on the left hand side of the desk	1	0	5.0%
Control/ reach	21	User misses target when it is at the edges of the screen	6	4	50.0%
	22	User would like to pan and position the statue	1	2	15.0%
	23	Difficult to select tool (three tools too close)	0	1	5.0%
Gesturing	24	User keeps hand open to apply gestures	6	0	30.0%
	25	User attempts to change hand	3	3	30.0%
	26	User would like to use both hands (bimanual manipulation)	1	0	5.0%
Gamification	27	Can we add tattoos?	0	3	15.0%
	28	Can we add my name (player)?	0	2	10.0%
	29	Can we paint the statue?	0	2	10.0%
	30	A better background image (sunset) and surroundings	0	1	5.0%
	31	Can we add clothes to the statue?	0	1	5.0%
	32	Can we add quests (go find the tool in the forest)	0	1	5.0%
	33	Funny sound, nice. Can we add more funny sounds?	0	1	5.0%
Visibility	34	Hand occludes a good view of the digital tool (carving, engraving)	6	0	30.0%
	35	User would like to zoom in/out the statue	1	0	5.0%
	36	During carving marble pieces fall onto parts of the statue	1	0	5.0%
		Total	75	77	

order to better position their hands in the scene, while others adopted an unusual orientation of the arm and hand (2/10 adults, 2/10 children) in order to be able to view both their hand and the digital tool used.

Most interaction design and UX issues are about the look & feel of the application (24 % of total issues for adults, 38 % for children). In this respect most users (4/10 adults; 9/10 children) reported that they did not have a good sense of depth and they often performed operations either in front of the statue or behind it. Furthermore, most users (5/10 adults, 7/10 children) reported arm fatigue especially during the engraving task. Another issue was that the virtual hand could move through (inside) the statue, which gave a strange feeling to some users. Other look & feel issues are listed in Table 2.

A considerable number of issues were about feedback (14.7 % for adults; 8.9 % for children). In this respect, users reported that they would like more elaborate audio feedback on some operations, especially during engraving when the sound of "scratching on marble" was the same regardless of whether the user was engraving in the correct part of the statue or not (5/10 adults; 4/10 children). Regarding visual feedback, four adult user reported that they would need some feedback on whether they have a good application of the gestures in terms or "rhythm" or velocity. Despite that we had provided a short animated tutorial at the beginning of each task, they would prefer dynamic visual feedback to adjust their moves.

A number of interesting findings were obtained regarding the user application of gestures. The most common (6/10 adults) was that users kept their palm open during some operations, especially during smoothing to enable a better view of the tool used. We had anticipated that, therefore we had designed the grasping of tools in a form of having the tool "attached" to the palm during the whole task (we did not want users to drop tools accidentally or by instant track losses). Notably, this behaviour was not observed in children interactions, because they did not have tool occlusion issues. In addition, we observed that some users (3/10 adults; 3/10 children) attempted to grasp the tool with their left hand, especially to work on the statue from the left side.

One area of findings was about the control and reach of all areas in the scene. We saw that many users (6/10 adults, 4/10 children) faced difficulties to reach to parts of the statue when these were at the edges of the scene; users moved their hand outside the Leap field of view and tracking was temporarily lost. Some user reported that they would like to hold and pan the statue (1/10 adult; 2/10 children), which would help them overcome issues of control and reach.

Another area of findings was about the gamification aspects of the application, which were reported by children alone. Various issues were proposed by children (like to add tattoos on the statue, to colour it, etc.), either spontaneously during think-aloud or at the brief interview at the end of the test.

The last group of findings was about the visibility of various elements of the scene during user interactions, which were reported only by adults. In this respect we identified that the virtual hand often occluded a comprehensive view of the tool in hand (6/10 users), which guided users to try several positions of the hand as discussed previously. One user remarked that an added ability to zoom in/out of the statue would be of convenience, while another reported that the parts of the statue they wanted to carve were occluded by previously removed parts (which was accidental for that user and could be easily removed with either hand).

6   Discussion

We have presented a detailed evaluation of the user experience of the Cycladic sculpture application which included both formative and summative assessments based on the concurrent think-aloud protocol, performance measurements and a short questionnaire. A total of twenty (20) participants tested the application; ten adults and ten children, who all reported a positive user experience. However particular UX issues remain, therefore we have identified the following set of guidelines about the design and development of this application, which may be relevant to similar development:

- User Positioning: Ensure that users can apply all required operations with comfort from the current setup and orientation of the screen, the controller and their stance.
- User Positioning: Ensure that users do not hold their whole hands on the air at a stretched position for long (not more than 20 s approximately).
- Feedback: Detailed and differentiated audio feedback is required for each (sub) task. A repertoire of sounds needs to be designed/produced/tested at design phase.
- Feedback: Detailed and differentiated visual feedback is required regarding: (a) the effect of gestures in the environment, and (b) the rhythm of gesture application.
- Error avoidance: Stick objects in user hand to avoid accidental drops.
- Gesturing: Let the user decide on the manner of holding an object, including the possibility to change hand.
- Control/reach: Ensure that the scene can be enlarged or scaled down, when the user applies detailed (or rough) operations.
- Gamification: Embed relevant gamification issues drawn on user requirements.

7   Further Work

The Cycladic sculpture application may be discretely seeded into the physical museum collections. In contrast to other kinaesthetic installations that are large in scale and require considerable free space for users to move and room for projected display, this application may be situated in a kiosk close to the figurines and crafting tools. This would allow a seamless coupling of physical exhibits and interactive technology in an affordable manner with regard to required space, budget and operational costs.

The application may be conceptually connected to Cycladic figurines that are present in the physical exhibition. In this way, for example a user might choose to create another figurine like that of a pregnant woman and in accordance to select appropriate tools and make respective operations. Furthermore, users could identify these tools or figurines in the physical collection and be motived to further seek for exhibits; the latter could be enhanced with mobile technologies and gamification scenarios.

Another area of further work is personalization: users can create some form of personal identity when they use the app, which can include not only their game scores but also individual content creations. The latter is related to recommendations made by many children about how they wanted to change the colours and texture of the figurines, as well as to make them wear clothes and jewellery. This extension could allow users to view a gallery of such creations made by previous visitors, as well as to share their own creations in social media or get a copy of that with 3D printing technology.

A further area of work is to enhance aspects of interactive storytelling features of this app. According to [11], the state of the art of storytelling in the field of cultural heritage and virtual museums is still very primitive, with a few good but isolated examples. An approach that can be adapted and extended for embodied interactions is outlined by the CHESS project [13] which offers an infrastructure for authoring cohesive narrations with carefully-designed references to the exhibits.

References

1. Anderson, E.F., McLoughlin, L., Liarokapis, F., Peters, C., Petridis, P., de Freitas, S.: Developing serious games for cultural heritage: a state-of-the-art review. Virtual Real. **14**(4), 255–275 (2010)
2. Dourish, P.: Where the Action Is: The Foundations of Embodied Interaction. MIT Press, Cambridge (2004)
3. England, D.: Whole body interaction: an introduction. In: England, D. (ed.) Whole Body Interaction, pp. 1–5. Springer, London (2011)
4. Fanini, B., d'Annibale, E., Demetrescu, E., Ferdani, D., Pagano, A.: Engaging and shared gesture-based interaction for museums the case study of K2R international expo in Rome. In: 2015 Digital Heritage, vol. 1, pp. 263–270. IEEE (2015)
5. Hein, G.E.: Learning in the Museum. Routledge, London (2002)
6. Hsu, H.M.J.: The potential of kinect in education. Int. J. Inf. Educ. Technol. **1**(5), 365 (2011)
7. Koutsabasis, P., Domouzis, C.: Mid-air browsing and selection in image collections. In: International Working Conference on Advanced Visual Interfaces (AVI 2016), Bari, Italy, 7–10 June 2016. ACM (2016)
8. Leap Motion App Store. https://apps.leapmotion.com/
9. Museum of Cycladic Art. http://www.cycladic.gr/
10. Papadimitriou, N.: How Were They Created? Materials and Techniques of Crafting Ancient Artefacts. A publication of the Museum of Cycladic Art (2015). ISBN 978-618-5060-12-1. (In Greek)
11. Pietroni, E., Adami, A.: Interacting with virtual reconstructions in museums: the Etruscanning project. J. Comput. Cult. Heritage **7**(2), 9 (2014)
12. Read, J.C.: Validating the fun toolkit: an instrument for measuring children's opinions of technology. Cogn. Technol. Work **10**(2), 119–128 (2008)
13. Vayanou, M., Katifori, A., et al.: Authoring personalized interactive museum stories. In: Mitchell, A., Fernández-Vara, C., Thue, D. (eds.) ICIDS 2014. LNCS, vol. 8832, pp. 37–48. Springer, Heidelberg (2014). doi:10.1007/978-3-319-12337-0_4
14. Von Hardenberg, C., Bérard, F.: Bare-hand human-computer interaction. In: Proceedings of the 2001 Workshop on Perceptive User Interfaces, pp. 1–8. ACM, November 2001
15. Vosinakis, S., Koutsabasis, P., Makris, D., Sagia, E.: A kinesthetic approach to digital heritage using leap motion: the Cycladic sculpture application. In: 8th International Conference on Games and Virtual Worlds for Serious Applications (VS-GAMES), Barcelona, 5–8 September 2016. IEEE (2016)
16. Vosinakis, S., Xenakis, I.: A virtual world installation in an art exhibition: providing a shared interaction space for local and remote visitors. In: Rethinking Technology in Museums (2011)

Researching Knowledge Concerns in Virtual Historical Architecture

S. Münster[1]([✉]), C. Kröber[1], H. Weller[2], and N. Prechtel[2]

[1] Media Center, TU Dresden, 01062 Dresden, Germany
{sander.muenster,cindy.kroeber}@tu-dresden.de
[2] Institute for Cartography, TU Dresden, 01062 Dresden, Germany
nikolas.prechtel@uni-wuerzburg.de

Abstract. 3D reconstructions have always been an important medium for teaching, illustrating and researching historical facts and items, especially architecture. Virtual representation is often created by cross-disciplinary workgroups, addressing a wide and heterogeneous audience. The authors investigated knowledge-related phenomena in four stages, using qualitative and quantitative research methods. The first stage focuses on the scope and overall relevance of virtual architecture within the field of digital heritage, and the second investigates phenomena related to the creation of virtual architectural representations. A third stage examines how skills and competencies for creating virtual architectural representations evolve during a project and whether teaching facilitates their development. Finally, a fourth stage evaluates how to design virtual building representations to make them comprehensible to a lay audience.

Keywords: Historic architecture · Digital 3D reconstruction · Cultural heritage · Visual communication · Knowledge representation · Information sciences

1 Introduction

Starting from the early 1980s, virtual 3D modeling technologies and computer- generated images have been used frequently in the context of cultural heritage. Related functions rely primarily on research, education and archiving, as well as the reproduction or management of sites and items. Architecture and built structures are key objects of both cultural heritage and digital modeling. In this context, our current research aim is to understand how digital methods correspond with architectural cultural heritage research and education and how this relates to the transfer and transformation of knowledge. Particular questions are (a) the importance of architecture in scholarly discourse on 3D modeling and (b) scenarios, phenomena and strategies for knowledge transfer and management related to the creation of virtual 3D reconstructions. Associated interests are identifying the implications for (c) appropriate teaching of digital 3D modeling methods in higher education as tools for knowledge communication and (d) designing virtual architectural models to support the perception of inherited knowledge of an object.

© Springer International Publishing AG 2016
M. Ioannides et al. (Eds.): EuroMed 2016, Part I, LNCS 10058, pp. 362–374, 2016.
DOI: 10.1007/978-3-319-48496-9_29

2   Theoretical Concepts

According to Barcelo, we "do not understand past social actions by enumerating [all possibilities]" [1, p. 414], but need a linkage between digital tools and human interpretation. Our research focuses on aspects of knowledge transformation and transfer, within and between humans as well as between humans and—as data—computers. This is closely related to concepts of intrapersonal knowledge such as reasoning or memorization, including how groups of people communicate and joint mental modeling [2]. Moreover, it is affected by human computer interaction and their explanatory approaches. Besides a perspective on knowledge holders, concepts like *visual reasoning* or *embodied knowledge* [3, 4] focus on an object which contains and represents knowledge, for example architecture.

Knowledge-Related Phenomena and Effects of Digital 3D Reconstruction. Why should we focus on knowledge? The main intention of both research and education is to gain and transfer knowledge. According to Müller [5], knowledge in the context of visual media relates to (1) the production of visual media, (2) the visual medium as object and (3) the reception of visual media. Against this background, digital 3D reconstruction models and visualizations act as (1) boundary objects—in terms of cross-culturally understandable media [c.f. 6]—for research and communication in the context of visual humanities. Furthermore they (2) embody substantial knowledge—in terms of psychological-physiological cognition, that is, about the proportions or dimensions of objects —during the creation of models and visualizations [7]. Last but not least, visual perception and reasoning is highly influenced by the properties or *Gestalt* of visual assets [8], for example its color or shape. The latter implicitly relates to the level of abstraction [9]. While semiotics focus on a function and Gestalt of signs, model theory focuses on the relation between an original and a model as its *abstraction* [10]. An established explanation schema illustrates Stachowiak's general model theory. This embodies a simplified or abridged image of an original, which is "pragmatic" in the sense of its subjective purpose orientation effect [11].

Digital 3D Reconstruction as a Catalyzer for Knowledge Transfer. As discussed above and verified empirically [12], digital 3D reconstructions rely on the transfer and incorporation of knowledge from various epistemic cultures. This raises questions about procedures and strategies for accessing, exchanging, and archiving digital assets along with the underlying knowledge base. One of the most common explanation models for cross-disciplinary understanding, the *common ground approach*, originates in cognitive psychology and explains factors and recommendations for successful communication [13]. Successful knowledge transfer between two individuals requires that their knowledge, beliefs, and assumptions are synchronized [14]. Especially in cross-disciplinary communication, issues include varying meanings of the same terms across disciplines or the opposite, usage of different terms for the same content [15]. These difficulties are exacerbated by the fact that differences are not known in advance, but usually show up only in the course of interdisciplinary cooperation. While the common ground theory focuses on communication between individuals, the *trading zones approach* focuses on modes of information exchange and collaboration in interdisciplinary working teams [16]. In these contexts, visualization techniques are important for gathering immediate visual feedback to sharpen and approve design visions. Visual media greatly support the formation of ideas within research and learning processes [4] and facilitate a deep learning effect [17].

Digital 3D Reconstruction and Visual Media to Enhance Learning Effects. Another aspect of interest is the best design for visual media to serve as outcomes of digital 3D reconstructions. This primarily depends on the type of visual media, whether physical objects, paper-based depictions, or digital media. Each medium has its own limitations and benefits: images can be easily remembered [18] and are well-suited to conveying information about spatial settings and shapes, but, unlike textsare not so suited to conveying blurry information, such as the various probabilities of reconstruction hypotheses of historical buildings. Another question concerns degrees of visual freedom, including qualities of visualization (whether realistic, abstract or schematic), and their role in knowledge communication and reasoning in certain scenarios [19]. Furthermore, an important question is how visual media are embedded in multi-sensory settings and accompanied by interaction—by gestures, pencils, or digital devices—or combined with auditory or olfactory impressions [c.f. 20].

3 Research Design and Results

Information sciences [21] and visual humanities are the disciplines best equipped to investigate knowledge-related phenomena associated with visual, virtual representations of historical architecture. We combined various theory-driven and empirical approaches for this research. The leading paradigm was to identify and explore phenomena and generate hypotheses using qualitative and quantitative research methods. The analysis was conducted in four stages. The first research stage focused on the scope and overall relevance of virtual architecture within the field of digital heritage. The second stage investigated phenomena in creating virtual architectural representations, especially the role of visual media. The third stage was a practice project to examine how cross-disciplinary skills and competencies for creating virtual architectural representations evolve during a project and whether teaching facilitates their development. A fourth stage evaluated how to design virtual architectural representations to make them comprehensible to a lay audience.

3.1 Discussing Virtual Representations of Historical Architecture

Research Design. The first step was to identify the scope and overall relevance of virtual architecture within the scholarly discourse. This included content analysis of publications in the field of digital heritage, examining both current projects and related objects. The data base was 452 journal articles and conference proceedings [12]. Qualitative content analysis was followed by the development of a categorization and its quantification [22].

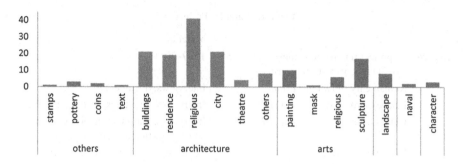

Fig. 1. Objects of reconstruction (n = 168, architectural objects highlighted).

Findings and Discussion. The investigated articles mention a total of 168 sites and items (Fig. 1). Of these objects, 41 are constructed structures, especially religious buildings like shrines, churches or temples, but also residence buildings and sometimes theater or opera houses (n = 4). A further 21 projects are dedicated to modeling various types of buildings including villas, city halls or cottages. Another 21 projects model parts of a city. Numerous projects focusing on modeling other architectural structures, including building parts like columns and vaults, were subsumed as "others" (n = 8). The current discourse on digital 3D modeling and reconstruction primarily focuses on architectural structures. Indeed, "architecture" is the second most important content-related keyword after cultural heritage used to tag articles in the field of digital reconstruction [23]. These findings explain why many attempts at standardization, documentation or—as shown in the next section—workflows focus specifically on architecture.

3.2   Creating Virtual Representations of Historical Architecture

Research Design. The second stage analysed production scenarios and workflows to examine knowledge transfer and related phenomena and workflows within project workgroups and creational processes [24]. This stage contained a survey of 26 project reports to examine current production scenarios of virtual 3D reconstructions for never built or no longer extant architecture (Table 1). An investigation took place via inductive and deductive qualitative content analysis to identify and classify project constellations and related phenomena. The leading paradigm for an evaluation of this stage was a mixed methods approach including heuristic frameworks and Grounded Theory [25].

For the four cases, a total of 9 interviews were conducted with key team members. In addition, 6 direct and participating observations of team meetings were carried out. A significant number of documents, including log files, communication data, protocols, sources, and model renderings, were also included in the investigation.

Findings and Discussion. Digital 3D reconstruction (Table 2) creates 3D models from various sources, such as photographs, plans, and historic drawings. In all observed projects, especially for architecture that is no longer extant or has never been built, historic plans and panoramas were by far the most important sources for creating a virtual reconstruction. A related phenomenon is that digital reconstruction projects require

Table 1. Sample (Projects)

	Project	Material
Reports	26 project reports describing interpretative 3D reconstruction projects	1999–2011
Cases	Roman City *(no longer extant)*	Interviews, documents
	Palace Gardens *(never realized)*	Interviews, direct observation, documents
	Church Interior *(never realized)*	Interviews, participating observation, communication data, documents
	Necropolis *(no longer extant)*	Published project report, interviews

skills in both highly specialized and complex software and interpretation techniques common within the humanities. For this reason, most projects are cross-disciplinary [29].

Table 2. Classification scheme: sources, modeling, and visualization. Based on [26, 27].

Sources	Modeling	Visualization
Historical sources • Hist. images: panoramas, plans • Additional hist. sources: e.g., text Contemporary sources • Visual: sites, plans, photography • Data: laser scans, photogrammetry Logical sources • Architectural systems • Analogies • Inner model logic	• Semi-automated modeling: algorithmic reconstruction • Procedural generators • Manual CAD/VR modeling	• Static images • Animations • Interactive Visualization: i.e. games • Data output: e.g., for manufacturing

Several factors influence a reconstruction process and lead to certain strategies for communication, cooperation, and quality management within these projects [28]. Especially when working groups with different disciplinary backgrounds are involved, extensive use of visual media fosters communication and quality negotiations (Fig. 2).

Common quality negotiation strategies deployed in the projects were based on a comparison between source images and images of the virtual reconstruction. While widely established symbols like arrows were used in all projects, some projects created their own graphical codices or metaphors for communication. Moreover, several projects successfully adopted highly standardized conventions from architectural drawings for interdisciplinary exchange. Regarding function, the generated 3D models support the preservation, reconstruction, documentation, research, and promotion of cultural heritage [37]. The aim is to present the virtual 3D models to an audience

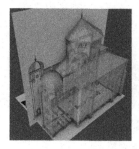

Fig. 2. Exemplified modeling and quality control techniques.

primarily as visual output, which could be static images, animations, or even interactive visualizations like computer games.

3.3 Learning Virtual Representations of Historical Architecture

Research Design. While the above research stages focused on ongoing or terminated projects in mostly professional contexts, this third stage investigates personal and organizational learning processes during a complete project lifecycle, as well as possibilities to facilitate these processes through education. Despite various attempts and projects to employ digital 3D reconstruction methods in education, teaching digital 3D reconstruction as a skill and as a research and visualization technology still plays just a minor role in academic instruction. Supported by the Saxon Centre for Teaching and Learning in Higher Education, an educational project was conducted to create an audio-visual guide for smartphones which describes certain places of interest and no longer extant construction parts of the cathedral in Freiberg in eastern Germany [29]. For the project-based work, 10 student teams were formed. The humanities students focused on the research and textual description of certain historical aspects, while geosciences students performed virtual reconstructions and animations to illustrate the results (Fig. 3). The course taught and trained relevant competencies, object-related knowledge about the cathedral, and best practice for project management and communication. The project was evaluated in several ways. Two joint group discussions—in the middle and at the end of the project—aimed to identify problems and to estimate the success of didactic guidance and the students' adaptation of practices and strategies. In addition, questionnaires at the beginning of the educational project, at the end of phase one, and at the end of phase two (n = 15; n = 11; n = 7) queried student satisfaction and their individual needs. All evaluations were analyzed via inductive and deductive qualitative content analysis [22].

Findings and Discussion. As a general finding, most of the students involved in the educational project were highly trained in methods of their own disciplines but had no previous experience of interdisciplinary teamwork.

The findings of the second stage, mirrored as an implication from our research activities, illustrate that the common ground and trading zones essential for cooperation within virtual architectural representation evolves slowly and mostly due to emerging

Fig. 3. Virtual reconstruction of the cloister

problems. According to cognitive load theory [30, 31], especially the early stages of project involved a high cognitive workload, affected by the high number of simultaneous tasks (e.g., team-building, task structuring, and improving the required professional competencies) [32, 33]. As highlighted in [17], mental processing and problem solving workflows are very different for textual and visual media. Moreover, the epistemic cultures [34] of art history and language studies are closer to each other, as humanities disciplines, than to geosciences. Consequently, synchronization between text and image related disciplines was especially challenging and time consuming. In problem solving, solution quality and progress greatly depend on the prior real or imagined experiences of individuals for a certain situation [35] and the availability of extant patterns for a solution [36]. This means that teaching implications and best practices prior to a project is less effective than coaching during it.

Related to the role of architecture within the educational project, several phenomena can be sketched. The cathedral in Freiberg functioned as a boundary object for communication between disciplines, facilitating cross-disciplinary discussion by making design and spatial relations of architecture directly feasible for all team members. Moreover, abstract, non-nomothetic information like multiple reconstruction alternatives or relational information could be properly transferred via media such as text or speech. Regarding the resulting application and the ambition to illustrate complex phenomena, mutual description and depiction enhanced the quality and clarity of information presentation [37]. The targeted application relied on various media, which required that the student team members develop competencies for selecting, processing and combining media, keeping in mind their suitability as a learning tool for visitors to the cathedral.

Encouraging students to research and explore historical objects by reproducing them virtually is an increasingly important issue [38]. Previous research has already focused on the role and effects of media in higher and museum education, especially visualizations as outcomes of digital 3D reconstruction processes [e.g. 39–41]. Other researchers have investigated the design of learning scenarios to educate about digital cultural heritage objects [e.g. 42, 43]. Sahle [44] has defined a core curriculum which is intended to serve as a blueprint for a design of academic digital humanities courses. While Liu [45] described general requirements for scholars in the field of humanities, Sprünker [46] defined a set of competencies required to cope specifically with digital 3D reconstruction and visualization. Despite all these activities, there is still no broad consensus on a specific digital visual humanities education paradigm, and there is still a lack of larger studies on teaching digital methods in visual humanities [c.f. 47, p. 405].

3.4 Designing Virtual Representations of Historical Architecture

Research Design. A fourth stage investigated the practical implications and user testing of a virtual architectural design. While game studies focus on final products [48] and their relation to an original, our interest was to explore how various levels of detail would affect the recognition of buildings and city structures. We developed six varying designs for a no longer extant block of buildings, which was formerly located in the city of Dresden in Germany and originally built in the late 19th century. The evaluation included two studies to (a) compare design alternatives for the buildings, and (b) verify the visual usability of the formerly preferred design alternative. Both studies employed a *thinking aloud* methodology from usability testing [49, 50], in which test users perform several given tasks within an application and comment on their activities and thoughts. In the first case 6 users (aged 23–52, 2 male and 4 female) compared and negotiated 6 design alternatives [51]. A second test involved 15 people with various levels of expertise concerning virtual architectural representation (5 experts, 4 novices, 6 no answer). This group performed tasks including identifying certain buildings within a virtual city model and describing their unique features, such as the type and certain attributes of the building.

Results and Discussion. A well-established approach to categorizing qualities of archi-tectural representation is the *level of detail* (LOD) scheme. LOD distinguishes between five different levels: LOD 1 is a block model or extruded footprint of a building and LOD 2 includes the block, its height and roof design. LOD 3 adds a photo texture of a facade, while LOD 4 stands for highly detailed modeling of the building hull, including all unique features. Finally, LOD 5 is highly detailed modeling of inner and outer building features [52]. While the LOD scheme provides just a rough classification, it may help define which features are most essential to identify a single building within a block and to identify a building as unique in comparison to others. The research literature suggests the following potentially influential features:

- Basic shape, including a simplified footprint of the building;
- Building height;
- Roof shape;
- Façade photo texture (e.g., windows, storeys);
- Building details (e.g., chimneys, balconies).

Expanding on this classification, six design alternatives with varying features were created (Fig. 4). All tests were performed within a modified Google Earth environment, including several degrees of freedom for the user to change the viewpoint. More gener-ally, identifying a building and estimating its scale in a virtual environment is highly dependent on the (virtual) context and any given information [53]. Especially block models (LOD 1) are insufficient by themselves. The additional information needed can be provided either by a higher level of detail in the case of a single building (e.g., by adding roof structures), by providing auxiliary visual clues (e.g., a map overlay as a ground plan for a building), or by combining various buildings with differing heights into blocks. Concerning the identification of individual buildings within a block, especially the basic shape, unique height, and individual roof colour foster recognition. An individual façade photo texture is perceptible only in close views. The basic geometry, height and individual roof shape of a building provide important visual clues to identify it as unique. The façade and additional building details influence this decision to a lesser extent. To sum up, little visual information is needed to identify a single building and to distinguish buildings from each other, (relatively) regardless of whether the users are novices or experts. How level of expertise and a professional background affect recognition of architecture is an interesting subject for future research.

Fig. 4. Design alternative example

4   Conclusion

The architecture of constructed structures is the most relevant object category for 3D modeling in cultural heritage and most prominent in academic discourse. Especially in the humanities, scholars do not yet have much competence in or affinity for digital research methods [56]. The key challenge is still to develop the skills of scholars and users in producing, evaluating and using digital reconstructions.

Creating a common ground for understanding is another major challenge in cross-disciplinary projects. Language is a sophisticated code pattern and requires the synchronization of individual interpretation and understanding. Architectural structures and their visual representation are highly suitable for creating common ground for interdisciplinary and expert-novice communication. They function as a boundary objects, similarly to shared metaphors. Especially for communication and negotiation, visual media are widely used within a creation workflow. Related competencies draw far more on implicit knowledge and experience than on theoretical implications and best practice. While project work, cross-disciplinary cooperation, and complex problem solving processes are an essential part of modern professional life and visualization projects, academic learning mostly focuses on explicit, theoretical knowledge and disciplinary ambition, rather than its practical application in complex scenarios. Paying more attention to project-based learning and related competencies in academic education in general would likely enhance cooperation quality and project progress.

Regarding the level of detail required to recognize architectural buildings, relatively little visual information is needed to allow viewers to distinguish buildings from each other or to identify a single building and to gain information about its spatial relation and shape. Therefore, architectural and landscape models provide an appropriate approach to structure and access further space-related information in a visual way, including historical sources, background information, and relationships [54]. As demonstrated in our research, even high levels of visual abstraction and schematic appearance can make architecture recognizable to an observer. This makes it possible to visualize different source qualities and levels of certainty, for example by schematic visualization [55–57]. This explorative study relies on methods from the social sciences. Various concepts and phenomena can be sketched, but the data available only allows for limited more general implications.

Acknowledgements. The Freiberger Dom educational project was funded by the Saxon Center for Higher Education in 2014 within the Learning in Transfer scheme. Research on Usability aspects was supported by Josefine Brödner and Katharina Hammel. The research activity described in this paper was funded by the German Federal Ministry of Education and Research (no. 01UG1520).

References

1. Barceló, J.A.: Towards a True Automatic Archaeology: Integrating Technique and Theory. Universitätsbibliothek der Universität Heidelberg, Heidelberg (2010)
2. Cannon-Bowers, J.A., Salas, E., Converse, S.A.: Shared mental models in expert team decision making. In: Castellan Jr., N.J. (ed.) Individual and Group Decision Making: Current Issues, pp. 221–246. Lawrence Erlbaum Associates Inc., Hillsdale (1993)
3. Arnheim, R.: Visual Thinking. Rütten & Loening, München (1969)
4. Gooding, D.C.: Cognition, construction and culture. Visual theories in the sciences. J. Cogn. Cult. **4**, 551–593 (2004)
5. Müller, M.G., Geise, S.: Grundlagen der visuellen Kommunikation: Theorieansätze und Analysemethoden. UVK Verlagsgesellschaft, Konstanz (2015)
6. Star, S.L., Griesemer, J.R.: Institutional ecology, 'Translations' and boundary objects. Amateurs and professionals in Berkeley's Museum of Vertebrate Zoology 1907–1939. Soc. Stud. Sci. **19**(4), 387–420 (1989)
7. Wilson, R.A., Foglia, L.: Embodied cognition. In: Stanford Encyclopedia of Philosophy, Stanford (2015)
8. Gerrig, R.J., Zimbardo, P.G.: Psychology and Life, 19th edn. Allyn & Bacon, Boston (2010)
9. Tversky, B.: Visuospatial reasoning. In: Holyoak, K., Morrison, R. (eds.) Handbook of Reasoning, pp. 209–249. Cambridge University Press, Cambridge (2005)
10. Mahr, B.: Das Wissen im Modell. Technische Universität, Fakultät IV, Berlin (2004)
11. Stachowiak, H.: Allgemeine Modelltheorie. Springer, Wien (1973)

12. Münster, S., Köhler, T., Hoppe, S.: 3D modeling technologies as tools for the reconstruction and visualization of historic items in humanities. A literature-based survey. In: Traviglia, A. (ed.) Across Space and Time, Papers from the 41st Conference on Computer Applications and Quantitative Methods in Archaeology, Perth, 25–28 March 2013, pp. 430–441. Amsterdam University Press, Amsterdam (2015)

13. Repko, A.: Integrating interdisciplinarity. How the theories of common ground and cognitive interdisciplinarity are informing the debate on interdisciplinary integration. Issues Integr. Stud. **25**, 1–31 (2007)

14. Clark, H.H.: Using Language. Cambridge University Press, Cambridge (1996)

15. Bromme, R.: Beyond one's own perspective. The psychology of cognitive interdisciplinarity. In: Weingart, P., Stehr, N. (eds.) Practising Interdisciplinarity, pp. 115–133. University of Toronto Press, Toronto (2000)

16. Galison, P.: Image & Logic: A Material Culture of Microphysics. University of Chicago Press, Chicago (1997)

17. Mintzberg, H., Westley, F.: Decision Making: It's Not What You Think. In: Nutt, P.C., Wilson, D. (eds.) Handbook of Decision Making, pp. 73–82. Wiley-Blackwell, Oxford (2010)

18. Nelson, D.L.: Remembering pictures and words. Appearance, significance, and name. In: Cermak, L.S., Craik, F.I.M. (eds.) Levels of Processing in Human Memory, Mahwah, pp. 45–76 (1979)

19. Bertin, J., Jensch, G.: Graphische Semiologie: Diagramme, Netze, Karten. de Gruyter, Berlin (1974)

20. Ch'ng, E.: Experiential archaeology: Is virtual time travel possible? J. Cult. Heritage **10**(4), 458–470 (2009). doi:10.1016/j.culher.2009.02.001

21. Stock, W., Stock, M.: Handbook of Information Science. De Gruyter Saur, Berlin/Boston (2015)

22. Mayring, P.: Qualitative content analysis. Forum Qualitative Sozialforschung **1**(2), Art. 20 (2000)

23. Münster, S., Kröber, C., Weller, H., Prechtel, N.: Virtual reconstructions of historical architecture as media for visual knowledge representation. In: Ioannides, M., Magnenat-Thalmann, N., Papagiannakis, G. (eds.) Mixed Reality and Gamification for Cultural Heritage. LNCS. Springer, Cham (in print)

24. Münster, S.: The role of images for a virtual 3D reconstruction of historic artifacts. In: International Communication Association (ICA) Annual Meeting, 17–21 June 2013, London (2013)

25. Bryant, A., Charmaz, K.: The SAGE Handbook of Grounded Theory. SAGE, Thousand Oaks (2010)

26. De Francesco, G., D'Andrea, A.: Standards and guidelines for quality digital cultural three-dimensional content creation. In: Ioannides, M., Addison, A., Georgopoulos, A., Kalisperis, L. (eds.) Digital Heritage: Proceedings of the 14th International Conference on Virtual Systems and Multimedia, Project Papers, pp. 229–233. Archaeolingua, Budapest (2008)

27. Hermon, S.: Reasoning in 3D. A critical appraisal of the role of 3D modelling and virtual reconstructions in archaeology. In: Frischer, B. (ed.) Beyond Illustration: 2D and 3D Digital Technologies as Tools for Discovery in Archaeology, vol. 1805, pp. 36–45. Tempus Reparatum, Oxford (2008)

28. Münster, S.: Workflows and the role of images for a virtual 3D reconstruction of no longer extant historic objects. In: ISPRS Annals of the Photogrammetry, Remote Sensing and Spatial Information Sciences (XXIV International CIPA Symposium), vol. II-5/W1, pp. 197–202 (2013)

29. Kröber, C., Münster, S.: Educational App creation for the Cathedral in Freiberg. In: Spector, J.M., Ifenthaler, D., Sampson, D.G., Isaias, P. (eds.) Competencies, Challenges, and Changes in Teaching Learning and Educational Leadership in the Digital Age. Springer, Switzerland (2016)
30. Collins, A., Brown, J.S., Newman, S.E.: Cognitive apprenticeship: teaching the craft of reading, writing and mathematics (Technical Report No. 403). University of Illinois, Cambridge (1987)
31. Hatcher, T., Hinton, B., Swartz, J.: Graduate student's perceptions of university team-teaching. Coll. Student J. **30**(3), 367–376 (1996)
32. Wegner, D.M.: Transactive memory. A contemporary analysis of the group mind. In: Mullen, B., Goethals, G.R. (eds.) Theories of Group Behavior, pp. 185–208. Springer, New York (1986)
33. Argyris, C., Schön, D.A.: Organizational Learning: A Theory of Action Perspective. Addison-Wesley, Reading (1978)
34. Knorr-Cetina, K.: Epistemic Cultures: How the Sciences make Knowledge. Harvard University Press, Cambridge (1999)
35. Tsoukas, H.: Complex Knowledge. Oxford University Press, Oxford (2006)
36. Simon, H.A.: Theories of bounded rationality. In: McGuire, C.B., Radner, R. (eds.) Decision and Organization, pp. 161–176. North-Holland Publishing Company, Amsterdam (1972)
37. Paivio, A.: Dual coding theory and education (Draft). In: Pathways to Literacy Achievement for High Poverty Children. The University of Michigan School of Education, 29 September–1 October 2006
38. Gerth, B., Berndt, R., Havemann, S., Fellner, D.W.: 3D modeling for non-expert users with the castle construction kit v0.5. In: Mudge, M., Ryan, N., Scopigno, R. (eds.) 6th International Symposium on Virtual Reality, Archaeology and Cultural Heritage (VAST 2005), pp. 49–57. Eurographics Association, Pisa (2005)
39. Sanders, D.H.: Virtual archaeology: yesterday, today, and tomorrow. In: Niccolucci, F., Hermon, S. (eds.) CAA 2004, Prato, 13–17 April 2004. p n.a.
40. Fisher, C.R., Terras, M., Warwick, C.: Integrating new technologies into established systems: a case study from Roman Silchester. In: Computer Applications to Archaeology 2009, Williamsburg, Virginia, USA, 22–26 March 2009
41. Flaten, A.: Ashes2Art: a pedagogical case study in digital humanities. In: CAA (2008)
42. Ferrara, V., Macchia, A., Sapia, S.: Reusing cultural heritage digital resources in teaching. In: Digital Heritage International Congress (DigitalHeritage), 28 October–1 November 2013, pp. 409–412 (2013). doi:10.1109/DigitalHeritage.2013.6744792
43. Gicquel, P.Y., Lenne, D., Moulin, C.: Design and use of CALM: an ubiquitous environment for mobile learning during Museum visit. In: Digital Heritage International Congress (DigitalHeritage), 28 October–1 November 2013, pp. 645–652 (2013). doi:10.1109/DigitalHeritage.2013.6744831
44. Sahle, P.: Auf dem Weg zu einem Kern- und Referenzcurriculum der Digital Humanities. Georg-August-Universität Göttingen, Göttingen (2013)
45. Liu, A.: Digital humanities and academic change. Engl. Lang. Notes **47**, 17–35 (2009). Special Issue on Experimental Language Education
46. Sprünker, J.: Educació patrimonial mitjançant recursos educatius en línia amb contingut de patrimoni cultural i xarxes d'aprenentatge, Ph.D. thesis, Barcelona (2011)
47. Sprünker, J.: Making on-line cultural heritage visible for educational proposes. In: Digital Heritage International Congress (DigitalHeritage), 28 October–1 November 2013, pp. 405–408 (2013). doi:10.1109/DigitalHeritage.2013.6744791

48. Torn, J.L.: The virtual cityscapes of rock star games. In: International Communication Association (ICA) Annual Meeting, London, 17–21 June 2013
49. Krug, S.: Don't Make Me Think! A Common Sense Approach to Web Usability, 2nd edn. New Riders Pub, Berkeley (2006)
50. Rubin, J., Chisnell, D.: Handbook of Usability TestingTesting, Second Edition: How to Plan, Design, and Conduct. Wiley Publishing Inc., Indianapolis (2008)
51. Weller, H.: Generalisierte 3D-Gebäuderepräsentation im Spannungsfeld von Primärinformation, Modellierungsaufwand und Wiedererkennbarkeit am Beispiel eines 3D-Stadtmodells von Dresdens um 1940 (Diploma thesis). TU Dresden, Dresden (2013)
52. Pomaska, G.: Web-Visualisierung mit Open Source - Vom CAD-Modell zur Real-Time-Animation. Herbert Wichmann Verlag, Heidelberg (2007)
53. Yaneva, A.: Scaling up and down. extraction trials in architectural design. Soc. Stud. Sci. **35**(6), 867–894 (2005). doi:10.1177/0306312705053053
54. Prechtel, N., Münster, S.: Cultural heritage in a spatial context – towards an integrative, interoperable, and participatory data and information management. In: Münster, S., Pfarr-Harfst, M., Kuroczyński, P., Ioannides, M. (eds.) How to Manage Data and Knowledge Related to Interpretative Digital 3D Reconstructions of Cultural Heritage? Springer, Cham (in print)
55. Danielová, M.: Visual reconstruction of archaeological data of the Sanctuary of Diana at Nemi, Italy (Master thesis), Munich (2014)
56. Lengyel, D., Toulouse, C.: Darstellung von unscharfem Wissen in der Rekonstruktion historischer Bauten. In: Heine, K., Rheidt, K., Henze, F., Riedel, A. (eds.) Von Handaufmaß bis High Tech III. 3D in der historischen Bauforschung. Verlag Philipp von Zabern, Darmstadt, pp. 182–186 (2011)
57. Apollonio, F.I., Gaiani, M., Sun, Z.: 3D modeling and data enrichment in digital reconstruction of architectural heritage. In: International Archives of the Photogrammetry, Remote Sensing and Spatial Information Sciences, XXIV International CIPA Symposium, 2–6 September 2013, Strasbourg, vol. XL-5/W2, pp. 43–48 (2013)

Project Paper: Data Acquisition, Process and Management in Cultural Heritage

Surveying Illusory Architectures Painted on Vaulted Surfaces

Matteo Flavio Mancini[1] and Marta Salvatore[2(✉)]

[1] Department of Architecture, Roma Tre University, Rome, Italy
matteoflavio.mancini@uniroma3.it
[2] Department of History, Representation and Restoration of Architecture,
Sapienza University of Rome, Rome, Italy
marta.salvatore@uniroma1.it

Abstract. This paper addresses the problem of surveying illusory architectures painted on vaulted surfaces. The survey of a *quadratura*, or a painting in general, requires recording the metric and chromatic characteristics of the subject and the typical characteristics of the painted surfaces, such as soot, engravings, and *giornate*. Our goals are the proposal of an "optimum" quality standard for surveying curved painted surfaces and testing a method to acquire and render the data that allows those standards to be met. The test, conducted on the corridor of Saint Ignatius of Loyola rooms in Rome depicted by Andrea Pozzo, shows how the quality of the texture can be measured in terms of overall sharpness and average resolution. It is also shown how it is possible to identify some reference standards that allow the quality of the final result to be determined already in the photography phase of the project.

Keywords: Architectural perspective · Photogrammetric survey · Resolution · Painted vault · Andrea Pozzo

1 Introduction

This paper addresses the problem of surveying illusory architectures painted on vaulted surfaces. As is known, illusory architectures, or *quadraturas*, are perspectives in a natural scale painted on the walls and ceiling of a room. They represent architectural subjects painted in continuity with the surrounding real space, thus altering the depth of the space to the eyes of the observer.

The survey of a *quadratura*, or a painting in general, requires recording the metric and chromatic characteristics of the subject and the typical characteristics of the painted surfaces, such as soot, engravings, and *giornate*, which are often invisible to the human eyes unless the artwork is viewed from very close.

The planar or curved morphology of the painted surface determines the survey method and the type of information it is possible to obtain.

In the case of paintings on flat surfaces, great results can be obtained by constructing High-Resolution Images (HRI) with metric value [1]. These images, which create a high-resolution reproduction in proper form of the wall, also contain metric and chromatic

© Springer International Publishing AG 2016
M. Ioannides et al. (Eds.): EuroMed 2016, Part I, LNCS 10058, pp. 377–386, 2016.
DOI: 10.1007/978-3-319-48496-9_30

information and allow the painting to be explored immersively, as if it were being observed up close; the closer it is observed, the higher the resolution.

In the case of vaulted subjects, however, the curvature of the surface requires the painting to be reconstruct in three-dimensional space. Although it is necessary to guarantee a close reading of the traces of the painting, HRI cannot provide any metric information in this case.

The experiments, which are still in progress[1], aim to highlight the main problems related to acquiring painted vaults. The objectives are the following:

- identify an "optimum" quality standard for surveying curved painted surfaces;
- test a method to acquire and render the data that allows those standards to be met.

2   Image-based 3D Models for Surveying Illusory Architectures

In the study of illusory architectures, it is generally necessary to be able to completely or partially redrawing the traces of the paintings. This requirement arises from different needs, which range from the study of the relationship between the illusory space of the perspective and real space to the study of hypotheses about the traces left in the painting when transferring the sketches onto the vault; to the construction of the flat developments of the painted surfaces; to the construction of thematic maps of the painting that highlight specific types of signs.

To carry out these steps, it is necessary to have a metrically accurate three-dimensional survey model that can render the proper form of the painting and the vaulted surface on which it lies without altering the chromatic characteristics. As well, a high overall resolution should be achieved to make the constructive signs of the painting legible. Finally, a model of this type should be manageable with common NURBS representation software in order to construct thematic vector maps.

Having to survey painted surfaces, we focused on techniques capable of faithfully revealing the chromatic characteristics of the surface. In particular, we used image-based 3D modelling photogrammetry techniques[2] aimed at constructing texturized three-dimensional models whose metric accuracy is entrusted to the images themselves [2–4].

The continual development of computational algorithms used by image-based software leads to increasing metric accuracy in building the discrete point cloud model. The correspondence between points in the cloud and the relative chromatic information is ensured by the fact that both are defined starting from the same set of data: the photographs[3].

---

[1] We are currently testing this methodology on similar paintings, such as on the vault of the Church of St. Ignatius and that on the hall of Palazzo Barberini (Rome), to confirm its validity.

[2] In this experimentation we chose to adopt one of the currently most popular photogrammetric software, Agisoft Photoscan 1.1, but the considerations of this paper are still valid by using any other similar software.

[3] The procedure is also advantageous if viewed in light of the time and cost entailed in the photography and processing phases, which make this technology a shared standard for quick survey campaigns.

Chromatic quality instead depends on the quality of the texture. Since the resolution and texture definition depend on those in the snapshots, it is currently possible to obtain a decidedly higher quality with this technique than with those obtainable with the cameras generally included with the most common laser scanners[4].

The overall texture quality is the main necessary characteristic of the survey models of the painted surface, which are destined for study, critical interpretation, and vector reconstruction of the illusory architectures. It is determined by the different parameters that intervene in the different steps to construct the model: acquisition, data processing, and vectorizing the traces.

For each of these steps, the main parameters that contribute to defining the overall quality of the survey model and its rendering were identified.

The experimentation was made on the *quadraturas* painted by Fr. Andrea Pozzo between 1681 and 1686 in the corridor that leads to the Saint Ignatius of Loyola rooms in the Church of the Gesù in Rome. This is a favourite case study because it is configured as a small immersive space in which the observer is completely enveloped by the illusory space, painted in part on the walls and in part on the vault (Fig. 1).

Fig. 1. Andrea Pozzo, corridor of the Saint Ignatius of Loyola rooms (Rome, 1681–1686).

---

[4] The resolution of cameras installed on today's commercially available scanners guarantee a maximum of 4 megapixels on average, compared to the 18 megapixels available on average for a full-frame professional camera.

3   Quality Parameters in the Photography Phase

In addition to its metric accuracy, the overall quality of an image-based survey is influenced by the photographic quality of the snapshots, which in turn depends on different factors including the sharpness and resolution.

If the overall sharpness is measured as a function of different parameters such as the resolution, acutance, and contrast, the resolution is highly dependent on the dimensions of the camera sensor. This is expressed as the common pixel/length ratio, and contributes to defining the quantity of informational content in an image, and therefore its level of detail [5].

The resolution of a snapshot is also influenced by the size of the sensor, the distance from the sensor to the subject, and the focal length. These quantities are related by the following simple relationship:

$$ls : f = x : d,$$

where ls is the length of one side of the sensor, f is the focal length, d is the object distance, and x is the length of the portion of wall in the picture (Fig. 2).

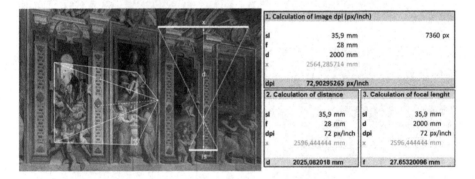

Fig. 2. The calculation of shooting resolution.

It is therefore possible to establish a priori the average resolution of a snapshot, which determines the average resolution of the model's texture, calculated based on the project to acquire the individual snapshots.

A decay, which is due to the curved morphology of the support and is difficult to quantify, should be considered when calculating the resolution. In fact, the sensor pixels record a variable unit of length as a function of the orientation of the plane tangent to the surface, which is different at each point with respect to the plane of the camera sensor in the case of vaulted surfaces; the higher the curvature of the surface, the greater the decay.

The corridor is shaped as a trapezoid covered by a segmental barrel vault. Its dimensions are similar to a prism of about 18 × 4.5 m, 3.5 m high imposts and 4.8 m high at the keystone. Dealing only with the painted surfaces, 174 snapshots were taken with a Nikon D800E, full-frame sensor (35.9 × 24 mm, 7360 × 4912 pixel, 36.3 megapixel), with fixed optics and a 28 mm focal length (AF-S NIKKOR 28 mm F/1.8 G).

Initially establishing an average distance of about 2 m from the painting, each individual snapshot recorded a 2.56-m-long portion of wall, with an average resolution of 72 dpi in 1:1 scale, so 30 pixels describe about 1 cm along the wall. This resolution is adequate for a video exploration of the painting, which is particularly effective in rendering the "surface" characteristics of the painting such as soot, engravings, and *giornate*, and which, operating in these dimensions, does not require particularly heavy computations.

The intrinsic parameters of the camera also contribute to the overall quality of a snapshot. These range from the use of low ISO to setting the aperture at a medium-high value to ensure great depth of field without introducing the diffraction typical of small apertures, the constant setting of white balance for the entire set of snapshots. The lighting conditions of the environment also greatly affect the quality of the model, and the texture in particular. The homogeneity of lighting in the environment is an important parameter because it guarantees the correct recognition of homologous points when processing the data and it permits construction of a relaxed surface mesh (characterized by a low level of noise) and the subsequent mosaicking of a homogeneous texture. Inhomogeneous exposure for the snapshots can instead cause errors when the software, which sets its algorithms based on the chromatic values of individual pixels, interprets the geometry. The rooms of the *quadraturas* have low lighting or, as in the case of the corridor of the Church of the Gesù, are lit by openings placed along a single wall, which light the environment inhomogeneously and make one of the walls strongly backlit.

Homogeneous lighting conditions can be obtained with artificial lighting systems, for example, inflatable lighting apparatus or flash systems [6] arranged in a fixed position in the rooms, or, by using high dynamic range (HDR) techniques to compensate zones with different lighting.

The cinematics of the photography also affect the quality of the model and the related texture. When we take a photo of a painting, the resulting image is a perspective. If we imagine taking two snapshots of the same subject, one very close and the other orthogonal to the wall, they will be rendered with a different number of pixels. One will therefore contain richer informational content than the other. To avoid this situation, it is useful to take snapshots such that the camera's sensor is parallel to the surface, thus guaranteeing greater execution of the structure from motion (SFM) algorithms and also a homogeneous quality of texture detail.

4   Quality Parameters for Data Processing

The photogrammetry software programs use SFM algorithms to reconstruct the three-dimensional coordinates of points starting with a set of structured images. The pipeline runs through the same steps in all software: camera calibration, internal and absolute orientation of the snapshots, reconstruction of geometries, and texture mapping[5].

---

[5] The calculations made by the software are statistical, which leads to variations of the results even when starting with identical datasets.

The geometric quality of the model depends on different parameters, which range from the snapshot quality to the development settings of the photographic set, to the computational capacity of the hardware used. Possible compressions of the source files made when converting the RAW format also influence the geometric quality of the model, but it is difficult to establish the amount.

The basic quality of the model is entrusted to the calibration and orientation phase. Making use of the computational characteristics required by the software, it is preferable to work with the highest accuracy possible. The resolution of the collinearity equations to recognize homologous points among the snapshots forms the basis of the calibration and orientation processes. The identification of notable points is made by analyzing the chromatic gradients around the points and this leads to a high sensitivity to strong-contrast situations. This is the case of shadows produced by strong natural or artificial lighting, but also by particularly contrasting chiaroscuro effects present in some *quadraturas*, as in the vault in the corridor of the Church of the Gesù, where the drawing on part of the vault and the corners of the beams produce a light relief in the 3D model that does not exist in reality [7] (Fig. 3).

Fig. 3. The light relief due to the contrasting chiaroscuro effects of the painting.

Texture creation constitutes the last phase of the process to generate the model. Photogrammetry software programs allow the UV mapping of the surface to be made, which is used to establish the resolution and method of fusion. In the case of the *quadraturas*, optimal results are obtained by using fusion methods that consider the normal to the texturized face. The information is used to choose the best snapshot to extract the chromatic data, that is, the snapshot made with the camera sensor as parallel to the surface as possible.

In the case of surveying illusory architectures or paintings in general, the texture is entrusted with rendering the entire informational content desired. The quality of the texture is measured mainly in terms of resolution, that is, the level of detail contained, which is configured as the main quality parameter to establish.

As mentioned above, a set of snapshots has an average resolution. This resolution, which we call acquisition resolution, decays more or less notably during data processing, even in relation to the dimensions of the set of snapshots.

Photogrammetry programs construct UV mappings of the acquired surface, which can be used to establish the dimensions compatible with the computational resources of the hardware. In the case of the corridor of the Church of the Gesù, the painted surface covers about 240 m^2, equal to a square of about 15 m on a side. It was acquired at 72 pixels/inch, which means that each cm^2 of surface was recorded on 900 pixels. If we wanted to construct a UV texture without losing quality and if it were possible to generate it by completely saturating the raster space available, the software would have to construct a map equal to 45000×45000 pixels.

If we also consider that a UV map cannot cover the entire square surface used[6], we would have to increase the number of required pixels, achieving dimensions that are even more onerous for common hardware to calculate.

To resolve this problem, photogrammetry programs allow the texture to be divided into multiple parts. Therefore, dividing a single texture into smaller maps, it would theoretically be possible to preserve the acquisition resolution. If we stay in the photogrammetry environment, the question could also be considered solved. Instead, having to export the model into a software environment dedicated to three-dimensional modelling, we would have to face the maximum resolution of the UV texture managed as a function of the software and the graphics cards used.

This resolution is generally limited to 8192×8192 pixels. Experimental tests have confirmed this limit; in fact, above these values, NURBS representation programs such as Rhinoceros, which was used in this experiment, generate a quadrangular tessellation of the texture that notably reduces the quality.

Therefore, in order to deal with these limits and maintain quality with respect to the acquisition resolution, in the case of the corridor we should required the photogrammetry software to construct about thirty textures. This is a heavy calculation that does, nevertheless, act as a useful reference to evaluate the quality. In fact, by reducing the number of textures, the resolution is also reduced proportionally, which can be calculated and evaluated qualitatively at this point using the acquisition resolution as the ideal reference.

The experimentation led to the construction of a model of the corridor of the Church of the Gesù with an accuracy equal to 8 mm, mapped with 10 textures with a resolution equal to one-third of the acquiring resolution (Fig. 4).

---

[6] A UV texture associates a raster image to each triangle of a mesh surface developed on the plane. Since the meshes are irregular polyhedrons, the constituent polygons tend to overlap in plane development. To avoid this superposition in the development phase, the surface is divided into multiple parts, and the developed polygons are situated in order to optimize the raster space available. The developed mesh obviously does not cover the entire square surface of the texture.

Fig. 4. Comparison between the acquisition resolution (left) and the 3D model resolution (right); loss of detail of the model texture with respect to the acquired resolution (centre).

5   Vector Reconstruction of Illusory Architectures

The texturized polygonal model serves as the survey basis to initiate the vector redesign of the traces of the painting on the mesh surface.

The geometric quality of the redrawing operation depends on the quality of the survey mesh, whose accuracy depends instead on the resolution and sharpness of the texture since this affects the possibility of identifying a greater number of signs.

Rhinoceros, the software used in this experimentation, includes two design tools capable of constructing both polylines and curves pertaining to a mesh surface. The procedure to construct the geometric entities is based on the projection of the entity represented above the reference mesh projected perpendicular to the plane of the computer screen. This procedure makes the redrawing operation rigorous. In fact, when we observe a three-dimensional texturized model, what we see is precisely an orthogonal projection of the texture drawing on the surface of the monitor. The use of a curve guarantees maximum adherence to the model because it requires continual input to select the entire chosen profile, but it also requires particular skill in execution. The use of a polyline instead provides a redrawing similar to what could be done years ago with an analogue photogrammetry instrument because the reconstruction of traces was made by selecting notable points on the surface in order to set the path of straight line segments. The intermediate segments are interpolated, which introduces a slight approximation, but the overall control is more accurate.

With these tools it is possible to obtain vector models of the painting or its parts, which lend themselves to different uses and which vary according to the texture resolution, like, for example, combination models of the painting or thematic maps that record particular signs present on the painted surface, such as soot, engravings, and *giornate* (Fig. 5). The vector model is also susceptible to reprojection operations and development useful to study the techniques of transferring the sketch to the painted surface; it is configured as a useful resource for informative applications.

Fig. 5. The 3D vector reconstruction of the corridor with the engravings of *graticola* (red lines). (Color figure online)

6   Conclusions

The experimentation, which is still underway, aimed to investigate the problem of surveying painted subjects, with particular reference to illusory architectures. The goal was to address the main problems related to the acquisition of this type of artwork and to test an acquisition and reconstruction method capable of producing metrically reliable three-dimensional models from which thematic vector models can be obtained.

Particular attention was dedicated to assessing the overall quality of these survey models, which depends on the quality of the surface geometry and the quality of the texture with which the model is mapped. It was shown how the quality of the texture can be measured in terms of overall sharpness and average resolution. It was also shown how, based on these parameters, it is possible to identify some reference standards that allow the quality of the final result to be determined already in the photography phase of the project, and therefore to plan the level of detail based on the aims of the survey.

Moreover the validity of this survey method is confirmed by the experimentation carried out on the corridor of rooms of Saint Ignatius where it leads to the identification of the engravings needed to apply the construction of the *graticola* (grid). This construction, well known for its application on the Glory of Saint Ignatius in the Church of Saint Ignatius in Rome, was also used here by Andrea Pozzo to draw the rough sketch on the surface of the vault. The studies on this topic are currently in progress.

References

1. Migliari, R., Fasolo, M., Baglioni, L., Salvatore, M., Romor, J., Mancini, M.F.: Architectural perspectives survey. In: Ioannides, M., Magnenat-Thalmann, N., Fink, E., Žarnić, R., Yen, A.-Y., Quak, E. (eds.) EuroMed 2014. LNCS, vol. 8740, pp. 463–472. Springer, Heidelberg (2014). doi: 10.1007/978-3-319-13695-0_45
2. Guidi, G., Remondino, F.: 3D modelling from real data. In: Alexandru, C. (ed.) Modelling and Simulation in Engineering. InTech (2012)
3. Luhmann, T., Robson, S., Kyle, S., Harley, I.: Close Range Photogrammetry: Principles, Techniques and Application, p. 528. Whittles Publishing, Dunbeath (2007)
4. Nguyen, H.M., Wünsche, B., Delmas, P., Lutteroth, C.: 3D models from the black box: investigating the current state of image-based modeling. In: Proceedings of the 20th International Conference on Computer Graphics, Visualization and Computer Vision (WSCG 2012), Pilsen, Czech Republic, 25–28, June, pp. 115–123 (2012)
5. Baglioni, L., Migliari, R., Salvatore, M.: Calcolo della risoluzione delle riprese panoramiche delle quadrature piane. In: Valenti, G.M. (ed.) Prospettive Architettoniche: conservazione digitale, divulgazione e studio, pp. 809–816. Sapienza Università Editrice, Roma (2014)
6. Baglioni, L., Fasolo, M.: Riflessioni sull'illuminazione artificiale di superfici con quadrature. In: Valenti, G.M. (ed.) Prospettive Architettoniche: conservazione digitale, divulgazione e studio, pp. 679–684. Sapienza Università Editrice, Roma (2014)
7. Chiabrando, F., Lingua, A., Noardo, F., Spanò, A.: 3D modelling of trompe l'oeil decorated vaults using dense matching techniques. Isprs Ann. Photogrammetry Remote Sens. Spat. Inf. Sci. **II**, 97–104 (2014)

The Application of Photogrammetry on Digitization and Promotion for Monuments and Temples in Taiwan - Taking Chua Family Ancestral Temple as an Example

Wun-Bin Yang[1,2(✉)], Tsung-Juang Wang[1], and Ya-Ning Yen[2]

[1] National Taipei University of Technology, 1, Sec. 3, Zhongxiao E. Rd., 106 Taipei, Taiwan
{t103859001,tjwang}@ntut.edu.tw
[2] China University of Technology, 56 Sec. 3 ShingLong Rd., 116 Taipei, Taiwan
{wunbin,alexyen}@cute.edu.tw

Abstract. In this study, the digitization projects of monuments and temples in Taiwan were conducted using photogrammetric technology along with 3D Laser Scanning Point Cloud Data to carry out accuracy assessment of photogrammetry and 3D laser scanning, and in addition, this study creates a standard operating procedure for the photogrammetry that can be used to map the cultural relic's facade of traditional temples in Taiwan. Moreover, a special workshop was established in order to promote the rapid modeling method for the photogrammetric technology by means of Chinese language version of CIPA 3 × 3 rules that was officially introduced at CIPA's 2015 Annual Meeting, so that this study can conduct the learning and educational programs to achieve the combination of cultural assets and public participation.

Keywords: Photogrammetry · Cultural heritage · Temple · Digital techniques · Learning

1 Introduction

Normally, the digitization of cultural property is more costly and takes much more time in terms of instruments and manpower. While comparing LiDAR with photogrammetry, the cost of LiDAR instrument is the most expensive, it is even up to ten times more expensive than photogrammetry. The process of post-production of digital images is more complicated and much more costly as well. On the other hand, these costs usually are deemed to be the critical factors affecting both the accuracy and usage of digital images. Thus, how to choose a suitable digital technology to satisfy different requirements has become one of the most important issues in this field.

Theoretically, the staff associated with cultural property wishes to get the most realistic 3d model with greater texture detail, shadowing and decoration effects for the historic monuments and heritage buildings, for instance, the application of ll3D laser scanning and digitization. However, the preservation of cultural property is always limited by the space, time, budget and manpower. It is, therefore, necessary to choose the suitable technology based on the work characteristics in order to build digital 3D

© Springer International Publishing AG 2016
M. Ioannides et al. (Eds.): EuroMed 2016, Part I, LNCS 10058, pp. 387–396, 2016.
DOI: 10.1007/978-3-319-48496-9_31

models with the best effects within limited resources. Comparing to highly accurate 3D laser scanning technology, the photogrammetry modeling technology can provide a rapid modeling method with low cost and low threshold, which is very suitable for preserving the digital records of historical sites, and hence, photogrammetry modeling technology has already become the main trend of rapid modeling technology.

There is some degree of difficulty in establishing SOP for various 3D image digitization, analyzing or studying various technologies related to the applications of cultural properties. Additionally, the digitization of cultural property usually takes longer and costs more than expected. This study, therefore, aims to contribute to the development of low-cost photogrammetric technology, and meanwhile, solving the problems of low accuracy and low usage of digital images affected by low-cost equipment. Under this circumstance, how to choose a suitable digital technology to meet the different requests from the users has become a bigger issue that needs to be resolved.

Relevant studies for applications of photogrammetry to historical monuments in Taiwan is still in the developing stage, in which, the other type of tangible cultural heritage is only a few cases. Main reason is that laser layer technology is popularly used for developing 3D images by the domestic industry, they seldom use the mature photogrammetric technology introduced by the foreign industry. However, in recent years, due to the high expenditure of advanced 3D laser scanning equipment and difficulty in operation due to its large dimension in addition to higher technology threshold, and this situation makes it impossible to be developed in Taiwan. Thus, this study would like to introduce photogrammetric technology to establish low-cost digital imaging technology to be used particularly for historic monuments.

Over the past several decades, Taiwan's rapid economic development totally ignored the importance of cultural preservation. At present, the national consciousness has urged the people in the whole country to take on the responsibility for preserving cultural properties. To enhance the local perspectives on conservation of cultural heritage, except the promotion programs sponsored by the government, actual activities involved in dynamic preservation should be conducted as well, which should be in conjunction with school education to create the community sense and public participation; it is hoping that we can achieve the sustainability and management of cultural properties through new digitization technology. To enhance and popularize the perspectives of digitization and preservation of cultural heritages, this study promotes the low-cost digital imaging technology used for recording historic monuments through the cultural activities held by a special workshop, aiming to accomplish the basic task for the promotion of education for cultural properties digitization.

2   Background

Photogrammetric technology contains aerial photogrammetry and close-range photogrammetry. The coverage area of the image developed by the aerial photogrammetry normally is large, which is suitable for reconstructing images for a large number of buildings in the large area. However, the photographing was taken vertically and moat of images were overlapped, the covered condition was more severe and it was hard to establish detailed models. In general, the distance for photogrammetry is limited to less than 300 m. The camera station can be set up on the ground or on a high tower. Having a good planning in advance, it still can take images for the building facades from every aspect and it will also completely cover each detailed structure of the buildings. So that it can build a detailed model for the buildings. Close-up images even can be used as the real image materials for posting the surface of buildings in order to build more realistic virtual reality scenes for buildings.

The earlier photogrammetry application used for historic monuments in Taiwan was the measurement for engineering drawings (Chien 1984). As to the study of 3D digitization of ancient temples and historic monuments, it is still in the phase of initial development. At present, relevant studies and applications related to the photogrammetric technology are growing towards maturity (Ioannides et al. 2013; Doulamis et al. 2015). The applications of 3D digitization for historic monument objects can be summarized as follows:

Currently, the automatic technology of photogrammetry is very popular, and 3D technology used for mapping the buildings having overall uncomplicated, geometric appearance along with fewer details is far more mature than before, which has significantly reduced the technology threshold and costs in the digitization and physical preservation of cultural properties. With a good method, so that ICT technology can be used to bridge the gap between cultural heritage and learning (Ott and Pozzi 2011). Furthermore, Lower threshold for photogrammetric technology in recent years has increased the level of affinity that will attract more users. While combining the power of public participation, it will effectively enhance the possibility of the digitization for cultural properties. In the future, photogrammetric technology will become a practical method for on-site digital recording of activities when the public is visiting the cultural properties. (De Reu et al. 2013; McCarthy 2014) (Fig. 1).

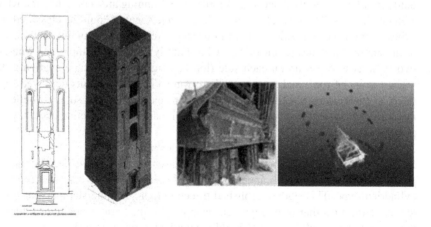

Fig. 1. Elevation and photographic 3D model of the minaret of the Qala of Beni Hammad (Almagro 2013; Almagro et al. 2015) and The documentation of traditional Batak Toba House (Hanan et al. 2015)

3   Digitization Work and Procedures

The subject of this study was Chua Family Ancestral Temple at the Chiung Lin Village, Kinmen County, Taiwan, which was built in 1840. It is an architecture of courtyard house with two-row and two-river and it is a national historic monument specified by the Taiwan government. The building materials were very elegant. In which, the roof of the main hall surpasses all other family temples in height in the same village and it has become one of the characters of Chua Family Ancestral Temple. At present, this temple is the only family temple in Chiung Lin area, which still keeps its construction monument. The building plane was adopted traditional architectural pattern, combining with obvious main axis and pattern in bilateral symmetry. The overall layout of the temple is developing and creating many flexible, smooth & internal spaces between reality and falsehood.

3.1   3D Laser Scanning

In this study, the 3D laser scanning technology was used firstly to establish overall coordinate system around the object. Then, the point cloud data generated by 3D laser scanning were used, based on original coordinate system and through specified locations, to relocate to a pre-positioned coordinate system in order to improve the accuracy of measurement. Moreover, after conducting the calibration of 3D point cloud coordinates, a 3D point cloud model was created, which could be used as the basis data and value-added application for performing the follow-up comparison and analysis.

a. 3D Outdoor Laser Scanning of Chua family Ancestral temple
    This study used Riegl LMS-Z420i scanner to implement digitized record for the outdoor of Chua Family Ancestral Temple. The scanning area contained the whole area on all sides. The marked points of long-range scanner could be classified into adhesive type and cylindrical type. In this study, ten ground scanning stations had been established in the area outside the Chua Family Ancestral Temple, and wherein, two stations were set up on each side (left and right) of building elevation at the highest point of roof; and moreover, there were 17 marked points deployed separately at the various positions either on the ground or the wall so as to build the marked point system that could improve the efficiency of integrating accuracy and point cloud data (Fig. 2).
b. 3D Indoor Laser Scanning of Chua Family Ancestral Temple
    Its interior space was scanned with a FARO Laser Scanner Focus3D. The marked points for the short-range scanner could be classified into the adhesive type and cylindrical type. This study established fifteen indoor scanning stations along with ten marked points that were deployed separately at the various positions either on the ground or the wall in order to build the marked point system (Fig. 3).
c. Results of 3D Scanning and Digitization of Chua Family Ancestral Temple
    In this study, the specific software was used for integrating the results of indoor point clouds with outdoor point clouds, which could be used as the basic information for implementing the digitization analysis of this study. The results are as follows (Fig. 4).

Fig. 2. Outdoor scanning work

Fig. 3. Indoor scanning work

Fig. 4. Results of indoor and outdoor point cloud, and CAD drawing

3.2 Digitized Photogrammetry

The operation of photogrammetry was implemented according to the Chinese-language version of CIPA 3 × 3 rules officially introduced at CIPA's 2015 Annual Meeting. Wherein, the cameras were set up vertically by facing the wall, and the cameras with featured members, which could be used for the photos overlapping, were moved from left to right along a horizontal track. At the corner of the wall, multiple photos should be taken additionally in order to set up the connection to transfer information between two walls.

As for the ground, because the ground of Chua Family Ancestral Temple is paved with bricks matching of repeated patterns, the difference between bricks is very little. While considering a higher probability of success at the stage of follow-up data processing, hence, the wide-angle lens were used to shoot the photos, because one single photo can cover a much larger area. The porch of the Chua Family Ancestral Temple is very narrow and it seems difficult to take better photographs via standard operation procedure. Under this circumstance, incomplete data may arise with regard to the inner portion of porch floor grating.

In the case study of Chua Family Ancestral Temple conducted in this year. While computing with about 1200 photos on the same computer, total running time for using VisualSFM is about 250 h, instead, Photoscan runs about 100 h only. Photoscan has a built-in module that can be used for the Mesh modeling. However, VisualSFM should be integrated with CMPMVS prototype. After testing, it was found that modeling function of CMPMVS could be applied to small objects only. It was not suitable for the building structure contained in the monuments. However, the mesh modeling function of Photoscan had a better integrity and applicability for such kinds of buildings (Fig. 5).

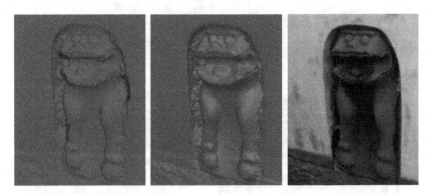

Fig. 5. Digitization of Wind-lion Gods at Chua Family Ancestral Temple

4   Comparison and Analysis for Digitization Results

This study used the images of scenes shot at the Chua Family Ancestral Temple and inputted them into Photoscan for scene reconstruction in order to build point cloud models. In addition, point clouds measured by 3D laser scanner were used as a basis for assessment for evaluating the point clouds. While comparing the point clouds of Photoscan with the point clouds of LiDAR, the coordinate system defined by each tool was belonging to a relative coordinate system, moreover, there is no any control point added in the procedure of point cloud establishment in Photoscan to be a scale basis, therefore the first task before starting to evaluate the point clouds was to transfer the point clouds of two groups into the same coordinate system. Thus, this study adopted the coordinate system and scale of LiDAR as a normative reference. So that the point cloud models generated by Photoscan were combined with the point could models generated by LiDAR and then all point cloud models would be transferred into the same coordinate system defined by LiDAR.

As to the accuracy analysis of point clouds, this study used the way of a fitting plane to evaluate the accuracy of 3D point clouds generated by two groups. On the flat surface such as wall or ground, point clouds of both groups would be cut synchronously so as to extract the point clouds of such flat surface. Also, the point clouds of LiDAR would be used as the fitting point of the said plane to find out the plane equation of such flat surface. After obtaining the plane equation, the deviation between the Photoscan's point clouds and such flat surface would be calculated in order to evaluate the accuracy.

In the part of the architectural appearance, it is divided into the outer wall (left, right and rear) and the courtyard house area. The extracted plane is shown in relevant figures, in which, it is divided into 13 plane areas. The total point clouds of each area are listed in Table 1. According to Table 1, it can be found that the number of point clouds generated by Photoscan is greater than the number of point clouds scanned by LiDAR. As a result, the texture of point cloud models can be seen clearly (Fig. 6).

Table 1. Number of point clouds

Partition of point cloud	Number of point cloud	
	LiDAR	Photoscan
S1_Left	98,982	4,402,590
S2_Right	216,568	3,104,981
S3_Back	125,423	1,963,125
1–1	3,784	133,034
1–2	3,802	107,779
2	1,004	275,643
3	1,662	459,100
4	14,804	1,430,267
5–1	703	29,492
5–2	998	29,251
6	912	68,865
7–1	795	94,283
7–2	677	96,329

Table 2 contains the accuracy analysis and the plane parameters of the fitting plane for each area obtained by means of LiDAR's point clouds. It can be found in Table 2 that the accuracy of the fitting plane of LiDAR is about 1 cm. However, on the partition of point cloud 1–2, a bigger flat error will appear, about 3.4 cm. While using the Photoscan's point clouds in such area to calculate the error of point clouds against the fitting plane, the most

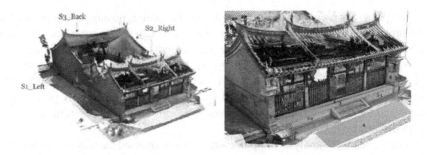

Fig. 6. Accuracy analysis of point clouds

errors are less than 5 cm. On the rear wall, there is a bigger error that is about 11 cm. There might be two reasons for such errors. One reason is that the error is produced by the point cloud, the other reason is that the error is occurring during the transferring procedure of the coordinates. In general, the average accuracy of the fitting plane of point clouds of Photoscan in the external area is about 3 cm.

Table 2. Accuracy analysis of point clouds (RMSE Unit: M)

Exterior	LiDAR (Surface equation Ax + By + Cz + 1 = 0)				Photoscan
Partition of point cloud	A	B	C	RMSE	RMSE
S1_Left	−0.1768	−0.2011	0.0074	0.0136	0.0407
S2_Right	−0.0407	−0.0463	0.0022	0.0100	0.0249
S3_Back	0.0236	−0.0207	0.0001	0.0118	0.1168
1–1	0.0832	−0.0732	−0.0039	0.0104	0.0028
1–2	0.0835	−0.0731	−0.0045	0.0344	0.0139
2	0.0559	−0.0333	0.3835	0.0199	0.0323
3	0.0480	−0.0171	0.5829	0.0160	0.0262
4	0.0216	0.0061	0.5845	0.0092	0.0329
5–1	0.0786	−0.0720	−0.0019	0.0081	0.0022
5–2	0.0825	−0.0730	−0.0019	0.0077	0.0172
6	−0.0416	−0.0474	0.0021	0.0072	0.0591
7–1	0.0622	−0.0555	−0.0021	0.0069	0.0118
7–2	0.0631	−0.0553	−0.0005	0.0082	0.0067
			AVG	**0.0126**	**0.0298**

5 Comparison Analysis of Costs of Producing Photogrammetric Products

The discussion related to photogrammetry cost will be divided into three portions: recording time of photos, data processing time (office work) and computer calculation processing time. Table 3 lists the real-time statistics information for shooting photos of the Chua Family Ancestral Temple during the photogrammetry operation.

The photos were shot by photogrammetric professionals who spent a whole day to complete his work. The light and climatic conditions on the site must be considered. The photo shooting on the site implemented according to SOP can reduce the time of field photography and data processing. However, existing SOP used for ancient monuments as well as middle and large scale buildings still needs to be improved. Thus, it is necessary to improve the SOP for photographing.

Table 3. Photogrammetry mapping work (Unit: hr)

Project	Photo shoot (Field)		Office work		Computer processing
	Professionals	General	Professionals	General	
Experimental	16	0	100	0	500
SOP work	4	4	24	0	200

6   Education and Promotion

CIPA 3 × 3 rules were established by Peter Whaldausl and Cliff Ogleby in 1994. The rules used photographic images as a feasible method for the implementation of measurements and applications in the future. The newest version (edition Nov. 2013) was updated by Bill Blake, Andreas Georgopoulos and José Luis Lerma (News posted in CIPA website). CIPA has compiled and produced "The Photogrammetry Documents related to the Simple Structure of 3 × 3 Rules" acting as a simple digitization method for cultural monuments and historical sites. The development principle of CIPA 3 × 3 can be applied to an easy and convenient photogrammetry method, which should be vigorously promoted in the domestic market.

The newest Chinese language version of CIPA 3 × 3 rules with additional correlation contents was officially introduced at CIPA's 2015 Annual Meeting. So that this study will use such rules to teach students and carry out simple training program of photogrammetry along with on-site operations in order to achieve the outcome of the promotion of low-cost digitization of cultural properties (Fig. 7).

Fig. 7. Photogrammetric workshop and on-site operation

7   Conclusions and Future Suggestions

This study aims to explore the feasibility, rough cost estimation, and initial accuracy analysis of photogrammetry that can be used for low-cost digital preservation of the monuments, historical buildings and ancient temples in Taiwan. After testing, the existing close-range photogrammetric operation procedures has good effects for small-middle sized objects or geometry objects, such as stone lion, stone carving and small pavilion. However, it is still necessary to further design SOP for middle-large sized buildings with curving shaping. Generally speaking, the higher accuracy of photogrammetric products, the higher operating costs. Thus, it needs to choose the most suitable equipment with appropriate accuracy level to meet the requirements as well as economic costs and benefits from various users. Based on the perspectives of preservation of monuments in Taiwan, the subsequent studies in the future, including: 1. Explore the simple and high precision photogrammetry techniques used for different types of monuments in Taiwan, and also compare the differences between each other; 2. Analyze the influence of adding control points, lights and shadows to same materials on the accuracy and integrity of different types of monuments; and 3. Study on the adaptability of photogrammetry combining with the public participation.

In the future, the possibility of using Mesh Model in the measurements and applications of historic monuments repair can be further discussed. The maturation and automation degree of photogrammetry will enhance the possibility of crossing the high threshold of digitization technology while carrying out digitization works and enhance the opportunity of public participation.

Acknowledgements. This study is sponsored by the Bureau of Cultural Heritage, Ministry of Cultural for 2015, 2016 Research and Development Project Plan (104-4, 105-3).

References

Almagro, A.: Surveying world heritage Islamic monuments in North Africa: experiences with simple photogrammetryic tools and no previous planning. In: ISPRS Annals of the Photogrammetry, Remote Sensing and Spatial Information Sciences, vol. II-5/W1 (2013)

Almagro, A., Tandon, A., Eppich, R.: First aid to cultural heritage: training initiatives on rapid documentation. In: The International Archives of the Photogrammetry, Remote Sensing and Spatial Information Sciences, vol. XL-5/W7 (2015)

Chien, H.K.: The Application of Historic Preservation by Photogrammetry, Master thesis. NCKU (1984)

De Reu, J., Plets, G., Verhoeven, G., De Smedt, P., Bats, M., Cherretté, B., DeMaeyer, W., Deconynck, J., Herremans, D., Laloo, P., Van Meirvenne, M., De Clercq, W.: Towards a three-dimensional cost-effective registration of the archaeological heritage. J. Archaeol. Sci. **40**(2), 1108–1121 (2013)

Doulamis, A., Soile, S., Doulamis, N., Chrisouli, C., Grammalidis, N., Dimitropoulos, K., Ioannidis, C.: Selective 4D modelling framework for spatial-temporal land information management system. In: Third International Conference on Remote Sensing and Geoinformation of the Environment, p. 953506. International Society for Optics and Photonics, June 2015

Hanan, H., Suwardhi, D., Nurhasanah, T., Bukit, E.S.: Batak Toba cultural heritage and close-range photogrammetry. Procedia Soc. Behav. Sci. **184**, 187–195 (2015)

Ioannides, M., Hadjiprocopi, A., Doulamis, N., Doulamis, A., Protopapadakis, E., Makantasis, K., Julien, M.: Online 4D reconstruction using multi-images available under Open Access. ISPRS Ann Photogramm. Remote Sens. Spat. Inf. Sci. **5**, W1 (2013)

McCarthy, J.: Multi-image photogrammetry as a practical tool for cultural heritage survey and community engagement. J. Archaeol. Sci. **43**, 175–185 (2014)

Ott, M., Pozzi, F.: Towards a new era for Cultural Heritage Education: discussing the role of ICT. Comput. Hum. Behav. **27**(4), 1365–1371 (2011)

3D Acquisition, Processing and Visualization of Archaeological Artifacts

The Samarra Collection of the Museum of Islamic Art in Berlin

Arie Kai-Browne[1]([✉]), Kay Kohlmeyer[1], Julia Gonnella[2], Thomas Bremer[1],
Susanne Brandhorst[1], Felix Balda[1], Sebastian Plesch[1], and Dennis Lehmann[1]

[1] Landscape Archaeology, Game Design, Computer and Media Sciences, University of Applied
Sciences Berlin, Berlin, Germany
{Arie.Kai-Browne,Kay.Kohlmeyer,Thomas.Bremer,
Susanne.Brandhorst,Felix.Balda,Sebastian.Plesch,
Dennis.Lehmann}@HTW-Berlin.de
[2] Museum für Islamische Kunst Berlin (SMB), Berlin, Germany
j.gonnella@smb.spk-berlin.de

Abstract. In the past decade there has been a steady increase in research projects dealing with the three-dimensional documentation of cultural heritage. While 3D-scanners and photogrammetry are widely used for documenting historical monuments and archaeological excavations, the application of this technology within museums has not yet been established within the daily work routine. Even though the benefits of 3D-documentation are quite manifold, usually only outstanding artifacts are being recorded in this manner due to the complex workflows for deriving datasets, which can be used for further research and knowledge transfer. The interdisciplinary research project MOSYS-3D has been dealing with the entire workflow ranging from data acquisition, pre- and postprocessing steps as well as testing different forms of visualizations.

1 Introduction

In general, museums and other institutions dealing with archaeological artifacts have been reluctant to integrate a 3D-digitization pipeline into their daily workflow due to the fairly complex and time consuming task of acquiring, processing and visualizing high resolution 3D-data. Even though the benefits of 3D-documentation are manifold for scientific research as well as educational purposes, usually only special finds are being digitally recorded in three-dimensions while large collections are mostly recorded using classical two-dimensional approaches.

The range of possibilities for the further use of high resolution 3D-data includes a variety of applications in the field of restoration/conservation, such as deformation analysis [1–3] the construction of fillings or supporting elements [4], or as the basis for condition mapping and archiving restoration information [5]. Of course, it is possible

© Springer International Publishing AG 2016
M. Ioannides et al. (Eds.): EuroMed 2016, Part I, LNCS 10058, pp. 397–408, 2016.
DOI: 10.1007/978-3-319-48496-9_32

to use rapid prototyping for creating replicas [6] or positives of molds [6]. For further scientific research 3D-data can be visualized in a standardized way, enabling the comparative study of shapes [7], while it is also possible to visually enhance fine structures, such as tool marks [8], fine carvings [9] or inscriptions. Furthermore the 3D-data can be manipulated, enabling the unwrapping of cylindrical objects, such as cylinder or similar artifacts [10]. Other interesting applications for scientific research include the automatic detection of cuneiform scripts [11], where the methodology itself is transferable to similar research question. Also automatically fitting large numbers of digitized single fragments [12, 13] offers a major benefit for the practical application of restoring fragmented artifacts.

The interdisciplinary research project "MOSYS-3D" (Mobile, modular System for highly accurate 3D Documentation of Cultural Heritage) is a cooperation of the University of Applied Sciences Berlin (HTW) and The Museum of Islamic Art Berlin (SMB), bringing together archaeologists, electronic engineers, game designers and computer scientists. The research aims at tackling different aspects of 3D-documentation, ranging from the efficient acquisition of 3D-data, automating pre- and post-processing steps and finding new ways for visualizing these data sets for knowledge transfer and scientific research questions.

We believe that utilizing interactive 3D-environments, such as game engines, offers manifold possibilities for the further usage of acquired 3D-data. The immediate interaction between the user and the digital data offers a new dimension of comprehending complex three-dimensional situations. Such environments do not only serve the purpose of displaying single 3D-models, but also enable the combination of different datasets, which have been derived from a multitude of different platforms with varying spatial scales, different resolutions and different accuracies. This allows, for example, visualizing small-scaled artifacts within their immediate archaeological context, such as the excavation area. Furthermore, the excavation site itself can be embedded within its surrounding landscape. Hence a combination of spatial scales can be achieved, which range from sub-millimeter to kilometers [14].

But for combining large amounts of 3D data, which have been derived from 3D-scanners, it is necessary to drastically reduce the file size, while retaining a certain degree of detail. Following we will show the necessary steps for efficiently processing high resolution data for combining large amounts of objects within one common environment, such as game engines or for web-based presentations.

2   Case Study - The Ancient City of Samarra

Samarra, located about 125 km north of Baghdad, is one of the outstanding sites in Islamic art history and archaeology. Here the first, more or less, systematic excavations took place in the years 1911–1913 under the supervision of Ernst Herzfeld. The Abbasid city of Samarra, extending over an area of 57 km^2, is one of the largest archaeological sites of the ancient world. Between 836 AD and 883 AD it was the administrative center of the Abbasid caliphate, from which the most significant and largest empire in Islamic history was governed. The Islamic culture and scientific achievements of this period had a lasting effect on later developments in Europe. Large parts of the Samarra finds excavated by Ernst Herzfeld were brought to the Kaiser-Friedrich-Museum Berlin and are currently in the Museum of Islamic Art Berlin. The finds include over 90 ornamented stucco panels, painted wood fragments, outstanding glass ware, pottery and stone artifacts. Unfortunately the current exhibition does not enable the observer to truly understand the importance and the historical context of the finds, therefore counteracting the actual purpose of a museum: Enhancing the understanding for our cultural heritage. Hence the Samarra finds in the Museum of Islamic Art in Berlin offer an ideal test case for demonstrating the potential but also the challenges of high resolution 3D-documentation, the further scientific analysis and possible ways of visualizing these datasets for knowledge transfer.

Therefore one aspect of the MOSYS-3D project was to digitize a large part of the Samarra collection at the Museum for Islamic Art Berlin, as groundwork for the virtual contextualization of the artifacts. For this purpose a vast array of historic photographs, excavation plans and Herzfeld's field notes have been collected and analyzed, enabling the exact localization of the digitized stucco panels within single rooms of different buildings. For the contextualization of the digitized finds, the archaeological excavation plans of Ernst Herzfeld form the groundwork for the complete three-dimensional reconstruction of selected buildings. For combining the reconstructed buildings and the stucco panels a game-engine serves as a common environment, where the final visualization can be realized in a way, that it enables easy access to researchers as well as laymen.

3   Methodology

Within the field of 3D-digitization of cultural heritage the applied methodology can vary immensely depending on the research questions at hand, the spatial scales involved, the type of objects to be recorded, the technical equipment used and so on [15, 16]. Furthermore the different types of 3D-digitizing technology applied require different approaches in regards of data acquisition and processing, therefore making it necessary to develop appropriate workflows to achieve the desired results.

Generally, data acquisition can be classified into active and passive techniques. Active methods, like 3D-scanners, rely on a self-induced signal to acquire spatial data while passive methods, such as photogrammetry or multi-spectral imaging, use ambient light. Both types of data acquisition strategies have their advantages and disadvantages, making it necessary to precisely define the cases in which one method should be preferred over another or if maybe the combination of both methods is beneficial [17]. In the case of digitizing the artifacts at the Museum for Islamic Art Berlin, it was determined that an active method of data acquisition would be necessary to ensure a ubiquitous data quality in regard to the accuracy. For a large extent the surfaces of the artifacts have a diffuse reflection, which is ideal for 3D-scanning as well as photogrammetry. But some areas do not have a sufficiently varying textured or structured surface, which can lead to an increase in noise when applying Structure-from-Motion based algorithms.

Also, dealing with 3D-aqcuisition methods, it is crucial to evaluate the functional principle, which determines whether the resolution, accuracy and range are sufficient for the research question at hand [18–20].

3.1 Data Acquisition

Hardware. For digitizing the Samarra finds the close-range 3D-scanner breuckmann smart SCAN3D-HE C5 was utilized, which is based on the fringe projection technique and uses two asymmetrically arranged 5 MP CCD-cameras for the data acquisition [21]. For each pixel the depth information is calculated, resulting in five million 3D-measurement points per scan. For the final computation of the 3D-data, it is possible to separate the input data according to the used camera/light-projection combination. The highest accuracy is achieved by using the data visible to both stereo-cameras (30° triangulation angle), though less surface of the object can be captured compared to using only a single camera and the light-projection. The distance between the object-of-interest and the 3D-scanner is static due to the functional principle, so only three different working ranges are available for this specific system. Given the static range between the object-of-interest and the scanner, the final spatial resolution of the 3D-scans is determined by the field-of-view of the lens. Therefore the lenses S-125, M-475 and L-950 were acquired, as a trade-off to capture small and large objects with a sufficient resolution in an appropriate time-frame. For most artifacts, including the stucco decoration, the 3D-scanner was used in combination with the M475 measurement field, delivering a spatial resolution of 0.17 mm and an accuracy of ±0.035 mm [21] (Fig. 1).

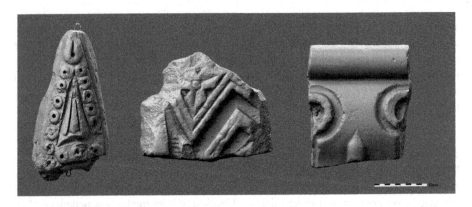

Fig. 1. Typical result of 3D-scanning; very accurate, high resolution mesh

Data Acquisition Strategies. The data acquisition strategies for digitizing artifacts using close-range 3D-scanners can vary to a certain degree. In general, each single 3D-scan represents one viewpoint, therefore making multiple, overlapping scans necessary to capture the entire surface of an object [22–24]. To acquire all necessary viewpoints, either the 3D-scanner itself or the artifact has to be re-positioned for every consecutive scan. Whether the 3D-scanner or the artifact has to be re-positioned depends mainly on the dimension and the fragility of the artifact. The individual viewpoints need to be aligned to create a single 3D-model of the object. There are diverse options on how to align all the single 3D-scans within the same coordinate reference system, which influences the data acquisition strategy. Nonetheless a certain amount of overlap between two scans is required for computing a best-fit match based on the geometrical features of the object.

One of the most common ways to align the individual scans is to manually define at least three overlapping correspondence points of two range maps, which act as a starting reference for a finer alignment based upon best-fit algorithms such as the well-known ICP (Iterative Closest Point) algorithm [25] (Fig. 2). This alignment step is usually part of the data acquisition process and is conducted after each single scan, adding a fairly significant increase of time required for capturing the entire object.

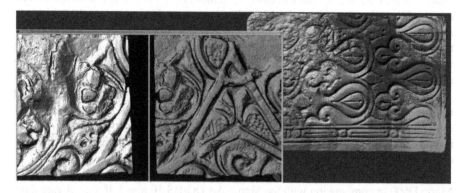

Fig. 2. Typical alignment of single scans using an ICP-based approach

Another possibility is the use of dedicated markers, which have to be distributed on or around the object-of-interest. These markers are automatically recognized by the scanning software, negating the need for manual definition of correspondence points [26]. Using this approach, it is necessary to keep the markers and the object-of-interest in the same orientation relative to each other. This method will not work with larger scaled, unmovable objects, such as the stucco decoration, where sticking the markers onto the objects surface cannot be done due to conservational considerations. Furthermore systems have been developed, which use an optical tracking system [27, 28] or that try to automatically align the 3D-scans based on texture features and geometrical properties of the object [26].

The approach of re-positioning the 3D-scanner on a tripod, especially when dealing with a large number of artifacts, becomes quite time consuming. Hence another part of the MOSYS-3D project was to develop a system for the efficient acquisition of 3D-data of unmovable objects. For this purpose a combination between a robotic system and the 3D-scanner was developed. The 3D-scanner was mounted onto the 6-axis robot arm pi4 UR10, which has a working range of 1300 mm and can record the position and the orientation with a repeatability of ±0.1 mm [29]. The positional information of each viewpoint is transferred to OPTOCAT 2015, where a macro was used to place the single scan within a common coordinate system, negating the need for additional markers or manual placement of correspondence points.

Color Information. In addition to the spatial data, the 3D-scanner is capable of capturing color information. The color information is recorded with the same imaging sensor as the depth information; hence an 8-bit RGB value is assigned to every 3D-point measurement. Due to the fairly small sensor size, the captured color information can show a fairly large amount of image-artifacts, which can be minimized through the possibility of capturing and averaging multiple color images [26].

For achieving high quality color data the lighting setup is essential. Preferably soft lighting should be setup in a way to minimize hard shadow casts and allow a uniform illumination of the object. This can easily be achieved when digitizing small finds under lab conditions but in case of the MOSYS-3D project the stucco panels, which are mounted to the walls of the depot and in the museum itself, the lighting situation was not controllable due to the changing natural lighting coming through large windows. It was not feasible to move the stucco panels to a controlled lab situation because the efforts to do so would have been out of the project's scope. But a major problem arises when using the ambient lighting for capturing color information: the shadows are baked into the colors, making the virtual relighting troublesome. Since the shadows are already captured within the color information, one is not able to virtually relight the scene because the direction of the virtual lighting and the captured lighting can be contradicting.

Therefore, additional photographic images were captured using the full-frame DSLR Nikon D600 in combination with the Sigma Art DG/HS 50 mm 1,4f lens. A ring flash was used in combination with appropriate exposure times to suppress the ambient lighting and to minimize shadows in the images. This approach enabled a uniform dataset of all stucco panels, enabling the comparative study of the color information.

3.2 Processing

Post-processing. The post-processing steps are crucial for deriving a continuous, high-resolution mesh from the acquired 3D-scans, which serves as basis for further analysis and visualizations. After the data acquisition the 3D-scans are already triangulated, negating the step of meshing a point-cloud. During the acquisition one already has to define certain parameters for the final computation of the depth-maps, for example whether only the data from the stereo-cameras should be used or whether data from all possible camera-light projector combinations should be used. This can be recalculated again in the processing phase, which can be especially useful when difficult surfaces, such as shiny materials, have been recorded. The individual viewpoints of the 3D-scans usually are already roughly aligned, following the previously mentioned acquisition-strategies. Nonetheless a global registration of all range maps is necessary to reduce the overall alignment error.

Quite often a manual clean-up of unwanted or unnecessary data, such as stray points or objects in the background is needed, which - depending on the content and acquisition strategy - can be automated to a certain degree. OPTOCAT offers the possibility to automatically mask dark areas with a definable threshold, so if one uses a dark surface for placing the artifacts, this area will be automatically excluded. It is also possible to take a scan of the background area and use this as a mask. After cleaning the unwanted parts of the 3D-data the single scans can be merged into a single, continuous mesh. Within OPTOCAT it is possible to define whether the mesh is supposed to be "watertight", meaning that all scan holes with a defined size will automatically be filled. Furthermore it is possible to decimate the mesh according to different filter parameters, such as the maximum spatial deviation to the original scan. After the final mesh has been computed, quite often additional repair work is necessary to eliminate self-intersecting triangles, small outliers, tunnels and spikes. This task was done using the Geomagic Studio Pro 12 software, where the mesh consistency is automatically analyzed and the mentioned errors repaired. After this step, the high resolution mesh can be exported to typical 3D-data formats, such as .ply or .obj, which can easily be imported to other 3D-modeling or visualization software.

For texturing the 3D-scans with external, high-quality imagery it is necessary to first do a photogrammetric reconstruction of the acquired digital images. The reconstruction is based on a common Structure-from-Motion/Multiview-Stereo approach implemented in the Agisoft Photoscan 1.2 software. The 3D-scan is subsequently aligned to the reconstructed dense point cloud using an ICP-approach implemented in the open-source software Cloudcompare [30]. The 3D-scan can then be imported to Agisoft Photoscan, where it is possible to use the computed camera positions to project the color information of digital imagery onto the mesh of the 3D-scan (Fig. 3).

Fig. 3. Combination of 3D-scanning and photogrammetry

Further Processing. Following the typical post-processing steps for deriving a high resolution, textured 3D-modell of the artifacts, various methods used in the field of gaming technology have been employed for drastically reducing the file size while maintaining a very high degree of detail. This is a necessary step for integrating large amounts of 3D-objects into an interactive real-time environment or for enabling the exchange of 3D-data via the web.

In the first step the high resolution mesh is decimated to approximately 1 % or less of its original spatial resolution. The decimation algorithm in OPTOCAT takes the curvature of the mesh into account, so flat surfaces will be decimated more than curved areas. After the decimation step, fine surface details, such as tool marks or fine carvings, are lost, and only the basic shape of the object is retained. For retaining the fine details, different texture maps have to be created, such as normal-, diffuse-, ambient occlusion- and curvature maps. Mapping textures i.e. pixel information, onto a mesh requires the computation of a UV-map, which means the mesh consisting of polygons has to be unfolded onto a two-dimensional plane. The UV-coordinates ensure the spatial link between the x, y, z coordinates of the mesh polygons and the image. After the UV-mapping the different textures can be computed, which is based on projecting surface information from the high resolution mesh onto the triangles of the decimated mesh, converting geometrical characteristics into pixel information. For example, for fine details a normal map contains the surface normal vector of the high-resolution mesh, which is stored as a RGB value in the pixel image. The RGB value represents the x, y, z value of the surface normal vector. This enables the interactive lighting of fine surface details. Ambient-occlusion maps store self-shadowing information, while curvature-maps define concave and convex areas of the mesh. When combined, these maps enable a realistic appearance of the decimated mesh, which visually is hardly distinguishable from the high-resolution mesh.

A major disadvantage of these post-processing steps is that for achieving optimal results a multitude of different software is required to be used. For example, the decimation can be done either in the manufactures software or, sometimes even with better results, in other software such as Meshlab, Geomagic Studio and many more. For UV-mapping a range of dedicated software, such as Ultimate Unwrap 3D, UVMapper or Headus UV Layout, are available. The computation of the texture maps again requires other software such as Xnormals or Blender. Therefore this workflow is quite labor-intensive, requiring a lot of manual intervention.

To reduce the time-frame required for drastically reducing high-resolution 3D-models while maintaining the fine details, a script was developed for Autodesk 3D Studio Max 2014 using MAXScript, which automates all the above mentioned steps. The script can be accessed via a user interface, where multiple 3D-models can be selected and the type of desired output can be defined. The selected data-sets are imported into 3D-Studio Max, where a modifier, which is a reversible modification of the mesh, is applied for decimating the mesh. After reducing the polygon count of the mesh, the model is automatically aligned to the coordinate axis, where an in-house developed algorithm tries to determine the correct orientation of the object. Afterwards, the MAXScript activates a Microsoft Windows batch script, which launches Z-Brush software and multiple scripts (Zscripts) for automatically creating a UV-Map. Following the unwrapping phase, the 3D-model is exported back to 3D-Studio Max, where another script is launched, which exports the 3D-model to Xnormals. In Xnormals the high- and low-resolution meshes are imported and the different maps are computed automatically based on the presets defined in the UI "Scan-Data Archive Helper". At the end of these processing steps, the finished decimated model is exported to a typical 3D-data format and can be used for a variety of purposes, ranging from web-based applications to the visualization within a game-engine.

This fully automated reduction process enabled to save an incredible amount of time. Manually processing a single, high resolution mesh took at least a couple of hours, depending on the complexity of the scanned object. Through the developed automated workflow described above, the time necessary for deriving a decimated mesh with different types of texture maps was reduced to around 10–15 min (Fig. 4).

Fig. 4. Visual difference between the high-resolution mesh and the decimated, textured mesh. Right: 9.700.000 polygons, filesize (.ply): 178 MB - Left: 30.000 polygons, filesize (.ply): 736 KB + 2 textures (.jpeg): 22 MB

4   Conclusions

Within the project MOSYS-3D different key aspects of 3D-documentation, ranging from the efficient acquisition of 3D-data, automated post-processing steps, and the final visualization, have been tackled within the case study of the Samarra collection at the Museum for Islamic Arts Berlin.

Regarding the acquisition of 3D-data, the use of a robotic arm for automatically positioning single 3D-scans turned out to be not as efficient as initially planned. This is due to different factors, ranging from the communication link between the proprietary software for controlling the scanner and the robotic arm as well as the time needed for eliminating vibrations caused by the movement of the robotic arm. Furthermore, the depot, where the artifacts and stuccos are stored, does not offer a lot of room for positioning the device and many objects are mounted fairly high on the walls, thus are not reachable. For a more efficient data capture some developments of the scanner-vendor are very promising. This includes reducing the time necessary for the actual scanning process as well as a recently implemented feature in OPTOCAT 2016, where the single scans are automatically aligned based on feature detection and depth information [26].

Significant achievements could be made in the area of processing the 3D-data. The time necessary for the data reduction and preparation for the use within game-engines or web-based viewer was reduced drastically, while still retaining high accuracy and fine details, which can be captured by modern close-range scanners. The manual labor was reduced to a fraction of the time spent before. The developed workflow enables an easy way to automatically reduce hundreds of objects with hardly any manual interference.

Furthermore, the benefits of utilizing real-time environments for displaying, interacting and contextualizing 3D-data has proven to be an efficient way of tackling certain research questions; some of which first emerged after combining various data sources within one environment. This also represents an ideal platform for knowledge transfer, enabling laymen to understand complex hypotheses and appealing especially to the younger generation, who are quite often rather reluctant to visit museums.

The use of real time environments for comprehending complex, multidimensional scenarios within a digital environment has tremendous potential and we believe this approach will be the future of working with 3D-data.

Acknowledgement. We want to express our sincere gratitude for the funding by the European Regional Development Fund (INNO 02-08/EDV. Nr. 2.1.6_0208_E) and the Regierender Bürgermeister von Berlin, Senatskanzlei, and the HTW Berlin University of Applied Sciences.

Furthermore we would like to thank Daniel Girardeau-Montaut (Cloudcompare) for his great contribution to the 3D-community.

References

1. Boochs, F., Huxhagen, U., Kraus, K.: Potential of high-precision measuring techniques for the monitoring of surfaces from heritage objects. In: International Workshop In-situ Monitoring of Monumental Surfaces, Florence (2008)
2. Bandiera, A., Alfonso, C., Auriemma, R.: Active and passive 3D imaging technologies applied to waterlogged wooden artifacts from shipwrecks. Int. Arch. Photogrammetry, Remote Sens. Spat. Inf. Sci. **40**(5), 15–23 (2015). Piano di Sorrento
3. Hess, M., Korenberg, C., Ward, C., Robson, S., Entwistle, C.: Use of 3D laser scanning for monitoring the dimensional stability of a Byzantine ivory panel. Stud. Conserv. **60**(sup1), 126–133 (2015). Sharjah
4. Arbace, L., Sonnino, E., Callieri, M., Dellepiane, M., Fabbri, M., Idelson, A.I., Scopigno, R.: Innovative uses of 3D digital technologies to assist the restoration of a fragmented terracotta statue. J. Cult. Heritage **14**(4), 332–345 (2013). Pisa
5. Scopigno, R., Cignoni, P., Callieri, M., Ganovelli, F., Impoco, G., Pingi, P., Ponchio, F.: Using optically scanned 3D data in the restoration of Michelangelo's David. In: Optical Metrology, pp. 44–53. International Society for Optics and Photonics, Munich (2003)
6. Wachowiak, M.J., Karas, B.V.: 3D scanning and replication for museum and cultural heritage applications. J. Am. Inst. Conserv. **48**(2), 141–158 (2009)
7. Saragusti, I., Karasik, A., Sharon, I., Smilansky, U.: Quantitative analysis of shape attributes based on contours and section profiles in artifact analysis. J. Archaeol. Sci. **32**(6), 841–853 (2005). Israel

8. Levoy, M., Pulli, K., Curless, B., Rusinkiewicz, S., Koller, D., Pereira, L., Ginzton, M., Anderson, S., Davis, J., Ginsberg, J., Shade, J., Fulk, D.: The digital Michelangelo project: 3D scanning of large statues. In: Proceedings of the 27th Annual Conference on Computer Graphics and Interactive Techniques (Siggraph 2000), pp. 131–144. ACM Press/Addison-Wesley Publishing Co., New York (2000)

9. Schäfer, A., Mara, H., Freudenreich, J., Bathow, C., Breuckmann, B., Bock, H.G.: Large scale Angkor style reliefs: high definition 3D acquisition and improved visualization using local feature estimation. In: Proceedings of the 39th Conference in Computer Applications and Quantitative Methods in Archaeology, pp. 70–80 (2011)

10. Pitzalis, D., Cignoni, P., Menu, M., Aitken, G.: 3D enhanced model from multiple data sources for the analysis of the cylinder seal of Ibni-Sharrum. In: VAST 2008: The 9th International Symposium on Virtual Reality, Archaeology, and Cultural Heritage, pp. 79–84. Eurographics Association, Braga (2008)

11. Fisseler, D., Weichert, F., Müller, G.G.W., Cammarosano, M.: Towards an interactive and automated script feature analysis of 3D scanned cuneiform tablets. In: Scientific Computing and Cultural Heritage, p. 16. Heidelberg (2013)

12. Zheng, S.Y., Huang, R.Y., Li, J., Wang, Z.: Reassembling 3D thin fragments of unknown geometry in cultural heritage. ISPRS Ann. Photogrammetry, Remote Sens. Spat. Inf. Sci. **2**(5), 393–399 (2014). Riva del Garda

13. Funkhouser, T., Shin, H., Toler-Franklin, C., Castañeda, A.G., Brown, B., Dobkin, D., Rusinkiewicz, S., Weyrich, T.: Learning how to match fresco fragments. J. Comput. Cult. Heritage (JOCCH) **4**(2), 7–13 (2011). New York

14. Goren, A., Kohlmeyer, K., Bremer, T., Kai-Browne, A., Bebermeier, W., Öztürk, D., Öztürk, S., Müller, T.: The virtual archaeology project - towards an interactive multi-scalar 3D visualisation in computer game engines. In: Across Space and Time, Papers from the 41st Conference on Computer Applications and Quantitative Methods in Archaeology, pp. 386–400. A. Traviglia Amsterdam University Press, Amsterdam (2013)

15. Rizzi, A., Voltolini, F., Remondino, F., Girardi, S., Gonzo, L.: Optical measurement techniques for the digital preservation, documentation and analysis of cultural heritage. In: VIII Conference on Optical 3D Measurement Techniques, Zürich, pp. 16–24, vol. 2 (2007)

16. Hassani, F., Moser, M., Rampold, R., Wu, C.: Documentation of cultural heritage; techniques, potentials, and constraints. Int. Arch. Photogrammetry, Remote Sens. Spat. Inf. Sci. **40**(5), 207–214 (2015). Göttingen

17. Gasparovic, M., Malaric, I.: Increase of readability and accuracy of 3D models using fusion of close range photogrammetry and laser scanning. ISPRS - Int. Arch. Photogrammetry, Remote Sens. Spat. Inf. Sci. **1**, 93–98 (2012). Melbourne

18. Boehler, W., Marbs, A.: 3D scanning instruments. In: Proceedings of the CIPA WG, vol. 6, pp. 9–18 (2002)

19. Iuliano, L., Minetola, P.: Rapid manufacturing of sculptures replicas: a comparison between 3D optical scanners. In: CIPA XX International Symposium, Turyn, pp. 384–389 (2005)

20. D'Apuzzo, N.: Overview of 3D surface digitization technologies in Europe. In: Proceedings of SPIE, the International Society for Optical Engineering, pp. 1–13. Society of Photo-Optical Instrumentation Engineers, San Jose (2006)

21. AICON 3D Systems breuckmann smartSCAN 3D- HE R5/C5 datasheet

22. Bernardini, F., Rushmeier, H.: The 3D model acquisition pipeline. Comput. Graph. Forum **21**(2), 149–172 (2002). Blackwell Publishers Ltd.

23. Farouk, M., El-Rifai, I., El-Tayar, S., El-Shishiny, H., Hosny, M., El-Rayes, M., Gomes, J., Giordano, F., Rushmeier, H., Bernardini, F., Magerlein, K.A.: Scanning and processing 3D objects for web display. In: 3DIM, Cairo, pp. 310–317 (2003)

24. Tucci, G., Cini, D., Nobile, A.: Effective 3D digitization of archaeological artifacts for interactive virtual museum. In: Proceedings of the 4th ISPRS International Workshop 3D-ARCH 2011, Florence (2011)
25. Besl, P.J., McKay, N.D.: Method for registration of 3-D shapes. In: Robotics-DL tentative, pp. 586–606. International Society for Optics and Photonics, Boston (1992)
26. AICON 3D Systems OPTOCAT Version 2016R1 User Manual
27. Mautz, R., Tilch, S.: Survey of optical indoor positioning systems. In: 2011 International Conference on Indoor Positioning and Indoor Navigation (IPIN), pp. 1–7. IEEE, Zürich (2011)
28. Barone, S., Paoli, A., Razionale, A.V.: Shape measurement by a multi-view methodology based on the remote tracking of a 3D optical scanner. Opt. Lasers Eng. **50**(3), 380–390 (2012)
29. UNIVERSAL ROBOTS UR10/CB3 Original instructions
30. CloudCompare (version 2.7) [GPL software] (2016). http://www.cloudcompare.org

PHOTOCONSORTIUM: Digitizing Europe's Photographic Heritage

Frederik Truyen[1(✉)] and Antonella Fresa[2]

[1] KU Leuven, Leuven, Belgium
fred.truyen@kuleuven.be
[2] Promoter, Pisa, Italy
antonella.fresa@promoter.it

Abstract. Photoconsortium is an association of photographic archives that contributed over 450.000 images of early photography to Europeana. In this contribution we discuss lessons learned, in particular on digitization and copyright issues and describe the activities involved in managing state-of-the-art digitized photographic archives. We discuss follow-on project activities such as Europeana Space, which focuses on creative reuse of digitized cultural heritage and the Europeana thematic photography channel.

Keywords: Photography · Digitisation · Europeana · Heritage · Cultural heritage · Metadata · Archives

1 Introduction

EuropeanaPhotography [1] was an EC funded project under the ICT Policy Support Programme of the Competitiveness and Innovation framework Programme, led by KU Leuven and Promoter, which started in 2012 and successfully completed its work in January 2015, delivering all the expected results.

The main outcome of the project was the delivery of hundreds of thousands of digitised masterpieces of early photography, coming from the most prestigious photographic archives and museums in Europe. These digital collections were ingested into Europeana [2], the European portal for digital cultural heritage, and are now accessible to researchers, students, and all the interested people.

The partners of EuropeanaPhotography decided wisely to give a "new life" to the outcomes of the project, and to make them alive beyond the end of the EC funded period. The partners agreed on a **long-term strategy**, transforming **cooperation synergies** into **PHOTOCONSORTIUM Association, the International Consortium for Photographic Heritage** [3].

PHOTOCONSORTIUM association was established on the 29th of October 2014 and its first General Assembly took place in Bratislava on the 6th of November 2014 where President Prof. Fred Truyen and Vice-president Dr. Antonella Fresa were elected together with the nomination of the members of the Steering Committee and of the Executive Council. The aim of the association is to **expand and enlarge the results of**

M. Ioannides et al. (Eds.): EuroMed 2016, Part I, LNCS 10058, pp. 409–419, 2016.
DOI: 10.1007/978-3-319-48496-9_33

EuropeanaPhotography, providing a sustainability model to ensure the long-term maintenance of the project results and to continue to cope with its original aims. In what follows, we describe the work of PHOTOCONSORTIUM, during and after the EuropeanaPhotography project.

2   Digitization of Photographic Cultural Heritage: Lessons Learned

Digitization of photographic cultural heritage involves many aspects, which we will shortly discuss in what follows. First of all, photographic archives contain a diversity of materials. Photographs can be kept as negatives, or as positive prints. The negatives can be individual glass negatives, but also paper negatives (e.g. in the calotype process), or they can be still part of celluloid film rolls, or cut out bands. Prints can be stand-alone photographs, often in folders or in albums, or be part of published books. Many photo houses also keep contact prints. The works in question could have been published or not. Often archives hold unselected materials relating to famous published photographs from famous photographers. Contact sheets are often revealing, as they show the selection process, in many cases not only performed by the photographer himself but also by the editor or publisher.

Managing a photographic archive hence involves a multitude of tasks, which have to do with **collection, documentation (metadata), curation, publication and preservation**. In all these tasks, digitization and digital technologies play a major role. These efforts need to keep in mind the key roles of an archive: protecting the authenticity and integrity of the stored documents, preserving this cultural heritage and on the other hand offering the public the means to exert their right to access this heritage. In EuropeanaPhotography, we gained several key experiences that we aim to provide as expert knowledge to other photographic archives.

3   Collection

In EuropeanaPhotography, we set up a content committee to oversee what collections were actually relevant to fit our goal, namely documenting the first one hundred years of photography. We had several kinds of archives: the world famous collections of Fratelli Alinari, Parisienne de Photographie, Imagno, Polfoto and TopFoto on the one hand, which are funded privately, and public archives such as Arbeijdersmuseet from Copenhagen, Denmark, ICCU/SGI in Italy or Gencat in Catalunya, Spain. Most of the masterpieces in these collections are widely known. We also had an important group of Central and Eastern European Archives which brought absolutely undiscovered material to the table. Archives such as Divadelny Ustav from Slovakia, the Museum of History of Photography in Krakow and ICIMSS from Poland, NALIS from Bulgaria, Lithuanian Art Museums from Lithuania brought in unseen collections. In the case of ICIMSS and NALIS, new material was researched and acquired from private family holdings. In Germany, United Archives specializes in acquiring unknown photographic collections to sell those to archives. Contributions were made by institutions that did not belong to the original partnership, such as the Cyprus University of Technology, the specialized centre Bali LTD, the Soviéta Géografica Italiana and the Israel Museum. The National Technical University of Athens provided technical support and the Koninklijke Musea voor Kunst en Geschiedenis in Belgium offered metadata expertise. The Centre for Image Research and Diffusion in Girona and the KU Leuven Imaging Lab took care of digitization research.

4   Documentation and Metadata

In any of these different cases, it is important to know that large parts of current archives are in fact undocumented, laying often unprocessed in maps and folders in their original packaging when they came from the donations. In large part, the activity in European-aPhotography thus resulted in actually discovering part of the reality of the first one hundred years of photography as it emerged from the archives. To have some consistency in the descriptions and to allow thematic organization we setup a metadata committee that developed a multilingual thesaurus in originally 13 – know 16 – languages describing the techniques, styles and themes of early photography. This thesaurus has been published as linked open data in skossified format [4]. Of course we are open to accept translations in other languages and further additions to the vocabulary. It was the first time that European photographic heritage was described using a common vocabulary. Since many of the established archives already used their own database and metadata system, this required a mapping which we did using an intermediate LIDO standard, which was the mapped to the Europeana Data Model using the widely used MINT tool developed at NTUA. The metadata standard committee oversees the consistent use and quality of the applied metadata. Besides correct photographic metadata we want good content descriptions allowing for clear identification of the author, subject, place and time of the photograph, which often poses serious problems as many photographs are poorly documented by the original donators. This is BTW one of the compelling reasons, as we will highlight further on, to publish these photographs in large databases such as Europeana, as background metadata enrichment can take place derived from similar photographs from other contributors. Problems with exact attribution of the author and lack of exact date information also brings some copyright issues as we will discuss.

5   Curation

As photographic archives contain a wide diversity of materials, we implemented a two-phased approach on curation. At first, each archive would look into its holdings and look what themes emerged from the yet to be digitized material. This was then brought together when partners showcased their collections to each other. This allowed us in a second phase to determine topics of interest that would be pursued further, so that there were transversal links between the partner collections. We decided e.g. not to focus too much on the first world war, as there was a specific Europeana project working on this. Themes would include a.o. leisure, sport, politics, art, culture, news and media. To make the large EuropeanaPhotography collection (currently at more than 450.000 images) more understandable and "tangible", a selection was made for a showcase exhibition,

"All our Yesterdays", [5] focusing on the lives in Europe in that era, with subthemes such as "The City Lives", "The Art of the Portrait", "Yesterday's Children", "Hardship and Drama", "The Eye of the Beholder", "Joy & Leisure" and "A Brave New World". A special subset "The Photographer at work" emerged from the finding that in many collections a kind of "selfies" avant-la-lettre were discovered. The focus on the average city lives was new to many of the archives, who usually focused on the important political, artistic and cultural heritage when curating collections. Rather than the famous poet of renowned prime minister we wanted to show people strolling the streets, enjoying a fair, going about their daily business. We discovered some lesser, more locally or even squarely unknown photographers that easily deserve a place among the world famous ones like Maurice Branger, Henry Cartier-Bresson and John Topham, such as Polish photographer Tadeusz Rząca or the unknown German photographer Karl Heinrich Lämmel (Fig. 1).

Fig. 1. Genre scene in the village, Krakow area. Rząca Tadeusz (1868–1928) – Museum of History of Photography, Poland

6   Publication

Digitization of cultural heritage allows for publication of this heritage in a multitude of formats and channels, thereby enhancing greatly access by the public. Communities have the cultural right to access their heritage, as has been advocated in important EC funded research such as Riches. The European Commission has made this goal one of its policies, hence its continuing support for Europeana, the portal to Europe's cultural heritage. This means there is some pressure on museums, libraries and archives to open up their content to the public. While this is quite natural for museums and libraries, this is not so evident for archives. The whole point of an archive is to protect the documents it keeps: it is absolutely essential that the very same, untampered document deposited at an archive can be retrieved unaltered decades later. This often means that archives have to shield documents in their holdings from changing moods and political turmoil. Many archives have been threatened in the past when revolutions or civil strife took place. Changes such as the move from Baltic countries out of the Soviet influence have an impact on the expectations the public has about what is being published out of the archive, and what is kept behind closed doors. There should be no illusion that there is ever a thing such as simply opening up the whole contents of an archive to the public. Besides societal pressures and political interference, two major problems are faced by archive professionals when envisaging publication of archive contents: copyrights and privacy.

As for copyrights, this is one of the toughest areas in digitization. While many legal systems have provisions for archives that allow to make copies for preservation ends – such as the US copyright law §108 – the same holds not true for publication. In particular, this is an issue for publication on Europeana. This is the very reason why Europeana developed a Licensing Framework, and provides in adapted Rights labels, partly based on Creative Commons Licenses. Anyway, it is a quite laborious effort to determine which works are in the Public Domain and which have rights attached to them that prevent publication. EuropeanaPhotography built extensive expertise in this matter and published useful tools and reports on this [6]. An even greater challenge is the so-called "orphan works", of which the author cannot be determined. Europe provides in an Orphan Works Directive, to be implemented by the national authorities, to make it possible for archives to publish these orphan works. Unfortunately, the procedure remains very cumbersome and anyway involves a time-intensive "diligent search", making it impractical. Collecting societies strongly oppose this idea and want to charge copyright indemnities, adding to the risk. Nevertheless, EuropeanaPhotography published a large volume of reusable content in the form of Public Domain marked and Creative Commons labelled works. In particular, readers might want to explore the open collections of Generalitat de Catalunya and Lithuanian Art Museum (Fig. 2).

Privacy is another issue that needs careful handling. Many archives document periods of strife and conflict. Certainly in smaller communities where families share long histories opening up an archive to the general public might stir up emotions and open old wounds. Serving the right of the public to access these testimonies of their shared past requires a professional, respectful and balanced approach, as collections themselves might be biased and do not necessarily reveal the whole story. It goes without saying that, e.g., the opening of archives on the Spanish civil war is an issue of much contention and debate.

Besides these two major issues other problems need some consideration. First of all not all objects that are safely kept in an archive are fit for publication. Some are legally forbidden, as is the case for some Nazi works, or would be perceived differently today as they were in the past. As communities and ethics have diversified and evolved, many documents or works that would have been perceived as neutral or harmless in past times could be felt quite offensive or divisive today, for example as being utterly racist. A related issue is the status of the original metadata. Depending on shifting ethics and sensitivities, past documentation of works, e.g. the assigned title or description, could be perceived today in a very different light. This is often the case with archives of colonial heritage. This poses a dilemma: the public, in particular also stakeholders and researchers, have a right to know the complete original metadata, while sometimes these cannot be published within the confinements of the law. EuropeanaPhotography members agreed in such cases to adapt the metadata, but to indicate that this has

Fig. 2. Portrait of the actress Míriam, dressed with Manila shawl and Cordovan hat. Antonio Esplugas National Archive of Catalonia (ANC).

happened and that the original ones are available for consultation at the archive. However, none of the partners has indicated that they actually had to use this procedure, probably given the fact that our collections did not focus on conflict documentation.

A particular problem faced by EuropeanaPhotography is the concern of many private contributors to archives about the moral integrity of the works or documents they deposit. Many people would love to donate family photo heritage to their local archive, but fear that when it becomes published online as public domain material, it could be reused without any moral restraint. Photos of their family might be altered, "defaced", ridiculed and republished. Or worse: they could be used in computer shooting games! The fear of desecration of personal or cultural heritage is important, and e.g. the Italian law has a provision protecting Italian Art works against such misuse. In many cases however, the owners think that only copyright protects them against such malpractice, and so are reluctant to donate when these copyrights do no longer exist, as with public domain works. However, in many jurisdictions there are solid protections of moral rights that can be successfully defended in court, regardless of copyright. Anyway Europeana-Photography was forced to develop rich documentation on these issues, and would recommend archives to provide similar information to their stakeholder communities.

7   Preservation

Digitization has become part of any serious preservation strategy. Often because original documents are prone to decay, and it is cheaper to preserve a digital copy. In the case of photography, glass negatives and metal plate positives such as daguerreotypes or tintypes preserve very well on their own, but the same certainly does not hold true for paper and celluloid negatives. For the original period worked on by PHOTOCONSOR-TIUM, the first 100 years of photography, the main issue are the calotypes and albumen prints, which are difficult to preserve and where digitization allows at least to keep the information that we have now. However, since the focus of PHOTOCONSORTIUM will move upwards in the 20th century, al lot of acetate and nitrate films in real danger of being lost forever urgently need to be digitized.

This means of course that this digitization needs to be done at the highest standards. For EuropeanaPhotography collections, with a large number of silver gelatine and wet collodion glass plates, specific digitization procedures with backlighting and multiple exposure in high dynamic range (HDR) were developed. For the KU Leuven collection, e.g., a dual exposure method was developed so that both the glass diapositive photograph as well as the surrounding frame with metadata could be captured in one image.

Current technology deployed amongst partners in PHOTOCONSORTIUM is very well suited for glass and celluloid negatives and diapositives. For Daguerreotypes, Ambrotypes and Tintypes research is being done with reflectance imaging techniques to yield better results and capture the true properties of the analogue object (Fig. 3).

Fig. 3. Rogier Van der Weyden 1436 – Art History collection – KU Leuven Imaging Lab

The consortium decided on the best suited file formats to store and preserve the photos, where more band more the Jpeg format comes into consideration as it has broad industrial support. PHOTOCONSORTIUM established a liaison with the Jpeg standard committee. In particular we are interested in encoding multispectral image data, in fingerprinting and invisible watermarking, and interoperability issues. But PHOTO-CONSORTIUM also looks into the digital preservation cycle as a whole, on the long term, and the physical storage and preservation. For this, common best practices were developed and shared. They are available to the larger community through the PHOTO-CONSORTIUM website.

On the other hand maybe the best preservation of photographic cultural heritage is to share it online, e.g. on Europeana. The more photographic testimonies are shared, the better they survive. For repressive authorities, it is easier to shut down a physical archive than to chase digital copies roaming the internet.

8   Results

The EuropeanaPhotography project produced excellent results. First of all, it digitised and delivered to the European portal of cultural heritage Europeana about 450,000 of the finest examples of early photography (1839–1939), increasing the value of the digitized photographic heritage retrievable via Europeana and accessible to everybody. These photographs provide a unique insight into the evolution of European society and the art of photography between the 19th and 20th centuries, which is a valuable source for understanding our history from multiple approaches (history, economics, sociology, anthropology, politics, art...). This extremely valuable source of information is promoted by PHOTOCONSORTIUM through narratives able to attract the attention of the general public and to contribute with novel information to the research. In this light, PHOTOCONSORTIUM participates in the second edition of the Digital Service Infrastructure project coordinated by Europeana Foundation (DSI-2), with the task to develop a photography channel in the Europeana portal. The new featured channel is planned to become available online for public access in 2017.

The Consortium includes both public and private bodies with complementary backgrounds and it diffuse the useful guidelines about digitization and cataloguing of early photography items which were produced in the European project. The Association also gives access and maintains the multilingual vocabulary released by the project and specifically tailored for photography, available in 16 languages[1]. PHOTOCONSORTIUM provides information IPR management and rights labelling of digital cultural content, exploiting and re-using the extremely valuable contribution to a very lively discussion which was carried out in the frame of the EuropeanaPhotography project. All the knowledge resources produced by the project continue to be available and to be maintained and updated by the PHOTOCONSORTIUM associates.

The project built a network of excellence on digitization and photographic heritage, which continues to be active in the framework of the PHOTOCONSORTIUM Association. All the relevant results produced by the EuropeanaPhotography project are kept updated in order to offer valuable solutions to the sector's needs and to prepare to face

---

[1] English, French, German, Dutch, Danish, Bulgarian, Slovak, Lithuanian, Polish, Spanish, Catalan, Italian, Russian, Ukrainian, Chinese and Hebrew.

new challenges. The members of the PHOTOCONSORTIUM Association represent a real aggregation of competences able to take care of updating technical documentation and guidelines, taking into account the latest research and technical advances, and promoting best practices and disseminating success stories. Cultural organisations, photographic archives, research and educational institutions and any other party interested in participating and contributing to the network can find in the PHOTOCONSORTIUM Association the right place to meet experts and share experiences.

The **purpose of the Association is the promotion and enhancement of the culture of photography and the photographic heritage**. To achieve its statutory goals, PHOTOCONSORTIUM aims to promote, organize and manage conferences, exhibitions, awards and training courses as well as to carry out publishing activities. The Association participates – and promote the participation of its members – in new projects and initiatives, including but not limited to the participation in the Programmes of the European Commission. All the initiatives of the association are primarily devoted to serving the interests of its members. In this light, it carries out and encourages research and studies on the themes of valorising and discovering photographic heritage, digitising early photographic content, communicating and sharing photographic collections. The association also continues to collect data and information of interest for the activities of the members. Through the expertise of its members, the association provides consultancy and personalised services both to its members and to third parties.

9   Current Projects

Digital cultural heritage is considered by the EU one of the key drivers of **economic growth and social innovation**. The Association is actively involved in European initiatives and projects. PHOTOCONSORTIUM represents a centre of expertise and knowledge on digitization, aggregation of content to Europeana and other portals, metadata standards, indexing, cataloguing and controlled vocabularies, best practices for the management of digital archives, and much more. This expertise and knowledge is the core to generate activities, provide services, organise training programs and seminars and participate in new research.

The Association is the framework for participation in **new initiatives and experimentation activities involving photographic heritage at the European level**. As an example, the digitized materials provided to Europeana through the EuropeanaPhotography project is the basis for the pilot activities in the Europeana Space [7] project. Europeana Space - Spaces of possibility for the creative re-use of digital cultural content - is a Best Practice Network project funded by the European Union under the ICT Policy Support Programme, whose project coordinator is Coventry University and technical coordinator is Promoter S.r.l. The network aims to increase and enhance the creative industries' use and re-use of Europeana and other digital collections. Multiple themed pilots present innovative models of digital cultural content exploitation in interactive TV, dance, games, publishing, museums, and, namely, photography.

PHOTOCONSORTIUM cooperates in the photography pilot of Europeana Space under the coordination of KU Leuven.

The pilot on photography is experimenting the reuse of the content aggregated through EuropeanaPhotography and demonstrating a range of possibilities offered by apps, the Europeana API[2], the Technical Platform of Europeana Space, and a multitude of tools developed by the open source community, to come up with innovative models involving photography. The experimentation activities include a hackathon (which took place in Leuven in February 2016), where developers of novel museum applications, storytelling and augmented reality apps met and proposed their projects. The best ideas were tunnelled through a monetization event and currently incubated to prepare for launch on the market in 2017.

At the same time, PHOTOCONSORTIUM Association cooperates with crowd-sourcing and citizen science initiatives. Photographic heritage is everywhere around us and helps us to enlighten personal and community stories, by visually transmitting ways of life and all kinds of experiences. The citizens' involvement in photographic heritage activities is a key element for the Association, not only as audience but also as an active actor in the activities promoted by PHOTOCONSORTIUM. An example of how to activate public participation in photographic heritage projects was the public digitisation activities carried out in the framework of "All Our Yesterdays" [8], the important photographic and multimedia travelling exhibition which showcases the best examples of the photographs digitised in EuropeanaPhotography. The first round of this exhibition was held in April–June 2014 in Pisa and the second in January–March 2016 in Leuven. Both editions included as a side element a digitisation station: a dedicated space provided with advanced digitisation technology and curated by professionals of photography, where visitors of the exhibition brought their own vintage photos to be digitised. In fact, a large part of our photographic cultural heritage is preserved and hidden in family albums, which not only include wedding pictures and grandfathers' portraits, but also reveal photographs of great historical and societal interest. It is of the utmost importance that citizens are encouraged to share this wealth of cultural heritage with the whole community. To explore more in depth how to address this participatory research, the association established a cooperation agreement with CIVIC EPISTEMOLOGIES [9], a successful European project, coordinated by the Italian Ministry of Economic Development. The main outcome of CIVIC EPISTEMOLOGIES is the roadmap for Citizen Researchers in the Age of Digital Culture. The collaboration between PHOTOCON-SORTIUM and CIVIC EPISTEMOLOGIES contributed to activate citizen involvement in photographic heritage research.

The participation of PHTOCONSORTIUM in the Digital Service Infrastructure project coordinated by Europeana Foundation is the most recent example of commitment of the Association to participate in European initiatives. The project, which lasts from July 2016 until beginning of 2018, foresees the creation of a range of thematic channels to promote access, use and re-use of digital cultural heritage content. Within the DSI-2 project, PHOTOCONSOTIUM curates the creation of the thematic channel on photographic heritage. This is a great acknowledgement of the value of Association within the European framework of research and development, which is expected to continue in the coming years through new initiatives.

---

[2] Application Program Interface.

The Association's **commitment to photographic culture and heritage** brings its members to proactively lead initiatives to value and transmit this rich heritage. The Association creates specific programs to reach all target audiences, including cultural institutions, photographic archives, specific research communities, the educational sector, younger and elder generations, the general public, and activists and amateurs in general.

The promotion and enhancement of photographic heritage finds in the Association a valuable tool to reach its objectives: a dedicated website giving visibility to all the digitised materials. Complementary to PHOTOCONSORTIUM website, a dedicated showcase was established in the *digitalmeetsculture* magazine edited by Promoter S.r.l. (one of the founding members of PHOTOCONSORTIUM) which counts currently more than 25,000 visits per month [10].

PHOTOCONSORTIUM was established as a non-profit association with a democratic structure, political independence, and unlimited duration. PHOTOCONSORTIUM allows membership to both natural and legal persons, public or private bodies, companies, and associations. It aims to enlarge its network internationally and welcomes new members sharing its aims.

More details about PHOTOCONSORTIUM and its future activities are available online at: www.photoconsortium.net and on our blog Digital Meets Culture.

Join our community by contacting info@photoconsortium.net.

Acknowledgements. EuropeanaPhotography funding grant European Union CIP-ICT-PSP-2011-5/297158; Europeana Space funding grant European Union CIP-ICT-PSP-2013-7/621037; CIVIC Epistemologies funding grant European Union FP7-INFRASTRUCTURES-2013-2/632694.

References

1. EuropeanaPhotography: http://www.europeana-photography.eu
2. Europeana: http://www.europeana.eu
3. PHOTOCONSORTIUM: http://www.photoconsortium.net
4. EuropeanaPhotography Multilingual Early Photography thesaurus: http://bib.arts.kuleuven.be/photoVocabulary/en.html
5. Exhibition "All our Yesterdays": http://www.earlyphotography.eu
6. Truyen, F., Waelde, C.: Copyright, cultural heritage and photography: a gordian knot? In: Borowiecki, K., Forbes, N., Fresa, A. (eds.) Cultural Heritage in a Changing World, pp. 77–98. Springer, Cham (2016). http://www.europeana-photography.eu/index.php?en/117/documents
7. Europeana Space: http://www.europeana-space.eu
8. http://www.earlyphotography.eu/
9. CIVIC Epistemologies: http://www.civic-epistemologies.eu/
10. Digital Meets Culture: http://www.digitalmeetsculture.net

Acquisition and Processing Experiences of Close Range UAV Images for the 3D Modeling of Heritage Buildings

Arnadi Murtiyoso[1], Pierre Grussenmeyer[1(✉)], Mathieu Koehl[1], and Tristan Freville[2]

[1] Photogrammetry and Geomatics Group, ICube Laboratory UMR 7357, INSA Strasbourg,
24 Boulevard de la Victoire, 67084 Strasbourg, France
{arnadi.murtiyoso,pierre.grussenmeyer,
mathieu.koehl}@insa-strasbourg.fr
[2] Drone Alsace, 4 Rue Sainte Cathérine, 67000 Strasbourg, France
contact@drone-alsace.fr

Abstract. The use of image-based techniques to document heritage sites has seen a resurgence in recent years with advancements in optical sensors as well as computing power. The rise of UAVs (Unmanned Aerial Vehicles) also complements this technique, by providing the advantage of aerial view over traditional terrestrial image acquisition. Recently UAVs began to become more and more specialized towards specific tasks, 3D modeling and reconstruction being some of them. In this study the use of state of the art UAV dedicated for close range inspection is analysed. Several case studies were performed on historical buildings in Strasbourg, France. Processing was done by utilizing both commercial and open source photogrammetry and SfM (Structure from Motion) solutions. Both the quality of the aerotriangulation and the dense matching were studied. The final objective of this project is to adapt existing terrestrial image acquisition and processing protocols for use by UAVs.

Keywords: UAV · Documentation · Photogrammetry · Close range · Protocols · Heritage buildings

1 Introduction

Since its first conception as military support, the UAV has seen a significant shift towards civilian use. In the fields of geomatics, this spread of small scale aerial technology means that it could be used to perform close range aerial photogrammetry. Coupled with the rapid development of optical sensors as well as computing power, this type of surveying becomes a very potential solution for various uses. The field of heritage documentation naturally benefits from these developments, as it complements the already established method of image-based terrestrial techniques [1].

Several types of UAVs exist in the market nowadays. A general classification of UAV types was given by [1, 2] which divides it into three main categories according to their physical features:

© Springer International Publishing AG 2016
M. Ioannides et al. (Eds.): EuroMed 2016, Part I, LNCS 10058, pp. 420–431, 2016.
DOI: 10.1007/978-3-319-48496-9_34

- Lighter than air platforms, such as balloons and kites. This category is low-cost but is more difficult to control due to its low wind resistance and low velocity.
- Fixed-wing platforms, with the capability of covering a large surface but may be limited in payload as well as wind resistance. The fixed-wing UAV is suited for larger-scale mapping resembling classical small-format aerial photogrammetry.
- Rotary-wing platforms, either with a single or multiple rotors. This type of UAV has a larger wind resistance, but its surface coverage can be significantly lower than that of the fixed-wing type. Hence its vast use in close-range applications.

In the field of geomatics, the optics as well as the sensor of the on-board camera plays an important role. Some UAV manufacturers have tried to accommodate these geometric demands by integrating better quality lenses, although it is still often limited by the payload. More recently, UAVs have started to specialize in various specific sectors such as agricultural mapping and close industrial (and heritage) inspection.

Progress in the field of computer vision has largely facilitated the classical photogrammetric workflow. As explained in [2, 3], the typical workflow involves automatic tie point feature extraction and matching. This is often followed by robust outlier detection and elimination and bundle block adjustment in order to retrieve the position and orientation of each camera station. Afterwards, dense matching algorithms enable the 3D reconstruction of a dense point cloud, up to one point for each pixel of the image [4].

2   Related Works

UAVs have seen wide use in the documentation of archeological sites, often to provide a general view of the surroundings [5]. This can be done either with a fixed-wing [6] or rotary-wing UAV [5, 6] depending on the dimensions of the site in question. Another use of the UAV is for close-range modeling or inspection of buildings by using the rotary-wing type. This type of acquisition is often performed in conjunction with terrestrial images and sometimes also with range-based techniques such as terrestrial laser scanning [7]. In these cases the UAV presents a natural advantage over other terrestrial techniques in its capability to capture aerial images, thus covering angles which would otherwise be impossible to cover from the ground.

In regards to acquisition and processing protocols, several procedures exist in the literature which deals mainly with terrestrial images. Often these protocols deal not only with the acquisition, but also with the calibration and recommendations for facilitating later processing steps. One of the objectives of this study is to adapt the existing established terrestrial acquisition protocols for use by UAVs.

The CIPA Heritage Documentation's 3 × 3 rules have existed since 1994 with several updates [8]. The latest version can be consulted in the CIPA website[1]. These rules concern not only the acquisition of images, but also recommendations for the calibration and procedures to be implemented during the survey.

Another protocol called TAPENADE (Tools and Acquisition Protocols for Enhancing Artifacts Documentation) was developed for the documentation of cultural

---

[1] http://cipa.icomos.org/.

heritage [9, 10]. These documents provide several different cases of objects and generally follow the image acquisition configuration suitable for the software Micmac. However, up until the writing of this article, only French versions of these protocols are available although a more general explanation of the recommendations in English is available in the TAPENADE website[2].

The University of Stuttgart's Institute for Photogrammetry has also developed their own protocol [11]. This protocol, called "One panorama each step", is targeted for producing a good dense matching result by using greatly overlapping images. This protocol was developed and tested for the dense matching software SURE and has also been tested on UAV data.

These existing protocols share some similarities. First, a good calibration using a convergent, controlled environment is always recommended rather than relying solely on *in situ* self-calibration. The importance of procedural documentation and description of the object is also stressed, something which may easily be forgotten but is nevertheless important. Finally, all three rules emphasize two kinds of image acquisition. The first involves general or global images with good convergence angles to ensure the precision of the resulting network while the second involves images with very large percentage of overlap (detailed stereo pairs) to facilitate the dense matching process.

3   UAVs and Software Solutions Employed

The first UAV used in this project is a multi-copter rotary wing platform manufactured by the company Sensefly and called Albris since April 2016 (previously known as Exom). The product first appeared in the market in May 2015 and was aimed to perform close-range high resolution inspections, mapping, and 3D modeling. It is equipped with multiple sensors, including a still 38 megapixels camera, a thermal and a video camera. Several ultrasonic sensors give an approximate distance measurement of its surroundings, enabling it to fly on a set distance from an object. The still camera itself is furnished with an 8 mm lens and a 10×7.5 mm sensor. This specification theoretically enables a GSD (Ground Sampling Distance) of up to 1 mm at a distance of 6 m.

Another UAV used is the DJI Phantom 3 Professional, also a multi-copter rotary wing type. This UAV was first released also in May 2015. The Phantom 3 is lightweight and relatively low-cost, but it is not geared for dedicated close-range inspection tasks. Unlike the previous versions, the Phantom 3 is no longer equipped with a fish-eye lens camera. This could potentially yield a better geometric result, but the sensor itself remains very small compared to most terrestrial cameras. It is equipped with a 4 mm lens and a 6.5×5 mm sensor. Figure 1 shows the main characteristics of these two UAVs.

The software solutions used in this study ranges from the commercial to the open source. From the commercial side Pix4D, Agisoft Photoscan and Photomodeler are used. Meanwhile open source solutions such as Apero-Micmac, SURE, and VisualSFM/ PMVS2 were tried.

---

[2] http://www.tapenade.gamsau.archi.fr/.

Sensefly Albris	
Platform	
Payload	1.8 kg
Flight autonomy	~22 minutes
Camera	
Focal length	8 mm
Sensor size	10 x 7.5 mm
	7152 x 5368 pixels
Horizontal FOV	63^0

DJI Phantom 3 Professional	
Platform	
Payload	1.3 kg
Flight autonomy	~23 minutes
Camera	
Focal length	4 mm
Sensor size	6.5 x 5 mm
	4000 x 3000 pixels
Horizontal FOV	94^0

Fig. 1. The UAV used in the study, Sensefly Albris and DJI Phantom 3 Professional as well as the main characteristics of their respective platforms and on board cameras.

From an algorithmic point of view, several approaches to the dense matching problem exist. The article [12] explains well the different types of dense matching algorithms. These different approaches towards dense matching may give different results in different scenarios.

Pix4D and Photoscan are two commercial solutions with a rather black-box nature. However, concurrent with the results of [12], Photoscan most probably performs a modified SGM (Semi-Global Matching) [13] of stereo pairs to generate depth maps, and then employs epipolar constraints at the end of this process to filter the results. Pix4D may have used a similar albeit different approach, since an SGM-based matching is offered as an additional plug-in.

Photomodeler has long been used by the architecture and archeology community for performing 3D image-based measurements [8]. This software has an advantage over other commercial solutions in that it provides more statistical information on its results, making it less black-box like. Photomodeler has since added a dense matching module based on stereo-pairs and more recently on a multi-view geometry.

The approach taken by SURE is well described in [14]. This software also uses a modified version of the SGM and computes a disparity map for each potential pair of images with a set value of overlap. The resulting depth-maps are then converted into a point cloud by employing geometric constraints to help reduce the number of outliers [12]. A free version of SURE is available for research or academic purposes.

Meanwhile, Micmac uses a multi-resolution and multi-image approach to dense matching [15]. The Micmac suite is modular and works with several levels of complexity and automation. The first module, Pastis, searches and matches tie points on the images.

Apero performs bundle block adjustment to retrieve the external orientation parameters of the camera stations. Finally, Micmac performs a pyramidal processing to search pixel correspondences. Results from a lower resolution matching are used to guide the matching at the higher resolution level, with the maximum resolution determined by a parameter [12].

PMVS (patch-based multi-view stereo) uses a different object-based approach [16]. It implements multi-view stereo-matching starting on a sparse point cloud generated by the SfM matched tie points. The matched "patch" around a tie point is then repeatedly expanded to nearby pixels and filtered using visibility constraints.

4   Case Studies

The UAVs were deployed to acquire images of two historical buildings located in the city of Strasbourg, France. The choice of objects was determined by their particularities and therefore also challenges, e.g. façades, painted walls, columns, etc.

4.1   The Josephine Pavilion

The Josephine Pavilion is a 19th century building located inside the Orangerie Park in the city of Strasbourg. It provides a good test object as the area around it is open without much vegetation. The back-façade is made from red sandstone, typical of the Alsace region while the front-façade is a relatively smooth wall painted in beige, giving little texture for the dense image matching step.

A test flight was performed in late 2014 before the project started using the Phantom 3 UAV. Close range images of each of the four façades from an average distance of 8 m were taken. A quick processing of these images (Fig. 2) shows dense matching problems on the front-façade, which has very little texture. A comparison of dense matching results of the central part of this façade using the employed matching algorithms is shown in Fig. 3.

Fig. 2. The textured mesh of the Josephine Pavillion data set generated by Photoscan. Note the meshing problem at the right side of the central façade due to lack of points.

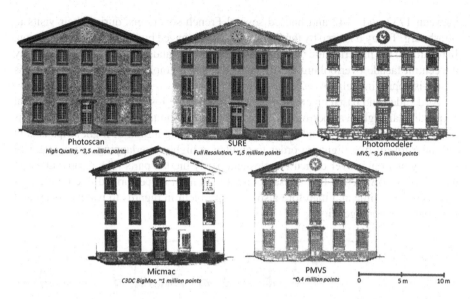

Fig. 3. Dense matching results of the central front-façade of the Josephine Pavilion, showing point clouds generated by the five dense matching algorithms employed.

Visually, Photoscan managed to retrieve points on the problematic beige wall. However, these points are noisy with up to 15 cm of dispersion on a wall which normally should be flat. Similarly with Photoscan, SURE also generates points on the painted surface with noises. On the contrary, processing on Photomodeler (using its MVS dense matching mode), Micmac, and PMVS detected only a sparse amount of points on this smooth surface.

Several preliminary analyses were taken from this pilot project. The first concerns the importance of image overlap of the object; indeed echoing the need for detailed images with large percentage of overlap mentioned in the existing protocols. A remark was made to acquire controlled oblique images in further projects in order not only to strengthen the image network geometry but also to better cover hidden parts (window sills, awnings, balcony, etc.). Oblique images will emulate the concept of detailed stereo pairs in a UAV acquisition scenario.

Furthermore, the problem of the object in question's material is also important to note. In the case of the pavilion, a textureless material hinders a proper pixel-by-pixel search for correspondence. Particular strategies should be taken to address this problem [12]. One strategy that can be employed involves changing the resolution of the images used in the dense matching; bearing in mind that in this case a better resolution matching does not necessarily produces a better result. Another involves changing the correlation coefficient threshold to allow more points (which may however be noisy) to be detected.

4.2 The Rohan Palace

The Rohan Palace is a historical landmark of the city of Strasbourg dating to the 18th century. Located next to the cathedral, the palace was built for the Cardinal Rohan between 1732 and 1742 and housed several French sovereigns during their visits to Strasbourg. Today it is used by three museums, all managed by the city's administration. In regards to the material, the palace is made of yellow sandstone. For this project, only the central façade overlooking the River Ill was photographed. The dimension of this façade is approximately 14 × 20 m.

As decided and based on previous experiences on the Josephine pavilion, a classical perpendicular flight was performed followed by four oblique flights with the cameras tilted to the right, left, up, and down (Fig. 4). The configuration of flight strips is kept the same for all five flights in order to emulate a highly overlapping and convergent geometry and thus cover difficult angles and partly hidden parts. The disadvantage of this method, however, is that the same flight plan must be performed five times. This increases flight time and therefore also poses problem in regards to battery issues and image texture homogeneity.

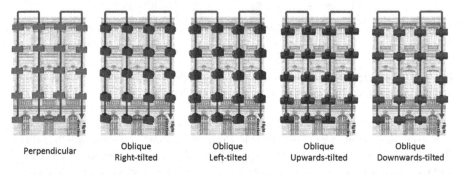

Perpendicular   Oblique Right-tilted   Oblique Left-tilted   Oblique Upwards-tilted   Oblique Downwards-tilted

Fig. 4. Perpendicular and oblique flight plans used for the façade.

In this project, the Sensefly Albris was used to acquire the images. Using its capability to fix camera-object distances, the UAV was flown at a fixed approximate distance of 5 m from the façade. In addition, 13 control and check points scattered on the façade are measured using a total station using the spatial intersection method in order to be able assess the precision and accuracy of the results. The 6 control points are placed on the limits of the flight zone following the classical aerial photogrammetry configuration. The remaining 7 points were used as check points, and are scattered evenly on the façade to represent changes of reliefs.

All algorithms succeeded in orienting the images except VisualSFM, which might be linked to the default number of detected tie points. Despite the theoretical GSD of 1 mm, here the precision of the aerotriangulation for all four solutions was on average 9 mm while the check point accuracy was 7 mm. It should be noted that the control and check points used are detail points (window edges, bricks, etc.) and not well defined targets. The precision and accuracy depend therefore on the quality of point marking. This however, was hampered by the noisy quality of the Albris' images. This noise problem has been acknowledged by Sensefly and an improvement of sensor quality is expected sometime soon.

As regards to the dense point cloud, the results as well as matching parameters employed for the four dense matching algorithms are shown by Fig. 5. The matching settings used in each algorithm correspond to the resampling of the input images to a quarter of their original resolutions. Note that this resolution setting is often employed in dense matching solutions in order to give the users a compromise between quality and processing time. The application of oblique images has effectively covered several difficult places such as the balcony and the lower part of the triglyph or the metope above it. However, the question of image noise still posed a problem. Indeed, a test performed with matching using half resolution images generated a sparser point cloud with many holes. On the contrary, a more complete point cloud was acquired using a lower resolution setting. This problem is most probably caused once again by the correlation coefficient threshold; in the higher resolution setting the algorithm calculates denser points which it assumes are noises and therefore deletes, leaving holes in the resulting point cloud.

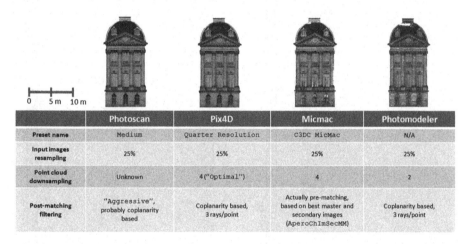

	Photoscan	Pix4D	Micmac	Photomodeler
Preset name	Medium	Quarter Resolution	C3DC MicMac	N/A
Input images resampling	25%	25%	25%	25%
Point cloud downsampling	Unknown	4 ("Optimal")	4	2
Post-matching filtering	"Aggressive", probably coplanarity based	Coplanarity based, 3 rays/point	Actually pre-matching, based on best master and secondary images (AperoChImSecMM)	Coplanarity based, 3 rays/point

Fig. 5. Dense point cloud generation parameters of the four algorithms tested.

Furthermore, in order to validate the accuracy of the dense matching results, a terrestrial laser scanning survey was performed on the façade concerned. This was done using a Faro Focus 3D laser scanner and the resulting point cloud has a resolution of about 6 to 8 mm. Evaluation was performed for a common portion of each result of the photogrammetric dense matching using the laser scanner point cloud as reference (see Fig. 6). All solutions gave standard deviations of around 1 cm compared to the reference. This corresponds more or less to the theoretical resolution of the point cloud at this image pyramidal level of matching (around 1.4 cm).

Larger histogram dispersion is observed in Photomodeler's results, which indicates a noisier point cloud. More holes are also observed in this point cloud. Photoscan and Pix4D gave more homogeneous i.e. less noisy results, with Photoscan detecting slightly more error. In addition, Micmac detects more holes in general compared to Pix4D and Photoscan, which may be related to the default correlation coefficient threshold in its semi-automatic C3DC matching mode.

In Fig. 7, the cross-section of one of the Corinthian columns is analyzed. The point cloud generated by Photomodeler presents the most noise. Micmac's results present a

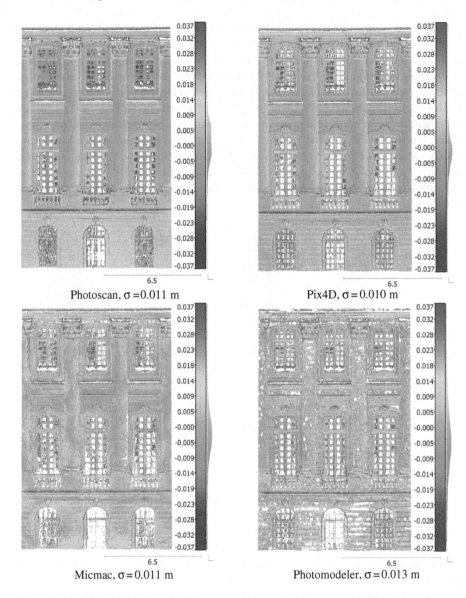

Fig. 6. Dense matching results analysis using laser scanning data as reference for a common part of the façade of the Rohan Palace.

circular trend for the cross-section albeit it is a rather rough, unsmooth representation. Photoscan and to some degree also Pix4D, present an almost smooth circular shaped point cloud profile. This suggests a form of interpolation and/or smoothing performed after the matching process to conform to certain geometric constraints. Furthermore, some solutions had difficulties in detecting points at the junctions where the column and the wall meet. Micmac, Photomodeler, and even the laser scanner (at the right junction)

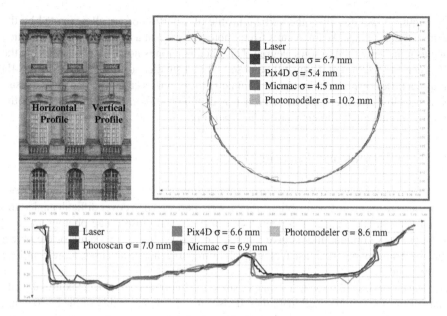

Fig. 7. A horizontal profile of one of the Corinthian columns (red square) and a vertical one of a part of the wall (green square). The blue lines represent laser scanner measurements. (Color figure online)

failed to detect points in this zone and therefore leave a hole. It is however interesting to note that both Photoscan and Pix4D still manage to detect points and close the hole in these difficult areas, although at the left junction Photoscan seems to have detected false points behind the column. Micmac and Photomodeler were also unable to reconstruct the left junction. However, Photoscan and Photomodeler are both less accurate in this case compared to Micmac and Pix4D.

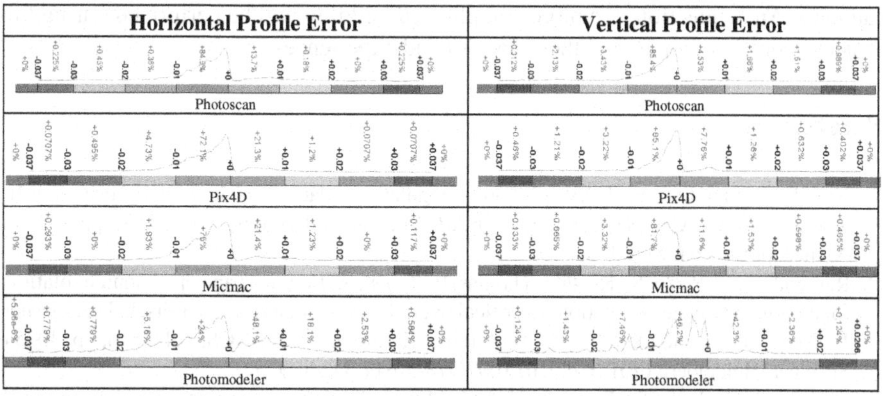

Fig. 8. Error graphs for the horizontal and vertical profiles using the same profiles from the laser data as reference.

Figure 7 also describes the vertical profile of a portion of a wall generated by the different algorithms. Again, results from Photoscan present a continuous surface which seems to be smoothed to some degree. This phenomenon is however less evident in the Pix4D profile although it can still be observed in a smaller scale. In this regard Pix4D is also a little noisier than Photoscan. Similar to the previous case, Micmac gives a result which follows the trend of the reference with minor noises. Photomodeler gives the noisiest point cloud with errors of up to 1 cm (Fig. 8).

5   Conclusions and Further Work

In this paper, the use of UAVs for the documentation of heritage buildings was assessed. In regards to the acquisition, oblique flights were performed to cover difficult angles and to emulate the detailed stereo pairs taken in terrestrial close range photogrammetry surveys. These oblique flights give a much larger overlap for each point of the object and therefore enable the dense matching algorithm to generate a denser, more complete point cloud.

The processing of these UAV images stress the importance of object textures despite state of the art pixel by pixel matching. It also stresses on the quality of the basic input, which is the images themselves. Even with more pixels in an image, image noises can render them useless and therefore reduce the quality of the matching. The comparison of several software solutions has also been addressed in this article. Even though all solutions give similar overall accuracies, the matching algorithms give differing results. A closer analysis showed that some algorithms may have added a point cloud post-processing step at the end of the matching.

In conclusion, the UAV has shown to be very potential to perform close range heritage inspections, being able to reach a centimetric (and theoretically even less) accuracy. It's capability to capture aerial images is a clear advantage compared to terrestrial techniques, and the use of oblique images in this study has been proven to be effective in covering otherwise difficult parts of the object. The software solution chosen should follow the cases encountered as they each have their own advantages and disadvantages. An acquisition of a more complicated building will be performed during this project in order to implement these lessons and experiences.

References

1. Nex, F., Remondino, F.: UAV: platforms, regulations, data acquisition and processing. In: Remondino, F., Campana, S. (eds.) BAR International Series, vol. 2598, pp. 73–86. Archaeopress, Oxford (2014)
2. Remondino, F., Pizzo, S., Kersten, Thomas, P., Troisi, S.: Low-cost and open-source solutions for automated image orientation – a critical overview. In: Ioannides, M., Fritsch, D., Leissner, J., Davies, R., Remondino, F., Caffo, R. (eds.) EuroMed 2012. LNCS, vol. 7616, pp. 40–54. Springer, Heidelberg (2012). doi:10.1007/978-3-642-34234-9_5
3. Chiabrando, F., Donadio, E., Rinaudo, F.: SfM for orthophoto generation: a winning approach for cultural heritage knowledge. In: International Archives of the Photogrammetry, Remote Sensing and Spatial Information Sciences, vol. XL-5/W7, pp. 91–98 (2015)

4. Achille, C., Adami, A., Chiarini, S., Cremonesi, S., Fassi, F., Fregonese, L., Taffurelli, L.: UAV-based photogrammetry and integrated technologies for architectural applications – methodological strategies for the after-quake survey of vertical structures in Mantua (Italy). Sensors **15**, 15520–15539 (2015)
5. Remondino, F., Barazzetti, L., Nex, F., Scaioni, M., Sarazzi, D.: UAV photogrammetry for mapping and 3D modeling – current status and future perspectives. In: International Archives of the Photogrammetry, Remote Sensing and Spatial Information Sciences, vol. XXXVIII-1/C22, pp. 25–31 (2011)
6. Suwardhi, D., Menna, F., Remondino, F., Hanke, K., Akmalia, R.: Digital 3D Borobudur: integration of 3D surveying and modeling techniques. In: International Archives of the Photogrammetry, Remote Sensing and Spatial Information Sciences, vol. XL-5/W7, pp. 417–423 (2015)
7. Grenzdöffer, G., Naumann, M., Niemeyer, F., Frank A.: Symbiosis of UAS photogrammetry and TLS for surveying and 3D modeling of cultural heritage monuments – a case study about the cathedral of St. Nicholas in the City of Greifswald. In: International Archives of the Photogrammetry, Remote Sensing and Spatial Information Sciences, vol. XL-1/W4, pp. 91–96 (2015)
8. Grussenmeyer, P., Hanke, K., Streilein, A.: Architectural photogrammetry: basic theory, procedures, tools. In: Kasser, M., Egels, Y. (eds.) Digital Photogrammetry, pp. 300–339. Taylor & Francis, London (2002)
9. Pierrot-Deseilligny, M., De Luca, L., Remondino, F.: Automated image-based procedures for accurate artifacts 3D modeling and orthoimage generation. In: Proceedings of the XXIIIrd International CIPA Symposium (2011)
10. Nony, N., Luca, L., Godet, A., Pierrot-Deseilligny, M., Remondino, F., Dongen, A., Vincitore, M.: Protocols and assisted tools for effective image-based modeling of architectural elements. In: Ioannides, M., Fritsch, D., Leissner, J., Davies, R., Remondino, F., Caffo, R. (eds.) EuroMed 2012. LNCS, vol. 7616, pp. 432–439. Springer, Heidelberg (2012). doi: 10.1007/978-3-642-34234-9_44
11. Wenzel, K., Rothermel, M., Fritsch, D., Haala, N.: Image acquisition and model selection for multi-view stereo. In: International Archives of the Photogrammetry, Remote Sensing and Spatial Information Sciences, vol. XL-5/W1, pp. 251–258 (2013)
12. Remondino, F., Spera, M.G., Nocerino, E., Menna, F., Nex, F.: State of the art in high density image matching. Photogram. Rec. **29**(146), 144–166 (2014)
13. Hirschmüller, H.: Semi-global matching – motivation, developments and applications. In: Photogrammetric Week 2011, pp. 173–184 (2011)
14. Wenzel, K., Rothermel, M., Haala, N., Fritsch, D.: SURE – the ifp software for dense image matching. In: Photogrammetric Week 2013, pp. 59–70 (2013)
15. Pierrot-Deseilligny, M., Paparoditis, N.: A Multiresolution and optimization-based image matching approach: an application to surface reconstruction from SPOT5-HRS stereo imagery. In: International Archives of the Photogrammetry, Remote Sensing and Spatial Information Sciences, vol. XXXVI-1/W41 (2006)
16. Furukawa, Y., Ponce, J.: Accurate, dense, and robust multi-view stereopsis. IEEE Trans. Pattern Anal. Mach. Intell. **32**(8), 1362–1376 (2009)

Internal 3D Printing of Intricate Structures

Théophane Nicolas[1], Ronan Gaugne[2], Cédric Tavernier[3],
Valérie Gouranton[4(✉)], and Bruno Arnaldi[4]

[1] Inrap/UMR 8215 Trajectoires, Cesson-Sévigné, France
[2] Université de Rennes 1/IRISA-Inria, Rennes, France
[3] Image ET, Mordelles, France
[4] INSA Rennes/IRISA-Inria, Rennes, France
valerie.gouranton@irisa.fr

Abstract. Additive technologies are increasingly used in Cultural Heritage process, for example in order to reproduce, complete, study or exhibit artefacts. 3D copies are based on digitization techniques such as laser scan or photogrammetry. In this case, the 3d copy remains limited to the external surface of objects. Medical images based digitization such as MRI or CT scan are also increasingly used in CH as they provide information on the internal structure of archaeological material. Different previous works illustrated the interest of combining 3D printing and CT scan in order to extract concealed artefacts from larger archaeological material. The method was based on 3D segmentation techniques within volume data obtained by CT scan to isolate nested objects. This approach was useful to perform a digital extraction, but in some case it is also interesting to observe the internal spatial organization of an intricate object in order to understand its production process. We propose a method for the representation of a complex internal structure based on a combination of CT scan and emerging 3D printing techniques mixing colored and transparent parts. This method was successfully applied to visualize the interior of a funeral urn and is currently applied on a set of tools agglomerated in a gangue of corrosion.

Keywords: Archaeology · Tomography · 3D printing

1 Introduction

Cultural Heritage professionals such as archaeologists and conservators regularly experience the problem of working on concealed artefacts and face the potential destruction of source material without real understanding of internal structure or state of decay. For example, artefacts may be encased in corroded materials or a block of ash, or integrated with, and inseparable from, larger assemblies, such as manufactured objects composed of several pieces.

The work presented in this paper aims to develop a non-destructive workflow for analysing and documenting the internal structure of artefacts, improving diagnostic techniques and knowledge by combining medical imaging technologies such as Computed Tomography (CT) with 3D printing. Our methodology allows to create digital

© Springer International Publishing AG 2016
M. Ioannides et al. (Eds.): EuroMed 2016, Part I, LNCS 10058, pp. 432–441, 2016.
DOI: 10.1007/978-3-319-48496-9_35

and physical 3D surrogates of objects to investigate, analyse and interpret their internal structure through volumetric scanning, 3D image rendering, and 3D printing.

Combinations of CT scan and 3D printing technologies have already been proposed in CH contexts. The projects presented in [1] and [2] both propose the use of 3D printers, combined with CT images, to reproduce high-value pieces, Chinese chess pieces in the first case, and Gold jewels in the second case. In [10], copies of fragile bones are used for sharing during study process and for exhibition.

This methodology was also successfully applied to physically access to encased artefacts through 3D images, and 3D printed replications without any irreversible physical action on the original material [3], even in the case of a disaggregated artefact [4]. In particular, in the first work, a removable copy of a Gallic weight illustrates how this technique allowed to better understand the internal structure of an artefact. This is also the case in the work of McKnight et al. [5] where a bones assembly from an animal mummy has been reconstituted for scientific analysis and public exhibition purpose. In both [2] and [6], a 3D print of the original shape of the archaeological material composed of an aggregate of several objects is proposed. This kind of production is useful to study the shape of disaggregated container.

In addition to these different works, it can also be interesting to have a view of both the external and internal structure of archaeological material in order to understand its production process, or to spatially localize the different notable internal items. The goal of the work presented in this paper is to propose a tangible representation of a complex intricate structure through advanced 3D printing. The process is applied to a funeral urn, and combines CT scan, 3D model processing, and 3D printing.

2   Archaeological Context

The excavation of the site of Domaine de la Bizaie in Guipry (Brittany, France, Fig. 1, Left) in a preventive archaeological context uncovered a trapezoidal shaped funerary enclosure. The central area housed ten cremation burials containing pottery vessels from the Iron Age (Excavation L. Aubry, Inrap, [7]). The exceptional state of preservation of some of these cremations prompted us to use tomography to analyse their contents. It allowed to highlight a number of metal objects as in the F42A cremation (Fig. 1, Right).

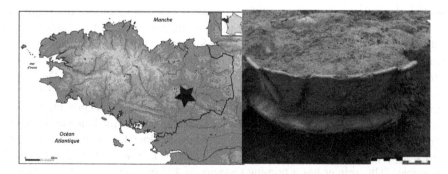

Fig. 1. Left: Domaine de la Bizaie, Guipry, France. Right: the F42 cremation, in situ

3   Description of the Work

The process used in this study is based on a combination of CT scan, 3D processing and 3D printing. The main goal of the process is to physically display the internal structure of the archaeological material. We thus chose to explore two possibilities offered by 3D printing: physical copy of a part of the initial material and global printing with transparency. The process follows these different steps:

1. A computed tomodensitometry of the archaeological material was performed generating a database of X-Ray images, with density data.
2. Surface 3D meshes are generated from the previous database. Each mesh corresponds to a density range.
3. The 3D models are processed to fit 3D printing constraints.
4. The resulting 3D models are 3D printed.

3.1   Technical Environment

CT Scan. The CT scanner used in this study is a Siemens SOMATOM sensation 16 owned by the French company Image ET (http://www.image-et.fr/) who delivers services and expertise on X-Ray images and associated tools.

The three-dimensional explorations were performed through two passes (acquisition) and 2D/3D images post-processing. The two acquisitions were a topogram (or radio mode) for positioning the slices to be realized and a helix scan.

The scan generates a dataset under DICOM format [8] of 512×512 pixels 2D slice images.

3D Data Processing. The data generated during the CT scan was processed with the free software Osirix, an image processing application for Mac dedicated to DICOM images. The 3D surface rendering functionality was used to generate 3D meshes corresponding to different density ranges. This functionality allows to generate the surface of a set of points whose density value is within a defined range.

The 3D model was then manually processed in order to remove unwanted data and automatically processed in order to get a ready-to print file.

3D Printing. We performed two different tasks of 3D printing on the urn, using two technologies: 3D printing of an internal artefact, and 3D printing of a whole material with transparency. The first 3D printer was a Stratasys Mojo owned by our institute. This 3D printer uses Plastic Jet Printing to print objects from ABS, in layers as thin as 178μ, with a maximum dimension of 12.7 cm × 12.7 cm × 12.7 cm. For the second printing, transparent 3D printing for complex objects appeared to be a not very developed technique. We contacted several Companies delivering advanced 3D printing services and only one, the CADindus Company (www.cadindus.fr), positively answered to our request. It uses a technology of multimaterial and multicolor additive manufacturing by resin polymerization for the production of the copies, on a Stratasys Objet500 Connex3 3D printer. This printer has a printing capacity of 49 cm × 35 cm × 25 cm, with an accuracy of 30μ.

3.2 Application of the Process to the Urn

Scan of the Urn. The urn was scanned as a whole at one time. As the sediments inside the urn were not too dense, the scan was performed with the values of 120 kV and 350 mAs. In order to scan the entire urn, the field of view was sized to 320 mm × 320 mm, resulting in a resolution of 625μ. We worked in an extended Hounsfield scale (from −10.000 to +40.000), in order to distinguish between fragments of bones and metallic parts and get a finer view of the metallic objects. A volume rendering is presented in Fig. 2.

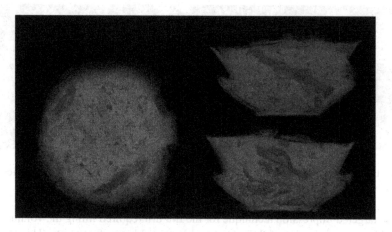

Fig. 2. Volume rendering of the urn (Color figure online)

The three views of volume rendering of the urn presented in Fig. 2 highlight the metal parts in blue, with two notable objects, a fibula and a knife blade. The red parts are fragments of bones. The sediments are displayed in transparent grey.

3D Data Generation and Processing. Three meshes were generated from the data with the Osirix software (Fig. 3). The first mesh, for the metallic parts, corresponds to the points whose radio-density is between 4500 and 10950, the second mesh, for the urn shape and sediments, between 700 and 1300, and the last mesh, for the bones parts, between 1600 and 2300.

Fig. 3. Left: meshes for the urn and sediments, Middle: metallic parts, Right: bones

Two issues arose after the generation of the meshes. First, corrosion gangues on the knife blade and fibula (Fig. 4, left) had a radio-density within the range of bones, visible in the mesh of the bones (Fig. 3, right). These gangues were easily removed as they were completely separated from other bones. Second, the mesh of the urn and ashes contained many galleries and cavities due to worms and insects (Fig. 4, right). All the galleries had to be manually removed and closed in order to get a clean transparency inside the urn. This task took several weeks, with many exchanges with the archaeologists in order to validate the modifications of the model.

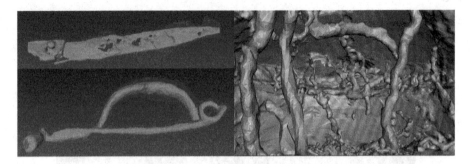

Fig. 4. Left: gangue of corrosion for the metallic parts. Right: worms and insect galleries inside the urn

The targeted impression technique for the full urn required filling the volume of the urn, with a negative print of the metallic objects and bones fragments. This task was performed with 3D Boolean operations in a 3D modeling tool.

Printing of the Fibula. The mesh of the fibula was isolated in order to propose a physical virtual extraction of this object whose shape appeared to be very well preserved. The process of producing the physical copy of the fibula from the digital data appeared to be very simple and fast (less than one day). The resulting copy of the fibula is presented in Fig. 5.

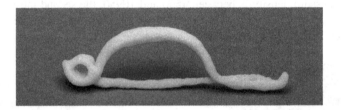

Fig. 5. 3D printing of the fibula

Printing of the Urn. In order to keep close to the initial volume renderings from tomography (Fig. 2), we chose to render the bones in magenta and the metallic parts in cyan. The printing phase took 50 h and required 8 kg of matter. It was printed with successive layers, bottom up (Fig. 6, left). The resulting printed object was covered with a pink support matter (Fig. 6, right)

Fig. 6. Left: on-going 3D printing of the urn. Right: the printed urn with its support matter (Color figure online)

Post-processing. An important post-processing of the object produced by the 3D printer is required to obtain a good transparency rendering (Fig. 7). This post processing, which lasted one week, consisted in four phases: (i) Removal of the support matter, (ii) Photo-bleaching during 72 h at 6500 kelvins («day light»), (iii) Sanding cycles with different size grit (from 180 to 800), (iv) Coating in sterile conditions.

Fig. 7. Transparency view in the 3D printed urn

4   Discussions on the Results

Before its actual excavation, the cremation 42A was the subject of a CT and a 3D reconstruction. 3D volume rendering informs on the preservation of the burial, the urn and the cremated bone block (its fragmentation and the deformations of the internal masses bioturbations…). It allows the identification, location and orientation in space of each artifact in a sustainable manner, the visualization and localization of the bone mass in its entirety and the observation of the nature of the sediment's components in the urn. These elements offer the possibility of taking immediate precautionary measures before any manual intervention. Furthermore, the digitization permits operations of "virtual" manipulation of artifacts to increase the observation providing the first interpretations before excavation. It also serves as supporting tangible "evidence" for elements that are difficult to characterize in 2D. With the segmentation tools, it is possible to obtain an independent 3D model of an artifact that can be virtually manipulated before its excavation. The additive techniques allow tangible handling and initial observations before the provision of the original. This process allows the provision of information within hours, which is not the case for the "operational chain" commonly implemented that can take months if protective measures are implemented, prior to the study of the archaeological material, as presented in Fig. 8.

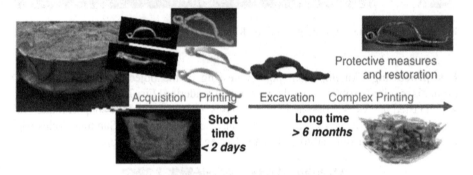

Fig. 8. Timelines of digital (blue) and physical (red) excavations (Color figure online)

Fig. 9. Left: the 3D printed fibula Right: the real fibula, after its excavation, and before the restoration process.

The CT scan provided information on the structural state of the object, and allowed the identification of the cluster type of the fibula. Nevertheless, the observation of 2D sections and 3D reconstruction did not make possible to truly characterize the number of turns of the spring and the pin holder. Different segmentations were performed resulting in a restitution of the object with an approximate resolution of the details, which requires a systematic return to the real object in fine. This model has been the subject of a 3D impression (Fig. 9, left) that allowed to corroborate a number of observations from CT scans but also to confirm with certainty the number of turns of the spring and the shape of the. Also of note is the tangible nature of 3D printing with respect to the digital model. These comments have all been confirmed after the implementation of protective measures (Figs. 9, right and 10, left). The characterization of the initial surface condition during manual cleaning by a conservator revealed a setting of longitudinal striations on the arc (Fig. 10, right). Only this manual intervention may allow detection of such a setting very difficult to determine virtually on a small object.

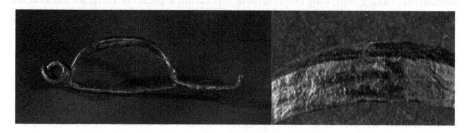

Fig. 10. Left: the fibula after restoration. Right: details of the etched patterns on the fibula

The CT scan reveals the different elements using an arbitrary color application (bone remains in red, metal in blue, biological indices in grey, etc.). For the neophyte, this palette can disturb, but is quickly understood. For the anthropologist, while ordinarily the information is supplied layer by layer in stratigraphic excavation, this comprehensive 3D visualization is more interactive. Translating from 2D to 3D, is none other than the transition from virtual to real and requires each expert to integrate this type of imaging. The complex 3D printing digital model overcomes this difficulty. After treatment, the printing transparency provides a 3D print of the container and contents (here funeral-deposit burned bones and iron objects knife rivet and fibula, Fig. 11).

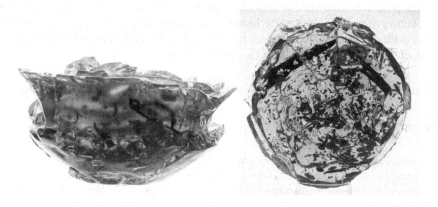

Fig. 11. Front and bottom views of the 3D printed urn (Color figure online)

Printing on both its tangible nature allows "direct" access to information and the physical handling of cremation deposit. It allows viewing and manipulation of the vessel and its contents in full and with integrity. Printing allows visualization of burned bones that are imperceptible when excavating (too small, fragile, or appearing negative, to be taken), but also some well-preserved bones (at least here, a long bone) and the determination of iron artefacts (here released from their mineralization). 3D printing also provides information for the reconstruction of the funerary urn. This tangible medium allows a manipulation/simple visualization to work on the analysis (such as the distribution of artifacts and the burial gestures) but also as a support for the excavation [2]. Indeed, 3D printing is the only tangible medium of context preserved after the excavation of the incineration.

5   Conclusion and Future Works

For the archaeologist, the first asset of the scanner remains the immediacy of information, essential in the case of diagnostics where time is short. Well before the excavation of a container (funeral vase…), imaging allows the establishment of a protocol, the scheduling of specialists' intervention, the possible solicitation of a conservator curator to keep the fluidity of the scientific treatment of the remains [9].

In this process, the substitution of the original by certified copies can be attractive for a valuation framework, given the fragility of unstable materials to exhibit. The archaeological sensitive materials suffer during traveling. Accidents due to manipulation (packaging, transport and installations) are inevitable. 3D printing offers promising perspectives regarding the diversity of materials faithful to the look, the weight, the texture of the original… From the image to the copy of an original, it takes an average a half-day with an easy correction of the design since we can re-intervene in the template file at any time. We also underline its importance in an educational setting with teaching kits embellished with 3D restitutions subject to multiple manipulations, but also for people with disabilities.

The processes used open up new exploratory research. For example, the possibility of obtaining a model of old or recent bioturbations (earthworms galleries…) in a funerary urn provides information on the presence of a perishable container and 3D printing of a model provides access to "all" of the skeletal remains.

Acknowledgement.   This project was funded by the CNRS Imag'In IRMA project, France.

References

1. Laycock, S.D., Bell, G.D., Corps, N., Mortimore, D.B., Cox, G., May, S., Finkel, I.: Using a combination of micro-computed tomography, CAD and 3D printing techniques to reconstruct incomplete 19th-century cantonese chess pieces. J. Comput. Cult. Herit. 7(4), Article 25, February 2015
2. Haßmann, H., Heintges, T., Rasink, B., Winghart, S., Wulf, F.-W.: Der bronzezeitliche Hortfund von Gessel, Stadt Syke, Landkreis Diepholz, Berichte zur Denkmalpflege in Niedersachsen Veröffentlichung des Niedersächsischen Landesamtes für Denkmalpflege Hameln: Niemeyer, vol. 32, no. 1, pp. 23–28 (2012)
3. Nicolas, T., Gaugne, R., Tavernier, C., Gouranton, V., Arnaldi, B.: Preservative approach to study encased archaeological artefacts. In: Ioannides, M., Magnenat-Thalmann, N., Fink, E., Žarnić, R., Yen, A.-Y., Quak, E. (eds.) EuroMed 2014. LNCS, vol. 8740, pp. 332–341. Springer, Heidelberg (2014). doi:10.1007/978-3-319-13695-0_32

4. Nicolas, T., Gaugne, R., Tavernier, C., Petit, Q., Gouranton, V., Arnaldi, B.: Touching and interacting with inaccessible cultural heritage. Presence: Teleoperators Virtual Environ. **24**(3), 265–277 (2015). MIT Press
5. McKnight, L.M., Adams, J.E., Chamberlain, A., Atherton-Woolham, S.D., Bibb, R.J.: Application of clinical imaging and 3D printing to the identification of anomalies in an ancient Egyptian animal mummy. J. Archaeol. Sci. Rep. **3**, 328–332 (2015)
6. Nicolas, T., Gaugne, R., Tavernier, C., Gouranton, V., Arnaldi, B.: Tomography and 3D printing for the study of archaeological artefacts. In: Proceedings of the Conference New Technologies for Cultural Heritage, Paris, musée du quai Branly, November 2014, Cambridge Scholars Publishing (to appear)
7. Aubry, L., Le Puil-Texier, M.: Un enclos funéraire de l'âge du Fer, Domaine de La Bizaie, Guipry, (Ille-et-Vilaine): rapport de fouilles, Cesson-Sévigné: Inrap GO, pp. 113–119 (2014)
8. Mustra, M., Delac, K., Grgic, M.: Overview of the DICOM standard. In: 50th International Symposium ELMAR, pp. 39–44 (2008)
9. Biron, M., Hurtin, S., Nicolas, T., Tavernier, C.: La tomographie des objets archéologiques complexes et/ou altérés: outil d'identification, d'analyse et d'aide à la décision pour les mesures conservatoires. In: Restaurer l'ordinaire. Exposer l'extraordinaire, Journée des Restaurateurs en Archéologie (JRA), Arles (2014)
10. Mitsopoulou, V., Michailidis, D., Theodorou, E., Isidorou, S., Roussiakis, S., Vasilopoulos, T., Polydoras, S., Kaisarlis, G., Spitas, V., Stathopoulou, E., Provatidis, C., Theodorou, G.: Digitizing, modelling and 3D printing of skeletal digital models of Palaeoloxodon tiliensis (Tilos, Dodecanese, Greece). Quat. Int. **379**, 4–13 (2015)

Towards Monuments' Holistic Digital Documentation: the Saint Neophytos Enkleistriotis Case Study

Marinos Ioannides[1], Charalabos Ioannidis[2],
Archimadrite Neophytos Enkleistriotis[3], David Castrillo[1],
Pavlos Chatzigrigoriou[1(✉)], Eirini Papageorgiou[1],
Georgios Leventis[1], Vasiliki Nikolakopoulou[1], Vasilis Athanasiou[1],
Fotis Bourexis[2], Sofia Soile[2], Styliani Verykokou[2],
Maria Costi de Castrillo[1], and Christian Sovis[4]

[1] Cyprus University of Technology,
31 Arch. Kyprianou Str., 3036 Limassol, Cyprus
{marinos.ioannides,p.chatzigrigoriou,e.papageorgiou,
georgios.leventis,v.nikolakopoulou,
vasilis.athanasiou}@cut.ac.cy,
david_jcz@edu.cut.ac.cy,
mariacosticastrillo@gmail.com
[2] National Technical University of Athens,
9 Iroon Polytechniou Str., 15780 Athens, Greece
{cioannid,ssoile}@survey.ntua.gr,
fotis.bourexis@gmail.com, st.verykokou@gmail.com
[3] The Holy, Royal and Stavropegic Monastery of Saint Neophytos,
Tala, 60289 Paphos, Cyprus
fr.neophytos.enkleistriotis@gmail.com
[4] 7Reasons, Hauptplatz 11, 3462 Absdorf, Austria
cs@7reasons.net

Abstract. The expansion of the term "monument" to include the surrounding area of the tangible cultural asset, its natural environment as well as the intangible data relating to its existence and use has gradually resulted the formation of the term "cultural landscapes". "Monument" has evolved into "monumental place" and a "place with its own soul" and nowadays into a "unity" incorporating the multiple and diversified views which regard the one and single object, the cultural asset. In this paper and through the presented case study of Saint Neophytos Enkleistriotis monument, we attempt to move further on, from the view of the "unity" and the interdiscipilinary approach to the "holistic" view, treating the cultural asset as a "whole"; a "whole" which will have been created from the harmonious merge of all the multifaced entities of which it is comprised.

Keywords: Holistic documentation · 3D model · Geometric documentation · Orthoimage · Structure from motion · UAV

© Springer International Publishing AG 2016
M. Ioannides et al. (Eds.): EuroMed 2016, Part I, LNCS 10058, pp. 442–473, 2016.
DOI: 10.1007/978-3-319-48496-9_36

1 Introduction

The emergence of a holistic approach to monument documentation is inextricably associated with the term 'monument', the quest of its meaning and its interpretation to the people involved in the documentation of the past. The term 'monument' has been transmitted many times following the evolutionary expansion of the concept of 'heritage' and its semantical transfer into 'Cultural Heritage' (CH). The main reason was the necessity to set tangible heritage in its wider context, and relate it with its physical environment and its intangible aspects (spiritual, political and social values) [1–3]. Both the existing natural and cultural diversity among the nations of the world and the appreciation of intangible heritage -as the primer fundamental element before its materialization into tangible heritage- led to a more anthropological, holistic heritage approach. Moreover, the infiltration of culture and nature in the concept of 'cultural landscape' as well as the broadened shift towards viewing historic buildings as an inseparable part of historic cities and sites, revealed the matter of 'monumental place'. In this way, a monument can be seen as a whole, within a place with a soul – a *genius loci* [4].

Monumental places are places of cultural identity and of great human achievement. While the tangible part of a monument may leave its material evidence in the course of time, the intangible part, which is more closely related to its creator, may never survive. The survival of intangible heritage is then depended on the onward (mainly oral) transmission of the knowledge behind its creation and the values it reflects: historical values, symbolical values, authenticity and quality. It is a transmission of practices, knowledge and skills that encapsulate a form of 'memory' of the built heritage and its relationship between the society and a normative system of ideas and beliefs. Consequently, 'values' and 'memory' are the substances that transform a built structure into a monument and are only a part of what the holistic documentation approach aims to capture. Due to the variety of its individual components (both tangible and intangible, material and immaterial, concrete and abstract, natural or artificial), monument documentation demands the coincidence of the effort of many scientific, engineering, and management disciplines to become a reality in order to gather all these kinds of professional data. Hence, interdisciplinary research and cross-sectorial approaches among the CH domain, that integrate knowledge and methods using real synthesis, can lead to the augmentation of documentation tools and standards in establishing holistic practices. Data collection for monumental buildings, complexes, settlements, areas, artifacts during documentation deals with "visible" data. This includes the documentation of past indications about monument's remains through geospatial surveying of its form, the recording of the materials used for its first creation and possible later interventions as well as the construction technology, which can lead to adequate pathology analysis and effective conservation of the building [5]. Along with the visible data, the "invisible" data, such as occurred past events, stories of the lives of the users and the local community, songs and lyrics written about it, liturgies in the case of religious monuments etc., will constitute the finishing layers that would deliver a unified information and knowledge hub.

Extending narrow and sterile considerations, the approach does not seek to "freeze" the intangible part of the monument, by reducing it into files, be in archives, inventories, museums, libraries, text, audio and video records [2]. Besides, it aims to creatively "revive" it by further exploiting every technological affordance of the present era. Eventually, holistic approach for monuments' digital documentation is oriented to provide the framework -a basis- for the ongoing adjustment and evolvement of the effective, multileveled and multi-perspective reuse of the documented information by the diverse user groups involved in the creation, use and dissemination of digital cultural heritage.

This paper focuses on holistic approach documentation activities partaken at St. Neophytos church; a church with tremendous monumental interest both of its tangible and intangible aspects as well as the unique blending of natural and man-made environment that bears the signs of human work and the effect of multicriterial factors that have shaped so far the history of the religious monument.

2 Methodology

The Digital Documentation of Monuments has met vast progress in recent years, since it develops parallel to the Information, Communication and Technology (ICT) sector. However, because of this fast development, digital documentation has also left many gaps and created challenges on data quality, accuracy, standards, archiving, copyrights and sustainability. There is a need to establish a methodology and a workflow, where various users (experts and non-experts) should follow, aiming to maximize collaboration, distribution and -at the end- capitalize the digital information of the monument. The proposed methodology of *holistic approach* presents a workflow that could (at the full end level) answer the requirements of the monuments' digital documentation, filling the above mentioned gaps, by involving all user needs from the beginning of the process. Counting users' needs on planning and implementing the holistic digital documentation is crucial due to the fact that the documentation sector as well as the whole life cycle of a digital cultural heritage asset, are by nature multidisciplinary (and during the documentation process become interdisciplinary). Therefore, before deciding *"what kind of data do I need (from them)"* it is essential to have an integrated image of the potential users' needs; their interrelationships, their intersectorial agendas (in which phase of the documentation process do they meet), the problems they are coming up against during the process and how they overcome those. This feedback, together with the required types of data, will enrich the *metadata* (data about data) and organize the *semantics* (information that needs to be interlinked) in order to shape system's *ontology* (monument's conceptual model), countering the above mentioned challenges (data quality, accuracy, standards, intellectual properties and sustainability).

The first step towards the proposed methodology of *holistic digital documentation* is the analysis of cultural heritage users and stakeholders. They can be categorized in two major teams: experts and non-experts [6] (Table 1); *"experts"* are users that create digital data from documenting monuments and *"non-experts"* are users that only use these data. Nevertheless, due to the fast development of the creative sector -especially in EU- the "non-experts" are creating new content that we cannot afford to leave outside the monuments' digital documentation, especially in the holistic approach. Hence, the boundaries of these teams are loose, leaving many non-experts to become experts due to their engagement, knowledge and creativity on specific cultural heritage assets (Fig. 1). On our proposed approach, expanding the boundaries between these teams is our aim; including more non-expert users in planning and digital documenting monuments augments the results, increases the coverage of the intangible heritage aspect, minimizes the possibility of faults and maximizes the prospects of reusing the digital data.

Table 1. Users' teams (expert and non-experts)

Experts	Non-experts
Anthropologists/Sociologists	Economists
Archaeologists	Electrical, Acoustic, Thermal Engineers
Architects	Exhibition designers
Archivists/Librarians	Fellows
Biologists	General Public
Civil Engineers	Tourists
Chemical Engineers	Students
Computer Scientists/ICT Specialists	Public Relation specialists
Conservators	Advertisers
Curators	Religion Authorities
Geologists	Administrative & Territorial Institutes
Geographers	Guides
Historians	Multimedia specialists
Material Engineers	Game developers
Structural Engineers	Decision makers
Geomatics Engineers	Police & Fire authority
Musicians/Artists	Owner
Neuroscientists (Psychologists)	Travel agents
Site managers	Local associations
Lawyers/Legal specialists	Local and Regional authorities
Physics	NGO's
Surveyors	Non-profit organisations

The second step is a parallel analysis of the cultural heritage information that we need to extract from the monuments' digital documentation. According to Core Data Index for historic buildings and monuments of the architectural heritage and its basic aim, a possible classification of individual buildings and sites is by: name, location, functional type, date, architect, building materials and techniques, physical condition, and protection status [7]. In addition, it should be taken under consideration the fact that depending on the country or the organization, the need for deeper levels of architectural, archaeological, environmental, historical, and planning information will vary; each one must define its own specific requirements. Towards the *digital holistic*

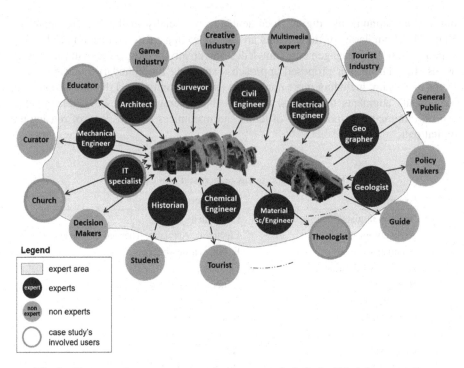

Fig. 1. Experts and non-experts users' engagement in holistic digital documentation

approach, the data (and metadata) that we need to document should expand and adjust to the quality restrictions given by ICT experts. A holistic unity of intellectual frameworks and approaches of information gathering beyond the disciplinary perspectives, is crucial for the sufficient implementation of an effective, transdisciplinary and collaborative work methodology that aims to define data collection process, case study setup, selection and utilization of systems and instruments, knowledge management, implementation of semantically enriched models, exploitation in education and business and the continuous advancement of the information gathered and reused. In Fig. 2, the proposed data and metadata scheme clearly presents the necessity for a horizontal connection of Digital Documentation with all data (and metadata) categories [5]. As digitalization is a procedure that could be applied in analogue data, it is necessary to clarify that the proposed holistic methodology requires the plethora of the documentation to be digital and not digitized. That said, obviously we can't avoid analogue data, especially during historic research, so digitalization will be applied following the same scheme of metadata. Last but not least, the 3D documentation of the monument is essential for holistic approach; documenting and creating the 3D model is a procedure that involves a number of users (experts and non-experts) that can directly benefit from the information covered by the 3D and many of them could (and should) offer data to upgrade the quality and enrich the information of the 3D model.

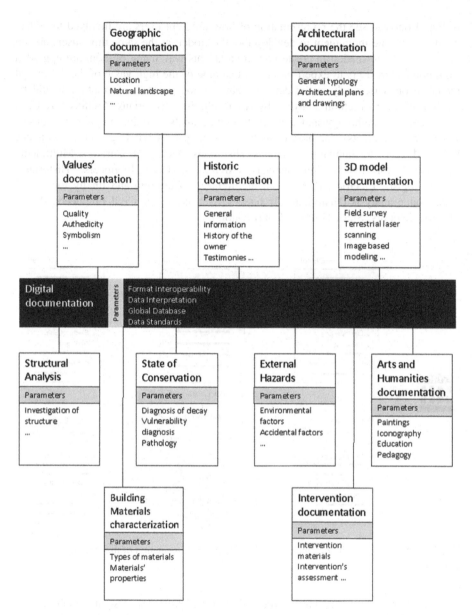

Fig. 2. Basic data and parameters documentation for holistic digital approach

In the case study of Saint Neophytos, the proposed methodology workflow was followed. At the beginning there was an effort to cover a number of users (experts and non-experts) in the process of documentation (Fig. 1). Since the approach is *digital*, various methods were discussed and the team developed a scheme of data collection aiming towards the holistic digital documentation methodology. In the first phase of the documentation the developing of the 3D Model was the crucial part of the workflow.

In Fig. 3 one can see the representation of how different users are involved to collect the data from the monument to develop the 3D Model; at the same time, users absorb the extracted information to create new content; this way many of them are upgraded from non-expert users to expert users. An example of the high value of the 3D digital model in our case study is the demand that the documented information should be vastly useful for structural analysis (by Archaeologists, Historians, Architects & Civil Engineers), for pathology and conservation state analysis (Civil Engineers, Conservators and Architects), for hazard analysis (Geologists, Civil Engineers, Architects, Policy Makers), for humanities analysis (Historians, Architects, Curators, Multimedia developers) for intervention analysis (Architects, Civil Engineers, Historians, Archaeologists, Electrical & Mechanical Engineers, Curators) and finally for monuments value analysis (Historians, Architects, Archaeologists, Civil Engineers, Policy Makers, Curators, Stake Holders, Conservators).

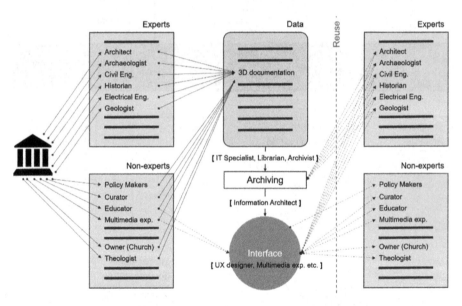

Fig. 3. Different Users' involvement in holistic digital documentation of the monument of Saint Neophytos.

The outcome of the digital documentation of the Enkleistra of Saint Neophytos is a highly-detailed 3D model, which may act as a reference point for the creation of applications in the field of Information Technology (IT). The specific 3D model provides incentives to developers in creating applications that will exploit model's full potentials in order to become useful tools to either experts or non-experts. However, the proper function of these applications relies on the existence of a corresponding database on a server and/or on cloud systems, where the acquired data needs to be stored in a format that will be accessible and easily interpreted by all. Towards the scope of proper interpretation, it is essential to establish standards for the collected data, leading this way to a qualitative data collection with improved integrity and decreased number of stored redundant data. Taking into consideration database's management, the stored data should follow the "Open Access" principles in order for its wider access and reuse to be ensured as different disciplines may enrich the database or even fulfill missing data. Parallel to that, a user friendly interface should be developed to help non-expert users to find the required information. The case study presented in this paper, is the first approach to Digital Holistic Documentation of Monument, using the proposed workflow. Obviously the project is ongoing and we are expecting interesting results, evaluation and limitations after the full deployment of user's engagement.

3   The Saint Neophytos Enkleistriotis Case Study

3.1   Values' Documentation

The Enkleistra of Saint Neophytos is an outstanding testimony of the Byzantine art and civilization at probably the most troubled and intense moments in this part of the Mediterranean: crusaders (English, Normans), byzantine and Arab elements are clearly reflected in the Enkleistra. The paintings (frescos) are characteristic of the "Komnenian" Byzantine art period (mid 12 century); one can identify strong emotions, mainly of passion and suffering, sophisticated proportions and movements of the figures who are dressed in rich clothes with wavy edges. There aren't many frescos saved in such good conservation state as the ones in the monument of Saint Neophytos Enkleistriotis. The preservation of the Enkleistra and the extensive documentation of its origin, development and further interventions provide clear information for its interpretation and confirm the authenticity of each element. This existing written documentation, the structure, organization and paintings of the Enkleistra are key to understanding the ways of the monastic life in the twelfth century.

The organic form of the Enkleistra and the plasticity of the cave carved in the rock differentiates it from any other religious building around the island. It is situated in a unique landscape, excavated in a cliff overlooking a valley and has withstood landslides and earthquakes for more than 800 years. It has additionally been continuously used for monastic life and as a pilgrimage destination for centuries. These factors add to its historic and cultural value and attract people from all the corners of the globe until this day. Function, symbolism, use and the natural shape of the mountain are interconnected in this monument, unified and understood into a unique example of Cypriot religious architecture.

The history, the uniqueness of the structural form and the amazing frescoes, make the Enkleistra of Saint Neophytos a monument of an exceptional tangible and intangible cultural Cypriot -and world- heritage.

3.2   Geographical Documentation

The Enkleistra is situated in the southwest part of the island of Cyprus, north of Paphos, 6 km away from the sea, at an altitude of 450 m. above sea level; a strategic position which offered control over the coast (Fig. 4). The monastery complex is located in a

Fig. 4. Geolocation of the Saint Neophytos' Enkleistriotis monastery complex in Cyprus, north of Paphos (left); the New Monastery (centre); the Old Monastery (right)

natural valley oriented south. There is a small waterfall on the northern side of the cliff that continues into a stream running south. The Enkleistra is situated on its west part. The mountain cliffs are of a white calcareous rock, a workable material which is easy to be eroded by natural phenomena (rain, vegetation, landslides) and/or hewed by man, thus facilitating the creation (natural or artificial) of caves.

3.3   Historical Documentation

Saint Neophytos Enkleistros ("The Recluse") (1134 A.D.–1219 A.D.), was born in the town of Lefkara, near Larnaca. His life runs parallel in time with one of the most unstable political periods in Cyprus [8]. At the age of 17 years old he chose the monastic life and for five years remained at the St. Chrysostom monastery near Kyrenia, cultivating the land and learning how to read and write. After two years he set off for Jerusalem and shortly afterwards attempted to go to Asia Minor in search of solitary life and enlightment. His attempt was unsuccessful and therefore decided to become an ascetic at the hilly area above Paphos [8, 9]. In 1159 A.D. he departed for his place of reclusion and formed his cell by modifying an already existing one, encurved on the body of the mountain.

In this section there will also be incorporated various information regarding the stakeholders, testimonies, bibliography, possible past uses as well as legal status.

3.4   Architectural Documentation

Ever since 1159 A.D. Saint Neofytos spend the rest of his life in Enkleistra, thus he had furtherly modified the place, gradually turning Enkleistra from a single cave into a complex of caves and constructions (Figs. 5 and 6). Between 1159 and 1160 [8] Saint Neophytos dug two caves: his Cell, in which he used to live until 1197 A.D. and where his grave also lies, and a consecutive-to-the-cell cave with an altar (Bema), which was dedicated to the Holy Cross. Both of these caves constitute the "**First Enkleistra**".

Fig. 5. Sketch of the Saint Neophytos' Enkleistriotis monastery complex in 1735 A.D.; the New Monastery (centre); the Old Monastery (left) (sketch: adapted by Barskij)

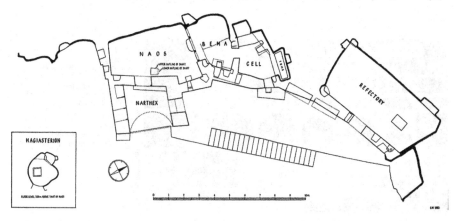

Fig. 6. Plan of various caves in the greater area of the old monastery complex - Level 1 (center), Level 3 (left) (plan: adapted by [8])

In 1170 A.D., due to his growing popularity, Saint Neophytos was obliged to accept a disciple, establish a monastery and adjust the mountain structure/rock constructions to monastic rules. Consequently, the First Enkleistra got extended. This extension included the excavation of a third cave towards northeast (**Naos**) around

1183 A.D. [8] and the construction of an extra space on the eastern side (**Exonarthex**), in order for the functional causes of the orthodox church to be fulfilled. Probably for functional reasons of the monastery the cave of the Refectory (dining room) was also excavated on the north side of the three-cave unity.

Due to the increasing number of pilgrims Saint Neophytos dug another cave at a higher level (the New Zion or Higher Enkleistra), which was completed by the end of 1197 A.D. and in which he moved and spent the rest of his life until his death around 1220 A.D. in search of solitude. Gradually more spaces have been added, thus expanding the complex of the **old troglodyte monastery**. A closed room with a dome was constructed above the Exonarthex, the **Sacristy**, another closed room at a higher level of the Sacristy, the **Holy Attendance and Sanctuary or Hagiasterion** which is connected to the Naos through a narrow hole on the floor, as well as one more cave on the northern part of the cliff, above the Refectory (probably formed in 1170 A.D.), the **Hermitage or Saint John Baptist Cave**, which is devoted to the Holy Cross.

The old troglodyte monastery is composed of five different levels (Fig. 7): *Level 0* (level of the bridge passing over the west stream), *Level 1* (approximately 5 m above Level 0) where the Narthex, Naos, Bema, the Cell of the Saint and the Refectory are situated, *Level 2* (Sacristy), *Level 3* (Hagiasterion), *Level 4* (the New Zion cell and the Saint John Baptist Cave). Because on the northeast (NE) side of the cliff there is a waterfall and a stream, the old monastery has expanded in the late twelfth century towards the southwest (SW), and as shown in the sketch made by Barskij (Fig. 5), some constructions already existed in 1735 A.D., possibly destroyed by a subsequent landslide. However, further to the SW, vestiges of other caves are traced, as well as stone building constructions used until not long ago by shepherds.

Fig. 7. Facade of the old monastery complex with all five levels (photo: David Castrillo, 2016)

In this section there will also be incorporated various information regarding the general typology, compared with other caves on a local and international level, possible evolution of typology, detailed architectural drawings on various scales based on the photogrammetric documentation.

3.5   Intervention Documentation

During the years 1963–1965 interventions of consolidation of the structure were carried out with the supervision of the Department of Antiquities of Cyprus. A covered veranda and five arches resembling the originals cited by the Saint were constructed (Level 1). Also stairs and paths from the Hagiasterion (Level 3) to the upper level (Level 4) were constructed.

In this section more detailed intervention data will be gradually added, in addition to a reference regarding intervention's materials and interventions' general assessment (actually solved problems or created new ones, successful or not successful, etc.).

3.6   3D Model Documentation

An important stage is the detailed documentation through the 3D recording of the monument; the products of this stage will be also used as the basemap for the studies of other specialists. First, the complete 3D geometric documentation of the Enkleistra via photogrammetric and surveying techniques is a fundamental step for addressing its structural and environmental problems. The results of the geometric documentation (sections, ortho-images, 3D models) will be provided to for its preservation and protection, as well as the planning of conservative repair operations. Furthermore, the generation of 3D printings or photorealistic 3D tours depicting in detail the internal and external parts of the Enkleistra is another objective of the 3D recording procedure and promotion of the monument.

3.6.1   Field Survey – Data Acquisition

As far as the geometric documentation of the Enkleistra is concerned, a combination of field surveying, terrestrial laser scanning, photogrammetric and computer vision techniques was applied. First, a geodetic network was established connecting the area in front of the rock, which includes the Enkleistra and the interior of all the rooms that exist inside the rock; so, all measurements and data collected can have a common georeference.

Scanning by a terrestrial time-of-flight laser scanner and image taking through terrestrial photography and the use of a small quadcopter UAV have been made at the external and surrounding area of the monument. A Canon EOS-1Ds Mark III camera was used for the acquisition of the terrestrial images (5616×3744 each) using two lenses of 24 mm and 16 mm focal length. Using the UAV, videos sequences depicting the external façade of the rock were taken by a GoPro camera, from a distance of 5 to 10 m from the object.

At the 4 rooms of the lower part of the Enkleistra, i.e., the old Enkleistra, which consists of the Naos dedicated to the Holy Cross (2 connected rooms) and the Cell of Saint Neophytos with his tomb, as well as the fourth separated room next to the Saint's cell, and at the outdoor corridor from which doors lead into the lower part of the Enkleistra, multiple laser scans and the acquisition of more than 1,500 terrestrial images took place. The combined use of images, for the application of image-based 3D modelling techniques, and laser scanning was necessary for the complete coverage of the complex areas inside these rooms (e.g., inside the tomb of the Saint, under and around the Altar in the Bema and the table in the cell, inside recesses in the walls of the Enkleistra, etc.) In the rooms of the upper part of the Enkleistra (Level 4) only the acquisition of photos (a few dozens for each room) was sufficient for the creation of 3D models.

More than 200 ground control points (GCPs), including both artificial targets and natural features easily recognizable in the imagery, were measured using Total Station equipment for the georeferencing of the images; also, the retroreflective targets of the laser scanner were measured to co-register the image-based and laser-based point clouds.

3.6.2   Data Processing

The automatic creation of 3D models using image sequences relies on photogrammetric and computer vision algorithms. The first step of the image-based modelling pipeline is the Structure from Motion (SfM) process [10], which refers to the method of simultaneous computation of the camera six degrees-of-freedom poses (i.e., the camera exterior orientation of the images) and the sparse 3D geometry of the scene. Feature extraction algorithms, like SIFT [11] or SURF [12], image matching and robust outlier rejection techniques [13] are used, usually in combination with a sequential (incremental) algorithm [12, 13] for metric reconstruction, in case of calibrated cameras, or projective reconstruction, in case of unknown interior orientation; in case of uncalibrated cameras an auto-calibration process is implemented [14–16]. The georeferencing of the SfM outputs is generally performed by estimating the 3D similarity transformation between the arbitrary SfM coordinate system and the coordinate reference system using GCPs [17]. The process of dense image matching [18] is applied for the creation of a dense 3D point cloud using the camera exterior and interior orientation of the imagery, estimated by the SfM process. Then, a 3D mesh model can be created using the generated dense point cloud [19] via a surface reconstruction algorithm. Finally, texture mapping may be applied to the mesh model using the oriented images. The result of the image-based 3D modelling process is a photorealistic textured 3D surface model of the scene depicted in the imagery that refers to the coordinate system defined by the GCPs or the arbitrary SfM coordinate system, in case of lack of such kind of information.

The Agisoft PhotoScan software was used for the creation of dense point clouds using images taken by the Canon EOS-1Ds Mark III camera as well as frames of the videos taken by the GoPro camera. The processing of each internal room of the Enkleistra was performed separately. Similarly, the outdoor corridor and the external facade of the Enkleistra were divided into separate projects. The alignment of the images was the first step performed by PhotoScan; it is a SfM process that generates a sparse point cloud of the scene and computes the camera interior and exterior orientation, using a modification of the SIFT algorithm for the extraction of feature points. GCPs were manually measured in the corresponding images to transform the camera poses and the sparse point clouds into the local coordinate reference system. Furthermore, some regions of a few images (e.g., retroreflective targets, obstacles due to measuring equipment) were masked in the images, in order to reduce the subsequent editing of the resulting dense point clouds. Dense image matching was the next step applied through PhotoScan; the software calculates depth information for each camera and combines it into a single dense point cloud.

Due to the complexity of the Enkleistra, some small areas without cloud points were observed in the generated 3D dense point clouds (i.e., under the Altar, inside recesses, etc.). 3D information for such areas was derived by the point clouds generated by the laser scanner. The processing of the scans was performed via the Leica Cyclone software, including their registration via the common targets as well as their georeferencing, using the measured coordinates of the targets. The Geomagic Studio was used for the registration and merging of the laser-based and image-based point clouds, separately for each room of the Enkleistra, as well as their editing, including the removal of wrong and noisy cloud points. Furthermore, this software was used for surface reconstruction for each separate point cloud, resulting in 3D mesh surfaces for each room of the Enkleistra. In areas where the image-based point cloud was sufficient (i.e., upper part of the Enkleistra, corridor and exterior regions), only the editing of the point cloud and the meshing were performed via Geomagic software.

The reconstructed surfaces were inserted again into the PhotoScan environment for texture mapping, using the oriented images. The outputs of these steps are 3D textured models for every internal and external part of the Enkleistra. Finally, the textured mesh surfaces were merged via the Geomagic software. Except for 3D products, orthoimages at a resolution of 1 mm were generated via PhotoScan software, using the oriented images and the derived point clouds, by manually determining the level of section for each orthoimage. The orthoimages as well as the texture atlases of the 3D models were processed via the Adobe Photoshop software.

3.6.3 The 3D Model

The main product of the geometric documentation of the Enkleistra monument is a detailed and accurate 3D model which includes both the external areas (the rock and the newer constructions, like the corridor, etc.) and the internals of the rooms (of the upper and the lower part of the Enkleistra) georeferenced in a unique coordinate system, so that their relative horizontal and vertical position will be correct. In the following figures typical 3D views, ortho-images and horizontal and vertical sections of the monument are illustrated (Figs. 8, 9, 10, 11, 12, 13, 14, 15, 16, 17, 18, 19, 20, 21, 22, 23, 24 and 25).

3.7 Structural Analysis

From a structural point of view, three different construction elements can be detected: the mountain rock, the stone masonry and the concrete. The mountain rock serves as back wall (western side) as well as ceiling of the caves, the stone masonry includes the walls, constructed to close the eastern façades of the excavated caves and which include openings for access or ventilation (doors and windows), while out of concrete are constructed all the contemporary interventions, namely the veranda (roof, arches, beams, columns) and possibly, the vertical reinforcement walls of the façade.

Regarding the structural condition, the latter additions in the period 1963–1965 (concrete beams, stone retaining walls) seem not to have helped to the stability of the

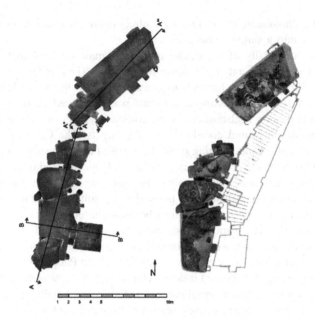

Fig. 8. Left: Projection on a single horizontal plane of the rooms of the Enkleistra that are at different levels (Level 1 up to Level 4) and the footprints of the vertical sections (AA and BB); Right: A view towards the ceiling at a horizontal section of the lower part of the Enkleistra

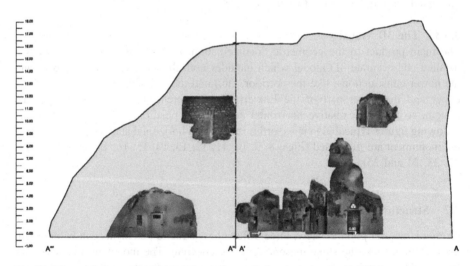

Fig. 9. The vertical section A–A‴ through the rock that includes the Enkleistra, with a metric scale of the relative elevations at the left (±0.00 m. at the entrance of Naos)

monument. On the contrary, it can be an added problem, since a theory for the deteriorated state of the monument is that below exist hollow areas (probably previous rooms or auxiliary spaces like stables, etc. described by the saint in his writings). These

Fig. 10. Left: The vertical section BB'; Right: The façade of the rock that includes the Enkleistra

Fig. 11. 3D view from the outside of the inside surfaces of the four rooms of the lower part of the Enkleistra (Level 1), as extracted from the point clouds of the laser scans.

voids, with the help of water infiltrated, seismic movements and the extra weight of the new interventions, could imply the displacement of the masonry stone walls and the evident detachment of the Narthex and the wall between them and also from the rest of the structure (Fig. 3). Moreover, the use of mortars rich in cement adds to the deterioration of the building structure.

In this section, the investigation of structure (description of bearing structure, construction techniques, distribution of building materials etc.) as well as mapping of structural state (e.g. mapping of structural cracks, disposition of elements, etc.) will gradually be included.

Fig. 12. 3D of the view from the outside of the inside of the Naos dedicated to the Holy Cross

Fig. 13. 3D view from the inside of the 3D textured model of the Naos

Fig. 14. Orthoimage of the western wall of the Naos

3.8 Building Materials' Characterization

This section will include information about the type of materials (e.g. stone, mortar, ceramic, metal, etc.), their physical properties, their composition (e.g. chemical, petrographic, mineralogical), their mechanical properties as well as their processing (e.g. cost and availability, production, etc.).

3.9 External Hazards

The Enkleistra, being an integral part of the natural environment of the area, presents a variety of problems mainly caused by landslides and the characteristics, properties and morphology of the area, weather conditions, lack of adequate maintenance or intensive human contact. Landslides could potentially change the morphology of the mountain side and the quality of the rock allows it to break down easily, a phenomenon which is accelerated by earthquakes, rain, fauna and flora creating an additional safety concern for visitors. Earthquakes of high intensity, from 5 to 7° on the Richter scale, are frequent in the Paphos area. One must also note that fire is a great potential threat of the monument due to its location. The shape of the valley where it is placed creates a 'no exit' situation in the event of a fire originating from the lower part of the valley. Winds from the south would aid in the acceleration of the dimensions of such a fire.

The large attraction of visitors results in the change of the interior atmospheric conditions due to accumulation of people inside the monument as well as physical contact and photographing of the frescoes. Additionally, interventions due to contemporary needs (electricity etc.) and maintenance are often damaging or irreversible

Fig. 15. 3D views from the outside of the inside of the Bema

Fig. 16. Orthoimages of Bema Left: the northwestern wall - Right: the eastern wall

Fig. 17. 3D view from the outside of the inside of the Cell of Saint Neophytos with his grave

due to use of inappropriate and incompatible materials and new elements (electrical installation, lighting etc.).

In this section the environmental factors, the accidental actions, the impact of particular human actions as well as the social and economic parameters will be further on analyzed.

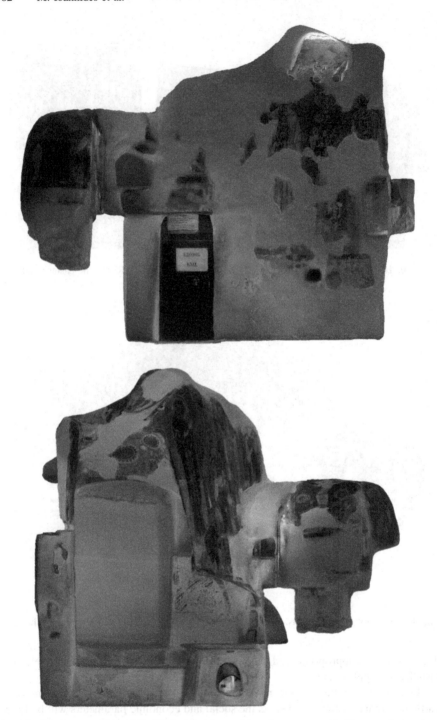

Fig. 18. Othoimages of the Cell of Saint Neophytos; Top: the eastern wall - Bottom: the western wall

Fig. 19. 3D view of the textured model of the grave of Saint Neophytos

Fig. 20. 3D view from the outside of the inside of the Refectory

3.10   Conservation State – Pathology Analysis

The level of humidity in the cell is also quite high, thus numerous frescoes in the lower parts of the walls have undergone extensive degradation. The main pathologies caused by the aforementioned problems are missing or detaching frescoe parts evident in the lower levels of the walls (frescoes degradation, large lacunas, lack of adherence and hollow areas under frescoes) as well as growing cracks.

Fig. 21. Orthoimage of the inside of the Refectory of the Enkleistra

Fig. 22. 3D views of the interior of the Sacristy; Left: Eastern wall - Right: Northern wall

Cracks are mostly evident on masonry reinforced by new walls or concrete columns (Fig. 26). The most recent earthquake in 2015 created displacements inside the cave and further expanded the already existing cracks (Fig. 26). Given that the back wall (mountain rock) does not show major damage and through the analysis of the cracks, the theory developed is that these cracks were created due to cavities below the existing cave. A more in-depth study reveals that the whole narthex is detached from the masonry walls, and that the masonry walls are detached from the rock mountain. This creates three separate structural elements which have different structural behavior.

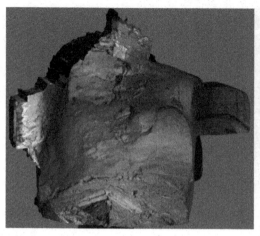

Fig. 23. 3D views of the interior of the Hagiasterion of St. Neophytos; Left: Southern wall - Right: Western wall

Fig. 24. 3D views of the interior of the New Zion; Left: Southern wall - Right: Western wall

More extensive research will reveal whether more caves (which seem to fail structurally) exist below Level 0, causing this type of extensive cracking (Fig. 27).

The diagnosis of decay which is derived from the usage of visual observations, non-destructive techniques, analytical testing, GIS decay mapping etc., the study of the mechanism of decay and the diagnosis of vulnerability (e.g. static and dynamic assessment, etc.) will be added to the provided aforementioned information.

3.11   Arts' and Humanities' Documentation

The architecture of the old monastery is inherently engaged with the layout of the frescoes and the presented iconographical themes. The digitally documented tangible structure is able to provide also a vast amount of intangible information, even life

Fig. 25. 3D views of the interior of the Hermitage or Saint John Baptist Cave; Left: southern wall - Right: western wall future work

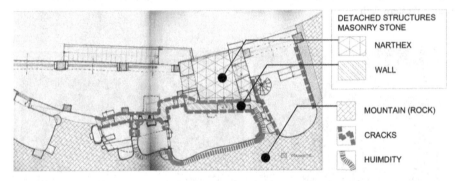

Fig. 26. Construction materials and structural conditions (architectural plan, David Castrillo 2016)

Fig. 27. Frescoes, conservation state with cracks and damaged areas (photos and graphic recreation of frescoes: David Castrillo 2016).

experiences, by incorporating various philosophical, educational and pedagogical meanings and interpretations.

In the case study of Saint Neophytos the 3D model provides detailed documentation also of the frescoes that exist in the Cell, the Bema and the Naos. According to written testimonies, the Enkleistra was painted in 1183 A.D. by Theodore Apseudes while the final phase of the paintings, mainly in the Naos, belonged to a different phase, after 1197 A.D. The paintings of the Enkleistra were completed and restored in 1503 A. D. through the commission of another monk, called also Neophytos [8, 9, 20].

The iconographical themes that were selected to cover the surfaces of the aforementioned spaces indicate that Enkleistra was meant to act as a "laboratory" for the study of the human soul's mechanisms and provide pilgrim with valuable pedagogical lessons. The knowledge of these mechanism offers human the capability to intervene upon them, in the pursue of victory upon the soul's passions and weaknesses. The pedagogical method of Saint Neophytos, which merges the content of the religious scenes with the cave architecture, comprises of three levels that comply with the three distinct zones of the iconographical programme.

The first level of the pedagogical training takes place inside the Cell of Saint Neophytos. In this room, where he was spending his everyday life Saint Neophytos had also engraved his own grave. The constant view of the grave trains the pilgrim about the concept of "death" and the perception of death's philosophical and spiritual essence. It is not only about the concept of the "inevitable end" of all humans, but furthermore about a training that sets human free, on one hand from the materialistic assets, and on the other hand from his desire to prevail upon other humans. When the pilgrim has reached to that point, then he experiences a grade of freedom that opens up his soul and enables him to profoundly love God.

Inside the Bema takes place the second level of the pedagogical training, due to the representation of Saint Neophytos between two Archangels, unique in the whole byzantine iconography. This representation expresses the loving bond between the human and his love object, namely God. But this road to Love and the unification of human with God is full of traps, deception, plausible phenomena which hide the truth and psychic projections of wishes (alike the projections of an oasis in the dessert), which constitute the "enemies" of the soul. At the same time the way is presented by which a human can cope with the aforementioned situations without damaging his own soul.

The third and last level of the training takes place in Naos. In Naos there are three zones of representations, the position and the general layout of the latter reveals to the eyes of the pilgrim a full life-cycle, through the pedagogical aspect of which the pilgrim can experience a profound spiritual situation.

The lowest zone of the iconographical programme presents ascetics as well as kings, all of them with a halo around their heads, in order to teach that both those who have abandoned the cosmic society and those who have reached the top of social pyramid and governed the world can defeat the human passions and conquer holiness. The presentation of the two opposites, the ones who have nothing (ascetics) and the others who have everything (kings) conveys the message that it is possible for the rest of the people who find themselves in the in-between zone to follow (if wanted) the path of spiritual life and (still) succeed their goals.

The road to reach the ultimate goal (union with God) is represented in the middle zone of the iconographical programme. It is the road of humility. This zone includes scenes from the last days of Jesus Christ, from Holy Wednesday until the Holy Resurrection. It concerns the conscious decision of human to choose forbearance and reconciliation with his co-humans through apologies.

The upper zone is covered by the scene of Ascension of Jesus Christ which is placed on the "roof" of the Naos, extending around the narrow hole that connects Naos with the Hagiasterion, from which Saint Neophytos used to provide the Holy Communion to the pilgrims. In these scenes, the mortal human body of Jesus Christ is lifted up to his Father, to be united with Him (God) and thus be transformed into immortal. In this way Jesus Christ prevailed over death and general decay, which is the success of the unification of humans with God.

Saint Neophytos used to provide the Holy Communion to the pilgrims through the narrow hole on the floor of Hagiasterion. In order for the pilgrims to receive the Holy Communion, they had to climb a ladder towards the narrow hole of Hagiasterion, through which Saint Neophytos was expecting on his knees to provide it to them. During this ascendance the pilgrims were experiencing initially, the approach to the way of life of the people around Jesus Christ in the scene of Ascension, afterwards the approach to Jesus Christ on the cloud presented in the upper zone of the iconographical programme and finally the union with Him through the offer of his body and blood (Holy Communion) executed by Saint Neophytos.

The aforementioned zones of iconographical programme with the architecture of the cave in combination with the service held in the church and the "road" of ascedance of each pilgrim towards the Holy Communion, thus the unification with God, were providing an exceptional pedagogical lesson to the people, through the combined cultivation of the senses, the feelings and the mind.

All the aforementioned aspects regard the intangible information that is incorporated in the monument of Saint Neophytos, which can provide pedagogical content and experiences to those who open up themselves to Christianity. They also serve as input for various educational purposes. The challenge of reusing and creating new digitized cultural heritage content is an issue that concerns scientists, practitioners, professionals and institutions in the field of culture and education. On the one hand, arts and cultural heritage education has been regarded as the key factors in development of the "knowledge society and creative ability" [21]. On the other hand, the ongoing development of ICTs is providing new opportunities of representation and interpretation of cultural heritage. Thus, learning about cultural heritage with the mediation of ICT tools and methods, such as an e-learning platform enriched with multimedia content, can be affective in all educational levels by using appropriately the available ICT affordances [22].

The aim is to engage learners from all ages, underage learners, adolescents as well as vocational trainers. Learning about the culture, the living conditions, the human creations and attitudes in the course of time, understanding the historic-cultural events and the evolution of society, and finally discerning what has survived at the socio-cultural surroundings, is the quintessence of arts and cultural heritage education. But in order to achieve the following learning approaches that take under consideration the benefits of using ICTs in cultural heritage education, we need to have a clear image of the range of the "knowledge" by which the present monument is dominated, so we can adjust it to our wide range of target learners. Learning approaches such as: (1) personalized, inquiry-based learning (2) on-site and anywhere learning experiences (3) interdisciplinary learning approaches and (4) collaborative learning experiences, demand prior presence and on-site experiential investigation in order to perceive the inherent value of Saint Neophytos monument, which will become the focus of the (e-) learning course.

An on-site analysis on Enkleistra's structure and its surrounding place was supplementarily conducted by research team's multimedia expert, while the required data were acquired through the use of state-of-the-art technological equipment. Moreover, a 360 camera facilitated the wide capture of Enkleistra's both internal and external landscape on video. The latter one can be used further on in the creation of VR video, while various audio recording devices were put near the cavern in order to capture the sounds caused by touristic engagement. Also, for the purposes of content enrichment several pictures along with video were taken, using not only smartphones with high-resolution cameras but also a UAV (drone) equipped with the latest GoPro 4 camera too. These acquired data will be represented in a digital installation of a physical interactive book, in which the story of Saint Neophytos will unfold before the eyes of readers encouraging them to engage with it using their hands, thus providing an educational approach of the monument's state. In order to accomplish this, the use of a computer software called VVVV is needed, where advanced programming skills in C# are required for its development.

Targeting at all audiences and lifelong learning experiences that can promote **sustainable** educational practices, we contribute to the **survival** of the monument's 'memory' and 'values'. In addition, by re-using its digital representation of its tangible and intangible aspects in such a context, we further provide its ongoing virtual and oral transmission of its history to the upcoming generations.

3.12   Digital Documentation's Parameters

As the holistic approach that it is proposed in this paper is digital, a member of the planning and research team is an ICT specialist. Having in mind the 3D models that are produced using survey means as well as their derived data, all the aforementioned set of information will be stored in an SQL relational database taking advantage of DB's capability in supporting plethora of data types (e.g. integer, chars, floats, strings) constituting it an ideal tool that will act as a reference point for the applications to run effectively. Additionally, this kind of database will be created on Microsoft's SQL Server, as it runs on programming extensions called Transact-SQL (T-SQL) expanding the common SQL standard to include more functions for the processing of string variables and procedural programming. Moreover, considering the fact that there may be compatibility issues for groups of experts who use open-source technologies, a MySQL database will be further considered as the primary common ground to be used. An important application that will exploit such a DB constitutes the development of an online learning system depicting the cultural significance of Enkleistra using CMS (e.g. WordPress, Joomla etc.) along with PHP code and various plugins enhancing platform's usability, where users will have the opportunity to be educated through interactive courses that will present the archived data in a user-friendly way. In addition to the proposed website, a mobile application will be considered for development in an IDE like Android Studio taking advantage of JAVA's capabilities towards the provision of useful information to users regarding Enkleistra's history and state through the use of 3D models. Assuming the existence of huge amount of data that will be generated over time, the use of data mining techniques to the aforementioned applications will be crucial for their analysis in order to improve their functionality. Towards that end, the collection of sufficient training data is most needed as Artificial Intelligence (AI) has reached a point, where advanced machine learning methods can be implemented in data mining techniques enriching their functionality. The creation of ML scripts that will either be built-in at the code or loaded externally using command(s) will provide the application the ability to "learn" by discovering various patterns that may exist in the data, targeting the enhancement of user experience and the designation of proper preservation methods for Enkleistra.

4 Conclusions and Future Work

A Holistic Documentation Approach to any Cultural Heritage element/monument requires an extensive and interdisciplinary research that considers its tangible and intangible aspects, complimented with a strong reflection in a wide variety of subjects. This is a pioneer approach in current documentation methodologies in the field. 'Building' plus 'memory', tangible plus intangible, is what transforms a simple structure into a monument, and this is what a holistic digital documentation aims to capture. The Saint Neophytos case study investigates the building's in-temporality which waits to be deconstructed and constructed again into a new form of communi-cation and will form pilot mechanism for other monuments. The application of a holistic approach can be the key to guarantee the uniqueness of the monument, and the documentation at several levels is the key to protect the cultural values of the place.

The approach followed focused on the documentation and the designation of appropriate preservation methods for the Enkleistra of St. Neophytos monastery, since it is a monument of great cultural significance. The outcome should act as a reference point for the application of restoration techniques that should be applied on Enkleistra's physical infrastructure in order to limit the risks that threaten its integrity. Nowadays it is difficult to finance these methods due to the economic crisis that exists in the Mediterranean countries, however an important measure that should be taken into consideration is the listing of Enkleistra on UNESCO's World Heritage Catalogue as a cultural heritage site of outstanding universal value from historical point of view by meeting certain criteria that should apply on its tangible form [23], leading this way in the raise of both domestic and global awareness towards its protection and conservation.

As technology has entered rapidly in peoples' daily lives, there are various digital online learning systems aiming to disseminate both tangible and intangible significance of historical monuments that are mentioned on UNESCO's World Heritage Catalogue. An online educational tool, created by [22], provides a new way of reusing Cultural Heritage data obtained from image-based and 3D modelling, terrestrial laser scanning techniques, photogrammetry methods etc. which could also be applied in St. Neo-phytos case. The proposed platform includes interactive lessons and activities using 3D representations of the cavern, where internet users are taught monuments' historic background in various multimedia ways (by solving digital puzzles that reenact hagiographies, watching dramatized videos that present the key elements of the monument). At the end of each lesson, users are asked to answer few comprehensive questions regarding the undertaken course awarding them with a ready-to-print state-ment of accomplishment. These online interactive courses could assist users in acquiring a better understanding of the existing risks that threaten Enkleistra's integrity. Furthermore, informative dissemination, such as publications, books, exhibitions, as well as re-creation of case study's digital content through 3d printing, screening, modeling, etc., will be helpful in the direction of raising public awareness about the monument and the necessity for its immediate conservation.

Although the expected increase of cultural tourism may constitute a beneficial side of raising awareness, it stimulates issues regarding its preservation as there are plenty of tourists that would like to interact with the already damaged hagiographies creating this way more detriment and degeneration on their surface. Fortunately, the use of Virtual, Augmented and Mixed Reality technologies have reached a point of evolution where they can offer realistic and interactive experiences to humans. Aiming at the decrease of touristic engagement inside the cave, an exploitation of these technologies can be achieved. More specifically, visitors would be "transferred" into a virtual rep-resentation of the cave where the Saint spent all of his life and could interact with the digital frescoes in a way that is both engaging and educational through their partici-pation in game(s), where they would be asked to fill the missing hagiographic segments in order for St. Neophytos to "come alive" and recite his story. Towards the afore-mentioned, an interactive analogue book can be located in the monastery's entrance where tourists may experience another form of educational environment grasping all the multimedia data (images, texts, 3D, videos etc.) that thrive from the monument while at the same time would be presented in a user friendly way.

Last but not least, creation of software and storage of the extracted cultural data along with its semantic interrelations, can be used in collaboration with modern advanced information systems like HBIM in depicting the optimal methods that can be exploited towards Enkleistra's preservation. This kind of management system can act as a reference point for the holistic digital documentation of this monumental cave, providing reverse engineering data to professionals from multidisciplinary areas that work together in the protection and preservation using detailed 3D models. By this way, academic research between various disciplinary sectors will be assisted too, and links with other methodological approaches and practices for monuments of similar characteristics or of common elements can be established.

Acknowledgements. 1. ITN-DCH (http://www.itn-dch.eu/) project has received funding from the European Union's Seventh Framework program for research, technological development and demonstration under GA n° 608013.

2. INCEPTION (http://www.inception-project.eu/) has received funding from the EU's H2020 Reflective framework programme for research and innovation under GA n° 665220.

3. Europeana Space (http://www.europeana-space.eu/) has received funding from the European Union's ICT Policy Support Program as part of the Competitiveness and Innovation Framework Program, under GA n° 621037.

4. 4DCH (http://www.4d-ch-world.eu/) project has received funding from the European Union's Seventh Framework program for research, technological development and demonstration under GA n° 324523.

5. Lo-Cloud (http://www.locloud.eu/) is co-funded under the CIP ICT-PSP program under GA n° 325099.

6. ViMM (http://www.vi-mm.eu/) has received funding from the EU's H2020 framework programme for support and coordination actions under GA n° 727107.

References

1. Ahmad, Y.: The scope and definitions of heritage: from tangible to intangible. Int. J. Herit. Stud. **12**, 292–300 (2006)
2. Bouchenaki, M.: A major advance towards a holistic approach to heritage conservation: the 2003 Intangible Heritage Convention. Int. J. Intang. Herit. **2**, 106–109 (2007)
3. Vecco, M.: A definition of cultural heritage: from the tangible to the intangible. J. Cult. Herit. **11**, 321–324 (2010)
4. Rodwell, D.: Sustainability and the holistic approach to the conservation of historic cities. J. Archit. Conserv. **9**, 58–73 (2003)
5. INCEPTION Project: D.1.3 - Project Report (2016)
6. ITN-DCH Project: D.1.1 - Project Report (2014)
7. Bold, J., Chatenet, M., Cortembos, T., Kovacec Naglic, K.: Guidance on inventory and documentation of the cultural heritage, Strasbourg (2009)
8. Mango, C., Hawkins, E.J.W.: The hermitage of St. Neophytos and its wall paintings. Dumbarton Oaks Papers 20, p. 119 (1966)
9. Tsiknopoullos, I.P.: The Encleistra and Saint Neophytos, Nicosia (1965)
10. Hartley, R., Zisserman, A.: Multiple View Geometry in Computer Vision, 2nd edn. Cambridge University Press, Cambridge (2003)
11. Lowe, D.G.: Distinctive image features from scale-invariant keypoints. Int. J. Comput. Vis. **60**, 91–110 (2004)
12. Bay, H., Tuytelaars, T., Gool, L.: SURF: Speeded Up Robust Features. In: Leonardis, A., Bischof, H., Pinz, A. (eds.) ECCV 2006. LNCS, vol. 3951, pp. 404–417. Springer, Heidelberg (2006). doi:10.1007/11744023_32
13. Fischler, M.A., Bolles, R.C.: Random sample consensus: a paradigm for model fitting with applications to image analysis and automated cartography. Commun. ACM **24**, 381–395 (1981)
14. Snavely, N., Seitz, S.M., Szeliski, R.: Photo tourism: exploring photo collections in 3D. ACM Trans. Graph. **25**, 835–846 (2006)
15. Klopschitz, M., Irschara, A., Reitmayr, G., Schmalstieg, D.: Robust incremental structure from motion. In: Third International Symposium on 3D Data Processing, Visualization and Transmission (2010)
16. Hemayed, E.E.: A survey of camera self-calibration. In: Proceedings of the IEEE Conference on Advanced Video and Signal Based Surveillance, AVSS 2003, pp. 351–357 (2003)
17. Nilosek, D., Walvoord, D.J., Salvaggio, C.: Assessing geoaccuracy of structure from motion point clouds from long-range image collections. Opt. Eng. **53**, 113112 (2014)

18. Remondino, F., Spera, M.G., Nocerino, E., Menna, F., Nex, F., Gonizzi-Barsanti, S.: Dense image matching: comparisons and analyses. In: Arqueologica 2.0, et al. (eds.) Proceedings of the DigitalHeritage 2013 - Federating the 19th International VSMM, 10th Eurographics GCH, and 2nd UNESCO Memory of the World Conferences, Plus Special Sessions from CAA, pp. 47–54 (2013)
19. Remondino, F.: From point cloud to surface: the modeling and visualization problem. Int. Arch. Photogramm. Remote Sens. Spat. Inf. Sci. **XXXIV**, 24–28 (2003)
20. Kakoulli, I., Fischer, C.: The techniques and materials of the wall paintings at the Enkleistra of St. Neophytos (Phase II) (2012)
21. Ott, M., Pozzi, F.: ICT and cultural heritage education: which added value? In: Lytras, M.D., Carroll, J.M., Damiani, E., Tennyson, R.D. (eds.) WSKS 2008. LNCS (LNAI), vol. 5288, pp. 131–138. Springer, Heidelberg (2008). doi:10.1007/978-3-540-87781-3_15
22. Ioannides, M., Bokolas, V., Chatzigrigoriou, P., Nikolakopoulou, V., Athanasiou, V.: Education use of 3D models and photogrammetry content; the Europeana space project for Cypriot UNESCO monuments. In: Proceedings of Fourth International Conference on Remote Sensing and Geoinformation of Environment, Cyprus, April 2016
23. UNESCO: Operational Guidelines for the Implementation of the World Heritage Convention. WHC.02/2 (2002)

Project Paper: Data, Metadata, Semantics and Ontologies in Cultural Heritage

First Experiences of Applying a Model Classification for Digital 3D Reconstruction in the Context of Humanities Research

Sander Münster[1(✉)], Cindy Kröber[1], Wolfgang Hegel[1],
Mieke Pfarr-Harfst[2], Nikolas Prechtel[3], Rainer Uhlemann[1],
and Frank Henze[1]

[1] Media Center, Technische Universität Dresden, Dresden, Germany
sander.muenster@tu-dresden.de
[2] Department of Architectural Design, Technische Universität Darmstadt,
Darmstadt, Germany
[3] Department of Cartography,
Technische Universität Dresden, Dresden, Germany

Abstract. While technological backgrounds, project opportunities, and methodological considerations for application are widely discussed, there is still no comprehensive classification scheme for digital 3D reconstruction in humanities research projects. Therefore we developed a prototype scheme in 2016. In this article we present the first results of applying this scheme and classifying five projects. Within this application we tested for intercoder reliability and for potential weaknesses of the scheme. While the reliability of the proposed scheme is generally good for categories with discrete values, qualitative categories result in highly differing coding.

Keywords: Cultural heritage · Information management · Classification models · Digital reconstruction

1 Introduction

Not untypically for research activities which cross disciplinary frontiers, it can be hard to formalize 3D reconstructions using standard indicators, such as a joint research object or explanatory approach. In contrast, considering the use of a common research method seems promising [1]. Since 3D reconstruction processes foster a nomothetic and holistic representation of the past, are they a methodological step backwards compared to modern problem-centered and constructionist approaches in the humanities [c.f. 2]? The humanities are facing various challenges in their use of digital reconstruction methods, which originate from architectural design, engineering, and geosciences, and are highly reliant on tools from computing. Examples include the need for simplification through model building, multiple authorship, or visual research strategies. These methods have been commonly used in both the academic and the private sector. Currently, digital reconstructions are mainly carried out in one single use context by interdisciplinary workgroups applying expert technologies.

© Springer International Publishing AG 2016
M. Ioannides et al. (Eds.): EuroMed 2016, Part I, LNCS 10058, pp. 477–490, 2016.
DOI: 10.1007/978-3-319-48496-9_37

Considering this background, the existence of numerous standards, guidelines and rules for dealing with historical content [3–7], which have only achieved limited practical relevance [8], has proven to be a challenge. In contrast, the concept of metadata in classification and descriptions of historical information has become widely established. Although one of these schemas, CIDOC-CRM [9], has gained popularity as a reference ontology (in terms of a generic concept of knowledge structure) in archaeology and museology to describe reconstructed objects, standards for metadata and its implementation as a whole remain highly heterogeneous [10, 11]. Current approaches to sustainable documentation of the creative process of digital reconstructions have not yet become sufficiently established in practice, despite diverse and innovative concepts [12, 13]. In this context, our interest is less in building another metadata scheme than in identifying general properties which characterize digital 3D reconstruction projects. Classification schemes need to be made easily applicable and their results comparable. Quantifiable categories would be helpful to achieve this aim, which relies on two concurring interests. On the one hand, an applicable classification scheme has to provide all variables of relevance to describe a certain object and a comprehensive set of values. On the other hand, an optimal scheme must be generic and slim to make it easily applicable—bearing in mind that schemes are often disregarded for the high workload involved—and consistent, that is, equipped with a full set of parameters. Moreover, an ideal classification scheme should also allow for classification ex post by non-insiders.

According to Merriam-Webster's dictionary, classification is a "systematic arrangement in groups or categories according to established criteria".[1] Classification aims at creating a taxonomy for a certain branch or aspect of information [14]. An ontology combines a taxonomy with the underlying principles of classification. Thus, an ontology sorts individual items into a specific scheme according to defined rules. Regarding the purpose of classification, it delivers "particular frame[s] of reference [which] help[s] us to make sense (both in passive and active meanings) of the world" and is widely discussed from philosophical as well as historical and practical points of view [e.g. 15, 16]. In the context of scholarly work, classification schemes are closely related to specific disciplines or—in a broader sense—epistemic cultures and supply a shared understanding of research objects, habits, methodologies, or publication bodies. This is an important prerequisite for further research-related tasks, such as the definition of best practice, implementation within academic curricula, shaping the scope of conference programs, and investigating funding and management responsibilities or cooperation networks [17].

In 2016 the authors proposed a preliminary classification scheme for digital reconstruction in humanities research [18]. Its development was based on the investigation of 2,931 journal articles and conference papers concerning the 3D reconstruction of historic objects, employing deductive and inductive methods of content analysis [19] and bibliometrics [20]. In order to examine project practices and their evolution, a qualitative content analysis of a further 26 international publications concerning digital reconstruction of lost objects was carried out. While such

---

[1] http://www.merriam-webster.com/dictionary/classification, accessed May 11, 2016.

publications provide records of past projects, follow-up research into four case studies was conducted and examined by a mixed-method approach, including heuristic frameworks and Grounded Theory [21]. While the development of the classification scheme and its elements were widely discussed in the previously mentioned article [18], the main research question here is whether the proposed scheme can be applied for various types of digital 3D reconstruction projects and handled by various individuals. So this article focuses on the following:

1. The application of the developed categorization scheme by different users in 6 example projects.
2. Evaluating the usability, eligibility, practicability and potential shortcomings of the scheme.

2 A Preliminary Classification Scheme for Digital Reconstruction in the Humanities

To briefly introduce the classification scheme, a related classification matrix distinguishes between (1) the research context in terms of the subject and the historic object and (2) the quality of digital 3D reconstruction (Fig. 1). The quality pertains to sources of reconstruction, technologies, the characteristics of the resultant computer model, documentation of reconstruction processes and—if created by an interdisciplinary team —a record of the collaboration between stakeholders.

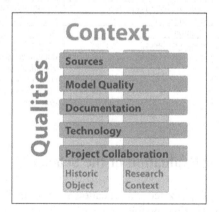

Fig. 1. General structure of a classification scheme for digital reconstruction

Taking into consideration that digital 3D reconstruction is highly heterogeneous in terms of objects, purposes, and workflows, we suggest a low-level compromise. Our proposed scheme contains some mandatory and widely quantified categories which are easily defined. A basic set of three variables has been identified: Technology (tools and geometry data type), project cooperation (project scale and date), and historical object (location, time of origin, and type of object). Most of the other descriptions (e.g., model qualities or documentation) are optional, not standardized, and qualitative only. Table 1 summarizes this classification scheme, the contained categories and variables.

Table 1. Overview of the preliminary classification scheme

Category	Variable	Characteristics, examples
Sources	type of source	original (material) evidence, acquired data, images, texts, "logical source"
	inherent knowledge	primary source, secondary source
Model quality	geometrical fidelity	accuracy, detail, coherence
	radiometric fidelity	properties, properties depending on accuracy, detail, coherence
	temporal fidelity	properties, properties depending on accuracy, detail, coherence
Documentation	result documentation	reference ontology, application ontology
	process documentation	approach
Technology	technological domain	GIS, VR, CAD, BIM
	model genetic workflow	semi-automated genesis, procedural generators, human-driven modeling approach
	tools	software
	geometry data type	point cloud, wireframe model, polygon model, voxel model, parametric model (program)
Project cooperation	project scale	employees, budget
	project dates	start and end date
	involved competencies	humanities, design, technologies
Historic object	type of object	static artifact, dynamic artifact
	general object properties	tangibility, temporality
	date of origin	year, period
	location	place
Research context	research object	source, historic object, system
	research function	documentation, data quality assessment, visualization, process investigation, conceptualization, contextualization, numeric analysis, hypothetical simulation

3 Application and Evaluation of the Scheme

This article evaluates the proposed classification scheme in the context of its application to various projects. Five people were asked to classify five projects (Fig. 2) according to the proposed classification scheme and to provide feedback on their experiences with an application of this scheme. To ensure independence from specific disciplinary backgrounds, we tested with individuals holding degrees in various disciplines, including history, architecture, geosciences, education, and informatics. For a categorization study, it is important to estimate whether application of a scheme by different individuals would lead to similar results. The effects and testing methods of this *intercoder reliability* are widely discussed especially in the context of social sciences [22]. Common practices to reduce the variance in classification entries include:

| Project 1: Uch Enmek | Project 2: Xi'an – 1st screenshot | Project 2: Xi'an – 2nd screenshot |
| Project 3: Zwinger 3D | Project 4: GEPAM | Project 5: Freiberg Cathedral |

Fig. 2. Examples of visualization outcomes

1. Providing well discernible and discrete sets of variants for all categories.
2. Providing anchor examples highlighting the application of the scheme.
3. Prior training of all coders on the application of the scheme [c.f. 23].

Aiming at a high level of awareness in our scenario, we supplied testers with both the classification scheme (Table 1) and published application examples. To evaluate differences between individuals in using the scheme, one of the projects was independently categorized by two individuals who were involved in the project (Project 1). As previously stated, the interest is in the applicability of the scheme, not only for project insiders. This issue was tested by asking project outsiders to describe projects only from published documents (Projects 2 and 5). The testers were directly involved in the other projects.

3.1   Project 1: Uch Enmek Ethno-Nature Park

The Altay Mountains boast outstanding cultural heritage. Remains of the once flourishing Scythian culture rank highest among the archaeological heritage found there, with the most famous being located in the Karakol and Ursul Valley. This is reflected in a conservation area called Uch Enmek Ethno-Nature Park. Archaeological expertise and data on the project's activities have been provided through a close collaboration with archaeologists from Ghent University. The working group led by Jean Bourgeois has been active in the Altay for some 15 years [24]. Courtesy of the GeoEye Foundation, the Dresden group was assigned four overlapping IKONOS high resolution satellite scenes of the Uch Enmek conservation site, forming an important data source.

3.2   Project 2: Xi'an – Emperor's Power in the Afterlife

The exhibition "Xi'an – Emperor's Power in the Afterlife", presenting the research results of 15 years of cooperation between Chinese and German institutions and scientists, was the occasion for a computer reconstruction and simulation that was embedded over three years in the ongoing scientific project. The 100×140 km area around the old imperial city of Xi'an is regarded as a cultural region in the 21st century. So far, in this region, two imperial tombs of the Qin Dynasty, 18 grave sites from the Han Dynasty, and eleven imperial tombs of the Tang Dynasty have been discovered and archaeologically investigated. Therefore, one primary objective of the project was to relay the immense spatial dimensions of the area and the almost unimaginable variety and number of archaeological sites. Simultaneously, the goal was to include details of individual exhibits based on the most recent, as yet unpublished excavations, surveys, findings, and research on the emperor and imperial tomb cities.

3.3   Project 3: Back to the Future - Zwinger 3D

The aim of the project is to virtually present the historical development of the Dresden Zwinger, which has experienced some 13 major phases in its 300 years of existence. Some of these were actually built, whilst others were merely ideas and ambitions of influential individuals. Models were presented as an animated film, which summarizes the project in an attractive way and provides a starting point for subsequent animations and illustrations on the construction history of the Dresden Zwinger (Table 2).

3.4   Project 4: GEPAM: Memorial Landscapes - Dresden and Terezín as Places to Remember the Shoah

The cities of Dresden and Terezín share the tragic history of the persecution of Jewish people during World War II. Memorials in both cities commemorate the victims of the Shoah. The purpose of 3D town models in the GEPAM project is to communicate the variety of documents and information concerning the Shoah and allow the user to evaluate events in terms of their location. Education concerning the Holocaust complements the process of remembrance. The target structure of the final presentation environment will allow access to documents and records related to the persecution of the Jews within a web-based city model and serve as a virtual memorial. The GEPAM project is financed by the EFRE scheme of the European Union supporting cross-border cooperation between the Czech Republic and Germany (Tables 3, 4 and 5).

3.5   Project 5: Freiberg Cathedral – Creating an Educational App

The project was a student seminar during which an app had to be created within an educational project. The outcomes of the individual efforts were bundled into a manual for interdisciplinary student projects. Supported by the Saxon Centre for Teaching and Learning in Higher Education, this seminar was a collaboration project between the

Table 2. Application of the proposed classification scheme: Project 1 – 1st and 2nd Coder

Category	Project 1: Uch Enmek Ethno-Nature Park – First Coder (Involved)	Project 1: Uch Enmek Ethno-Nature Park – Second Coder (Involved)
Sources		
Type of source	acquired data (satellite images, digital elevation models (DEM)), excavation plans, contemporary photographs, physical remains	excavation documentation (here: site type and extent), photographs, satellite imagery, aerial photographs, topographic reference, scientific texts, field visits
Inherent knowledge	primary source with probability of changes: kuragan (burial mounds) remains secondary sources: excavation plans, satellite images	primary sources: contemporary 21/2D landscape model compiled from topographic references and remote sensing imagery, archaeological site documentation from recent archaeological field work (text, photographs) secondary sources: scientific literature on Scythian burial mounds (for reconstruction)
Model quality		
Geometrical fidelity	level of detail (LOD) 2 models and generalized land use	LOD1 of rural landscape, LOD2 of rural buildings (prototypes representations according to building taxonomy), LOD2 of archaeological objects (kuragans)
Radiometric fidelity	generalized color scheme	NPR model (not aiming at true color representation)
Temporal fidelity	no temporal changes	shows present state only (time reference by imagery), multi-temporal extension possible
Documentation		
Process doc.	textual within thesis	periodical protocols
Results doc.	not indexed by metadata	XML classification scheme of landscape objects
Technology		
Technological domain	GIS-based modeling of landscape, VR modeling of obstacles, based on acq. data	GIS-based modeling as a basis, VR-modeling for 3D objects (buildings and archaeological objects)
Model genetic workflow	semi-automated modeling of landscape, human-driven modeling of obstacles	GIS landscape model as a synthesis of map digitization and interpretation of remote sensing imagery, 3D object generation by 3D modeling software
Tools	ArcGIS, SketchUp, Maxon Cinema 4D	ArcGIS, SketchUp, Maxon Cinema 4D
Geometry data type	shapefiles, polygon models	shapefiles, polygon models
Project Cooperation		
Project scale	~800 person-hours (modeling and data)	~1500 person-hours (modeling only)
Project dates	2007-2014	2011-2014
Involved competencies	geoscientists, archaeologists, historians	geoscientists, archaeologists
Historic Site		
Original location	Uch Enmek , Russia	Uch Enmek Conservation Site (Siberia, Russian Federation)
Time of origin	~ 600 A.D.	present situation, archaeological objects: 5th–7th century BC
General object properties	(partially) no longer extant tangible object	kuragans in different states of conservation, most of them destroyed by illicit digging
Type of object	landscape with obstacles	3D landscape model including schematized 3D archaeological sites
Research context		
Research function	visualization, conceptualization of land use (e.g., forest, settlements, or kuragans)	documentation of sites, public attention and awareness, education, workflow development for automated transfer from GIS-based landscape models to 3D interactive, clickable model objects (POIs) with context balloons, NPR landscape visualization

Table 3. Application of the proposed classification scheme: Project 2, 1ˢᵗ and 2ⁿᵈ Coder

Category	Project 2: Xi'an – Emperor's Power in the After-life – First Coder (Involved)	Project 2: Xi'an – Emperor's Power in the Afterlife – Second Coder (not involved)
Sources		
Type of source	historical texts, texts, photographs, plans, results of excavation, sketches, comparable buildings or build structures, findings, data from archaeological prospection	photographs, excavation plans
Inherent knowledge	primary sources: remains of 11 buildings, 18 lost buildings, data from archaeological prospections secondary sources: excavation plans, sketches, texts, comparable buildings or structures, photographs, discussion with archaeologist	primary source: remains, excavation data secondary sources: interpretation by archaeologists
- Model quality		
Geometrical fidelity	LOD0: model of region of Xi´an LOD1: model of the complete structure of the whole mausoleum with 3 parts LOD2: models of the 3 parts of the mausoleum (north, south, hill) LOD3: models of 29 buildings LOD4: detailed model of the tomb inside the hill	not applicable
Radiometric fidelity	detailed textured models	textured models
Temporal fidelity	time span of Tang Dynasty	not applicable
- Documentation		
Process documentation	published: http://tuprints.ulb.tu-darmstadt.de/2302/	published dissertation
Results documentation	published: http://tuprints.ulb.tu-darmstadt.de/2302/; film projection	exhibition
Technology		
Technological domain	not named	VR modeling of buildings based on sources
Model genetic workflow	human-driven modeling	human-driven modeling of buildings
Tools	Maya, After Effects, Adobe Premiere	Maya
Geometry data type	polygon models	polygon models
Project Cooperation		
Project scale	~ 4,160 person-hours (with students)	not applicable
Project dates	2004-2006	2005-2006
Involved competencies	architects, archaeologists, geoscientists, historians	architects, archaeologists
Historic Site		
Original location	Zhaoling, China	Zhaoling, China
Time of origin	~ 6ᵗʰ-7ᵗʰ century AD	~ 6ᵗʰ-7ᵗʰ century AD
General object properties	(Partially) no longer extant tangible object	no longer extant tangible object
Type of object	landscape, city structures, buildings	buildings
Research context		
Research function	digital reconstruction and simulation	not applicable

Table 4. Application of the proposed classification scheme: Projects 3 and 4

Category	Project 3: Back to the Future - Zwinger 3D	Project 4: GEPAM Memorial Landscapes
Sources		
Type of source	text, pictures, photographs, plans, remaining buildings	text, pictures, photographs, plans, remaining buildings
Inherent knowledge	primary source: historical drawings, plans, sketches and paintings secondary source: remaining buildings	primary sources: 34 remaining buildings with modifications, 58 lost buildings secondary historical sources: artistic pictures, photographs, plans secondary contemporary sources: photographs, plans, texts
Model quality		
Geometrical fidelity	LOD3 of buildings relevant for the subject, LOD1 of city buildings	LOD1 of city landscape, LOD3 of buildings relevant for the subject
Radiometric fidelity	architectural white paper color scheme	generalized color scheme
Temporal fidelity	no temporal changes	transitions: per year, binary (display/no display)
Documentation		
Process documentation	no documentation	periodical protocols and changelogs
Results documentation	no documentation	XML metadata: time, author, location for LOD 1 objects according to GIS
Technology		
Technological domain	human-driven modeling of LOD3 objects GIS-based modeling of LOD1 objects	GIS-based modeling for LOD1 objects VR-modeling for LOD 3 objects
Model genetic workflow	human-driven modeling of landscape	human-driven modeling of obstacles
Tools	Autodesk 3ds Max, Blender, Maxon Cinema 4D	ArcGIS, SketchUp, Maxon Cinema 4D
Geometry data type	polygon models	shapefiles, polygon models
Project Cooperation		
Project scale	~7200 person-hours (modeling only)	~3200 person-hours (modeling only)
Project dates	2006-2012	2012-2014
Involved competencies	historians, architects, information scientists	geoscientists, information scientists, historians, linguists
Historic Site		
Original location	Dresden, Germany	Dresden, Germany
Time of origin	~1700–1900	1935–1945
General object properties	partially no longer extant tangible object	(partially) no longer extant tangible object
Type of object	buildings, landscapes, city	buildings (3D city model)
Research context		
Research function	visualization, documentation of the history, presentation, exhibition	documentation of sources and information, visualization, conceptualization of building functions, contextualization (city model), process investigation (change of use of buildings and devastation due to WWII)

Table 5. Application of the proposed classification scheme: Project 5, 1st and 2nd Coder

Category	Project 5: Freiberg Cathedral – First Coder (involved)	Project 5: Freiberg Cathedral – Second Coder (not involved)
Sources		
Type of source	remains, terrestrial laser scans, photographs, texts, pictures, plans	physical/ material evidence, iconographical interpretations
Inherent knowledge	primary source: remaining late Gothic building from ~1500 and several other remaining objects, lost building from 1180 secondary historical sources: pictures, photographs, plans secondary contemporary sources: photographs, plans, texts, architectural investigations by e.g., Magirius (1972)	primary source
Model quality		
Geometrical fidelity	LOD3 for exterior of both buildings, Simplified reconstruction of interior, Detailed modeling of relevant objects	very accurate due to 3D scanning technology (exact measurements or fidelity data not available)
Radiometric fidelity	generalized color scheme	non color scan
Temporal fidelity	9 different models with no temporal changes within one model	one state, no changes
Documentation		
Process doc.	textual within student assignment	further documentation besides text and images not available on the website
Results documentation	not indexed by metadata	unknown
Technology		
Technological domain	VR modeling based on acquired data and plans/pictures	semi-automated genesis on the basis of scan data; manual rework for illustrational purposes.
Model genetic workflow	human-driven modeling of obstacles, semi-automated for triangulation of point clouds (ceiling, Goldene Pforte [Golden Portal]), photo texture for ceiling	unknown
Tools	RiScanPRO, FARO SCENE, Maxon Cinema 4D	most probably polygon model based on point cloud.
Geometry data type	polygon models	semi-automated genesis on the basis of scan data; manual rework for illustrational purposes.
Project Cooperation		
Project scale	~400 man hours for acquisition, modeling and output	3 university professors, unknown number of technical professionals and a group of students
Project dates	2014	April 1, 2014 – September 30, 2014
Involved Competencies	art history, linguistics, geodesy, cartography	art history, German studies, geodesy, cartography, 3D design
Historic Site		
Original Location	Freiberg, Germany	Freiberg, Saxony, Germany
Time of origin	1180–2014	around 1225-1230, deconstructed and rebuilt at the end of 15th century
General object properties	(partially) no longer extant tangible object	tangible object
Type of object	building, building parts and smaller objects (e.g., pulpit)	sculpting and stonemasonry, sandstone, original color lost
Research context		
Research function	visualization, conceptualization of functions	visualization, illustration of iconography and architectural concepts process investigation (change of use of buildings and devastation due to WWII)

Institute of Art and Music Studies and the Media Center of the Technische Universität Dresden with the Chair for German Literature and Medieval Studies of the Technische Universität Chemnitz. The project took place in 2014 with 30 student participants at both bachelor and master level. The project included students in the fields of art history, linguistics, and geoscience. The humanities students researched aspects of architecture within the cathedral and its purpose for communication with the visitors. Visualizations by the geoscience students, such as reconstructions and animations, illustrated the results.

4 Implications

The experience with the applications of the proposed scheme for projects [cf. 8] was as follows: All testers shared the overall assessment that application was easy and the categories were easily distinguishable. Comprehension problems of specific criteria, however, were also recorded: For example, a "technological domain" could not always be determined due to its non-accordance to any specific domain. Likewise, the category "inherent knowledge" was not intuitively applicable, and the testers could only identify the requested concepts after consulting the provided examples. In a broader perspective some general problems seem to result from different meanings of technical terms and concepts within different disciplines, for example the term level of detail (LOD) [25]. Distinction between primary and secondary sources of information makes more sense since reconstructions also comprise projects which deal with complex time layers and variable cultural impacts on the objects of study. Once temporal change is proved or at least likely, primary sources have to be combined with secondary sources to meet the demand for comprehensive final information. As evaluated practically, satisfying completion of the table will only be likely for people very familiar with the project. It cannot be done based solely on publications and project records as many of the requested aspects are not reflected in documentations or reports. In other words, project outsiders looking at an overview of reconstructions with a certain research focus may find it difficult to arrive at a comprehensive and consistent set of application tables. As is predictable, categories with discrete values such as date or location lead to perfectly comparable results. Supposedly due to the provided anchor examples, some other categories were also interpreted similarly by the encoders. The project scale was—with one exception—generally described as an amount of person-hours, object types by object classes (e.g., buildings or landscapes), and available competence, indicated by the professional background of the staff. Geometric fidelity was mostly quantified using the LOD scheme, but nonetheless interpreted heterogeneously. Qualitative categories, for example "inherent knowledge", were partly misinterpreted, having been filled with duplicates of the preceding category "sources". Another category with highly hetero-geneous interpretation was "research function". For projects 2 and 5 we had tested coding by both insiders and external individuals. It was found that 80–90 % of cate-gories could be clarified without direct project involvement. While descriptions by external persons were rarely incorrect, both quality and level of detail fell significantly below that of the description by insiders. Unsurprisingly, the retrieval of information on the project scale from documentation alone was fairly limited. Information on research function and inherent knowledge may be derived from project descriptions, but is not comprehensive or sufficient in many cases.

5 Conclusion

Some general remarks can be made regarding application of the proposed scheme. All involved coders assessed the scheme as easily applicable. It reportedly took 10–15 min to fill in all the categories. Sufficient completion required insider knowledge of the project, but approximately 80–90 % of categories could also be completed—in reduced detail and complexity—by outsiders. With regards to the reliability of coding, approximately one third of all categories required discrete values like time, location, or object classes, leading to fully comparable results. For another major group of categories, coders employed well-established classification methods, such as staff disciplinary background to describe involved competencies, media types to classify sources, or LOD to distinguish between various geometric fidelities. One shortcoming is that schemes such as the LOD classification were not interpreted identically by all coders and should be further explained by anchor examples. Finally, some qualitative categories like research function or inherent knowledge were handled highly heterogeneously and may require either further standardization or reclassification as optional. Another important remark from one of the testers was that spatial scale, a key factor which determines all reconstruction processes, was not included in our scheme. While we tested for the quality of the output, we did not focus on usage. As stated before, no alternative metadata scheme should be proposed as an outcome of our research. In fact, the intention was to identify generic properties of digital 3D reconstruction projects. The aim was to provide a determining framework to assist investigations, for example into the evolution of a disciplinary identity or the historical development of digital 3D reconstruction. Moreover, the scheme might provide guidance for methodological assessment and discourse. Nevertheless a future task would be to synchronize with extant reference ontologies, especially as many elements for describing projects in general and objects in particular are highly elaborated within these schemes. Therefore, we encourage researchers to adapt the scheme according to their needs. Moreover, we would like to invite other researchers to assess, amend, extend, and further develop the proposed core scheme.

Acknowledgements. The research activity described in this paper was funded by the German Federal Ministry of Education and Research (no. 01UG1520).

References

1. Krishnan, A.: What are Academic Disciplines. Some Observations on the Disciplinarity vs. Interdisciplinarity Debate. National Centre for Research Methods, University of Southampton, Southampton (2009)
2. Wengenroth, U.: Was ist Technikgeschichte? (1998)

3. Beacham, R., Denard, H., Niccolucci, F.: An introduction to the London charter. In: Ioannides, M., Arnold, D., Niccolucci, F., Mania, K. (eds.) Papers from the Joint Event CIPA/VAST/EG/EuroMed Event, pp. 263–269 (2006)
4. Bendicho, V.M.L.-M.: The principles of the Seville Charter. In: Proceedings of XXIII CIPA Symposium, Prague, Czech Republic, 12–16 September 2011 (2011)
5. Sürül, A., Özen, H., Tutkun, M.: ICOMOS digital database of the cultural heritage of Trabzon. In: Proceedings of XIX CIPA Symposium, Antalya, Turkey, 30 September–4 October 2003 (2003)
6. Kiouss, A., Karoglou, M., Labropoulos, K., Moropoulou, A., Zarnic, R.: Recommendations and strategies for the establishment of a guideline for monument documentation harmonized with the existing European standards and codes. In: Proceedings of XXIII CIPA Symposium, Prague, Czech Republic, 12–16 September 2011 (2011)
7. Pfarr, M.: Dokumentationssystem für Digitale Rekonstruktionen am Beispiel der Grabanlage Zhaoling, Provinz Shaanxi, China, Ph.D. Thesis, Darmstadt (2009)
8. Münster, S., Köhler, T.: 3D reconstruction of cultural heritage artifacts. A literature based survey of recent projects and workflows. In: Virtual Palaces, Part II. Lost Palaces and their Afterlife. Virtual Reconstruction between Science and the Media, München (2016)
9. Doerr, M.: The CIDOC conceptual reference module. An ontological approach to semantic interoperability of metadata. AI Mag. 24(3), 75–92 (2003)
10. Felicetti, A., Lorenzini, M.: Metadata and tools for integration and preservation of cultural heritage 3D information. In: Proceeding of XXIII CIPA Symposium, Prague, Czech Republic, 12–16 September 2011 (2011)
11. Ronzino, P., Niccolucci, F., D'Andrea, A.: Built heritage metadate schemas and the integration of architectural datasets using CIDOC-CRM. In: Boriani, M., Gabaglio, R., Gulotta, D. (eds.) Online Proceedings of the Conference BUILT HERITAGE 2013 Monitoring Conservation and Management, Milano, pp. 883–889 (2013)
12. Pfarr-Harfst, M.: Documentation system for digital reconstructions. Reference to the Mausoleum of the Tang-Dynastie at Zhaoling, in Shaanxi Province, China. In: 16th International Conference on "Cultural Heritage and New Technologies", Vienna, 2011, pp. 648–658 (2011)
13. Niccolucci, F.: Setting standards for 3D visualization of cultural heritage in Europe and beyond. In: Bentkowska-Kafel, A., Denard, H., Baker, D. (eds.) Paradata and Transparency in Virtual Heritage, pp. 23–36. Ashgate, Burlington (2012)
14. Rasch, R.F.R.: The nature of taxonomy. Image 19(3), 147–149 (1987)
15. Bowker, G.C., Star, S.L.: Sorting Things Out: Classification and Its Consequences. MIT Press, Cambridge (1999)
16. Huvila, I.: Sorting the metaverse out and how metaverse is sorting us out. In: Power, D., Teigland, R. (eds.) The Immersive Internet: Reflections on the Entangling of the Virtual with Society, Politics and the Economy, pp. 192–203. Palgrave MacMillan, Basingstoke (2013)
17. Münster, S., Kuroczyński, P., Pfarr-Harfst, M., Grellert, M., Lengyel, D.: Future research challenges for a computer-based interpretative 3D reconstruction of cultural heritage – a German community's view. In: ISPRS Annals of the Photogrammetry, Remote Sensing and Spatial Information Sciences (XXV International CIPA Symposium) II-5-W3, pp. 207–213 (2015)
18. Münster, S., Hegel, W., Kröber, C.: A classification model for digital reconstruction in context of humanities research. In: Münster, S., Pfarr-Harfst, M., Kuroczyński, P., Ioannides, M. (eds.) How to Manage Data and Knowledge Related to Interpretative Digital 3D Reconstructions of Cultural Heritage? LNCS. Springer, Cham (in print)
19. Mayring, P.: Qualitative Content Analysis. Forum Qualitative Sozialforschung 1(2), Art. 20 (2000)

20. Münster, S., Ioannides, M.: The scientific community of digital heritage in time and space. In: Guidi, G., Scopigno, R., Torres, J.C., Graf, H. (eds.) 2nd International Congress on Digital Heritage 2015, Granada (2015). 978-1-5090-0048-7/15

21. Kelle, U.: The developement of categories different Documentation system for digital approaches in grounded theory. In: Bryant, A., Charmaz, K. (eds.) The SAGE Handbook of Grounded Theory, pp. 191–213. SAGE (2010)

22. Lombard, M., Snyder-Duch, J., Bracken, C.C.: Content analysis in mass communication: assessment and reporting of intercoder reliability. Hum. Commun. Res. **28**, 587–604 (2002)

23. Lamnek, S.: Qualitative Sozialforschung. Lehrbuch, Weinheim (2005)

24. Bourgeois, J., De Wulf, A., Goosens, R., Gheyle, W.: Saving the frozen Scythian tombs of the Altai Mountains (Central Asia). World Archaeol. **39**, 458–474 (2007)

25. Luebke, D., Watson, B., Cohen, J.D., Reddy, M., Varshney, A.: Level of Detail for 3D Graphics. Elsevier Science Inc., Atlanta (2002)

Digital Preservation of Cultural Heritage: Balinese *Kulkul* Artefact and Practices

Cokorda Pramartha[✉] and Joseph G. Davis

School of Information Technologies, The University of Sydney, Sydney, Australia
{cokorda.rai,joseph.davis}@sydney.edu.au

Abstract. One of the goals of digital preservation of cultural heritage is to gather, refine, maintain, and share cultural resources that can subsequently be used and developed by scholars, members of the community, and future generations. We present the details of our research dealing with one aspect of Balinese culture, the Balinese traditional communication system (*kulkul*), undertaken in the Indonesian island of Bali. We introduce a new framework based on Balinese cultural principles (*Tri Hita Karana* and *Desa Kala Patra*) to capture, classify, and organize cultural artefact and practice knowledge, and design and develop an online digital portal prototype to enable the sharing and growth of knowledge related to the Balinese *kulkul*. This knowledge is held largely in tacit form in the Balinese community, poorly documented, and fragmented, which makes the preservation difficult and yet crucial. The aim of the project is to document, preserve, and educate the Balinese community and the younger generations in particular on an important aspect of Balinese culture. This community will be encouraged not only to learn about *kulkul* and related practices but also contribute their own knowledge to enable the online digital portal to evolve into a living repository of Balinese cultural knowledge. The basic *kulkul* knowledge and understanding was obtained through in-depth interviews with selected Balinese cultural experts and knowledgeable community members (Professors from a Balinese University, spiritual leaders, senior community leaders, and craftsmen). As part of the digital portal, our project also includes the development of a basic ontology of key *kulkul*-related concepts and terms, and their inter-relationships to support the semantic searching and browsing of online resources.

Keywords: Balinese *kulkul* · Digital heritage · Digital portal · Ontology · Living cultural repository

1 Introduction

Over the past few decades, digitization of cultural heritage and natural history has gained much attention from researchers, practitioners, and memory institutions (galleries, libraries, archives, museums, and natural history institutions). Digital preservation of cultural heritage is a complex and interdisciplinary task involving computer science, history, library, literature, information science and art. One of the goals of digital preservation is gathering, refining, maintaining, and sharing the cultural resources that subsequently

© Springer International Publishing AG 2016
M. Ioannides et al. (Eds.): EuroMed 2016, Part I, LNCS 10058, pp. 491–500, 2016.
DOI: 10.1007/978-3-319-48496-9_38

can be used and developed by scholars, members of the community, and younger generations. Moreover, digitization is used for creating new means of accessing cultural information, where the users and/or future generations have the ability to learn, understand, and further develop the digital resources through the Internet.

Many countries all around the world face the problem of cultural heritage extinction or depletion, and many of the objects and cultural practices are poorly documented, largely tacit, and fragmented [1–4]. These contribute in making the preservation project difficult, and yet crucial. The fragmentation of cultural knowledge presents a major challenge for cultural preservation, rendering it time-consuming and labor-intensive. Technological developments such as the Internet, smartphones, and advances in IT allow for a unique and crowd driven solution to this problem. By undertaking a crowd driven, systematic approach to gather, store, check and organize cultural information, we aim to integrate the diverse knowledge, make it widely available through appropriate framework and platforms, and test the accuracy and validity of our approach towards preserving and extending cultural heritage.

1.1 Aims and Significance

This project aims to enhance the Balinese community understanding and the younger generations in particular on an important aspect of Balinese culture. Much of this knowledge is deeply tacit and collectively held within the Balinese community. This is the first stage of our digital project which externalizes the complex body of knowledge and makes it available through an online digital portal for the benefit of the Balinese community as well as the large number of people with deep interest in Balinese culture and traditions.

The objective of this paper is to propose a knowledge organization and classification framework for Balinese cultural heritage, and to design and develop an online digital portal prototype system for preserving, archiving, and sharing knowledge related to unique Balinese culture artefacts by tapping into the community-level understanding and knowledge of cultural heritage.

1.2 Research Problem

A problem encountered in cultural digitization projects is the preservation of information beyond the actual object, such as contextual and cultural practice-related information. UNESCO identified such practices as very fragile by their very nature and easily forgotten, making the digitization of this cultural information is vital for preservation.

Bali is renowned of worldwide tourist destination because of its highly developed culture such as art, traditional dance, painting, music, language, etc. The information relating to the Balinese cultural knowledge is complex. Even for cultural and community experts it is far from straightforward to model this domain of knowledge. Much of this knowledge is held largely in tacit form and rooted in the Balinese community. Furthermore, without clear documentation of Balinese culture [5, 6] specifically Balinese *kulkul*, makes this study even more challenging and significant. Also, the fact that *kulkul* practices are diverse and not standardized makes it particularly important to understand and capture the information as much as possible in the right context, and putting it together in the right form of an online digital portal.

2   Background and Related Literature

2.1   Bali and Balinese Culture

The island of Bali is one of thousands island, and one of the smallest provinces of the Indonesia archipelago. The Balinese culture is maintained through daily practice and religious rituals that keeps the traditions of the past alive [5]. This tradition passes from one generation to another by letting the next generation learns through experience every process that related to the local Balinese culture.

The Balinese culture built on the top Balinese traditional community such as custom village (*desa adat* or *desa pekraman*), *banjar*, and *sekaa*. Religious ceremonies which are integral thinking and attitudes of the Balinese, continue as frequently and as importantly as ever, and remain relatively unchanged over the years in spite of modernization trends [7].

Kenthongan is an ancient traditional communication tool which is made of bronze with elongated holes [8], which is widely known in the Indonesian archipelago. In Bali this *kethongan* is known as *kulkul* (Fig. 1) that is owned by every traditional Balinese community (*desa adat, banjar adat,* and *sekaa*). *Kulkuls* are made of wood or bamboo and are installed in the *Bale kulkul* (typically near temples, village, and *banjars*) in every village. These objects, the cultural practices, and messages surrounding the different *kulkul* sounds represent a distinct and unique dimension of Balinese cultural heritage. The *kulkul* acts as an alarm in the community for ceremonies and hazard e.g. gatherings the community, fire, flood, murder, etc. [9], and it vary from one Balinese village to another.

Fig. 1. Balinese *kulkul*

2.2   Digital Preservation Within Cultural Heritage

Cultural heritage tends to be seen as the product of the physical cultural traditions and spiritual achievements in the form of the value of the past. Turning towards the digital age, cultural heritage institutions such as Galleries, Archives, Museums and Libraries

(GLAM) started to identify the need for digitizing their various collections and making them available online [10].

There are many reasons why cultural heritage collections should be available online. The most important purpose is to make legacy cultural knowledge accessible, further developed, and passed on to future generations. Also, this will allow students, researchers, teachers, and the public to explore and connect with their past. These cultural heritage collections include sites, objects and intangible things that have cultural, historical, aesthetic, archaeological, scientific, ethnological or anthropological value to groups and individuals [11]. Several digital works and project initiatives have been carried out to prevent cultural knowledge erosion in Indonesia [1, 3, 12].

3   Methodology

This study is based on design science research methodology (DSRM) [13]. It will assess the ability of experts' and non-experts' contributions to preserve, and experiment with the prototype system to be created. The DSRM (Fig. 2) consist of several stages: (1) Problem identification and motivation; (2) Objectives for solutions; (3) Design and development; (4) Demonstration and Evaluation; and (5) Communication.

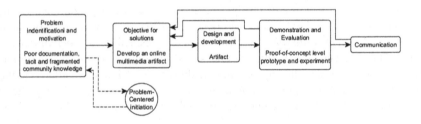

Fig. 2. Design Science Research Methodology (DSRM)

This research employs a problem-centered approach in which the research entry point is the problem identification and motivation activity. We proceed in this sequence because of the idea for the research resulted from observation of the problem. The system design and development on this project (Fig. 3) is using prototyping method and involves three activities: 1. Cultural experts interview, 2. Prototyping, and 3. Implementation and testing the online digital portal.

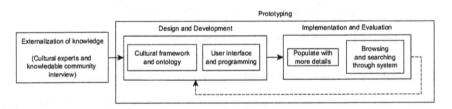

Fig. 3. System Development Life Cycle

3.1 Externalization of Knowledge

The first part of this study involved exploring and gathering knowledge from Balinese cultural heritage experts and knowledgeable community members about the Balinese traditional communication tool (Balinese *kulkul*). This exploratory phase of our research project is to externalized the knowledge, help to design an online computer web-based digitization system, and create a basic model of ontology that can be utilized by computer-based system to facilitate the browsing and searching for information included in the online digital portal.

The *kulkul* community knowledge exists in somewhat tacit form, and this knowledge is shared through socialization (tacit to tacit) of Balinese community social systems from generation to generation. Tacit knowledge is a knowledge that based on individual experience, deeply embedded, hard to express and explain, not yet articulated, and equals as practical know-how knowledge. Thus, one way to represent it is through metaphors, drawings, and other method that not require any formal language [14]. Furthermore, the externalization of tacit knowledge is one of the most challenging steps of knowledge conversion [14–16].

Over a period of two months prior to the interviews, an extensive review of the literature was performed to help frame the interview questions and explore the key issues in the context of Balinese *kulkul*. Interviews using snowball strategy has been chosen for the method on externalization of this community tacit knowledge. The snowball strategy is a form of purposeful sampling when the researchers asks participants to recommend other individuals to the study [17]. This method is appropriate for our project when we were initially unfamiliar with the topic and the complexity of the research central phenomenon. The sampling process initiated by an independent expert in each group exclusively triggers getting the different snowballs rolling. We stopped the snow-ball rolling whenever the group of participants repeats the same answers corresponding to the questions.

Semi-structured interview approach was selected as the means for information collection. This format of interview allows for specific questions and topics to be addressed while offering the respondents an opportunity to give additional feedback and elaborate further on any aspect of their experience they considered relevant to this study [18]. The semi-structured interview questions consisted of 23 questions, and fall into three main categories: (a) history of *kulkul*, (b) *kulkul* artefact, and (c) *kulkul* practices.

The interviews took place during the period of 03rd of August to the 12th of November 2015. In order to collect accurate data and to enable verbatim transcription, they were audio-recorded, always with the interviewee's consent. The interviews used a combination of Bahasa and Balinese language. The participants' age was between 47 – 65 years old, their average experience in their field is more than 10 years, all participants were male. They came from the west, east, south, and central regions of Bali.

The basics of *kulkul* system was collected incrementally from four groups of experts. These groups of interviewees consisted of five Professors from a Balinese University (who are acknowledged experts in methods of traditional communication), four Balinese spiritual leaders (who are identified because they have the knowledge about the spiritual significance of these traditions), eight senior community leaders in Bali (identified as key leaders who are the person in charge to ring the *kulkul* in *banjar* or village), and two *kulkul* craftsmen (identified because they possess practical knowledge in making the *kulkul* artefact).

Each interview session took for about 30 min up to 120 min. Many of the respondents had difficulties in expressing the knowledge surround the *kulkul* domain. They understood how the *kulkul* is practiced in the community, however it was sometimes hard for them to express it in the formal language. Therefore, occasionally researchers had to repeat the interview due to the complex and relatively tacit knowledge related to the *kulkul* domain.

We used the knowledge externalization method proposed by Nonaka and Takeuchi Fig. 4. First, metaphor is a method to express what the interviewees know, but hard to say by asking them to create a symbol and synthesis to find the distance between symbols. This method is used to merge two different and distant areas of experience into single image or understanding. Second, analogy is used to reconcile contradictions and make distinctions between symbols. Finally, the knowledge was crystalized into a model by constructing the basic *kulkul* domain ontology.

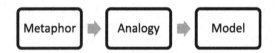

Fig. 4. Externalization knowledge methodology

During the interview we asked some of the interviewees to demonstrate how they practice the *kulkul* in the community to help us understand the different practices of kulkul. For example, two of the interviewees literally said that they practice two frames (*duang tulud bulus*) for the situation of hazard, nevertheless the way they sounded the kulkul are completely different (the total number of beat and the rhythm) as shown on Fig. 5.

Fig. 5. Two frames of *kulkul bulus* at (a) Gianyar region, and (b) Karangasem region

3.2   Knowledge Classification and Organization

Our digital portal framework (Fig. 6) to capture, classify, and organize the richness of *kulkul* knowledge is based on the outcome of the interviews which enabled us to elaborate on the key Balinese cultural principles (*Tri Hita Karana* and *Desa Kala Patra*) as they relate to *kulkul*. *Tri Hita Karana* is the Balinese belief or philosophy of balance and harmony [19–21] including three factors: (1) Universal (*parahyangan*), (2) environment *(palemahan)*, which refers to harmony with nature, and (3) people *(pawongan)*, which implies harmony among people. This first set of concepts is related to the *kulkul* practices where *kulkul* sound is a part of every Balinese religious ceremony *(parahyangan)* that is mainly held in the temple area. Also, this sound is used for any type of activities that involve a large number of people in the Balinese traditional community *(pawongan)*. The second set of concepts called the space *(desa)*, time *(kala)*, and circumstances *(patra)* [21] dictates that humans are not passive individuals but who will always try to adapt themselves to their environment that influences their lives. The *Desa Kala Patra* concept can be used to explain the variations in *kulkul* practices in the Balinese community.

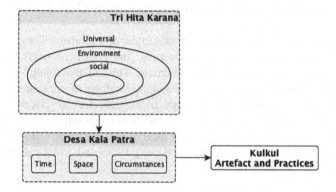

Fig. 6. The Balinese *kulkul* framework

The *kulkul* knowledge classification cannot separate the interdependence between the artifact (tangible) and its practices (intangible). Also, this kind of cultural heritage classification systems are still being debated by the UNESCO on the Preamble of the 2003 Convention for the Safeguarding of the Intangible Cultural Heritage [22].

Information can be viewed at two different levels: syntactic where this information based on the volumes of the information, and semantic more focus on the meaning of the information and how it related to the other concept. Ontology is a formal, explicit specification of a shared conceptualization [23], and have been developed to provide a machine-processable semantics of information sources that can be communicated between different agents (software and humans) [24]. Moreover, ontology is one of alternatives to representing the domain of knowledge, where this method helps us to do semantic modeling of concepts, and the axioms in ontology are represented in logic languages [25].

The CIDOC CRM[1] is a well-known cultural ontology that enables information integration, mediation and interchange of heterogeneous cultural heritage data and their correlation with digital library and archive information, and this cultural ontology has been studied for this project. The CIDOC-CRM has been used to abstract hundreds of schemata (80 classes and 130 relationships) in various museum disciplines, and helps improve the semantic of knowledge from distributed database of cultural heritage

---

[1] http://www.cidoc-crm.org.

[26–28]. However, less than five percent of its concept has been used by museum [29], and the CIDOC-CRM is too museum centric [30].

The ontology development falls into two categories: (i) developed from scratch [31], and (ii) reusing and integrating with an existing ontology [32] based on the knowledge representation needed. In this project we develop the ontology from scratch, and the purpose of applying ontological approach is to enable flexibility of the knowledge growth, as the collecting of *kulkul* knowledge was done incrementally. Therefore, a formal reasoning can be applied when this knowledge evolves.

4   Prototyping, Design, and Implementation of Digital Portal

The online digital portal prototype is currently under development. The development of basic *kulkul* ontology (class, object properties, and data properties) Fig. 7 used a protégé[2] ontology editor, and the OWL2 language. This kulkul ontology serves as backbone to support semantic browsing and searching facilities of our system. The apache Jena[3] framework was chosen as ontology triple store for our development, while Fuseki[4] is used as a middleware layer to interfacing our web application to the ontology. In addition to that, the EasyRdf[5] API was used to provide a PHP API to Fuseki. The browsing results are retrieved and displayed using JSON and AJAX calls. Our application supports the following facilities:

- Populate: allows multiple online users to contribute by populating more details of Balinese *kulkul*.
- Browsing: allows users to browse through different part of the ontology by navigating through *kulkul* classification hierarchies.
- Searching: allows users to construct a query relating to one or more attributes of the *kulkul* artifact and practices as inputs and displaying a selected attribute for the output.

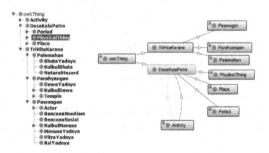

Fig. 7. Kulkul ontology

---

[2] http://protege.stanford.edu/.

[3] http://jena.apache.org/.

[4] https://jena.apache.org/documentation/serving_data/.

[5] http://www.easyrdf.org/.

5   Conclusion and Future Work

We have presented the details of our research dealing with one aspect of Balinese culture, the Balinese traditional communication system (*kulkul*). Our contributions include externalizing the largely tacit and fragmented *kulkul* knowledge, and developing an ontology to represent this knowledge. The *kulkul* framework based on Balinese cultural principles (*Tri Hita Karana* and *Desa Kala Patra*) is to capture, classify, and organize cultural artefact and practice knowledge, and design and develop an online digital portal prototype to enable the sharing and growth of knowledge related to the Balinese *kulkul*.

We are currently working on analyzing and testing the usability of our online digital portal system by having community-based crowdsourcing to contribute more details in order to refine and update community cultural resources. The users' feedback will be used as inputs to expand the *kulkul* ontology and to enhance the digital portal.

Acknowledgement. This project received funding from The Indonesia Endowment Fund for Education (LPDP) grant no. PRJ-02/LPDP/2013 and Competitive Research Grant Ristekdikti grant no. 486.24/UN14.2/PNL.01.03.00/2016.

References

1. Sanabila, H.R., Manurung, R.: Towards automatic wayang ontology construction using relation extraction from free text. In: EACL 2014, p. 128 (2014)
2. Rosner, D., Roccetti, M., Marfia, G.: The digitization of cultural practices. Commun. ACM **57**, 82–87 (2014)
3. Hasibuan, Z.A.: An overview of integrated approach to digital preservation: case study of Indonesian e-Cultural heritage and natural history information retrieval system. In: International Conference on Advanced Computer Science and Information System (ICACSIS), pp. 31–36 (2011)
4. Hui, D., Siwei, Y., Ying, J.: Knowledge representation of Chinese genealogical record of VIPs in KMT and CPC. In: Ninth International Conference on Hybrid Intelligent Systems, HIS 2009, vol. 3, pp. 116–120 (2009)
5. Walker, B., Helmi, R.: Bali Style. Thames and Hudson, London (1995)
6. Covarrubias, M.: Island of Bali. Periplus Editions (HK) Limited, Singapore (2008)
7. Suryani, L.K., Jensen, G.D.: Trance and Possession in Bali: A Window on Western Multiple Personality, Possession Disorder, and Suicide. Penerbit ITB, Bandung (1999)
8. Kebudayaan, D.P.: Ensklopedia Musik Indonesia. Departemen Pendidikan dan Kebudayaan, Proyek Inventarisasi, dan Dokumentasi Kebudayaan Daerah (1985)
9. Goris, D.R., Dronkers, D.P.L.: Bali Atlas Kebudayaan. Pemerintah Republik Indonesia (1955)
10. Zlodi, G., Ivanjko, T.: Crowdsourcing digital cultural heritage. izlazi u samo elektroničkom izdanju: NE (2013)
11. http://www.unesco.org/new/en/brasilia/culture/world-heritage/heritage-legacy-from-past-to-the-future/
12. Pramartha, C.R.A., Dwidasmara, I.B.G.: The composition approach non-QWERTY keyboard for Balinese script. In: 2014 IEEE Canada International Humanitarian Technology Conference - (IHTC), pp. 1–4 (2014)
13. Peffers, K., Tuunanen, T., Rothenberger, M.A., Chatterjee, S.: A design science research methodology for information systems research. J. Manage. Inf. Syst. **24**, 45–77 (2007)

14. Koskinen, K.U., Pihlanto, P., Vanharanta, H.: Tacit knowledge acquisition and sharing in a project work context. Int. J. Proj. Manage. **21**, 281–290 (2003)
15. Abidi, S.S.R., Cheah, Y.N., Curran, J.: A knowledge creation info-structure to acquire and crystallize the tacit knowledge of health-care experts. IEEE Trans. Inf. Technol. Biomed. **9**, 193–204 (2005)
16. Nonaka, I., Takeuchi, H.: The Knowledge-Creating Company: How Japanese Companies Create the Dynamics of Innovation. Oxford University Press, Now York (1995)
17. Creswell, J.W.: Educational Research: Planning, Conducting, and Evaluating Quantitative and Qualitative Research. Merrill, Upper Saddle River (2005)
18. Louise Barriball, K., While, A.: Collecting data using a semi-structured interview: a discussion paper. J. Adv. Nurs. **19**, 328–335 (1994)
19. Jensen, G.D., Suryani, L.K.: The Balinese People: A Reinvestigation of Character. Oxford University Press, Singapore (1992)
20. Windia, W., Pusposutardjo, S., Sutawan, N., Sudira, P., Supadmo Arif, S.: Transformasi sistem irigasi subak yang berlandaskan konsep TRI Hita Karana. SOCA (Socio-Economic of Agriculturre and Agribusiness) 5 (2005)
21. Pitana, I.: Tri Hita Karana – the local wisdom of the balinese in managing development. In: Conrady, R., Buck, M. (eds.) Trends and Issues in Global Tourism 2010, pp. 139–150. Springer, Heidelberg (2010)
22. http://www.unesco.org/culture/ich/en/convention
23. Gruber, T.R.: A translation approach to portable ontology specifications. Knowl. Acquisition **5**, 199–220 (1993)
24. Fensel, D.: Ontologies: A Silver Bullet for Knowledge Management and Electronic Commerce. Springer, Heidelberg (2004)
25. Martinez-Cruz, C., Blanco, I.J., Vila, M.A.: Ontologies versus relational databases: are they so different? A comparison. Artif. Intell. Rev. **38**, 271–290 (2012)
26. Hong-Zhe, L., Bao, H., Jing, W., Jun-Kang, F.: An information flow based approach to semantic integration of distributed digital museums. In: International Conference on Machine Learning and Cybernetics, pp. 4430–4437 (2006)
27. Guoxin, T., Tinglei, H., Zheng, Z.: A knowledge modeling framework for intangible cultural heritage based on ontology. In: Second International Symposium on Knowledge Acquisition and Modeling, KAM 2009, vol. 1, pp. 304–307 (2009)
28. Hong-Zhe, L.: Global ontology construction for heterogeneous digital museums. In: International Conference on Machine Learning and Cybernetics, vol. 7, pp. 4015–4019 (2007)
29. Doerr, M., Iorizzo, D.: The dream of a global knowledge network: a new approach. J. Comput. Cult. Herit. **1**, 1–23 (2008)
30. Brownlow, R., Capuzzi, S., Helmer, S., Martins, L., Normann, I., Poulovassilis, A.: An ontological approach to creating an andean weaving knowledge base. J. Comput. Cult. Herit. **8**, 1–31 (2015)
31. Cristani, M., Cuel, R.: A survey on ontology creation methodologies. Int. J. Seman. Web Inf. Syst. (IJSWIS) **1**, 49–69 (2005)
32. Gómez-Pérez, A., Rojas-Amaya, M.D.: Ontological reengineering for reuse. In: Fensel, D., Studer, R. (eds.) EKAW 1999. LNCS (LNAI), vol. 1621, pp. 139–156. Springer, Heidelberg (1999). doi:10.1007/3-540-48775-1_9

Interconnecting Objects, Visitors, Sites and (Hi)Stories Across Cultural and Historical Concepts: The CrossCult Project

Costas Vassilakis[1], Angeliki Antoniou[1], George Lepouras[1],
Manolis Wallace[2(✉)], Ioanna Lykourentzou[3], and Yannick Naudet[3]

[1] Human-Computer Interaction and Virtual Reality Lab,
Department of Informatics and Telecommunications,
University of the Peloponnese, 22 131 Tripolis, Greece
{costas,angelant,gl}@uop.gr

[2] Knowledge and Uncertainty Research Laboratory,
Department of Informatics and Telecommunications,
University of the Peloponnese, 22 131 Tripolis, Greece
wallace@uop.gr

[3] Luxembourg Institute of Science and Technology,
5 avenue des Hauts-Fourneaux, 4363 Esch/Alzette, Luxembourg
{ioanna.lykourentzou,yannick.naudet}@list.lu
http://hci-vr.dit.uop.gr/, http://gav.uop.gr, http://www.list.lu/

Abstract. Human History, is a huge mesh of interrelated facts and concepts, spanning beyond borders, encompassing global aspects and finally constituting a shared, global experience. This is especially the case regarding European history, which is highly interconnected by nature; however, most History-related experiences that are today offered to the greater public, from schools to museums, are siloed. The CrossCult project aims to provide the means for offering citizens and cultural venue visitors a more holistic view of history, in the light of cross-border interconnections among pieces of cultural heritage, other citizens viewpoints and physical venues. To this end, the CrossCult project will built a comprehensive knowledge base encompassing information and semantic relationships across cultural information elements, and will provide the technological means for delivering the contents of this knowledge base to citizens and venue visitors in a highly personalized manner, creating narratives for the interactive experiences that maximise situational curiosity and serendipitous learning. The CrossCult platform will also exploit the cognitive/emotional profiles of the participants as well as temporal, spatial and miscellaneous features of context, including holidays and anniversaries, social media trending topics and so forth.

Keywords: Adaptation · User profiles · Mobile applications

1 Introduction

"CrossCult: Empowering reuse of digital cultural heritage in context-aware crosscuts of European history" is a newly started project, supported by the European

M. Ioannides et al. (Eds.): EuroMed 2016, Part I, LNCS 10058, pp. 501–510, 2016.
DOI: 10.1007/978-3-319-48496-9_39

Union under the H2020-REFLECTIVE-6-2015 "Innovation ecosystems of digital cultural assets" funding scheme. The CrossCult project aims to help European citizens understand and perceive their common past and present in an holistic manner, while fostering retention and promoting reflection. To this end, the CrossCult project adopts guidelines formulated in recent research [5,6] regarding the design of the interactive experiences and their narratives; these guidelines can be codified as four major principles as follows:

- Raise consciousness about the importance of History
- Tackle the study of History from a multi-faceted perspective
- Approach History not only through the written texts from successive eras, but also through all the traces left by those societies (archaeological remains, iconography, epigraphy, numismatics, architecture, art, etc.)
- Reckon that there are no absolute truths in History, but various possible interpretations of the archaeological remains and contrasting viewpoints

In this light, the cultural heritage sites, historic events and (digital) cultural assets are not presented as disconnected but rather they target at increasing understanding of the interrelated nature of culture and history. In doing so, the CrossCult project and platform allows the interconnections of objects, resources, visitors, sites and (hi)stories across European Cultural and Historical concepts and events. In addition, CrossCult uses an extensive knowledge base, using existing cultural repositories (e.g. Europeana) and a specially designed technological platform to maximize situational curiosity, serendipitous learning and reflection on different historical and social phenomena, like for example the place of women in societies, the movement of populations historically and today, establishment of healing practices, etc.

The project is using cutting edge technology to allow meta-history research from pilot experience with narratives built from cross-border connections and crosscutting topics. Furthermore, new technologies for smart venues and whole cities allow the multi-level, cross-repository interconnection of venues and digital cultural heritage resources. Personalized, adaptive and context-aware experiences are at the heart of the project in attempt to increase the Quality of Visitor Experience [13].

The project approach will be implemented and validated through a number of pilots, designed to operate under different parameters (individual vs. collaborative participation; authoritative vs. crowdsourced content; narrative vs. exploratory vs. serendipitous content delivery; intra-venue vs. inter-venue connections; temporal, vs. spatial vs. topic-related connections; physical presence vs. virtual presence), and will provide valuable insight on the effect that these parameters have on cognitive aspects, such as reflection, (re)interpretation, relation and comparison.

The remaining of this paper is organized as follows: Sect. 2 focuses on the personalization aspects in CrossCult, considering that personalization is considered a key feature to achieve the goals listed above and Sect. 3 describes the CrossCult infrastructure, outlining the architectural modules of the platform and their functionality. Finally, Sect. 4 concludes the paper and outlines future research.

2 Personalization in Cultural Heritage

Previous research has shown the importance of personalized applications for cultural heritage since they are found to increase the quality of visiting experience [1,12]. Personalized applications in cultural heritage are not only increasingly popular among cultural institutions [3] but visitors also seem to prefer them [7]. Personalized content can target the needs of a diverse audience and allow the targeted presentation of big amounts of available cultural information, providing different information to different people [19]. Cultural heritage institutions also use personalized applications as means to attract visitors. For a detailed survey on the use of personalization approaches in cultural heritage institutions one may refer to [4].

Within our project personalization goes beyond the current state of the art, aiming to appropriately tailor content, functionalities and presentation so as to foster reflection, (re)interpretation, relation and comparison, taking into account aspects such as the users cognitive profile, the current group dynamics, non-typical connections of cultural objects and so forth.

2.1 The Cold Start Problem and the Role of Social Media

However, although personalization in cultural heritage is useful, creating correct visitor profiles is a rather demanding task basically due to the short duration of most visits and the fact that most visitors might only visit a specific space only once. Within these time restrictions, visitor profiles need to be created quickly and effectively in terms of their appropriateness for the different visitors. The question raised though is how to start creating these profiles and where to find the necessary information.

Different approaches have been employed like using heuristic techniques [9], probability-based algorithms [11] or user prototypes/personas [15]. The problem is that although visitors enjoy the benefits of personalized applications in cultural heritage, they are at the same time reluctant at dealing with form-filling activities and researchers have to become more creative in applying indirect approaches for the collection of the needed information for the creation of user profiles.

Over the last years, more and more people are using social media for social interaction, information seeking, pass time, entertainment, relaxation, communicatory utility, convenience utility, expression of opinion, information sharing, and surveillance/knowledge about others. While interacting with these media, people provide vast amounts of personal information that can be further exploited for the creation of user profiles.

It has been demonstrated that peoples behavior on social networks reflects actual personality traits [17]. Therefore social media can be rich sources of information to efficiently create user profiles for personalized content in cultural heritage, also dealing with the cold start problem.

Recently a European project explored the potential of Facebook in providing the necessary information for the creation of museum visitor profiles [2]. However, research is still at the early stages and algorithms are not always reliable [16]. In this framework, CrossCultCrossCult aims at providing the necessary infrastructure for the effective elicitation of user profiles using different means, including social networks.

2.2   Group Adaptation

Although the above may apply for individuals and the elicitation of individual user profiles, adaptation for group visitors and elicitation of group profiles is a whole different story. Visitors rarely visit alone [14], yet most cultural heritage technologies, such as the ones discussed in the previous paragraphs, are made for individuals.

Early approaches have provided group visitors with a shared device for a common experience, but in more recent studies although each visitor has her own device, the experience is cooperative; for example the CHESS system that uses interactive storytelling for group visitors [18]. Context-aware applications for small groups have been also discussed [10] and the mobility of visitors has been also taken into account [8].

2.3   Personalization and Adaptation in CrossCult

The CrossCult platform will address personalization and adaptation by realizing both *item recommendations* and *path recommendations*.

Item recommendations include points of interest, exhibits, or even individual resources. Content-based recommendation techniques will be used here to match the candidates for recommendation (POIs, exhibits or resources) against the profile of the visitor; additionally, matching the candidates for recommendation against the current context (e.g. semantics of currently viewed collection, characteristics of exhibits viewed so far within the visit etc.) may provide opportunities for re-contextualization of entities and increased serendipity. Collaborative filtering techniques will also be employed, to enhance the visitors experience using information from the visits of other users with similar profiles (e.g. similar preferences, interests, visit goals and so forth). The recommender system will exploit the full set of semantic information that will be available for candidates for recommendation, by accessing the relevant ontological descriptions that are stored in the CrossCult repository (Fig. 1).

Path recommendations will not only arrange for suggesting routes that include exhibits that are deemed of high interest to the user, but also arrange for making the visiting experience meaningful. To this end, path formulation will strive to lead the visitor through routes in which the exhibits tell a certain story (e.g. they relate to social aspects of life in antiquity) or allow the visitor to reinterpret History from the items that s/he will view along the suggested route. Furthermore, path formulation will take into account real-time data regarding the location of other visitors, so as to avoid annoyances, such as high waiting times or overly crowded areas; due to the real-time nature of crowd location data, routes may be re-planned to adapt to the current situation. Finally, route planning will consider the visiting style of the visitors, i.e. their usual pattern of movement into cultural venues as well as constraints on their available or planned time; an initial estimate for the duration of the visit can be projected from previous visits, considering both the venue statistics and the individual visitor statistics, while the user may modify the estimated value.

All recommendation techniques require that user characteristics, interests and interaction history are recorded in a user profile, so as to match them either against the data and metadata of recommendation candidates (for content-based recommendations) or against profiles of other users (for collaborative filtering-based approaches). Users however may not offer to directly enter information through profile completion pages since the related for them is high and the benefits are not always apparent; moreover, for users that have been recently registered with the system, formulation of successful recommendations will be inhibited due to the cold start problem. To tackle these issues, techniques for implicit profile population and interest extraction are employed complementary to explicit input. Mini-games and quizzes are used to offer an insight to characteristics and interests of the users, while mapping visitors to personas or stereotypes is used to assist in identifying recommenders (i.e. other people with similar interests or characteristics, often called nearest neighbors) for collaborative filtering recommendations. Mini-games and quizzes will be delivered through social network platforms, exploiting their widespread and dissemination dynamics to maximize the potential of information gathering.

Recommender systems in CrossCult will exploit trending topics information from social media to allow venue content curators to promote exhibits or collections relevant to topical issues; this feature will enable venues to take advantage of subjects publicity, turning it into interest on their content. In this context, trending topics are read from social media and matched against the metadata of exhibits and collections; subsequently, the highest matches are presented to venue content curators who can then choose how (and if) these matches can be best used to trigger visitor interest and promote the venue content.

Regarding the aspect of group adaptation, the CrossCult project is in line with recent developments in museum/visitor studies listed earlier and it recognizes the need for the development of collaborative applications targeting group visitors as well as individuals. For this reason, group profiles will be created and content will be adapted according to the groups requirements. To this end, the personalization mechanisms in the CrossCult project include algorithms to determine whether an individual is visiting alone, or in a group. While this can be extracted using a direct question, additional technological means will be exploited to facilitate user profiling, such as near-field communications, identification of previously paired Bluetooth devices, identification of users that have an established friend relationship in social networks and so on.

Finally, recommenders in CrossCult will foster the creation of sporadic social networks by recommending connections among people that co-visit a venue. In

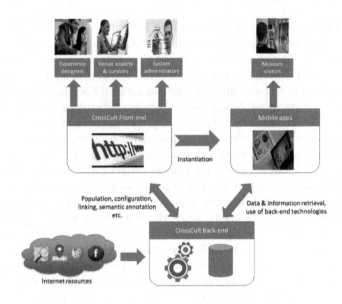

Fig. 1. The CrossCult platform overall architecture

this respect, the profiles of current venue visitors will be analyzed and groups of people with related interests and matching personalities will be determined; then suggestions will be forwarded to members of each group to join an online group through which they can engage in collaborative live discussion, participate in educational games or even formulate a physical group. These recommendations will respect user anonymity, and only after explicit consent of all interested parties the electronic IDs of the users will be exchanged.

We expect that user interaction within the context of sporadic social networks will promote the creation of new views on the venue content and the connections between exhibits, enriching the venues informational content. Some of the connections are expected to outlive the duration of the visit (e.g. through an establishment of a friend relation in social networks), supporting post-visit actions (including discussions, diffusion of information to other social network members and so forth), which could extend the benefits of the visiting experience.

3   CrossCult Infrastructrure

To accommodate the functionalities listed in the previous section, the CrossCult platform employs a layered approach targeting all stakeholders in the user experience delivery process. These include experience designers, venue experts and curators, system administrators and visitors.

In this process, venue experts and curators undertake the tasks of (a) curating digital content, providing textual and multimedia descriptions for exhibits as well as the associated metadata, and (b) establishing semantic links between exhibits/exhibit elements. Semantic links may be either established directly, e.g. by linking a painting depicting a loom to a statue of woman under the relationship uses, or indirectly by linking two items to the same ontology concept (e.g. two exhibits representing a loom and a horse are linked to the everyday life ontology concept). Furthermore, semantic links may be established among exhibits of different venues, or venue exhibits may be linked to resources in cultural repositories such as Europeana.

Experience designers employ user profiling tools to arrange for user profile population, mainly through mini-games and quizzes. Experience designers identify the opportunities for personalization and exploit exhibit data/metadata, user profile information and data from analysis of previous visits to the venue to offer a personalized experience to the visitor. Experience designers also arrange for offering suitable opportunities to visitors to enter comments as well as personal views on exhibits and their relations; these inputs may then be presented to subsequent visitors as personal views of previous users or be reviewed and accepted by venue experts and curators, and be integrated into the venues officially delivered information. In this respect, user input handling constitutes a form of crowdsourcing. Experience designers finally cater for choosing data from external sources, such as trending topics, calendar information (such as holidays or events), external sources with POI evaluations and so forth, which will be exploited to promote personalization and foster topicality.

The last category of the venue-side stakeholders is system administrators, who will provide the necessary computing and communication infrastructure for the operation of the applications and the storage and retrieval of information.

All venue-side stakeholders perform their tasks from the CrossCult front-end, which constitutes a powerful and intuitive web-based environment within providing the above-listed features. The data entered through the front-end are stored and organized at the CrossCult back-end which hosts the information repository, as well as all services needed to support the visitors application runtime (the back-end is detailed below). Once all required elements have been entered and configured via the CrossCult front end, the mobile apps which the visitors will use can be instantiated.

App instantiation is an automated procedure within which the mobile app code is generated, using predefined code templates and venue-specific options. Options mainly pertain to the functionalities that will be available to the users of the mobile app (i.e. venue visitors), such as entering comments and personal views, formulating sporadic networks, participating in mini-games and quizzes, sending messages to other users and so forth; in all cases, content (both official and user-contributed, such as comments and texts entered by other users) is retrieved dynamically from the CrossCult back-end. The mobile apps also arrange for receiving from the back-end recommendations, notifications and messages from other users and communicating them accordingly to the visitors.

The CrossCult back-end encompasses a repository for the storage, organization and retrieval of cultural information and pertinent metadata, while it additionally hosts modules for delivering the needed functionalities to both the front-end and the mobile apps. In particular, the back-end arranges for the following tasks (a) storing user profiles and unifying user profile information obtained from different sources (e.g. explicit input, mini-games, quizzes etc.); (b) gathering contextual data (including time of day, calendric information such as holidays, trending topics and related information from the internet); (c) collecting information about the number of visitors within each venue sub-location; (d) performing semantic reasoning over the ontological representations to deduce new relationships from the existing ones, augmenting thus the informational content; new relationships may be also detected among exhibits of different venues or exhibits of a venue and external cultural information repositories through metadata matching; (e) using all the previous listed information to generate recommendations for the users, regarding the exhibits to see, the paths to follow and venues to visit, and (f) supporting sporadic social network formulation (including identification of groups of visitors with common interests and generation of recommendations for joining sporadic social networks) and communication between their members,

4   Conclusions

In this paper we have outlined the main vision of the CrossCult project, which aims to provide the means for offering citizens and cultural venue visitors a holistic view of history, breaking cultural, local or viewpoint siloes in History-related experiences. In this respect, the CrossCult project approaches History as a huge mesh of interrelated facts and concepts, spanning beyond borders, encompassing global aspects and finally constituting a shared, global experience.

The main instrument to achieving this goal is personalization, through which narratives will be created for the interactive experiences that maximise situational curiosity and serendipitous learning. Personalization will exploit information in user profiles, either directly entered or more typically implicitly inferred and a semantically rich network of cultural information items; these items can be hosted in a single cultural venue, be dispersed among multiple venues or even be hosted in cultural repositories, such as Europeana. The CrossCult platform will also exploit the cognitive/emotional profiles of the participants as well as temporal, spatial and miscellaneous features of context, including holidays and anniversaries, social media trending topics and so forth. The CrossCult project will finally promote group exploration and group activities by employing group adaptation techniques and fostering the creation and operation of sporadic social networks, which will interconnect people with similar interests.

The CrossCult project is currently at its development stage. The platform components, which capitalize on the participants existing technologies, are being built and will be integrated to form the front-end and back-end components. Within the CrossCult project four pilot applications will be built, each one targeting to a specific category of History-related experiences: pilot 1 targets large multi-thematic venues; pilot 2 targets a setting with many small, interconnected venues; pilot 3 targets a single venue that promotes non-typical cultural connections among exhibits; and pilot 4 targets a setting involving multiple cities, offering cross-cultural interplay with their past and present. Through these pilots, the CrossCult approach will be validated and further enhanced with new features, taking into account the reactions comments and requests of the users.

Acknowledgment. Part of this work has been funded by the CrossCult H2020 project, Grant #693150.

References

1. Antoniou, A., Lepouras, G.: A study to investigate adaptation aspects for museum learning technologies. J. Comput. Cult. Herit. **3**(2), Article 7, October 2010
2. Naudet, Y., Antoniou, A., Lykourentzou, I., Tobias, E., Rompa, J., Lepouras, G.: Museum personalization based on gaming and cognitive styles: the BLUE experiment. Int. J. Virtual Communities Soc. Netw. **7**(2), 1–29 (2015). Special Issue on Social Media and Networks for Multimedia Content Management
3. Aoidh, E.M., Bertolotto, M., Wilson, D.: Towards dynamic behavior-based profiling for reducing spatial information overload in map browsing activity. GeoInformatica **16**, 409–434 (2012)
4. Ardissono, L., Kufli, T., Petrelli, D.: Personalization in cultural heritage: the road travelled and the one ahead. User Model. User-Adap. Inter. **22**(1–2), 73–99 (2012)
5. Berglund, S., Ekman, J., Deegan-Krause, K., Knuten, T. (eds.): The Handbook of Political Change in Eastern Europe. Edward Elgar Publishing, Cheltenham (2013)
6. Burton, A.: Ten Design Principles. Duke University Press, Durham (2011)
7. Findlater, L., McGrenere, J.: A comparison of static, adaptive, and adaptable menus. In: Proceedings of the SIGCHI Conference on Human Factors in Computing Systems (CHI 2004), pp. 89–96. ACM, New York (2004)
8. Fosh, L., Benford, S., Reeves, S., Koleva, B., Brundell, P.: See me, feel me, touch me, hear me: trajectories and interpretation in a sculpture garden. In: Proceedings of the SIGCHI Conference on Human Factors in Computing Systems (CHI 2013), pp. 149–158. ACM, New York (2013). http://dx.doi.org/10.1145/2470654.2470675
9. Hameed, M.A., Ramachandram, S., Al Jadaan, O.: Information Gain Clustering Through Prototype-Embedded Genetic K-Mean Algorithm (IGCPGKA): a novel heuristic approach for personalisation of cold start problem. In: Proceedings of the Second International Conference on Computational Science, Engineering and Information Technology (CCSEIT 2012), pp. 390–395. ACM, New York (2012)
10. Kuik, T., Stock, O., Zancanaro, M., Gorfinkel, A., Jbara, S., Kats, S., Sheidin, J., Kashtan, N.: A visitor's guide in an active museum: presentations, communications, and reection. J. Comput. Cult. Herit. **3**(3), Article 11, February 2011. 25 pages, http://dx.doi.org/10.1145/1921614.1921618
11. Lin, C., Xie, R., Li, L., Huang, Z., Li, T.: PRemiSE: personalized news recommendation via implicit social experts. In: Proceedings of the 21st ACM International Conference on Information and Knowledge Management (CIKM 2012), pp. 1607–1611. ACM, New York (2012)
12. Lykourentzou, I., Claude, X., Naudet, Y., Tobias, E., Antoniou, A., Lepouras, G., Vassilakis, C.: Improving museum visitors' quality of experience through intelligent recommendations: a visiting style-based approach. In: Intelligent Environments (Workshops), pp. 507–518 (2013)

13. Naudet, Y., Lykourentzou, I., Tobias, E., Antoniou, A., Rompa, J., Lepouras, G.: Gaming and cognitive profiles for recommendations in museums. In: SMAP 2013, pp. 67–72 (2013)
14. Petrelli, D., Not, E.: User-centred design of flexible hypermedia for a mobile guide: reflections on the HyperAudio experience. User Model. User-Adap. Inter. 15(3–4), 303–338 (2005)
15. Roussou, M., Katifori, A., Pujol, L., Vayanou, M., Rennick-Egglestone, S.J.: A life of their own: museum visitor personas penetrating the design lifecycle of a mobile experience. In: CHI 2013 Extended Abstracts on Human Factors in Computing Systems (CHI EA 2013), pp. 547–552. ACM, New York (2013)
16. Theodoridis, T., Papadopoulos, S., Kompatsiaris, Y.: Assessing the reliability of Facebook user profiling. In: Proceedings of the 24th International Conference on World Wide Web (WWW 2015 Companion), pp. 129–130. ACM, New York (2015)
17. Tkalcic, M., Chen, L.: Personality and recommender systems. In: Ricci, F., Rokach, L., Shapira, B. (eds.) Recommender Systems Handbook, pp. 715–739. Springer, New York (2015)
18. Vayanou, M., Katifori, V., Chrysanthi, A., Antoniou, A.: How to coordinate visitor actions? In: Proceedings of the 19th ACM Conference on Computer-Supported Cooperative Work and Social Computing, San Francisco, 27 February–2 March 2016
19. Walczak, K., Wojciechowski, R., Cellary, W.: Dynamic interactive VR network services for education. In: Proceedings of the ACM Symposium on Virtual Reality Software and Technology (VRST 2006), pp. 277–286. ACM, New York (2006)

Project Paper: 3D Reconstruction and 3D Modelling

Debate and Considerations on Using Videos for Cultural Heritage from Social Media for 3D Modelling

Kyriacos Themistocleous[✉]

Cyprus University of Technology, 2-6 Saripolou, 3036 Limassol, Cyprus
kt33@cytanet.com.cy

Abstract. Social media can be used as a new source of information by archaeologists and cultural heritage experts to access cultural heritage-related videos for creating 3D models using Structure for Motion techniques. There is a vast amount of data now available on social media, which are posted every day on the internet. However, there is confusion regarding if such data is considered fair use, public domain, creative commons or copyrighted. Indeed, social medias, such as Facebook, Twitter, Instagram and YouTube, have different regulations regarding ownership and republishing videos. This paper will discuss how social media can be used for cultural heritage research, especially if video data is used, transformed or repurposed for 3D modelling.

Keywords: Social media · Video · Documentation · Cultural heritage · Fair use · Copyright · Public domain · Creative commons

1 Introduction

There is a wealth of information on social media, including images and videos of cultural heritage sites, which provides a unique opportunity to cultural heritage specialists. From photos uploaded to Facebook by tourists to videos taken with UAVs posted to YouTube, cultural heritage specialists have a plethora of data that can be used study cultural heritage sites around the world. However, the issue of copyright remains a constant question. With the use of state of the art photogrammetry techniques, video can be used to create 3D models [1, 2]. This paper will examine the implications of copyright and fair use rules for cultural heritage specialists regarding transforming videos posted from social media into 3D visualization models.

2 Social Media

In recent years, social media is proving to be a very valuable resource for researchers from a variety of disciplines [3]. The photos and videos available through social media constitute a valuable source of information for Cultural Heritage professionals. Indeed, there are several projects that incorporate open data to promote the digital preservation of lost cultural heritage due to natural disasters, wars, military campaigns, and terrorism using social media data in a cooperative, open-source project, including Project Rekrei

© Springer International Publishing AG 2016
M. Ioannides et al. (Eds.): EuroMed 2016, Part I, LNCS 10058, pp. 513–520, 2016.
DOI: 10.1007/978-3-319-48496-9_40

(http://projectmosul.org), the Zameni Project (http://zamaniproject.org), the Democratization of Sciences project (http://aist.usf.edu) and the digital reconstruction of the Bamiyan Buddhas [4]. It is now possible to use video imaging from social media such as YouTube, Facebook and Twitter to create 3D models of cultural heritage architectures and monuments [2, 5]. Indeed, the 3D-ICONS project (3dicons-project. eu/eng/) digitises in 3D architectural and archaeological monuments and buildings identified by UNESCO as being of outstanding cultural importance.

Social media are online communication channels that allow people, companies and other organizations to create, share, or exchange information, ideas, images and videos in virtual communities and networks. Social media has transformed our means of communication by providing instant information to publish and publicize almost anything [6]. Digital technology and the new ways to use and reuse content are challenging society's notion of what is fair use and what is copyrighted [7]. Social networking sites such as Facebook, Twitter, YouTube, etc. allow users to share their writings, photos, videos and other creations with the world. Using open media such as YouTube, Facebook, Tumblr, Spotify, Pinterest, or personal blogs of various types, billions of online users are sharing, linking, embedding, cutting and pasting as common practice. Today, every social media user is a publisher of sorts and many publish without consideration of existing copyright laws.

One of the difficulties in using social media for cultural heritage purposes concerns the issue of copyright and fair use. There is a vast amount of data now available on social media, which are posted every day on the internet. As well, sharing text on social media is an accepted part of social media and to do so would not be an infringement of copyright unless the text comes from a third party source. However, there is confusion regarding copyright and the risk of infringement with social media data and if such data is considered fair use, public domain, creative commons or copyrighted. Indeed, social media such as Facebook, Twitter, Instagram and YouTube have different regulations regarding ownership and republishing images and videos. In order to understand the importance of copyright in social media, it is important to first define what is copyright, fair use, public domain and creative common and how this applies to using videos from social media to create 3D models for cultural heritage purposes. As well, it is important to realize that the laws governing copyright, fair use, public domain and creative common differ depending on the country. The majority of laws referring to copyright come from the United States, the United Kingdom and Australia. Due to the different legal regulations regarding copyright, fair use, etc. between different countries as well as the different social media terms of use, cultural heritage specialists should verify with their local laws prior to publication of their work.

2.1 Copyright

Copyright refers to the protection given to any created work from being copied or distributed without permission. Copyright attaches as soon as the original work is created, and applies to both published and unpublished works. Copyright is an automatic right and does not require the author to file special paperwork, as is the case for trademark and patent. Derivative works, where an original created work is modified through additions and changes (such as adapting a book for film, or translating a document) are also covered by copyright.

Copyright covers works that are created or shared on social media websites. However, the website's terms and conditions may change the author's rights to the work. For example, Facebook, YouTube, Google, Twitter, Flickr and Tumblr gives itself the right to use anything that is posted, including photos, videos, art work and text. According to YouTube, copyright owners of the posting can use Content ID to identify and manage their content on YouTube to protect against copyright infringement. However, YouTube offers Fair Use protection for posting that borrow small bits of material from an original work, are transformative in nature and do not affect the market of the original product. In this case, copyright is not violated since the video is not reproduced by any means but instead select content is transformed into another media.

2.2 Fair Use

Fair Use refers to the legal right to use copyrighted work in a reasonable manner without the owner's consent for purposes such as teaching, scholarship and research. The purpose of the Fair Use Doctrine is to allow for limited and reasonable uses as long as the use does not interfere with owners' rights or impede their right to do with the work as they wish [8]. Fair use is not the same as free use. Fair use is a legal exception to the exclusive rights an owner has for his or her copy-righted work.

There are four factors that must be considered when making a fair use claim:

- Purpose - The purpose of the use
- Nature - The nature of the copyrighted work
- Amount - The amount and substantiality of the work that is used in relation to the work as a whole
- Effect - The effect on the potential market for or value of the copyrighted work

Fair use applies if the original image is repurposed or transformed in such a way that there is a complete change in meaning and purpose. A particular use of a copyrighted work may be considered transformative if it uses the copyrighted work in a completely new way or with a new purpose that the original work's creator never intended. When the purpose for using the copyrighted content is not commercial and where the use is somehow transformative from the copyright holder's original use, a fair use argument is strong. The purpose for linking on social media is usually non-commercial and is transformative, in that the purpose of sharing interesting content is different than the copyright holder's purpose for creating and placing it online. Additionally, because the use is transformative, the act of sharing links to copyrighted content likely will not have a negative effect on the copyright holder's market [9]. For example, using videos of a cultural heritage site to create a 3D model can be considered transformative use. The most important factor in fair use is *purpose*- is the use transformative from the original use? Courts are more likely to uphold the fair use doctrine if the creation is transformative, meaning that the end product adds something new, with a different character, expression, meaning or message.

Figure 1 provides a guideline for Fair Use for using images to create 3D models.

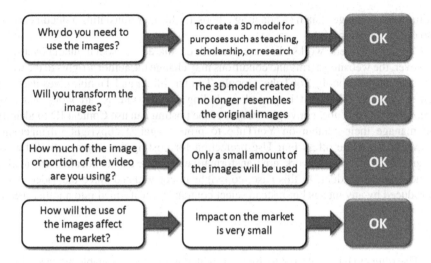

Fig. 1. Guidelines for Fair Use for using images to create 3D models

According to the fair use criteria, using social media for research or educational use, as is often used by cultural heritage specialists, is acceptable and does not constitute copyright infringement. Fair use applies in cases where a portion of the images are used and transformed in such a way that they no longer resemble the images, such as transforming a video into a 3D model. Although fair use applies to such cases, it is not mandatory but it is considered good practice to reference the source of the image or video (if known).

2.3 Creative Commons

Creative commons refer to material that are copyrighted but the creator has put provision on their use. For example, a creative commons license might stipulate that the image can be used as long as it is not changed in any way. As of 2015, there were 1 billion creative commons works on the internet free for the public to reuse [10]. For example, in the case of YouTube, users can check the video license as "Creative Commons Attribution License," which means users can download and reuse the video legally.

2.4 Public Domain

Public domain refers to material that no long has copyright restrictions and no one owns the copyright. It refers to ideas, facts, and works that have not been fixed in a tangible medium, works created by the government are not eligible for copyright protection Works in the public domain are free to be copied and used without restriction. When a work's copyright expires, it also becomes a part of the public domain. Copyright does not apply to works in the public domain; words, names, slogans or short phrases (those may have protection in trademark law); blank forms; works that are not original; and government works. Therefore, if the work is not protected by copyright, then there is no concern whether the Fair Use Doctrine will apply [8].

Figure 2 provides a detailed flowchart for how to decide to use images from another source for 3D modeling.

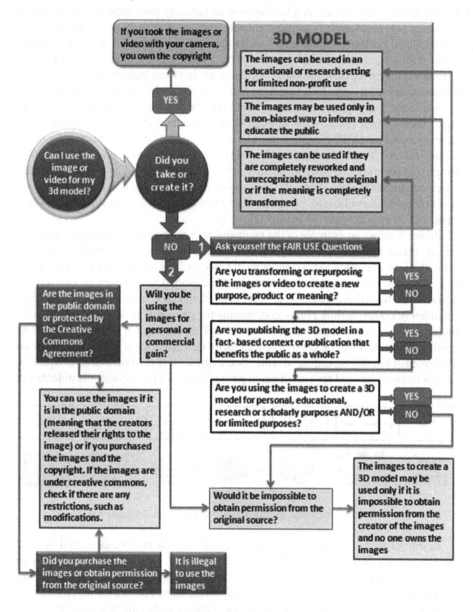

Fig. 2. Flowchart for deciding to use images for 3D modeling

3   Methodology

During the last 20 years, cultural heritage and archaeology have experienced a technical revolution [11] as researchers use the combination of aerial imagery for 3D reconstruction of the cultural heritage sites. Advances in 3D scanning techniques, drone use and tourist's online postings and videos are giving cultural heritage experts and archaeologists a new set of tools to prevent the permanent loss of cultural artefacts and landscapes. Today, most of the videos uploaded onto social media are high resolution, which facilitates the use of this method. These techniques provide a set of new tools for cultural heritage experts to capture, store, process, share, visualize and annotate 3D models in the field [12–19]. The implementation of image-based 3D modeling provides a time- and cost-effective manner for digital documentation [20–23]. Advances in the fields of Photogrammetry and Computer Vision have led to significant breakthroughs such as the Structure from Motion (SfM) algorithm which creates 3D models of objects using sequences of 2D images [1, 2]. There is also a wealth of research available for using uncalibrated image sequences from video and without camera calibration to create 3D models [2].

Figure 3 shows an example of the methodologies to create a quality geo-referenced digital surface model (DSM) using videos of a cultural heritage site from social media using the SfM algorithm [2]. To generate 3D models from social media, a sequence of images need to be captured from a video [2]. The captured images then undergo quality analysis and distortion correction, in order to be aligned and related to each other to get a number of corresponding points to determine the geometric relationship between the images. A 3D point cloud is then generated and modelling and texture mapping are applied. The model can be geo-referenced using Ground Control Points to display the completed 3D model according to scale. Due to the lack of field measurements, the 3D models can only be used for visualization purposes and not for accurate documentation.

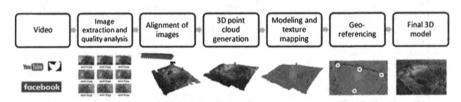

Fig. 3. Methodology for creating 3D models from social media images [2]

In the 3D reconstruction, the image undergoes several modifications and the final product is completely transformed from the original. As mentioned above, the process of using the SfM method changes the video, which is the original media source, and completely transforms and changes the media, so it clearly falls within into the fair use guidelines. According to the fair use guidelines (Figs. 1 and 2), the transformation from video to 3D model described constitutes fair use, since the images captured from video are repurposed and transformed by digitally changing the distortion, balance, tone, exposure, contract and clarity to create a new product and media, which is the 3D model. Also, the sequence of images captured and used to create the 3D model are from a small portion of the video and are digitally transformed in order to change the media to a 3D model, which conforms to the fair use guidelines in Figs. 1 and 2. The manipulation of the images captured from the original video produces a product that is significantly different from the original media; therefore, it can be regarded as a new work.

4   Conclusions

Although social media provides an opportunity for cultural heritage experts to have access to a vast amount of data available on the internet, the issue of copyright remains a constant question regarding how to use this information. This paper clarifies the difference between copyright, fair use, public domain and creative commons for cultural heritage experts who are using videos posted to social media to create 3D models. The use of videos from social media to create 3D models conforms to the fair use guidelines, since the sequence of images used are transformed to a new media and purpose. The SfM technique can be used so that videos of cultural heritage sites from social media can be transformed into 3D models by adhering to fair use guidelines, since the videos undergoes several modifications and the final product is completely transformed from the original. The final result, which is a 3D model, can be considered a new work since it undergoes a specialized process and is transformed from the original media.

References

1. Kyriakaki, G., Doulamis, A., Doulamis, N., Ioannides, M., Makantasis, K., Protopapadakis, E., Hadjiprocopis, A., Wenzel, K., Fritsch, D., Klein, M., Weinlinger, G.: 4D reconstruction of tangible cultural heritage objects from web-retrieved images. Int. J. Herit. Dig. Era. **3**(2), 431–452 (2014)
2. Themistocleous, K.: Model reconstruction for 3D vizualization of cultural heritage sites using open data from social media: the case study of soli cyprus. J. Arch. Sc. (2016). doi:10.1016/j.jasrep.2016.08.045
3. Kietzmann, J., Silvestre, B., McCarthy, I., Pitt, L.: Unpacking the social media phenomenon: towards a research agenda. J. Pub. Aff. **12**(2), 109–119 (2012)
4. Grun, A., Remondino, F., Zhang, L.: Photogrammetric reconstruction of the great Buddha of Bamiyan, Afghanistan. Photogr. Rec. **19**(107), 177–199 (2004)
5. Alsadik, B., Gerke, M. Vosselman, G.: Efficient Use of video for 3D modelling of cultural heritage objects. BISPRS Ann. Photogramm. Remote Sens. Spatial Inform. Sci., vol. II-3/W4, 2015 PIA15 + HRIGI15 (2015)
6. Cuddy, R.H.: Copyright issues for social media (2013). https://www.legalzoom.com/articles/copyright-issues-for-social-media
7. Rodriguez, J.E.: Social media use in higher education: key ares to consider for educators. Merlot J. Online Learn. Teach. **7**(4) (2011). http://jolt.merlot.org/vol7no4/rodriguez_1211.htm
8. Hawkins, S.: Copyright fair use and how it works for online images, 3 November, 2011 (2011). http://www.socialmediaexaminer.com/copyright-fair-use-and-how-it-works-for-online-images/
9. Gutierrez Alm, J.: Sharing copyrights: the copyright implications of user content in social media Hamline University's School of Law's. J. Publ. Law Policy **35**(1), 2 (2014). Transcending Intellectual Property Rights: an Exploration into the Unchartered Territories of the Intangible, Infringed, and the Internet

10. Creative Commons (2015). https://stateof.creativecommons.org/report/

11. Macheridis, S.: Image-based 3D modeling as a documentation method for Zooarchaeological remains in waste-related contexts. Ethnobiol. L. **6**(2), 242–248 (2015). doi:10.14237/ebl.6.2.2015.342

12. Ioannides, M., Hadjiprocopis, A., Doulamis, N., Doulamis, A., Protopapadakis, Eft., Makantasis, K., Santos, P., Fellner, D., Stork, A., Balet, O, Julien, M., Weinlinger, G., Johnson, P.S., Klein, M., Fritsch, D.: Online 4D reconstruction using multi-images available under open access. ISPRS Ann. Photogramm. Remote Sens. Spatial Inform. Sci., **II-5/W1**, 169–174 (2013)

13. Themistocleous, K., Agapiou, A., King, H.M., King, N., Hadjimitsis, D.G.: More than a flight: the extensive contributions of UAV flights to archaeological research–the case study of curium site in cyprus. In: Ioannides, M., Magnenat-Thalmann, N., Fink, E., Žarnić, R., Yen, A.-Y., Quak, E. (eds.) EuroMed 2014. LNCS, vol. 8740, pp. 396–409. Springer, Heidelberg (2014). doi:10.1007/978-3-319-13695-0_38

14. Themistocleous, K., Agapiou A., Cuca, B. Hadjimitsis, D.G.: Unmanned aerial systems and spectroscopy for remote sensing applications in archaeology. In: Proceedings of the 36th International Symposium on Remote Sensing of Environment (ISRSE–36) (2015a)

15. Themistocleous K., Agapiou A., Lysandrou, V., Hadjimitsis, D.G.: The use of UAVs for remote sensing applications: case studies in cyprus. In: Proceedings of SPIE 9644, Earth Resources and Environmental Remote Sensing/GIS Applications VI, 96440T (20 October 2015). doi:10.1117/12.2195027 (2015b)

16. Themistocleous, K., Ioannides, M., Agapiou, A., Hadjimitsis, D.G.: The methodology of documenting cultural heritage sites using photogrammetry, UAV and 3D printing techniques: the case study of Asinou Church in Cyprus. In: Proceedings of the Third International Conference on Remote Sensing and Geoinformation of Environment, SPIE 953510 (June 19, 2015). doi:10.1117/12.2195626 (2015c)

17. Themistocleous K., Ioannides M., Agapiou A., Hadjimitsis D.G.: A new approach for documenting architectural cultural heritage: the case study of Asinou Church in Cyprus. In: Proceedings of International Conference on Sustainability in Architecture and Cultural Heritage (2015d)

18. Fiorillo, F., Jimenez, B., Remondino, F., Barba, S.: 3D surveying and modeling of the archaeological area of Paestum, Italy. Virt. Archaeo. Rev. **4**, 55–60 (2012)

19. Eisenbeiss, H.: UAV Photogrammetry, Ph.D. Thesis. Institute fur Geodesie und Photogrammetrie, ETH-Zurch. Zurich, Switzerland (2009)

20. de Reu, J., de Smedt, P., Herremans, D., van Meirvenne, M., Laloo, P., De Clercq, W.: On introducing an image-based 3D reconstruction method in Archaeological excavation practice. J. Arch. Sc. **41**, 251–262 (2014). doi:10.1016/j.jas.2013.08.020

21. de Reu, J., Plets, G., Verhoeven, G., de Smedt, P., Bats, M., Cherrette, B., de Maeyer, W., Deconynck, J., Herremans, D., Laloo, P., van Meirvenne, M., de Clercq, W.: Towards a three-dimensional cost-effective registration of the archaeological heritage. J. Arch. Sc. **40**, 1108–1121 (2013). doi:10.1016/j.jas.2012.08.040

22. Dellepiane, M., Dell'Unto, N., Callieri, M., Lindgren, S., Scopigno, R.: Archeological excavation monitoring using dense stereo matching techniques. J. Cult. Her. **14**, 201–210 (2013). doi:10.1016/j.culher.2012.01.011

23. Verhoeven, G., Doneus, M., Briese, C., Vermeulen, F.: Mapping by matching: a computer vision-based approach to fast and accurate georeferencing of archaeological aerial photographs. J. Arch. Sc. **39**, 2060–2070 (2012). doi:10.1016/j.jas.2012.02.022

Investigations of Low-Cost Systems for 3D Reconstruction of Small Objects

Thomas P. Kersten[✉], Daniel Omelanowsky, and Maren Lindstaedt

Photogrammetry and Laser Scanning Lab, HafenCity University Hamburg,
Überseeallee 16, 20457 Hamburg, Germany
{Thomas.Kersten,Maren.Lindstaedt}@hcu-hamburg.de,
omelanowsky@gmx.de

Abstract. In this paper geometric investigations are presented, which demonstrate the potential of the low-cost recording systems DAVID SLS-1 and Microsoft® Kinect for sustainable use in applications for architecture, cultural heritage and archaeology. From the data recorded with DAVID SLS-1 and Microsoft® Kinect 3D models were produced by different programs and these were examined in relation to handling, quality and reliability in further post processing. For the investigations a number of 3D objects with different surface forms, including a test body, were scanned using the structured light system ATOS I 2M from GOM as references. To compare the results of the Kinect and the SLS-1, digital surface models of this test body were automatically generated using image-based low-cost recording systems (Nikon D7000). As a result of these 3D comparisons to the ATOS reference data a standard deviation of 1.5 and/or 1.6 mm was obtained with the structured light system SLS-1 and/or with the Kinect, while with the image-based 3D reconstruction methods of VisualSFM/CMVS a higher standard deviation of up to 0.2 mm was achieved. Although the introduced low-cost structured light system David SLS-1 could not show the geometrical accuracy of a high end system (ATOS I) of approx. 0.04 mm, it is useful for the 3D recording of smaller objects (size up to 50 cm) with a reduced accuracy for several different applications.

Keywords: 3D · Automation · Comparison · Image matching · Modelling · Point cloud · Reconstruction

1 Introduction

For 3D shape recording of small and complex objects modern systems typically work according to the triangulation principle. For a long time these systems were only available at the expensive, high-end of the market, but in recent years affordable options have become increasingly available for users with smaller budgets. Current low-cost systems are available on the market but neither the quality nor the quantity of the recorded data is often considered in public discussion. However, contributions from Hieronymus et al. [1], Wujanz et al. [2], Khoshelham [3] and Boehm [4] present test results of 3D sensors from the low-cost field and the gamer market. Since the market for 3D consumer sensors

© Springer International Publishing AG 2016
M. Ioannides et al. (Eds.): EuroMed 2016, Part I, LNCS 10058, pp. 521–532, 2016.
DOI: 10.1007/978-3-319-48496-9_41

is constantly growing, an examination of this equipment regarding reliability and accuracy for measuring tasks is an obvious requirement. Results of empirical accuracy tests are presented in [5], in which models from image-based low-cost 3D reconstruction methods are compared with reference data of higher accuracy.

The applications of so-called low-cost systems are to be found predominantly within the field of archaeology and cultural heritage, in which the structured light projection procedure is often used by preference. Thus, Sablatnig and Menard [6], Akca et al. [7], McPherron et al. [8], Bathow and Breuckmann [9] described that structured light scanners are widely adopted for these applications, since the contactless procedure is particularly well suited for the 3D documentation of small objects. First test results with Microsoft Kinect were presented by Wujanz et al. [2], Khoshelham [3] and Smisek et al. [10], while Mankoff and Russo [11] have also reported on experiences with the Kinect in glaciological, bathymetrical and geomorphological applications.

In the present contribution the potential of both low-cost systems DAVID SLS-1 and Microsoft® Kinect has been evaluated in comparison to image-based reconstruction procedures using several test objects as practical examples. Reference measurements of the different test objects were recorded with a structured light system (GOM ATOS I 2M).

2 Low-Cost Systems Evaluated

In these investigations a total of three low-cost recording systems was evaluated: (a) the Microsoft® Kinect [12], (b) the DAVID SLS-1 [13], which both work with an active (projector) and a passive (camera) sensor using the triangulation method, and (c) an image-based recording system (using different digital SLR cameras).

The Kinect was used in combination with the ReconstructMe software [14] which is freely-available for non-commercial applications. This sensor, which originates in the gaming market, offers a resolution of 640×480 pixels with a measuring distance of 0.8 to 3.5 m. The Kinect costs approximately €100. The operational and functional principle is described in [15]. The SLS-1 is a low-cost structured light system from DAVID Vision Systems GmbH in Koblenz, which commercially distributed this product including the software DAVID Laserscanner as a complete 3D recording solution at a price of approximately €1700 (Nov. 2012). The integrated camera consists of a monochrome CMOS image sensor with a fixed focal length of 12 mm and an image resolution of 744×480 pixels. The projector used in this system, which projects the structured light, is a commercial Acer K11. The base distance between camera and projector can be determined by system calibration in the software DAVID Laserscanner. Although the camera is monochrome, it is possible to texture the 3D models with colour by projecting several colours onto the object with the projector and by measuring the respective reflections from the object surface with the monochrome camera. DAVID software offers the whole workflow from object recording through scan registration to the export of the model, while with ReconstructME only recording and data export are possible. In principle, the measuring volume is unlimited for the MS Kinect, if certain conditions are considered as described in [14]. With the DAVID SLS-1 the maximum expanse of the object surface is 30–500 mm. For image-based reconstruction procedures the digital SLR camera Nikon D7000 (4,938 × 3,264 pixels) was used, which can be very flexibly used for object recording. The following automatic generation of 3D point clouds and/or 3D object models was carried out with the open-source software Bundler [16] and PMVS2 [17], with the free available non-commercial software VisualSFM [18] as well as with the Autodesk Web service 123D Catch [19]. These three image-based 3D reconstruction methods are already briefly introduced in [5].

The evaluated recording systems are represented in Fig. 1; for detailed technical specifications the relevant manufacturers' web pages are referenced.

Fig. 1. Evaluated low-cost systems (f.l.t.r.): Nikon D7000, DAVID SLS-1 and MS Kinect

3   Evaluation Criteria and Methods

3.1   System Stability

The measuring systems DAVID SLS-1 and MS Kinect can be calibrated and prepared for data recording (the digitization procedure) within a few minutes by an experienced user. In order to be able to meet a statement about the stability of the SLS-1, as the first investigation camera calibration was conducted twenty times every ten minutes. The interior (intrinsic) and exterior (extrinsic) parameters of the camera are summarized in the calibration report. The SLS-1 uses a camera model of Tsai [20]. Which includes the following interior orientation parameters: focal length f, radial distortion coefficient $\kappa 1$, scale factor sx and the coordinates of the principle point cx and cy.

Figure 2 illustrates the SLS-1 calibration setup (left) and the computed focal length C in pixels (px) for the observation period of 200 min, in which 20 calibrations were carried out with the software DAVID Laserscanner (version 3.4.0).

For system calibration the camera acquires images of an orthogonally constructed calibration field provided with targets (Fig. 2 left) and whose geometry is known. The lowest and highest value of the calibrated focal length in the calibration series has a wide margin of 3.5 pixels, whereby the largest deviation was registered in minute 150. Unlike the other values, the series of measurements in minutes 30–60, 90, 110, 160 and 200 match each other well since their deviations are only approx. one pixel. In principle all values are evenly distributed, but a descending trend is clearly observable. Additionally,

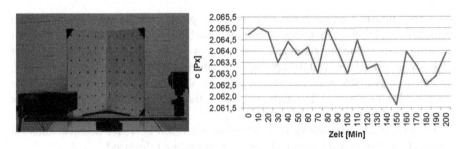

Fig. 2. DAVID SLS-1 (software version 3.4.0) – Calibration setup (left) and the variation of the focal length (right) over the time period of 200 min

observation of the remaining intrinsic parameters (parameters of interior orientation) took place during these tests. It was observed that the location of the principle point in x-direction varies by only approximately 2.5 pixels. On the other hand, a span of 4 pixels is shown in the y-direction and it rises continuously starting from the first measurement. The scale factor varies around the value 0.084; it has the largest deviation of 0.0001 from the average value in minute 70. Although the temperature environment in the laboratory was constant, the computed parameters of interior orientation appeared to vary arbitrarily. This demonstrates a minor instability of the SLS-1, which also might affect the geometrical results of data recording.

In order to evaluate the stability of the Kinect on the basis of system calibration results, 20 photographs were manually taken from different positions and were stored in a log file (protocol of results). This procedure was repeated in a series of five measurements. The intrinsic parameters of the Kinect include the camera constant in x and y-direction (fx/fy) and the coordinates of the principle point (px/py). The results of the series of measurements are illustrated in Fig. 3, which cannot be compared with the series of measurements in Fig. 2.

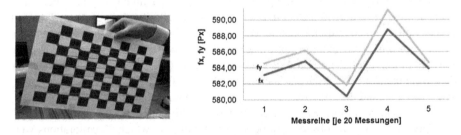

Fig. 3. MS Kinect – calibration pattern (left) and the variation of the focal length (right)

The span of the focal length is up to 10 pixels (see measurement series 3 and 4 in Fig. 3) for all series of measurements, whereby the largest deviation is approximately 3.5 pixels between fx and fy. On the other hand the values of the measurement series 1, 2 and 5 vary only approximately 1 pixel. Exactly the same results were achieved for the coordinates of the principle point. The largest deviation compared to the average value is registered in measurement 4 at approx. 4 pixels. Due to the fact that the values of interior orientation vary substantially despite calibrations under constant laboratory conditions, high system stability can also not be certified for the Kinect.

Investigations with DAVID SLS-1 and MS Kinect have demonstrated that the calibration results seem very arbitrary and are often inexplicable. However, the following measurements and 3D comparisons to reference data show that the differences for small objects are in the sub-millimetre range. Both the camera and the projector of the DAVID system were calibrated. The workflow and the results of the projector calibration are described in detail in [21].

3.2 Repeatability (Precision)

Repeatability (precision) is a criterion relating to the quality of a measuring procedure. It is also called as internal accuracy of a measurement, and is determined by the repetition of measurements. Using a gypsum figure, whose body size corresponds to the usual recording volume (91 mm × 156 mm × 91 mm) of the system, the repeatability of the DAVID Systems was analysed.

In addition, the data capture of the gypsum figure was performed every six minutes during a time period of two hours. These six minutes correspond to the recording time of a real scanning object. In this way 19 different models were computed for analysis in Geomagic, each consisting of approximately 104,000 triangle points. A precision of 0.007 mm resulted from the mean of the average deviations of the 19 difference models. The largest deviations to the master scan (first scan of the SLS-1 is set as reference) of +0.032/−0.041 mm occur after half of the recording time and/or measurement series. In order to guarantee that the master scan meets the precision needs of the SLS-1 (0.2 % of the measuring volume according to the manufacturer specifications), a 3D comparison to the reference model of the ATOS I was generated.

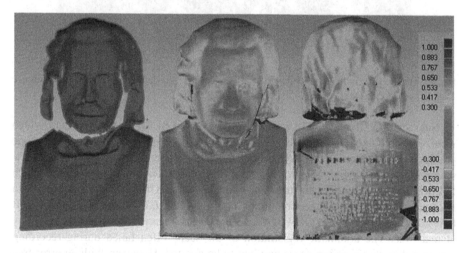

Fig. 4. Deviation between master scan (SLS-1) and scan 10 (left) as well as 3D comparison (centre and right) of both models (green = better than 0.3 mm) (Color figure online)

In Fig. 4 one can see that the average deviations of 0.23 mm meet the precision needs of the SLS-1. The maximum deviation of 1 mm at the edge results from measuring noise or light reflection. This can be ignored for the data analysis, since boundary regions can be smoothed and shrunken by edge operators within DAVID Software to ensure that they do not distract from the finished 3D model. In Fig. 4 (right) the 3D comparison makes it obvious that the generated model shows patch errors (registration of the scans) on the back of the gypsum figure with particularly bad results in the shoulder region where the deviations are up to a millimetre.

3.3 Analysis of Deviation by Comparison with Reference

In order to give a statement about the geometrical quality of the three systems used, the test body "Testy", which was introduced by Reulke and Misgaiski [22], from the Institute for Computer Science of the Humboldt university in Berlin was used (Fig. 5). First, as a reference, the test body was recorded in 52 scans with the ATOS I (17 mm lens) (approx. 225,000 points). In particular, the surfaces of the model in the indentation and in the twist were difficult to scan.

Fig. 5. Test body testy from the Humboldt University in Berlin (left and right) and the reference scan using ATOS I 2M (centre)

Subsequently, the test body was measured with the SLS-1 by twelve scans, which were registered to each other using the David software. During measurement the same problems occurred as with the ATOS I due to the occlusion of certain model areas. The scanning was carried out in approx. 15 min, while the production of a 3D model which followed took 105 min. For the recording with the system Kinect/ReconstructMe, seven attempts on a high performance computer (Intel Xeon CPU E5540 with 2.53 GHz, 12 GB RAM, NVIDIA GeForce GTX 690) were necessary in order to reconstruct the test body in real time. The automatic registration of the scans often failed during recording meaning that the recording procedure had to be aborted. However, with an error free recording process the 3D model of Testy was generated within three minutes. Co-registration as a post-processing step is not possible since the two data records cannot be registered on-line. The acquisition of 54 photos with the Nikon D7000 (18 mm lens) for the image-based 3D reconstruction procedure with Bundler/PMVS2, VisualSFM and 123D Catch was conducted within 15 min. For scaling of the object, two points on the test body were measured with a total station Leica TCRP 1201+. The distance between the two object points was determined with a standard deviation of 0.2 mm. For the subsequent scaling of the different models Geomagic Qualify was applied using the computed distance between the two points. The speed of the subsequent 3D reconstruction of Testy depended upon soft- and hardware. A standard computer (Intel core 2 duo CPU T7700 with 2.40 GHz, 12 GB RAM and a NVIDIA GeForce 8600M GT) needed approx. 60 min with VisualSFM for generation of the 3D point cloud, while with Bundler/PMVS2 a point cloud was produced after 480 min. On the other hand after the photos were uploaded on the server the Autodesk web service 123D Catch needed approx. 10 min to make the computed 3D model available for download. In order to support the measuring algorithms for image orientation by providing appropriate textures in the object background, the photographs were taken after putting the test body on a newspaper (Fig. 5). In post processing triangle meshes were computed in Geomagic using the point clouds from Bundler/PMVS2 and VisualSFM. Finally, all meshed models of Testy were compared with the reference data from ATOS I in Geomagic Qualify. Firstly a rough registration of the five models to the reference model was manually undertaken using identical points. This was later refined using the ICP algorithm with the best fit method. The results of 3D comparisons between the reference model from the high-end system ATOS I, the two evaluated low-cost systems and the image-based reconstruction procedures are represented in Fig. 6.

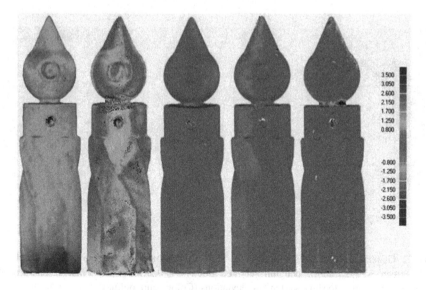

Fig. 6. Generated 3D models of testy in comparison to ATOS I 2M (f.l.t.r.): DAVID SLS-1, MS kinect, VisualSFM/CMVS, Bundler/PMVS2 and autodesk 123D catch (green < 0.8 mm) (Color figure online)

In the results of 3D comparison between SLS-1 and the reference systematic effects (negative deviations) are clearly consistently distributed over the entire body (see Fig. 6 left). It is to be assumed that these systematic deviations are caused by a scaling error in the SLS-1 data. In contrast the deviations between the Kinect model and the reference are unevenly distributed, since the data capture with ReconstructMe was also carried out very unevenly (recording start and stop). However, the models from image-based 3D reconstruction procedures show only very small deviations.

In Table 1 the results of the 3D comparison, which were generated in Geomagic, are summarised. They show that the image-based reconstruction procedures achieved significantly better results for maximum and average deviation as well as for standard deviation as the two tested systems SLS-1 and MS Kinect. Similar good results for image-based reconstruction procedures were shown by Kersten and Lindstaedt [23] for small to medium sized objects in archaeology and cultural heritage.

Table 1. Deviations to reference for the models of the test body Testy generated by different systems [mm].

System/Software	# triangles	Max. dev.	Av. dev. +	Av. dev. −	Std. dev.
DAVID SLS-1	1.650.404	21.5	2.3	1.5	1.5
Kinect/ReconstMe	389.628	15.3	0.9	0.9	1.6
VisualSFM	464.246	2.7	0.1	0.1	0.2
Bundler/PMVS2	405.980	4.0	0.1	0.1	0.3
123D Catch	14.034	5.2	0.5	0.3	0.7

Fig. 7. Generated 3D models with DAVID SLS-1 in comparison to ATOS I 2M – wheel hub (left, green = ±0.5 mm), penguin (centre, green = ±0.2 mm) and Einstein bust (right, green = ±0.3 mm) – to show systematic deviations (Color figure online)

Additionally, three more objects were used for a 3D comparison of the results from the DAVID SLS-1 and the data from the ATOS I 2M (reference). The three objects were composed of different materials: cast iron for the wheel hub, bronze for the penguin, and gypsum for the Einstein bust. These objects were scanned as follows: wheel hub – 70 scans with ATOS, 24 scans with SLS-1, penguin – 70 scans with ATOS, 6 scans with SLS-1, and Einstein bust – 21 scans with ATOS, 17 scans with SLS-1. The results of the 3D comparison are illustrated in Fig. 7 and summarised in Table 2. The difference plots in Fig. 7 show that the problematic surface areas for scanning with the SLS-1 are the edges of the object. Nevertheless, some systematic effects (indicated in blue) are also illustrated in the difference plots.

Table 2. Deviations to reference for the models of three test objects generated by DAVID SLS-1 [mm].

Test body	Size [cm^3]	# triangles	Max. dev.	Av. dev. +	Av. dev. −	Std. dev.
Wheel	23 × 12 × 23	4.057.057	11.1	0.5	−0.7	1.2
Penguin	22 × 46 × 28	2.229.541	16.5	0.2	−0.2	0.4
Einstein	11 × 16 × 10	912.320	−13.6	0.3	−0.4	0.6

3.4 Polygon Decimation

Usually the modelling of object surfaces as polygon networks creates large data volumes, which makes representation of such data on terminal devices with low performance (e.g. Smartphones with 600 MHz processor) or on the Internet problematic. For this reason polygon decimation of meshed 3D models is the solution for such a task to guarantee fast access to the data. Results on polygon decimation of meshed models from terrestrial laser scanning data were already published in [24]. These results showed that one can reduce the data set of 3D models up to 10 % without having significant losses to geometrical or visual quality.

To verify this, the test body Testy was examined in relation to polygon decimation using the data from the DAVID SLS-1. A file size of approx. 120 MB (1.7 million triangles) corresponds to 100 % of the original data recorded for Testy. The percentage of polygon decimation can be defined by the user in the DAVID Laserscanner software. Up to a polygon decimation of 20 % (approx. 290,000 triangles) there is no significant geometrical deviation to the original. However, the visual comparison of the test body reduced to 20 % already shows smoothing effects at edges and at the targets. Nevertheless, the meshed models can be reduced up to 20 % of the volume of data without accuracy losses. The results of the polygon decimation are represented in Fig. 8 for four 3D models of the test body Testy (100 %, 20 %, 6 % and 4 %).

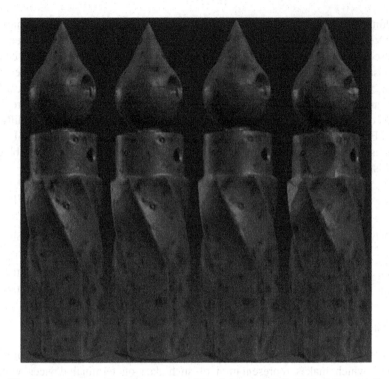

Fig. 8. Results of polygon decimation (f.l.t.r.): Testy 100 %, 20 %, 6 % and 4 %.

4   Conclusion and Outlook

In this paper geometrical investigations under laboratory conditions showed that the two low-cost systems DAVID SLS-1 and Microsoft Kinect generate significantly worse results compared to image-based reconstruction procedures using digital SLR cameras. The 3D models generated from image-based reconstruction procedures are characterized by a high degree of automation and by very good quality. However, the two evaluated low-cost systems offer the advantage of on-line control of completed recording of the object and/or of the object space during the digitization process. On the other hand image-based reconstruction procedures automatically compute 3D point clouds and/or 3D surface models without direct access by the user meaning that gross errors become visible only after the computation from the photos. Nevertheless, the quality of the SLS-1 results corresponds to the accuracy after system calibration specified by the manufacturer (0.2 % of the measuring volume). Unfortunately, no information about the algorithms used in the DAVID Laserscanner software is available to the user (e.g. registration, triangle meshing, etc.). The complete package DAVID SLS-1 is suitable for users who would like to produce digital 3D models with limited accuracy of small objects for various applications and within a short time. A further decisive criterion for the purchase of a SLS-1 is the attractive price, which is 25 times less than for high-end products (e.g. ATOS I 2M). The results of the system Microsoft Kinect/ReconstructMe were better than from the SLS-1; however there is still substantial optimization potential in hard- and software for both systems. Efficient and successful 3D object recording with the Kinect requires repetition and/or practical experience by the user. Thus, several approaches are often necessary in order to achieve a useful result. Furthermore, a good computer with high performance graphics processor is necessary when using Kinect/ ReconstructMe in order to obtain results at all. Generally, this low-cost system offer an economically accessible product for many users for providing contactless 3D object recording for digitization of objects (including in the field of education).

References

1. Hieronymus, J., Misgaiski, M., Reulke, R.: Genauigkeitsvergleich von 3D-Sensoren aus dem Freizeit- und Spielemarkt. Photogrammetrie – Laserscanning – Optische 3D-Mess-technik, Beiträge der Oldenburger 3D-Tage 2011, T. Luhmann/C. Müller (eds.), Wichmann Verlag, Heidelberg, pp. 232–234 (2011)
2. Wujanz, D., Weisbrich, S., Neitzel, F.: 3D-Mapping mit dem Microsoft® Kinect Sensor – erste Untersuchungsergeb-nisse. Photogrammetrie – Laserscanning – Optische 3D-Mess-technik, Beiträge der Oldenburger 3D-Tage 2011, T. Luhmann/C. Müller (eds.), Wichmann Verlag, Heidelberg, pp. 274–283 (2011)
3. Khoshelham, K.: Accuracy analysis of kinect depth data. In: The International Archives of the Photogrammetry, Remote Sensing and Spatial Information Sciences, vol. XXXVIII-5/W12, pp. 133–138 (2011)
4. Böhm, J.: Accuracy investigation for structured-light based consumer 3D sensors. Photogrammetrie – Fernerkundung – Geoinformation, (2), 117–127 (2014)
5. Kersten, T.P., Lindstaedt, M.: Automatic 3D object reconstruction from multiple images for architectural, cultural heritage and archaeological applications using open-source software and web services. Photogrammetrie – Fernerkundung – Geoinformation, (6), 727–740 (2012a)
6. Sablatnig, R., Menard, C.: Stereo and structured light as acquisition methods in the field of archaeology. In: Fuchs, S., Hoffmannm, R. (eds.) Mustererkennung 1992, pp. 398–404. Springer, Heidelberg (1992)
7. Akca, D., Remondino, F., Novák, D., Hanusch, T., Schrotter, G., Gruen, A.: Recording and modeling of cultural heritage objects with coded structured light projection systems. In: 2nd International Conference on Remote Sensing in Archaeology, Rome, Italy, December 4-7, pp. 375–382 (2006)
8. McPherron, S.P., Gernat, T., Hublin, J.J.: Structured light scanning for high-resolution documentation of in situ archaeological finds. J. Archaeol. Sci. 36(1), 19–24 (2009)
9. Bathow, C., Breuckmann, B.: High-definition 3D acquisition of archaeological objects: an overview of various challenging projects all over the world. In: 23rd CIPA Symposium, pp. 12–16 (2011)
10. Smisek, J., Jancosek, M., Pajdla, T.: 3D with kinect. In: Fossati, A., Gall, J., Grabner, H., Ren, X., Konolige, K. (eds.) Consumer Depth Cameras for Computer Vision, pp. 3–25. Springer, London (2013)
11. Mankoff, K.D., Russo, T.A.: The Kinect: a low-cost, high-resolution, short-range 3D camera. Earth Surf. Proc. Land. 38(9), 926–936 (2013)
12. Microsoft: Kinect for Windows® (2015). www.microsoft.com. Accessed 20 Sep 2015
13. David: DAVID 3D Scanner (2012). www.david-laserscanner.com. Accessed 6 Dec 2012

14. Profactor: technology to capture 3D models in real time (2016). www.reconstructme.net. Accessed 21 Mar 2016
15. Garcia, J., Zalevsky, Z.: Range Mapping using speckle decorrelation. United States Patent, Patent No. US 7,433,024 B2 (2008)
16. Snavely, N., Seitz, S.M., Szeliski, R.: Modeling the World from internet photo collection. Int. J. Comput. Vis. **80**(2), 189–210 (2008)
17. Furukawa, Y., Ponce, J.: Accurate, dense and robust multi-view stereopsis. IEEE Trans. Pattern Anal. Mach. Intell. **32**(8), 1362–1376 (2010)
18. Wu, C.: VisualSFM: A Visual Structure from Motion System (2011). http://ccwu.me/vsfm/doc.html#dep. Accessed 21 Mar 2016
19. Courchay, J., Pons, J.P., Monasse, P., Keriven, R.: Dense and accurate spatio-temporal multi-view stereovision. In: Zha, H., Taniguchi, R., Maybank, S. (eds.) ACCV 2009. LNCS, vol. 5995, pp. 11–22. Springer, Heidelberg (2010). doi:10.1007/978-3-642-12304-7_2
20. Tsai, R.Y.: An efficient and accurate camera calibration technique for 3-D machine vision. In: IEEE International Conference on Computer Vision and Pattern Recognition, Miami, USA, pp. 364–374 (1986)
21. Omelanowsky, D.: Untersuchungen der Low-Cost 3D-Aufnahmesysteme DAVID SLS-1 und Microsoft Kinect. Unpublished Master Thesis in Master Study Programme Geomatics, HafenCity University Hamburg, January (2013)
22. Reulke, R., Misgaiski, M.: Test body "Testy" for laser scanning and optical systems. Photogrammetrie – Fernerkundung – Geoinformation, (6), zum Titelbild (2012)
23. Kersten, T.P., Lindstaedt, M.: Image-based low-cost systems for automatic 3D recording and modelling of archaeological finds and objects. In: Ioannides, M., Fritsch, D., Leissner, J., Davies, R., Remondino, F., Caffo, R. (eds.) EuroMed 2012. LNCS, vol. 7616, pp. 1–10. Springer, Heidelberg (2012). doi:10.1007/978-3-642-34234-9_1
24. Kersten, T.P.: 3D scanning and modelling of the bismarck monument by terrestrial laser scanning for integration into a 3D city model of hamburg. In: Ioannides, M., Fellner, D., Georgopoulos, A., Hadjimitsis, D.G. (eds.) EuroMed 2010. LNCS, vol. 6436, pp. 179–192. Springer, Heidelberg (2010). doi:10.1007/978-3-642-16873-4_14

Digital Documentation: Villa Borghese

Martina Attenni[1], Cristiana Bartolomei[2], and Alfonso Ippolito[1(✉)]

[1] Sapienza University of Rome, Rome, Italy
{martina.attenni,alfonso.ippolito}@uniroma1.it
[2] Alma Mater Studiorum University of Bologna, Bologna, Italy
cristiana.bartolomei@unibo.it

Abstract. The knowledge of historical and architectural heritage is today reinforced by the growing use of digital instruments serving the purpose of documenting and disseminating data. The development techniques to build 3D models made them pivotal elements in popularizing information on objects on the scale of architectonic structures. Digital archives supplement 3D models with heterogeneous data (2D models, images, texts, video materials, bibliographical documents) with the purpose to preserve, evaluate and popularize cultural heritage (CH) by devising an open system of knowledge. This study puts forward a critical operative method and some guidelines to record, construct, manage, visualize and navigate 3D models with a view to achieving a full comprehension of the architecture in their own context, permitting to discover their inter-relationships through a digital archive.

Keywords: Villa Borghese · Cultural heritage · Survey · 3D/2D models · Digital archives

1 Introduction

Evaluation and preservation of CH is connected with the innovative processes of gaining, managing and using knowledge. For several years now, data archiving has been a central issue insofar as works of cultural heritage are concerned. It is precisely in this domain that the methodologies of digital 3D models representation were significantly applied. The ever-growing number of digital models as well as the diversity of processes and objects involved impose the necessity to define new modalities for documentation, managing and sharing information. Nowadays the techniques and instruments of digitalization have made possible the large scale production of 3D objects belonging to CH. The main feature that transforms physical objects into digital ones involves the construction of photorealistic 3D models close to geometric, metric, structural, chromatic models geometrically, metrically, structurally, chromatically closely resembling real objects. These models provide a much more articulated and complex representation than others because they can be used as bases to construct knowledge systems. Digital visualization makes possible an integrated interpretation of heterogeneous data and a redefinition of the very concept of representation by linking it to the concept of information. 3D models are the central point as representation of existing artifacts and as metaphors for navigation inside other types of data. This study

© Springer International Publishing AG 2016
M. Ioannides et al. (Eds.): EuroMed 2016, Part I, LNCS 10058, pp. 533–543, 2016.
DOI: 10.1007/978-3-319-48496-9_42

describes an integrated system to record, construct, manage, visualize and navigate 3D reality based models of architectural object into a digital archive. Constructing such a system has to overcome problems of creating a model based digital archive: how to obtain 3D reality based models of objects which are different but homogeneous as to their scale [1], uncertainty level and visualization typology; how to structure the 3D database able to display documentary materials (documents, photos, drawings) digitally; which criteria to apply in order to make the procedure repeatable in case studies with analogous characteristics; the standardization of 3D/2D model. Surveying operations, indispensable when the aim is to construct models of real objects are linked to the characteristics of the case studies analyzed, on the level of detail representation and of communicative aims. In order to address these problems, we defined, a-priori, and verified, a-posteriori, standardized characteristics of 3D and 2D models, able to evaluate both the quality and the fidelity with accurate pre-defined metric standards. 3D models were built with the purpose to identify the architecture and their related resources (images, 2D models, text, etc.) as elements connected with the 3D geometry. Through the recent surveying technologies is possible to obtain models that include all fine details of the original artifact such as a photo-realistic representation of the surface. In recent years there have developed new research areas concerned with the speedy acquisition of data that contain a high quantity of information; use of low cost instruments that ensure results comparable to those obtained with the 3D laser scanner within a single acquisition and restitution campaign. This is precisely the principal area of enquiry of our research, which aims primarily at realizing models obtained through a survey that integrates traditional and low cost methodologies for non-contact surveying. The study seeks to integrate the process of surveying with that of cataloguing by structuring out models obtained through digital photographic images in a documentary archive.

2 Villa Borghese Architectures: Data Capture and Processing

The Villa Borghese covers the area of approximately 80 ha in the very center of Rome. Its construction as a suburban residence started around the year 1606 but today it is an open-air museum containing buildings, architectural complexes, monuments and fountains, all works of outstanding baroque, neoclassical and eclectic artists. The study of the architecture of Villa Borghese started with a careful and detailed cataloguing of existing structures. The park is dotted with elements representing various architectural typologies of grand, medium and small scale. The buildings erected for the purpose of representation function today as venues of cultural events and intellectual activity: art galleries, museum, academies. Others, conceived as forms of embellishing the gardens, have not changed their original function and identify important places in the park like entrances or intersections between main alleys. The present research concerns only objects of the medium scale (entrances or architectural décor) and on the small scale (fountains and sculptures). The choice is related to the experimental aspect of the surveying methodology adopted, considered especially suitable for artifacts of this type.

The survey operation, as a process involving *extensive knowledge*[1], aims at the accurate representation of the analyzed subject and its goal goes beyond the consideration of the technique and the specific instrument, making the ultimate result of this process broader and more amplified. For this reason, drafting a procedure based on the interaction between direct and indirect[2] high cost and low cost methodologies for the elaboration of 2D and 3D models would be a topic of great interest. The definition and managing of the 3D model become the crucial point of the problem for the solution of which it is fundamental to define an operative methodology that could be referred to in a standardized manner. The concepts of data quality[3] and scientificity[4] [2] alongside that of uncertainty control turn out to be fundamental in the processes of acquisition and elaboration. Nowadays the integration of surveying methods has proved to be necessary, and can now be considered a standard practice. It is thanks to this integration that we are capable of understanding the object of study and analysis, in both general and detailed terms. Surveying is thus to be intended as a rigorous methodological process that, through operations of selection, measurement and representation of important points, is capable of describing the geometric-spatial, dimensional and formal qualities of the object of study and, in absolute, allowing for the achievement of the profound awareness of the aforementioned object. Preparing a survey campaign for a huge architectonic site such as the one discussed here obviously entails an initial stage of rigorous planning and analysis in order to optimize the information that is then acquired. This stage must be regarded as fundamental for two reasons: first, because it is precisely the results of this preparatory effort that will provide the material which will be worked on to produce the survey's deliverables; second, because this is the only stage in which the data will have all of the numerical information deriving from the measurement operations, and that can always be used as a critical data as it has not been processed or interpreted in any way. This work discusses the possibilities offered by the integration of heterogeneous methods, traditional and innovative, for massive

---

[1] René Descartes distinguishes between normal knowledge, achieved only by our senses, and profound knowledge, achieved by scholars using only study methods and techniques that can demonstrate to the mind what is precluded to the senses.

[2] All operations that envisage the gathering of knowledge need to have a reference framework both vis-à-vis the data acquisition method (surveying) and the selection, processing and restitution of the acquired data (survey).

[3] Quality is here understood as a description of contingent or permanent properties of an object. It designates any concretely determined formal aspect of a given reality. Thus, a meteorological setting is qualitatively described by an aggregate of parameters that define the characteristic of measure: uncertainty, repeatability, accuracy.

[4] "The stage of data acquisition [...] should always be considered as an application of a scientific method [...] based on a collection of empirically observable and measurable data [...] which can be archived [...] subjected to external verification [...] to be validated; the applied procedure should be replicable in order to acquire a new aggregate of data comparable to the preceding one".

surveying[5] and digital technologies for representation and communication. To optimize data captured at Villa Borghese in surveying campaigns, it was decided to combine different surveying methods and instruments with the objective to control error in order to be better confront problems involved in surveying architectural and sculpture elements of medium and small scale. The study of villa Borghese architecture is based on a process that integrates traditional surveying techniques with those of low cost, non-contact ones. This methodology makes it possible to ascertain that the direct survey control the measurements and the image based modeling[6] techniques the model construction [3]. The experimented procedure was aimed at constructing qualitatively controllable 3D and 2D graphic models where it is essential to define the uncertainty level of the model scale. The surveying procedure yielded a numeric model (point cloud) – an objective datum which avoids conscious schematization done by the operator and is configured as the departure point for further elaborations. The quality of the data obtained with various software which work with this technology has been verified by attributing to each model a scale reference that describes its capacity to reproduce reality digitally in relation to its geometric features and those related to surface qualities. The sequence of works started with data acquisition (surveying) to collect some sets of photographs[7]. It was decided at the outset to proceed with data acquisition applying the same criteria for all the objects analyzed doing general and detailed photo shots with 30 % of overlapping to obtain as full coverage as possible. In order to describe the characteristics of each type of element and to define survey accuracy, tolerances, methods and output the following step was performed for choosing the most appropriate technique taking the following into account: object characteristics (its dimension/volume, size threshold at micro- and macro-scale), material characteristics; capture instrument characteristics (accuracy and resolution required, recovery area dimensions); lighting conditions; presence or absence of lambertian materials; aim of the survey (size and minimum level of detail to be returned). Data obtained were elaborated with Agisoft Photoscan, commercial software to obtain 3D model from photographic images. Data have been processed to reconstruct a low density point cloud that became very dense in the successive phase. Finally, 3D mesh model of the object was obtained with an algorithm called SIFT (Scale Invariant Feature Transform). Photo elaboration with Photoscan ensured the identification of the object's salient points, which made it also possible to control the uncertainty level of metric values, always <3 mm. In the majority of cases we were able to obtain a complete reconstruction of the object overcoming major problems of coverage (Fig. 3). It becomes clear now how the data acquired with different surveying methodologies

---

[5] Technologies that make it possible to capture millions of points on surfaces without the requiste of establish the measured distances. The result of their application differs qualitatively and quantitatively from that obtained with traditional instruments, which always assume the operator's selection of the salient points to measure of the object of study (3D laser scanning, Structure from Motion technology, Gigaphoto).

[6] This technique offers the possibility to generate 3D content from photographic images without the need of high-cost hardware. This technology originates in the theory of photogrammetry and makes it possible to build 3D models on the basis of photographs.

[7] NIKON D300 camera with CMOS sensor of 12 MP.

became comparable and indispensable for a heterogeneous information database structure that yields an ever more detailed rendition of the object analyzed [4]. Data elaboration belongs with the stage of survey. 3D textured models worked out were taken as the point of departure for devising standard 2D models[8]. A low cost survey conducted with quick methodologies enabled us to acquire highly flexible data which could define the characteristic features of the object (its geometry, topology, texture) in geometrical-proportional and architectural drawings, degradation and color analyses. The definition of such 2D and 3D models is the result of considerations prompted by the will to defining a standard for communicating the characteristics of all the objects surveyed in the same manner [8]. The choice is related to the experimental aspect of the surveying methodology adopted, considered especially suitable for artifacts of this type (Figs. 1 and 2).

3 Database Management System

Modeling proved considerably advantageous in the stage of documentation: the output being an informative model which lead to critical interpretations [5]. An information system that divulges connections and links between high definition 3D models and heterogeneous data turns out to be an extensively articulated structure [6]. It must be able to acquire and modify spatial data in order to archive, maintain, analyze and present them in the alphanumeric and/or graphic form. Building up an archive whose objective is to preserve and popularize objects of CH involved some problems in working out the conceptual model, data acquisition modalities, visualization, navigation and access to the contents [7]. The concept of information structured within a database lies at the very centre of the present research. The Archive of Villa Borghese architecture aims at identifying the kind of information of the architectural object and classifying them into distinctive and characteristic categories, which make it possible to cognize the given object. Such knowledge can be achieved only after cognizing the precise geometry of the architectural structure in close relation to other univocal and selective information, concern the structure, construction techniques, the state of preservation and the materials of which the object was built. Moreover, it transcends the metadata[9] generated during the surveying campaign as well as all the documentation collected so far derived from historical-architectural inquiries and surveys conducted on the objects in question. One modality to popularize objects of CH has been

---

[8] Geometric (1:100) and architectural (1:50) plans, elevations and sections.

[9] Metadata, considered as data about data, can help to organize information and provide digital identification and to understand the process through which one or more artifacts were processed or interpreted (The London Charter, version 2.1).

Fig. 1. Cataloging of Villa Borghese architectures. From huge (Buidings) to medium (Monumental entrances, Street furniture, Fontains) and small scale (Monuments).

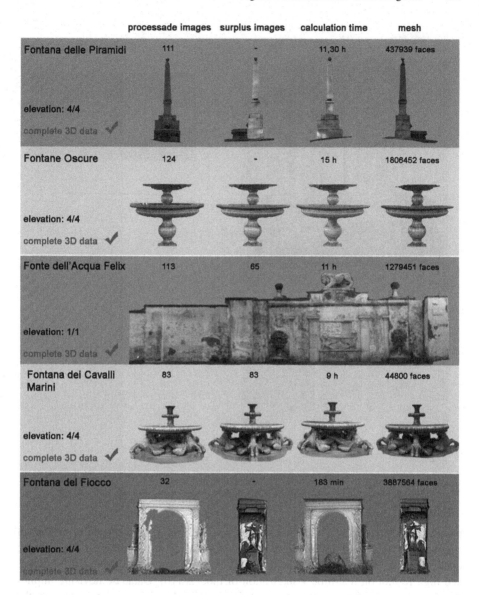

Fig. 2. Cataloging and analysis of obtained results. Software Agisoft Photoscan. Case study: Fontains.

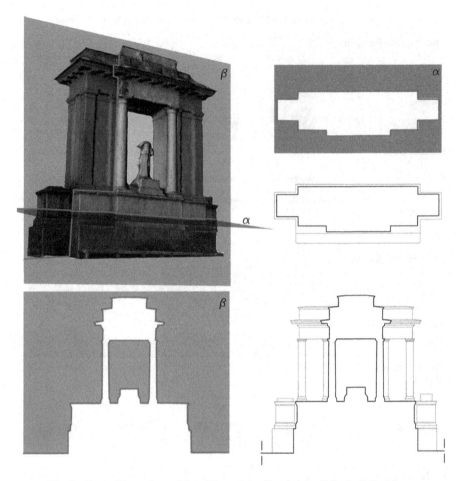

Fig. 3. From 3D mesh model to 2D models. Case study: Edicola della Musa.

provided by software 3DHOP[10] that ensures visualization, with the ultimate goal of sharing and spreading information. It allows data entry by different cataloguers, qualification of 3D models in relation to different levels of detail, semantic structure and high resolution real-time visualization of models [10]. Database devising implies an attempt at answering some questions involved in designing compartments of the informatics system in order to guarantee its use with the passage of time; the ability to sustain diverse formats in order to ensure data integration; connection with

---

[10] 3DHOP (3D Heritage Online Presenter) is an open-source software package for the creation of interactive Web presentations of high-resolution 3D models, oriented to the Cultural Heritage field. It allows the creation of interactive visualization of 3D models directly inside a standard web page, just by adding some HTML and JavaScript components in the HTML code. The 3D scene and the user interaction can be easily configured using a simple "declarative programming" approach, and by a series of provided JavaScript functions (Retrieved from: http://3dhop.net/).

heterogeneous information. It integrates successfully the descriptive aspects with the spatial nature of the real object and their formal characteristics expressed by models. Clicking on the selected part of a model, is possible to obtain a wide gamut of information. Special tables have been drawn up while the database fields and the graphic interface of the web page contains a form for inserting data. These sections are interconnected, so that it is possible to move from one section to another using simple hyperlinks that connect the different areas (Fig. 4).

EDICOLA DELLA MUSA
Litografia di F. benoist, 1870

Costruita tra il 1833 e il 1842, l'edicola è costituita da una basamento in travertino all'interno del quale si trova la statua di Baccante,facilmente riconoscibile dalla pelle di cerbiatto appoggiata sulla veste, nonostante la maschera in cemento l'abbia trasformata in una musa. La statua attuale non è quella originale ma una copia, collocata sul posto nel 1900. Dalla litografia si nota come originariamente l'edicola fosse corredata da due statue poggiate sui dadi in travertino posti lateralmente.

Fig. 4. Structuring digital archive to manage heterogeneous data. Case study: Edicola della Musa.

4 Conclusions

Digital archives are considerably advantageous for disseminating information related to CH: they can be used alongside of or complementary to physical archives; they offer photorealistic visualizations of models of existing objects; they can be used by different clients (specialists, generic) since it is possible to filter the contents; data are ready to be used directly for analyses based on geometric and formal information provided by different representation scale; it is possible to get to know the object completely moving with ease from the general to the particular, from the simple to the complex (and vice versa) by breaking down the objects into sub-components organized hierarchically [9]. Taking advantage of the newest technologies, languages and communication protocols that facilitate information exchange and sharing, it is possible to manage information on a much larger scale as well as construct instruments thanks to which information can be really exchanged and fully shared. Today digital objects have become a tradition in the cultural production and a business cycle with the objective to disseminate and communicate cultural data. The management of CH is linked with the development of new methods of acquisition and transmission of knowledge, and it passes through an ever- increasing quantity and complexity of metadata. The application of ICT to cultural heritage is certainly one of the most interesting frontiers of activity since object characteristics can be extracted from 3D images and models and can be made interactive.

References

1. Bianchini, C., Borgogni, F., Ippolito, A., Senatore, L.J., Capiato, E., Capocefalo, C., Cosentino, F.: From surveying to representation: theoretical background, practical issues, possible guidelines. In: 18th International Conference on Virtual Systems and Multimedia, VSMM 2012, pp. 507–513 (2013)
2. Bianchini, C.: L'approccio scientifico al rilevamento del teatro di Mérida. In: La documentazione dei teatri antichi del mediterraneo, pp. 22–37. Gangemi, Roma (2012)
3. De Luca, L.: La fotomodellazione", Flaccovio Editore, Palermo (2011)
4. Remondino, F., Campana, S.: 3D Recording and Modelling in Archaeology and Cultural Heritage - Theory and Best Practices. Archaeopress BAR Publication Series, Oxford (2014)
5. Siotto, E., Callieri, M., Pingi, P., Scopigno, R., Benassi, L., Parri, A., La Monica, D., Ferrara, A.: From the archival documentation to standardised web database and 3D models: the case study of the camaldolese abbey in Volterra (Italy). In: 18th International Conference on Cultural Heritage and New Technologies, CHNT 18, pp. 1–9 (2014)
6. Minto, S., Remondino, F.: Online access and sharing of reality-based 3D models. SCIRES-IT SCientific RESearch and Information Technology Ricerca Scientifica e Tecnologie dell'Informazione **2**(2), 18–27 (2014)
7. Bartolomei, C., Ippolito, A.: Low-cost cataloguing methodologies for architecture: the system of gates in Bologna. In: Ioannides, M., Magnenat-Thalmann, N., Fink, E., Yen, A., Quak, E., Way, E. (eds.) Digital Heritage: Progress in Cultural Heritage, Documentation, Preservation and Protection, EuroMed 2014, pp. 249–257. Multi-Science Publishing Co. Ltd., United Kingdom (2014)

8. Bianchini, C., Borgogni, F., Ippolito, A., Senatore, Luca, J.: The surveying and representation process applied to archaeology: a quest for invariants in a highly variable context. In: Di Giamberardino, P., Iacoviello, D., Jorge, R.N., Tavares, J.M.R.S. (eds.) Computational Modeling of Objects Presented in Images. LNCVB, vol. 15, pp. 1–29. Springer, Heidelberg (2014). doi:10.1007/978-3-319-04039-4_1

9. Gaiani, M., Benedetti, B., Apollonio, F.I.: Teorie per rappresentare e comunicare i siti archeologici attraverso modelli critici. SCIRES-IT SCientific RESearch and Information Technology Ricerca Scientifica e Tecnologie dell'Informazione 1(2), 37–70 (2011)

10. De Luca, L., Busarayat, C., Stefani, C., Renaudin, N., Florenzano, M., Véron, P.: An iconography-based modeling approach for the spatio-temporal analysis of architectural heritage. In: Shape Modeling International Conference (SMI 2010), Washington, USA, pp. 78–89 (2010)

Digital 3D Reconstructed Models – Structuring Visualisation Project Workflows

Mieke Pfarr-Harfst[1(✉)] and Stefanie Wefers[2]

[1] TU Darmstadt, Darmstadt, Germany
pfarr@dg.tu-darmstadt.de
[2] i3mainz – Institute for Spatial Information and Surveying Technology,
Mainz University of Applied Sciences, Mainz, Germany
stefanie.wefers@hs-mainz.de

Abstract. Cultural Heritage (CH) visualisations have to be understood as a combination of research sources, the contemporary historical and cultural context (Zeitgeist), project background and work process. All available information is collected, consolidated, filtered and assembled into a coherent picture. In case of digital 3D reconstructed models, the result is a digital data set that can be processed for different application fields. They are understood as a result of a complex creative process and as a synthesis of a CH research project, its CH context, the available research source material, and the modeling process itself. For all visualisation types in CH different conditions, factors, and basic rules apply to achieve a high quality result. Two examples are presented illustrating the structured view on visualisation projects as such. This paper seeks to differentiate the various research sources being the basis for digital 3D reconstructed models and defines work phases allowing a quality assessment. Furthermore, the potentials of including this structured view into the ontology COSCH^{KR} currently under development is discussed. In combination with traditional guidelines COSCH^{KR} platform could open up new and flexible approaches.

Keywords: Visualisation · 3D reconstruction · Cultural heritage · Workflow

1 Introduction

Visualisation is "the act or process of interpreting in visual terms or of putting into visible form" [1]. This universal definition encompasses all kind of figurative display (digital and physical) such as 2D images, drawings, paintings, but also 3D representations, 3D point clouds, 3D models, and 3D print-outs. Such kind of visualisations are used within CH disciplines to convey a specific message with respect to a research result which is not clearly visible in the material CH itself since it is e.g. only partly preserved or lost its context of usage. Therefore, a CH visualisation combines facts and interpretations [2]. They are a result of an interdisciplinary, collaborative process in which mostly architecture, archaeology, and the history of art and architecture are involved. However, due to recently evolving digital technologies, more disciplines are involved in this process such as computer science and surveyors.

© Springer International Publishing AG 2016
M. Ioannides et al. (Eds.): EuroMed 2016, Part I, LNCS 10058, pp. 544–555, 2016.
DOI: 10.1007/978-3-319-48496-9_43

Digital 3D reconstructed models (further on "digital models") are used as a new medium in the field of transfer of knowledge since about 25 years [3]. The benefit of these data sets is that various output formats can be chosen depending on the aimed application. In the last decade the application fields and possibilities of these digital models are, however, under discussion: In addition to a transfer of knowledge which very often is only linked to one event such as a film sequence shown in one exhibition, the value of these digital reconstructed models is acknowledged through their application already during research and in a long-term perspective also for preservation and documentation of condition status and processes. As such CH visualisations have to be understood as a combination of research sources [4], the contemporary historical and cultural context (Zeitgeist), the project background and the work process. All available information can be collected, consolidated, filtered and assembled into a coherent picture. In the case of digital models, the result is a digital data set that can be processed for different application fields.

As soon as digital models are not only understood as a mere visualisation but also as a tool documenting the generation process, the project planning and handling of all information gets very complex. The overall aim of all projects creating a digital 3D representation should be to enable a continuous re-use also for later projects. One essential part for this aim is a structured view on such projects creating a conceptual basis. Therefore, in a first attempt this paper seeks to differentiate the various research sources being the basis for digital models and define project work allowing a quality assessment.

2 Definition of Terms

The term "visualisation" summarises in the field of CH various types of display and application. All these types display complex relationships and aspects using a variety of visual media ranging from simple 2D applications to digital models including drawings, 3D point clouds or meshs. Technologies such as laser scanning or SfM acquire or generate 3D data, whereas digital models usually combine heterogeneous data sources including 3D data representing material CH and results from hand-made, artificial modeling processes.

We focus on digital models as they are a result of a complex creative process including various disciplines. As soon as they are used in the context of a CH research project or as a tool to visualise the results of such projects, they have to be understood as a synthesis of the project, its context, the available research source material, and the modelling process itself. For all visualisation types in CH different conditions, factors, and basic rules apply to achieve a high quality result.

Terms such as "computer-based visualisation" and "(3D) reconstructed model" are suggested by Daniele et al. [5] and Denard [4]. The first is defined as "The process of representing information visually with the aid of computer technologies" [4] being a general term for all kind of digital visualisations. And the second is defined as "A 3D model that has been created based on the shape and appearance of a real object. The reconstruction is done either by technological means as 3D scanning (see [Sampled Model]) or by scientific data such as architectural designs and reference images" [5] being more specific and reflecting our understanding of 3D models. It takes the need into account to differentiate the various digital data sets which are used as a supporting tool in the generation of a 3D model or which are integrated in the 3D model. The "Sampled Model" is "A 3D model that has been created through means of digital scanning from a real world existing object. The scanning is done with a device that analyses the real-world object and collects data on its shape and nowadays its appearance" [5]. However, it is also necessary to be able to name those parts of a digital 3D reconstructed model which are not sampled models but are the result of a hand-made modelling process. For these digital data sets we suggest the term "hand-made digital reconstruction".

Furthermore, we suggest adding the following more detailed definition to the above cited definition of the term "digital (3D) reconstructed model": digital models are computer-based models of landscapes, buildings, building structures, material objects and/or structural elements in which the object-based knowledge is gathered, consolidated, compacted and visualised. The consequence of this process is the visualisation of knowledge, why these models are mirrors of recent research and an object of future research; as such they are an innovative and future-orientated tool in the field of research, preservation and transfer of knowledge.

3   State of the Art: Visualisations Through Digital 3D Reconstructed Models

For more than 20 years, visualisations and especially digital models have been applied in the field of CH research [6, 7] merging and visualising object-related knowledge. Being a synthesis of research results, the historio-cultural context, and modelling processes, the 3D data set is used as a basis for a variety of display modes, output and presentation formats in various fields of application [3, 8]. 3D models are mainly used as a visualisation of CH assets in the context of exhibitions [8]. However, they are also present in other media representations such as TV documentaries [9] or web-based applications [10, 11] and affect the image of the past. Through recent technological developments it has become possible that everybody can create such models. However, the evaluation of the scientific quality of these models often remains sidelined [12, 13]. In the current and future field of research, visualisations in the CH domain become more and more important due to their potentials and possibilities of application [8, 14]. This is associated with a number of challenges: issues such as the development of a methodology or process-related guideline or generally applicable strategy and the documentation of the underlying resources and the processes in terms of a scientific justification are present in the current discussion. For digital reconstructed models no solutions are defined, yet [15]. Current topics under discussion on a national and international level are basic principles, methodology, documentation, knowledge representation, and appearance; in Germany a working group "Digital reconstructions" was founded in 2013. The idea is to create a community network on a national level giving the basis for a common understanding on the above mentioned topics.

Two of the above mentioned aspects of visualisation in CH will be discussed in this paper: methodology and documentation. In the area of methodology theoretical studies have been previously carried out. One of the most important results of these studies is, that goal, intention, and application context always belong together and affect the process and result of a visualisation project [3, 8, 16]. First ideas of guidelines are provided by the London and Seville Charter [17].

In the last five years, knowledge evidence of 3D data sets with respect to the development of documentation strategies has become more and more relevant. Projects such as "colonial3D" [18], "Bamberg 4D" [19], and "MayaArch3D" [20] as well as the still ongoing project "Virtual reconstructions in transnational research environments - The portal: palaces and parks in the former East Prussia" [21] and "Toporaz topography in space and time" [22] deliver first approaches to the establishment of spatial virtual platforms combined with the annotation of research sources and process data to the 3D models. For quality assurance it is also necessary to develop a system assisting the reconstruction process. The aspect of usability is one of the most important ones in this context. The system to be developed must be practicable, easy to understand, and developed on the basis of the user needs. Other projects are dedicated to the theoretical discussion of this topic as a basis for the development of a practical documentation system [23, 24].

In 2010, a 4-level system was developed as a documentation strategy, which reflects the complexity of the process and the basics of scientific visualisations [12]: Level 1 is the background of the project which is, the knowledge of the models: project partners, intention, technology, results; level 2 contains the project context, the knowledge that is represented by the models, aside from the knowledge about the models; level 3 defines the data structure including all available research sources and their nomenclature. This should be done individually as every project has its own specifications; level 4 describes the connection of all research sources to the reconstructed model and the final product of a modelling process. The essential point is to document both research sources and hand-made reconstructed models as well as the sampled model. Main decisions and milestones should be depicted. Starting point is the text-based construction description, an overview of the key data on the building with cross references to the so-called source and methods catalogues. In a building's research source catalogue, the research source is assigned directly to a specific object or building of the entire visualisation project, and in the methods catalogue the project is linked to the research sources and the process. This 4-level system reflects a documentation strategy saving the knowledge contained in a CH visualisation project and additionally its modelling process by archiving e.g. interim modelling results.

An important contribution to the theoretical discussion can be found in Bentkowska-Kafel et al. [25]: two necessary aspects "transparency" and "paradata" are discussed in the context of quality assurance of CH visualisation. Both terms focus on evidence of knowledge, sustainability of data, but also the presentation of hypotheses and findings. Nevertheless, the scientific debate regarding scientific quality assurance of visualisations in CH has just started.

4   Structuring the Creation of Digital 3D Reconstructed Models

CH visualisations, especially digital models, and their creation process are influenced by a high number of factors. Analysing 19 CH 3D visualisation projects of three different institutions (King´s College London, University of Sarajevo, Technische Universität Darmstadt), it is possible to define a first framework of such a working process through the identification of similarities and differences of typical processes and methodologies [26].

The following research questions were the basis for the investigation: Are there any similarities between the different workflows and methods? What are the similarities (definition), what are the differences (definition)? What are the reasons for the differences and the similarities relating to context of the 3D model? Are there any dependencies between properties, potentials, and application scope and possibilities? Is it possible to define some general phases of a workflow?

Together with results from earlier studies [12] the following factors influencing the process of 3D modelling were defined: background of the project; context of the project; timeline; involved people; intention/aims of the project (research, transfer of knowledge, preservation); application field; application/preservation format; application possibility; type of 3D visualisation method; technical system/aspects; methodology and steps of processes; results.

Based on this, it was possible to define a framework of a workflow. It consists of four main phases and the background of the project as a general frame. The four project phases are "preparation", "data acquisition", "data processing", and "finishing" [26]. All parameters such as involved people, timeline, intention, expected result, financial condition as well as available research sources and technical systems, which are necessary realising a project, are fixed within the preparation phase. The output of this phase generates the input for the phase "data acquisition" affecting the methods and techniques for generating the data.

The input of the phase "data processing" is based on the results of "data acquisition" and the selected method. Within the 3rd phase the acquired data are used in various ways depending on the project intention and purpose. Both phases are therefore linked as the quality and content of the data sets acquired in the 2nd phase have to meet the requirements of the phase "data processing". Through harmonisation of both phases the entire project benefits. The result of this phase is a digital data set (2D or 3D), which is the basis for the "finishing" phase providing data formats which serve the needs of the application defined by the project aim. Various application fields and possibilities require a great scope of processing the digital data set.

Within and in-between the phases an input-output principle exist determining the next step and the way how work packages (WP) as part of the phases interact (iterative or linear). Actually, this depends on the project background such as the purpose, involved people, available techniques, timeline, and funding. Therefore, the background of the project generates the frame and working process.

Three main milestones exist: The first one is the defined background of the project being the basis and input for all phases and WPs. The second is reached when all necessary data are acquired being an input for the phase "data processing". The third milestone is the digital data set - the digital reconstructed model - available after the data processing phase being the input for the finishing phase creating the result. At the beginning of a project (within preparation phase) it is necessary to define further milestones depending on individual parameters.

The complexity of the work process is particularly evident in the phase "data processing". As examples, the projects "Body and Mask in ancient Space" [27] and "Oplontis Visualisation Project" [28] are described in more detail. The focus of the first project was identifying conditions and actualities of ancient theatre as well as the roll of body and masks in the context of theatres using digital visualisation methods. Within the interdisciplinary collaborative research project, different digital techniques such as 3D scanning, 3D modelling, 3D motion capturing, and rapid prototyping were used. The following different CH visualisation types were applied in a virtual research environment: film sequences, hand-made 3D reconstructions (theatre), sampled models of objects (masks) and characters (actors), 3D point clouds acquired with laser scanners. The process consisted of eight different WPs connected in various ways not following a linear order. It was rather the case that the input or output of a WP fixed single steps bringing out a non-linear working process (Fig. 1).

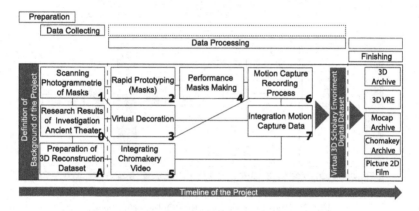

Fig. 1. Working process of project "Body and Mask".

It becomes clear that the various output data that were generated in the phase of "data acquisition" were incorporated in various WPs within the phase "data processing". The digital reconstruction of the theatre as a setting of the subsequent performances of the actors has been resorted to an existing digital 3D model of an ancient theatre. Furthermore, digital 3D models of masks were generated using a 3D laser scanner. The digital masks were again transferred into a physical format through 3D print-outs. The 3D print-outs of the masks were coloured and used by the actors in the simulation of the performance. The performance was recorded by the motion capture process and inserted into the digital 3D model of the theatre.

The entire digital 3D reconstructed model was used to generate various output formats such as film sequences and 2D renderings (finishing phase). This process is characterised within "Data Processing" of the further processing of data in several ways. The WPs were linked in an iterative and linear process, too.

The main issue of the Oplontis project was to bring all research results and bibliographic references together in an interactive, real-time 3D model. This model should be used as a virtual research environment, a documentation of the actual status quo of the research and a systematic multidisciplinary study of Villa A and Villa B at Oplontis. Research questions were e.g. the chronological understanding of the villas, the relation of building and ancient landscape, the function of the villas as well as the social structure of the inhabitants. The following different CH visualisation types were used in the virtual research environment: hand-made 3D reconstructed models (villa), sampled models (3D point clouds).

The workflow of the project Oplontis was non-linear, iterative, and intersecting. Interlinking the single WPs is a very popular workflow (Fig. 2). However, it is also noticeable that within the phase "data processing" the results of different WPs are always a basis for other WPs.

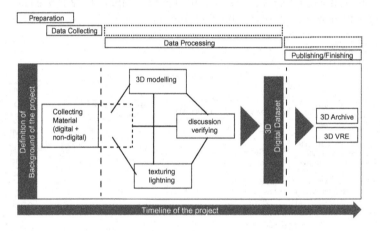

Fig. 2. Working process of the "Oplontis" project.

For most dissemination projects creating digital models, a circular interaction between WPs is observed. Additionally, within the phase "data processing" four tasks can be defined: basic research, 3D modelling, verification, and texturing. The basic research is not limited to the phase of project preparation; in fact it accompanies the entire process. This includes not only the classic source research and evaluation, but also the preparation and processing of digital output data such as 3D point clouds generated e.g. by laser scanners. The 3D modelling together with the verification forms the core of the actual process. A decisive factor is that the 3D modelling needs to be understood as a craft, which is dependent on the modeller, the technical system, and the basics. Through verification the quality in scholarly and content sense of the digital 3D reconstruced model is assured. Additionally, a need for quality assurance within the data processing with respect to technical aspects exists. The texturing usually happens at the end of the modelling process of each singular model being part of an entire 3D reconstructed model. Therefore, the texturing task is interlinked with all WPs.

Between the tasks an input-output principle exists in all directions. The available sources (ranging from 3D point clouds to drawings) are e.g. input for the 3D modelling which produces as output a 3D model. This output in turn is used as input for the verification or texturing task. The output of the verification is a result which in turn can serve as input for the 3D modelling or for basic research.

5 Discussion

By structuring visualisation projects as described above, factors having impact on the entire workflow, content or output are made visible. A more detailed structuring will support the project planning as knowledge gaps between various involved experts will be bridged. Especially the phase "data acquisition" encompassing the digitisation of maps, ground plots etc. as well as the spectral and/or spatial recording of physical objects allows a workflow optimisation as a deterministic connection between the physical characteristics of the object, the capabilities of the recording device and the required data content and quality exists.

Currently, the so-called COSCH^{KR} platform is under development which is intended to give recommendations for spatial and spectral recording strategies with respect to CH objects, CH applications, external influences and required data [29–31]. The COST Action TD1201: "Colour and Space in Cultural Heritage (COSCH)" gives the opportunity to develop such kind of a platform structuring and linking the knowledge of the various disciplines involved in the recording of CH objects as through this Action a European network exists bringing all experts together which are necessary for such kind of a discussion and structuring (conservators, CH experts, engineers, surveyors, IT experts, etc.). The platform envelops an ontology so-called COSCH^{KR} (Knowledge Representation; for technical details see [29, 30]) which is expressed with Web Ontology Language (OWL) [32]. It is a domain ontology with hierarchically structured classes which are interlinked through rules defining dependencies of the technical parameters (such as object size, measurement accuracy etc.) required to set-up a reliable 3D or spectral digitisation strategy for a specific CH application. Due to this intention this domain ontology is completely different to formal ontology CIDOC-CRM developed for archives and museums. It enables the structuring of all biographical information about CH (e.g. provenance). The entire ontology is built-up upon the following five top-level classes: Technologies, Data, CH Application, Physical Thing, and External Influences (Fig. 3). The sub-classes of Technology were created through a global view on expert knowledge [33]. Through logical rules and dependencies a link is established between CH Application and Data requirements which allows exploiting the ontology and retrieving recommendations.

For the definition of the class "Physical Thing" we refer to the CIDOC-CRM class E18 "Physical Thing": "This class comprises all persistent physical items with a relatively stable form, man-made or natural. [...]" [34]. The subclasses and characteristics which define the "Physical Thing" within COSCH^{KR} ontology in more detail are all

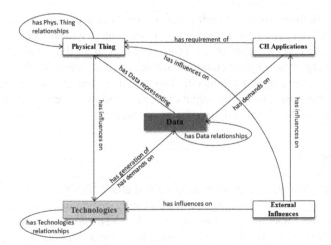

Fig. 3. Top-level classes of the ontology enveloped by the COSCH^KR platform. The classes are linked through rules (arrows) and dependencies.

technology oriented. They describe the physical appearance and shape of a physical thing and do not refer to terms describing their function or purpose in the real world (such as church, fibula, ceramic etc.). To give a short impression on the structure, e.g. the death mask of Tutankhamun would be characterised as a small to medium sized "Physical Thing" (class "Size") with a complex 3D shape (classes "Structure" and "Shape") and a partly highly reflective (gold; class "Reflectance") and partly translucent (glass and precious stone inlays; class "Transparency") surface. With respect to a visualisation project the "Physical Thing" could be a ground plot or the ruins of a building. However, the object which should be digitised has to be put in the context of the "CH Application" and its requirements on the "Data". Each "CH Applications" requires different data quality and content (Fig. 3), e.g. a CH application requires a high spatial accuracy or a high spectral quality. Therefore, the "CH Application" provides a statement of requirements (a) with respect to the "Physical Thing" and (b) with respect to "Data" which are needed for the "CH Application".

"A manner of accomplishing a task especially using technical processes, methods, or knowledge" [35] defines the scope of the class "Technologies" (Fig. 3). Through its subclasses, dependencies, and rules the acquisition and processing of the "Data" with tools required by the "CH Application" are described. Since the ontology so far focuses on spectral and spatial recording and data usage, the classes contain information about spectral and spatial devices, data acquisition and processing. For visualisation projects further digitisation devices including the description of their capabilities would need to be integrated. The generated "Data" (Fig. 3) are digital representations of the "Physical Thing". Its physical characteristics determine the choice of the recording device as they have major influence on the data quality. Furthermore, the acquisition and processing of data is affected through "External Influences" (Fig. 3) such as site illumination, visibility or staff competence.

The scope of the class "Data" (Fig. 3) is understood as "facts or information used usually to calculate, analyse, or plan something" [36]. Its subclasses describe all kind of acquired or processed data including data about the "Physical Thing", e.g. published in a book. As the class "Technologies" also might have demands on the class "Data" it is a 2-way relationship (Fig. 3): E.g. for the generation of digital reconstructed models all kind of source materials might play a role and have to be included in the data processing.

Through the 5 top-level classes all aspects relevant within the two phases of a digitisation and visualisation (data acquisition and processing triggered by the finishing phase) are covered. The intention is to implement mainly the phases "data acquisition" and "data processing" of visualisation projects in the above described ontology (COSCH^{KR}). The essential part is to define and structure the requirements of the phase "data processing" on the acquired data within visualisation projects. E.g. a 3D point cloud used as basis for the spatial dimension of a hand-made reconstructed model does not need a high point density, whereas a high point density with colour information would be needed if the intention would be to integrate the 3D point cloud in the digital 3D reconstructed model. Finally, the COSCH^{KR} platform will be able to give recommendations for the set-up of visualisation projects. On the one hand it will be possible to check if available data sets meet the requirements of the data processing and application. On the other hand it will support the data acquisition (especially 3D data and spectral data), which are satisfying the project's needs.

6   Conclusion

Through the investigation of 19 visualisation projects the interaction between WPs was identified and structured as linear, iterative or both. The differences are a result of the project background. The circular, alternating process is best suitable for projects with a complex content or intention and uncertain research sources. Often questions or queries occur during complex 3D modelling projects that can be answered only in the course of the project in cooperation with all partners. Therefore, it is recommended to use a linear process for less complex digital models containing an easy manageable content with a clear project intention. At the beginning of a project it should be decided on the basis of all available facts and parameters which working process fits best. In the future, the project planning phase could be supported not only through traditional guidelines but also through the above suggested COSCH^{KR} platform.

Acknowledgement. This work was partly supported by COST under Action TD1201: Colour and Space in Cultural Heritage (COSCH). Furthermore, we would like to thank Prof. Dr.-Ing. Frank Boochs and Dr. Ashish Karmacharya (i3mainz) for discussions and support.

References

1. Merriam-Webster. http://www.merriam-webster.com/dictionary/visualization
2. Rizvić, S., Tsiafaki, D.: Interim Report 2012–2014. COSCH WG5: Visualisation of CH Objects and its Dissemination. COSCH e-Bulletin 3, Mainz (2016)
3. Pfarr-Harfst, M.: 25 years of experience in virtual reconstructions - research projects, status quo of current research and visions for the future. In: Giligny, F., Djindjian, F., Costa, L., Robert, S. (eds.) CAA 2014: 21st Century Archaeology: Concepts, Methods and Tools. Proceedings of the 42nd Annual Conference on Computer Applications and Quantitative Methods in Archaeology, pp. 585–592. Archaeopress, Oxford (2015)
4. Denard, H.: The London Charter for the computer-based Visualisation of cultural heritage. Draft 2.1, 7 February 2009. http://www.londoncharter.org/
5. Daniele, F., Alfonsina, P., Mohamed, F.: Terminology, definitions and types of virtual museums. V-must Experience the future of the past. Deliverable report D2.1c (2014). http://www.v-must.net/library
6. Grellert, M., Koob, M., Pfarr, M.: Ephesos - Byzantinisches Erbe des Abendlandes. Digitale Simulation und Rekonstruktion der Stadt Ephesos im 6. Jahrhundert. In: Daim, F., Drauschke, J. (eds.) Byzanz - das Römerreich im Mittelalter: Pracht im Alltag eines Weltreiches. Teil 2,2, Schauplätze, pp. 731–744. Verlag des RGZM, Mainz (2010)
7. Pfarr-Harfst, M., Grellert, M.: 25 years virtual reconstructions - actual challenges and the comeback of physical models. In: Proceedings of Digital Heritage International Congress, pp. 91–94. IEEE Press, New York (2013)
8. Münster, S.: Entstehungs- und Verwendungskontexte von 3D-CAD-Modellen in den Geschichtswissenschaften. In: Meissner, K., Engelien, M. (eds.) Virtual Enterprises, Communities and Social Networks, pp. 99–108. TUDpress, Dresden (2011)
9. Unsere Geschichte: Ostpreußens vergessene Schlösser, project description. www.ndr.de/-fernsehen/sendungen/unsere_geschichte/Unsere-Geschichte-Ostpreussens-vergessene-Schloesser,sendung514286.html and video: www.youtube.com/watch?v=Pxe7YgAEs2w
10. Forschungsarbeiten des RGZM in Ephesos. www.rgzm.de/ephesos/
11. DHOP – 3D Heritage Online Presenter. http://3dhop.net/
12. Pfarr, M.: Dokumentationssystem für digitale Rekonstruktionen am Beispiel der Grabanlage Zhaoling, Provinz Shaanxi, China. TUprints, Darmstadt (2010)
13. Dwarehouse. https://3dwarehouse.sketchup.com/?hl=de
14. Grellert, M.: Immaterielle Zeugnisse – Synagogen in Deutschland: Potentiale digitaler Technologien für das Erinnern zerstörter Architektur. Transcript-Verlag, Bielefeld (2007)
15. Münster, S., Kuroczynski, P., Pfarr-Harfst, M., Lengyel, D.: Future research challenges for a computer-based interpretative 3D reconstruction of cultural heritage - a german community's view. In: Proceedings of 25th International CIPA Symposium 2015 on SPRS Annals of the Photogrammetry, Remote Sensing and Spatial Information Sciences, 31 August – 04 September 2015, Taipei, vol. II-5/W3, pp. 207–2013 (2015)
16. Münster, S.: Interdisziplinäre Kooperation bei der Erstellung virtueller geschichtswiss enschaftlicher 3D-Rekonstruktionen. Springer, Heidelberg (2016)
17. Lopez-Menchero, V., Grande, A.: The principles of the Seville Charter. In: Proceedings of the XXIII CIPA Symposium, Prague, Czech Republic, 12–16 September 2011. http://cipa.icomos.org/fileadmin/template/doc/PRAGUE/096.pdf
18. Colonia 3D. http://colonia3d.de/colonia3d-home/
19. Bamberg4D. https://www.uni-bamberg.de/bauforschung/forschung/projekte/digitales-stadtmodell/4d/
20. MayaArch3D. http://www.mayaarch3d.org/language/en/sample-page/

21. Virtual reconstructions in transnational research environments - The portal: palaces and parks in the former East Prussia. http://www.herder-institut.de/index.php?id=585
22. Toporaz topography in space and time. https://www.fiz-karlsruhe.de/de/forschung/projekte/toporaz-topographie-in-raum-und-zeit.html
23. Kuroczyński, P., Hauck, O., Dworak, D.: Digital reconstruction of cultural heritage – questions of documentation and visualisation standards for 3D content. In: Ioannides, M., Mageanat-Thalmann, N., Fink, E., Zarnic, R., Yen, A., Quak, E. (eds.) Proceedings of 5th International Conference on Digital Heritage. Progress in Cultural Heritage: Documentation, Preservation and Protection, EuroMed 2014, Limassol, Cyprus, 3–8 November 2014, Springer, Heidelberg (2014). http://www.academia.edu/9189049/
24. Bruschke, J., Wacker, M.: Neuartige Werkzeuge für die Entwicklung und Dokumentation digitaler Rekonstruktionen. In: TU Dresden Forschungsförderung und Transfer, TechnologieZentrumDresden GmbH, Industrie- und Handelskammer Dresden, GWT-TUD GmbH (eds.) Dresdner Transferbrief, p. 9. TUDpress, Dresden (2015)
25. Bentkowska-Kafel, A., Denard, H., Baker, D. (eds.): Paradata and Transparency in Virtual Heritage. Ashgate, Farnham (2012)
26. Pfarr-Harfst, M.: Evaluation of selected projects at the Faculty of Electrical Engineering Sarajevo and King's College London. In: Rizvić, S., Tsiafaki, D. (eds.) Interim report 2012–2014. COSCH WG5: Visualisation of CH Objects and its Dissemination. COSCH e-Bulletin 3, Mainz (2016). http://cosch.info/bulletin-3-2015
27. The Body and Mask in Ancient Theatre Space. http://www.kvl.cch.kcl.ac.uk/masks/
28. The Oplontis Visualization Project. http://www.oplontisproject.org/index.php/people/the-oplontis-visualization-project/
29. Boochs, F., Bentkowska-Kafel, A., Degrigny, C., Hauta-Kasari, M., Rizvic, S., Trémeau, A.: Towards optimal spectral and spatial documentation of cultural heritage. COSCH – an interdisciplinary action in the COST framework. In: Proceedings of XXIV International CIPA Symposium 2013 on Recording, Documentation and Cooperation for Cultural Heritage. ISPRS Archives, Strasbourg, France, 2–6 September 2013, vol. XL-5/W2, pp. 109–113. Curran Associates, Inc., Red Hook (2013)
30. Wefers, S., Karmacharya, A., Boochs, F.: I need high-quality data of my cultural heritage object – Development of a platform recommending 3D and spectral digitization strategies. In: Proceedings of the 8th International Congress on Archaeology, Computer Graphics, Cultural Heritage and Innovation 'ARQUEOLÓGICA 2.0' in Valencia (Spain), 5–7 September (2016, in press)
31. COST Action TD1201 COSCH. www.cosch.info/coschkr
32. OWL. https://www.w3.org/2001/sw/wiki/OWL
33. Wiemann, A.-K., Boochs, F., Karmacharya, A., Wefers, S.: Characterisation of spatial techniques for optimised use in cultural heritage documentation. In: Ioannides, M., Magnenat-Thalmann, N., Fink, E., Žarnić, R., Yen, A.-Y., Quak, E. (eds.) EuroMed 2014. LNCS, vol. 8740, pp. 374–386. Springer, Heidelberg (2014). doi:10.1007/978-3-319-13695-0_36
34. Le Boeuf, P., Doerr, M., Ore, C.E., Stead, S.: Definition of the CIDOC Conceptual Reference Model. Produced by the ICOM/CIDOC Documentation Standards Group, Continued by the CIDOC CRM Special Interest Group. Version 6.2, May 2015. http://new.cidoc-crm.org/Version/version-6.2
35. Merriam-Webster, technology. http://www.merriam-webster.com/dictionary/technology
36. Merriam-Webster, data. http://www.merriam-webster.com/dictionary/data

Reconstruction of Wooden "Polish Manor"

Anna Rozanska[1(✉)] and Wojciech Koryciński[2]

[1] Wood Technology Department,
Warsaw University of Life Sciences WULS-SGGW, Warsaw, Poland
annamaria.rozanska@gmail.com
[2] Department of Industrial and Medicinal Plants,
University of Life Sciences in Lublin, Lublin, Poland
wojciech.korycinski@up.lublin.pl

Abstract. Historical manor houses form an important part of Polish cultural heritage. Manors referred to one storey bricked or, more frequently, wooden buildings. The aim of this study consists in a historical, stylistic, structural and functional analysis of Polish manors and in the reconstruction design of a wooden manor house forming part of a homestead in the Museum of Folk Culture in Kolbuszowa.

Keywords: Reconstruction · Manor house · Decorative wooden floors · Parquet

1 Research Aim and Background

The term "cultural substance" often appears in the context of conservation and restoration. In accordance with the definition, it refers to what is constant and remains the same, independently of the changes in its features or external transformations. The term "cultural substance" refers fully to architecture, including the architecture of Polish wooden manor houses. Historical manor houses form an important part of Polish cultural heritage. A publication dated 1659, entitled "A Short Treatise on the Construction of Polish Manor Houses, Palaces and Castles" describes the characteristic features of Polish architecture, taking into account three kinds of residential buildings: manor houses, palaces and castles. Manors referred to one storey bricked or, more frequently, wooden buildings.

The aim of this study consists in a historical, stylistic, structural and functional analysis of Polish manors and in the reconstruction design of a wooden manor house forming part of a homestead in the Museum of Folk Culture in Kolbuszowa.

2 Methods

The restoration design consisted in creating a model (a scheme) for the reconstruction of the manor house. It had to take into account the historic patterns and the typical structures, material characteristics, usage functions, conservation requirements and technologies of manufacture. The reconstruction was based on a systematic method of

© Springer International Publishing AG 2016
M. Ioannides et al. (Eds.): EuroMed 2016, Part I, LNCS 10058, pp. 556–563, 2016.
DOI: 10.1007/978-3-319-48496-9_44

industrial design, following the phases of designing: the analytical phase including programming and data collection (observation, measurements, inductive reasoning), creative phase including analysis, synthesis and preparation (evaluation, judgement, deductive reasoning and decision) and the phase of implementation understood as communication (including descriptions, explanations and transfer) [1]. The restoration design was based on a historical, stylistic, structural and functional analysis of the Polish manor house, taking into account the scope of reconstruction and research concerning the patterns, structures and technologies of manufacture of the manor houses in South-Eastern Poland, both preserved and not.

3   Research Results

3.1   "Polish Manor" as a Cultural and Architectural Phenomenon

A manor homestead is a closed and logical functional layout of elements that are mutually related in view of space and composition. It includes the manor house itself with the access road, outbuildings and other residential structures, as well as farm buildings that often went together with ponds, a network of roads and vegetation: decorative gardens, crops and parks. It also included fences or other elements connecting it with its immediate surroundings. A manor homestead forms an urbanistic whole.

There were two basic types of manor homesteads that developed in Polish lands from the second half of the 16th century till the 20th century. The first one is the practical type, resembling an agricultural farm, with its elements grouped around the central yard. This type, popular since the second half of the 16th century, in the baroque period, limited the domination of manors in the composition. It was transformed under the influence of foreign architectural designs, secular culture and lifestyle, pursuing a more stately, sumptuous appearance and following fashionable trends. Manor homestead transformation was also due to their demilitarisation. The new type was characterised by the domination of the manor house and an axial layout. When feudal castles became obsolete in the 17th century, manor houses achieved a dominant position and started to look similar to palace layouts, just at a smaller scale (e.g. the representative, residential part was reduced to one storey). The type of classicistic manors for middle-income and poorer nobility was developed in Poland in the 4th quarter of the 18th century. Its characteristic features include a rectangular plan without protruding corner rooms, a porch or portico on the axis of the front facade supported by 4 pillars, and a high roof - often a monitor roof.

The great popularity of the Polish manor house as an architectural model is also related to its universal functionality. The Polish manor is a residential building fit for a wide spectrum of users. It is functional - with one storey, often built of wood on a rectangular plan, easy to make, open to modifications or expansions.

3.2   Development of Manor Construction in South-Eastern Poland

The disappearance of defensive elements in the architecture of late 17th and early 18th century was associated with the devaluation of old military and fortification methods;

and in the area of Sandomierz Wilderness, interesting for us, it was also due to the end of Tatar raids. The development of socage estates at that time meant that many new buildings had to be erected - manor houses, outbuildings, administrative buildings and the so called folwarks. They were built on a rectangular plan out of wood - a resource that was easily accessible in Sandomierz Wilderness - and their roofs were covered with shakes. In South-Eastern regions of Poland, 80 % of buildings were built of wood. The manor houses in that part of the country had a hall in the centre (preceded by a porch), whose floor was usually made of bricks and walls covered with lime, while the ceilings were made of sawn lumber or linen. On both sides of the hall there were guest rooms, bedrooms, studies, closets, chambers and oriel rooms (protruding corner rooms). Floors in the rooms were usually made of sawn timber, similar to the ceilings that sometimes were covered with lime. Sometimes there were also linen ceilings in these rooms. They were heated with tile stoves or fireplaces. The timber for doors and windows was cut manually into logs and rather was not planed, and only the boards were sawn in the sawmills. Windows and doors had single wooden wings mounted on hinges or pivots and closed with locks. The outbuildings were constructed in a similar but more humble way. The folwarks (serfdom-based farm estates) also included humble residential buildings with 1 or 2 rooms and a hall, where the servants lived.

3.3 Scope of Reconstruction of Kolbuszowa Manor Homestead

In the 18th and 19th century, in the area of Sandomierz Wilderness and the contemporary powiats: kolbuszowski, leżajski, mielecki, niżański and tarnobrzeski, manor homesteads existed in: Bielice, Chorzelów, Dzikowiec, Kiełkowo, Kolbuszowa, Niwiska, Piskoro-wice, Sadkowa Góra, Trześnia near Tarnobrzeg, Trześnia near Niwiska, Trzęsówka and Wilcza Wola. In Brzeziny, two manor houses were documented with drawings, while the third one (not included in the documentation, so probably the least interesting as to its architecture) has been preserved until today. Those manor houses were used as the basis for reconstruction of a manor homestead that is currently under way in the Museum of Folk Culture in Kolbuszowa.

The scope of manor homestead reconstruction includes the manor house with its front, stately part and a small decorative garden, together with the part pertaining to the farm and the administrator's house (moved from the manor homestead in Rudna Wielka) as well as the granary (moved from the manor homestead in Bidziny) [2]. The plan of the estate had to admit the possibility of further expansion with such buildings as: stable and carriage building, smithy, cowshed, brewery, etc. The design was prepared in three versions made around the main element - a manor house based on the existing manor from Brzeziny. Only the translocation and reconstruction of the manor house assumes that a real building will be recreated. The entire estate is a compilation of elements and features characteristic for manor homesteads, adapted to local conditions. The part pertaining to the farm will be shown through the relocated: farm manager's house, granary and in the future other buildings, grouped around the yard. This part is connected to the manor part through a crop garden. The manor part has an axial layout (that was popular in the 18th and 19th centuries independently of the region) with an access avenue, a round lawn surrounded by the driveway, the manor house, a French garden with symmetrical planting beds and a less formal garden.

3.4 Description of the Reconstructed Manor House

19th century publications contain detailed descriptions of countryside cottages of that region. Cottage layouts are discussed in detail together with the materials of manufacture, the types of foundations, floors, wall structures, wall protection, ceilings, kinds of doors and windows, roof structures and covering materials, galleries, porches and stoves. They also enumerate and describe non-residential buildings such as: barns, granaries, stables, cellars, lumber mills, carriage houses, horse mills, sheds, pigsties, chicken houses, dovecotes, wells and windmills. We can also find there synthetic descriptions of the settlements on these lands, as well as plans of local farms. The topic of decorations and ornaments is also discussed there, including flower gardens, orchards and fences around the cottages. Nonetheless, 19th century texts do not contain any information about the manor homesteads in that region, although sometimes manor facades, cross sections and plans are published, suggesting large building volumes.

We can only deduct from those publications that Polish manor houses were usually built of pine or fir wood, using the popular log house technique. Especially sumptuous buildings were made of larch. On the corners, the logs were connected with interlocking notch joints. After World War I, dovetail joints started to appear, perfect for smooth walls required to apply boarding, which was very popular at that time. The posts at log connections in very long walls had grooves, similarly to the vertical jambs of doors and windows.

The wood used in building construction in Brzeziny was taken from the Brzezinski forest and its diameter could reach 20 in. (12 in. on average). It was used in the form of logs with round or square section, cut with axes or hatchets due to the better durability of those tools in comparison with saws. Only boards and planks were sawn. Manor houses, similarly to cottages, could be built on foundations dig in the ground and made of very thick trees that served as support for the first log of each wall, much thicker than the other ones, creating the frame of the sill plate. In order to protect the building against sinking into the ground, oak rootstocks with bark (but also pine or fir saturated with resin) or stones were placed in the ground on hard rock under the house corners. In this case, the sill plate had to be replaced every couple of years. This is why, due to swampy or at least wet ground, proper foundations started to be built some time later. At the beginning, they were made of stones taken from the fields that were simply loosely placed under the sill plates, while the corners were supported by rootstocks dug into the ground. The usage of stones was limited due to local superstitions and the fact that rootstocks gave better stability in boggy areas. Also stone and brick foundations started to appear, made of irregular stones bound with mortar with one layer of bricks placed on them (and two layers under the gable walls). The bricks, connected with mortar, were placed in two layers, with their narrower and longer surfaces facing outside, and the sill plate was placed directly on top of them. Under the corners, bigger stones or locally produced cement blocks were placed. The third type of foundation was made of regularly shaped mortar bound stones. On top of them a layer of bricks was often placed, and on them - rarely - tar paper insulation. In houses built on slopes such high stone and brick foundations were used as cellars. Countryside cottages usually did not have floors, only logs longitudinally cut in halves in the part of the dwelling room devoted for cattle. The first floors appeared in those buildings at the end of the 19th century and were made of planed, unpainted planks placed on round beams with their top side cut, lying directly on scattered sand. In manor houses, floors were made of beams covered with planks, while in more stately (richer) buildings sometimes panel parquets could be found already at the end of the 18th and beginning of the 19th century.

The manor house from Brzeziny is a wooden, one storey building with a non-habitable attic, hip roof with jerkinheads, without cellar and built on a bricked foundation (Fig. 1). It was built using the log house technique, with dovetail corners, on the plan of a rectangle (dimensions: 21.75 m × 17.63 m), porch on the front and veranda/gallery on the garden side. The building is quite big, with seven axes and two rows of rooms. On each of its longer walls there are six-seven high, two-wing, symmetrically placed windows with jamb structure. At the shorter walls on the garden side with two two-wings windows, foundations of protruding corner rooms were found. The corner rooms were accessed by one-wing doors that have been preserved only on the side of the northern current kitchen. Each window wing is divided with horizontal structural battens (muntins) into six square glass panes.

Fig. 1. Brzeziny manor house overview [3]

The section of the manor house shows the structural features of the building. Both external and internal walls have log structure, while the core of the manor (the chimneys and the central part of internal walls) is bricked (Fig. 2). The wall is connected with the log structure by gradually sliding on the subsequent logs. Wooden parquets were placed on joists lying on the sand. The beams supported boarding or very decorative wooden panel parquets (of the Versailles type), whose patterns developed together with new developments in interior design. Wooden ceilings are made of planks placed on top of the beams that, in all the rooms, are placed transversally to the longer side of the rectangle, supported by binding joists. The visible ceiling beams are decorated with chamfers. The ground floor is 3 m high (from floor to ceiling) and the attic 4.75 m. The hip roof with jerkinheads, with two-tier collar beam structure and crown posts, was probably covered with shakes. This is deducted from dense roofing battens (used to install the boarding) on the rafters. The rafters had sprockets supported by the protruding ends of ceiling beams that changed the roof slope angle and elongated the eaves that protected walls against water stains. The porch was covered with a saddleback roof with boarding on the gable, and the gallery covering continued the line of the roof slope.

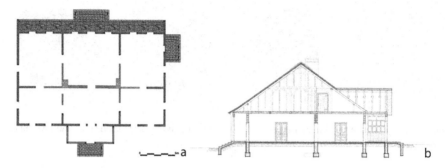

Fig. 2. Functional layout (a) and section (b) of Brzeziny manor house [3]

3.5 Room Functionality

The above-mentioned two-wing entrance door leads to a spacious Hall (Fig. 2). Another two-wing doors lead from the Hall to side rooms of the front row of rooms on the left and on the right. On the main axis, there is a two-wing door leading to the most stately room of the manor, which could be a dining room or a living room. From the Dining Room one may pass through a two-wing door to a side room of the garden row on the left, and on the right to the kitchen that was recently installed there. The side rooms of the front row and the garden row can be connected with one another.

The functional layout of the manor house is clear and logical. It is an enfilade layout with two rows of rooms. The Hall is in the middle and behind it there is the dining/living room - the centre of life in the manor. The rooms placed on the axis that starts with the porch lead us further to side rooms.

Two doors in each room facilitate the circulation of traffic inside the manor house. Initially the protruding corner rooms connected on both sides to the side rooms of the garden row probably contained bedrooms. Their remains can be seen in the shape of the foundations of the corner room and the door opening closed with bricks on the Southern wall, as well as the one-wing door opening that has been preserved on the Northern side.

3.6 Study of the Patterns and Structures of Wooden Floors

The manor house in Brzeziny was definitely created in accordance with a perfect symmetrical plan, stressing its representative function. The manors could be more or less sumptuous, depending on the ambitions or the social status of their owners, or on the architect. The decorative parquets that have been preserved in the Witkowice manor house, located nearby, include a representative rosette in the Banquet Room, evoking the style of rich piano nobile parquets of the neighbouring Łańcut Castle. The parquets preserved in two other rooms in Witkowice have a more practical character, although some aesthetical ambitions can be seen in them as well (Fig. 3).

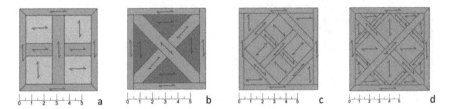

Fig. 3. Parquet patterns in manor houses in: Witkowice (a and b), Bieżdziedza (c) and Dydnia (d); scale: 1:100 mm

The manor in Kolbuszowa is a typical wooden manor of late baroque, built in the 18th century, with a traditional layout of room functions (apart from the kitchen that was introduced at the end of the 19th century). The stately rooms of the garden row should have more sumptuous, decorative parquets. The side rooms of the front row should have more humble decorative parquets. The last room of the garden row that has been changed into a kitchen can receive a wooden "frieze" (with a pattern of squares made of planks and battens) that will be both practical and decorative.

4 Summary

The patterns of high-class architecture passed to vernacular architecture with certain delay. In existing manor houses, the shape of the building would be transformed and improved, exterior walls would be covered with boarding and interior design would be changed, covering the ceiling beams with a stylish lower ceiling (planks on the bottom part of the beams), placing wooden panelling on the walls and changing parquet patterns. Nonetheless, considering that manors had sentimental value for Polish nobility as the seats of their families, their attachment to tradition and respect for the creations of their ancestors limited the interventions in the shape of those buildings. On the other hand, interiors were often modified, in order to follow the most fashionable trends in architecture. In Polish manor houses since the beginning of the 19th century, panel parquets and even decorative rosettes (e.g. Witkowice Manor) started to replace parquets made of boards or boards organised in a pattern of squares separated with battens (the so called frieze floors).

As a result of the introduction of collective property and the appropriation of manor houses after World War II, the interior furnishing was irreversibly destroyed. At this moment, only iconographic materials can show us the richness of many of those houses. There is an urgent need of stock-taking and documenting the buildings that have been preserved, as well as reconstructing the non-existing buildings together with their interior furnishing. This problem is also very important due to the ongoing deterioration of the interiors of historical buildings caused by continuous usage, changes of owners and refurbishment works [4, 5].

References

1. Archer, B.L.: Systematic method of industrial design. In: Biblioteka Wzornictwa, Vol. 7. Instytut Wzornictwa Przemysłowego, Warsaw (1987)
2. Fortuna-Marek, A., Gliwa, A., Potera, B.: Manor homestead as a functional layout and its realisation in the Ethnographic Park of the Museum of Folk Culture in Kolbuszowa. Biuletyn Muzeum Kultury Ludowej w Kolbuszowej **1**, 113–141 (2009)
3. Sobolewski, H.: Detailed Design for a Manor Homestead - Brzeziny Manor House, Rzeszów (2014)
4. Rozanska, A., Burawska, I., Policińska-Serwa, A., Koryciński, W., Mazurek, A., Beer, P., Swaczyna, I.: Study of antique wooden floor elements of chosen buildings from south-eastern Poland. In: Proceeding of the 8th International Conference on Structural Analysis of Historical Construction SAHC 2012, Wrocław, Poland, 15–17 October 2012
5. Rozanska, A., Sudol, E., Wierzbicki, J., Mazurek, A., Beer, P.: Antique wooden floor construction solutions and the possibilities of using them in reconstructions. In: 2nd International Conference on Structural Health Assessment of Timber Structures (SHATIS 2013), Trento, Italy, 4–6 September 2013

Project Paper: Heritage Building Information Models (HBIM)

Digital Tools for Heritage Preservation and Enhancement

The Integration of Processes and Technologies on 20th Century Buildings in Brazil and India

Luca Rossato[✉]

Department of Architecture, University of Ferrara, Ferrara, Italy
rsslcu@unife.it

Abstract. Currently the 20th century architectures are all over the world in danger and under attack: these buildings (in many cases designed by international renowned professionals) are facing a silent destruction. Day by day they are slowly modified in terms of materials, volumes, colours or even demolished. These architectures are still used for public purposes or as residential buildings but they are usually in bad conditions and their state of materials conservation is quite poor. This on-going research explores in depth the possibility to preserve and valorize modern heritage in Brazil and India by the integration of 3D tools, processes and technologies in order to face the future preservation challenges. Soon after the research process the main topics of the project were evaluated and studied to create the bases for a structured research path. In parallel the case study assessment was able to identify suitable buildings (both in Brazil and India) on the which the chosen topics are now being applied in order to improve the knowledge on the design process and reach a guidelines proposal for the preservation and enhancement of these architectures.

Keywords: 20th century architecture · Modern architecture · 3D tools · Technologies · Heritage enhancement

1 Subject of the Scientific Research

1.1 State of the Art

The global research on modern architecture started few decades ago but it has already involved many historians, academics, curators, writers, archivist and journalist: people who lent their knowledge and time in order to better understand a miscellaneous phenomenon. In this wide research field the global exchange of architectural ideas and forms over the 20th century is an important characteristic to be highlighted which came from the geographical movements and migrations of architects and engineers.

Modern buildings are apparently less sensitive to minor changes as those of earlier historic periods. To preserve this massive built heritage it is essential to understand their history and fundamental design principles. If we really want to cure the buildings diseases, like doctors do, we should know the anamnesis of patients, their background

© Springer International Publishing AG 2016
M. Ioannides et al. (Eds.): EuroMed 2016, Part I, LNCS 10058, pp. 567–578, 2016.
DOI: 10.1007/978-3-319-48496-9_45

and causes of illness. The design of windows, for example, often is the most interesting part of their architectural characterization. Modern buildings are, for their concepts, shapes, materials, perfect case studies to explore the integration of 3D technologies and heritage conservation (and valorization toward the transmission of knowledge to future generations).

The design of windows, for example, often is the most interesting part of their architectural characterization[1]. Modern buildings are, for their concepts, shapes, materials, perfect case studies to explore the integration of 3D technologies and heritage conservation concepts.

Despite the wide range of modernist buildings in global south countries (previously known as developing countries), architecture history books focus on the Western scenario of this style. As stated by Lu (2010, p. 1) "with the exception of the work of a very small number of acclaimed architects, little attention was devoted to modern architecture in third world which was considered merely lesser forms of Western modernism".

1.2 Anthropological Background

The research on the strong relation between the new modernism principle influence in South America and Asia and the anthropological effect on local societies and styles could help to better understand this tangible (and also intangible) heritage toward its preservation and enhancement. A more anthropological approach is needed to identify the transcultural principles underlying the design of modern buildings in India and Brazil: as recently stated by the Italian sociologist Domenico De Masi, these are currently the last two countries bringing a sort of humanism within their deep cultures. On the one hand Brazil is the land of the corporal humanism due to its image of "country of happiness", where things are very often related to the curves of human body (for instance Oscar Niemeyer architectures[2]), on the other hand India is the country of spiritual humanism, a place where souls and thoughts merge and spread out a sense of deep personal involvement in every visitor[3].

Transformation/adaptation process on modernism buildings in Brazil and India could be defined as a kind of architectural transculturation phenomenon. The term transculturation has been coined by Cuban anthropologist Fernando Ortiz in 1947 to describe the transition process of merging and converging cultures. Transculturation does not consist merely of acquiring another culture (acculturation) or of losing or uprooting a previous culture (deculturation). Rather, it merges these concepts and additionally carries the idea of the consequent creation of new cultural phenomena (neoculturation)[4].

Brazil and India have strong relations with migration influxes or outflows that influenced local art and culture. Also the architectures of this countries have always reflected

---

[1] Macdonald (1996).

[2] Philippou (2008).

[3] De Masi (2014).

[4] Ortiz (2002).

this views, especially the ones from the twentieth century buildings designed by the great masters of modernist architecture in a period of incredible flow of ideas and concepts and sharing of cultural backgrounds.

In this wide scenario the nationalist movements coincide with the modernist architectural thinking and the promotion of an international style. Architects responded to the increasing challenges in different ways, some employed technological innovations, others got inspired from vernacular solutions to design regional interpretations modern architecture principles[5].

2   Methodology

The research is exploring by deep study 3D technologies for the heritage conservation, highlighting the current state of art, opportunities, processes and possible future challenges.

The research themes are:

- Twentieth century architecture framework in India and Brazil
- Documentation processes and technologies

The Research process is based on the evaluation of:

- Architects migration flows and related transculturation phenomenon
- Materials of modern architectures in Brazil and India
- Preservation framework on modern architectures in Brazil and India
- Digital archives and database use for heritage enhancement
- 3D modelling for documentation
- Non-invasive technologies

In selection process the main topics of the research project were evaluated and studied in order to create the bases for a structured research path. In parallel the case study assessment identified suitable buildings as possible case studies. The main selection process steps were:

- Selection of case studies (200 buildings analyzed)
- Selection of the most suitable topic to be applied on case studies

In application process the chosen topic are currently being applied to the most suitable case studies in order to reach a design proposals guidelines based on local context and environmental issues. The research main topics are:

- Data sheet and representation techniques (applied on 80 buildings out of 200)_Sect. 3.1
- BIM approach (applied on 20 buildings out of 200)_Sect. 3.2
- 3D laser scanner survey (applied on 3–4 buildings out of 200)_Sect. 3.3

---

[5] Lang et al. (1997).

The innovative building materials and structural systems of these modern architectures are at the same time warts and all. On one hand modern architects were brilliant and very creative on the other they not always had enough knowledge on the nature and behavior of new materials.

This research could actually help towards the creation of local management plans that could guide long-term maintenance of buildings and the transmission of modern design principles (Fig. 1).

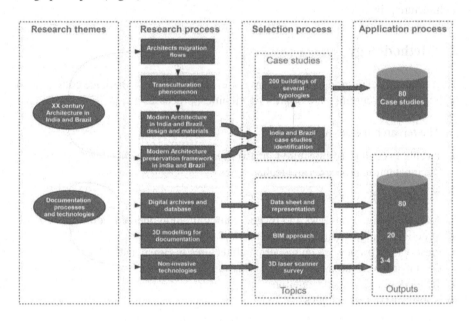

Fig. 1. The research methodology

3   An Heritage in Danger: Topics Application

3.1   Representation Techniques: The Redrawing Process of Modern Architecture in India and Brazil

If time has slowly switched off the power of the transformer dreams of modernist architects, their buildings are a legacy of extraordinary value that should be protected and enhanced as it is a collection of real lessons of architecture. For this reason, the in-charge teachers of the course of Techniques of Architectural Representation (TRA) a discipline of the second year of Architecture Curriculum at the Department of Architecture of the University of Ferrara, decided to analyze by different groups of students the heritage built in the vast and heterogeneous Indian and Brazilian contexts.

In 2016, for the third consecutive year, through the works of the greatest architects of the period it is possible to browse an important slice of history of architecture, passing by the national identity search for specific local features, an architecture that is eclectic, hybridized, which addresses the theme of living, of dwelling, with a completely new and varied language of a different symbolism from that of the past, redesigned with poetry and sharpness.

The use of drawings in order to carry out analytical reviews of the archival heritage of 20th century architectures in India and Brazil can reveal design experiences that reflect the different territorial contexts from which they emerged and the cultural forces behind them. The so called "survey of the project" was the adopted methodology: by analyzing and redrawing the original documents using innovative graphic layouts the research can highlight the potentials of these built heritage.

The aspects taken into account in this phase describe the complexity of the study and the need of well-structured data. The process led to a very good understanding of the designer's work by the interpretation of original drawings, scheme and pictures, that reveal the design process behind the construction.

The deep knowledge of the buildings, carefully selected and analyzed with a precise methodology and representation techniques, had as outputs an exceptional variety of ideas for further research and reinterpretations. For example the study of demolished modern buildings or the reconfiguration of different design hypothesis for the most important buildings of this period (Fig. 2).

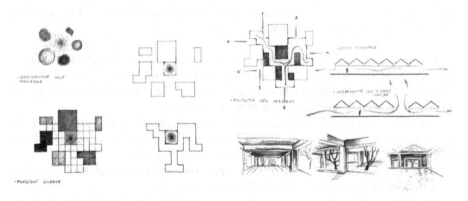

Fig. 2. Redrawing and understanding the modern architecture: Gandhi Ashram in Ahmedabad by Charles correa. Research and drawings by A. Sousa, I. Bulgaru, M. Abdelhaj

3.2 BIM Approach: Modelling Ramkrishna House House in Ahmedabad, India, by Charles Correa

The elaboration of digital models by Ferrara University Architecture Department staffs has gone through a careful planning and guided process in the field of BIM (Building Information Modeling), a virtual three-dimensional space in which each component can be called full-scale, integrating all information related to the geometry with details concerning the materials employed, the phases of realization, costs, technical charac-teristics, and by linking the building with environmental factors (Fig. 3).

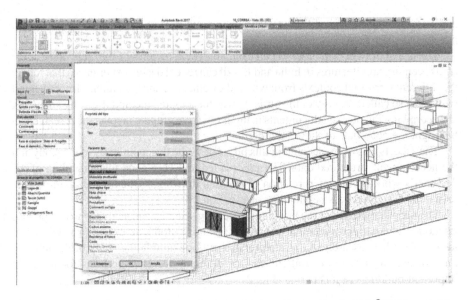

Fig. 3. Ramkrishna House in Ahmedabad, by Chalres Correa, Revit 2017® BIM model by E. Ranuzzini, O. Ballardini, D. Felloni.

In this framework, the Development of geometrical single-disciplinary Building Information Model (BIM) of the Ramkrishna House in Ahmedabad gave to research team basic shared knowledge of the data harvested from the documentation analysis and it will help to manage all information about the building.

The house, designed by Charles Correa, presents parallel walls which form the backbone of its plan, a structure divided into 4 main zones: living areas, guest rooms with private garden, service area and bedrooms on the upper floors.

Built between the 1960 and 1962 the house explores the ideas related to dwelling issues in India in strong relation with climate challenges[6].

The BIM model of this architecture has been created taking advantage of the documentation research on Charles Correa drawings. The picture of the original construction were thus utilised in order to study the materials framework. Beside being a strong base spatial research and study by this model was also used in order to create a virtual reality (VR) model. Software as V-Ray use a proprietary stereoscopic rendering camera to generate a 3D environment with existing Revit cameras, lighting and materials. With this environment it was so possible to generate photo-realistic images of the Correa project to give to the public a sense of what the house look like by creating a VR "map" of a building inside and out (Fig. 4).

The key passages of the BIM creation were focused on: acquisition of building data, integration of other sources of information able to describe the built heritage, definition of reference geometries for architectural components, development/detailing of the

---

[6] Scriver and Srivastava (2015).

Fig. 4. Ramkrishna House in Ahmedabad, by Chalres Correa: original pictures (left side) and photo-realistic views (right side). Rendering by E. Ranuzzini, O. Ballardini, D. Felloni.

building as 3D digital reconstruction, and implementation of instruments for the exploitation of the model between valorization and management.

The advantages associated to the approach proposed concern the flexibility of the instruments adopted, the quality of the results obtained in terms of precision and level of detail, and the possibility of communication between the product developed and other solutions oriented on the exploitation of the building through the model.

The final output of this 3 years BIM research highlighted a strong synergy between building management and valorization approaches through the workflow. Future perspectives of this scenario are related to the diffusion of accurate methods for the acquisition of building data and the development of 3D models. Building Information Modelling methodology is increasingly penetrating into building design. Currently laser scanning appears to be the ideal solution for data acquisition on existing buildings. It allows the quick and precise high definition capture of 3D data. The challenge here is to create a parametric 3D BIM model from the precise depiction of the real world, in the form of a point cloud. For instance point snapping allows the precise remodelling of the point cloud regions with 3D BIM elements.

This diffusion may bring a wide and common evolution, influencing management strategies of cultural heritage currently adopted in India and Brazil with the optimization of management strategies and improvement of knowledge on modern heritage.

3.3   3D Laser Scanner Integrated Survey of Casa das Canoas, by Oscar Niemeyer, Rio de Janeiro, Brazil (1951)

Designed by Niemeyer in 1951 as his family home, Das Canoas House is considered one of the most significant examples of modern architecture in Brazil and is well recognized by specialists in art history as a synthesis of modern architecture and authorial self-creation that flourished in Europe and in America (Fig. 5).

Fig. 5. Casa das Canoas (Rio de Janeiro) by Oscar Niemeyer

The most interesting feature is the fusion of organic architecture and minimalist architecture. As it is an obvious tribute to the Farnsworth House, Das Canoas puts geometric regularity in crisis, but does not alter the formal purity. From Mies design to Niemeyer's Das Canoas, its possible to see the evolution of reinforced concrete into a modern building material[7].

The house is currently facing bad problems of materials deterioration and lack of maintenance. Main degradation issues are vegetation, that is growing very fast on external walls and on horizontal surfaces due to the local climate; structural, because part of the house is slowly moving towards the hill slope and an intervention need to be urgently planned; big cracks cross the bedrooms ceiling and rain water is leaking inside the house, plaster is becoming very fast darker and weaker; swimming pool pavement shows cracks and deterioration and further analyses are required to better understand the causes of this problem; great geological instability of the slope subject to strong storms is a serious degradation factor.

The documentation of the architectural masterpiece by Niemeyer has been intended priority to analyse the current condition and the state of conservation of the building, which currently suffers from a lack of maintenance. The integrated survey was carried

Fig. 6. Casa das Canoas: points cloud section CAD ready for architectural drawings

---

[7] Weinstraub and Hess (2012).

out by the DIAPReM centre at Ferrara University and started from the architectural analysis: Oscar Niemeyer's ideologies in terms of society, politics and architecture had formed a unique style, which he expressed to the full in the architecture of the house at Canoas, which in itself was a remarkable achievement of Modernist architecture (Fig. 6).

The documentation of the architectural masterpiece by Niemeyer has been intended priority to analyse the current condition and the state of conservation of the building, which currently suffers from a lack of maintenance. The integrated survey was carried out by the DIAPReM centre at Ferrara University and started from the architectural analysis: Oscar Niemeyer's ideologies in terms of society, politics and architecture had formed a unique style, which he expressed to the full in the architecture of the house at Canoas, which in itself was a remarkable achievement of Modernist architecture.

The "reading" of the architecture composition focused three main themes of investigation: the shape of the space and its three-dimensional use, the study of the relationship between architecture and sculpture and the visual connections between interior and exterior, the relationship of architecture with the surrounded green landscape (Fig. 7).

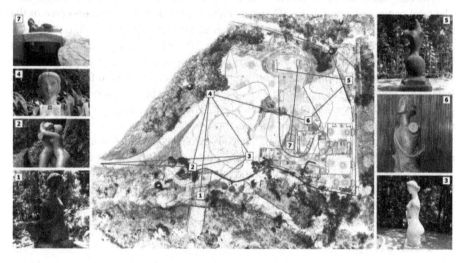

Fig. 7. Locations of main sculptures on point cloud plan and their relation with the Casa das Canoas' main openings

Niemeyer adopted this idea and throughout his career he not only designed sculptural buildings, but he also insisted for the right sculptures and paintings to go with them. In the Casa das Canoas are placed sculptures by his friend Alfredo Ceschiatti. For the first time a 3D survey with this level of detail (3 mm) allows to identify new ways of "reading" and cross interpretation, such as the triangulation perspective between the artwork placed by Oscar Niemeyer into the enclosed and not enclosed space. Thanks to the detailed data capturing it was possible to identify the axes of relationship that develop from the placement and orientation of the female bodies to encourage to share the environmental and architectural experience.

An integrated survey methodology was applied in order to obtain set of data to be critically analysed to examine in depth the research themes on the architecture by Niemeyer (Table 1).

Table 1. Main data of the instrumental survey campaign.

Total station	Leica TS06
Matched targets	53
Polygon vertexes	7
3D laser scanner	Leica C10
Number 3D scan stations	128
Acquired targets	142
Point cloud coordinates	1.717.862.695
Work schedule	10 days (about 75 h)

The integrated survey project involved 10 days on field working, about 8 h per day. The total computed area for the 3D survey campaign included the external area of the house and the garden. This is because the landscape project was an essential part of the overall design process by Oscar Niemeyer. The 3D survey has been carried out with Leica C10 Laser Scanner (Lidar technology) and topographic survey was performed by Leica Total Station TS06 plus 2″. Topographical main connection to the network and framework, consisting of a polygonal closed or opened to bench marks at the ends and with polygonal rods with no longer than 80 m. The survey campaign has been documented by a detailed photographic survey.

The great opportunity to document and survey one of the most significant architectures by Oscar Niemeyer, developed in cooperation with the Oscar Niemeyer Foundation, has shown how the integrated methodology is able to reveal new aspects of the building and to analyze spaces and surfaces by means of innovative methods that have allowed to track intellectual avenues completely unexplored and unpublished.

4   Future Steps

The series of documentation developed by the masters of the modernism in India and Brazil that have been deeply analyzed during this research, have been reconfigured and utilized in order to achieve the creation process of 3D study models. These models enable greater and more effective understanding of the masterpieces of modern architecture in these countries and thus a possible stronger preservation policy. Future steps should be the creation of a digital platform by the which it will be possible for researchers and experts to have access at this database.

On the other hand it has been highlighted that three-dimensional survey has proved to be essential to represent buildings/areas that would be otherwise impossible to analyze, for example elevations deeply immersed in very green areas, and to find plans matches that are essential to understand the architectural "philosophy" of the modernism masters.

In this representative phase there is a motivational value, which makes the survey-representation a real project itself, with significant critical implications aimed at the determination not only of geometric precision but, especially in architecture, of visualization and conceptual representation of reality.

At the moment integration of 3D survey and BIM approach seems to be the strongest base for future conservation plans and valorization projects. Furthermore, in case of demolition or unexpected events (such us natural disasters, etc.) this methodology will also preserve the memory of this extraordinary heritage.

To address these challenges, the Getty Foundation in Los Angeles, USA, developed *Keeping It Modern*, a grant initiative that aims at the conservation of modern buildings. The programme is already supporting modern buildings grant projects of outstanding architectural significance that promise to advance conservation practices: the University of Ferrara is deeply involved in the preservation masterplan of three of this buildings. The cooperation between the Getty initiative and the on-going research could actually help towards the creation of conservation management plans that guide long-term maintenance policies and the testing and analysis of modern architecture materials (Fig. 8).

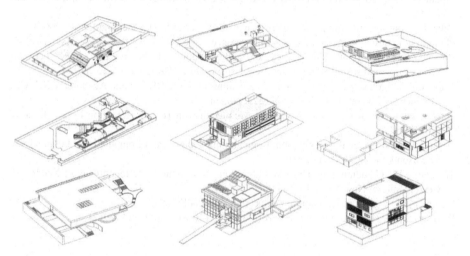

Fig. 8. Some examples of 3D database of Indian and Brazilian modern architectures developed by the research carried out at the University of Ferrara Architecture Department

References

Baan, I., Muller, L., Nooteboom, C., Stierli, M.: Brasilia-Chandigarh: Living with Modernity. Lars Muller Publisher, Zurich (2010)

Bahga, S., Bahga, S.: Le Corbusier and Pierre Jeanneret: Footprints on the Sands of Indian Architecture. Galgotia Pub. Co., New Delhi (2000)

Balzani, M., Sasso, D.F., Rossato, L.: The architectural survey for the revitalization of Villa Itororó in São Paulo. Paesaggio Urbano-Urban Design **5–6**, 68–75 (2015)

Belluardo, J., Ashraf, K.K.: An Architecture of Independence. Princeton Architectural Press, New York (1999)

Bhargava, M.L.: Architects of Indian Freedom Struggle. Deep & Deep, New Delhi (1981)

Bhatt, V., Scriver, P.: Contemporary Indian Architecture After the Masters. Mapin Publishing. Pvt. Ltd, Ahmedabad (1990)

Brusaporci, S.: Emerging Digital Tools for Architectural Surveying Modelling and Representation. Hershey, IGI Global (2015)

Cairo, A.: The Functional Art: An Introduction to Information Graphics and Visualization. Pearson Education, Inc., New York (2012)

De Masi, D.: Mappa mundi: Modelli di vita per una società senza orientamento. Rizzoli, Milan (2014)

Lang, J.T.: A Concise History of Modern Architecture in India. Permanent Black, Delhi (2002)

Lang, J.T., Desai, M., Desai, M.: Architecture and Independence: The Search for Identity - India 1880 to 1980. Oxford University Press, Oxford (1997)

Lu, D.: Third World Modernism: Architecture, Development and Identity. Taylor & Francis, New York (2010)

Macdonald, S.: Modern Matters: Principles and Practice in Conserving Recent Architecture. Donhead, London (1996)

Model House Research Group (ed.): Transcultural Modernisms. Sternberg Press. Wien (2014)

Montaner, J.M.: Arquitetura e crítica na América Latina. Romano Guerra Editora, São Paulo (2014)

Ortiz, F.: Contrapunteo cubano del tabaco y el azúcar (Letras His). Catedra, Madrid (2002)

Philippou, S.: Oscar Niemeyer: curves of irreverence. Yale University Press, New Haven (2008)

Rossato, L.: The architectural survey and representation of the modern project between preservation and sustainability. Paesaggio Urbano-Urban Design **4**, 12–19 (2015)

Salonia, P.: Which is the right direction? Proceedings of the XVIII General Assembly ICOMOS, Florence, 9 November 2015, pp. 521–523. Napoli (2015)

Scriver, P., Srivastava, A.: India: Modern Architectures in History. Reaktion Books, London (2015)

Sowa, J.F.: Knowledge Representation: Logical, Philosophical and Computational Foundations. Thomson Learing, Boston (2000)

Theoharis, D.: Contemporary Third World Architecture, Search for Identity. Pratt Manhattan Center Gallery, New York (1983)

Waisman, M.: O interior da história. Perspectiva, São Paulo (2013)

Weinstraub, A., Hess, A.: Oscar Niemeyer Casas, GG Brasil, São Paulo (2012)

From Integrated Survey to the Parametric Modeling of Degradations. A Feasible Workflow

Massimiliano Lo Turco$^{(\boxtimes)}$, Federico Caputo, and Gabriele Fusaro

Department of Architecture and Design, Politecnico di Torino, Turin, Italy
massimiliano.loturco@polito.it,
{federico.caputo,gabriele.fusaro}@studenti.polito.it

Abstract. This work fits into an international research field about 3D modeling to evaluate the Building Information Model performance for infographic representation of Cultural Heritage. Modeling an historic building involves the creation of parametric objects library starting by data survey. The primary purpose of the research is the translation of these information into a parametric model, through the definition of a proper methodology. The main focus of the research is the creation of parametric object representing the preservation status of material and building components: some recurring schemes of the traditional representation have been identified, in order to find a methodology that leads to link these data to the HBIM (Historic BIM) model, improving their capabilities.

Keywords: Cultural heritage · Point cloud · H-BIM · 3D decay · Data representation

1 Introduction

In the last period Building Information Modeling is emerging as the most reliable method to manage architectural design and building processes. Literature supplies both theoretical approaches and several practical applications. However, very little research regards to BIM applied to historical architecture, even if some initial results indicate the actual HBIM (Historic BIM) capability for the conservation of Cultural Heritage [1].

Since the architectural heritage has taken advantages from the development of data capturing technologies, an open issue is the integration of BIM systems and data source for existing buildings, supporting the creation of 3D knowledge and management systems [2].

At this regard, after various heuristic processes, a novel workflow that starts from point cloud and image survey data was defined: it was needed to define different steps:

1. Focus on the issue of accuracy between point cloud and modeled objects [3] Contrary to what usually was done, the control on the level of geometrical accuracy was directly done in the BIM environment, as shown below on Sect. 4.
2. Creation of historical libraries of building object that currently do not exist. Also in this case, the current workflows do not provide for a direct upload of "cropped"

© Springer International Publishing AG 2016
M. Ioannides et al. (Eds.): EuroMed 2016, Part I, LNCS 10058, pp. 579–589, 2016.
DOI: 10.1007/978-3-319-48496-9_46

point cloud into the design component environment. Several approaches were tested; two of these were adopted (later explained on Sect. 4).

3. Finally, we focused on the chance to model 3D decays in the BIM platform, enriching the related database with graphic, geometric and alphanumeric data that can be effectively used to design and manage future interventions (Sect. 5). This issue is considered by the authors as the most innovative part of the entire work, because no instances related to these theme were found.

2   The State of the Art: A Brief Overview

According to the main statements of the London Charter for the computer-based visualization of Cultural Heritage (that establishes internationally-recognized principles for the use of computer-based visualization by researchers, educators and Cultural Heritage organizations) it is necessary to take into account several types and degrees of access that computer-based visualization can uniquely provide to cultural heritage stakeholders, including the study of change over time, magnification, modification, manipulation of virtual objects, embedding of datasets [4]. Basically, the accurate and detailed reconstruction of geometric models of real objects has become a common process. Most of the published works are mainly focused on data survey processing, through a comparison between point clouds and models. Some others critically discuss about the meaning of "rigorous" BIM protocols [5]. In literature, other works show several steps in HBIM modeling, pursuing several aims, such as:

- energy evaluations and the searching for a new database for the construction industry, as in InnovANCE project, which was also attended by some researchers of the Politecnico di Torino [6].
- structural simulations and conservation analysis [7].
- monitoring processing, characterized by a strong contribution of Geomatics [8].
- More conceptual considerations on the rules of classical architecture [9, 10].

The proposed work relates to the validation of an effective system constituted by graphical and alphanumeric representation; this usual BIM approach is implemented by the infographic description of the materials and their preservation status that belong to a historical heritage.

3   The Case Study of "Torino Smistamento" Roundhouse

The analyzed case study is a property of the Ferrovie dello Stato, now abandoned and originally used for storage of locomotives, for which it has been proposed a specific intervention. The building was created to adapt standard the railways for the Universal Exhibition of 1911, to celebrate the 50th anniversary of the establishment of the Unification of Italy. It is composed by two different areas: the first one is used for the maintenance and the parking of the trains; the other one is used for the goods switching, coming by railway. The maintenance area was constituted by a roundhouse containing 51 shelted railroad tracks (Fig. 1), next to two sheds for the most complex interventions (A and B parts) (Fig. 2).

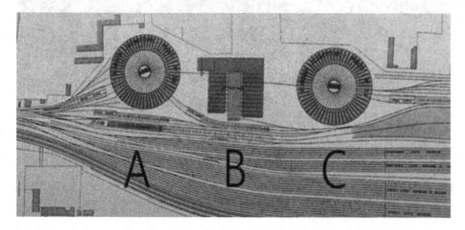

Fig. 1. Detail of the site plan, developed in 1905, compared with the existing situation. Development of the wares staging area of Torino Smistamento (nearby Lingotto) [11].

Fig. 2. The 1st December 1943 bombardment: birdseye view of bombings concentrated in via Nizza [12].

The bombings of 1943 caused huge damage to the circular structure, knocking down some of the 51 aisles, reducing the overall number to 32. The roundhouse is made of a structural repeated module constituted by three bays, sized to host a railroad-car. All rails are linked to a junction turning platform, in order to allocate the wagons inside the module. Actually the building is partially used (Fig. 3).

Fig. 3. Perspective birdseye view of the roundhouse, taken from Google Earth, Turin, acquisition date: 08/07/16, 45°02′28.66″N 7°40′00.37″E elev. 239 m alt. 353 m.

4   Description of the Survey and Parametric Modeling Activities

After the historic research, the design survey has been realized; the work was characterized by combined techniques, mostly based on TLS. As known, the Terrestrial Laser Scanner can acquire a large amount of data in a very short time, automatically recording geometric, radiometric and photographic information, later georeferenced into a unique coordinate system.

The point cloud is described through statistical precision indicators that do not actually define the true overall accuracy of the cloud. To do that, the reliability has been verified through a test procedure which evaluates the differences between point coordinates measured with the total station and point coordinates extracted from the cloud. This process allowed to assess the overall tolerance, which is the parameter that really matters to the user survey.

The point clouds are then imported into the BIM software to start with the modeling phase. The production of an "As-Is" model involves the need to model the existing architecture components, which do not belong to the objects contained into the usual software libraries.

The creation of new elements implicates a reading of the geometric rules followed to define the shape of the building components. It is therefore necessary to semantically interpret the geometrical rules and then to parameterized them. As previously mentioned, a method for the creation of parametric objects starting from the point cloud was experienced: that procedure is not feasible in the classic versions of BIM platforms, because it is not allowed to import segmented point clouds within the interface used to model single components.

Moreover, the main parameters of certain system families have also been customized, such as the walls and slabs layering. At the same time, a geometric layout of the building structure was defined: this was done replicating the module with a polar array, setting the reference system of radial axes and determining the center of the structure. These assumptions were validated after the comparison with the point cloud (Fig. 4).

Fig. 4. Top view of the entire point cloud. In red, the distances between the points used for the testing of measures. (Color figure online)

In order to achieve a better validation of the digital model, new parameters were added: some for the GRADE (GRAphic DEtail that define the detail level of the graphic representation) and LOD controls (Level of Development, meant as the degree of reliability of information associated with different elements). These usually are used in the design phase, when the information assets increase together with the design development; some new variables were added to assess the reliability degree and completeness of information element detected. Finally, this data can be viewed through thematic representations.

The geometric validation of the model was performed experimenting the use of a software for the metric control: at this regard, it was used Pointsense, a plugin for the management of point clouds within Revit environment (BIM application used). This plugin allows to evaluate the accuracy of the proposed virtual reconstruction, providing some tools about flatness, verticality and horizontality controls, directly working with BIM software. This control is explained in detail in most of the works previously mentioned [2, 3, 5] (Fig. 5).

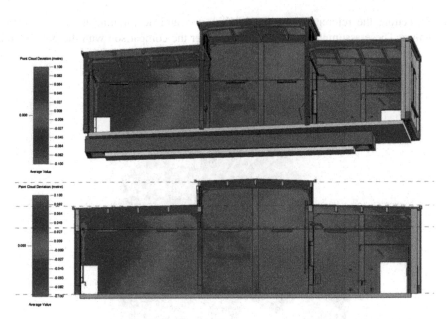

Fig. 5. The graphs provided by Pointsense allow to assess qualitatively the deviation between the point cloud and parametric model: most of the points that belong to the surface of the walls have a deviation that does not exceed 3 cm. The color changes on the wall surface are an index of non-planarity. (Color figure online)

They actually use different software, managing the exported 3D model with a loss of information; in other word the metric accuracy is evaluated by duplicating data with a high risk of making mistakes: the process is not bidirectional, so it is not possible to reimport this data into the BIM platform. But the proposed innovation identifies a more interoperable workflow, as we proceed to calculate the difference between the virtual position of an element and the data survey readable by the point cloud: if this difference is less than the predetermined tolerance, the geometric reconstruction can be considered reliable.

5 New Strategies for Representing Parametric Decays

The last part of testing involved research and critical analysis of the most innovative representation of the internal decays. A useful method to define new ways of working in BIM environment has been identified. The test focused on a sample form of the structure: there, the preservation status has been detected, firstly plotted using the traditional representation techniques. The methodology used refers to the handbook of Mario Dalla Costa [13] which can still be considered a reference point for the Restoration area. In this approach we have added some changes for entering alphanumeric and graphic data into the parametric modeling environment. Regarding to the usual representation method proposed in the manual, all the information on dating and the consistency of the building are actually shown on the usual 2D drawings in orthogonal projections, applying a pattern element connected to a legend containing added data.

Within the BIM model, geometries are represented through well-defined mathematical rules. The geometries of pathologies instead can be very complex. We have tested several approaches (for instance: the implementation of the functionality through programming languages such as API and Python, or a mixed use of algorithmic design software, to name only the main ones). Then, it was decided to use an "adaptive component" (for Revit is a particular object that can be adapted to a surface using movable vertex) able to be associated with flat and curved surfaces (Fig. 6).

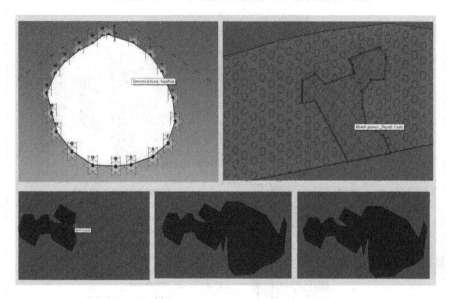

Fig. 6. On the top, left side: adaptive component based on 20 vertices. On the right, parametric decays readable in 3D views. Below, the editing process and merge of the various parts.

Doing this, the vertex can be modified, and the decay components are visible in the 3D environment, supporting new ways of viewing and analysis. The added value consists on the ability to associate new parameters that describe the pathology, the working procedure to restore the building components, photos, data materials and quantities (i.e. extensions of the decay, expressed in square meters).

So, multiple analysis can be done, making them more evident through multicriteria schedules defined by qualitative and quantitative data, preserving the production of traditional graphic drawing. At the end of this process a specific template has been set up for future restoration works, containing all settings used for this pilot project.

6 Conclusions and Future Developments

This paper proposes a method able to describe, classify and organize information assets concerned with Architectural Heritage, through the use of integrated survey procedures [14].

The research constitutes a very little part of several studies already known by the Scientific Community; however we are fully convinced of our innovative ideas for the introduction of BIM methodology for documentation of architectural heritage, with a specific focus on the restoration works (Fig. 7).

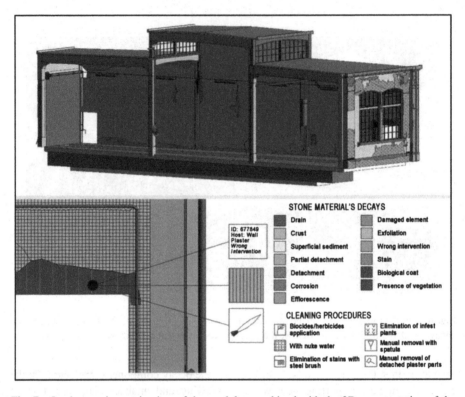

Fig. 7. On the top: isometric view of the modulus combined with the 3D representation of the decays. Below, sample labels applied to a 3D decay, with the corresponding legend.

The work demonstrates that it is possible to develop a HBIM, starting from the checking of the metric accuracy: in particular, the transfer from numerical model (cloud of points) to a mathematical model (3D modeling) is a process that involves simplifications and deductive hypothesis. Furthermore, these hypotheses depend both on the object of the study and from the survey purposes: therefore these options must be individually evaluated [15]. From the geometric point of view, the BIM platform manages mathematical models, choosing the rule and not the form: introducing

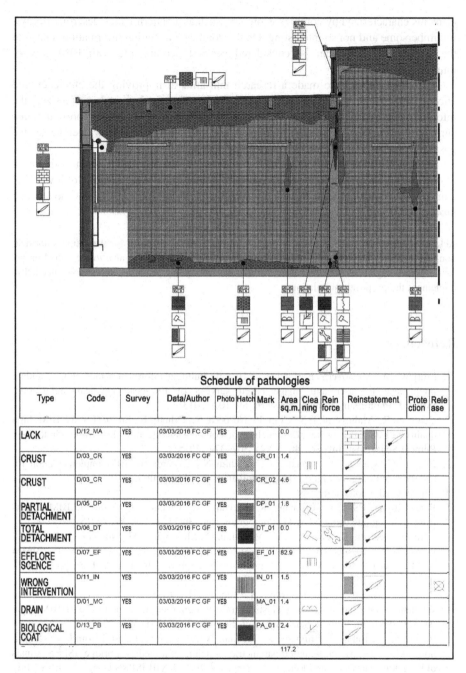

Table: Schedule of pathologies

Type	Code	Survey	Data/Author	Photo	Hatch	Mark	Area sq.m.	Clea ning	Rein force	Reinstatement	Prote ction	Rele ase
LACK	D/12_MA	YES	03/03/2016 FC GF	YES			0.0					
CRUST	D/03_CR	YES	03/03/2016 FC GF	YES		CR_01	1.4					
CRUST	D/03_CR	YES	03/03/2016 FC GF	YES		CR_02	4.6					
PARTIAL DETACHMENT	D/05_DP	YES	03/03/2016 FC GF	YES		DP_01	1.8					
TOTAL DETACHMENT	D/06_DT	YES	03/03/2016 FC GF	YES		DT_01	0.0					
EFFLORE SCENCE	D/07_EF	YES	03/03/2016 FC GF	YES		EF_01	82.9					
WRONG INTERVENTION	D/11_IN	YES	03/03/2016 FC GF	YES		IN_01	1.5					
DRAIN	D/01_MC	YES	03/03/2016 FC GF	YES		MA_01	1.4					
BIOLOGICAL COAT	D/13_PB	YES	03/03/2016 FC GF	YES		PA_01	2.4					
							117.2					

Fig. 8. Thematic sheet of the current preservation state: section that shows the internal facade with description of the degradation pathologies, realized through BIM application: any information present on the sheet is directly associated to the 3D degradation element.

elements characterized by complex geometry, such as a pattern which describes decays, is cumbersome and not so interesting. On the contrary, managing information related to the preservation state can be considered perfectly compatible with BIM way of thinking.

It is assumed to have made a research that aims at improving the efficiency and effectiveness of more conventional procedures. The final model synthesizes the information usually fragmented (firstly because belong to different representations) enriching it with new methods of analysis and management of data, opening up the possibility for new scenarios of "knowledge" [16].

Finally, we have argued about the replicability of the process, thought as the reuse of objects that belongs to the architecture of the past, and for the creation of a working template for future reusable surveys, to achieve the infographic sharing of models and procedures (Fig. 8).

Acknowledgements. The authors would like to thank Kubit software for their kind authorization to use Pointsense for Revit plug-in for research purposes. Thanks also to the Faro Europe, (with specific regard to Alberto Sardo) for the availability, by providing the support needed to implement the proposals simulations.

References

1. Murphy, M., McGovern, E., Pavia, S.: Historic building information modelling – adding intelligence to laser and image based surveys of European classical architecture. ISPRS J. Photogram. Remote Sens. **76**, 89–102 (2013)
2. Quattrini, R., Malinverni, E.S., Clini, P., Nespeca, R., Orlietti, E.: From TLS to HBIM: high quality semantically-aware 3D modeling of complex architecture. Int. Arch. Photogram. Remote Sens. Spat. Inf. Sci. **40**(5/W4), 367–374 (2015)
3. Biagini, C., Capone, P., Donato, V., Facchini N.: Towards the BIM implementation for historical building restoration sites. Automation in Construction (2016)
4. http://www.londoncharter.org/
5. Barazzetti, L., Banfi, F., Brumana, R., Previtali, M.: Creation of parametric BIM objects from point clouds using NURBS. Photogram. Rec. **30**(152), 339–362 (2015)
6. Caffi, V., Daniotti, B., Lo Turco, M., Madeddu, D., Muscogiuri, M., Novello, G., Pavan, A., Pignataro, M.: Il processo edilizio supportato dal BIMM: l'approccio InnovANCE - BIMM enabled construction processes: the InnovANCE approach. In: ISTeA, Bari, pp. 91–109, 10–11th July 2014
7. Dore, C., Murphy, M., McCarthy, S., Brechin, F., Casidy, C., Dirix, E.: Structural simulations and conservation analysis-historic building information model (HBIM). Int. Arch. Photogram. Remote Sens. Spat. Inf. Sci. **40**(5/W4), 351–357 (2015)
8. Barazzetti, L., Banfi, F., Brumana, R., Previtali, M., Roncoroni, F.: BIM from laser scans… not just for building: nurbs-based parametric modeling of a medieval bridge. ISPRS Annals of the Photogrammetry and Remote Sensing, vol. III-5, XXIII ISPRS Congress, 12–19 July 2016, Prague, Czech Republic (2016)
9. Dore, C., Murphy, M.: Semi-automatic generation of as-built BIM facade geometry from laser and image data. ITcon **19**, 20–46 (2014)

10. De Luca, L.: Relevé et multi-représentations du patrimoine architectural Définition d'une approche hybride de reconstruction d'édifices. Thèse de l'ecole doctorale Arts et Metiers ParisTech, Aix-en-Provence, mars (2006)
11. Ballatore, L., Masi, F.: Torino, Porta Nuova: storia delle ferrovie piemontesi. Abete, Roma (1988)
12. Bassignana, L.: Torino sotto le bombe. Nei rapporti inediti dell'aviazione alleata. Edizioni del Capricorno, Torino (2003)
13. Dalla Costa, M.: Il progetto di restauro per la conservazione del costruito. Celid, Torino (2000)
14. Inzerillo, L., Santagati, C.: Using dense stereo matching techniques in survey. Disegnare Idee Immagini **47**, 82–91 (2013)
15. Lo, Turco M., Sanna, M.: La modellazione digitale ricostruttiva: il caso della chiesa della Misericordia a Torino. Disegnare Idee Immagini **41**(2010), 42–51 (2010)
16. Docci, M., Maestri, D.: Manuale di rilevamento architettonico e urbano. Laterza, Bari (2009)

INCEPTION Standard for Heritage BIM Models

Peter Bonsma[1(✉)], Iveta Bonsma[1], Anna Elisabetta Ziri[2], Silvia Parenti[2(✉)],
Pedro Martín Lerones[3], José Luis Hernández[3], Federica Maietti[4], Marco Medici[4],
Beatrice Turillazzi[5], and Ernesto Iadanza[5]

[1] RDF Ltd., Iskar 25, 1000 Sofia, Bulgaria
{peter.bonsma,iveta.bonsma}@rdf.bg
[2] Nemoris srl, Via Decumana 74 A, 40133 Bologna, Italy
{annaelisabetta.ziri,silvia.parenti}@nemoris.it
[3] Fundación CARTIF, Parque Tecnológico de Boecillo, P. 205,
47151 Boecillo, Valladolid, Spain
{pedler,josher}@cartif.es
[4] Department of Architecture, University of Ferrara,
Via Ghiara 36, 44121 Ferrara, Italy
{federica.maietti,marco.medici}@unife.it
[5] Consorzio Futuro in Ricerca,
Via Saragat 1, 44122 Ferrara, Italy
beatrice.turillazzi@unife.it, ernesto.iadanza@unifi.it

Abstract. The EU Project INCEPTION will create a platform that is able to exchange content according to state-of-the-art available open BIM standards. This INCEPTION open Heritage BIM platform is not only exchanging data according to existing state-of-the-art standards, but it is based on a new Heritage BIM model using Semantic Web technology. This allows applications to retrieve content according to modern query languages like SPARQL and allows user defined 'on-the-fly' extensions of the standard. This paper describes the structure and development of this new Heritage BIM standard. The Heritage BIM standard is developed by several Semantic Web and BIM standardization specialists in combination with top experts in the field of Cultural Heritage, all of them partners within the INCEPTION project.

Keywords: 3D · BIM · IFC · ifcOWL · GIS · H57 · H-BIM · OWL · OWL2 · Semantic web · RDF · RDFS

1 Introduction

The European Project "INCEPTION - Inclusive Cultural Heritage in Europe through 3D semantic modelling"[1], funded by EC within the Programme Horizon 2020, focuses

---

[1] The INCEPTION project, Grand Agreement no.: 665220 started the last June 2015, is developed by a consortium of fourteen partners from ten European countries led by the Department of Architecture of the University of Ferrara. More information can be found on [http://www.inception-project.eu/].

© Springer International Publishing AG 2016
M. Ioannides et al. (Eds.): EuroMed 2016, Part I, LNCS 10058, pp. 590–599, 2016.
DOI: 10.1007/978-3-319-48496-9_47

on three main objectives: to create an inclusive understanding of European cultural identity and diversity by stimulating and facilitating collaborations across disciplines, technologies and sectors; to develop cost-effective procedures and enhancements for on-site 3D survey and reconstructions of cultural heritage buildings and sites; to develop an open-standard Semantic Web platform for accessing, processing and sharing interoperable digital models resulting from 3D survey and data capturing.

This inclusive approach includes open-standard format for cultural Heritage Building Information Modelling (H-BIM) as part of the overall procedure aimed at enriching and enhancing the changing role of 3D representations for knowledge, reconstruction, preservation and exploitation of Cultural Heritage.

The integration of semantic attributes with hierarchically and mutually aggregated 3D digital geometric models is essential for management of heritage information. The development of tools for 3D automatic delineation depending on acquisition technologies, from point clouds to photo-based data, allows to achieve a common standard interoperable output for BIM environment. Therefore, starting from advanced procedures aimed at handling multi-data point clouds and triangle meshes into BIM software, the INCEPTION procedure advances BIM approach for Heritage knowledge, going a step forward the usual procedure to locate/define 2D or 3D primitive shapes onto the point clouds. INCEPTION develops methodologies and algorithms to recognize these shapes. Results will be constructed in BIM software avoiding the oversimplification of the shapes. When used in models of Cultural Heritage, semantic BIM will be able to be connected to different users (e.g. scholars, technicians, citizens, etc.) in support of the user's needs for interpretation of the cultural heritage model, in addition to the common BIM features of 3D visualization, technical specifications and dataset.

The recent earthquake in central Italy (23 August 2016), causing about 300 victims, almost destroyed the beautiful towns of Accumoli and Amatrice. The last one was inserted in 2015 among the "most beautiful villages of Italy". Both the towns date back to XI–XII centuries and are home to beautiful churches and sanctuaries, heavily damaged by the earthquake. The same fate has befallen many houses of historical interest. Similarly, in 2009, the same region was hit by a big earthquake that fatally wounded the wonderful ancient city of L'Aquila, still undergoing a slow process of architectural recovery, causing 309 victims.

One of the aims of the INCEPTION procedure is protecting the cultural heritage of seismic areas with scopes of classification, prevention and reconstruction.

The paper starts exploring the state of the art within existing open standards, focusing on available H-BIM solutions up to explaining INCEPTION implementations.

2   Existing Open Standards

In the area of BIM, GIS, Cultural Heritage and Semantic Web, a lot of valuable work is already done. INCEPTION has taken existing state-of-the-art open standards and technology as a starting point. In this chapter we will just name a few relevant open standards in the area of BIM and Point Clouds, without being complete in number of standards nor in the areas (for example GIS was removed completely keeping the paper size reasonable). A complete reference can be found in D4.1 from the INCEPTION project.

2.1 Existing BIM Standards

This paragraph will explain the main open BIM standards expected to be used for data providers of BIM.

IFC (ifcXML, ifcOWL, ifczip). The first developments for the IFC format dates back to 1985. The name IFC (Industry Foundation Classes) was first introduced in 1994 led by Autodesk. In 1995 it became a vendor independent standard and had several releases, IFC 151 and IFC 20LF (Long Form) were popular releases for the academic world. Since IFC 2 × 3 released in 2006 (and later improvements IFC 2 × 3 Final and IFC 2 × 3 TC1) it was also becoming more popular for use in real life projects. Nowadays IFC 2 × 3 TC1 is still the most popular version although for INCEPTION the new version IFC4 (formally known as IFC 2 × 4) has some important improvements for both 3D representation and scheduling.

IFC is meant to be used by all the disciplines in the Building & Construction industry and the only widely used open standard supporting so many different disciplines. All major CAD vendors and a wide variety of other applications offer support for IFC. Most of the applications supporting IFC are not certified, although most CAD systems with IFC support have a certification from buildingSMART. IFC carries an object-based view of the model, including geometry in 3D (and 2D) as well as properties and interrelationships between objects. It is a well thought through standard with relatively high complexity for software vendors to support. IFC support includes schedule data, quantities and many other construction related data.

The standard exchange format for IFC is STEP/EXPRESS. As serialization support for this format is limited the past few years other serializations are defined also. It started with support for ifcXML, with an alternative 'simple' ifcXML format. More recently also ifcOWL serialization is created, this last format is compatible with Semantic Web RDF, RDFS and OWL2 standards. Although there is a small data loss the fast majority of knowledge is kept in these alternative serializations. A different format is ifczip and is nothing more than the zipped version of an original IFC file.

bSDD. Building Smart Data Dictionary is like the semantic extension of the IFC schema. Although IFC in combination with its property sets (and about 3000 properties) has already a lot of semantics in it, to cover the complete Building & Construction industry the semantic definition has to be far larger (numbers differ but we could expect that 100.000 object definitions are required where even the latest IFC schema has less than 1000 entities). bsDD is the standard from Building Smart defining how such extensions of the semantics can be stored and defined.

2.2 Existing Point-Cloud Standards

E57. Most 3D imaging systems for data exchange today takes place using one of three types of file formats: proprietary formats (not an efficient approach to data exchange in the long term), ad-hoc formats (not space or time efficient and no widespread usage), or the LAS format (limited file size and features). The E57 format is intended to overcome these issues, being a more general format that is well-suited for storing data across a variety of application domains. It is able to store point clouds and also other information from 3D scanners like images. The file format is specified by the ASTM, an international standards organization, and it is documented in the ASTM E2807 standard Huber (2011).

Next to the standard a 'reference implementation' is created to make more attractive and easy the use of the standard. The reference implementation is called libE57 and is written in C++ and sources are available [http://www.libe57.org/]. The libE57 application contains an API that can be used by parties that like to import or export files in E57 format.

2.3 Available H-BIM Solutions

Several H-BIM Solutions are already available. One thing we can notice in many of these solutions is use of Semantic Web techniques or use of BIM related standards. For example the vendor specific standard Graphisoft GDL language (Graphical Description Language) allows parametric modelling of components, something very useful in the area of geometry for Cultural Heritage content.

One typical behavior of most currently available H-BIM solutions is that they are clearly focused on one or two areas of the core of a Semantic Web based solution:

- Cultural Heritage
- Semantic Web technology
- BIM /3D /Point Cloud knowledge

3 Semantic Web

3.1 RDF

RDF (Resource Description Framework) supports creating and processing metadata by defining a default structure. This structure can be used for any data, independent of their character. Thus, the application areas of RDF are numerous, e.g., web-based services, peer-to-peer networks, and semantic caching models; they all have in common that huge amounts of data have to be processed when querying RDF data. RDF data can be represented using XML, a triple structure or a graph. Only the graph representation enables the semantic interpretation of the RDF schema.

All of the elements of the triple are resources with the exception of the last element, object, that can be also a literal. Literal, in the RDF sense, is a constant string value such as string or number. Literals can be either plain literals (without type) or typed literals typed using XML Datatypes. These triples together form RDF graph. A normative syntax for serializing RDF is RDF/XML.

3.2 RDF Schema (RDFS)

RDFS extends RDF vocabulary to allow describing taxonomies of classes and properties. It also extends definitions for some of the elements of RDF; for example it sets the domain and range of properties and relates the RDF classes and properties into taxonomies using the RDFS vocabulary.

The RDF schema statements are valid RDF statements because their structure follows the structure of the RDF data model. The only difference to a pure "resource - property - value" - triple is that an agreement about the specific meaning for reserved terms and statements has been made. Next to that, the RDF schema provides a vocabulary for defining the semantics of RDF statements.

3.3 Web Ontology Language (OWL)

OWL is a W3C standard. The abbreviation stands for Web Ontology Language and is a language for processing information on the web. It is built on top of RDF and RDFS. OWL was designed to be interpreted by computers and parsed by applications. It is not meant for being read by people. OWL is written in XML and has three sublanguages - OWL Lite, OWL DL (includes OWL Lite) and OWL Full (includes OWL DL). The Ontology is about the exact description of things and their relationships. For the web, ontology is about the exact description of web information and relationships between web information. The standard OWL is a part of the "Semantic Web Vision", a future web where:

- Web information has exact meaning
- Web information can be processed by computers
- Computers can integrate information from the web

3.4   Web Ontology Language 2 (OWL2)

OWL 2 adds new functionalities with respect to OWL 1. Some of the new features are syntactic sugar (e.g., disjoint union of classes) while others offer new expressivity, including keys, property chains, richer data types, data ranges, qualified cardinality restrictions, asymmetric, reflexive, and disjoint properties, and enhanced annotation capabilities. OWL 2 also defines three new profiles and a new syntax. Some of the restrictions applicable to OWL DL have been relaxed resulting in a slightly larger set of RDF Graphs that can be handled by Description Logics reasoners.

3.5 Reasoning

OWL enables "reasoning", as mentioned above. That means it gives the possibility to check the logical correctness of statements and add statements that are implied by other statements

A "semantic reasoner", "reasoning engine", "rules engine", or simply a "reasoner", is a piece of software able to infer logical consequences from a set of asserted facts or axioms. The notion of semantic reasoner generalizes that concept of inference engine, by providing a richer set of mechanisms to work with. The inference rules are commonly specified by means of an ontology language, and often a description language. Many reasoners use first-order predicate logic to perform reasoning; inference commonly proceeds by forward chaining and backward chaining. There are also examples of probabilistic reasoners, including Pei Wang's non-axiomatic reasoning system, and Novamente's probabilistic logic network.

3.6 SPARQL

SPARQL is the reasoning language for Semantic Web. Servers support in many cases out-of-the-box SPARQL queries.

The gate for the access to the Inception ontology will be a SPARQL endpoint. SPARQL 1.1 is a semantic query language and a recommendation of W3C. Its adoption in Inception project is important to access to the CH semantic storage. Multiple programming languages, libraries and semantic repositories implement SPARQL queries. The 1.1 standard also allows to write queries which directly update the RDF graph. Being SPARQL syntax based on graph traversal, it is also easy to visualize SPARQL results graphically. Although repositories could be navigated and examined with different tools, a SPARQL endpoint is one of the powerful tools to open semantic data to main exploitation.

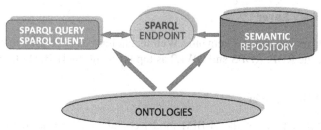

4 H-BIM Ontology

This chapter describes the architecture of the H-BIM Ontology as well as some examples of the content. The H-BIM Ontology is the core of the INCEPTION Platform. The content of the Ontology will be developed together with the specialists that are partners within INCEPTION. By definition the content will however be incomplete; the architecture therefore allows users to extend the H-BIM Ontology either for projects or for larger aggregations, like countries, styles etc.

4.1   Background

The architecture of the H-BIM Ontology is defined to enable storage of semantic information from any cultural heritage object. A clear distinction between tangible and non-tangible content is defined and, in line with the base concepts behind Semantic Web technology, it allows layered extension of the ontology itself. Typical for the H-BIM Ontology is the close connection with existing state-of-the-art BIM standards like IFC/ifcOWL and the link with 3D content defined in Semantic Web (i.e. open standard CMO with Extensions).

4.2   Architecture Overview

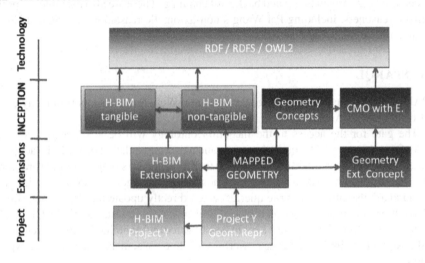

4.3   Technology Layer

Within this layer we use the Semantic Web technology as described in Sect. 3. This means use of the RDF, RDFS and OWL2 as top layers of the H-BIM Ontology.

4.4   INCEPTION Layer

The INCEPTION layer of the H-BIM model contains the real knowledge from the specialists within the INCEPTION project. This is knowledge about Cultural Heritage but also knowledge from existing state-of-the-art open BIM and open GIS standards.

One important part of the INCEPTION layer is the difference between tangible and non-tangible results. Since this is a known term in the area of Cultural Heritage and distinction is not always clear, much time and effort is put in defining what is covered by the terms.

4.5 Extensions Layer

As soon as new concepts within the extension layer are defined the queries can be used. Extension could concern new relations between existing content and therefore applied on all existing content, but extensions can also be specific for dedicated content. Some examples:

Example of Extensions Applicable on Existing Content. The INCEPTION H-BIM standard has embedded parts of the semantic structure of IFC (and therefore ifcOWL). This means classes Wall, WallStandardCase and Cur-tainWall exist. Adding a super class Walls and the knowledge that above named classes inherit from this new class Wall is an extension that works on all available content. A SPARQL query can be created to get all instances of new class Walls and it will directly have content for the majority of the Cultural Heritage H-BIM models stored in the INCEPTION platform.

Example of Extensions Applicable on New Content. It is allowed to add a class to the H-BIM model in the extension layer with a new name and no relation to any existing part of the H-BIM model. A query on this class is only relevant for new content incorporating the knowledge that this new class is existing.

4.6 Project Layer

Within the project layer the real content is defined, this content is arranged according to the layers above. All content can be queried according to the SPARQL queries defined on top of the INCEPTION layer. It is also possible to create solution specific queries as well as queries dedicated to certain extensions as defined in the extension layer.

5 Implementation

The INCEPTION standard is the base for the platform that will be developed within INCEPTION. As the INCEPTION standard is developed.

5.1 Server Solutions

The core of the INCEPTION platform will be a server that is able to handle the INCEP-TION standard and offer basic functionality like support for SPARQL. During writing of this paper the selection of the server handling this Semantic Web data is not finalized yet, there are several options and the most promising solutions at this moment seem to be RDF4 J and Fuseki 2.

As not only Semantic Web data needs to be stored, but many different file formats including open standard BIM formats as well as point cloud data a file server will be part of the INCEPTION platform also.

Sesame /RDF4J 2.0. The official name is RDF4J and its current release is 2.0, however this solution is best known under its former name OpenRDF Sesame framework. It became part of the Eclipse Foundation and has no official first version at this moment after this important change.

Fuseki 2. Fuseki server is already existing for a while and although especially Fuseki 2 would be of interest for INCEPTION also Fuseki 1 is still actively maintaine. Fuseiki 2 is a server solution on top of Apache and Jena and also called Apache Jena Fuseki. It is a SPARQL server and an open source project.

5.2 SPARQL Queries

Technology choices and implementation will be driven by the accessibility of data through SPARQL queries addressed to a SPARQL endpoint. This means that a running REST web service should respond to data queries and produce as results a set of triples serialized on one of the most used RDF serialization (RDF/XML, Turtle, N3) or an RDF graph. This should include queries both on tangible and non-tangible data and their specific relations.

SPARQL queries are "data-oriented" so there is no inference in the query language itself, all the data manipulation and inferencing has to be done by a layer on storage or on in memory RDF data. Thanks to its structure and many converters present in the market SPARQL queries can be applied not only to native RDF data but also on any data that could be mapped to RDF, like other kind of well-formed relational data.

6   Conclusion

The use of BIM for Cultural Heritage is becoming more and more an effective tool to manage 3D representations at different layers and for multiple purposes, pursuing the common vision, at European level, to apply research, technology and innovation in innovative media to expand understanding and access of the heritage assets.

One of the main challenges is how to manage the complexity of heritage buildings and sites, fostering the collaboration across disciplines through semantic-aware representations, able to solve interoperability issues and avoiding the segmentation of knowledge. The technology of Semantic Web and integration with 3D and BIM are the drivers behind H-BIM Ontology. The H-BIM Ontology in its turn is the core of the INCEPTION H-BIM Platform.

The INCEPTION procedure could be conveniently exploited for protecting the cultural heritage of seismic areas with scopes of classification, prevention and reconstruction.

References

Bonsma, P.: Semantic web platform and interfaces. In: Deliverable 6.2 of the EU Project Proficient (2014)

Huber, D.: The ASTM E57 file format for 3D imaging data exchange. In: Proceedings of the SPIE, Electronics Imaging Science and Technology Conference (IS&T), 3D Imaging Metrology, vol. 7864A, January 2011

Dore, C., Murphy, M.: Integration of Historic Building Information Modeling (HBIM) and 3D GIS for recording and managing cultural heritage sites. In: 2012 18th International Conference on Virtual Systems and Multimedia (VSMM), pp. 369–376. IEEE (2012)

Hichri, N., Stefani, C., De Luca, L.; Veron, P.; Hamon, G.: From point cloud to BIM: a survey of existing approaches. In: International Archives of the Photogrammetry, Remote Sensing and Spatial Information Sciences, vol. XL-5/W2 (2013)

Volk, R., Stengel, J., Schultmann, F.: Building Information Modeling (BIM) for existing buildings - literature review and future needs. Autom. Constr. **38**, 109–127 (2014)

Kauppinen, T., Paakkarinen, P., Mäkelä, E., Kuittinen, H., Väätäinen, J., Hyvönen, E.: Geospatio-temporal Semantic Web for Cultural Heritage (2010)

BauDenkMalNetz – Creating a Semantically Annotated Web Resource of Historical Buildings- Anca Dumitrache and Christoph Lange

Mantegari, G., Palmonari, M., Vizzari, G.: Rapid prototyping a semantic web application for cultural heritage: the case of MANTIC. In: Aroyo, L., Antoniou, G., Hyvönen, E., Teije, A., Stuckenschmidt, H., Cabral, L., Tudorache, T. (eds.) ESWC 2010. LNCS, vol. 6089, pp. 406–410. Springer, Heidelberg (2010). doi:10.1007/978-3-642-13489-0_33

Pauwels, P., Verstraeten, R., De Meyer, R., Van Campenhout, J.: Architectural Information Modelling in Construction History (2009)

From SfM to Semantic-Aware BIM Objects
of Architectural Elements

Massimiliano Lo Turco[1] and Cettina Santagati[2(✉)]

[1] Department of Architecture and Design, Politecnico di Torino, 10125 Turin, Italy
massimiliano.loturco@polito.it
[2] Department of Civil Engineering and Architecture, Università di Catania, Catania, Italy
cettina.santagati@dau.unict.it

Abstract. The huge diffusion of Building Information Modeling approaches in the field of architectural design has characterized the research of the last decades; however very little research has been undertaken to explore the advantages and criticalities of BIM methodologies in Cultural Heritage domain. Moreover, the last developments in digital photogrammetry lead to easily generate reliable low cost 3D textured models, that can be used to create semantic-aware objects of reusable library of historical architectural elements. The aim is to test a novel workflow practitioner centered, based on the use of the latest solutions for point cloud managing into BIM.

Keywords: Cultural heritage · Point cloud · H-BIM · Structure From Motion (SfM) · Data representation

1 Introduction

The use of digital technologies has totally changed and improved the working methods applied to architectural heritage domain. Nevertheless, most operators, trusting in the progressive automation of data acquisition, believe they are be able to manage the complexity of reality without having the required cultural background. Only after a scholar's interpretation, data turn into an evaluated and recognizable information, distinctive for the knowledge of the studied object.

The capabilities of Historical Building Information Modeling (H-BIM) need to be explored, giving centrality to the critical interpretation of the acquired data: this is a field of research always more essential and critical, also considering the copious presence of historical buildings in Europe and in Italy and the lack of BIM protocols and procedures on this topic. BIM approach can be defined as a "shared digital representation of physical and functional characteristics of any built object [...] which forms a reliable basis for decisions" [1]. However, the suitability of BIM platforms for historical architecture is still considered a great challenge. The first relevant issue is the relationship between 3D data acquisition and their conversion in parametric semantic-aware components, hierarchically organized.

© Springer International Publishing AG 2016
M. Ioannides et al. (Eds.): EuroMed 2016, Part I, LNCS 10058, pp. 600–612, 2016.
DOI: 10.1007/978-3-319-48496-9_48

The latest 3D acquisition techniques (laser scanning, digital photogrammetry) supports easy and quick data acquisition. The obtained point cloud contains geometrical, material and color data of the acquired objects, as well as information related to the state of conservation. Nevertheless, the point cloud is constituted by a huge number of points, ontologically indistinct until they are geometrically interpreted [2]. To this day, there is no automatic processing tool available that allows for the identification of complex shapes (such as the ones that characterize historical buildings) and turns them into geometric parametric models.

It is a fact that the use of a commercial BIM package is mandatory to fulfill basic BIM requirements [3]. However, the existing BIM platforms were developed for architectural design; this means that the parametric objects inside them, often are not suitable for the modeling of existing historical architecture elements such as walls, portals, windows, cornices and string courses that use the elements of architectural language.

Furthermore, dealing with a historical building, in addition to geometrical information, a lot of heterogeneous data have to be organized and managed. The BIM database is able to recover such information, becoming an indispensable resource for different professionals involved in the restoration, intervention or management of existing buildings.

Therefore, it is necessary to create a shared parametric semantic-aware library of architectural elements that belong to the different historical ages [4, 5]. These objects have to be created as external components (families according to Revit). If well modeled and generalized, these components can be reused in similar contexts. One chance is to use the architectural treatises that describe the architectural classical elements, another one is to start from the survey of architectural elements.

We apply this last approach, reasoning for single architectural components, developing and testing a workflow that exploits the advantages of low cost digital photogrammetry and of a specific plugin able to manage point clouds into commercial BIM platform, thus useful to create parametric semantic 3D models of an architectural element. We will reflect on data conversion (level of abstraction and generalization, level of accuracy), Grade and LoD requirements in the case of "as-built" H-BIM. The aim is to discuss these open issues, testing a novel workflow based on the use of the latest available solutions for point cloud managing.

Here the structure of the paper: Sect. 2 will mark the state of the art and will analyze different approaches and results; Sect. 3 describes the proposed workflow in detail; while Sect. 4 refers to a chosen case study; then we will critically discuss the obtained results, taking into account some feasible future research.

2   The State of the Art

In the last years, the use of BIM in the field architectural design field has brought to a consolidation in the procedures and the identification of standard methods. However, the challenge is still open if considering the conservation, management and enhancement of the architectural heritage. It is required to review and update data acquisition process, the standardization and structuring of acquired data in a 3D semantic model and the subsequent representation and usability of the model.

Together, the digital recording of cultural heritage sites using laser scanning and photogrammetry has become a topic of great interest in the field of conservation and cultural heritage. Although data collection technologies are now very efficient and automated, the processing of this data is still time consuming [6].

The spread of Image-based 3D modeling techniques, through digital photogrammetry free, low cost and open source packages, have drastically increased in the past few years, especially in the field of Cultural Heritage [7]. Many researchers have carried out several tests that have demonstrated the metric reliability of Structure from Motion (SfM) techniques for architectural elements where other techniques (such as Terrestrial Laser Scanning- TLS) are costly, not sufficiently dense or not easy to access [8, 9]. Moreover, tests performed by several research teams have demonstrated that these techniques are strictly dependent on the quality of the dataset (network, image resolution, radiometric quality). [10] and are suitable for medium size objects, such as architectural elements and details.

At present, we can distinguish between desktop and web based packages. If the first ones need a high performance computer for data processing, the second ones use the power of cloud computing to carry out a full-automatic data processing. In both cases, the output is a dense textured point cloud of the analyzed object that can be easily turned into a 3D mesh model.

Regarding to H-BIM methodology, very little research has been undertaken to understand the potential of BIM for heritage buildings [11]. The efforts of researchers are currently focused on two basic questions:

- Can be effectively used a BIM-based approach for the investigation on historical buildings using commercial BIM platforms?
- How turn point clouds into rigorous BIM?

The first question deals with the lack of specific components/tools for historical architecture available for commercial BIM platforms. The reconstruction of complex shapes seems a challenging task. Once having obtained the point cloud and identified the single elements and their mutual relationship, the operator could [12]:

- built an in-place family directly in the project environment;
- create a family that could be reused in other projects (usually BIM platforms don't allow to import point clouds into family editor except using specific plugins [13]);
- create 3D external objects and import them in the BIM model as surface models.

In literature, other works show several steps in 3D HBIM modeling [5]; these workflows use different software with the necessary format conversion and we mainly observe a 2D simplification with slices of point clouds to build up the 3D model.

The second question is linked to the meaning of "rigorous BIM". In literature we find several studies [3–5] that address the crucial transition from the point cloud to the intelligent parametric object, introducing the concept of level of accuracy. In other words, the point cloud can be considered a digital copy of the object that preserves its geometric features (irregularities, deformations, etc.): are we able to guarantee the metric accuracy captured by digital survey in the BIM modeling phase? Is the level of abstraction too high for an appropriate geometry reconstruction? Some authors carry out a comparison - point cloud to model - to evaluate if the deviation is in keeping with the scope of the H-BIM. Others prefer to perform the 3D modeling in other platforms able to create and manage NURBS surfaces [3, 5]: they use proper protocols to convert NURBS into parametric surfaces then uploaded in BIM platforms. Other studies refer to "rigorous BIM", meaning as the complete exploitation of BIM approaches for Cultural Heritage buildings not only in terms of geometric accuracy, but also considering other features (parametric objects, relations, attributes, correct setting of Grade and LoD).

2.1 Process and Product Taxonomies

Some samples of reconstruction of the existing condition often suggest to generate a semantic model [14] based on a constant comparison between the information included in the historical treatises and the profiles achievable from a point clouds. Some others are focused on the issues of accuracy between building objects models (walls, pillars, vault) and point clouds. Others, instead, suggest creating a historical library of building object models currently not available.

Moreover, others propose a different classification of the whole approach, shifting the focus from general to specific issues. In this regard, "as-built" BIM characterization involves three aspects, allowing building a structured point cloud: shapes, relations and attributes [15]. Regarding the shape of the object it can be classified according to three variable: parametric or non-parametric/global or local/explicit or implicit [16]. In a global representation, the entire object is described, while in a local one only a portion of the object is characterized.

Regarding to the taxonomies of each single building component, a further important consideration must be pointed out before developing this topic: as said, 3D models that contain only 3D (metric) data are not BIM models [17]. This means that a model generated from point clouds is not a BIM unless are added: parametric intelligence/relationships/attributes. Therefore, our challenge is to set up new digital components that belong to cultural heritage, working on parametric through explicit modeling (CSG), and preparing the field for corresponding data population.

3 A Workflow Centered on Data Critical Interpretation for the Creation of Parametric Semantic Components

As highlighted in the previous works, the transition from the discrete (point cloud) to the continuous (parametric 3D model created on the photogrammetric surveys imported into BIM platform) still retain a certain stiffness. The first problem lies in the limited usability of parametric components available in libraries and websites, because they provide large amounts of material mainly focused on new constructions.

The evaluation of BIM capabilities applied to Cultural Heritage is a relevant field of investigation, through heuristic approaches that could open new research avenues. Our workflow starts from the acquisition phase: the point cloud survey requires a series of pre and post processing stages, which involve cleaning, sorting and combining of different sets of point cloud data. Then, point cloud data can be considered as a skeletal framework, which is mapped using parametric elements to shape the H-BIM component [5]. It must be said that BIM software mostly used, (Revit 2016), does not allow you to import point clouds portions, in the family design interface, to be used as the basis for the virtual reconstruction of the building components (doors, windows, pillars, beams, …), the only vector formats that can be imported are .dwg or .dwf. The idea to create "in-place family" has been voluntarily discarded, because such elements, directly realized into the model, can only be saved in the .rvt project (Revit file format), without generating any .rfa external (and reusable) family. This last step is mandatory to set up any library of reusable objects for subsequent interventions.

An elementary solution, although very time-consuming, consists on the use of applications that handle point clouds to make a controlled selection, a subsequent conversion into a text file and a further file processing to obtain the file format requested. The first attempt considered a step for converting the point cloud into a .dwg file. This involved the coding of a Python script able to permit the importation in Rhinoceros several extensions point file (.xyz, .pts, .csv) and the subsequent saving into .dwg file. However, once imported into family design interface, the .dwg point cloud has some stiffnesses, making the virtual modeling of certain items that needs to be visualized, analyzed and measured in lateral views (sections) extremely arduous.

Then, we moved on commercial plugins that have been released in the last years (such as Pointsense and Cloudworks for Revit). These tools make the management and processing of point cloud easier in Revit family interface for example by extracting orthophotos or segmenting point clouds. In this research work we tested the use of PointSense for Revit, a Kubit plugin resell by Faro [21] that allows the user to import the whole point cloud or a part of it directly into Revit family editor (Fig. 1).

Fig. 1. From right to left: RGB point cloud available on Revit interface; the point cloud loses the RGB property when imported into Revit family interface; Pointsense xray ortho-view.

Furthermore, this plugin allows you to easily extract x-ray ortho-view from the point-cloud which are georeferenced in the same reference system. So, ortho-images and segmented/cropped point cloud are the basic data imported for further processing within the family editor. Doing that, the critic interpretation of data is favored because point data redundancy is abstracted to the essential object skeleton lines. This approach is similar to the use of *in situ* eidotype as trace, with the advantage to have a point cloud as reference that can be visualized, cropped and consulted in realtime. This brings to a proper data interpretation and discretization: through the use of reference planes and reference lines the skeleton of the new parametric component can be outlined; the following dimension and conversion into parametric variables will guarantee the geometric flexibility of BIM components.

Furthermore, each single element, if modeled in three dimensions, is able to store a plurality of heterogeneous type information. This can be considered the added value of using BIM instead of more established conventional approaches.

Model components and decorations were modeled through family design interface: for each windows, doors and all the decoration and ornaments, we cropped the point cloud to extract 2D profile useful to outline complex shapes drawn from classical orders. According to Murphy [5] and De Luca [19], a bottom-up approach is adopted which starts with the smallest building objects such as ornamental mouldings and profiles. These uniform objects are created from a shape vocabulary of 2D shapes usable for all configurations of the classical orders [20]. This approach is considered the best one, because usable in future interventions, as it allows to identify the regulatory geometric rules (invariants) (Fig. 2).

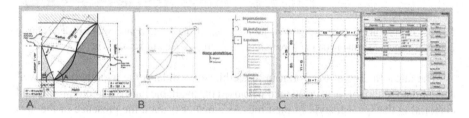

Fig. 2. Cima parametrization according to Aubin (A), De Luca (B), and family editor (C).

After the modeling phase we worked on the database to better organize the different information gathered. All documents used for modeling, in fact, were linked to their virtualized components, associating an image parameter to the different elements categories. This implementation allows to link together in a unique virtual environment the various original sources. The virtual reconstruction permits multiple queries and the production of thematic drawings (such as the identification of the different measurement instruments, the evaluation of the types of degradation, the fourth dimension control, etc...).

4   A First Case Study Application

To test our workflow, we choose a 15th century gothic portal, characteristic of Catalan-Aragonese architecture in the Etnean area of Eastern Sicily as case study. This portal is one of the few memories that survived the catastrophic events at the end of the 17th century in Eastern and South-eastern Sicily: the disruptive Mount Etna eruption (1669) that covered and erased 16 etnean towns and the earthquake (1693) that destroyed almost all the towns of the Val di Noto. The portal belongs to the old church of S. Maria delle Grazie in Misterbianco (5 km far from Catania) which was covered by the eruption of 1669 and was brought to light in the last years thanks to the excavations carried out by the Superintendence to Cultural Heritage of Catania. This portal represents a recurrent typology of the catalan-aragonese architecture in Etnean area (Catania), other very similar examples can be found in Mascalucia (church of S. Annunziata in Mompilieri and the church of S. Antonio Abate) as well as in the remaining area (Randazzo, Francavilla, S. Lucia del Mela, Taormina, etc.) (Fig. 3).

Fig. 3. 15th century Catalan-Aragonese gothic portals (from left to right): S. Maria delle Grazie in Misterbianco; S. Annunziata in Mompilieri; S. Antonio Abate in Mascalucia.

The latest finding of the portal in Misterbianco, validates the hypothesis of a well consolidate school of local craftsmen who used the available materials, interpreting and elaborating the spanish style of the time. As a matter of fact, the presence of the lava stone as construction material together with white limestone brings to a distinctive bichromatism typical of these areas: the portal in Misterbianco is a round arch portal whose jambs are in lava stone; the springing cornice ashlar is realized in white limestone as well as the archivolt, the cordon and the conclusive corbel.

4.1   3D Survey

The photos were taken with a SONY DSC-W310 digital camera, 35 mm lens and at a resolution of 12 Mpix. The shot project took in consideration the geometrical features of the portal and the presence of the decorations for a total of 30 shots.

In order to design a workflow compliant with the most used commercial BIM platform (Revit) among all the available SfM packages we choose Autodesk cloud-based photogrammetry service Recap 360. Taking advantage of the photogrammetric approach and algorithms of Computer Vision, the service reconstructs the internal parameters of the camera and the position in space of homologous points between frames starting from the correspondence between a sequence of images. The user creates the project, adds survey points or reference distances to scale the model, chooses the resolution of the model (low, ultra), the smart cropping and/or texturing option, the export format (e.g. rcs, rcm, obj). Then the images are uploaded and sent to the cloud. When the model is ready, the user can improve the results by adding survey points and resubmitting the project. The obtained point cloud in rcs format was imported in Recap PRO, then cropped and prepared for the following importation in Revit. Together, the obj model (mesh textured model) was opened in Rhinoceros and the first textured orthophotos were extracted (Fig. 4).

Fig. 4. View of the dataset, the reconstructed point cloud and orthophoto of the portal.

4.2 Geometrical Interpretation of Architectural Elements

The point cloud provides a digital replica of the portal, a mass of raw data that describes the object but needs to be interpreted in order to be transformed into a parametric semantic-aware model. To do this, the geometrical rules that generate the complex surfaces have to be recognized as well as the corresponding mathematical law. The construction of the geometric model requires a deep knowledge of the shapes and the language of historical architecture. In this phase the scholar works consciously, recognizing the different elements and proceeding from general to particular by identifying the architectural elements that characterize the object of study, gradually destructuring the elements that constitute them up to the mouldings, the atoms of the architectural lexicon [19].

Therefore, it is mandatory the rigorous identification of: the elements that geometrically describe the investigated surfaces; the geometric genesis of studied surface (translation, rotation, interpolation); the mathematical law (Revolution, Estrusion); the construction planes for each 2D profile and path and their extrapolation from the point cloud by means of cutting planes. The architectural elements need to be decomposed in their formal, material and structural features, to extract the geometrical rules that generate the several surfaces/elements (invariant features) and a set of 2D profiles (variant features).

In this sample, the portal presents some relevant features of Catalan Architecture: a simple round-arch archivolt ended by a cordon and corbels (in limestone); straight jams (in lava stone), and an ashlar that holds the arch spring cornice (in limestone).

Thinking on the invariant and variant elements, we can assume that not always is the arch spring cornice present (as in the case of Mompilieri), and in some cases the cordon profile is inside the external jamb line (once again in Mompilieri); furthermore, the cornice and cordon 2D profiles varies according to the creativity of the craftsmen.

Therefore, portal invariant features are: the presence of a limestone archivolt ended by a cordon (extrusion along a curve path), the presence of lava stone jambs (extrusion); the presence of a corbel, the use of limestone ashlar in correspondence of arch springer; the variant elements are the 2D profiles of the cordon, the presence of arch springer cornice, the position of the 2D profile of the cordon (inside or outside the external jamb line). All these issues have to be considered during the modeling phase, choosing properly the reference planes, the origin of 2D profiles, the generating rules (extrusion) in order to create a H-BIM component that generalize this type of Catalan-Aragonese portal so that it can be re-used in other projects (Fig. 5).

The last step is the verification of the so called level of accuracy, that is the adherence of the modeled component to the point cloud irregularities at the required scale of representation. This test can be directly carried out into BIM environment by using Pointsense plugin or external software such as Geomagic, Cloud Compare, Meshlab.

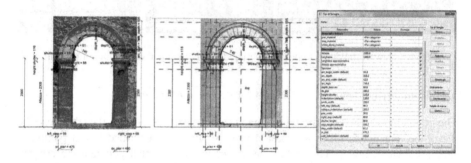

Fig. 5. Modeling of the portal through the interpretation of the data contained in the point cloud and list of type and instance parameters associated with the modeled family.

4.3   Focus on Grade and LoD Specification

As known, the BIM platform allows to associate multiple data to a single virtual component. The first group controls graphic contents: international guidelines identify the Grade level to manage the graphical representation of building components in orthogonal projection and spatial views, congruent with different levels of detail.

The second group concerns with alphanumeric data: the international standard identify the LoD parameter (meant as Level of Development) as the degree of reliability of information that can be expected from data contained into the digital model.

For what concerns the graphical views associated to different levels of detail, we based the modeling procedure on the basis of eidotypes drawn during the survey, consistent to the different representation scales (Fig. 6); it was decided to set up:

– at Grade 1: displaying the jambs and the frame of the archivolt, highlight the different material of springer cornice and jambs (consistent to 1:200 scale);
– at Grade 2: 2D schematic drawings of corbel and cordon were added (1:100 scale);
– at Grade 3: 3D modeling of the corbels, cordon; the ashlars of the archivolt and jambs were more defined (1:50 scale).

Referring to LoD specification, it must be said that such classifications are closely useful for new buildings interventions, where the measurement of the LoD level is linked to economic, topological, construction and maintenance information. In the case of interventions on historical buildings, it is needed to include other variables, critically analyzing the richness of information available; this is done to measure the reliability degree of the survey. More the survey is complete, greater the integration with the various stakeholders who participated in the study can be arranged.

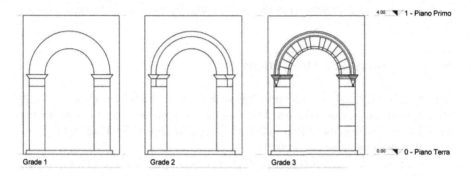

Fig. 6. Proposed Grade levels associated to the portal family.

This procedure includes the retrieval of design archives, the photos of the state-of-art, the metric survey techniques, the degradation surveys. Through the creation of shared parameters (usable to multiple types of components, and on several projects) we are able to associate new data to the element detected. Then, the added information will therefore be made evident in the model through labels, schedules or thematic views (Fig. 7).

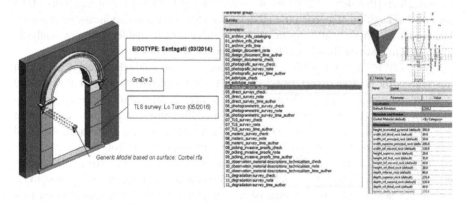

Fig. 7. 3D Family and list of shared parameters relating to survey procedures used to tag elements. On the right, the corbel family uploaded on the portal and used as a nested family.

4.4 Results and Future Works

We tested our workflow on a single case study to fully apply our procedure, verifying both theoretical and practical outlined issues. The promising obtained results lead us to plan for the future. We will expand this work comparing our workflow applied to the same object using several software and workflows from SfM object (point cloud) importation to BIM, critically evaluating the results.

Moreover, we will test our workflow on more objects characterized by different kind of complexity using the same approach, comparing the results and taking into account the advantages and weakness.

5   Conclusions and Open Items

Regarding to existing H-BIM library objects, both the methods for semi-automatically plotting building facades and manual plotting methods can be used. The approach used with H-BIM is to map the objects in 2D onto segmented point clouds and orthographic images in elevation, plan and section.

The sub-elements (mouldings, profiles, symbols, etc.) become the architectural vocabulary; the whole composition relates to a linguistic structure, this linguistic analogy offers architecture a basis for analysis and understanding. As a matter of fact, ontology can be intended as a particular conceptual framework or as a specification of a conceptualization. It enables aggregation, topological and directional relationships.

Aggregation (i.e. part of, belong to, etc.), could be modeled with a hierarchical-based tree representation that permits to describe the composition in a local-to-global way. Accordingly, it is possible to develop semantics and management procedures in order to determine the correct LoD of the surveying and of the model. This can be surely considered an open research topic, because of a current lacking in regulation systems (or guidelines) that define the levels of LoD according to the degree of reliability of the survey. The creation of a geometric model allows for many more applications of survey data, such as semantic and information modelling which enables complex analysis, management and visualization of heritage data.

Finally, it is crucial to make a general thought on the methodological accuracy: at this regard, the London Charter [21], defines the principles to be followed for the 3D representation of the Cultural Heritage, in line with the values of transparency, communicability of the methods and results of this modeling process. So, this guarantees a repeatability of the scientific process where the variable element is the data, the fixed one is the process [22]. The application of these principles will allow to define a methodology for the knowledge (and the representation) of the Cultural Heritage that makes the virtual reconstruction, the processing and communication of data more transparent. The understanding of cultural dimension is thus a greater formal qualification in a permanent relationship between architectural space and information space. It therefore guarantees a repeatability of the scientific process where the variable element is the data, the invariant one is the process.

Acknowledgements. The authors would like to thank Kubit software and Faro Europe (Alberto Sardo) for their kind authorization to use Pointsense for Revit plug-in for research purposes.

References

1. ISO Standard, ISO 29481-1:2010(E): Building Information Modeling — Information Delivery Manual — Part 1: Methodology and Format (2010)
2. Santagati, C.: 3D laser scanner aimed to architectural heritage survey: from the point's cloud to the geometrical genesis determination. Int. Arch Photogramm. Remote Sens. Spat. Inform. Sci. 36 (5) (2005)
3. Barazzetti, L., Banfi, F., Brumana, R., Previtali, M.: Creation of parametric BIM objects from point clouds using NURBS. Photogram. Record. **30**(152), 339–362 (2015)
4. Quattrini, R., Malinverni, E.S., Clini, P., Nespeca, R., Orlietti, E.: From TLS to HBIM: high quality semantically-aware 3D modeling of complex architecture. Int. Arch. Photogramm. Remote Sens. Spat. Inform. Sci. **40**(5/W4), 367–374 (2015)
5. Murphy, M., McGovern, E., Pavia, S.: Historic building information modelling – adding intelligence to laser and image based surveys of European classical architecture. ISPRS J. Photogram. Remote Sens. **76**, 89–102 (2013)
6. Dore, C., Murphy, M.: Semi-automatic generation of as-built BIM facade geometry from laser and image data. ITcon **19**, 20–46 (2014)
7. Remondino, F., El-Hakim, S.: Image-based 3D modelling: a review. Photogram. Rec. **21**(115), 269–291 (2006)
8. Santagati, C., Inzerillo, L., Di Paola, F.: Image-based modeling techniques for architectural heritage 3d digitalization: limits and potentialities. Int. Arch. Photogramm. Remote Sens. Spat. Inform. Sci. **XL-5/W2**, 550–560 (2013)
9. Kersten, T., Lindstaedt, M.: Automatic 3D object reconstruction from multiple images for architectural, cultural heritage and archaeological applications using open-source software and web services. Photogrammetrie - Fernerkundung - Geoinformation **2012**(6), 727–740 (2012)
10. Gaiani, M., Remondino, F., Apollonio, F.I., Ballabeni, A.: An advanced pre-processing pipeline to improve automated photogrammetric reconstructions of architectural scenes. J. Remote Sens. **8**(3), 178 (2016)
11. Fai, S., Graham, K., Duckworth, T., Wood, N., Attar, R.: Building information modelling and heritage documentation. In: 23rd CIPA Symposium, Prague, Czech Republic, 8 p. (2011)
12. Biagini, C., Capone, P., Donato, V., Facchini N.: Towards the BIM implementation for historical building restoration sites. Automation in Construction (2016)
13. Garagnani, S., Manferdini, A.M.: Parametric accuracy: building information modeling process applied to the cultural heritage preservation. Int. Arch. Photogramm. Remote Sens. Spat. Inform. Sci. **XL-5/W1**, 87–92 (2013)
14. Apollonio, F.I., Gaiani, M., Sun, Z.: 3D modeling and data enrichment in digital reconstruction of architectural heritage. Int. Arch. Photogramm. Remote Sens. Spat. Inform. Sci. **XL-5/W2**, 43–48 (2013)
15. Hichri, N., Stefani, C., De Luca, L., Veron, P.: Review of the "as-built BIM" approaches. Int. Arch. Photogramm. Remote Sens. Spat. Inform. Sci. **40**(5/W1), 107–112 (2013)
16. Tang, P., Huber, D., Akinci, B., Lipman, R., Lytle, A.: Automatic reconstruction of as-built building information models from laser-scanned point clouds: a review of related techniques. Autom. Constr. **19**, 829–843 (2010)

17. Arayci, Y.: Towards building information modelling for existing structures. Struct. Surv. **26**(3), 210–222 (2008)
18. http://faro-3d-software.com/CAD/Products/PointSense/3D_Laser_Scanner_Revit.php
19. De Luca, L.: Relevé et multi-représentations du patrimoine architectural Définition d'une approche hybride de reconstruction d'édifices. Thèse de l'ecole doctorale Arts et Metiers ParisTech, Aix-en-Provence, mars (2006)
20. Aubin, P.: Renaissance Revit: Creating Classical Architecture With Modern Software. G3B Press, Oak Lown (2013)
21. http://www.londoncharter.org/
22. Novello, G., Lo Turco, M.: Which drawing to deliver more information? In: Less More Architecture Design Landscape, Le vie dei Mercanti X Forum Internazionale di Studi, Aversa-Capri (ITA) Napoli: La scuola di Pitagora editrice, pp. 690–699 (2012)

Project Paper: Novel Approaches to Landscapes in Cultural Heritage.

Observing Landscape Changes Around the Nicosia Old Town Center Using Multi-temporal Datasets

Branka Cuca[✉], Athos Agapiou, and Diofantos G. Hadjimitsis

Department of Civil Engineering and Geomatics,
Cyprus University of Technology, Saripolou 2-8, Limassol, Cyprus
{branka.cuca,athos.agapiou,d.hadjimitsis}@cut.ac.cy

Abstract. In 1980s a significant boom in construction industry was witnessed in Cyprus. This paper explores the changes of land use that have occurred over the past 30 years around the historical capital of Nicosia, in particular around the core of the historic city defined by the Venetian walls. Further to some Open geospatial Data available within the national and regional geo-portals, the research has focused on the use and exploitation of freely accessible satellite imagery (such as Landsat and Sentinel imagery) and other archive aerial datasets in order to observe the most recent modifications of the urban landscapes. The changes occurred over time were observed using multi-spectral multi-temporal dataset with main aim to create thematic maps for further interpretation. The changes were hence identified, mapped and structured so as to emphasise different types and density of urban development affecting the surrounding landscapes and potential "hot-spots". Such observations could be a valuable input to the future urban development of Nicosia.

Keywords: Historical cities · Nicosia · Cyprus · Earth observation · Landsat · Changing landscape

1 Introduction

Geo-spatial information is increasingly being used for purposes of territorial management as it has been recognized to be crucial when it comes to informed decision making processes that regard landscapes and environment. The nature of geo-information is in fact twofold - on one side the elaboration of such data is capable to describe phenomena that has already occurred (i.e. impact assessment purposes) and on the other side to provide us with simulations of possible further effects or occurrence (scenario modelling). In this paper authors opted for a combined and integrated use of multi-spectral, multi-temporal and multi-source data available over Cyprus in order to explore the contribution of freely available satellite imagery for monitoring of changes around the city of Nicosia and to suggest possibilities offered by such data for implementing the Open geospatial information available through national and EU repositories. Open geospatial Data approach was also of interest due to the recently established national INSPIRE platform, implemented by the Department of Land and Surveying of the Republic of Cyprus [1]. In the framework of Open Government

© Springer International Publishing AG 2016
M. Ioannides et al. (Eds.): EuroMed 2016, Part I, LNCS 10058, pp. 615–624, 2016.
DOI: 10.1007/978-3-319-48496-9_49

initiative, experts consider geospatial data to be significantly important category [2]. The possibility to access publicly collected and available data is retained crucial for the development of new and innovative applications useful for a variety of social domains [3]. Such approach that promotes the use and re-use of publicly collected data is actually encouraged by public policies for economic purposes [4].

This paper investigates the contribution of satellite imagery to non-space sectors such as built environment and urban development. The interaction between urban (built) environment and the surrounding landscapes was observed applying a combined and integrated use of multi-spectral and multi-temporal data (Sect. 2). Section 3 illustrates the methodology applied on the satellite remote sensing data with focus on change detection, with illustration of the results in Sect. 4. A discussion on the method and its use for purposes of decision making in urban contexts is provided in Sect. 5. Paper concludes with inputs on the land use changes around the city of Nicosia and on possible contribution of the information deriving from the satellite imagery in the future decision-making processes that regard the island's capital.

2   Datasets

The main data used to observe the changes in landscape around Nicosia's walls were freely available satellite imagery Landsat (LT), described in Table 1.

Table 1. Landsat imagery used in the study

Year (date-month)	Satellite (Sensor)	Spatial resolution (m)		Spectral resolution (nm) (only VIS-VNIR listed)
		Panchromatic	VIS	
1987 (22-April)	LT5 (Thematic Mapper – TM)	15	30	450–900
2003 (25-Sept)	LT5 (Thematic Mapper – TM)	15	30	450–900
2016 (5-April)	Landsat8 Operational Land Imager (OLI)	15	30	433–885

The images were accessed and downloaded from the geo-portal of the Geographical Survey of United States (USGS) for the years 1987, 2003 and 2016. This choice was made in order to investigate changes in the period of 80s and 90s (years of construction sector "boom" recorded in Cyprus) [5] and to observe possible modifications in urban fabric in the years after Cyprus accession to the European Union in 2004. PCA methodology was applied as it is frequently used to understand interactions between landscape and urban sprawl. In 2015, for example, Agapiou et al. [5], use PCA to determine areas of Paphos municipality that have undergone dramatic change in their land use for the period 1984–2010.

Figure 1 above shows Nicosia observed in all three images in Red – Green – Blue (RGB) bands i.e. the band combination that corresponds to the human vision. Below the same area as seen in band combination NIR – R – G that enhances the presence of vegetation (in red). This paper concentrates on the changes occurred in the part of Nicosia under administration of Republic of Cyprus, south of the buffer zone area.

Fig. 1. Nicosia Municipality seen in RGB (above) and as NIR – green – blue (below). (Color figure online)

3   Methodology

3.1   Creation of Multi-spectral Multi-temporal Imagery Using Landsat Data

In order to observe the land changes using this multi-spectral imagery over a period of time, first it was necessary to build "stack layers" composed of two images. This was performed for three pairs (1984–2003; 1984–2016 and 2003–2016) using ERDAS Imagine 2010 software©. The images obtained in such a way are hence referred to as multi-spectral multi-temporal imagery. However, it is important to mention that a selection of bands for every image was made, according to their suitability for observing changes of construction and vegetation areas i.e. the urban development and possible landscape changes around inhabited spaces. Table 2 reports these combinations for all three pairs used.

For experiment purposes an additional image combining all three images was built following the same procedure. In this case, a composite image of 19 bands was obtained, as illustrated in Table 3.

Figure 2 shows two scenarios A and B with hatched buffer zone (left) and with buffer zone show as outline (right). The couple of images A refer to a stack image pair 1987–2016 observed with a combination 1,8, 14 i.e. showing the blue bands of both

Table 2. Landsat satellite imagery and respective bands used for creation of multi-spectral multi-temporal pairs.

Image pair	Single satellite image per year	Band number in the original image (wavelength)	Band number in multi-temporal image
Pair 1987–2003	LT5 1987	Band 1 – blue (0.45–0.52)	1
		Band 2 – green (0.52–0.60)	2
		Band 3 – red (0.63–0.69)	3
		Band 4 – Near Infrared (0.77–0.90)	4
		Band 5 – short-wave Infrared (1.55–1.75)	5
		Band 6 – Thermal Infrared (10.40–12.50)	6
		Band 7 – red (2.09–2.35)	7
	LT5 2003	Band 1 – blue (0.45–0.52)	8
		Band 2 – green (0.52–0.60)	9
		Band 3 – red (0.63–0.69)	10
		Band 4 – Near Infrared NIR (0.77–0.90)	11
		Band 5 – short-wave Infrared SWIR (1.55–1.75)	12
Pair 1987–2016	LT5 1987	Band 1 – blue (0.45–0.52)	1
		Band 2 – green (0.52–0.60)	2
		Band 3 – red (0.63–0.69)	3
		Band 4 – Near Infrared (0.77–0.90)	4
		Band 5 – short-wave Infrared (1.55–1.75)	5
		Band 6 – Thermal Infrared (10.40-12.50)	6
		Band 7 – red (2.09–2.35)	7
	LDCM 8 2016	Band 2 – blue (0.45–0.51)	8
		Band 3 – green (0.53–0.59)	9
		Band 4 – red (0.64–0.67)	10
		Band 5 – NIR (0.85–0.88)	11
		Band 6 – short-wave Infrared (1.57-1.65)	12
		Band 7 – SWIR (2.11–2.29)	13
		Band 8 Panchromatic (0.50–0.68)	14
Pair 2003–2016	LT 5 2003	Band 1 – blue (0.45–0.52)	1
		Band 2 – green (0.52–0.60)	2
		Band 3 – red (0.63–0.69)	3

(*continued*)

Table 2. (*continued*)

Image pair	Single satellite image per year	Band number in the original image (wavelength)	Band number in multi-temporal image
		Band 4 – Near Infrared NIR (0.77–0.90)	4
		Band 5 – short-wave Infrared SWIR (1.55–1.75)	5
	LDCM8 2016	Band 2 – blue (0.45–0.51)	6
		Band 3 – green (0.53–0.59)	7
		Band 4 – red (0.64–0.67)	8
		Band 5 – NIR (0.85–0.88)	9
		Band 6 – short-wave Infrared (1.57–1.65)	10
		Band 7 – SWIR (2.11–2.29)	11
		Band 8 Panchromatic (0.50–0.68)	12

Table 3. Landsat satellite imagery and respective bands used for creation of a composite multi-spectral multi-temporal image.

Composite image	Single satellite image per year	Band at the origin and its wavelength domain	Band number in the multi-temporal image
1987 – 2003 – 2016	LT5 1987	Band 1 – blue (0.45–0.52)	1
		Band 2 – green (0.52–0.60)	2
		Band 3 – red (0.63–0.69)	3
		Band 4 – Near Infrared (0.77–0.90)	4
		Band 5 – short-wave Infrared (1.55–1.75)	5
		Band 6 – Thermal Infrared (10.40–12.50)	6
		Band 7 – red (2.09–2.35)	7
	LT5 2003	Band 1 – blue (0.45–0.52)	8
		Band 2 – green (0.52–0.60)	9
		Band 3 – red (0.63–0.69)	10
		Band 4 – Near Infrared NIR (0.77–0.90)	11
		Band 5 – short-wave Infrared SWIR (1.55–1.75)	12
	LDCM8 2016	Band 2 – blue (0.45–0.51)	13
		Band 3 – green (0.53–0.59)	14
		Band 4 – red (0.64–0.67)	15
		Band 5 - NIR (0.85–0.88)	16
		Band 6 – short-wave Infrared (1.57–1.65)	17
		Band 7 – SWIR (2.11–2.29)	18
		Band 8 Panchromatic (0.50–0.68)	19

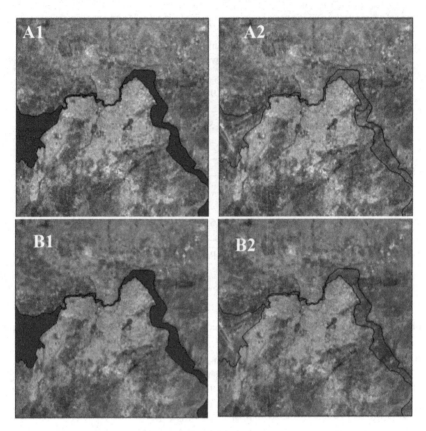

Fig. 2. Blue band combinations: (A) 1987–2016 image observed in band combination 1, 8 and 14 (above) and (B) 1987-2003-2016 image observed in band combination 1, 8, 13 (below). (Color figure online)

images and using panchromatic band to enhance the spatial resolution. Couple B refers to a stack of all three images (Table 2) observed with a band combination 1, 8, 13 i.e. the blue bands in all three years. Such visualization criteria was chosen because man-made structures (and materials such as cement) are more easily distinguished in this range of spectrum.

3.2   3.1 Principal Component Analysis of Multi-spectral Multi-temporal Data

In order to analyze these first observations, a spectral enhancement technique was performed using a Principal Component Analysis (PCA). The parameter of 5 elements was used in order to have a significant qualitative gradient of changes in a range from 1 to 5 (with 1 referring to the most and 5 referring to least significant changes, respectively). Equivalent analysis was made for a multi-temporal image combining all three datasets. The image obtained however results in a complicated set of information that regards almost 30 years. In order to comment such image a more thorough background in terms of historical information and documentation is needed (Fig. 3).

4 Results

The results obtained using the PCA is illustrated in Fig. 4. It is to be noted that such images appear in false-colour meaning that RGB channels are attributed to single elements of the PCA. Here the band combination used was 1, 2, 4 meaning that higher changes are observed in channels of Red and Green (1 and 2 respectively) while milder changes are observed in Blue channel (4 on the scale of 1–5).

Hence, the colours seen on the image do not have an absolute value but are an indication of landscape change in the cover (and hence use) observed and it requires further qualitative and quantitative interpretation. A closer look on the walled city of Nicosia and its southern area within the PCA image 1987–2016 (Fig. 5) show some significant changes around the city walls (white dashed lined), just out of the walls and along the main transport arteries of the city (red colour).

Such observations were identified as 'hot-spots' and were further examined observing the values of sample pixels across all the bands used in both images.

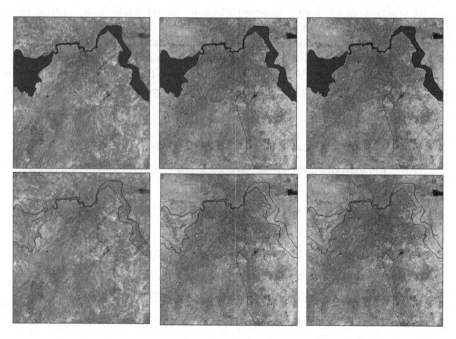

Fig. 3. Principal Component Analysis for image pairs: 1987–2003 (left); 2003–2016 (middle) and 1987–2016 (right). Buffer zone is shown as hatched (above) and as outline only (below).

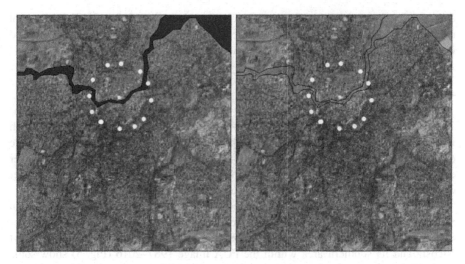

Fig. 4. PCA of the image pair 1987–2016, a close-up on southern Nicosia. (Color figure online)

Using 1987–2016 PCA image as a reference, a sample of 9 points was selected (points within the walled city, on the walls and out of the walls on 'hot-spots' and on areas with medium and low change-rate). Choosing the blue band as the most suitable one for observations of changes in construction, the absolute differences in reflectance values were observed in bands 1 and 8 of the image pair 1987–2016 (Table 2), shown in Fig. 5. The difference value is not steady but shows fluctuation: such behavior could indicate changes in the urban environment (such as demolition or new construction) for example in point 3 (around Venetian walls) or in point 6 (hot-spot 3). Further, the four pixel samples corresponding to 'hot-spots' were examined for their reflectance values

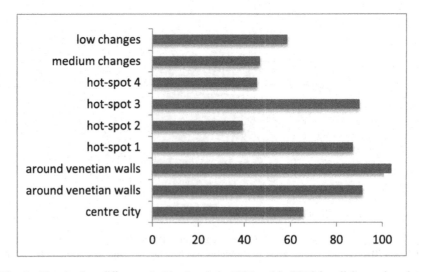

Fig. 5. The absolute difference in blue bands in 1987 and in 2016 for all 9 sample points

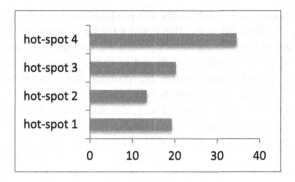

Fig. 6. The absolute difference in NIR bands in 1987 and in 2016 for all 'hot-spots'

in Near Infrared (NIR) band in both years (i.e. bands 4 and 11 from Table 2). Figure 6 shows that differences in reflectance of 'hot-spots' 1, 2 and 3 have a similar trend, while it is different for 'hot-spot' 4. NIR range of the spectrum this band is particularly suitable for detecting changes in vegetation. This observation could hence be an indication of change in vegetation cover in the 'hot-spot 4'.

5 Discussion

The results illustrated show that quite a few areas in Nicosia have been subject to land cover change and hence probably their land use. The PCA seems to be an adequate method for qualitative analysis and useful for identification of 'hot-spots' i.e. areas mostly subject to change. The limits of this approach is that areas cannot be assumed as 'hot-spots' only upon the investigation of satellite imagery but they need to be further examined using urban masterplans or technical maps. In addition to reflectance pixel values, the assumptions made on the type of land cover change are to be further elaborated using historic data and in-situ measurements, also due to the limit of the image spatial resolution. The method proposed can be however suitable for two reasons: (1) it can provide an overview of the changes on a territorial scale of entire municipalities (or even larger areas) and (2) it can help to identify specific areas of the city that have been subject to change and that require further investigation.

6 Conclusions

The study here illustrated was an attempt to observe changes in urban environment of the Nicosia municipality, in particular in the southern area around the walled historic city. The methodology employed regards the use of freely available satellite imagery that was examined using multi-spectral multi-temporal pairs of images. Further to the visual interpretation, the study illustrates a spectral enhancement method using a PCA. The results show some clear changes in the urban fabric in southern area of the walled city of Nicosia, helping to identify several significant 'hot-spots'. Possible use of such result could be seen in the development and implementation of the urban masterplans or planning the construction works that could have high impact on the historic urban structure e.g. new high speed transport connections, proximity of larger constructions to sensitive areas such as Venetian walls and so forth. However, it is important recall that in order to quantify and describe the changes more precisely, further in-situ measurements and comparison with historic information such as maps and aerial images needs to be performed. In such a way, it would be possible correlate in an even more significant manner the observations coming from satellite imagery with changes in the urban scenario that have occurred over the past three decades.

Acknowledgements. The present communication is under the "ATHENA" project H2020-TWINN2015 of European Commission. This project has received funding from the European Union's Horizon 2020 research and innovation programme under grant agreement No. 691936.

References

1. Neocleous, N., Papantoniou, A.: The implementation of the DLS portal and the INSPIRE geoportal of Cyprus. In: Proceedings of Fourth International Conference on Remote Sensing and Geoinformation of Environment (RSCy2016), Pafos, Cyprus (2016)
2. Janssen, K.: Open government data and right to information: opportunities and obstacles. J. Community Inf. **8**(2) (2012)
3. Cuca, B.: Geospatial future is open: lessons learnt from applications based on open data. In: Gervasi, O., Murgante, B., Misra, S., Rocha, A.M.A.C., Torre, C., Taniar, D., Apduhan, Bernady O., Stankova, E., Wang, S. (eds.) ICCSA 2016. LNCS, vol. 9788, pp. 491–502. Springer, Heidelberg (2016). doi:10.1007/978-3-319-42111-7_39
4. Directive 2003/98/EC on the re-use of public sector information (2003)
5. Agapiou, A., Alexakis, D.D., Lysandrou, V., Sarris, A., Cuca, B., Themistocleous, K., Hadjimitsis, D.G.: Impact of urban sprawl to archaeological research: the case study of Paphos area in Cyprus. J. Cult. Heritage **16**(5), 671–680 (2015)

Towards the Sustainable Development of Cultural Landscapes Through Two Case Studies on Different Scale

Eirini Papageorgiou[✉]

Cyprus University of Technology, CY 3036 Limassol, Cyprus
e.papageorgiou@cut.ac.cy

Abstract. Since the beginning of the twentieth century the definition of Cultural Heritage has gradually expanded from the scale of individual monument to the scale of cultural landscapes. The broadening of the term has at the same time increased the complexity of the information originating from different domains and being on different scales and forms. In this context, the objectives as well as the challenges involved in the Cultural Heritage sector have become highly diversified, often leading to fragmented and less successful interventions which do not conform with the principles of Sustainable Development. Therefore Cultural Heritage and Sustainable Development should correlate with each another. Pursuing the achievement of sustainable models of development for cultural landscapes, this paper investigates how the factor of scale can act as a linkage between the fields of Cultural Heritage and Sustainable Development.

Keywords: Cultural landscapes · River valleys · Network of settlements · Scale factor · Sustainable development · Heritage management · Strategic planning · Cultural Heritage

1 Introduction

1.1 Key Considerations

The concept of a historic monument embraces not only the single architectural work but also the urban or rural setting in which is found the evidence of a particular civilization, a significant development or a historic event. This applies not only to great works of art but also to more modest works of the past which have acquired cultural significance with the passing of time [1]. The above definition indicates that a number of characteristics are incorporated in the concept of Cultural Heritage (CH) which relate to time, space, scale, as well as tangible and intangible properties [2, 3]. The concept of CH nowadays refers not only to a variety of constructions offering physical evidence of the past, but embraces also places and surroundings [4]. This expansion of the concept allows not only monuments, groups of buildings and sites [5] to be considered as CH assets, but also urban centers, natural, mixed and cultural landscapes [6]. The gradual shift of the concept of CH asset from individual building to group of buildings, buildings' surroundings, districts, sites and whole areas indicates a parallel shift from the scale of the individual building and building complex to the scale of urban, town

© Springer International Publishing AG 2016
M. Ioannides et al. (Eds.): EuroMed 2016, Part I, LNCS 10058, pp. 625–644, 2016.
DOI: 10.1007/978-3-319-48496-9_50

and regional planning. In this context, the bigger the scale, the bigger the integration of "environment" in the concept of CH gets. In addition to the concept of "environment", the Burra Charter clearly states that cultural significance is embodied in the place itself, providing emphasis on the physical location of a place, which may have a range of values [7]. Landscape is considered to be an autonomous entity and a key element for the achievement of sustainable development, *based on a balanced and harmonious relationship between social needs, economic activity and the environment* [8]. Futhermore, the man-made environment correlates with the natural one, within it has been created and evolved, as well as with the society which has generated this CH asset on the one hand by providing funds and creativity and on the other hand by depending its livelihood on the beneficial uses of it. In this context, CH is regarded as one of the four interdependent elements, namely economic, social, cultural and environmental [9, 10].

On the other side, environment, society and economy are the three pillars, on the common grounds of which lies "Sustainable Development". According to the European Commission[1], *sustainable development stands for meeting the needs of present generations without jeopardizing the ability of future generations to meet their own needs – in other words, a better quality of life for everyone, now and for generations to come. It offers a vision of progress that integrates immediate and longer-term objectives, local and global action, and regards social, economic and environmental issues as inseparable and interdependent components of human progress.* In this context, CH is an element of Sustainable Development, as an integral part of each one of the environmental, social and economic components of the latter; a part that should be protected and *transmitted to the future generations to guarantee their development* [4].

Therefore CH acts at the same time both as an asset to be protected and supported in order for its existence to be safeguarded through time, and as a provider of *the tools and framework which help to shape, delineate and drive the development of tomorrow's societies* [11]. This twofold role of CH and its bidirectional relation to the parameters of environment, society, economy and the overall concept of Sustainable Development are illustrated in the figure below (Fig. 1).

Since the role of CH has been recognized to be an active one and due to its multifaceted nature, the need for CH management has been created [4, 8]. This management is also necessary to be assessed under the prism of sustainability, and towards that direction different methodological approaches have been developed [10, 12–15]. At the same time the role of strategic planning, as the process of *designing a desired future and identifying ways to bring about it* [18], has been highlighted [16, 17].

1.2   Case Studies – Selection and Goals

The large amount of information included in the field of CH, its multilevel interrelations as well as the complexity of the objectives and the challenges it faces, make any decision-making process difficult, often leading to fragmented and less beneficial

---

[1] http://ec.europa.eu/environment/eussd/ (accessed: 09/2016).

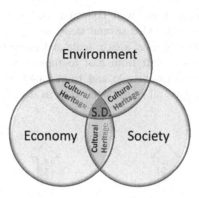

Fig. 1. Cultural Heritage and Sustainable Development (S.D.): a relation of mutual contribution

interventions. The bigger the scale of the CH asset, the bigger gets the problem of managing it and conform the interventions applied upon it to the principles of sustainability.

Through the consecutive presentation of two real case studies of cultural landscapes in mountain regions, which differ in scale, this paper aims to investigate the research question whether it is possible to achieve sustainable development on each one of these two scales of CH independently or only through the parallel and complementary survey of both spatial scales, in the context of regarding space and its components as a "whole".

The first case study refers to a network of nineteen riparian rural settlements along the axis of the river Karpenisiotis in Evritania prefecture (central Greece). The second case study refers to a single traditional settlement situated in the mountain region of Zagori in Epirus (northwest Greece). Both of the surveyed areas represent the *combined works of nature and man* [5], strongly influenced by the geomorphology, which has played a catalytic role in the definition of their boundaries as well as in the formation of their character. They are *illustrative of the evolution of human society and settlement over time, under the influence of the physical constraints and/or opportunities presented by their natural environment and of successive social, economic and cultural forces, both external and internal* [6], thus are characterized as cultural landscapes.

The purpose of this paper is the correlation of two multiparametric fields (CH, Sustainable Development) though an approach that extends in time, space, scale and properties, by using a variety of tools originating from different scientific domains. The goal of the aforementioned approach is to maximize the management capacity of the complex and diversified data of cultural landscapes, secure the efficiency of the research outcomes and safeguard the sustainability of the proposed interventions.

2   Methodology

2.1   The Method

Attempting to comprehend the character of the surveyed area the research in both case studies was conducted in four phases. In these phases the data from the sectors of environment, society and economy were collected, analyzed, assessed and formulated into proposals. Each phase included several steps, sectoral and intersectoral ones. In this context the parameters of time, space, scale and properties were taken into consideration. The bidirectional shift from past to future, from individual building to region, from microscale to macroscale and from tangible to intangible was a key element across all phases and all steps of the way, as depicted in Fig. 2.

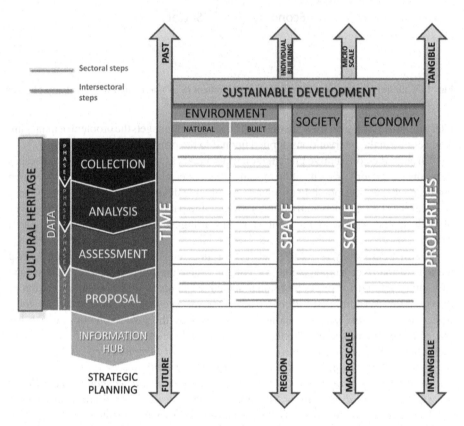

Fig. 2. Data management in correlation with time, space, scale and properties.

The first phase was the data collection phase, in which all the related documents and data that describe the spatial and economic evolution as well as the social changes through time were retrieved through research in archives and various sources. In the course of this procedure the engagement and the active participation of the local key players has been proven catalytic for the completeness of all information. Also during this phase extensive field work has been carried out.

The second phase was concerning the analysis of the collected quantitative and qualitative data. All the past studies and surveys as well as the implemented actions and projects were also analyzed, in order to understand the successes but also the failures and deficiencies of the existing policies. In this phase the combination of various information management tools which facilitate the depiction of the extensive thematic information, such as the ones used in the domain of architecture, urban and regional planning, have been proven to be highly supportive.

Following the phase of analysis, in the next phase the data were assessed also with the use of tools originating from the business sector, which have facilitated the classification of the latter into groups of strengths, weaknesses, opportunities and threats.

In the fourth phase, the information retrieved from the previous stages was used to formulate the proposals.

In any case, the aforementioned data that have been collected, analysed and assessed, can be considered as an "information hub" about the region (Fig. 2); an "information hub" which can support any decision-making process in terms of strategic planning. This "information hub" can also act as a fertile platform, upon which a *pool of knowledge* [19] can be created, in the meaning that all the involved parties (i.e. stakeholders, policy makers, local communities etc.) can complementarily and coherently create their own knowledge and added value for the region.

The above described methodology is presented in the following Sects. 2.1.1 and 2.1.2 in more detail for each one of the selected case studies. The steps taken as well as the tools used are different, depending on the scale of the surveyed area. In the case of the network of settlements, the scale extends from the one of regional planning to the one of urban planning, while the case of the individual rural settlement is presented through the shift from the scale of urban planning up to the scale of individual building.

2.1.1 Network of Settlements - *from the Scale of Regional Planning to the Scale of Urban Planning*

Environment. In Step 1, the boundaries of the surveyed area were defined according to specific criteria (Fig. 3 in Sect. 3).

In Step 2, data were gathered concerning the natural characteristics of the area such as climate, fauna and flora, aquatic resources, geomorphology, environmental zones, etc.

In Step 3, data about the typology of each settlement on the basis of urban planning, the building capacity and the land uses were gathered.

In Step 4, data regarding the built environment were collected, such as general architectural typology of the buildings, important constructions (bridges, watermills etc.) as well as significant locations and paths around the settlements.

In Step 5, the correlations between the natural and the built environment were surveyed.

In Step 6, data were gathered which concern the infrastructures.

In Step 7, a survey about the past and current administrative organization of the area and the prefecture has been conducted (Fig. 5 in Sect. 3), as well as the past and current legislative framework that is related to the urban and regional development.

In Step 8, data about the interconnections of the settlements are gathered, such as paths and trails that connect them etc.

Society. In Step 1, data about the characteristics of the population were gathered such as gender, age, schooling, density etc., as well as their change within a time span of a decade, in order to understand the nature of the inhabitants and their potential contribution to the actions proposed (Fig. 4 in Sect. 3).

In Step 2, data were gathered concerning historical facts, local traditions, festivals etc.

Economy. In Step 1, data regarding the three main production sectors (primary, secondary, tertiary) were gathered.

In Step 2, data regarding the labor status of the population were collected, as well as their change within a time span of a decade.

Intersectoral (Environment – Society – Economy). In Step 1, an extended analysis of all past studies and surveys, as well as of the implemented projects and actions has been conducted, for documentation as well as for assessment reasons.

In Step 2, there has been a contact with the representatives of the local communities as well as with the ones of the local and central authorities, in order to document their view regarding the problems, the deficiencies and the needs as well as the possible solutions. Moreover, in order to take into account their future vision for the area.

In Step 3, the Strengths and the Weaknesses of the region were highlighted alongside with the Threats that it faces and the Opportunities to be considered.

In Step 4, historic data were detected and interrelated with the partial abandonment of the settlements (Society-Environment) and the negative impact on Economy.

2.1.2   Individual Settlement - *from the Scale of Urban Planning to the Scale of Individual Building*

Environment. In Step 1, the already existing boundaries of the surveyed area were highlighted.
In Step 2, data were gathered regarding the natural environment, namely geomorphology, climate, fauna and flora, rainfalls, protected environmental areas etc.

In Step 3, data about the built environment were gathered, concerning the classification of the settlement within the wider network of settlements to which it belongs.

In Step 4, data about the settlement's typology on the basis of urban planning, its building capacity and the land uses were gathered.

In Step 5, built and non-built plots, built and free spaces as well as their indicators were defined (Fig. 9 in Sect. 4). Also the building uses were identified. Moreover, the role of landscape in the formation of the plots, of the urban units and of the road system was surveyed.

In Step 6, the architectural plans of the dwellings and of other special buildings of the settlement (church, school etc.) were collected and their form, design, construction materials and bioclimatic attributes were detected.

In Step 7, data regarding the connection of the settlement with the surrounding area were gathered, such as networks of paths, bridges etc.

Society. In Step 1, data about the characteristics of the population were gathered, such as gender, age, schooling, density etc., as well as their change within a time span of the last decade, for the same reason mentioned in Sect. 2.1.1.

Economy. In Step 1, data regarding the labor status of the population were collected, as well as their change within a time span of the last decade.

Intersectoral (Environment – Society – Economy). In Step 1, historic data were detected, in particular the ones interrelated with colonization (Society-Economy) and the gradual increase of the number of dwellings (Environment), thus concerning the transformation of the built space through time.

2.2   The Tools

The different scale of the case studies imposed the combined use of different tools, in order to manage and process the large amount of the collected information. These tools are briefly presented below:

2.2.1   Network of Settlements - *from the Scale of Regional Planning to the Scale of Urban Planning*

(1a) *GIS,* as a spatial analysis tool which facilitates the spatial distribution of various indicators, **(1b)** *Thematic maps,* which illustrate various information deriving from the phase of analysis, **(1c)** *Overall maps* for the surveyed area, **(2)** *Databases,* **(3)** *Aerial photographs* (scale 1:30.000), **(4)** *Site photographs,* **(5)** *Geophysical maps* (scale: 1:50.000), **(6)** *Topographic maps* (scale 1:5.000), **(7)** *Charts,* depicting the analyzed data, **(8)** *Documentation sheet* for each settlement (Fig. 6 in Sect. 3), with visual and descriptive information regarding the following data: name of the settlement, municipality, prefecture, altitude, total area (ha), settlement's typology, population characteristics and their change within the time span of a decade, special historical data with spatial impact, tangible and intangible cultural data (festivals etc.), special buildings and constructions (churches, watermills etc.), special locations and routes close to the settlements' boundaries, topographic map, aerial photograph and site photograph of the settlement, **(9)** *Documents,* which include data that can only be described in text form, **(10)** *SWOT analysis.*

In particular, SWOT analysis has been proven to be a very useful tool for the combination of the multiple information of the surveyed area and has provided a good basis for the formation of the strategic planning of the latter. In the spatial context of the particular case study, SWOT analysis has also been supplemented by the use of GIS, which has enabled *the spatial distribution of the indicators under analysis and highlighted environmental aspects and human interactions with the natural environment, thanks to the overlaying of thematic layers* [15]. This kind of spatial SWOT analysis is a tool which has also been used in other case studies [20–22] and includes data from the phase of analysis, regardless if they can be quantified or not.

2.2.2 Individual Settlement - *from the Scale of Urban Planning to the Scale of Individual Building*

(1) *Aerial photopraphs* (scale 1:5.000), (2) *Site photographs*, (3) *Topographic maps* (scale 1:5.000), (4) *Thematic maps*, which illustrate various information regarding the built and the free space of the settlement as well as its buildings (scale: 1:1.500), (5) *Charts,* depicting the statistic data, (6) *Documentation sheet* (Fig. 11 in Sect. 4) for each one of the buildings of the settlement, with visual and descriptive information regarding the following: name of the settlement, municipality, prefecture, number of the building and number of the urban unit to which it belongs, past and present building use, dating of the building, names of owners and their social characteristics, photograph and topographic map of the building and its plot, urban planning indicators, photographs and architectural drawings per elevation, short architectural description, buildings' typological characteristics and general architectural typology, construction materials, state of preservation, evaluation of importance and proposed protection grade, (7) *Architectural drawings*, (8) *3D sketches,* (9) *Typology table* (Fig. 10 in Sect. 4), which includes the classification of the settlement's buildings into the main identified categories (types and subtypes), alongside their architectural and dimensional variations.

In the following Sections (Sects. 3 and 4), the two case studies are presented along with a short description and a sample of the work done throughout the four phases of data management. This presentation acts complementarily to the facts that have already been described in Sects. 1 and 2, as well as to the ones that will be analyzed in Sect. 5 (Results).

3 Case Study 1: Network of Settlements – Development Perspectives for the Settlements of Karpenisiotis River Valley in Evritania Prefecture

The nineteen riparian settlements along the axis of Karpenisiotis river, belonging nowadays to three different municipalities, constitute a unity of special interest that has been surveyed in this dissertation of 2004 [23]. In particular, the river is situated at an altitude zone of 500 m.– 600 m. above sea level while all settlements are situated at an altitude zone between 700 m. and 1000 m. above sea level (Fig. 3).

In addition to the landscape characteristics, according to which a zone has been defined, the network of the settlements is established by the dense mesh of man-made paths that unites them and also from many historical facts, such as that in 1836 A.D. these settlements used to belong to the same municipality, which means that the area was considered to be homogeneous. Due to their location, their proximity to the river and the river valley which supported the existence of the settlements and the habitants' living, as well as their common characteristics in various other fields of tangible and intangible CH, these settlements are recognized to be a unity with common problems and needs and therefore be treated as a network with similar development potentials. The boundaries of the network are defined in such way, in order to align to geomorphological characteristics (natural boundaries) (Fig. 3), thus surpassing the existing

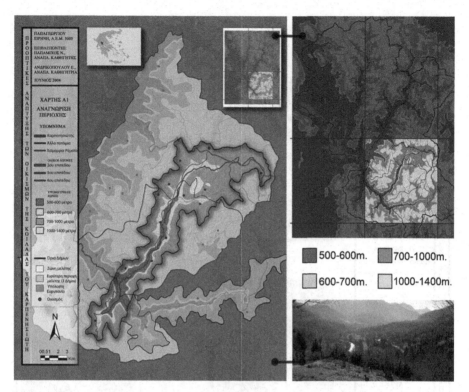

Fig. 3. Identification of the surveyed riparian area (valley of Karpenisiotis river)

ones, which have been defined according only to strict authority and administrative criteria (artificial boundaries) (Fig. 5).

Target of this project is the sustainable development of the area along the Karpenisiotis river through the judicious management of its resources and potentials. Fundamental belief is that the development of this (river) axis can serve as a model for the contiguous riparian valleys and their settlements, thus disseminating the development in the whole region. Worthmentioning is that all collected information was found scattered in various archives and authorities, while this project managed to gather the multiple and multifaceted information into one place, acting for the first time as an *information and knowledge hub* [24] about the region.

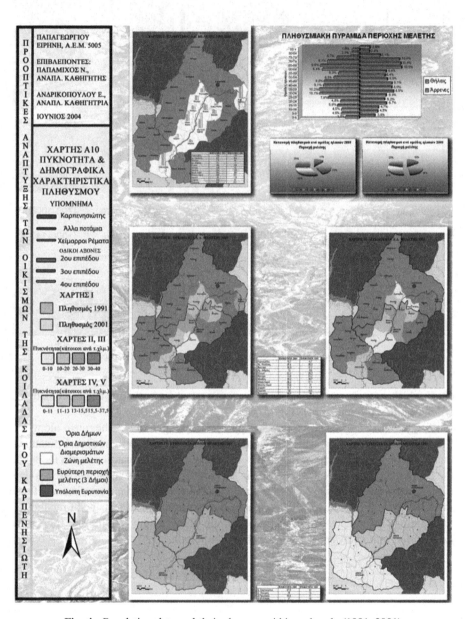

Fig. 4. Population data and their changes within a decade (1991–2001)

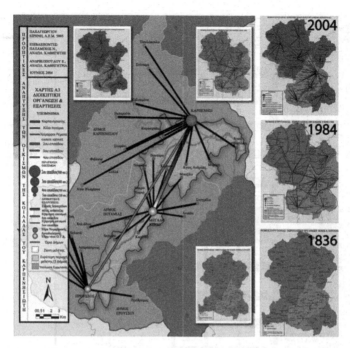

Fig. 5. Administrative structures and correlations in different time periods (1836, 1984, 2004)

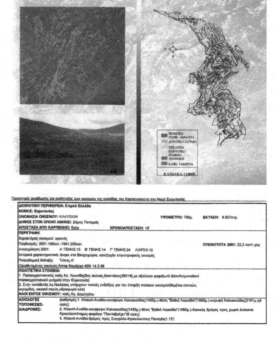

Fig. 6. Typical settlement's documentation sheet

636   E. Papageorgiou

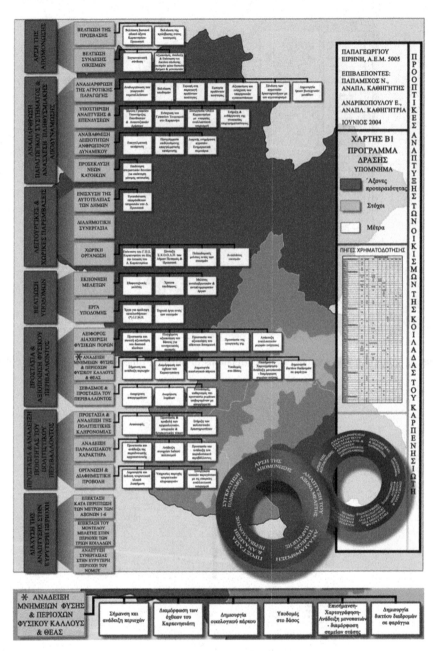

Fig. 7. Strategic axes for the development of the wider region (below, right); Strategic masterplan with axes, targets and actions specifically for the surveyed area and funding opportunities for their implementation (center); Detail of a proposed target with its supplementary actions (below)

4   Case Study 2: Individual Settlement - Conservation and Redevelopment of the Traditional Rural Settlement of Koukouli in Zagori of Epirus

After the study of a "network of settlements", the scale shifts from regional to urban. This case study refers to a single rural settlement with already defined boundaries and was surveyed in the context of a M.Sc. dissertation in 2006 [25]. The settlement of Koukouli in Zagori of Epirus (northwest Greece) is a traditional village situated on Tymfi mountain at an altitude of 880 m. above sea level, close to the Vikos gorge (Fig. 8) and the valley of Voidomatis river. It is surrounded by outstanding natural environment, which is protected by national and international laws. Moreover, it belongs to a wider network of settlements in the territory, called 'Zagorochoria', which according to national laws is recognized to be a *network of settlements carrying ancient traces of regional, urban and spatial organisation that have to be safeguarded.*

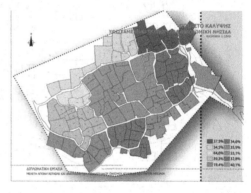

Fig. 8. The Vikos gorge in the wider region (Copyright: Geozah (CC BY-SA 4.0, https://commons.wikimedia.org/w/index.php?curid=49173760)

Fig. 9. Urban units and indicators about the built and non-built space of Koukouli (Figure created by the author; site plan adapted by [26])

Worthmentioning in this case is that the existing administrative boundaries of the settlement (illustrated in Fig. 9 with a strict outline) do not comply neither with the formation of the landscape nor with the boundaries that are distinctively formulated by the outline of the existing urban plots.

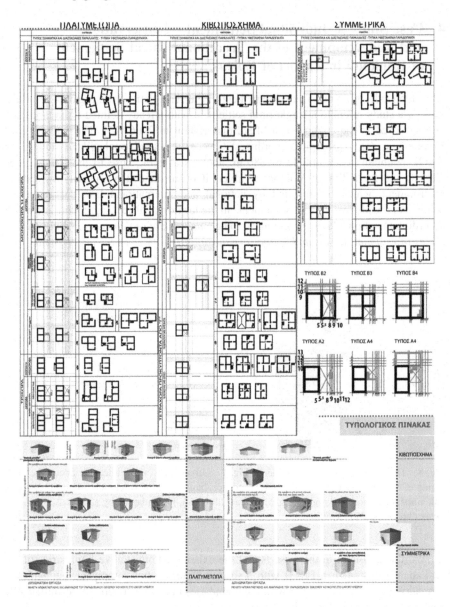

Fig. 10. Typology table with schematic representation of the dwellings' plans alongside their architectural and dimensional variations, classified in three basic categories (upper part); Schematic 3D sketches representing the evolution and variations of the dwellings' volume types (lower part). (Figures, schematic 2D-3D representations and concept created by the author; dwellings' survey plans adapted by [26])

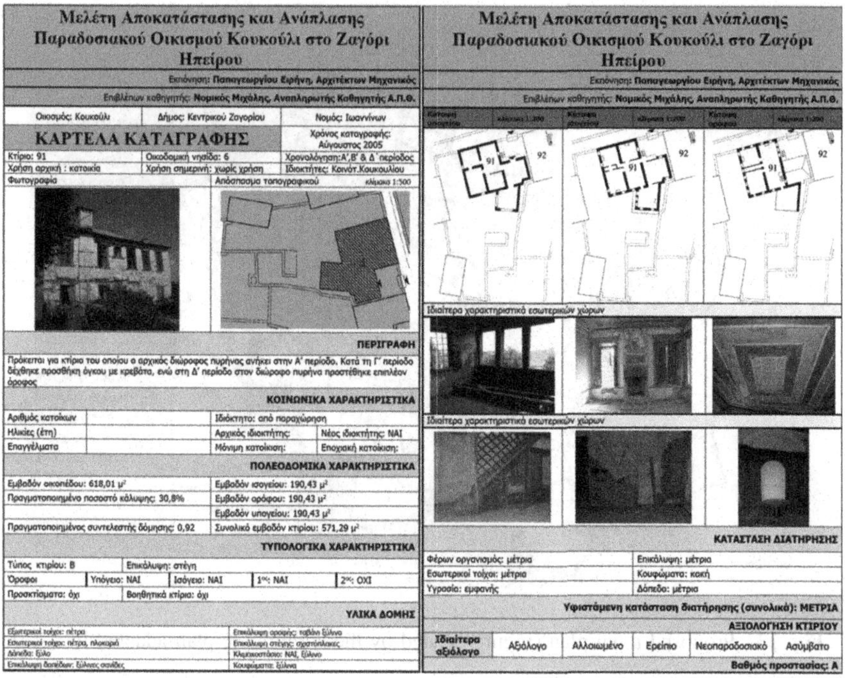

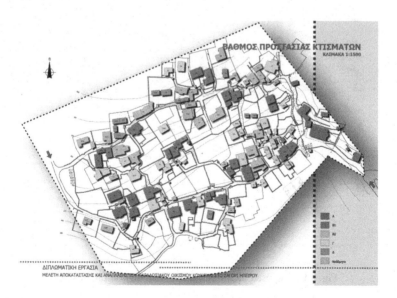

Fig. 11. Typical building's documentation sheet (Figure created by the author; dwellings' survey plans adapted by [26])

Fig. 12. Map of the proposed protection grade of the buildings, following the preservation state assessment in 2005 (Figure created by the author; site plan adapted by [26])

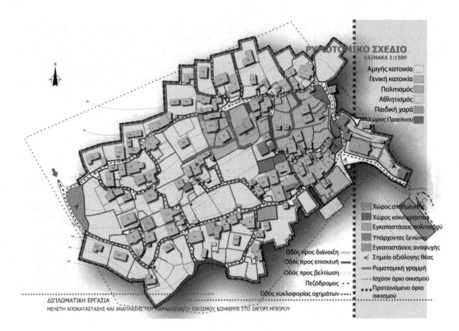

Fig. 13. Proposed town plan (Figure created by the author; site plan adapted by [26])

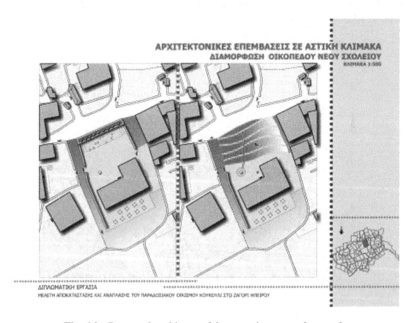

Fig. 14. Proposed architectural interventions on urban scale

5 Case Studies Results

Depending on the scale of the area surveyed in each case study, the research results differ and are presented below:

5.1 Network of Settlements - *from the Scale of Regional Planning to the Scale of Urban Planning*

In Step 1, a strategic masterplan for the development of the region was defined, as illustrated in Fig. 7 (see Sect. 3). Seven strategic axes were specified, each one of them was subdivided into targets and each one of the targets was further on subdivided into distinct actions.

In Step 2, funding opportunities were detected for all proposed actions included in the masterplan, thus confirming that the latter one is applicable within the current financing framework.

In Step 3, a series of thematic maps were produced, which illustrated the suggested spatial interventions, such as transportation network, infrastructures, environmental interventions, interventions for touristic development etc.

The aforementioned maps were complemented by a book of 220 pages, which included a full text description of the research procedure in all phases and the steps followed, as well as of the proposed strategic plan.

5.2 Individual Settlement - *from the Scale of Urban Planning to the Scale of Individual Building*

In Step 1, a new detailed Building Regulation was defined, aligned with the actual state of the particular settlement, its building and land use capacity and development potentials. This new Building Regulation was formulated specifically for the particular settlement, in contrast to the existing general Building Regulation which was the same for all the settlements belonging to the network of 'Zagorochoria', without having taken into account the particularities of each one of them. The proposed Building Regulation included also guidelines for the restoration of the old traditional buildings and the permitted interventions upon them according to their protection grade, the construction of new buildings in order to comply to the character of the settlement, construction materials, urban equipment etc.

In Step 2, a new town plan was proposed, which included all the building and land uses, the interventions on urban scale, the redefinition of the settlement's boundaries etc. (Fig. 13 in Sect. 4).

In Step 3, various thematic maps were produced in order to illustrate the spatial interventions, regarding the protection grade imposed on the buildings (Fig. 12 in Sect. 4), the planning of public spaces etc. (Fig. 14 in Sect. 4).

The data about the settlement throughout the phase of collection, analysis, assessment and proposal alongside with documentation sheets (Fig. 11 in Sect. 4), maps and charts have been included and extensively described in a book of 240 pages. This book supplemented in text form all the aforementioned (data and procedure).

Furthermore, the town plan alongside with the Building Regulation were the operational guidelines of the strategic planning, to which any intervention conducted within the settlement, should be aligned.

6 Conclusion

In both aforementioned case studies the exhaustive procedure of data collection, analysis, assessment and proposal in the context of time, space, scale and tangible-intangible properties in each one of the fields of environment, society, economy and culture has provided exceptional input for the strategic planning of each one of the two regions. Despite the fact that the same procedure was followed on each one of the two different scales (same four phases, same parameters of time, space etc. taken into consideration), diversified outcomes and distinct strategic planning proposals have been developed, which have subsequently led to different kind of interventions on each scale. Looking at the bigger picture, the interventions proposed on one scale stop at the point where the interventions of the next scale begin and do not disrupt each other. Minor overlapping of them on the urban scale can only be regarded as a "buffer zone" which enables the assimilation of the interventions and the smooth bidirectional shift from one scale to the other.

Through the case studies presented, it has become clear that the survey of every settlement individually is, in principle, positive, because all the data that have contributed to the formulation of the settlement and its character are gathered and assessed, its particularities are identified and therefore taken into consideration along the process of decision making and planning of the interventions upon it. However, for the interventions not to be fragmented and for the development of each settlement to be actually successful and beneficial, its planning should be incorporated into the planning of the broader spatial network to which it belongs (network of settlements), and reverse. Both of these scales act complementarily, enhancing each other with data and safeguarding the efficiency of the decisions taken on each scale, thus ensuring sustainability.

Under this prism the answer to the research question whether it is possible to achieve sustainable development on each one of these two scales of cultural landscapes independently, regarding each case as individual case study, or through the parallel and complementary survey of both spatial scales, in the context of regarding space and its components as a "whole", has also become clear.

Acknowledgments. The research leading to these results has received funding from the People Programme (Marie Sklodowska-Curie Actions) of the European Union's Seventh Framework Programme FP7/2007-2013/under REA grant agreement no. 608013. Special thanks also to my supervisors Dr. Eleni Andrikopoulou, Professor of Architecture, Dr. Nikos Papamichos, Assistant Professor of Architecture and Dr. Michael Nomikos, Assistant Professor of Architecture at the Aristotle University of Thessaloniki (AUTH) for the scientific support and guidance throughout the aforementioned projects.

References

1. ICOMOS: International Charter for the conservation and restoration of monuments and sites (The Venice Charter) (1964)
2. ICOMOS: The Nara document on authenticity (1994)
3. Vecco, M.: A definition of cultural heritage: from the tangible to the intangible. J. Cult. Heritage 11, 321–324 (2010)
4. UNESCO/ICCROM/ICOMOS/IUCN: Managing cultural world heritage (2013)
5. UNESCO: Convention concerning the protection of the world cultural and natural heritage. In: General Conference Seventeenth Session, vol. 1, pp. 135–145 (1972)
6. UNESCO: Operational guidelines for the implementation of the world heritage convention (2015)
7. Australia ICOMOS: The Burra Charter (1999)
8. Council of Europe: European landscape convention (2000)
9. Vernieres, M., Patin, V., Mengin, C., Geronimi, V., Dalmas, L., Noel, J.-F., Tsang King Sang, J.: Methods for the economic valuation of urban heritage: a sustainability-based approach (2012)
10. Dalmas, L., Geronimi, V., Noël, J.F., Tsang King Sang, J.: Economic evaluation of urban heritage: an inclusive approach under a sustainability perspective. J. Cult. Heritage 16, 681–687 (2015)
11. ICOMOS: 17th general assembly and scientific symposium "Heritage, driver of development". ICOMOS News, vol. 18 (2011)
12. Ferretti, V., Bottero, M., Mondini, G.: Decision making and cultural heritage: an application of the multi-attribute value theory for the reuse of historical buildings. J. Cult. Heritage 15, 644–655 (2014)
13. Ferretti, V., Comino, E.: An integrated framework to assess complex cultural and natural heritage systems with multi-attribute value theory. J. Cult. Heritage 16, 688–697 (2015)
14. Oppio, A., Bottero, M., Ferretti, V., Fratesi, U., Ponzini, D., Pracchi, V.: Giving space to multicriteria analysis for complex cultural heritage systems: the case of the castles in Valle D'Aosta region, Italy. J. Cult. Heritage 16, 779–789 (2015)
15. Comino, E., Ferretti, V.: Indicators-based spatial SWOT analysis: supporting the strategic planning and management of complex territorial systems. Ecol. Indic. 60, 1104–1117 (2016)
16. Cerreta, M., Panaro, S., Cannatella, D.: Multidimensional spatial decision-making process: local shared values in action. In: Murgante, B., Gervasi, O., Misra, S., Nedjah, N., Rocha, A.M.A.C., Taniar, D., Apduhan, B.O. (eds.) ICCSA 2012. LNCS, vol. 7334, pp. 54–70. Springer, Heidelberg (2012). doi:10.1007/978-3-642-31075-1_5
17. Fusco Girard, L., De Toro, P.: Integrated spatial assessment: a multicriteria approach to sustainable development of cultural and environmental heritage in San Marco dei Cavoti, Italy. Cent. Eur. J. Oper. Res. 15, 281–299 (2007)
18. Steiner, G.: Strategic planning: what every manager must know, a step-by-step guide (1979)
19. Žarnić, R., Rajčić, V., Moropoulou, A.: Identity card of cultural heritage: how to collect and organize data. In: Ioannides, M., Fritsch, D., Leissner, J., Davies, R., Remondino, F., Caffo, R. (eds.) EuroMed 2012. LNCS, vol. 7616, pp. 340–348. Springer, Heidelberg (2012). doi:10.1007/978-3-642-34234-9_34
20. Baycheva-Merger, T., Wolfslehner, B.: Evaluating the implementation of the Pan-European criteria and indicators for sustainable forest management – a SWOT analysis. Ecol. Indic. 60, 1192–1199 (2016)

21. Geneletti, D., Bagli, S., Napolitano, P., Pistocchi, A.: Spatial decision support for strategic environmental assessment of land use plans. a case study in southern Italy. Environ. Impact Assess. Rev. **27**, 408–423 (2007)
22. Sanò, M., Fierro, G.: Integration of the SWOT analysis as a coastal management tool with a geographical information system: two approaches to the problem and first results Dipartimento per lo studio del Territorio e delle sue Risorse (Dip. Te. Ris.) Università di Genova. Univ. Genova (2003)
23. Papageorgiou, E.: Development perspectives for the settlements of Karpenisiotis river valley in Evritania prefecture, Dissertation, AUTH (2004). (Original in Greek)
24. Ioannides, M., Davies, R., Chatzigrigoriou, P., Papageorgiou, E., Leventis, G., Niko-lakopoulou, V., Athanasiou, V.: 3D Digital Libraries and their contribution in the documentation of the past. In: Mixed Reality and Gamification for Cultural Heritage. Springer, Heidelberg (2016)
25. Papageorgiou, E.: Conservation and reformation of the traditional rural settlement of Koukouli in Zagori of Epirus. M.Sc. dissertation, AUTH (2006). (Original in Greek)
26. Christidis, V.: The architecture of the village of Koukouli in the area of Zagori, Epirus, vol. 1, 2, Rizareio Foundation, Athens (2004) (Original in Greek)

The Fortification System of the City of Urbino: The Case Study of Valbona Gate from 3D Surveys to GIS Applications for Dynamic Maps

Sara Bertozzi, Laura Baratin[✉], and Elvio Moretti

Conservation and Restoration School – DiSPeA,
University of Urbino Carlo Bo, Urbino, Italy
{sara.bertozzi,laura.baratin,elvio.moretti}@uniurb.it

Abstract. The city walls of the city of Urbino, originally Metaurense Urvinum, today represent the result of an evolution that has antique origins, from proto-historic settlements to the first Roman ruins, up to its current conformation, expression of the important Renaissance period. We present a study of documentation, survey and analysis of the various parts of the walls, analysed in their entirety and in individual elements, among these we focus on the main access gate to the historic centre, Valbona Gate. The integration of avant-garde technologies during all the phases, from the survey to the graphic rendering, up to advanced management with GIS instruments allows us to have a picture of the architectural reality both of the present and the past, fundamental for scheduled maintenance and for planning future conservation interventions. The geometric and morphological survey brought the process to completion with the problems relating to deterioration, the understanding of the situation of the pathologies and the descriptive dimension of the architectural elements in a complete bi- and tri-dimensional GIS system that allows us to take advantage of a complete series of processing and statistical assessment capabilities. The project is part of a wider program of research on the walled city of Urbino, wherein the analysis of the city walls integrates with the diachronic analysis of its expansion and the geomorphological context in which it is found as well as a 3D City Model and the analysis and management of the built environment, current and archaeological.

Keywords: 3DGIS · Walled city · Urbino

1 Introduction

The management, evaluation and maintenance capabilities of the architectural heritage are currently based on the immense capacity of reading and interpretation of knowledge concerning the use of innovative computing instrumentation. In particular, a fundamental concept that is exalted by the integrated use of organic surveying techniques with those for the management of data is that of documentation. It serves as a tool to make information accessible to those who cannot investigate the property itself and it becomes an integral part of the conservation process that should be based on thorough

© Springer International Publishing AG 2016
M. Ioannides et al. (Eds.): EuroMed 2016, Part I, LNCS 10058, pp. 645–656, 2016.
DOI: 10.1007/978-3-319-48496-9_51

research, physical and analytical surveys [1]. The study of a walled city provides a thorough assessment of its historical evolution and the relationship that the architectural composition and its development may have had with the very life of the city and its inhabitants. It is therefore necessary to define and organise all the information concerning both the internal living apparatus, which constitutes the historical core of the city, and the walls themselves that delimit it, defensive structures that over the centuries became a historical testimony and physical delimitation of the cultural and vital centre of the city. The walls had functioned as a protection for the inside inhabitants from outsiders, identified the city's boundary, and in some cases defined powerful families' or rulers' territory [2]. The entire documentation process involves a painstaking phase of identification and recording of the information that is useful in defining an appropriate planning strategy for conservation and intervention. The complex nature of the historic city requires a detailed documentation and the mapping of its cultural and natural characteristics, a thorough knowledge of its urban morphology, historical evolution, physical and functional characteristics and socio-economic processes.

Several works have been carried out on the analysis of the walled cities and on city walls, for a deeper understanding of the city and to preserve elements of such great importance [3–5]. For some years now in the city of Urbino, UNESCO World Heritage Site, there has been a series of research programmes that have allowed us to carry out various levels of investigations [6–9], from the geomorphological evolution of the territory on which the town is located to a diachronic analysis of the metamorphosis of the city walls from the preurban phase to the current state, up to a detailed definition of the urban apparatus through the 3D City Model and an integrated analysis of plans and elevations of individual architectural buildings of interest [10, 11], all managed in the GIS environment for a possibility of advanced management.

We now define, in the proposed work, a thorough analysis of the city walls, to proceed to an operation of documentation and assessment of the possible deterioration and impairment due to events which have taken place in the course of time, evaluating the various levels of risk and the applicable interventions. The analysis of the built environment in elevation can also be carried out through a stratigraphic reading of the archaeological type, in fact, the sequence with which various parts of the architectural object were built or restored can be documented with methods similar to those applied to deposits that have been buried. Indispensable for rendering this process operational is the high reliability and resolution of the survey, because, even if the artefact is still the primary source of information, there is the absolute necessity to record every consideration that derives from direct observation in a scientifically correct way. Naturally, the three-dimensional model produced by a series of laser scans remains the best way to implement this virtuous process. Its management through GIS technology allows us to implement the organisation and the interrogation of the data supplied by the survey by means of a relational database. To implement the project on the city walls of Urbino, a series of laser scanner surveys have been carried out, starting from the main Gates, allowing us to read the individual stones or bricks, determine the various types or characteristics, establish the conservation status and record all previous restoration interventions to which it had been subject over time. The result is a dynamic mapping of the "GIS based" prospectuses made available to the management entities, in order to provide scheduled maintenance that limits the maintenance or reconstruction interventions over time. In order to implement an effective scheduled conservation action, it is not enough to have a thorough physical knowledge of the object one seeks to preserve, but it is necessary to know and analyse historical events connected to it and to accurately reconstruct all the previous interventions of restoration that the object has undergone in the course of time.

2 Urbino Walled City

The birth of the Duchy of Urbino dates back to 1443, in virtue of the nomination of Oddantonio II da Montefeltro to Duke of Urbino by Pope Eugene IV. He reigned for less than a year. In 1444, he was in fact assassinated following a popular uprising, which brought his older half-brother Federico to power, who will prove himself to be one of the greatest princes on the Italian chessboard of the era, as famous for his role as commander in battle as he was renowned as a cultured patron of the arts. Under his guidance, from 1444 to 1482, the duchy soon became one of the focal points of the Italian Renaissance. During this brief period the city underwent a radical transformation, induced especially by the decision of Federico to build his residence on the Poggio, already seat of the first settlement in the Roman epoch. The Palace would become over the centuries a true manifesto of Renaissance architecture and has been defined by the critic Kenneth Clark as: "the prototype of the Renaissance palaces and the most beautiful in the world".

The urban structure that the city assumes after the interventions carried out during this period and which has come down to us still intact, even now represents the summit of Renaissance architecture, harmoniously adapted to its physical environment and to its past, making it an entirely exceptional place, which since 1998 has been registered in the list of Unesco World Heritage sites. The main actors of urban transformations were mainly the architects Luciano Laurana and Francesco di Giorgio Martini who would leave their mark, still visible today in the architectural structure of the city.

In 1508 the duchy passed to the della Rovere family, who transferred the seat of the duchy to Pesaro and then passed to the State of the Church in 1631. In 1621, on the occasion of the marriage of the last Duke of Urbino, Federico Ubaldo della Rovere who married Claudia de' Medici, Porta Valbona was erected. A new golden age for the city of Urbino arrived at the beginning of the eighteenth century, following the election to the papacy of Clement XI, part of the Albani family. This figure, with enlightened patronage, promoted the construction of civil and religious buildings, contributing to giving a more modern structure to the city, without however changing the development of the walls in a significant way. In the course of the 1860s only a small portion of the wall was demolished in order to build a Toll Barrier, named after the then Princess Margaret of Savoy, erected in part also on the Bastion of Belisario. This change, however modest, still resulted in the rebuilding of the section of the walls between the Bastion of San Polo and the small Bastion of San Girolamo, demolished during these works. Built at the same time was the new road that, passing along the walls, connects the Barrier Margherita to the current Piazza della Repubblica square that led to the closing of the San Polo Gate. In 1906, again with the aim of further improving access to the city, the Del Monte Gate was demolished and buried or most of the bastion was knocked down to create a lookout on which the monument to Raphael was erected. Taking into account these changes, the historic city walls of Urbino, as shown on the the chorographic plan of 1841 of Fig. 1, include seven city gates, thirteen bastions and the Albornoz Fortress.

Lastly, in the sphere of the reorganisation and restructuring plan of the historic centre launched by the city of Urbino in 1964, which included the restoration of the patrol walkways on the walls, the reopening of the Francesco di Giorgio ramp and the recovery of the old stables of the Duke called the "La Data", also included was the transformation of the Mercatale into underground parking for cars below the level of the plaza. The works began in 1969 and were concluded in 1972 by the architect Giancarlo De Carlo. With the parking lot and the closure of the railway line that connected Urbino to Fano in 1987 the Mercatale saw a vast increase also of the number of buses arriving, and the square continues to carry out its function as the main access to the city of Urbino, even if today the bus station has been moved to the complex of Santa Lucia Gate.

3 Valbona Gate

The most important of the changes that have been imposed following the construction of Palazzo Ducale was not the demolition of many old buildings located on the Poggio, where the ancient Roman city once had risen, but the urgent need to acquire new spaces for the expansion of the entire urban nucleus.

Palazzo Ducale, which exemplifies this theme, stands on the Roman forum (altitude 450 m) but the western side acquires space with an almost vertical development, conquering the entire escarpment and individuating two fundamental levels, that of the foundation of the Torricini (small thin towers) (altitude 433 m) and that of Mercatale, delineated by the Renaissance walls on one side and by the great work that is the "Risciolo" by Francesco di Giorgio Martini on the other. The huge substructure wall is composed of seven masonry vaults that support the Mercatale Plaza that, as local tradition dictates, was created over the rubble and soil that was moved there so as to build the foundation of Palazzo Ducale itself and that, upon its completion at ground level, reaches an altitude of 410 m. The base of the substructure wall is located at the minimum altitude of 384 m and then, in its maximum elevation, covers a vertical drop of no less than 26 m. The section of Fig. 2 shows the altitude profile starting from the Albornoz Fortress on the left, to Palazzo Ducale, with the positioning of the square of Piazzale Mercatale, Valbona Gate, the substructures of the Risciolo and the Spiral Ramp.

In the vast Piazzale del Mercatale (Market Square), which owes its name to the fairs and markets that were held there in the past, rises Valbona Gate, the architectural construction connected to the city walls, designed and built by the Urbino architect, Sigismondo Albani. It is the only Gate of Urbino with a monumental face directed outwards, opening toward the main access route to the city. It is an architectural product that is perfectly up-to-date with the examples of the late Mannerist and Baroque period, very probably derived from the models of the Treatise by Sebastiano Serlio, with the face having smooth ashlars to act as a background to the pairs of lateral

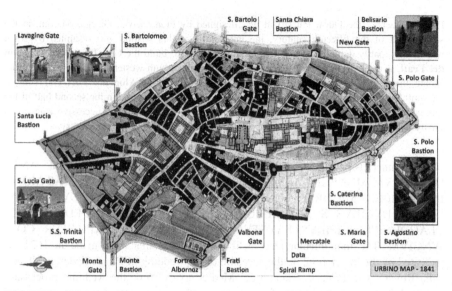

Fig. 1. The chorographic plan of the city of Urbino with all the gates, bastions and the Albornoz Fortress indicated. These artefacts have constituted the defensive apparatus of the city and still today the majority of them are conserved. **Valbona Gate**, even today the main point of access to the city; **Santa Lucia Gate**, situated on the south-eastern slope of Colle del Monte, north of the city walls; **Lavagine Gate**, rebuilt in the seventeenth century, following the demolition of the homonymous bastion adjacent to the city gate, is located at the bottom of the south-eastern slope of Colle del Monte; **Del Monte Gate**, no longer existing, was located on the hilltop of Colle del Monte, at the summit of the current Via Raffaello, north-west of the ancient city, was demolished in the early years of the twentieth century in order to improve the viability of the area and access to the historic center; **San Bartolo Gate**, located on the eastern slope of Colle del Poggio, east of the city walls; **Santa Maria Gate** or Sant'Agostino, located on the western slope of Colle del Poggio, close to the bastion of Sant'Agostino; **San Polo Gate**, situated on the southern slope of Colle del Poggio but, from the 1860s no longer accessible to public transit, after the construction of the nearby Toll Barrier; the **Bastion of Santa Lucia**, it is the northernmost tip of the boundary wall, not accessible to the public, because it hosts a private garden; **Bastion del Monte**, semi-destroyed during the early years of the twentieth century, only the base has survived because it is underground, was adjacent to the homonymous city gate; the **Bastion of San Bartolo**, located close to the homonymous city gate, collapsed in February 1928 and rebuilt in the early 1930s; the **Bastion of Santa Chiara**, situated on the south-eastern slope of Colle del Poggio; the **Bastion of Belisario**, in the south-east of the city walls, was restored in the 1860s, it conserves part of the buildings of the old Barrier Margherita; the **Bastion of San Polo**, representing the extreme southern tip of the walls, was restored in the nineteenth century; the **Bastion of Sant'Agostino**, situated on the western side of the walls and of the Colle del Poggio; the **Bastion of Santa Caterina**, located on the western slope of Colle del Poggio, rebuilt in 1963, following a partial collapse due to erosion of the underlying ground; the **Bastion della Santissima Trinità**, situated on Colle del Monte, to the north of the city walls between the Del Monte and Santa Lucia Gates; the **Bastion of Lavagine**, demolished in the seventeenth century, was adjacent to the homonymous city gate; the **Bastion of San Girolamo**, demolished in the 1860s, was a small bastion of semicircular shape on the south-eastern slope of Colle del Poggio, between the bastions of Belisario and Santa Chiara; the **Bastion of the Spiral Ramp**, its principal feature is a large spiral staircase that connects the ducal stables known as "La Data" that are located adjacent to the section of the walls between this bastion and that of Santa Caterina, at

Palazzo Ducale, (the Ducal Palace). It was designed by Francesco di Giorgio Martini, in the second half of the fifteenth century, the upper part of this bastion was occupied by some warehouses, partly demolished in the nineteenth century to build the City Theatre; the **Bastion dei Frati**, a small bastion of semicircular shape, on the south-western side of the Colle del Monte, under the Albornoz Fortress and above Valbona Gate; the **Albornoz Fortress**, rising in the south-western corner of the city walls, on Colle del Monte, erected in the second half of the fourteenth century by Cardinal Anglico Grimoard, modified in several successive stages and finally restructured in its current form toward the first half of the sixteenth century.

semi-columns supporting the inscription: VRBINVM ROMANORVM ANTI-QVISSIMVM MUNICIPIVM VMBRIA OLIM VETVSTISSIMA CIVITAS MODO INTER PICENI MAIORES, LONGE TAME HISCE TEMPORIBVS SVB SEREN-ISSIMIS DVCIBVS SVIS CLARIOR, SED ILLARIOR NVQ; FEDERICO ET CLAUDIA PRINCIPIBVS FAVSTVM ET SAECVNDVM PRECATVR CON-IVNGIVM. The monumental face, deliberately spectacular, was made in 1621, as indicated by the inscription, on the occasion of the wedding of Prince Federico Ubaldo della Rovere with Princess Claudia de' Medici, to welcome the wedding procession and the bride and groom coming from Florence. Placed along the route were triumphal arches enriched with figurations, most of them were precarious works. This Gate is the exception, built with stone and bricks despite the fact that it was known that the wedding procession and the bride and groom would stay in Urbino just one night. The Duke established his residence in Pesaro where in February 1622, Vittoria was born, destined to be the last descendant of Della Rovere family. In fact, Federico Ubaldo would die the next year in Urbino, having just reached the age of 18, on 28 June 1623. Still today and not only because it is linked to these historical facts, but also for its important function as the main access to the city, Valbona Gate is the most important of the seven gates that are part of the city walls of Urbino.

Valbona Gate has always created many problems linked to deterioration, especially of the stone material, for which various interventions of restoration were carried out, indispensable for reaching the current state of conservation. The first was carried out by Mastro Silvio Tommasini in 1755 and it focused mostly on the ornamental part and on the stabilisation of the two eagles, work by the architect Giovan Francesco Buonamici. Included in the context of the same restoration, reinforcements were made to the wall alongside the Gate. In 1825 it was Giuseppe Corsini who undertook some repairs and restoration on the external monumental part. It was then the turn of the Technical Officer of the Municipality of Urbino who, on 27 September 1873 approved a project for the removal of a public fountain which was close to the door. The reason for the intervention was essentially of an aesthetic nature because the fountain was used as a drinking trough for animals. However, a subsequent appraisal dated 17 October 1873 highlighted the severe conditions of deterioration involving the entire gate and he ensured that work of a structural type of restoration would be carried out with extreme urgency. Despite the work carried out, in 1784 there was the need once again for a major intervention of consolidation and maintenance. Also in the 1950s, it was nec-essary to intervene with other structural work, a result of which was the walkway above the gate being created, by removing some houses the two ends of via Mazzini were

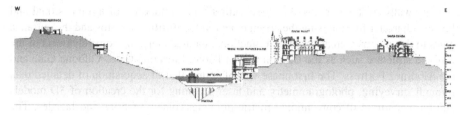

Fig. 2. Section circa W-E of the city of Urbino which shows the difference in height on which the main buildings of the city are located: from right to left the Albornoz Fortress, Piazzale Mercatale with the substructures of Risciolo and Valbona Gate, the Spiral Ramp, Palazzo Ducale and the complex of Santa Chiara.

connected, as well as other minor changes including the insertion of an epigraph at the summit of the pediment that testified the restoration work carried out in those years; the text reads: ANNO JVBILAEI MCML AERE PVBBLICO PRINISTINI OPERIS AD EXEMPLAR RESTITUTUM. The last restoration interventions in order of time date back to 1985–1986 and were carried out by the firm Carli and again in 1995 by the same company on indications of Croci.

4 Survey and GIS Projet

The analysis and management of data relative to the walls of Urbino for different levels of users takes place through various steps and the integration of a series of methodologies and technologies that find in GIS the optimal support for complex and diverse needs. The initial input data are obviously the base cartographies, in particular the 1:1.000 maps supplied by the Municipal administration, showing all of the elements that compose the historical centre of Urbino and the areas adjacent to the fortified system, both as urban fabric (buildings, roads, walls etc.) and as territorial characteristics (contour lines outside the urban centre, topographic points, boundaries of green areas, etc.). Integrated with them are the CTR, (Regional Technical Map), having a 1:10.000 scale, thematic geological and geomorphological maps, acquired by the CARG project, again at the 1:10.000 scale in Raster format, which are the basis for a reconstruction of the orography of the terrain in current terms and in those of historical evolution, in addition to maps of various historical eras and the iconographies for the transformation of the urban area both in the historical centre and along the city walls.

The project concerning the walls of Urbino aims at providing an effective instrument in the framework of scheduled maintenance that can manage not only the restoration interventions, but also serves as continuous monitoring of the current situation and a means for future evaluations that also take into account the future valorisation of this historical segment of the city.

As indicated, the project is part of a wider programme of research on the management of the heritage of the city's historical centre, part of the UNESCO heritage, both in its current connotations and in those of the past.

The walls are then analysed in their entirety for evaluations of a dimensional and logistic character by analysing the arrangement of the fortified systems and the entrance gates to the city, as well as those of a functional nature, analysing some elements of the fortified structure such as the Bastion of San Paolo, Lavagine Gate, Valbona Gate and the Albornoz Fortress. The first phase was of course that of acquisition of detailed data through surveying, photogrammetry and laser scanning for the creation of 3D models and the restitution of conventional metric drawings: plans, sections and facades. The initial process is therefore based on a series of surveying operations, aimed at controlling the dimensional consistency, the characterisation of the various descriptive typologies (history, techniques, materials, form and nature of deterioration, etc.) and to the creation of the basis on which to operate the subsequent analysis and study of the themes, to then move to a stage of display and fruition of the data, within which it is possible to manage a reconstruction of reality in a highly flexible way, that is, one that is useful for diverse types of end users.

Direct and photographic surveys have led to aerial photography renderings that shall integrate the topographical survey through total station, carried out through topographical points identified by architectural targets and the point clouds deriving from the laser scanner. The entire step of alignment and cleaning of the clouds has led to the creation of the grid and the 3D model, allowing the insertion of horizontal and vertical planes that define plans, prospectuses and sections of the final architectural and metric surveying. The graphic rendering, all the iconographic documentation and information on the material characteristics and on the various surveys executed in the course of time on the gate and on the evolution of its conformation, were integrated into a GIS system (ArcGIS in its latest version 10.3.1) which allows the analysis and management in two- and three-dimensional environments. The 3D surveys were also modelled to define the various phases of evolution of the architectural shape of the gate, starting from the second half of the fifteenth century to its current definition (Fig. 3).

The structuring of the GIS project starts in the 2D environment, then in ArcMap where a series of methodological steps were defined in order to bring together all the data available in map, section and prospectus into a single project, connecting them to one another through complete relational databases, to finally bring about the three-dimensional environment only as data management and query. The idea is to start from the georeferenced maps, in this case in Monte_Mario_Italy_2 (WKID: 3004; Authority: EPS; Projection: Transverse_Mercator; False_Easting: 2520000.0; False_Northing: 0.0; Central_Meridian: 15.0; Scale_Factor: 0.9996; Latitude_Of_Origin: 0.0; Linear Unit: Meter (1.0), for a general and territorial framework of the elements being studied. Particular attention is paid in this phase to the organisation of the walls in the map, organised as polygonal features but subdivided into various segments that identify the areas targeted for intervention to which the reliefs refer. This subdivision already allows dimensional analysis of the structural elements of the fortifications and the first statistical evaluations to be performed, bringing about their connection with the rest of the in-depth information through the organisation of a relational database. Inserted in the attributes table is an identifier field of the particular section of the wall, which is used as a key field in a Join operation with prospectuses and sections of detail, always managed within the same project, but spatially placed in a completely different position. The GIS is in fact used as a management programme of

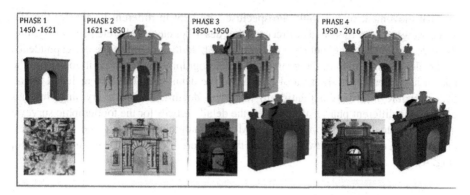

Fig. 3. 3D reconstruction of the various building phases that have affected Valbona Gate. The first gate was built in conjunction with the construction of the walls of the Federico period at 2,67 m from the current level of the road surface, whose foundations have been brought to light during some excavations. On the occasion of the extension works of Palazzo Ducale, the walls and the gate were rebuilt, however defining a very simple form with a vault bricks and without ornaments. On the occasion of the wedding of Federico Ubaldo della Rovere with the Princess of Tuscany Claudia de' Medici the gate was adorned with a giant order of twin columns in Tuscan style, two niches with statues, a frieze and a swan-neck pediment. Over the next three centuries a series of restoration works were carried out that had not radically modified the monument, with the exception of two eagles in massif limestone in the first half of the eighteenth century, in place of the shrines placed above the niches, whose statues had been stolen between the late seventeenth and early eighteenth centuries. In the course of the centuries, various dwellings were built against the rear side of the gate, taking advantage of the spaces where the sentinels stood guard, during the period of the reign of the Montefeltro family. During the last phase in 1950, an epigraph was placed at the centre of the swan-neck pediment certifying some restoration of the artistic type carried out on the Gate. In those years there was also the project which involved the demolition of the homes built onto the gate for the realisation of the walkway that extended on the eastern part of the walls until the Spiral Ramp of Francesco di Giorgio Martini.

geographical maps, but its development in relation to spatial elements that cannot undergo classic georeferencing is still of great interest. In this case, the use of the workspace, therefore the XY plane, is utilised as a simple work plan to manage metrically correct spatial data such as prospectuses and sections which can be applied to all the typical analyses of the Spatial Analyst tools. This XY plane becomes a hypothetical XZ plane, as if the elevation could be handled in its vertical plane, so as to allow the transformation of every element in the 3D feature and then subject each one into a subsequent georeferencing for management in 3D, in the ArcScene environment, in their correct geodetic position.

However, the entire phase of organisation and data processing takes place in ArcMap, so that coexisting in a single project are the georeferenced cartography and the data arising from the reliefs, prospectuses and sections, brought together in a separate area of the workspace. For the sake of convenience, a linear feature is used that starts from the 0.0 coordinates by creating the X axis definition line (considering the workspace as the XZ plane) on which all polygonal features are placed that describe the vertical movement of the walls. Prospectuses are kept in different layers, for the elevated weight of the thousands of records that describe, element by element, everything down to the single stone, but each of them has a field that identifies the correspondence to the element in a map in the georeferenced cartography. In this way, it goes from the spatial identification of the area of interest, to the detailed relief. Also included are all the mappable information relative to historical documents and everything that has covered the different phases of the relief, the detail vertices for the topographic surveys, the orthophotos, the photoplanes, etc. All information is stored in the Geodatabase environment, divided into two parts, one that is georeferenced and the other that is not (Fig. 4).

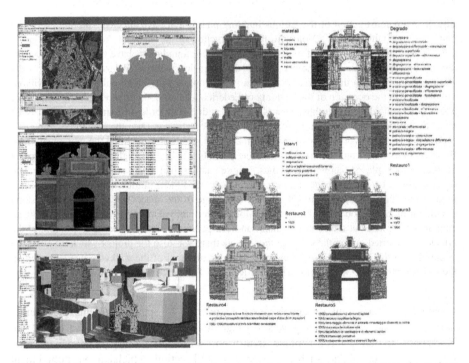

Fig. 4. The image shows the methodological approach used with GIS to manage the various components of the walls of Urbino, taking Valbona Gate as an example. At the top, the georeferenced walls are divided into segments that identify the elements of interest, listed in the table of attributes with the field NameID, that serves as a key field for the relational database with which to move directly to the prospectus of interest, in this case that of Valbona Gate. Each element of the prospectus is associated with a series of information in a table that can provide a number of different views, with the creation of dynamic cartography, which also allows the processing of graphs and statistical analyses. The management and the final querying of the whole project is carried out, after appropriate placing and georeferencing, in the 3D environment, where maps, models and prospectuses coexist.

Of essential importance was an accurate analysis phase of the types of construction materials and of the current deterioration that, in some portions of the walls, such as that from the Albornoz Fortress to the Bastione dei Frati, has brought about outlining a mapping of the surface deterioration, of the infesting weeds and of the biological colonisation, leading to identifying the effects that these have had on the masonry, the major causes that may have led to certain critical issues and the types of intervention needed to restore optimum conditions. The percentage of coverage of the different biological forms in the various sections analysed and a thorough assessment of the characteristics and impact of each of these on the masonry types present has allowed us to identify a danger index, indicative of the areas on which to intervene with greater urgency. Sampled and analysed, by means of the mass spectrometer, were also a series of in-depth samples. Summary data sheets were created to describe the spectra present and the main descriptive information, transforming them into images to insert in the attributes table. A special layer, a feature class, indicates the mapping of the samples, indicating in the database the type of biological species referenced and returning a field in Raster format that allows the insertion of images that can be directly queried by the geometric element in the workspace.

5   Conclusions

The project brings about an accurate definition of the walls of Urbino, in particular Valbona Gate, through a well-defined process that allows us to carry out a detailed study to acquire knowledge about the historical, artistic and architectural characteristics of the artefact and its evolution over the centuries, arriving at a complete plan for currently surveying and managing these characteristics. The integration of advanced instrumentation allows us to combine the geometric and morphological data with descriptive qualitative information that leads to the use of final management in two- and three-dimensional GIS environments. Thanks to the capacity of organising all data into a single Geodatabase system, the information relating to the conservation status and to deterioration, restoration interventions carried out, comparisons with other similar types of gates, the constructive evolution, the mapping of the pathologies, previous and scheduled interventions, all layers become searchable and stackable, so that they may be subjected to queries and statistical analysis, the basis for a thorough scheduled maintenance.

Acknowledgements.   We acknowledge students and professors of the First Level Master "Instruments and Methodologies for Cultural Heritage Conservation and Valorization" of the University of Urbino Carlo Bo for your cooperation and Municipality of Urbino for all available materials for research purposes.

References

1. Husseini, B., Bali, Z.: Documentation, using GIS techniques in conservation of a World Heritage Site, a case study of "The Old City of Jerusalem". In: The International Archives of the Photogrammetry, Remote Sensing and Spatial Information Sciences, 25th International CIPA Symposium 2015, Taipei, Taiwan, 31 August – 04 September 2015, vol. XL-5/W7 (2015)
2. Bennison, A.K., Gascoigne, A.L.: Cities in the Pre-Modern Islamic World: The Urban Impact of Religion. State and Society. Taylor & Francis, Abingdon (2007)
3. Shah, K.: Documentation and cultural heritage inventories, case of the historic city of Ahmadabad. In: ISPRS Annals of the Photogrammetry, Remote Sensing and Spatial Information Sciences, 25th International CIPA Symposium 2015, Taipei, Taiwan, 31 August – 04 September 2015, vol. II-5/W3 (2015)
4. Mohareb, N., Kronenburg, R.: Arab Walled Cities: investigating peripheral patterns in historic Cairo, Damascus, Alexandria, and Tripoli. In: Proceedings of Eighth International Space Syntax Symposium, Santiago, PUC (2012)
5. Guley, K., Abbasoglu, S.: Proposal for the revitalisation of the Walled City Famagusta. In: 2005 WSEAS International Conference on Environment, Ecosystems and Development, Venice, Italy, 2–4 November, pp. 90–95 (2005)
6. Bertozzi, S., Baratin, L., Moretti, E.: L'evoluzione delle trasformazioni di un centro storico tramite GIS: la città di Urbino. In: Proceedings of ESRI Italia 2016, Rome, Italy, 20–21 Aprile 2016
7. Baratin, L., Bertozzi, S., Moretti, E.: Le trasformazioni della città di Urbino durante il periodo dei Montefeltro: tecniche innovative per lo studio delle trasformazioni urbane. In: Processi di analisi per strategie di valorizzazione dei paesaggi urbani. I luoghi storici tra conservazione e innovazione, Proceedings. 29 Gennaio 2016, Rome, Italy. A cura di Gerardo Maria Cennamo. Ermes. Servizi editoriali integrati S.r.l., Ariccia (RM), pp. 105–115 (2016). ISBN 978-88-6975-094-6
8. Baratin, L., Bertozzi, S., Moretti, E.: GIS intelligence for a cutting-edge management of 3D Cities. In: Proceedings of Digital Heritage – International Congress 2015, Granada, Spain, 28 Settembre – 2 Ottobre 2015 (2015)
9. Baratin, L., Bertozzi, S., Moretti, E.: The Geomorphological transformations of the City of Urbino: the design of the city analysed with GIS tools. In: SCIRES it, SCIentific RESearch and Information Technology, vol. 5, no. 1, pp. 41–60 (2015). e-ISSN 2239-4303, doi 10.2423/i22394303v5n1pp41 © CASPUR-CIBER Publishing, http://caspur-ciberpublishing.it
10. Bertozzi, S., Moretti, E.: Gestione integrata dei rilievi del Portico di San Francesco ad Urbino. In: Baratin, L, Acierno, M, Muratore, O. Strumenti e Metodi per la Conservazione e la Valorizzazione dei Beni Culturali. Ancona, IL GABBIANO S.r.l., pp. 114–121 (2015). ISBN: 978-88-905347-7-5
11. Bertozzi, S., Baratin, L., Moretti, E.: Cultural Heritage: restituzione reale di prospetti e piante in ArcScene. In: Proceedings of 15 Conferenza Italiana Utenti ESRI, Rome, Italy 09–10 aprile 2014, Supplemento a GEOMEDIA, vol. 2–2014, ISSN: 1128-8132
12. Mazzini, F.: I mattoni e le pietre di Urbino, pp. 62–64, Argalia editore, Urbino (1982)
13. Luni, M.: Archeologia nelle Marche - Dalla preistoria all'età tardoantica, pp. 195–196, Nardini editore, Firenze (2003)

Project Paper: Innovative Methods on Risk Assessment, Monitoring and Protection of Cultural Heritage

Disaster-Risk Indicators and Their Evaluation, Communication for Traditional Settlement

Alex Ya-Ning Yen and Chin-Fang Cheng[✉]

China University of Technology, 56 Sec. 3 ShingLong Rd., Taipei 116, Taiwan
{alexyen, aabbyy}@cute.edu.tw

Abstract. Disaster-risk management has become an important issue in the conservation of cultural heritage since the beginning of 21st century. However the implementation procedure of the disaster-risk management was mainly focused on single monument and short of the research for the settlements which is still a big challenge for us. In 2005, to comply with the international trend, Taiwan amended the Cultural Heritage Conservation Act, in which settlements as a new category of monuments were declared – *"Settlement: a group of building s, street houses, settlements which have architectural style, landscape, historical, artistic or scientific value."* This research develops disaster-risk indicators for the traditional settlement and takes Quion-lin settlement, a World Heritage potential site as an example, analyzing the procedure to set up a network of conservation value and the disaster-risk indicators for traditional settlement. GIS will play as an important tool for the integration and communication within the stakeholders.

Keywords: Disaster-risk indicators · Traditional settlement · Cultural heritage · GIS

1 Introduction

In 1989, the General Assembly of the United Nations proposed a natural disaster reduction plan (IDNDR, 1990–1999) for next decade. Yokohama Strategy Plan In 1994 released an action program on the prevention, preparedness as well as mitigation for the prevention of natural disasters. In 2005, United Nations Department of International Strategy for Disaster Reduction (UNISDR) announced the Hoygo Framework for Action 2005–2015, HFA, for disaster mitigation extending to the level of national and community resilience. The overall goal was trying to establish a global strategy for disaster mitigation.

In the beginning 20 years, the objects of world cultural heritage sites were mainly in single buildings. However, under the influence of the Washington Charter, 1987, Cultural landscape Charter, 1992, Xian Declaration, 2005 and Quebec Charter, 2008, the concept of conservation has extended to the site and place of heritages. The conservation of Historic Urban Landscape had been noted as an important challenge in the "Operational Guidelines for the Implementation of the World Heritage Convention, OG." A management approach methodology has been discussed in recent years and the disaster-risk management has been identified as one of the important parts of this

© Springer International Publishing AG 2016
M. Ioannides et al. (Eds.): EuroMed 2016, Part I, LNCS 10058, pp. 659–668, 2016.
DOI: 10.1007/978-3-319-48496-9_52

approach. However, the tools on the risk assessment and monitoring for the implementation of traditional settlements are important research issues.

In 2005, to comply with the international trend, Taiwan amended the Cultural Heritage Conservation Act, and declared settlements as a new category of monuments. *"Settlement: a group of buildings, street houses, settlements which have architectural style, landscape, historical, artistic or scientific value"*.

This research takes Quion-lin settlement, a World Heritage potential site as an example, analyzing the procedure to set up a network of conservation value and the risk indicators for traditional settlement. GIS will play as an important tool for the integration and communication within the stakeholders.

2   Literature Review

2.1   Disaster-Risk Indicator

Based on the concept for disaster-risk management of cultural heritage, some integration framework had been established by important international organizations which is a top down idea and helps to construct a more comprehensive network with the relevant disaster prevention system. Under the above effort[1], some useful tools were developed to help the evaluation. 5 important impacts for the World Heritage, (pressure from the developing, environment, disaster-risk, tourist/recreation and the number of resident) were identified in the "Format for the nomination of properties for inscription on the World Heritage List, 2015". In 2011, the ICCROM had released a toolkit for the risk assessment and 14 risk indicators were noticed in this document. Which are buildings and Development, transportation Infrastructure, utilities or Service Infrastructure, pollution, biological resource use/modification, physical resource extraction, local conditions affecting physical fabric, social/cultural uses of heritage, other human activities, climate change and severe weather events, sudden ecological or geological events, invasive/alien species or hyper-abundant species, management and institutional factors, and other factor(s).

2.2   Public Participation

The World heritage Committee released the Budapest Declaration in 2002. A 4C strategy (Credibility, Conservation, Capacity building and Communication) was announced to help the conservation of the WH. In 2007, the 31st World Heritage Committee was held in Christ Church City, New Zealand. In this meeting the fifth C (Community) was added and became a 5Cs strategy. This issue was put in the article 26 of OG (Fig. 1).

---

[1] Ya-Ning Yen, Chin-fang Cheng, 《Research on the GIS as a communication platform in the risk management of traditional settlement》, 2014.

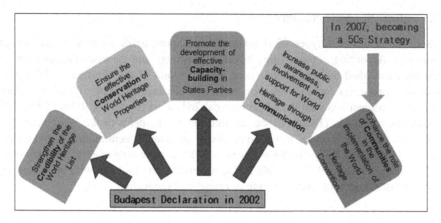

Fig. 1. 5Cs strategy

The ICOMOS Charter for the Interpretation and Presentation of Cultural Heritage Sites, 2008, made clear definition and provided efficiency for the general public to understand the CH.

- *Interpretation refers to the full range of potential activities intended to heighten public awareness and enhance understanding of cultural heritage site. These can include print and electronic publications, public lectures, on-site and directly related off-site installations, educational programmer, community activities, and ongoing research, training, and evaluation of the interpretation process itself.*
- *Presentation more specifically denotes the carefully planned communication of interpretive content through the arrangement of interpretive information, physical access....... and multimedia applications and websites.*

2.3   The Experiences of Taiwan

A value based conservation and management approach were key concepts of the Conservation Act, 2005; public participation was identified as an important part of implementation. Based on this Act, a self-management plan for the site manager was developed. Through a 4 years' research, 18 potential risk indicators of the monument were identified and put in the management plan. However, a boarded scope research on the settlement and environment is still needed.

3   Execute Process

Firstly, from the literature review, this research will establish the risk-disaster indicators for the historic settlement. Secondly, through AHP method (Analytic FDM (Fuzzy Delphi Method)) we can set up a working table for evaluating those indicators. To the end, under the concept of 5Cs strategy, a GIS based cultural mapping will be developed as a tool for the communication within the stakeholders.

3.1 Risk-Disaster Indicators

There are 2 different types of risk-disaster indicators needs to prepare for certain purposes. According to the existing research, indicators and the assessment weighting can be established for single monument. Take 5 topics of the "Format for the nomination of properties for inscription on the World Heritage List (2015)" as a reference and make comparison with the 14 disaster-risk indicators by the ICCROM (2009)[2], 18 indicators in Taiwan (Table 1)[3]; we can find the requirements of the WH monitoring are far beyond the practical needs especially in the management affairs. Based on the result of Table 1, a similar tool was developed for the reviewing of entire settlement by AHP (Table 2). Basically, the table includes 3 main parts together with indicators for the risk assessment: disaster prevention, rescue and recovering.

3.2 Public Participation and GIS

This research takes 5 steps for the implementation (Fig. 2).

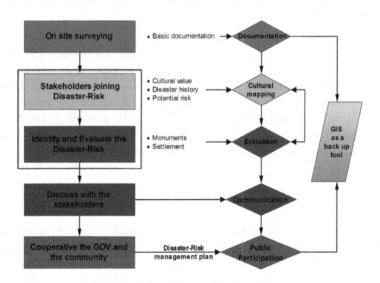

Fig. 2. Public communication, participation and GIS

- Build up a basic documentation of the settlement and transfer all the information into the GIS as a basic platform on site surveying.

---

[2] These 14 indicators were taken in the ICCROM workshop on the monitoring of WH in Suzhou, China, 2009.

[3] Ya-Ning Yen, Chin-fang Cheng, Hung-Ming Cheng, 《Disaster Risk Management and Measurement Indicators for Cultural Heritage in Taiwan》, 2015.

Table 1. Disaster-risk indicators

Format for the nomination of properties for inscription on the World Heritage List (2015)	ICCROM (2009)	Disaster-Risk indicators in Taiwan (2016)
1. Development Pressures	1. Buildings and Development 2. Transportation Infrastructure 3. Utilities or Service Infrastructure	10. Disaster history 11. Improper placement of items
2. Environmental pressures	4. Pollution 5. Biological resource use/modification 6. Physical resource extraction 7. Local conditions affecting physical fabric	16. Pests or ants Road 17. Increased moisture, wall seepage serious
3. Natural disasters and risk preparedness	10. Climate change and severe weather events 11. Sudden ecological or geological events 12. Invasive/alien species or hyper-abundant species	18. Other factor(s)
4. Responsible visitation at World Heritage sites	2. Transportation Infrastructure 3. Utilities or Service Infrastructure 9. Other human activities	18. Other factor(s)
5. Number of inhabitants within the property and the buffer zone	8. Social/cultural uses of heritage 9. Other human activities	1. The use of fire 2. Improper placement of items 3. Undated environmental clean-up 4. Excessive electrical facilities, lines of old (including extension cords)

(*continued*)

Table 1. (*continued*)

Format for the nomination of properties for inscription on the World Heritage List (2015)	ICCROM (2009)	Disaster-Risk indicators in Taiwan (2016)
	13. Management and institutional factors	1. The use of fire 2. Improper placement of items 3. Undated environmental clean-up 4. Excessive electrical facilities, lines of old (including extension cords) 5. Management organization and lack of staff 6. Failure in regularly attending relevant courses or lack of certificates 7. Cooperation with community 8. Lack of fire-fighting equipment 9. Lack of monitoring alarm 12. Insufficient entrances (including those are often closed) 13. Unused to be repaired/repair/repaired 14. Gutters are not smooth 15. Doors and windows damaged
	14. Other factor(s)	18. Other factor(s)

- Invite the stakeholders joining a cultural mapping exercise mainly on the identification of the cultural value (tangible, intangible and their locations), disaster history and potential risk. All the results will integrate into GIS.
- Survey and evaluate all the possible risk-disaster indicators of the monuments, settlement and mark in the GIS.
- Discuss with the stakeholders on the results of step 2, 3 which process can help them to get community awareness on the risk preparedness and the necessity of its management.
- Establish a cooperative based on the information from the GIS of the GOV and the community. At this moment, GIS will become a tool to help the management, education, communication and monitoring.

Table 2. Risk assessment in settlement

A. Disaster prevention	
Nature, Environment	(1) Climate Change, (2) Typhoon, (3) Flooding, (4) Earthquake, (5) Fire, (6) Biological, Microorganism
Manmade disasters	(1) Military, (2) Fire, (3) Burglar, (4) Traffic accident
Development pressures	(1) Illegal development, (2) Traffic
Usage behavior	(1) Tourist, (2) Improper use, (3) Festival
Mitigation	(1) Exercises, (2) Education
B. Disaster rescue	
Evacuation	(1) General evacuation, (2) Tourists evacuation
Roadside Assistance	(1) Main road, Secondary roads, (2) Evacuation Site
Natural resources	(1) Water, (2) Well
Equipment	(1) Fire hydrant, (2) Alarm device, (3) Monitoring, (4) Water Supply
C. Recovering	
Physical	(1) Resettlement sites, (2) Materials, (3) Craftsman, (4) Administrative Support
Psychological	(1) Tutor, (2) Resettlement

4   Quion-Lin Settlement Example

4.1   Background

Kinmen is one of the 18 potential sites of World Heritage sites in Taiwan with "various threats of war in 1600 years' history in-between continuing to pursue the values of peace" as its major value. Quion-lin settlement is one of the main strongholds of the Kinmen inscription. Tsai clan based in Quion-lin settlement has more than 1,000 years of history and many ancestors in the family became government officials or made glorious military achievement. Currently the settlement has about 1,800 residents, 8 national monuments, 1 county cultural settlement, 2 historic buildings, 2 intangible cultural heritages (Wind Lion God, Quion-Lin Ancestor worship), 332 traditional settlements, accounting for 43.92 % of all, is known as a living traditional culture settlements. Quion-Lin settlement was registered as cultural settlement in December 2011.

4.2   Procession

This research takes 5 steps to implement the survey of disaster-Risk indicators and their assessment, communication with the stakeholders (Fig. 3). After the advanced survey and analysis, a disaster- risk map (Fig. 4) was developed together with several important issues.

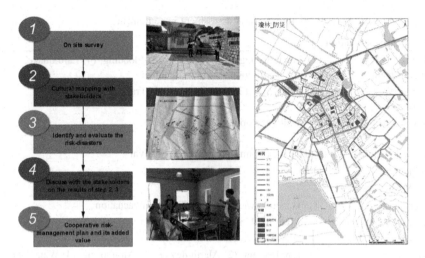

Fig. 3. Procession of disaster-risk indicators

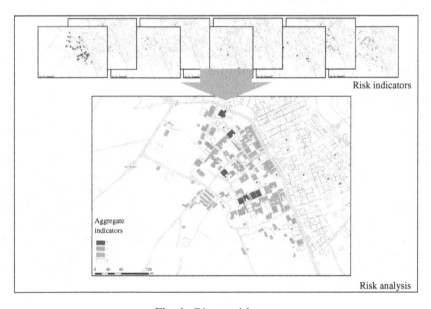

Fig. 4. Disaster-risk map

1. People's understanding of the disaster mostly restricted to individual homes. Important factors relevant whole settlement, such as spreading risk, relief roads, as well as emergency water was lack of pervasive awareness.
2. GIS is an efficient tool for risk communication and as a platform for the advanced researches' implementation such as the simulation by FDS, PATH FINDER etc.

4.3   Discussion

- Through a 3 years' processing in Quion-lin (2013–15), a clear risk management plan has been established which can help the advanced researches. However the following implementation framework such as legal, training, monitoring and integrative exercise is still needed (Fig. 5).

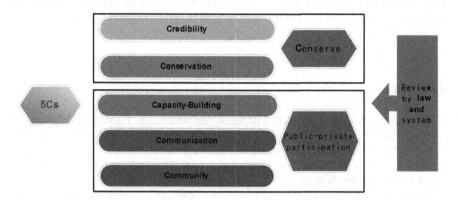

Fig. 5. Popular participation in safety management system

- In this case, the residents of Quion-lin can understand the importance of risk management. On the other hand, how to balance the contradiction within the conservation and developing pressure is still a big challenge.

5   Conclusion

In the era of 21 century, the challenge for the conservation is not only to proceed with the monument or its culture content, but also focuses on the additional value resulted from public participation, education and management during the process of conservation. There are many researches on the enforcement of awareness for public participation in conservation. Various topics have been discussed in those papers, such as method, tool, medium, value, assessment, etc. for risk management. Moreover, how these efforts can be applied on site?

This research finds,

- By referring the existing document and experiences, we can establish the risk-disaster indicators and the relevant information of traditional settlement as a foundation for building the risk management plan. From onsite surveying, assessment (monuments, entire environment) and the message from the cultural mapping with the stakeholders can make a great help to integrate various ideas. GIS is an efficient tool in this process.

- Disaster prevention and management should not only relay on some physical monitoring of cultural heritage (such as electronic devises' monitors), but also strengthen cooperation between the public and private sectors. Integrating the information from public participation, the GIS system can play as a communication platform for risk management as to linking the private community with other public departments to make added value.

Acknowledgements. Special thanks to the project "Research on the risk communication and resilience of historic district" (MOST 103-2625-M-163-001), sponsored by the Ministry of Science and Technology.

References

1. Klir, G.J., Folger, T.A.: Fuzzy Sets, Uncertainly and Information. Prentice Hall, Upper Saddle River (1988)
2. ICCROM, Wijesuriya, G.: Approaches to condition assessment (2009)
3. China University of Technology: Kinmen County Settlement King Lam preservation and redevelopment plan, Kinmen County Department of Cultural Affairs (2014)
4. China University of Technology: Monuments built and settlements district calendar professional services centre (II), Bureau of Cultural Heritage (2016)
5. UNESCO: Operational Guidelines for the Implementation of the World Heritage Convention (2015)
6. Yen, Y.-N., Cheng, C.: Research on the GIS as a communication platform in the risk management of traditional settlement. In: Euromed 2014, Cyprus (2014)
7. Yang, W.-B., Cheng, H.-M., Yen, Y.-N.: An application of G.I.S on integrative management for cultural heritage- an example for digital management on Taiwan Kinmen cultural heritage. In: Euromed 2014, Cyprus (2014)
8. Yen, Y.-N., Cheng, C., Cheng, H.-M.: Disaster risk management and measurement indicators for cultural heritage in Taiwan. In: 25th International CIPA Symposium (2015)
9. http://www3.rits-dmuch.jp/anshinanzen/. Accessed May 2016

Pervasive Wireless Sensor Networks for the Monitoring of Large Monumental Structures: The Case of the Ancient City Walls of Siena

Alessandro Pozzebon[✉], Tommaso Addabbo, Ada Fort, Marco Mugnaini, Enza Panzardi, and Valerio Vignoli

Department of Information Engineering and Mathematical Sciences, University of Siena, Via Roma 56, 53100 Siena, Italy
alessandro.pozzebon@unisi.it,
{addabbo,ada,mugnaini,panzardi,vignoli}@ii.unisi.it
http://www.iism.unisi.it

Abstract. In this paper, a solution for the pervasive monitoring of large monumental structures based on the use of Wireless Sensor Networks is presented. In particular, the paper focuses on the case of the Ancient City Walls of the city of Siena, Italy, that still surround the whole historic centre and require a real time monitoring of the cracks present in several points.

Two different network topologies are presented for the deployment of a pervasive monitoring infrastructure, and a novel sensing platform based on the use of Hall effect based sensors is presented. The architecture of the whole sensor node is described, together with the laboratory test phase that proves the effectiveness of the proposed solution. The proposed solution is expected to be deployed in a 1.8 Km section of the city walls in the next months.

Keywords: Wireless Sensor Network · Monumental structures · Hall Effect sensor · Mesh network · Distributed network

1 Introduction

The monitoring of the static of vast monumental buildings poses several problems in terms of system design, pervasive coverage and data reliability. With the term "Monumental buildings" we indicate all these structures that are characterized by large dimensions and a high historical, artistic and cultural value, like castles, cathedrals or palaces. These buildings can be in some cases centuries old, and present structural cracks that can evolve leading to permanent damages or even collapses.

The monitoring of these structures and the realization of alert systems is a complex activity due to many factors. The biggest one is the dimension: large

© Springer International Publishing AG 2016
M. Ioannides et al. (Eds.): EuroMed 2016, Part I, LNCS 10058, pp. 669–678, 2016.
DOI: 10.1007/978-3-319-48496-9_53

buildings may present several critical points, thus requiring a large quantity of sensing devices. This means that the realization of a pervasive infrastructure can be expensive and depends on the number of sensors to be deployed. Moreover, data acquisition can be complex with a wired sensor network: reaching all the sensors with a cable would mean to cover the surface of the building with a wide network of wires.

The second factor that affects the deployment of a sensing infrastructure in a large monumental building is its high historical and artistic value: this implies that the instrumentation to be positioned on the structure must have a low visual impact. Small sensors should be employed, possibly choosing devices that could be embedded inside the walls. Similarly, wirings should be avoided or minimized.

Finally, the last factor that must be taken in account concerns the effectiveness of the monitoring infrastructure as an alert system to warn against possible risk situations. This means that the monitoring infrastructure should be able to provide data in real time and then remotely: commonly used visual systems like crack meters require the intervention of an operator to manually detect possible changes in a crack and may not be sufficient to detect possible collapses.

Wireless Sensor Networks (WSN) [1] can represent the ideal solution to face all the problems listed before. The term WSN is widely used to indicate all the monitoring infrastructures composed by a variable number, from few unities to even some thousands, of sensing devices, called Sensor Nodes, provided with wireless connectivity, and then able to transmit, locally and remotely, all the collected data sets. Sensor nodes can be deployed in large quantities, thus covering even large structures, they can be designed to reduce as much as possible (even down to some tens of euros) their cost, and their wireless connectivity prevents from the installation of wires. Sensor nodes are usually small, and their shape can be designed to be adapted to the final installation environment, thus reducing as much as possible their visual impact. Finally, Sensor Nodes can be provided with global connectivity, allowing the real time data transfer to a remote data collection centre in charge of providing alerts in case of critical situations.

The use of WSNs for Structural Health Monitoring has been widely studied [2,3]. The most part of the described systems focus on the monitoring of civil infrastructures [4]: for example in [5] the use of WSN in bridge health monitoring is described, while in [6] the use of intelligent WSNs fior the evaluation of concrete buildings is presented. Some solutions focusing on the use of WSNs for the monitoring of historical buildings can also be found [7,8]: in particular, in [9] a Wireless Sensor Network for the monitoring of the medieval Torre Aquila in the city of Trento, Italy is described, while [10] presents a WSN to be deployed in the Basilica S. Maria di Collemaggio in the city of L'Aquila, Italy, badly damaged by the 2009 earthquake.

The solution proposed in this paper focuses on the monitoring of an historic structure of huge dimensions, the City Walls of the city of Siena, Italy, and proposes the use of novel, high-precision, low-cost sensors, that can be employed in large quantities, thus allowing the deployment of a truly pervasive monitoring infrastructure. The paper is structured as follows: in Sect. 2 the case study, i.e.

the City Walls of Siena, are briefly presented, together wit their peculiar structural problems. Section 3 describes the proposed Network architectures, while the structure of the sensing device is presented in Sect. 4. Section 5 presents the result of the first tests carried out in the last months while in Sect. 6 some final conclusions are presented together with the work to be carried out in the next future.

2   The Case Study

As already told, the proposed monitoring infrastructure has been shaped to be deployed on the ancient City Walls of the city of Siena, Italy (Fig. 1). This huge architecture still surrounds the whole historic centre of the city and is one of the most imposing witnesses of the importance of the city during the Middle Ages. It was built along several centuries, even if the walls that can be seen today were mostly built in the thirteen and fourteen century. The path of the walls runs for about 7 km, enclosing an area of about 180 ha: it is interrupted only by 8 monumental gates. The structure reaches in some points a height of 15 m, and a thickness of about 2 m.

While the whole structure is currently in a good state of preservation, it presents several hundreds of cracks that require continuous monitoring to avoid possible collapses which may also occur as a result of critical meteorological phenomena. In particular, the Municipality of Siena is currently focusing its attention on a 1.8 Km section of the walls in the south-east corner of the city, moving from the *Porta Romana* monumental gate to the *Porta Ovile* monumental gate. This is the section that will be interested by the first deployment of the monitoring infrastructure and where a test campaign has been started in August, 2016. In this section, two sites have been identified for the first tests, the *Porta Romana* test site (Fig. 2(a)) and the *Porta Ovile* test site (Fig. 2(b)): in these sites cracks moving along the three dimensions can be found, requiring the design of three different sensor layouts. Moreover, this section is surrounded by green areas, without connection to the electricity line: this means that an energy harvesting solution has to be set up to allow the continuous operation of the system.

3   Network Architecture

In order to develop a monitoring infrastructure able to cover the whole section of the City Walls under study, two different network topologies have been proposed, all based on the use of IEEE 802.15.4 XBee radio modules, providing a maximum transmission range of around 100 m in line of sight. While the thickness of the Walls could reduce this range, all the sensors are expected to be positioned on the same side of the walls: this means that they are ideally always on line of sight.

The first network topology is a centralized architecture based on a mesh topology, while the second one is a distributed topology composed by a set of

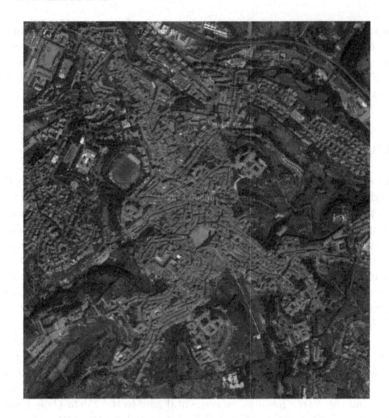

Fig. 1. The historic centre of Siena with the City Walls.

(a)   (b)

Fig. 2. The two test sites: *Porta Romana* (a) and *Porta Ovile* (b).

autonomous sub-networks based on a star topology. These two different topologies are due to the main features of the structure to be monitored: the City Walls extend in length and the deployment section is around 1.8 Km long, and then a centralized star topology has to be discarded due to the impossibility to reach the farthest nodes. Similarly, a tree topology was discarded due to the high dependence on failures to intermediate nodes.

The first topology (Fig. 3(a)) foresees the realization of a single Gateway node provided with both local (IEEE 802.15.4) and global (GPRS) connection. This node is in charge of receiving all the data transmitted by the other nodes and transmit them to the remote data collection centre. The nodes are arranged according to a mesh topology based on ZigBee protocol, that allows multi-hop: this solution is especially fault tolerant and it allows the operation of the system in the event of failure of a single node. On the other side, the system is strictly dependent on the operation of the Gateway node: if this node fails, the whole infrastructure can no longer operate.

The second topology (Fig. 3(b)) is based on the deployment of more than one Gateway, in charge of collecting the data from all the nodes in line-of-sight around it. Such a solution has higher costs due to the need of more than one GSM transmission module, but is more resistant to failures: in particular, the autonomy of the single star networks allows each sub-system to operate autonomously and not depend on the functioning of the other sub-systems.

4   Sensor Node Structure

The wall crack monitoring is performed by a low-cost dedicated displacement sensor developed by the authors that is based on a commercial Hall sensor. The device is based on a permanent magnet placed in front of an integrated Hall sensor and insures the required measurement range of 4 mm and an accuracy of 10 μm.

Figures 4 and 5(a) show the crack monitoring node and the sensor structure respectively.

In Fig. 5(b) the sensing principle is illustrated: the permanent magnet mounted on one side of the crack generates the magnetic flux density field which, far from its surface on its axis, can be approximated by the following equation:

$$B_x = \frac{2\mu_0\mu}{4\pi x^3},\tag{1}$$

where x is the distance, μ is the magnetic field moment and μ_0 is the magnetic permeability of vacuum. The Hall sensor, mounted on the opposite side of the crack, trasduces this field into a Hall voltage, namely $Vout_{sens}$, which is related to the magnetic flux density field B as follows:

$$Vout_{sens} = K_H I B_x,\tag{2}$$

where K_H is the Hall constant, I is the current in the sensor, and B_x is the component of the magnetic flux density perpendicular to current flowing in the sensor.

Since the overall displacement provides a voltage output non-linearly related to the distance x between the magnet and the sensor surface, the working point

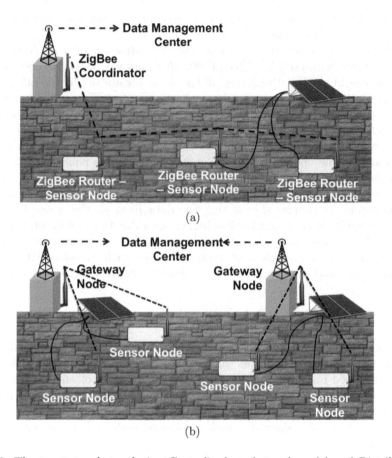

(a)

(b)

Fig. 3. The two network topologies: Centralized mesh topology (a) and Distributed star topology (b).

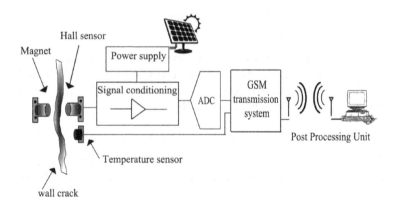

Fig. 4. Schematic diagram of the overall measurement system.

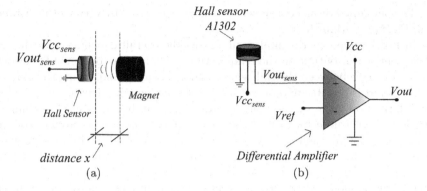

Fig. 5. Structure of the displacement sensor for crack monitoring (a). The linear circuit to adapt the sensor output voltage range to the input full scale of the ADC in Fig. 4(b).

was carefully selected in order to grant a large sensitivity and a sufficient measurement range. The Hall voltage is amplified with a linear conditioning system (Fig. 5(b)), providing the voltage

$$V_{out} = (V_H - V_{ref})A_0, \tag{3}$$

where A_0 is the overall gain and V_{ref} is an offset voltage. The ADC resolution sets the basic constraint to the overall design, whereas the voltage full-scale sets a limit to the distance range (x_{MIN}, x_{MAX}).

5   Test and Validation

The proposed proof of concept system shown in Fig. 4, has been designed using the Hall-effect sensor A1302 by Allegro Microsystems and a neodymium magnetic disk (NdFeB) with dimensions 8 mm (height) and 10 mm (diameter), and a magnetization grade N45, suitable to operate up to 80 °C. The output voltage range of the Hall sensor has been adapted to the input full scale 0−5 V range of a 10−bit ADC converter. It is important to mention that the variation of the environmental temperature becomes an issue in a long-term monitoring of the crack width. Indeed, temperature variations affects both the response of the electronic devices and mechanical structure of the sensor causing possible alterations in the measurements. For this reason, the sensing system has been equipped with an integrated-circuit for temperature sensing, namely the LMT84 by Texas Instrument. This sensor provides an analog output voltage proportional to the temperature in the range from −50 °C to 150 °C.

The Hall sensor and the magnet are coupled by a 3D printed ABS holder (see Fig. 6(a)), which allows for fixing the magnet and the Hall sensor to the two sides of the crack, maintaining the alignment and housing also the front end electronics and the temperature sensor.

The developed displacement sensor was characterized by varying the distance x in Fig. 5(a) within the range 0–30 mm.

In Fig. 7 some experimental results show the overall dependence of the displacement sensor output on the temperature. The data are obtained by keeping a fixed distance between the Hall sensor and the magnet and letting the temperature vary. It is possible to observe that this dependence is fairly linear, therefore the information given by the temperature sensor can be easily used to compensate for the measurement drift of the displacement sensor. The proof of concept monitoring system was tested placing two sensors on field. In Fig. 8 some measurement results are shown. Data are related to a measurement time of about two days (measurements are transmitted with time intervals of 1 min) and come from a sensor mounted on the city wall in the month of August. In the upper plot both raw distance data (blue line) and data compensated for temperature (red line) are reported.

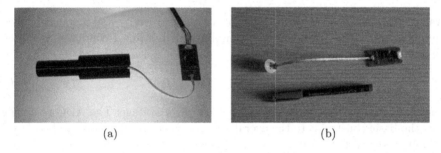

(a)   (b)

Fig. 6. Printed ABS holder for the magnet, the Hall and temperature sensors (a). Printed circuit boards hosting the sensors and the conditioning electronics (b).

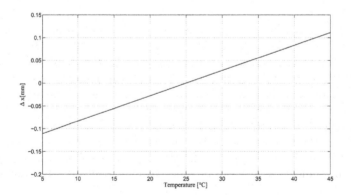

Fig. 7. Dependence of the sensor output on the temperature. The distance between the magnet and the Hall sensor was kept at a fixed distance and the temperature was varied.

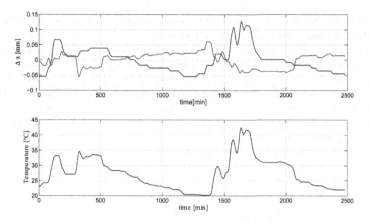

Fig. 8. Distance and temperature variations measured by the device under test (blue line). The compensation of the effect of the temperature variations on the displacement measurements is reported in red line. (Color figure online)

6   Conclusion

In this paper the realization of Wireless Sensor Node based on the use of Hall Effect sensor for the high precision monitoring of crack displacement in monumental structures has been presented. The proposed solution has been tested in laboratory providing the required accuracy. At the same time, a network architecture has been studied to allow the deployment of the proposed node in large quantities in order to set up an alert system covering all the structure to be monitored. While the architecture has been thought for a specific deployment site, it can be easily adopted for any kind of situation where the monitoring of large monumental structures is required.

The laboratory tests proved the effectiveness of the solution. A test campaign has been started in August and sensors have been placed in two test sites. The on field test is preliminary to the deployment of the whole monitoring infrastructure that is expected to be completed in 2017.

References

1. Yick, J., Mukherjee, B., Ghosal, D.: Wireless sensor network survey. Comput. Netw. **52**(12), 2292–2330 (2008)
2. Federici, F., Alesii, R., Colarieti, A., Graziosi, F., Faccio, M.: Design and validation of a wireless sensor node for long term structural health monitoring. In: 2013 IEEE SENSORS, pp. 1–4 (2013)
3. Torfs, T., Sterken, T., Brebels, S., Santana, J., van den Hoven, R., Spiering, V., Zonta, D.: Low power wireless sensor network for building monitoring. IEEE Sensors J. **13**(3), 909–915 (2013)
4. Yun, C.B., Min, J.: Smart sensing, monitoring, and damage detection for civil infrastructures. KSCE J. Civil Eng. **15**(1), 1–14 (2011)

5. Zhou, G.D., Yi, T.H.: Recent developments on wireless sensor networks technology for bridge health monitoring. In: Mathematical Problems in Engineering (2013)
6. Amditis, A., Stratakos, Y., Bairaktaris, D., Bimpas, M., Camarinopolos, S., Frondistou-Yannas, S., Torfs, T.: An overview of MEMSCON project: an intelligent wireless sensor network for after-earthquake evaluation of concrete buildings. In: Proceedings of 14th European Conference Earthquake Engineering (2010)
7. Capella, J.V., Perles, A., Bonastre, A., Serrano, J.J.: Historical building monitoring using an energy-efficient scalable wireless sensor network architecture. Sensors 11(11), 10074–10093 (2011)
8. Rodriguez-Sanchez, M.C., Borromeo, S., Hernndez-Tamames, J.A.: Wireless sensor networks for conservation and monitoring cultural assets. IEEE Sens. J. 11(6), 1382–1389 (2011)
9. Zonta, D., Wu, H., Pozzi, M., Zanon, P., Ceriotti, M., Mottola, L., Corr, M.: Wireless sensor networks for permanent health monitoring of historic buildings. Smart Struct. Syst. 6(5–6), 595–618 (2010)
10. Potenza, F., Federici, F., Lepidi, M., Gattulli, V., Graziosi, F., Colarieti, A.: Long-term structural monitoring of the damaged Basilica S. Maria di Collemaggio through a low-cost wireless sensor network. J. Civil Struct. Health Monit. 5(5), 655–676 (2015)

Project Paper: Digital Applications for Materials' Preservation and Conservation in Cultural Heritage

The SACRE Project: A Diagnosis Tool of Built Heritage

Sarah Janvier-Badosa, Kévin Beck, Xavier Brunetaud, and Muzahim Al-Mukhtar[✉]

PRISME Laboratory UPRES EA 4229, University of Orleans,
8 rue Leonard de Vinci, 45072 Orleans, France
{sarah.janvier,kevin.beck,xavier.brunetaud,
muzahim.al-mukhtar}@univ-orleans.fr

Abstract. The SACRE project is a research project which aims to create a tool to help the professionals in charge of preservation and restoration of cultural heritage buildings. The objective of this project was to develop a working methodology and create the technological tools necessary to implement this methodology. This project describes the steps the development of the digital health record of a building. This project focused on the study and understanding of the mechanisms of degradation of limestone, the main material for building construction. The Castle of Chambord was chosen to be the subject of this study.

Keywords: Castle of Chambord · Limestone · Degradation · Preservation · Digital health record

1 Introduction

In the field of heritage preservation, the practice of restoration of historical monuments requires to make a diagnosis of the state of conservation before any restore operation.

The SACRE project (Degradation monitoring, characterization and restoration of limestone monuments) is a research project funded by the Region Centre of France, between 2008 and 2012. The objective of this project is to provide a tool diagnosis for preventive conservation and the establishment of a timetable of restorations to preserve a significant monument: the Castle of Chambord. This project aims at the creation of a monument health record.

The concept of health records of a monument is an analogy with the medical vocabulary, which aims to study aspects of the monument health. The health record is both the support and the result of the diagnosis of the building, as defined by Fitzner [1] and Smith and Prikryl [2]. The challenge is to synthesize our knowledge of past, present, and what we can predict of its future.

Creating this health record meets the need of professionals in the conservation and restoration of historical monuments: know the history of the monument and understand its current state, in order to predict its evolution. A heterogeneous corpus of historical and scientific data was collected. The data collected during the study is needed to establish a detailed diagnosis of the state of the building, the location of the damage, weather, historical and architectural archives... The characterization of tuffeau degradation and understanding of these degradation mechanisms is also a component of this project, as

© Springer International Publishing AG 2016
M. Ioannides et al. (Eds.): EuroMed 2016, Part I, LNCS 10058, pp. 681–690, 2016.
DOI: 10.1007/978-3-319-48496-9_54

a basis for numerical simulation of weathering processes and so in predicting the evolution of degradation.

After presenting the administrative and scientific organization of the SACRE project, this paper will attempt to present the process of constitution of the health record of a building, by illustrating the methodology with a current type of degradation in the Loire Valley on tuffeau stone: spalling. A continuation of this part will be the presentation of the technical tools and specifications for the establishment of a health record that can be described as "digital". Finally, this paper will open on different applications and continuation of this tool and this research project.

2   Project Presentation

2.1   The Castle of Chambord and the Studied Facades

The Castle of Chambord was chosen to be the subject of this project. François 1er begins its construction in 1519. After several stops and starts of construction, the castle was partially unfinished at the death of the king in 1547.

His successors will provide various additions, modifications and repairs over the centuries. The interest of this building is that it is built in tuffeau, the limestone most commonly used at this period for constructions of the Loire Valley. Posterior restorations report various types of limestone used instead of tuffeau. In contrast to many buildings located in urban areas, the Chambord castle is located in rural areas, in the center of a park of 5500 ha. The study of degraded limestone phenomena is made simpler by freeing an additional degradation parameter.

The SACRE project focuses on three identified parts of the Domaine national de Chambord: the South Façade, the East Tower and the Stables of Marshal of Saxe (Fig. 1). These facades were selected for different characteristics, making them representative of different states of preservation and restoration of the castle. The interest of the South Façade is that it is the castle entrance facade. It has often been reorganized and restored over the centuries, and presents a variety of dates and types of stones. Conversely, for the East Tower, only five of its spans are accessible to visitors, others have little has been restored and much more damage than the South Facade. Finally, the

Fig. 1. Location of the studied façades in the SACRE project

Stables of Marshal of Saxe, located near the entrance of the castle, are later, the start of construction dating from the late seventeenth century. They are now mostly in ruins.

2.2 Objectives and Organization of the Project

The SACRE project was carried by a CNRS laboratory, the CRMD (now ICMN) in collaboration with the PRISME (laboratoire Pluridisciplinaire de Recherche en Ingénierie des Systèmes, Mécanique, Energétique), the Domaine national de Chambord and the LRMH (Laboratoire de Recherche des Monuments Historiques).

This fundamental and applied research program is divided into 5 parts:

1. The CAD modelling of monument aims at constructing a graphic base used to gather all data acquired during the project.
2. The realization of the health record will reference all the information necessary to establish a detailed diagnosis of the state of alteration of the monument: mapping of degradations, weather conditions, architectural and historical archives.
3. The simulation and prediction of degradations, which is the most fundamental step of this research program, is to simulate the process of degradations both in experimental aging tests in laboratory and in numerical modelling in order to understand the evolution and to estimate the kinetics of degradations.
4. The creation of a tool for decision support is the application of simulation, and aims to estimate the rate of degradation. Added to that a costing of restoration, this software tool will provide a rational schedule of restoration work.
5. The valuation of the project to the public will be achieved by giving an access to a simplified version of the software, presented at an exhibition at Chambord castle.

3   The Health Record: From the State of the Art to Diagnosis

3.1   Referencing of Historical Data

The first stage of this work was to inventory the historical archives of the castle to find the different stages of construction and restoration. The data attempting to be accurate at the scale of the stone. Mappings were performed, which allow to report the extent of restoration done on these façades. The analysis of this information allows for example to assess the proportion of visible stones replaced for each of the restoration periods. On the East tower, nearly 20 % of the stones have been replaced (against 50 % for the South Façade).

From in situ observations and a summary description of the types of damage, degradation mappings have also been drawn to scale of the stone (Fig. 2). The spalling was identified as specific of tuffeau stone, and most destructive. By correlating the mappings produced, with environmental conditions, it was possible to identify the environmental factors statistically associated with these degradations. These factors are varied and can be climatic, anthropogenic and/or related to the nature of the stone and its position in the building [3]. Textual and graphic data from historical research have completed the previous analysis by introducing a temporal notion: these texts and images were used to evaluate the development time of a degradation in a new stone and assert the existence of this degradation at a particular time. And if not, it was possible to estimate the onset period. Thanks to the comparison of historical data and surveys of the present state of degradation, a first order of size of these kinetics was estimated: the time required for a degradation to grow up to become visually observable [4].

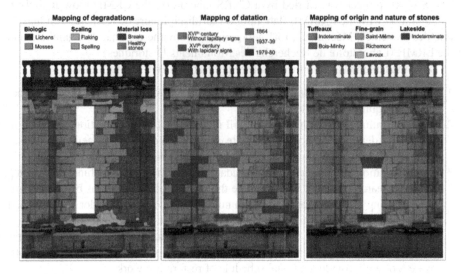

Fig. 2. Mappings of origin, dating and state of degradation of stones, East Tower of the castle (Janvier-Badosa *et al.*, 2016)

3.2 Sampling and Characterization of Degradations

The continuity of this work of visual diagnosis was laboratory characterization of samples from the castle. The tuffeau is a calcium-silicate stone with high porosity (45 %), containing clay minerals (10 %) [5]. The most damaging degradation for the monument is the spalling. This degradation is characterized by a crack parallel to the surface of the stone to 1 or 2 cm depth. Over time, a plaque several centimetres in thickness gradually forms under the stone surface and eventually falls away, leaving the resulting new surface powdered.

This degradation formation mechanisms are subject to assumptions not yet validated [6]. The analyzes performed on all samples by X-ray diffraction and by ion chromatography showed the significant presence of gypsum ($CaSO_4$, $2H_2O$ exogenous mineral) with a maximum systematically located in the cracks. Its concentration is maximum at the fracture, approximately 1 cm depth: 1.6 weight-% of gypsum. When other networks cracks develop parallel to the surface, greater depth the gypsum concentration increases again locally before being zero beyond 50 mm. This gypsum distribution profile was observed in both stones areas already engaged in a process of spalling, and in healthy areas (Fig. 3) [7].

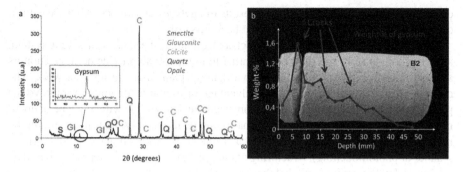

Fig. 3. Example of a diffractogram with gypsum detection (a), and example of the distribution of weight-% of gypsum, depending on the depth (b).

3.3   Understanding the Spalling Process?

Artificial ageings and numerical tests were then conducted to clarify, this gypsum development mechanisms and to assess its role in the training process of spalling. Various parameters were studied: the pollutant transport mode, pre-cracking of the sample, isolation of the sample during drying. The results suggest that the test "water+gypsum" does not allow migration of a significant amount of gypsum inside the stone.

The sulfuric acid imbibition is the method that maximizes the amount of gypsum formed, but mainly in the 1 mm below the surface, and very little depth. Finally, the SO_2 gas followed by partial imbibition of water is the only protocol that allowed the precipitation of a large amount of gypsum in the center of the stone, with a maximum level on the water front (Fig. 4). The parameters linked to drying are secondary, and pre-cracking plays only when the crack is orthogonal to the surface, allowing the sulfuric acid to form gypsum along this crack. The distribution of gypsum, as characterized on a flaking, seems to result from an attack by sulfuric acid (acid rain), while that characterized on a spalling appears to be from atmospheric SO_2 followed by rainy periods. But the role of the gypsum in the phenomena of scalling is not elucidated. An overall process describing the various stages of the degradation has been proposed. This process involves both the atmospheric SO_2 and fatigue of the area subject to moisture variations by thermal-water differential expansion. It is not possible to specify with certainty the relative importance, or chronology. The combination of these two factors seem to be the most probable hypothesis for the initiation and propagation of a crack parallel to the surface, symptomatic of a spalling [8].

4   The Necessity of a Digital Tool

4.1   Specifications

Among all the data collected in this study, some data concern the building or the facade as a whole, such as environmental or weather data. Others relate a stone or a part of the wall, such as dating or degradation mappings. Finally, others are more specific and concern only part of the stone, such as results of analyzes of samples. All these data, at different scales, constitute the monument health record.

However, it was necessary to collect and organize the data in a single system, allowing both to store and link them in order to interpret and provide heritage curators a digital tool to better control the known data, to plan future restoration work. The concept of digital health record takes advantage of digital technology to improve the potential of the health record: make it more accurate, compatible with any type of document, easier to complete and update, analysable quantitatively, and finally usable by many people. In this digital health, "digital" is due to 3D acquisition technologies (laser scanner or photomodelling), structuring of data (database with 3D referencing based on a 3D model of the monument), and the solution of work and data visualization (free and open web interface, searchable by all professionals in heritage preservation) [9].

4.2 The 3D Model as Graphical Representation

The graphical representation should satisfy various requirements: it should be convenient to achieve, scientifically accurate and precise, and of acceptable image quality to ensure a correct visualization of the smallest required component: a stone. So,

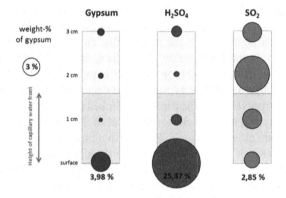

Fig. 4. Summary of results of aging tests.

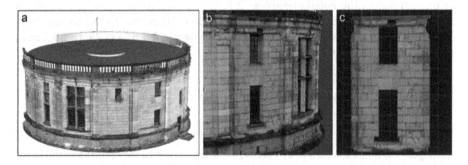

Fig. 5. 3D model of the tower of Chaudron, with photomodeling technic (a). Selection of a 3D entity (b) and unfolded in 2D (c).

photomodeling technique has been adopted [10, 11]. After the acquisition of geo-referenced points using a tachometer, we took pictures on a regular basis all around the tower. The ImageModeler software has been used to calibrate and orient photographs to each other. The building volumes were then defined as precisely as possible by the juxtaposition of geometric shapes. Textures, extracted from oriented photographs, have been applied to the faces of the 3D model. Finally, the building was divided into coherent architectural entities (windows, spans pilasters, capitals…) (Fig. 5).

4.3 The Database

Developed by the MAP-GAMSAU laboratory (Marseille, France), NUBES is a web-based open source platform for the representation, documentation and analysis of architectural features [12]. Originally, NUBES did not include the necessary features for the creation of a digital health record on the state of conservation of buildings, and therefore it has been adapted to match the needs of the SACRE project [13]. Once all entities are registered, it is possible to navigate through the 3D model, and to select an entity whose unfolded texture can be displayed in a 2D interface for semantic annotation purposes. In order to accomplish this task, a vector graphics editor was adapted and integrated into the NUBES platform to draw/edit mappings using hierarchical layers (Fig. 2). Compared to a conventional mapping from a photography or drawing of a facade, all the reliefs, so all surfaces, are mappable, including the hidden parts on an orthogonal view. Among mapping features, a statistical analysis tool allows the automatic calculation of areas concerning drawn surfaces (Fig. 6).

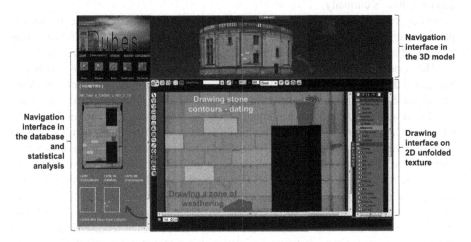

Fig. 6. The NUBES interface: drawing forms on 2D unfolded texture, displaying mappings on the 3D model, and possibilities of statistical analysis of drawing surfaces

5   Towards a Project Application

After the SACRE project, a new project started: the MONUMENTUM project (2013–2016). This project aims to offer curators, architects, restorers, a 3D acquisition tool, mapping and data processing, which is both technically accessible, intuitive, and a provider of new data that enrich the diagnosis. The SACRE project has provided the basis for the development of MONUMENTUM project, and allowed to establish the specifications for the implementation of the new tool. The support of these maps was revalued, and annotations of dating, nature materials, and degradation, are made directly on photos that allow build the model 3D photogrammetry, generating a point cloud [14]. The creation of the 3D model is thus greatly facilitated. Indeed, the technique of photo-modelling presented previously is very long, tedious for complex architectures and carved parts, and sometimes cause errors during area calculations. The project also plans to integrate the structural aspect of the building, a concept not taken into account in NUBES and the SACRE project.

A second project, VOLUBILIS (2015–2018), also benefits progress and methodologies developed during the SACRE project. The steps of diagnosis and the establishment of the health record, identified during the SACRE project, are applied to the ancient site of Volubilis.

Finally, during the SACRE project, several tourism improvements ideas have been considered and made to present this new tool and improve the perception of the restoration by the general public in Chambord. Several web reports, regional, and newscasts were broadcast, on the SACRE project and its implications, in order to stimulate interest and the public's curiosity.

Other projects were also planned: educational seminars for school, an exhibition to present scientific results, including 3D media on computers and tablets representing Chambord and restorations and a consultation version of the digital health record.

The issue is to convince visitors that heritage preservation is everyone's responsibility, and that everyone can make a contribution. If these projects were not completed during the SACRE project, these animations and exhibitions devices are now being developed and will take place in the next months, until 2019, the anniversary of the construction of the castle. A final project has also been created in support of this valuation activity: VALMOD project (2014–2017). This project aims to tourism improvements of the Castle of Chambord from the collection of architectural and historical data made during the SACRE and MONUMENTUM projects, and their digital processing via distribution media to different audiences. It is to work at an edutainment valuation of knowledge gathered or produced. The public will be able to navigate through different interpretations of the Castle of Chambord in a 3D virtual format representing different periods to the present state and even suggestions for future states, particularly in terms of material degradation or restorations, while accessing according to the type of audience, in more or less popularized versions of the various sources used to offer these interpretations.

6 Conclusions

The Castle of Chambord, emblematic monument of the Loire Valley, is the most visited monument in the Région Centre in France. The SACRE project, providing the manager of cultural heritage, a tool to optimize the expenses of restoration, contributed to maintenance of good state of this building and ensure a sustainable tourist attraction.

The SACRE project helped drawing up the concept of the monument health record as a tangible principle within the historical heritage conservation studies.

The three concepts of health records (past, present and future) of the monument, are structured around a 3D graphic model, graphic support of the building and information about it. The past of the monument is based on the history of the construction, alterations and restorations with the various materials used. This reflects the types of degradation observed on the castle, and extent. The future state of the monument presume the evolution thanks to experimental and numerical studies of the mechanisms and kinetics of degradation.

And thanks to the digital health record, quantitative statistics can be carried out on degraded surfaces and stones: their nature, their history and their environment. The methodology developed during the SACRE project provided the creation of new research projects, being in line with the conclusions of the SACRE project. being in line with the conclusions of the SACRE project.

References

1. Fitzner, B., Heinrichs, K., La Bouchardière, D.: Damage index for stone monuments. In: Protection and Conservation of the Cultural Heritage of the Mediterranean Cities, Proceedings of the 5th International Symposium on the Conservation of Monuments in the Mediterranean Basin, Seville, Espagne, 5–8 April 2000, pp. 315–326 (2002)
2. Smith, B.J., Prikryl, R.: Diagnosing decay: the value of medical analogy in understanding the weathering of building stones, building stone decay: from diagnosis to conservation. Geol. Soc. London **271**, 1–8 (2007)
3. Janvier-Badosa, S., Brunetaud, X., Beck, K., Al-Mukhtar, M.: Kinetics of stone degradation of the Castle of Chambord – France. J. Archit. Heritage **10**(1), 96–105 (2016)
4. Janvier-Badosa, S., Beck, K., Brunetaud, X., Al-Mukhtar, M.: A historical study of Chambord castle: a basis for establishing the monument health record. Int. J. Archit. Heritage **7**(3), 247–260 (2013)
5. Beck, K., Al-Mukhtar, M., Rozenbaum, O., Rautureau, M.: Characterisation, water transfer properties and deterioration in tuffeau: building material in the Loire valley-France. Int. J. Build. Environ. **38**(9), 1151–1162 (2003)
6. Rautureau, M.: Tendre comme la pierre, ouvrage collectif sous la direction de Michel Rautureau, Ed. Conseil régional, Centre & University of Orléans (2001)
7. Janvier-Badosa, S., Beck, K., Brunetaud, X., Al-Mukhtar, M.: The occurrence of gypsum in the scaling of stones at the castle of Chambord (France). J. Environ. Earth Sci. **71**(11), 4751–4759 (2014)
8. Janvier-Badosa, S., Beck, K., Brunetaud, X., Guirimand-Dufour, A., Al-Mukhtar, M.: Gypsum and spalling decay mechanism of Tuffeau limestone. J. Environ. Earth Sci. **74**(3), 2209–2221 (2015)

9. Janvier-Badosa, S., Stefani, C., Brunetaud, X., Beck, K., De Luca, L., Al-Mukhtar, M.: Documentation and analysis of 3D mappings for monument diagnosis. In: Toniolo, L., Boriani, M., Guidi, G. (eds.) Built Heritage: Monitoring Conservation Management, pp. 347–357. Springer International Publishing, Cham (2015)

10. Brunetaud, X., Stefani, C., Janvier-Badosa, S., Beck, K., Al-Mukhtar, M.: Comparison between photomodeling and laser scanning applied to realizing 3D model for digital health record. Eur. J. Environ. Civil Eng. **16**(Supp. 1), 48–63 (2012)

11. Brunetaud, X., De Luca, L., Janvier-Badosa, S., Beck, K., Al-Mukhtar, M.: Application of digital techniques in monument preservation. Eur. J. Environ. Civil Eng. **16**(5), 543–556 (2012)

12. De Luca, L., Busayarat, C., Stefani, C., Veron, P., Florenzano, M.: A semantic-based platform for the digital analysis of architectural heritage. Comput. Graph. **35**(2), 227–241 (2011)

13. Stefani, C., Brunetaud, X., Janvier-Badosa, S., Beck, K., De Luca, L., Al-Mukhtar, M.: Developing a toolkit for mapping and display stone alteration on a web-based documentation platform. J. Cult. Heritage **15**(1), 1–9 (2014)

14. Manuel, A., Stefani, C., De Luca, L., Veron, P.: 2D/3D semantic annotation towards a set of spatially-oriented photographs. In: XXIV International CIPA Symposium, Strasbourg, France (2013)

Pigments Identification Using Raman Spectroscopy of the 16th Century Printed Book "Osorio"

Igor Lukačević[1], Theodore Ganetsos[2(✉)], and Thomas Katsaros[3]

[1] Department of Physics, University J. J. Strossmayer, Trg Ljudevita Gaja 6, 31000 Osijek, Croatia
[2] Laboratory of non-destructive techniques, Department of Automation, Piraeus University of Applied Science, P. Ralli & Thivon 250, 12244 Egaleo, Greece
ganetsos@teipir.gr
[3] Byzantine and Christian Museum of Athens, Athens, Greece

Abstract. Croatia has possessed books continuously since the Middle Age. One of the most beautiful examples of the 16th century Prandau-Normann collection is the description of the reign of the King of Portugal Emanuel (1st) has been written by Hieronymus Osorio – Hieronymi Osorii Lvsitani Silvensis in Algarbiis episcope, printed in the printing house of Arnold Birckmann, one of the three most famous Middle Age printers in Köln. Dr. Igor Lukačević, in his experimental work [1] showed that a pigment palette is a common one for the period between 16th and 19th century. Three complementary, non-invasive spectroscopic techniques were used: micro-Raman spectroscopy, PIXE spectroscopy and UV-VIS FORS spectroscopy. Several pigments were identified, like vermilion or cinnabar and minium, white lead and massicot. However, pigments from blue, light blue and green coloured regions could not be determined uniquely, leaving the authors' palette incomplete. Fluorescence, coming from the usage of the Ar+ laser, was the main negative factor during the Raman experiments. For some of the pigments, it was so intense that it covered all of the pigments spectral lines. Dr. Theodore Ganetsos, during his visit in Croatia, used a portable Raman Spectrometer (laser 785 nm) [2, 3], which would not induce such fluorescence and, consequently, more Raman lines are presented, making the pigment identification more definite and authors' palette complete. We identified ponsjakite to the dark blue area, from the results of PIXE and the Raman peaks.

Keywords: Pigments · Raman · Osario · Identification · Fluorescence

1 Introduction

Lorem In the fundus of the Department of printed books in the Museum of Slavonijai in Osijek, Croatia, the library of Prandau-Normann family stands out by its worth both in quantity and historical significance. Almost 9000 books were brought to the Museum from their county chateau in Valpovo by the act of the Croatian Commission for the gathering and preservation of cultural goods (KOMZA). Their family library is an unavoidable fund for studying the cultural history of Slavonija, and the spring of

© Springer International Publishing AG 2016
M. Ioannides et al. (Eds.): EuroMed 2016, Part I, LNCS 10058, pp. 691–700, 2016.
DOI: 10.1007/978-3-319-48496-9_55

numerous social studies, for it testifies about the fields of interest, social developments and activities of its owners, and its content is equivalent to the contents of the collections from other castles in Croatia and Central Europe.

One of the most beautiful examples of the 16th century Prandau-Normann collection is the description of the military campaign of the Spanish king Emanuel Hieronymus Osorio – Hieronymi Osorii Lvsitani Silvensis in Algarbiis episcopi..., printed in the printing house of Arnold Birckmann, one of the three most famous Middle Age printers in Köln. The binding of the book is covered with brown leather and decorated with what on sight seems to be a golden oval medallion with an oriental motif. ''Osorio'' is decorated with seven foreedge miniatures, which were the centerpoint of our research: two on the upper and lower fore-edges and three on the side fore-edge.

The sizes of miniatures are about 5 × 4 cm and their author utilized several different colors: red, green, light blue, dark blue, yellow, pink and brown. They are all placed on a what appears to be a gilded fore-edge. The miniatures represent (two upper, two lower and three on the side, respectively): the four Evangelists, the Adoration of the Magi, an aristocratic coat of arms of an unknown origin and the Birth of Jesus (Fig. 1). The inner side of the book cover is filled with the hand written notes of, now, light brownish color.

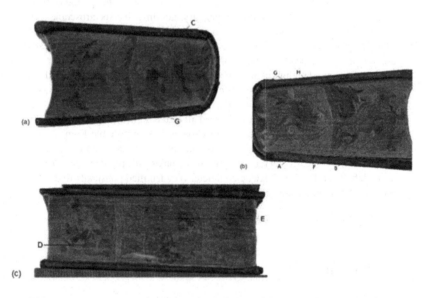

Fig. 1. Miniatures on the upper (a), lower (b) and side of the fore-edge (c). Black circles and labels denote the areas which were used in the experiments: A – gold, B – red, C – pink, D – dark blue, E – light blue, F – green, G – yellow, H – brown. (Color figure online)

2   Experimental Results - Discussion

Fluorescence, coming from the usage of the Ar+ laser, was the main negative factor during the Raman experiments in a previous work. For some of the pigments, it was so large that it covered all of the pigments spectral lines. For these pigments, we could only bring assumptions based on the PIXE results. Fluorescence has, thus, prevented us to obtain the pigment identification with certainty for several colors. We presumed that using the laser with the large wavelength (785 nm) would not induce such fluorescence and, consequently, more Raman lines would be visible, making the pigment identification more definite.

For this reason we used the DeltaNU 785 nm portable Raman Spectrometer. (Fig. 2) Fluorescence emission stems from sample molecules or trace impurities that absorb the laser excitation and emit a broad background at the same energies as the Raman scattering. One way to eliminate or reduce the fluorescence emission is to select a laser excitation wavelength that does not have enough energy to excite molecular fluorescence. The advantage of 785 nm reduces competing fluorescence interference in compounds through this process.

Fig. 2. The 785 nm DeltaNu Raman spectrometer.

It has 35 micron laser spot size, resolution 5 cm^{-1} and spectral range 200–2000 cm^{-1}. A digital microscope and a color video camera used to define the best distance between substrate and the laser beam.

2.1 Raman Experimental Data

The 785 nm excitation appears to be the most efficient laser line. It also has the great advantage that it can be used to perform "out of the lab" measurements with the portable Raman set up. The recording is difficult because of a huge fluorescence, in some cases, but not higher than that observed with the fixed instrument. A baseline subtraction is mandatory to make the specific signatures visible. The instrument support a power of ~5–10 mW with x50 objective, which is an important limitation for measurements with a mobile set-up. There is a lot of ambient light collected even when a black textile is used to cover the setup.

Gold Color. We measured several positions and especially for the gold pigment two of them, the position A (Fig. 3) (main peaks at 1641, 1218, 755, 537 and 348 cm^{-1}) and the position A1 (Fig. 4) (main peaks at 1627, 1218, 813, 424 and 348 cm^{-1}); the peaks may correspond to the degradation of an alloy copper, zinc, gold and iron in very good agreement with bibliography [6].

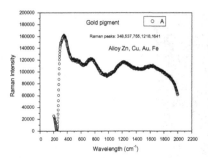

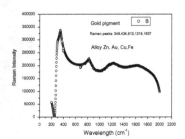

Fig. 3. Raman spectra of position A   **Fig. 4.** Raman spectra of position A1.

Red Color. We measured several positions and especially for the red pigment two of them, the position B (Fig. 5) (main peaks at 336, 353, 408 and 548 cm^{-1}) and the position B1 (Fig. 6) (main peaks at 336, 353, 410 and 548 cm^{-1}); in very good agreement with the results of PIXE (Fe, Hg, Pb). We can't specify the form of the sulfide of mercury because the mineral and the artificial form haven't any chemical difference. On the other hand in PIXE we found Fe and an amount of this, is perhaps related to the mineral form of the mercury sulfide as cinnabar. According to the Raman peaks and the PIXE results we suggest the mixed of minium-cinnabar and red ochre. This way of application (minium and cinnabar) is a common painting technique in medieval times.

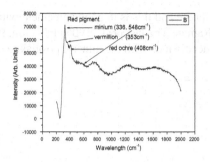

Fig. 5. Raman spectra of position B

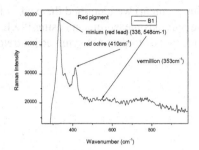

Fig. 6. Raman spectra of position B1.

Pink Color. We measured several positions and especially for the pink pigment two of them, the position C (Fig. 7) (main peaks at 543, 1056 cm^{-1}) and the position C1 (Fig. 8) (main peaks at 549, 1053 cm^{-1}); the bold peaks may correspond to minium and lead white) in very good agreement with the PIXE results.

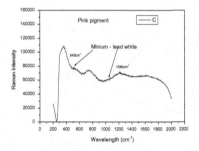

Fig. 7. Raman spectra of position C.

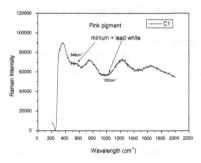

Fig. 8. Raman spectra of position C1.

Blue Color. We measured several positions and especially for the blue pigment two of them, the position D – dark blue pigment (Fig. 9) (main peaks at 335, 403, 746, 767, 1093, 1580 and 1623 cm^{-1}) and the position E – light blue pigment (Fig. 10) (main peaks at 401, 746, 769 and 1623 cm^{-1}); the peaks (665, 667, 687 and 1050 cm^{-1}) may correspond to Lead white) in very good agreement with bibliography. To the Fig. 9 (dark blue pigment) we identified the peaks of posnjakite and this is in good agreement with the previous measurements using PIXE and Raman. The last peak (1906 cm⁻¹) Fig. 9, corresponds to the SO4 symmetric stretch in accordance with the mineral posnjakite.

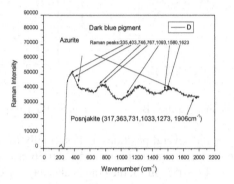

Fig. 9. Raman spectra of position D

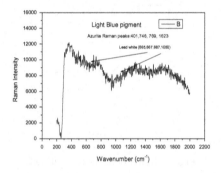

Fig. 10. Raman spectra of position E.

Green Color. We measured especially for the green pigment one position, the position F (Fig. 11) (main peaks at 348, 436, 532, 755, 1054, 1086, 1232, 1498 cm⁻¹); the most peaks correspond to malachite) in agreement with Clark [5]. This result is in accordance with PIXE results [1].

Yellow Color. We measured several positions and especially for the yellow pigment three of them, the position G (Fig. 12) (main peaks at 289 and 360 cm⁻¹), the position G1 (Fig. 13) (main peaks at 292 and 364 cm⁻¹) and the position G2 (Fig. 14) (main peaks at 284 and 360 cm⁻¹); these peaks may correspond to massicot - PbO) in agreement with bibliography and PIXE measurements [5].

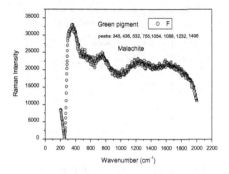

Fig. 11. Raman spectra of position F

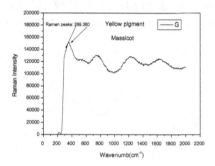

Fig. 12. Raman spectra of position G.

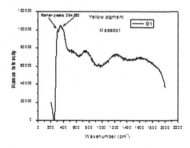

Fig. 13. Raman spectra of position G1.

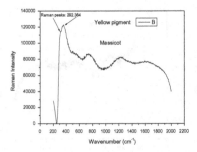

Fig. 14. Raman spectra of position G2.

Brown Color. We measured several positions and especially for the brown pigment two of them, the position H (Fig. 15) (main peaks at 551,1322,1580 cm^{-1}) and the position H1 (Fig. 16) (main peaks at 543, 1325, 1579 cm^{-1}); the first peaks may correspond to the minium and the bold peaks corresponds to carbon [4].

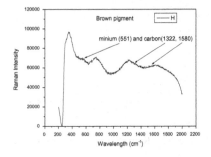

Fig. 15. Raman spectra of position H.

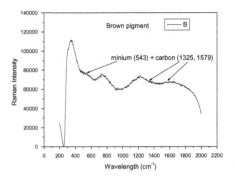

Fig. 16. Raman spectra of position H1.

2.2   Results - Identification

In comparison with other work we summarize our experimental results. Using the 785 nm we identify the pigments in several position to this artefact. We present our results as shown in Table 1.

Table 1. Comparison with results from other work [1].

Area	PIXE [1]	Raman (514 nm) [1]	Area (this work)	Raman (785 nm) (this work)
A (gilded)	Gold		A and A1	Alloy Zn, Cu, Au, Pb,Fe
B (red)	Vermilion and minium	Vermilion and minium	B and B1	Red ochre, minium and (HgS) vermilion
C (pink)	Minium and white lead	Minium and white lead	C and C1	Minium + lead white
D (dark blue)	Any copper blue pigment	Any copper blue pigment	D	Azurite + posnja kite
E (light blue)	Any copper blue pigment and white	Any copper blue pigment	E	Azurite + Lead white
F (green)	*Malachite or verdigris or a mixture of copper blue pigment and massicot*		F	Malachite $CuCO_3.Cu(OH)_2$
G (yellow)	*Massicot*		G, G1, G2	(PbO) Massicot
H (brown)		minium	H, H1	Minium + carbon

3   Conclusion

In this research work we used 785 nm Raman spectrometer in order to identify the pigments. It was a successful procedure and we have very good agreement with related bibliography and with other similar techniques and authors [1, 4–7].

Acknowledgements. Th. Ganetsos would like to thanks the Head of the University J. J. Strossmayer, Department of Physics and the partners in Croatia for this useful collaboration and the support during his stay in Osijek.

References

1. Lukačević, I., Ergotić, I., Vinaj, M.: Non-destructive analyses of 16th century printed book "Osorio" with the colorful fore-edge miniatures. Croat. Chem. Acta **86**(2), 207–214 (2013)
2. Katsaros, T., Ganetsos, T.: Raman characterization of gemstones from the collection of the Byzantine & Christian Museum. Archaeology **1**(2), 7–14 (2012)

3. Ganetsos, T., Katsaros, T., Vandenabeele, P., Greiff, S., Hartmann, S.: Raman spectroscopy as a tool for garnet analysis and investigation on samples from different sources. Int. J. Mater. Chem. **3**(1), 5–9 (2013)
4. Colomban, P., Mancini, D.: Lacquerware pigment identification with fixed and mobile Raman microspectrometers: a potential technique to differentiate original/fake artworks. In: Arts, vol. 2, pp. 111–123 (2013). doi:10.3390/arts2030111
5. Bell, I.M., Clark, R.J.H., Gibbs, P.J.: Raman spectroscopic library of natural and synthetic pigments. Christopher Ingold Laboratories, University College London, 20 Gordon Street, London WC1H 0AJ, UK
6. Deneckerea, A., Leeflang, M., Bloemc, M., Chavannes-Mazel, C.A., Vekemans, B., Vinczed, L., Vandenabeelee, P., Moensa, L.: The use of mobile Raman spectroscopy to compare three full-page miniatures from the breviary of Arnold of Egmond. Spectrochim. Acta, Part A **83**, 194–199 (2011)
7. Martens, W., Frost, R.L., Kloprogge, J.T., Williams, P.A.: Raman spectroscopic study of the basic copper sukphates – implications for copper corrosions and bronze disease. J. Raman Spectrosc. **34**(2), 145–151 (2003)

Design and Application of a Data System for the Comparative Study of Historic Mortars

Vasiliki Pachta[(✉)] and Ioanna Papayianni

Laboratory of Building Materials, Department of Civil Engineering, Aristotle University Thessaloniki, Thessaloniki, Greece
{vpachta,papayian}@civil.auth.gr

Abstract. Mortars are among the first building materials used in constructions and have played a significant role in building technology's evolution. A large number of mortar samples were systematically analyzed, leading to the need of a flexible data system in order to evaluate and comparatively study all results. This system allowed recording and classifying the data input (physico-mechanical, chemical characteristics), according to the mortar type (structural, renders-plasters, mosaic-mural substrates). With a specific toolbox all information could be easily sorted and comparatively - statistically evaluated, while the data input could be updated for future needs. The basic goal of the data system was to manage the information regarding historic mortars, but throughout its use it seems that a lot of other parameters could be also envisaged. It could therefore become a necessary tool for any scientist engaged to the field of restoration materials and techniques.

Keywords: Data system · Historic mortars · Statistic evaluation · Properties

1 Introduction

Mortars are among the primer materials used in construction, firstly as coverings of wooden huts, later as bonding materials of adobe houses and stone masonries, and finally as renders and plasters. They were often used as substrates for decorative elements such as murals, wall or floor mosaics. Each mortar type (structural, renders-plasters, substrates of murals, wall-floor mosaics) presents specific characteristics that are mostly related to their functional role and application, the available raw materials, as well as the building technology of each era [1–4].

The use of computational methods for the statistical evaluation of research results is a well known process with many applications [5–8]. However their use for the comparative evaluation of building materials' properties and especially of historic materials is rather limited and usually focuses on the study of a limited number of results [9–12].

With the help of an expert system, all data of the analytical study can be easily evaluated in giving a better profile of the analyzed mortar. The benefits of such a consideration provide:

© Springer International Publishing AG 2016
M. Ioannides et al. (Eds.): EuroMed 2016, Part I, LNCS 10058, pp. 701–710, 2016.
DOI: 10.1007/978-3-319-48496-9_56

- comparative study of great sources of information that could not be otherwise implemented
- extraction of crucial conclusions related to historic materials' structure,
- contribute to the optimum design of the suitable repair mortar.

A further step could be the recording of similar expert systems of the characteristics of mortars used for the repair of historic structures. By this way, comparisons could be allowed about the characteristics and properties of existing/old/new mortars.

This paper concerns the design and application of a flexible data system for the comparative study of a high number of historic mortars research results, analyzed during the last two decades in the Laboratory of Building Materials of the Aristotle University of Thessaloniki. The management of this source of information emerged many difficulties, due to the high number of samples and the large range of results. The tools that technology provides were therefore necessary for their classification and exploitation. By this way valuable information concerning the technological evolution of mortars was revealed.

The study includes the description of the system's functionality and use, as well as indicative results from the statistical approach of historic structural mortars' properties.

2 Design and Application of the Data System

During the last two decades more than 3000 historic mortars were analyzed in the frame of National and European projects, according to a holistic methodology developed in the Laboratory of Building Materials [2, 3, 13–15]. According to the methodology the microstructural, physico-mechanical and chemical characteristics of mortars were determined through a series of tests. Microstructure observation was performed with stereoscope (Leica Wild M10) assisted by image analysis (ProgRes), aggregates granulometry by sieving after decomposition and granulation of the original sample by hand (EN1015-1:1998), porosity and apparent specific gravity were according to RILEM CPC 11.3, while mechanical strength was evaluated in sound, shape modified samples by applying crushing test. Finally, wet chemical analysis assisted by Atomic Absorption was performed in a fine fraction of the sample (<63 μm).

The comparative study of this source of information emerged many difficulties, due to the high number of samples and the large range of results. Therefore, a logic system of the classification of all data was of great importance. For example, which of the characteristics of monuments, apart from their dating could be related to the mortars? The type of the structure, such as castle, theatre? Which of the results of the chemical results of the mortars would be considered for their characterization? Should relevant indices be used? How the position of the mortar in the structure influences its characteristics?

The major outcome of the data system was that through the statistical analysis, numerous conclusions could be extracted, regarding the technological characteristics of mortars (i.e. binder/aggregate ratio, aggregates' type and gradation, binder system, preservation state). Remarks in relation to other parameters, such as historic period, type of mortar, type of monument could also be made.

The main goal of the expert system was to be easily applicable by any user, include a great number of results, allow statistical evaluation of the data and permit modifications according to future needs. By this way, important information for scientists dealing with the conservation and restoration of monuments (restorers, architects, civil engineers, conservators) could be easily drawn, since all that information could be used for the design of compatible repair materials and for understanding the construction philosophy of old masons.

The system was designed in Microsoft Office ACCESS 2003 and in its present form includes the results from the analysis of totally 1500 mortar samples. It is still updated, and it is believed that in its final form it will consist of the results of more than 3000 mortar samples.

2.1   Structure of the Data System

The data system was designed in order to upload and manage a great number of mortars' results of various types, historic periods and monuments. Its proper design led to its limited size (1.5 GB), so as not a central PC for its use to be necessary, but in order for all archives to be easily transferred to any computer. It totally includes it 839 folders and 8.069 files, from which 2.500 photos, 2.209 tables and 850 diagrams, which are all added in the form of hyperlinks, so as not to increase its size.

The basic axes of its design were the 'tables' and 'forms' which were interrelated. In the tables, all data was input and could be classified according to a parametric statistic analysis, while forms were the tools for the presentation of the data [3]. The function and usage of the data system can be graphically depicted in Fig. 1.

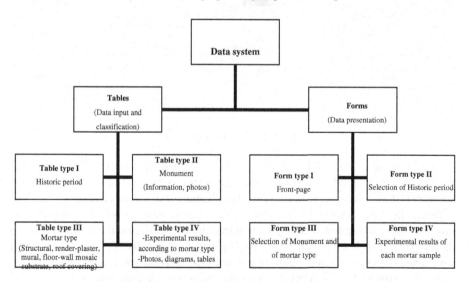

Fig. 1. Graphic design of the data system usage and functionality

In the data system totally 1381 mortar samples were recorded which referred to 985 structural, 300 renders-plasters, 55 floor mosaic substrates, 15 floor substrates, 18 mural substrates, 4 wall mosaic substrates and 4 roof coverings. These samples were taken from totally 122 monuments mainly of Greece, which were dated from the Hellenistic up to the pre-cement modern period (beginning of the 20th century).

2.2 Data Input. Tables and Forms

The data system consisted of totally 4 types of tables (Fig. 1), which were all interrelated [3, 9]. The first type (Table I) included the historic periods from of the mortar samples (Hellenistic, Roman, Byzantine, Ottoman, Medieval, Modern). The second one (Table II) gave all relevant information concerning the monuments from which the mortars have been sampled, such as name, constructional type (castle, church, sanctuary, bath, private house, public building), constructional period and subsequent phase etc. (Fig. 2). Additionally, figures and architectural designs have been hyperlinked in order to enrich all input.

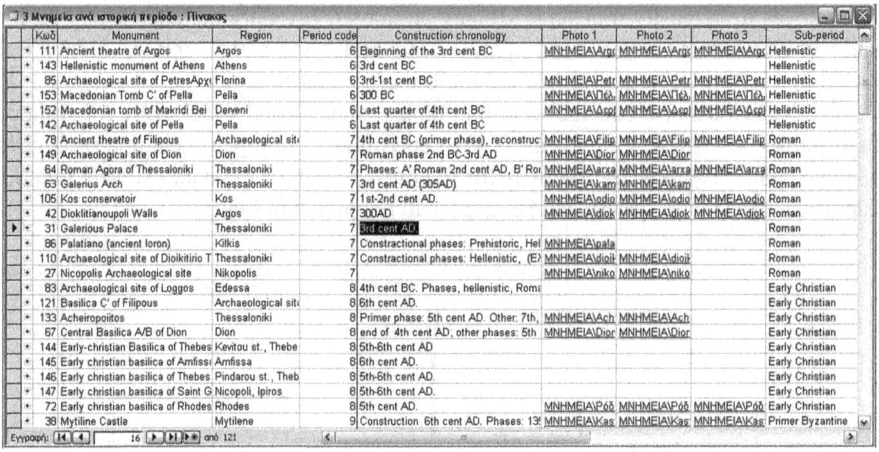

3 Μνημεία ανά ιστορική περίοδο : Πίνακας

Κωδ	Monument	Region	Period code	Construction chronology	Photo 1	Photo 2	Photo 3	Sub-period
111	Ancient theatre of Argos	Argos	6	Beginning of the 3rd cent BC	MNHMEIA\Argo	MNHMEIA\Argo	MNHMEIA\Argo	Hellenistic
143	Hellenistic monument of Athens	Athens	6	3rd cent BC				Hellenistic
85	Archaeological site of PetresΑρχ	Florina	6	3rd-1st cent BC	MNHMEIA\Petr	MNHMEIA\Petr	MNHMEIA\Petr	Hellenistic
153	Macedonian Tomb C' of Pella	Pella	6	300 BC	MNHMEIA\Πέλ	MNHMEIA\Πέλ	MNHMEIA\Πέλ	Hellenistic
152	Macedonian tomb of Makridi Bei	Derveni	6	Last quarter of 4th cent BC	MNHMEIA\Δερ	MNHMEIA\Δερ	MNHMEIA\Δερ	Hellenistic
142	Archaeological site of Pella	Pella	6	Last quarter of 4th cent BC				Hellenistic
78	Ancient theatre of Filipous	Archaeological sit	7	4th cent BC (primer phase), reconstruc	MNHMEIA\Filip	MNHMEIA\Filip	MNHMEIA\Filip	Roman
149	Archaeological site of Dion	Dion	7	Roman phase 2nd BC-3rd AD	MNHMEIA\Dior	MNHMEIA\Dior		Roman
64	Roman Agora of Thessaloniki	Thessaloniki	7	Phases: A' Roman 2nd cent AD, B' Ro	MNHMEIA\arxa	MNHMEIA\arxa	MNHMEIA\arxa	Roman
63	Galerius Arch	Thessaloniki	7	3rd cent AD (305AD)	MNHMEIA\kam	MNHMEIA\kam		Roman
105	Kos conservatoir	Kos	7	1st-2nd cent AD.	MNHMEIA\odio	MNHMEIA\odio	MNHMEIA\odio	Roman
42	Dioklitianoupoli Walls	Argos	7	300AD	MNHMEIA\diok	MNHMEIA\diok	MNHMEIA\diok	Roman
31	Galerious Palace	Thessaloniki	7	3rd cent AD.				Roman
86	Palatiano (ancient Ioron)	Kilkis	7	Constractional phases: Prehistoric, Hel	MNHMEIA\pala			Roman
110	Archaeological site of Dioikitirio T	Thessaloniki	7	Constractional phases: Hellenistic, (E	MNHMEIA\dioik	MNHMEIA\dioik		Roman
27	Nicopolis Archaeological site	Nikopolis	7		MNHMEIA\niko	MNHMEIA\niko		Roman
83	Archaeological site of Loggos	Edessa	8	4th cent BC. Phases, hellenistic, Roma				Early Christian
121	Basilica C' of Filipous	Archaeological sit	8	6th cent AD.				Early Christian
133	Acheiropoiitos	Thessaloniki	8	Primer phase: 5th cent AD. Other: 7th,	MNHMEIA\Ach	MNHMEIA\Ach		Early Christian
67	Central Basilica A/B of Dion	Dion	8	end of 4th cent AD, other phases: 5th	MNHMEIA\Dior	MNHMEIA\Dior		Early Christian
144	Early-christian Basilica of Thebes	Kevitou st., Thebe	8	5th-6th cent AD				Early Christian
145	Early christian basilica of Amfiss	Amfissa	8	6th cent AD.				Early Christian
146	Early christian basilica of Thebes	Pindarou st., Theb	8	5th-6th cent AD.				Early Christian
147	Early christian basilica of Saint G	Nicopoli, Ipiros	8	5th-6th cent AD.				Early Christian
72	Early christian basilica of Rhodes	Rhodes	8	5th cent AD.	MNHMEIA\Ρόδ	MNHMEIA\Ρόδ	MNHMEIA\Ρόδ	Early Christian
38	Mytiline Castle	Mytilene	9	Construction 6th cent AD. Phases: 13	MNHMEIA\Kas	MNHMEIA\Kas	MNHMEIA\Kas	Primer Byzantine

Εγγραφή: 16 από 121

Fig. 2. Table type II. Monuments' information

The third table (Table III) included the list of the various mortar types (structural, renders-plasters, mural substrates, roof coverings, wall mosaic substrates, floor substrates, floor mosaic substrates). The classification of the research results according to the mortar types was significant, since as it has been formerly concluded the selected raw materials and the followed application techniques are diachronically interlinked to their type [3, 13]. For example renders and plasters are usually applied in 2 to 3 well compacted layers of reduced width, aggregates gradation and increased Binder/Aggregate ratio to the surface, which influences the physico-mechanical aspects of the layers (porosity, mechanical strength) [15].

Table III was directly linked to the fourth table type (Table IV) which was divided in as many tables as the mortar types, in order for the results input to be according to the specific characteristics of each type and the samples of each category to be easily comparatively evaluated. In Table IV (Fig. 3) the analysis results of each mortar sample were presented (figures macro-micro were added), concerning:

- sample data (number, type, monument, historic period, sampling area)
- microstructural characteristics (type and origin of aggregates, inclusions, structure stability, cracks and voids, salt presence etc.)
- physico-mechanical properties (porosity, apparent specific gravity, compressive strength)
- aggregates gradation
- chemical characteristics
- other interrelated properties such as Binder/Aggregate ratio and binding system

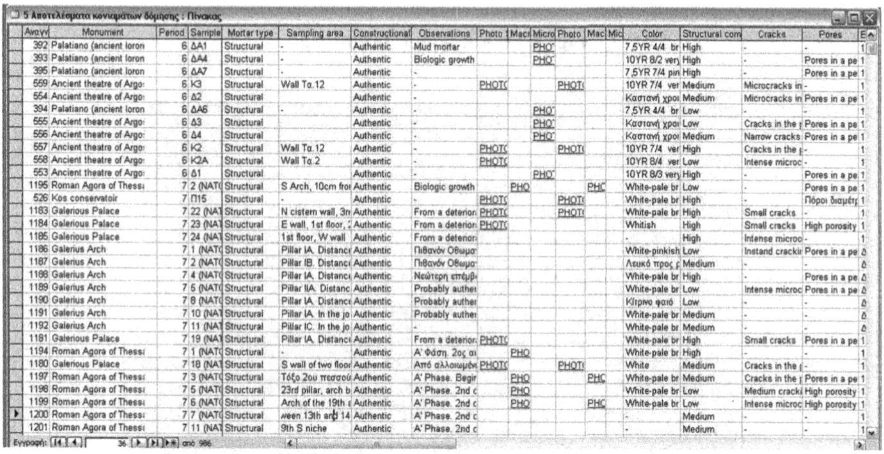

5 Αποτελέσματα κονιαμάτων δόμησης : Πίνακας

Αναγν	Monument	Period	Sample	Mortar type	Sampling area	Constructional	Observations	Photo	Macr	Micro	Photo	Mac	Mic	Color	Structural com	Cracks	Pores	E
392	Palatiano (ancient loron	6	ΔΑ1	Structural	-	Authentic	Mud mortar			PHO				7,5YR 4/4 br	High	-	-	1
393	Palatiano (ancient loron	6	ΔΑ4	Structural	-	Authentic	Biologic growth			PHO				10YR 8/2 very	High	-	Pores in a pe	1
395	Palatiano (ancient loron	6	ΔΑ7	Structural	-	Authentic	-							7,5YR 7/4 pin	High	-	Pores in a pe	1
559	Ancient theatre of Argo	6	K3	Structural	Wall Τα.12	Authentic	-	PHOT			PHOT			10YR 7/4 ver	Medium	Microcracks in	-	1
554	Ancient theatre of Argo	6	Δ2	Structural		Authentic	-							Καστανή χρο	Medium	Microcracks in	Pores in a pe	1
394	Palatiano (ancient loron	6	ΔΑ6	Structural	-	Authentic	-			PHO				7,5YR 4/4 br	Low	-	-	1
555	Ancient theatre of Argo	6	Δ3	Structural		Authentic	-			PHO				Καστανή χρο	Low	Cracks in the	Pores in a pe	1
556	Ancient theatre of Argo	6	Δ4	Structural		Authentic	-			PHO				Καστανή χρο	Medium	Narrow cracks	Pores in a pe	1
557	Ancient theatre of Argo	6	K2	Structural	Wall Τα.12	Authentic	-	PHOT			PHOT			10YR 7/4 ver	High	Cracks in the	-	1
558	Ancient theatre of Argo	6	K2A	Structural	Wall Τα.2	Authentic	-	PHOT						10YR 8/4 ver	Low	Intense microc	-	1
553	Ancient theatre of Argo	6	Δ1	Structural		Authentic	-			PHO				10YR 8/3 very	High	-	Pores in a pe	1
1195	Roman Agora of Thess	7	2 (NAT	Structural	S Arch, 10cm fro	Authentic	Biologic growth		PHO			PHC		White-pale br	Low	-	Pores in a pe	1
526	Kos conservatoir	7	Π15	Structural	-	Authentic	-	PHOT			PHOT			White-pale br	High	-	Πόροι διαμέτ	1
1183	Galerious Palace	7	22 (NAT	Structural	N cistern wall, 3r	Authentic	From a deterior	PHOT			PHOT			White-pale br	High	Small cracks	-	1
1184	Galerious Palace	7	23 (NAT	Structural	E wall, 1st floor,	Authentic	From a deterior	PHOT						Whitish	High	Small cracks	High porosity	1
1185	Galerious Palace	7	24 (NAT	Structural	1st floor, W wall	Authentic	From a deterior							-	High	Intense microc	-	1
1186	Galerius Arch	7	1 (NAT	Structural	Pillar IA. Distanc	Authentic	Πιθανόν Οθωμα							White-pinkish	Low	Instand crackir	Pores in a pe	Δ
1187	Galerius Arch	7	2 (NAT	Structural	Pillar IB. Distanc	Authentic	Πιθανόν Οθωμα							Λευκό προς	Medium	-	-	Δ
1188	Galerius Arch	7	4 (NAT	Structural	Pillar IA. Distanc	Authentic	Νεώτερη επέμβ							White-pale br	High	-	Pores in a pe	Δ
1189	Galerius Arch	7	5 (NAT	Structural	Pillar IIA. Distanc	Authentic	Probably auther							White-pale br	Low	Intense microc	Pores in a pe	Δ
1190	Galerius Arch	7	8 (NAT	Structural	Pillar IA. Distanc	Authentic	Probably auther							Κίτρινο φαιό	Low	-	-	Δ
1191	Galerius Arch	7	10 (NAT	Structural	Pillar IA. In the jo	Authentic	Probably auther							White-pale br	Medium	-	-	Δ
1192	Galerius Arch	7	11 (NAT	Structural	Pillar IC. In the jo	Authentic	-							White-pale br	Medium	-	-	Δ
1181	Galerious Palace	7	19 (NAT	Structural	Pillar IA. Distanc	Authentic	From a deterior	PHOT						White-pale br	High	Small cracks	Pores in a pe	1
1194	Roman Agora of Thess	7	1 (NAT	Structural	-	Authentic	Α' Φάση. 2ος αι		PHO					White-pale br	High	-	-	1
1180	Galerious Palace	7	18 (NAT	Structural	S wall of two floo	Authentic	Από αλλοιωμένι	PHOT			PHOT			White	Medium	Cracks in the	-	1
1197	Roman Agora of Thess	7	3 (NAT	Structural	Τόξο 2ου πεσσού	Authentic	Α' Phase. Begir		PHO			PHC		White-pale br	Medium	Cracks in the	Pores in a pe	1
1198	Roman Agora of Thess	7	5 (NAT	Structural	23rd pillar, arch b	Authentic	Α' Phase. 2nd c		PHO					White-pale br	Low	Medium cracki	High porosity	1
1199	Roman Agora of Thess	7	6 (NAT	Structural	Arch of the 19th	Authentic	Α' Phase. 2nd c		PHO			PHC		White-pale br	Low	Intense microc	High porosity	1
1200	Roman Agora of Thess	7	7 (NAT	Structural	ween 13th and 14	Authentic	Α' Phase. 2nd c							-	Medium	-	-	1
1201	Roman Agora of Thess	7	11 (NAT	Structural	9th S niche	Authentic	Α' Phase. 2nd c							-	Medium	-	-	1

Εγγραφή: 36 από 986

Fig. 3. Table type IV. Experimental results of each mortar sample

On the other hand, forms were divided in four types. The first one (Form I) concerned the front page of the data system (Fig. 4), while the second one (Form II) was interrelated to Table type I and introduced the historic periods (Hellenistic, Roman, Byzantine, Ottoman, Medieval, Modern) that the user could select in order to see the results of specific mortar samples.

In the third form type (Form III), which was interrelated to Tables II and III, one could select a specific monument and a specific mortar type and be automatically transferred to the form type IV (interlinked to Table IV), where the analysis results of mortars were shown (Fig. 5).

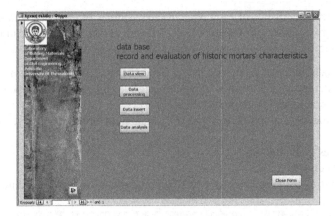

Fig. 4. Form type I. Front-page

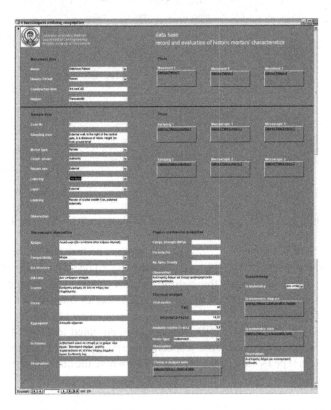

Fig. 5. Form type IV. Analysis results from a specific mortar sample (Galerius Palace, render)

The basic advantage of the data base was that the user could sort the preferred information (i.e. the results from a specific mortar type of a monument) or take general
information regarding a whole category of samples (i.e. results regarding the structural

mortars of a specific historic period) and statistically evaluate them. The statistic analysis of the results was realized through the queries that enable the user to track down and handle specific information. These queries could be based in one or more relevant tables and accumulate data from them.

3   Statistical Evaluation of Experimental Results

The application of the data system allowed evaluating comparatively all results, according to the parametric classification of inputs, by grouping specific parameters [13–15]. This parametric classification could be realized in the tables, where all results have been uploaded. Per example, one could compare the mortars' properties according to the mortar types, the historic periods, specific monuments and proceed to a statistical evaluation of results, in order to take different pieces of information.

The major goal was that through the analysis numerous conclusions could be asserted, regarding several topics relevant to the technological evolution of historic mortars. Indicatively, some general conclusions from the comparative study of structural mortars are presented in this paper (binding system type, gradation of aggregates, binder/aggregate ratio), in order to understand the data base's functionality and effectiveness. Figure 6, depicts the samples' frequency according to the era to which they are dated.

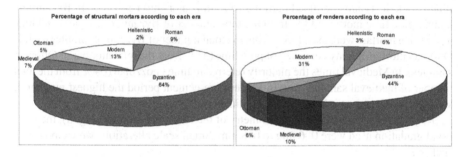

Fig. 6. Frequency of mortar samples (structural, renders) according to the era to which they are dated (total number of analyzed samples 1381)

The use of the data system, six years after its construction proved that a lot of parameters could be comparatively studied, while due to the high number of results, one could lead to safe conclusions about historic mortars' properties. The statistical evaluation of all results can therefore depend on the user's interest that can configure all data.

From the statistical evaluation of the analysis results of structural mortars dated from the Hellenistic period (4th century BC) until the beginning of the 20th century the following observations arose [3, 13]:

The binding system type of the analyzed structural mortars throughout the historic periods was mainly based on lime (Fig. 7). From the Hellenistic period, mixed binding systems (lime+pozzolan) were used (8 % from the total number of Hellenistic samples consisted of lime+pozzolan), while the majority of Hellenistic mortars (69 %) consisted of lime+clayish material with pozzolanic reaction.

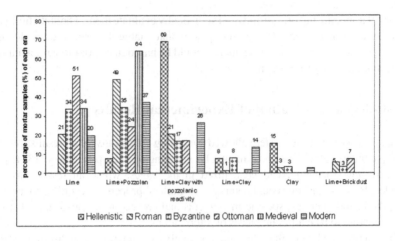

Fig. 7. Binding system of structural mortars of all eras

The use of pure lime mortars firstly presented during Roman times (21 % from the total number of Roman samples), while the highest percentage of Roman structural mortars consisted of lime+pozzolan. Brick dust also started to be added in the matrix during the Roman period (5 % from the total number of Roman samples consisted of lime+brick dust) and continued until the Byzantine and Ottoman years. In Byzantium, mainly pure lime mortars (34 % from the total number of Byzantine samples) and lime +pozzolan mortars were used (35 % from the total number of Byzantine samples), while Ottoman mortars mainly consisted of pure lime (51 % from the total number of Ottoman samples). In Medieval times the majority referred to lime+pozzolan (64 % from the total number of medieval samples) and in Modern pre-cement period the highest number of samples concerned pure lime (20 %) and lime+pozzolan (37 %).

Regarding the aggregates' granulometry of the structural mortars (Fig. 8), the most usual gradation used were 0–6 mm to 0–8 mm. Small scale alterations were envisaged, such as:

Hellenistic mortars presented a variety in aggregates granulometry ranging from 0–2.5 mm to 0–16 mm, but mainly consisted of aggregates of 0–4 mm size (38 % from the total number of Hellenistic mortars). Roman mortars mainly concerned 0–8 mm size aggregates (45 %), while 0–6 mm and 0–16 mm size were also seen (20 % and 26 % respectively); the same was asserted for Byzantine mortars. Ottoman mortars followed the same criteria, with mainly 0–6 mm aggregates (46 % of the total Ottoman samples), Medieval presented a wider range from 0–1 mm to 0–16 mm and finally modern mortars consisted of aggregates of 0–2.5 mm to 0–16 mm.

4 Conclusions

The use of computational methods for the statistical approach of research results, regarding historic mortars seems to be a significant tool for the comparative study of large sources of information that could not be otherwise exploited. Flexible data systems

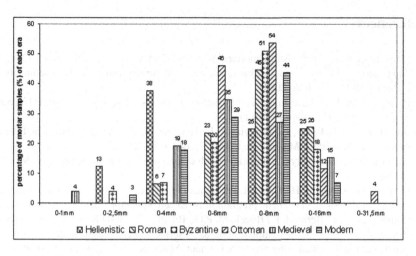

Fig. 8. Aggregates' granulometry of structural mortars of all eras

can therefore become important tools for the evaluation of results and the assertion of conclusions concerning the properties and consistency of materials. Their proper design and construction could lead to:

- archiving of a great source of information,
- presentation of all data in an easily comprehendible format,
- easy applicability by any user,
- possibility of alterations according to future needs,
- interrelation with other data systems.

In addition, these systems could act as interdisciplinary tools among scientists dealing with the conservation of monuments, in order to disseminate knowledge and draw valuable information regarding building materials and techniques. The collaboration among research centers and institutions through a network of databases concerning historic building materials, could be therefore an overall and ambitious aim, that could lead to the evaluation of a wide range of results, such as materials characteristics, monuments types, environmental aspects, pathology symptoms etc. These networks could become significant tools for any scientist dealing with restoration issues, while it could contribute to the selection of proper intervention materials and techniques, for the benefit of Cultural Heritage.

Acknowledgments.   The authors would like to thank the Hellenic Cement Industry Association for supporting the project entitled "Study of the technological evolution of mortars and concretes" (2006-2009).

References

1. Elsen, J.: Microscopy of historic mortars - a review. Cem. Concr. Res. **36**, 1416–1424 (2006)
2. Papayianni, I.: Design of compatible repair materials for the restoration of monuments. Int. J. Restor. **10**(6), 623–636 (2004)
3. Pachta, V.: Study of the technological evolution of mortars. Dissertation, Aristotle University of Thessaloniki, Thessaloniki (2011)
4. Van Hees, R.P.J., Binda, L., Papayianni, I., Toumbakari, E.: Characterisation and damage analysis of old mortars. Mater. Struct. **37**(273), 644–648 (2004)
5. Ashlock, D.: Evolutionary Computation for Modelling and Optimization. Springer, New York (2006)
6. Baykasoğlu, A., Güllü, H., Çanakçı, H., Özbakır, L.: Prediction of compressive and tensile strength of limestone via genetic programming. Expert Syst. Appl. **35**(1–2), 111–123 (2008)
7. Comby-Peyrot, I., Bernard, F., Bouchard, P.O., Bay, F., Garcia-Diaz, E.: Development and validation of a 3D computational tool to describe concrete behaviour at mesoscale. Application to the alkali-silica reaction. Comput. Mater. Sci. **46**, 1163–1177 (2009)
8. Dimitriu, R.C., Bhadeshia, H.K.D.H., Fillon, C., Poloni, C.: Strength of ferritic steels: neural networks and genetic programming. Mater. Manuf. Processes **24**(1), 10–15 (2009)
9. Papayianni, I., Pachta, V., Iliadou, K.: A data base system for managing information concerning historical mortars. In: Ioannides, M., Addison, A., Georgopoulos, A., Kalisperis L. (eds.) VSMM 2008, pp. 271–277 (2008)
10. Moropoulou, A., Polikreti, K., Bakolas, A., Michailidis, P.: Correlation of physicochemical and mechanical properties of historical mortars and classification by multivariate statistics. Cem. Concr. Res. **33**, 891–898 (2003)
11. Miriello, D., Barca, D., Bloise, A., Ciarallo, A., Crisci, G.M., De Rose, T., Gattuso, C., Gazineo, F., La Russa, M.F.: Characterisation of archaeological mortars from Pompeii (Campania, Italy) and identification of construction phases by compositional data analysis. J. Archaeol. Sci. **37**, 2207–2223 (2010)
12. Anzani, A., Binda, L., Carpinteri, A., Invernizzi, S., Lacidogna, G.: A multilevel approach for the damage assessment of Historic masonry towers. J. Cult. Heritage **11**, 459–470 (2010)
13. Pachta, V., Stefanidou, M., Konopissi, S., Papayianni, I.: Technological evolution of historic structural mortars. J. Civ. Eng. Architect. **8**(7), 846–854 (2014)
14. Stefanidou, M., Pachta, V., Konopissi, S., Karkadelidou, F., Papayianni, I.: Analysis and characterization of hydraulic mortars from ancient cisterns and baths in Greece. Mater. Struct. **47**(4), 571–580 (2013)
15. Stefanidou, M., Pachta, V.: Technological characteristics of coatings applied in monuments of the 4th C BC in Greece. Rev. Rom. Mater. / Rom. J. Mater. **45**(1), 35–42 (2015)

GIS Applications for a New Approach to the Analysis of Panel Paintings

Laura Baratin[✉], Sara Bertozzi, Elvio Moretti, and Roberto Saccuman

DiSPeA, Conservation and Restoration School,
University of Urbino Carlo Bo, Urbino, Italy
{laura.baratin,sara.bertozzi,elvio.moretti}@uniurb.it

Abstract. A work of art, considered in its complexity and in its evolution over time, requires knowledge and thorough study in order to arrive at its correct interpretation, a prerequisite for any conservation and maintenance interventions. The evaluation of the preliminary information on the work of art and its analytical reading are closely interrelated to a careful and critical use of the technical and operational instruments defined in a comprehensive and focused methodological programme. Information technology and the integration of multidisciplinary knowledge lead to making even more powerful forms of support available for a phase of documentation, as a means of investigation and organisation of the information, followed by analysis and processing that implement the knowledge of the work of art. Instruments for the 3D surveys of the panels and software for processing and post-processing allow us to obtain digital models of the surveyed surfaces, which are implemented in the GIS environment. We take advantage of the advanced analytical and management capacities, normally applied to the territory, with a simple change of scale, allowing us to carry out detailed investigations on the painting, on the paint film and on the supporting panel. Quantitative evaluations of the metric/statistical type on the spatial distribution of the elements are flanked both by colourimetric analysis, vectorising the RGB components and extrapolating the useful information, and by graphic analysis of the iconographic composition and on the conservation status. We then process the three-dimensional data relative to the morphology of the panel, allowing the identification of any critical aspects or elements of deterioration, until reaching a geometrical comparison among subsequent acquisitions that allows us to identify any displacement due to modifications of the support. The application of the method also allows us to define a comparison between diverse sensing systems to verify their accuracy and effectiveness, in a perspective of programmed management of interventions that will optimise costs and benefits and predispose the elevation profiles to study the morphological evolution along particular lines of interest. The GIS application in a field which is so different from the usual context of usage provides innovative scenarios and various potentials of data analysis and processing.

Keywords: GIS analysis · Spatial Analyst · 3D Analyst · Paintings

© Springer International Publishing AG 2016
M. Ioannides et al. (Eds.): EuroMed 2016, Part I, LNCS 10058, pp. 711–723, 2016.
DOI: 10.1007/978-3-319-48496-9_57

1   Information Technology and Works of Art

A comprehensive path of evaluation and analysis of a work of art, in particular a panel painting, provides complete and in-depth preliminary knowledge of the object and a thorough definition of historical data connected thereto. The instruments offered today by Information Technology lead to specific methodological paths that are well defined, applicable with greater frequency to the entire field of the Cultural Heritage, but also specifically to the analysis and management of painted works of art on supports such as canvas or wooden panels. The entire process of study, documentation and in-depth study on the work of art, on its validity and historical importance, on techniques etc., then passes to diagnostic investigations and the surveying phase, and lastly to the relationship between the content and its representation, which respects the metric and space characteristics. The survey "as a discipline that uses all the sciences and of all the techniques that can contribute to the reading, to the measurement, to the analysis of the objects in their morphological, material and structural aspects, whether overt or hidden" [1] allows us to reach the definition of the image that is corrected, with graphic renderings and 3D models. The image of the painting itself, if surveyed and represented with repeatable criteria, becomes the object of a series of branches of Information and Communication Technology defined as Image Processing, Pattern Recognition and Computer Vision [2]. In the context of restoration these concepts can take on a certain importance if you thinks about the possibility of acting virtually on the work of art in all the operating phases, from the preliminary study, to the evaluation on the conservation status, up to applying various tests for a complete and correct restoration intervention. Instrumental analysis automatically highlights and extrapolates criticalities that are barely detectable to the naked eye with an added value of a certain importance, objectivity, integrating the specific expertise of various disciplines applied synergistically [3]. Among the various software applicable to the study of these works of art, of great interest and innovation is the application of GIS systems. We speak of tools for analysis and management of the territory that, using various types of data, can perform spatial, statistical, morphological and morphometric analyses, identifying the characteristics that define the territory. Applying the tool to the analysis of paintings on wood means simply changing the dimensions of the subject under investigation. From the conceptual point of view, there are no significant differences, since GIS operates without the scale ratio normally applied in cartography, replacing it with the concept of accuracy, for which the absolute dimensions of the object represented are not as important as the quality with which it is surveyed. In the case of a territory, a survey in which the metre is used as the unit of measurement can be considered as excellent resolution, just as a tenth or a hundredth of a millimetre is data of absolute precision in the analysis of the morphometric characteristics of a painted panel. Another element of difference only in appearance is the georeferencing data. In a territorial context, data concerning a defined portion of the territory are placed in "Overlay", using the coordinates that refer to a specific geodetic reference system, while in analysing mobile objects, data are all positioned according to a layer of reference, however maintaining their spatial and elevation components intact. This creates a series of digital maps of the work of art that can be represented in the two- or three-dimensional manner, by parameterising the type and the display algorithm as an aid for the identification of sensitive areas, such as for problems of deterioration or to highlight problems of deformation of the substrate which can have an impact even on the paint film.

Analytically studying the morphology of a panel always tends to give a "synchronous" reading of its condition, that is to say, it is analysed for what it is in that moment and not for what was previously was or will be in the future. It is therefore clear that such an operation is always possible for the object under examination, regardless of its evolution over time. If instead we want to have a different approach, it is necessary to proceed to a "diachronic" analysis, that is, surveys in successive moments with the same methods and subsequent data comparison. Precisely because a study of this kind implies a strong interdisciplinary approach and an indispensable interoperability of data, the maps that are obtained are always themed, calibrated and customised in order to also make the analysis scientifically accurate, clear and understandable even to non-experts of the GIS system.

2 GIS Methodology

The acquisition of all the data relating to the panel and the painting necessarily pass through a painstaking phase of surveying and data processing. The creation of 3D digital models, that accurately describe the surface of the object under examination, passes through a process called 3D Scanning, with the creation of point clouds and the definition of models on triangular grids to obtain a faithful representation of the shape and colour characteristics of an actual object, for the study of errors of measurement, inconsistencies of the shapes, accurate up to a few tenths of a millimetre. We then proceed to the acquisition of high-resolution images, rendered along with the calibration of the camera, map of the depth and the quality of each image, which are reworked during post-processing and used as the basis for the creation of graphic bases and for the subsequent phases of pictorial and colour analysis. The digital data becomes a complex and precise set of measures in the space from which it is possible to extrapolate the significant elements for geometric interpretation.

The passage into a GIS environment allows a very delicate phase of data acquisition, wherein all files defined by the various stages of surveying and processing must be standardised, translated and possibly georeferenced, to obtain a single homogeneous project and the overlay of the information layers. We use the release of ESRI ArcGIS 10.3, proceeding in the two-dimensional ArcMap environment, for the entire phase of organisation and data processing, to move then into ArcScene for viewing and managing 3D data. ArcCatalog allows the structuring of the apparatus of the project and the management of the various types of layers, while the diverse instruments offered by ArcToolbox and the various extensions and toolbars enable us to carry out a series of in-depth analyses and data processing to obtain information and quantitative and statistical assessments.

All input data inserted in the project passes through two main stages, a first stage for the general management of the data organisation and georeferencing of the features, along with an organic structure of the databases, to proceed to spatial processing through the Patch Analyst and Spatial Analyst extensions and a colourimetric analysis of the paint film vectorising the image pixels to proceed to statistical evaluations of distribution and frequency. The second phase focuses on the files of the rendering of the 3D reliefs, by performing a series of operations that allow us, after organisation and harmonisation of the data, to obtain three-dimensional processed images for the morphological and morphometrical analysis of the panel, to make diachronic comparisons using the same instrument or synchronic ones to evaluate the reliability of the various instruments (Fig. 1).

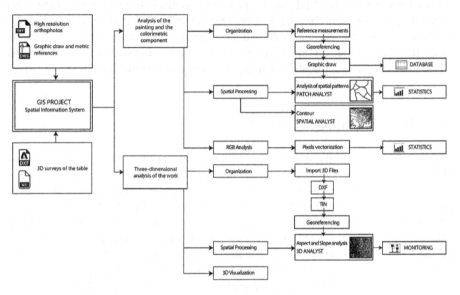

Fig. 1. The GIS project is structured by means of the methodological steps defined, involving two major phases of action structured in repeatable and standardised steps.

2.1   The Painting and the Paint Film

The organisation of the whole GIS project starts from the input process of all useful data in ArcMap and their positioning in the same spatial context. We are not referring to a geographic information system but one that will use the workspace as a spatial plan. The Layer System is not georeferenced according to a geodetic reference system but instead is only attributed units of measure. In this step, the interoperability of the software is crucial. The descriptive layers of the graphic base and the geometric conformation of the panel are normally created in Autocad, where it is necessary that the design is developed in 1:1 scale, clearly defining the units of measure used. The same must be done when the 3D relief is carried out and if the various files do not coincide as units, it will be fundamental to scale the DWG files or the DXF 3D files (possibly created by the WRL or by 3DS) so that everything is standardised. Obviously, it is best to always maintain files of greater detail by scaling the rest in order not to lose the accuracy of the best data. The units of measurement of the work plan are therefore indicated as well as those of the display by proceeding to "georeference" everything, translating the various files to place them in the overlay, by means of Georeferencing or Spatial Adjustment. The procedure involves moving all the files by positioning them on a layer that defines the X axis, approximately at the 0.0 coordinates, but the weight of the 3D files is also an important factor to consider. Often this file is of extreme detail, and therefore, very heavy. In this case, it is opportune to maintain the latter in the position attributed to their insertion and shift all the other files in the overlay. These operations are often delicate, because the three-dimensional file, once placed in the plane, loses the defined contours of the edges and it can be difficult to interpret, for example, where the frame or support ends. In this case, it may be useful to open these files first ArcScene in order to understand their conformation, and then use them in ArcMap, overlaying the contour, graphic base, orthophotos, etc. The organisation of all data prepares the project for the processing.

The graphic base or any reliefs of criticalities, such as, lacunae, loosening and detachment, abrasions, etc., define the patches with certain attributes listed in tables and as such can be treated through the Patch Analyst extension. This is an extension that allows us to perform spatial analysis of the coverage of a landscape, based on the conformation of the patches and their associated attributes. The idea of comparing the patterns present on the surface of the painting to those defining a landscape has derived from the work of Henriques and Goncalves [4] readapted and developed for specific situations. The metrics characteristic and conformations of the fragments that compose the painting are evaluated with statistical indexes in relation to the attributes that define them and/or to the total area of the painting, to highlight the evolution of the discontinuities present, quantify their distribution and make any stylistic comparisons. The lacunae or abrasions present or any applications of gesso, if graphically delineated, are statistically evaluated on the basis of homogeneity/heterogeneity of distribution, regularity/irregularity of the shapes and dimensions. We then proceed to the application of the Contour, a Spatial Analyst tool that automatically creates vector lines that join continuous phenomena on a raster, identifying the pixels with the same value. Again, according to a geographic concept, we are talking about an instrument of creation of the contour lines, level curves, which allow us to identify discontinuity on the panel or on the painted surface, due therefore also to different thicknesses of colour. The evolution of the analysis then continues to the paint film as colour analysis. The painting is given resolution according to the pixels that make up the image, of very high resolution, that is, defined by their RGB values. We do not act on the entire painting because it would involve quite elaborate and heavy operations for the processor, but we identify the details of attention on which to perform the analysis. To be able to extract them, we use the vector elements that define them, so the ideal is a good graphic base, polygonal if possible.

A series of steps enable allow us to get the details still as raster and subject them to vectorisation processes, first for single-band to ultimately bringing everything together in a single layer where the polygonal pixels, individual or grouped by the same value, correspond to the same number of polygons with information relating to the three bands in different fields of the attributes on which we can rapidly view statistical reports, creating a bar graph of the distribution of values, indicating the values of counting, sum, maximum, minimum, mean, median, and standard deviation. It also creates an RGB field with the unit value, to then proceed to frequency analysis that helps us individuate the most widespread colourimetric triads and their spatial location making it possible to compare these data with reconstructions performed instead in the diagnostic phase, which gives information regarding what was supposed to have been the original colour for that detail.

2.2 Processing on Three-Dimensional Surfaces

Renderings of the 3D surveys are acquired in ArcGIS to analyse the distribution of the data and perform calculations that allow us to rapidly individuate the morphological evolution of the panel and any changes in diachronic investigations. The file formats, normally VRML, are transformed into DXF and imported into ArcMap, georeferencing all the data (if the weight of the file is excessive, for an expeditious handling we can also directly import the *.wrl, transforming it into Multipatch and later into 3D raster to be subjected to spatial processing, however losing some of the quality of the results). In this phase, a very useful element is the verso of the panel, both as image and as the vectorial rendering of the principal geometries, in order to compare any disconnection or discontinuous movement from the support structure. For the overlay analysis these elements are first mirrored then georeferenced, in order to superimpose on them layers of the front as if they were being seen in transparency.

By means of the DXF we proceed directly to the creation of TIN files (Triangulated Irregular Network). These are models that consent the representation of an area in its three dimensions through a network of contiguous triangles, defined as nodes and lines that are unevenly distributed, built through a technique known as Triangulation of Delauney. For a numerical representation of the surface of the object under examination, we use a mathematical relationship of the type $z = f(x, y)$, whereby the surface of the support with the paint film is described by a function that to each pair of position coordinates (x, y) associates a value in the elevation of the surface itself. The surface is then represented through a series of triangles (TIN model) starting from a discrete number of elevation measurements (samples consisting of x, y, z triplets) obtained from the survey with the laser scanner, photogrammetry or photomodelling. The TIN allows us to immediately obtain a clear visualisation of the morphology of the panel, based on the Elevation symbology, but it also allows us to observe spatial analyses displayed by the Symbology menu, without the need of further data processing stages, avoiding data redundancy and taking advantage of the concept of dynamic cartography typical of the GIS system, unique spatial information with which to associate different views based on the same attributes of the file. The representation for Elevation highlights the height modifications of the TIN elements through special colour scales, algorithms of definition of the intervals and the number of classes, to then switch to the Slope and Aspect type of analyses, which are based on the calculation of the derivative before the elevation. The analysis of the steepness or the descent of the slopes, SLOPE, defines the slope of the triangulations, in degrees or percentage, always with colour scales, definition of the break interval and number of classes. The slope value for each cell is calculated as the ratio between the height difference (rise) between the current cell and its immediate neighbour and the distance (run) between the centres of the two cells, expressed in degrees or as a percentage. When the input data is a TIN, the system will automatically convert into a GRID model to obtain a homogeneous distribution of the cells over the entire area. The slope also assumes different values depending on the direction considered, given that the calculation, for each cell, evaluates the variation in elevation between it and the eight adjacent cells, which are 3 × 3 floating windows, but the distance between the centres of two adjacent cells will be different depending on the direction considered. The slope at any surface can then assume different directions that can be grouped into classes using the ASPECT tool. Aspect identifies the direction in the downslope of the maximum rate of change in value from each cell compared to its neighbouring cells. It can therefore be thought of as the display of the direction of the slope, where the values of each output raster cell are displayed as if a compass were being used and measuring clockwise in degrees from 0 (north or the pinnacle) to 360 (again at the northern pinnacle), coming back to the starting point. To the flat areas that do not have a descending direction is assigned the default value of −1, and always displayed in grey with the indication of "flat".

The diachronic analysis is an operation that allows the Restorer to make a qualitative assessment of his or her intervention on an overall scale, but it is also possible to make a quantitative assessment using the elevation profiles. In fact, it is not a given that a deformation distributed in a more even way on the panel is not to the detriment of the increase of the curvature. To evaluate this specific problem, it is possible automatically derive the application of elevation profiles from templates starting from TIN or DEM modes, thanks to a specific function of the 3D Analyst for ArcGIS. The "Interpolate Line" tool leads to the definition of a shape file that follows the morphological trend of the model along a line of defined length that can be reapplied to various TINs in overlay, allowing timely comparisons. Customisable graphics are created with the elevation profile, which can be subjected to exaggeration to better highlight the discontinuities.

3   Results

The Spatial Statistics menu of the Patch Analyst allows us to define a series of indexes on the panel of the Madonna and Child with Saint Monica, Saint Augustine and the Trinity by Vittore Belliniano, both for the analysis of the application of gesso carried out on the lacunae, and of the iconographic base allows us to define how the artist may have worked in the context of a stylistic comparison and/or of the activity of the "bottega" (workshop) (Fig. 2). The first 4 indexes, SDI (Shannon's Diversity Index), SDE (Shannon's Evenness Index), AWMSI (Area Weighted Mean Shape Index) and MSI (Mean Shape Index), apply only to the landscape level and evaluate the number, form and complexity of the patches. We see in this case, for example, an SDI of 0.203, an SEI of 0.2936 and an MSI of 1.4666. The SDI is equal to 0 if there is only one patch and grows with the increase of the number, the SEI is equal to 0 when the patch distribution observed is low and approaches 1 when the distribution of types of patches becomes more uniform and the MSI is equal to 1 when all patches are circular and increases with the increasing of the irregularity of the shape. Already it is possible to identify a certain presence of patches, a rather heterogeneous distribution and a certain unevenness of the shapes. In the analysis for the classes of the application of gesso on the total area, it detects the presence of 4037 patches (NumP), an average perimeter per patch of 0.0329 (MPE), an average size of 0.000042 (MPS) and total areas of all the patches defining the application of gesso amounting to 0.17108 on a total of 3.30832 m. Then there are the indexes indicating the median, standard deviation, coefficient of variation of the patches, etc.

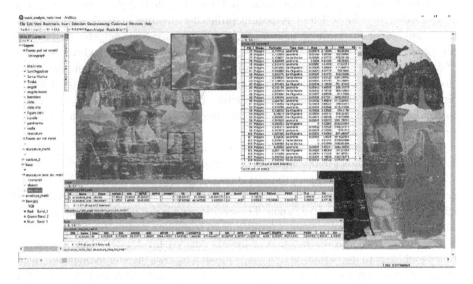

Fig. 2. The Patch Analyst extension allows us to apply a series of indexes for statistical evaluations of both the criticalities present on the panel and of the conformation of the patches that make up the iconographical base.

The automation of the recognition of the values helps us to rapidly identify discontinuities, assess the depth according to the proximity of the contour lines and define the contours objectively. In Fig. 3 the Contour application on the panel by Lorenzo Lotto.

Vectorialization of pixel also offers the possibility of managing the three fields separately allows us to assume a digital restoration, carrying out restoration tests on the screen with the inclusion of the values that the finished intervention should have and evaluating the quality of the rendering without having to act directly on the painting. It reproduces a virtual reality of the painting, in which the machine and not the human eye, identifies the colours that are present. The vectorial pixels, original or restored, can be associated with the correct symbology as correspondence of colour through the attribution of a specific script.

In Fig. 4, for example, a detail of the Carlo Crivelli Altarpiece shows that the triad of greatest distribution in the bodice examined is 75.71.73, while diagnostic investigations have revealed that the original colour should have corresponded to an ultramarine blue, therefore 18.10.143.

An interesting case study examined with this method is the "Hermit Saints Triptych" by Hieronymus Bosch where the panel was surveyed with different techniques, laser scanning, photogrammetry and photomodelling, and in three different campaigns which allowed us to carry out an analytical study of a diachronic type.

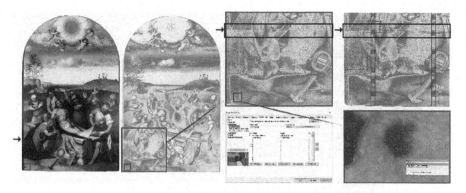

Fig. 3. The Contour tool of the Spatial Analyst leads to the creation of contour lines which bring together the elements of equal value recognised by the raster with the orthophotos of the painting, enabling us to both already highlight the demarcation of the junction between the wooden boards (as you can clearly see from the layer of the verso placed in overlay), and to delineate contours of highlighted details or of criticality (stains, lacunae…).

In Fig. 5 there is a comparison between the three successive campaigns, the first made on 4/10/2013, the second on 12/12/2013 and the third on 18/11/2015 at the conclusion of the restoration, using a Faro laser. Between the first and second interventions, there had been an intervention on the panel involving the removal of the wood block structure and the result already shows evident differences, clearly identifiable from the processing carried out. The left edge of the panel in the second campaign appears lower and quite uniform from the bottom to the top. The upper right corner is still the lowest area but it is certainly less imbalanced compared to the first campaign. The right edge of the panel also looks more uniform and continuous. Considered overall, the morphological trend in the second campaign is more homogeneous and regular. The data obtained with the third campaign tend to confirm the anomalies already detected but the panel appears with a more uniform morphology, perhaps related with the cleaning done on the paint film. Therefore, the diachronic analysis confirms that there has been some adjustment of the panel although the anomalies on the top part still persist, lower than the bottom section, while the imbalance of the left side seems to have been reduced, at least in the lower part. The analysis of the data obtained using the Aspect tool of ArcGIS, in Fig. 5 at the bottom, viewing with the same settings values through 8 classes plus the Flat one, leads to a number of conclusions:

1. The panel as a whole has a general deformation that extends along the diagonal direction from the upper left corner to the lower right corner.
2. Still very evident is the disconnection located along the entire strip of about 3 cm positioned at the top of the panel.
3. The diachronic analysis shows a much more homogeneous pictorial surface in the third campaign compared to the first two, which can be related to a successful cleaning intervention. All this of course makes it possible to positively assess the operations implemented during the intervention and demonstrates how the proposed methodology is able to record the operations that have been carried out.

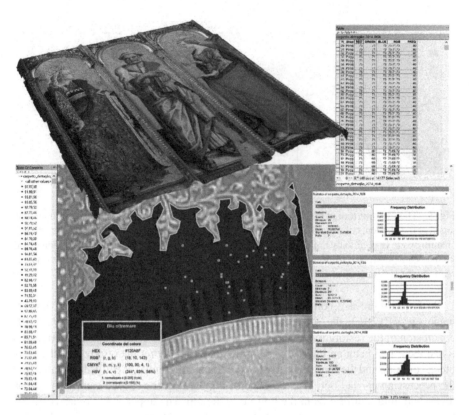

Fig. 4. The detail of the bodice of one of the figures of the Crivelli Altarpiece panel is vectored to perform statistical and distribution analyses of the RGB values and any digital restoration operations by comparing the actual values with the original ones identified through diagnostic investigations. (Color figure online)

4. The right panel of the support is slightly more irregular than the one on the left, but overall the support appears homogeneous, with both parts facing outwards, creating a panel that is curved and slightly warped.

The Slope indicates that the database contains the values that also refer to the thickness of the panel and not only of the painted surface, which, dimensionally much larger, tend to blend together all the differences found on the surface in question. Notice how the red colouring is arranged exclusively on the edges. All this, however, does not prevent us from confirming the anomalies due to warping and those due to the 3 cm strip on the top part of the object. The third campaign highlights anomalies that are not easily explainable with diachronic analysis.

The interpretation of the processing is also supported by a comparison with the image and the graphic base of the verso of the panel, mirrored and placed in overlay. In this case it has been useful for making clear how the reversal of direction does not take place at the junction of the panels in the verso, located in the perfect centre about 30 cm from

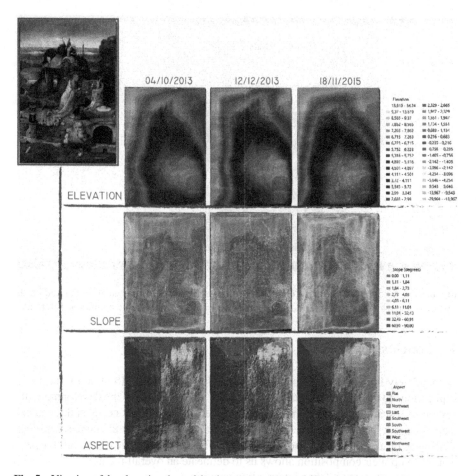

Fig. 5. Viewing of the elevation data of the three campaigns conducted with the Faro laser scanner on the central panel of the Hermit Saints Triptych by Hieronymus Bosch. The 3D surveys have been subject to processing that have enabled the creation of a TIN from which to obtain data on elevation (at their peak), on the slopes (at their centre, Slope) and on their direction (ASPECT, at their base) to make diachronic comparisons between the three successive campaigns.

the edge, but is shifted by about 3 cm to the left of the centre, which can easily be explained by the thinning it underwent in 1838.

In Fig. 6 are shown for comparison the profiles derived from the first two campaigns carried out with laser, in this case Minolta, to highlight the comparison. The interpolation lines are positioned in the lower part of the panel, the part that presents the maximum convexity, having a progression from left to right and naturally they have been obtained always along the same track. The comparison shows that the highest part of the panel, corresponding to the central zone, has not undergone significant differences, while recording a clear lowering of the external areas already on the right, but even more apparent on the left and this of course entails a greater total convexity. The scale on the axes X and Y is in mm.

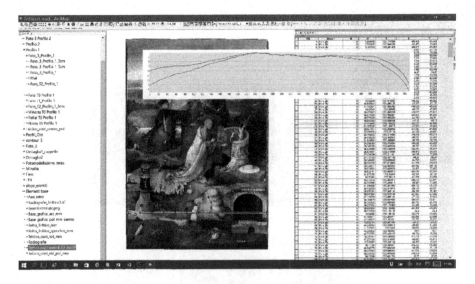

Fig. 6. The automatic creation of elevation profiles along lines of interpolation defined on the surface of the panel help identify the morphological evolution to highlight significant differences.

4   Conclusions

A completely innovative methodology both in the context of GIS systems and in the applications to the cultural heritage is presented, which has led to the development of a system of research which attempts to bring together the various needs and technical-theoretical competence to develop a system that is repeatable and standardised. The possibility of analysing the panels in their diverse artistic-historical-structural aspects that make up their composition allows us to delineate an overall picture of the work of art in its current state to define intervention operations.

Certainly fundamental in the development of a research of this entity has been the possibility of working on various highly prestigious works of art, such as the triptych of the Martyrdom of St Liberata and the Hermit Saints Triptych by Hieronymus Bosch, undergoing restoration by the Gallery of the Accademia of Venice and by the Dutch Bosch Foundation, the Polyptych Altarpiece by Carlo Crivelli of Montefiore dell'Aso (Ascoli Piceno), the Madonna and Child in Glory with the Saints Martin, Michael the Archangel and George by Vincenzo Pagani of the Civic Museum of Ripatransone (Ascoli Piceno) and the Madonna and Child with St Augustine, Saint Monica, All Saints and the Trinity by Vittore Belliniano, of the Civic Museum of Feltre (Belluno).

To make diachronic comparisons between surveys carried out with the same methodology in different periods also directs attention to any deformations and transformations of the panel while it is possible to use the processing carried out also for comparing synchronic surveys, but made with different instruments, such as laser scanners, photogrammetry or photomodelling, evaluating the reliability of the data to assess the best practices in terms of cost/accuracy.

References

1. Baratin, L., Bertozzi, S., Moretti, E., Saccuman, R.: Monitoring of the deformation of the support with laser technologies and analysis of the pictorial surface with GIS systems. In: Proceedings of APLAR 5, Vatican City, Rome, 18–19 September 2014 (2014)
2. Bertozzi, S., Baratin, L., Moretti, E.: Pictorial surfaces and supports: GIS analysis, characterisation and monitoring. In: Proceedings of ESRI Italia 2015, Ergife Palace Hotel, Rome, 15–16 April 2015 (2015)
3. Bennardi, D., Furferi, R.: Il Restauro Virtuale tra ideologia e metodologia. Edifir (Edizioni Firenze S.r.l.), Florence (2007)
4. Henriques, F., Gonçalves, A.: Analysis of lacunae and retouching areas in panel paintings using landscape metrics. In: Ioannides, M., Fellner, D., Georgopoulos, A., Hadjimitsis, D.G. (eds.) EuroMed 2010. LNCS, vol. 6436, pp. 99–109. Springer, Heidelberg (2010). doi: 10.1007/978-3-642-16873-4_8

References

...

Project Paper: Visualisation, VR and AR Methods and Applications

'Translation' and Fruition of an Ancient Book Through Virtual Reality in the Case of Lost Cultural Heritage

Case Study: "*Inscriptiones*" by Emmanuel Thesaurus

Sanaz Davardoust[1(✉)], Anna Osello[1], and Rosa Tamborrino[2]

[1] Department of Structural, Geotechnical and Building Engineering,
Polytechnic of Turin, Turin, Italy
{sanaz.davardoust,anna.osello}@polito.it
[2] Department of Architecture and Design, Polytechnic of Turin, Turin, Italy
rosa.tamborrino@polito.it

Abstract. This article presents a methodology for historical information fruition, such as ancient books texts, in the tourism field. The case study highlights the great possibility that virtual reality (VR) offers to Cultural Heritage professionals in terms of communication and awareness raising of end users. This methodology, applied to the rare 17th century book by Emmanuel Thesaurus "*Inscriptiones quotquot reperiri potuerunt Opera ed diligentia Emmanuelis Philiberti Panealbi*", allows us to show the lost seventeenth-century traits of the Marble Hall in Palazzo di Città (Turin). Tourists can be immersed in a virtual space based on the words of the ancient book within the real space of the Hall, which let him relive the early baroque project atmosphere.

Through this work, it is possible to show how the use of cutting-edge ICT, such as BIM, can impact both on research and society, by arousing the public interest for Cultural Heritage and shared understanding.

Keywords: Digital history · Virtual reality · Information fruition · Historical building · Digital/virtual documentation · Digitized book · Protection · Valorization · Interoperability · BIM

1 Introduction

The subject of the historical and artistic heritage protection is currently the focus of many debates since it concerns a field having one of the greatest economic potential, especially in Italy: the tourism. [10] Italy possesses a very rich and interesting multi-millenial history, providing the community of a wide range Cultural Heritage, consisting of building, spaces, paintings, books and an almost unlimited source of information and written and physical documentation.

Nevertheless this abundance poses many management, degradation prevention and effective communication problems while ensuring economic sustainability investments in this field. Moreover, in most cases, the information is guarded in barely accessible and readable manuscripts and rare books. The original language is often Latin, which

© Springer International Publishing AG 2016
M. Ioannides et al. (Eds.): EuroMed 2016, Part I, LNCS 10058, pp. 727–736, 2016.
DOI: 10.1007/978-3-319-48496-9_58

was kept in use in some fields until late 20th century, for example in homily and religious inscriptions, but is not used anymore except from an elite inner circle of scholars and intellectual (People usually can't understand Latin although some Italians continue to study it at school). Besides, many ancient and original books are preserved in historical libraries, whose access and fruition is often limited, particularly for non-professionals users. Digitization started to bridge this gap allowing the access also to rare books and documents difficult to reach (i.e. the ongoing digitization of the Archivio di Stato in Venice by a project of Ecole Polytechnique de Lausanne [12], or the realization of Search engines and databases, such as "data.bnf.fr." or "Europeana", which inform about where to find different prints and libraries around the world.

Another important aspect concerns the communication of such information, which mostly are just readable words, which need interpretation by highly specialized scholars and professionals. In fact, this information can be enigmatic for most of the people, since they were directed to an audience of other epochs and with specific interpretative capabilities based on profound knowledge of a historical, social, artistic, and political context. Nevertheless, these documents often include much more than simple notions for disciplines: they are witness of a space and a time of civilization, becoming especially important for lost Cultural Heritage.

This state of art makes necessary the figure of experienced professionals with specific skills in reading, interpreting, filtering and processing information, in order to show the data to end users in the most effective way.

In this sense, the extremely rapid and stable development of ICT is constantly providing innovative solutions both to facilitate research operations and to elaborate new prospects of development and protection of the Cultural Heritage, especially when Data interpretation need to be also visualized. Most books in fact were not illustrated and now they are perceived with an incomplete use of the sense of the view.

In recent years, for example, the Virtual Reality is increasingly imposing thanks to its ability to communicate tangible (physical and geometrical elements) and intangible information (historical data, energy, structural, etc.) through a three-dimensional reconstruction of the descriptions taken by historical sources. VR is the artificial reconstruction of both real and imagined - or no longer existing [17, 18] - environment with the support of software and devices for three-dimensional modeling and user/model interaction. This innovative technology uses cutting-edge digitization and visualization tools to immediately and effectively show tangible and intangible aspects.

Many projects, since late 90 s and still in our days, highlighted the possibilities of VR models in the field of tourism, dissemination and sensitization of common users; among the most advanced it's possible to cite the virtual tours of Casa Batlló (Barcelona) [15], Valle del Tevere and Teramo [16]. But the implementation of ICT in CH could go beyond the simple 3d restitution, and help the communities in Historic Estate management. BIM methodology is an important example of how to integrate powerful database management, interoperability with other software and complete support to technical users involved in a historical building preservation, while providing highly communicative 3d models and data for VR environment modelling.

For this reason, BIM and VR can now work translating information coming from ancient and cryptic sources into highly understandable and immersive ambient made of colors, shapes and sounds. The resulting visualization of such works is usually entrusted to various kinds of computer devices, from the traditional monitors of computer platforms to the most modern immersive navigation systems, such as Oculus Rift.

The treated case study in this article, *Inscriptiones* by the Count Emmanuel Thesaurus, is a collection of the paintings descriptions once belonging to Palazzo di Città, Municipality of the City of Turin since 1659.

2 The Aula Maior of Palazzo di Città as Described in "Inscriptiones" by Emmanuel Thesaurus

The Inscriptiones quotquot reperiri potuerunt opera et diligentia Emmanuelis Philiberti Panealbi of the Jesuite Emanuel Thesaurus o Tesauro (Turin 1593–1677), were published in Turin in 1666. Among the several editions of the books in libraries around the world, there is its copy in the National Library in Turin, Biblioteca Reale. This issue is very rare and precious, and its contents is very relevant for the history of the city and its lost Cultural Heritage (CH).

This book, after the restoration of the Town Hall in 19th century, is the last direct source that historian can examine to find evidence of the original baroque appearance of the once called Aula Maior. In fact, the building went through constant expansions and transformations until 20th century and often was at the center of dramatic events of the city.

The sieges who threatened the city, the economic crisis due to the numerous wars of the XVII e XIX centuries and finally the Napoleonic army's entrance in the capital of the Savoy State had affected a negative effect on the public coffers, often precluding the possibility of maintaining the original structure of buildings and urban image (See Fig. 1).

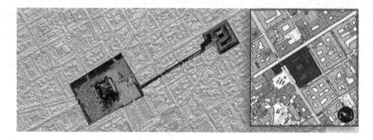

Fig. 1. Town hall and its square, the relationship with piazza castello in a satellite view.

In some rooms of the Town Hall, the degradation reached advanced stages and forced the Municipality to radical interventions, which did not always correspond to a simple restoration, but rather, in some cases, led to deeper transformation.

The Marble Hall–the current name of Aula Maior - is the most significant example in this sense, because the roof infiltration irremediably disfigured the sumptuous ceiling paintings, made by the Flemish painter Jean Miel. The majority of the surfaces were

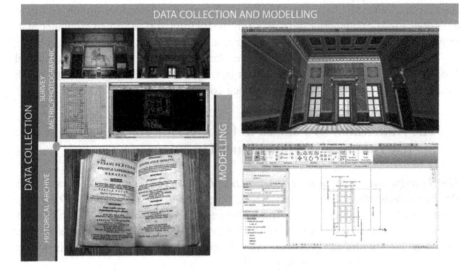

Fig. 2. Data collection and modeling of the marble hall

irreparably damaged, suggesting the whole restoration of the room in a neoclassical design, which reflected the most used style of early nineteenth century [2].

The intervention completely transfigured the Baroque style and its characteristics, replacing the wooden finishing and the ancient frescoes with the marble finishing (from which the hall takes its actual name) and wooden ceilings decorated with gray pigmentation to simulate marble. The austere and dignified character of the hall where citizens can meet the Mayor has finally buried the seventeenth-century image of the Hall hiding precious and antique tales. In fact, as Cravero recalls in the first modern study published on the history of this building, "(…) the magnificent frescoes cycle (…), illustrated the most striking episodes of the ancient history of Turin" - "(…)l'imponente ciclo d'affreschi illustravano gli episodi più salienti dell'antica storia di Torino."- and he goes on to say, "fortunately, a precise and direct testimony of the lost paintings was conserved by (…) Count Emanuele Filiberto Thesaurus, - "Per fortuna delle pitture scomparse ci è stata serbata una precisa testimonianza, (…) del Conte Emanuele Filiberto Tesauro" - who probably inspired the choice of the themes and the Latin mottos, which, very didactically, described the depicted scenes [4].

Thesaurus was an important figure of the period, who received the entrustment of the frescoes themes choice for many rooms of the Municipality. He was a "Vir nobilissimus, in Aula Taurinensi celeberrimus" since the 18th Century *Storia Letteraria d'Italia* by Zaccaria and became the tutor of the sons of the Carignano Duke, being a very reputed erudite by the Savoy aristocracy. He wrote in Latin, but he also translated from the Latin adapting ancient texts. This book, which is now preserved in the Royal Library of Turin, and other important historiographical sources, give us other important hints on the disposition of those paintings in the hall. [6].

Some of Thesaurus' writings have been reprinted by Doglio [7]. In this context we aim to underline how the fruition of the original book and its related information can be accessed by a wide range of readers for enhancing the understanding of CH. Information can be found in libraries and museums, also by using important new digital sources. For example, through Europeana, European Digital Library, we can search the portrait of the author, Thesaurus, and we can find it in the Austrian National Library. [13, 14] Nowadays we can link Thesaurus's iconography to its biography through the web and databases, such as French National Library dbs, which contains some of his books. [9] With this research we aim to connect written description with the lost pictures in order to visualize - within the space of the room - how visitors at that time had to feel the previous designed baroque vision of this painted space. The room was a visual narrative, and we translated the book in a rich narrative by integrating words and space, and iconography.

Cravero himself quoted Eugenio Olivero –author- hypothetic scheme, which was the basis for the reconstruction of the frescoes disposition.

These lost pictorial narrations are also important for a profound comprehension of the path to nobility of the City of Turin since they visualized the mythological origins of the Savoy family. As many other Italian lordship previously made during the Renaissance, the Savoy family, even if in belated epoch, used mythological tales of its own born as a propaganda tool in an European field, to magnify its own dignity and right to reign.

From this direct source, a meticulous reconstruction of the image of the hall begins. This research, therefore, has a double purpose: on one hand, telling how the room appeared before the nineteenth-century intervention, highlighting the profound stylistic transformation and the resulting change in the visual impact on its visitor, compensating the lack of iconographic documents with the manuscript description. On the other hand, bringing back to tourist and visitors an insight into past Turin culture and history, valorizing an important but neglected and hidden written source.

Palazzo di Città and Aula Maior have been modelled in the context of the project "Digitization of the Buildings of Turin" which aims to realize a virtuous and innovative model for managing Public Estate through BIM. This methodology allows the integration of both tangible and intangible information (such as Thesaurus' book descriptions) inside a 3d information model; these data, which are now conserved in expensive and hardly accessible papery archives, can be thus dematerialized, becoming available for many typologies of users. Moreover, this source will contribute to the enrichment of a digital web supporting the actors involved in the building and its historic heritage conservation.

This goal is achieved through progressively structured activities: building survey, historic, management, architectonic and plant data retrieving, 3d and information modelling of the whole building in BIM environment and, finally, use of dedicated software for specific activities such as energy analysis, Facility Management and, as deepened in the next paragraphs, 3d immersive VR modelling for tourism, dissemination and sensitization activities.

3   Interpretation and Translation of the Book into a 3dimensional Virtual Space

After a long process of careful reading and interpretation of the information retrieved from the book and the other written sources, it was foreseen the possibility to translate the words of the manuscript into a better communicating device.

Among the different opportunities provided by ICT developers, the virtual reality has been chosen for its economic sustainability, rapidity of realization, great perceptive impact and power of suggestion, and high usability by any end-users.

The first step was the definition of narrative character for the Hall modeling. Undeniably, the lack of iconographic documentation of the lost paintings discouraged the project from taking a photorealistic approach; the peculiarity of these scenes, and the consequent scarce diffusion of these subjects in the paintings by contemporary artists to Miel, indeed does not permit to identify similar paintings that would allow a plausible and philological reconstruction of the real images. Therefore, the focus is put on the evocative appearance of the project and its cultural and political message, limiting the choice to preserved seventeenth-century paintings, contemporary and with similar characteristics to those of Miel, conserved in Turin museums. For this reason, in the virtual model, the paintings are deliberately blurred, while the descriptions in the book by Thesaurus, being reliable and first-hand, were directly re-used and accurately shown.

Nevertheless, the carried out research on the ancient system of the room and their comparison with the Latin text, provided a number of information at least on the distribution of the images. The erudite person, in fact, gives precise description on both subjects of the paintings, and their subdivision: the top 5 histories described the origins of Turin. At the four corners were immortalized four episodes where history and myth were blended, from the Roman period while at the center we could admire the Egyptian myth of Phaeton founding the city. The believing in this legend built a great interest in Egyptian civilization and brought a humongous amount of archeological findings to Savoyard capital. This immense collection is now conserved in one of the most admired and visited attraction of the city: the Egyptian Museum [8].

A description of other 10 boards on the upper strip of the wall, and 8 in the lower, follows. The first ones carry ten further significant historical moments in the evolution of Turin, while the latter illustrate eight emperors who, for different reasons, were important for the city; in this case, the figures were conventionally represented between columns, like in other examples of the time (image of Emperors between columns) [3].

The division of the strips of the wall most likely remained the same also in the later nineteenth century restoration, which sets a sharp color change between the marbles below the access doors transom and those above it.

Some of the hypotheses about a more precise disposition of the paintings, made by successive historical sources, were rejected after a comparison between baroque environments and other seventeenth-century rooms of the palace, which survived until the present day.

The methodology of this work involves the restitution of the certain information through a realistic modeling, while all the uncertain data were translated into evocative images. For example, all measures (width, height, length of the room and of the

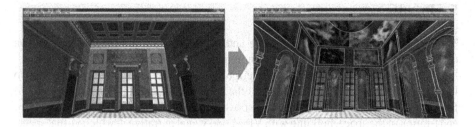

Fig. 3. Covering the neoclassical surfaces and showing the baroque style

windows) of the virtual environment are identical to those of the real room. In fact the basis of the 3d virtual model is the actual Marble Hall while the baroque style is visualized as a painted veil, covering the neoclassical surfaces and showing the ancient appearance. (See Fig. 3) The starting sources were the Historical Archives projects, the historical documents that tell the story of the Hall, computer material delivered by the Town Hall of Turin, consisting of a.dwg file of the existing and security plan, and finally, a rich bibliography about the building, its square and generally the history of Turin.

This information was verified and compared with the metric and photographic survey of existing building, allowing very detailed modeling of the framework up to a 1:1 scale. After updating.dwg, it was possible to begin the modeling phase with Revit 2014, BIM software whose tools like schedules, parametric families, information on materials or else, enable the implementation of an enriched three-dimensional model with easily generated, exportable database, always consultable by the different actors who are involved in the project [1] (See Fig. 2).

4   From BIM to VR for the Visualization of Data

Another important feature that was added to the 3d model is the possibility of reading the words of the book from an animated pop up screen, which show the original pages of the manuscript, preventing its degradation. To do this, the Aula Maior was specifically characterized for the environment visualization in the virtual reality, taking advantage of the interoperability of BIM software, and exporting the model to 3ds Max, which can manage in a fast and efficient way, the rendering and navigation operations of the environment. Subsequently the file was exported to Unity, software used for gaming to create environments where characters move. This gaming platform allows managing graphic renderings, light effects, creating soil, physical simulation, sound effects and options for customizing of the project (scripting systems). For example, through this last procedure, it is possible to set an automatic pop up of the information relating to the paintings and to objects when the user moves closer to them [5, 11].

5   Results

The result of such work is a suggestive and evocative environment that provides an overall idea of space to the visitors by an immersion in the room.

The project brings the paintings descriptions back into their contest, the room; so that the users can visualize the content of the book in the same ambient they were born from (the Marble Room). In such way it is possible to recreate the lost ancient appearance and fruition of the space, building with VR a good visual narrative in which virtual space, text and images combine.

Moreover, the tourist can make a comparison between the Marble Hall and the Aula Maior, moving in the real room and visualizing the ancient look through the Oculus or other VR devices. In addition, the user can select any wanted information, personalizing his experience and enjoying the simple visual involvement or deepen the knowledge about Turin myths and history. The possibility of interaction with the modeled elements in this virtual environment is one of the most important strengths of VR, because any object can contain extra information selected and provided by designers about the epoch, the protagonists of the histories once depicted in the paintings and the historical context in which Thesaurus moved (Fig. 4).

Fig. 4. Displaying of the marble hall using unity

6   Conclusion

In conclusion, this research highlighted some important aspects for any other work involving Digital History, emphasizing the innovative approach to both buildings and books valorization. The ICT tools can in fact be a great ally in the communication of any kind of source belonging to Cultural Heritage, thanks to their power of involving tourists and non-professionals into highly immersive experiences, stimulating curiosity and interest for artistic and historical richness. These technologies can be a support to overcome any difficulty that both professionals and visitors might face in reading the sources of first-hand information, such us manuscript, building inscriptions and any other written data. The digitalization of our CH libraries and archives can undoubtedly be one of the main fields of research for both scholars and professionals, providing a solution to the conservation and managing of incalculable numbers of public heritage treasures. Nevertheless, the project shows how the informatics technology can't substitute the traditional phase of reading, filtering and interpretation of the historical sources, emphasizing the important role of human factor in the crucial choices of the right tools for the final communication of the data. The role of the designer is also determinant in finding a reading key assisting the end-user in concentrating on the hidden details, finding the history laying in all those environment and buildings we take for granted.

References

1. Osello, A. (ed.): Buiding Information Modelling: Geografic Information System, Augmenred Reality for Facility Management. Dario Flaccovio, Palermo (2015)

References from books

2. AA.VV.: Il Palazzo di Città a Torino, The City Palace in Turin, Vincenzo Bona S.p.A., Turin (1986) (in Italian)
3. Thesauri, E.: Inscriptiones quotquot reperiri potuerunt Opera ed diligentia Emmanuelis Philibeti Panealbi, editio secunda, Taurini (1666)
4. Cravero, D.G.: Trecento anni di vita Del Palazzo Civico di Torino 1663–1963, Three hundred years of City Palace life in Turin 1663–1963. Città di Torino, Turin (1964). (in Italian)
5. Sherman, W.S., Craig, A.B.: Understanding Virtual Reality-Interface Application and Design. Morgan Kaufmann, San Francisco (2003)
6. Zaccaria, A.: Storia letteraria d'Italia, literary history of Italy, pp. 690–691, vol. III. Poletti, Venice (1750) (in Italian)
7. Luisa, DM., (ed.): Emanuele Tesauro, Scritti, Emanuele Tesauro, Writing. Edizioni dell'Orso, Alessandria (2004) (in Italian)
8. Cibrario, L.: Storia di Torino, history of Turin. Alessandro Fontana, Turin (1846). (in Italian)
9. Tamborrino R., Rinaudo F.: Translating urban history, research and sources, into interactive digital libraries. In: Geomatics Workbooks, no 12, pp. 175–183. Como (2015)

References from other literature

10. MiBAC, 2006/2008. Ministero per i Beni e le attività culturali, CulturaItalia. http://www.culturaitalia.it

References from websites: (Accessed 18 May 2016)

11. http://www.realtavirtuale.net/oculus-rift/
12. http://dhlab.epfl.ch/
13. http://data.bnf.fr/atelier/12182716/emanuele_tesauro/
14. http://www.europeana.eu/portal/record/92062/BibliographicResource_1000126200534.html
15. http://mobileworldcapital.com/508/
16. http://www.itabc.cnr.it/pagine/progetti-ricerca-itabc-cnr

17. http://www.raiscuola.rai.it/articoli/la-domus-aurea/21345/default.aspx
18. http://journalofdigitalhumanities.org/3-1/transforming-the-object-of-our-study-by-john-n-wall/

An Interdisciplinary Study on the Ancient Egyptian Wines: The Egywine Project

Maria Rosa Guasch-Jané[✉]

Mondes Pharaoniques (UMR 8167 "Orient et Méditerranée"),
Université Paris-Sorbonne, Paris, France
Maria-Rosa.Guasch_Jane@paris-sorbonne.fr

Abstract. This article presents the research results of the 'Irep en Kemet' Project that studies the Ancient Egyptian wine culture and the newly developed website of the research project [www.wineofancientegypt.com] to transfer the knowledge and disseminate the results. For the first time, the corpus of the viticulture and winemaking scenes in the ancient Egyptian private tombs has been developed, together with the bibliographical and scene-detail databases. The second phase of the 'Irep en Kemet' website includes an interactive archaeological map of Egypt with the viticulture and winemaking scenes, and also the databases and the results of the research. Moreover, the objectives and preliminary results of the EGYWINE project that investigates the wine jars and wine inscriptions, and the ancient DNA of the Egyptian wines, are presented.

Keywords: Ancient egypt · Grapes · Wines · Wine jars · Inscriptions · Paleogenomics

1 Introduction

The research on the subject of Ancient Egyptian wines is an interdisciplinary research including several studies and research projects.

The 'Study of the viticulture and oenology scenes in the Egyptian tombs' scientific project (2011–2014) is a scientific project, directed by Dr. Maria Rosa Guasch Jané, was hosted by the *Faculdade de Ciências Sociais e Humanas* of the *Universidade Nova* in Lisbon (Portugal), and funded by the *Fundação para a Ciência e a Tecnologia* (FCT) of the Portuguese Ministry of Education and Science. The research project has created the corpus of the viticulture and winemaking scenes in the ancient Egyptian tombs.

The "Ancient Egypt's Wine Rebirth" Egywine project (2016-2018) is the Marie Sklodowska Curie Grant number 699858 (H2020-MSCA-IF-2015) funded by the European Comission, and hosted by the *Mondes Pharaoniques* (UMR 8167 "*Orient et Méditerranée*") directed by Professor Pierre Tallet at the *Université Paris-Sorbonne* in Paris, France. Egywine project studies the ancient Egyptian wine jars and wine inscriptions and is carrying out the first ever paleogenomic analysis of the ancient DNA (aDNA) of Egyptian wines. Egywine addresses the viticulture origins, production and preservation of the ancient Egyptian wines, and the diffusion of the Egyptian wine culture legacy to

© Springer International Publishing AG 2016
M. Ioannides et al. (Eds.): EuroMed 2016, Part I, LNCS 10058, pp. 737–748, 2016.
DOI: 10.1007/978-3-319-48496-9_59

Europe. To transfer the knowledge and disseminate the research results, the website 'Irep en Kemet' [www.wineofancientegypt.com] has been developed and is now updated with the recent research on this subject.

2   Study of the Colour of the Egyptian Wines

The symbolism of the wine in ancient Egypt was based on its red color, not only because of the relation established between wine and the blood of the resurrection god Osiris, but also because of the reddish color of the River Nile during the annual flood-with ferruginous sediments coming from the Ethiopian mountains-, when the harvest time for grapes started [1, 2]. The Egyptian mythology related the wine only to the red color, and no textual references to white wine–or to red wine- from the Dynastic period (3100–343 BC) have been found in Egypt up to now. The first mention of white wine in Egypt is from Athenaeus of Naucratis, who lived during the 3rd century BC, in his book *The Deipnosophistae*, where he explains that Mareotis wine, in the area of the lake Mariut near the city of Alexandria, was "excellent, white and enjoyable, aromatic..." [3].

During my PhD at the Nutrition and Food Science Department, Pharmacy Faculty of the *Universitat de Barcelona*, the kind (color) of the wines that were made in ancient Egypt was investigated. An analytical method [4, 5] for archaeological residues of wine was developed using the liquid chromatography mass spectrometry in tandem (LC/MS/MS) technique. Two compounds were identified in archaeological residue samples from Tutankhamun's amphorae using the LC/MS/MS method: tartaric acid, as grape marker, and syringic acid derived from malvidin, the latter being the main compound responsible for the red color of grapes and wines, as red grape marker [4, 6, 7]. The results of analysing residue samples from Tutankhamun's amphorae revealed that in ancient Egypt red and white wines were given the name *irp* [5, 7].

The analytical results added new information to the inscription on the amphorae: about the type of wine contained. There was a red wine in Tutankhamun's amphora number *Journal d'Entrée (JE)* 62314 [5, 7] at the Egyptian Museum in Cairo, with the inscription "Year 9, wine of the Estate of Aten of the Western River, chief vintner Khaa", and a white wine was contained in Tutankhamun's amphora *JE* 62316 [5, 7] with the inscription "Year 5, wine of the Estate of Tutankhamun, ruler of Thebes in the Western River, chief vintner Khaa". The results of the analyses also confirmed that in Egypt, during the New Kingdom period, three kinds of grape products were made [5]: red wine, white wine and the *shedeh*, a red wine with a different preparation.

The origin and nature of the *shedeh*, which has no translation, was a mystery since a century ago, with pomegranates or grapes having been proposed as a raw material. According to Papyrus Salt 825 (BM 10051) of the Late period (715–332 BC), the only text found so far that mentions the elaboration of the *shedeh*, it was filtered and heated; nevertheless, due to a damage in the Salt papyrus, the botanical source of *shedeh* remained unknown [5, 8–10].

The results of analyzing a sample of a residue from the *shedeh* amphora found in Tutankhamun's burial chamber (*JE* 62315, Carter number 206 [11]), bearing the inscription "Year 5, *shedeh* of very good quality of the Estate of Aten of the Western River, chief vintner Rer" [12] confirmed that *shedeh* was a red grape wine [5, 6]. Further research suggested the use of the three different wines found in Tutankhamun's Burial chamber were for the King's three-step resurrection ritual [13].

3   The Corpus of the Viticulture and Winemaking Scenes

Viticulture and winemaking scenes were depicted on the walls of the private tombs in Egypt from the Old Kingdom period (2575–2150 BC) through the Graeco-Roman times (332 BC–395 AD).

The 'Study of the viticulture and oenology scenes in the Egyptian tombs' scientific project (2011–2014) has documented and studied the viticulture and winemaking scenes in the Egyptian private tombs [14, 15].

For the first time, the scenes have been documented and studied together, including the texts associated to the images, and photographed. The scenes depicted on the walls of the tombs represent the main steps of the harvest and the wine production and are unique (see Fig. 1).

Fig. 1. Grape harvest scene from the tomb of Khnumhotep III (BH3) at Beni Hassan, Egypt. © 'Irep en Kemet' Project 2016

A bibliographical researchable database (Fig. 2) relevant to wine, viticulture and winemaking in the ancient Egypt has been completed, with 200 entries including articles, books, chapters in book, academic thesis, essays, abstracts, on-line articles and websites.

Furthermore, a scenes-detailed database with 92 records of tombs dated from the 4th Dynasty (2575–2450 BC) of the Old Kingdom until the 30th–31st Dynasties (380–332 BC) of the Late period has been developed [15].

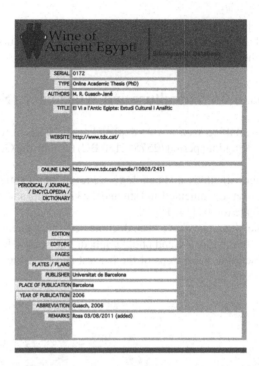

Fig. 2. Bibliographic database on the Ancient Egyptian wine. ©'Irep en Kemet' Project 2016

The database of the scenes of viticulture and winemaking in the ancient Egyptian private tombs (Fig. 3) includes for each scene: record number, scene description with the different steps according to the theme, that is, viticulture or winemaking.

In the viticulture scenes, the steps represented are: vinery, taking care of the vine, grape harvest and counting the baskets.

In the winemaking scenes, the steps represented are: transporting grapes to a press, pressing grapes, heating and filtering, pressing the remains in a sack press, filling wine jars, fermentation, offerings to goddess Renenutet, wine tasting, sealing the wine jars, labelling wine jars, counting wine jars, transporting wine jars to a cellar, refrigerate during fermentation, and store wine jars in a cellar.

The scene-detail database (Fig. 3) also includes: scene details, annotations, scene type and scene condition, text (inscriptions and translation) and image/photo. Moreover, the dating (period, dynasties and kings), location (provenance, governorate, archaeological site), provenance (governorate, archaeological site, tomb name and number, and location inside the tomb) and present location (if it is the same as provenance, if it's a museum then location inside the museum and inventory number, and others if it's not a museum) are detailed.

The project methodology included data collection analysis of the archives, compilation of documents and all the information associated with the Egyptian tombs having scenes of viticulture and winemaking, such as location, tomb owner names and titles, dating, among others [15].

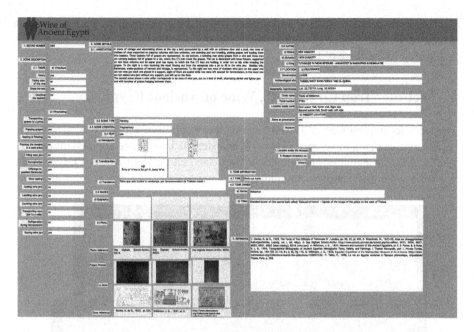

Fig. 3. Scenes-detailed database of the Ancient Egyptian tombs with viticulture and winemaking scenes. ©'Irep en Kemet' Project 2016

This comprehensive study of all scenes and associated texts, combined with a photographic survey in Egypt during 2013, have permitted to record and analyze all the scenes, including some unpublished ones.

The bibliographical research of the scenes of viticulture and winemaking has resulted in the identification of unpublished scenes. Furthermore, some of the scenes of viticulture and winemaking are not available for publication, because of copyrights or because they were never drawn or photographed. For this reason, and with permission of the Permanent Committee and Foreign Mission Affairs Department of the Supreme Council of Antiquities (SCA) of Egypt, we carried out a photographic survey for the tombs.

The 2013 photography mission to the Egyptian necropolises included the identified tombs to check the information obtained from historical documents and to take updated photographs of the scenes. The photographic mission allowed us to have access to almost all the tombs with scenes of viticulture and winemaking to study the images and associated text, and to identify unpublished data. It also permitted us to detect the current state of conservation of the already published scenes.

The photography mission work was divided into three phases, based on the geographic location (Upper Egypt, Middle Egypt and Lower Egypt) allowed taking detailed, high-resolution photos of the viticulture and winemaking scenes, which will be presented in the scenes-detailed database [15].

Furthermore, our successful photography mission also gave a great opportunity to explore the tombs, in which these scenes were depicted and learn about their contexts and current conditions.

This research study on the viticulture and winemaking scenes in the ancient Egyptian private tombs is an important tool for the future documentation and conservation of the archaeological heritage of Egypt.

4   Website "Irep En Kemet", Wine of Ancient Egypt

The website 'Irep en Kemet' (=Wine of Ancient Egypt) project [www.wineofancien-tegypt.com] is being developed (Fig. 4) to transfer the knowledge and disseminate the results of our research on the subject of the wine culture from Ancient Egypt to the scientific and non-scientific community.

Fig. 4. The 'Irep en Kemet' (=Wine of Ancient Egypt) website on the study of the Ancient Egyptian wine culture. ©'Irep en Kemet' Project 2016

The creation of the website in 2013 was financially supported by the VINSEUM, *Museu de les Cultures del Vi de Catalunya*, in Vilafranca del Penedès (Barcelona, Catalonia) [www.vinseum.cat] and developed by *Sistemes de Gestió de Patrimoni* (SGP) [www.sgponline.net].

The website content includes the general information about the research on the viticulture and winemaking scenes and including: introduction, history, objectives and methodology, the team members, bibliography (Fig. 5), news (Fig. 6), links, collaborations and contacts.

Fig. 5. Published articles and congresses in the website. ©'Irep en Kemet' Project 2016

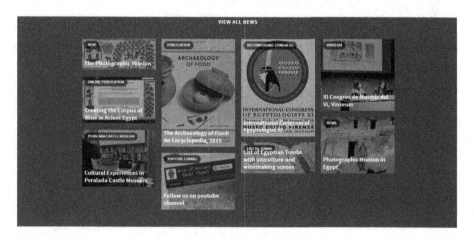

Fig. 6. Photographic mission, lectures, articles and congresses presented in the website news. ©'Irep en Kemet' Project 2016

In 2015 a second stage of the website, funded by Perelada Fine Estates in Perelada (Girona, Catalonia) [www.perelada.com/en], is developed to include the project results, the bibliography and scenes-detailed databases, and the interactive archaeological map of Egypt for the tombs with viticulture and winemaking scenes (Figs. 7 and 9).

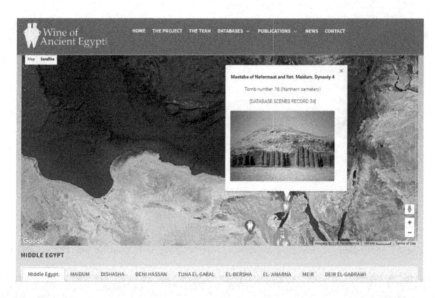

Fig. 7. Archaeological map of Egypt with the tombs having viticulture and winemaking scenes on the 'Irep en Kemet' website. ©'Irep en Kemet' Project 2016

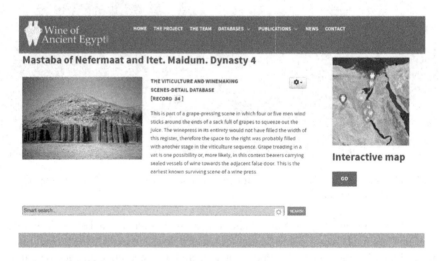

Fig. 8. Database of the tombs having viticulture and winemaking scenes presented in the website. ©'Irep en Kemet' Project 2016

Furthermore, the website includes our publications on the topic of wine in Ancient Egypt, freely accessible on-line.

The website will include all the collected data, studies and analysis. Currently, the on-line access to the scene-detail and bibliographic databases, and to the georeferenced tombs' map is being developed (Fig. 8).

Fig. 9. The viticulture and winemaking scenes presented in the website. © 'Irep en Kemet' Project 2016

Regarding the technical aspects, the website is multiplatform and available for consultation through mobile devices: tablets and 3G mobiles. The Qr codes have been generated to allow the consultation through these devices. The platform language is based on XML (eXtensive Markub Language). The web interface is designed using Content Management System (CMS) with open code, a free software under General Public Licence, allowing an intuitive navigation and actualization of the contents of the website.

Fig. 10. Tutankhamun's amphora *Journal d'Entrée* number 62303. ©Maria Rosa Guasch Jané, with permission of the Egyptian Museum in Cairo

The web platform gives visibility to our research on the Ancient Egyptian wine culture, an open access to the scenes-detailed and bibliography databases, which will be georeferenciated, and the dissemination and socialization of the archaeological knowledge in relation to wine in antiquity as well as bibliography and multimedia material (images, audiovisual) and 3D reconstructions. The use of the Information and Communications Technology (ICT) will allow dissemination and on-line consultation.

5   Egywine Project

The Egywine project studies how the Egyptian wines were made to understand the ancient traditional elaboration methods for the knowledge advancement and heritage conservation.

Egywine is an interdisciplinary project that collects and documents evidences (pottery and organic material) for the entire process of grape cultivation and wine production in Egypt interrelating various scientific disciplines (archaeology, paleogenomics, history and semantics).

The EGYWINE project aims are to:

- Identify what is linked with wine from the Predynastic (3800–3300 BC) to the New Kingdom (1550–1069 BC) period;
- Study the Ancient Egyptian wine jars;
- Analyze ancient wine residues from pharaonic Egypt through paleogenomics.

5.1   Egyptian Wine Jars and Wine Inscriptions

Since the Predynastic Period (4000–3100 BC), wine jars were placed in the Egyptian tombs as funerary offerings. During the New Kingdom Period (1539–1075 BC), two-handled wine jars (amphora type) were inscribed in hieratic to indicate: the year, the name of the product, the quality, the provenance, the property (royal or private) and the name and title of the wine-maker (Fig. 10).

The inscription on the amphora *JE* 62303 (Fig. 10) of the Cairo Egyptian Museum, from Tutankhamun's tomb (KV62) at Thebes, reads: "Year 4, wine from the Estate of Aten, in the Western River, chief vintner Nen" [12]. The clay seal of this amphora is broken and it is open on the upper part, as Fig. 10 shows. Like the labels in the modern wine bottles, the inscriptions on the New Kingdom wine jars give us information about the harvest and wine production [16] revealing that the ancient Egyptians considered this information relevant and necessary to be able to distinguish between wines. It was extremely important to know the vintage and the provenance of the product.

The method of wine production and preservation of the ancient Egyptian wines, and the diffusion of the Egyptian wine culture legacy to Europe is investigated through the analysis of the pottery and the wine inscriptions.

5.2 Paleogenomic Analysis

The paleogenomic analysis aim to identify possible relations with current grape varieties, wine yeasts, and grape vine origins.

Egywine project offer multiple perspectives of study: (i) vine genome evolution since its initial domestication; (ii) fermentation yeasts evolution; (iii) wine making process evolution, through a metagenomic analysis of the multiple microorganisms used during, or along, the wine making process.

Acknowledgements. The 'Study of the viticulture and oenology scenes in the Egyptian tombs' scientific project (2011–2014) was funded by the *Fundação para a Ciência e a Tecnologia* (FCT) of the Portuguese Ministry of Education and Science.

The "Ancient Egypt's Wine Rebirth" Egywine research project (2016–2018) number 699858 is a Marie Sklodowska Curie grant financially supported by the European Comission (H202-MSCA-IF-2015). We would like to thank the Vinseum and the Perelada Fine Estates for the financial support of the website.

References

1. Poo, M-Ch.: Wine and wine offering in the religion of ancient Egypt. In: Helck, W., Westendorf, W. (eds.), pp. 149–151. Kegan Paul International, London (1995)
2. Poo, M-Ch.: Weinopfer. In: Helck, W., Westendorf, W. (eds.) Lexikon der Ägyptologie, vol. 6, pp. 1186–1190. Harrassowitz, Wiesbaden (1986)
3. Athenaeus (I, 33 d-f): Athenaeus, the deipnosophists, with an English translation by Charles Burton Gulick. In: Loeb Classical library, vol. 1, pp. 146–147. London Harvard University Press, Cambridge-Massachusetts (1961)
4. Guasch-Jané, M.R., Ibern-Gómez, M., Andrés-Lacueva, C., Jáuregui, O., Lamuela-Raventós, R.M.: Liquid chromatography mass spectrometry in tandem mode applied for the identification of wine markers in residues from ancient Egyptian vessels. Anal. Chem. **76**, 1672–1677 (2004)
5. Guasch-Jané, M.R.: Wine in ancient Egypt: a cultural and analytical study. In: British Archaeological Reports S1851, pp. 11, 29–30, 53–54, 56–59. Archaeopress, Oxford (2008)
6. Guasch-Jané, M.R., Andrés-Lacueva, C., Jáuregui, O., Lamuela-Raventós, R.M.: The origin of the ancient Egyptian drink *shedeh* revealed using LC/MS/MS. J. Archaeol. Sci. **33**, 98–101 (2006)
7. Guasch-Jané, M.R., Andrés-Lacueva, C., Jáuregui, O., Lamuela-Raventós, R.M.: First evidence of white wine in ancient Egypt from Tutankhamun's tomb. J. Archaeol. Sci. **33**, 1075–1080 (2006)
8. Derchain, P.: Le papyrus Salt 825 (B.M. 10051), Rituel pour la Conservation de la Vie en Égypte. Mémoires vol. LVIII: 137 (II, 1), (no. 10), pp. 137, 147–149. Académie Royale de Belgique, Bruxelles (1965)
9. Tallet, P.: Le *shedeh*, etude d'un procédé de vinification en Égypte ancienne. BIFAO **95**, 459–492 (1995)
10. Tallet, P.: De l'ivresse au dégrisement, à propos d'un article récent sur le vin *shedeh*. Göttinger Miszellen **227**, 105–112 (2010)
11. Carter Archive: Tutankhamun: anatomy of an excavation, The Howard Carter Archives. The Griffith Institute, Oxford. http://www.griffith.ox.ac.uk. Accessed 15 June 2016

12. Černy, J.: *Wine jars*. In: Baines, J. (ed.) Hieratic Inscriptions from the Tomb of Tutankhamun, Tutankhamun's Tomb Series, vol. II, pp. 1–4. Griffith Institute, Oxford (1965)
13. Guasch-Jané, M.R.: The meaning of wine in Egyptian tombs: the three amphorae in Tutankhamun's burial chamber. Antiquity **85**(329), 851–858 (2011)
14. Guasch-Jané, M.R., Fonseca, S., Ibrahim, M.: The 'Irep en Kemet' project, documenting the corpus of wine in ancient Egypt. In: Proceedings of 4th International Conference (Euromed 2012) on Cultural Heritage and Digital Libraries, Amathus (Cyprus), Oct 29-Nov 3 2012, International Journal of Heritage in the Digital Era Suppl 1, 1, pp. 181–186. ISBN 2047–4970, Multi-Science Publisher, UK (2012)
15. Guasch-Jané, M.R., Fonseca, S., Ibrahim, M.: The complete corpus of viticulture and winemaking scenes from the ancient Egyptian private tombs. In: Proceedings of the XIth International Congress of Egyptologists, Florence, Italy, 23–30 August 2015 (in revision)
16. Guasch-Jané, M.R.: On Egyptian wine marketing. In: Hudecz, A., Petrik, M., (eds.) Commerce and Economy in Ancient Egypt, Proceedings of the 3rd International Congress for Young Egyptologists 25–27 September 2009, Budapest. BAR S2131, pp. 63–69. Archaeopress, Oxford (2010)

ArchaeoInside: Multimodal Visualization of Augmented Reality and Interaction with Archaeological Artifacts

Kadar Manuella and Domsa Ovidiu[✉]

Department of Computer Science and Engineering, 1 Decembrie 1918 University of Alba Iulia,
Alba Iulia, Romania
manuellakadar@yahoo.com, domsaddd@yahoo.com

Abstract. This paper reports on a system named **ArchaeoInside** designed in order to offer a virtual environment for archaeological exploration with large access to public, researchers and museum curators. **ArchaeoInside** project aims at recording, classifying, digitizing, accessing and presenting archaeological sites and artifacts in Augmented Reality.

Keywords: Augmented reality · 3D interaction · VR systems · Archaeological artifacts

1 Background

Virtual Reality (VR) and 3D modeling projects involving archaeological data started at the end of the eighties, the beginning of the nineties. First attempts into establishing standards and methodologies for the use of VR and 3D modeling techniques in archaeology, particularly data communication by means of such techniques, the historical credibility of VR and 3D products, the accuracy of the products from the archaeological point of view or the need for a transparency of data have been widely discussed in [1–4].

Other methodological and theoretical aspects of VR and 3D modeling applications in archaeology have been developed [5] and new approaches of archaeological research using VR and 3D models have been proposed in [6–8]. Issues such as: should archaeologist bother at all with VR and 3D modeling, what is the gain of the archaeological research from VR or why should archaeologist deal with VR have received pertinent answers in well-documented research works that emphasized the need of multi-disciplinary collaboration. In the last five years, projects that integrate cultural contents, interfaces and technological devices have been launched by interdisciplinary teams, in order to have a holistic vision of information. The emphasis is given to perception, capacity of learning, 3D behaviors, connectivity, dynamic processes of learning, embodiment as fundamental factors of virtual communication.

Innovative multimodal visualization technology has opened the possibility of creating augmented reality that integrates 3D content into a museums website, thus enhancing the experience of learning acquired by a visitor's interaction with an online exhibition, either within the museum or in the Internet [9, 10]. Further, virtual reality interfaces offer curators new technological tools for preservation and access. The curator

© Springer International Publishing AG 2016
M. Ioannides et al. (Eds.): EuroMed 2016, Part I, LNCS 10058, pp. 749–757, 2016.
DOI: 10.1007/978-3-319-48496-9_60

may utilize such tools to extend the already existing digital preservation techniques by adding digital 3D models of artifacts to their digital archives, and then reuse these digital surrogates for presentations in visualization systems that also allow online access [10].

This paper reports on a system, named ArchaeoInside which has been designed by an interdisciplinary team of archaeologists, computer graphics specialists, programmers who have collaborated to offer a virtual environment to the large public and to researchers and curators.

ArchaeoInside has been designed by taking into consideration key issues when designing museum interactive system. Key issues as have been presented in [10], are:

1. Museum interactive systems should be as cost effective as possible given the limited funds available to museums.
2. 3D content should be created as cheaply as possible in addition to digitization of supporting data.
3. Consideration should be given to the costs of maintaining the museum interactive systems because this implies new skills that need to be acquired by the museums, staff etc. The museum may in effect be converting itself from a learning institute to a so called hybrid institution where the institution exhibits are not only analogue (i.e. the physical artifact), but also the digital surrogate or resources. In this context, it is important that authoring tools contain all tools necessary for proper digital curation.
4. Appropriate interaction techniques should be devised to augment the digital resource so as to effectively engage the user. In order to identify suitable interaction techniques for the end-user but also to the curator, formal usability evaluation studies are necessary. Therefore, relevant skills are needed.
5. Any museum interactive system should present the information as a story that reinforces the heritage behind the artifact that is on display targeting at different users and age groups. Using the new opportunities that digital storytelling [11] offers it is required to extend the skill set of museum curators and staff.
6. Perceived 'presence' is shown to be enhanced when modalities such as sound and 3D content are added in a museum interactive system in order for the visitor to feel part of the virtual exhibition.

2   ArchaeoInside Model

ArchaeoInside deals with recording, classification, digitization, access and presentation of elements that belong to archaeological excavations. The way the data are organized and accessed follows the territorial standards logic and it is directly connected with its contents. It is a concrete -not theoretical- open and evolving model.

The objectives of the system are: (i) documentation of the identity and value of the prehistoric sites, (ii) gathering and preservation of historic evidence that are scattered in public and private archives, (iii) conveying of findings and data to the local public, competent authorities, student population through museums and to the international academic community through web integration, (iv) development of a digital platform for recording and documentation of the cultural heritage.

The system was designed to manage various types of data such as: temporal data (description of historical periods), description of spatial data (description of places of the archaeological site), different kind of maps that have been digitized (axonometries, maps, sections, plans, elevations, excavation profiles and plans), digital photos or ancient photos digitized, videos, scanned drawings, scanned texts, vectorial plans (generated in SVG), 3D models. The Use Cases are detailed in UML schema in Fig. 1. Figure 1 presents various operations for an efficient exploitation of the ArchaeoInside system. All UML schemas help the user (visitors and experts) to query interfaces by keywords and images.

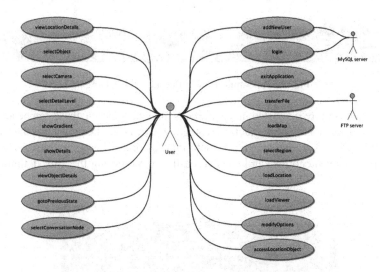

Fig. 1. Use Cases of ArchaeoInside

3   ArchaeoInside System

The user has the option to explore the virtual environment starting from a 3D map that is chosen from the main menu of the application, further one can obtain information on the region selected and can continue to ask for information on objects discovered in the archaeological site (Fig. 2).

Fig. 2. Selection menu

The example provided here is the Seusa-Gorgan site from Alba County representing an archaeological complex site dated to the Late Chalcolithic. The site is a settlement belonging to Cotofeni Culture. General Information is provided on dialogue base. The user can explore the now-a-days site (Fig. 3) through a virtual panoramic view and then can immerse into the excavation, namely the chalcolithic village. In the prehistoric scene the user has the option of exploring the 3D location of the chalcolithic site.

Fig. 3. Panoramic view of the site –Seusa Gorgan

If the user is more interested in the artefacts than the location, these can be accessed directly from the menu. The artefacts are categorized by large classes such as the material and then in more specific categories such: type of object, usage, culture, size. New categories or subcategories can be added easily by modifying the xml. definition file (Fig. 4).

Fig. 4. The Seusa-Gorgan site excavation

Interaction is provided through sound, interactive conversation, video presentations or interaction with artifacts situated in the location. There are several *detail* zones within the location that provide accurate information on different types of materials and made techniques belonging to the referred period.

Visualization and manipulation of 3D objects are facilities integrated into the Object Viewer. The user can rotate, move, and resize selected objects. Several levels of detail are provided for textures and for the 3D models of the artifacts that can be changed by accessing the graphical interface within the Object Viewer (Fig. 5). New objects can be loaded without recalling another state of launch. The user has the option to select the background gradient, object's details and type of visualization camera.

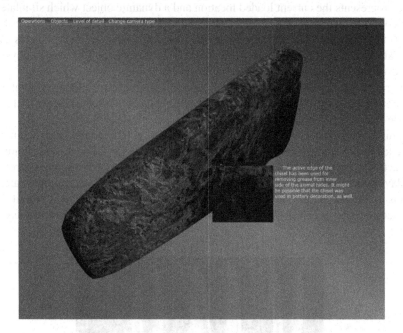

Fig. 5. Digital bone chisel with surface details in Object Viewer

4 Methodological and Technological Approach

The challenges in generating virtual worlds are connected to performances versus natural behavior and aspect of the environment. Such requirements are often in contradiction: convincing models and high level physical simulation implies better hardware and software, meaning an increased computational level that has effects on the global performance. The ArchaeoInside system has been achieved by using open source or shareware software such as: Irrlicht Engine [12], irrKlang Audio Library [13], Newton Game Dynamics Physics Engine [14], LibCurl Multiprotocol File Transfer Library [15], Ffmpeg Audio/Video conversion tool [16]. Using the Irrlicht Engine and irrKlang, ArchaeoInside integrates event analysis and contextual media in its 3D interfaces.

In the engine selection process several factors have been considered: speed, stability and usability. The Newton Game Dynamics engine was chosen due to its popularity and because has strong community development, is fast, and has a simple API. Newton Game Dynamics is an integrated solution for real time simulation of physical environments. The API provides scene management, collision detection, and dynamic behavior and yet it is small, fast, stable and easy to use. The engine implements a deterministic solver, which is not based on traditional Link Control Protocol (LCP) or iterative methods, but possesses the stability and speed of both, respectively. This feature makes the product a tool not only for games, but also for any real-time physical simulation. In the current version of the application only the collision component is used. The application calculates in real-time collisions between two objects. First is the static object which represents the current loaded location and a dynamic object which simulates the user controlled avatar. For each object specific materials can be set which describe the interaction parameter. In future versions the interaction between more objects can be simulated, such as the interaction with artefacts, so the user will be able to physically interact with them besides other interaction modes.

For data acquisition, 3D modeling of the artifacts, image processing, UV mapping, texture mapping various software has been used such as: Autodesk Maya 2012 [17], Adobe Photoshop CS 3 Extended [18].

Museum artifacts can be digitized accurately using 3D scanners, photogrammetry and cheap software that creates photo realistic 3D models for online display. Innovative interaction systems have been designed to expand the traditional museum approach of displaying an artifact in a show case with curators' point of view on a simple card. The idea is to liberate the physical artifact by a digital surrogate and interact with it. It has been considered the ability to create interaction systems composed of replicas of a

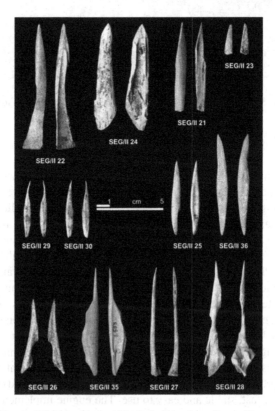

Fig. 6. Display of bone chisels findings from Seusa-Gorgan

physical artifact linked to a 3D model (digital surrogate) of that artifact in order to deliver a contextual heritage view on the artifact [10].

The show case (Fig. 6) can be considered an example for integrating Augmented Reality (AR) through computer-generated virtual information into the real physical environment [19]. One can imagine such a system in a museum whereby the actual artifact is displayed in its show case, perhaps on a wall (Fig. 6), and a large display is situated next to the case. Further, a robust physical replica of the artifact is linked to the display, which presents a virtual environment containing a 3D model of the artifact. Thus, the visitor will obtain tactile information that is traditionally impossible, and by selecting attached sensors on the replica they can also explore a 3D world that digitally narrates the story of the artifact on the display [10].

Figure 7 presents a Chalcolithic bone chisel which was imported into Maya development environment for model building.

Fig. 7. Chalcolitic bone chisel

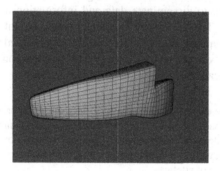

Fig. 8. Bone chisel wireframe

Many developers find this arrangement to be a much better way to work because one can ultimately create a more precise model. Attempting to model from memory or by referring to hard copy references will ultimately lead to errors, and the proportions of the final models will likely be off. A polygonal model has been used due to its mathematical simplicity: by providing a piecewise linear approximation to shape, polygonal meshes lend themselves to simple, regular rendering algorithms in which the visibility and colors of most pixels are determined by interpolating across the polygon's surface. Such algorithms embed well in hardware, which has in turn led to widely available polygon rendering accelerators for every platform. In addition, polygons serve as a sort of lowest common denominator for computer models, since most model representations (spline, implicit-surface, volumetric iso-surface) may be converted with arbitrary accuracy to a polygonal mesh. For these and other reasons, polygonal models are the most common representation for every application from video games to visualization of medical, scientific, and CAD data sets [20].

In order to import a 3D model into an engine like Irrlicht the model has to be made up of polygons (Fig. 8). A primary concern when modeling 3D models for applications is the polygon count and efficiency. Models have to be more efficient to maintain a manageable data set to render. The reasoning here is that an efficient streamlined environment composed of the lower poly assets will render more smoothly and give better frame to frame renders. The modeling methods applied can generate also low polygon resolution version of the meshes without modifying the perception of the model [20].

5   Conclusions and Future Work

The ArchaeoInside project is still in progress but the work done up to now already allows us to draw methodological conclusions for the creation of a virtual reality system based on a unique model with high accuracy and detailed data. The entire reconstruction of the virtual site is next to be achieved. Further improvements to the system will be the addition of input devices such as virtual reality gloves and extending the system so that it can be used with mobile devices. Through the 3D reconstruction of the Calcholitic village we approach an accurate and suggestive interpretation that involves the public and transmits the importance of cultural heritage and thus its conservation.

Such models allow to disseminate data and information that often belong to the scientific community. The possibility to interact with cultural heritage increases the respect and the understanding of the public. The use of advanced applications and freely shared technologies gives the possibility to make the common heritage accessible to everyone in its historical, artistic and scientific dimensions.

Acknowledgements.   Special thanks are granted to Mr. Mihai Gligor, the principal investigator of the Seusa-Gorgan archaeological site for providing access and valuable information and to the enthusiastic team of students hearing Computer Science, namely Robert Iancu and Vlad Buda who have volunteered in gathering data from site, have widely contributed to the programming and digital representations of artefacts.

References

1. Ryan, N.S.: Computer-based visualization of the Past: technical realism and historical credibility. In: Main, P., Higgins, T., Lang, J. (eds.) Imaging the Past: Electronic Imaging and Computer Graphics in Museums and Archaeology, No. 114 in British Museum Occasional Papers, pp. 95–108 (1996)
2. Kanter, J.: Realism vs. reality: creating virtual reconstructions of prehistoric architecture. In: Barceló, J.A., Forte, M., Sanders, D.H. (eds.) Virtual Reality in Archaeology. BAR International Series, vol. 843, pp. 47–52. Archaeopress, Oxford (2000)

3. Frischer, B., Abernathy, D., Favro, D., Liverani, P., De Blaauw, S.: Virtual reality and ancient rome: the UCLA cultural VR labs Santa Maria Maggiore project. In: Barceló, J.A., Forte, M., Sanders, D.H. (eds.) Virtual Reality in Archaeology. BAR International Series, vol. 843, pp. 155–162. Archaeopress, Oxford (2000)
4. Forte, M.: About virtual archaeology: disorders, cognitive interactions and virtuality. In: Barceló, J.A., Forte, M., Sanders, D.H. (eds.) Virtual Reality in Archaeology. BAR International Series, vol. 843, pp. 247–259. Archaeopress, Oxford (2000)
5. Vanaten, I.: Argumentation paths in information infrastructure of the archaeological virtual realities. In: Burenhult, G. (ed.) Archaeological Informatics: Pushing the Envelope CAA 2001. BAR International Series, vol. 1016, pp. 494–499. Archaeopress, Oxford (2004)
6. Beex, W., Peterson, J.: The Arminghall henge in space and time: how virtual reality contributes to research on its orientation. In: der Stadt Wien, M. (ed.) Enter the Past – The E-Way into the Four Dimensions of Cultural Heritage CAA 2003 Proceedings. BAR International Series, vol. 1127, pp. 490–493. Archaeopress, Oxford (2004)
7. Wendrich, W.Z., Bos J.E.M.F., Pansire, K.M.: VR modeling in research, instruction, presentation and cultural heritage management: the case of Karanis (Egypt). In: Ioannides, M., Arnold, D., Niccolucci, F., Mania, K. (eds.) The Evolution of Information Communication Technology in Cultural Heritage. Where Hi-Tech Touches the Past: Risks and Challenges for the 21st Century, Nicosia, pp. 225–230 (2006)
8. Meyer, È., Grussenmeyer, P., Perrin, J., Durand, A., Drap, P.: Intra-site level cultural heritage documentation: combination of survey, modeling and imaginary data in web information systems. In: Ioannides, M., Arnold, D., Niccolucci, F., Mania, K. (eds.) The Evolution of Information Communication Technology in Cultural Heritage. Where Hi-Tech Touches the Past: Risks and Challenges for the 21st Century, Nicosia, pp. 129–134 (2006)
9. Mourkoussis, N., Mania, K., Petridis, P., White, M., Rivera, F., Pletinckx, D.: An analysis of the effect of technological fidelity on perceptual fidelity. In: Proceedings of the IEA 2006 (International Ergonomics Association), 16th World Congress on Ergonomics, The Hague, Netherlands (2006)
10. Petridis, P., Pletinckx, D., Mania, K., White, M.: The EPOCH multimodal interface for interacting with digital heritage artefacts. In: Zha, H., Pan, Z., Thwaites, H., Addison, Alonzo, C., Forte, M. (eds.) VSMM 2006. LNCS, vol. 4270, pp. 408–417. Springer, Heidelberg (2006). doi:10.1007/11890881_45
11. Pletinckx, D., Silberman, N.A., Callebaut, D.: Heritage presentation through interactive storytelling: a new multimedia database approach. J. Vis. Comput. Anim. 14(4), 225–231 (2003). Wiley
12. Irrlicht Engine, http://irrlicht.sourceforge.net/
13. irrKlang Audio Library, http://www.ambiera.com/irrklang/
14. Newton Game Dynamics Physics Engine, https://code.google.com/archive/p/newton-dynamics/downloads
15. LibCurl Multiprotocol File Transfer Library, https://curl.haxx.se/libcurl/
16. Ffmpeg Audio/Video conversion tool, https://ffmpeg.org/
17. Autodesk Maya 2012, http://www.autodesk.com/products/maya/overview
18. Adobe Photoshop CS 3 Extended, http://adobe-photoshop-cs3-extended.soft112.com/
19. Azuma, R.: A survey of augmented reality. Presence: Teleoperators Virtual Environ. 6(4), 355–385 (1997)
20. Luebke, D., Reddy, M., Cohen D.J., Varshney, A., Watson, B., Huebner, R.: Level of Detail for 3D Graphics. In: Barsky, B.A. (ed.) University of California, Berkeley. Morgan Kaufmann Publishers, Elsevier Science (USA) (2003)

DICE: Digital Immersive Cultural Environment

Stelios C.A. Thomopoulos[(⊠)], Adam Doulgerakis, Maria Bessa,
Konstantinos Dimitros, Giorgos Farazis, Eftichia Georgiou,
Tassos Kanellos, Christina Karafylli, Maria Karafylli,
Dimitris M. Kyriazanos, Vassilios I. Kountouriotis,
Vassilis Lampropoulos, Christos Margonis, Christos Maroglou,
Dionisis Motos, Alexandra Papagianni, Manolis Paterakis,
Katerina Skroumpelou, Giorgos Konstandinos Thanos,
Ino-Eleni Theodorou, Christina Phobe Thomopoulos,
Panagiotis Tsimpiridis, Dimitris Zacharakis, and Andreas Zalonis

Integrated Systems Laboratory, Institute of Informatics and Telecommunications,
National Center for Scientific Research "Demokritos", 15310 Athens, Greece
{scat,adoulgerakis,mbessa,k.dimitros,gfarazis,
efgeorgiou,tassos.knl,ckarafilli,mkarafilli,dkyri,
bkoutoutiotis,vlamp,chris.margonis,cmaro,d.motos,
alexpapagianni,mpaterakis,ksroumbelou,giorgos.thanos,
itheodorou,cpt,ptsimpiridis,dzacharakis,
azalonis}@iit.demokritos.gr

Abstract. A Digital Immersive Cultural Environment (DICE) consists of a
VR/AR (virtual & augmented reality) platform, a CMS (Content Management
System) and a GIS (Geographic Information System) for geo-referencing both
space and content and for providing immersive navigation in the VR/AR space.
Such a platform offers 3D reconstruction of space, geo-coding of the virtual
space in actual geographic coordinates and overlay capabilities with real georeferenced space. The coupling of a CMS with a GIS associates information and
data with the geographic coordinates of the VR/AR space, thus making available
content on demand in accordance to spatial point of interest within the VR/AR
space and immersive navigation in both VR and AR spaces. Incorporation of
simulation platforms, localization technologies, motion tracking technologies
and VR UI's, creates a fully interactive immersive VR/AR ecosystem, beyond
the state of the art, with augmented capabilities in education, training, entertainment, content creation, etc.

Keywords: Virtual reality · Augmented reality · Digital cultural space · GIS ·
Indoor localization · Immersive navigation · Simulation

From the second author, names are in alphabetical order.

M. Ioannides et al. (Eds.): EuroMed 2016, Part I, LNCS 10058, pp. 758–777, 2016.
DOI: 10.1007/978-3-319-48496-9_61

1 Introduction

The concept of the DICE as a means of creating a sustainable ecosystem for the development of 3D digital (virtual and augmented reality) immersive cultural environments for a wide range of activities, from education, to research, to entertainment and leisure, was first introduced by S.C.A. Thomopoulos in 2014 [1] and was refined in 2015 [2]. The DICE concept was motivated and initially introduced by the need for the creation of a comprehensive and sustainable ecosystem for smart specialization in the area of Culture and Tourism. As it can be seen in Fig. 1, the "Wheel on innovation" (to be referred to as WOI in what follows) consists of three sectors (or elements) that it is necessary to work in concertation in order to maintain its spin.

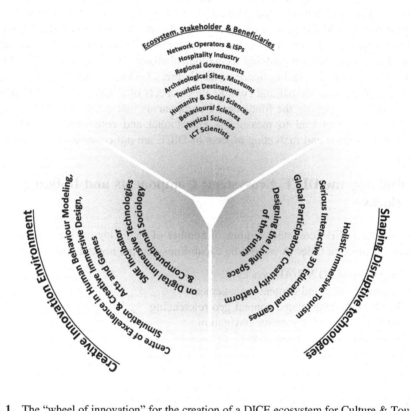

Fig. 1. The "wheel of innovation" for the creation of a DICE ecosystem for Culture & Tourism

The most critical element of WOI is the Ecosystem of Stakeholders & Beneficiaries that includes (and the list is not exhaustive): Creators of Digital Immersive Environments (e.g. architects, digital artists, digital designers, etc.), Historians, Archaeologists, Humanity & Social Scientists, Behavioral Scientists, Information & Communication Technologies, Physical Scientists, Mathematicians & Analysts, Archaeological Sites & Museums, Touristic Destinations, Regional Governments, Network Operators & ISPs, etc. All these together acting as the scientific, technological and business catalysts will enable the creation of a DICE platform capable of delivering the functionalities that are necessary for an immersive cultural environment.

The second critical element of WOI is the Creative Innovation Environment: In order to coherently and over time coordinate the development in the complex WOI ecosystem, it is necessary to have in place a Center of Excellence in Creative Immersive Design, Arts & Games, Human Behavior Modeling, Computational Sociology and Simulation, and Creative Story Boarding. Furthermore, an SME Incubator is necessary as a complementary ingredient of the Center of Excellence in order to facilitate, expedite and catalyze the fast transition of the technological developments into the market and the expedient extraction of the added value within them.

Last, but not least, the third pillar "Shaping of Disruptive Technologies" is required to foster an environment for creating disruptive technologies with exponential benefits to the economy and the generation of new added value through a Holistic Immersive Tourism approach, Serious Interactive 3D Educational Games, and a Global Participatory Creativity Platform enabling technological crowd sourcing, and, as an ultimate goal, the Design of the Living Space of the Future. Due to the limitation in space and the focus on the educational and collaborative aspects of DICE, we will only present our efforts in developing the fundamental components that can make DICE a reality and how these can lead to measurable educational and collaborative results. The financial, economic and marketing aspects of DICE are not covered in this paper.

2   Building the DICE Ecosystem: Components and Building Blocks

Building the DICE Ecosystem requires a number of technological elements ad components in place in order to ensure the capabilities that are needed for:

- Generation of 3D VR/AR spaces
- Content creation and content management
- VR/AR space and related content geo-referencing
- Storyboarding and immersive navigation
- Automated Content Adaptation
- Content DB specification
- Narrative and Content Delivery Method Authoring Tools
- Simulation, gamification and visualization tools
- UI/UX for intuitive and immersive VR/AR interfaces and devices
- Crowdsourced Content Aggregation, Validation and Recommendation
- Collaborative research, education and co-creation tools
- Personalized access to content based on preferences, user profile, disabilities, etc.
- Personalized Storytelling
- Social Media Platform Integration
- Common Specifications towards a unified UI providing access to all content types, including specifications concerning accessibility limitations due to disabilities.

The above are some of the elements that are required in order to be able to accommodate the stakeholders of the DICE ecosystem as delineated in Fig. 1. Analyzing the above, possibly non-exhaustive list of requirements for a DICE ecosystem as a technological, collaborative, inclusive and immersive platform, the following key building blocks emerge:

#1 A platform for the creation of 3D virtual environments that it is either based on commercial, popular 3D design platforms or interfaces with them, a set of tools and plague-ins for embedding content (in the form of text, audio, video, animations, immersive navigation, etc.), a gamification engine, either as an internal engine or a plague-in to a commercial engine, an interface with a powerful simulation engine for the creation of necessary animations within the immersive VR/AR environment, and powerful UI/UX's to guarantee integration of VR equipment and devices for immersive experiences.

#2 A platform for geo-referencing 2D/3D architectural and geolocating indoor and outdoor 2D/3D and their content so that they can be georeferenced on a map, thus allowing information retrieval based on location information, access and navigation in VR and AR spaces using locative services, and geographical alignment of virtual 2D/3D reconstructions with actual 2D/3D buildings and artifacts.

#3 A platform for allowing general purpose simulations, including human behavior, motion and dynamics of human, animal and physical system, and device modelling and simulation to allow scenario-based animations, immersive interactions of the users within the platform through avatars, gamification and interactivity.

#4 A platform of a distributed simulation environment for coupling different simulators of events, spaces, behaviors, and physical phenomena or man-made mechanisms, devices or processes, and embedding the output of these simulators in the DICE environment.

#5 A platform for crowd-sourcing (multimedia) content, allowing aggregation, validation and recommendation of the crowd-sourced content and interface for integration with different social media platforms.

#6 A platform for collaborative research, education and training to include co-creation tools, personalized access to content based on preferences, user profile, disabilities, etc., personalized storytelling, and UI/UX for intuitive and immersive VR/AR interfaces and devices.

ISL has already developed the first four platforms required for creating the DICE ecosystem, and is in the process of completing platforms #5 and #6. The first four platforms are, namely:

(a) **i-Guide**, a 3D VR/AR creation and navigation platform for building block #1 [3];
(b) **wayGoo**, a platform for geolocating and managing indoor and outdoor 3D spaces and content within for building block #2 [4];
(c) **OCULUS Sim** distributed simulation platform consisting of two key components:
   a. **i-Crowd** a general purpose simulation engine for behavior, motion and dynamics of human, animal and physical system, and device modelling and simulation for building block #3 [5]; and

b. **Pyrones**, a distributed simulation environment of coupling simulators of different phenomena and events with different visualization capabilities as required by different application domains for building block #4 [6]; and

(d) **i-Rescue** 3D immersive & interactive gamification platform for building block #4 [6].

have reached a stage of maturity between TRL7 and TRL9 (Technological Readiness Level 7 to 9) and are described next, whereas the other two for #5 and #6 are in the process of development.

In addition to its contributions through the each one of the six different platforms that constitute its key building blocks, DICE offers an integrated platform that goes beyond the current state of art in digital immersive environments for culture, education, entertainment, collaborative working, and tourism.

The first four of the six platforms are described briefly in the next Section whereas examples of their usage in the context of promoting the DICE ecosystem are given in Sect. 5.

3   Description of the Four DICE Platforms

The four platforms that are described next have been built in a modular way so that can either be used as separate applications or in conjunction with each other as building blocks of a **modular and distributed DICE** architecture that integrates various platform components to deliver an ecosystem that accommodates the needs and requirements of all stakeholders involved in the ecosystem.

(a) i-Guide [3], a 3D VR/AR creation and navigation platform: i-Guide aims at enhancing the user experience as a "digital" visitor to archaeological sites and monuments. Through the detailed 3D reconstruction of the monument the visitor is offered a first person navigation in the original form of the monument. The platform offers a number of features that allow the systematic development of immersive digital cultural environments and digital tours that enable the creator of such spaces to design them in a non-ad hoc but methodical manner, thus accelerating their productions and allowing for a signature UI-UX look-and-feel. Knossos i-Guide is the first 3D immersive "digital" visit to the Palace of Knossos in Crete entirely developed within the i-Guide platform. Figure 2 depicts the modular elements of the Knossos i-Guide platform that allow the management of any multimedia digital content in a uniform way by simply replacing the core 3D VR Knossos reconstruction by any other, actual or imaginary, 3D VR reconstruction and a simple content adaptation of the content to the relevant artifact.

(b) wayGoo [4], a platform for geolocating and managing indoor and outdoor 3D spaces and content within: wayGoo is a platform for Geolocating and Managing indoor and outdoor spaces and content with multidimensional indoor and outdoor Navigation and Guidance. Its main components are a Geographic Information System, a back-end server, front-end applications and a web-based Content Management System (CMS). It constitutes a fully integrated 2D/3D space and content management system that creates a repository that consists of a database, content components and administrative data

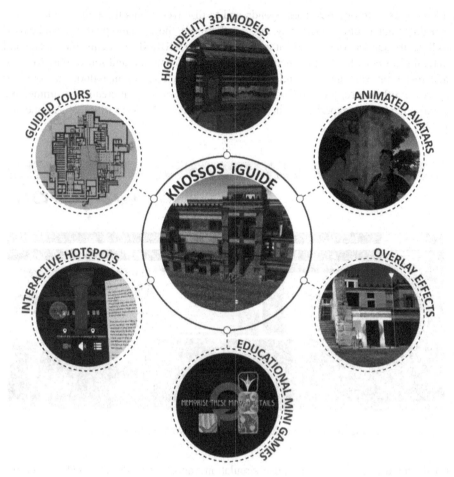

Fig. 2. Knossos i-Guide platform

(Figs. 3 and 4). wayGoo can connect to any third party database and event management data-source. The platform is secure as the data is only available through a Restful web service using https security protocol in conjunction with an API key used for authentication. To enhance user experience, wayGoo makes the content available by extracting components out of the repository and constructing targeted applications. The wayGoo platform supports geo-referencing of indoor and outdoor information and use of metadata. It also allows the use of existing information such as maps and databases. The platform enables planning through integration of content that is connected either spatially, temporally or contextually, and provides immediate access to all spatial data through interfaces and interactive 2D and 3D representations. wayGoo constitutes a mean to document and preserve assets through computerized techniques and provides a system that enhances the protection of your space, people and guests when combined with wayGoo notification and alert system. It constitutes a strong marketing tool providing staff and visitors with an immersive tool for navigation in indoor spaces and allowing users to organize their agenda and to discover events through wayGoo event scheduler and recommendation system. Furthermore, the wayGoo platform can be used in Security applications and event management, e.g. CBRNE incidents, man-made and natural disasters, etc., to document and geolocate information and sensor data (off line and real time) on one end, and offer navigation capabilities in indoor and outdoor spaces. Furthermore, the wayGoo platform can be used for the creation of immersive environments and experiences in conjunction with VR/AR (Virtual & Augmented Reality) technologies.

Fig. 3. wayGoo platform server-side working environment

(c) i-Crowd [5], a general purpose simulation engine: Initially designed as a crowd behavior simulator for simulating, testing and visualizing evacuation scenarios, the i-Crowd Simulation platform has evolved into a complete domain-independent agent-based behavior simulator with an emphasis on crowd behavior and building evacuation simulation. Under continuous development, it reflects an effort to implement a modern, multithreaded, data-oriented simulation engine employing latest state-of-the-art programming technologies and paradigms. It is based on an extensible architecture that separates core services from the individual layers of agent behavior, offering a concrete simulation kernel designed for high-performance and stability. Its primary goal is to deliver an abstract platform to facilitate implementation of several Agent-Based Simulation solutions with applicability in several domains of knowledge, such as: (i) crowd behavior simulation during [in/out] door evacuation; (ii) non-player character AI for game-oriented applications and gamification activities; (iii) vessel traffic modeling and simulation for Maritime Security and Surveillance applications;

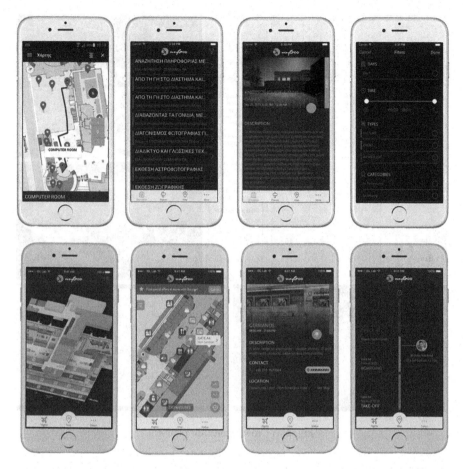

Fig. 4. UI/UX mobile implementation of wayGoo for different application domains

(iv) urban and highway traffic and transportation simulations; (v) social behavior modeling and simulation; and in general, (vi) behavior, motion and dynamics of human, animal and physical system and device modelling and simulation platform (Fig. 5).

Some notes on the simulator:

- The simulator itself is designed as an abstract Agent-Based System, and it is based on the Entity-Component design paradigm.
- The Entity is the main architectural unit of the simulator, being the only object that resides directly inside the simulation kernel.
- Complex behaviors are built by populating Entities with Components provided by Layers that reside outside the core, as plug in systems.
- Thus, the main processing kernel that deals with resource allocation and processing synchronization is separated from the individual behavior implementations that usually deal with higher level functionalities (steering, path finding, intelligence, communications etc.).

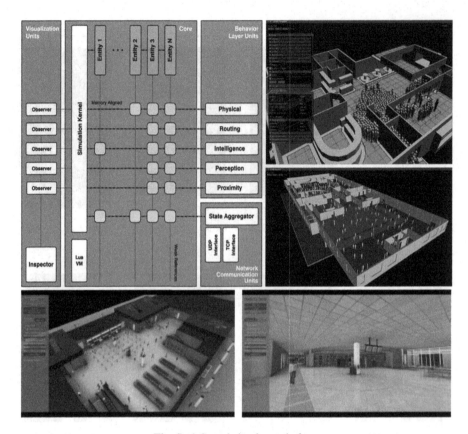

Fig. 5. i-Crowd simulator platform

(d) PYRONES [6], developed in the context of modeling and simulating large structural fires continue that pose a great threat towards human life and property, PYRONES has become a modular, distributed and highly integrated platform for building and human behavior modeling platform under any catastrophic events. Due to the complexity and non-deterministic characteristics of a building fire disaster, it is not a straightforward task to assess the effectiveness of fire protection measures embedded in the building design, planned evacuation strategies and potential modes of response for mitigating the fire's consequences. Additionally, there is a lack of means that realistically and accurately recreate the conditions of building fire disasters for the purpose of training personnel in order to be sufficiently prepared when vis-a-vis with such an environment.

The PYRONES system has been developed to address all these aspects through a comprehensive approach that relies on accurate and realistic computer simulations of the individual phenomena and their interactions. PYRONES offers innovative tools and services to strategically targeted niches in two market domains. In the domain of building design and engineering, PYRONES is seamlessly integrated within existing engineering Building Information Modelling (BIM) workflows and serves as a building performance assessment platform, able to evaluate fire protection systems. On another front, **PYRONES** penetrates the building security management market, serving as a holistic training platform for specialists in evacuation strategy planning, firefighters and first responders, both at a Command & Control and at an individual trainee level. The overall **PYRONES** architecture, simulation and visualization modes are shown in Figs. 6 and 7.

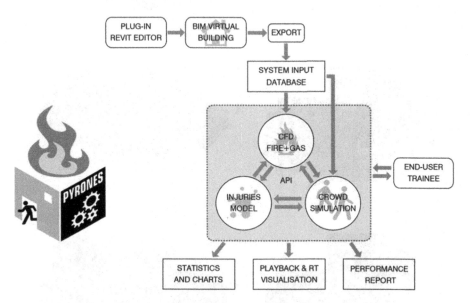

Fig. 6. PYRONES distributed modular architecture

iRescue is an immersive 3D game platform developed as an active game (ex-ergame), using the Kinect sensor for the tracking of the player's movement and position. It also available for passive game playing for various game and mobile platforms.

Figure 8 shows a scene for an i-Rescue game that takes place at an airport after a catastrophic event has occurred. iRescue immersive 3D game places the player within an airport after a disastrous event. As a member of an elite paramedic corps, the player's objective is to guide the evacuating panicked crowd towards a safe pathway. Diverse and unpredicted simulated crowd behaviours, gradually advancing crowd density and difficulty, as well as special actions, aim to capture the player's interest in an entertaining and challenging experience. Due to control system malfunctioning during landing, the n crashes on the main terminal building causing serious damages to the airport building structure. Rifts and debris are everywhere raising havoc among the passengers.

Only an elite paramedic can deal with the situation and is the first to respond to the site by motorcycle, in order to guide the passengers to safely evacuate the building without falling in a rift. The main objective of the player, is to save as many persons as

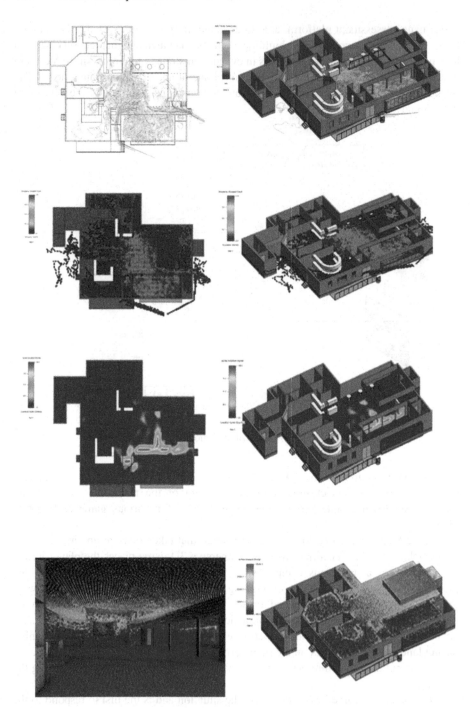

Fig. 7. PYRONES simulation and visualization modes

Fig. 8. A scene for the i-Rescue airport rescue game

she can, in order to achieve a better score and rank. Using the Kinect sensor for the tracking of the player's movement and position, the player interacts with the VR environment in a natural way trying to save as many people as possible.

For additional information about the different platforms DICE is made up of, the reader is referred to [15] as well.

4 DICE Architecture: The DICE System/Platform and Innovation

The DICE architecture aims at the development of an innovative, integrated yet modular platform for improving access to multimedia content and facilitating the creation of 3D digital immersive environments, by using the latest advances in visual representation technologies and a combination of advanced and novel features that facilitate deeper cultural learning and understanding, by immersing visitors into social aspects of the culture associated with the exhibition.

The digital content (both tangible and intangible) is: (a) organized using various multi-dimensional hyper structures and topologies, such as neural networks, hyper-spaces and clusters overlaid on the 4D space-time continuum; (b) related through dynamic semantic synapses; (c) presented/curated through a variety of curating, storytelling and editing tools for organizing and curating a collection of digital assets with a specific, yet dynamically experienced and interactive context; (d) visualized through a variety of information visualization techniques, VR/AR technologies and affective interfaces; and (e) experienced through a variety of modalities that allow remote and on-site access, first and third person visits, individual and group tours, and direct interactivity through social media or indirect through gamification and avatars.

The content is delivered through an immersive mixed reality user experience, referring both to the relevant physical and virtual cultural spaces and artefacts. The cultural assets are geo-temporally linked to their context and accessed through virtual (for remote access) and/or augmented reality (for in-situ access) technologies. The platform enables access to reconstructions of shattered or broken artefacts, identification and reunification of contextually related assets that have been scattered across multiple museum collections.

DICE exploits the technology, not only towards the optimum presentation of the digital content, but also towards societal and educational dimension. As presented in various studies, VR holds considerable potential as a powerful medium for learning: it gives users the ability to carry out tasks that could be difficult or impossible in the "real world" due to constraints such as cost or location; allows for continuing and growing social interactions which can serve as a basis for collaborative education; allows individuals – especially children – to learn from non-symbolic first-person experience. Along these lines, the platform combines VR/AR with a novel gamification layer that allows the VM visitor to participate in stories and events related to the VM collection exhibits: the visitor may select a virtual character and communicate with other visitors (virtual or real); interact with characters of that era and immerse into their everyday life; learn a skill and engage in the creation of an artefact or product of that era; play games based on historical facts or on fictional histories related to the exhibits. This gamification layer is built with the engagement of cultural heritage professionals and learning experts in order to effectively achieve the education of all VM visitors on the subject matter.

Social Media and blogging tools (such as Facebook and Twitter) are integrated into the platform to invite end-users to share their personal experience, effectively converting it to a virtual meeting and learning place. The DICE is a space that can offer visitors – and especially young people – opportunities for participation, sharing, conversation, interaction that allows a more effective contextualization and interpretation of cultural assets and assist professionals in assessing the understanding of cultural content in VR/AR environments by broader audiences.

Within this framework, the main attributes of the DICE architecture/platform, as shown in Fig. 9, are:

(1) State-of-the-art front-end components which incorporate the best available technology that will assure the optimum visual quality and user experience, using all relevant ICT tools (VR - Oculus Rift/Google Cardboard, AR – Vuforia/Wikitude, gesture-based Interactivity, 3D modelling, high quality lighting and shading, Spatial 3D sound, animations);

(2) An innovative and intuitive authoring tool that provides unique ways to organize, relate, present/curate, visualize and experience the digital content and information, allowing the efficient usage and/or further development of the platform from the cultural heritage professionals.

(3) A flexible and scalable back-end component that can synthesize diverse information from various sources, by also incorporating semantic tools that allow the use of diverse information from different databases, and also assists the front-end components in the creation of visual narratives, histories, games, matched to the curator's objectives, the individual visitor's characteristics, and the available content;

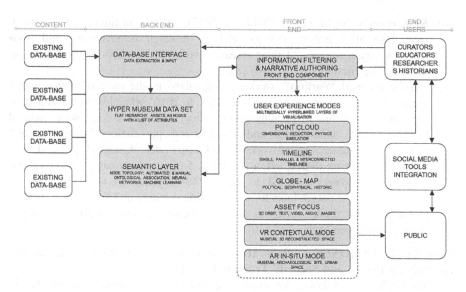

Fig. 9. DICE Architecture adapted to the creation and curation of a Virtual Museum

(4) A gamification layer for learning and education purposes – the developed games will be incorporated into the platform as additional assets for exploitation by the curator.

(5) The holistic approach on personalized narration/storytelling and behavior-based adaptation with the inclusion of a large number of available information for the individual visitor, including social media interactions, sentiment analysis, personal information, experience from prior visits;

(6) Social Media integration.

5   DICE Use Cases in Education and Collaborative Working

Next we present three use cases of pilot projects that took place within the DICE ecosystem.

Use-Case 1: Knossos i-Guide Education and Gaming Platform [3]

Knossos i-Guide (Fig. 2), has been developed as a platform for education and gaming aiming at achieving an educational immersive tour guide in the virtually reconstructed archaeological palace of Knossos enriched with animated content, narrations, manual and automatic tour guides, validated rich historical and archaeological content, info-points within the tour, overlay of pictures of today site through the patent-pending "gelatin™ mechanism," educational digital art games and puzzles, and related adventure games. The Knossos i-Guide platform has been tested in various (informal) educational events and activities such as the:

(a) **Athens Science Festival** (ASF 2015/2016 http://www.athens-science-festival.gr/ en/) [7];

(b) **Researcher's Night** (2013, 2014, & 2015), an EU instituted annual event throughout all member-states to celebrate research achievements and open research organizations and their research work to the public (https://www.iit. demokritos.gr/news/ren2015_post) [8];

(c) **"Archaeological Workout"** workshop organized in the context of the annual event "Archaeological Dialogues" in 2015 & 2016, whereby digital and conventional approaches to learning about history and archaeology were coupled harmoniously to achieve better understanding and appreciation of culture, art and history (http://archaeological-workout-workshop.iit.demokritos.gr/) [9]; and

(d) **SMART Camp on digital art**, a fast-track, 5-day summer camp organized and taught by researchers from ISL to students 13-18 years old, where students are taught how to use design tools for creating virtual spaces and animation, and how to present their digital creations using projection mapping techniques (http:// smart-camp.iit.demokritos.gr/) [10].

Use-Case 2: PYRONES Collaborative Distributed Simulation Platform for Engineering Design and Security Training [6, 11]

PYRONES is a collaborative distributed real-time simulation platform that is motivated by the threat that structural fires continue to pose towards human life and property and the need to understand how these fires interact with the materials building are built of and how they propagate; what health threat these fires impose on tenants of a building; how effective escape mechanisms and design are; how evacuation plan function; and last, but not least, how active fire extinguishing mechanisms, e.g. sprinklers, retardants, etc., help in preventing the fire from reaching life threatening levels. Due to the complexity and non-deterministic characteristics of a building fire disaster, it is not a straightforward task to assess the effectiveness of fire protection measures embedded in the building design, planned evacuation strategies and potential modes of response for mitigating the fire's consequences. The PYRONES platform (Figs. 6 and 7) has been developed to address all these aspects through a comprehensive approach that relies on accurate and realistic computer simulations of the individual phenomena and their interactions. The platform offers collaboration at different levels, as presented in Fig. 10: (a) at the simulation level by offering integration of simulation modules from different providers and for different eventualities; (b) at the integration level by offering plug-ins for commercial software tools, such as Revit from Autodesk; and (c) at the application/market level: to engineering for building designing and testing and to security for training of first responders.

The PYRONES simulation platform was tested by performing a simulation of the Station Nightclub structural fire incident, which took place in West Warwick, Rhode Island in 2003. The specific event is considered to be a benchmark simulation scenario as it was one of the most lethal and well-studied fire accidents, which caused 96 deaths. The National Institute of Standards and Technology (NIST), in the report of the technical investigation of the incident, estimates the maximum safe population limit for the specific building to be 420. Based on press reports for the number of occupants at the station nightclub the night of the incident, the testing of the PYRONES system considered a distribution of 460 people within the building.

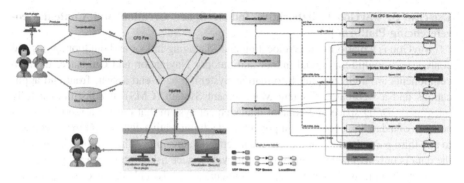

Fig. 10. PYRONES Overall architecture and collaborative environment

Three scenarios were tested [11]. While in the first scenario implementation fire advancement and crowd evacuation were examined as two independent phenomena, in the other two scenarios these phenomena were considered as interconnected processes. The first scenario implementation followed the scenario of the first simulation conducted by NIST, which did not couple fire and evacuation and the results of the PYRONES simulation were compared to the NIST's simulation results. The second scenario coupled fire and evacuation simulation and the results of the PYRONES simulation were compared to the actual incident's results as reported by Rhode Island Attorney General's Office. The third scenario coupled fire with evacuation and it was further assumed that sprinklers were installed in the building. This scenario was used to assess the effectiveness of a plausible enhancement in the building fire security measures.

The results of the PYRONES simulations were compared to the NIST's simulation results, in terms of temperature, carbon monoxide and heat flux.

- The results of the execution of the scenario with a delay of 40 s under predict the actual number of victims by a mere 9 % (the number of predicted fatalities was 87 ± 3), providing a low error margin.
- The estimated number of people remaining at 90 s for the second scenario (with fire) was 295 which is considerably more than that in scenario 1 (228 people, without fire). Thus, it is important to couple fire and crowd, injuries models in order to calculate the average safe evacuation time.
- The main threats to the occupants were the toxic gases and the heat release. Most of the locations in the simulated station nightclub became untenable due to the toxic gasses concentrations14 (CO concentration exceeded 3200 ppm after 80 s), as well as the temperature9 (temperatures exceeded the 120 °C threshold after 60 s). This conclusion is in accordance with the conclusions drawn in the NIST report.
- Most of the fatalities in PYRONES simulation were caused by the toxic gases (specifically most of the fatalities were caused by the concentration of CO, approximately 62 % of fatalities). This also agrees with the NIST report, where most fatalities are described to be caused due to toxic gas inhalation.

Use-case 3: wayGoo Collaborative Indoor Space Creation and Content Geo-referencing Platform [4]

wayGoo is a platform for Geolocating and Managing indoor and outdoor spaces and content with multidimensional indoor and outdoor Navigation and Guidance. Its main components are a Geographic Information System, a back-end server, front-end applications and a web-based Content Management System (CMS). It constitutes a fully integrated 2D/3D space and content management system that creates a repository that consists of a database, content components and administrative data. wayGoo can connect to any third party database and event management data-source. The platform is secure as the data is only available through a Restful web service using https security protocol in conjunction with an API key used for authentication. To enhance user's experience, wayGoo makes the content available by extracting components out of the repository and constructing targeted applications. The wayGoo platform supports geo-referencing of indoor and outdoor information and use of metadata. It also allows the use of existing information such as maps and databases. The platform enables planning through integration of content that is connected either spatially, temporally or contextually, and provides immediate access to all spatial data through interfaces and interactive 2D and 3D representations. wayGoo constitutes a means for documenting and preserving assets through computerized techniques and provides a system that enhances the protection of your space, people and guests when combined with wayGoo notification and alert system. It constitutes a strong marketing tool providing staff and visitors with an immersive tool for navigation in indoor spaces and allowing users to organize their agenda and to discover events through wayGoo event scheduler and recommendation system. Furthermore, the wayGoo platform can be used in Security applications and event management, e.g. CBRNE incidents, man-made and natural disasters, etc., to document and geolocate information and sensor data (off line and real time) on one end, and offer navigation capabilities in indoor and outdoor spaces. Furthermore, the wayGoo platform can be used for the creation of immersive environments and experiences in conjunction with VR/AR (Virtual & Augmented Reality) technologies.

The wayGoo platform has been used to geolocate various events, exhibits and fairs, such as the Mobile World Congress 2015 in Barcelona, Spain; the campus of NCSR Demokritos, the 2nd Hellenic Forum for Science and Innovation, the Researcher's Night exhibit in 2014 and 2015, and the Athens Science Festival 2015 & 2016. A virtual tour of these event can be downloaded from both AppStore and PlayStore by searching for wayGoo and downloading the mobile apps.

The use of wayGoo in the context of DICE is quite apparent for it allows the accurate georeferenced of content and building (actual and virtual), thus enabling: (a) immersive navigation in a cultural space and location-based services associated with a virtual or physical visit or tour of the site; (b) innate geographical alignment between virtual reality and actual/physical reality artifacts for the creation of truly immersive VR/AR experiences.

Summing up, the three use cases described above offer precious experience for addressing similar issues, such as immersive and interactive education in culture and the arts, impact analysis of hazardous events in cultural monuments and means to address and mitigate them, and content management and navigation in cultural spaces in conjunction with the use of VR/AR technologies.

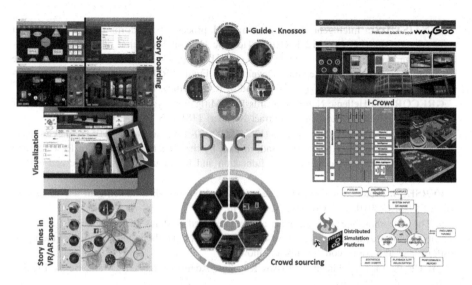

Fig. 11. DICE Ecosystem block diagram implementation with the key components shown as modular building blocks

6 Conclusions

The DICE ecosystem described in Fig. 1 is gradually being translated into a technological platform (of platforms) through a modular approach, by developing a distributed architecture that allows major components of the DICE puzzle, each built separately and in a modular way, to be integrated into one common DICE Platform of Platforms (PoP). ISL has developed already four critical platforms described in this paper and tested them in a variety of pilot and commercial use cases. Furthermore, using its prior Systems of Systems (SoS) design and implementation experience from the PERSEUS demonstration project [12, 13], ISL is integrating all these platforms into one common but flexible DICE platform while working to develop and complete the remaining building blocks for content creation, storyboarding and storytelling, gamification, personalization and crowd sourcing integration (Fig. 11).

Acknowledgments. a. The work and results presented in this paper has been supported by the following research projects [14]:

AF3: Advanced Forest Fire Fighting, Grant Agreement No. 607276, funded under FP7-SECURITY - Specific Programme "Cooperation": Security of the European Commission.

FLYSEC: Optimising time-to-FLY and enhancing airport SECurity, Grant Agreement No. 653879, funded under programme H2020-EU.3.7. – "Secure societies - Protecting freedom and security of Europe and its citizens" of the European Commission.

PYRONES: PYRo-mOdelliNg and Evacuation Simulation system: This project was supported by the Programme: NSRF/ESPA (EPAN II), Contract Number: ISR 2866, funded by the General Secretariat for Research and Technology (GGET), Hellenic Ministry of Education, Religious Affairs, Culture and Sports, and the Israeli Industry Center for R&D, Matimop, under the "Greece-Israel Bilateral R&T Cooperation 2013–2015".

SYNAISTHISI: Intelligent data collection and processing platform for energy efficient applications, Contract No. 2012 KRHPIS, Hellenic General Secretariat of Research & Technology, Duration: 32 months (02/04/2013 – 12/31/2015), Co- financed by Greece and the European Union- European Regional Development Fund (ERDF), under the O.P. "Competitiveness and Entrepreneurship" (OPCE II) and of R.O.P Attica, R.O.P Macedonia- Thrace.

GRECORISK: Hellenic Natural-Hazards Risk-Mitigation System of Systems, funded under Programme: SYNERGASIA 2011, Contract Number: 11SUN 8 1696, 2013–2015.

TASS: Total Airport Security System (FP7-SEC-2010- Contract No. 241905) research project funded by the European Commission and, in part, by the General Secretariat of Research and Technology (GSRT) of the Ministry of Education and Religious Affairs, Culture and Sports, Greece.

PERSEUS: Protection of European seas and borders through the intelligent use of surveillance, FP7-SEC-2010.3.1-1-Contract No. 261748.

b. The co-authors are all colleagues at the Integrated Systems Laboratory (ISL) and have contributed towards the enhancement of the DICE concept and the implementation of the DICE platform and its various components as follows:

• **DICE** Platform Architecture: Tassos Kanellos, Adam Doulgerakis, Maria Bessa, Eftichia Georgiou and Andreas Zalonis.

• **i-Guide** 3D VR/AR visualization, tour guide, navigation platform & story boarding platform: Giorgos Farazis, Christos Maroglou, Panagiotis Tsimpiridis, Alexandra Papagianni, Ino-Eleni Theodorou and Christina Phobe Thomopoulos.

• **wayGoo** indoor geocoding & navigation platform: Christina Karafylli, Maria Karafylli, Dionisis Motos, Vassilis Lampropoulos, Manolis Paterakis, Christos Maroglou, Konstantinos Dimitros, Dimitris Zacharakis, Giorgos Konstandinos Thanos, Katerina Skroumpelou and Dimitris M. Kyriazanos.

• **i-Crowd** human behavior ssimulator: Vassilios I. Kountouriotis, Manolis Paterakis

• **PYRONES** distributed simulation platform: Vassilios I. Kountouriotis, Manolis Paterakis, Tassos Kanellos and Adam Doulgerakis.

• **i-Rescue** gamification platform: Adam Doulgerakis, Tassos Kanellos, Betty Evangelinou and Dafni Polyzos.

References

1. https://prezi.com/mvja6fyp3ldq/copy-of-2014-copyright-isl-ncsr-demokritos-all-rights-reserv/
2. https://prezi.com/embed/zx-bzzmmvy5s/
3. Knossos i-Guide video teaser v4 and educational games. https://vimeo.com/105324264, https://vimeo.com/120785074, https://vimeo.com/120784644
4. Thomopoulos, S.C.A., Karafylli, C., Karafylli, M., Motos, D., Lampropoulos, V., Dimitros, K., Margonis, C.: WayGoo: a platform for geolocating and managing indoor and outdoor spaces. In: Proceedings of SPIE, Baltimore, USA, 18–20 April 2016, vol. 9842 (2016)
5. Kountouriotis, V.I., Paterakis, M., Thomopoulos, S.C.A.: iCrowd: agent-based behavior modeling and crowd simulator. In: Proceedings of SPIE, Baltimore, USA, 18–20 April 2016, vol. 9842 (2016)

6. Kanellos, T., Doulgerakis, A., Georgiou, E., Kountouriotis, V.I., Paterakis, M., Tho-mopoulos, S.C.A., Pappou, T., Vrahliotis, S.I., Rekouniotis, T., Protopsaltis, B., Rozenberg, O., Livneh, O.: PYRONES: pyro-modelling and evacuation simulation system. In: Proceedings of SPIE, Baltimore, USA, 18–20 April 2016, vol. 9842 (2016)
7. Athens Science Festival 2015. https://vimeo.com/126392686
8. Researcher's Night (2013, 2014 and 2015). https://www.iit.demokritos.gr/news/ren2015_post
9. Archaeological Workout. https://vimeo.com/159943241
10. SMART Camp on digital art. https://vimeo.com/150669087, https://vimeo.com/161189858
11. PYRONES use case scenario simulation video. https://vimeo.com/137834302, https://vimeo.com/163534330, https://vimeo.com/154047986
12. PERSEUS: Protection of European seas and borders through the intelligent use of surveillance. http://www.perseus-fp7.eu/, https://vimeo.com/135040978, https://vimeo.com/118606731
13. Kanellopoulos, S., Katsoulis, S., Motos, D., Lampropoulos, V., Margonis, C., Dimitros, K., Thomopoulos, S.C.A.: OCULUS Sea: integrated maritime surveillance platform. In: SPIE Defense and Security, Signal Processing, Sensor/Information Fusion, and Target Recognition XXIV, Paper 9474-23, 21 April 2015
14. https://www.iit.demokritos.gr/isl/projects
15. http://claret.gr/

Project Paper: The New Era of Museums and Exhibitions: Digital Engagement and Dissemination

Imaging Novecento. A Mobile App for Automatic Recognition of Artworks and Transfer of Artistic Styles

Federico Becattini, Andrea Ferracani(✉), Lea Landucci, Daniele Pezzatini, Tiberio Uricchio, and Alberto Del Bimbo

NEMECH - New Media for Cultural Heritage, University of Florence, Viale Morgagni 65, 50124 Firenze, Italy
{federico.becattini,andrea.ferracani,lea.landucci,daniele.pezzatini, tiberio.uricchio,alberto.delbimbo}@unifi.it
http://nemech.unifi.it

Abstract. *Imaging Novecento* is a native mobile application that can be used to get insights on artworks in the "Museo Novecento" in Florence, IT. The App provides smart paradigms of interaction to ease the learning of the Italian art history of the 20th century. *Imaging Novecento* exploits automatic approaches and gamification techniques with recreational and educational purposes. Its main goal is to reduce the cognitive effort of users *versus* the complexity and the numerosity of artworks present in the museum. To achieve this the App provides automatic artwork recognition. It also uses gaming, in terms of a playful user interface which features state-of-the-art algorithms for artistic style transfer. Automated processes are exploited as a mean to attract visitors, approaching them to even lesser known aspects of the history of art.

Keywords: Cultural heritage · Mobile application · Visual recognition · Artistic style transfer · Convolutional neural networks

1 Introduction

Modern museums can provide new paradigms for experiencing artworks. Thanks to the technological development, novel initiatives include pervasive uses of tech to create interactive experiences for visitors throughout a museum. However, making content relevant and appealing through these modern technologies is a difficult problem, requiring more and more interactivity as the audience is shifting towards a 'multimedia point of view'. Moreover, while the massive amount of available artworks constitutes a huge resource for education and recreation purposes, it can also be a cognitive burden for visitors.

The cognitive process related to learning has been an active subject of study in recent decades. According to cognitive load theory, learners must cope with a certain level of cognitive effort to process new information [22]. In this regard, multimedia education, defined as "presenting words and pictures that

© Springer International Publishing AG 2016
M. Ioannides et al. (Eds.): EuroMed 2016, Part I, LNCS 10058, pp. 781–791, 2016.
DOI: 10.1007/978-3-319-48496-9_62

are intended to foster learning" [19], can be an effective remedy because it facilitates the activation of sensory and cognitive perceptions (e.g. visual and notional memory), avoiding visitors from information overloading. This can also be reinforced by gamification, that is the use of playful experience to help a user find personal motivations and engagement with serious content [24]. This combination can enhance the visitor's involvement and further lower its cognitive effort. Using gamified applications, museum visitors have the opportunity to feel the emotion of a game, share results with friends on social networks or become part of a game community [20]. This aspect of learning through gaming is even more valuable in the context of the "Bring Your Own Device" (BYOD) approach [3] that allows on demand access to digital content on personal devices. The BYOD approach and gamification have been identified in the NMC Horizon Report 2015 to be increasingly adopted by museums in one year's time or less for mobile and online engagement [15].

In this paper we report our experience in embedding these concepts into *Imaging Novecento*, a system built around a mobile application developed for the museum "Museo Novecento" in Florence, IT. We aimed at improving the learning process of the visitors by exploiting a simple gamification paradigm, and at reducing visitors cognitive load. To this end, we also developed a state-of-the-art computer vision system that is able to (1) recognize artworks from photos; (2) apply their style to user photos.

1.1   The Museo Novecento in Florence and Innovecento

The "Museo Novecento" in Florence, IT, is a museum opened on June 24, 2014. The museum is dedicated to the Italian art of the 20th century and offers a selection of about 300 artworks distributed in fifteen exhibition halls on two levels. The venue is located in the former hospital of the "Leopoldine" in Piazza Santa Maria Novella. The museum has been an example of innovation since its genesis, thanks to the prompt adoption of the latest multimedia technologies.

In March 2015, in order to improve the visitor experience, the Municipality of Florence has published an open call "INNOVecento - Novecento Museum Innovation Lab" inviting companies and professionals to propose ideas and solutions based on ICT. Five companies specialized in technologies applied to cultural heritage have already responded to the call which, at the time of writing, is still open. As NEMECH, centre of competence of the Tuscany region in Italy, we proposed *Imaging Novecento*. The App features automatic recognition of artworks through the visitor's smartphone and automatic transfer of artistic styles from artworks. These styles can be applied to user images.

1.2   Motivations and Design

The target of the App is rather wide. Although *Imaging Novecento* can be used by anyone (e.g. tourists and residents), during the design process we identified a specific audience. We mainly target the App towards people in a relatively young age (between 14 and 30 years old), more accustomed to digital technologies, open to technological innovation and to gamification.

One of the main ideas of the App is to exploit the pervasiveness of mobile cameras in modern smartphones to reduce the cognitive effort required to museum visitors. In fact, despite themed rooms and the ubiquitous explanatory cards, users can still be overwhelmed by the great number of artworks present in the museum. Labels in museums can be very concise or, on the contrary, can be filled with lots of explanation, often generic, not highlighting salient features of individual paintings. By using *Imaging Novecento*, the visitor can take a picture of the artwork he is interested in. The App will automatically recognize the painting and provide related information. Another reason for the adoption of this automatic process is the resistance of museums' curators to place or attach additional materials, such as QR codes or BLE iBeacon [12], next to artworks.

Furthermore, tourists and school groups are usually 'hit-and-run' visitors who tend to rapidly forget or do not have the time to process the overload of information. To solve this issue, *Imaging Novecento* leverages a playful feature that employs state-of-the-art algorithms for transferring artistic styles from recognized artworks to user images. This is done using a gamification paradigm at the interface level. Gamification techniques have been proved to be useful in engaging students in the learning process, improving their skills and maximizing their long-term memory [27].

1.3   Previous Work

Several previous works have addressed the problem of providing an engaging experience to museum visitors. Rapid technological development has led to the implementation of a lot of applications. There are several active trends for virtual museums: immersive reality [10,18], natural interaction installations [4,9], mixed reality, mobile applications [5,31]. While they all offer increasing engagement of visitors, only recently studies on the effects of audience have been carried out [15,21]. In particular, a recent audience study has been conducted on the case of the "Keys to Rome" international exhibition, hosted at the "Imperial Fora Museum" in Rome in 2015, to assess the impact of these technologies on cultural heritage. The exhibition was made up of 11 digital installations and applications, installed in the museum [21]. The study highlights some fundamental aspects that must be taken into account when designing applications for virtual museums: (1) the majority of museum visitors are tourists and school groups; (2) visitors generally require applications with an high level of interactivity, particularly on their mobile devices; (3) it is essential for the UX design to use metaphors of informal learning capable to stimulate attention, memory and engagement (e.g. through gamification) in visitors.

Automatic Artwork Recognition. Automatic artwork recognition is a long standing problem in applications for cultural heritage. Descriptors such as SIFT and SURF have been used for years in order to address this task [25,28] due to their accuracy in recognizing paintings. Crowley and Zisserman [6] retrieve artworks finding object correspondences between photos and paintings by using a deformable part based method. More recent approaches for artwork recognition adopt Convolutional Neural Networks (CNN) as in [2], where a holistic and a part based representation are combined. Peng and Chen [23] exploit CNNs to extract cross-layer features for artist and artistic style classification tasks. Artistic style recognition is also performed in [16] on two novel large scale datasets. Similarly to these works, we explore the use of CNNs features but we aim to obtain a global representation that is semantically meaningful and also capable of retaining low level visual content information. Artwork recognition has also been used with wearable devices, as in [4] where the user's position is jointly estimated with what he is looking at.

Artistic Style Transfer. Regarding the application of artistic style to photos, a lot of research has been done in the past. The problem of rendering a given photo in the style of a particular artwork is known in literature as a branch of non photorealistic rendering [17]. This class of works use texture transfer [7,30] to achieve style transfer. These techniques are non-parametric and directly alter image pixels of the content image into pre-defined styles. Another direction of work focuses on the idea of separating style and content in order to 'remix' them together in different configurations. First works were evaluated on much simpler images such as characters in different handwritings [29] or images representing human body configurations [8]. Only recently, the breakthrough paper from Gatys *et al.* [11] showed the possibility of disentangling the content from the style of natural images by using a convolutional neural network based representation. The advantage of this approach is the capability of performing style transfer from any painting to any kind of content images. The approach was recently extended with a more advanced perceptual loss [14] and also applied to movies [1] by considering the optical flow.

2   The System

The system is composed by two main components: a mobile App and a computer vision system responsible to address the two tasks of automatically recognize artworks and apply artwork styles to user photos. The mobile App is used by the visitor in the museum and is the *fulcrum* of the user interaction. Once installed by the user in his mobile phone, it allows to take pictures, deliver artwork information and request the style transfer to new photos. Due to the limited amount of computational power available on most mobile devices, the computer vision system is deployed on a scalable web server system that processes requests from the mobile App. Since the two tasks use quite different technologies, we discuss them separately in the following sections.

2.1   The Mobile App

Imaging Novecento has been developed as an Android application using Ionic[1].
Ionic is a framework, based on Sass and AngularJS, for building highly interactive native web apps through mobile-optimized HTML, CSS and JS components and tools. *Imaging Novecento* is a contextual App that can be used exclusively inside the Museo Novecento in Florence. An information flyer of the App is delivered to the visitor at the ticket office. In the flyer there are a QR code, through which the visitor can download the App from the Google Play store, and the list of the artworks on which the App can perform the automatic recognition and style transfer processes. The list comprises a selection of twenty artworks for which the museum's curators have provided multimedia materials. The App interface (Fig. 1) is quite simple and is organized in two main views: (1) the Camera View and (2) the Artwork Details view.

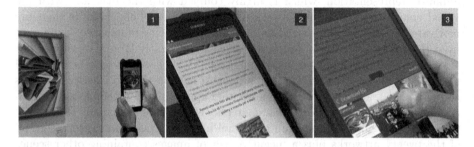

Fig. 1. *Imaging Novecento* in action: (1) the user takes a picture of an artwork; (2) the artwork is recognized and insights are shown; (3) the user selects a photo from his own gallery in order to apply that artwork style and to share the results on social networks.

The Camera View allows the visitor to frame one of the artworks on the list in order to have it immediately recognized by the automatic system. Proper feedback is given in case the recognition is not successful. Once the artwork is recognized, the Artwork Details view is activated. In this view, exhaustive but concise information about the author, the history of the artwork and its artistic style are given. An infographic is presented to the user. It works as a "call to action" for enabling the transfer of the recognized painting style to a photo from the user's device gallery. The infographic provides an animated preview that shows the result of the artistic style transfer on a predefined picture. After the image has been successfully uploaded, the remote process for style transfer is performed. The result of the elaboration is then sent to the user in a few minutes by email. The image has a resolution of 900 px wide preserving the original image aspect ratio and can be shared on the most popular social networks (e.g. Facebook).

---

[1] http://ionicframework.com/.

2.2 Automatic Artwork Recognition

Artwork recognition is performed through a Python web server with a REST interface. The server processes the image and returns the ID of the recognized painting. The recognition step combines modern deep features with classical Support Vector Machines (SVM) in order to classify photos of paintings. Image features are extracted using a deep convolutional neural network (CNN), and are then evaluated using a set of classifiers, one for each recognizable artwork. The neural network we adopted is the Caffe reference model [13], fine-tuned for style recognition using the FlickrStyle dataset [16][2].

In order to obtain a representation which is at the same time semantically meaningful and capable of retaining low level visual content information, we extract image features from an intermediate level of the network. In particular, we adopt the *pool5* feature map, the latest one before the fully connected (FC) layers of the CNN. In fact, FC layers trade spatial information for a more semantic representation, which is highly coupled with the task and with the visual domain on which the network has been trained. This choice is therefore motivated by the fact that our visual domain, while being quite close, is different from the one of FlickrStyle. Moreover, since a sufficiently large dataset was not available to perform a further fine-tuning step, SVM classifiers have been trained to adapt the framework to the App's domain and be able to classify artworks correctly. For training the classifiers we used approximately 1,800 images, gathered at the museum using different smartphones and tablets, namely Galaxy S4, Galaxy Tab, iPhone 6, iPad Mini and OnePlus One. These images represent all of the twenty artworks plus a 'negative' set of images containing other scenes and paintings inside of the museum. They are used to reduce the false positive rate when the user accidentally attempts to recognize other paintings. All the classifiers are One vs All SVMs. During the evaluation phase, the ID of the highest scoring one is returned to the mobile App, if it scores above a cross validated threshold. Details about the recognized artwork are then provided to the user, who can upload a personal photo to get the style of the painting transferred on to it. Calls to the webserver are handled asynchronously and each request takes approximately 300 ms on a CPU.

In order to test the recognition accuracy we collected an additional set of photos which were not used for training. For each one of the twenty artworks in our system, we collected approximately 30 photos taken from different viewpoints, with different scales and degrees of occlusion. Figure 2 shows some of the photos from the test set. Some of them are "difficult" in a sense that might be blurred or taken from challenging viewpoints and artworks may be partially occluded by other visitors. Despite these difficulties our system achieves an overall good performance with a mean accuracy of 94.01 %. In detail, in Fig. 3 we report the confusion matrix for the twenty artworks in the test set, showing how often each painting is correctly classified or confused with other artworks. As can be seen,

---

[2] The network is available online at http://caffe.berkeleyvision.org/gathered/ examples/finetune_flickr_style.html.

Fig. 2. Samples from the dataset collected at the museum. On the first row standard pictures are shown, depicting the painting in their entirety. On the second row instead, are reported more challenging photos, due to blur, occlusion or rotation.

.91	.00	.02	.00	.00	.00	.00	.02	.00	.00	.00	.00	.00	.00	.00	.00	.04	.00	.00	.00
.00	.96	.00	.00	.00	.00	.00	.00	.00	.00	.00	.00	.00	.00	.00	.00	.04	.00	.00	.00
.00	.00	1.0	.00	.00	.00	.00	.00	.00	.00	.00	.00	.00	.00	.00	.00	.00	.00	.00	.00
.00	.00	.00	1.0	.00	.00	.00	.00	.00	.00	.00	.00	.00	.00	.00	.00	.00	.00	.00	.00
.00	.00	.00	.00	.91	.00	.09	.00	.00	.00	.00	.00	.00	.00	.00	.00	.00	.00	.00	.00
.03	.00	.09	.00	.00	.86	.03	.00	.00	.00	.00	.00	.00	.00	.00	.00	.00	.00	.00	.00
.00	.00	.00	.00	.00	.00	.92	.00	.00	.00	.00	.00	.00	.00	.00	.04	.04	.00	.00	.00
.00	.00	.00	.00	.00	.00	.00	1.0	.00	.00	.00	.00	.00	.00	.00	.00	.00	.00	.00	.00
.00	.00	.00	.00	.00	.00	.00	.00	1.0	.00	.00	.00	.00	.00	.00	.00	.00	.00	.00	.00
.00	.00	.07	.00	.00	.00	.00	.00	.00	.87	.00	.00	.06	.00	.00	.00	.00	.00	.00	.00
.00	.00	.00	.00	.00	.00	.00	.05	.00	.00	.95	.00	.00	.00	.00	.00	.00	.00	.00	.00
.00	.00	.00	.00	.00	.00	.00	.09	.00	.00	.00	.78	.00	.00	.00	.13	.00	.00	.00	.00
.00	.00	.00	.00	.00	.00	.00	.08	.00	.00	.00	.00	.92	.00	.00	.00	.00	.00	.00	.00
.00	.00	.00	.00	.00	.00	.00	.00	.00	.00	.00	.00	.00	.93	.07	.00	.00	.00	.00	.00
.00	.00	.00	.00	.00	.00	.00	.00	.00	.00	.00	.00	.00	.04	.96	.00	.00	.00	.00	.00
.00	.00	.00	.00	.00	.00	.00	.00	.00	.00	.00	.00	.00	.00	1.0	.00	.00	.00	.00	.00
.00	.00	.00	.00	.00	.00	.00	.00	.00	.00	.00	.00	.00	.00	.00	1.0	.00	.00	.00	.00
.00	.03	.00	.00	.00	.00	.03	.03	.00	.00	.00	.00	.00	.00	.00	.03	.00	.86	.00	.00
.00	.00	.00	.00	.00	.00	.00	.00	.00	.00	.00	.00	.00	.00	.00	.00	.00	.00	1.0	.00
.00	.00	.00	.00	.00	.00	.00	.00	.00	.00	.03	.00	.00	.00	.00	.00	.00	.00	.00	.97

Fig. 3. Confusion matrix for the artwork recognition module. Each row indicates the percentages of correct and incorrect classifications for a given artwork.

the majority of artworks are perfectly recognized. Only four artworks have performance slightly inferior to 0.9, due to the difficult lightening conditions present in their specific locations at the museum.

2.3   Artistic Style Transfer

From the Artwork Detail view of the mobile App, the user has the possibility to upload a personal image on which the style of the artwork will be applied. In this way, entertaining personal pictures that share similarities with the artworks can be obtained and shared on social networks. As a result, a visit at the museum can become a playful experience, combining gaming and learning aspects for young visitors. We base our approach on that of Gatys *et al.* [11], that is capable of freely mixing style and content of two different photos. The main advantage of this approach is its broad applicability to different styles, in contrast to fixed handcrafted styles [7,30]. This allows a museum curator to easily add new artworks in the system without requiring the development of a new transfer style algorithm. Following [11], our approach uses a CNN to derive a neural representation of content and style. The feature responses of a pretrained network on object recognition (VGG-19 [26]) are used to capture the appearance of an artwork image and the content of a user photo under the form of texture information. We start from a blank novel image that is altered with back-propagation until its neural representation is similar in terms of euclidean distance to the style and content representations (Fig. 4).

Fig. 4. Two examples of image stylization: (1) Baccio Maria Bacci, "Il tram di Fiesole", applied to a picture of the Battistero in Florence, IT; (2) Alberto Moretti, "Malcom X ed altri", applied to a picture of Piazza della Repubblica, also in Florence.

Unfortunately, the generation of the image is quite computational intensive. For an image of 900 pixel large, it takes about ∼90 seconds on a K80 NVIDIA GPU. As a result, the requests have to be handled offline since it is not possibile to obtain the output image in few seconds. Considering also that multiple requests can be made at the same time from multiple users, we implemented a scalable web server that is able to be easily deployed on several interconnected nodes. Web requests are handled in Python and enqueued to a distributed queue run by a Celery[3] server. By treating each request as a single unit task, it allows to process the images in a distributed batch fashion on several GPUs and several servers if available. After completing the computation, each output image is sent to the user via email, together with a description of the artwork. We also include links to share the image to several social media, with the aim of enabling viral publicity of the museum.

3 Conclusion

We presented the *Imaging Novecento* App, recently developed for the "Museo Novecento" in Florence, IT. Following previous studies on cultural heritage audience and applications, the App aims at enhancing the experience in the museum reducing cognitive load and exploiting gamification. The App automatically recognizes a selection of paintings and provides insights on artworks and their authors. The user can upload a personal picture with his smartphone to get it stylized with the recognized artwork style. He also has the possibility of sharing it on social networks. In the paper we show how computer vision technologies can be exploited to increase interactivity and reduce cognitive load. This can attract the targeted audience to the museum and further engage people with content.

Acknowledgments. We acknowledge the support of the "Museo Novecento" in Florence, IT, and the Municipality of Florence, IT. This research was supported by "THE SOCIAL MUSEUM AND SMART TOURISM", MIUR project no. CTN01_00034_23154_SMST.

References

1. Anderson, A.G., Berg, C.P., Mossing, D.P., Olshausen, B.A.: Deepmovie: using optical flow and deep neural networks to stylize movies. arXiv preprint arXiv:1605.08153 (2016)
2. Anwer, R.M., Khan, F.S., van de Weijer, J., Laaksonen, J.: Combining holistic and part-based deep representations for computational painting categorization. In: Proceedings of the 2016 ACM ICMR, pp. 339–342. ACM (2016)
3. Ballagas, R., Rohs, M., Sheridan, J.G., Borchers, J.: Byod: bring your own device. In: Proceedings of the Workshop on Ubiquitous Display Environments, Ubicomp, vol. 2004 (2004)
4. Baraldi, L., Paci, F., Serra, G., Benini, L., Cucchiara, R.: Gesture recognition using wearable vision sensors to enhance visitors Museum experiences. IEEE Sens. J. **15**(5), 2705–2714 (2015)
5. Chen, C.Y., Chang, B.R., Huang, P.S.: Multimedia augmented reality information system for Museum guidance. Pers. Ubiquit. Comput. **18**(2), 315–322 (2014)
6. Crowley, E., Zisserman, A.: The state of the art: object retrieval in paintings using discriminative regions. In: BMVC (2014)

---

[3] http://www.celeryproject.org.

7. Efros, A.A., Freeman, W.T.: Image quilting for texture synthesis and transfer. In: Proceedings of the 28th Annual Conference on Computer Graphics and Interactive Techniques, pp. 341–346. ACM (2001)

8. Elgammal, A., Lee, C.S.: Separating style and content on a nonlinear manifold. In: Proceedings of the 2004 IEEE Computer Society Conference on Computer Vision and Pattern Recognition, CVPR 2004, vol. 1, pp. I–478. IEEE (2004)

9. Fanini, B., d'Annibale, E., Demetrescu, E., Ferdani, D., Pagano, A.: Engaging and shared gesture-based interaction for museums the case study of K2R international expo in rome. In: 2015 Digital Heritage, vol. 1, pp. 263–270. IEEE (2015)

10. Fineschi, A., Pozzebon, A.: A 3D virtual tour of the Santa Maria della Scala Museum Complex in Siena, Italy, based on the use of Oculus RIFT HMD. In: 2015 International Conference on 3D Imaging (IC3D), pp. 1–5. IEEE (2015)

11. Gatys, L.A., Ecker, A.S., Bethge, M.: A neural algorithm of artistic style. arXiv preprint arXiv:1508.06576 (2015)

12. He, Z., Cui, B., Zhou, W., Yokoi, S.: A proposal of interaction system between visitor and collection in Museum hall by iBeacon. In: 2015 10th International Conference on Computer Science & Education (ICCSE), pp. 427–430. IEEE (2015)

13. Jia, Y., Shelhamer, E., Donahue, J., Karayev, S., Long, J., Girshick, R., Guadarrama, S., Darrell, T.: Caffe: Convolutional architecture for fast feature embedding. In: Proceedings of the 22nd ACM MM, pp. 675–678. ACM (2014)

14. Johnson, J., Alahi, A., Fei-Fei, L.: Perceptual losses for real-time style transfer and super-resolution. arXiv preprint arXiv:1603.08155 (2016)

15. Johnson, L., Adams Becker, S., Estrada, V., Freeman, A.: The NMC Horizon Report: 2015 Museum Edition. ERIC (2015)

16. Karayev, S., Trentacoste, M., Han, H., Agarwala, A., Darrell, T., Hertzmann, A., Winnemoeller, H.: Recognizing image style. arXiv preprint arXiv:1311.3715 (2013)

17. Kyprianidis, J.E., Collomosse, J., Wang, T., Isenberg, T.: State of the "Art": a taxonomy of artistic stylization techniques for images and video. IEEE Trans. Vis. Comput. Graph. 19(5), 866–885 (2013)

18. Malomo, L., Banterle, F., Pingi, P., Gabellone, F., Scopigno, R.: Virtualtour: a system for exploring cultural heritage sites in an immersive way. In: 2015 Digital Heritage, vol. 1, pp. 309–312. IEEE (2015)

19. Mayer, R.E., Moreno, R.: Nine ways to reduce cognitive load in multimedia learning. Educ. Psychol. 38(1), 43–52 (2003)

20. Negruşa, A.L., Toader, V., Sofică, A., Tutunea, M.F., Rus, R.V.: Exploring gamification techniques and applications for sustainable tourism. Sustainability 7(8), 11160–11189 (2015)

21. Pagano, A., Armone, G., De Sanctis, E.: Virtual Museums and audience studies: the case of "Keys to Rome" exhibition. In: 2015 Digital Heritage, vol. 1, pp. 373–376. IEEE (2015)

22. Park, S.: The effects of social cue principles on cognitive load, situational interest, motivation, and achievement in pedagogical agent multimedia learning. J. Educ. Technol. Soc. 4, 211–229 (2015)

23. Peng, K.C., Chen, T.: Cross-layer features in convolutional neural networks for generic classification tasks. In: 2015 IEEE International Conference on Image Processing (ICIP), pp. 3057–3061. IEEE (2015)

24. Reiners, T., Wood, L.C. (eds.): Gamification in Education and Business. Springer International Publishing, Switzerland (2015)

25. Ruf, B., Kokiopoulou, E., Detyniecki, M.: Mobile Museum guide based on fast SIFT recognition. In: Detyniecki, M., Leiner, U., Nürnberger, A. (eds.) AMR 2008. LNCS, vol. 5811, pp. 170–183. Springer, Heidelberg (2010). doi:10.1007/978-3-642-14758-6_14

26. Simonyan, K., Zisserman, A.: Very deep convolutional networks for large-scale image recognition. arXiv preprint arXiv:1409.1556 (2014)

27. de Sousa Borges, S., Durelli, V.H., Reis, H.M., Isotani, S.: A systematic mapping on gamification applied to education. In: Proceedings of the 29th Annual ACM Symposium on Applied Computing, pp. 216–222. ACM (2014)

28. Temmermans, F., Jansen, B., Deklerck, R., Schelkens, P., Cornelis, J.: The mobile Museum guide: artwork recognition with eigenpaintings and SURF. In: WIAMIS 2011, Delft, The Netherlands, April 13–15, 2011. TU Delft; EWI; MM; PRB (2011)

29. Tenenbaum, J.B., Freeman, W.T.: Separating style and content with bilinear models. Neural Comput. **12**(6), 1247–1283 (2000)

30. Xie, X., Tian, F., Seah, H.S.: Feature guided texture synthesis (FGTS) for artistic style transfer. In: Proceedings of the 2nd International Conference on Digital Interactive Media in Entertainment and Arts, pp. 44–49. ACM (2007)

31. Yoon, S.A., Wang, J.: Making the invisible visible in science museums through augmented reality devices. TechTrends **58**(1), 49–55 (2014)

Towards the Design of a User-Friendly and Trustworthy Mobile System for Museums

Kostas Koukoulis and Dimitrios Koukopoulos[✉]

Department of Cultural Heritage Management and New Technologies, University of Patras,
Agrinio, Greece
{kkoukoulis,dkoukopoulos}@upatras.gr

Abstract. Designing mobile applications for enhancing user visiting experiences in museums is a current trend. This paper discusses the current work on mobile applications that are dedicated to museums. Following a specific methodology, we propose specific user and app classification requirements. Based on those requirements, we present the design of a user-friendly and trustworthy mobile system prototype that includes functionality needed from such institutions. We adopt suitable authorization mechanisms permitting specific operations to various user groups. We evaluate the proposed system design comparing it with other known systems following a specific usage scenario. We feel that this study could help on the design and implementation of trustworthy mobile-based museum visiting applications.

Keywords: Cultural heritage · Museum mobile applications · Digitization · Multimedia databases · Web smartphone-based services

1 Introduction

Museums are in a rush to follow the trend of our era. According to the Museums Association [1] they started providing specialized mobile applications to the users of the museums respecting the fact that the use of mobile smartphones has exploded over the past years. This trend is being extensively adopted by large institutions for the profound reason that they have the funds to finance such a change. Their intensions are to offer extra content to the visitors, to make them more energetic during their tour, to attract new visitors, to expand the access to people with special needs and finally to make visitors participants of their activities [1]. Ambrose and Paine [20] insist that a museum should know its users and should have answers on questions such as: why will people visit my museum, who will visit, how much time they will spend etc. The fact is that today museum visitors, like everybody else, use a smartphone. But the adaption of technology should not be made blindly. Some skeptics think that the museum transforms in the base of database design [13]. Others support the use of technology as a need for the new generation [14].

An important challenge in cultural web-based systems is long-term availability that includes digital rights management and content preservation from unauthorized access

© Springer International Publishing AG 2016
M. Ioannides et al. (Eds.): EuroMed 2016, Part I, LNCS 10058, pp. 792–802, 2016.
DOI: 10.1007/978-3-319-48496-9_63

[28]. This problem is even worse in mobile systems that support management, collection and dissemination of multimedia content in cultural environments due to the inherent characteristics of mobile devices (operating systems gaps and absence of access control and data security mechanisms) [27, 29].

In this work, we demonstrate a methodology of designing and evaluating a mobile system for cultural institutions, like museums. The goals of our approach are two-fold: enhancing visit experience for end-users and facilitate management and preservation actions for the institution personnel concerning museum visits. Thus, we investigate user requirements and mobile application capabilities that can be exploited for the design of a friendly, useful and trustworthy mobile system serving visiting and management purposes. We analyze the basic system usage scenario targeting on the study of specific user groups (personnel or visitors), specifying cultural content types, attributes and relations, limiting permitted user operations on cultural content for security purposes and supporting specific services that can be applied before, during and after a museum visit. Having these potentials in mind, we propose a system architecture for the trustworthy and user-friendly adaptation of mobile services into the everyday life of a museum. Furthermore, we investigate operationally the proposed system in order to understand the communication interactions and needs of the various entities participating in system's design. Finally, we make an attempt to evaluate our system design involving specific experts in museum technologies and environments. In this attempt, we compare the proposed system to other well-known museum visiting applications [3, 4, 6] following s specific simple usage scenario.

2 Related Works

In 2006 there was a big challenge for the digitalization process [15], the majority of the museums already had web sites and also used other technologies such as accounting software, broadband internet connection, computerized catalogs, computerized collections management systems etc. Nowadays a museum includes not only a website, but also a social media presence, mobile tools and apps, electronic fundraising [16], and much more such as some management system for its assets [17, 18]. The Acropolis Museum [12] has released digital applications for home users regarding the exhibits, has created a digital repository for educational purposes and provides on site visual material in portable electronic media. The Smithsonian Institute [19] provides applications for educational purposes and a vast amount of material is digitized, categorized and provided for researchers, kids and educators. A large number of apps exist already in Google's play store and the majority is being built by independent companies containing specialized material [21, 22]. A small amount of them were built by the institutions but the documentation is unavailable to the public. The British Museum Lite [23] allows a virtual tour at British Museum and provides maps, high resolution images and thematic catalogues of exhibits. Smithsonian Institution [24] provides its own app. It contains visit planning, search on museums assets, AR and information about the museum. The full version costs a few dollars and provides full functionality. A lot of research has been done in the field of authorization mechanisms concerning access control in multimedia content [25–27]. An authorization model specialized for multimedia content stored in digital libraries is described in [25]. Content-based access control is applied on multiple files of digital art projects in a collaborative web-based environment [26]. An authorization mechanism based on role-based access control is applied on smartphone devices for protecting multimedia content which is disseminated though multimedia guiding services in a cultural environment in [27]. Considering the fact that Museum Mobile Apps are being built for such a short period, evaluation methods are not yet published. Some work has been done in the past few years in designing mobile applications for cultural institutions. Chess project makes efforts to use AR, digital storytelling and personalized tour with the use of personas [3]. Another implementation made by researches in Korea proposed a system that provides a unified presentation of the content of the museums in a whole region [6]. Other researchers proposed a system that implements a tour based on the knowledge of other people providing again functionality such as AR [4].

3   User Requirements and App Classification

Till now there are a few works that deal with the investigation of user requirements for applications offering services in environments of cultural interest (museums, archaeological sites, city centers, etc.) [5, 7, 8]. Hui-Ying and Chao-Chien [5] talked about visitor's expectations of a visit to an archeological site and this work was the base for structuring our user requirements. Palumpo et al. [7] started a study to identify the key factors related to visitor satisfaction. They ended up with six must have functionalities. Along with these requirements, there were placed data from a Smithsonian's [8] wide research that aimed to investigate their visitors needs regarding to their visits at the institution. Analyzing all these data we ended up with a set of axes that a mobile application should implement. Based on the Smartphone functionalities (camera, microphone, Wi-Fi connection, Bluetooth, touch screen capabilities, GPS sensor) and interviews taken from museum experts we propose a number of user requirements for a mobile application (Fig. 1).

Educational environment	Usefulness	Type of application
■ Provides an easy way to obtain information about activities recently made.	■ Provide information on hours of operation, instructions for accessing the site, calendars etc.	■ Presentations, guided tours, temporary - fixed exhibitions
■ Contains or promotes related educational activities.	■ Information about other facilities (parking, restrooms, metro access, security services, wheel chair accessibility)	■ Museum highlights, topics, exhibits, must see
■ The exhibits are presented in an attractive way.		■ Dedicated points on individual exhibits
■ The way the narrative is easy to understand.		■ Create user content
■ The content of the app is educational.		■ Games based on exhibits, treasure hunts, multiplayer games, daily trivia
■ The display mode enhances understanding.	■ Provided amenities such as a	
■ Visitors retrieves the information in front of the exhibit	simple system for ticketing (ticketing, crowd information)	**Ease of use**
■ Provides information from the experts, artists and scientists (interviews)	■ Summary information for contiguous areas of interest	■ The app contain functionality for the user before, during and after the visit to the museum.
■ Contains bibliographic info (authors, curators, creators, artists, scientists)	■ Way finding (location, directions, floor plans)	■ The app meets the needs of visitors
		■ The app provides help

Fig. 1. User requirements

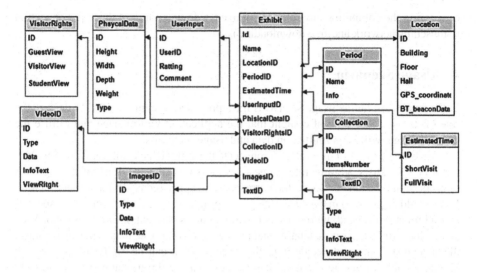

Fig. 2. Basic tables in composite DB

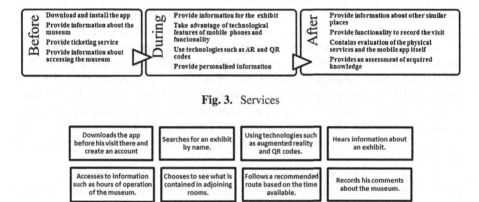

Fig. 3. Services

Fig. 4. Simple usage scenario

Some work has been done in order to classify the applications regarding their features [2]. Their classification includes axes such as general characteristics (free or paid app), type of the application (guided tours, devoted to specific artworks, games, content creation by user), use of the app (during, before or after their visit) and functionality (contains web 2.0, AR, various views). Data was also taken from Smithsonian's research [8]. App classification parameters based on technological characteristics that specialize the application environment can be classified in three categories: (i) technology and features (like installations on all mobile environments, use network capabilities and mobile sensors, AR, interaction and personalization), (ii) security (like user different rights and functionalities, existence of security mechanism capabilities or not), and (iii) app reliability concerning the computing environment (like easy downloading of the app, connection to museums network and free downloading).

4 Usage Scenario

In the process to define usage scenarios for a proposed system we need to declare the role of its users, the type of content that the application will manage and diffuse the operations that will be permitted on data and usage scenarios.

There are six types of users able to connect to the app and have different functionality: curators, specialists, administrators, guests, visitors and students. Each of these groups of users should be able to access the corresponding app screens, data and functionality. Users could be grouped in two basic categories project team members (curators, specialists, administrators) and internet users (visitors, guests, students). *Curators:* Should be able to have full access of databases and produce the composite data. They also choose the specialists team and decide with the director what can be digitized. *Specialists:* Should be able to manage content data of the database through app screens, to alter database data, to add new exhibitions, to create tour routes and to add information about the museum. Their contact info should be also in the database. In real, they are artists, creators or scientists. *Administrators:* Provide to other types of users the corresponding screens and maintain the database and the hardware that supports the app. *Visitors:* Museum visitors or just the users of the app. Some researchers indicate that the users' needs are relevant to their background [8]. These needs differentiate according to their place of residence, frequency of visits, use of museum aids, reasons for using their phones and their styles of accessing information. *Guests:* They can access limited functionality and data in order to have a clear view for using the proposed app. *Students:* Could access all the functionality assigned to visitors and also view primitive data, specialist's comments, contact info of specialists etc. Guests and students are a subtype of visitor.

The app content refers to all kind of data that will be held in the database concerning places of the museum and users. *Images:* Images of exhibits, collections, museum halls and its exteriors, architectural drawings, floor and hall plans containing the exact position of the exhibits and city area maps. *Audio: not* a main exhibition item, but a way to provide the visitor information about an exhibit and to facilitate persons with disabilities in their tour in an advanced version of the system. *Video:* from excavations, maintenance, exhibit transportations to other museums or from any special time of the course of the exhibit. Video of specialist interviews, visitor's experiences, future visitor's comments and virtual tours. *Text:* in-depth object info, descriptions of exhibits and collections, specialist interview transcripts, museum info and user's comments. All entities included in the database should have a text. *GPS/routing data:* outdoor routing data like positions and routes of exhibits, places of interest, public transportation stations and data for indoor routing using Bluetooth and beacons [9].

All content should be classified in a number of main categories and should be placed in separate databases. *Primitive museum data (Primitive DB):* Specialists provide data regarding the exhibits and collections (images, texts, sound, video and multimedia).

Composite museum data (Composite DB): Produced by primitive data and data provided by visitors (comments, photos, videos) and guests like personalized tours content. Visitors and students material along with the recorded path of their visit to the museum could constitute the basis for a collection of stories referring to different user interests. *User credentials (User Credential DB):* Login information and user preferences. *Logistic data (Logistics DB)*: Information regarding the ticketing service, way finding, security services, hours of operation, parking or metro access, restrooms and crowd information (data provided by special trained personnel). *User-generated content (User Content DB):* Data to be stored by internet users. These data are kept separately from the composite data but are connected with the corresponding exhibition id. *Security Data (Security DB):* Any access to the database will be recorded.

Data are kept in separate databases as shown in Fig. 5. The basic work that is made on the data could be divided in a number of categories: insert, delete, view, search, annotate and relate. Specialists have full access to their own data on primitive content database. Curators may also annotate these data and are responsible for creating composite data on a distinct database. Content created by internet users is placed on a different database. The administrator of the system does not manipulate data regarding museum assets. He should only be able to assign privileges to users and to keep the system running, doing whatever is needed from the technological side.

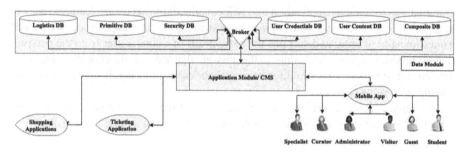

Fig. 5. System architecture

For internet users the main action is viewing. The app should give them the option to choose among different kinds of views. For example, they should be able to view a full time video or a portion of it or just a scene. Some of the services devoted to visitors are a part of the dissemination. The system should contain games related to the museum content, give visitors the right to publish some of the content to social networks such as recorded visits structuring their own scenarios like story-telling process or even to give them the functionality to buy goods from the museum store. Internet users are able to create their own material and their data should be stored in a separate DB following the schema of "Basic tables in composite DB" (Fig. 2).

A guest should be able to view the smaller amount of information. He may become a visitor and the provided information needs to meet that need. He should be able to view informational data about the museum such as opening hours and navigation to the museum, data regarding to the museum exhibits and collections in order to decide if he wants to visit it and to just gain some knowledge. The only insert that he could do on data is some rating. Visitors should be able to access and view data regarding the exhibits and the collections, to see personalized routes to follow on their visit, to hear audio descriptions, use augmented reality etc. Also, they can input data taken during their visit such as photographs and put their comments and ratings. A more demanding visitor is the type of student. Students have the same rights as visitors plus the option to view scientific papers and specialist comments and data. Students can store locally certain data that the curator permits. The main objective of the app is to provide them with material for their studies and researches. Permissions for accessing this material should be given to them for a specific data set from the curator.

The main issue was to assign privileges to internet users. The data manipulation is made through the app's services. Each user type is assigned to a number of screens in his app and de facto with the corresponding services. In the assigned screens there was a need to show or hide data. The publication right field on podcast, video, images and text contains the rights for viewing the corresponding data for each subtype of internet users. The estimated guide time is a model based characteristic. It is needed in order to automatically calculate tours on demand based on visitor's available time.

5   Services and Scenarios

Our goal was to build an application that will contain all the necessary features that will help the visitors of a cultural institution to have an integrated tour experience. We created a questionnaire in order to determine the basic needs of a simple user from the perspective of museum experts. According to the answers that we had, we classify application services for the internet user in three main categories: pre-touring, in-touring and post-touring operations (Fig. 3).

A simple scenario is created for the evaluation of the proposed app. This scenario contains basic actions that a visitor usually performs visiting a museum (Fig. 4).

6   Proposed System Architecture

The proposed mobile app delivers services for both internet users and project team members. An application connected to the database is also used for ticketing and shopping services by museum staff. The system is separated in modules. The first module of the system contains a database set (Security DB, Primitive DB, User credentials DB, User content DB, Composite DB) and a broker in order to facilitate their use (Database management module). Data will be accessed only through services and the direct database will be prohibited. Any access to the main application data will be recorded by the security database. The second module is the Application Server where is installed all the logic of the proposed system in order to access our data with safety. Complementary the application server can support commercial transactions between users and museum, like user ticketing and shopping that are necessary functionalities in modern museums for funding purposes. The third module contains Mobile Services and its role is to interact successfully and efficiently with the users. Also, users through the app can make commercial transactions with museum. The proposed system is implemented as a three-tire application. For the data layer we use a DBMS like SQL Server. The application layer uses an application server (such as Microsoft's IIS). The presentation layer contains the mobile app which operates in Android smartphones that use SDK 24.4.1 and systems for ticketing and shopping that are based on HTML5 and angularJS.

7   Operational Design Scenarios

Search for an exhibit by name: The visitor stands before the exhibit and read its label. His main objective is to find information regarding the specific item. The application has simple search functionality for cases like this. He touches the menu and tap on the search icon. Immediately the screen gets blare and a single line search input field appears on the top. The visitor enters the exhibit name. The mobile app passes the search keyword to the corresponding functional unit which in its turn request information from the broker. The broker routes the question to one or more databases and returns a list of items to the functional unit that is provided to the visitor.

Visitor chooses to see what is contained in adjoining rooms: The visitor is in the museum and located to a hall. He doesn't want to be in that specific area anymore and wants to have an overview of the halls next to him. He taps on the apps menu and chooses "What's next to me". Immediately the action goes to the Application server along with his position data. Broker chooses the composite database and asks for hall plans of places next to his position. These plans are being forwarded to the Application Server who sends them to the app.

Following a recommended route based on the time available and personal interests: The visitor finds out that he hasn't got much time. He decides to let the system propose a route defining the available time and his interests. From his screen he chooses "Give me a proposed tour". Then the app asks him to fill in information about his interests (like era, artists, value of the exhibits). Visitor has one hour left and wants to see the most popular exhibits. Then a request is being made to the application server. The application server does a query to databases asking information about popular exhibits (rated by visitors). For each exhibit the application server asks databases for the estimated time needed for viewing it. Subsequently, it creates a route considering his position and the criteria mentioned above. The route is provided to the visitor.

8   Evaluation

In order to evaluate the proposed system, we adopt the method proposed by Lewis et al. known as cognitive walkthrough [10]. The basic advantage of this method relies on the fact that there is no need of fully implementing the system you need to evaluate [11]. There are two phases in this method: preparation and evaluation. In the preparation phase there is a need to determine a set of representative tasks that the application is intended to support. We selected the tasks of the simple usage scenario on Fig. 4. In the second phase, a small number of specialists from fields related to museum technologies and environments, read the application specifications and grade each user action. Grades varied from 0 to 4. Zero indicates the absence of the service. The grades 1 to 4 correspond to the familiarity of users towards specific acts (the percentage of users who know to use a system service). Four is the maximum degree and 1 is the minimum one. In our evaluation, we compare the proposed system with systems presented in [3, 4, 6]. The proposed system seems to get the highest score (Fig. 6).

User can	Proposed System			System A			System B			System C		
	E1	E2	E3	E1	E2	E3	E1	E2	E3	E1	E2	E3
Searches for an exhibit by name.	4	4	4	3	3	3	4	4	3	0	0	0
Using technologies such as augmented reality and QR codes.	4	3	4	3	4	3	0	0	0	4	4	4
Hears information about an exhibit.	4	4	4	4	3	4	4	3	3	3	4	3
Access to information such as hours of operation of the museum.	4	3	4	0	0	0	0	0	0	0	0	0
Chooses to see what is contained in adjoining rooms.	4	4	4	0	0	0	0	0	0	0	0	0
Following a recommended route based on the time available.	4	4	4	4	4	4	4	3	4	4	3	4
Records his comments about the museum.	4	4	4	0	0	0	4	4	4	4	4	4

Fig. 6. Walkthrough evaluation

9   Conclusions

The proposed system attempts to satisfy the needs of users, experts or not, concerning the visit experience in a museum. It exploits the functionalities of modern smartphone devices in order to offer efficient visiting services in a friendly manner. We have taken into account user requirements (and app classifications requirements), usage scenarios (users, content classification and permitted content operations) to build services and scenarios that would be served by the proposed system. After system design, we started to implement the proposed system services in order to support the basic usage scenario. A first primitive evaluation indicates success on the design of the proposed system and the produced comparison validates it. Following we are going to implement the full system functionality targeting specific museum environments (like general, technology, history and art museums [30]) and distribute our mobile app to the broad community through the App Store. In this process, we are going to ask user community for continuous feedback in terms of ease of use, potential usefulness, perceived usefulness and security of use.

Acknowledgement. This work is an internal project of Cultural Technology Laboratory of the Department of Cultural Heritage Management and New Technologies of the University of Patras having as target group the local museums and cultural heritage environments of Aitoloakarnania, a prefecture in Greece.

References

1. Atkinson, R.: 2013 MA mobile survey. Technical report, Museums Association (2013)
2. Economou, M., Meintani, E.: Promising beginning? evaluating museum mobile phone apps. In: Ciolfi, L., Scott, K., Barbieri, S. (eds.) Rethinking Technology in Museums 2011: Emerging Experiences, pp. 87–101. University of Limerick, Ireland (2011)

3. Pujol, L., Katifori, A., Vayanou, M., Roussou, M., Karvounis, M., Kyriakidi, M., Eleftheratou, S., Ioannidis, Y.: From personalization to adaptivity–creating immersive visits through interactive digital storytelling at the Acropolis Museum. In: Botia, J.A., Charitos, D. (eds.) IE 2013, pp. 541–554. IOS Press, Athens (2013)

4. Huang, W., Kaminski, B., Luo, J., Huang, X., Li, J., Ross, A., Wright, J., An, D.: SMART: design and evaluation of a collaborative museum visiting application. In: Luo, Y. (ed.) CDVE 2015. LNCS, vol. 9320, pp. 57–64. Springer, Heidelberg (2015). doi:10.1007/978-3-319-24132-6_7

5. Shi, H.Y., Chen, C.C.: A study of service quality and satisfaction for museums-taking the national museum of prehistory as an example. J. Hum. Res. Ad. Learn. 4(1), 159–170 (2008)

6. Bae, E.S., Im, D.U., Lee, S.Y.: Smart museum based on regional unified app. Int. J. Soft. Eng. Appl. 7(4), 157–166 (2013)

7. Palumbo, F., Dominici, G., Basile, F.: Designing a mobile app for museums according to the drivers of visitor satisfaction. In: Raguz, I.V., Roushdy, M. (eds.) Recent Advances in Business Management and Marketing, pp. 159–166. WSEAS Press, USA (2013)

8. Smart phone services for Smithsonian visitors. Technical report, Smithsonian Institution (2010)

9. Chawathe, S.: Beacon placement for indoor localization using bluetooth. In: 11th International IEEE Conference on Intelligent Transportation Systems, pp. 980–985. IEEE Press, Beijing (2008)

10. Lewis, C., Polson, P., Wharton, C., Rieman, J.: Testing a walkthrough methodology for theory-based design of walk-up-and-use interfaces. In: CHI 1990, pp. 235–242. ACM Press, New York (1990)

11. Polson, P., Lewis, C., Rieman, J., Wharton, C.: Cognitive walkthroughs: a method for theory-based evaluation of user interfaces. J. Man Mach. Stud. 36(5), 741–773 (1992)

12. Learning resources, Acropolis Museum. http://www.theacropolismuseum.gr

13. Pepi, M.: Is a museum a database?: institutional conditions in net utopia. e-flux 60 (2014)

14. Connecting museums with generation Z. Technical report, Smack Agency (2013)

15. Status of technology and digitization in the nations' s museums and libraries. Technical report, Institute of Museum and Library Services (2006)

16. Johnson, L., Adams Becker, S., Estrada, V., Freeman, A.: NMC horizon report: 2015 museum edition. Technical report, The New Media Consortium (2015)

17. Koukopoulos, D., Tsolis, D., Heliades, G.: Ionian music archive: application of digitization, management and dissemination technologies for musical cultural heritage. In: IISA 2014, pp. 239–244. IEEE Press, Chania (2014)

18. Chaplin, E., Tullock, J.: Successfully managing archives in museums. Technical report, AIM Success Guides (2015)

19. Smithsonian. https://www.si.edu

20. Ambrose, T., Paine, C.: Museum Basics, 3rd edn. Routledge, Oxford (1993)

21. Museums in NYC. https://play.google.com

22. Rodin museum. https://play.google.com

23. The British Museum Lite. https://play.google.com

24. Smithsonian mobile. https://play.google.com

25. Kodali, N., Farkas, C., Wijesekera, D.: An authorization model for multimedia digital libraries. J. Dig. Libr. 4(3), 139–155 (2004)

26. Koukopoulos, D., Styliaras, G.: Security in collaborative multimedia web-based art projects. J. Mult. 5(5), 404–416 (2010)

27. Koukopoulos, D., Styliaras, G.: Design of trustworthy smartphone-based multimedia services in cultural environments. J. Electron. Commun. Res. 13(2), 129–150 (2013)

28. Arnold, D.: Paster's quadrant: cultural heritage as inspiration for basic research in computer science. J. Comput. Cult. Her. **2**(1), 1–10 (2008)
29. Oberheide, J., Jahanian, F.: When mobile is harder than fixed (and vice versa): demystifying security challenges in mobile environments. In: HotMobile 2010, pp. 43–48. ACM Press, New York (2010)
30. Types of Museum. http://www.britannica.com/topic/types-of-museums-398830

Project Paper: Serious Games for Cultural Heritage

Project iMARECULTURE: Advanced VR, iMmersive Serious Games and Augmented REality as Tools to Raise Awareness and Access to European Underwater CULTURal heritagE

D. Skarlatos[1(✉)], P. Agrafiotis[1,2], T. Balogh[3], F. Bruno[4], F. Castro[5], B. Davidde Petriaggi[6], S. Demesticha[7], A. Doulamis[2], P. Drap[8], A. Georgopoulos[2], F. Kikillos[12], P. Kyriakidis[1], F. Liarokapis[9], C. Poullis[10], and S. Rizvic[11]

[1] Cyprus University of Technology, Limassol, Cyprus
dimitrios.skarlatos@cut.ac.cy
[2] National Technical University of Athens, Athens, Greece
[3] Holografika Hologrameloallito Fejleszto Es Forgalmazo Kft, Budapest, Hungary
[4] 3D Research s.r.l., University of Calabria, Rende, Italy
[5] Universidade Nova de Lisboa, Lisbon, Portugal
[6] Ministero dei Beni e delle Attività Culturali e del Turismo, ISCR, Rome, Italy
[7] University of Cyprus, Nicosia, Cyprus
[8] Aix-Marseille University, Marseille, France
[9] Masaryk University, Brno, Czech Republic
[10] Concordia University, Montreal, Canada
[11] Sarajevo University, Sarajevo, Bosnia and Herzegovina
[12] Pierides Foundation, Larnaca, Cyprus

Abstract. The project iMARECULTURE is focusing in raising European identity awareness using maritime and underwater cultural interaction and exchange in Mediterranean Sea. Commercial ship routes joining Europe with other cultures are vivid examples of cultural interaction, while shipwrecks and submerged sites, unreachable to wide public are excellent samples that can benefit from immersive technologies, augmented and virtual reality. The projects aim to bring inherently unreachable underwater cultural heritage within digital reach of the wide public using virtual visits and immersive technologies. Apart from reusing existing 3D data of underwater shipwrecks and sites, with respect to ethics, rights and licensing, to provide a personalized dry visit to a museum visitor or augmented reality to the diver, it also emphasizes on developing pre- and after- encounter of the digital or physical museum visitor. The former one is implemented exploiting geospatial enabled technologies for developing a serious game of sailing over ancient Mediterranean and the latter for an underwater shipwreck excavation game. Both games are realized thought social media, in order to facilitate information exchange among users. The project supports dry visits providing immersive experience through VR Cave and 3D info kiosks on museums or through the web. Additionally, aims to significantly enhance the experience of the diver, visitor or scholar, using underwater augmented reality in a tablet and an underwater housing. The consortium is composed by universities and SMEs with experience in diverse underwater projects, existing digital libraries, and people many of which are divers themselves.

© Springer International Publishing AG 2016
M. Ioannides et al. (Eds.): EuroMed 2016, Part I, LNCS 10058, pp. 805–813, 2016.
DOI: 10.1007/978-3-319-48496-9_64

Keywords: Underwater · Archaeological sites · Shipwrecks · Maritime · Virtual museums · Serious games · Immersive · Holography · European identity

1 Introduction

The area of Virtual Museums, Virtual Guides and Virtual Reconstruction of Cultural Heritage, has a number of past and currently important active projects of this scope (e.g. V-MUST, F-MU.S.EU.M., VENUS, MINERVA, MINERVA PLUS, MINERVA EC, THE MICHAEL PLUS, ATHENA, ATHENA PLUS, ARCHEOGUIDE, 3DMURALE etc.). However, these projects do not address the real challenge of an Underwater Virtual Museum. In addition, projects related to underwater cultural heritage and environments are not engaged with the challenge of Virtual Museums and Immersive Technologies. These projects (e.g. SASMAP, WRECKPROTECT, ARROWS, STACHEM, 3D-UNDERWORLD, NOPTILUS, CURE) are focusing on the development of tools and techniques to survey, assess, stabilize, monitor and preserve underwater archaeological sites using robot systems and scanners. It is important to note that the majority of these projects are not dealing with dissemination and wider public awareness of underwater cultural heritage. In particular, in the Mediterranean Sea where most of the oldest underwater assets exist, are at most in risk due to the marine environment, trawlers, looting and wood degrading marine borers. Hence recording and promoting CH is most important in the Mediterranean Sea than any other place.

1.1 Scope

Project's iMARECULTURE scope is to raise public awareness of European identity by focusing in maritime cultural heritage, which by default brings together different civilizations. In particular, it aims in bringing inherently unreachable underwater cultural heritage, within digital reach of the wide public, by implementing virtual visits, serious games with immersive technologies and underwater augmented reality. Scope of the project is to design, analyze, develop and validate pioneer applications and systems in the context of Virtual Museums through collaborative and innovative research from a diverse group of scientists, researchers, archaeologists, experts and museums.

The project combines the two aforementioned groups of research projects into one by merging advancements in VR with the underwater environment. It will accomplish it by using existing technology to create breakthrough applications and digital experiences in the area of Virtual Museums in order to empower different types of users to engage with European underwater cultural heritage digital resources by exploiting re-use and re-purposing of existing data.

1.2 Approach

Submitted in the call 'Virtual museums and social platform on European digital heritage, memory, identity and cultural interaction' (CULT-COOP-08-2016), the projects investigate new ways to personalize the museum visit to a digital of physical visitor, while support social cohesion and European identity. Virtual museums are particularly strong in visualizing CH that it either intangible, does not exist anymore, it is partially destroyed or it is remotely located. Ancient maritime commerce is a perfect example of civilizations' interaction and cultural exchange, but unfortunately not easily exhibited to the wider public. Ships, shipwreck sites and underwater sites in general, are far from public's reach and understanding. Enabling immersive technologies to allow for content enhanced dry visits of visitors on such sites, it will inevitably raise public's awareness and stir further interest about maritime culture.

The goal is to bring shipwreck sites to the reach of the wider public, so that they can have a personalized and interactive dry visit using VR googles from the comfort of their house. Museum visits could be further enhanced, using immersive technologies, such as VR caves and holographic screens. The latter allow for all visitors to witness an interactive 3D experience of another visitor, while they carry no special glasses or any other equipment, while freely walking around the objects under investigation. Moreover, the project will enhance the underwater experience of diver visitors, as there are submerged archaeological sites, that support such visits. Especially designed underwater tablets using Augmented Reality (AR) will superimpose information about specific finds and architectural designs on the screen of a specially designed underwater tablet. The information will be provided in real time, and on user's demand, in order to avoid overloading the diver.

Following the need to extend any visit, pre- and after- the visit serious games and storytelling, encourage and surrounds the physical visit. As a pre-visit experience, social platform users will be able to participate in a seafaring game, sailing between ancient ports for commerce, trying to confront all natural and human hazards the ancient crew had to face, using the limited resources and limitations of that specific time period. Similarly, as an after-visit experience, the social platform users will be able to partner up for a virtual excavation dive on an ancient shipwreck, with all limitations and problems that such dives have, and enjoy the 'discovery' and surfacing of new artifacts, while appreciate the work done by underwater archaeologists.

Three sites have been carefully selected for project's implementation, based on their ability to support the context of each action, as well as their data availability, so that no assets were to be allocated on data acquisition.

Mazotos shipwreck site: The site [1], when discovered, was virtually undisturbed, so its archaeological importance, as well as the immediate need for its protection, triggered the organization of the first Cypriot underwater archaeological project. The wreck lies at a depth of −44 m, some 14 nautical miles south-west of Larnaca, 1.5 nm from the shore, near Mazotos village. The main visible feature of the site is a concentration of amphorae on a sandy, almost flat sea-bed. Its maximum vertical relief measures 1 m and its maximum dimensions are 17.5×8 m. The oblong concentration, almost in the form of a ship, has a north-south orientation and consists of 500–800 Chian amphorae partly or totally visible, which date to the middle of fourth century BC.

Xlendi shipwreck site: The Phoenician shipwreck off Gozo Xlendi. resting at a depth of 110 m, it is probably the oldest ancient shipwreck in the central Mediterranean (700BC). Xlendi Bay is a narrow inlet on the south-west coast of Gozo, close to the island's south-western point Rasil-Wardija and to the capital Rabat, which is 2.5 km away.

Rabat is a hilltop town that is thought to have been the main settlement area throughout Gozo's history. Xlendi lies at the mouth of a valley which runs from the Rabat hill to the coast. The valley is bounded by high rock walls but opens into a floodplain, which is the site of the modern village, before meeting the sea. There is a good, fresh water source in the village of Fontana, on the road between Rabat and Xlendi [2, 3].

Baiae underwater archaeological park: The Baiae site is of particular interest, it was created in 2002 and it is together a Marine Protected Area and an Underwater Archaeological Park. Environmental aspects of this area are related to a peculiar volcanic and deformational history. The submerged area includes part of the territory of the ancient city of Baiae and Portus Iulius, comprising the roman harbour and numerous constructions used as warehouses. The archaeological remains include luxurious maritime villas and imperial buildings, more modest houses, private thermae, tabernae and all those structures that characterize the cities of the Roman age. The itineraries of "Villa con ingresso a protiro" (selected for this Project) with black and and white and white mosaic floors, and thermae; the Villa of Pisoni, the Nymphaeum of Punta Epitaffio (with copies of statues of the Imperial families and of Roman gods); the Portus Iulius with the remains of mosaics floor of a republican Villa and a building with a porticos. The Baiae underwater archaeological park will serve also as a demonstration site for the developed Augmented Reality systems.

All actions will be evaluated in order to attain measurable results, and enhanced by appropriate storytelling.

2   Project Approach and Methodology

2.1   Objectives

Being an interdisciplinary project, the first step is the clear definition of targets, goals, test sites and wrecks to be used. Several decisions about the serious games, the age, the era and data to be gathered, will be taken. Discussions about existing VR and AR technologies [4] and implementation will clarify the roadmap towards milestones and goals.

Data gathering and pre-processing phase: Is the fundamental pillar for the project. Both 3D as well as supporting data will be accumulated by partners, from open sites, published journals and books and partner's archives to support storytelling, narratives, 3D models of sites [5–9], ships [10], cargos, probabilistic geospatial analysis about ship routes [11], wreck site formation processes, etc. Having all the necessary information, iMARECULTURE will create and re-use a plethora of 3D models for both the ship wreckages and the amphorae, allowing people to examine the 3D underwater environment and objects on it. Similarly, a site of Baiae underwater archaeological park where a complete 3D model exists [12, 13], will be used for the implementation of the AR supported dives.

Virtual reality phase: This phase offers the users more than underwater tour, at a safe environment. Additionally, this phase offers the enhanced experience of the diver, visitor or scholar, using underwater augmented reality in a tablet and an underwater housing. In VR people around the world can access any environments using immersive technologies and internet access. Supportive narrative and multimedia tools [14] will provide interactive information about the site and objects allowing for a personalized experience, both in terms of navigation as well as in objects' queries. At the same time, emphasis will be given towards the creation of a universal standard for storytelling presentation [15]. End-users will be in position to interfere/adjust the excavation discovery story, according to their liking.

Serious games in platforms: All the knowledge acquired through this project will lead to the creation of serious games in platforms [16, 17]; actual and high detailed environments will be presented, allowing the gamers to fully explore and interact with them. The main focus will be on the two imperative aspects of the serious games: storytelling and interaction; both of which are essential in engaging the users and inspiring further intrinsic learning.

Additionally, the knowledge base will cover, under a unified framework, a variety of underwater CH sites of different properties and characteristics. Holistic records enable rich and generic characterization of the aforementioned cultural heritage elements into well-defined and structured components and machine-readable formats that allow the utilization of multi-domain information in an automated way. This holistic knowledge is built upon the CIDOC/CRM protocol and it extends the standard to include historic documentation, geometric survey, material survey, as well as critical environmental parameters. Furthermore, the project will extent BIM protocol, which is a process involving the generation and management of digital representations of physical and functional characteristics of places and objects, in order to describe and manage knowledge about underwater sites and CH assets.

Finally, diagnostic schemes for site formation analysis will be bullied by incorporating (i) underwater changes profiling, (ii) non-invasive/non-destructive analysis methods while (iii) documenting the sensor acquired spatio-temporal data and (iv) supporting data aggregation strategies. Protocols developed in past EU projects will form the basis for the project protocols and will be adapted according to specifications.

3   Methodology

3.1   IMARECULTURE Methodology Steps

Figure 1 is presenting the methodology steps adopted for this project. The project starts with the project scenario and use case definition. The cultural heritage items of the three involved underwater cultural sites will be selected in a way that covers all iMARECULTURE challenges. Then, an iterative process is adopted to specify a concrete architecture that can fulfil all user requirements and pilot sites demands. The design is performed at two cycles. The first gives the first form of the algorithms needed to be applied.

1 • Scenarios, Cultural Analysis & Requirements

2 • Initial Architecture design

3 • Definition IRP issues

4 • Launch of the first set of algorithms

5 • The Final i-MareCulture Architecture

6 • Launch of the second set of algorithms

7 • First integrated and validated prototype

8 • Launch of the final set of algorithms

9 • Pilot Setup design and evaluation

10 • Final integrated and validated prototype

11 • Pilot Execution

12 • User acceptance

Fig. 1. The i-MareCulture methodology steps

Additionally, are specified and defined the IPR issues involved in the project. Then the first set of algorithms is launched and the updated architecture takes into account results from the previews step. Subsequently the second set of algorithms is launched. At the next step the first integrated and validated is created: All the aforementioned research components are integrated to launch the first initial prototype.

Then we launch the final set of algorithms and we design the pilots and the evaluation frameworks used for objectively assess the performance and acceptance of the architecture. Finally, the final iMARECULTURE platform will be assessed by different types of users.

3.2 Description of "Virtual Sites"

The project exploits 3 different "Virtual Sites" (Fig. 2) (existing sites for virtual and augmented reality applications) in order to implement its multidisciplinary approach and accomplish the described objectives. The proposed sites are representative of different kind of Underwater Cultural Heritage, of different states of environmental and geomorphologic conditions (i.e. water depth) and of different periods, in order to present the users a wide range of the common European maritime culture. Consequently, our selection of 3 virtual sites includes: (1) Mazotos shipwreck site, Cyprus; (2) Xlendi shipwreck site, Malta and (3) Baiae underwater archaeological park, Italy. These cover the Mediterranean basin from center to east. We have also taken care that these sites cover a wide chronological span from 700BC to 400AD.

(a)   (b)   (c)

Fig. 2. (a) The main concentration of Mazotos shipwreck site (photo: MARELab, University of Cyprus), (b) Amphorae laying on the seabed at the Xlendi wreck (Photo: The University of Malta/COMEX/CNRS, (c) The Nymphaeum of Punta Epitaffio

3.3   Description of Demonstration Sites

Thalassa Museum: Thalassa Municipal Museum was opened in August 2005, and it is directed by the Pierides Foundation, in association with the Hellenic Institute for the Preservation of Nautical Tradition and the Tornaritis-Pierides Marine Life Foundation. The Museum is located at the centre of Agia Napa in Cyprus and it has the sea as a subject-matter. It is the first museum of its kind across the Mediterranean region with main principle to present to the audiences, the local and foreign visitors, the impact and the significance of the sea upon the history of the island.

The main exhibit at the fourth level and of the museum itself is the 'Kyrenia II' vessel (Fig. 3). A life size exact replica of the ancient ship of Kyrenia of the Classical period (400 B.C.), which was built in 1985 for scientific experimental purposes by the Hellenic Institute for the Preservation of Nautical Tradition of Athens. At the same level the visitor walks on a glass floor where a reconstruction of the old shipwreck is displayed.

Fig. 3. The life size exact replica of the ancient ship of Kyrenia, the reconstruction of the old shipwreck

4   Specific Innovations

The project connects education, research and industry by supporting and boosting innovative enterprise to develop their technological breakthroughs into viable products in
the area of Virtual Museums and Digital Heritage, with real commercial potential.
Furthermore, based on the scope and specific aims of the project, significant research
will be conducted in

- Developing the outline and short population of a 3D Library as tools for Maritime
  Archaeology using ontological schemes
- Digitization of naval engineering models and shipbuilding content
- Geospatial analysis of naval routes among main ancient commerce centers
- Multimedia storytelling and interaction
- Underwater Augmented Reality Interfaces
- Hybrid underwater tracking solution based on acoustic sensors and computer vision
- Virtual Reality Interfaces on VR glasses, VR caves and holographic screens
- Serious games through social platforms

The tools will be validated and tested across real-world application scenarios and
cases and under a number of different participants. This way, we will prove the innovation potential of our platform over diverse and challenging environments. The serious
games platform, the AR/VR interfaces will be assessed in real cases and will include
scenarios coming from maritime archaeology research so as to achieve a great mixture
between entertainment, informal educational, and underwater/maritime CH understanding. The project supports concrete plans and exploitation activities at certain times
to further improve innovation potential.

5   Conclusions

The project iMARECULTURE combines different research disciplines, namely experts
in 3D acquisition, Virtual and Augmented reality, serious games developers, geo-statis-
tics and GIS, archaeologists, story tellers, along with technology of underwater tablets,
holographic screens, in underwater sites and museums into one group. This way it will
accomplish existing technology to create breakthrough applications and digital experiences in the area of Virtual Museums in order to empower different types of users to
engage with European underwater cultural heritage digital resources by exploiting re-
use and re-purposing of existing data.

References

1. Demesticha, S.: The 4th-Century-BC Mazotos Shipwreck, Cyprus: a preliminary report. Intl.
   J. Naut. Archaeol. **40**(1), 39–59 (2011)
2. Drap, P., Merad, D., Hijazi, B., Gaoua, L., Nawaf, M.M., Saccone, M., Chemisky, B.,
   Seinturier, J., Sourisseau, J.-C., Gambin, T.: Underwater photogrammetry and object
   modeling: a case study of Xlendi Wreck in Malta. Sensors-Basel **15**, 30351–30384 (2015)

3. Azzopardi, E.: The shipwrecks of Xlendi Bay, Gozo, Malta. Intl. J. Naut. Archaeol. **42**, 286–295 (2013). doi:10.1111/1095-9270.12020
4. Liarokapis, F.: An augmented reality interface for visualizing and interacting with virtual content. Virtual Reality **11**(1), 23–43 (2007). Springer
5. Poullis, C.: A framework for automatic modeling from pointcloud data. IEEE Trans. Pattern Anal. Mach. Intell. **35**(11), 2563–2575 (2013)
6. Demesticha, S., Skarlatos, D., Neophytou, A.: The 4th-century BC shipwreck at Mazotos, Cyprus: new techniques and methodologies in the 3D mapping of shipwreck excavations. J. Field Archaeol. **39**(2), 134–150 (2014)
7. Georgopoulos, A., Agrafiotis, P.: Documentation of a submerged monument using improved two media techniques. In: 2012 18th International Conference on Virtual Systems and Multimedia (VSMM), pp. 173–180. IEEE (2012)
8. Balletti, C., Beltrame, C., Costa, E., Guerra, F., Vernier, P.: 3D reconstruction of marble shipwreck cargoes based on underwater multi-image photogrammetry. Digit. Appl. Archaeol. Cult. Heritage **3**(1), 1–8 (2016)
9. McCarthy, J., Benjamin, J.: Multi-image photogrammetry for underwater archaeological site recording: an accessible, diver-based approach. J. Marit. Archaeol. **9**(1), 95–114 (2014)
10. Castro, F., Gomes-Dias, D.: Moulds, Graminhos and Ribbands: a pilot study of the construction of saveiros in Valença and the Baía de Todos os Santos area. Brazil. Intl. J. Naut. Archaeol. **44**(2), 410–422 (2015)
11. Leidwanger, J.: Modeling distance with time in ancient Mediterranean seafaring: a GIS application for the interpretation of maritime connectivity. J. Archaeol. Sci. **40**, 3302–3308 (2013)
12. Bruno, F., Lagudi, A., Gallo, A., Muzzupappa, M., Davidde, B.P., Passaro, S.: 3D documentation of archaeological remains in the underwater Park of Baiae. Intl. Arch. Photogramm. Remote Sens. Spatial Inf. Sci. - ISPRS Arch. **40**(5W5), 41–46 (2015)
13. Petriaggi, B.D., de Ayala, G.G.: Laser scanner reliefs of selected archaeological structures in the submerged Baiae (Naples). Intl. Arch. Photogramm. Remote Sens. Spatial Inf. Sci. **5**, 79–83 (2015). doi:10.5194/isprsarchives-XL-5-W5-79-2015
14. Balogh, T., Forgacs, T., Agocs, T., Bouvier, E., Bettio, F., Gobbetti, E., Zanetti, G.: A large scale interactive holographic display. In: IEEE VR2006 Conference, Virginia, USA (2006)
15. Rizvic, S., Skalonjic, I.: Reconstructing cultural heritage objects from storytelling - virtual presentation of Sultan Murat's Fortress in Sjenica. In: Proceedings of 2nd International Congress on Digital Heritage, vol. 2, ISBN:978-1-5090-0047-0 (2015)
16. Anderson, E.F., McLoughlin, L., Liarokapis, F., Peters, C., Petridis, P., de Freitas, S.: Developing serious games for cultural heritage: a state-of-the-art review. Virtual Reality **14**(4), 255–275 (2010). Springer
17. Mortara, M., Catalano, C.E., Bellotti, F., Fiucci, G., Houry-Panchetti, M., Petridis, P.: Learning cultural heritage by serious games. J. Cult. Heritage **15**(3), 318–325 (2014)

Immersivity and Playability Evaluation of a Game Experience in Cultural Heritage

Roberto Andreoli, Angela Corolla, Armando Faggiano, Delfina Malandrino[✉],
Donato Pirozzi, Mirta Ranaldi, Gianluca Santangelo, and Vittorio Scarano

Department of Computer Science, University of Salerno,
Via Giovanni Paolo II, 132, 84084 Fisciano, SA, Italy
angelacorolla@gmail.com, armando.faggiano@gmail.com,
ranaldi.mirta@gmail.com, giansant77@gmail.com,
{dmalandrino,dpirozzi,vitsca}@unisa.it

Abstract. The introduction in the market of head-mounted displays (HDMs), originally used for gaming, opens the door to a wide set of application fields that could benefit of characteristics, such as immersivity, presence as well as a high degree of realism. In the field of Cultural Heritage, an immersive virtual experience can enhance playfulness and involvement in the fruition of a cultural experience, by determining a more efficient knowledge absorption and retention of the learnt content.

In this work we introduce a prototype of a Serious Game in Cultural Heritage, named *HippocraticaCivitasGame*, designed and implemented to foster playfulness and learning effectiveness. We also performed an evaluation study to assess users' perceived immersivity and playability, as well as the effectiveness when analyzing the acquired knowledge about the archaeological site structure and the proposed learning goal.

Keywords: Virtual reality in cultural heritage · Serious game technologies · Evaluation

1 Introduction

Immersive Virtual Reality (VR) has been widely used in several domains ranging from entertainment and gaming to education and training (military, aerospace and defense, health, and so on), from heritage and archeology to architectural design, from therapy to retail and interactive media [1,3,8].

According to a new forecast from market research firm Gartner [10], wearable electronic device sales will increase 18.4 % year over year to hit 322.7 million shipments in 2017 ($6.31 million coming from head-mounted displays, with a percentage increase of 341 % from 2016 to 2017). The demand for virtual reality devices will grow rapidly in the coming years owing to the wide availability of technologically advanced virtual reality devices, their increased computational power and reduced costs, and their increasing utility in a variety of applications. Indeed, some of the big technology giants have entered the virtual reality market. Facebook, Inc. acquired *Oculus VR*, in March 2014 for approximately $2

M. Ioannides et al. (Eds.): EuroMed 2016, Part I, LNCS 10058, pp. 814–824, 2016.
DOI: 10.1007/978-3-319-48496-9_65

billion. Sony, HTC and Microsoft Corporations released their virtual displays, that is the *PlayStation VR* headset, the *HTC Vive* and the *Microsoft HoloLens* devices, respectively. The aim for all is the same: *"to further extend virtual reality into verticals beyond gaming, such as communications, media, entertainment, education and other areas"*.

Moreover, the 2016 Horizon Report from the New Media Consortium [12] predicted that immersive virtual reality technology is likely to have a large impact on teaching and learning in higher education worldwide in the next years. The compelling aspect of virtual reality is its ability to transport learners into environments and situations that they otherwise may never have access to, being able *to be* in the present, but *projected* in the past. Serious Games (SGs) [23], which are focused on the learning aspect of games, combined with immersive technologies are able to improve players' experience, therefore contributing to a more effective knowledge acquisition and retention [7].

The objective of this work is to present *HippocraticaCivitasGame*, a prototype of a Serious Game in Cultural Heritage, designed and developed to foster the understanding and the learning of an archaeological site, set at *Palazzo Fruscione-San Pietro a Corte* in Salerno, and of its historical elements in effective and enjoyable way. We also performed an evaluation study to assess effectiveness in terms of knowledge acquisition of a specific learning goal, the game playability, and finally users' appreciation and acceptance of the developed SG.

2   Related Work

Several relevant works are available in literature, including works addressing immersivity and effectiveness of knowledge acquisition and retention. Immersion, in its several acceptations, has been studied in different works [18,20]. Moreover, some other works addressed other interesting game characteristics, such as, perceived presence and usability [11,14].

Park et al. [21] designed a system mediated by HMD technology to experience an immersive tour in Cultural Heritage. Immersiveness was positively rated by players when using virtual devices compared to the traditional tour method.

About the correlation among immersivity, emotions and knowledge retention, Chittaro et al. [7] considered the use of a visor for a SG in aviation safety, allowing players experiencing an emergency evacuation on an aircraft compared with the traditional safety card. Authors observed that the immersive game increases the knowledge retention as well as the user engagement.

Bellotti et al. [2] proposed a model abstracting the SandBox SG, which offers a generalization of task-based learning theory. The authors developed a SG in CH field, named *Travel in Europe*, assessing the knowledge acquisition and concluding that SGs represent a significant opportunity for learning.

A well-known and crucial limit to mention is the cybersickness effect caused by virtual reality devices during their usage. Specifically, cybersickness is caused by a disagreement between visually perceived movement and the vestibular system's sense of movement.

Various studies indicate it can affect 50 % to 80 % of people, depending on the fidelity of the digital content and how it is presented [6]. Works in this field state that the problem can often be improved with habituation [16] or by intervening on the field of view of used displays [5]. Lee et al. [17] investigated the *cross-dimensional virtual reality* coupling the Leap Motion for the hand tracking with the Oculus Rift. As result, the mixed technology with the seated position, significantly reduced nausea.

3   A Serious Game for CH

In this section we present the prototype of our immersive Serious Game, named *HippocraticaCivitasGame*(a screenshot is shown in Fig. 1). First, we introduce the game design, and then we discuss about some technical details of the game implementation.

3.1   Game Design

In the old town of Salerno, there is the historical structure of *S. Pietro a Corte-Palazzo Fruscione*. It is an archaeological site that shows how the city developed since Roman times until nowadays. The most important elements are the remains of the palace of the Longobard Prince Arechis II, which constitutes a rare preserved example of civil architecture of the eighth century A.D. [22]. The site was investigated through excavations from 1988 to 1990, and recently in 2011 and 2012. The archaeologists unearthed the remains of Roman buildings interpreted as Thermae of I-II century A.D. to above which was erected the Arechis's palace with a richly decorated chapel. In the Norman period, just to the north, was built another mansion, which was expanded under the Angevin kings and then it was transformed to the present day.

Fig. 1. *HippocraticaCivitasGame* snapshot of the male *frigidarium.*

In order to design the game, we identified the game macro learning goal, which is the understanding of archaeological site pluri-stratification. Indeed, it

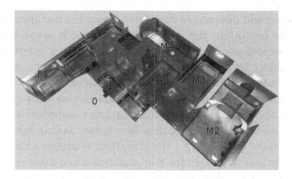

Fig. 2. Thermae level map. Atrium, vestibule and room with cabinet (0-1-2); female *apodyterium* (F1), *frigidarium* (F2), *tepidarium* (F3), *caldarium* (F4); male *apody-terium* (M1), *frigidarium* (M2), *tepidarium* (M3), *caldarium* (M4); *praefurnium* (P).

has different historical periods, the Roman, Longobard, Norman and Angevin periods, with different architectural styles as well as a variety of archaeological and historical elements. When playing, users through the posed challenges can experience, visit and hopefully grasp such a variety. In particular, the game is divided in three levels, one for each historical period. Micro learning goals are single challenges to solve during the game to learn specific environment, historical or archaeological elements. All the micro learning goals together contribute to the whole archaeological site understanding.

In order to evaluate game immersivity, we focused on the first level which corresponds to the Roman Thermae. Therefore, the game starts in the vestibule of the the Virtual Thermae environment (Fig. 2, room 1). The environment, is divided into female and male parts; each part is composed of four rooms: the changing room (*apodyterium*), the cold room (*frigidarium*), temperate room (*tepidarium*) and hot room (*calidarium*). This level, firstly, aims to show how thermal environments were structured. Thus, as narrative pretext we introduced the challenge to bring an object from one place to another. This challenge, a well-known game design pattern [4], can be exploited to foster the visit of the places in a map. The object to find was the *strigil* (i.e., a tool for body cleansing) placed within a cabinet (Fig. 2, room 2) and to move in one of the two *apodyterium*.

3.2 Game Implementation

The *HippocraticaCivitasGame* is based on Unity, a cross-platform game engine that offers many features and extensions to develop games. In addition to the game engine features, we designed a collection of reusable building blocks to facilitate the future extensions. The main building blocks are: *Controller Manager*, *Game Logic*, *Game State*, *Storage*, and *Display Manager*.

Players interact with our Serious Game using the Oculus Rift (DK2) and the gamepad XBOX 360 controller devices. Inputs from those devices are forwarded to the *Controller Manager*, which is responsible for their processing, and for generating a command directed to the *Game Logic*. For instance, when the player presses a specific button on the gamepad, this input is associated to an avatar action; the same action can be triggered by a different input device, such as the Microsoft Kinect by envisioning a specific gesture. Therefore, the *Controller Manager* is an interface between the input devices and the *Game Logic*. Of course, the action may change the world and the avatar state (e.g., rotating it).

The *Game Logic* coordinates the different game components and defines the game rules. It handles the starting of a new game, avatar initial position, and initialisation of game objects (e.g., the strigil). It contains a timer to keep track of the game duration, that lasts for five minutes; when time expired the avatar is blocked and the data structure that contains avatar's statistics (e.g., movements on the map) are saved in a file; for performance reasons, this operation is performed, only once, at the end of the game.

The *Game State* contains the entire game status in terms of avatar state and world state. It stores, every second, the avatar position, rotation and time in the *Storage*; it also keeps track of objects' gathering and positioning, e.g., the strigil object in our Serious Game. Finally, the main goal of the *Display Manager* is to render the game; it shows textual and image information during the immersive experience. Finally, a demo of *HyppocraticaCivitasGame*, with a three-minutes visit in *Palazzo Fruscione-San Pietro a Corte*, is available online[1].

4   Evaluation

In this section we first describe the methodology that we employed for our evaluation study, defined according to the standard HCI methodology [13], afterwards we discuss the results obtained when a group of 72 people was involved in testing our Serious Game.

4.1   Methodology

Our study took place in a large, dedicated space in a research laboratory at the University of Salerno. The workstation used for rendering the environment was equipped with an i7-4770K 8-CPU, a Nvidia GTX770 Graphics card, and 16 GB of main memory. The input device used was a wireless Microsoft XBOX 360 Controller. The virtual reality headset supported was based on the Oculus Rift.

The study envisioned three different phases in which we carried out: (a) a Preliminary Survey (b) a Testing Phase and (c) a Summary Survey, as defined and implemented in other contexts [9,19].

As first step, participants filled out a preliminary survey questionnaire about their demographics (i.e., gender, age, education level), video gaming experience, and eventual sensitivity to the kinetosis or motion sickness problem, that is the disagreement that exists between visually perceived movement and the vestibular system's sense of movement. Thereafter, participants were briefly informed about

---

[1] http://www.di.unisa.it/~delmal/research/usability/Euromed2016/Demo/.

the task to perform. Specifically, the challenge for the players is to find the *strigil* in the game environment and place it in one of the two *apodyterium*, as described in Sect. 3.1. They had a fixed amount of time to complete the task (i.e., 5 min). When this time expired, interested participants were anyway allowed to continue the virtual experience. At the end of the testing phase we asked users to fill in a questionnaire, adapted from [24], aiming at assess the perceived degree of presence, control and motivation, and playability characteristics. Performance data were collected during the gaming experience. Specifically, we logged, for each participant, the time when she started the experience, the time when she found the strigil, the time when it was arranged in the requested place, and finally, the time when the experience finished. In the last phase we asked users to fill in a summary survey aiming at assess the effectiveness of the knowledge acquisition with regard to the performed task. We also gathered users' perceptions about the usefulness of the serious game for educational purposes and their propensity to recommend the game to a friend.

To analyze the opinions of participants in terms of immersion and their overall subjective experience we used the standard Presence Questionnaire (PQ) [24]. It measures in what degree users feel as they are actually part of the experienced environment. From this questionnaire we extracted questions that allow to obtain sub-scores in terms of three factors: realism (RF), control factor (CF), and involvement (INV). We also studied cybersickness, the digital version of the motion sickness, by administering a questionnaire adapted from [15]. All questionnaires, translated into Italian, are available online[2], while the whole evaluation study lasted approximately 40 min.

Subjects were students, teachers, and employers at several departments of the University of Salerno. They were recruited through flyers and word of mouth advertising. Their participation was voluntary and anonymous. They were also informed that they could stop at any time during the evaluation process. For data analysis, non-parametric tests (Kruskal-Wallis and Mann-Whitney) were applied to study differences between groups. The Shapiro-Wilk goodness-of-fit test. Finally, questionnaire responses were analyzed using SPSS.

4.2 Results

A total of 72 participants were recruited from the general campus population (49 % Human field study, 51 % Scientific field study). In detail, the education level included 25 % with bachelor degree, 69 % with a master degree, and 6 % with a PhD. The sample was mostly male (64 % male, 36 % female) with a mean age of 27 (SD = 8). 67 % of participants reported intermediate or higher experience with videogames, 21 % stated to be expert, while only 12 % reported a low experience in that field. 35 % reported to be prone to motion sickness (we did not find any statistical difference with regard to the gender factor). Finally, the entire sample had no confidence with the Oculus Rift device.

---

[2] http://www.di.unisa.it/~delmal/research/usability/Euromed2016/Questionnaires. pdf.

Results of the Testing phase showed that 80 % of participants was able to find the strigil, but only 64 % was able to put it in the right place. On average, it took about 2.5 min to find the strigil, and about 63 seconds to put back it in the right place. However, almost all participants (96 %) were able to successfully respond to the question about the definition of the strigil (among three different provided answers). This result suggests that participants paid attention to the messages conveyed during the experience, although they stated to be very involved in the game. The overall result indicated a positive learning outcome for the knowledge question posed.

Results about the SG quality characteristics are shown in Fig. 3(a) and Table 1. Specifically, in Fig. 3(a) we report the results of users' perceptions about playability, the control they had within the game, and their motivation. Participants enjoyed the experience (M = 6.0, SD = 1.0). They also rated positively the aesthetics of the Serious Game (M = 5.9, SD = 1.3). We did not find any statistical differences with regard to these metrics when considering the gender factor. About the *Control* factor, our sample agreed with how easy was to use the Oculus (*"I found the field of view rotation using Oculus Rift - head movement - very easy to perform"*, M = 6.1, SD = 1.4) and expressed high satisfaction in terms of the sensitivity of the controller (*"The game controller sensitivity in the virtual experience was adequate"*, M = 6.0, SD = 1.1). Similarly, the *Motivation* factor was positively rated by our sample (M = 6.5, SD = 0.7).

As shown in Table 1, the Presence questionnaire is aggregated in four factors, all positively rated. Participants found out responsive the overall system (M = 6.5, SD = 0.8), and they perceived very natural the interactions within the game (M = 6.0, SD = 1.0). What is really remarkable is that, despite participants had few time to play, they rated very positively their involvement as well as their increased ability at the end of the experience (M = 5.6, SD = 1.5), highlighting the easiness of the controls that we designed for the game. The *Realism Factor* was highly positively rated, as also derived by informal suggestions at the end of the evaluation process. 35 % of participants, in fact, provided as positive aspect of the overall experience, the quality of the rendering and how much "real" the virtual experience was perceived. Finally, we did not find any statistical differences with regard to these metrics when considering the gender factor. Instead, we found out a significant correlation among all the analyzed subscales.

Results about cybersickness, showed that dizziness was the symptom most felt by the participants at the study (44 %). Nausea was the second most felt symptom, with the highest degree of severity (7 % felt the nausea with a sever level). Only 20 % of participants did not suffered of any type of problem. Moreover, when comparing kinetosis results (question posed in the Preliminary survey) with cybersickness results (question posed in the Summary Survey) we found out that 43 %, out of 65 % who reported do not suffer of any motion sickness problem, experienced cybersickness during the immersive experience. We did not find differences when analyzing cybersickness in terms of demographic factor.

As further analysis, we classified participants in three groups, namely, *"Young"* (with the age range 19–25), *"Young Adults"* (with the age range 26–31),

Table 1. Presence and Immersion. 7-Point Likert scale.

ID	Question	Factor	Mean	SD
1	How responsive was the environment to actions that you initiated (or performed?)	CF	6.5	0.8
2	How natural did your interactions with the environment seem?	CF	6.0	1.0
3	How much did your experiences in the virtual environment seem consistent with your real-world experiences?	RF	5.6	1.1
4	How involved were you in the virtual environment experience?	INV	6.3	1.0
5	How proficient in moving and interacting with the virtual environment did you feel at the end of the experience?	CF	5.6	1.5
6	Were you involved in the experimental task to the extent that you lost track of time?	INV	5.6	0.5

and "*Adults*" (with the age range 31–60). Our *Adults* users were also the less familiar with video games and immersive systems (4 experts in the older group against 11 in the young one). Interestingly, we found out a correlation between age and reported sense of general discomforts due to cybersickness. We also found out a correlation between the feeling of discomforts due to cybersickness and the experience of the users with virtual immersive environments. Oculus Rift devices have not completely penetrated the consumer market, but as discussed in Sect. 1, they will become more and more popular in the next few years. As a consequence, users will start to get used to them, and therefore, cybersickness

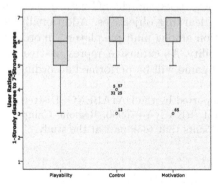

(a) Playability, control & motivation.

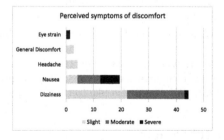

(b) Data about perceived cybersickness, organized according to 3 severity levels.

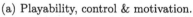

Fig. 3. Results of the presence and simulator sickness questionnaires.

could be reduced through training and established experience. However, a longitudinal study, with a large and diversified sample of participants, is needed to study these effects. Finally, we did not find any statistical differences among the three groups of users in terms of playability, control and motivation factors.

Results of the Summary survey showed that the use of games for Cultural Heritage was highly accepted by participants. Specifically, on average, both the usefulness of the idea of using the SG for learning ($M = 6.5$, $SD = 0.8$), and the propensity to recommend to other the experience ($M = 6.7$, $SD = 0.6$) were positively rated.

5   Conclusion and Future Work

This paper proposed *HippocraticaCivitasGame*, a Serious Game prototype designed and developed to foster learning and understanding of the Roman Thermae in the *Palazzo Fruscione-San Pietro a Corte*, in Salerno. The performed evaluation study showed that our SG was able to convey important information about the structure of the site and the micro learning goal analyzed. Indeed, 96 % of participants successfully responded to the question about the definition of the strigil, among the three different provided answers.

Results about presence and immersion revealed that participants enjoyed the experience and they also rated positively the aesthetics of the whole Serious Game. 35 % of participants provided as positive aspect of the overall experience, the quality of the rendered environment, and how much real the virtual experience was perceived. Moreover, despite they had few time to play, they rated very positively their involvement as well as their increased ability at the end of the experience, highlighting the easiness of the controls that we designed for the game. Furthermore, the idea of using our SG for learning was highly accepted by participants. Specifically, on average, both usefulness and the propensity to recommend to other the experience were positively rated.

Finally, we are currently working on how to extend the SG with other game levels and with the corresponding micro learning objectives. Additionally, we are enhancing the SG to allow collaboration among multiple players, in order to further guarantee involvement and playability. An extensive, representative, and longitudinal evaluation study of the final game will be performed accordingly.

Acknowledgments. This research was supported by the DATABENC (Distretto ad Alta Tecnologia per i Beni Culturali) project, REA NA-876990, Regione Campania, Italy. We would also like to thank all participants that took part at the study.

References

1. Adding a level of reality to online shopping. http://www.starthub.org/news/adding-level-reality-online-shopping. Accessed 10 Jun 2016
2. Bellotti, F., Berta, R., De Gloria, A., D'ursi, A., Fiore, V.: A serious game model for cultural heritage. J. Comput. Cult. Heritage (JOCCH) 5(4), 17 (2012)

3. Bellotti, F., Berta, R., Gloria, A.D., Panizza, G., Primavera, L.: Designing cultural heritage contents for serious virtual worlds. In: International Conference on Virtual Systems and Multimedia, pp. 227–231 (2009)
4. Bjork, S., Holopainen, J.: Patterns in game design (2004)
5. Carnegie, K., Rhee, T.: Reducing visual discomfort with hmds using dynamic depth of field. IEEE Comput. Graph. Appl. **35**(5), 34–41 (2015)
6. Chang, C.H., Pan, W.W., Tseng, L.Y., Stoffregen, T.A.: Postural activity and motion sickness during video game play in children and adults. Exp. Brain Res. **217**(2), 299–309 (2012)
7. Chittaro, L., Buttussi, F.: Assessing knowledge retention of an immersive serious game vs. a traditional education method in aviation safety. IEEE Trans. Vis. Comput. Graph. **21**(4), 529–538 (2015)
8. Cukor, J., Gerardi, M., Alley, S., Reist, C., Roy, M., Rothbaum, O.B., Difede, J., Rizzo, A.: Virtual reality exposure therapy for combat-related PTSD. In: Ritchie, E.C. (ed.) Posttraumatic Stress Disorder and Related Diseases in Combat Veterans, pp. 69–83. Springer International Publishing, Switzerland (2015)
9. Fish, A., Gargiulo, C., Malandrino, D., Pirozzi, D., Scarano, V.: Visual exploration system in an industrial context. IEEE Trans. Ind. Inf. **12**(2), 567–575 (2016)
10. Gartner: Worldwide Wearable Devices Sales Forecast (2016). http://www.gartner.com/newsroom/id/3198018. Accessed 13 Jun 2016
11. Hupont, I., Gracia, J., Sanagustín, L., Gracia, M.A.: How do new visual immersive systems influence gaming QoE? a use case of serious gaming with Oculus Rift. In: International Workshop on Quality of Multimedia Experience, pp. 1–6 (2015)
12. Johnson, L., Adams Becker, S., Cummins, M., Estrada, V., Freeman, A., Hall, C.: NMC Horizon Report: 2016 Higher Education Edition (2016)
13. Jonathan, L., Feng, J.H., Hochheiser, H.: Research Methods in Human-Computer Interaction. Wiley, Hoboken (2010)
14. Kalawsky, R.S.: The validity of presence as a reliable human performance metric in immersive environments. In: proceedings of the Presence Workshop 2000 (2000)
15. Kennedy, R.S., Lane, N.E., Berbaum, K.S., Lilienthal, M.G.: Simulator sickness questionnaire: an enhanced method for quantifying simulator sickness. Int. J. Aviat. Psychol. **3**(3), 203–220 (1993)
16. Kennedy, R.S., Stanney, K.M., Dunlap, W.P.: Duration and exposure to virtual environments: sickness curves during and across sessions. Presence Teleoper. Virtual Environ. **9**(5), 463–472 (2000)
17. Lee, P.W., Wang, H.Y., Tung, Y.C., Lin, J.W., Valstar, A.: TranSection: hand-based interaction for playing a game within a virtual reality game. In: Proceedings of the 33rd Annual ACM Conference Extended Abstracts on Human Factors in Computing Systems, CHI EA 2015, pp. 73–76 (2015)
18. Lugrin, J.L., Cavazza, M., Charles, F., Le Renard, M., Freeman, J., Lessiter, J.: Immersive FPS games: user experience and performance. In: ImmersiveMe 2013, pp. 7–12 (2013)
19. Malandrino, D., Scarano, V., Spinelli, R.: How increased awareness can impact attitudes and behaviors toward online privacy protection. In: International Conference on Social Computing, SocialCom 2013, pp. 57–62 (2013)
20. McMahan, R.P., Bowman, D.A., Zielinski, D.J., Brady, R.B.: Evaluating display fidelity and interaction fidelity in a virtual reality game. IEEE Trans. Vis. Comput. Graph. **18**(4), 626–633 (2012)
21. Park, D., Nam, T.J., Shi, C.K.: Designing an immersive tour experience system for cultural tour sites. In: CHI 2006 Extended Abstracts on Human Factors in Computing Systems, pp. 1193–1198 (2006)

22. Peduto, P., Fiorillo, R., Corolla, A.: Salerno. Una sede ducale della Langobardia meridionale. Spoleto: CISAM (2013)
23. Susi, T., Johannesson, M., Backlund, P.: Serious games: an overview (2007)
24. Witmer, B.G., Singer, M.J.: Measuring presence in virtual environments: a presence questionnaire. Presence Teleoper. Virtual Environ. **7**(3), 225–240 (1998)

Tirolcraft: The Quest of Children to Playing the Role of Planners at a Heritage Protected Town

Bruno Amaral de Andrade$^{(\boxtimes)}$, Ítalo Sousa de Sena,
and Ana Clara Mourão Moura

Geoprocessing Laboratory, School of Architecture,
Federal University of Minas Gerais, Belo Horizonte, Brazil
{deandradebruno,italosena,anaclara}@ufmg.br

Abstract. The main goal of the article is to explore the potential of Minecraft as a platform to engage children into participatory planning. The game enables the players to easily design using blocks to build structures like houses, playgrounds, lakes, vegetation, agriculture, etc. The area of study is a town called Tirol, a heritage protected settlement built by austrian immigrants in the municipality of Santa Leopoldina, State of Espírito Santo, Brazil. This article advances on the state of the art by articulating the potential of Minecraft as a game-based learning into urban participatory planning with children as protagonists actors of rethinking the city. Also, the game enables children to design appropriating themselves on the concept of "child-friendly city" and discussing their design ideas with each other collaboratively. The results indicate that children can learn and work on a playful way to collaborate on urban planning processes, and widens open new researches possibilities.

1 Geogaming: Serious Games & Urban Planning

The development and application of Serious Games in Urban Planning are on its first steps, but have been through an exponential growth as means to help citizen enhance competences like playing the role of designers of their city. The central reference on the hybrid theme "Serious Games & Urban Planning" is Alenka Poplin[1], whose researches and publications helped and guided us develop our own research structure, like the new concept of *Geogames* (Vemuri et al. 2014).

Hence, this article aims to explore the potential of Minecraft as a serious gaming platform to acquire knowledge to engage civic participation on redesigning the place, especially giving the children a leading role. The participatory design was conducted through an intuitive psychogeographic input of non-expert users, and as a digital instrument we used an existing game to get straight to the planning phase.

---

[1] Assistant Professor, Department of Community and Regional Planning, College of Design, Iowa State University. Research interests: GeoGames for urban planning & Serious games for civic engagement, User experience with interactive maps & GeoVisualization.

© Springer International Publishing AG 2016
M. Ioannides et al. (Eds.): EuroMed 2016, Part I, LNCS 10058, pp. 825–835, 2016.
DOI: 10.1007/978-3-319-48496-9_66

With the support of free and open source software *World Painter*[2] and *MicroDEM*[3] using real world data of the study area to analyze and visualize a territory model to export to Minecraft. Then, in Minecraft there was an opportunity to provide learning processes and rapid meaningful feedback. This experience was an opportunity to come up with important analyzes in co-creating personalized and pervasive games for planning.

Therefore, elects an empirical approach as a concrete-object, the town of Tirol, in Santa Leopoldina, State of Espírito Santo. First, we built a digital elevation model of the territory and then make it thematic with anthropic and landscape elements. With the modeling of a real case study on a virtual platform, seeks an empathic relationship of the children with their territory so that they feel engaged to perform specific interventions, where their range of scale reaches, for example, the home to school route, and other routes and places they visit constantly (Poli 2006).

Furthermore, this article also seeks on a broader perspective come up with relevant questions that will be pursued during the sequence of the research in geogames, such as: How could geogames better work on benefiting citizen on knowledge and awareness about the territory? Serious games as a game-based learning can really be a more attractive instrument to participatory design? What are the stories of games that best fit children's participation in urban planning? What kind of a pilot geogame be like to reach and attract more engagement and participation of social actors?

2   Serious Games and Geogames

Vemuri et al. (2014) expatiating on the differences between the concepts of games, serious games and geogames. The last one that interests us the most for this article is conceptualized as serious games focused on learning about the territory and the different ways of representing and visualizing it in a game-based environment. The authors refers by the same tolken of the concept of geogames to Ola Ahlqvist[4] and Christoph Schlieder[5], who conducts researches on geogames, extolling the movements of players involving locomotion and thereby the physical effort characteristic of any sportive activity as a missing element in interactive console games. Interestingly, Schlieder et al. (2005, p. 168) defines what is not a geogame, that is "(…) games that do not satisfy the spatio-temporal coherence constraints in which resources magically jump around the board – are not geogames".

---

[2] Available on http://www.worldpainter.net/, accessed in 20 May 2016.

[3] Available on http://www.usna.edu/Users/oceano/pguth/website/microdem/microdem.htm, accessed in 20 May 2016.

[4] AHLQVIST, Ola; SCHLIEDER, Christoph. Geogames and Geoplay Game-based Approaches to the Analysis of Geo-Information. "GeoGames – a virtual simulation workbench for teaching and learning through real-world geography". Available on http://geogame.osu.edu/, accessed in 18 May 2016.

[5] Assistant Professor of Computing in Cultural Geosciences, Head of the Geogames Team, Laboratory for Semantic Information Processing, Otto-Friedrich-University Bamberg, Germany.

Basically, the goal of geogames is to be one or a series of decision-making game-based models capable to support participatory processes in urban planning (Tóth and Poplin 2014).

3 Why Use Minecraft as a Game-Based Learning Tool?

Until August of 2016 Mojang, company that developed the game, has sold more than 24 million Minecraft (PC version), what shows the importance of this game in the world scene. This success is primarily related to the possibility of the player interact with digital world on an experience to build or destroy anything. This characteristic also make this game an endless one, leading to an infinity of possibilities. The block logic brings to the player an experience of endogenous connection to learn, when the environment drives the player to explore the territory to gather supplies from the nature and build structures like houses, castles, mines, vegetation, etc. These aspects of the game have an intrinsic potential to a game-based learning, because of the way that the player interact with the environment.

Colin Gallather organized in 2015, with others teachers, a manual that shows how Minecraft could be used in classrooms. They explain that this game develop concepts like creativity, collaboration (in multiplayer online servers), digital citizenship, fun, leadership, differentiation, engagement, independence, also others aspects of the learning process. Sean Dikkers (2015) published a book called Teachercraft, where he explains the possibilities of applying Minecraft in educational approach, exploring the usefulness of the game in the knowledge-based students' formation, but also in the approximation of the teachers with the digital environment. This potential shows that Minecraft also can be used as a tool to develop others topics by the flexibility of the game structure logic.

4 Why Tirol in Brazil to Play a Participatory Game with Children?

The reason of choosing Tirol as the study area is in the fact that the municipality of Santa Leopoldina be a territory of heritage interest, for having an architectural and urban perimeter protected by the State Council of Culture, and farms buildings of sugarcane and coffee cultures from the nineteenth century in the rural areas, such as Tirol. It is done both a justification through analysis of historic cartography mapping, referring to the territorial cycles that shaped the palimpsest of Santa Leopoldina, and the emergence and consolidation of immigrants occupying cores not Lusitanian, in particular Austrians in Tirol (Andrade 2012).

From the standpoint of the cartography analyses (Fig. 1), the black color highlights the area of the Imperial Government's project delimitation called Colony of Santa Leopoldina, and the stars in yellow demarcate and reveal the names of the countries of origin of immigrants, from top to bottom, there is *Luxemburgo, Pomerania, Tyrol, California* e *Hollanda*. In fact, the urban center of Santa Leopoldina is outside the area delimited for the colony, thus raises the hypothesis that the city center is built to give privilege to the Luso-Brazilian residents for commercial uses, while rural areas were reserved to non-Lusitanian immigrants as specified above. This hypothesis can be confirmed in the contemporaneity according to the architectural legacy and diffuse settlement in the region, related to the former colony (now splitted in various munic-ipalities, one of them still keeps the name of Santa Leopoldina), so that the immigrants cultural heritage is located mainly in rural areas, just like Tirol (Andrade 2015).

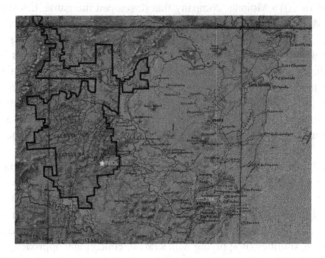

Fig. 1. Tirol's location (in yellow) in the municipality of Santa Leopoldina, State of Espírito Santo, Brazil. (Color figure online) Source: Adapted from Planta da Parte da Província Espírito-Santo, 1978 (Andrade 2015).

Data updated by the IBGE[6] (Instituto Brasileiro de Geografia e Estatística) shows that the municipality of Santa Leopoldina has an estimated population of 12,885 inhabitants, in 2015, a territorial area of 718.097 km^2, and a population density of 17.05 inhabitants/km^2. According to the IBGE 2010 census, 21.5 % of the population lives in the urban center, and 78.5 % live in the rural area (Fig. 2).

This reasoning justifies the interest of this study in the town of Tirol, based on the assumption of its notorious landscape, its singular history, its citizen, and its now-a-days problems like the rupture of cultural values and consequently a population exodus (Andrade 2015). That are, therefore, why we chose to work with the children as social actors who has the potential to be empowered to *Geodesign* (Steinitz 2015) alternative futures to solve the struggles of Tirol.

---

[6] Source http://cidades.ibge.gov.br/painel/painel.php?codmun=320450, Accessed in 11 July of 2016.

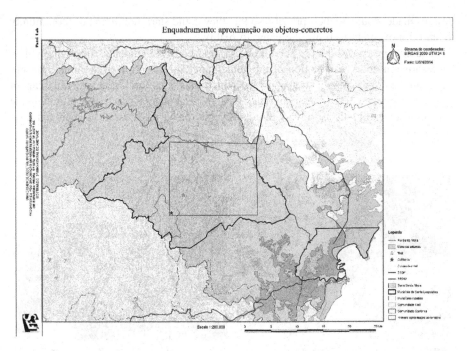

Fig. 2. Tirol's location. Source: Andrade (2015, p. 54)

5 Tirolcraft: Children's Participatory Design

The activity is developed at the Tirol School for children from pre-school until the fifth year of the fundamental school, about 04 to 11 years old. We worked with all the students, which are 30 students divided in two groups: the pre-school and the fundamental school. The methodology steps followed: (1) Presentation of the Minecraft game and its functionalities; (2) The objective of the activity: "Redesigning Tirol"; (3) One by one every student played the game an put one's own spin on it; (4) Final discussion of the projects and what could really be done in Tirol.

The step 1 of the method we designed in the game some structures using blocks, we showed how the game works and the principal functions of using it on a computer, which is different from when you play the game on a video-game console. The step 2 consisted in explaining carefully the main objective of this experiment that is Redesigning Tirol as they would like to see it become. We explained that they could relate some structures as it is presented now, or was settled historically, or they could propose something new. The step 3 allowed every student to play the game and build something ones though it could be built in Tirol to make a better place to live, always trying to show them how important it is to think and design collectively to reach a maximum consensus as it is possible. The step 4 we provoked a discussion about the results of their interventions in the place, what they really thought it could be built and how the community would have liked it. In addition, we asked which one of the designs made would be their priority, so that they could start mobilizing the community to start a movement to bring the game to reality.

The first group was the pre-school one, composed by 12 students. Surprisingly they have shown a good exploitation of the game, since the attention to the initial presentation and as long as the activity flowed. Which makes us think that we really cannot judge a younger child to reaching the goal of a geogaming activity, although the territorialist school tells us to work more with children between 9 and 12 years old (Poli 2006) (Fig. 3).

Fig. 3. Pre-school children playing Minecraft

In the meantime, of the development of the activity, the pre-school children got distracted, because of the availability only of the researcher's notebook. The five computers that the informatics laboratory has only one works but it does not have the minimum capacity to play Minecraft, and the other four are new but not working. Besides, we had to play offline, because the school does not have internet anymore, and the one they had the professors told us it had a bad speed quality (Fig. 4).

Henceforth, some of the projects that the pre-school children projected were (Fig. 5): (a) buildings with materials coming from the local environment, like wood and stone; (b) playgrounds with equipment for playing activities; (c) lakes; (d) cavern; (d) square in front of the school and the church, with lake, trees, flowers, animals, and a child playground.

Fig. 4. Children getting distracted by the fact of having only one computer to play

Fig. 5. Minecraft design made by pre-school children

The second group was the fundamental-school one, composed by 18 students. They have shown a desirable exploitation of the game, and have made some very interesting suggestions, collaboration to each other ideas and most importantly designs. They did not show any issue on non-concentration like the pre-school ones.

Henceforth, some of the projects that the fundamental school children projected were (Fig. 6): (a) new buildings like a bigger school; (b) vegetation trees, and gardens with flowers; (c) cavern; (d) a new square in front of the school and the church, with lake, trees, flowers, animals and child playground with a places for bicycle, roll-erblades, kick scooter, and skate (Fig. 7).

Fig. 6. Fundamental-school children playing Minecraft

6   Final Considerations and Further Research Steps

First of all, it is incredible how children can quickly learn a game, by its inherent motivational aspect of being fun, other than being an innovative method of teaching at school, the fact that their own territory is modeled urging an affective reaction concerning the place as it matches their own mental maps, and the empowerment aspect of decision about future scenarios for their town.

Notwithstanding, some of the ideas of the Tirolcraft experiment remained only on the discourse, like the will to design paved streets and sidewalks, a big square to reunite the community, a shopping mall, and an amusement park. Speaking of that, in Tirol

Fig. 7. Minecraft design made by fundamental-school children

there are almost no pavements, most of it are still on dirt roads with no regular maintenance. Which could be explained that as much as they would take the game seriously on a specific purpose, the fun aspect, the innovation activity at the school, and the fact that most of them never played Minecraft were distracting for them.

On a broader perspective, the development and application of this methodology, technology and model aims to favor cultural landscape maintenance, both by identifying heritage values and developing civic consciousness. This first step of the approach is to strengthen the involvement of the children, to listen and hear them, as a way to approximate to the whole community. Then it becomes possible to the next step on a game-based learning approach to rebuild digitally the cultural landscape and lead the community to identify values for furthering guidelines and best practices related to spaces for protection and planning. Hence, this second step relates to the following works in progress provisionally entitled "3D Virtual Cultural Landscape Navigation of Tirol" and "The Sticker Album of Tirol".

Concerning the questions that moved us to this experiment, geogames appears to better work, both from this experiment with children and from the lessons learned specially from Alenka Poplin, when it has a playful environment with a tight objective focus. Alongside, game-based learning could be a powerful instrument to be used on participatory design regarding its engaging flavor. The stories to be told on a game seems to be on the direction of best representing and visualizing a real world case study, with elements that come from mental maps of the local community.

Overall, it was a successful experiment since the modeling using mostly free and open source GIS software, although some adjustments had to be made like fixing from inside Minecraft the smaller parcel of the center town, the location that they have in domain in their mental maps. The children showed and proved to be relevant social actors to be considered in urban planning processes coming up with ideas, even detailed ones, from a delicate perspective that could enrich a participatory design of a place.

Finally, a geogame pilot that could be developed to reach and attract more engagement and participation is one capable of engaging and motivating the citizen on a real world tridimensional modeling. Adding the most elements as possible from mental maps of its own community, like even sounds of the place, real people dialogues, little quests to best known and recognize the place. The format should be one played on various digital devices, with the social actors online being able to talk to each other and find a consensus to reach at the end of the process alternative futures for their city.

References

de Andrade, B.A.: Uma rota patrimonial para o rio Santa Maria da Vitória, como instrumento de conservação, valorização, requalificação e/ou transformação do patrimônio territorial. Graduation Thesis, Department of Architecture and Urbanism, Federal University of Espírito Santo, Vitória, Brazil (2012)

de Andrade, B.A.: Representando o Patrimônio Territorial com tecnologia da geoinformação. Experimento em Santa Leopoldina, Espírito Santo, Brasil. Master Thesis, Post-Graduation Program in Architecture and Urbanism, Federal University of Espírito Santo, Vitória, Brazil (2015)

Poli, D.: Il bambino educatore: progettare con i bambini per migliorare la qualità urbana, p. 270. Alinea Editrici, Florence (2006)

Poplin, A.: Games and serious games in urban planning: study cases. In: Murgante, B., Gervasi, O., Iglesias, A., Taniar, D., Apduhan, B.O. (eds.) ICCSA 2011. LNCS, vol. 6783, pp. 1–14. Springer, Heidelberg (2011). doi:10.1007/978-3-642-21887-3_1

Poplin, A.: Digital serious game for urban planning: "B3 – Design your Marketplace!". Environ. Planning B Planning Des. 41(3), 493–511 (2014). Pion Ltd., London

Poplin, A.: Playful public participation in urban planning: a case study for online serious games. Comput. Environ. Urban Syst. **36**(3), 195–206 (2012). Elsevier

Schlieder, C., Kiefer, P., Matyas, S.: Geogames: a conceptual framework and tool for the design of location-based games from classic board games. In: Maybury, M., Stock, O., Wahlster, W. (eds.) INTETAIN 2005. LNCS (LNAI), vol. 3814, pp. 164–173. Springer, Heidelberg (2005). doi:10.1007/11590323_17

Steinitz. Um framework para o Geodesign. Alterando a Geografia através do Design, p. 208. Esri Press, California (2015)

Tóth, E., Poplin, A.: ParticiPécs – a cooperative game fostering learning about the built environment and urban planning. In: 17th AGILE Conference on Geographic Information Science (AGILE), Workshop Geogames and Geoplay, Castellón, Spain (2014)

Vemuri, K., Poplin, A., Monachesi, P.: YouPlaceIt! a serious digital game for achieving consensus in urban planning. In: 17th AGILE Conference on Geographic Information Science (AGILE), Workshop Geogames and Geoplay, Castellón, Spain (2014)

Pervasive Game Utilizing WiFi Fingerprinting-based Localization

Filip Maly, Pavel Kriz[(✉)], and Michael Adamec

Faculty of Informatics and Management,
Department of Informatics and Quantitative Methods,
University of Hradec Kralove, Hradec Kralove, Czech Republic
{Filip.Maly,Pavel.Kriz}@uhk.cz

Abstract. The ability to find out a geographical position of a user is one of the unique features of today's mobile devices. The aim of this work is to suggest and implement a pervasive game for the Android operating system which will utilize two methods of the localization of the mobile device simultaneously. The application should guide the user through historical sites and other places of interest in the town. It could increase their attendance as well. The combination of the two ways of the localization will allow us to achieve two goals. First, to verify if the user is really located at the given place (i.e. that he/she did not mock his/her position via Developer Options at the Android system). Second, to create and update our own database of WiFi fingerprints usable for faster WiFi-based localization.

Keywords: Localization · Fingerprinting · WiFi positioning · Geofencing · Gamification · Pervasive game · Android · GPS

1 Introduction

A mobile phone is no longer a tool for making phone calls and sending SMS messages only. Similar to human beings, today's mobile phones are able to receive and process information from the surrounding environment. Various types of sensors have been added to the mobile phones.

A sensor for determination of the geographical position is one of the most important sensors today. Most devices contain a chip able to receive a signal of *GPS* (Global Positioning System). The *Assisted GPS* (A-GPS) technology is often supported by the online devices. To speed up the localization of a device, A-GPS downloads data necessary for the localization quickly from the Internet instead of downloading them from the GPS satellites via a slow data-link. Despite this, the time-to-first-fix of an A-GPS receiver may vary from approx. 10 to 30 s which may be a frustrating period for users [1].

Information about the user's geographical position is very valuable for developers of mobile applications. These data can be used for navigation on the map, for suggestion of the nearest bus stops when looking for transport connection, for sharing the position with friends at the social networks, etc. [2,3].

© Springer International Publishing AG 2016
M. Ioannides et al. (Eds.): EuroMed 2016, Part I, LNCS 10058, pp. 836–846, 2016.
DOI: 10.1007/978-3-319-48496-9_67

The main goal of this work is to suggest and implement a pervasive game for the Android operating system which will use more options to determine the geographical position of the mobile device and to test the feasibility of the solution. The application will show the most famous Places of Interest (POI) in the town guiding the user to them. The user will be assigned certain amount of points when he/she visits the POI. The players will then compete with other participants to achieve a higher score. At the same time, the application will enable to synchronize the user's game profile among multiple devices and a web portal. Thus, the user will be able to log in at any of his/her mobile devices and will always have the up-to-date data about the places visited and about the amount of points assigned. It will also be possible to provide special offers (for example a reduced entrance fee) to the users based on their score or their choice of the previous POIs (personal preferences). It can increase attendance of more POIs involved in the game.

Our work will deal with the issue of the multiple-source localization of devices in the Android operating system, geofencing and synchronization of the profile.

The rest of this paper is organized as follows. We formulate the problem in Sect. 2. Section 3 describes the existing positioning techniques and related work. In Sect. 4, we analyze the requirements of the proposed application. Section 5 describes the proposed solution. Several details regarding the implementation are shown in Sect. 6. We present the results of the testing in Sect. 7. Section 8 concludes the paper.

2 Problem Formulation

The main objective of our mobile application is to guide the user on the map to the historical site or another POI. Then, the application will verify if he/she really is at the given place. This verification will be done in two ways – using GPS and using fingerprints of WiFi networks. Owing to this, it will be possible to find out if the user is or is not cheating, for example with the aid of location-mocking enabled by the Developer Options in the Android operating system. Thanks to this solution, our own database of WiFi networks fingerprints will also be filled. This database will serve for the WiFi-based localization that is faster than A-GPS and improves the User Experience (UX) thus.

The application will consist of two parts. The first part is a web-based application interface (API) which will enable to download information about POIs into the device, to log into the service, to synchronize the user's profile and to compete with the other users. The second part is the mobile application for the Android system. The Android platform has been chosen because it is the most wide-spread mobile system at the market [4].

3 Positioning Techniques and Related Work

3.1 Positioning Using Cellular Networks

The positioning based on cellular networks is the least precise, but on the other hand the most energy-efficient method. To localize the device, the information about the communication of the mobile phone with the Base Transceiver Stations (BTS) are used. Currently, the trilateration (multilateration in general) is often used [5]. Depending on the particular solution and the density of base stations, its accuracy is about hundreds of meters. It is necessary to know the exact geographical position of all base stations of the cellular network. The localization based on cellular networks is available through the *LocationAPI* service. There are also free alternatives, such as the *OpenCellId* service [6].

3.2   WiFi-Based Positioning

The positioning based on the surrounding WiFi transmitters is another option for the localization of the mobile device. This way of the localization is the most accurate in cities with a large number of WiFi networks.

Each WiFi access-point (AP) has its own MAC address. The principle of the localization itself is very similar to the determination of the position using the cellular networks. The mobile phone is able to find out the received signal strength (RSS) and the MAC addresses of the individual APs of the surrounding WiFi networks.

The calculation of the position itself can be done in different ways depending on the method used [7]. Multilateration and fingerprinting are the main methods. As for multilateration, it is necessary to know the position of the particular APs. As for fingerprinting, it is necessary to build a database of fingerprints in advance and then to search for the most similar (or k of the most similar ones) fingerprint with the known position. In the ideal case, the localization using WiFi can have accuracy of meters at the cost of very low energy consumption [8].

3.3   Bluetooth-Based Positioning

Bluetooth transmitters can be used for the localization in a similar way as the WiFi access points [9,10]. Due to the limitation of the original Bluetooth specification (such as a lengthy process of the device discovery), this approach has not been used much. The situation changed with the advent of Bluetooth 4.0 in 2010. Due to low energy consumption and fast device discovery, the utilization of this technology is much more promising [11,12]. But still, there are not as many Bluetooth transmitters (called beacons) in the public space as WiFi access points.

3.4   Global Navigation Satellite Systems

GPS is the oldest public Global Navigation Satellite System (GNSS), with the aid of which it is possible to determine the position and the precise time anywhere on the Earth. The GPS can be divided into three segments.

The *space segment* currently consists of 32 orbiting satellites [13]. The *Control segment* monitors and controls the cosmic segment of the system and updates the satellites' movement model [14]. The *user segment* is the last part. Users receive signals from the individual satellites with the aid of the GPS receiver. The receiver can derive its position based on the time of flight (TOF) of the signals (corresponding with the distance among the satellites and the receiver).

The accuracy of the publicly available part of the GPS may vary from meters to tens of meters, depending on many factors [15].

3.5 Related Work

The WiFi-based localization is not a novel idea. RADAR [16] is one of the first systems based on WiFi fingerprints. This topic becomes hot in recent years due to widespread smart-phones [8] and ubiquitous location-based services. Most authors focus on indoor localization [17], because GPS usually fails indoors.

There are also location-based mobile applications with gamification aspects such as Foursquare. Unfortunately, they are not proof against cheating because they use a common location service on the mobile device, which can provide mocked coordinates.

In contrast to the existing solutions, we present a novel approach to check the presence outdoors using the cross-verification between the GPS-based and the WiFi-based localization.

4 Analysis

In the previous section, we have described the ways of the localization of a mobile device outdoor. Each way has its own advantages and disadvantages. While the cellular-network-based localization is the most energy efficient, is not suitable for navigation in the pervasive game because of the insufficient accuracy. The localization based on WiFi has an improved accuracy while requiring the database of access-points or their fingerprints near points of interest at the beginning of operation. It would also be required to update the database because of changes in the wireless networks. The localization using GPS is the last option. This method is precise enough for navigation on the map and for decision if the user had really visited the given place. Its drawbacks are the longer time necessary for carrying out the localization, higher consumption of the electric energy and the possibility of relatively easy faking of the GPS coordinates by the user. It could happen that the user could get points for visiting POIs without physically being there.

5 Proposed Solution

The aim of the application is to guide the user at for example historical sites and other interesting places in the city. Navigation built into the Google Maps will be used in the guidance phase. We have designed the following work-flow. First, the player logs into the application. Then, the list of the cities is offered to him/her, from which he/she can download one to the mobile phone using the web API.

Thanks to this initial phase, a large amount of data can be downloaded via WiFi avoiding speed and data limits forced by the user's cellular data plan. Later on, the mobile connection is used only when "activating" the place (the sight) itself by the user, for downloading the current leader-board and for displaying the map (if not cached). Nevertheless, the volume of the data transferred can be minimized by the use of cache.

5.1 Verification of the Presence

We have to be able to verify the user's physical presence at the place prior to the assignment of the points for visiting it. Of course, it is possible to check the distance from the place based on the GPS coordinates only. Then, if the user is close enough, he/she can acquire the corresponding number of points. But there are Android applications that can mock the GPS coordinates reported to other applications, especially for rooted devices. In this way, the user could get points (and potential rewards) for visiting a place without actually being there. This issue is solved by scanning the surrounding WiFi networks and creating a so called fingerprint at the given place.

It is necessary to scan the surrounding WiFi networks (including their MAC addresses and RSS) near the POI before filling the data about the POI into the database. This initial phase can also be performed by scanning WiFi fingerprints additionally by the application's users themselves. This is a certain form of crowd-sourcing. The scanned fingerprints from the first users are used as a base for further verification. Later fingerprints may keep the database up-to-date when cross-verified among multiple users at the same place.

The procedure of verification of the presence at a given POI is the following: after activating the place by the user, the distance is checked using the GPS coordinates. This distance has to be shorter than the distance in the database which is defined individually for each place. Than, the presence of the sufficient number of WiFi networks with the significant RSS at the particular place is verified. If there were not enough significant WiFi networks near the place during the scanning, the points for visiting the place should be assigned directly. This situation has to be always verified by the data from more users. If the user does not receive any networks at a given place and the others do, it is a highly suspicious situation. If a sufficient number of networks is received, the surrounding wireless networks are compared with those in the database using their MAC addresses. In this way it is verified if the user is really present near the given place. Then, the corresponding number of points is assigned to him/her.

5.2 Profile Synchronization

The user should be allowed to play the game on any of his/her devices and should always see the up-to-date data at it. This especially means to have marks at the already visited places and the number of points that he/she has got for the visiting. Thus the synchronization of the user's profile has to be implemented.

To send the profile changes from the server to the mobile device using Push Notifications, we could utilize the Google Cloud Messaging (GCM) [18]. But finally, our own way of synchronization technique has been designed. During the logging into the application, the unique API key is generated for the user. If the user logs in the application from another device, another API key will be generated. The API key acquired for the first device becomes invalid at that time and the application logs out automatically. This means it is possible to play the game on one device only in a given moment. In this way it is ensured that it is enough to download the user's profile data at login-time only and they do not have to be synchronized continuously while the game is played on the particular device.

6 Implementation

The application consists of two parts; server-side and client-side. The server-side is written in the PHP scripting language and the data are saved in the MySQL database. Figure 1 shows the database model. The REST architecture (Representational State Transfer) has been chosen for the API [19].

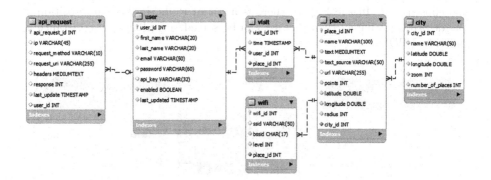

Fig. 1. Database model

The client-side application is supposed to run at the Android version 4.0.3 or later. The application utilizes several libraries; the *Support Library* that ensures the compatibility with older versions of the Android operating system, the *Picasso* library handling the pictures, the *Retrofit* library with the *OkHttp* HTTP client for communication with the web API, and the *Material-ish Progress* library.

6.1 Localization Implementation Details

For the GPS-based localization, we use the *Fused Location Provider* at the Android platform. We also use the *geofencing* feature via the *GeofencingAPI*. It may fire an event when the user enters or leaves a certain defined area on the map. Each POI is assigned with the latitude, the longitude and the radius of the monitored area. If the user enters this area, the button appears on the screen with the aid of which it is possible to activate the POI by the user and then to get points for visiting it. The GeofencingAPI is not able to add more than 100 monitored areas [20]. But this was taken into account in the design of the application and individual POIs are distributed grouped by the towns in order to circumvent this restriction.

6.2   Graphical User Interface

The user interface is localized into Czech and English language. Major components of the Graphical User Interface (GUI) will be described in the text.

In the Fig. 2a, the main screen of the whole application with the game map is shown. On the map there are red spots representing the unvisited POIs. There are transparent blue circles around the unvisited POIs indicating the area where user can activate the POIs and receive the points. The detail of the POI (see Fig. 2b) contains the information whether the POI has or has not been visited (activated), the distance from the POI, the number of points which will be assigned to the user for activation and the text with the basic information about the chosen POI. In the Fig. 2c, there is a list of POIs. If the valid position of the device is available, then this list can be sorted according to the distance to individual POIs.

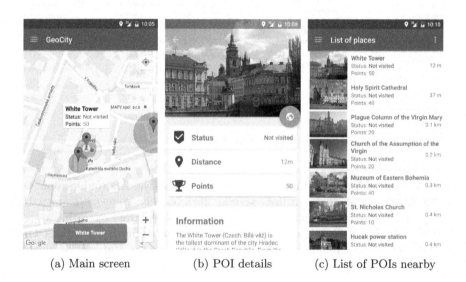

(a) Main screen   (b) POI details   (c) List of POIs nearby

Fig. 2. Screenshots

7   Initial Measurements

Testing of the application was divided into several phases. In the first phase, the presence of a sufficient number of wireless networks with an acceptable strength of the broadcasted signal near individual sights (POIs) had to be found out. Seven most important sights in Hradec Kralove, Czech Republic, were chosen based on [21]. Near these sights, thorough measurement of surrounding wireless networks was done. The results in the Table 1 show that there are more than 10 wireless networks near majority of sights in the town. The St. Nicholas Church is the only place where the number of networks is extremely low having low RSS values. Thus, this place is not suitable for the proposed cross-verification.

Table 1. Number of wireless networks and their signal strengths around the chosen sights in Hradec Kralove, Czech Republic

Name of the sight	# of WiFis	Mean RSS [dBm]	Median RSS [dBm]
White Tower	10	−88,50	−89,0
Holy Spirit Cathedral	14	−88,43	−90,5
Church of the Assumption of the Virgin	19	−91,42	−92,0
St. Nicholas Church	3	−92,67	−94,0
Hucak power station on the Elbe River	12	−91,01	−92,0
Plague Column of the Virgin Mary	19	−89,16	−91,0
Muzeum of Eastern Bohemia	37	−90,65	−92,0

Figure 3 shows a histogram of the particular AP's RSS values in the White Tower location. During comparison of fingerprints, one should consider using a filter that ignores unstable APs with RSS lower than a threshold value. Note that different devices may report different RSS values. This should be taken into account introducing a normalization function that will be device-specific. Based on our measurement, RSSs lower than 92 dBm (measured with Samsung Galaxy S4 Mini) are reflected and/or unstable.

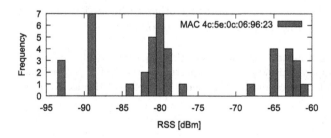

Fig. 3. A histogram of an AP's RSS values in the White Tower location

8   End-to-End Tests

In the second phase of testing, the application was installed to five users' mobile phones for a detailed qualitative testing based on one-on-one interviews. All users were asked to log in the application, download the POIs in Hradec Kralove and visit at least one sight. During this trial, several minor issues were revealed.

After log-in, the list of towns available to download is displayed. Based on the users' responses, the dialog warning against the excessive data download has been added. Then, the timeout regarding the communication with the server had to be adjusted from 10 to 20 s. After elimination of these issues, the users were satisfied with the application. They appreciated its graphic arrangement, low consumption of the mobile data and overall speed of the response.

9   Conclusion

In this paper, we have described the design and implementation of the novel Android application for tourists having unique features; the fingerprint-based localization and the location verification. The application is currently in closed beta testing but the APK is available[1]. The aim of the application is to guide the user to chosen places of interest (e.g. historical sites) in the town and to give him/her the interesting information about them. The application could also contribute to a higher attendance of these places by incorporating the gamification approach.

The use of the WiFi fingerprinting for validation of users' presence at the area of the POI is the main contribution. In contrast to other similar applications, the fingerprints of wireless networks are used for localization besides the GPS. Thus, the user is prevented from manipulating his/her geographic coordinates on the map and from cheating. The fingerprint database may also be used for the faster localization at the POI before the GPS receiver reaches the time-to-fix. The presented approach represents an effective way for WiFi data collecting.

The application was thoroughly tested in different versions of the Android. For the real deployment it is necessary to create a sufficiently extensive database of places so that the application is as attractive for the users as possible. In future work, we will focus on incorporating other technologies such as the promising Bluetooth Low Energy Beacons into the solution.

Acknowledgements. The authors of this paper would like to thank Tereza Krizova for proofreading. This work was supported by the SPEV project, financed from the Faculty of Informatics and Management, University of Hradec Kralove.

---

[1] http://edu.uhk.cz/~krizpa1/doku.php?id=geocity.

References

1. Zhang, J., Li, B., Dempster, A.G., Rizos, C.: Evaluation of high sensitivity GPS receivers. In: International Symposium on GPS/GNSS, Taipei, Taiwan (2010)
2. Singhal, M., Shukla, A.: Implementation of location based services in android using GPS and web services. IJCSI Int. J. Comput. Sci. Issues **9**(1), 237–242 (2012)
3. Vanjire, S., Kanchan, U., Shitole, G., Patil, P.: Location based services on smart phone through the android application. Int. J. Adv. Res. Comput. Commun. Eng. **3**(1), 4982–4987 (2014)
4. IDC: Smartphone OS market share, 2015 Q2 (2016). http://www.idc.com/prodserv/smartphone-os-market-share.jsp
5. Kan, K.K.H., Chan, S.K.C., Ng, J.K.Y.: A dual-channel location estimation system for providing location services based on the GPS and GSM networks. In: 17th International Conference on Advanced Information Networking and Applications, AINA 2003, pp. 7–12, March 2003
6. Trevisani, E., Vitaletti, A.: Cell-ID location technique, limits and benefits: an experimental study. In: Sixth IEEE Workshop on Mobile Computing Systems and Applications, WMCSA 2004, pp. 51–60, December 2004
7. Honkavirta, V., Perala, T., Ali-Loytty, S., Piche, R.: A comparative survey of WLAN location fingerprinting methods. In: 6th Workshop on Positioning, Navigation and Communication, WPNC 2009, 243–251, March 2009
8. Machaj, J., Brida, P.: Using of GSM and Wi-Fi signals for indoor positioning based on fingerprinting algorithms. Adv. Electr. Electron. Eng. **13**(3), 242–248 (2015)
9. Bruno, R., Delmastro, F.: Design and analysis of a Bluetooth-based indoor localization system. In: Conti, M., Giordano, S., Gregori, E., Olariu, S. (eds.) PWC 2003. LNCS, vol. 2775, pp. 711–725. Springer, Heidelberg (2003). doi:10.1007/978-3-540-39867-7_66
10. Muñoz-Organero, M., Muñoz-Merino, P.J., Delgado Kloos, C.: Using Bluetooth to implement a pervasive indoor positioning system with minimal requirements at the application level. Mob. Inf. Syst. **8**(1), 73–82 (2012)
11. Budina, J., Klapka, O., Kozel, T., Zmitko, M.: Method of iBeacon optimal distribution for indoor localization. In: Christiansen, H., Stojanovic, I., Papadopoulos, G.A. (eds.) CONTEXT 2015. LNCS (LNAI), vol. 9405, pp. 105–117. Springer, Heidelberg (2015). doi:10.1007/978-3-319-25591-0_8
12. Kriz, P., Maly, F., Kozel, T.: Improving indoor localization using Bluetooth low energy beacons. In: Mobile Information Systems (2016). http://www.hindawi.com/journals/misy/2016/2083094/
13. El-Rabbany, A.: Introduction to GPS: The Global Positioning System. Artech House Mobile Communications Series. Artech House, London (2002)
14. Seppänen, M., Ala-Luhtala, J., Piché, R., Martikainen, S., Ali-Löytty, S.: Autonomous prediction of GPS and GLONASS satellite orbits. Navigation **59**(2), 119–134 (2012)
15. Modsching, M., Kramer, R., ten Hagen, K.: Field trial on GPS accuracy in a medium size city: the influence of built-up. In: 3rd Workshop on Positioning, Navigation and Communication, pp. 209–218 (2006)
16. Bahl, P., Padmanabhan, V.N.: RADAR: an in-building RF-based user location and tracking system. In: INFOCOM, pp. 775–784 (2000)
17. Rai, A., Chintalapudi, K.K., Padmanabhan, V.N., Sen, R.: Zee: zero-effort crowdsourcing for indoor localization. In: Proceedings of the 18th Annual International Conference on Mobile Computing and Networking, Mobicom 2012, pp. 293–304. ACM, New York (2012)

18. Sneps-Sneppe, M., Namiot, D.: Spotique: a new approach to local messaging. In: Tsaoussidis, V., Kassler, A.J., Koucheryavy, Y., Mellouk, A. (eds.) WWIC 2013. LNCS, vol. 7889, pp. 192–203. Springer, Heidelberg (2013). doi:10.1007/978-3-642-38401-1_15
19. Masse, M.: REST API Design Rulebook. O'Reilly Media, Inc., Sebastopol (2011)
20. Google Android Developers Portal: Creating and monitoring geofences (2016). http://developer.android.com/training/location/geofencing.html
21. Hradec Kralove Offical Webpages: History and heritage - Significant Hradec Kralove Monuments (2016). http://www.hradeckralove.eu/tourists/history-and-heritage

Project Paper: Digital Cultural Heritage in Education, Learning and Training

ErfgoedApp

An Educational Experiment with Augmented Reality, Cityscapes and Campusscapes in Brussels

Marc Jacobs[1,2(✉)], Morien Schroyen[2], and Joke Vanderschoot[2]

[1] FARO, Flemish Interface for Cultural Heritage, Brussels, Belgium
Marc.jacobs@faro.be
[2] HARP, Vrije Universiteit Brussel, Brussels, Belgium
{mmjacobs,morien.schroyen,joke.vanderschoot}@vub.ac.be

Abstract. In 2015 in Flanders (Belgium) an ErfgoedApp (heritage app) was launched. It was developed by Vidinoti and FARO with PixLive. The program allows to construct and use Augmented Reality applications, linked to heritage items, collections and institutions. In 2015–2016 master students in archaeology, arts sciences and archivists experimented with the app, as part of the course work. They managed to produce applications that work, provided feedback to further develop the App and offered reflection on the relation between heritage work, cityscapes and augmented reality and the differences between working with or towards texts or visual information. Low or no cost for distributing and using the applications in practice in heritage and academic contexts proved possible.

Keywords: Erfgoedapp · Heritage app · Augmented reality · Cityscapes · Campusscapes · Heritage studies

1 ErfgoedApp

First we briefly present the ErfgoedApp, an app that is introduced for free in Flanders not only for users but also for heritage institutions and students, as a tool to generate and experience Augmented Reality linked to heritage items and representations in the form of images. Then we will discuss the context in which the tool was launched, the organization that was the driving force and the underlying goals. In the third section we will discuss the context of the courses and some feedback that was provided. In the fourth part we will present one example and some issues related to it.

What is the ErfgoedApp (heritage app) and how does it work [1]? On the one hand, for the user (the visitor, the public, the student, …), it is a tool that one can use with an iPhone or another smartphone or an iPad or another tablet.[1] It is first necessary to download the app (10 MB) from the mayor app stores, via i-tunes store or the play.google.com/store/apps. This is for free. This has to be done only once: please try it out yourself. The

---

[1] The app requires iOS 7.0 or more recent for iPad or iPhone and 4.0 for phones and tablets that function on Android.

© Springer International Publishing AG 2016
M. Ioannides et al. (Eds.): EuroMed 2016, Part I, LNCS 10058, pp. 849–858, 2016.
DOI: 10.1007/978-3-319-48496-9_68

second necessity is that Bluetooth is activated, a standard feature on smartphones or tablets. Thirdly, one needs a wifi connection or access to mobile internet. There are however possibilities to also use the app in spaces where no wifi or mobile internet is available, e.g. via the option of downloading all the information on the smartphone or tablet.

What can users do? First it is necessary to make a connection between the app and the heritage item (or representation of it). This can be done by scanning a QR-code. An alternative method is by receiving and accepting a signal of an iBeacon. An iBeacon is a small Bluetooth transmitter powered by a battery (life span: two years, price 40 euros for the heritage institution). It sends a UUID: a universal unique identifier, triggering a specific scenario connected to one or more heritage items. It can be attached, via a simple paste or sticky substance, to the wall, floor or ceiling, to a fire extinguisher, near a painting, sculpture or window. Or, in an out-door version of the iBeacon, against a wall or a sign, somewhere in a garden or in front of a monument, etc. The range can be specified, ranging from a few centimeters to 200 m. It allows for negotiating or forcing a specific viewpoint, listening distance or perspective of the user. The version that will be released in December 2016 will also work on GPS-locations outdoors, a powerful combination with the iBeacon indoors.

Once the signal is received, then the app should be self-explanatory, offering visual and text information linked to an item, to a collection or a location or land- or cityscape. Scanning a QR code, or specific images or accepting the signal of an iBeacon allows to synchronize the content. This can yield the desired effect of augmented reality. This could be in an interaction with a painting, a photo or another work of art through smartphone or a tablet. But it could also involve the scanning of a picture, a drawing or a page in a book or magazine, on a postcard or sticker, or on a computer screen, with access to additional content in the form of a video or audio file or as a text.

For the heritage actor or mediator (a museum, an archive, volunteer organizations, professionals, students,...) the backend of the system is presented as a free tool to construct an experience and application for the users. The ErfgoedApp was developed by FARO. Flemish Interface for cultural heritage, sponsored by the Department of Culture, Youth, Sports and Media of the Flemish government (in Belgium), in collaboration with a spin-off of the Ecole Polytechnique de Lausanne (EPFL), called Vidinoti. The Swiss partner developed PixLive Maker, a CMS (Content Management System) that allows to create and manage augmented reality content. A connection is made with an image (pdf or jpg, or a QRcode) or iBeacons, and then scenarios can be activated. PixLive Maker provides a GUI-based scripting interface for building scenarios. The program allows to monitor the way the app is used (by tracking clicks and iBeacon activity), to follow-up and adapt the content. The state of the batteries can be monitored at a distance. The metrics allow to track the traffic and the pushed and demanded content. These iBeacons can work as a complement to GPS and Google maps, reaching users in indoor areas, tunnels, basements and spaces beyond the reach of satellite signals. Since 2016 the use of multiple languages to present and consult the content is available, a must in the Belgian context.

2   Interface, Brokers and Mediators

The Erfgoedapp is developed and distributed by FARO. In particular FARO's talented ICT specialist and project manager Bram Wiercx, is also providing basic and advanced training in museums, archives and other heritage institutions in Flanders. Learn to DIY (do it yourself) is the moto of those courses but also the title of a (regularly updated) self-study module in Dutch that FARO has been developed and made available for free online [2]. Via erfgoedapp.be experiences are shared, new launches or use in exhibitions are announced. Important is the feature of www.erfgoedkaart.be. This was a result of a massive survey of the whole cultural heritage sector in the so-called Prisma project in 2011–2012. More than 1700 museums, libraries, archives, heritage cells or associations and volunteer organizations in Flanders are presented on Google Maps, with data and coordinates of those actors. They have priority access to the courses, are attributed a login on simple request and can obtain iBeacons to use.

The Cultural Heritage Decree (2008, updated 2012, to be revised in 2016) of the Flemish Community explicitly gave the task to FARO as a Flemish Interface for Cultural Heritage to inspire, propose, develop and support measures, networks and programs for museums, archives, libraries, centres of expertise, volunteer organizations, and so on. FARO also gives advice about safeguarding policy and practice for local, regional and (inter)national civil servants, politicians and other policy makers. FARO is called a "steunpunt" (pivot), an institution is up to now located and mediating between the government, the academic world, international networks and the field of cultural heritage (museums, archives, associations, networks,…): an in-between and thus interestingly ambiguous position. "Cultural brokerage", "mediation" or "boundary spanning" are concepts used by heritage workers in FARO to describe their individual functions and "interface" the word for the combined effect. Underlying are theoretical and methodo-logical choices, that are related among others to actor-network theory, participatory methods, reflexivity and the emerging paradigm of critical heritage studies. Cultural brokerage is a crucial factor here [3, 4]. Every year FARO organizes the Cultural Heritage Day in Flanders, on the second Sunday after Easter, which reaches on average 250.000 persons, see www.erfgoeddag.be., also a yearly chance to promote the heritage app. A tool like the ErfgoedApp illustrates the mission to introduce and translate inno-vation, to generate DIY applications at low cost and to invite as many actors and sectors as possible to collaborate in heritage work and reach a large public or audience, or even better to invite others to participate or co-create.

3   Context of the Courses with an ErfgoedApp Experiment

In 2015–2016, an experiment was conducted at the Vrije Universiteit Brussel in two courses: "Heritage and ethnology" on the one hand and "Forum: Contemporary issues in Art History and Archaeology" on the other, both offered by professor Marc Jacobs, on the master and the master-after-master level, at which in total 30 students participated. One third were students of the master-after-master archives sciences and (documentary) heritage management, usually with a previous training as historian (at the master level).

The rest were students aspiring to become master in arts sciences and archaeology. Six of these students are older, working students that bring much experience, only one trained and active as a visual content producer. The participants share the characteristics that they are of course computer literate but not specialists, highly trained in heuristics and interpreting historical sources, specialists in retrieving information and critically assessing and using those texts, images and objects. None of them are programmers. In both courses the students were challenged to use the ErfgoedApp, to develop an application that will be tested and if possible made available publicly by non-specialists. The participants agreed that at least first years students arriving on campus in September would be able and seduced to try it out.

Two types of projects were selected. In the course "heritage and ethnology" the university campus was used as the site where augmented reality constructions had to be developed. On the one hand special attention was devoted to works of art on campus, not only statues and art-work in open-air but also the enormous painting of Renaat Braem and his wife, spread over five flours and the basement in the central building M, where the rector and most of the central university services are based. That painting evokes the evolution from the Big Bang to the 20th century (inspiring one student to find inspiration in the trailer of the Big Bang Theory series). On the other hand the focus was on that M building itself, a piece of architecture developed by architect Renaat Braem and classified as a protected monument in Brussels. The students developed apps for the (freemasons' and other) symbols at the entrance of the building, the statues of the founders and the building plans. They also developed apps for the Q building and the Kultuurkafee. The last decades the big aula Q was not only used for academic lectures and honorary doctorates, but also for music performances of pop musicians and concerts of classical music, and an annual singing feast of the students. The Kultuurkafee was famous for performances, wild parties and, in dark periods in the past, also for drug abuse. It was demolished two years ago and a building trajectory to replace it with new students homes, cultural spaces and a new Culture Café is going on now. The students conducted interviews with people who used to work, drink, party or meet there and integrated that material, together with photos and film footage in the app.

A specific requirement was to use archives and/or oral history. Therefore a close collaboration with the university archives (CAVA) was organized. They welcomed the students and helped to find the archival sources. The mixed group of arts students and archivists saw it as a particular challenge to use scans or original archive material in the app (even adding augmented reality to the archive material by scanning them and synchronizing with the QRcodes). This provided new challenges about permissions, copyright, on how to refer to original sources in a visual application. The choice to focus on festivities and cultural manifestations led the students to track down archive collections on campus that were not yet in the university archives, hence contributing to a win-win-situation with CAVA. Each student made a functioning app, and a research report on the story told, the sources found and used and the experience with the app. There were three groups that decided to make a collective presentation, of the buildings M, of the in between spaces outdoors and the building Q.

In another course called Forum, in 2016 the theme was "cityscapes". A number of lectures on that notion in architecture, urban planning but also cultural studies, on applications on for instance the interpretation of photographs or the representation of cities and towns in the paintings of Peter Bruegel or the Flemish Primitives were given as an introduction. Also a two hour introduction was given by Bram Wiercx on using the ErfgoedApp. The students had to select a location in the city of Brussels and develop an Augmented Reality experience. An extra challenge for the students that participated in the Forum course was that they had to integrate and discuss the theory and practical applications of "cityscape" in a paper accompanying their app. Several students opted to work on the university campus (in Brussels), as mentioned above. One group worked on the neighborhood of the Rijksadministratief Centrum in the heart of Brussels, where also the Nationaal Stripmuseum (national museum for comic books, ranging from Kuifje to Guust Flater) is located. They developed a very nice application to discover several streets, statues and gardens in the city using tools from the comic books in the app, including for instance the use of text balloons. Other students decided to work on the North South train connection (Gare du Midi - North Station). In order to build this trainline, many houses in the city center had to be demolished: an excellent topic to deal with in Augmented reality. All these apps will be developed further in the course of 2016 and made available for a larger audience.

The general feeling and feedback of the students was that it took an investment of time, sweat and frustrations, to get past the first hurdles of using a new program and experimenting with it. But after many hours of experimenting, the participants were satisfied that they could realize something that looked professional and that actually worked in tablets and phones. They could apply the skills they had learned, including the disposition not to be satisfied with easily available information online, in Wikipedia or brochures or publications. They tried to discover, use, interpret and present new material and insights. Some of the participants tried to add several layers and contradicting versions and interpretations or they attempted to generate eye-opener experiences. They struggled with the format, e.g. of not resorting to the classical annotation systems like using footnotes and they found ways around this, by smuggling in solutions via PDFs and reference systems. They were happy to learn that the classes.

The students experimented with but often finally did not opt for iBeacons. This is of course also partly due to the fact that they did not operate from within a heritage institution or organization, with own buildings and other infrastructure. Most of the participants opted for augmented reality experiments by uploading jpeg-, png-images or pdfs. They could easily generate these records or QR codes. What the students particularly appreciated was the fact that the software suggested appropriate formats or sections when using images. They also found the next step, connecting "content name" to the images and then building scenarios a feasible step. The PixLive editor allows to connect scenarios and to add different kind of buttons. Remarkable is that the art history students repeatedly decided to use a number of the visual gimmicks available, like the "scratch and win" option. Most of them used the scratch tool for making the user discover other versions, other images and variations. It will be interesting to see how the game dimension of the Scratch, Win or Lose possibility will be used, making random options possible.

The most successful results made a kind of storyboard first, on paper or in a drawing program before starting to build the app. The promoters of the program claimed that the application was intended more to make connections with one or a series of objects or image and connect tours or a story to each of them. The students preferred to build complex tours and deep layers and scenarios, testing the limits of the program. A popular choice was the easy to use image carousels that user can swipe away. Here again the suggestion to carefully think about the order of the images first was emphasized by the students (chronological or by contrasts, organized in regions, per family or age group, per type of object, materials or significance, ...). The present generation of students had no problems to work with YouTube-, Vimeo- or DailyMotion-videos (available online) and MP4-videos made, for instance with a smartphone, iPad or video cameras. Here again the choice was made to mobilize publicly available free software like http://handbrake.fr.

4   The Project of Morien and Joke

Let us present one example, a project developed in one month time, or better in about 60 working hours each, by two VUB-students in art sciences Morien Schroyen and Joke Vanderschoot [5]. As participants in the Forum course, they found inspiration in the lecture and the book by Isabelle Doucet (University of Manchester): "*The Practice Turn in Architecture. Brussels After 1968*". She argued that late-20th (and 21st) century Brussels was composed of a number of layers and styles and she demonstrated and explained this on the basis of one very rich photograph of a contemporary cityscape. The students decided to repeat that experiment, to make a long walk in Brussels and ended up in what they considered as a suitable location. They opted to develop the idea of cityscape, by finding a vantage point in the center of Brussels, from a location with a distance of less than 400 meters of touristic hotspots like Manneken Pis, the Central Market and the Central Station of Brussels. The location they chose was not one of the places where foreign or domestic tourists normally come. They selected a view from alongside the Brussels North-South train axis, near the elite high school of the Sint-Jans Bergman-scollege and the graffiti rich skateboard ramp and transjunction near Kapellekerk. They shot the following panorama shot and went looking for different historical links and layers (Fig. 1).

From left to right they chose entry points, a new skatepark, the Anneessens tower and the remnants of the old city walls, the Hoogstraat, the Kappelekerk and the Bruegel sites. To demonstrate the potential they connected virtual tours to each of the sites. For the Anneessens tower abundant historical information could be found, both on the construction itself as about the historical figure of Anneessens. The remnants of the old city walls linked up with other remaining parts in several parts of the city offered another challenge. The vantage point of the train north south-connection in the 1950s and 1990s made it possible to mobilise that story of heavy disturbance of the cityscape [6]. It also allows to foresee a bridge to other apps of other students focusing on that issue, apps that were not yet available when writing the paper. The skatepark was constructed as a result of a commission by Leefmilieu Brussel granted to Recyclart in 2003 and realized via a participatory project. This opened the space during day time and in the evening for young people between 14 and 24 years old; a skater generation. All these examples are documented in other types of source material, hence providing challenges to find consistency. The fourth part explores the Kapellekerk, that originally was located outside the

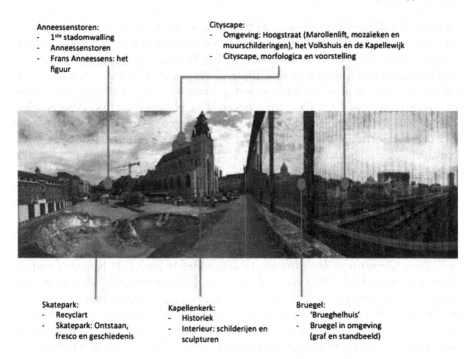

Anneessenstoren:
- 1ste stadomwalling
- Anneessenstoren
- Frans Anneessens: het figuur

Cityscape:
- Omgeving: Hoogstraat (Marollenlift, mozaïeken en muurschilderingen), het Volkshuis en de Kapellewijk
- Cityscape, morfologica en voorstelling

Skatepark:
- Recyclart
- Skatepark: Ontstaan, fresco en geschiedenis

Kapellenkerk:
- Historiek
- Interieur: schilderijen en sculpturen

Bruegel:
- 'Brueghelhuis'
- Bruegel in omgeving (graf en standbeeld)

Fig. 1. Basic scheme for the storyboard of the app developed by Morien Schroyen and Joke Vanderschoot (Forum course VUB, 2016)

city core but developed as the central point of a vibrant quarter. It was the neighborhood where the famous artist Pieter Bruegel was located. The internal history and the restauration of the church proved to be quite interesting.

Joke and Morien made an assessment of the risks of using iBeacons. The chance for theft or vandalism in the skate park was deemed too high. They negotiated with the person responsible for the Kapellekerk and obtained the permission to attach iBeacons in the church but also to consider putting sign or board to offer QR codes. Also leaflets could be made. They decided to develop a brochure that can be multiplied, and hence the QR-codes and images.

In the project of Morien and Joke the so-called Bruegelhuis was part of the application. Although there seems to be no hard evidence, the claim is made by Brussels officials that it was the house where Bruegel allegedly lived during the last days of his life. In 2019, the 450th anniversary of the death of the famous painter will be the occasion for big festivities. The Flemish community has opted to turn this into one of its main events, for attracting tourists, resulting in major exhibitions, connected to the blockbuster exhibition project in Vienna in 2019. The city of Brussels, but also the Royal museum of fine arts in Brussels, will also organize activities, focusing on the Bruegelhuis. Today, that 16th century house still has to be developed, constructed if one might say. It cannot be visited yet. In May 2016 Interpret Europe and Herita organized a congress in Belgium. From the congress venue in Mechelen they organized a number of workshops in Flanders, including Brussels. One of the workshops was about

"Interpreting Bruegel" in Brussels. On the one hand the Bruegel Box, an installation powered by Google Cultural Institute in the Royal Museum of Fine Arts in Brussel was visited and tested. On the other hand the so-called Bruegel house in de Hoogstraat was visited. Afterwards a workshop took place in the offices of FARO, located nearby. During the discussions of the international specialists gathered there, it became clear that there was a lot of doubt about the potential of the place and the risks about building such an installation using vague source material. The two students were not convinced and decided not to go for a full-fledged story, but kept a critical distance when constructing the augmented reality. They presented it as a potential story that could be constructed and played out in the house. Two weeks after finishing their assignment an article was published in the heritage journal OKV that was picked up by the Belgian press. In the article the link between Pieter Bruegel and the house in the Hoogstraat was rejected and new sources located the place of residence in another street in Brussels.

During the exam and subsequent discussions, a new dimension was explored. Morien and Joke got hold of a study made by heritage students in 2009–2010, Pieter-Jan De Vos, Koen Aertgeerts, Audrey Dussaard and Sandrine Herinckx. They made a study to develop the attic of the college at the site into a new heritage attraction. Their work "The Sint-Jan Berchmanscollege and it's Urban Environment in Brussels" offers a lot of possibilities. Their drawings and suggestions are interesting material to present to people looking at the (for outsiders) inaccessible building and huge roof, imagining what is in there and what could be in there. A 360 photo and a virtual visit of several of the potential developments could be offered. In the exam that turned into longue conversations, we concluded that several of the locations had similar stories to tell: not realized but potential heritage attractions.

Just like the other students, Joke and Morien provided several pages of feedback on what they liked and what they regretted, in particular voicing the request for better text processing facilities. This and other feedback was used in the summer of 2016 to improve the system, and to add a performant text editor to the app.

5   Conclusion

Even in – or precisely because of – the experimental phase of the app, inviting last year master students in heritage studies to use this device has proven to be interesting. It is empowering to be able to realize something that works in real life and that is more than only a paper. The students experienced that the same archival and heuristic work they are used to do can have a huge added value, that accompanying texts can be made and provided as PDF. They understood the power of mobilizing their skills with creativity, but also the importance of taking into account the role of end-users, readers and the public. Because the app is actually intended to be used, they also had to exercise their mediating skills and propose a marketing strategy. In the forum course of 2016–2017 the experiment will be repeated. The challenge we will use then is to also work with processes of assessing and formulating a statement of significance. At the end of the course, they will have experimented with two techniques that will be on the agenda in most heritage institutions in Flanders the next five years, augmented reality and frameworks of significance (Figs. 2 and 3).

Fig. 2. QR code used to synchronize the panorama photo

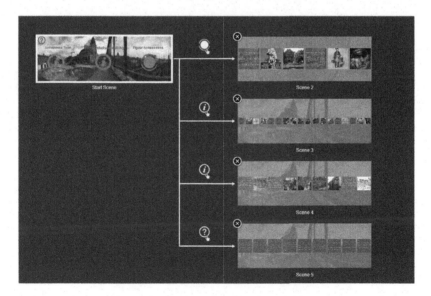

Fig. 3. Screenshot of basic structure developed by Schroyen and Vanderschoot

References

1. Wiercx, B.: De ErfgoedApp, Innovative met iBeacons & Augmented Reality, Faro. Tijdschrift over cultureel erfgoed, 8, nr. 3, pp. 37–39 (2015). www.erfgoedapp.be
2. Wiercx, B.: De Erfgoedapp DIY, Brussel, FARO (2015). https://s3-eu-west-1.amazonaws.com/faronet/erfgoedapp/ErfgoedappDIY.pdf
3. Jacobs, M.: Brokerage, addressing boundaries and the new paradigm of safeguarding intangible cultural heritage. Folklore studies, transdisciplinary perspectives and UNESCO. Volkskunde **115**, 265–291 (2014)
4. Jacobs, M.: Development brokerage, anthropology and public action. Local empowerment, international cooperation and aid: safeguarding of intangible cultural heritage. Volkskunde **115**, 299–318 (2014)
5. Begeleidende tekst bij opdracht Erfgoedapp Samenwerking: Morien Schroyen – Joke Vanderschoot. Brussel, VUB (2016)
6. Van Meerten, M.A.O.: Buiten-sporig Brussel. 50 jaar Noord-Zuidverbinding, Tielt, Lannoo (2002)

Contextualizing 3D Cultural Heritage

James Lloyd(✉)

Ancient History Encyclopedia, Horsham, UK
james.lloyd@ancient.eu.com

Abstract. An increasing number of cultural heritage 3D models are being made public via the 3D-party platform, 'Sketchfab'. This is a hugely popular way to share cultural heritage with a wide audience. The British Museum's model of the Granite head of Amenemhat III has been viewed online 61,500 times and downloaded 3,000 times (as of writing). This paper will explore Ancient History Encyclopedia's project to include 3D models on their website, and how doing so helps contextualize an object, creating a deeper learning experience for the reader of our content and the viewer of a model.

Keywords: Sketchfab · 3D model · Ancient History Encyclopedia · Contextualization · Digital pedagogy

1 Introduction

An increasing number of cultural heritage institutions are creating 3D models and uploading them to Sketchfab, "the leading platform for publishing and sharing 3D cultural content online" [1] and Sketchfab actively encourages museums and cultural heritage institutes to use its service to host their 3D models by providing them with a free business account, enabling to make the most of the service that Sketchfab offers. Because this field of cultural publication (open access 3D models) is still quite new though, there are many pedagogical issues that need to be thought-through. What is being achieved, and what do museums want to achieve, by uploading 3D cultural heritage?

This paper will focus on just one of these issues: context. A museum gallery is a space that seeks to enhance the understanding of the objects included in it. This could be achieved by placing objects in some form of chronological, geographical, or other thematic order, but many more creative approaches exist. In sum, the space of the museum gallery is a vital factor in how we engage with cultural heritage [2]. Despite this, when we make a 3D model of a heritage object, its wider context can be over-looked by a viewer as it is removed from the spatial context provided by a museum. As such, this paper will focus on a questionnaire run by Ancient History Encyclopedia [3], in order to better understand some of the issues users have with contextualizing 3D models of cultural heritage as they appear on Sketchfab.

2 Why Sketchfab?

One of the reasons why Sketchfab is such a popular interface for cultural heritage institutions to use (in addition to those reasons already mentioned) is its ease of use. The website supports over 30 file types, and provides exporters for 49 different

M. Ioannides et al. (Eds.): EuroMed 2016, Part I, LNCS 10058, pp. 859–868, 2016.
DOI: 10.1007/978-3-319-48496-9_69

programmes [4, 5]. When a model is uploaded, a number of 3D settings can easily be adjusted, such as camera field of view and lighting. Further, users are able to add annotations to their models, enabling cultural heritage institutions to create 'digital museum labels'. In addition to this ease of use, studies such as that undertaken by Adriana D'Alba and Greg Jones conclude that "*using a 3D virtual environment can create a positive impact in visitors before, during, and after a visit, and it can be a viable alternative for those who cannot attend and learn from museums exhibitions around the world*" [6]. By categorizing and tagging their models, this virtual environment is also searchable, but, so far, but is not as advanced as the system of 3D Semantic Annotations as outlined by Chih-Hao Yu el al. [7]. Nevertheless, all of these factors seem to make Sketchfab the interface of choice for open access dissemination of 3D models of cultural heritage and are the reasons why models found on this website were used for the questionnaire.

However, there are some limitations. In order for the 3D models to load correctly, modern internet browsers are required. This is because Sketchfab uses the WebGL plugin to display 3D models online, and while this plugin is inbuilt in most current internet browsers, it is not in older versions. As one teacher commented in response to Question 15: "*My browser and OS are not up to date (I'm using Windows XP) and I can't see the annotations. I'm not saying they don't work, and I'm not saying they should work on my operating system, but if your annotations have to be viewed by an up-to-date machine will this work in the average High School classroom?*". The fact that not all schools will have access to computers with internet browsers or internet connections to facilitate a whole classroom browsing a 3D cultural heritage database is perhaps a current limiter to the reach of 3D cultural heritage as an educational tool, but nevertheless, I still agree with Benedetto et al. that there is "*enormous potential brought by WebGL for CH applications development*" [8].

3 The Questionnaire

As mentioned above, this questionnaire was carried out by Ancient History Encyclopedia, a non-profit organization whose mission is to improve history education worldwide. We aim to do this by creating the most complete, freely accessible and reliable history resource in the world. With over 2 million monthly readers, and over 300,000 social media followers we are most-read ancient history publication (online or in print) in world. This large user-base makes us well equipped to conduct research into how users are currently interacting with 3D models cultural heritage.

While the aim of this paper is to explore issues of context and contextualization regarding the use of 3D models, the scope of the questionnaire was wider. As such this paper will focus on the questions asked that were most relevant to this topic (Table 1 provides a full list of all questions).

Table 1. Copy of the questionniare

	Question	Multiple choice/ranking option
Demographic		
1	How old are you?	
2	Are you...?	Male/female/other
3	What country do you live in?	
4	Would you describe yourself as a...?	Teacher/school student/undergraduate/postgraduate/history enthusiast/other
5	What is your highest qualification?	High school/BA/MA/PhD/other
6	Why do you use Ancient History Encyclopedia?	Personal interest/professional interest/research for university/my teacher asked me?
7	Which of the following topics interest you?	IT/computer games/photography/cultural heritage/history
Interacting with 3D models		
8	What is your prior experience of 3D models	None/aware of them/occasionally use them/regularly use them/know how to create 3D models?
9	How easy is it to navigate this 3D model?	1–10
10	How would you rate the overall quality of this 3D model?	1–10
11	How does using the 3D model compare to viewing a photograph of the same object?	
12	How could this 3D model be improved?	
13	How easy is to navigate this 3D model?	1–10
Type of 3D model		
14	How does using a 3D model of a place compare to using a model of an object?	
Using annotations		
15	How useful were the annotations to understanding this model?	
Contextualizing 3D models		
16	How important to understanding an object is viewing it within its wider historical/archaeological context?	1–10
17	How does viewing a 3D model compare to viewing an object in a museum?	
18	Have the various annotations provided enough information about the model to understand its wider historical context?	
19	How useful (for studies/research) do you find these 3D models?	1–5
20	Any further comments...	

3.1   Layout of the Questionnaire

Respondents were asked to follow links to three different models currently on Sketchfab. The first was the British Museum's model 'Granite head of Amenemhat III' [9], the second was the South Etruria Tomb Survey at the Swedish Institute in Rome's model of 'Tomba della Sedia at San Giovenale' [10], and the third was Nestor F. Marque's model 'Coliseo de Roma/Roman Colosseum' [11].

The first section of the questionnaire asked general demographic questions, the second section enquired after users' experience in interacting with 3D models, asking respondents to interact with the British Museum's model 'Granite head of Amenemhat III' (Fig. 1). The third section asked users to compare the experience of using a 3D model of a cultural heritage place, compared to using a 3D model of a cultural heritage object. Here respondents were asked to interact with the South Etruria Tomb Survey at the Swedish Institute in Rome's model of 'Tomba della Sedia at San Giovenale'. Section four asked users to comment on the use of annotations with a 3D model. Here respondents interacted with Nestor F. Marque's model 'Coliseo de Roma/Roman Colosseum'. The final section asked users a number of questions concerning 3D models and historical/archaeology context. Since this data was solicited (the questionnaire was advertised on www.ancient.eu and Ancient History Encyclopedia's social media) most respondents already had an interest in history and the answers to Question 7 show that respondents' interests were primarily historical rather than technological. Out of 203 respondents who answered the question, 'Which of the following topics interest you?', 177 answered 'history'; 121 'cultural heritage'; 80 'photography'; 49 'computer games; and 35 IT/programming. This data, and all following data, was collected between 27/8/2016 22:52 and 30/8/2016 22:38. As such, the main limitation of this questionnaire is that it was only conducted over three days, and while it gained enough responses over that time period, a larger dataset is always welcome.

Additionally, respondents did not have to answer every question; hence why certain questions have a higher or lower number of answers than others. There were twenty different questions in total (Table 1). I will now focus on the answers to those questions which are most directly relevant to exploring issues concerning 3D models and contextualization.

4   Data

The[1] majority of users thought that annotations were very useful for understanding a 3D model (Fig. 2), and thought that an object's wider historical and archaeological context were important to understanding an object (Fig. 3). While those responses were perhaps expected, less than half of the respondents thought that annotations provided enough information all of the time (Fig. 5). This helps place in context one respondent's response to Question 20 that *"...the quality of the annotations are [sic] critical to the value [of the model]."*

---

[1] For Questions 15, 17–18, which elicited a short response from respondents, answers have been summarised with a single word or short phrase for the purposes of representation.

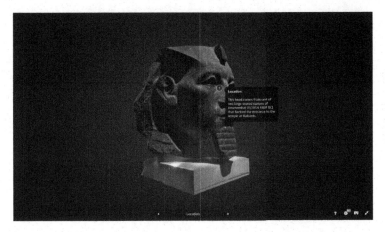

Fig. 1. Screenshot of Granite head of Amenemhat III by The British Museum (CC Attribution NonCommercial) showing Sketchfab's interface, with one of the annotations selected.

While Sketchfab enables a level of contextualization (in that models can be categorized and tagged), respondents thought it was sometimes lacking. Some of the answers to Question 16 included the comments that: *"Good, but it would be better with context of other objects"*; *"Viewing it as an individual object allows one to see its purpose and appreciate its existence, while viewing it with other historically contemporary objects enables one to get a general idea of what was going on at the time and appreciate that period as a whole"*; *"It works on its own, but it would be a richer educational experience if the object was given some historical context."*

However, responses were mixed, *"It's still very cool. A small amount of historical context would be nice but comparative items would be unnecessary"*; *"Pay more detail to the one and not overwhelmed by all the other artefacts."*

The responses to Question 17 are not surprising, with the majority of respondents choosing to highlight that 'ease of access' was a major positive difference between conventional museum visits and viewing 3D models of cultural heritage online (both in terms of the physical freedom of viewing such models, and that they can be viewed in 360°, unlike the majority of objects on display in museums).

Further, it seems that respondents interpreted 'context' and 'contextualization' in a variety of ways. Out of forty-eight responses to Question 20, one respondent commented: *"I would have liked for instance to know the situation of the tomb in the landscape or to be able to situate the Colosseum as opposed to the Forum or the Egyptian head in its place of origin, if possible?"*. Sadly, visually contextualizing 3D cultural heritage within its wider archaeological landscape is at the moment a financially unfeasible option for us (Figs. 4 and 6).

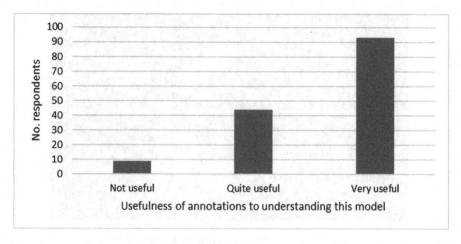

Fig. 2. Question 15 (146 responses)

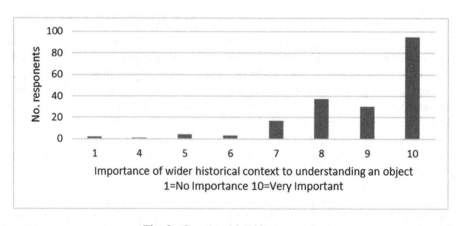

Fig. 3. Question 16 (189 responses)

5 Reflections on the Data

As such, it seems that the majority of respondents wanted to understand these 3D models within their wider historical and archaeological context, but that there was minimal desire for this to be done visually. In order to achieve this we decided to enable users to contribute 3D models from Sketchfab to Ancient History Encyclopedia. This means that 3D models can be embedded in our definitions and articles and be viewed within their wider historical and archaeological context. For example, a 3D model of a Cypriot Poppy flask created by the Ure Museum of Greek Archaeology [12] can be embedded in a definition of Cyprus under the subheading of Bronze Age Cyprus (Fig. 7). Users can then interact with the model while reading about its wider context, while the model's annotations can be used to access object specific details.

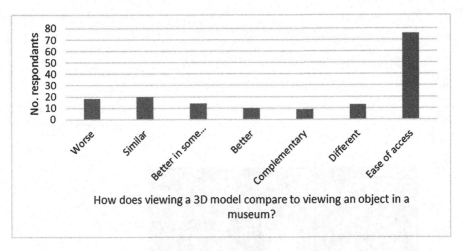

Fig. 4. Question 17 (160 responses)

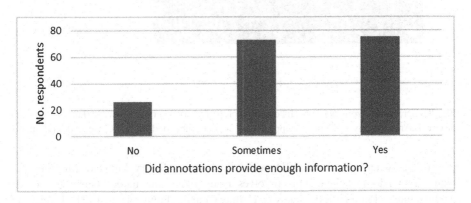

Fig. 5. Question 18 (174 responses)

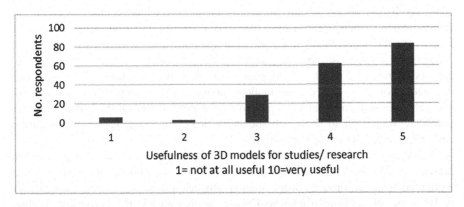

Fig. 6. Question 19 (183 responses)

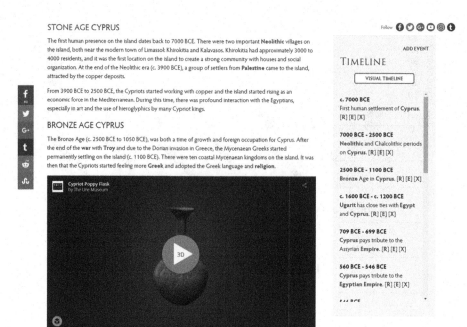

STONE AGE CYPRUS

The first human presence on the island dates back to 7000 BCE. There were two important **Neolithic** villages on the island, both near the modern town of Limassol: Khirokitia and Kalavasos. Khirokitia had approximately 3000 to 4000 residents, and it was the first location on the island to create a strong community with houses and social organization. At the end of the Neolithic era (c. 3900 BCE), a group of settlers from **Palestine** came to the island, attracted by the copper deposits.

From 3900 BCE to 2500 BCE, the Cypriots started working with copper and the island started rising as an economic force in the Mediterranean. During this time, there was profound interaction with the Egyptians, especially in art and the use of hieroglyphics by many Cypriot kings.

BRONZE AGE CYPRUS

The Bronze Age (c. 2500 BCE to 1050 BCE), was both a time of growth and foreign occupation for Cyprus. After the end of the **war** with Troy and due to the Dorian invasion in Greece, the Mycenaean Greeks started permanently settling on the island (c. 1100 BCE). There were ten coastal Mycenaean kingdoms on the island. It was then that the Cypriots started feeling more **Greek** and adopted the Greek language and **religion**.

The Cypriot Archaic Era (c. 750 BCE to 475 BCE) was a problematic time for the island's inhabitants, as the Assyrians, Egyptians, and Persians succeeded one another as rulers of the island. Around 709 BCE **Sargon II** of **Assyria** extorted submission taxes from Cyprus in exchange for the island's independence. By 699 BCE the Assyrians were involved in other conflicts and had to leave Cyprus. **Pharaoh** Amasis of Egypt used the same policy as the Assyrians, when he claimed to be ruler of the island, around 560 BCE.

Fig. 7. Screenshot from Ancient History Encyclopedia's dev server, showing the Ure Museum of Greek Archaeology's 'Cypriot Poppy Flask' model embedded in the 'Cyprus' definition.

Further, when users add a 3D model to Ancient History Encyclopedia they are required to add metadata. This involves categorizing the model (such as 'Art & Architecture', 'Places', and 'States & Cultures') and adding tags to it which relate to the object itself, but also to other content on Ancient History Encyclopedia, and content is categorized into a rough world region. This process is reviewed and ultimately controlled by our editors in order to maintain consistency and accuracy. As such, our search feature enables users to filter their search criteria based on these factors. This enables the 3D models to be viewed in relation to other articles, images, videos that are contextually related. Additionally, utilizing this metadata, an object automatically appears as 'related content' on any page with which it shares tags. However, one of Ancient History Encyclopedia's limitations, in that it is a virtual platform, is that we do not have access to original cultural heritage objects in the same way as museums uploading 3D models to Sketchfab, the above process is a way which we can further contextualize the 3D models of others.

While this is in many ways similar to how the Europeana database organizes and presents its 3D models of cultural heritage [13, 14] we include 3D models with a written context - an obvious differentiation between a database and an encyclopedia. A 3D model of the Roman goddess Cybele, as presented in the Europeana database [15] provides the viewer with plenty of information about the object (dimension, provenance, chronology, and a certain amount of textual contextualization via a short description of the object), but displays it very differently to Ancient History Encyclopedia. If that model were to be uploaded to Ancient History Encyclopedia, it would be embedded in an article about Cybele or Roman religion, enabling a contextualization of the object that would enable viewers to better understand the importance of the object to a Roman worshipper, to give just one example. Further, there is a certain immediacy of integration provided by WebGL and the Sketchfab model.

In the future, we plan to further contextualize our content by date and geography/location. We also intend to link our content with the Pelagios [16, 17] and (possibly also) Period0 databases [18], however, such plans are in their early stages. It is hoped that the research drawn from this questionnaire will help to inform the process.

By embedding 3D models within definitions or articles, we change the focus from solely the object to understanding how it relates to a wider body of historical and archaeological material, but because 3D models are such a visually and interactively stimulating medium, they additionally provide a greater understanding of the object than a conventional 2D photograph would.

This is Ancient History Encyclopedia's response to contextualizing 3D models, and it will be reviewed with a follow-up survey in order to assess how successfully it has achieved its goals, and how it might still be further improved. As such, I hope that this paper might prompt further discussion as to the pedagogy of 3D models in cultural heritage.

Acknowledgements. Thanks to Jason Moser for developing the integration of Sketchfab models into Ancient History Encyclopedia, and Jan van der Crabben and James Weiner. Many thanks to the anonymous reviewers for their constructive suggestions and corrections, any mistakes of course remain the author's own. Thanks too to all the cultural heritage institutes who upload their models to Sketchfab.

References

1. https://sketchfab.com/museums. Accessed 30 Aug 2016
2. Hillier, B., Tzortzi, K.: Space syntax: the language of museum space. In: Macdonald, S. (ed.) A Companion to Museum Studies, pp. 282–301. Blackwell, London (2006)
3. https://www.ancient.eu
4. https://help.sketchfab.com/hc/en-us/articles/202508396-3D-File-Formats?utm_source=website&utm_campaign=upload_hints. Accessed 30 Aug 2016
5. https://sketchfab.com/exporters. Accessed 30 Aug 2016
6. D'Alba, A.: Jones, G: Analyzing the effects of a 3D online virtual museum in visitors' discourse, attitudes, preferences, and knowledge acquisition. In: Nettleton, K., Lennex, L. (eds.) Cases on 3D Technology Application and Integration in Education, pp. 26–47. Information Science Reference, Hershey (2013)
7. Yu, C.-H., Groza, T., Hunter, J.: High speed capture, retrieval and rendering of segment-based annotations on 3D museum objects. In: Xing, C., Crestani, F., Rauber, A. (eds.) ICADL 2011. LNCS, vol. 7008, pp. 5–15. Springer, Heidelberg (2011). doi:10.1007/978-3-642-24826-9_5

8. Benedetto, M., Ponchio, F., Malomo, L., Callieri, M., Dellepiane, M., Cignoni, P., Scopigno, R.: Web and mobile visualization for cultural heritage. In: Ioannides, M., Quak, E. (eds.) 3D Research Challenges in Cultural Heritage. LNCS, vol. 8355, pp. 18–35. Springer, Heidelberg (2014). doi:10.1007/978-3-662-44630-0_2

9. https://sketchfab.com/models/64d0b7662b59417986e9d693624de97a. Accessed 31 Aug 2016

10. https://sketchfab.com/models/554b3a527ccf4a869584f219b959555c. Accessed 31 Aug 2016

11. https://sketchfab.com/models/544c64b6445e4899a17350c949b7766a. Accessed 31 Aug 2016

12. https://sketchfab.com/models/1e6cdc4882d04fc5a4535ae8163c1ac6. Accessed 31 Aug 2016

13. http://www.europeana.eu/portal/en. Accessed 2 Sept 2016

14. Santos, P., Serna, S.P., Stork, A., Fellner, D.: The potential of 3D internet in the cultural heritage domain. In: Ioannides, M., Quak, E. (eds.) 3D Research Challenges in Cultural Heritage. LNCS, vol. 8355, pp. 1–17. Springer, Heidelberg (2014). doi:10.1007/978-3-662-44630-0_1

15. http://www.europeana.eu/portal/en/record/2048709/object_HA_942.html. Accessed 2 Sept 2016

16. http://commons.pelagios.org/

17. Rainer, S. Elton, S., Leif, I.: Exploring Pelagios: a visual browser for geotagged datasets. In: International Workshop on Supporting Users' Exploration of Digital Libraries, Paphos, Cyprus, 23–27 September 2012 (2012)

18. http://perio.do/

Crowdsourcing Cultural Heritage: From 3D Modeling to the Engagement of Young Generations

Laura Inzerillo[1] and Cettina Santagati[2(✉)]

[1] Department of Architecture, University of Palermo, Palermo, Italy
laura.inzerillo@unipa.it
[2] Department of Civil Engineering and Architecture, University of Catania, Catania, Italy
cettina.santagati@dau.unict.it

Abstract. Monitoring, digitizing and archiving museum artworks represent an important socio-cultural accomplishment and an overcoming in digital preservation today. Cultural heritage is constantly under threat of terrorist attacks and natural disaster. The high costs related to documentation task have prevented a constantly and massive survey activity. The low cost 3D image based acquisition and elaboration techniques of an object, allow to carry out a 3D photorealistic model in a short time. Therefore, a lot of museum adopted these techniques for the artworks archiving. Crowdsourcing activities can significantly speed up survey and elaboration procedures. If, on the one hand, these initiatives can have a positive impact, on the other hand involve the online user with a marginal role. In this paper we demonstrate how it is appropriate thinking the museum visitor as "museum operator/maker" of the digital model overstepping the outcomes achieved so far.

Keywords: Cultural heritage · 3D modeling · Structure from Motion (SfM) · Museum collections · Crowdsourcing

1 Introduction

Dissemination, conservation and knowledge of cultural heritage are essential elements in its life cycle analysis (LCA), whether it is a museum, archaeological, architectural or urban site. The possibility to schedule the updates on the state of conservation of an artwork, ensures its own preservation for future generations. We could bear in mind cataclysms, earthquakes, terrorist attacks, etc. that endanger the life of a physical reality like a museum and its artworks.

The virtualization of an artwork guarantees the digital preservation and its passing down to future generations. That is, history, identity and culture of a community are strictly related to their cultural roots and signs of the past.

The high costs due to 3D acquisition of an artwork whether it is a sculpture, an archaeological site, an architectural element, have not, so far, allowed a cyclical and scheduled monitoring to guarantee a reliable analysis of the work itself. Several attempts have been put in place to support the delicate and utterly titanic undertaking aimed at 3D archiving and reconstruction of museum collections, e.g. 3D icons project, the latest

© Springer International Publishing AG 2016
M. Ioannides et al. (Eds.): EuroMed 2016, Part I, LNCS 10058, pp. 869–879, 2016.
DOI: 10.1007/978-3-319-48496-9_70

Uffizi museum in Florence 3D digitization ect. [1–3]. On the other hand, today there are praiseworthy initiatives seeking in different ways to engage the online user to a museum site, assigning him tasks to help the museum itself in some important digital goals (Egyptian Museum of Turin, Heritagetogether project). However, the online user often has a role still marginal and it is a small piece in the enormous reconstruction mechanism. Our research tends to overrun the goals achieved so far. The source of cooperation is identified in the museum or site visitor: he becomes the creator of the 3D content, acting as a digital maker rather than a mere spectator.

Building on the results obtained from the state of the art we will demonstrate that through the use of existing low cost 3D acquisition techniques (very easy to use and available on the market) it is possible to create an organized system of a production cycle that starts from the museum, involves the visitor, returns to the museum and moves to the community.

2   The State of the Art

The last years have seen several technological innovations in the field of photogrammetry and computer vision techniques for the creation of useful and accurate 3D models of objects, by combining robust algorithms, powerful computers or cloud computing platforms. Several studies have been addressed to the exploitation of SfM algorithms for the creation of 3D models of cultural heritage objects and sites [4–7]. The power of Structure from Motion (SfM) techniques lies in the low learning curve for the realization of a good dataset and in the totally automatic or semi automatic pipeline for the subsequent realization of the textured 3D model. Furthermore, compact or mobile phone cameras can also be used, with good visualization results.

One interesting project that exploits the power of SfM techniques for 3D reconstruction is 4D-CH-World [8]. The main goal of the project, funded under the VII European framework, is to enable historians, architects, archaeologists, urban planners and affiliated professionals to reconstruct views of historical structures starting from millions of images floating around the web and interact with them. Furthermore, the project foresees semantic enrichment of the end results and their subsequent export to Europeana, the European digital library, for integrated, interactive 3D visualisation within regular web browsers.

On the other side, there is an increasingly attention in the power of crowdsourcing for Cultural Heritage: volunteers called to absolve simple tasks that cannot be carried out automatically by a computer and are time consuming for museums employees. However, dealing with cultural heritage, we could consider this a niche crowdsourcing, due to the cultural skills required to the volunteers [9].

One meaningful projects directly managed by a museum is Micro-Pasts project [10]. The project is co-led by UCL and the British Museum, since may 2016 it involves also a pilot experience at the Egyptian Museum in Turin. The platform's goal is to engage traditional academics, archaeological societies, interested individual members to create new, high quality archaeological and historical data about the human past. The project foresees the engagement of volunteers on line assigning them simple tasks such as transcription and photo-masking on British Prehistory and British Museum collections. As regards photo-masking, the goal is to create masks that isolate the object, improving the 3D reconstruction (Photoscan).

Another interesting project is Heritagetogether [11]. It uses crowd-sourced digital photographs to produce 3D models of Neolithic and Bronze Age remains from Gwynedd and Anglesey area. It is a collaborative Arts and Humanities Research Council project, with academic partners at Manchester Metropolitan, Bangor and Aberystwyth universities. The inspiration for the project was the prevalence of digital camera use in the UK, not least on mobile phones, to crowd-source archaeological research data and to create fully textured digital 3D models using SfM techniques. Volunteers find on the web site tutorials and a list of available software.

If the previous projects are aimed by a cultural-social instance, Stone Bridge Plaka project and Project Mosul answer to our empathic feeling after a catastrophic event to react and try to reconstruct lost heritage sites in order to preserve, also if virtually, the memory and the identity of a place.

Crowdsourcing the traditional stone bridge of Plaka project [12] was aimed to collect images on a lost heritage with the aim to virtually reconstruct it by means of SfM algorithms. On the 1st of February 2015, the central section of the Plaka stone bridge's unique arch collapsed due to extreme weather conditions. Then a web site has been developed for collecting images and videos by volunteers contributors. They were processed both with free and open source solutions (VisualSfM) and commercial ones (Agisoft Photoscan).

As regards Project Mosul [13], it rises at the end of February 2015 after the shocking news of IS destructions of Mosul Museum. The reaction of heritage community brought to the attempt to digitally reconstruct lost heritage starting collecting pictures and using photogrammetry to carry out this task. It was created a platform to manage crowd-sourced images 3D model generation, giving citizen scientists the tools they needed to undertake this task (tutorial, available software). However, the output is a 3D textured model which lacks of geometric fidelity, but constitutes a valuable source for visualization, memory and documentation. Nowadays the platform has been moved to www.rekrei.org and includes a global focus on lost or at risk heritage.

All the highlighted projects are developed on online platforms, one of the major difficulty is the engagement of the online visitor.

However, our idea detaches from these previous experiences because directly engages a museum visitor on site, changing and enhancing his visit experience, transforming him into a 3D cultural content creator during the visit. As will be described in the following sections.

3   A Simple Idea for Museum Collections

The idea of identifying in the museum/archeological-site visitor, a bottom source aimed at dissemination, enhancement and knowledge of Cultural Heritage, got leverage both from the above described projects and the experimentation results on SfM techniques. Although SfM 3D models have less metric accuracy and geometric precision of laser scanning models - especially if integrated with other sophisticated techniques such as flood-lighting instruments, X-Ray investigation, etc.-, the SfM 3D model quality improves significantly if pictures are taken according to photogrammetric criteria, paying attention to enlightenment conditions, and it is carried out an advanced pre-processing before 3D reconstruction [14].

The potential of Micro-Past, Heritagetogether, Project Mosul (Rekrei) platforms, let us to verify the practicability of a more arduous idea: to encourage the museum/site visitor to give a personal contribution either through the creation of a data set or the final 3D model.

Nevertheless, it was necessary to test our idea on a first target of young visitors. The opportunity provided by the national event #invasionidigitali (thanks to which the involved museum allows the tablet, camera, cellphone to make photos and videos) allows us to involve our students of Palermo and Catania Engineering Schools.

The students just turned in real "digital 3D invaders", without any cultural and technological difficulty. The professors trained the students with the necessary technical and critical tools on SfM techniques, so they could work on their own. The carried out models showed expertise in the use of these techniques and capacity to investigate. Below are showed the phases of the experimentation.

3.1   Engagement and Students/Visitors Training

At this step, thanks to the visibility provided by the national event #invasionidigitali [15] the students felt involved in a bottom-up system of cultural heritage enhancement through the use of social media (facebook, twitter, instagram). This has facilitated their active participation in our project idea also thanks to the introductory seminars on #invasionidigitali held by Dr. Elisa Bonacini, ambassador for the project in Sicily. In addition, the simplicity and easiness in the construction of the 3D model (from the dataset to the 3D reconstruction) encouraged the student to have a social and cultural role, being aware of the final objective: with a little effort, the student/visitor promotes architectural heritage and co-creates 3D cultural content of great value [16].

3.1.1   #Digitalinvasions

#invasionidigitali (#digitalinvasions) is an Italian bottom up project started in 2013 [15]. This initiative was a reaction to the cancellation, for economic reasons, of the "Culture Week" event that allowed for free entrance to museums. Each 'invasion' is a mini-socio digital event in itself with its own poster, Facebook event and hashtag. Social and digital communication are the key to the invasions: 'invaders' are bloggers, amateur archaeologists artists, photographers, Instagrammers, communication experts, but also common people with a wide range of backgrounds, all with the same desire to promote their cultural heritage through social media. By joining the Manifesto (www.invasionidigitali.it), people decided to support Italy's cultural institutions by "invading" them with cameras, smartphones and tablets and share their cultural experiences through the web and social media.

3.1.2   SfM Techniques

In our experiment, students were free to adopt one of the available suggested solutions (Agisoft Photoscan or Recap360 Autodesk platform). If the first one needs a high performance computer for data processing, the second one use the power of cloud computing to carry out a semi-automatic data processing instead of considerably slowing-down the computer.

A fundamental step is the realization of the photographic network of the object: it is recommended that the angle between one shot and another is about 5–10° so that the overlapping between neighboring frames is of about 70 %; furthermore the images around the object should be taken with different rotations and different heights so as to vary the angle of the shoot.

In Agisoft Photoscan the user can give inputs to the several steps of 3D reconstruction (alignment, dense reconstruction, meshing, texturing) concerning the kind of reconstruction, the accuracy, the number of faces, etc. While using Recap 360 the user uploads the images and waits the service for completing the task. The output is a 3D polygonal textured model that can be exported for further usage in external programs according to different formats (OBJ, Ply).

4   Results at Salinas Museum in Palermo and Civic Museum of Castello Ursino in Catania

The students involved in the experimentation were from Drawing Course of the first year of Environmental Engineering of University of Palermo and from Digital Survey Course of the fourth and fifth year of Building Engineering-Architecture of University of Catania. The students of both classes, consisting of about 80 students, lived with enthusiasm and attractiveness the event.

In both cases students were divided into groups to any one of which was assigned a work of art. The following images show the 3D models made by students, chosen by different typologies and dimensions. They are visualized according 4 different modes: textured, solid, x-ray, wireframe. This choice has been made with the intent to show lack of holes, deformations, etc. and meshes face resolution.

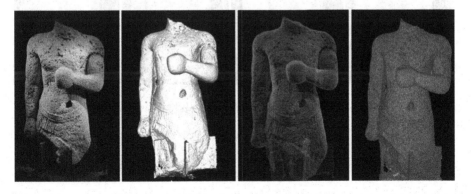

Fig. 1. Torso of the Stagnone (Salinas Museum)

The data set have been made with mobile devices, digital compact camera and reflex camera; the reconstruction resolution variable from low to high values; the data set are made by 40–70 photos (Figs. 1, 2, 3, 4, 5, 6, 7 and 8).

Fig. 2. Statue of Zeus Ourios (Salinas Museum)

Fig. 3. Sarcofago in alabastro: Hasti the dead (Salinas Museum)

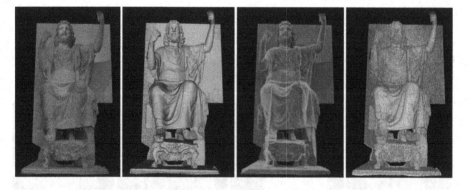

Fig. 4. Statue of Zeus sitting on a throne (Salinas Museum)

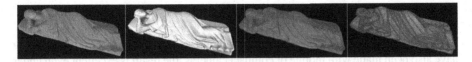

Fig. 5. Sepulchral statue end of XIV-beginning of XV century (Castello Ursino Civic Museum)

Fig. 6. Marble bust Agrippina Maggiore (Castello Ursino Civic Museum)

Fig. 7. Head of Arpocrate (Castello Ursino Civic Museum)

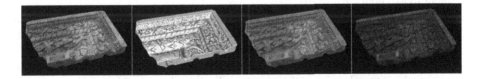

Fig. 8. Fragment of door cornice (Castello Ursino Civic Museum)

5 Discussion and Proposal

The models produced by the students are very impressive and, if you consider that some have also been made with mobile or compact cameras, the result is excellent even under the geometric profile.

Moreover, the heterogeneity of our target (students) in terms of age and cultural background should not be underestimated: those of Palermo attend the course of Drawing which is delivered at the 1st year of degree course in Environment Engineering (18–19 years of age), those of Catania attend the course of Digital Survey which involves students of 4th and 5th year of the degree course in building engineering-architecture (22–23 years of age).

Some of the students involved, especially those of the 4th and 5th year have followed up to the experience within the university courses also in their personal life experience: we refer to students who have produced 3D models of artworks exhibited in European museums (Louvre, Villa Borghese, etc.) visited during personal trips.

The results have given our idea strength aimed at identify a potential creator of 3D cultural content in the young visitor; therefore, visitor, appropriately engaged, becomes an indispensable resource for the development, dissemination, preservation and knowledge of the cultural heritage of society as a whole.

The crucial point is to identify how the results achieved from other crowdsourcing experiences and our experience can find an operational synthesis within an existing museum reality. Below the synthesis of the full process (acquisition, storage, valorization of the models) considering some technical and economic issues:

- **Technical features of the objects/models:** The geometric characteristics of the object do not affect the 3D reconstruction of the model. Problems were found attributable to the material that constitutes the object: for example glass and reflective metals. Particular attention should be paid in the acquisition of objects inside showcases. The features of the model in terms of graphics and metric accuracy are closely related to the resolution of the digital camera. Therefore it would be desirable that the museum could consider as initial investment the acquisition of two–three digital cameras with the same technical specifications.
- **Efforts/time required to the visitors:** It is desirable that on average a dataset does not exceed hundred images, so the time for the creation of a data set takes from 5 to 20 min. The timing of the loading and processing of the data set vary depending on the hardware features/power of cloud computing. Generally, the range is from one hour to five hour.
- **Copyright issues:** In order to guarantee the paternity of the creation of a model, models will be released in CCBY license, that include in metadata the name/s of the model creators.
- **Business rationale:** The business rationale has two main objectives: the first is to realize the 3D cataloguing of the museum collection, the second is to achieve a return in terms of number of visitors due to the media echo both of the initiative itself and of visual/cultural/creative impact of created models.

– **Operational rationale for the institutions:** The digital models will be stored for the conservation and will be disseminated as Open Data by using social media also by video, animations, interactive navigations, etc.; each visitor will have assigned a specific task, so there should not be any possibility of annoyance of the operation during the acquisition process.
– **Overall technical infrastructure and features of the system:** The museum will achieve the following features: digital database of photo archive of the collections items, 3D repository enriched by metadata linked to the objects, a team of experts that will design, check the quality of the models, maintain the technical infrastructure and give tips to visitors. Furthermore, the museum should foresee the use of a laboratory for workstations where the visitor could upload the data set and start the elaboration. And 3D prints of the model should before see.

Below we highlight some of the operational arrangements-to be implemented along the visitor's path so that he can be engaged and turns himself into a creator of 3D cultural content:

– Visitor must feel involved in the role of actor from his first step at the museum entrance: led lighting spots invite the visitor to become the 3D model author, addressing him towards the vision of a video tutorial;
– The video tutorial, following the introductory/emotional part, is divided in three main parts: creation of the data set, upload and configuration of software/platform parameters, upload of the 3D model;
– The visitor, who participate in the digital reconstruction campaign, could get rewarded thanks to compensation package as free tickets to the museum, score recognition, etc.;

To ensure that the integrated system can ensure an effective response from the visitor, it would be appropriate that the museum activates a promotional campaign through social media and involving school students too.

6   Conclusion

The integrated system structured as above, becomes a potential enrichment not only for the museum and the visitor/maker but also for the community and future generations. The museum experiences a continuous updating of its data fed from a cultural, technological and cognitive ferment bottom-driven, according to the ideals of participatory museum. The visitor/3D maker is involved in the enrichment of the digital cultural heritage with a starring role in a continuous upgrade of the 3D acquisition techniques, until then unknown to him, thus contributing to the growth of knowledge.

The community and future generations will benefit from the outcomes of such large archive, knowledge, dissemination and exploitation of artworks whose 3D visualization may solve museums remote reachability problems or, in the future, collections digital preservation. The operating methodological model described so far could also be extended to the works that are conserved in warehouses stock giving them the possibility to be disseminated and studied; to museum environments; to architectural and civil infrastructure assets, and more generally to cultural heritage.

Acknowledgements. Authors would like to thank Marianna Marcucci, Fabrizio Todisco and Elisa Bonacini, Digital Invasions project; Giovanna Spadafora and Sandro Garrubbo, Salinas Museums in Palermo; Valentina Noto, Museo Civico Castello Ursino in Catania.

References

1. http://3dicons-project.eu/eng/News
2. Guidi, G., Barsanti Gonizzi, S., Micoli, L.L., Russo, M.: Massive 3D digitization of museum contents. In: Toniolo, L., Boriani, M., Guidi, G. (eds.) Built Heritage: Monitoring Conservation Management, pp. 335–346. Springer International Publishing, Cham (2015)
3. Maschner, H., Schou, C.D.: Virtualization and the democratization of science: 3D technologies revolutionize museum research and access. In: 2013 Digital Heritage International Congress, pp. 265–271 (2013)
4. Inzerillo, L., Santagati, C.: Using dense stereo matching techniques in survey. Disegnare Idee Immagini. **47**, 82–91 (2013)
5. Lerma, J., Navarro, S., Cabrelles, M., Villaverde, V.: Terrestrial laser scanning and close range photogrammetry for 3D archaeological documentation: the Upper Palaeolithic cave of Parpallo as a case study. J. Archaeol. Sci. **37**, 499–507 (2010)
6. Lo Turco, M., Sanna, M.: Reconstructive digital modelling: the Church of Mercy in Turin. Disegnare Idee Immagini. **41**, 42–51 (2010)
7. Remondino, F.: Advanced 3d recording techniques for the digital documentation and conservation of heritage sites and objects. Change Over Time **1**(2), 198–214 (2011)
8. Ioannides, M., Hadjiprocopis, A., Doulamis, N., Doulamis, A., Protopapadakis, E., Makantasis, K., Santos, P., Fellner, D., Stork, A., Balet, O., Julien, M., Weinlinger, G., Johnson, P.S., Klein, M., Fritsch, D.: Online 4D reconstruction using multi-images. ISPRS Annals of Photogrammetry Remote Sens. Spat. Inf. Sci. **II-5/W1**(1), 169–174 (2013). Available Under Open Access
9. Biella, D., Sacher, D., Weyers, B., Luther, W., Baloian, N., Schreck, T.: Crowdsourcing and knowledge co-creation in virtual museums. In: Baloian, N., Zorian, Y., Taslakian, P., Shoukouryan, S. (eds.) CRIWG 2015. LNCS, vol. 9334, pp. 1–18. Springer, Heidelberg (2015). doi:10.1007/978-3-319-22747-4_1
10. Bonacchi, C., Bevan, A., Pett, D., Keinan-Schoonbaert, A., Sparks, R., Wexler, J., Wilkin, N.: Crowd-sourced archaeological research: the micropasts project. Archaeol. Int. **17**, 61–68 (2014)
11. Griffiths, S., Edwards, B., Karl, R., Labrosse, F., Miles, H., Moeller, K., Roberts, J., Tiddeman, B., Wilson, A.: Crowd-sourcing archaeological research: HeritageTogether digital public archaeology in practice. Internet Archaeol. **40** (2015). http://dx.doi.org/10.11141/ia.40.7.3
12. Stathopoulou, E.K., Georgopoulos, A., Panagiotopoulos, G., Kaliampakos, D.: Crowdsourcing lost cultural heritage. ISPRS Annals of Photogrammetry Remote Sens. Spat. Inf. Sci. **II-5/W3**, 295–300 (2015)
13. Vincent, M.L., Flores Gutierrez, M., Coughenour, C., Lopez-Menchero Bendicho, V.M., Remondino, F., Fritsch, D.: Crowd-Sourcing the 3D digital reconstructions of lost cultural heritage. In: 2015 Digital Heritage, vol. 1, pp. 171–172 (2015)

14. Gaiani, M., Remondino, F., Apollonio, F.I., Ballabeni, A.: An advanced pre-processing pipeline to improve automated photogrammetric reconstructions of architectural scenes. J. Remote Sens. **8**(3), 178 (2016)
15. Bonacini, E., Marcucci, M., Todisco, F.: #DIGITALINVASIONS. A bottom-up crowd example of cultural value co-creation. In: Proceedings of the First EAGLE International Conference 2014 on Information Technologies for Epigraphy and Digital Cultural Heritage, 29–30 September and 1 October 2014, Paris, pp. 265–284. Sapienza Università Editrice (2014)
16. Bonacini, E., Inzerillo, L., Marcucci, M., Santagati, C., Todisco, F.: 3D #Digital Invasions: a crowdsourcing project for mobile user generated content. Furnace J. **2** (2015)

Training Schools for Conservation of Cultural Heritage: Between Expertise, Management and Education

Anna Lobovikov-Katz[1]([✉]), Gumersindo Bueno Benito[2], Vanesa Marcos Sánchez[2], Joao Martins[3], and Dalik Sojref[4]

[1] Faculty of Architecture and Town Planning, Technion - Israel Institute of Technology, Technion City, 32000 Haifa, Israel
anna@technion.ac.il
[2] Foundation Santa María la Real Historical Heritage, Aguilar de Campoo, Palencia, Spain
{gbueno,vmarcos}@santamarialareal.org
[3] Faculty of Sciences and Technology (UNL) and UNINOVA, Lisbon, Portugal
jf.martins@fct.unl.pt
[4] WTTC, Berlin, Germany
dalik.sojref@wttc.de

Abstract. Training schools make an important feature of the European research landscape, fostering exchange in frontier research, and building basis for further research and development. How the cross-area, management and educational issues can be effectively put together in training schools, and specifically, for the benefit of a multi- and interdisciplinary field of conservation of cultural built heritage? This paper showcases the experience from the first lessons of the COST (European Cooperation in Science and Technology) Action i2MHB (Innovation in Intelligent Management of Heritage Buildings), to examine and suggest tools useful for further multidisciplinary synergies and networks in this and other frameworks.

Keywords: Training school · Conservation of cultural built heritage · Education · Interdisciplinary

1 Introduction - EU Training Schools in the Frameworks of Cost Actions

Training schools are a valuable tool in order to enrich sustainable development. They can be used as a lifelong learning tool or as a fast track to scientific updating. Either use is valuable, with its own singularities, but targeted to quite distinct audiences. According to UNESCO, "Every person, at every stage of their life should have lifelong learning opportunities to acquire the knowledge and skills they need to fulfill their aspirations and contribute to their societies". The UNESCO's new education agenda strategic objectives for 2014–2021 encompass three major strategic objectives: (1) Developing education systems to foster quality and inclusive lifelong learning for all; (2) Empowering learners to be creative and responsible global citizens and (3) Shaping the future education agenda [1]. On the other hand, rather than

© Springer International Publishing AG 2016
M. Ioannides et al. (Eds.): EuroMed 2016, Part I, LNCS 10058, pp. 880–890, 2016.
DOI: 10.1007/978-3-319-48496-9_71

providing general training or education, training schools should provide intensive training in emerging research topics.

The issue of education and training, along with youth and sport, is addressed in the European Commission through the Erasmus+Programme [2]. Europe recognizes that providing citizens with the necessary skills will allow them to play an active society role and achieve personal fulfillment. The Erasmus+Programme has three major key actions: (1) Mobility of individuals; (2) Cooperation for innovation and the exchange of good practices and (3) Support for policy reform. Regarding training schools key action 1 is the most interesting vector; thus it considers mobility of learners and staff, Erasmus Mundus Joint Master Degrees and Erasmus+Master Loans. Regarding the mobility of learners and staff a Vocational Education and Training (so called VET) traineeship abroad is considered up to a maximum of 12 months. These vocational training schools are set for both apprentices and students. It is mandatory that the vocational training takes place in another country, where trainees are hosted at a workplace (in an enterprise or other relevant organization) or at a VET school (with periods of work-based learning in an enterprise or other relevant organization). Several H2020 projects offer training schools, within their activities, dedicated to early-stage researchers including internationally renowned scientists and leading industrials. These training schools allow young researchers to further training and allow them to acquire new complementary skills in order to enhance their career development (Fig. 1).

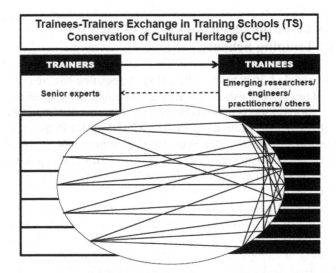

Fig. 1. COST Training Schools: the main focus of trainees-trainers knowledge and ideas' exchange in Training Schools (TS) in Conservation of Cultural Heritage (CCH) © A. Lobovikov-Katz

European Cooperation in Science and Technology (COST organization) is the longest-running European framework. It has been supporting trans-national cooperation across Europe since 1971 [3]. In its role as the breeding ground for trans-sectoral multi-national co-operation projects, COST delivers the best frame to set an effective platform to share the knowledge on related research topics. Through COST Actions, COST supports networking activities with particular attention to research training and exchange. The COST Action functions to accomplish a true multidisciplinary effort and consequently intends to overcome the fragmentation within dedicated scientific and technological research field and thus deliver to the young members of the Action a new horizon to nourish innovative flagship initiatives in an international context. COST Actions have several networking tools at their service:

- Conferences
- Workshops
- Dissemination activities
- Short-term scientific missions

These networking tools let researchers improve their ideas by sharing them with their colleagues, providing valuable inputs for their research, career and innovation. The COST Association view of a training school is an instrument that provides intensive training in emerging research topics within the laboratories and organizations involved in a particular COST Action. Their participants are mainly, but not exclusively, young researchers involved in COST Actions. However, training Schools can also cover appropriate re-training as part of life-long learning. In the year of 2014, COST has financed 370 Actions and 367 training schools have been organized [4].

2 Content and Management Outline of the First i2MHB Training School

Currently composed of 36 countries, the COST Association has created a multidisciplinary team of researchers, experts, companies and public administrations of 23 countries linked to various aspects of heritage management, aimed at implementing actions to more intelligently manage heritage. COST ACTION TD1406 Innovation in Intelligent Management of Heritage Buildings Training School took place in Aguilar de Campoo, Palencia (Spain) on January 27th to 29th 2016. This Training School was based on work from COST Action TD1406, supported by COST (European Cooperation in Science and Technology).

COST (European Cooperation in Science and Technology) is a Pan-European, intergovernmental framework whose mission is enabling breakthrough scientific and technological developments leading to new concepts and products, thereby contributing to the strengthening of Europe's research and innovation capacities. Foundation Santa María la Real Historical Heritage is strongly interested in creating awareness of the current challenges of the heritage sector, and here is where this kind of Training School has its origins. Foundation Santa María la Real Historical Heritage, a Project from Castile and León, emerged in 2014 as the result of the union between two reference entities with extensive experience in the field of heritage: Foundation Santa María la Real Historical Heritage. While maintaining the character of its predecessors, the new institution provides services at the national and international level, with its main focus on the study, restoration, conservation and promotion of social, natural and cultural heritage. The combined efforts of the two participating institutions bring together a wide range of interests and ongoing or past activities, of which more than 500 involve the restoration and enhancement of heritage assets in the nine provinces of Castile and León, as well as at the national level, in different regions.

Triggered by the opening of the COST ACTION call, the necessary efforts for the organization of the activities that would take place during three days were made, and the request to the involved experts for their collaboration was carried out. The next step was the selection of the most suitable trainees, which was accomplished by a board of COST ACTION members. The applicants were carefully selected, on the basis of the motivation letter and CV that they had previously submitted.

English was the second language in the headquarters of Foundation Santa María la Real Historical Heritage during the Training School. 13 students and doctoral students from Spain, and 13 additional ones from different European countries were awarded a scholarship by the European COST association to participate in a training school on innovation in the field of heritage. The Training School enabled the learning of new techniques, methods and advances in heritage management, while working to generate research areas and create networks for specialized contacts.

During the first working day, the participants were able to get close to the Foundation experience in the field of heritage management, as the entity director, Juan Carlos Prieto, explained them how the entity has worked "for more than thirty years on the study, restoration, conservation and dissemination of heritage". They were told that later, owing to the addition of other entities and administrations, the entity acquired new skills, and evolved from restoration to *preventive* restoration and intelligent heritage management. Projects like Monitoring Heritage System (MHS), installed with success in about fifty buildings, enabled the transition. With regards to MHS, not only were the trainees told how the system works, but Dr. M. Chiriac, the engineer of Foundation Santa María la Real Historical Heritage, explained them how the system was developed, the way the sensors act, and their application in heritage building monitoring.

On the second day, the students had the opportunity to see *in situ* how the system works: they visited MHSLab, an intelligent lab created by Foundation Santa María la Real Historical Heritage, which was established in the Romanesque chapel of Canduela. The objective of MHSLab, as the trainees were told, was to test the effectiveness of different types of techniques and materials used in the field of heritage. They also had the opportunity to get to know the Iberian Peninsula Romanesque Encyclopaedia experience, a true cultural project where more than a thousand researchers have collaborated to catalogue many of the Romanesque remains in the Peninsula. The Encyclopaedya can be found in international bookstores and libraries.

Pedro Martín (OMG), a researcher at Cartif Technology Center, gave a talk of his work on 3D documentation of historic buildings. Marija Damjanović, from Croatia, focused her presentation on the transformation of historic landscapes; and Laura Daví, from the University of Barcelona, introduced her research focus on the monastery of San Cugat del Vallés.

Later that day, the Exhibition Centre ROM was visited, and the Israeli architect Anna Lobovikov-Katz, who had developed a new method to improve heritage conservation analysis through technical methods of drawing, participated as a speaker.

On the third day, trainees learned from the following interventions:

The impact of cultural infrastructures. The case of the Human Evolution Museum in Burgos. Alejandro Sarmiento. Manager of Atapuerca System and HE Museum.

A conference on a Digital Information Model for the Knowledge and Management of Immovable Cultural Heritage. Patricia Ferreira Lopes. Architect. Phd student at Higher Technical School of Architecture of Seville. Research group HUM799 "Strategies for the heritage knowledge". A talk on Tourism and Heritage: Building Smart Destinations. Juan Vicente Calle Lamelas. Phd student in Tourism. University Rey Juan Carlos Madrid.

The results of the previous day's practical, conclusions and demonstration of application of Rapid Learning Methodology for Conservation (Preservation) of Cultural Heritage – Understanding through Drawing. Dr. Anna Lobovikov-Katz, Arch., PhD, Technion, Israel.

And finally we ended with a round table discussion on Conclusions of the training school: Challenges for the Early Career Investigators (ECI). During those three days, different topics were addressed: for example, the methods developed by technicians from the University of Belgrade to counteract the effects of earthquakes on heritage, or to fight biological problems affecting conservation. In addition, some speakers explained practical cases, such as the management of Monsalud monastery and the Roman site of Ercávica in Cuenca.

The quality of the Training School was assessed by means of an anonymous survey to the trainees. General results of the survey are shown in Figs. 2, 3, 4 and 5.

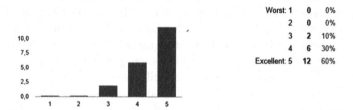

Fig. 2. Q: Did the content and activities carried out in the training school correspond to your expectations?

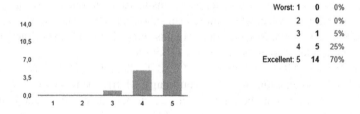

Fig. 3. Q: Did the trainers explain in a clear and concise way the activities in each section?

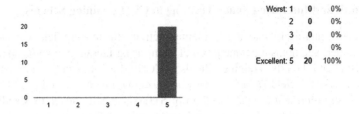

Fig. 4. Q: Were the professionals responsible for the training school close to the students, fostering a good work ambience and participation?

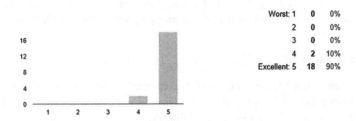

Fig. 5. Q: Were the installations' conditions adequate for the seminar?

Both trainers and trainees of this Training School represent wide range of the areas of knowledge in research and practice within the field of conservation of cultural heritage (CCH).

3   Interdisciplinary Research and Education in Conservation of Cultural Heritage - The Interdisciplinary "Language" for Training Schools (TS)

This section of the paper examines the selected aspects of TS in CCH and their educational value, keeping the following issues in mind:

- Multi- and interdisciplinary character of CCH and CCH training schools
- Main lines of inter-area contributions of education value within the CCH complex
- CCH training schools and contemporary education.

As mentioned in the *Introduction*, training school is an instrument that provides intensive training in emerging research topics within the laboratories and organizations involved in a particular COST Action. This section focuses on the trainee as the main beneficiary of a Training School, through direct instruction. Analysis of the leading role of COST Action management and of local organizers of TS is beyond the scope of this paper, while trainers-related issues are mentioned here merely in the context of trainee-centered analysis.

3.1 Multi- and Interdisciplinary Training in CCH Training Schools

Among many interdisciplinary areas of human activity, the modern field of conservation of cultural heritage holds a unique position, comprising literally the entire spectrum of STEM, SSH and the arts. Training schools in CCH reflect the multi- and interdisciplinary character of this field Therefore, many organizations involved in a single CCH COST action, usually represent a wide spectrum of STEM and SSH fields, thus adding their input to the interdisciplinary structure and content of COST training schools in general, including those in the framework of COST ACTION TD1406 Innovation in Intelligent Management of Heritage Buildings (i2MHB). Analysis of the COST i2MHB training schools showed a wide range of CCH areas of expertise of both trainers and trainees, along with multi- and interdisciplinary cross-area topics introduced in the school program.

3.2 The Audience

Actors. With a view to contribution to CH conservation through educational activities, several main types of actors and their inter-area contribution can be defined. The following main groups of actors can be delineated:

- CCH researchers
- CCH practitioners
- CCH students
- Non-CCH public of diverse background.

Conservation Community. In conservation of CH, research is an integral part of restoration practice, and at the same time, contribution of education to research in CCH has been examined in several publications [5]. With regard to actors from the conservation community (CCH researchers, CCH practitioners and CCH students), we come up with the following scheme (Fig. 6). It presents a multi-beneficial contribution between and within different departments of CCH-activity (practice, research, education) and CCH-actors (practitioners, researchers, students).

Some inter-area contributions are well-explored phenomena, e.g. a dually-beneficial CCH students-CCH practice exchange. Experience in exposure of learners to actual conservation process in curricula or courses in conservation of cultural heritage, has shown good results [6, 7]. Thus, students contribute to actual conservation of cultural heritage, and at the same time enrich their knowledge and understanding in a way which could be hardly achieved in the classroom, through e-learning. In training schools, combined participation of researchers and practitioners, both on the side of lecturers and trainees, reinforces such exposure to the diverse areas of activities. In long-term education, even in a usual semester course, it contributes to the development of cross-area abilities, which might be of benefit to the main area of interest of a trainee, e.g. a conservation practitioner, exposed to a research project, could develop typical research qualities. According to the COST rules, the duration of a training school ranges between 3 days to one week. This short duration of training schools adds to the intensity of inter- and intra-area exchange between diverse groups of actors involved.

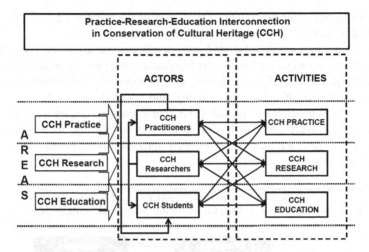

Fig. 6. "Areas-Actors-Activities" scheme: practice-research-education Interaction in Conservation of Cultural Heritage (CCH) © A. Lobovikov-Katz

Non-conservation Public of Diverse Backgrounds. With regard to multiple types of actors in CCH complex, another group should not be overlooked: the non-conservation public. Generally, its members can be subdivided into several sub-groups including (a) general public; students of different levels of education, especially (b) secondary and (c) tertiary levels; (d) non-conservation researchers. The groups "c" and "d" are of particular interest, especially because of inter- and multidisciplinary nature of conservation of cultural heritage. Involvement of sub-groups "c" and "d" (university students and non-conservation researchers) might open new horizons for emerging researchers and engineers, and also contribute to their understanding of interdisciplinary cooperation in the modern reality. CCH learning contributes to understanding of interdisciplinary cooperation in all areas, also those non-related to conservation, among both "c" and "d" groups. Inclusion of non-conservation researchers in the field of conservation of cultural heritage is not a new phenomenon. Their active participation in training schools allows their re-training as part of life-long learning.

3.3   Multiple and Diverse Roles of Trainees in Training Schools

Following good TS practices, and specifically in the course of COST Action MP1004: "Hybrid Energy Storage Devices and Systems for Mobile and Stationary Applications", 2011–2015, different types and levels of involvement of trainees have been encouraged in the COST Training School in Aguilar de Campoo.

In addition to their usual learning role, young participants can be encouraged to propose topics for lectures and for round tables sessions which might be of interest, chairing the round tables discussions (community of young researchers as a breeding ground for new ideas and approaches). They can be also encouraged to suggest the trainers or "invited speakers" etc. In the COST Training School in Aguilar de Campoo trainees were encouraged to give talks/lectures along with their trainers. These correspond to one of the main COST ideas - to pave the way for active involvement of young researchers.

Figure 7 outlines multiple optional roles of trainees (versus trainers) in a Training School (TS) which might include their involvement in the planning stage before TS (a), active participation in the TS activities (b), and evaluation of results after the completion of TS (c). Exposure of trainees to planning, and undertaking activities of combined content-management character provides excellent training ground for the contemporary research reality. Performing such diverse roles as trainee and trainer, student and lecturer, allows the TS trainees to widen their horizons, and to improve their learning abilities through active learning.

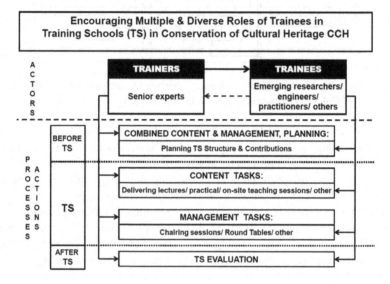

Fig. 7. Encouraging multiple and diverse roles of trainees in training schools before, during and after TS activities © A. Lobovikov-Katz

3.4   Training Schools (TS) and Education

Modern education theory and practice provide a wide range of learning approaches and practices. Several types of learning relevant to CCH training schools can be outlined:

- Class learning activities
- Laboratory
- In-situ learning on historic or conservation sites
- E-learning
- Blended learning (combining frontal instruction with online learning activities).

Bringing TS trainees together in real environment, thus allowing their immediate communication with other trainees and trainers, - is an important advantage of training schools. Therefore, distance learning and e-learning - the innovative contemporary ways of learning - are less relevant to CCH Training Schools. However, blended learning might be helpful, and especially through the inclusion of online activities before or after the TS period, and in non-virtual instruction which takes place on TS venue. Such delayed-in-time linkage of online and offline learning would be a complex multi-disciplinary education development. In addition, blended learning might be also instrumental for real-time blended learning during TS period, in order to facilitate understanding between trainees and trainers of diverse conservation backgrounds. In this case, on-line tasks might be differentiated to suit the diverse parts of target audience, and involve "flipped classroom" methods.

On-site learning activities are indispensible in CCH, which is in line with innovative development in education of recent decades [8]. Pre-planned combination of "passive" and "active" learning activities in diverse types of learning and in different learning situations, and especially the in-situ learning in CCH research and practice held on heritage conservation sites, can result in innovative results [9].

Training School (TS) in CCH comprises diverse components, and gives trainees a unique access to:

- Diverse types of learning activities (class/on-site/laboratory; active/passive)
- Inter- and multidisciplinary learning material
- Local cultural heritage and its conservation
- Diverse types of knowledge (CCH research; actual CH projects)
- Immediate learning and scientific exchange with senior CCH experts
- Diverse teaching methods showcasing educational trends from different universities and other organizations
- Combining several roles in TS (optional), e.g. learning (trainee), teaching (giving a presentation), scientific management (contributing to a TS planning; moderating a session)

TS goals can be easily formulated as deriving from the contemporary CCH requirements and EU policy in research, education and training. However, the open-end character of TS activities can complicate defining and achieving specific learning objectives. The application of educational theories and approaches, commonly used in "regular" education on different levels, should be specifically adjusted to CCH TS. According to the authors' experience, TS trainees are often characterized by high learning motivation and multi-disciplinary educational background. These and other data often contribute to effective learning and creative knowledge exchange between trainees, and trainers, and support the overall dynamic character of training schools in the conservation of cultural heritage.

4   Conclusions

The summarizing document of COST strategic Workshop *The Safeguard of Cultural Heritage* pointed out that 'the need for trans-disciplinary cooperation and training of young scientists to strengthen the European research arena in the field of cultural heritage is a recurrent theme' [10]. Ultimately interdisciplinary character of modern conservation of CH, involving different fields of science, technology, humanities and arts, tight connection between research and practice typical of this field, along with often multi- and interdisciplinary profile of CCH experts, have a challenging impact on CCH Training Schools.

Following the continuing development in conservation of cultural heritage, and education, there would be a lasting need for reviewing and re-developing CCH training. Training Schools in conservation of cultural heritage can provide a unique testing ground for improvement and development of training in interdisciplinary research and development outside the CCH domain, and, in turn, contribute to the preservation of the world heritage through training researchers, engineers, architects, archaeologists and conservators.

Acknowledgements. This article is based upon work from COST Action TD1406 i2MHB - Innovation in Intelligent Management of Heritage Buildings, supported by COST (European Cooperation in Science and Technology).

References

1. UNESCO Education Strategy: United Nations Educational, Scientific and Cultural Organization (2014)
2. Erasmus+Programme Guide: European Commission (2016)
3. About COST: C. Halén, COST Office (2014)
4. COST Annual Report 2014: COST Association (2015)
5. Lobovikov-Katz, A.: Heritage education for heritage conservation (contribution of educational codes to study of deterioration of natural building stone in historic monuments). Strain Int. J. Exp. Mech. **45**(5), 480–484 (2009)
6. Lobovikov-Katz, A.: The virtual and the real: e-learning in interdisciplinary education – the case of cultural heritage. In: The 13th Annual MEITAL National Conference "New Technologies and Their Evaluation in Online Teaching and Learning", Technion - Israel Institute of Technology, Haifa, June 2015 (2015). http://meital.iucc.ac.il/conf2015/papers15/A3_3.pdf
7. Keith, D.A.: Reflections on eight semesters of employing service learning in an undergraduate historic preservation course. Preserv. Educ. Res. **4** (2011)
8. Levin-Peled, R., Sagy, O., Lobovikov-Katz, A., Chitaiad, T.: Guidelines and tips for creating an interesting and appealing learning process for young students. In: Educational Linkage Approach in Cultural Heritage, ELAICH, ENPI 150583 (2010)
9. Lobovikov-Katz, A., et al.: Tangible versus intangible in e-Learning on cultural heritage: from online learning to on-site study of historic sites. In: Ioannides, M., Magnenat-Thalmann, N., Fink, E., Žarnić, R., Yen, A.-Y., Quak, E. (eds.) EuroMed 2014. LNCS, vol. 8740, pp. 819–828. Springer, Heidelberg (2014). doi:10.1007/978-3-319-13695-0_84
10. Fioravanti, M., Mecca, S. (eds.): Proceedings of COST Strategic Workshop on the Safeguard of Cultural Heritage: A Challenge From the Past for the Europe of Tomorrow, 11th–13th July 2011 Florence, Italy (Proceedings e report; 80). Firenze University Press, Firenze (2011)

Educational Creative Use and Reuse of Digital Cultural Heritage Data for Cypriot UNESCO Monuments

Marinos Ioannides[1], Pavlos Chatzigrigoriou[1(✉)], Vasilis Bokolas[1],
Vasiliki Nikolakopoulou[1], Vasilis Athanasiou[1], Eirini Papageorgiou[1],
Georgios Leventis[1], and Christian Sovis[2]

[1] Cyprus University of Technology, CY 3036 Limassol, Cyprus
{marinos.ioannides,p.chatzigrigoriou,v.nikolakopoulou,
vasilis.athanasiou,e.papageorgiou,georgios.leventis}@cut.ac.cy,
vmpoko@yahoo.gr
[2] 7Reasons, Hauptplatz 11, 3462 Absdorf, Austria
cs@7reasons.net

Abstract. Nowadays, there is a rising demand of reusing the constantly enriched information from heritage digitalization in different ways. One of the objectives of the EU Europeana Space project is the development of a holistic approach for educating people (grown-ups and kids) on Monuments that are listed at UNESCO world heritage list, in Cyprus. The proposed model action is based on the cross cultural approach which, at the same time, responds to the contemporary pedagogical and methodological directions. The system uses innovative digital heritage resources to help the user learn about the different phases of the monument, the history, the architectural value and the conservation stage. The result is a responsive educational platform, where every Monument is a different course and every course is addressed to different age groups. Moreover, part of our future work is the evaluation of the platform by particular groups of our target users.

Keywords: 3D models · Education · Digital heritage · Cross-cultural · CH data reuse

1 Introduction

Objective of the project is the holistic approach of a listed UNESCO World Heritage Monuments in Cyprus, for development of a platform to educate people (grown-ups and kids). The system uses innovative digital heritage resources, in order to help the user, in a UX friendly way, to learn about the different phases of the monument, the history, the architectural value and the conservation stage. The resulting platform is accessible through smart devices and desktop computers, (in the frame of "Bring Your Own Device" a.k.a. BYOD). The main challenge was the reuse of Europeana Data (Pictures and 3D objects) in a way that the information on the platform would be comprehensible. Computer technologies allow various visualizations and digital re-constructions of archaeological monuments and sites. These models can be integrated in a demonstration as an educational user friendly platform, a tool that addresses Cultural Heritage (CH)

© Springer International Publishing AG 2016
M. Ioannides et al. (Eds.): EuroMed 2016, Part I, LNCS 10058, pp. 891–901, 2016.
DOI: 10.1007/978-3-319-48496-9_72

artefacts' reconstruction by using the Europeana (and other creative commons) collections. The work started with a preliminary search on Europeana and other online management galleries and the identification of objects/monument for the demonstration. It then used the images and models that can be found on Europeana as thumbnails and that can be reached through Europeana on the holders' web-sites. When the object is of high quality and ready, then it can be offered for free use to education, architecture, historians, civil engineers, students, etc. The tool will be available by the end of the project as a Pilot test platform for primary, secondary, tertiary educational levels, and also to support vocational training (for archaeologists, preservation, protection of monuments and sites), and the tourist industry (for example guides). Also, an evaluation plan has been set up in order for us to have the first results from our target users, their reactions to the content and how the platform could be implemented as a teaching procedure.

2   Aims - Limitations

The basic aim of the project is the development of a completed system of a digital information, education and entertainment (edutainment) for adults, adolescents and teenagers concerning the most representative monuments and landmarks of Cyprus, reusing existing data from Europeana.

The proposed UNESCO monuments digital learning system will further aim to:

1. Help users to learn the history of the UNESCO monument
2. Educate users in architecture and cultural heritage
3. Raise awareness on protecting and conserving our heritage
4. Promote the UNESCO monuments
5. Inform on risks that threaten the monuments

For the development of the Educational Tool, we are re-using Digital Heritage Data (DHD), starting from simple pictures of the Monuments and - at the highest end - 3D objects. A complete recording of a monument requires the first step to be a digitization to develop the 3D model. 3D objects can be presented by plethora of methods and technologies depending on factors that influence the monument and the suitability. Three most common factors that need to be calculated before initializing an approach to a 3D reconstruction are the following: (a) Complexity in size and shape, (b) Morphological complexity (level of detail) and (c) Diversity of raw materials.

Since in this project's aim is the re-use of CH data that thrive through Europeana collections, we contacted an in depth research for this content in Europeana's Repositories. Apparently, Europeana's content is inefficient for 3D image reconstruction. Furthermore, the Digital Heritage Surveying Data (DHSD) is also limited as well as several other techniques that are also helpful in the 3D reconstruction procedure of a monument, as empirical techniques, topographic techniques and rectified photography.

3 Educational Approach

Taking into consideration all the aforementioned limitations, we adopted our project to the content we had available. Certain images and 3D models of UNESCO's monuments in Cyprus were used in order to form the educational content of the platform. The presented educational tool responds to the multicultural features of present era but at the same time to the contemporary pedagogical and methodological directions.

Nowadays, the challenge of re-using digitized cultural heritage content from Open Repositories is an issue that concerns scientists, practitioners, professionals and institutions of the related field. One of the areas that re-use can yield fruit is education. On the one hand, arts and cultural heritage education has been regarded as the key factors in development of the knowledge society and creative ability [1]. On the other hand, the ongoing development of Information and Communication Technologies (ICTs) is providing new opportunities of representation and interpretation of cultural heritage. Thus, learning about cultural heritage with the mediation of ICT tools and methods - in our case the e-learning platform enriched with multimedia content - can be affective in all educational levels by using appropriately the available ICT affordances.

Information technology and the 'culture of the image' gradually and steadily gain a key role in school learning while at the same time there is a constant fervent effort in the modern educational systems to functionally and effectively integrate the 'new media' both as teaching tools and as a distinct separate school subject (in ventures of a reformation/review of the content of the existing curricula). Besides all this, the most important reason for using digital tools in education is because it constitutes an entraining way for the acquisition of knowledge and it can compose a refreshing change to the daily school routine enhancing children's enthusiasm [2]. Apart from underage learners, we also aim to engage adolescents, adults as well as vocational trainers in learning and becoming aware of these historic monuments. Learning about the culture, the living conditions, the human creations and attitudes in the course of time, understanding the historic-cultural events and the evolution of society, and finally discerning what has survived at the sociocultural surroundings, is the quintessence of arts and cultural heritage education. But in order to achieve the favorable learning outcome, there are four learning approaches that we employed for ensuring the values of ICTs in cultural heritage education: (1) Personalized, inquiry-based learning approaches (2) On-site and anywhere learning experiences (3) Interdisciplinary learning approaches and (4) Collaborative learning experiences [1].

Each one of these approaches has its origins to the main changes brought by the massive and precise digitalization of Cultural Heritage in the recent years. Every single cultural artifact becomes digital in a way that its primary ontological value is expanded. For instance, images of such artifacts are no longer bi-dimensional; their detailed and zooming abilities allow users to study and interact with them in any preferred dimensional level. What is more, zooming out of those images puts cultural artifacts into a wider context that reveals where they lie on or have been created. These are perspectives that can adopt innovative approaches to teaching and learning [1]. In the sections below, it is analyzed how we manage to approximate the aforementioned approaches to the online educational platform.

4   Methodology

First of all, it was very important that the design of the online educational platform would follow the "bring your own device" (BYOD) [3, 4] approach, as the most common and easier to apply method. BYOD refers to "technology models where students bring a personally owned device to school for the purpose of learning" [5]. There has been an increasing interest in supporting BYOD in schools by growing support from students, parents, and teachers. A US survey conducted by Project Tomorrow, shows that over 60 % of middle and high school students prefer to use their own devices for learning unlike school supplied laptops or netbooks [6]. Another survey by Bradford Networks for educational institutes in US and UK [7] showed that 78 % use devices in their school systems "for personal use by teachers and students," while 72 % stated that students use the devices to complete class assignments. The results indicate great acceptance of BYOD approach and that might be due to the very purpose of any educational sector to provide knowledge with every means of information possible. Nevertheless, although BYOD is generally considered to help promote better outcomes via a more personalized learning and act as a connection between home, school and other spaces, how BYOD can offer to inquiry-based pedagogical practices in authentic learning environment is still immature [3].

Therefore, in order to achieve a more personalized and possible on-site and anywhere learning experience, we developed a platform compatible to all smart devices (android, iPhone, iPad, windows tablets). A responsive web site was decided to be used, with the

Fig. 1. Screenshot of the web site of Panagia Assinou online course. Orthophotographs, photogrammetric pictures, 3D sections and other surveying products were used for educational purposes.

capability to run on desktop and portable devices. The design of the platform is based on an Educational Theme (WordPress) with CSS reconfiguration. The decision for an Educational Theme was taken in order to use an environment familiar to most of the visitors (both students and teachers). Since it is widely regarded that the most common used educational platforms at the internet are Coursera, Udacity, edX etc. [8, 9], we use similar User Interface design so that is familiar to the users. This way we cover the UX Design requirement (Fig. 1). Having in mind that the challenge is to use the Europeana Data (mostly photogrammetric pictures and 3D objects) in a way that the information on the platform will be comprehensible by the users, data should be presented in an appropriate way so to cover all the users' spectrum. Most of the data have little metadata information and they lack history and cultural value description (semantics). Even when we have this information, we need to adjust the data to make the information useful for educators and people

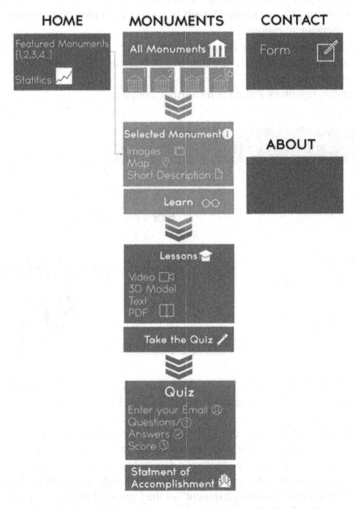

Fig. 2. A detailed site map was the first step to design the site.

that are not familiar with cultural heritage. The first step was to design a detailed Site Map, taking under consideration the UX Design guidelines (Fig. 2).

As one can see at the demonstrator site (wp.digitalheritagelab.eu), every monument is a different "Course". Every course has a number of lessons, just like in any online education portal. The information about the monument is divided to separate lessons, as follows (Fig. 3):

1. Lesson about the History of the Monument.
2. Lesson about the Local History: short reference on the local history through the literature study.
3. Video: short dramatized video, which presents on a descriptive and communicative dimension the key elements that anyone should know about the monument (in an understandable form, suitably subtitled for both adults and children).
4. Glossary: important words that are used at the text.
5. The 3D object (downloadable in a pdf file and in a simple online version).
6. Comprehension questions.
7. Activities: puzzles, hotspot images, games.
8. Quiz: a short quiz (usually 10–20 Questions) about the Monument. You need to score 70 % in order to pass.
9. References: resources and links for further studying

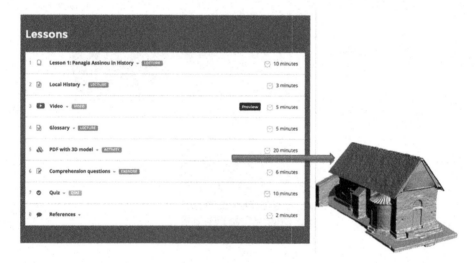

Fig. 3. Example of lessons' structure. The 3D file is used for download purpose, encouraging the schools to use it for 3D printing and then painting it in classrooms by the kids.

In every lesson, there is a time estimation, to help educators and users to manage their own time and pace when studying about the monument. At the end, there is a "Review" section. Every visitor can write a review and choose 1–5 stars for the course. This way, courses with better score will be proposed at the Home Page. Finally, users can print a "statement of accomplishment" of the Course, if they pass the Quiz.

The web site, as an educational tool, uses different digital heritage data depending on the age of the users. For kids aged between 6 and 10 years old, the ortho-rectified pictures were used as a puzzle game (Fig. 4). For older kids the same pictures can be used as "find the hot-spot" game, were useful information is hidden under different hot-spots of the image (Fig. 5). In all ages, 3D models of the Monument are used to encourage interaction but - most important - to give the teacher the opportunity to download and 3D print the model. This way, the kids can touch, paint and interact with the Monument's model, enriching the overall learning experience. Furthermore, students could be divided into groups (either e-course is a lesson inside the classroom or homework assignment)

Fig. 4. Using ortho-rectified pictures for developing interesting online games for educational purposes. In this case, a picture was used for an online puzzle game, addressing kids aged 6 years old

Fig. 5. Using photogrammetric or panorama pictures for developing interesting online games for educational purposes. These pictures cover bigger areas than usual pictures and more "hot spots" could be applied on them, with more information.

so to foster collaboration among them to produce shared ideas and form knowledge through communication and interaction. What is also achievable via the e-learning platform is the collaboration between students from different schools, either Cypriot or International. These collaborative learning experiences are available by the proper use of such ICT tools.

At the same time, the content of every lesson is different, depending on the ages of the users. For users aged over 16 years old, for life-learning users and for vocational training, the content is more advanced; the glossary is more complex and the demands (quiz, comprehensive questions) are higher. The courses (monuments) that are addressed for younger children, the content is simplified according to their age. In order to organize the courses and improve the user experience of the site, three virtual teachers were developed. Each teacher has different ages in her/his virtual classroom and different courses (monuments). This way, if an educator teaches i.e. elementary school, she/he would follow the elementary school virtual teacher, using fast and efficient the correct courses for the classroom.

5   Results - Conclusions

Today is obvious that we have a lot of digital data (especially from crowdsourcing platforms like Europeana) with controversial information. If any student, educator or simple user needs to learn or study the history of a monument, usually she/he ends up (through google search) to huge number of information, text, picture (with no obvious connection or order) and without the semantics or the metadata that they need to study the Monument.

In order to achieve rigid results, we combined the Europeana and Open Source Data on the Internet, with an educational tool. The model construction is based on the cross-cultural approach, which responds to the multicultural features of present era but at the same time to the contemporary pedagogical and methodological directions.

The result is an online learning user-friendly experience, where visitors (educators, students and simple users) have the opportunity to read, watch, interact (3D model) and test their knowledge in cultural heritage. The information is adjusted to their needs and, if they finish the course successfully, they can use the references to deepen their knowledge.

The affordances described above: personalized content for different ages, roles (teachers - students), professionals, can be furthered integrated with interdisciplinary learning dimensions. Specific objects can be linked with external or internal data to related sources from various relevant disciplines. An existed network could be broadened with historical, socio-cultural, economical and other geographical links, which allow a stronger interpretation of the presented cultural artifact itself [10].

Moreover, one of the future features of the platform would be the ability to provide a 3D model of the monument constructed by photographs taken by actual users being on the site's physical environment. For cultural e-courses this kind of personalized e-learning functionality, and therefore personalized interaction, is one of the most important requirements [10].

Last but not least, Europeana's content enrichment with Image Based Modeling Data is considered to be vital in order to overcome the existing obstacles and limitations and to provide the user with superior robusting experiences.

6 Future Work

An evaluation of the platform is planned to be conducted with (a subset of) our target users participating at the procedure. Students, teachers as well as teaching inspectors in two schools, one in Greece and the other one in Cyprus, will evaluate the platform. In order to cover the cross-cultural aspect of the application, it is important to engage both the users that know the monuments and can visit them on site (Cypriots) and the users that might have some information about the monuments but they are not capable of visiting those (Greeks). The evaluation of the educational aspect of the platform will follow a methodology of joint techniques, in order to have a more integrated and overall view of the evaluation results.

In this phase a prototype of the platform is completed and running successfully and we intend to run a formative evaluation. Formative evaluation, is usually taking place during the development or improvement of an educational program or product [11], in order to make it more effective and make any changes appropriate as well as to check whether it meets the learning needs of the users [12, 13]. It is a user-centered approach [14].

Before evaluating the platform, some definitions of the terms involved must be clear. First, educational software is considered any application used for the computational support of education and teaching. Evaluation of educational software is the systematic collection, analysis and interpretation of information of any aspect of a product, with direction to the ascertainment of its effectiveness and efficiency or the estimation of any other parameters relevant to its applicability [15]. Generally, in the evaluation process of educational software, the educational environment where the software is used, the perceptions of the students as well as other parameters involved in the learning process (stakeholders, environment), should be taken into consideration [16].

Regarding the collection of research data, it has been noted that the persistence with one technique can influence or misrepresent the image of the subject that the researcher has dealt with [17]. So, it is necessary to use combinatorial methods, such as interview, focus groups, and/or (e-)questionnaires. Those three methods are planned to be employed in our evaluation process. The teaching inspectors will evaluate the platform through interviews, teachers will use questionnaires and finally, students will evaluate the software in focus groups. These pairs of method-user were assigned according to the types of users and the quality/quantity of the data we want to receive from each one type.

In detail, interview is particularly prevalent and effective in the case of 'qualitative' surveys. In this research, semi structured interviews on subjects that promote, teach and communicate historical knowledge, are directed to 'capture' ideas, thoughts and representations that the subject has on the particular research topic [18–20]. The questions will be categorized into: (a) demographic (general nature and on the expertise of individuals), (b) cognitive (knowledge held by people on the subject), (c) experience and (d) personal opinion [21]. Sampling and analytical issues of data resulting from the interviews will be handled based on the international relevant literature [22].

The planned questionnaires will take account both specific ethical issues (informed consent, understanding of the opportunities provided by the research, confidentiality, anonymity and non-traceability, reliability and validity) and basic functionality criteria, structure and usability. The aim is to create a short, focused and easy to use tool, which will be distributed and (at the best case scenario) completed electronically through the Internet [17].

Last but not least, students are the most important evaluators with the, most difficult and intensive to design, evaluation technique. The "special group session" (focus group) is a technique of qualitative data collection, in which a small number of participants (usually 4–9 people) discuss and comment on a specific topic, under the guidance of a trained mediator. Participants are distinguished by some common characteristics, such as their relationship with the matter under investigation, but also by the growing dynamic between them during the session [23]. The value of this technique is based on the interaction and the 'chemistry' that can be developed between the participants, which encourages them to express freely and with intimacy, unobstructed views, attitudes and ideas they have about the subject matter, agreements or disagreements with the opinions or attitudes of the other attendees [24]. All these are describing a full educational context when learning is taking place inside the classroom. Such forms of rich interactions and dialogs we are expecting to record from students.

Acknowledgements.   1. Europeana Space (http://www.europeana-space.eu/) has received funding from the European Union's ICT Policy Support Program as part of the Competitiveness and Innovation Framework Program, under GA no. 621037.

2. ITN-DCH (http://www.itn-dch.eu/) project has received funding from the European Union's Seventh Framework program for research, technological development and demonstration under GA no. 608013.

3. INCEPTION (http://www.inception-project.eu/) has received funding from the EU's H2020 Reflective framework programme for research and innovation under GA no. 665220.

4. 4DCH (http://www.4d-ch-world.eu/) project has received funding from the European Union's Seventh Framework program for research, technological development and demonstration.

5. Lo-Cloud (http://www.locloud.eu/) is co-funded under the CIP ICT-PSP program.

6. ViMM (http://www.vi-mm.eu/) has received funding from the EU's H2020 framework programme for support and coordination actions under GA no. 727107.

References

1. Ott, M., Pozzi, F.: ICT and cultural heritage education: which added value? In: Lytras, M.D., Carroll, J.M., Damiani, E., Tennyson, Robert, D. (eds.) WSKS 2008. LNCS (LNAI), vol. 5288, pp. 131–138. Springer, Heidelberg (2008). doi:10.1007/978-3-540-87781-3_15

2. Stafford, T.: Teaching Visual Literacy in the Primary Classroom: Comic Books, Film, Television and Picture Narratives. Routledge, London (2010)

3. Song, Y.: "Bring Your Own Device (BYOD)" for seamless science inquiry in a primary school. Comput. Educ. **74**, 50–60 (2014)
4. Afreen, R.: Bring Your Own Device (BYOD) in higher education: Opportunities and challenges. Int J Emerg Trends Technol Comput Sci **3**, 233–236 (2014)
5. Alberta Education: Bring your own device: a guide for schools (2012). Accessed 25 June 2012
6. Palmer research white paper: best practices for enabling BYOD in education (2013)
7. Bradford Networks: The impact of BYOD in education
8. Yuan, L., Powell, S.: MOOCs and disruptive innovation: implications for higher education. eLearning Pap. In-depth. **33**, 1–7 (2013)
9. Zutshi, S., O'Hare, S., Rodafinos, A.: Experiences in MOOCs: the perspective of students. Am. J. Distance Educ. **27**, 218–227 (2013)
10. Styliadis, A.D., Akbaylar, I.I., Papadopoulou, D.A., Hasanagas, N.D., Roussa, S.A., Sexidis, L.A.: Metadata-based heritage sites modeling with e-learning functionality. J. Cult. Heritage **10**, 296–312 (2009)
11. Postlethwaite, T.N.: Educational research: some basic concepts and terminology 1. Comp. Educ. **1**, 1–55 (2005)
12. Maslowski, R., Visscher, A.J.: Formative evaluation in educational computing research and development. J. Res. Comput. Educ. **32**, 239–255 (1999)
13. Reeves, T.C.: Evaluation of the design and development of IT tools in education. In: Voogt, J., Knezek, G. (eds.) International Handbook of Information Technology in Primary and Secondary Education, pp. 1037–1051. Springer, Heidelberg (2008)
14. Pintelas, P., Karatrantou, A., Panagiotakopoulos, C.: The evaluation of educational software and its content. Deukalion (2012)
15. Panagiotakopoulos, C., Pierrakeas, C., Pintelas, P.: The Educational Software and Its Evaluation. Metaichmio Publishing, Athens (2003)
16. Squires, D.: An heuristic approach to the evaluation of educational multimedia software (1997). http://www.media.uwe.ac.uk/~masoud/cal-97/papers/squires.htm
17. Cohen, L., Manion, L., Morrison, K.: Methodology of Educational Research. Ekfrasi, Athens (1997)
18. Patton, M.Q.: Qualitative Evaluation and Research Methods. SAGE Publications Inc., Newbury Park (1990)
19. Opie, C.: Research Procedures Doing Educational Research. A Guide to First Time Researchers. Sage Publications, London (2004)
20. Rubin, H.J., Rubin, I.: Qualitative Interviewing: The Art of Hearing Data. Sage Publication, Thousand Oaks (1995)
21. Wallen, N.E., Fraenkel, J.R.: Educational Research: A Guide to the Process. Psychology Press, Cambridge (2001)
22. Mertler, C., Charles, C.: Introduction to Research. Pearson Education Inc., New York (2005)
23. Litosseliti, L.: Using Focus Groups in Research. A&C Black, London (2003)
24. Goldenkoff, R.: Using focus groups. In: Wholey, J., Hatry, H., Newcomer, K. (eds.) Handbook of Practical Program Evaluation, pp. 340–362. JosseyBass, San Francisco (2004)

Time-Travelling with Mobile Augmented Reality: A Case Study on the Piazza dei Miracoli

Mihai Duguleana[1(⊠)], Raffaello Brodi[2], Florin Girbacia[1], Cristian Postelnicu[1], Octavian Machidon[1], and Marcello Carrozzino[2]

[1] Faculty of Mechanical Engineering, Department of Automotive and Transport Engineering, University Transilvania of Brasov, 500036 Brasov, Romania
{mihai.duguleana,garbacea,cristian-cezar.postelnicu, octavian.machidon}@unitbv.ro
[2] PERCRO – TECIP, Scuola Superiore Sant'Anna of Pisa, 56017 San Giuliano Terme, Italy
{raffaello.brondi,m.carrozzino}@sssup.it

Abstract. This paper presents a new application in the field of cultural heritage, allowing outdoor site exploration throughout different periods of time, based on Mobile Augmented Reality (MAR) technology. The purpose of this research is to allow a free interaction metaphor between users and heritage landmarks, and to enrich their travel experience with important historic facts. We use Metaio SDK to implement this concept within an Android application. We take the specific case of the Leaning Tower of Pisa, the Cathedral and the Baptistery, all key landmarks from Piazza dei Miracoli in Pisa, to prove the usefulness of this paradigm. Five epochs are presented within the application, together with key data about each of them. We assess the usability and engagement of this application by conducting a study with 15 users. The results obtained from the user evaluation show that the concept is not only valid, but also attracting to most of the people. The findings suggest that this kind of applications may attract more visitors while also enhancing their visiting experience.

Keywords: Cultural heritage · Augmented Reality · Mobile phones · UNESCO World Heritage · User experience

1 Introduction

Today, Augmented Reality (AR) is widely used in several contexts including Cultural Heritage. By combining real and virtual worlds, AR aims at enriching the user experience. The current research trends regard AR developments in the broader field of tourism (including visiting historical landmarks and cultural heritage sites) as instruments capable of providing extended information about the visualized items while also being able to maximize the visitors' satisfaction and enhance their experience [1]. There is a comprehensive research activity within the field of AR in museums, with applications targeting the improvement of the visitor's experience by creating an informational synergy between the real and digital world, providing additional digital

© Springer International Publishing AG 2016
M. Ioannides et al. (Eds.): EuroMed 2016, Part I, LNCS 10058, pp. 902–912, 2016.
DOI: 10.1007/978-3-319-48496-9_73

material (3D data, images, videos) about the cultural assets. The stated goal of many heritage studies that use AR is to offer, by the means of digital restoration, a historical accurate visual/audio perspective on landscapes, items and activities no longer available (either totally or partially).

There are many initiatives that use AR as a starting point, and build over this technology. For example, in [2] is proposed the use of serious games (enhanced with immersive technologies such as virtual environments and augmented reality) to improve the cultural heritage experience, bringing it closer to the large public and enabling learning cultural content in an engaging way. Other studies use the metaphor of a "flash-light" to provide AR content [3], or 3D audio content as means to augment the reality [4].

However, despite such a wide spreading of AR systems and guides in the field of cultural heritage, time-based applications are scarcely exploited, and their influence on the visitor's behavior has not been properly evaluated so far. Ha, T. et al. proposed a semantic model based on meta-data rather than actively using multiple planes for each era [5]. In [6], authors use a display bar and 2D images, instead of 3D models, to display the augmented content. Moreover, most of the literature focuses on indoor applications (museum guides, virtual and augmented installations and exhibitions for a museum). This paper proposes an AR-based time-travel guide and analyzes the effectiveness of the system on visitors/tourists of the largest landmark from Pisa, the Piazza dei Miracoli. Based on this analysis, we summarize a few guidelines for future AR applications used as outdoor time-based guides, in order to raise their effectiveness and improve the user interaction.

1.1 Related Works

There are a lot of studies and experimental implementations developed for integrating virtual or augmented reality systems in cultural heritage sites.

In [1] the researchers present the implementation of a mobile-AR educational game for iPhones destined to aid the visitor's understanding about an archeological site and exhibition. A flexible 3D semi-immersive platform for the virtual recreation of Cultural Heritage monuments with educational applications is presented in [7]. The authors also conducted a survey to evaluate the impact of the platform usage on students, and the results showed that it had the potential to raise student interest in cultural heritage and while also easing the learning process.

Immersive systems have a great potential in improving the learning process, and are thus targeted as having possible applications in the cultural heritage field. Researchers in [8] have created an information landscape-based immersive system intended to allow a fast and easy navigation among a large volume of various types of cultural heritage information (text, audio, and video).

Other works in this area [9–11] include the development of immersive tour experience systems for cultural tour sites. These are basically observation posts enhanced with audio/video augmented reality to provide the immersive experience by superimposing virtual cultural heritage artifacts on their historical accurate position in the real world (thus being able to virtually reconstruct lost landscapes, buildings, etc.).

In [12] the visitor experience was also evaluated using a questionnaire, the users rating it as positive and appreciating the novelty of the AR system.

Most recent research targets implementing augmented reality systems on mobile devices, for raising their availability and ease-of-use [13]. A smartphone 3d model visualization system based on augmented reality is presented in [14] as being a novel approach for implementing such visualization systems for outdoor environments, such as the one proposed in this paper.

Another example is the work described in [15], where a mobile application designed to improve the user's cultural experience during the sightseeing of a city of art is described. This app basically detects the POIs inside the mobile device's camera's video feed and composes an augmented scene with a virtual image slider, providing thus the user with additional digital content regarding the specific item retrieved using a cloud computing service.

There are several other related papers [16] that describe similar applications of interactive augmented reality systems for enhanced exploration of cultural heritage sites and artifacts. As mentioned above, all these papers present the design and implementation of various AR/VR systems in cultural heritage environments but lack a proper evaluation of how their usage impacts the visitors of such sites.

The authors of [17] are among the first to follow such a direction by showing the potential role of embodied AR experience in changing thoughts and beliefs about a certain place (from a cultural/social point of view). Also, [18] presents a MAR travel guide and evaluates the relation between this system and the user's emotion, adoption behavior and other cognitive implications. Regarding the user adoption of such AR systems, in [19] are identified three factors as being very influential in encouraging cultural heritage visitors to use AR apps: technology readiness, visual factor of the AR and situational factor.

2 Methods and Materials

2.1 MAR Setup

The AR application presented in this paper is called TowerAR. It is an Android based application that uses MAR to present historical information (3D models and photographs) from Piazza dei Miracoli, Pisa. The application was developed using Metaio SDK library (www.metaio.com). The MAR experience is provided via a Samsung Galaxy Tab S2 tablet. In order to augment the video stream from the camera, the user can point the tablet to a monument and can select the information related to it that will be displayed registered on the target. Users can select to display just 2D information on top of the video or the full 3D reconstruction of the building. The main functionalities of the AR system are:

- **AR view of 3D models:** This is the main view of the TowerAR application where the 3D models are displayed co-located with the real monument, based on the selected time period. The view is presented in the Fig. 1.

Fig. 1. The TowerAR app main components

- **Detailed information view:** Shows detailed information as historical images displayed close to the selected monument. Each of the photographs contains a description of the monument from the specific historic period.
- **Timeline selection:** Allows selecting different periods using specific buttons.
- **Landmark selection:** Allows selecting between the 3 different landmarks: the Tower, the Cathedral or the Baptistery (Fig. 2).

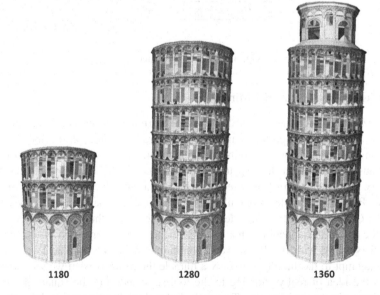

Fig. 2. The 3D models of the Leaning Tower used for the time-based guide (years 1180, 1280 and 1360)

2.2 Application Architecture

TowerAR has a relatively simple design, which is flexible enough to be customized for any heritage site with multiple landmarks (Fig. 3). The user can navigate through 3 separate panels. In the dashboard area, users can choose among the monuments which are closer to their location. As soon as a monument is selected, the camera turns on and the users can point the mobile device towards the monument which they want to learn more about. Using a timeline bar, users can choose the time in history during which they want to visualize the augmented stream. Based on the Metaio SDK, the mobile device identifies the landmark and overwrite the output with information collected from the 3D models and the content databases.

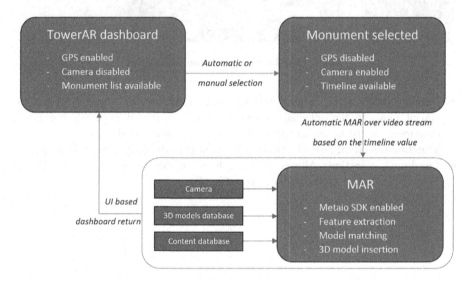

Fig. 3. TowerAR architecture

2.3 Case Study: Piazza dei Miracoli

The Piazza dei Miracoli is an UNESCO World Heritage Site located in center of Pisa, Tuscany, Italy. This important landmark is regarded as one of the most beautiful European medieval centers due to its fine architectural elements. The square consists of 4 religious structures: the leaning tower, the Cathedral, the Baptistry and the Sacred Cemetery. The evolution of these edifices has been well documented over time. The tower of Pisa, for example, was built in 3 stages, over a time span of 177 years [20]. Both the Cathedral and the Baptistery evolved a lot since they were first completed. Given the extent of happenings that could influence the present form of the Piazza dei Miracoli (starting with the Pisan wars, continuing with World War Two and Mussolini's attempt to fix the tilt), it is truly a miracle the result is what we see today. This gave us the idea of really showing to the tourists wandering the square the way the tower changed over the centuries. The Cathedral and the Baptistery also have their own stories. The Cathedral's construction started in 1064, almost 120 years before the construction of the tower begun. The building evolved over the next hundreds of years to the form we can witness today. The Baptistery is the largest building of its kind in Italy, and was not originally thought to sustain a dome. The most recent roof form was given by Nicola and Giovanni Pisano, by the XIV century.

3 Evaluation

A user study has been conducted in order to assess the usability and appreciation of the developed application. The system has been proposed to several tourists visiting Piazza dei Miracoli, and the impressions of the participants have been collected using an online questionnaire.

3.1 Procedure

The experimenters asked people visiting the square to participate in the experiment. After an explanation of the purpose of the experiment and an introduction to the TowerAR application, a tablet has been given to the participants who were left free to visit the square. In order to get information about the surrounding monuments, they only needed to point the tablet towards the points of interest. Participants were allowed to use the tablet as much as they wanted (each participant used the app between 3 and 10 min). After they tried the application, participants were asked to fill a questionnaire which collected their impressions.

3.2 Participants

The participants to the experiment have been recruited among tourists visiting the square. A total of 15 subjects, 11 males and 4 females subjects, aged between 17 and 48 (31.14 ± 7.95) years took part at the experiment. During the recruitment we asked the participants to rate their usage of mobile devices on a Likert-scale (from 1 to 7) and if they have ever previously used an AR application. Each one of them uses a smartphone or tablet almost every day (6.6 ± 0.71) but just a third of them have ever used or seen an AR application.

3.3 Questionnaire Design

The questionnaire proposed to the users (Table 1) was composed by a first section intended to collect some demographic information (gender and age) and the degree of familiarity of the subjects with mobile devices and AR applications. The second section (Q3–Q17) aims to assess the usability of the application using the Handheld Augmented Reality Usability Scale (HARUS) [21]. The HARUS questionnaire has been purposely developed to evaluate the comprehensibility and manipulability of Handheld Augmented Reality (HAR) applications. Comprehensibility refers to the "ease of understanding the information presented" by an HAR application. The manipulability refs to "ease of handling the AR application as the user performs a task". HARUS questionnaire contains eight statements for the comprehensibility scale and eight statements for the manipulability scale. We decided to remove one of the manipulability questions ("I found it easy to input information through the application") because it is not relevant in the evaluation of the proposed application. The last section (Q18–Q26) aims to assess the enjoyment and usefulness of the application. The questions

Table 1. Evaluation questionnaire

Personal Skills	Q1: How often do you use mobile devices (tablet, smartphone)?
	Q2: Have you experienced Augmented Reality before this test?
Comprehensibility	Q3: I thought that interacting with this application requires a lot of mental effort
	Q4: I thought the amount of information displayed on screen was appropriate
	Q5: I thought that the information displayed on screen was difficult to read
	Q6: I felt that the information display was responding fast enough
	Q7: I thought that the information displayed on screen was confusing
	Q8: I thought the words and symbols on screen were easy to read
	Q9: I felt that the display was flickering too much
	Q10: I thought that the information displayed on screen was consistent
Manipulability	Q11: I thought that interacting with this application requires a lot of body muscle effort
	Q12: I felt that using the application was comfortable for my arms and hands
	Q13: I found the device difficult to hold while operating the application
	Q14: I felt that my arm or hand became tired after using the application
	Q15: I thought the application is easy to control
	Q16: I felt that I was losing grip and dropping the device at some point
	Q17: I thought the operation of this application is simple and uncomplicated
Enjoyment	Q18: I enjoyed using the application
	Q19: I found the application unpleasant
	Q20: I found the application exciting
	Q21: I found the application boring
Usefulness	Q22: By using the app, I could quickly and easily find historical pictures and information
	Q23: By using the app, I learned more about the history of Piazza dei Miracoli
	Q24: By using the app, I could quickly find historical pictures and information from places nearby
	Q25: By using the app, I am more likely to find historical pictures and information that interests me
	Q26: I found useful being able to browse different historical ages with the application

have been extracted from the questionnaires proposed by Haugstvedt and Krogstie [22] using the "Perceived usefulness" and "Perceived enjoyment" constructs. Q26 has been added in order to evaluate the feature which allows users to switch between different augmented views linked to different epochs.

All the questions, except Q2 which is a True/False question, use a 7-point Likert scale, ranging from 1 – "strongly disagree", to 7 – "strongly agree".

3.4   Results

The questionnaires results have been analyzed in order to evaluate the developed application in terms of usability and appreciation. Following the instructions provided by the authors in [21, 22], the answers have been aggregated in order to obtain a value for each one of the four constructs defined by the two questionnaires: Comprehensibility, Manipulability, Enjoyment and Usefulness. To compute the construct outcomes, for each user, we first invert the results of negatively stated items and then we sum all the values related to the specific construct. The obtained score is mapped to a range of 0 to 100.

Figure 4 shows the outcomes of the questionnaire for each of the questions. The values reported here have not been inverted yet. The values obtained for each question

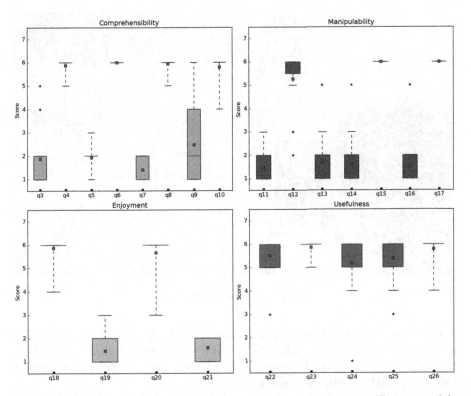

Fig. 4. The plot shows the outcome for each question proposed to the users. The mean and the interquartile values are reported in the boxplots. Outliers are reported as asterisks

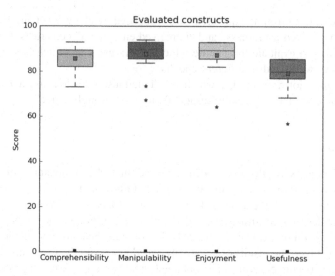

Fig. 5. The plot displays the results for the four constructs. The mean and the interquartile values are reported in the boxplots. Outliers are reported as asterisks

Fig. 6. Using the TowerAR app

indicates a positive evaluation. This can be seen more clearly in Fig. 5 where the values for each construct – Comprehensibility ($M = 85.59$; $SD = 4.98$), Manipulability ($M = 87.61$; $SD = 7.58$), Enjoyment ($M = 87.38$; $SD = 7.12$) and Usefulness ($M = 79.42$; $SD = 7.89$), are reported.

4 Conclusions and Future Developments

In this paper, we presented TowerAR, an application which allows MAR-based time-travelling for the monuments of the Piazza dei Miracoli, Pisa. Historical information (3D models and images) is visible when the users point the mobile device towards the edifices. A preliminary user study was conducted to evaluate the comprehensibility, manipulability, enjoyment and usefulness of TowerAR. After plotting the results, we have found a high score for all analyzed constructs. The results of experiments show that users not only were satisfied by the application, but also felt excited when using it (Fig. 6). Further developments can be made in improving the 3D models, adding more locations, testing the application with a larger user base, implementing an automatic selection based on GPS coordinates or linking the AR content to web-based libraries.

Acknowledgements. This paper is supported by European Union's Horizon 2020 research and innovation programme under grant agreement No. 692103, project eHERITAGE (Expanding the Research and Innovation Capacity in Cultural Heritage Virtual Reality Applications).

References

1. Angelopoulou, A., Economou, D., Bouki, V., Psarrou, A., Jin, L., Pritchard, C., Kolyda, F.: Mobile augmented reality for cultural heritage. In: International Conference on Mobile Wireless Middleware, Operating Systems, and Applications, pp. 15–22 (2011)
2. Mortara, M., Catalano, C.E., Bellotti, F., Fiucci, G., Houry-Panchetti, M., Petridis, P.: Learning cultural heritage by serious games. J. Cult. Heritage **15**(3), 318–325 (2014)
3. Ridel, B., Reuter, P., Laviole, J., Mellado, N., Couture, N., Granier, X.: The revealing flashlight: interactive spatial augmented reality for detail exploration of cultural heritage artifacts. J. Comput. Cult. Heritage **7**(2), 1–18 (2014). Association for Computing Machinery (ACM)
4. D'Auria, D., Di Mauro, D., Calandra, D.M., Cutugno, F.: A 3D audio augmented reality system for a cultural heritage management and fruition. J. Digit. Inf. Manag. **13**(4), 203–209 (2015)
5. Ha, T., Kim, Y., Kim, E., Kim, K., Lim, S., Hong, S., et al.: K-Culture time machine: development of creation and provision technology for time-space-connected cultural contents. In: Proceedings of the International Conference on Human Interface and the Management of Information, pp. 428–435 (2015)
6. Fiore, A., Mainetti, L., Manco, L., Marra, P.: Augmented reality for allowing time navigation in cultural tourism experiences: a case study. In: International Conference on Augmented and Virtual Reality, pp. 296–301 (2014)
7. Bustillo, A., Alaguero, M., Miguel, I., Saiz, J.M., Iglesias, L.S.: A flexible platform for the creation of 3D semi-immersive environments to teach cultural heritage. Digit. Appl. Archaeol. Cult. Heritage **2**(4), 248–259 (2015)
8. Ruffaldi, E., Evangelista, C., Neri, V., Carrozzino, M., Bergamasco, M.: Design of information landscapes for cultural heritage content. In: Proceedings of the 3rd International Conference on Digital Interactive Media in Entertainment and Arts, pp. 113–119 (2008)

9. Carrozzino, M., Bergamasco, M.: Beyond virtual museums: experiencing immersive virtual reality in real museums. J. Cult. Heritage **11**(4), 452–458 (2010)

10. Gaugne, R., Gouranton, V., Dumont, G., Chauffaut, A., Arnaldi, B.: Immersia, an open immersive infrastructure: doing archaeology in virtual reality. Archeologia e Calcolatori, Supplement **5**, 1–10 (2014)

11. Malomo, L., Banterle, F., Pingi, P., Gabellone, F., Scopigno, R.: VirtualTour: a system for exploring cultural heritage sites in an immersive way. In: 2015 Digital Heritage, vol. 1, pp. 309–312 (2015)

12. Olsson, T., Kärkkäinen, T., Lagerstam, E., Ventä-Olkkonen, L.: User evaluation of mobile augmented reality scenarios. J. Ambient Intell. Smart Environ. **4**(1), 29–47 (2012)

13. Casella, G., Coelho, M.: Augmented heritage: situating augmented reality mobile apps in cultural heritage communication. In: Proceedings of the 2013 International Conference on Information Systems and Design of Communication, pp. 138–140 (2013)

14. Han, J.G., Park, K.W., Ban, K.J., Kim, E.K.: Cultural heritage sites visualization system based on outdoor augmented reality. AASRI Procedia **4**, 64–71 (2013)

15. Vecchio, P., Mele, F., De Paolis, L.T., Epicoco, I., Mancini, M., Aloisio, G.: Cloud computing and augmented reality for cultural heritage. In: International Conference on Augmented and Virtual Reality, pp. 51–60 (2015)

16. Seo, B.K., Kim, K., Park, J., Park, J.I.: A tracking framework for augmented reality tours on cultural heritage sites. In: Proceedings of the 9th ACM SIGGRAPH Conference on Virtual-Reality Continuum and its Applications in Industry, pp. 169–174 (2010)

17. Oleksy, T., Wnuk, A.: Augmented places: an impact of embodied historical experience on attitudes towards places. Comput. Hum. Behav. **57**, 11–16 (2016)

18. Kourouthanassis, P., Boletsis, C., Bardaki, C., Chasanidou, D.: Tourists' responses to mobile augmented reality travel guides: the role of emotions on adoption behavior. Pervasive Mobile Comput. **18**(7), 1–87 (2015)

19. Chung, N., Han, H., Joun, Y.: Tourists' intention to visit a destination: the role of augmented reality (AR) application for a heritage site. Comput. Hum. Behav. **50**, 588–599 (2015)

20. Burland, J.B., Jamiolkowski, M., Viggiani, C.: The stabilization of the leaning tower of Pisa. Japan. Geotechn. Soc. **43**(5), 63–80 (2003)

21. Santos, M.E.C., Polvi, J., Taketomi, T., Yamamoto, G., Sandor, C., Kato, H.: Toward standard usability questionnaires for handheld augmented reality. IEEE Comput. Graph. Appl. **35**(5), 66–75 (2015)

22. Haugstvedt, A.C., Krogstie, J.: Mobile augmented reality for cultural heritage: a technology acceptance study. In: 2012 IEEE International Symposium on Mixed and Augmented Reality (ISMAR), pp. 247–255 (2012)

Author Index

Printed in the United States
by Baker & Taylor Publisher Services